HIGH WAY TO HEAVEN

STUDIES
IN MEDIEVAL AND
REFORMATION THOUGHT

FOUNDED BY HEIKO A. OBERMAN †

EDITED BY

ANDREW COLIN GOW, Edmonton, Alberta

IN COOPERATION WITH

THOMAS A. BRADY, Jr., Berkeley, California
SUSAN C. KARANT-NUNN, Tucson, Arizona
JÜRGEN MIETHKE, Heidelberg
M. E. H. NICOLETTE MOUT, Leiden
ANDREW PETTEGREE, St. Andrews
MANFRED SCHULZE, Wuppertal

VOLUME LXXXIX

ERIC L. SAAK

HIGH WAY TO HEAVEN

HIGH WAY TO HEAVEN

THE AUGUSTINIAN PLATFORM BETWEEN REFORM
AND REFORMATION, 1292-1524

BY

ERIC L. SAAK

BRILL
LEIDEN · BOSTON · KÖLN
2002

This book is printed on acid-free paper.

Library of Congress Cataloging-in-Publication Data

Saak, Eric Leland.
 High way to heaven : the Augustinian platform between reform and Reformation, 1292-1524 / by Eric L. Saak.
    p cm. — (Studies in medieval and Reformation thought, ISSN 0585-6914 ; v. 89)
 Includes bibliographical references and indexes.
 ISBN 9004110992
  1. Augustinians—History. 2. Church history—Middle Ages, 600-1500. I. Title. II. Series.

BX2906.3 S33 2002
271'.4—dc21   2002066558

Die Deutsche Bibliothek - CIP-Einheitsaufnahme

Saak, Eric Leland:
 High way to heaven : the Augustinian platform between reform and reformation, 1292 - 1524 / by Eric L. Saak. – Leiden ; Boston ; Köln : Brill, 2002
    (Studies in medieval and reformation thought ; Vol. 89)
    ISBN 90–04–11099–2

ISSN 0585-6914
ISBN 90 04 11099 2

© *Copyright 2002 by Koninklijke Brill NV, Leiden, The Netherlands*

All rights reserved. No part of this publication may be reproduced, translated, stored in a retrieval system, or transmitted in any form or by any means, electronic, mechanical, photocopying, recording or otherwise, without prior written permission from the publisher.

*Authorization to photocopy items for internal or personal use is granted by Brill provided that the appropriate fees are paid directly to The Copyright Clearance Center, 222 Rosewood Drive, Suite 910 Danvers MA 01923, USA.
Fees are subject to change*

PRINTED IN THE NETHERLANDS

*I'd rather learn from one bird how to sing
than teach ten thousand stars how not to dance*
e.e. cummings

If salvation and help are to come, it is from the child
Maria Montessori

For Jonas
(b. 15 September 1998)

And for his mother
Anja

In memory of his Grandma

Dolores Saak
(25 May 1929–7 January 1998)

And in memory of

Heiko Augustinus Oberman
(15 October 1930–22 April 2001)

CONTENTS

Acknowledgments xi
Abbreviations xv
Note on Citation of Sources xvii

Introduction   The Heart of the Matter 1

Chapter One   Power Politics and the Emergence of the
Augustinian Platform: The Myth of Christendom 15
  I. Popes, Princes, Prelates, and Patres 16
    A. The Power of Privilege 19
    B. One Holy, Catholic, and Apostolic Church 28
  II. The War for Rome 41
    A. The Eternal City and the Church Body 44
    B. Battle Fronts 55
    C. The Sovereign Church 70
    D. The Fallible Pope 106
  III. The Augustinian High Way 138

Chapter Two   Creating Religious Identity: The Myth
of Augustine 160
  I. From Reality to Myth: The Politics of
    Augustine's Body 163
  II. The Medieval Augustine 175
    A. Possidius 176
    B. Philip of Harvengt 179
    C. The *Legenda Aurea* 183
  III. The Creation of the Augustinian Myth 187
    A. The *Vita Aurelii Augustini Hipponensis Episcopi* 189
    B. The *Initium sive Processus Ordinis Heremitarum*
        Sancti Augustini 194
    C. Nicholas of Alessandria's *Sermo de beato Augustino* 201
    D. Henry of Friemar's *Tractatus* 209
    E. Jordan of Quedlinburg's *Collectanea Sancti Augustini* 218

Chapter Three Precepts and Practice: Jordan of Quedlinburg
and the Defining of Augustinian Life 235
  I. Frater Jordanus 243
    A. The Pleasures of Paris 245
    B. The Making of a Lector 253
    C. Murder and the Cathedral: The Realities of
       Religious Life 256
    D. Theologian, Preacher, Administrator 264
  II. Living as a Son of Augustine: The *Liber Vitasfratrum* 267
    A. Origins, Context, and Structure 268
    B. The Genuine *Vita Apostolica* 276
    C. De-Sexing Augustine 286
    D. Compelling Observance 306
  III. Regulating Daily Life: The Generalate of Gregory
     of Rimini 315

Chapter Four Ethics and Erudition: The Theological Endeavor
of the Augustinian *Studia* 345
  I. Augustinian Pastoral Theology 347
  II. Spiritual Knowledge: The Augustinian Theological Core 356
  III. The Augustinian Educational System 368
    A. The Least of Scholars 369
    B. Theology in the *Studia*: Jordan's Lectures in Erfurt 383
  IV. The Mendicant Theology of the Augustinian *Studia* 387
    A. Divine Dialectic 388
    B. The *Lector Gratie* 394
    C. Grace Given Gratuitously 398
    D. The Direction of Grace 408
    E. Becoming Saints 412
    F. Attaining the Blessed End 417
    G. Divine Geography 422
    H. The City of God in Exile 430
    I. Election and Predestination 436
    J. Between God and the Devil 445
    K. The Law Old and New 449
    L. Paying What is Owed 455
    M. Fighting the Devil 462
    N. In The Trenches 465

Chapter Five   Passion and Piety: Catechesis and
The Power of Images in the Later Middle Ages 467
  I. Passion for the Passion 470
  II. Jordan of Quedlinburg's *Meditationes de Passione Christi* 476
  III. Reading the Passion: Exegesis, Catechesis, and
     Devotion to the Passion in the Later Middle Ages 505
    A. Passion and Devotion 511
    B. Teaching and Preaching the Passion 520
      i. *Ons heren passie* 521
      ii. *Fasciculus Morum* 523
      iii. Antonius Rampegolus' *Figure Bibliorum* 529
      iv. Ulrich Pinder's *Speculum Passionis* 535
  IV. Passion Hermeneutics 543
  V. Beyond the Walls: From Exegesis to Catechesis 561
  VI. The Truly Religious 576

Chapter Six   Between Reform and Reformation 584
  I. Apocalypse Now: The Origins of the Augustinian
    Observance 587
    A. Schism and the Antichrist 588
    B. Antonius Rampegolus and the Observant Mentality 594
      i. *Inimicus crudelissimus* 596
      ii. *Ecclesia Concussa* 601
      iii. *Veri Religiosi* 612
  II. Beatus Vir 618
    A. Entering the Black Hole: The Reformation
      Discovery 623
    B. The Black Satan: From Reformation to Reform 628
      i. *Misericordia dei* 630
      ii. *Pater et Praeceptor* 637
      iii. *Vestes Nuptiales* 660
      iv. *Frater Martinus* 670
  III. The Sons of Augustine 673

Epilogue 676

Appendices 681
  A. Terms, Concepts, and Definitions 683
  B. Bonifacii VIII *Bullae selectae spectantes ad ordinem
     eremitarum sancti Augustini* 736

    C. Augustini de Ancona *Summe de potestate ecclesiastica Littera Dedicatoris et Tabula* 743
    D. Jordani de Quedlinburg *Vita Sancti Augustini* 774
    E. Gregorii Ariminensis *Ordinationes et Litterae* 811
    F. Jordani de Quedlinburg *Meditationum de Passione Christi Momentum et Expositio Arboris eius* 823

Bibliography 837
Index 865

ACKNOWLEDGMENTS

The appearance of the present study has been made possible by far more than the efforts of the one who bears the name of author. It was conceived in late December of 1989 in an apartment in Rome near the Colosseum, though its earliest origins can be traced back to the early 1980s and the stacks of the Doheny Library of the University of Southern California. It began to grow beyond embryonic form in the University of Arizona's Division for Late Medieval and Reformation Studies, and in Tübingen during the academic year 1992/1993, where I worked in the *Institut für Spätmittelalter und Reformation*, and in the *Abteilung für philosophische Grundfragen der Theologie* of the Catholic Theological Faculty, benefiting from the context of the longstanding, Tübingen-Arizona tradition of research focused on the historical problematic of the transition from medieval to early modern culture. Having achieved its first trimester of development in my doctoral dissertation, it thereafter matured in the environment provided by the Centre for Classical, Oriental, Mediaeval, and Renaissance Studies of the Rijks*universiteit* Groningen, and underwent further gestation in the peaceful settings of The Hague and the Medieval Institute of the University of Notre Dame. It finally came to fruition in the rich surroundings of the *Institut für Europäische Geschichte, Abteilung Abendländische Religionsgeschichte* in Mainz. With conviction I avow that the disharmony, dissonance, and atonal errors in what follows are there due only to the cracking of my own voice and to my inability to have learned my lessons better. Yet public acknowledgment does very little actually to communicate my gratitude or to repay my debts, which I remain unable to explain or express adequately. Thus the acknowledgments that follow remain to a large extent in the private realm, and all the better; some things simply should not be made public.

Two individuals in particular have influenced my work on the Augustinians from its very beginning, not only by their own formidable scholarship, but also by their personal encouragement, support, and inspiration: the late Damasus Trapp, OSA and Adolar Zumkeller, OSA.

For their tutelage, support, and advice, I am indebted to Alan Bernstein, William J. Courtenay, Richard C. Dales, Kaspar Elm, the late Gordon Griffiths, Richard Jensen, Paul W. Knoll, Hans-Christoph Rublack, and Donald Weinstein. Deserving of special thanks are Manfred Schulze, Walter Simon, and Georg Wieland. Ernest B. Koenker was the one who formed me as a scholar, and to him my gratitude is matched only by my affection.

In addition, for reasons as diverse as the individuals here listed, I thank Maria Luisa Betterton, Dorothea A. Christ, Robert Christman, Peter Dykema, Neal Erlenborn, Brad Gregory, Peter Hatlie, Berndt Hamm, Jos. M.M. Hermans, Katja Himanen, Hilly Hommes, Norry Horlings-Brandse, Femke Kramer, Ron Love, Tom McCreight, E. Ann Matter, Iris Petrakopoulos, Darleen Pryds, Suse Rau, Jonathan Reid, Angeniet Reinink-Sirag, Justa Renner-van Niekerk, Manuel Santos, Marion Torringa, Jacoba Van der Velden, Markus Wriedt, Eelcko Ypma, OSA, and Elsie Vezey.

To C.H. Kneepkens, Alberic de Meijer, OSA, and especially to Martijn Schrama, OSA, I am more grateful and indebted than words can begin to convey.

Standing apart as one who has merited unique acknowledgment for so many reasons is Heiko A. Oberman, whose unfathomable depth of humanity, scholarship, knowledge, wisdom, and patience has informed this work throughout. It is one of my deepest regrets that he is not able to read the published version, having too soon embarked on his own "high way to heaven." Though it may be proverbial and somewhat trite, it is nevertheless most true, sincere, and an understatement to say that his death was a loss for us all.

Without the support, encouragement, and friendship of John Frymire and Andrew Gow, this book would never have reached its present form, and to Andrew I am most grateful as well for his acceptance of this book in the series *Studies in Medieval and Reformation Thought*.

In a category all her own is Anja Petrakopoulos, whose love, insistence, persistence, and perseverance have been fundamental. This book is for her.

And finally to my parents, Robert and Dolores Saak, I owe far more than I am even aware. Their unceasing and unconditional love, combined with their financial, emotional, spiritual, and parental support, has sustained me throughout many years of quandary, uncertainty, and despair. My mother especially took an intimate interest in my work and the sadness will always remain that she did not live long enough to be able to hold this book in her hands, or to have the opportunity to hold in her arms her grandson, Jonas, to whom this book is dedicated.

For financial support of the research for this book I am indebted to the Graduate College of the University of Arizona and to the same University's Division for Late Medieval and Reformation Studies. In addition, grants from the German Historical Institute of Washington, D.C. and the German Fulbright Commission enabled me to carry out foundational research in Germany in the summer of 1990 and during the academic year 1992/93 respectively. A generous postdoctoral fellowship from the Netherlands Organization for Scientific Research allowed me to continue work and to refine my findings during the years 1994 to 1998, which I spent at the Rijks*universiteit* Groningen and the Netherlands Research School for Medieval Studies. The Medieval Institute at the University of Notre Dame, and its director at the time, Patrick Geary, opened to me their amazing resources and facilities during my time as a Visiting Scholar at the Institute in the Fall of 1999. And finally, a special word of gratitude for support, financial and otherwise, is due Gerhard May and Rolf Decot, and to the *Institut für Europäische Geschichte* in Mainz.

I am indebted to the staffs of the Biblioteca Angelica in Rome, the University Library of Villanova University, the Herzog August Bibliothek in Wolfenbüttel, the Staatsbibliothek Preussischer Kulturbesitz in Berlin, the Bayerische Staatsbibliothek in Munich, the Universitätsbibliotheken of Tübingen and Basel, the Bamberg Staatsbibliothek, the Newberry Library of Chicago, the Bibliothèque nationale de France, the Bibliothèque de l'Arsenal in Paris, the Biblioteca Apostolica Vaticana, the Hesburgh Library of the University of Notre Dame, the Stadtsbibliothek of Mainz, the Martinus Bibliothek and the Bibliothek of the Gutenberg Museum in Mainz, and an especial acknowledgment of gratitude is due to the staff of the Koninklijke Bibliotheek in The Hague. Special thanks are merited as well by the Bibliotheek Augustijns Instituut in Eindhoven and its librarian, Ingrid van Neer, and to the *patres* and *fratres* of the Augustijnenklooster Mariënhage.

Much of Chapter Two and parts of Chapter Three originally appeared in different form in *Augustiniana* 49 (1999), 109–164, 251–286, under the title, "The Creation of Augustinian Identity in the Later Middle Ages." I would like to thank the editors for permission to reprint that material here.

I can only hope that what follows will reflect in some respects, however insufficient, a modicum of my gratitude to those who have contributed so much, in so many ways, to this work's realization.

E.L. Saak
Mainz
12 November 2001

ABBREVIATIONS

AAug.	*Analecta Augustiniana*
AHR	*American Historical Review*
ARG	*Archiv für Reformationsgeschichte*
Aug(L)	*Augustiniana*
AWA	*Archiv zur Weimarer Ausgabe der Werke Martin Luthers*
BGPhThMA	Beiträge zur Geschichte der Philosophie und Theologie des Mittelalters. Texte und Untersuchungen
BhTh	Beiträge zur historischen Theologie
BnF	Bibliothèque nationale de France
BSIH	Brill's Studies in Intellectual History
BStB	Bayerische Staatsbibliothek
CCCM	Corpus Christianorum, Continuatio Mediaevalis
CCSL	Corpus Christianorum, Series Latina
CSA	Corpus Scriptorum Augustinianorum
CSEL	Corpus Scriptorum Ecclesiasticorum Latinorum
CTM	*Concordia Theological Monthly*
DAChL	*Dictionnaire d'Archeologie chrétienne et de Liturgie*
DSp	*Dictionnaire de spiritualité*
ESMAR	Education and Society in the Middle Ages and Renaissance
FTS	Freiburger Theologische Studien
Hümpfner, intro.	Jordani de Saxonia *Liber Vitasfratrum*. Ed. Winfridus Hümpfner and Rudolph Arbesmann. Cassiciacum 1. New York, 1943, Introduction.
JEH	*Journal of Ecclesiastical History*
JEMH	*Journal of Early Modern History*
LexMA	*Lexikon des Mittelalters*
L&S	Lewis and Short, *A Latin Dictionary*. 1879; Oxford, 1980.
LThK	*Lexikon für Theologie und Kirche*
MGH.SS	*Monumenta Germaniae Historica: scriptores*, Berlin, 1826–
NB	Nationalbibliothek
NDB	*Neue Deutsche Biographie*
NKZ	*Neue kirchliche Zeitschrift*

OGE	*Ons Geestelijk Erf*
PL	*Patrologiae cursus completus: series latina.* Ed. J.-P. Migne. Paris, 1841–1864.
PG	*Patrologiae cursus completus: series graeca.* Ed. J.-P. Migne. Paris, 1857–1866.
RThAM	*Recherches de théologie ancienne et médiévale*
SdB	Stadtbibliothek
SHCT	Studies in the History of Christian Thought
SMRT	Studies in Medieval and Reformation Thought
StB	Staatsbibliothek
STGMA	*Studien und Texte zur Geistesgeschichte des Mittelalters*
SuR	Spätmittelalter und Reformation Texte und Untersuchungen
SuR.NR	Spätmittelalter und Reformation Neue Reihe
TRE	*Theologische Realenzyklopädie*
UB	Universitätsbibliothek
VerLex	*Die deutsche Literatur des Mittelalters Verfasserlexikon*
VIEG	Veröffentlichungen des Instituts für Europäische Geschichte Mainz
ZKTh	*Zeitschrift für Katholische Theologie*
ZThK	*Zeitschrift für Theologie und Kirche*
Zumkeller *MSS*	Adolar Zumkeller, *Manuskripte von Werken der Autoren des Augustiner-Eremitenordens in mitteleuropäischen Bibliotheken.* Cassiciacum 20. Würzburg, 1966.

NOTE ON CITATION OF SOURCES

In the documentation for this study I have employed two series of abbreviations. The first are those given above. The second are found in the bibliography, and concern the primary source material. I have cited all sources in the study that follows according to the list of abbreviations there given, together with complete bibliographical information. For previously edited works, I have used the edition as given in the bibliography, with page and/or column reference, and line numbers when available, given in the notes in parenthesis; manuscripts are cited in the notes according to the list of abbreviations given in the bibliography, followed by foliation; early printed editions are cited likewise according to the abbreviations, with the place and date of publication given in parenthesis, followed by foliation or pagination. Where I have used and listed in the bibliography multiple manuscripts or editions of a single work, the primary reference is to the first listed; when I cite the secondary reference, this is indicated in the notes themselves. For the abbreviations of classical and patristic sources, I have followed those given in the *Thesaurus linguae latinae, Supplementum* (Lipsiae, 1958). Regarding the presentation of text in the notes, I have standardized the orthography based on the individual manuscripts and early printed editions used, and have modernized the punctuation. Biblical references are to the Vulgate; *Biblia Sacra iuxta Vulgatam Versionem*, eds. Bonifatio Fischer, H.I. Frede, Johannes Gribmont, H.F.D. Sparks, W. Thiele, and Robert Weber, Deutsche Bibelgesellschaft (Stuttgart, 1985), cited according to the abbreviations there used; the translations are either my own directly from the Vulgate, or those of *The New English Bible with The Apocrypha* (Oxford, 1970). All other translations are my own unless otherwise noted.

INTRODUCTION

THE HEART OF THE MATTER

> *There is a voice that cries:*
> *Prepare a road for the Lord through the wilderness*
> *Clear a highway across the desert for our God.*
> Is. 40:3

On 3 May 1512, the Prior General of the Augustinian Order, Giles of Viterbo, delivered the inaugural oration of the Fifth Lateran Council. Twenty years previously he had preached to all Italy the explanation of the Gospels, Prophets, and Apocalypse: his audience "would see both disturbances and disasters of the Church, but eventually would witness amelioration."[1] Such a reform had now come to pass: "the one who so often cried out, *My eyes will see the days of salvation* (Lk. 2:30), now finally exclaims: My eyes have seen salvation and the sacred beginnings of the expected renewal."[2] According to Giles, Christ would enable the Council "to extirpate vice, to foster virtue, to trap the foxes swarming to destroy the holy vineyard in this raging storm," and would "call back our fallen religion to its former purity, its ancient light, its native splendor, and its sources."[3] Six months later, Giles preached in the Augustinian church of Santa Maria del Popolo in Rome on the occasion of the treaty negotiated between Pope Julius II and the Emperor Maximilian. Giles praised Julius, in his presence, for having subdued the twin monsters that

---

[1] "Nam cum annis ab hinc circiter viginti, quantum in me fuit, et per exiguae vires tulere, evangelia populis interpraetatus sim, prophetarum vaticinia aperuerim, Ioannis Apocalypsim de successu ecclesiae universae ferme Italiae enarraverim, ac saepenumero affirmaverim eos qui tunc audiebant ingentes ecclesiae et agitationes et clades visuros, illiusque emendationem aliquando conspecturos." Aeg.Vit. *Or.Lat.* (185,15–20).

[2] "Nunc par esse visum est, ut qui haec dixerat ventura, idem venisse testetur, et qui toties exclamaverat, *Videbunt oculi mei salutaria tempora* [Lc. 2:30], iam tandem exclamet: Viderunt oculi mei salutare sanctumque principium expectatae instaurationis." *Ibid.*, (185,21–24).

[3] "... ipsa re, veri, sancti, exacti Concilii celebrandi, extirpandi vitia, virtutes excitandi, vulpes quae ad sanctam demoliendam vineam hac tempestate scatent capiendi; ac denique collapsam religionem, in veterem puritatem, in antiquam lucem, in nativum splendorem, atque in suos fontes revocari." *Ibid.*, (185,27–31).

had been devastating Italy and destroying the Church—schism and war: "Beyond all hope and all belief, beyond what anyone could have conceived possible, you extricated yourself and your ship and brought her safely into harbor. At one and the same time, and with amazing speed, you delivered Italy from the burden of war and the Church from schism."[4] The pope offered the only hope for the Church and for the salvation of true religion, for only the pope, working through the Council, could ensure, as Giles preached in St. John the Lateran, that humans are to be changed by the holy, not the holy by humans.[5]

Humans are to be changed by the holy, *homines per sacra*: this was the encapsulation of Giles' reform program.[6] As Christ's vicar on earth, only the pope could effect such a reform, such a passive reform. This did not, however, yield a passivism, at least certainly not on the part of Giles. Giles fought incessantly for the reform of his Order, which he saw as an urgent necessity. On 13 January 1517, Giles wrote a letter to the entire Order in which he emphasized the immediate need for the Order to reform itself: "Gather everyone together," Giles instructed, "order prayers, intercessions, fasts. Then, trusting in God, take counsel with one another, summoning the wisest of the fathers of the province, and promptly write to me a report of what takes place. For the situation is at boiling point, so that whatever is to be done must be done with equal amounts of speed and wisdom."[7] As Giles was mustering all his religious and political clout in Rome to safeguard the rights and privileges of his Order, seemingly unaware of the storm brewing north of the Alps, a theology of passive reform, of passive righteousness, was being developed by the German Augustinian friar, Martin Luther.

---

[4] "... quod nemo speravit, nemo credidit, nemo unquam fieri posse cogitavit—non modo te ac naviculam tuam eripueris atque in portum adduxeris, sed mira celeritate simul et Italiam iugo et ecclesiam scismate vindicaveris." Aeg.Vit. *Or.foed.* (111).

[5] "... quod homines per sacra immutari fas est, non sacra per homines." Aeg.Vit. *Or.Lat.* (186,35).

[6] See Francis X. Martin, *Friar, Reformer, and Renaissance Scholar. Life and Works of Giles of Viterbo, 1469–1532* (Villianova, PA, 1992); and John W. O'Malley, *Giles of Viterbo on Church and Reform. A Study in Renaissance Thought*, SMRT 5 (Leiden, 1968).

[7] "Convocate omnes, indicite orationes, preces, ieiunia, inde deo freti consilium capite, patribus provincie sapientioribus accersitis, et ad me quid occurrerit cito scribite. Fervent enim ita omnia ut quam maxime fieri potest occurri oporteat tum sapientia tum celeritate." Aeg.Vit. *Lett.Fam.* 338 (220,101–105).

In 1518, Frater Martin appealed to Pope Leo X, a very close friend of Giles, asking the most blessed father to judge the validity of his theses against indulgences. Luther, prostrating himself at the pope's feet, offered all that he had and all of himself, and sought the blessed father's protection against his detractors, for, as Luther affirmed, "I acknowledge your voice as the voice of Christ residing and speaking in you."[8] A higher road to reformation cannot be imagined than the one taken by the Augustinians, a passive reform, led by the voice of the pope as the embodiment of the voice of Christ—*except* for the even higher way of reform that the Augustinian high way to heaven itself produced. For Giles the agent of 'reformation' was the pope; for Luther, 'reformation' lay in the realm *supra papam*: the agent of 'the Reformation' could only come from God on high.[9] The Augustinian platform in the later Middle Ages contained within itself the currents that surged into floodwaters in the early sixteenth century. The longed-for renewal never came. Giles of Viterbo may have praised Pope Julius II for having saved Italy from war and schism in 1512, but little did he see that the platform which he represented and for which he so vigorously fought, was soon to throw Europe into war and schism on a magnitude never previously imagined.

This book is the first of a planned trilogy tracing the emergence, development, and impact of the Augustinian platform in late medieval and early modern Europe.[10] It is a story not previously told. It is a story of religion and politics, of theology and piety, a story of the highest ideals and of the most mundane strivings to be religious in a world of intrigue, temptation, war, famine, exploitation, and greed. It is a story of the fight of the "old Adam" with the "new," of the struggle to enforce and impose obedience, and of the battle for the souls of late medieval society caught between God and the devil. On 9 October 1524, Frater Martin Luther appeared in

---

[8] "Quare, beatissime pater, prostratum me pedibus tuae beatitudinis offero cum omnibus quae sum et habeo. Vivifica, occide, voca, revoca, approba, reproba, ut placuit, vocem tuam vocem Christi in te praesidentis et loquentis agnoscam." *WA* 1.529,22–25; see also Chapter Six below.

[9] See Heiko A. Oberman, *Luther. Mensch Zwischen Gott und Teufel* (Berlin, 1982).

[10] The project extends from Giles of Rome to Jerome Seripando. The forthcoming second volume is titled: *The Failed Reformation. The Reform of Religion and the Augustinian Observance in the Later Middle Ages*; which will then be followed by the third and final volume: *The True Church. The Augustinian Platform as an Instrument of Catholic Reform*.

public for the first time without his cowl. A week later he was never to don it again, and the late medieval Augustinian "high way to heaven" was buried by the entrenchment of Catholic and Protestant confessionalization.

This is by no means to imply, however, that the Augustinians, much less Augustine, ceased to play a role in the development of Western culture. Indeed the overwhelming influence of Augustine on the intellectual life of the West needs no debate or proof. From his own day into modern times, Augustine has stood as a formidable authority in theology, philosophy, literary theory, and politics, appealed to by medieval scholars, Renaissance humanists, reformers both Catholic and Protestant, and dedicated members of Port-Royal. In fact, the entire theological tradition in the West can be regarded as a "series of footnotes" to Augustine.[11] Yet the Augustinian high way to heaven, which at times in the later Middle Ages was simultaneously a "highway to heaven" with connotations not only of elevation and hierarchy, but also of speed and ease, fundamentally changed with the rest of European society in the course of the sixteenth century so that at some point we can no longer speak of the Middle Ages, but must use the designation early modern Europe. The *high way* and the *highway*, both intended to be reflected in the title of this study, symbolize the inherent tensions within the Augustinian platform between its precepts and its practice, between the theoretical expression of its ideals and the actual day to day life of the Augustinian friar. When Europe became early modern, the stress of the polarization of theory and praxis was not overcome or left behind, but the world had become another. The high way to heaven of the Augustinian platform was a medieval phenomenon, which was being developed nearly two hundred years before Giles wrote to all the provinces of the Order that the efforts to reform must continue, "until there is but one way of life and one standard of observance throughout the Augustinian Order."[12] Such was never achieved, and such unified observance there had never been, even in the beginning, even in the time of the creation of the Order, its platform, and its myth.

---

[11] Jaroslav Pelikan, *The Christian Tradition. A History of the Development of Doctrine*, v. 1: *The Emergence of the Catholic Tradition (100–600)* (Chicago, 1971), 330; see also Gareth B. Matthews, ed., *The Augustinian Tradition* (Berkeley, 1999).

[12] "... numquam satisfaciemus donec in Augustinensi republica unus fiet vivendi modus, una mandatorum observatio..." Aeg.Vit. *Lett.Gen.* 156 (269,39–41).

On 15 July 1255, Pope Alexander IV summoned representatives from the Orders of St. Augustine and St. William, from the followers of Friar John Bonus, the Brethren of Favali, and the Brictinenses to convene at Sancta Maria del Popolo in Rome, to discuss the union of these eremetical groups.[13] The result was the foundation and first General Chapter of a new Order, which "... legitimized for the first time the imposition of a certain rule on diverse religious groups and the change from rules already approved."[14] From this time forward, the diverse members constituting the union were to be brought "into a single observance of the way of life and a uniform regulation of living."[15] Thus the *Ordo Eremitarum Sancti Augustini* (O.E.S.A.; today, O.S.A.) came into existence, confirmed by the Bull *Licet ecclesiae catholicae*, issued by Alexander IV on 9 April 1256.[16] From its very inception, the OESA was the creation of the pope. Yet the question that we must address is the extent to which in the later Middle Ages the pope, or the papacy, became the creation of the Augustinian Hermits.

It is, certainly, nonsense to consider the papacy as a creation of the OESA, since papal monarchy had been well-established long before the Bull of Alexander IV through the policies and efforts of popes from Gregory VII to Innocent III.[17] Yet with their institutional origins having been based on papal fiat, the Augustinians' very existence as a religious Order was dependent upon legitimizing such a decree. Individual Augustinian authors, such as Giles of Rome, James of Viterbo, and Augustinus of Ancona, have long been recognized

---

[13] See Rafael Kuiters, "Licet Ecclesiae Catholicae," *Aug(L)* 6 (1956), 9–36 and the text of the Bull edited by Albericus de Meijer, *Aug(L)* 6 (1956), 9–13; A. Kunzelmann, *Geschichte der deutschen Augustiner-Eremiten*, v. 1: *Das dreizehnte Jahrhundert* (Würzburg, 1969); Kaspar Elm, *Beiträge zur Geschichte des Wilhelmitenordens*, Münstersche Forschungen 14, (Köln, 1962), ch. V: "Die Union zwischen Wilhelmiten und Augustiner-Eremiten (1256–1266)," 108–119; Cyril Counihan, "Lay and Clerical Elements in Early Augustinian History," *AAug.* 43 (1980), 304–333; and especially Balbino Rano, "San Agustín y los orígenes de su Orden. Regla, Monasterio de Tagaste y Sermones ad fratres in eremo," in *San Agustin en el XVI Centenario de su Conversion 386/87–1987, La Ciudad de Dios. Revista Agustiniana* CC (1987), (Salamanca, 1987), 649–727.

[14] Kuiters, "Licet Ecclesiae Catholicae," 14.

[15] "... in unam ordinis observantiam, et vivendi formulam uniformem..." *LEC* (12).

[16] For an analysis of *Licet Ecclesiae* and a discussion of the historical developments leading up to and stemming from the Great Union, see Kuiters, "Licet Ecclesiae."

[17] See Colin Morris, *The Papal Monarchy. The Western Church from 1050–1250* (Oxford, 1989).

as major contributors to late medieval political philosophy as proponents of papal hierocratic theory.[18] What has not been noted, however, is the extent to which such political theory was fundamental to the corporate identity of the OESA. The late medieval Augustinians from Giles of Rome to Giles of Viterbo enunciated a high way to heaven whereby the salvation of Church and Empire, of individual souls and Christian society as such, was predicated on the preeminence of papal power. It was not as individual political theorists, but as members of the OESA constructing a corporate platform for their Order's religious mission in late medieval society, that members of the Order became the very architects of the theoretical construction of papal sovereignty.[19] The Augustinians may not have been the creators of the pope, or of the papacy, but they were the creators of the late medieval papal political theory that provided the legitimization and justification of the Augustinian identity, an identity that became the foundation of the Augustinian platform for the reform of Christian culture.

Almost a century ago, Ernst Troeltsch argued that Augustine was the first theologian to develop a Christian cultural ethic.[20] This cultural ethic was based on the pursuit of the highest good and brotherly love, and found its most complete expression in Augustine's monasticism.[21] According to Troeltsch, however, the culture of Augustine's ethic was limited to the culture of late antiquity. Augustine

---

[18] See Richard Scholz, *Die Publizistik zur Zeit Philipps des Schönen und Bonifaz' VIII. Ein Beitrag zur Geschichte der politischen Anschauungen des Mittelalters* (Stuttgart, 1903); Michael Wilks, *The Problem of Sovereignty in the Later Middle Ages. The Papal Monarchy with Augustinus Triumphus and the Publicists* (Cambridge, 1963); and most recently Jürgen Miethke, *De Potestate Papae. Die päpstliche Amtskompetenz im Widerstreit der politischen Theorie von Thomas von Aquin bis Wilhelm von Ockham*, SuR.NR 15 (Tübingen, 2000), esp. 94–108.

[19] See Chapter One below.

[20] Ernst Troeltsch, *Augustin, die christliche Antike und das Mittelalter. Im Anschluss an die Schrift "De Civitate Dei,"* (Berlin, 1915); *cf.* Hannah Arendt, *Love and Saint Augustine*, edited with an interpretive essay by Joanna Vecchiarelli Scott and Judith Chelius Stark (Chicago, 1996). It should also be noted that before his studies on the theology of the Augustinian school, Adolar Zumkeller first had written works on the social and spiritual teachings of the Augustinians; see Zumkeller, *De Doctrina Sociali Scholae Augustinianae Aevi Medii*, AAug. 22 (1952), 57–84; *idem*, "Die Lehrer des geistlichen Lebens unter den deutschen Augustinern vom dreizehnten Jahrhundert bis zum Konzil von Trient," in *Sanctus Augustinus, Vitae Spiritualis Magister*, 2 vols. (Rome, 1959), 2:239–338.

[21] "Das mönchische Leben ist ganz einfach das Christentum an sich..." Troeltsch, *Augustin*, 153–154.

had no followers.[22] Though recognizing the vast temporal and geographical space that separated fifth-century northern Africa from fourteenth-century Europe, we can nevertheless find a new expression of Augustine's cultural ethic in the religious culture of Augustine's late medieval sons, with their pastoral mission of pursuing a transformational sanctity.[23] The historical, as distinct from the theological referent for what has been called the "Augustinian Renaissance" of the later Middle Ages, is fundamentally the renaissance of Augustine's cultural ethic, founded on the monastic life, the highest good, and brotherly love in imitation of Augustine himself. This cultural ethic in the later Middle Ages was referred to as Augustine's religion, the *religio Augustini*. In the chapters that follow, we will begin to trace the story of Augustine's religion in the later Middle Ages and the consequences of that religion for the emergence of early modern Europe.[24]

Our present task is four-fold: 1.) To understand the Order's self-understanding and self-representation; 2.) To analyze how that self-understanding and representation were developed in context of the Order's self-presentation in working to establish itself within its social world; 3.) To evaluate the means and structures employed to create a corporate identity; and 4.) To evaluate how the attempt to enforce uniformity played itself out within the Order, analyzing the tensions between the Order's ideals, and the practical day to day reality of living as an Augustinian. To do so, I have employed the concept of the Augustinian platform. The 'Augustinian platform' does not refer

---

[22] "Er ist die letzte und größte Zusammenfassung der absterbenden antiken Kultur mit Ethos, Mythos, Autorität und Organisation der frühkatholischen Kirche und konnte mit seinem Wesentlichsten gar nicht auf den Boden einer anderen Kultur übernommen werden." *Ibid.*, 7. *Cf.*: "Denn was man auch sagen mag von einer Krisis des Augustinismus, seiner Sünden- und Gnadenlehre seit dem 18. Jahrhundert, die in Wahrheit mehr eine Krisis des Paulinismus als eine solche des Augustinismus war und ist, die eigentliche Seele des Augustinismus liegt in seiner Ethik des höchsten Gutes und damit hat er die Grundfragestellung aller religiösen Ethik auch noch für die Gegenwart formuliert." *Ibid.*, 173.

[23] See E.L. Saak, "*Quilibet Christianus*: Saints in Society in the Sermons of Jordan of Quedlinburg, OESA," in *Models of Holiness in Medieval Sermons*, Fédération Internationale des Instituts d'Études Médiévales, Texts et Études du Moyen Âge 5, ed. Beverly Mayne Kienzle, with Edith Wilks Dolnikowski, Rosemary Drage Hale, Darleen Pryds, and Anne T. Thayer (Louvain-la-Neuve, 1996), 317–338.

[24] For the understanding of 'religion' as used throughout this study, see Appendix A.3. The analysis of and argument for the impact of Augustine's religion on the emergence of early modern Europe will be continued in the second and third volumes of this trilogy.

to any specific historical document. It is intended to stand for the complex of the Order's ideals, institutions, programs, structures, and directives that provided the Order with the means to establish itself as a unique religious group within late medieval society. The 'high way to heaven' refers to the general hierocratic ideology, of which the Augustinian platform was a specific expression. The Augustinians were not the only religious who took the high way to heaven. Yet in their unique pursuit thereof, in following their platform, they not only were able to create a place for themselves within late medieval ecclesiastical culture, but thereby they also became the primary architects of the high way itself.

The historical role of Augustine's hermits, however, has been overshadowed by the wealth of scholarship devoted to the Franciscan and Dominican Orders.[25] The Augustinians have been allowed to speak primarily in the fierce debates over the relationship between late medieval theology and the Reformation,[26] with the result that their broader impact on the political and cultural life of Europe from the fourteenth to the sixteenth centuries has remained vague, if

---

[25] See, for example, C.H. Lawrence, *The Friars. The Impact of the Early Mendicant Movement on Western Society* (London, 1994), who gives the Augustinians and Carmelites only very brief treatment. The extent to which the OESA is under-represented in scholarship can be garnered from the *International Medieval Bibliography*; for January through June 1995 for example, the IMB lists twenty-eight entries under the general category, "Dominican order", fifty-six entries for "Franciscan order", and only one entry for "Augustinian hermits, order of friars"; IMB v. 29, part 1 (Leeds, 1996), 414, 419, and 398 respectively. This distribution is paralleled by subsequent volumes, as well as by mention of the various mendicant Orders in the most recent over-view of religious life in the Middle Ages, Arnold Angenendt's *Geschichte der Religiosität im Mittelalter* (Darmstadt, 1997). In the index, the Dominicans are given fourteen entries, the Franciscans, twenty-one, and the Augustinians, one, and this one, on page 77, is simply a reference to Luther having been a member of the Observant Augustinians, and the importance of the Augustinian Observance for the Reformation. Likewise, in Marcia L. Colish's, *Medieval Foundations of the Western Intellectual Tradition, 400–1400* (New Haven, 1997), whereas Augustine is given primacy of place, there is no discussion of the Augustinian Order, though the index gives substantial references to both the Franciscan and Dominican Orders in addition to Francis and Dominic. Even the excellent volume edited by Gert Melville and Jörg Oberste gives no mention of the OESA; *Die Bettelorden im Aufbau. Beiträge zu Institutionalisierungsprozessen im mittelalterlichen Religiosentum*, Vita Regularis. Ordnung und Deutung religiosen Lebens im Mittelalter 11 (Münster, 1999). A notable exception to this general trend is Bernadette Paton's *Preaching Friars and the Civic Ethos: Siena, 1380–1480* (London, 1992), where Augustinian preachers are given a prominent place.

[26] For an overview of the scholarship focusing on 'late medieval Augustinianism,' see Appendix A.1.

acknowledged at all. In the theological context, historians have indeed noted a revitalized Augustinianism in the later Middle Ages, and have looked for its origins in the commentaries on the *Sentences* of Peter Lombard composed by members of the Order of Hermits of St. Augustine. These texts offer evidence for the resurgence of a strong anti-Pelagianism, combined with a previously unmatched erudition with respect to Augustine's works.[27] Yet the meaning of the term 'Augustinian' is not exhausted by theological abstractions. The impact of this Augustinian renaissance cannot be grasped fully with reference to the highest echelons of late medieval scholasticism alone. The works of the Augustinian doctors of theology reflect only a small part of the Augustinian tradition. The teaching of the instructors in the Order's heretofore neglected network of schools (*studia*) reveals the wide array of tenets operative within the Order, which cannot be limited to those contained in the treatises and commentaries composed in Paris and Oxford.[28]

The Augustinian Hermits formed one of several religious organizations in the Middle Ages whose members looked to Augustine as the source for their individual and corporate life. The Hermits, together with the Dominicans, Premonstratensians, Augustinian Regular Canons, and various female religious, including the Second Order of the Hermits, comprised the family of religious groups in the later Middle Ages that followed Augustine's monastic Rule.[29] Yet the Augustinian Canons and the Augustinian Hermits laid special claim to being in the direct line of descent from Augustine himself. Though the Canons considered themselves to be the heirs of the Bishop of Hippo,[30] the Hermits identified with the model of Augustine as did

---

[27] See E.L. Saak, "The Reception of Augustine in the Later Middle Ages," in *The Reception of the Church Fathers in the West*, ed. Irena Backus, 2 vols. (Leiden, 1997), 1: 367–404.

[28] See Chapter Four below.

[29] For the Augustinian Rule and its complex textual and historiographical traditions, see L. Verheijen, *La Règle de saint Augustin*, I, *Tradition manuscrite*; II, *Recherches historiques* (Paris, 1967); see also *idem, Nouvelle Approche de la Règle de saint Augustin* (Abbaye de Bellefontaine, 1980). *Cf.* George Lawless, OSA, *Augustine of Hippo and His Monastic Rule* (Oxford, 1987), and especially pages 127–135. Thirty years after the publication of Verheijen's exhaustive study, erroneous comments concerning the Rule are still made, and made as assertions without taking into account the state of the scholarship on the Rule, or offering evidence to the contrary. Thus Marcia Colish can still claim that the Augustinian Rule was originally a letter to nuns; see Marcia L. Colish, *Medieval Foundations*, 52.

[30] For the Canons, see Jean Châtillon, *Le Mouvement Canonial Au Moyen Age. Réforme*

no other religious group. The Hermits' conscious propagation of the ideals of Augustine's religious life combined the Order's mission in both cloister and commune with a new academic Augustinianism. In the course of the fourteenth century, the Augustinian Hermits, asserting themselves indefatigably to be Augustine's true sons, articulated a religious Augustinianism based on their appropriation of the Church Father in thought and deed; they developed and transmitted a clearly profiled group identity as the true sons and heirs of Augustine, which in turn served as the pith of both the Order's academic theology and its social endeavor.[31]

The imitation of Augustine's created *persona* served as the standard by which the authenticity of Augustine's lineage was determined.[32] This was a multifaceted image, consisting of the combination of Augustine as *Pater Noster, Preceptor Noster*, and *Sapiens Architector Ecclesie*. These three symbols coalesced in the emergence of the Augustinian myth, the representations of the Order's earliest history whereby Augustine was portrayed as the founding father of the OESA. The Order's mythic origins were generated in the early 1330s, when the Hermits were in fierce debate with the Canons over which Order was the genuine heir of Augustine. With their identity at stake, members of the OESA provided the necessary documentation to prove that they alone could claim Augustine as their true father. The effort culminated in the *Collectanea Augustiniana* and *Liber Vitasfratrum* of the fourteenth-century Augustinian hermit, Jordan of Quedlinburg.[33] In both works, Jordan sought to establish that the Hermits were the only legitimate sons of Augustine. Moreover, from Jordan's pen came more sermons, extent in more manuscripts, than from that of any other Augustinian before Martin Luther.[34] Thus Jordan, lector in the

---

de l'église, spiritualité et culture, ed. Patrice Sicard (Paris, 1992); Bernard McGinn, *The Presence of God. A History of Western Christian Mysticism*, v. 2: *The Growth of Mysticism. Gregory the Great Through the 12th Century* (New York, 1996), 363–418; and the discussion on the debates between the Canons and the Hermits in Chapter Two below.

[31] See E.L. Saak, "The Creation of Augustinian Identity in the Later Middle Ages," *Aug(L)* 49 (1999), 109–164, 251–286.

[32] For the concept of *persona*, see Aaron Gurevich, *The Origins of European Individualism*, trans. Katherine Judelson (Oxford/Cambridge, MA, 1995), 89–99, and *passim*. "The *persona*," Gurevich explained, drawing on the sermons of Berthold of Regensburg, "was a *socially determined* individual." *Ibid.*, 166.

[33] See Chapters Two and Three below.

[34] See Saak, "Saints in Society," 319.

Order's *studium* at Erfurt and then later at Magdeburg, will receive special attention in the story to be told.[35]

Yet Jordan is by no means the only late medieval Augustinian author who has been virtually ignored by modern scholarship. To understand Augustinian theology in the later Middle Ages, scholars must return to the numerous texts of the tradition that have never been edited. Even given the advances made in the past thirty years, we still know relatively little.[36] Consequently, the breadth and depth of the Augustinians' influence on late medieval culture have been missed, a contribution so evident from their extant works, most of which are still awaiting readers, interpreters, and editors. As we will see, the religious world of the late medieval Augustinians was one integrated with society at large. The Augustinians were writing in confrontation with and in response to the pastoral challenges they met in their social world. The religious ideas of society, which were inseparable from political and economic tensions and turmoil, needed to be shaped and formed in keeping with Church doctrine. In addition to philosophy and theology, the basis for molding and (in)forming social life was the production and inculcation of catechetical literature.

The intensified enterprise to indoctrinate society with the fundamental precepts of Christianity stemmed from the social platforms and preaching campaigns of various religious groups, yielding a concurrent upsurge in devotion. Late medieval Passion devotion, most often labeled as "Franciscan" or "Carthusian" spirituality, was central to the Augustinian pastoral program. In this context, the catechetical nature of works on Christ's Passion is brought to the fore.[37] How the Passion of Christ was read in the later Middle Ages determined Christian identity, which went hand in hand with an increasing demonization of the Jews.[38] The hermeneutic operative in late medieval Passion discourse was created by religious ideologies, which included both religion-specific theologies, and the more general catechetical endeavor to shape lay piety. The analysis of the

---

[35] For a biographical and historiographical overview of Jordan's life and works, see E.L. Saak, *Religio Augustini. Jordan of Quedlinburg and the Augustinian Tradition in Late Medieval Germany*, Unpublished Ph.D. dissertation, University of Arizona, 1993, 13–41.
[36] See Saak, *Religio Augustini*, 82–84.
[37] See Chapter Five below.
[38] See Miri Rubin, *Gentile Tales. The Narrative Assault on Late Medieval Jews* (Yale, 1999).

catechetical nature of late medieval Passion texts places the relationship between Christ's Passion, the demonization of the Jews, and the theology of the Christian pastoral mission in new light. Personal, individualized Passion devotion cannot be separated from the clerical catechetical program. Rather than amorphous examples of a general, late medieval piety, catechetical works often arose from specific, programmatic theologies. This was certainly the case for Jordan of Quedlinburg's *Meditationes de Passione Christi*, one of the most widely disseminated works on the Passion in the later Middle Ages.[39]

The Augustinian catechetical endeavor, however, was grounded not only in the recognized need to instill orthodoxy; it also had its source in the Order's religious life, its distinctive spirituality and theology, which were central to the Augustinian platform. By the mid-fourteenth century, the Order had effected an institutionalization of Augustine's religion in its educational program, with the lectorate as its core. The theology of the lectorate, moreover, was unabridgedly Augustinian.[40] The theology taught in the Order's *studia* was a fundamental component of the Order's social mission. Yet to function as the spiritual and religious catalyst for society, Augustine's hermits needed a clear understanding of their own religious heritage, which served as the source of their religious life; they needed to recognize how and why they were a unique religious group. In other words, to fulfill their religious and social mission, the Augustinians first had to understand the meaning, goal, and purpose of their own religion.

In charting the Augustinian platform in late medieval and early modern Europe, we will see throughout the struggle inherent between the defining of the Order's identity, and its enforcement. This is not a story of heroes and heretics, of regulators and rebels, though it is that too in part: it is a story of striving to live up to the ideals of following in the footsteps of Augustine, even when that entailed deviation from the institutionalized Order. From the political battles between Pope Boniface VIII and King Philip IV of France, to those of Pope John XXII and Louis of Bavaria; from the Great Schism, to the birth of the Augustinian Observance, and finally to Luther's Wittenberg, the Augustinians struggled existentially and corporately in their attempts to be the genuine sons of their father. To polar-

---

[39] See Chapter Five below.
[40] See Chapter Four below.

ize the story between the "good and the bad," the "faithful and lax," the "Observants and Conventuals," or the "Catholics and Protestants," is to side with the rhetoric of one of the factions and to miss the complexity of the platform's matrix. Luther's ponderous existential *Angst* of finding the righteousness of God had been prepared for centuries by the Augustinian endeavor to be a religious, and a true son of Augustine. This was no simple over-scrupulousness of individual conscience, for salvation was at stake—for oneself, for the Church, and for society. From Giles of Rome to Giles of Viterbo, the Order's underlying motivation stemmed from the same religious identity and its multifarious interpretations.[41] Reform, Counter-Reform, and Re-Formation were all various lanes of the Augustinian high way to heaven from the late thirteenth to the mid-sixteenth centuries. Politics and theology, preaching and practice, devotion and deviation were all inseparable facets of following Augustine. "To have one heart and soul in God," was the central precept of the Augustinian Rule. It is, perhaps, one of the greatest paradoxes of history that based on this ideal, and based on this dictum, the hearts and souls of Western Europe became divided irreparably. That too, is part of our story.

For over a century, Augustine's theology has been a recognized factor in the origins of the Reformation. Yet much scholarly conflict and debate has produced no consensus concerning its precise influence.[42] By adopting an interdisciplinary approach that combines perspectives and methods from theology, religious studies, history, literature, and sociology, I have endeavored to return the theology of the Augustinian Order in the later Middle Ages to the historical context of the Order's religion to further our understanding of Augustine's heritage. In so doing, the scope extends beyond the boundaries of describing the ideals of a particular religious group. The analysis of the Augustinians' high way to heaven exposes the artificiality of the walls that have been constructed separating theology from religion and

---

[41] Francis Martin argued: "The paradoxical picture emerges of an Order with its members apparently divided between their traditional allegiance to Rome and on the other hand a strong attraction to Luther... What emerges... is a paradox, not a contradiction. The Catholic and the Protestant reforms were both products of the same movement... Luther began something momentous but he in his turn was the product, one might say the end product, of a much earlier religious process." Martin, *Friar, Reformer*, 76–77.

[42] See Appendix A.1.

society, and official religion from civic religion and popular piety.[43] Moreover, the interpretation of the Augustinian platform here presented contributes to the understanding of religious orders, and of the dynamics of religious groups. Yet above all, the story of the Augustinians' high way to heaven is an indispensable factor for tracing the transition from medieval to early modern culture. For Augustine's religion, theology was essential, politics was inescapable, devotion and spirituality were vital, and the pastoral mission was undeniable, as the ideology of the Augustinian platform transformed the hearts, souls, consciences, and territories of medieval Europe from the ideal of having one heart and soul in God (*cor unum et anima una*) to the religion of the prince determining that of his subjects (*cuius regio, eius religio*). As Augustine's city of God metamorphosed into the city Reformation, the late medieval high way to heaven became a relic of the past. Yet the heart of the matter remains: to live with one heart and soul in God, even if only as a dream, even if only as a dream past and failed, is nevertheless an ideal and heritage that bears remembering. This ideal and heritage, of living truly with one heart and soul in God, stripped of the ideological content of its religious platform, is perhaps worthy of a new harmonization of meaning with reality, whereby in the qualitative time of myth, rather than in the quantitative time that "crushes and kills,"[44] humans can indeed be changed by the holy.

---

[43] In his Introduction to an excellent collection of essays, Nicholas Terpstra wrote: "Religion itself has such a complex range of dimensions and forms that a focus on the formal hierarchy of the Catholic church seems almost quaint, if not peripheral to an understanding of how faith animated local communities." Nicholas Terpstra, "Introduction: The Politics of Ritual Kinship," in *The Politics of Ritual Kinship. Confraternities and Social Order in Early Modern Italy*, ed. Nicholas Terpstra (Cambridge, 2000), 1–8; 3. In some ways I certainly agree, but I would phrase it a bit differently: 'Religion itself has such a complex range of dimensions and forms that an exclusion of the formal hierarchy of the Catholic church seems almost ignorant, if not detrimental to an understanding of how faith animated local communities.'

[44] Marcia Eliade, *Myth and Reality*, trans. Willard R. Trask (New York, 1963), 193.

CHAPTER ONE

POWER POLITICS AND THE EMERGENCE OF THE AUGUSTINIAN PLATFORM: THE MYTH OF CHRISTENDOM

Christendom is a myth, and always has been. It was an idea and an ideal, a mental construct, a hoped for dream. As such, Christendom was perhaps the most powerful myth that has ever been created. One can no longer point to the politico-geographical demarcations of "Christian Europe" in any meaningful way, and the fantasies of a universal empire have done sufficient damage to the consciousness of the West that one can only hope that they will forever remain dead in their graves, existing only as memories reminding of the horrors they had caused. Perhaps no other myth has been responsible for as much bloodshed, for as much cruelty and inhumanity, for as much destruction, for as much evil, as has the myth that is temporally measured by the years of "Our Lord." For the greater part of the two thousand years since the days of Jesus of Nazareth, Christendom was the dominant myth that shaped and determined reality.

Christendom was a myth, even when princes were willing to die for its defense and prelates legitimated the pernicious persecution of its perceived parasites. Yet Christendom was a myth with boundaries and borders for much of its history, built on the backs of peasants, women, Jews, Turks, heretics, witches, deviants, the poor, the devout, and the pious, all of whom were victims of the battle to define and enforce religious obedience in service to the ideal championed by pope and by emperor. All the while Christendom never existed, but the impact of its reality lit the funeral pyres of heretics and sent armies on their paths of destruction. For as long as Christendom persisted, politics and religion could not be distinguished, for Church and State were interdependent if not synonymous, whether as a Church-State, or as a State-Church. As an ideal, as a myth, Christendom was founded on ideas and their defense, on theory and practice, on theology and ideology.[1]

---

[1] For the concept of ideology as employed in this study, see Appendix A.2.

Ideology is knowledge, even if skewed. It forms the basis for processing understandings of reality, and thus points to the fact that knowledge is never pure, even knowledge of the divine. Knowledge is power, and power is politics.[2] And for our story, the story to be told in the pages that follow, politics is power, and power is theology, and theology is a part of ecclesiology. It is not so much that "ideas have legs" as it is that ideas form the blood and the bones of social and political action. And it was the ideas germinated in speculation, meditation, and contemplation that formed the basis of the Augustinian theological imperative to reform Christian society. The Augustinian platform was a political platform; it was a religious platform; it was a theological platform; and it was a platform that was emerging in the early fourteenth century when the myth of Christendom was in danger of disintegration.

I. Popes, Princes, Prelates, and Patres

It was not a good year for Benedict Caetani. Perhaps, though, it came as no surprise. There had, after all, been signs of impending doom already the year before, when news finally reached Rome of the fall of Acre in August of 1291. Moreover, on 18 June 1291 Alfonso of Aragon died. Alfonso had been the key to Benedict having diplomatically brought about the Treaty of Tarascon, establishing peace after ten years of conflict between Aragon, Sicily, and Naples that had begun with the Sicilian Vespers of 30 March 1282. With Alfonso's death, it appeared that all was for naught and one of Benedict's greatest triumphs had overnight been completely dismantled. And now, in August of 1292, the heat of the Roman summer burned stronger than usual, and malaria was running rampant through the streets of the eternal city. Benedict himself was ill, but not from malaria. He left Rome for his home in Anagni, where he would try in peace to recuperate from yet another attack of stones, though his prospects were not looking good. If ever there was a time when Benedict needed to be at the height of his strength, this was

---

[2] *Cf.* Michel Foucault, *Power/Knowledge: Selected Interviews and Other Writings, 1972–1977*, ed. C. Gordon (New York, 1980).

it, for the previous April the year had begun on a continuing ominous note when Pope Nicholas IV died.[3]

It might have offered Benedict a hoped for opportunity, when the Franciscan Pope, Nicholas, gave up the ghost. After all, even with the recent rumblings of misfortune, Benedict had reasons to be positive. Two years earlier, in 1290, Benedict had silenced the notoriously verbose theologians of the University of Paris, putting the secular masters in their place in defending the rights and privileges of the mendicants.[4] Then came the triumph of Tarascon in February of 1291, and shortly thereafter, during the Easter elections, Benedict's brother Roffred become a Roman senator. By October of the same year, Benedict himself had been named cardinal by Pope Nicholas.[5] Perhaps his career would soar even higher with the papal vacancy. Benedict was certainly an ambitious sort. But the continued political struggles within the College of Cardinals, and in Rome in general, between the Orsini and the Colonna come to the fore in that summer of 1292 and Benedict was in any case out of the immediate fray, resting in Anagni. He had to find ways to further the cause of his own family, the Caetani, and something had to be done about finding a new pope. Yet ill health, recent defeats, and continuing power struggles were on Benedict's mind while at his country home. 1292 was not going to go down as one of his stellar years. His fortunes, however, were soon to change, and were to change for the better, or—for the worse.

It was not a good year for Pope Boniface VIII. During his eight years in office since his election on Christmas Eve of 1294 after the abdication of Celestine V, when Benedict Caetani assumed the name of Boniface, he had faced trials and tribulations more than he cared to remember. Aragon, Naples, England, Hungary, Genoa, Florence, the Empire, Scotland, and the Knights Templars, had all given Boniface thorns in his side, but none stung as sharply, or penetrated as deeply as the thorn that was France. Philip IV, King of France, Philip the Fair, *Philippe le Bel, Philipp der Schöne*, was for Boniface

---

[3] See the still unparalleled biography of T.S.R. Boase, *Boniface VIII* (London, 1933), 3–33.
[4] Boase, *Boniface VIII*, 20–22; for the account of Benedict's mission to Paris, see Heinrich Finke, *Aus den Tagen Bonifaz VIII. Funde und Forschungen* (Münster, 1902), 9–24, Quellen, iii–vii.
[5] Boase, *Boniface VIII*, 25–26.

more bastard than beauty.[6] The right to tax ecclesiastical incomes had ignited the controversy, but even though money was certainly at issue, the larger question was who had control of the Church in France, the king, or the pope? What was, after all, the nature of princely sovereignty and on what law was it based, natural law, Roman law, divine law? And where and how did the King of France fit in? Lawyers had been debating such questions for some time,[7] but the theoretical discussions became ideological artillery in the political battles that began in earnest when Boniface issued his Bull *Clericis laicos*, promulgated on 24 February 1296.[8] Moreover, during the course of the controversy it became clear that Boniface had greater, more dangerous, and more pernicious adversaries than even the French: the Colonna of Rome, among whom were a number of cardinals who began plotting with the French against Boniface, resenting the rise of his family, the Caetani, at their expense.[9] And now, in the autumn of 1302, Boniface wanted to settle matters once and for all. He had been fortunate that just as it seemed his enemies were to triumph and Philip IV would win the day, the Flemish revolted against French incursions, and did so most successfully. Moreover, the French Chancellor, Peter Flotte, who had done so much damage to Boniface, even having circulated widely within France a forged version of his Bull *Ausculta fili*, lay dead on the battle field.[10] Boniface had called for a council to meet in Rome to deal with the problems. It opened on 30 October 1302, with thirty-six of the seventy-eight French bishops in attendance, including Giles, Archbishop of Bourges, who had long been in residence at Rome and was a faithful supporter of Boniface. The council condemned Flotte and his memory, depriving his family of all ecclesiastical privileges, but refrained from attacking Philip IV directly. By mid-November it disbanded, without having achieved all that much.

---

[6] In addition to Boase, see Jean Rivière, *Le Problème de l'Église et de l'État au Temps de Philippe le Bel. Étude de Théologie positive* (Paris, 1926); Scholz, *Die Publizistik*.

[7] Kenneth Pennington, *The Prince and the Law, 1200–1600. Sovereignty and Rights in the Western Legal Tradition* (Berkeley, 1993), esp. 38–164.

[8] Scholz, *Die Publizistik*, 4–7; Boase, *Boniface VIII*, 131–156.

[9] Boase, *Boniface VIII*, 165, and *passim*.

[10] *Ibid.*, 301–312; and Tilmann Schmidt, *Der Bonifaz-Prozess. Verfahren der Papstanklage in der Zeit Bonifaz' VIII. und Clemens' V*. Forschungen zur Kirchlichen Rechtsgeschichte und zum Kirchenrecht 19 (Cologne, 1989), 17–54. For Flotte, see Scholz, *Die Publizistik*, 355–363.

Boniface had to take matters into his own hands and sat down to write his response to all the issues he was facing. He must have been glad to have on his desk a treatise recently composed and sent to him by his good friend, the Archbishop of Bourges, on ecclesiastical power. With repose, even when his enemies on all sides were plotting as fiercely as ever, Boniface took up his pen and began: *Unam sanctam ecclesiam catholicam*...

A. *The Power of Privilege*

It was a good year for Frater Giles of Rome. On 4 January 1292, three months before the death of Pope Nicholas and seven months before Benedict Caetani retired to Anagni, Giles had been elected prior general of his Order, the Order of Hermits of St. Augustine. Giles was a renowned theologian and already in May of 1287 at the Order's General Chapter meeting in Florence, Giles' works were made the standard for the entire Order. Every lector and student of the Order was to follow Giles' teachings, opinions, positions, and his written works, including those yet to be written, in order to be illumined themselves, to instruct others, and to be assiduous defenders of the faith.[11] Three years later, when Benedict Caetani came to Paris to deal with the disputes between the secular and the mendicant theologians, he called on Giles, together with the Franciscan John of Murro, to remove the impudent Henry of Ghent from office, letting the Parisian masters know very clearly that "before the Roman Curia would abolish the privileges of the mendicants, it would bring the University of Paris to its knees."[12] Benedict and Giles would at least from that point on remain close, and in April of 1295, just a little over two months after Benedict was elected as Pope Boniface VIII, Boniface appointed Giles to the archbishopric of Bourges.

---

[11] "Quia venerabilis magister nostri fratris Egidii doctrina mundum universum illustrat, diffinimus et mandamus inviolabiliter observari, ut opiniones, positiones et sententias scriptas et scribendas predicti magistri nostri, omnes ordinis nostri lectores et studentes recipiant eisdem prebentes assensum et eius doctrine omni qua poterunt sollicitudine, ut et ipsi illuminati alios illuminare possint, sint seduli defensores." Esteban, *AAug.* 2 (1908), 275. The scholarship on Giles is extensive, though there is no comprehensive study of his life and works; see E.L. Saak, "Aegidius Romanus," in *Augustine Through the Ages. An Encyclopedia*, ed. Allan D. Fitzgerald, O.S.A. (Grand Rapids, 1999), 14–15, and the literature there cited.

[12] "Unde dominus Benedictus vocans magistrum Johannem de Murro et magistrum Egidium precepit eis, quod predictum magistrum Hinricum ab officio lectionis suspenderent. Quod factum fuit... dixit dominus Benedictus: Vos magistri

Yet when Giles assumed the leadership of his Order in 1292 he was not only a highly respected theologian and friend of Cardinal Caetani. He was also very well connected with the King of France. Philip III had asked Giles to care for the education of his son and heir. Giles readily took to the task, and composed for Prince Philip a treatise on princely rule, *De regimine principum*, completed before 1285, when upon the death of his father, Prince Philip became King Philip IV at age seventeen.[13] Giles' *De regimine principum* became "one of the most widely spread books of the Middle Ages,"[14] translated into French, Italian, Spanish, Catalonian, Portuguese, English, Low German, and even into Hebrew.[15] The king's favor for Giles was explicit when in 1293 Philip transferred the cloister of Santa Maria de Pontoise, a few kilometers northwest of Paris, from the Brothers of the Sack to the Augustinian Hermits, and then in 1294 made it possible for the Augustinians to purchase land in Paris for their general house of studies and did so "on account of our greatest favor for our beloved Frater Giles of Rome, professor of theology, member of our household, and of the same Order of Hermits of St. Augustine."[16] Soon, however, Giles would find himself caught in the middle of the vicious conflict between his two great beneficiaries, Philip IV and Boniface VIII. He could no longer serve two lords. He was already archbishop of Bourges when the problems began and he knew where his primary loyalties lay, as well as those of his Order. Giles sided with Boniface, becoming his staunchest supporter. Nevertheless, in 1292, Giles still enjoyed the closest of ties with both the royal household and the Church hierarchy. He was in a posi-

---

Parisienses, stultam fecistis et facitis doctrinam scientie vestre, turbantes orbem terrarum, quod nullo modo faceretis, si sciretis statum universalis ecclesie. Sedetis in cathedris et putatis, quod vestris rationibus regatur Christus... Vere dico vobis: antequam curia Romana a dictis fratribus hoc privilegium ammoveret, potius studium Parisiense confunderet." Finke, *Aus den Tagen*, Quellen, vi–vii.

[13] Scholz, *Die Publizistik*, 37–38, 43–44.
[14] "... eines der verbreitesten Bücher des Mittelalters..." *Ibid.*, 38.
[15] *Ibid.*, 44.
[16] "ob favorem potissimum dilecti et familiaris nostri fratris Egidii Romani eiusdem ordinis, sacre pagine professoris." *Chartularium Universitatis Parisiensis*, II. No. 583, as cited by Scholz, *Die Publizistik*, 38, n. 23. Scholz claimed that Philip gave the piece of land to the Augustinians as a gift. Gutiérrez, however, states that Philip gave the Order permission to purchase the land, as well as having mentioned the transfer of Santa Maria de Pontoise to the Augustinians, which Scholz did not; Gutiérrez, *Geschichte des Augustinerordens*, v. 1/1: *Die Augustiner im Mittelalter, 1256–1356* (Würzburg, 1985), 89.

tion politically as well as theologically to lead his Order as none other could, and that he did.

We do not know much about the details of Giles' generalate, which lasted for only three years. His register during his time as prior general has not survived. Yet Giles' leadership of the Order extended beyond his time in office. He was the dominant and most influential member of the Order until his death in 1316. And already in 1292, Giles set the Order on a path that it would follow for the next two centuries.

Shortly after his election as prior general, Giles sent a circular letter to all the provincial priors of the Order.[17] The overarching theme was the need to establish, effect, and enforce regular observance (*observantia regularis*),[18] and the provincial priors were the key. They were the ones who were to visit every house of their province to make sure the stipulations of the Order's *Rule* and *Constitutions* were being followed, the *Constitutions* that had just two years previously been ratified at the General Chapter at Regensburg (1290). On their visitations, the provincial priors were to confirm that correct procedure was being followed regarding meals and that the divine office was properly celebrated. Any misuse found was forcefully to be corrected.[19] The provincial priors themselves were to follow such regulations above all, for otherwise regular observance would never be achieved. Furthermore, the provincial priors were responsible for ensuring that such stipulations were upheld by the local priors and by the Order's lectors, for they too served as examples for the

[17] *AAug.* 4 (1911), 202–204.

[18] "Inter cetera que pulcritudinem et decorem religionibus largiuntur et in agro dominico atque in vinea Domini Sabbaoth fructus ubique germinante producunt, et que in dei ecclesia ordinibus statum tribuunt, ac etiam firmitatem, potissime esse cernuntur observantia regularis, discipline rigor, studii fervor, vite munditia, pax et concordia absque acceptione aliqua personarum." *AAug.* 4 (1911), 202.

[19] "In primis ergo precipimus et mandamus quod vos, provincialis, cum omni diligentia observetis que in Constitutionibus continentur et eadem faciatis sollicite ab aliis fratribus in vestra provincia observari, et cum per provinciam pergitis, non eques, sed pedes incedere studeatis. Quando autem ad loca ordinis perveneritis, servetis refectorium, intretis oratorium ad horas diurnas et nocturnas, sicut in Constitutionibus continetur; insolentes et male se gerentes, cuiuscumque et qualiscumque conditionis existant, omni timore postposito viriliter corrigatis, habendo dictos pre oculis, zelum ordinis et rigorem iustitie absque omni partialitate et sine acceptatione persone; priores autem conventuales, ut teneant communitatem, frequentent refectorium, continuent oratorium penitus obstringatis, contra autem facientes, nisi moniti resipiscant, a prioratus officio absolvatis." *AAug.* 4 (1911), 202.

common brothers.[20] Every house of the Order was to have a copy of the *Constitutions*, which were to be read frequently in the refectory and in chapter, so that no one could claim ignorance as an excuse for misconduct.[21] Schools were also to be maintained and established. Schools for grammar were mandatory, and Giles exhorted the provincial priors to set up schools for theology as well, since theology schools, together with regular observance, were the means for the Order to grow in humility and to rise in honor.[22] Furthermore, diligent efforts were to be made both to recruit new, worthy members, and to find suitable places for establishing new houses.[23]

Giles' letter is not elaborate and he did not go into great detail. Yet we see here already the seeds of what would become the Augustinian platform: stress on the need for regular observance in strictly following the *Constitutions*, focusing especially on the common life, a noted emphasis on study, combined with a hierarchical organizational structure, and a concerted campaign for growth, all placed under the leadership and directives of the prior general.[24] This was

---

[20] "Nunquam etiam in vestra provincia regulares observantie tenebuntur, nisi vos, provincialis, observetis eas et eas faciatis a prioribus, et etiam lectoribus quasi a maioribus observari iuxta modum in Constitutionibus pretaxatum, ut ex hoc minores fratres ad observandum eorum moveantur exemplo; Lectores quidem si suas non continuent lectiones, sicut in Constitutionibus est expressum, debita provisione priventur." *AAug.* 4 (1911), 203. On the role of the lectors, see Chapter Four below.

[21] "In quolibet etiam loco vestre provincie Constitutiones Ordinis habeantur, quam citius fieri poterit bono modo, et ipsas Constitutiones novas, vel saltem veteres, quamdiu non habent novas, in capitulo et in refectori legi crebro crebrium procuretis, ut nullus, quia ignoratum, se valeat excusare." *AAug.* 4 (1911), 203. It is unclear to what Giles was referring by the *Constitutiones veteres*; the editor notes: "Textus Constitutionum, quas Aegidius appellat veteres, editus non est; fortasse eum refert Codex Verod. 41, qui certe hac in re speciale studium meretur." It could be, however, that Giles was referring to earlier versions of the Regensburg *Constitutions*, which had already been proposed at the General Chapter of Orvieto in 1284; see Gutiérrez, *Geschichte*, 1/1, 62ff.

[22] "Sane gramaticales scole in vestra provincia teneantur et durent per totum annum, sicut de aliis studiis in Constitutionibus declaratur. Ipsi etiam studia theologie toto vestro conamine manuteneatis ac etiam foveatis, quia per ea, simul cum observantia regulari, oportet nostrum ordinem in humilitate crescere ac etiam exaltari." *AAug.* 4 (1911), 203. See Chapter Four below regarding the various levels of schools within the Order.

[23] "Ad hec detis et dari faciatis pro viribus omnem operam cum effectu, ut boni novitii possint in vestra provincia recipi, recepti, religiose tractari, informari, morum modestia et studii disciplina. In bonis siquidem civitatibus atque burgis, ubi non sunt fratres nostri, loca nobis apta capere studeatis, et in locis que habetis priores bonos preficere atque sanctos." *AAug.* 4 (1911), 203.

[24] "... decernimus ad singulos provinciales nostri ordinis, seu ad eius vicarios,

a conscious program, designed to strengthen the Order and give it a firm foundation. Though not extensive or unique, at least it was a beginning.

When Giles assumed his Order's highest office, the Order had only been in existence for thirty-six years. It was still a new Order, struggling to find its place and still fighting for its legitimacy. The Augustinians' two biggest competitors, the Franciscans and the Dominicans, were already well established. They had received papal confirmation from Pope Innocent III, and by the end of the thirteenth century had not only received numerous privileges, but had also created their own foundational myths upon which they constructed their respective corporate identities as the Order of Friars Minor and the Order of Preachers. Moreover, they had developed institutional structures for perpetuating those identities, and had achieved a secure place in the Church and society.[25] The Augustinians lagged behind. Giles' programmatic letter for establishing a unified observance throughout his Order enunciates little that distinguishes the Augustinians from competing religious organizations. The Augustinian hermits had not developed their own identity, nor had they found their own mythic origins that would enable them to differentiate themselves from all other religious, giving them a unique place and role in the religious culture of their world. That would come, but it was not a factor for Giles in 1292. Giles was general when the Order was still in a stage of building itself from the ground up and this Giles knew very well. He sent out his letter with the stated purpose that "our entire desire and effort most of all concerns how our religion might shine forth, bear fruit, grow, and achieve a firm place in God's

---

presentis pagine seriem destinare, eisdem in virtute sancte obedientie districte mandamus, quatenus omnes et singulos articulos hic contentos ipsi in seipsis quantum sinit humana fragilitas, inviolabiliter servent et alios sibi subiectos faciant observare; et, quod absit, si circa hic iniuncta relatione veridica ad aures nostras de vestra provincia defectus notabiles pervenirent, ad suspensionem vestri officii et ad alias graves penas tarditate submota procedere niteremur." *AAug.* 4 (1911), 202.

[25] For the Dominicans, see Markus Schürer, "Die Dominikaner und das Problem der *generationes venturae*. Zu Traditionsbildung und -vermittlung in der Frühphase der Institutionalisierung des Predigerordens," in *Die Bettelorden im Aufbau*, 169–214; for the Franciscans, Achim Wesjohann, "*Simplicitas* als franziskanisches Ideal und der Prozeß der Institutionalisierung des Minoritenordens," in *Die Bettelorden im Aufbau*, 107–168; and for both see also Thomas Füser, "Vom *exemplum Christi* über das *exemplum sanctorum* zum 'Jedermannsbeispiel'. Überlegungen zur Normativität exemplarischer Verhaltensmuster im institutionellen Gefüge der Bettelorden des 13. Jahrhunderts," in *Die Bettelorden im Aufbau*, 27–105.

church."[26] The Order had been the creation of the pope, and if the Order was to flourish, it needed continued papal support to carve for itself its own unique niche in the ecclesiastical structure. Giles knew the lay of the land. When conflict arose between Philip IV and Boniface VIII, Giles, who had been appointed as archbishop of Bourges by Boniface, and yet as such was one of Philip's highest ranking ecclesiastical dignitaries,[27] continued to lead his Order in the direction that he saw was required. The Order could not survive without the favor of the pope. Defending the pope became synonymous with the cause of the Order, and Giles continued to lead.

In 1297 Giles began his unmitigated support for Boniface with his treatise *De renuntiatione papae*.[28] Boniface had issued *Clericis laicos* the previous year and the counterattack was not long in coming. In May through June of 1297, Boniface's greatest enemies, the Colonna, issued three documents denying the very legitimacy of Boniface's papacy.[29] Celestine V, not Boniface, was the true pope.[30] The saintly Franciscan Peter Marone had been elected on 5 July 1294, which finally ended the papal vacancy after the death of Nicholas IV. Yet Celestine V was not the sort of man who was suited to the hardball politics required of Christ's vicars, and resigned the papacy on 13 December, after only five months in office.[31] According to the Colonna, however, Celestine had been coerced into resigning by Benedict Caetani, who was calling himself pope. Moreover, the pope was pope by divine election and by divine law, and thus the papacy was not the type of office from which one could resign.[32] Consequently,

---

[26] "... totus noster animus totusque conatus ad id potissime tendat, ut nostra religio decore fulgeat, fructum faciat, augmentum suscipiat et in dei ecclesia habeat firmum statum." *AAug.* 4 (1911), 202.

[27] It is possible that Giles was appointed to Bourges at the express wish of Philip, and he certainly had Philip's approval; Scholz, *Die Publizistik*, 37.

[28] For discussions of *De renuntiatione*, see Finke, *Aus den Tagen*, 71–76; Scholz, *Die Publizistik*, 44; and Boase, *Boniface VIII*, 175; for a treatment of the conflict within the context of political theory and its development, including Giles, see Miethke, *De Potestate Papae*, 45–82.

[29] Heinrich Denifle, "Die Denkschriften der Colonna gegen Bonifaz VIII. und der Cardinäle gegen die Colonna," in *Archiv für Literatur -und Kirchengeschichte des Mittelalters*, ed. Heinrich Denifle and Franz Ehrle, vol. 5 (Freiburg im Breisgau, 1889), 493–529. The three documents of the Colonna are found on pages 509–515; 515–518; and 519–524, with the response of the Cardinals found on pages 524–529.

[30] *Ibid.*, 515–516.

[31] See Boase, *Boniface VIII*, 29–51.

[32] See, for example, Denifle, "Denkschriften," 511.

Boniface's attempts to exert his authority were clear evidence of his usurpation and tyranny and held no force whatsoever.

A reply from Boniface was certainly needed. This came in two forms: the first, was a formal response signed by seventeen cardinals that supported Boniface and his legitimacy;[33] the second, was Giles' treatise *De renuntiatione papae*, which provided the theoretical foundations of the papal position. On 8 April of the following year, 1298, in his Bull *Sacrae religionis merita*, Boniface granted the privilege to the OESA to elect their own prior general based on his favor for the Order;[34] on 5 May 1298, Boniface issued his Bull *Tenerem cuiusdam constitutionem*, which added the Augustinian Hermits and the Carmelites to the exemption granted to the Franciscans and Dominicans regarding the prohibition against the multiplication of religious Orders that was issued by Pope Gregory X at the Second Council of Lyon in 1274;[35] on 21 January 1299 Boniface issued *Sacer ordo vester*, which placed the Augustinian Hermits, his "beloved sons in the Lord," under his direct protection and authority.[36] Giles knew what he was doing.

Yet even before *Clericis laicos* and Giles' *De renuntiatione papae*, Boniface had already begun bestowing privileges on the OESA. Three years after Giles sent his letter outlining the Order's program to all the provincial priors, and only two months before Boniface appointed Giles to the archbishopric of Bourges, Boniface issued his Bull *Ad consequendam gloriam* on 19 February 1295. Giles had stated that his concern was above all to make a place for the Augustinians, and with Boniface's *Ad consequendam* the Order was beginning to make headway. At issue was the competition between the Augustinians and other religious Orders. Rivalry, jealousy, and disputes over property and privileges were at issue, frequent reports of which, Boniface affirmed, were most distressing. Other Orders were not playing fair, and were building houses and churches very near those of the Augustinians, thus encroaching upon the Augustinians' territory. Boniface, therefore, prohibited any religious Order, including the Franciscans, the Dominicans, and the Carmelites, from building churches, oratories, monasteries, or any other buildings within 140

---

[33] *Ibid.*, 524–529.
[34] Appendix B.2.
[35] Appendix B.3.
[36] Appendix B.4.

rods of an Augustinian Church.[37] That such was indeed going on seems to be indicated by Boniface's letter to the archdeacon of Agen of 14 March 1299, in which Boniface informed the archdeacon that he, Boniface, had sent Cardinal John of Saints Marcellinus and Peter to hear the case between the Augustinians and the Franciscans in Agen, the latter of which, the Augustinians had asserted, were planning on building a monastery within the 140 rod limit of the Augustinian oratory. Boniface explained that Cardinal John had summoned the Franciscans to appear before him in public for the case to be heard, as was custom, but that the Franciscans were stalling and the case could not proceed. Therefore Boniface instructed the archdeacon to subpoena the Franciscans to appear for arbitration within a two month period, and to write back to Boniface telling him of the date and terms.[38] Boniface addressed the same problem once again two years later in his Bull *Exhibita nuper nobis* of 15 January 1301. The dispute was likewise between the Augustinians and the Franciscans, but this time in Quedlinburg, in the Augustinian province of Saxony-Thuringia. The controversy, however, had already been going on for years. In 1295 the Augustinians had built a monastery in Quedlinburg on the northwest bank of the river Bode in the new settlement (*castro novo*) in the diocese of Halberstadt. The Franciscans already had a house on the opposite bank, in the old settlement (*castro antiquo*) under the jurisdiction of Halle, and claimed that the Augustinian house had been built within the 140 rod limit surrounding their property, a privilege that they too had supposedly been granted (*pretextu privilegii eis ab apostolica sede concessi*), and thus they tried to demolish the new Augustinian edifice, whereupon, the Augustinians appealed to Boniface. Boniface admitted the 140 rod limit, but, since the Augustinian house was located in a separate political jurisdiction from that of the Franciscan, and since the Bode flowed between the two, the geographical constraints did not apply. Consequently, Boniface granted permission for the Augustinians to

---

[37] Appendix B.1. It is unclear precisely what a rod (*canna*) was. The *OED* gives two lengths: between 5 and 10 feet; or, sixteen and one half feet; *The Oxford English Dictionary*, prepared by J.A. Simpson and E.S.C. Weiner, 2nd Edition (Oxford, 1989), vol. 14, 28C, II.6a and II.7a. Taking the larger estimation as the basis, and converting feet to meters, Boniface granted the OESA a "free area" of 704.238 meters from an Augustinian church, or approximately seven-tenths of a kilometer, or, converting kilometers to miles, a little less than a half mile (.437 mile).

[38] Appendix B.5.

remain in their present location, and prohibited any further interference.[39] It was good to have a pope on one's side. And that the Augustinians did, and on 16 January 1303 Boniface granted the Hermits their most extensive privileges yet in his Bull *Inter sollicitudines nostras*.

Boniface's Bull *Inter sollicitudines* had not come unprepared. The Augustinians had by 1303 succeeded in gaining protection and support from the papacy over-against incursions from any other religious Order, and especially against the Franciscans. Boniface had already exempted the Augustinians from the ban on new religious Orders of the Second Council of Lyon, and had taken the Order under his own protection. And now, in 1303, it was time to solidify the rights and privileges of the OESA. Giles' program for the Order as enunciated in his circular letter of 1292 had come to fruition. Giles had stated that regular observance and theological studies were the means for the Order to grow and prosper, and these two factors were the ones Boniface explicitly mentioned as reasons for granting the privileges he did. According to Boniface, the OESA abounded with learned priests and preachers, who were bearing great fruit for the Church, based as much on the quality of their lives as on their knowledge. Thus Boniface granted the Order the rights and privileges of preaching, hearing confessions, absolving sinners, administering penance, and of burying the faithful in their cemeteries. Moreover, he explicitly forbade any other religious from any Order, as well as secular priests, from burying parishioners in an Augustinian Church without the express consent of the Order. He further bestowed the Augustinians with the rights and privileges that had been granted to the Franciscans and Dominicans.[40] By 1303, the Augustinians had achieved a legal basis equal to that of their

---

[39] Appendix B.6; cf. Kunzelmann, *Geschichte*, 1: 223–224.
[40] Appendix B.7. Boniface, however, also had his realistic side. On 13 February 1302 a group of Augustinians were present at a public consistory, protesting the actions of the Franciscan Bishop of Ancona, Nicholas, who apparently had been trying to reform the observance of the Augustinians, which he found lacking. The report relates: "XVII kal. Marcii fuit publicum consistorium et proposuerunt fratres sancti Augustini contra episcopum Anconetanum, quia ceperat eos et vituperaverat verbo et facto, et papa dixit: Multi ribaldi et vili homines recipiuntur in ordinibus. Contraria audivimus de illo vestro priore et adhuc non intelleximus, quod fecerit aliquam correctionem sed bene comedit et bibit et devorat. Et tu, Francisce [i.e., the Cardinal Deacon, Francis Caetani], dixit nepoti, scribas illi episcopo, quod bene eos corrigat..." The text thereafter is missing; Finke, *Aus den Tagen*, Quellen, xli.

two largest competitors, and were under the special protection of the pope. Giles' program had been most successful indeed, and Boniface had gained much as well. Not only had Giles provided the theoretical defense of the legitimacy of Boniface's election in his treatise *De renuntiatione papae*, but a year before Boniface issued *Inter sollicitudines*, Giles had dedicated and sent to Boniface his treatise *De ecclesiastica potestate*, which established the hierocratic papal political position on firmer theoretical ground than ever before. This, moreover, was a treatise of which Boniface made good use. Giles' *De ecclesiastica potestate* was the major source for Boniface's most famous Bull, issued in November of 1302, *Unam sanctam*.[41]

B. *One Holy, Catholic, and Apostolic Church*

It would be easy to view the events transpiring during the decade 1292 to 1302 as a process of political *quid pro quo* between Boniface and the Augustinians. And that it was. Giles wrote in defense of the papal position, and Boniface in return increasingly secured the rights and privileges of the OESA. Moreover, between the winter of 1301 and the spring of 1302, James of Viterbo had likewise composed a work espousing in no uncertain terms the primacy of the see of St. Peter. His *De regimine christiano* has been called the first treatise on the Church as such, and was dedicated to Boniface.[42] Boniface had reason to praise the Augustinians' learning and way of life, and on 3 September 1302 Boniface appointed James as archbishop of Benevento, though on 12 December, at the request of King Charles II, Boniface transferred James to the archbishopric of Naples.

Yet more was going on than mutual defense and support. Though the Augustinians were by no means the only authors who were espousing hierocratic theory—the names of such theologians as the Franciscan Alvarus Pelagius, the Domincan Peter de la Palu, and Henry of Cremona readily come to mind—they were the ones who developed the papal political theory to its highest degree in

---

[41] For an analysis of the textual parallels between *Unam Sanctam* and Giles' *De ecclesiastica potestate*, see Rivière, *Le Problème de l'Église*, 394–404; Scholz, *Die Publistik*, 126–129. For *Unam sanctam*, see Denzinger *Ench.* nrs. 870–875 (384–387).

[42] H.-X. Arquillière, *Le plus ancien traité de l'église, Jacques de Viterbe, De Regimine Christiano (1301–1302)* (Paris, 1926); see also Rivière, *Le Problème de l'Église*, 228–251; Scholz, *Die Publizistik*, 131–152; and Antony Black, *Political Thought in Europe, 1250–1450* (Cambridge, 1992), 49–54.

composing its classic expressions. Three of the four authors Brian Tierney mentioned as representatives of "the extreme papalists" were Augustinians; in addition to Henry of Cremona, Tierney lists Giles of Rome, James of Viterbo, and Augustinus of Ancona, without noting that these were all Augustinian friars.[43] It is tempting to pass over that fact and to approach the political theory of the late thirteenth and early fourteenth centuries as falling roughly into three general camps: the hierocrats, those arguing for a limited papal monarchy, and the supporters of lay supremacy,[44] and this in a time when, as Michael Wilks has argued, "[t]he less that the popes could achieve in the world of fact, the more far reaching were the claims of their supporters, who, relieved of the necessity for maintaining some sort of relationship between theory and practice, were able to give full expression to that juristic desideratum, the omnicompetent sovereign."[45] Divorced from reality, authors such as Giles can then be treated purely on the level of ideas, and his *De ecclesiastica potestate* can be reduced to an abstract theoretical treatise that combined the traditional Gelasian theory with Pseudo-Dionysian hierarchy and the corporate ideals of John of Salisbury, that then, drawing on Hugh of St. Victor and with Thomistic influence, was a restatement of traditional Augustinian political theory.[46] On one level, a level "relieved of the necessity for maintaining some sort of relationship between theory and practice," such an analysis is both illuminating and not that far from the truth. For the history of political thought, when the "relationship between theory and practice" can be sidestepped in charting the grand march of abstract, disembodied ideas, Giles' treatise stands as "probably the first complete teaching of Absolutism,"[47] and as such merits our attention. Yet Giles' political

---

[43] Brian Tierney, *Origins of Papal Infallibility, 1150–1350. A Study on the Concepts of Infallibility, Sovereignty and Tradition in the Middle Ages*, SHCT 6 (Leiden, 1972), 6; *cf.* Jürgen Miethke, "Die Rolle der Bettelorden im Umbruch der politischen Theorie an der Wende zum 14. Jahrhundert," in *Stellung und Wirksamkeit der Bettelorden in der städtischen Gesellschaft*, ed. Kaspar Elm, Berliner Historische Studien 3/Ordensstudien 2 (Berlin, 1981), 119–153; and *idem, De Potestate Papae*, 94–108, where Miethke focuses explicitly on the Augustinians, though still treating them as individual authors rather than as working within the context of their Order's ideals.

[44] This is fundamentally the approach taken by Michael Wilks, *The Problem of Sovereignty*.

[45] Wilks, *The Problem of Sovereignty*, 151.

[46] Aeg.Rom. *De eccl.pot.*, ix–x.

[47] "Es ist wohl die erste vollständige Lehre des Absolutismus, die Aegidius geschrieben hat." *Ibid.*, xiv.

sensitivities were anything but naïve; he was no "arm-chair" political theorist. Giles' entire concern, as he explicitly informed his Order, was to provide for the Order's growth and prosperity, creating a firm place for it in God's church. In doing so, Giles, together with James of Viterbo and, as we will see shortly, Augustinus of Ancona, was constructing a place for his Order within the Church by simultaneously constructing the theory of the Church. Whereas statements of papal supremacy had developed since the time of Gregory VII's *Dictatus Papae*, Giles and his confreres were no mere papal publicists. Giles did not write a work *De potestate papae*, but *De ecclesiastica potestate*, and James of Viterbo, *De regimine christiano*, and Augustinus of Ancona, *Summa de potestate ecclesiastica*. In order to ensure their Order a firm status within the Church, the Augustinians first had to develop a doctrine of the Church. They were in no way "relieved from the relationship between theory and practice," even if such a disjunction was a historical fact. Boniface VIII could no more make his claims reality in the political battle with Philip IV than could twenty years later Pope John XXII in his conflict with the Emperor Louis of Bavaria. Yet the same was true for the other side as well. Both Philip IV and Louis of Bavaria had their theorists too: Pierre Dubois and William Nogaret, Marsilius of Padua and William of Ockham, whose political constructs formed the basis for their princely patrons' political platforms, which remained as unfulfilled as did those of the popes. Yet for the early fourteenth century, political theory was an essential part of political practice, as the war of words was conducted as indispensable support for the troops in the field, whether in Paris and Flanders, or in Milan and Rome. And in the midst of it all, a religious Order was creating itself as it was developing its own identity and ideals by politically maneuvering on the playing field of power politics between pope and prince in order to establish and secure its own existence, which was indissolubly linked with that of the Church itself. In the early fourteenth century, the Augustinian platform was founded upon the doctrine of the Church, which was becoming ecclesiology in the political pursuits of an Order that would come to refer to itself as of the sons of Augustine.

Giles' *De ecclesiastica potestate* is far more than a political treatise espousing papal sovereignty. It is an essay on Christian society. Though Giles dedicated the work to Boniface VIII, Giles' intended audience was every member of Christendom. He opened with a statement of purpose: to teach people from the Gospels what is to be known concerning faith and morals, lest anyone be condemned by their ignorance at the last judgment.[48] He repeated this assertion in chapter twelve of book two to defend what might seem to be needless repetition of material and arguments. The goal of the work was the education of all Christians (*Finis autem huius operis est omnes fideles sive totum populum christianum erudire*), and thus Giles wanted to be sure that he would reach those of varying intellectual capacity. Therefore he was not bothered by the rehashing of his points.[49] Christians, all Christians, must not be ignorant of the essentials concerning faith and morals, for eternal salvation is at stake. Yet faith and morals are finally determined for the Church as a whole by the head of the Church, the supreme pontiff and his fullness of power (*plenitudo potestatis*).[50]

It was a vision of society that Giles enunciated, whereby the reign of God, the reign of Christ, imbued all levels and aspects of temporal life.[51] The pope possessed fullness of power as God's vicar, the embodiment of Christ's heavenly reign on earth. As such, it was not so much the individual pope that was at issue, but the office itself. "For the pope is the same," Giles argued,

> and the Supreme Pontiff is the same, now as in the time of Peter, just as the Roman people is the same now as it was a thousand and more years ago, and the Tiber also is the same Roman river as it was from the beginning. The men who comprise the Roman people are different at different times, for they come and go, yet the Roman people is the same... Thus, the Supreme Pontiff is always the same, even though the man appointed to the office is not always the same. Peter, therefore, had nothing more in the way of power than the Supreme Pontiff has now. And just as the power of the Church was entrusted to Peter inasmuch as the Church was founded upon Christ, and, consequently, power over souls, over bodies and over all the temporal goods which they possess was entrusted to him, since all faithful men are founded upon Christ in their whole selves and in all that is theirs, so also he who is now Supreme Pontiff, since there has been the same Pontiff from the beginning, even though not the same man, is entrusted with the government of all such things. And just as Peter received the government of the Church immediately from Christ, so too he who is now Supreme Pontiff, since the Supreme Pontiff is the same now as

---

[48] Aeg.Rom. *De eccl.pot.* 1,1 (5).
[49] Aeg.Rom. *De eccl.pot.* 2,12 (100–101).
[50] Aeg.Rom. *De eccl.pot.* 1,1 (5–6).
[51] *Cf.* Miethke, "Die Rolle," 147.

then, is known to have received such power immediately from God or from Christ, who was the True God.[52]

Giles' treatise offers nothing less than a comprehensive view of reality, and a way of thinking corresponding to that reality that extends from the throne of God to the seat of Satan. This mode of thought was founded upon a hierarchical construct of being, that dichotomized existence into body/soul, temporal/spiritual, heaven/hell. Such polarizations are not dualistic oppositions. They are hierarchically organized realms of being that exist in tension in human existence, but that cooperate harmoniously within the created divine order. Only when this order is circumvented or undermined by human or diabolical corruption does the opposition make itself apparent. The goal of Giles' treatise was to make known this structure and to explicate its implications so that harmony might prevail, the harmony of divine order, righteousness, and justice.

The body/soul hierarchy is one of the foundational principles of Giles' work. God created humans as composites of body and soul, or spirit and flesh. There is a threefold union of body and soul. The first regards the composite nature of human beings, whereby the individual is one, but is so comprised of both physical and spiritual elements. The second union then is the proper relationship between body and soul, whereby the body is subordinated to the soul, and

---

[52] "Idem est enim nunc papa et idem summus pontifex qui fuit a tempore Petri, sicut idem est populus Romanus nunc, qui fuit iam sunt plus quam mille anni; et eciam idem est Tiberis, et idem Romanus fluvius, qui fuit a principio. Homines enim sunt alii et alii, quia hii fluunt et refluunt, qui constituunt Romanum populum, attamen idem est Romanus populus... Sic semper est idem summus pontifex, licet non semper sit idem homo in huiusmodi officio constitutus. Non ergo plus habuit de potestate Petrus, quam nunc habeat summus pontifex. Et sicut Petro fuit commissa potestas ecclesie, prout ecclesia est fundata super Christum, et per consequens fuit ei commissa potestas super animas, super corpora et super omnia temporalia que habent, quia omnes fideles secundum se totos et secundum omnia sua fundati sunt super Christum: sic et summo pontifici qui nunc est, quia est idem pontifex qui prius fuit, licet non sit idem homo, omne huiusmodi regimen est commissum. Et sicut Petrus immediate habuit a Christo regimen ecclesie, sic et summus pontifex qui nunc est, quia est idem summus pontifex qui tunc fuit, immediate a Deo sive a Christo, qui erat verus Deus, habere huiusmodi noscitur potestatem." Aeg.Rom. *De eccl.pot.* 2,4 (51–52; trans. 46–47). For the theme of the eternal existence of Rome, expressed juridically in Gratian's *Decretum* with the maxim *Ecclesia nunquam moritur*, combined with the sempiternity of the Roman Empire and the *populus romanus*, see Ernst H. Kantorowicz, *The King's Two Bodies. A Study in Mediaeval Political Theology* (Princeton, 1957), 291–310.

the flesh to the spirit. The third, however, is evil and reprehensible: the rebellion of the flesh against the spirit.[53]

The body has such a relationship to the soul because it is one that reflects the order of the universe itself:

> We see in the government of the universe that the whole of corporeal substance is governed through the spiritual. Inferior bodies are indeed ruled through superior, and the more gross through the more subtle and the less potent through the more potent; but the whole of corporeal substance is nonetheless ruled through the spiritual, and the whole of spiritual substance by the Supreme Spirit, that is, by God.[54]

This distinction then becomes the basis for the further hierarchy of temporal/spiritual and their respective order of governance:

> And just as there are two elements in man, body and spirit, so does man need a twofold food, bodily and spiritual; and so the Lord says in Matthew IV, *Man shall not live by bread alone, but by every word that comes out of the mouth of God*. Indeed, because he is not only body, but is body and soul or body and spirit, man therefore shall not live by bread alone (that is, by bodily food alone, for 'bread' may be taken to mean any kind of bodily food), but he shall live by the word of God: that is, by spiritual food. For just as the body needs bread as its bodily food, so does the spirit need the word of God as its spiritual food. Thus, because he is not simple, but is composed of two elements, man is therefore not nourished by a single, but by a twofold food: namely, bodily and spiritual. And so he is governed and ruled under a twofold sword: earthly and ecclesiastical; royal and priestly; material and spiritual.[55]

---

[53] Aeg.Rom. *De eccl.pot.* 1,7 (23–24).

[54] "Videmus autem in gubernacione universi, quod tota corporalis substancia per spiritualem gubernatur. Reguntur quidem inferiora corpora per superiora et grossiora per subtiliora et minus potencia per potenciora. Tota tamen corporalis substancia regitur per spiritualem, et universa spiritualis substancia per summum spiritum, videlicet per Deum." Aeg.Rom. *De eccl.pot.* 1,5 (16; trans. 12).

[55] "Et sicut duo sunt in homine, corpus et spiritus, sic homo indiget duplici cibo, corporali et spirituali; ideo dicit dominus Matthei quarto: *Non ex solo pane vivit homo, sed in omni verbo quod procedit de ore Dei* [Mt. 4:4] Homo quidem, quia non est corpus tantum, sed est corpus et anima, sive corpus et spiritus, ideo non vivit ex solo pane, idest in solo cibo corporali, ut per panem intelligatur quilibet corporalis cibus, sed vivit ex verbo Dei, idest ex cibo spirituali; quia, sicut corpus indiget pane tanquam suo cibo corporali, ita spiritus indiget verbo Dei tamquam suo cibo spirituali. Homo itaque, quia non est simplex, sed est compositus ex duobus, ideo non nutritur uno solo cibo, sed duplici: corporali videlicet et spirituali; sic gubernatur et regitur sub duplici gladio, terreno et ecclesiastico, regali et sacerdotali, materiali et spirituali." Aeg.Rom. *De eccl.pot.* 1,7 (23; trans. 19); *cf.* Aeg.Rom. *De eccl.pot.* 2,13 (111–129).

Here Giles has moved from the governance of the individual to the governance of society. The temporal/spiritual hierarchy forms the central argument for Giles to relate political to ecclesiastical authority. Humans have been created in God's image, and as such have dominion over lower forms of being. Yet within humans, the spiritual soul is to rule the physical, material body.[56] And thus,

> Since there is no doubt that the divine is more perfect than the human and the heavenly than the earthly and the spiritual than the bodily, nothing is more consistent, therefore, than that royal power, which is a human and earthly power and over bodies, should be subject to and ordered towards the service of the priestly power, and especially the power of the Supreme Pontiff, which is in some measure a divine and heavenly power and over spiritual things.[57]

The same relationship that exists between body and soul is valid for the realms of temporal and spiritual lordship, the spiritual sword and the temporal or material sword.[58] Thus temporal lordship, as represented by the emperor, is subordinate to and is to serve the spiritual lordship, which is the Church and the Church as embodied in the pope.[59]

Giles' presentation of temporal authority as the servant of spiritual authority, the sovereignty of priestly, ecclesiastical lordship governing material, kingly lordship, reflects the divine order of the universe.[60] Earthly life is lived between God and the devil: one is either a servant of Christ, or a servant of Belial, a faithful member of Christ's Church living in God's light, or a son of darkness.[61] The proper order of spiritual and material, of body and soul, distinguishes the faithful from the impious. Giles by no means equates earthly sovereignty as such with the realm of darkness. It can become so, however, when placed in opposition to ecclesiastical lordship, which

---

[56] Aeg.Rom. *De eccl.pot.* 2,4 (50); Aeg.Rom. *De eccl.pot.* 3,5 (172).
[57] "Et quia nullus dubitat, quin divina sint perfectiora humanis et celestia terrenis et spiritualia corporalibus, ergo nil conveniencius, quam quod potestas regia, que est potestas humana et terrena et super corporalia, subsit et sit ordinata in obsequium potestatis sacerdotalis et potissime potestatis summi pontificis, que est potestas quodammodo divina et celestis et super spiritualia." Aeg.Rom. *De eccl.pot.* 2, 4 (53; trans. 48).
[58] Aeg.Rom. *De eccl.pot.* 2,5 (57–58).
[59] Aeg.Rom. *De eccl.pot.* 1,7 (27); 2,4 (50–52); 3,4 (167).
[60] Aeg.Rom. *De eccl.pot.* 2,6 (67–69).
[61] Aeg.Rom. *De eccl.pot.* 2,11 (96).

imitates the divine hierarchy of angels. Drawing from Pseudo-Dionysius, Giles sets forth a threefold angelic hierarchy that governs the universe. This hierarchy is then mirrored by the ecclesiastical hierarchy with the pope as God's vicar. Temporal authority, or the material sword, exists within the lowest level of the governing hierarchy. The only realm that exists independently from the divine hierarchy is the demonic hierarchy with Lucifer at the helm. Yet even though the demons oppose the divine hierarchy, they nevertheless work towards the salvation of the elect and God's final judgment when all rule will cease. If temporal lordship therefore is not subservient to spiritual lordship, it serves the powers of Satan by perverting God's created order of the universe.[62] In short, the emperor is either the pope's faithful servant, or the devil's minion.

One would misread Giles' treatise if one read it only as a defense of papal power. That it surely is, but for Giles far more is at issue. It is an explication of Christian society, a construction of Christendom, drawing implications based on God's governance of the universe as revealed to humankind. And the Passion of Christ is the point of departure, for Christ's Passion established the law of grace and the holy sacraments, without which there is no salvation:

> But under the law of grace, the sacraments are not only distinct and defined by precept, but they are also universal... it is commanded that the Gospel be preached in all the world and to every creature, that is, to every human being, whether male or female. Baptism, therefore, is a universal sacrament for all time... since no one may obtain salvation without having received it either in fact or by desire. And since this sacrament is conferred in the Church, the Church is therefore catholic, that is, universal, and is the mother of all, since no one may obtain salvation unless he is subject to the Church and unless he is her son. And the Church has received this universality, and she has received this sacrament, from the Passion and after the Passion of Christ... And so the Church is said to have been formed from the side of Christ, because it is from the Passion of Christ that the Church's sacraments derive their power. And because it was then, when Christ had suffered, that the Church began to be universal, so that no one could be saved except through the Church's sacraments... Adam is called the form of Christ because just as he was the father of all according to the flesh, so Christ is the father of all according to faith. And just as Eve was formed from the side of the sleeping Adam, so

---

[62] Aeg.Rom. *De eccl.pot.* 2,13 (121–129).

from the side of the sleeping Lord upon the cross there flowed the sacraments through which the Church is saved.[63]

The Church is the body of Christ, and thus salvation comes only through membership in the Church.[64] The Church is equated with Christian society and what lies outside the Church exists in the realm of Satan. Only as faithful members of the Church can one truly possess one's own soul, body, and worldly goods, for all right of possession comes from God:

> Therefore through the sacrament of baptism, which is the direct remedy against original sin, and through the sacrament of penance, which is the remedy against actual sin, you will be made a worthy lord and a worthy prince and possessor of things. And since these sacraments are not conferred except in the Church and through the Church, since no one is able to receive baptism unless he is willing to subject himself to the Church and to be a faithful son of the Church, since the Church is catholic, that is universal, without which salvation is not possible, and since no one receives the sacrament of penance, except within the Church, since the Lord said to Peter, *Whatever you shall bind*, etc., no one thus can be a worthy lord or a worthy prince or a worthy possessor of goods except under and through the Church.[65]

---

[63] "Sed in lege gracie sunt sacramenta non solum distincta et sub precepto, sed eciam sunt universalia... mandatur quod predicetur evangelium in universo mundo et omni creature, idest omni homini, tam masculo quam femine. Sacramentum ergo universale est baptismus omni tempore... cum nullus potest consequi salutem sine eo vel in re vel in voto. Et quia sacramentum hoc datur in ecclesia, ideo ecclesia est catholica idest universalis, et est mater omnium, cum nullus possit consequi salutem, nisi sit subiectus ecclesie et nisi sit eius filius. Hanc autem universalitatem habuit ecclesia et habuit hoc sacramentum a passione et post passionem Christi... Ideo ex latere Christi dicitur esse formata ecclesia, quia a passione Christi habent virtutem sacramenta ecclesie. Et quia tunc cepit ecclesia esse universalis, ut nullus salvaretur, nisi per sacramenta ecclesia... quod Adam dicitur forma Christi, quia sicut ille est pater omnium secundum carnem, sic Christus est pater omnium secundum fidem; et sicut ex latere Ade dormientis formata est Eva, sic ex latere domini dormientis in cruce fluxerunt sacramenta per que salvatur ecclesia." Aeg.Rom. *De eccl.pot.* 2,7 (72–73; trans. 67–68).

[64] Aeg.Rom. *De eccl.pot.* 2,12 (109).

[65] "Ergo per sacramentum baptismi, quod est directum remedium contra originale, et per sacramentum penitencie, quod est remedium contra peccatum actuale, efficeris dignus dominator et dignus princeps et possessor rerum. Et quia hec sacramenta non nisi in ecclesia et per ecclesiam tribuuntur, quia nullus potest suscipere baptismum, nisi velit se subiecere ecclesie et esse filius ecclesie, cum ecclesia sit catholica, idest universalis, sine qua salus esse non potest, et cum nullus recipiat sacramentum penitencie, nisi sub ecclesia et per ecclesiam, dicente domino Petro: *Quodcumque ligaveris* etc, nullus efficitur dignus dominator nec dignus princeps nec possessor rerum, nisi sub ecclesia et per ecclesiam." Aeg.Rom. *De eccl.pot.* 2,8 (78–79; trans. 73–74).

Giles espoused a thorough-going dominion of grace, whereby one only exercises authority justly when done so in good-standing with the Church, and for the well-being of the Church. God is the true possessor of all goods, of all sovereignty, authority, and justice, and only those who are subject to God, justly and rightly hold possessions and lordship as stewards of God's gifts.[66] Moreover, the same applies to the rights of inheritance. Property can only be transferred from father to son rightly by the authority of the Church, which determines just ownership:

> Thus ... the heirs of mighty princes and the sons of all faithful men must acknowledge that they receive the inheritance, power and lordship which they possess rather from the Church, through whom, spiritually regenerated, they are made worthy of such honors, powers and riches, than from the carnal parents through whom they were born unworthy. And all faithful men, as often as they are plunged into mortal sin and absolved through the Church, must acknowledge that they hold all their goods, all their honor, all their power and riches, from the Church, through whose absolution they have been made worthy of those things of which, when they served sin, they were unworthy. And since none are worthy of honor or lordship of power or of any other good except through the sacraments of the Church and by the Church and under the Church ... no one is worthy of any power unless he is made worthy under the Church and through the Church.[67]

God is the origin of all goods, of all possession, of all authority, all power, and of all justice, and only in harmony with God's established order can humans make proper use of the goods they have received from God.[68] Christ is the ruler and founder of the commonwealth, and no just government can exist that is not governed by Christ.[69] Christ's reign, Christ's lordship, which makes all justice

---

[66] Aeg.Rom. *De eccl.pot.* 2,8 (75–81).

[67] "Potentum itaque principum heredes et quorumcumque fidelium filii hereditatem quam habent, potenciam et dominium ... magis debent recognoscere ab ecclesia, per quam spiritualiter regencrati fiunt talibus honoribus, potestatibus et facultatibus digni, quam a parentibus carnalibus, a quibus nascuntur indigni; et quilibet fideles, quociens in peccatum mortale habuntur et per ecclesiam absolvuntur, tociens omnia bona sua, omnes honores, omnes potestates et facultates suas debent recognoscere ab ecclesia, per quam absoluti facti sunt talibus digni, quibus cum peccato serviebant, erant indigni. Et quia nulli sunt digni nec honore nec dominio nec potestate nec aliquo alio bono, nisi per sacramenta ecclesiastica et per ecclesiam et sub ecclesia ... nullus tamen est dignus aliqua potestate, nisi sub ecclesia et per ecclesiam fiat dignus." Aeg.Rom. *De eccl.pot.* 2,9 (85; trans. 80).

[68] Aeg.Rom. *De eccl.pot.* 2,9 (83–84); *cf.* 2,1 (32–33); 2,6–8 (67–73).

[69] Aeg.Rom. *De ecl.pot.* 2,7 (73); 3,11 (200–206).

possible, is present on earth through the lordship of the Church, and God's vicar, the pope. The Church, therefore, possesses universal lordship, and all rule, all just rule, is through the Church, for the Church, as the commonwealth of grace and love, is God's established order and reign on earth.[70]

This is the main point and thrust of Giles' treatise. His theory of papal hierocratic sovereignty is based upon his view of ecclesiastical sovereignty, the earthly reign of Christ, corresponding to the reign of God in heaven. Just as God sits at the helm of the angelic hierarchy, so does the pope, as God's vicar on earth, preside over the ecclesiastical hierarchy, which is synonymous with Christian society.[71] As God's vicar, the pope is the spiritual being that judges all and can be judged by no one.[72] And just as God has complete and supreme sovereignty over all creation, so does the pope have complete sovereignty on earth, a true fullness of power.[73] Moreover, the pope possesses the same divine discrimination in the exercise of his authority as does God. Just as God by his absolute power can do whatever God chooses to do immediately without secondary causes, so the pope, who in the usual administration of his authority employs secondary causes as his instruments, can by his absolute power affect whatever he chooses immediately and directly in his plenitude of power. Only thus, based on the pope's ordained powers, does temporal sovereignty come into being and exercise a distinct realm of jurisdiction.[74] The emperor, and indeed every prince, even Philip IV, King of France, administers authority from the appointed jurisdiction of the universal sovereign, the pope, as an expression of the papal, and divinely ordained, created order. Such an order does not detract from or undermine the foundational reality of the absolute power and sovereignty of God's vicar. The pope is not a mere official of the Church, and is certainly not a simple administrator. The pope, as pope, is the embodiment of the Church, the embodiment of God's reign on earth, exercising the authority of Christ himself, through

---

[70] Aeg.Rom. *De eccl.pot.* 2,4 (48–54).
[71] Aeg.Rom. *De eccl.pot.* 2,13 (126–127).
[72] Aeg.Rom. *De eccl.pot.* 2,12 (102).
[73] Aeg.Rom. *De eccl.pot.* 3,2 (155–156).
[74] Aeg.Rom. *De eccl.pot.* 3,9 (191–192); cf. 3,7–8 (181–190). Regarding the distinction between papal *potentia absoluta* and *ordinata*, see William J. Courtenay, *Capacity and Volition. A History of the Distinction of Absolute and Ordained Power* (Bergamo, 1990).

whose Passion all will be saved who will be saved, in the final triumph of the kingdom of God.[75]

Giles' *De ecclesiastica potestate* has so often been seen as the exemplary expression of extreme papalism. Yet it was so only as the first complete expression of extreme ecclesiasticism, written to defend the Church against the King of France, who was trying to usurp just sovereignty. The Church, not the pope as such, stands central in Giles' work, which is not to take away from his exaltation of papal power. Based on his ascending hierarchies, Giles' doctrine of the pope is a corollary to his doctrine of the Church. His treatise presents a view of reality, of universal reality, and as such, as all his other writings, was to be normative for his Order.

"One holy, catholic, and apostolic Church...": these are not the words of Giles, but of Boniface VIII, and of the Creed. They do nevertheless encapsulate Giles' central vision in the work he dedicated to Boniface, and which Boniface used as a major source for his Bull *Unam sanctam*. Moreover, this was a vision that Giles imparted to his Order. It was an Augustinian vision that only much later began to show signs of disintegration. Yet what was true for the Order, was not as valid for the Church as such. Boniface may have been pleased with his assertions issued in November of 1302, but little did he know that *Unam sanctam* was to have such an impact.

In the early morning of 7 September 1303, William of Nogaret, the successor to Peter Flotte as the French Royal Chancellor, together with a band of conspirators consisting, among others, of Colonna, led a force of 300 horses and 1,000 foot soldiers through the city walls and into the heart of Anagni. Pillage and plunder was the goal, and the prize victim was Boniface. By mid-afternoon, the bandits had broken the defenses of the papal residency and entered Boniface's private chamber itself. Nogaret had to decide whether to kill Boniface then and there, or to bring him captive back to France. Yet the former option Nogaret realized might not work to his best interest and besides, renewed defenses were forming outside in the city. Nogaret was needed, and left Boniface to his own deserts. The resistance was finally able to put the bandits to flight, and Boniface was led to the marketplace to absolve all those who had come to his defense from all wrong doing. Yet the conspirators had had their affect. Boniface

---

[75] Aeg.Rom. *De eccl.pot.* 3,12 (206–209); 3,2 (152–153).

was broken. A month later, on 12 October 1303, Benedict Caetani died.[76] So much for God's vicar on earth. So much for the theoretical construction of Christendom. One holy, catholic, and apostolic Church brought to its knees by a band of thugs.

Even if the debacle of Anagni gave it a greater shock than ever before, and perhaps than ever since, the papacy, and Church, remained.[77] Giles' *De ecclesiastica potestate* was written for Boniface, but it looked over the pope's shoulders to all Christians. God's vicar, God's sovereignty and reign, was not dependent on any one person, or even on any individual pope. There is no question that Giles was a staunch supporter of Boniface, but it was not for Boniface that Giles was writing. He was writing to explicate the divinely revealed nature of Christendom, which was grounded in the community of love and grace through the Passion of Christ. He was writing as an archbishop, and as an Augustinian friar, who was bringing Augustine's teaching to bear on the issue at hand, citing Augustine far more often than any other authority. Giles knew his writings were to be normative for his Order, his Order that had recently received many privileges from the pope, confirming it in its status. He took up his pen in continuing his own program for his Order as explicated in 1292. Giles provided the foundation of a platform designed to ensure that his Order's religion would continue to flourish. And flourish it did.

Shortly after Giles' *De ecclesiastica potestate*, yet another Augustinian friar, Augustinus of Ancona, wrote in defense of Boniface.[78] Twenty years later, Augustinus was still at work, authoring what has been

---

[76] Boase, *Boniface VIII*, 341–351.

[77] The event of Anagni was a shock not only for the Church, but for Europe as a whole. *Unam sanctam* had posed a direct threat to the emerging French patriotism; see Kantorowicz, *The King's Two Bodies*, 249–267. It was a contest between two competing and irreconcilable ideologies, and something had to give. That something, was Anagni. Yet even one who viewed Boniface as worthy of the tortures of hell as did Dante, still considered the attack on the pope in Anagni to be abhorrent, equivalent to a new flagellation of Christ; Kantorowicz, *The King's Two Bodies*, 454–455.

[78] Augustinus composed two early treatises, which Wilks dates to the period 1307–1309; Wilks, *The Problem of Sovereignty*, 5. The first, is his *Tractatus contra articulos inventos ad diffamandam Bonifacium*, edited as an anonymous treatise by Finke, *Aus den Tagen*, Quellen, lxix–xcix; the second, is his *Tractatus de facto Templariorum*, edited by Scholz, *Die Publizistik*, 508–516. Another early work of Augustinus is his *Tractatus contra divinatores et sompniatores*, not mentioned by Wilks, but dated to c. 1310 by Scholz, *Unbekannte Kirchenpolitische Streitschriften Aus der Zeit Ludwigs des Bayern (1327–1354)*,

called one of the "most influential and most important books ever written on the nature of the papal supremacy in the Middle Ages,"[79] his *Summa de potestate ecclesiastica*, dedicated to another pope with problems on his hands, Pope John XXII. It had only been twenty-four years since *Unam sanctam* when Augustinus completed his *Summa* in 1326,[80] and times had not changed all that much, at least on the surface. The pope was still in conflict with the prince, though it was no longer the king of France, but the emperor, who was challenging papal primacy. The Augustinians, nevertheless, were still writing treatises espousing hierocratic theory, even if neither the papal nor the imperial party was clearly emerging the victor. Appearances, however, can be deceiving. The arguments on both sides may have had a familiar ring to them, but the world of Augustinus and Pope John XXII was a very different one from that of Giles and Boniface VIII.

II. The War for Rome

The days of the fourteenth century were not halcyon. Not long after the debacle of Anagni, Pope Clement V moved his court to Avignon in 1305, which began what became known as the Babylonian Captivity of the Church.[81] Nevertheless, the ghost of Boniface VIII still lingered, as Philip IV and the Colonna repeatedly used the threat and actual proceedings of a posthumous heresy trial of Boniface as a

---

2 vols., 1:191–197; Scholz partially edited this work; *ibid.*, 2:481–490. For Augustinus, see above all, P.B. Ministeri, "De Augustini de Ancona, O.E.S.A. (d. 1328) Vita et Operibus," *AAug.* 22 (1951/52), 7–56, 148–262. For analyses of Augustinus' *Summa de potestate ecclesiastica*, see Wilks, *The Problem of Sovereignty*, and more recently the work of Ulrich Horst, "Die Armut Christi und der Apostel nach der Summa de ecclesiastica potestate des Augustinus von Ancona," in *Traditio Augustiniana. Studien über Augustinus und seine Rezeption*, Festgabe für Willigis Eckermann OSA zum 60. Geburtstag, ed. Adolar Zumkeller and Achim Krümmel, Cassiciacum 46 (Würzburg, 1994), 471–494; *idem*, "Die Lehrautorität des Papstes nach Augustinus von Ancona," *AAug.* 54 (1991), 271–303; and Miethke, *De Potestate Papae*, 170–177.

[79] C.H. McIlwain, *The Growth of Political Thought in the West* (London, 1932), 278; as cited by Wilks, *The Problem of Sovereignty*, 2.

[80] For the dating of Augustinus' *Summa*, see the introduction to Appendix C. Antony Black confused Augustinus' death date with that of the completion of his *Summa*; Antony Black, *Political Thought*, 49.

[81] See G. Mollat, *The Popes at Avignon. The 'Babylonian Captivity' of the Medieval Church*, trans. from the ninth French edition by Janet Love (New York, 1963).

political card in their ongoing battles with the pope.[82] On 1 June 1310 the first formal *auto-da-fé* took place at Paris when Marguerite Porete was burned at the stake as a relapsed heretic.[83] Just the year before, Henry, count of Luxembourg, had been crowned King of the Romans at Aachen, and on 29 June 1312 Henry was crowned emperor in Rome by Clement V in the basilica of St. John the Lateran. Less than a year later, on 26 April 1313, Henry condemned King Robert of Naples, the papal vicar in Italy, to be beheaded and his lands to be confiscated for the crime of insubordination, a controversy "of the first rank in legal history," which focused "more precisely on the authority of the emperor over other Christian kings than any earlier confrontation between emperor or king, and pope." Robert escaped prosecution by Henry's sudden death the following August, which led to a disputed election of his successor.[84] Two years later began the Great Famine, which decimated northern Europe from 1315–1322.[85] For much of the century, war plagued Italy, England, and France. In 1328 Pope John XXII was himself declared a heretic and deposed by Emperor Louis of Bavaria, who set up in opposition the anti-pope Nicholas V. Louis' own claims to the imperial throne, however, were by no means uncontested, a fact that John XXII exploited to his utmost. Yet the theoretical basis of papal sovereignty had already by 1324 been undermined by Marsilius of Padua's *Defensor Pacis*, and the pope had pronounced as heretical what had been seen as the highest expression of Christian perfection, the Franciscan ideal of poverty.[86] The hope for a new crusade was ever being renewed,[87] even as anticlericalism was on the rise. On 15 September 1325 the citizens of Magdeburg murdered their archbishop, a case that came to involve both pope and emperor.[88] The previous year in Erfurt, a group of citizens had hanged a priest

---

[82] Boase, *Boniface VIII*, 355–379; Schmidt, *Der Bonifaz-Prozess*.

[83] See Katharina M. Wilson, ed., *Medieval Women Writers* (Athens, Georgia, 1984), 204–210.

[84] Pennington, *The Prince and the Law*, 165–201; quotations from page 171 and 166.

[85] William Chester Jordan, *The Great Famine. Northern Europe in the Early Fourteenth Century* (Princeton, 1996).

[86] For a discussion of the politics of the Franciscan Poverty Controversy, see Tierney, *Origins*.

[87] See Norman Housley, *The Avignon Papacy and the Crusades, 1305–1378* (Oxford, 1986).

[88] See Chapter Three below.

they had convicted by fiat of theft, which led to what has been called a *Pfaffenkrieg*.[89] In 1327 Louis was preparing for his D-Day campaign on Rome, and many of the Lombard cities under the Visconti were gleefully under interdict. Chaos and confusion ruled the day. And looming on the horizon was a new pestilence, the Black Death, that beginning in 1348 ravaged Europe as no war ever had previously or since. Thirty years later Christendom was split by the onslaught of the Great Schism. For the fourteenth century, the myth of Christendom was a joke, and would have been seen as such if the situation had not been so serious, and if the stakes had not been so high.

This was the world of Pope John XXII, and this was the context in which the Augustinian platform was developed. Given all the crises, the traumas, the conflicts, and confusion, answers were needed, and answers that offered comprehensive solutions. And answers came. This was, after all, the century of law, the century of Bartolus of Sassoferrato, Giovanni Andrea, Pierre Bertrand, and Baldus de Ubaldis.[90] It was the century of the rise of the nation state, ringing the deathknell of the imperial *dominium mundi*.[91] This was, moreover, the century of humanism, the century of Dante, Petrarch, and Boccacio, the century of renaissance, the century of Giotto and Simone Martini. There is so much that renders the fourteenth, far more than the thirteenth, truly the "greatest of centuries."[92] And in the midst of it all, there came an answer that was the most comprehensive and ambitious expression of papal supremacy ever attempted, Augustinus' *Summa*, a treatise that led Michael Wilks to comment that "the 'Babylonian captivity,' often regarded as being in fact the nadir of the medieval papacy, was in theory its crowning triumph."[93]

---

[89] See Chapter Three below.

[90] For an overview of the development of law and politics in the fourteenth century, see Albert Rigaudière, "The Theory and Practice of Government in Western Europe in the Fourteenth Century," in *The New Cambridge Medieval History*, vol. VI: c. 1300–c. 1400, ed. Michael Jones (Cambridge, 2000), 17–41.

[91] "Everywhere, civil and canon lawyers made a case for the rediscovered sovereignty of their own country and made the famous formula *rex in regno suo imperator est* (the king is emperor in his kingdom), victorious from Sicily to England... The empire did not disappear, but it fragmented while the national monarchies triumphed a little everywhere, except in the Italian peninsula where the city-states secured their success to varying degrees." *Ibid.*, 21.

[92] *Cf.* James J. Walsh, *The Thirteenth, Greatest of Centuries* (New York, 1924).

[93] Wilks, *The Problem of Sovereignty*, 407.

Yet Augustinus accomplished even more: his *Summa* is the first treatise that argued for the Augustinian way of life, the Augustinian *Rule*, as the highest and most perfect form of the apostolic life.[94] Augustinus explicitly combined his Order's cause with that of the pope, offering a genuinely Augustinian solution to all the crises and conflicts, paving the way of his Order's high way to heaven, and doing so in midst of the power struggles between the emperor, the pope, and another religious Order whose members became embroiled in politics to an extent unforeseen and unimagined by their humble founder, the *poverello*, St. Francis of Assisi. Augustinus' *Summa* is not an abstract treatise of papal hierocratic theory. It is a comprehensive treatment of ecclesiastical society. As such it is unique, but it was not an isolated endeavor. Augustinus' *Summa* was the most extensive expression of a common Augustinian campaign that had begun with Giles of Rome: the theoretical construction of Christendom and the creation of the Augustinians' religious identity.[95]

A. *The Eternal City and the Church Body*

The Via Merulana is a tree-lined, dreamy street, one that makes fantasies seem possible. Transported out of its setting, it could almost, but not quite, be a street in the suburban midwest of America, with its shops, coffee bars, ice cream parlors, and quaint restaurants, where one can still on a summer night be served a fabulous pasta by a waiter named Antonio, who in his youth had aspirations of becoming a famous actor. Yet such dreams are illusions, and even if the appearance strives to give another impression, the Via Merulana is perhaps uniquely down to earth among the streets of Rome, connecting as it does St. John the Lateran on the south and Santa Maria Maggiore on the north. The Via della Concilliazione leading into St. Peter's cannot compare, at least in its present manifestation with its all too stinking odor of Mussolini, which is perhaps only paralleled by the interior of the Teatro dell'Opera. The Via Merulana

---

[94] "... sicut nulla regula potest esse perfectior regula apostolorum, sic nulla regula potest esse perfectior regula beati Augustini, que non aliud essentialiter continet quam apostolorum documenta." Aug.Anc. *Summa* 97,5 (ed. Rome, 1479), fol. 270rb.

[95] For an impressive study of the concept and practice of reform in the early fourteenth century, focusing on, though by no means limited to, the pontificate of Benedict XII, see Jan Ballweg, *Konziliare oder päpstliche Ordensreform. Benedikt XII. und die Reformdiskussion im frühen 14. Jahrhundert*, SuR.NR 17 (Tübingen, 2001).

unites the church of the great medieval councils, Lateran III, Lateran IV, and the abortive Lateran V, the pope's church, where popes were crowned, with the Roman church of Our Lady, where snow still falls in August.[96] The papacy and the mother of God, joined by a link the length of which one can still walk leisurely in less than an hour, and if one tries, the trek can be made in thirty minutes, a path taken assuredly by the likes of Pope Innocent III in the thirteenth, and by the Augustinian General Giles of Viterbo in the sixteenth century. And from the Via Merulana the Roman Forum and Colosseum are close by, most doable for an evening stroll by moonlight, reminding one of Rome's imperial past, before the times of popes and Germans, welling up conjectures and memories of what was, of what had been, before the fall.

The Villa Borghese is across town, and the time needed to reach it from the Via Merulana on the metro seems on occasion nearly to equal that required to arrive at Santa Maria Maggiore from the Lateran by foot. Yet when once there, one has been transported to another side of Rome, of contemporary Rome, and of late medieval Rome, when the Villa had not yet achieved its present form, and was just outside the Aurelian walls. Then there was no question of the romance of the parks, ampitheaters, and statuary as they now exist, foreshadowing in a different vein the splendors to be had in the Vatican, its museum, and its gardens. What is now the Villa Borghese was in the fourteenth century mere wilderness, and the Sistene Chapel had not yet been erected, and St. Peter's did not have its dome. Even within the walls there were farms and animals, fishmongers and cloth merchants, shoemakers, pilgrims and garbage, sewers and stench.[97] Though what is now the Villa Borghese was

---

[96] Robert Brentano, *Rome Before Avignon. A Social History of Thirteenth-Century Rome* (2nd edition, London, 1991), 87.

[97] For a description of medieval Rome, see Brentano, *Rome Before Avignon*, 13–70. Even in 1500, Rome, as Peter Partner described it, "was pervaded by rusticity. Cows ruminated in the Forum; horses cropped the grass round the Columns of Trajan and Marcus Aurelius; sheep roamed over at least four of the seven Hills. The Palatine Hill was covered by vineyards; the Circus Maximus was a market garden. For all its echoes of the Empire of the Caesars, for all the clerical pageantry of its priestly residents, Rome was only a large, medieval village, smelling of cows and hay." Peter Partner, *Renaissance Rome, 1500–1559* (Berkeley, 1976), 4. Partner notes as well: "In 1450 Rome had been even more bucolic than it was in 1500." *Ibid.*, 5, where he also then gives examples from two delightful reports on the condition of the city from Spanish travellers. This, then, gives some idea of what the Rome of the early fourteenth century must have been.

then wilderness, it was wilderness only by its existence on the edge of eternity, the eternity that was Rome, with the city's wall drawing the boundary between chaos and order, barbarity and civilization, at least by design. The line was thin indeed, and if one descended from the hilltop that only much later was to become cultivated and developed into a momument of the Baroque, one would enter Rome via the Porto del Popolo, coming into the palazzo where just on the left-hand side one would find, and still does, the medieval Augustinian church of Santa Maria del Popolo.[98]

Rome was the city of the Augustinians, and it was to remain so. Yet that is not saying very much. Rome was the city of Christendom, as the awe-inspiring remains of Constantine's Basilica forever impress on one's conscious and unconscious mind. It was an Augustinian city only to that extent. Milan, Ostia, or even Pavia, where Augustine's body was brought and buried in the eighth century, have better claims to be the 'Hippo of Italy' than does Rome, whose sack by Alaric in 410 C.E. led Augustine to compose his magnificent *De Civitate Dei*, arguing against attaching any ultimate significance to such a pagan city of empire. Yet despite Augustine's attempt to persuade otherwise, Rome remained what it always had been, the earthly city of God, the center of the world for both popes and emperors, for Church and Empire. Like it or not, for better and for worse, in sickness and in health, till death do us part, the Church and Roman Empire, holy or otherwise, were inseparably married, and as often happens with spouses, began to resemble each other. As Ernst Kantorowicz put it,

> Infinite cross-relations between Church and State, active in every century of the Middle Ages, produced hybrids in either camp. Mutual borrowings and exchanges of insignia, political symbols, prerogatives, and rights of honor had been carried on perpetually between the spiritual and secular leaders of Christian society. The pope adorned his tiara with a golden crown, donned the imperial purple, and was preceded by the imperial banners when riding in solemn procession through the streets of Rome. The emperor wore under his crown a mitre, donned the pontifical shoes and other clerical raiments, and received, like a bishop, the ring at his coronation. These borrowings affected,

---

[98] Walking down the steep path from the Villa Borghese today, one enters the palazzo directly, not needing to go around to the Porto, and thus, Santo Maria del Popolo is on one's right.

in the earlier Middle Ages, chiefly the ruling individuals, both spiritual and secular, until finally the *sacerdotium* had an imperial appearance and the *regnum* a clerical touch.[99]

The Via Merulana, at least south of the Esquiline, and the Palazzo del Popolo were in the thirteenth and fourteenth centuries situated in areas dominated by two competing families, the Annabaldi and the Colonna. The Colonna touted their daughter Margherita as a saint,[100] and had special clout since in the early 1220s Giovanni Colonna, who had been made cardinal-priest of Santa Prassede by Innocent III, brought back to Rome from the East the very column to which Christ himself had been bound and on which he had been scourged, which is still to be viewed, together with the indescribable mosaics, in Giovanni's church, just a stone's throw away from the church where one could find part of Christ's crib, Santa Maria Maggiore.[101] The Colonna, however, had already risen to power in Rome by the mid-twelfth century,[102] whereas the Annabaldi were in comparison newcomers, achieving ascendency only a half-century later, rising "on the back of Conti greatness" when Annibaldo Annibaldi married a sister of Innocent III.[103] Riccardo Annibaldi, who is of particular importance for our story, was, as the son of Annabaldo, "by blood as much Conti as Annibaldi,"[104] the legitimate nephew of the pope. By 1238 Riccardo was made cardinal-deacon by Gregory IX, another Conti relative.

In the thirteenth century there was no Annabaldi pope, and the only Colonna pope was so only indirectly, when the virtual family chaplain became Nicholas IV.[105] Yet both families cultivated their religious devotion by patronage of religious Orders. The Colonna to be sure considered Margherita to be a saint, and because she had striven to live as a Franciscan tertiary, the family had a special affinity for the Order of Friars Minor; the Annabaldi, on the other hand, thanks to Riccardo, had, and in some very real ways had created,

---

[99] Kantorowicz, *The King's two Bodies*, 193.
[100] Brentano, *Rome Before Avignon*, 174–183.
[101] Brentano, *Rome Before Avignon*, 180. Brentano most accurately remarked parenthetically, "The column was, and is, a beautiful little object, although it is very difficult to understand how a man could have been scourged at it." *Ibid.*
[102] *Ibid.*, 179.
[103] *Ibid.*, 190.
[104] *Ibid.*, 191.
[105] *Ibid.*, 147.

the Augustinians. Riccardo, Brentano asserted, "more than anyone else, formed the Augustinian Hermits into the Order they became."[106] He was the Order's cardinal protector, and already by 1256, the year of the Order's foundation by the Conti pope Alexander IV, Riccardo had secured for the Hermits the church of Santa Maria del Popolo. To do so, however, was no easy task. Riccardo had to arrange for the Franciscans, who had been in residence at the people's church in the territory of the Colonna, to be transferred to Santa Maria in Aracoeli, while the Benedictines of Aracoeli were simply dispersed.[107] This gave the Augustinians a firm foothold in Rome, which was then expanded by Honorius IV in 1287 when he established the Augustinians in the church of San Trifone.[108] Once having secured a base, the Augustinians never left, and neither did their cardinal protector. Riccardo Annabaldi still stands entombed in the wall of St. John the Lateran.

Family politics, papal politics, imperial politics: these are what formed the Augustinian Order, and they all meshed in the city that was eternal. Rome left its mark. Rome was, after all, the same Rome as had always existed, the Tiber was the same river, and the Roman people, the *populus Romanus*, was the same as it had always been, as Giles of Rome affirmed.[109] The city of Cicero and Vergil, of Caesar and Augustus, of Peter and Paul, of Constantine and Sylvester, not only symbolized, not only represented, but in fact *was* Christendom, and both pope and emperor unceasingly wooed their beloved to capture her heart, her soul, and her body.

The pope, however, was uniquely Roman, more so than the German emperor, and Rome was uniquely the pope's. She was his Church, he was her bishop, and to her must he remain true, for otherwise, were he to abandon Rome for another, it would be as involving her in adultery, as Augustinus of Ancona put forth in his *Summa*.[110] Only in Rome could the pope best serve Christendom, and only in Rome could the pope exercise his full authority and

---

[106] *Ibid.*, 194.
[107] *Ibid.*, 257–258.
[108] *Ibid.*
[109] See note 52 above.
[110] "Papa singulariter est Romanus episcopus, sed sicut vir non debet adulterari suam uxorem, ita nec episcopus ecclesiam suam, ut illam dimittat." Aug.Anc. *Summa* 21,1 (ed. Rome, 1479), fol. 74va; *cf.* Mt. 5:32–33.

jurisdiction. Anywhere else, the pope would be subject to being cowed into capitulating with the local prince, either from affection or from fear, thus falling away from equity and justice.[111] Human weakness of the flesh though it may have been, adultery can be found in popes too, and the pope to whom Augustinus dedicated his *Summa* was residing in Avignon.

Augustinus wrote about Rome, her bishop, and her Church, yet he himself did so only from a distance. His *Summa* was composed in Naples, where Augustinus had been even before John XXII excommunicated Louis of Bavaria. In 1321 Augustinus succeeded Pietro de Narnia as the court chaplain and regent master of the Order's *studium generale*.[112] Augustinus had special ties with the heir to the thrown, Charles of Calabria, son of King Robert d'Anjou, and the king referred to Augustinus as *consiliarius, cappelanus, familiaris, et fidelis noster*.[113] Naples was where James of Viterbo had served as archbishop, and Giles of Rome had dedicated the second book of his commentary on the *Sentences* to Robert. There was a tradition of Augustinian patronage in Naples, and Robert was the temporal ruler closest to the pope. He was the papal vicar in Italy, having the responsibility to maintain the Church and her peace by the exercise of the material sword. Robert, moreover, had early on plotted an Italian strategy for Pope Clement V, which then became the general program of John XXII: there should not be another imperial election, or at least if one could not be avoided, the pope should make sure that the emperor would have to come to Rome to be confirmed and crowned by the holy pontiff.[114] Robert was a pious king, a preaching king, and he consciously propogated his image of sanctity, even

---

[111] "In nulla enim patria papa potest uti tanta libertate et tanta iurisdictionis potestate, nec tantam pro populo Christiano facere utilitatem sicut Rome et in patrimonio beati Petri. Residendo enim in alia patria supponit se sub dominio regum et principum et sic vel timore vel amore non libere potest uti iustitia et equitate, sed cogitur ab ipsa deviare. Sed cum presit Rome papa et in partibus Italie per immediatam administrationem temporalibus et spiritualibus in nulla patria potest uti suo dominio universaliter sicut ibi, nec tantam utilitatem pro populo Christiano facere, cum sit patria maioris affluentie et maioris convenientie pro convenientibus ad eius curiam quam aliqua alia." Aug.Anc. *Summa* 21,1 (ed. Rome, 1479), fol. 75vb.

[112] Ministeri, "De Vita et Operibus," 53.

[113] Regesto Angioino 271 (1327–1328 B), fol. 17^r, as reproduced by Ministeri, "Vita et Operibus," 236, nr. 2.

[114] K. Müller, *Der Kampf Ludwigs des Baiern mit der römischen Curie. Ein Beitrag zur kirchlichen Geschichte des 14. Jahrhunderts*, v. 1: *Ludwig der Baier und Johann XXII* (Tübingen, 1879), 36–40. Müller noted: "Diese Forderung des Königs bildete, wenn wir schon

as he harbored radical Franciscans at court.[115] He was by no means a papal pawn and has remained a rather enigmatic figure. Yet Robert's court in Naples provided Augustinus with first-hand experience in observing the machinations of a papal defender of the peace, though one who was not quite a model of princely perfection in the eyes of the pope. Augustinus, however, was not writing for Robert. Naples offered Augustinus the opportunity to see both sides, so to speak: to be a member of a princely court, and given that this was the court of Robert, to have intimate contact with the papal court in Avignon. And it was the prince of the latter for whom Augustinus wrote his work.

Augustinus' *Summa de potestate ecclesiastica* is an extensive treatise, counting over 600 double-column pages in the early printed editions.[116] It consists of 112 questions, divided into three major parts.[117] There are at least twenty-four extant manuscripts of the complete work, and another fifteen containing fragments.[118] The *Summa* received five editions in the fifteenth century, and then four successive editions in Rome, beginning in 1582 and ending in 1585, which was also the last edition of Augustinus' work.[119] Augustinus' sources, aside from the Bible, are primarily patristic, with citation to the works of Augustine above all; and canonistic, though Huguccio of Pisa and his *Summa* is the only canonist Augustinus mentioned by name. Hugh of St. Victor's *De Sacramentis* and Bernard's *De Consideratione* are also formidable authorities.[120] Augustinus' *Summa* could be considered his

---

hier anticipieren, was sich erst aus dem Verlauf der ganzen Regierung des Papstes ergeben kann, das Programm, dem Johann XXII. im allgemeinen getreu blieb." *Ibid.*, 37. Robert, according to Müller, ". . . auf die Politik des Papstes einem hervorragenden Einfluß ausgeübt habe." *Ibid.*

[115] Darleen N. Pryds, *The King Embodies the Word. Robert d'Anjou and the Politics of Preaching*, SHCT 93 (Leiden, 2000). For Robert's relationship with the OFM, see especially *ibid.*, 104–121; for Angevin rule in general, see *L'État Angevin. Pouvoir, Culture et Société entre XIIIe et XIVe Siècle*, Collection de l'École Française de Rome 245, Istituto Storico Italiano Per il Medio Evo, Nuovi Stuid Storici 45 (Roma, 1998); for an in depth study of Angevin iconography, see Tanja Michalsky, *Memoria und Repräsentation. Die Grabmäler des Königshauses Anjou in Italien*, Veröffentlichungen des Max-Planck-Instituts für Geschichte 157 (Göttingen, 2000).

[116] I have used the Rome, 1479 edition of this work in the Koninklijke Bibliotheek in The Hague, signature Inc. 170 F 24, which has modern foliation totaling 324 folios.

[117] For the list of questions, together with Augustinus' letter of dedication to John XXII, see Appendix C.

[118] Ministeri, "Vita et Operibus," 209–212; *cf.* Zumkeller *MSS* nr. 141 (77–78).

[119] Ministeri, "Vita et Operibus," 212.

[120] *Cf.* Wilks, *The Problem of Sovereignty*, 9–10. No comprehensive analysis of

magnum opus, though even as great as it is, and even given the influence it had, such a designation would not be fair to Augustinus, who authored thirty-one other titles that have been authenticated, with an additional thirty works of spurious or dubious authorship that were attributed to the Neapolitan court chaplain.[121] Yet his *Summa* stands apart from his *Sermones de tempore et sanctis*, his lectures on Matthew, his glosses on the Pauline epistles and on the Apocalypse, to name just a few, as the work in which Augustinus presented as such his vision of Christian society. While Augustinus is generally acknowledged as having been of major importance for the development of fourteenth-century political thought, his *Summa*, not to mention Augustinus himself, has only been the focus of a single major study, which explicates Augustinus' views in the abstract context of the contemporary political theory.[122] The *Summa* is still a work largely unknown and misunderstood. It deserves more attention.

The Church was the state, and the state was the Church. That was Augustinus' position, even though the Emperor Louis of Bavaria viewed the Church as his own, and with good reason. The myth of Christendom was by no means an exclusively papal construct. The popes had, in fact, over the centuries slowly appropriated for themselves the imperial ideology, changing it, shaping it, molding it, and transforming it into their own. In the early thirteenth century Riccardo Annabaldi's uncle, Innocent III, began desacralizing kingship by

---

Augustinus' sources however has ever been made, and no critical edition has been undertaken. This is a major lacuna. Here I have focused on the historical context of Augustinus' work, and make no pretense nor attempt to analyze it in that of the canonist tradition. Such an investigation, however, would surely shed much light on Augustinus' work. I hope such blind-spots are compensated for, or at least excused by, the present approach. For an analysis of the basic canonistic traditions upon which Augustinus was drawing, see B. Tierney, *Foundations of the Conciliar Theory. The Contribution of the Medieval Canonists from Gratian to the Great Schism*, Cambridge Studies in Medieval Life and Thought 4 (Cambridge, 1955); Augustinus does not make an appearance in Tierney's foundational study (he is mentioned three times in passing as a "papal publicists"), which however makes clear that a parallel work dealing with the influence of the canonists on the hierocratic authors and the so-called "publicists" would be most welcome.

[121] Ministeri, "Vita et Operibus," 154–156, 233.

[122] Wilks, *The Problem of Sovereignty*, which was published in 1963; there are, however, two doctoral dissertations by Dutch scholars that focused on Augustinus; the first, written in French, was never published, E. van Moé, *Les Ermites de St. Augustin au début du XIVe siècle. Agostino Trionfo et ses théories politiques*, see *Position de thèses* (Paris, 1928), 101–114; and R. van Gerven, *De wereldlijke macht van den paus volgens Augustinus Triumphus* (Antwerp-Nijmegen, 1947); see Wilks, *The Problem of Sovereignty*, 2.

refusing to annoint the emperor with chrism on the head, a privilege he reserved for bishops.[123] It was the same pope who for the first time officially designated his own office, rather than that of king or emperor, as being the vicar of Christ,[124] although the emperor was still styled as 'God on earth,' *deus in terris, deus terrenus, deus praesens*.[125] Nevertheless, whereas in 1100 the Anonymous Norman considered the emperor to be "one who has become God and Christ by grace,"[126] by the time of Frederick II, with inspiration drawn from Roman Law, the emperor began conceding somewhat his divine titles by fashioning himself as the vicar of Justice, the *vicarius Iustitiae*, responsible for preserving the *patria*.[127]

The Church, however, had a slightly different view of what the *patria* entailed. For the Christian, the true *patria* was paradise, the heavenly Jerusalem, and the pope as Christ's vicar was its defender.[128] *Pater patriae, vicarius Christi, vicarius dei*: all terms that at various times had been applied to both pope and emperor, both of whom applied them as well to the practical exercise of their office. Yet the pope as the defender of the *patria* had connotations to which the emperor could not pretend. The papal appropriation of the title *vicarius Christi* was intimately connected to liturgical and theological developments. The eucharist became dogmatically defined as the true body of Christ at the Fourth Lateran Council, with Innocent III presiding. Regardless of imperial claims and traditions, the clergy had always been in charge of the sacraments, and now, as never before, in the sacrament of the eucharist, the true body of Christ, the *corpus verum*, was present. This led to a shift in terminology and concepts. Previously the eucharist had been referred to as Christ's mystical body, the *corpus mysticum*, unifying all members of the Church. Now, however, what was the *corpus mysticum*, had become the *corpus verum*, and the *corpus mysticum* became identified with the Church as in institution. By the time of Boniface VIII, the Church itself had become a body, a corporation, possessing juridical and sociological implications as much as liturgical and sacramental.[129] The Church had become incorporated. As Kantorowicz argued,

---

[123] Kantorowicz, *The King's Two Bodies*, 319.
[124] *Ibid.*, 91.
[125] *Ibid.*, 92; 160–161; *cf.* Rivière, *Le Problème de l'Église*, 435–440.
[126] Kantorowicz, *The King's Two Bodies*, 42–61; 48.
[127] *Ibid.*, 191–192.
[128] *Ibid.*, 232–272.
[129] *Ibid.*, 194–202. Kantorowicz writes: "The consecrated bread now was termed

The new term *corpus mysticum*, hallowing, as it were, simultaneously the *Corpus Christi Juridicum*, that is, that gigantic legal and economic management on which the *Ecclesia militans* rested, linked the building of the visible Church organism with the former liturgical sphere; but, at the same time, it placed the Church as a body politic, or as a political and legal organism, on a level with the secular bodies politic, which were then beginning to assert themselves as self-sufficient entities. In that respect the new ecclesiological designation of *corpus mysticum* fell in with the more general aspirations of that age: to hallow the secular polities as well as their administrative institutions.[130]

The Church as a corporation, a legal entity, a sociological body, a political and economic organization, had, in some ways, always been such, but only with Boniface VIII had it become explicitly so, and the only question that remained to be answered was who was the chief executive? Both pope and emperor had valid claims, though the sacramental and liturgical aspects weighted the answer in favor of the pope as the vicar of Christ, the head of the Church, the highest priest, and the bishop of Rome, even if the emperor was never willing to concede in full; Constantine's basilica was there to remind. The pope's temporal rule and all its required apparatus, as Augustinus of Ancona termed it, was actually derived from Constantine. Thus all imperial privilege, dignity, and splendor were due the pope. Yet because he was to give glory to Christ, the pope was not only to be glorious, but also humble, and cautious that his external apparatus not be the cause of scandal.[131] The pope, after all, had an especial affect on Rome. As Bretano noted, the pope's

---

significantly the *corpus verum* or *corpus naturale*, or simply *corpus Christi*, the name under which also the feast of *Corpus Christi* was instituted by the Western Church in 1264. That is to say, the Pauline term originally designating the Christian Church now began to designate the consecrated host: contrariwise, the notion *corpus mysticum*, hitherto used to describe the host, was gradually transferred—after 1150—to the Church as the organized body of Christian society united in the Sacrament of the Altar. In short, the expression 'mystical body' which originally had a liturgical or sacramental meaning, took on a connotation of sociological content. It was finally in the relatively new sociological sense that Boniface VIII defined the Church as 'one *mystical* body the head of which is Christ.'" *Ibid.*, 196; see also Tierney, *Foundations*, 106–153; Otto Gierke, *Political Theories of the Middle Ages*, trans. with an introduction by Frederic William Maitland (Cambridge, 1900; Beacon Paperback edition: Boston, 1960³), 22–30.

[130] Kantorowicz, *The King's Two Bodies*, 197.
[131] Aug.Anc. *Summa* 101,4–5 (ed. Rome, 1479), fol. 281rb–283vb; "Dicendum <est> quod sicut omnis gloria filie regis puta ipsius ecclesie sponse Christi est ab intus, sic omnis gloria pape ministri Christi principalis sponsi ecclesie ab intus esse debet. Est autem tunc gloria ab intus... quando omne bonum quod quisque Christi munere facit et de omni honore sibi impenso in Christi gloriam refert. Potest

54   CHAPTER ONE

... attitude toward Rome, the city, the length of time he spent there, could alter a huge list of rents, prices, and incomes. In electing a pope the cardinals were electing the employer (although he might be a reemployer) of cooks and poulterers, of warriors and castellans, of clerks and confessors, the selector of cardinals, the favorer of religious orders, of nationalities.[132]

The corporate Church claimed the constitution of Christendom no less than did the emperor, who reached back to an earlier age of sacral lordship when the emperor could fashion himself as more than a German prince. Innocent III was one turning point and Boniface

---

autem papa exteriorem apparatum honoris et magnificentie in Christi gloriam referre tripliciter. Primo propter Christi sacerdotii honoris reverentiam; secundo propter populi subiecti obedientiam; tertio propter malorum reprimendam malitiam. Planum est enim quod longe maioris dignitatis et excellentie est sacerdotium Christi quam fuerit sacerdotium Leviticum, cum hic non carnes vitulorum et hircorum sed vera Christi caro immoletur et sumatur. Quanta autem exteriori paratura fuerit honoratum et orantum illud sacerdotium longus tractatus fit in Exodo et in aliis libris canonis sacri ... quod in veste poderis quam habebat Aaron totus erat orbis terrarum et parentum magnalia in quatuor gradibus lapidum erant sculpta, et magnificentia dei in dyademate capitis illius erat scripta. Multo ergo magis dignum est Christi sacerdotium omni paratura honoris et glorie adornari. Secundo debet eius paratura ordinari ad populi subi<e>ctam obedientiam. Despecto enim prelatorum in subditis quandoque parit contemptum et ideo debet Christi vicarium gloriosum in conspectu populi apparere nedum apud illos quos oportet esse subiectos si nimie deiectionis servaretur humilitas regendi frangeretur auctoritas. Tertio ordinanda est talis paratura quandoque propter malorum reprimendam malitiam, ne aliqui malivoli attemptarent tyrannicam rabiem exercere in illum qui loco Christi positus est in malleum et tyrannorum flagellum. Semper tamen in tali exteriori apparatu temperantia et modestia est servanda ne in Christiano populo materia scandali tribuatur et ambitio et mundi gloria queratur ... est dicendum quod papa succedit Petro in exteriori apparatu quantum ad iurisdictionem. Statim enim receptis clavibus Petrus loco Christi verus et legitimus dominus fuit omnium temporalium et spiritualium, sed quantum ad actualem possessionem et administrationem verum est quod in tali exteriori apparatu successit Constantino, ita quod illa que Constantinus dei beneficio recepit de manu domini hec ipsa tribuit Silvestro vicarius eius ... est dicendum quod papa debet esse Christi imitator in mentis humilitate, sic enim Christus dixit Mathei undecimo: *Discite a me quia mitis sum et humilis corde* [Mt. 11:29]. Exteriorem tamen honoris et reverentie potestatem in Christi gloriam ipse debet recipere et referre ut quantum Christus in cruce fuit humiliatus, tantum propter crucem in eius vicario sit honoratus et exaltatus ... Modestia tamen in ipsa apparatura et equitatura est servanda propter scandalum pusillorum vitandum ... est dicendum quod si debita modestia servetur in exteriori apparatu non datur occasio scandali, cum talia non impendantur homini sed Christo cuius vicarius existit, summo tamen opere strepitus armatorum vitandus est a papa, cum arma militie sue non carnalia sed spiritualia esse debeant, nisi forte in casu cum timerentur insidie malignorum." Aug.Anc. *Summa* 101,4 (ed. Rome, 1479), fol. 281[va]–282[ra].

[132] Brentano, *Rome Before Avignon*, 142.

VIII another of a slow development whereby the Church, or rather the *sacerdotium* headed by the pope, appropriated for itself the ideology of Christendom. Yet the new legal, economic, and sociological construct of the term *corpus mysticum* was before Boniface first put forth in the treatise he had used as the source for his *Unam sanctam*, Giles of Rome's *De ecclesiastica potestate*.[133] Moreover, Giles, as did the Augustinians William of Cremon, Augustinus of Ancona, and Hermann of Schildesche after him, applied the traditionally imperial term *vicarius dei* to the pope. The pope was no longer only the vicar of Christ, but the vicar of God as well, reigning as God on earth.[134] The pope had become indeed, as Augustinus repeatedly asserted, both king and priest, after the order of Melchesidech.[135] It was a fitting image.

B. *Battle Fronts*

> If it appears that what we have put forth in the above as settled, defined, or what in any other way we have asserted or written, is less than catholic, it was not said with a lack of respect, and we submit it for correction and determination to the authority of the catholic church or to a general council of the faithful.[136]

It came as a shock. On 24 June 1324 Marsilius of Padua completed his *Defensor Pacis* with the above quoted passage. This, however, was a treatise that had as its primary goal "to destroy the temporal power of the papacy."[137] While it might seem that Marsilius' statement here

---

[133] Aeg.Rom. *De eccl.pot.* 2,4 (50); 2,14 (132); 3,2 (152). It should also be noted that Giles used the image of the body thoroughout his treatise.

[134] "... quod sumus pontifex se habet sicut dei vicarius..." Aeg.Rom. *De eccl.pot.* 2,13 (126); "Sed summi pontifices sunt in terra sicut dii." Will.Crem. *Repr.* 2,1 (65,749); "... papa qui dei vicarius est..." Aug.Anc. *Summa* 101,8 (Rome, 1479), fol. 284rb; "Quia sicut [papa] desinit esse dei vicarius per renuntiationem... ita forte desinit esse dei vicarius per mortem..." Herm.Schild. *cont.neg.* 2,4 (67,38–41).

[135] "Papa gerit vicem Christi saltem quatum ad potestatem et iurisdictionem officii... sacerdotium et regale dominium Christi... figuratum... per sacerdotium et dominium Melchisedech, qui fuit simul rex et sacerdos... Potestas ergo regalis est in papa...'" Aug.Anc. *Summa* 1,7 (ed. Rome, 1479), fol. 8vb–9va.

[136] "... supradictis a nobis adicientes quod, si quid in ipsis reperiri contingat determinatum, diffinitum, aut aliter quomodolibet pronuntiatum vel scriptum minus catholice, id non pertinaciter dictum esse; ipsumque corrigendum atque determinandum supponimus auctoritati ecclesiae catholicae seu generalis concilii fidelium Christianorum." Marsilius *Def.pac.* 3,3 (501,15–20).

[137] Alan Gewirth, *Marsilius of Padua, The Defender of Peace*, vol. I: *Marsilius of Padua*

regarding his appeal to the authority of the Catholic Church is out of place with the tenor of the work as such, his formulation equates the Church's authority with that of a general council of the faithful, the latter of which represents the *universitas fidelium* as coterminous with the *universitas civium*, "the 'legislator' of the Marsilian state."[138] For Marsilius, no less than for Augustinus, "the church *is* the state, and vice versa."[139] In this light we come to realize that Marsilius' *Defensor Pacis*, which is so often treated as a unique and revolutionary treatise of political theory, is also, if not primarily, a work of revolutionary ecclesiology.[140]

---

and Medieval Political Philosophy (New York, 1951), 255; Marsilius *Def.pac.*, xiii; Marino Damiata, *Plenitudo Potestatis e Universitas Civium in Marsilio da Padova* (Florence, 1983), 48. See most recently Miethke, *De Potestate Papae*, 204–221. Gewirth pointed to Marsilius' "Augustinianism," as a foundational aspect of his political theory; see Gewirth, *Marsilius of Padua*, 37–39, and *passim*. Though critical of Gewirth's position and those who have in modified form followed him, Joanna Vecchiarelli Scott still notes that: "Marsiglio could mine Augustinianism for a wealth of remarks concerning law and obedience to duly constituted authorities, while easily turning a blind eye to the saint's less numerous comments on the internal hierarchy of the church... the radical extremity of Marsiglio's conclusions do not invalidate the possiblity that he may have accurately reproduced the saint's attitudes toward political authority." Scott, "Influence or Manipulation? The Role of Augustinianism in the *Defensor Pacis* of Marsiglio of Padua," *Augustinian Studies*, 9 (1978), 59–70; 78–79.

[138] Gewirth, *Marsilius of Padua*, 300.

[139] *Ibid.*, 292. For Marsilius' view of the church, see *ibid.*, 260–302; Gierke, *Political Theories*, 16; Damiata, *Plenitudo Potestatis*, 235–236.

[140] "Der umfängliche zweite Hauptteil des Traktats dient der polemischen Applikation der gewonnenen Grundsätze auf die Strukturen, die die kirchenpolitischen Diskussionen der zwanziger Jahre des 14. Jahrhunderts beherrscht haben. Vielleicht kam es Marsilius für den aktuellen Konflikt stärker auf diese eingehende und sorgfältige Darlegung an als auf die Konstruktion der staatlichen Gewalt, die für heutige Leser so viel aufregender wirkt." Miethke, *Die Potestate Papae*, 220. To argue comprehensively for Marsilius having primarily advocated an ecclesiology would require a separate study. His identification of the church with the state, nevertheless, makes it possible to view his work from one or the other perspective. The work appears in much different light when read as an ecclesiological tract, rather than as one establishing on purely rational grounds the sovereignty of the secular state. He is clear that to "live well" is to be understood both as referring to this life and to the future life; Marsilius *Def.pac.* 1,4,3 (12,20–13,15), and that knowing what is required for the future life is "useful" for living in the present life, and thus is necessary for the state; Marsilius *Def.pac.* 1,4,4 (13,16–14,5). He is further clear that only the Christian faith is the true faith which leads to the blessedness of the future life; Marsilius *Def.pac.* 1,5,13 (21,5–16). Marsilius attempts to show that the temporal jurisdiction of the church is a perversion of the true church and its structure and function. His point is to establish the 'true church', which consists of all Christians and thus is equated with the state, led by the emperor. When Marsilius analyzes the role of the *valentior pars*, the *pars principans*, or the *legislator*, it is as much *ecclesiastici* he is referring to as it is *cives*. Thus he uses Aristotle as an aid for defining

It could not have been otherwise. Even if Marsilius was far ahead of his time, he was still a product of his age.[141] The ideal of universal empire was not one that could simply be cast aside at will. Marsilius' republicanism is present throughout, a republicanism molded by the Lombard city states.[142] Yet still he addressed his treatise to the emperor, Louis of Bavaria. Louis was to exterminate heresy, uphold and serve the catholic truth as well as all worthy disciplines, correct vice, propagate virtue, put an end to quarrels and to secure peace and tranquillity, for Louis was the minister of God.[143] Louis was indeed to be the defender of peace, and peace was the highest goal of communal life. Christ had come to bring peace and this was Marsilius' point of departure, which he stated with reference to

---

the true Church and its structure, of which the *sacerdotium* is a single, but not singular, function.

[141] Miethke has noted: "Es ist bemerkenswert, wie Marsilius hier die politische Philosophie des Aristoteles an einem bestimmten historischen Punkt der menschlichen Entwicklung verortet, wie er aber zugleich auch die heilsgeschichte Erlösungstat des Gottmenschen Christus geradezu historisiert und damit in die Allgemeingültigkeit einer aristotelischen Wissenschaft hinein, wenn nicht einebnet, so doch einordnet. Marsilius will, so macht er dem Leser deutlich, Aristoteles nicht wiederholen, er will ihn auch nicht, wie das in Paris damals verschiedentlich geschehen war, ausschließlich kommentieren, er möchte noch Ausweis dieser programmatischen Erklärung den griechischen Philosophen um eine entscheidende Dimension ergänzen und auf die Gegenwart, seine eigene Gegenwart des 14. Jahrhunderts anwenden, weil das Aristoteles selbst noch nicht hatte tun können. Aristoteles vermag aber die wissenschaftliche Methode zu liefern, die nun auch für die politische Analyse der Gegenwart des Marsilius fruchtbar gemacht werden kann und soll, denn deren Unterschiede zur Welt des Aristoteles waren in dem einen Punkt, der Existenz der christlichen Kirche und ihrer Ansprüche, dem Verfasser so klar, daß er das schon in der Bestimmung seines Ausgangspunktes, in den ersten Zeilen seines umfangreichen Textes, als evident einführen konnte." Miethke, *De Potestate Papae*, 207; "Daß Marsilius der politischen 'Krankheit' seiner Tage mit Hilfe der politischen Theorie des Aristoteles beikommen will, heißt natürlich nicht, daß er die Texte des griechischen Philosophen etwa nicht mit den Augen des 14. Jahrhunderts und durch die Brille seiner eigenen Erfahrungen läse." *Ibid.*, 211.

[142] Gewirth, *Marsilius of Padua*, 23–31.

[143] "... in te quoque respiciens singulariter tamquam Dei ministrum huic operi finem daturum, quem extrinsecus optat inesse, inclitissime Ludovice, Romanorum Imperator, cui sanguinis antiquo speciali quasi quodam iure, nec minus singulari heroica tua indole ac praeclara virtute insitus et firmatus est amor haereses extirpare, catholicam veritatem omnemque aliam studiosam disciplinam extollere atque servare, vitia caedere, studia propagare virtutum, lites extinguere, pacem seu tranquillitatem ubique diffundere ac nutrire; sequentium sententiarum summas, post tempus diligentis et intentae perscrutationis, scripturae mandavi, ex ipsis arbitrans iuvamentum quoddam evenire posse tuae vigili maiestati, praescriptis lapsibus atque contingentibus aliis reliquisque utilitatibus publicis providere curanti." Marsilius *Def.pac.* 1,1,6 (5,15–27); *cf.* Marsilius *Def.pac.* 2,26 (397–423).

Cassiodorus, Job, and the Gospels.[144] Whereas papal hierocratic authors such as Giles of Rome and James of Viterbo, against whom, at least in part, it has been argued Marsilius was writing,[145] had considered the state as a function of the Church, one can see Marsilius' position as a mirrored opposite: the church as a function of the state. Yet such an interpretation does not adequately capture Marsilius' vision. For Marsilius the priesthood, the *sacerdotium*, is indeed a function of the state, but the Church is not to be equated with the priesthood. The *sacerdotium* is also a function of the Church, for the Church is comprised of all the faithful, the *universitas fidelium*.[146] Therefore "ecclesiastics, in keeping with this most true and proper meaning of the term, are and ought to be considered as all the faithful of Christ, the priests as much as the laity, in that Christ with his own blood gathered to himself and saved all."[147] Marsilius set the hierocratic theory on its head, based on a radical reinterpretation of the scriptures and the theological tradition. He saw the temporal power of the ecclesiastical hierarchy as the greatest obstacle to peace, and therefore as the greatest threat to the well-being of society, and consequently to the well-being of the Church. Whereas for Giles of Rome, the doctrine of the pope was a corollary of his doctrine of the Church, for Marsilius, the *legislator* and the *valentior pars* of civic society[148] were corollaries of his ecclesiology, with the emperor as head of the Church and the preserver of peace.[149]

---

[144] Marsilius *Def.pac.* 1,1 (1–2).

[145] "In Marsilius' direct doctrinal opponents, who upheld the 'church' side of the conflict at the end of the thirteenth century and the early years of the fourteenth—such largely forgotten men as Egidius of Rome, James of Viterbo, Henry of Cremona, Augustinus Triumphus, Alexander of St. Elpidius—the claims and arguments in behalf of the papal plenitude of power brought the whole conception of political power to an unparalleled degree of development." Gewirth, *Marsilius of Padua*, 8. Moreover, as did Tierney, Gewirth looked over the fact that all of the opponents of Marsilius he mentioned, except for Henry of Cremona, were Augustinians. It was an Augustinian front against which Marsilius was reacting, which could also explain in part Marsilius' 'Augustinianism'.

[146] Marsilius *Def.pac.* 2,2,3 (117–118).

[147] "Et propterea viri ecclesiastici, secundum hanc verissimam et propriissimam significationem, sunt et dici debent omnes Christi fideles, tam sacerdotes quam non-sacerdotes, eo quod omnes Christus acquisivit et redemit sanguine suo." Marsilius *Def.pac.* 2,2,3 (117,16–19).

[148] For Marsilius' concept of the *legislator*, see Gewirth, *Marsilius of Padua*, 167–175; for that of the *valentior pars*, see *ibid.*, 182–199.

[149] Once again it depends on perspective and how one reads Marsilius, namely, whether he started from the position of a purely rational, Aristotelian view of the

This was not a challenge that could be ignored.[150] Pope John XXII had already begun his campaign against Louis of Bavaria in 1323 when on 8 October John ordered Louis to cease acting as emperor until the disputed election of 1314 between Louis and Frederick of Austria could finally be settled and legitimately confirmed by the Holy See, prohibiting all ecclesiastical and temporal rulers from supporting Louis until such a time.[151] Louis remained unmoved, feeling secure in his support at home as well as among the Ghibelline cities of northern Italy, including Milan and its Duke, Galeazzo Visconti, whom John had already excommunicated on 23 January 1322. Now it was Louis' turn, and John promptly placed the interdict on Louis and his adherents on 23 March 1324; not quite four years later, in January of 1328, John called for a crusade against the still unrepentant Duke of Bavaria.[152] The last thing John needed in 1324 was more propaganda undermining his authority, including the claim that the pope had no right to excommunicate anyone without the consent and directive of the imperial Church.[153] John was already in a heated controversy with the Franciscans, and could not leave unanswered a treatise as thoroughly opposing his position as Marsilius' *Defensor Pacis*. The very Church was at stake. Thus between 1324

---

state and then applied such a position to the Church, or, whether he started from the development of his ideas on the Church, which then had consequences for political structure. *Dictio* 2 comprises the overwhelming majority of the work, even if it is preceded in presentation and argument by *Dictio* 1. If one reads the *Defensor Pacis* from the perspective of *Dictio* 3, especially 3,2 where Marsilius gives his conclusions, the ecclesiological emphasis of the work comes to the fore.

[150] H.S. Offler has, however, questioned the explosive nature of Marsilius' reception, arguing that the *Defensor Pacis* only became widely enough known to make a significant impact a century later, during the conciliar debates; see Offler, "The 'Influence' of Ockham's Political Thinking: The First Century," in *Die Gegenwart Ockhams*, ed. Wilhelm Vossenkuhl and Rolf Schönberger (Weinheim, 1990), 338–365; 346–347. Yet the first reaction to Marsilius was indeed very strong. Even if the *Defensor Pacis* as such was not widely known, some of its most challenging positions were. One could argue that neither John XXII nor William of Cremona (see below) knew Marsilius' text, but while that is an important point to make, it does not detract from the impact the text had, even if only by hearsay. Influence and impact can be measured on other bases than precise textual knowledge. For an argument that William did indeed know the text of the *Defensor Pacis*, see the introduction to Appendix C below.

[151] For a thorough discussion of the issues, see Müller, *Der Kampf Ludwigs des Baiern*, 56–75, and for the earlier background, *ibid.*, 1–56. For the text of John's Bull, see Bert. *KVA* (34–43).

[152] Müller, *Der Kampf Ludwigs des Baiern*, 171–175; Bert. *K VA* (29).

[153] Marsilius *Def.pac.* 3,2,16 (495,23–25); 2,6,10–14 (167–174); 2,21,8–9 (334–336).

and 1327 John solicited responses from a number of theologians to six articles drawn from Marsilius' work. The most important refutation that provided the justification for the condemnation of the *Defensor Pacis* in John's Bull *Licet iuxta doctrinam* of 23 October 1327, was the *Reprobatio Errorum* of William of Cremona, the prior general of the Augustinian Hermits.[154]

William's treatise is a point by point refutation of the articles in question, and thus, lacks a sense of coherency. It is by no means a thorough response to the *Defensor Pacis*, which is far more detailed and in-depth than the six positions extracted therefrom for condemnation. Neither in the six articles, nor in William's *Reprobatio* is Marsilius met on his own terms, and the majority of his most central arguments are ignored.[155] The six articles are, nevertheless, revealing of the nerves that Marsilius had hit, and William's reply goes to the heart of the issues separating Marsilius from the papal position.[156] The condemned positions are as follows:

1. That all temporal possessions of the Church are subject to the emperor and that he can therefore appropriate them as his own property;
2. That it falls to the emperor to correct and punish the pope, as well as to establish the pope in office, or to remove him from office;
3. That St. Peter the apostle was not the head of the Church any more than was any other of the apostles, nor did Peter have more authority than did the other apostles; moreover, Christ left no head of the Church, nor did he establish his own vicar;

---

[154] For a discussion of William's work, see Scholz, *Unbekannte Kirchenpolitische Streitschriften*, 1:13–22. The only other treatise that we know was commissioned by John XXII was that of the Carmelite Sybert von Beek, *Reprobatio sex errorum*; see Syb.B. *Repr.* However, the Praemonstratensian Petrus de Lutre wrote a treatise against Marsilius in 1328, as did the Augustinian hermit, Hermann of Schildesche. For Petrus, see Scholz, *Unbekannte Streitschriften*, 1:22–27; 2:29–63; for Hermann, *ibid.*, 1:50–60; 2:130–153; Herm.Sch. *cont.neg.*, vii–xiv; and Zumkeller, *Schrifttum und Lehre des Hermann von Schildesche O.E.S.A. (d. 1357)*, Cassiciacum 15 (Würzburg, 1959), 135–143, 168–217. For *Licet iuxta dotrinam*, see Denzinger *Ench.* Nr. 941–946 (398–399).

[155] *Cf.* note 150 above, and the introduction to Appendix C.

[156] That the six articles William addressed were selected by John XXII is confirmed not only by their correspondence to *Licet iuxta doctrinam*, but also by the parallel text given by the Carmelite Sybert of Beek in his refutation; see Will.Crem. *Repr.* Prologus (3,5–4,44); Syb.B. *Repr.* (3–4). *Licet iuxta doctrinam*, however, only includes five articles; Denzinger *Ench.* nr. 941–946 (398–399).

4. That all priests whatsoever, whether pope, archbishop, or parish priest, are equal in authority and jurisdiction based on the institution of Christ. Yet if one priest were to have more authority than the others, it would come about only from his having been granted such by the emperor, and thus the emperor can revoke such authority;

5. That the pope or the Church can punish no man for any crime whatsoever with coercive authority unless the emperor grants the authority to do so;

6. That any priest is fully able to absolve sinners from any crime or sentence imposed, or from any dangerous state of being to the same extent as is the pope.[157]

It is clear from William's treatment, as well as from the text of the articles themselves, that article four was perceived as the most pernicious. In the text of the articles, the only comment given in addition to presenting the position to be condemned, is in article four, where it is noted that from such a thesis it follows, in keeping with

> the blasphemy of those foolish heretics, that for the last three hundred years, during which they have infected the world with their idolatry, there has been no one among those holy popes whom the Church venerates as saints, who was truly a pope or pontiff. And that the Church has most terribly erred the entire time in all its offices in calling Peter the prince of the apostles and by saying that he was legitimately the vicar of Christ, as well as considering the Roman church to be the mother and teacher of all other churches. So many absurd conclusions come from such a thesis that they are too numerous to mention here.[158]

---

[157] Will.Crem. *Repr.* Prologus (3,5–4,44). The editor, Mac Fhionnbhairr, also gives references to the passages in the *Defensor Pacis* upon which the articles drew. He does not, however, list Marsilius *Def.pac.* 3,2 (493–500), where Marsilius gives his own list of 42 conclusions drawn from his work. Yet articles 1,2,4, and 5 could have been taken either directly or summarily from Marsilius' own conclusions, with the first drawing from Marsilius' list numbers 23, 27, and 28; article 2: Marsilius' 10, 18, and 29; article 5 from Marsilius' numbers 14, 15, 16, 21, and 30; and article 4 is a virtual restatement of Marsilius' conclusion number 17: "Omnes episcopos aequalis auctoritatis esse immediate per Christum, neque secundum Legem Divinam convinci posse, in spiritualibus aut temporalibus praeesse invicem vel subesse." Marsilius, *Def.pac.* 3,2,17 (495,26–28); article 4 reads: "Quarto dicunt, quod omnes sacerdotes, sive sit Papa, sive archiepiscopus sive sacerdos simplex, quicumque sunt aequales in auctoritate et iurisdictione ex institutione Christi." Will.Crem. *Repr.* Prologus (4,26–28). Mac Fhionnbhairr lists *Defensor Pacis* 2,15; 2,17; 2,25,4, and 2,28,2 as the sources.

[158] "Ex hoc sequitur secundum blasphemiam istorum stultorum haereticorum,

After going into various arguments refuting the position of sacerdotal equality, William concluded by asserting that: "To posit no distinction among the clergy with regard to the power of jurisdiction, is to pervert the entire Church and the entire ecclesiastical order."[159] This, naturally, was precisely Marsilius' point. From the Church's perspective, article four was more dangerous than was article three or article one, which denied the primacy of St. Peter and the right of the Church to temporal possessions respectively. While the other articles William certainly considered to be heretical, and thus inimical to the Church, or vice versa, article four cut to the core. At issue was the very architecture itself of the Church.[160] It was one thing to debate the power of the pope over against the power of the emperor, or even to question whether the pope did indeed have primacy within the Church, but it was another matter to undercut the hierarchical structure upon which all further arguments of papal primacy were based. This William well understood, and if there is any unifying principle in his treatise, it is his consistent defense and espousal of the hierarchical Church and his implicit vision of Christian society, a mode of thought that followed in the footsteps of Giles of Rome.

William's treatment of the first article is the longest of his treatise. There at the outset William launched into a discussion of the Church as such, how it was defined and on what it was based.[161] Marsilius had argued that the *viri ecclesiastici* should not be limited to members of the clergy, but included all faithful Christians, *omnes Christi fideles*.[162] William was in complete agreement, as had the canon-

---

quod in trecentis annis, quibus idololatrae praefuerunt mundo, nullus de illis sanctis Papis, quos colit Ecclesia sicut sanctos, fuerit Papa vel pontifex. Et quod Ecclesia turpiter erravit semper in suis officiis vocando Petrum principem apostolorum et dicendo eum legitimum vicarium Jesu Christi vel Romanam ecclesiam esse aliarum matrem et magistram. Et tot absurda sequuntur, quot numerari non possunt in hoc scripto." Will.Crem. *Repr.* Prologus (4,30–37); *cf.* Syb.B. *Repr.* (3–4).

[159] "Nullam enim ponere distinctionem inter sacerdotes quoad potestatem jurisdictionem est pervertere totam Ecclesiam et totum ordinem ecclesiasticum." Will.Crem. *Repr.* 4,4 (91,304–306).

[160] Syb.B. *Repr.* (12–13). Sybert did recognize the importance of article four, concluding that it was heresy and led to schism, because it would entail that the emperor had spiritual power over the Church, rather than the pope, yet Sybert did not address the fundamental issue at stake, the hierarchical structure of the Church itself.

[161] Will.Crem. *Repr.* 1,1–2 (5,37–11,221). No such ecclesiological treatment is found in Sybert's work.

[162] Marsilius, *Def.pac.* 2,2,2–3 (116–118); see also note 147 above.

ists been all along. Not only the clergy, but the laity as well, all Christians, the *universitas fidelium*, the *communitas omnium fidelium*, are *ecclesiastici*.[163] Yet this was only one way of defining the Church. The second way of understanding the Church is by the more potent members of the *universitas fidelium*, the *pars potior*, which may have been William's counter to Marsilius' *valentior pars*. The *pars potior* of the Church, is the *universitas clericorum*, the clergy, the more noble part of the Church, and thus the Church can be understood as consisting of the clergy alone.[164] And yet in both ways of understanding the Church there is hierarchy.

Drawing from Hugh of St. Victor's *De Sacramentis*, and in complete agreement with Giles' *De ecclesiastica potestate*, William argued that in the Church as the *universitas fidelium* there is still the distinction to be made between the body and the soul. The body lives from the soul, and the soul lives from God. Each has their respective goods and nourishment, and in each, justice is served. Thus, in the Church, there is the temporal power that corresponds to the body, and the spiritual power that corresponds to the soul. These two powers are the two swords of the Church, the material sword and the spiritual sword, whereby the first is that of the temporal, lay power, and the second resides with the spiritual power, which is the clergy.[165] The distinction between body and soul, forms the basis

---

[163] "Uno modo pro communitate omnium fidelium.... Ergo primo modo accipitur ecclesia pro tota communitate et universitate fidelium.... Non quin laici non sint ecclesiastici, immo sunt..." Will.Crem. *Repr.* 1,1 (5,38–6,74). See also Tierney, *Foundations*, 134–141, 202–206.

[164] Will.Crem. *Repr.* 1,1 (6,70–7,83); the term *pars potior* was later used by Zabarella as loosely analogous to *valentior pars*, which stemmed not only from Marsilius, but also from William of Moerbeke's translation of Aristotle's *Politics*. Zabarella, however, used it to refer to the *potior pars* of a General Council, which could embody the entire authority of the Council; he did not use it in terms of the Church as such; Tierney, *Foundations*, 223–237. Tierney notes that Zabarella's terminological echo of Marsilius "has sometimes been unduly emphasized." *Ibid.*, 223. William, however, was writing in direct response to the six articles and may very well have known the *Defensor Pacis* directly, though there is no concrete proof; the term *pars valentior* in any case is not found in the six articles, and William chose to use a distinct term from the *pars valentior* of Aristotle, or the common *sanior pars*, when explicating his view of the Church in his condemnation of the articles. There is further nothing about the first article as such that would necessitate an ecclesiological statement such as William gives. Though it remains speculative, it is also persuasive that William knew the *Defensor Pacis* and used the term *potior pars* as referring to the clergy as a direct reply to Marsilius; see also the introduction to Appendix C.

[165] Will.Crem. *Repr.* 1,1 (6,43–70).

for the second understanding of the Church, whereby the spiritual power, the clergy, is taken as definitive thereof as the more powerful and more noble part of the Church.[166] William then continued by basing all right of lordship on an Augustinian theory of dominion, whereby all possession is just only when subservient to God, from whom all lordship is derived, and consequently all lordship resides in the Church.[167]

The relationship between the body and soul, for William as it was for Giles, was based on the divine order. Just as the universe exists according to the divinely established order, so does the Church, and thus, the temporal power is to be ordered in relation to the spiritual power whereby the material sword serves the spiritual sword in the same way that the body serves the soul.[168] Hence, it is only fitting that within the Church there is only one head, and that head is the pope, Christ's vicar, who rules the Church, and all Christian society, spiritual as well as temporal, as God on earth.[169] Thus the emperor is the subject and servant of the pope.[170]

Such an analysis was music to John's ears. William had responded to the six articles with depth, and he had done so based on the ecclesiological vision of Giles of Rome. Moreover, William was only one Augustinian writing in defense of the papal Church. By 1324 Alexander of San Elpidio had completed his treatise *De ecclesiastica*

---

[166] Will.Crem. *Repr.* 1,1 (6,70–7,83); cf. Will.Crem. *Repr.* 2,1 (48,190–49,234).

[167] Will.Crem. *Repr.* 1,2 (7,96–11,221); 1,3 (12,266–13,284) William's Augustinian approach to the issue of lordship is seen further in his treatment of the second part of the first article, namely, whether the emperor can appropriate Church property for himself. Sybert had treated this question in terms harkening back to the legal question of the emperor's authority surrounding the legislation of Roncaglia of Frederick II, namely, that the Church's temporal goods were in the possession of the Church in the same fashion as a private individual's possessions. Since the emperor could not justly appropriate the goods of one of his subjects, so could the emperor not appropriate the temporal goods of the Church; Syb.B. *Repr.* (7–9); cf. Pennington, *The Prince and the Law*, 15–37. William, on the other hand, based his response on the dominion of grace; Will.Crem. *Repr.* 1,5–7 (20–38), stating explicitly that the question of ecclesiastical lordship is determined based on the doctrine of creation; Will.Crem. *Repr.* 1,7 (35,1034–1050).

[168] Will.Crem. *Repr.* 2,1 (48,190–49,234; 58,518–537); 2,2 (66,779–799); 3,1 (68,15–72,157); 4,1 (82,18–84,89).

[169] Will.Crem. *Repr.* 2,1 (65, 747–761); cf. Will.Crem. *Repr.* 3,2 (76,259–265), where William argued that Peter possessed both the temporal and the spiritual sword based on John 18:10 where Peter cut off the ear of the soldier.

[170] "Imperator vero est eius [*scil.* papae] subditus et servus." Will.Crem. *Repr.* 4,3 (90,293–294); cf. 5,1 (91,9–93,65).

potestate, which was essentially a restatement of James of Viterbo's *De regimine christiano*, and dedicated the work to Pope John XXII.[171] Three years later Hermann of Schildesche had dedicated and sent a treatise to John, which he then later expanded into his *Tractatus contra haereticos negantes immunitatem et iurisdictionem sanctae ecclesiae*.[172] And by 1326, Augustinus of Ancona had finished his *Summa de potestate ecclesiastica*, also dedicated to John XXII.

There can be little doubt that Augustinus directed his *Summa* against Marsilius' *Defensor Pacis*.[173] In his letter of dedication to John, Augustinus states his intent to counter the errors of those who do not believe in the power of the Roman pontiff, who is the true successor to Peter and Christ's vicar on earth, possessing universal lordship over all temporal and spiritual goods. Those believing such falsehood, usurp divine authority, having based themselves on prideful curiousness, following the superstitions of the Athenians, who were interested only in learning about novelties.[174] Augustinus never explicitly mentioned Marsilius or the *Defensor Pacis*, but neither did the six articles nor William in his *Reprobatio*.[175] Yet in its breadth and depth Augustinus' *Summa* responds to the *Defensor Pacis* on a scale far greater and far more directly than had previously been done, even in the articles of condemnation and the theological treatises they elicited.

Marsilius, however, was not the only opponent facing the Augustinian-papal ecclesiology in 1326. A month before Marsilius completed his *magnum opus*, and two months after he had been excommunicated, Louis of Bavaria issued a document that has become known as the *Sachsenhausen Appeal*, dated 22 May 1324.[176] Louis, referring to John

---

[171] Alexander de Sancto Elpidio, *De ecclesiastica potestate*, ed. J.T. Rocaberti, *Bibliotheca Maxima Pontifica*, vol. 2/7 (Rome, 1698), 1–40.

[172] The earliest part of the work is the third, which Hermann sent to the pope. This part, however, has not survived, and we only have the first two parts of Hermann's treatise, which were completed before 1332. See Herm.Schild. *con.neg.*, viii–ix.

[173] Ministeri, "De Vita et Operibus," 54. Wilks makes no mention hereof, treating Augustinus' *Summa* only in the context of political theory, though he does discuss Marsilius.

[174] Aug.Anc. *Summa* Epist. (Rome, 1479), fol. 2vb–3ra; for the text of Augustinus' letter of dedication, as well as the table of questions he treats in his *Summa*, see Appendix C.

[175] *Licet iuxta doctrinam*, however, does explicitly condemn the positions it attributes to Marsilius and John of Jandun; Denzinger *Ench.* nr. 946 (399).

[176] See Lud.IV. *App*. According to Damiata, Marsilius at least knew of the *Sachsenhausen Appeal*; Damiata, *Plenitudo Potestatis*, 145.

as "he who calls himself pope,"[177] condemned John for the unjust excommunication of himself, the emperor, as well as of the Visconti and the Lombard cities, all of which had caused havoc and disturbed the peace.[178] John's political machinations against the rightful emperor, God's servant, were an usurpation of authority and power.[179] Moreover, by doing so John was preventing the Gospel from being spread, and thus was the enemy of the true Church.[180] For these reasons, Louis called for a general council of the Church to depose John as a heretic, and as a rebel against Christ.[181]

Even more, however, was at issue. Louis portrayed himself as the defender and protector of the Catholic Church and Christian faith, but he did not directly attack the position of the pope as such. Indeed, the office of the papacy is fiercely defended in the *Sachsenhausen Appeal*. This is a document of central importance for the history of the papacy, for it is here, for the first time, that the argument is made for papal infallibility.[182]

It might seem incongruous that the infallibility of the pope was put forward in a work attacking Pope John XXII in no uncertain terms, and one that exalted the position of the emperor. But that is precisely what we find, and there are good reasons. After Louis had presented his case at some length regarding John's usurpation of

---

[177] "... proponimus contra Iohannem, qui se dicit papam vicesimum secundum..." Lud.IV *App.* 1 (386); Bert. *KVA* (44).

[178] "... [Johannes] quod inimicus sit pacis et intendit ad discordias et scandala suscitanda non solum in Italia, quod notorium est, sed etiam in Alemania, suscitando prelatos et principes commovendo per nuncios frequentes et litteras et sollicitando, ut contra sacram imperium et nos debeant guerram movere et pro viribus rebellare." Lud.IV *App.* 1 (386–387); Bert. *KVA* (44); 6 (388); Bert. *KVA* (48); 15 (392–394); Bert. *KVA* (58–62). In *Appellatio* 6 Louis makes the procedural point that one cannot be condemned without a trial, which had been a fundamental point Clement V had made against Henry VII in his Bull *Pastoralis Cura*; see Pennington, *The Prince and the Law*, 187–188.

[179] Lud.IV. *App.* 13–14 (390–392); Bert. *KVA* (52–58).

[180] Lud.IV. *App.* 7 (388); Bert. *KVA* (48).

[181] Lud.IV. *App.*[2] (411–425). The text of Berthold does not correspond to that in Baluzius. Baluzius gives two documents as Louis' *Appellatio*. The first is found on pages 386–410, with the second following on pages 411–425. Each document has its separate paragraphicization, and both are dated 22 May 1324. Berthold gives the text of the first document through to Baluzius page 410, but then omits the concluding sentence in the Baluzius text, and skips to presenting the last paragraph of the second text given by Baluzius on page 425. Moreover, Berthold omits paragraphs 29 and 30 of the first text presented in Baluzius (Baluzius, page 408; Berthold, page 100).

[182] See Tierney, *Origins*, 182–186.

authority, there follows a portion of the text that then turns to condemn John of heresy. This section of the work has been referred to as a Franciscan excursus, or even a separate treatise, that was then inserted into the *Sachsenhausen Appeal*.[183] According to Tierney, the most likely author of the excursus was Bonagratia of Bergamo.[184] Yet in 1324, Bonagratia, together with his close friend Michael of Cesena, the minister general of the Franciscan Order, had not yet made their definitive break with the pope. It was only in 1326 that Michael began secret negotiations with Louis, having been summoned to Avignon by John. In December of 1328, Michael and Bonagratia finally arrived in Avignon. After a series of conflicts with John, the two Franciscans, together with another of their coreligious, William of Ockham, who at that time was also in Avignon having been summoned by the pope, fled in April of 1329 and took refuge at the court of Louis in Pisa.[185] Yet regardless who the author might have been, the Franciscan excursus is a fierce defense of the Franciscan doctrine of apostolic poverty, which John had condemned in 1323 in his Bull *Cum inter nonnullos*.

And that was the point. John had condemned as heretical the very basis of the Franciscan *Rule* and way of life, the doctrine that Christ and the apostles held no property either individually or in common. The author of the excursus was flabbergasted. This was a position that popes from Gregory IX to Nicholas IV had upheld, and that had been confirmed by Nicholas III's Bull *Exiit*.[186] This was the doctrine, moreover, the foundational bulwark, upon which Francis, the *seraphicus vir*, had established his Order. The Franciscan was the highest form of the evangelical life, and the closest to imitating truly that of Christ and the apostles themselves. To claim otherwise, is to profane the very Gospel, for the entire Gospel, as well as all the sayings of the apostles and of all up to the present day affirm that Christ and the apostles lived in the highest form of perfect poverty.[187] Then came the central argument. What the popes have proclaimed based on the key of knowledge to be true in the realms of faith and morals, is eternally and unchangeably true, for the catholic faith is

---

[183] Lud.IV. *App.* 28,1–11 (398–408); Bert. *KVA* (74–100).
[184] Tierney, *Origins*, 183.
[185] *Ibid.*, 200–201.
[186] Lud.IV. *App.* 28,1 (398–399); 28,3 (405–406).
[187] Lud.IV. *App.* 28,1 (398–399).

68   CHAPTER ONE

based on eternal and unchangeable truth. Thus once such doctrine has been defined, it cannot be called into question or overturned by any succeeding pope, for to claim otherwise, would be to throw all catholic teaching into doubt, and any one doing so should be considered a heretic.[188] Moreover, to claim that the Franciscan doctrine of poverty is not that of Christ and the apostles is to claim that Christ was not truly the Christ and messiah whom the prophets proclaimed, and the claim that Christ was not truly Christ is the foundation of the sect of the antichrist.[189] The author did not go so far, and neither did Louis, as to list John himself as a member of this sect, but the implication was clearly made. John had condemned as heretical an eternal truth of the catholic Church, which therefore rendered him a heretic, and in fact, an antichrist.

John, however, held his ground. As Tierney put it, John

> reacted to the Sachsenhausen Appeal with all the glee of a wily old tactician who sees his adversary stumble into an unnecessary blunder. Good canonist that he was, John knew very well that the idea of the pope's possessing an unerring key of knowledge was a novelty, probably nonsensical and certainly unacceptable to all sound Catholic opinion.[190]

A blunder on the part of the Franciscan author it might have been, but it was one that had serious consequences for John, who was not to remain all that gleeful for very long. When Michael of Cesena, Bonagratia of Bergamo, and William of Ockham fled Avignon in early 1329 to Louis' court in Pisa, they would have met another member of Louis' entourage who had been at his court in Munich already since 1326, and who had accompanied Louis on his march on Rome: Marsilius of Padua. In his *Defensor Pacis* Marsilius had

---

[188] "Quod enim per clavem scientie per romanos pontifices semel determinatum est in fide et moribus recte vite, est immutabile, eo quod ecclesia romana est inerrabilis in fide et veritate nec potest dare regulam falsam vel malam in recte vivendo nec in veritatis judicio ecclesia romana potest sibi esse contraria. Si enim in uno esset falsa vel sibi contraria, in omnibus vacillaret. Et super hoc fundamento generale capitulum se in predicta littera stabilivit. Nam quod semel per summos pontifices dei vicarios per clavem scientie est diffinitum esse de fidei veritate, non potest per successorem aliquem in dubium revocari vel eius quod diffinitum est contrarium affirmari, quin hoc agens manifeste hereticus sit censendus. Cuius veritatis ratio et fundamentum est, quia fides catholica est de vero perpetuo et immutabili prorsus. Et ideo quod semel est diffinitum verum esse in ipsa fide vel moribus, in eternum verum est et immutabile per quemcumque." *Ibid.* (403).

[189] Lud.IV. *App.* 28,2 (404–405).

[190] Tierney, *Origins*, 186.

advocated the poverty of Christ and the apostles as the basis for denying the clergy the right to temporal lordship. Even if Marsilius' arguments in general were not ones the Franciscans would have stomached, they joined forces on the fundamental issue of the poverty of Christ, and did so, as adherents and supporters of Louis.[191] The emperor now counted as members of his court two of the most penetrating minds of the century, if not of the entire Middle Ages: Marsilius and William of Ockham. When Louis returned to Munich the following year, he brought them both with him, and in Munich, Ockham began his attacks on John.[192]

Yet already in 1324, even if John knew he could handle the assertion of papal immutability, he did not take the matter lightly. The *Sachsenhausen Appeal* was after all not an isolated, renegade treatise of a radical Franciscan, even if it included such in part. It was a frontal attack put forth by the emperor, calling for a Church council to depose the heretic who was calling himself pope, and undermining papal sovereignty by posing the doctrine of papal infallibility. Moreover, it reasserted the Franciscan as the highest form of Christian life, that closest to Christ and the apostles, which implies that if a pope were not a Franciscan, the Franciscan Order would be more perfect than the pope.[193] John recognized the threat the Franciscan pretensions posed, and had condemned them as heretical in *Cum inter nonnullos*. Yet here they had raised their ugly head most aggressively, couched within an imperial manifesto. And to make matters worse, shortly after the *Sachsenhausen Appeal*, John became aware of an even greater threat, Marsilius' *Defensor Pacis*, a treatise that used the doctrine of apostolic poverty to dislegitimate the temporal authority of the Church. These two documents of 1324 were a double-barrel blast against the ecclesiastical structure as John knew it. Two years later, there came a reply: Augustinus of Ancona's *Summa*.

---

[191] Marsilius *Def.pac.* 3,2,38 (499); 2,13,22 (231–232) 2,13,30 (237); 2,13,33 (238–239); 2,14,3 (245); 2,14,14 (252–253); 2,14,23–24 (261–263).

[192] Tierney, *Origins*, 205–237; for Ockham's political works, see also Jürgen Miethke, *Ockhams Weg zur Sozialphilosophie* (Berlin, 1969), esp. 348–427 regarding the conflict with John XXII, and *idem*, *De Potestate Papae*, 248–295; A. Stephen MacGrade, *The Political Thought of William of Ockham. Personal and Institutional Principles* (Cambridge, 1974); and H.S. Offler, "The 'Influence' of Ockham's Political Thinking." For a cogent discussion of the relationship between the property of religious Orders and papal jurisdiction, see Ballweg, *Ordensreform*, 106–124.

[193] Tierney, *Origins*, 175; Horst, "Die Armut Christ," 488–491.

C. *The Sovereign Church*

When Louis of Bavaria invaded Rome in 1328, he did so as the defender of the Church, as the defender of peace and of orthodoxy, as the minister of God, all bearing echoes of an earlier age. One, however, would err, if one saw in Louis' pretensions merely an ideological superstructure, a legitimation that was required by his time. He believed his story. He was fighting for Christendom no less than was his arch-enemy Pope John XXII. John too had troops in the field, battling in the north against the Visconti and the Estensi, as well as against the communes in the March of Ancona of Montefeltro, Speranza, Osimo, Urbino, Recanati, and Spoleto having called for a crusade against these cities in December of 1321. Three years later Fermo and Fabriano were added to the list,[194] before John launched his military campaign against Louis in early 1328. Augustinus had cautioned against papal use of military force except in the case of extreme need, and had done so with good reason.[195] Yet the need was there. What they were fighting for, on one level at least, was a myth: the idea of a unified universal government, the idea of Christendom, and who was to be its champion.[196] This is not, however, to claim that Louis and John were idealistic dreamers, Don Quixotes fighting for some etherial principle—far from it. They were both down to earth politicians as few have been and they both knew the stakes, and they both knew the issues, and what was to be gained, or lost: the eternity that was Rome, and all the power, privilege, and prestige that entailed. One must not be a reductionist, viewing the matter as either a contest between ideologues, or crass oportunists. Both made for the reality. Louis and John were fighting for ideas and beliefs, fighting for wealth, fighting for power, and for control; even if it was still fighting for windmills, the Christendom that was Rome was a windmill with a lot of substance. And in the midst of it all, in the rockets' red glare, with bombs bursting in air, Augustinus of Ancona constructed his summation of the sovereign

---

[194] Housley, *The Italian Crusades*, 25–26.
[195] See note 131 above.
[196] "Hence the prevailing belief in the necessity for an inviolate social order, culminating in the institution of absolute monarchy. To this end society was given a religious character: it became a church and its monarch a god... Man repeatedly demonstrates his inability to survive without his myths, and the most potent of these is the myth of the state." Wilks, *The Problem of Sovereignty*, 524.

Church, offered to Pope John, and thereby contributed to the reality of the conflict, of the blood that was shed and of the destruction inflicted, in the name of the justness, and righteousness of the cause.

Augustinus' fight for Christendom was, as had been Giles of Rome's, a battle that was synonymous with the cause of the Order. Giles and Augustinus were as opportunistic as were Popes Boniface and John, as were Princes Philip and Louis. The pen may not have been as powerful as the sword, as Anagni seemed to prove, but it was anything but impotent. And of all the pens taken up in battle, that of Marsilius of Padua, of an anonymous Franciscan, of William of Ockham, of William of Cremona, and of Hermann of Schildesche, among all the others, that of Augustinus stands above the rest in its comprehensive vision.

Augustinus' *Summa* remains something of a paradox. Michael Wilks claimed that Augustinus "alone amongst the publicists of the thirteenth and fourteenth century gives a really complete and adequate account of the maturer stages of papal-hierocratic doctrine," while at the same time argues that Augustinus "had in fact anticipated almost the whole of William of Ockham's conciliar theory."[197] Augustinus to be sure on occasion seems to assert contradictory positions, such as on the one hand claiming that the pope can be judged by no one but God alone, yet on the other, should the pope decree something that is directly against divine law, he is to be strongly opposed.[198] Ulrich Horst has referred to such tensions in Augustinus' work as resulting from an ambiguity in Augustinus' view of the teaching authority of the papacy, pointing out that "the question of truth was

---

[197] Wilks, *The Problem of Sovereignty*, 2 and 11; "Zu den Paradoxien der Ekklesiologie des Augustinus von Ancona gehört eben auch, daß man ihn—wieder seine Intentionen—zu den Wegbereitern konziliaristischer Ideen gerechnet hat." Ulrich Horst, "Die Lehrautorität des Papstes nach Augustinus von Ancona," *AAug.* 54 (1991), 271–303; 302.

[198] "Papa omni lege humana posita per eum vel per alium solutus est, quia a nulla lege potest iudicari iudicio condemnationis, sed a sola lege eterna secundum quam verissime dictum est per apostolum, oportet nos omnes presentari ante tribunal Christi." Aug.Anc. *Summa* 44,8 (ed. Rome, 1479), fol. 144ra; "Si [papa] mandaret aliquid contra illam [*scil.* contra legem divinam] puta si preciperet quod creatura aliqua honore latrie adoraretur vel quod nomen dei in vanum assumeretur aut quod tempus deditum ad cultum dei sibi subtraheretur, sibi non esset obediendum, immo fortiter resistendum." Aug.Anc. *Summa* 22,1 (ed. Rome, 1479), fol. 77va–b.

not seen to be the real problem," given Augustinus' distinction between truth and justice as they exist in God, and as they are to be determined in the current situation (*secundum praesentem iustitiam*).[199] Augustinus never addressed such questions of conflict within his work. Yet one still stumbles across them, though they are far more harmonious than they may seem at first when Augustinus' vision of the Church as a whole is taken into account. He was not writing a systematic treatise on papal sovereignty and authority *per se*, but was explicating the extent and boundaries of ecclesiastical power.[200] The lordship of Christ is the central theme and had Augustinus given an alternative title to his work, it would have been *De regno Christi*. Christ was the head of the Church, and it was the task of drawing the implications and consequences of that recognition in context of the papal-imperial battle for Christendom that Augustinus set for himself in his *Summa*.

Augustinus did not pull any punches, even if some of them surely missed their mark. He opened straight off with a response to his opponents, Louis and Marsilius, by beginning with a question dealing explicitly with the power of the pope. Here Augustinus touched on many of the themes that he would elaborate later on in his work, and set forth a distinction that is fundamental for understanding the entire *Summa*: the difference between the pope's power of ordination (*potestas ordinis*) and power of jurisdiction (*potestas iurisdictionis*). The pope's power of ordination is that of his office as priest and bishop; his power of jurisdiction inheres in his office as pope. Regarding the former, the pope, and indeed every ordained priest and bishop, receives from the grace conferred in the sacrament of ordination a divine imprint (*character*), which enables him to perform his duties. Thus the power of ordination is related to Christ's true body (*corpus verum*), for the primary function of the priest, whether parish

---

[199] "... daß die Wahrheitsfrage nicht als das eigentliche Problem empfunden wurde." Horst, "Lehrautorität des Papstes," 302–303; 303.

[200] "In omni negotioni ignorantia est periculosa quia multa mala sequuntur ex ipsa ... Si ergo ignoratur quanta est et que est potestas pape est valde periculosum et ex parte eius qui preest et ex parte illorum qui sibi subiiciuntur. Cum enim papa presit fidelibus ecclesie mediantibus clavibus sibi a Christo collatis, si scitur quanta est potestas eius et circa que, tunc scitur quod preest eis clavem potentie non excedendo et circa clavem scientie non errando. Sed si talis potestas ignoratur, tunc preest subditis suis ignoranter et illa que facit, agit potestate excedente et clave scientie errante, quod sine periculo sui et subditorum esse non potest." Aug.Anc. *Summa* 1,10 (ed. Rome, 1479), fol. 11vb.

priest, bishop, or pope, is consecrating the host in celebrating mass. To this extent, all bishops and priests are equal to the pope.[201] The power of jurisdiction, however, is uniquely the pope's, in so far as the pope receives immediately from Christ the power of the keys, and thus the pope is Christ's vicar. As such, the pope possesses universal jurisdiction of both the temporal and spiritual realms, and all are subject to the sovereignty of the pope, who governs Christ's mystical body (*corpus mysticum*).[202]

---

[201] "Omnis potestas ordinis vel respicit characteris impressionem vel respicit characteris perfectionem. Nam characteris impressio fit in septem ordinibus, quia in quolibet ordine imprimitur character. In episcopatu vero licet non imprimatur character, perficitur tamen character iam impressus, ut per talem perfectionem possit episcopus, qui est perfectus sacerdos, sibi similes generare. Sed omnes episcopi habent characteris impressionem et characteris perfectionem. Ergo omnes episcopi sunt equales pape in potestate ordinis." Aug.Anc. *Summa* 1,4 (ed. Rome, 1479), fol. 6rb; "Dicendum quod in papa est duplex potestates: una respectu corporis Christi veri et ista vocatur potestas ordinis; alia est respectu corporis Christi mystici et ista vocatur potestas iurisdictionis vel administrationis. Si ego loquimur de potestate pape respectu corporis Christi veri que est potestas ordinis, talis non est nisi una unitate reali, quia in omnibus sacerdotibus et episcopis talis potestas non plurificatur nec ex parte ipsorum sacerdotum vel episcoporum offerentium quia omnes offerunt in persona unius sacerdotis puta Christi; non enim illa verba *hoc est corpus meum* proferuntur in persona sacerdotis vel episcopi consecrantis, sed in persona Christi ... quod Christus, qui mensam illam ornavit, discipulorum in ceno presto est mense nostre quam consecrat, quia non est homo qui proposita panem et vinum corpus et sanguinem facit. Sed ille qui crucifixus est pro nobis Christus cuius virtute consecrantur, licet sacerdotis ore proferantur. Nec plurificatur ex parte rei oblate, quia non aliud corpus offertur per unum episcopum vel per unum sacerdotem et aliud per alium. Sed illud idem corpus numero offertur per unum quod per omnes alios. Nec tertio plurificatur ex parte passionis commemorate quia una et eadem passio Christi semel recepta commemoratur per omnes ... Potestas ergo ordinis que est respectu corporis Christi veri una est realiter in papa et in omnibus sacerdotibus et episcopis, quia in tali potestate omnes sacerdotes non sunt nisi unus sacerdos et omnes episcopi nisi unus episcopus per unitatem unius sacerdotis consecrantis et unius rei oblate et unius passionis commemorate." Aug.Anc. *Summa* 1,6 (ed. Rome, 1479), fol. 8^{ra-b}.

[202] "Sed loquendo de potestate iurisdictionis tam spiritualium quam temporalium talis est in papa immediate ... auctoritas iurisdictionis non conceditur nisi per claves ecclesie; sed claves ecclesie christus non concessit nisi Petro singulariter, sicut patet Mathei sexto decimo: *dabo tibi claves celorum* [Mt. 16:19] ... Christus solum unum vicarium et unum caput vult esse in ecclesia ad quod diversa membra recurrent, si forte ab invicem dissentirent." Aug.Anc. *Summa* 1,1 (ed. Rome, 1479), fol. 3vb; "Si loquamur de potestate iurisdictionis sive accipiatur talis potestas iurisdictionis in spiritualibus sive in temporalibus nullus est equalis pape in tali potestate, quia omnes alii episcopi vocati sunt in partem sollicitudinis et administrationis; solus autem papa habet administrationem universalem toto orbe." Aug.Anc. *Summa* 1,4 (ed. Rome, 1479), fol. 6va; "Si vero loquamur de potestate pape respectu corporis Christi mystici, que est potestas iurisdictionis, talis similiter est una <potestas> in papa unitate cuiusdam ordinis. Nam in corpore mystico triplicem ordinem distinguere

74   CHAPTER ONE

Augustinus was not the first to make the distinction between the pope's two powers, but he was the one to develop it to its fullest.[203] It was his answer to Marsilius. If one were to factor out of Augustinus' *Summa* the pope's power of jurisdiction, one would find a view of the Church not so dissimilar to that advocated in the *Defensor Pacis*. Marsilius too recognized the priesthood's divine imprint at ordination (*character*), and used the sacramental function of the priesthood to argue for the equality of the *sacerdotium*.[204] Yet Marsilius denied the pope's power of jurisdiction. He based his argument on the imitation of Christ. The apostles were the true imitators of Christ and they taught their successors to be so as well.[205] Christ, however, rejected all temporal lordship and together with his apostles, wanted to be subject to the jurisdiction of the secular ruler. Moreover, the apostles taught that this was an essential doctrine, the contravention of which would lead to eternal damnation.[206] Marsilius called on the

---

possumus: unum quo clerici ordinantur ad clericos; alium quo laici ordinantur ad clericos; tertium quo laici ordinantur ad laicos." Aug.Anc. *Summa* 1,6 (ed. Rome, 1479), fol. 8rb.

[203] The distinction can be traced back to Gratian; Tierney, *Foundations*, 32–33. Innocent III then claimed that Peter was not only superior to the other apostles in terms of the *potestas jurisdictionis*, but was also the source of the jurisdiction of all other prelates; *ibid.*, 243. See also Wilks, "*Papa est nomen iurisdictionis*: Augustinus Triumphus and the Papal Vicarate of Christ," *Journal of Theological Studies* 8 (1957), 71–91, 256–272. William of Cremona also used the distinction as the basis for his arguments in his *Reprobatio*, but Giles of Rome did not in his *De ecclesiastica potestate*.

[204] Marsilius *Def.pac.* 2,15 (263,9–272,32).

[205] "Idem quoque ostendam apostolos praecipuos tamquam Christi veros imitatores fecisse quosque successores facere docuisse." Marsilius *Def.pac.* 2,4,3 (130,2–4).

[206] "... amplius quoque [ostendam], tam Christum quam ipsos apostolos voluisse subesse atque subfuisse continue coactive iurisdictioni principum saeculi, realiter et personaliter, aliosque omnes, quibus legem veritatis praedicaverunt aut per scripturam mandaverunt, idem facere docuisse atque praecepisse sub poena damnationis aeterna." Marsilius *Def.pac.* 2,4,3 (130,4–9). Marsilius then goes on to say that he will also deal with power of the keys of the kingdom, and then comments: "Ipsius etenim ignorantia extitit hactenus, et impraesentiarum est, origo multarum quaestionum et damnosarum litium inter Christi fideles." Marsilius *Def.pac.* 2,4,3 (130,13–15). Augustinus had a similar view, though coming from the opposite position: "Disputare de potestate pape hac intentione ut homo eam minuat et minorem quam sit credere faciat vel hac intentione ut causa favoris vel complacentie ultra quam debet extendat, est causa litis et discordie quia semper extrema in materia morali sunt vituperabilia et culpabilia. Sed disputare de tali potestate hac intentione ut sciatur quanta sit et ut sibi suis subiectis veritas clarius elucescat qualiter cuncta ipse faciat et disponat secundum rectum usum clavium potestate non excedente et scientia non errante, non est causa litis et discordie sed pacis et veritatis." Aug.Anc. *Summa* 1,10 (ed. Rome, 1479), fol. 12ra.

proof text of John 18:36, Christ's words to Pilate, "my kingdom is not of this world."[207] Harkening back to an imperial ideology already since past, Marsilius considered the emperor, or the prince, not the pope, to be the *vicarius dei*,[208] whereas Christ and the apostles were the example for the function of the *sacerdotium*, subject to the temporal, secular power.

This was an argument that Augustinus met head-on.[209] Whereas Marsilius based his analysis on Christ's earthly life, Augustinus took as his point of departure a much broader view of Christ that held together the life of Christ, with the glorified Christ. Augustinus argued that Christ clearly had both regal and sacerdotal power, and this can be seen in his incarnation, in his life on earth, and in his resurrection.[210] Furthermore, Christ said that his kingdom was not *of*

---

[207] Marsilius *Def.pac.* 2,4,4–13 (130–143). Marsilius treats the issue at length, bringing in numerous authorities from scripture and the fathers to prove that Christ shunned all worldly, temporal rule, for which John 18:36 served as his point of departure. He concludes: "Ex adductis itaque veritatibus evangelicis, et sanctorum et aliorum approbatorum doctorum interpretationibus earum, apparere debet omnibus evidenter, Christum seipsum exclusisse seu excludere voluisse, tam sermone quam opere, ab omni principatu seu regimine, iudicio seu coactiva potestate mundana, ipsumque seipsum principibus et saeculi potestatibus coactiva iurisdictione voluisse subiectum." Marsilius *Def.pac.* 2,4,13 (143,14–20).

[208] Marsilius *Def.pac.* 2,30,5 (487,3–18).

[209] Augustinus never mentioned the *Defensor Pacis* nor the *Sachsenhausen Appeal*, and many of his questions and arguments could have been drawn from the canonist tradition. Yet Augustinus was not an academic canon lawyer teaching in the schools. His dedicatory letter to John XXII places his work within the context of contemporary issues. In this light, his opponents were Marsilius and the *Sachsenhausen Appeal*. It is very likely that he knew the documents themselves, though he couches his arguments in abstract, even though most practical and pertinent, form. Neither did Marsilius name his opponents. See the introduction to Appendix C.

[210] "Respondendo dicendum <est> quod papa gerit vicem Christi saltem quantum ad potestatem et iurisdictionem officii. In Christo autem planum est fuisse potestatem regalem et sacerdotalem quod ostensum est primo in eius incarnatione; secundo in eius conversatione; tertia in eius passione et in eius resurrectione. Nam in eius incarnatione potestas regalis ei ostensa est quia ex tribu regali trahit originem secundum carnem; potestas vero sacerdotales quia suum adventum per Iohannem baptistam qui fuit filius sacerdotis voluit nunciare . . . quia Christus futurus erat rex, propheta, et sacerdos. Ideo divina providentia factum est ut tres evangeliste qui Christum quantum ad humanam naturam assumptam notificare scripserunt hac ordine eorum evangelia inceperunt, quia Matheus incipit a semine regali dicens: *Liber generationis Iesu Christi filii David regis* [Mt. 1:1]; Marcus vero a vaticinio prophetali dicens: *Initium evangelii Iesu Christi sicut scriptum est in Isaia. Propheta* [Mc. 1:1]; sed Lucas a sacrificio sacerdotali dicens: *Fuit in diebus Herodis sacerdos quidam nomine Zacharias* [Lc. 1:5]. Secundo ostensus est in eius conversatione, cum enim Mathei septimo decimo: Illi *qui accipiebant dragma* dicerent Petro *quare magister vester non solvit dragma*, Christus preveniens cum volentem interrogare dixit, *quid tibi videtur Petre, reges terre a*

this world (*de hoc mundo*); he did not say that his kingdom was not *in* this world (*in hoc mundo*). Christ's kingdom is indeed in this world, for both in this world and in the future, Christ reigns over all his faithful: in this world by grace and in the future heavenly kingdom in glory. In his response to Pilate, Christ was not abdicating his temporal lordship, but was making clear that his kingdom was not to be the tyrannical lordship of unregenerate human nature.[211] Christ was king and priest after the order of Melchisedech, and the dominion of Christ is that of his vicar, the pope.[212]

Augustinus is clear that Christ is the head of the Church, and it was for the singular honor of the Church that Christ became human and was crucified. It was for the Church that Christ chose

---

quibus accipiunt tributum a filiis suis an ab alienis? quo respondente *ab alienis* conclusit: *Ergo liberi sunt filii regum* [Mt. 17:23–25]. Super quo verbo dicit Hieronimus quod dominus noster et secundum carnem et secundum spiritum filius regis erat, quia secundum humanitatem ex David stirpe erat generatus; secundum vero divinitatem omnipotentis patris erat verbum et ideo tanquam regum filius tributa solvere non debebat. Tertio ostensum est hoc in eius passione, nam potestatem regalem ostendit quando intrans Ierusalem cum diabolo spugnaturus regalem reverentiam suscepit ab apostolis sternentibus vestimenta et ramos de arboribus in via. Unde et estimo verbum Zacharie inductum est per evangelistam Matheum dicentem Zacharie nono: *Ecce rex tuus veniet mansuetus sedens super asinam et pullum eius* [Mt. 21:5; Za. 9:9]. Potestatem vero sacerdotalem ostendit tunc quando seipsum obtulit in ara crucis. Idem enim fuit sacerdos offerens et oblatum... Idem ipse unus verusque mediator Christus per sacrificium pacis reconcilians nos deo unum cum illo mansit cui offerebat; unum in se fecit pro quibus offerebat ipse unum esse qui offerebat et quod offerebatur. Quarto hoc ostensum est in eius resurrectione quia potestatem regalem ostendit in diaboli expoliatione quando multa corpora sanctorum surrexerunt cum eo et introierunt in sanctam civitatem in signum victorie obtente. Sacerdotalem vero ostendit in spiritus sancti dantione quando dixit Johannis vicesimo: *Accipite spiritum sanctum quorum remiseritis peccata remittuntur eis* [Io. 20:22–23]. Unde Mathei ultimo dicit: *Data est mihi omnis potestas scilicet sacerdotalis et regalis in celo et in terra* [Mt. 28:18]." Aug.Anc. *Summa* 1,7 (ed. Rome, 1479), fol. 8vb–9rb.

[211] "Christus ergo non dixit: regnum meum non est in hoc mundo, quia et in hoc mundo et in futuro regnat super fideles suos, hic per gratiam et in futuro per gloriam, sed dixit: non est de hoc mundo, quia de hoc mundo est quicquid homini est a deo creatum et ex vitiata stirpe Ade generatum. Sed iam factum est regnum non de hoc mundo quicquid de ipsis hominibus per ipsum Christum regeneratum est dicente apostolo: eripuit nos de potestate tenebrarum et transtulit nos in regnum filii caritatis sue. Vel potest dici... quod regnum Christi non fuit de hoc mundo quia non fuit modo mundano quo modo sunt alii regni qui ex fortitudine ministrorum accipiunt potestatem regnandi." Aug.Anc. *Summa* 1,7 (ed. Rome, 1479), fol. 9rb. For the issue of tyrannical lordship, see below.

[212] "Papa gerit vicem Christi saltem quatum ad potestatem et iurisdictionem officii... sacerdotium et regale dominium Christi... figuratum... per sacerdotium et dominium Melchisedech, qui fuit simul rex et sacerdos... Potestas ergo regalis est in papa...." Aug.Anc. *Summa* 1,7 (ed. Rome, 1479), fol. 8vb–9va.

his apostles; it was for the Church that the prophets prophesied; it was for the Church that God parted the Red Sea and provided manna for the Israelites; and for the Church the world was created and heaven established. Such is God's care for his Church, and such is his care for his popes.[213] Yet Christ still remains the head of the Church, the *caput ecclesie* and the prince of the world: "In the entire functioning of the world," Augustinus explained,

> there is only one government (*principatus*), for it is fitting that there be only one. Therefore, there should only be one universal ruler (*princeps*)... Thus one ruler and one government. The ruler, however, of the world government is Christ himself, whose vicar is the pope.[214]

The pope is Christ's vicar and rules in Christ's place, *in loco Christi*, but he does so only instrumentally. Christ is the head of the Church

---

[213] "Quamvis enim deus habeat curam generalem de gubernatione omnium rerum, singulari tamen modo habet curam de potestate summi pontificis regentis et gubernantis suam ecclesiam... Nam propter ecclesiam celum extensum est, aer sparsus est, mare diffusum est, terra fundata est, paradisus plantatus est, et multa mirabilia facta sunt propter ecclesiam: mare dividebatur et iterum suebatur, petra scindebatur et iterum coniungebatur; manna pluebat de celo et tanquam prunosa ponebatur mensa; propter ecclesiam prophete, propter ecclesiam apostoli, propter ecclesiam unigenitus dei filius factus est homo, ego ipsam statui qui celum fundavi et angelos creavi, sed propter celum crucifixus non sum, propter celum celeste corpus non accepi nec naturam angelorum assumpsi ut dicas quoniam celo angelis et omni creatura singularior et honorabilior est ecclesia." Aug.Anc. *Summa* 1,5 (ed. Rome, 1479), fol. 7^{rb-va}.

[214] "Tota machina mundialis non est nisi unus principatus scilicet quia non debet esse nisi unus principatus. Ideo non debet esse nisi unus universalis princeps... Ideo unus princeps et unus principatus; princeps autem totius principatus mundi est ipse Christus, cuius papa vicarius existit." Aug.Anc. *Summa* 22,3 (ed. Rome, 1479), fol. 78va. This form of argument can be traced back to Alanus Anglicus in the early thirteenth century. Alanus had argued: "Est enim corpus unum ecclesia, ergo unum solum caput habere debet." Alanus Anglicus, *Glossa ad Compilationem primam*, II.XX.7, as quoted by Tierney, *Foundations*, 139. At issue was corporate law, and from where the head of the corporation derived its jurisdiction and authority. Innocent IV argued that the head of a corporation had the authority, and not the corporation itself, a position Hostiensis disputed; see Tierney, *Foundations*, 106–131; for Innocent IV and Hostiensis, *ibid.*, 107f. Augustinus would have sided with Innocent IV, and used the argument to claim a single world government headed by Christ, whose vicar was the pope. Augustinus also made the argument for the pope's world supremacy based on the hierarchy of communities drawn from Aristotle: the village, lead by the local parish priest; the city, headed by the bishop; the province, governed by the archbishop; the kingdom, ruled by patriarchs or primates; and finally the entire world, ruled by the pope. Aug.Anc. *Summa* 1,6 (ed. Rome, 1479), fol. 8va; *cf.* Wilks, *The Problem of Sovereignty*, 28–30.

principally. As such, Christ is both the Church's heart and head, vivifying his mystical body.[215]

Within the governance of the mystical body, there is a threefold relation: a relationship between the various orders of the clergy; the relationship between the laity and the clergy; and that regulating the laity amongst themselves. Augustinus placed these relationships in an ascending order based on the body/soul and temporal/spiritual hierarchies as found in Hugh of St. Victor and Giles of Rome. The bodily, temporal realm, is to be ruled by the spiritual.[216] Thus the relationship among the laity is determined by the relationship between the laity and the clergy, which is itself in turn governed by the relationship among the clergy. Citing Augustine, and echoing Giles of

---

[215] "Dicendum <est> quod caput respectu membrorum quatuor conditiones habet. Nam primo in situ habet eminentiam; secundo in effectu habet influentiam; tertio in natura habet convenientiam; quarto in perfectione habet abundantiam. Propter istas igitur quatuor conditiones Christo principaliter et pape qui est vicarius eius instrumentaliter convenit esse caput ecclesie... Papa igitur est caput ecclesie... potest tamen <papa> cor appellari propter alias conditiones... Primo quod est communicativum vite a natura bene custoditum; secundo quod corrupto eo non est aliud ex quo fiat auxilium aliis membris; tertio quod est principium omnium venarum et nervorum; quarto quod est primum principium sensitivum ex quo discernitur vivum a non vivo. Verum quia has conditiones cor habet respectu membrorum secundum quandam ordinem possit comparari Christus principaliter vel papa instrumentaliter secundum quod invisibiliter vivificat ecclesiam, magis tamen comparatur capiti secundum visibilem naturam qua homo homini prefertur... sicut corpus Christi fuit unitum personaliter divinitati mediante anima, ita quod tota humanitas Christi coniuncta divinitati est caput ecclesie et influit in ipsa, sic membra ecclesie spiritualia principaliter recipiunt huiusmodi capitis influxum, corporalia vero quasi secundario in quantum membra corporalia existunt arma iustitie deo in presenti ecclesia militante... Et in quantum gloria anime derivabitur ad corpora in ecclesia triumphali quando vivificabat corpora nostra propter inhabitantem spiritum eius in nobis ut... in capite sunt aliqui sensus interiores et aliqui exteriores. Esse ergo caput ecclesie secundum interiorem influentiam non convenit nisi soli Christo quia interior fluxus gratie non est nisi ab ipso; sed esse caput ecclesie secundum exteriorem presidentiam universaliter convenit pape particulariter autem potest convenire aliis prelatis." Aug.Anc. *Summa* 19,2 (ed. Rome, 1479), fol. 71[ra-b]. For the pope ruling *in loco Christi*, see note 131 above, and note 231 below. The distinction between Christ as the head of the Church *principaliter* and the pope as the head of the Church *instrumentaliter* can be traced to Huguccio's gloss on Mt. 16:16–19, where he makes the distinction between the Church being founded on Christ *principaliter* and on Peter *secundario et quasi ministrum*; Tierney, *Foundations*, 27.

[216] "[Hugo d. sancto Victore] distinguit duplicem vitam: spiritualem et corporalem; duplicem populum: laicorum er clericorum; duo bona: spiritualia et temporalia; et duplicem potstatem: spiritualem et secularem... quantum vita spiritualis dignior est quam terrena et spiritus quam corpus, tantum spiritualis potestas terrenam potestatem et secularem et honore et dignitate precedit." Aug.Anc. *Summa* 1,3 (ed. Rome, 1479), fol. 5[va-b].

Rome, Augustinus argued that since the more crass, inferior bodies are to be ruled by the spiritual, and since the spiritual bodies are ruled by the creator of the universe, the clergy are to be hierarchically ordered in relationship to the highest priest, the pope.[217] The pope has received his authority and power directly from Christ himself. Bishops, on the other hand, receive both their power of ordination and their power of jurisdiction from the pope, whereas temporal rulers, princes, kings, and emperors, possess only temporal jurisdiction, which is given them by the pope for the service of the Church. Yet insofar as temporal rulers have the immediate exercise of temporal authority and administration, they have a power exceeding that of the pope and can claim that they receive their jurisdiction directly from God, for they have received their authority from God's vicar, and are to use such power for the good of the Church.[218] The pope, however, has received power directly from Christ himself, and the pope is the source of all further spiritual and temporal

---

[217] "Si vero loquamur de potestate pape respectu corporis Christi mystici que est potestas iurisdictionis talis similiter est una <potestas> in papa unitate cuiusdam ordinis. Nam in corpore mystico triplicem ordinem distinguere possumus. Unum quo clerici ordinantur ad clericos; alium quo laici ordinantur ad clericos; tertium quo laici ordinantur ad laicos. Et quia ordinatio qua laici ordinantur ad laicos est potestas corporalis, cum semper corporale et temporale debeant regulari per spirituale, necessarium est quod talis potestas laicorum reguletur per potestatem spiritualem qua ipsi clerici ordinantur ad laicos. Similiter potestas clericorum qua ordinantur ad laicos regulanda est et ordinanda per potestatem qua clerici ordinantur ad clericos et potissime per potestatem illam qua clerici ordinantur ad summum clericorum qui est papa, ita quod papa per unam potestatem ordine quodam habet ordinare clericos ad clericos et laicos ad laicos inter se. Et ista est deductio beati Augustini tertio <libro> de trinitate capitulo quatuor ubi ait quod quemadmodum corpora crassiora et inferiora per subtiliora et potentiora quodam ordine reguntur, ita omnia corpora reguntur per spiritum vite, et spiritus vite irrationalis regitur per spiritum vite rationalem et spiritus vite rationalis desertor atque peccator regitur per spiritum vite rationalem pium et iustum et spiritus iustus et pius regitur per ipsum deum, et sic universa creatura regitur per summum creatorem ex quo et per quem et in quo condita atque instituta est." Aug.Anc. *Summa* 1,6 (ed. Rome, 1479), fol. 8rb. Augustinus cites Aug. de trin. 3,4 (135,16–136,23). Giles of Rome cited the same passage for the same purposes; Aeg.Rom. *De eccl.pot.* 1,5 (16). Yet Augustinus cites a longer portion of the text, and more accurately, than did Giles, which indicates that he used Augustine directly. Augustinus further employed the body/soul hierarchy, and more extensively, in *Summa* 1,8 (ed. Rome, 1479), fol. 9vb–10ra.

[218] "Est dicendum quod verum est potestatem imperialem esse a deo, quia non est a papa ut est homo sed est a papa ut gerit vicem Christi in terra, qui fuit verus deus et verus homo." Aug.Anc. *Summa* 1,1 (ed. Rome, 1479), fol. 4va.

jurisdiction, which flows from the pope as a river from its font, for the origin of all jurisdiction is the lordship of Christ.[219]

Augustinus made a further distinction regarding the lordship of Christ, and consequently that of the pope, between Christ's immediate workings within the Church, and Christ's governing his Church through the mediation and administration of his vicar. The latter corresponds to Christ's temporal power; the former, to his eternal and perpetual power.[220] Christ's temporal power is thus equated with the pope's power of jurisdiction in governing the *corpus mysticum*, of which there are three principal functions: fighting against tyrants; ordering his subjects; and teaching and upholding the divine commandments.[221] This power will only last as long as is needed in the present life. When all tyrants have been subdued and when all Christ's subjects are brought under Christ's lordship in peace, there will no longer be a need for Christ's temporal power, or for his vicar, for then, in the future life, Christ will rule immediately by his eternal and perpetual power. Yet until that time comes, the pope remains "the teacher of the divine commandments; the priest and prelate ordaining and employing his subjects; and the king fighting against

---

[219] "In illo residet immediate potestas iurisdictionis spiritualium et temporalium, cuius auctoritate fit prelatorum electio et confirmatio; sed auctoritate pape fit prelatorum electio et confirmatio; ergo . . . talis potestas immediate residet solum in papa. Sed potestas episcoporum et prelatorum iurisdictionis temporalium et spiritualium est derivata et non immediata. Derivata enim est in eis a Christo mediante papa quod patet tali ratione: sicut se habent rivuli ad fontem et radii ad solem, rami ad arborem, sic se habet potestas episcoporum ad potestatem pape . . . sic ecclesia una est que in multitudinem latius mire fecunditatis extenditur et episcopatus unus est cuius a singulis pars in solidum tenetur. Sed constat quod aqua rivulorum non est aqua fontis immediata sed derivata; ergo potestas iurisdictionis episcoporum non est immediata a Christo, sed derivata in eis mediante papa." Aug.Anc. *Summa* 1,1 (ed. Rome, 1479), fol. 3vb–4ra. The metaphors here of jurisdiction flowing from the pope as rays from the sun, roots from a tree, and rivers from one source, is from Cyprian via the *Decretum*; Tierney, *Foundations*, 134.

[220] "Dicendum <est> quod pape potestas, cum sit collata sibi a Christo, dupliciter potest accipi: primo ut est a Christo mediante papa administrata; secundo ut est ab ipso Christo immediate operata. Nam aliter est loquendum de potestate Christi qua regnat super suos fideles ut est ab eo mediante papa tanquam mediante suo vicario et mediatore administrata, et alia est loquendum de tali potestate ut est ab ipso tanquam a principali auctore immediata operata, quia primo modo potestas Christi est temporalis; secundo modo perpetua et eternalis." Aug.Anc. *Summa* 1,9 (ed. Rome, 1479), fol. 10vb.

[221] "Nam potestas Christi qua nunc regnat mediante papa suo vicario consistit principaliter in tribus: primo in debellatione tyrannorum; secundo in ordinatione subditorum; et terto in ammonitione et exhortatione divinorum mandatorum." Aug.Anc. *Summa* 1,9 (ed. Rome, 1479), fol. 10vb.

tyrants."[222] Through the pope Christ rules his people, for the pope is as Mount Sinai; as God descended to his people from Sinai, so does Christ come to the entire Christian people through the pope.[223] Christ is the head of the Church and the lord of the world.

It was all for the Church. Christ's incarnation and Passion, the creation of the world and of heaven, were all brought about for the Church, for the Church is Christ's body. As such, Christ committed the temporal governance of the Church to his vicar, Peter and his successors, giving Peter the keys of the kingdom and commanding him to feed his sheep. Peter's jurisdiction, and consequently that of his successors, was a temporal jurisdiction, the temporal jurisdiction of Christ, which encompassed both the temporal and spiritual realms, Christ's reign in heaven and Christ's reign on earth.

---

[222] "Ista autem tria non sunt necessaria nisi in <presenti vita>; presenti vita terminata non erit amplius necessarium ut tyranni et mali homines compescantur, iam pace data fidelibus Christi et quando iam omnes inimici eius positi erunt sub scabello pedum eius nec amplius erit necessarium ut subditi disponantur et ordinentur cum iam omnes ordinati et presentati erunt sub dominio Christi... potestas ergo Christi ut est in presenti vita mediante papa tanquam mediante suo vicario et mediatore administrata est temporalis quia solum quamdiu durat mundus est necessarium quod papa sit doctor in exhortatione divinorum, et sit sacerdos et prelatus in ordinatione et dispositione subditorum, et sit rex in debellatione tyrannorum. Sed presenti vita terminata non erit amplius necessaria exhortatio divinorum nec dispositio vel ordinatio subditorum nec debellatio tyrannorum. Si vero loquamur de potestate Christi qua in futura vita erit ab ipso tanquam mediante principali auctore immediate operata, tunc talis potestas eterna erit et perpetua." Aug.Anc. *Summa* 1,9 (ed. Rome, 1479), fol. 10vb–11ra; "Nam quamdiu sumus in hoc mundo sumus in via et sumus in quodam bello. In bello autem necessario sunt aliqui principantes et aliqui subservientes. Et ideo quamdiu sumus bellatores et sumus in exercitu tamdiu angeli dominabuntur angelis et homines hominibus quia tota ecclesia militaris est terribilis ut castrorum acies ordinata. Sed cum pervenerimus ad deum tanquam ad terminum et finem felicitatis nostre, non erimus amplius bellatores, nec erit amplius necessaria dominatio vel prelatio. Unde dicitur prime ad Corinthios quindecimo quod cum ipse filius *tradiderit regnum* idest suos electos *deo patri* tunc erit finis quia tunc evacuatus erit omnis principatus et omnis potestas [1 Cor. 15:24]... Omnis ergo potestas a deo finaliter ratione eius reductionis." Aug.Anc. *Summa* 1,2 (ed. Rome, 1479), fol. 5ra.

[223] "Significatur enim summus pontifex per montem Sinai de quo dicitur Exodi undevicesimo quod *die tertio descendit dominus coram omni plebe super montem Sinai* dicens filiis Israel *ne ascendatis in montem nec tangatis fines eius. Omnis enim qui tetigerit montem morietur* [Ex. 19:11–12]. Significatur etiam summus pontifex per talem montem ratione eius generalitatis quia sicut mediante tali monte descendit deus corum toto populo iudeorum, sicut Christus mediante potestate summi pontificis in lege nova descendit super toto populo christanorum. Et ratione sublimitatis, quia sicut ille mons sublimior erat omni alio, sic papa sublimior est omni alio prelato. Et ratione legalis auctoritats: quia sicut de illo monte data est lex sic de ipso papa omnes leges et omnia iura exquirenda sunt." Aug.Anc. *Summa* 1,5 (ed. Rome, 1479), fol. 7va.

Furthermore, Christ ordained Peter and all the apostles to be his successors in terms of his own priesthood. All the apostles were given the responsibility and authority, both temporal and spiritual, of governing Christ's true body on the altar, the *corpus verum*; to Peter alone, however, Christ gave the responsibility and authority of ruling in his place and of serving as his instrument for the governance of his mystical body, the *corpus mysticum*. Thus the pope is the head of the Church, the *caput ecclesie*.[224]

This was the basis for Augustinus' distinction between the pope's power of ordination (*potestas ordinis*) and his power of jurisdiction (*potestas jurisdictionis*). Though they are held together in the being of Christ, within Christ's temporal jurisdiction they are completely separate. Only the later makes the pope the pope, the vicar of Christ, whereas by the former, the pope is the bishop of Rome equal to all other bishops. Thus a layman could be elected pope, and were this to happen, he would have all power of jurisdiction and would truly be Christ's vicar, even though he would not have the power of ordination.[225] With this distinction, the papacy had become disconnected

---

[224] "Dicendum <est> quod omnis status reducitur ad unum caput aliter non esset dicendum status sed casus. Ubicunque autem est capitis unitas, ibi est status. Ubicumque autem pluralitas casus est non status. Totius autem status episcopalis et ecclesiastice hierarchie caput est episcopatus Christi ad quem omnes episcopatus et prelationes omnes ecclesiastici ordinis reducuntur iuxta illud primi Petri secundo, *Conversi estis nunc ad pastorem et episcopum animarum vestrarum* [I Pt. 2:25] Unde super illo verbo Johnnis vicesimo primo, *Pasce oves meas* [Io. 21:17] dicit glosa quod finito prandio commissionem ovium soli Petro commendavit Christus et nulli alteri, cuius commissionis reminiscens primi Petri quinto dicit *Pascite qui in vobis est gregem dei* [I Pt. 5:2] super quo verbo etiam dicit glosa quod sicut dominus soli Petro totius gregis curam habere iussit, ita Petrus sequentibus pastoribus ecclesie iure mandat ut cum quisque, qui secum est, gregem dei sollicita gubernatione pascere tueatur aliquis teneatur ... ergo est dicendum quod verum est in illa sufflatione spiritus sancti apostolos esse factos a Christo sacerdotes et episcopos et in sacerdotio receperunt potestatem ordinis respicientem Christi corpus verum et in episcopatu receperunt potestatem ordinis respicientem Christi corpus mysticum. Unde totam potestatem ordinis immediate a Christo recipiunt. Verumtamen potestatem iurisdictionis qua possent potestatem ordinis exequi in tanta vel in tali materia non receperunt nisi a Petro post missionem spiritus sancti ... soli autem Petro potestas clavium commissa est, ut patet Mathei sexto decimo [*scil.*: *Tibi dabo claves regni celorum*, Mt. 16:19]." Aug.Anc. *Summa* 88,1 (ed. Rome, 1479), fol. 248[va-b]; this is also a reply to Marsilius *Def.pac.* 2,16,2 (274, 1–19).

[225] "Et dico potestas iurisdictionis temporalis quia loquendo de potestate spirituali quantum ad potestatem ordinis que respicit corpus Christi verum, et que est respectu ipsorum sacramentorum, puto quod talis est in papa in quantum est episcopus et in omnibus episcopis immediate a deo. Cuius ratio est quod talis potestas non convenit pape in quantum papa, quia si aliquis eligatur in papam nullum

from the see of St. Peter, the Roman episcopate, for not only can the pope truly be the pope and the vicar of Christ while not being the ordained bishop of Rome, but the pope as pope is not necessarily required to reside in Rome; the pope rules in Christ's place, whose residence and throne is heaven.[226] As Michael Wilks has argued, "This theoretical separation of papacy and Roman church represents the last stage in the erection of the papal monarchy into a truly universal power."[227]

And universal it was. Wilks claimed that "the pope, Christ, and the *Ecclesia* are all fundamentally one and the same thing."[228] While for Augustinus this is certainly not the case as such, his exposition of Christ's vicarate does associate, though does not equate, the pope, Christ, and the Church. In philosophical terms, one could say that there is a real distinction between Christ, the pope, and the Church, but there is no formal distinction. The temporal reign of Christ is coterminous with both the sovereignty of the Church militant and the jurisdiction of the pope, which extends from heaven to purgatory. The pope's jurisdiction exceeds that of any angel,[229]

---

ordinem habens erit verus papam et habebit omnem potestatem iurisdictionis in spiritualibus et temporalibus et tamen nullam habebit potestatem ordinis. Convenit ego talis potestas ordinis pape inquantum est sacerdos vel episcopus." Aug.Anc. *Summa* 1,1 (ed. Rome, 1479), fol. 3[va–b]. See also Wilks, *The Problem of Sovereignty*, 391–407, who discusses this distinction in Augustinus, though with respect of other passages in the *Summa*, placing it in context of the contemporary political theory.

[226] "Papa non necessitatur residere in aliquo determinato loco, quia vicarius est illius cuius sedes celum est, et terra scabellum pedum eius." Aug.Anc. *Summa* 21,1 (ed. Rome, 1479), fol. 75[va].

[227] Wilks, *The Problem of Sovereignty*, 405. While Wilks had made a penetrating analysis of the development in political theory in the early fourteenth century based on Augustinus' *Summa*, he at times over-emphasizes. Thus he write: "Christ's office, not Peter's see, was now held to be the basis of papal power, because a direct successorship to Christ alone could emancipate the papacy from the Petrine heritage with all its local Roman ties. With the development of papal sovereignty the papal identification with Christ had to be emphasised at the expense of the sucessorship to Peter, and this could not be done whilst papal power was dependent upon the Roman church. Above all others Augustinus Triumphus saw how the vicariate of Christ could be made to achieve this result. But he also realised that in order to free the pope from the Roman bishopric it was necessary to rid him of his episcopacy altogether." Wilks, *The Problem of Sovereignty*, 406. There is certainly truth here, but Wilks overlooks the extent to which Augustinus did argue for the central importance of Rome and the Roman church for the pope. Moreover, it was precisely the pope as Peter's successor that established the vicarate of Christ. For the "ties that bound" the pope to Rome, see the following section below.

[228] Wilks, *The Problem of Sovereignty*, 356.

[229] "Dicendum <est> quod maior est iurisdictio pape quam cuiuslibet angeli...

84　　　　　　　　　　　　CHAPTER ONE

and the pope can virtually empty purgatory by means of granting indulgences.[230]

The pope, moreover, determines the correct interpretation of scripture, and is indeed himself the interpreter of scripture.[231] Here Augustinus was again replying directly to Marsilius. Marsilius had argued that Constantine, by imperial authority, called together the

---

nulli ergo angelo commissa est iurisdictio et cura totius orbis, sed pape totius mundi iurisdictio et cura commissa est, non solum ut nomine mundi importetur terra, sed etiam ut nomine mundi importatur celum, quia super celum et terram iurisdictionem accepit." Aug.Anc. *Summa* 18,1 (ed. Rome, 1479), fol. 68rb. Augustinus argued though that every individual and every city has a guardian angel; *ibid.* The angels, however, are greater than the pope in terms of lordship; Aug.Anc. *Summa* 18,3 (ed. Rome, 1479), fol. 69^{ra-b}.

[230] "... iudicare de his qui sunt extra ecclesiam prelatis ecclesie non est concessum, quia ergo multi possunt esse in purgatorio et forte sunt qui non fuerunt de foro ecclesie militantis dum viverent, sed immediate deus eos salvos fecit per suam gratiam quam sacramentis ecclesie non alligavit. Vult tamen deus eos punire in purgatorio secundum taxationem sue iustitie, quantum ad tales qui non subiciuntur iurisdictioni pape secundum meritum sacramentale, communicatio indulgentie non habet locum. Ita quod puto duo genera personarum esse in purgatorio vel saltem posse esse que proprie non subiiciuntur iurisdictioni pape et quibus indulgentie applicari non possunt per papam quantum ad satisfactionem pene. Primo illi qui carent merito conditionali et qui carent illis que pro eis faciant illa propter que ordinate sunt indulgentie valere. Secundo illi qui carent merito sacramentali, ut qui salvati sunt preter communem legem et gratiam sacramentorum. Tales enim immediate salvantur per gratiam dei sacramentis non alligatam. Ita ut immediate a deo puniantur et pena purgatorii relaxantur secundum taxationem sue iustitie. Preter istos ergo duos gradus personarum quantum ad omnes alios puto quod papa possit purgatorium expoliare." Aug.Anc. *Summa* 32,3 (ed. Rome, 1479), fol. 112vb. Wilks argued that Augustinus conceived "of the pope as ruler in heaven, earth and hell." *The Problem of Sovereignty*, 357. This is a further example of Wilks' exaggeration. Augustinus was clear that the pope's power did not extend to hell, since those in hell were damned, and thus not under his jurisdiction, although the pope could lessen their torture; Aug.Anc. *Summa* 34,4 (ed. Rome, 1479), fol. 118ra–119va. Giles had specifically denied the pope's jurisdiction over souls not only in hell, but also in purgatory; Aeg.Rom. *De eccl.pot.* 2,5 (58).

[231] "Dicendum quod eius est interpretari cuius est condere; Christi autem est sacram scripturam condere quia de ipso est tota scriptura subiective et fundamentaliter... Ad eum [*scil.* Christum] ergo pertinet auctoritative sacram scripturam interpretari... Planum est autem quod Christi vicarius in tota ecclesia est papa. Unde loco Christi ad eum principaliter pertinet sacram scripturam exponere in cuius signum iam eius passione appropinquante pro Petro cuius successor est papa rogavit ut non deficeret fides sua sicut scribitur Luce vicesimo duo [Lc. 22:32]... planum est in ecclesia multos esse et fuisse dono spiritus sancti repletos super expositione et interpretatione sacre scripture; quia tamen angelis Sathane potest se transfigurare in angelum lucis, ideo quid tenendum et quid non tenendum sit de illis interpretationibus non nisi auctoritate summi pontificis terminari potest. Unde qualiter interpretatio sententialiter sit tendenda in sacra scriptura solum ad papam spectat." Aug.Anc. *Summa* 67,2 (ed. Rome, 1479), fol. 201vb–202ra.

first general council of the Church. The general council was to determine and define any ambiguities in scripture, and to separate false and erroneous understandings from the genuine and true meaning.[232] Furthermore, it was for the general council alone to determine and define all questions regarding the articles of faith, the divine commandments, the rites and rituals of the Church, and the jurisdiction of divine law, and once such definitions had been given, no bishop or any authority less than a subsequent general council can change such definitions by adding to them, by subtracting from them, or by suspending their effect.[233] Augustinus had a very different opinion.

All law, righteousness, and justice is to be found in Christ, who administers his jurisdiction through his vicar. Thus the pope is the interpreter and source of all human law: ecclesiastical, canon law and civil, imperial law. In cases of necessity, the pope can even make dispensations in divine law.[234] All law is valid only when its origin is in divine law, and consequently, only through the authority of the pope.[235] Stating a position that would have made Marsilius cringe,

---

[232] Marsilius *Def.pac.* 2,25,4 (383,1–7); 2,19,2 (312,15–313,21); 2,20,1–14 (318–326); 3,2,1 (493,10–15).

[233] Marsilius *Def.pac.* 2,20,1 (318,24–319,24); 2,21,10 (336,18–31).

[234] "Dicendum <est> quod quadruplex interpretatio legis civile pertinet ad papam. Prima est quantum ad eius correctionem. Multa enim permittit et multa impunita relinquit lex civilis que per divinam legem cuius papa minister est corriguntur... Secunda est quantum ad eius obligationem ad papam. Namque spectat interpretari quas controversias et que ecclesiastica negotia vult ligari vel solvi legibus imperatorum et que non... Tertia est quantum ad eius confirmationem. Non enim potest esse magis exempta lex quam legislator. Unde si examinatio et confirmatio imperatoris spectat ad papam, oportet quod imperialum legum confirmatio vel reprobatio similiter ad ipsum spectat. Quarta quantum ad eius declarationem et suppletionem, sicut enim omnis scientia humaniter inventa est imperfecta et quedam umbra respectu divine scientie, sic papa qui est armarium sacre scripture debet imperiales leges declarare et supplere per noticiam et sufficientiam divine scientie cuius minister est." Aug.Anc. *Summa* 67,3 (ed. Rome, 1479), fol. 202[rb]. The pope is also the interpreter of natural law in terms of its application; *Summa* 67,4 (ed. Rome, 1479), fol. 202[va]–203[ra]; "Prima vero regula vocatur lex nature communiter et large. Secunda vero magis proprie. Tertia maxime proprie. Quamvis ergo papa non possit dispensare in lege nature communiter sumpta, dispensat tamen in lege nature secundum quod restringitur ad humanam naturam agentem cum electione et discretione." *Summa* 60,1 (ed. Rome, 1479), fol. 172[vb]. In general, Augustinus' position is that the pope is bound by divine and natural law, but has free reign regarding all human, positive law; see *Summa* 60,2–4 (ed. Rome, 1479), fol. 173[rb]–174[va]; "Sed casum necessitatis, nec lex divina nec humana in dispensando excludit." Aug.Anc. *Summa* 97,3 (ed. Rome, 1479), fol. 268[vb].

[235] "Dicendum <est> quod secundum Augustinum primo libro de libero abitrio, lex eterna est summa divina ratio qua iustum est ut omnia sint ordinatissima cui

86   CHAPTER ONE

Augustinus argued that the pope is to correct imperial law in the same way that divine law corrects imperial law.[236] Imperial law, though based on divine law, is not always binding since it does not always reflect the intention of the law giver. Local circumstances, customs, and times vary, and therefore human law may not always lead to virtue and the common good, which is its purpose. The pope, therefore, is to ameliorate such discrepancies.[237]

---

semper obtemperandum est [*cf.* Aug. lib.arb. 1,6,48–51 (220,42–74)]. Secundum quam omnnis lex recte fertur recteque imitatur. Omnis ergo lex dummodo iusta sit, quia secundum Augustinum libro supradicto, mihi lex non videtur esse dicenda que iusta non est, dependet a lege divina dupliciter. Primo effective et derivative, eo ipso quod iusta est, cum non aliter discernatur quid sit iustum et quid iniustum nisi lege divina mediante, iuxta illud Proverbio octavo: *per me reges regnant et legum conditores iusta discernunt* [Prv. 8:11]. Secundo materialiter et subiective, quia ex divinis sermonibus prime leges imperiales materialiter composite sunt. Nam Numma Pompilius qui Romulo successit in regno per decim viros leges ex libris Salomonis conscribi decrevit et in latinum sermonem translatas in duodecim tabulas exposuit... et iurisconsultus ponit quod cum aliquid addimus vel detrahimus iuri divino et naturali tunc ius civile efficimus. Illo ergo iure lex imperialis dependet ab auctoritate pape quo iure dependet a lege divina, cuius ipse papa est vicarius et minister potissime... Medius autem inter deum et populum christianum est ipse papa. Unde nulla lex populo christiano est danda nisi ipsius pape auctoritate. Sicut nec aliqua lex fuit data populo Israelitico nisi mediante Moyse ipso attestante Deutronomii quinto: *Ego sequester et medius fui inter deum et vos, ut annuntiarem vobis verba eius* [Dt. 5:5]." Aug.Anc. *Summa* 44,1 (ed. Rome, 1479), fol. 140^{rb-va}.

[236] "Papa est principaliter executor legis divine, sicut imperator est executor legis humane. Eo ergo modo papa potest corrigere imperatoris legem, quo modo lex divina habet corrigere legem humanam." Aug.Anc. *Summa* 44,4 (ed. Rome, 1479), fol. 141^{va-b}.

[237] "Lex imperialis includit multas conditiones quas non oportet ab omnibus servari, quia nec ista fuit intentio legislatoris, ut lex eius secundum omnes conditiones illas ab omnibus servaretur. Includit namque lex primo omnium actuum humanorum directionem eo quod omnis intentio legislatoris ad hoc tendit, ut per legem datam actus humani dirigantur ad virtutem et ad bonum inducantur. Secundo includit consuetudinis loco et tempore convenientis observationem. Dicit enim iurisconsultus quod que longa consuetudine comprobata sunt, ac per annos plurimos observata, velut tacita civium conventione non minus quam iura scripta servantur. Tertio includit superioris et inferioris ordinationem. Secundum enim Augustinum, si proconsul mandat uni aliquid observandum et in illo dispensatum sit cum eo per imperatorem vel superiorem, non stringitur ad illud servandum, dispensatione superioris facta. Quarto includit violentam coactionem, ad hoc enim facte sunt leges, sicut dicit Isidorum ut eorum metu humana coherceatur audacia, tuta que fit inter improbos innocentia et in ipsis improbis formidata supplitio refrenetur nocendi facultas. Quantum ergo ad actuum humanorum directionem et quantum ad superioris et inferioris ordinationem, omnes leges imperiales servare debent. Sed quantum ad consuetudinis observationem vel violentam coactionem, non omnes leges predictas servant. Sed solum illi qui consuetudine illa approbata stringuntur et qui dominio potestatis alicuius regis vel principis subduntur." Aug.Anc. *Summa* 44,2 (ed. Rome, 1479), fol. 140vb–141ra.

The pope himself, however, is to recognize the justice of imperial law and to abide by it, but he is in no way bound coercively by any human law. The pope is the spiritual man who judges all and can be judged by no one, save God alone; the pope is indeed free from the law (*legibus solutus*).[238] Arguments to the contrary, such as that made by Marsilius, that the Gospels prove that the pope is bound by the law since Christ had bound himself to the law by giving tribute to Ceasar, do not hold water.[239] The pope is above all human law, and indeed is the source of all human law. All imperial law is valid only by the authority of the pope.[240]

Augustinus' discussion of the pope as the interpreter, corrector, and authenticator of civil law re-emphasized his position regarding the emperor holding jurisdiction only from the pope and for service to the Church. Yet he not only put forth a legal argument for the primacy of the papacy, but also a historical argument. In responding to the position that kingship preceded the priesthood and thus the emperor historically preceded the papacy, and consequently has primacy, Augustinus replied that the question needs to be answered with regard to a distinction between imperial dominion as usurpation

---

[238] On the concept of the *princeps legibus solutus*, especially as it related to the pope in the works of the canonists, particularly Hostiensis, see Pennigton, *The Prince and the Law*, 64–90.

[239] Marsilius *Def.pac.* 2,4,9–13 (134–143); 2,9,9 (193,1–27).

[240] "Omnis iustitia implenda est per prelatum tam legis quam nature; papam ergo solutum esse lege quancumque iusta et iuste posita, dupliciter potest intelligi. Primo quantum ad condemnationis iudicium, et si<c> papa omni lege humana posita per eum vel per alium solutus est, quia a nulla lege potest iudicari iudicio condemnationis, sed a sola lege eterna secundum quam verissime dictum est per apostolum, oportet nos omnes presentari ante tribunal Christi. Secundo quantum ad operationis exemplum et sic ipse tanto verius ligatus est omni lege iusta, quanto verius ipse vicem illius gerit, qui exemplo implevit quod verbis docuit... quod iustum est principem legibus suis obtemperare, quia tunc iura sua ab omnibus custodienda existimet, quando et ipse illis reverentiam prebet... nec papa vel imperator legibus solutus est quantum ad iustitiam directivam, immo quantum ad hoc voluntarius ipse tenetur talem iustitiam implere. Est autem solutus a lege quantum ad violentiam coactivam, quia non cogitur ab aliquo, et quantum ad virtutem potestativam, quia potest legem imitare pro loco et tempore quod non possunt alii. Et secundum hoc eodem modo papa solutus est a lege multo fortius quam ipse [*scil.* imperator]... quod spiritualis homo non iudicatur ab aliquo homine, sed bene iudicatur per legem divinam a quo iudicio nec ipse papa nec aliqua creatura excluditur... non obstante Christum liberum esse a lege tributali, solvit tamen tributum ad vitandum scandalum infirmorum, sic ipse papa vicarius eius legem per eum positam vel confirmatam servare tenetur, ne alii exemplo eius scandalizentur." Aug.Anc. *Summa* 44,8 (ed. Rome, 1479), fol. 144[ra–b].

and tyranny, and as natural, political dominion. The first is allowed for the punishment of the damned and of sinners, as well as for the correction of evil, whereas the second is given to the emperor or prince for the remission of sin for the peace of the righteous.[241] Regarding dominion as usurpation and tyranny, such dominion preceded the priesthood, for it began with Cain and his son Enoch.[242] With respect to natural, political dominion, however, the priesthood preceded kingship, for political kingship was derived from the priesthood of Melchisedech, who was the founder of the priesthood. All first born males, from Noah to Aaron, were high priests (*summi pontifices*), and only therefrom was rightful, political kingship established for the peace of the church.[243] All such high priests prefigured the papacy.

---

[241] "Dicendum quod de dominio legali seu imperiali dupliciter possumus loqui. Primo ut est usurpatum et tyrannicum; secundo ut est naturale et polliticum. Primum est permissum in penam damnantium et in penam peccantium atque in correctionem malorum. Secundum est concessum in remedium peccati propter pacem iustorum." Aug.Anc. *Summa* 36,1 (ed. Rome, 1479), fol. 123vb.

[242] "Primum ego dominium usurpatum et tyrannicum fuit ante sacerdotium... quod primus regum terre fuit ipse Cayn; secundus eius filius Enoch in cuius nomine ubi regnaretur condita est civitas... postmodum omnes geniti ex maledicto semine Cayn usurpative et tyrannice dominium sibi acquisiverunt." Aug.Anc. *Summa* 36,1 (ed. Rome, 1479), fol. 124vb.

[243] "Sed dominium naturale et politicum et recto et iusto titulo acquistum secutum est sacerdotium, quia tale dominium in ministerium sacerdotii et in tuitionem et defensionem ecclesie concessum est. Unde dicit Isidorus in libro de summo bono: Cognoscant principes seculi deo debere rationem reddere propter ecclesiam quam a Christo tuendam suscipiunt. Nam sive augeatur pax ecclesie per fideles principes, sive solvatur. Ille ab eis rationem exigit qui eorum potestati suam ecclesiam credidit. Planum est autem quod sacerdotium statim post diluvium institutum fuit in persona Melchisedech, qui summum sacerdotem qui nunc est significabat... quod Melchisedech aiunt Hebrei fuisse secundum filium Noe et computatione annorum ostendunt eum usque ad Isaac vixisse et omnes primogenitos a Noe usque ad Aaron summos pontifices fuisse. Ita ut omnes qui iusto titulo dominio naturali et politico sumpserunt dominium ad rei publice defensionem et ecclesie dei tuitionem vere per summos sacerdos ordinati sunt." Aug.Anc. *Summa* 36,1 (ed. Rome, 1479), fol. 123vb–124ra. Augustinus further dismisses the arguments that 1) there was *dominium* in the state before the fall based on the distinction between the intellect and the other powers of the soul, 2) the argument that according to Genesis 15 kings were established and existed before the papacy, and 3) that Saul was chosen as king before the institution of the papacy, by countering that while such dominion in the state of grace was there in principle, it was not so with coercive power or with subjection of one power to the others, which only came about as the result of sin which made humans the slaves of sin; further, the kingship of which Genesis 15 speaks was tyrannical kingship, not based on the end of political dominion, which is to serve the priesthood in the extirpation and correction of sin; and finally, that Saul

Here Augustinus made a further distinction whereby the papacy is to be understood in three ways, according to: 1.) its prefiguration (*figura*); 2.) the person of the pope (*persona*); and 3.) the office of the papacy (*officium*). With regard to its prefiguration, the papacy, and the priesthood as such, preceded all rightful lordship of temporal rulers, for it began with Melchisedech. Even more to the point is the papacy in terms of the person of the pope. Personally, Peter was the first pope, yet although in temporal administration there were many kings and emperors before Peter, in jurisdiction, Peter's lordship is eternal, for it is the same lordship as that of Christ. Thus it not only preceded all temporal dominion, but all temporal dominion is derived from Christ, and consequently from the person of the pope. Yet with regard to the immediate administration of the office of the papacy, that, according to Augustinus, only began at the time of Constantine, and thus, kingship preceded the priesthood.[244] Augustinus was, however, quick to make clear that all such kingship was usurpation and tyranny. The only truly natural and political lordship is that as an instrument and minister of the pope, and thus of the Church.

The distinctions between usurpatory and tyrannical lordship on the one hand, and natural, political lordship on the other, combined with the further distinction between the prefiguration, person, and office of the pope, are central for understanding Augustinus' view of the relationship between the emperor and the pope. This is

---

was appointed king by Samuel, who acted as the high priest, and thus Saul's kingship was derived from the priesthood; Aug.Anc. *Summa* 36,1 (Rome, 1479), fol. 123va–124ra.

[244] "Dicendum <est> quod dominium papale possumus considerare tripliciter: Vel quantum ad figuram; vel quantum ad personam; vel quantum ad officium. Quantum ergo ad figuram, officium papale precessit omnes imperatores et omnes reges qui iusto titulo naturaliter et politice dominium sumpserunt, quia summum sacerdotium in Melchisedech figuratum et significatum est... Quantum vero ad personam verum est quod dominium papale in beato Petro incepit qui fuit primum papa quem planum est plures imperatores et reges precessisse in temporalium administratione, non autem quantum ad ipsius dominium iurisdictionem, quam nec ante nec post nullus rex vel imperator habere potest nisi a Christo et per consequens nisi a papa, quia potestas Christi eterna est, que non auferetur et regnum eius quod non corrumpetur ut scribitur Danielis septimo [Dn. 7:26–27]. Sed quantum ad officium secundum immediatam administrationem aliquorum temporalium et secundum liberam executionem omnium spiritualium in toto orbe terrarum officium papale post Constantinum imperatorem incepit." Aug.Anc. *Summa*, 36,1 (ed. Rome, 1479), fol. 124ra–b.

especially so for his interpretation of the importance of the Emperor Constantine, and what had become known as his donation. Marsilius had noted that all Roman bishops trace the origin of their temporal jurisdiction to Constantine's donation of the western empire to Pope Sylvester. He then pointed out that were this indeed a valid grant of power, it should be realized that what this entails is that the power was Constantine's to begin with, and thus, no temporal jurisdiction is properly that of the priesthood, but of the emperor or prince.[245] Such power included that of investing bishops. Thus, early on when the Church had granted the right to invest bishops with their temporal jurisdiction to princes, it was simply returning a right that had been that of the prince to begin with, and which the prince, in any case, had first granted to the Church. Yet once the bishop of Rome had returned the right of investiture to the prince, no succeeding Roman bishop could revoke that right without the consent of the people.[246] Moreover, Louis of Bavaria had sought to remind John XXII that whatever liberty and honor the Church possessed, had originally been granted by Constantine to Sylvester. John, however, as the successor to Sylvester, was trying to destroy the *sacrum imperium*, abusing his plenitude of power, which is only for the edification of the Church.[247]

Augustinus replied by first asserting that the papacy is not derived from the emperor,[248] before posing the question as to whether the pope should acknowledge the emperor's temporal lordship at all. Here Augustinus made a further threefold distinction regarding lordship between: 1.) the restitution of lordship that had been tryannically usurped, either in terms of acquisition or of use, namely, the use of temporal goods not placed in service of the Church; 2.) the

---

[245] Marsilius *Def.pac.* 2,11,8 (212,4–25).
[246] Marsilius *Def.pac.* 2,25,9 (389,12–390,13).
[247] "Item non recogitat, quod beato Silvestro pape latenti tunc temporis in spelunca magnificentissime contulit Constantinus quicquid Ecclesia libertatis hodie obtinet vel honoris. Ipse autem Silvestri successor ut dicit male respondet imperio de predictis, immo sacrum imperium exterminare conatur per fas et nefas et per omnem modum suos fideles et devotos destruere, sicut patet in processu nuper contra sacram imperium et nos et iustitiam nostram facto. In quo etiam abutitur notorie plenitudine potestatis, que nonnisi ad edificationem Ecclesie datur." Lud.IV. *App.* 5 (388).
[248] Aug.Anc. *Summa* 36,2 (ed. Rome, 1479) fol. 124rb–124vb. Augustinus' argument here is not very indepth, relying most of all on the Gelasian distinction between the greater and lesser lights; the pope is the sun, while the emperor is the moon.

immediate administration of temporal lordship; and 3.) universal jurisdiction. With regard to the first two forms, the pope indeed recognizes the temporal lordship of the emperor, for in both cases the Church receives from the emperor, or from any other king, its temporal possessions and their immediate administration. Yet with regard to universal jurisdiction, the pope recognizes no one but God. Even if the pope receives temporal goods unjustly, or uses temporal goods unjustly, unlike an emperor, a king, or a prince, based on his universal jurisdiction he cannot be called before any earthly authority to answer such charges, for he is to be judged by God alone.[249]

This, then was the context of Augustinus' treatment of the donation of Constantine. In his acceptance of Constantine's grant, Pope Sylvester recognized Constantine's lordship in the first two senses, namely, as the immediate administration of temporal goods, and as the restitution of temporal goods acquired or used tyrannically. Before his baptism, Constantine had persecuted the Church and thus did not possess natural, political lordship, but usurpative and tyrannical. After his baptism, Constantine conferred temporal goods on the Church, but did so in terms of restitution, and exercised temporal

---

[249] "Dicendum <est> quod dominium temporale quantum ad presens tripliciter possumus considerare. Primo quantum ad ipsorum temporalium tyrannice et usurpative ablatorum restitutionem. Possunt enim aliqui tyrannice et usurpative dominium temporale habere vel quantum ad acquisitionem, quia iniusto titulo et tyrannice huiusmodi dominium acceperunt, vel quantum ad usum et executionem, qua non utuntur ad protectionem et defensionem ecclesie, sicut ministerialiter uti debent. Multi namque imperatores ante Christi adventum dominium temporalium forte iusto titulo acceperunt et si per electionem populi vel eorum ad quos pertinebat domini effecti sunt, quia tamen tali dominio non ministerialiter utebantur in obsequium ecclesie et in defensionem ecclesiastice discipline, sed potius eius impugnationem, tale dominium tyrannicum et usurpatum censendum erat... Secundo temporalium dominium possumus considerare quantum ad immediatam administrationem quam imperatores et reges et alii principes seculi habent et habuerunt, aliter domini temporales non appellarentur nisi temporalium immediatam administrationem haberent. Tertio tale dominium possumus considerare quantum ad universalem et totalem iurisdictionem. Totalis enim et universalis dominus spiritualium et temporalium est ipse Christus et vicarius eius summus pontifex. Columne enim celi contremiscunt et pavent ad nutum eius et sub eo curvantur qui portant orbem, ut scribitur in Iob. Primis ergo duobus modis papa bene potest recognoscere dominium temporale ab imperatoribus et regibus, quia quantum ad eorum tyrannice et usurpate ablatorum restitutionem et quantum ad eorum immediatam administrationem ecclesia ab imperatoribus recepti et recipit temporalia. Sed quantum ad universalem iurisdictionem cominium temporale a nullo recognoscit nisi a deo. Huius signum est, quia si papa iniuste temporalia reciperet vel quod iniuste uteretur coram nullo principe posset conveniri et a nullo posset iudicari nisi a deo solo." Aug.Anc. *Summa* 36,3 (ed. Rome, 1479), fol. 125^{ra-b}.

lordship as a minister of God in service to the Church.[250] What Constantine gave to the Church, he gave to the Church as restitution for what had not been rightfully his, that which he had acquired by tyranny and usurpation. Consequently, when popes then in turn grant temporal goods or rights to the emperor or to kings, it should not be taken as a recognition of lordship, but rather as means for preserving the peace of the Church.[251]

The donation of Constantine, however, was of central importance for it marked the beginning of the papacy's immediate administration of its office. It did not, however, signify the beginning of papal jurisdiction, temporal or otherwise, since Augustinus distinguished between the papacy's jurisdiction, and the papacy's actual exercise of that jurisdiction in its temporal administration. Constantine had restored to the Church what he had usurped tyrannically from the legitimate dominion of the Church. Having thus been granted, such a donation was binding on all imperial successors of Constantine by natural and divine law. Using a similar logic as had Marsilius, Augustinus then argued that once relinquished, the emperors could not take back from the Church what had become once again the Church's rightful possession. Anyone trying to do so, according to the words of Constantine himself, would be in contempt of divine law and worthy of damnation.[252] Constantine was the first emperor

---

[250] "Quia beatus Silvester non recepit illa temporalia a Constantino quantum ad dominii recognitionem, sed quantum ad immediatam aliquorum temporalium administrationem, quorum ecclesia ante non habebat et quanto ad ipsius ecclesie et fidei catholice defensionem. Quia sicut dictus Constantinus ante receptionem baptismi utebatur dominio temporalium tyrannice et usurpative ad ecclesie impugnationem et christianorum persecutionem, ita postmodum sicut dei minister usus est tali dominio ad ecclesie exaltationem et christiane fidei defensionem. Nam multa privilegia concessit ecclesie in favorem christiane fidei." Aug.Anc. *Summa* 36,3 (ed. Rome, 1479), fol. 125rb.

[251] "Et si inveniatur quandoque aliquos imperatores dedisse aliqua temporalia summis pontificibus sicut Constantinus dedit Silvestro, hoc non est intelligendum eos dare quod suum est sed restituere quod iniuste et tyrannice ablatum est. Eodem modo si legatur quandoque aliquod summos pontifices dare bona temporalia imperatoribus et regibus hoc non est intelligendum eos facere in dominii recognitionem sed magis in pacis ecclesiastice conservationem quia servum dei non oportet litigare sed mansuetum esse ad omnes." Aug.Anc. *Summa* 1,1 (ed. Rome, 1479), fol. 4rb; "Constantinus autem reddidit ecclesie et vicario Christi illa que ab ipso receperat, cum dictum sit supra, omnia esse dei et per consequens pape vicarius eius, quantum ad honoris venerationem et dominii recognitionem." Aug.Anc. *Summa* 43,3 (ed. Rome, 1479), fol. 139vb.

[252] "Illa que sunt iuris naturalis et divini omnes obligant presentes et sequentes

or prince to exercise truly natural and political dominion by recognizing and initiating the immediate administration of the pope's rightful jurisdiction. As Augustinus constantly repeated, the emperor is the pope's minister and servant, and any other relationship is one that is tyrannical and revolts against God, destroying the peace of the Church, which is precisely what the emperor is to protect. In the immediate administration of his office, the *pope* is the true *Defensor pacis*.

Augustinus' view of the relationship between pope and emperor was by no means restricted to theoretical legal and historical discussion. It was also directed at the practical implications of governing Christendom. In keeping with his view that all lordship is derived from Christ and thus from the pope, Augustinus asserted that it falls to the pope to elect the emperor,[253] whereas Marsilius saw things rather the other way around.[254] The pope was, moreover, empowered to establish the empire as he saw fit, and had already done so, having effected the translation of the empire from the Romans to the Greeks, and from the Greeks to the Germans.[255] Thus he could

---

quo iure Constantinus talem obligationem fecit. Unde scribitur capitulo supradicto quod Constantinus talem obligationem fecit dicens: Coram deo vivo qui nos regnare precepit, et coram terribili eius iudicio obtestamur, omnes nostros successores imperatores et cunctos optimates amplissimumque senatum et universum populum in toto orbe terrarum nunc et in posterum nulli eorum quoquo modo hec concessa infringere vel aliquo modo conveli. Si quis autem quod non credimus in hoc temerator aut contemptor extiterit, eternis condemnationis subiaceat innodatus." Aug.Anc. *Summa* 43,3 (ed. Rome, 1479), fol. 139vb.

[253] Aug.Anc. *Summa* 35,1 (ed. Rome, 1479), fol. 119vb–120rb; "Unde puto quod papa qui universos fideles in presenti ecclesia ad pacem habet ordinare et ad supernaturalem finem consequendum dirigere et destinare et iusta et rationabili causa existente per seipsum possit imperatorem eligere, ut propter eligentium neglegentiam vel discordiam aut propter electi bonitatem et condecentiam vel propter populi christiani pacis providentiam seu propter cohercendi hereticorum, paganorum, et scismaticorum potentiam et audaciam posse enim pape fulcitum debet esse veritate iustitia et equitate. Non enim potest adversus veritatem, sed pro veritate ut dicit apostolus secunde ad Corinthios ultimo. Et ideo cum subest causa rationabilis et iusta, puto quod potest." Aug.Anc. *Summa* 35,1 (ed. Rome, 1479), fol. 120ra.

[254] Marsilius *Def.pac.* 2,21,5 (331,7–332,5). Marsilius found the assertion that popes could elect emperors was to conclude "falsum ex veris et malum ex bonis." Marsilius *Def.pac.* 2,26,5 (401,1–2); for his treatment of the papal claims to elect the emperor, see Marsilius *Def.pac.* 2,26,4–5 (399,18–401,28).

[255] Aug.Anc. *Summa* 37 (ed. Rome, 1479), fol. 127vb–131ra; "Illud quod sit auctoritate summi pontificis fit auctoritate Christi cuius sacerdotium eternum fuit et in eternum durabit. Unde quod factus est de translatione regnorum Christi auctoritate permissive vel effective auctoritate summi sacerdotis dicitur esse factum." Aug. Anc. *Summa* 37,2 (ed. Rome, 1479), fol. 129ra; "Dicendum <est> quod postquam

take away what he had granted and transfer the empire from the Germans to any other people.[256] Though it was historically understandable and viable that the seven electors were all German, it was not so by eternal decree. The pope could appoint as imperial electors those whom he considered to be worthy of the office regardless of nationality.[257] The empire does not have to be German, and neither do the electors. In direct answer to both Marsilius and Louis of Bavaria, Augustinus furthermore argued that the pope is the one who confirms the election of the emperor, and no emperor can exercise authority without the confirmation and approbation of the pope, which was the issue that had begun the conflict between John XXII and Louis in the first place, and had been the policy advocated by Robert d'Anjou.[258] The emperor is to govern the empire as the pope's

---

imperator Constantinus baptizatus est per beatum Silvestrum, imperio occidentali cessit et urbem sibi in Gracia elegit que Bisanzium vocabatur, quam Rome potentia et meritis coequavit. Ibidemque sedem imperialem constituit et extunc imperium a Romanis ad Grecos translatum est, ita ut imperator de partibus occidentalibus non debeat se intromittere nisi expressa auctoritate et mandato summi pontificis... Constantinus huiusmodi translationem fecit auctoritate summi pontificis qui tanquam vicarius dei filius celestis imperatoris iurisdictionem habet universalem super omnia regna et imperia." Summa 37,3 (Rome, 1479), fol. 129^{rb-va}; "... predictus rex [Otto I] a Leone summo pontifice cum toto clero et populo christiano imperator est constitutus forma et modo quo Carolus Magnus per Adrianum constitutus fuerat... et extunc imperium a Grecis dicitur ad Germanos esse translatum." Summa 37,4 (Rome, 1479), fol. 129vb–130ra.

[256] Aug.Anc. Summa 37,5 (Rome, 1479), fol. 130^{ra-va}: "Nulli tamen dubium esse debet quin summus pontifex, quem Constantinus vicarium esse dei filii firmiter confessus est, imperatorem possit eligere quemcumque et undecumque sibi placet in auxilium et defensionem ecclesie." Aug.Anc. Summa 37,5 (Rome, 1479), fol. 130rb.

[257] Aug.Anc. Summa 35,1–5 (ed. Rome, 1479), fol. 119vb–122ra; "Quamvis ergo novitates sint timende, ubi tamen evidens et manifesta apparet utilitas potestati pape subesse dinoscitur mutare et innovare omne quod expedit reipublice utilitati nec mutationes canonum et statutorum predecessorum vel suorummet attribuendum est eius animi levitati, quando videtur esse expediens reipublice utilitati et pacis populi Christiani unitati... potestas eligendi imperatorem ad sedem apostolicam pertinere, sicut ergo a sede apostolica potestas eligendi imperatorem electoribus est concessa ita a predicta sede potest eis auferri." Summa 35,3 (ed. Rome, 1479), fol. 121ra; "potestates seculares intra ecclesiam necessarie non essent nisi ut quod non prevalet sacerdos efficere per doctrine sermonem, potestas hoc imperet per discipline terrorem, quia sepe celeste regnum per regnum terrestre proficit ut quando aliqui intra ecclesiam positi contra fidem et disciplinam ecclesie agunt rigore principum conterantur. Quando ergo summus pontifex hoc videret ad talem finem magis valere personas alicuius regni vel regionis quam alterius posset iuste huiusmodi transmutationem facere." Summa 35,4 (ed. Rome, 1479) fol. 121va; cf. Marsilius Def.pac. 2,30,7 (488,10–489,22).

[258] Aug.Anc. Summa 38–39 (ed. Rome, 1479), fol. 131ra–134ra; "Dicendum quod ad illum pertinet immediate imperatoris confirmatio ad quem pertinet imperii imme-

minister and servant, and whereas the papacy is eternal as the vicar of Christ's reign, the empire will only last until the last days, when Gog and Magog assume all earthly power in the time directly before the last judgement.[259]

Though couched in theoretical terms, Augustinus' arguments had very practical implications for John's battles with Louis. Yet Augustinus did not restrict himself to discussions of papal/imperial relations. His explication of ecclesiastical power extended to all facets of temporal and spiritual life. Christ's reign on earth was at issue, and knowing

---

diata iurisdictio. Postquam enim Constantinus cessit imperio occidentali, nulla sibi reservatione facta in civitate Romana, in partibus Italie, et in omnibus occidentalibus regionibus, plenum ius totius imperii est acquisitum summis pontificibus non solum superioris dominationis verum etiam immediate administrationis, ut ex ipsis tota dependeat imperialis iurisdictio quantum ad electionem et quantum ad confirmationem. Ita ut extunc nullus de iure potuerit se intromittere de regminie occidentalis imperii absque expressa auctoritate et mandato sedis apostolice, nisi usurpative et tyrannice, sicut fecit Iulianus apostata et multi alii. Igitur sicut ad summum pontificem pertinet imperii universalis iurisdictio sic ad ipsum spectat imperatoris confirmatio et approbatio." *Summa* 38,1 (ed. Rome, 1479), fol. 131[rb]; "Per electionem enim imperator generatur et acquiritur esse, per confirmationem vero acquirit virtutem per quam agat. Sed per administrationem exequitur ipsum agere et ipsum operari mediante substantia et mediante virtute sibi per electionem et confirmationem acquisita. Unde sicut nulla creatura potest agere immediate sine virtute superaddita, quia tunc sua substantia esset sua virtu quod soli deo convenit, sic imperator per solam electionem non potest administrare nisi beneficium confirmationis recipiat, quia tunc sequeretur quod sua electio esset eius confirmatio quod solum veritatem habet de summo pontifice qui superiorem non habet." *Summa* 39,1 (ed. Rome, 1479) fol. 133[ra]. The emperor could, however, exercise administrative authority in Germany without the confirmation and approbation of the pope, but he could do so only as a king, not as an emperor (*magis ut rex quam ut imperator*); *Summa* 39,3 (ed. Rome, 1479), fol. 133[vb]–134[ra]. This issue had been the start of the conflict between Louis and John; Louis considered having to have his election confirmed by the pope to be ". . . de summe malitie emanasse et contra deum et justitiam et contra jura imperii atque nostra et contra consuetudines approbatas predictas et contra sacri imperii libertatem et dignitatem et utilitatem et contra jura et libertates principum imperii electorum et aliorum principum et Alemanie totius et omnium imperii subditorum et vasallorum . . ." Lud.IV. *App.* 13 (390–391). Marsilius agreed; Marsilius *Def.pac.* 2,26,7–11 (403,1–406,26), where Marsilius concludes with asserting the rights of Louis to rule completely despite what the pope had tried to impose. Louis was on good ground here, at least in terms of other princes. Edward I of England and Philip III of France both had assumed their rule at the time of their accession to the crown, not upon their confirmation or coronation; see Kantorowicz, *The King's Two Bodies*, 328–329. Popes, however, had since Innocent III claimed that the empire reverted back to the lordship of Christ during an interregnum, and thus, the governing of the empire fell to the pope when there was no valid, or recognized, emperor; *ibid.*, 335f.

[259] Aug.Anc. *Summa* 42,1–2 (ed. Rome, 1479), fol. 137[ra]–138[rb]; see also note 365 below.

the extent of the power and authority of Christ's vicar was imperative for every Christian, as it had been for Giles of Rome.

The legal jurisdiction of the pope surpassed that of the relationship between imperial law, natural law, and divine law. The pope was bound by the latter two forms of law, but had free reign regarding all human law: all positive law, all imperial law, all royal law, and all Roman law; all the law that served as the foundation of princely rule. Yet in specific cases it was often uncertain precisely what law was at issue, and thus Augustinus delved into the extent to which the pope can alter, or grant dispensation from, what appears to be divine law: the Ten Commandments, the sacraments, the articles of faith, and the creed, which Marsilius had claimed was the unique perogative of a general council. Canon law too was human law, even if ecclesiastical law, and thus it was subject to the authority of the pope. But divine law was divine law, and the pope, even as Christ's vicar, could not go as far as to redefine or annul the dictates of the divine, and of the divine as it impinged upon the daily lives of the faithful.

In his discussion of issues that had been debated by canonists for at least a century, Augustinus posed the question of whether the pope can make dispensation regarding the Ten Commandments.[260] Augustinus held firm to his position that the pope cannot contravene divine law, and the Ten Commandments are exemplary divine law. In his discussion of the first commandment, *You shall have no other god to set against me... You shall not bow down to them or worship them, for I, the Lord your God, am a jealous god*, Augustinus was clear that the pope cannot make dispensation, which Augustinus explored with regard to those consulting with demons, astrologers, witches, and idolaters.[261] Beginning with the second commandment, however, Augustinus made distinctions regarding in what respect the pope could make dispensation.[262] Thus, after having determined six ways God's name can be taken in vain,[263] Augustinus argued that the pope

---

[260] Tierney, *Foundations*, 48–53, 88–91.
[261] Aug.Anc. *Summa* 48 (ed. Rome, 1479), fol. 151ra–153va; "... cum talibus ergo idolatris papa dispensare non potest, sicut non potest dispensare contra primum preceptum quo precipitur quod unus deus adoretur et colatur." *Summa* 48,3 (ed. Rome, 1479), fol. 153rb.
[262] Aug.Anc. *Summa* 49 (ed. Rome, 1479), fol. 153va–155va.
[263] Aug.Anc. *Summa* 49,1 (ed. Rome, 1479), fol. 153vb.

cannot make dispensation regarding taking God's name in vain as such, but can regarding the reasons for having done so.[264] Similarly, the pope can make dispensation regarding the fourth commandment. A member of a religious Order is not excused from the commandment to honor your father and mother in terms of providing for their material well-being, but can receive dispensation from the actual personal execution of such care if other means can be found for meeting the obligation.[265] Indeed, the obligation of the commandment takes precedence over fulfilling the counsels, and thus a religious can be excused from his vows in order to provide the required care to his parents.[266]

Yet the room for the pope to make dispensations regarding the commandments was limited indeed. Thus the fifth commandment,

---

[264] "Omnibus istis sex modis iuramentum est indispensabile, quia dispensari non potest ut aliquo istorum modorum nomen dei in vanum assumatur. Sed secundo modo materialiter, ut illud quod iuratur sub iuramento non includatur, papa potest dispensare. Potest enim homo tale quid iurare quod repugnat iustitie equitati, ut si quis iurat male agere puta hominum velle occidere vel adulterari vel quod est boni impeditivum et contra caritatem, ut religionem non intrare. Quandoque vero repugnat iudicio discretionis et deliberationis maturitati, et sic omnia iuramenta que dubia sunt an sint licita vel illicita et an expedientia vel non expedientia, que incauta vocantur sunt dispensabilia. Quandoque vero repugnat testificande veritati ad cuius assertionem iuramentum inducitur et sic falsum iuramentum est dispensabile. Quandoque etiam repugnat superioris potestati, et sic cum puella sit sub potestate patris et uxor sub potestate viri iuramentum factum sine eorum consensu dispensabile est. Sed quandoque repugnat rei publice utilitate et sic cum papa totius reipublice utilitatem et communitatem habeat videre considerare et dispensare, ideo omnia iuramenta contraria rei publice utilitati per eum dispensabilia sunt." Aug.Anc. *Summa* 49,1 (ed. Rome, 1479), fol. 153vb–154ra.

[265] "Planum est enim quod per impotentiam exequendi preceptum homo excusatur ab executione et potissime quando impotentia exequendi est temporalis quandoque ad actum reductibilis, quia si esset perpetua non remaneret obligatio precepti exquo nunquam posset impleri. Nunc autem est quod status religionis non impedit semper hominem a subventione parentum quia multi casus possunt occurre in quibus potest parentibus subvenire vel per licentiam superioris de proprio suo labor vel per administrationem communium rerum. Puto ergo quod religiosus propter statum religionis non absolvitur ab obligatione precepti dati de subventione parentum sed ab executione potest excusari donec adsit sibi possibilitas subvendiendi." Aug.Anc. *Summa* 51,1 (ed. Rome, 1479), fol. 159ra.

[266] "Dicendum <est> quod in preceptis est iustitia sufficiens et necessaria. In consiliis vero iustitia habundans et expediens. Est enim preceptum magis ncessarium quam consilium; consilium vero magis bonum licet minus necessarium... Ideo puto quod in casi in quo obligat preceptum dei de honore parentum ut quando aliter impleri non posset eorum subventio quam manendo in seculo, tunc non habet locum consilium de intrando religionem, sed potius esset peccatum eo quod in tali casu consilium esse contrarium precepto dei." Aug.Anc. *Summa* 51,2 (ed. Rome, 1479), fol. 159^{rb-va}.

Thou shall not kill, is an absolute principle of divine law and the pope can do nothing about it, although Augustinus did recognize four cases in which killing is permitted without breaking the commandment: 1.) when one kills one's enemies in a just war; 2.) when God commands one to kill, as God did Abraham; 3.) when judges justly condemn criminals to death; and 4.) when one receives a private, hidden counsel and inspiration from the Holy Spirit to kill, as did Samson.[267] All other instances of killing human beings are disallowed, even killing in self-defense.[268] The same holds true for the sixth com-

---

[267] Aug.Anc. *Summa* 52,1–5 (ed. Rome, 1479), fol. 161[ra]–163[va]; "Excipiuntur tamen quatuor casus in quibus cadit dispensatio ut homo iuste occidatur absque transgressione illius precepti... Primo: si illi qui deo auctore bella iusta gerunt hostes interficiunt, non transgrediuntur divinum preceptum. Secundo: si expresso iussu dei et precepto hoc fiat. Unde Abraham excusatur qui filium innocentem voluit occidere, non enim fecit contra preceptum illum, non occides, quia ex dei precepto illud facere voluit. Tertio: si iudices qui publica potestate funguntur, malefactores puniunt <qui> homicidium crimen incurrunt. Quarto: si illud fiat privato consilio et occulta inspiratione spiritus sancti. Sic excusatur Sampson, qui seipsum cum hostibus occidit. Similiter Iepthe qui filiam suam unigenitam de victoria revertenti occurrentem occidit, ut habetur Iudicium undecimo [Idc. 11: 34–40]. Ipsi enim privato consilio hoc fecerunt." Aug.Anc. *Summa* 52,1 (ed. Rome, 1479), fol. 161[rb].

[268] "Ideo puto quod culpa sit hominem occidere ne ipse occidatur, quacunque inevitabili necessitate hoc fiat, quia animam proximi plus teneor diligere quam corpus proprium, quod me invito possum perdere. Planum est atque quod anima proximi perditur ex quo in actu iniuste me occidentis per me occiditur... qualiter inculpati esse queant occidentes alios ne ipsi occidantur non video, et qualiter excusari possint a culpa non invenio... est dicendum quod licet prius homo teneatur diligere animam suam quam proximi, plus autem tenetur diligere animam proximi quam proprium corpus. Planum est autem quod occisio volentis me iniuste occidere non est sine periculo damnationis anime proximi. Ideo non solum perfecto viro verumetiam cuilibet private persone magis expedit permittere se occidi quam occidere." Aug.Anc. *Summa* 52,3 (ed. Rome, 1479), fol. 162[ra-b]. Augustinus also addressed the illegitimacy of suicide, *Summa* 52,4 (ed. Rome, 1479), fol. 162[va-b]; and the discrepancy between civil and divine law, whereby civil law permitted a father to kill his adulterous daughter in four instances, none of which Augustinus saw as fitting with divine law: "Planum est autem quod minus malum est adulterium quam quod mulier in adulterio deprehensa sic per patrem interificiatur. Nam melius est quod tale quid impunitum dimittatur quam post interfectionem eius pater interficiens pena parricidii puniatur, presertim cum paterna pietas que semper consilium capit, pro liberis liberandis potius quam interficiendis non sine inconsulto dolore et magno incitativo ad interfectionem adultere filie moveatur quamvis tamen lex penam non apponat, a culpa tota parricidii excusari non potest propter duo: Primo quia lex divina que principaliter precipit non occides, humanis legibus astricta non est, ideo talis tanquam transgressor legis divine pene ecclesiastice est subiiciendus tanquam parricida, licet eius culpa posset excusari seu alleviari et aggravari secundum conditionem circumstantie occurrentis. Secundo quia secundum promissionem legis magis ostenditur quod pater interficiens filiam adulteram ex dolore et ira vindicte et iniurie et eam irrogate quam ex zelo iustitie fecerit, secundum quem modum

mandment against committing adultery, for even "simple fornication" is a mortal sin and the pope cannot change that.[269] The pope can, however, make dispensation regarding the degrees of consanguinuity required for legitimate marriage, except for that between parents and their children, and thus he can make a marriage that normally would be considered incestuous, to be legitimate and sacramental.[270] Yet the Ten Commandments are in general not subject to papal dispensation because they are divine law, by which even the pope is bound.

The same holds true for the sacraments.[271] The pope cannot institute new sacraments, for this is a power Christ has reserved for himself.[272] Similarly, although Christ could grant sacramental grace without the actual sacrament, as the case of the thief on the cross testifies,

---

non solum privata persona verumetiam minister legis interficiens maleficum a culpa homicidii non excusatur. Non enim lex permittit patri filiam adulteram occidere, nisi quatuor conditionibus appositis: Primo quod in ipso actu et operatione adulterii eam occidat; Secundo quod simul interficiat adulterum cum adultera; Tertio quod non ubique sed solum in domo quam inhabitat vel in domo mariti ipsam occidat. Maiorem enim iniuriam putavit legislator quod in domo patris aut mariti ausa fuit filia adulterium committere; Quarta quod in continenti inconsulto dolore et dum est in actu acerbi doloris filiam adulteram occidat. Planum est autem quod omnes iste conditiones secundum quas permittitur patri adulteram filiam occidere ostendunt quod talis occisio non sit zelo iustitie sed magis dolore illate iniurie, ac per consequens culpa parricidii carere non potest." *Summa* 52,5 (ed. Rome, 1479), fol. 163ra–b.

[269] "Fornicatio simplex est peccatum mortale." Aug.Anc. *Summa* 53,4 (ed. Rome, 1479), fol. 165ra.

[270] Aug.Anc. *Summa* 53,5 (ed. Rome, 1479), fol. 165va–166ra; "Dicendum <est> quod licet consanguinitas sit naturale vinculum, non tamen tollit matrimonium impediendo carnalem copulam, nisi secundum determinatum gradum, quem determinare spectat ad ecclesiam in quo gradu copula talis carnalis sit licita et in quo illicita." *Summa* 53,5 (ed. Rome, 1479), fol. 165vb.

[271] Aug.Anc. *Summa* 58,1–8 (ed. Rome, 1479), fol. 198rb–200vb; 169ra–170ra. In the copy of the Rome, 1479 edition of Augustinus' *Summa* that I have used in the Koninklijke Bibliotheek in The Hague, signature: Inc. 170 F 24, a quire has been mis-bound. The edition was printed without pagination or foliation, but has a modern, continuous foliation. Question 55,1–4, dealing with the issue of papal dispensation regarding the eighth commandment breaks off toward the end of q. 55,2 at the end of fol. 168vb. The ending of q. 55,2 through to the mid-point of q. 58,6 is found on fol. 193ra–200vb. One must then return to fol. 169ra for the rest of q. 58,6. From q. 58,6 to q. 66,3 the text is continuous from fol. 169ra–192vb, with q. 66,4 beginning then after the mis-bound quire on fol. 201ra.

[272] Aug.Anc. *Summa* 58,1 (ed. Rome, 1479), fol. 198rb–199ra: "Ex quibus omnibus patere potest quod sacramentorum institutio non convenit pape nec alicui puro homini, sed soli Christo." Aug.Anc. *Summa* 58,1 (ed. Rome, 1479), fol. 198va; "Sed Augustinus exponens illud verbum Johannis undevicesimo, *Unus militum lancea latus*

the pope can not do so. Christ could have granted this power to his vicar, but he in fact did not.[273] The pope, however, can make dispensation regarding the accidents of the materials used for the sacraments, such as leavened or unleavened bread, but not regarding the substance itself or its form.[274] Yet whereas the sacraments are part of the divine law Christ has instituted, and thus the pope can neither create new sacraments, nor abolish the old ones, this does not extend to the sacramentals, regarding which the pope can do basically as he sees fit for the Church, creating new sacramentals, or decreasing the number of the established ones.[275]

---

eius aperuit [Io. 19:34], dicit quod vigilanti verbo evangelista usus est ut non diceret latus eius percussit aut vulneravit, sed aperuit, ut illic quodammodo vite ostium panderetur. Unde sacramenta ecclesie emanarunt sine quibus ad vitam que vere vita est non intratur. Sicut ergo a solo Christo virtus et efficacia sacramentorum emanavit, sic ab ipso Christo solum institutio sacramentorum facta est." Aug.Anc. *Summa* 58,1 (ed. Rome, 1479), fol. 198vb.

[273] Aug.Anc. *Summa* 58,2 (ed. Rome, 1479), fol. 199ra–199va: "Sic non debemus negare Christum hanc potestatem conferre potuisse, quamvis collata non sit." Aug.Anc. *Summa* 58,2 (ed. Rome, 1479), fol. 199rb.

[274] Aug.Anc. *Summa* 58,3–4 (ed. Rome, 1479), fol. 199va–200rb; "Puto ergo quod in formis sacramentorum non cadit dispensatio, sed illis debet uti ecclesia quibus ipse Christus immediate usus est vel apostoli qui ab ipso acceperunt." Aug.Anc. *Summa* 58,3 (ed. Rome, 1479), fol. 199vb; "Dicendum <est> quod sicut videmus in rebus naturalibus sic suo modo est in signis sacramentalibus. In naturalibus autem sic est quod in his que differunt specie materia est diversa propter diversitatem forme. Membra enim leonis et cervi differunt quia anime eorum differunt ... sed in his que sunt eiusdem speciei forma non est diversa, nisi propter diversitatem materie, ita quod manet unitas forme specifice cum diversitate materie diversificate per diversa accidentia, sic in signis sacramentalibus oleum et aqua et panis differunt sacramentaliter propter diversitatem formarum sacramentorum. Sed unum et idem sacramentum potest habere materiam diversificatam per diversa accidentia ut quod sit aqua dulcis et amara non diversificat speciem sacramenti baptismi et quod sit azimus panis vel fermentatus non diversificat materiam sacramenti eucharistie. In materia ergo ordinata essentialiter ad formam sacramenti non cadit dispensatio, sed in diversificatione materie penes diversa accidentia non mutantia ipsius materie speciem vel entitatem, dispensari potest." Aug.Anc. *Summa* 58,4 (ed. Rome, 1479), fol. 200^{ra-b}.

[275] "Dicendum <est> quod tria sunt genera sacramentorum ... Quedam enim sacramenta sunt proprie dicta, que per se faciunt ad hominis salvationem et sine quibus salus hominis haberi non potest. Quedam vero sunt que faciunt ad hominis exercitationem, ut aqua aspersionis et susceptio cineris et similia sine quibus salus hominis quamvis haberi possit, occulpata tamen in his humana mens aliquam sanctificationem et gratiam ampliorem per ea acquirere potest. Alique vero faciunt ad eorum que sunt vera sacramenta devotam preparationem, sicut omnia sacramentalia, ut consecratio vestium altarium et ecclesiarum ac ministrorum. In numero ergo primorum sacramentorum papa dispensare non potest, quia ab illo instituta sunt qui omnia posuit in numero, pondere, et mensura. Sed in numero aliorum que non sunt proprie sacramenta, sed magis quedam sacramentalia, papa potest

In complete opposition to Marsilius' assertions, Augustinus placed the creed and articles of faith as well under the pope's jurisdiction, in that neither are as such divine law. Thus the pope, as the head of the Church, can create new creeds and add articles of faith to meet the needs of the Church, although he cannot subtract from the articles, nor can he alter the substance of the creed.[276] Both the creed and the articles of faith were established for the good of the Church, since they teach what is to be believed. As such, if the pope were to create new articles of faith or new creeds, all the better, since the entire glory of ecclesiastical power lies in the building up of the Christian faith. The Church furthermore, Augustinus argued calling on Augustine, has three characteristics: universality, unity, and authority. Creeds and articles of faith contribute to each by spreading the faith and establishing the Church's authority, which is unified in the head of the Church, the pope. Thus the pope can create new creeds and articles of faith for the glorification of ecclesiastical power and the edification of the Church.[277]

---

dispensare multiplicando vel diminuendo secundum quod videt ecclesie utilitati et devotioni fidelium expedire." Aug.Anc. *Summa* 58,6 (ed. Rome, 1479), fol. 169ra.

[276] Aug.Anc. *Summa* 59,1–4 (ed. Rome, 1479), fol. 170ra–172ra. The issue of whether the pope could create new articles of faith had been debated since at least Alexander III and the canonist Alanus Anglicus, and became the cause for more of John XXII's headaches. John was reluctant to admit that the pope could create new articles of faith except in a restricted sense; see Tierney, *Origins*, 193–196.

[277] "Dicendum <est> quod hunc questionem determinat Augustinus in libro de symbolo ubi vult quod omnis symboli condendi et ordinandi in sancta dei ecclesia terminatur auctoritas. Habet enim fides christiana tria secundum eundem Augustinum. Primo universalitatem, unde dicitur catholica, quia non docetur in angulis sicut doctrina hereticorum, sed publice et universaliter diffusa est per universum orbem. Secundo unitatem, quia una fuit fides antiquorum et modernorum... Tertio auctoritatem, dicit enim Augustinus contra epistolam fundamenti, ego non crederem evangelio si non crederem ecclesie. Ex his tribus patere potest quod novum symbolum condere solum ad papam spectat, nam symbolo ponuntur in illa que universaliter pertinent ad christianam fidem. Illi ergo incumbit auctoritas huiusmodi symbolum condere qui est caput fidei christiane et in quo tanquam in capite omnia membra ecclesie uniuntur et cuius auctoritate omnia que ad fidem spectant firmantur et roborantur... ergo est dicendum quod semper symbolum cum de novo conderetur breviter colligeret que essent de salute credendi et ideo semper memoria iuvaretur et non confunderetur; nec oporteret omnes credentes omnia symbola et que in predictis symbolis continerentur actualiter in memoria retinere, sed illa dumtaxat que essent ad necessitatem salutis. Alia autem minores tenerentur credere in fide maiorum ad quos pertinet fidem defensare et in symbolis ipsam explicare contra insurgentes errores. Aliud est enim scire tantummodo quod homo credere debeat propter adipiscendam vitam beatam que non nisi eterna est et aliud est scire quemadmodum hoc ipsum et piis opituletur et contra impios defendatur." Aug. Anc. *Summa* 59,1 (ed. Rome, 1479), fol. 170^{rb-va}; "Tota enim gloriatio ecclesiastice

Not only creeds and articles of faith, but also the propagation of the faith in all aspects was the pope's task. Thus Augustinus explicitly addressed the issue as to whether and to what extent, given the Church's authority, not only the members of Christendom, but pagans and Jews as well, owed obedience to the pope. Christians certainly owe their primary obedience to the pope, and were the pope and the emperor to issue contradictory commands, that of the pope is to be obeyed. Yet although the pope establishes and regulates all government, Augustinus stated once again that the pope is to respect and uphold the justice of temporal lordship and rule.[278]

Pagans, however, were in a different situation, for although they were *de jure* subject to the universal lordship of Christ, *de facto* they were, or could be, outside the political jurisdiction of Christendom.[279] While the pope can use coercive force against those pagans living within the jurisdiction of imperial law, he cannot remove dominion or jurisdiction from pagan kingdoms.[280] They are, nevertheless, still subject to natural law, and thus the pope, as the administrator of all justice, has the right to punish pagans contravening natural law, punishing their sins *contra naturam*.[281] There was, however, a desired

---

potestatis debet esse in edificatione et augmentatione fidei christiane, non in destructione vel diminutione, quia in hac nullum est posse." Aug.Anc. *Summa* 59,3 (ed. Rome, 1479), fol. 171rb.

[278] Aug.Anc. *Summa* 22,1–7 (ed. Rome, 1479), fol. 77rb–81rb; "Eodem modo si aliud mandat papa et aliud imperator, obediendum est pape et non imperatori. Verum quia iustitia per fidem Christi est confirmata non extirpata... ideo sicut papa debet esse omnis iustitie observator et omnium principatuum institutor et ordinator, sine quibus iustitia minime servari posset, sic debet omnem debitam subiectionem et obedientiam subditorum ad principes et reges seculi manutenere et gubernare non tollere vel subtrahere." Aug.Anc. 22,3 (ed. Rome, 1479), fol. 78vb.

[279] Aug.Anc. *Summa* 23,1–6 (ed. Rome, 1479), fol. 81rb–84ra; see especially Aug.Anc. *Summa* 23,2 (ed. Rome, 1479), fol. 82^{ra-b}.

[280] Aug.Anc. *Summa* 23,3 (ed. Rome, 1479), fol. 82^{rb-vb}; 2,5 (ed. Rome, 1479), fol. 83^{rb-vb}.

[281] "Dicendum quod quantum ad presens triplex est lex: eterna, naturalis, et positiva. Lex eterna <nec> ponitur nec deponitur; lex vero naturalis ponitur, sed non deponitur. Sed lex positiva ponitur et deponitur. Legis igitur eterne et divine papa debet esse imitator, quia ab ipso omnis lex et omnis iustitia derivatur... Legis vero naturalis papa debet esse observator, non enim potest ipsam mutare, quia sicut ab ipso non ponitur, ita ab eo non deponitur. Sed immediate talis lex a deo menti rationali imprimitur, nec sibi per legem nec prophetas contradicitur, sed potius assentitur... Sed legis positive papa debet esse lator et imitator pro temporum congruentia, quia sicut ab ipsa ponitur, ita ab ipsa deponi potest. Quia igitur legis naturalis papa debet esse observator, omnes paganos et transgressores talis legis iuste potest punire. Nam unusquisque iuste potest puniri pro transgressione illius legis quam recipit et quam profitetur observare... Pagani vero et omnes barbare nationes

level of toleration, for even though pagans were *infideles*, they were still nevertheless part of Christ's lost sheep for whom he had died. There was a chance that they could be converted and become faithful members of Christ's Church.[282] Thus even their superstitious rites were to be allowed should the pope deem it to be of benefit for the faithful, but otherwise such rites should be avoided at all costs, if not obliterated.[283]

Augustinus espoused a similar attitude towards the Jews, combining tolerance with clear lines. The Jews are the perpetual servants of the faithful, yet their conversion is ever to be hoped. Nevertheless,

---

per legem divinam veteris vel novi testamenti convinci non possunt. Nec per legem positivam cum neutram recipiant. Unde sicut per legem nature qua coguntur profiteri convinci possunt, ita per ipsam possunt iuste puniri... est dicendum quod papa non iudicat de interiori conscientia, sed de exteriori operum evidentia, contra que si lex naturalis reclamet, ipso facto convincuntur esse puniendos, quia evidentia patrati sceleris non indiget clamore accusatoris. Unde super illo verbo Genesis duodevicesimo, *Clamor Sodomorum [...] venit ad me* [Gn. 18:20–21], dicit glosa Gregorii: Mala proximorum nostrorum non prius iudicemus quam videamus." Aug.Anc. *Summa* 23,4 (ed. Rome, 1479), fol. 83ra.

[282] "Dicendum <est> quod Christus per passionem suam meruit iudiciariam potestatem super omnem creaturam... Vide quam latum sit regnum Christi, quia a mari usque ad mare id est a quolibet fine terre usque ad quemlibet finem terre diffundetur tam late dilatabitur ecclesia. Vicarius autem Christi est papa. Unde nullus potest se subtrahere ab eius obedientia de iure, sicut nullus potest de iure se subtrahere ab obedientia dei... omnes creature rationales sunt oves Christi iure creationis et sufficienter iure redemptionis, quia ipse pro omnibus sufficienter passus est. Sed pagani et infideles non sunt ex ovibus Christi fidei adhesione... Secundum enim Augustinum de nullo est diffidendum quia qui hodie sunt iudei vel pagani, cras poterunt esse christiani. Omnes enim possunt esse oves Christi ex parte ecclesie per eius charitatem quia pro omnibus orat ut convertantur et per eorum potestatem quia omnibus datum est velle et liberum arbitrium quo converti possunt... Nam [catholica ecclesia] utitur paganis et gentilibus ad materiam operationis sue, hereticis ad probationem doctrine sue, scismaticis ad documentum stabilitatis sue, iudeis ad comparationem pulchritudinis sue. Omnibus tamen gratie dei participande dat potestatem sive illi formandi sint sicut pagani, sive reformandi sicut heretici, sive recolligendi sicut scismatici, sive admittendi sicut iudei." Aug.Anc. *Summa* 23,1 (ed. Rome, 1479), fol. 81^{va-b}.

[283] "Ecclesia quasi quinque modis debet se habere in correctione vitiorum. Primo per dissimulationem; secundo per maturam tolerationem; tertio per subtilem investigationem; quarto per duram increpationem; quinto per omnimodam exterminationem. Imitatur enim ecclesia iudicium dei, qui multa mala in presenti dissimulat, multa mature tolerat, multa subtili investigatione ad lucem deducit, multa vero duris flagellis fortiter increpat, multa vero omnimode exterminat. Unde si papa videat conversationem paganorum prodesse fidelibus vel per ipsorum conversationem vel ipsorum christianorum dissidii et aliorum malorum vitationem potest et debet eorum ritum et superstitionem tolerare, alias debet omnino vitare, potessime nunc iam fidelibus multiplicatis non expedit ritum paganorum et aliorum infidelium cum fide christiana admisceri." Aug.Anc. *Summa* 23,6 (ed. Rome, 1479), fol. 83vb–84ra.

given their ingratitude, they must be prevented from harming the Christian faith.[284] Yet the pope is not to use coercive power to effect their conversion, since true conversion comes from God alone. If, however, Jews have already converted, then force is to be used to make sure they fulfill their obligations made to the Church, and indeed, force can be used to compel Jews to accept the faith, though forced conversions as such are not valid. Faith comes from the will and can only truly be infused by God. Nevertheless, Augustinus pointed out, a coerced will is still a will.[285] Thus in hope for the conversion of the Jews, Augustinus allowed Christians to socialize with Jews, though with limitations.[286] Yet Jews were not to hold offices of authority over Christians,[287] nor were they allowed to hold Christian slaves.[288] In general, however, the pope was to enforce the toleration of the Jews and their religion, and no Christian was to harm Jews bodily nor materially. If their synagogues were vandalized or destroyed, the Jews were to be allowed to repair or rebuild them to their former state.[289] Augustinus did not say, however, that

---

[284] "Dicendum <est> quod propria culpa iudeorum eos summisit perpetue servituti fidelium, pietas tamen christiana que desiderat omnes homines salvos fieri, sperans de eorum conversione, quamvis eos receptet et sustineat in eorum cohabitationem, considerans tamen eorum ingratitudinem que semper abundavit in eis, tollit eis omnem occasionem seviendi et ledendi christianam fidem." Aug.Anc. *Summa* 24,5 (ed. Rome, 1479), fol. 86rb.

[285] "Respondendo <est> dicendum quod aliqui respondent ad istum articulum tali distinctione premissa. Infidelium quidam sunt qui nunquam susceperunt fidem, sicut gentiles et iudei, et tales ut dicunt nullo modo sunt ad fidem compellendi ut credant, quia credere voluntatis est. Alii vero sunt infideles qui quandoque fidem susceperunt et eam profitentur, et tales sunt corporaliter compellendi ut impleant quod promiserunt et teneant quod semel susceperunt ne nomen domini blasphemetur et christi fides viliis ac contemptibilis habeatur... Ideo puto absque preiudicio dicendum quod vel queritur de facto vel de modo fiendi. Si vero queritur de facto ita quod aliqui ad fidem suscipiendam violentia compulsi sunt, si talis violentia fuit absoluta, non sunt cogendi ipsam tenere. Si vero fuit mixta et conditionalis, fidem susceptam tenere compellendi sunt, quia secundum Augustinum voluntas coacta voluntas est... Sed si queritur de modo fiendi, puto quod si speretur aliqorum infidelium conversio per terrores et flagella compellendi sunt. Non quidem ad fidem suscipiendam, cum fidem infundere sit solus dei, sed ad consentiendum et obicem non prebendum per obstinatam voluntatem, nam in conversione infidelium ecclesia debet dei iudicium imitari." Aug.Anc. *Summa* 24,1 (ed. Rome, 1479), fol. 84rb. Augustinus was also clear that the pope was not to force Jewish babies to be baptized; Aug.Anc. *Summa* 24,3 (ed. Rome, 1479), fol. 85^{ra-va}.

[286] Aug.Anc. *Summa* 24,7 (ed. Rome, 1479), fol. 87^{ra-va}.
[287] Aug.Anc. *Summa* 24,5 (ed. Rome, 1479), fol. 86^{ra-va}.
[288] Aug.Anc. *Summa* 24,6 (ed. Rome, 1479), fol. 86va–87ra.
[289] "Nullus Christianus eorum quemlibet sine iudicio terrene potestatis vel occidere

synagogues were not to be vandalized or destroyed in the first place, which points to the ambiguity inherent in the Church's policy towards the Jews. Yet the Jews, as the pagans, posed different considerations for the Church's jurisdiction than did those rebellious to the faith. Heretics, schismatics, tyrants, and the excommunicated were all subject to the direct authority of the pope and were to be punished and forced to be brought back into the fold.[290]

There is one, holy, catholic, and apostolic Church. This was the position of Augustinus no less than it was that of Boniface VIII and Giles of Rome. The Church's glory was in the augmentation and expansion of the Christian faith, the building of the mystical body of Christ, who ruled his Church both directly and through his vicar, the pope. The sovereignty of the Church was that of Christ, its head. As such it extended from the issues of whether a monk could leave his Order to care for his parents; whether sex outside of marriage was a mortal sin; who could sacramentally marry whom; whether the pope could punish pagan sins against nature; how to deal with the Jews; or whether leavened or unleavened bread should be used for the eucharist; to regulating the relationship between all temporal and spiritual jurisdiction, the relationship between the pope and princes, kings, and emperors, establishing the political administration of society; and finally descending to the depths of purgatory and reaching to the celestial realm of the angels. It encompassed both the bedroom and the boardroom, this world and the next, sin and salvation. This was the entity that was the Church, and the entire world was subject to its authority, for the pope, as the vicar of Christ, was to fight as a king against tyrants, to administer his subjects as their priest and prelate, and to be the teacher of God's law. This was Christendom. As the head of the Church, as Christ's vicar, the pope's jurisdiction spanned the ends of the earth and beyond. It was his responsibility to govern the Church in Christ's stead. This was an ominous task, for the sovereignty and jurisdiction of Christ were

---

vel vulnerare vel suas pecunias auferre presumat, aut bonas quas hactenus habuerunt consuetudines immutare, presertim in festivitatum suarum celebratione, quisquam fustibus vel lapidibus eos nullatenus perturbet neque aliquis ab eis coacta servitia exigat, nisi que ipsi tempore preterito facere consueverunt. Synagoge vero ipsorum si destruantur, possunt absque contradictione ipsas reparare in eadem qualitate et mensura in qua prius fuisse noscuntur... quod papa non imitatur iudeos in iudasimo, sed tolerat eorum ritum per rationem dictam."Aug.Anc. *Summa* 24,2 (ed. Rome, 1479), fol. 85ra.

[290] Aug.Anc. *Summa* 25–28 (ed. Rome, 1479), fol. 89ra–102va.

truly universal. The pope was indeed the king of kings and the lord of lords, for his reign was the reign of Christ.

There is, however, throughout Augustinus' treatment of the pope's power and the Church's sovereignty an inherent tension. On the one hand, the sovereignty of the Church is the temporal jurisdiction of Christ, who governs through his vicar, whereby the pope is the instrument and administrator of Christ's kingdom. On the other hand, the sovereignty of the Church is embodied in Christ's vicar, whereby the pope is the possessor of Christ's temporal jurisdiction. It is the tension between Christ as the *caput ecclesie* and the pope as the *caput ecclesie*, the tension between the eternal person of the pope, and the office of the pope, and it becomes all the greater when one begins to realize, as Augustinus was very much aware, that the pope, even as the source of all human justice and law, as the interpreter of law and of the scriptures, as the maker of kings and of emperors, as the highest priest of God's Church, who could be judged by no one save God alone, could, nevertheless, err.

D. *The Fallible Pope*

That the pope was fallible had long been both assumed and asserted. The novelty was the claim for the opposite, put forth by some "unknown, rebellious friar."[291] Tierney included Augustinus with authors espousing the traditional opinion, but found his treatment "particularly interesting because . . . he overtly raised the question of papal infallibility in connection with the papal key of knowledge."[292] Yet that was precisely the point of the *Sachsenhausen Appeal*, to which Augustinus was responding.[293] Moreover, Tierney touches on Augustinus only cursorily, quoting a brief passage as representing Augustinus'

---

[291] Tierney, *Origins*, 185.
[292] *Ibid.*, 184.
[293] The third argument *pro* is that made by the Franciscan Excursus in summary form: "Videtur enim quod papa in potestate clavium non possit excedere vel errare quia in eo quod est infinitum non potest esse excessus; sed potestas clavium in papa est infinita; ego in ea non potest esse excessus. Preterea excessus est usurpando potestatem alterius; sed papa non potest alterius potestatem usurpare cum sit dominus omnium; ergo non potest in potestate excedere. Preterea ecclesia non potest errare . . . sed papa est caput ecclesie; ego non potest errare in clave scientie. In contrarium est commune dictum doctorum quod papa omnia potest clave potentie non excedente et clave scientie non errante." Aug.Anc. *Summa* 20,6 (ed. Rome, 1479), fol. 74vb–75ra; "Quod enim per clavem scientie per romanos pontifices semel determinatum est in fide et moribus recte vite, est inmutabile, eo quod ecclesia

position, in which Augustinus relates the common opinion of theologians.[294] The text in question is from article six, question twenty of Augustinus' *Summa* and is not a statement of Augustinus' position, but is his argument *contra* after having first posed three arguments for the position of infallibility in typical scholastic fashion. One, however, cannot simply take the arguments *contra* as representing the position of Augustinus. In every article of every question, Augustinus proceeds by resolving arguments *pro* and *contra* in a more intricate treatment than either side of the opposition he had set up. And this is the case for question twenty, article six.

For Augustinus the pope is indeed infallible: "since such power [of the keys] has been given to the pope by God, the pope is not able to use it to excess nor to err." The power of the pope is in fact infinite.[295] He did, however, qualify such statements. Essentially his position is that as long as the pope does not err, he is infallible. It is perhaps most clearly stated in his reply to the second argument he posed for infallibility, which runs: "Furthermore, it is an excess to usurp the power of another; but the pope is not able to usurp the power of another since he is the lord of all; therefore, he is not able to use his power excessively."[296] Augustinus responded by arguing that "the pope is not able to usurp the power of another by the use of his own power since his power extends to all; but he is able to usurp the power of another by the abuse of his power."[297] The pope is not able to err formally as such (*per se et formaliter*) but he can indeed err circumstantially and materially (*per accidens et materialiter*).[298] When it comes down to it, Augustinus uses his distinctions

---

romana est inerrabilis in fide et veritate... Nam quod semel per summos pontifices dei vicarios per clavem scientie est diffinitum esse de fidei veritate, non potest per successorem aliquem in dubium revocari..." Lud.IV. *App.* 28,1 (403).

[294] Tierney, *Origins.*, 185.

[295] "... cum talis potestas sit sibi a deo collata, non potest in ipsa excedere neque errare... dicendum quod in potentia pape, que est infinita, non potest esse excessus..." Aug.Anc. *Summa* 20,6 (ed. Rome, 1479), fol. 75rb.

[296] "Preterea, excessus est usurpando potestatem alterius; sed papa non potest alterius potestatem usurpare cum sit dominus omnium; ergo non potest esse excessus." Aug.Anc. *Summa* 20,6 (ed. Rome, 1479), fol. 74vb–75ra.

[297] "Ad secundum est dicendum quod papa non potest usurpare potestatem alterius per sue potestatis usum, cum eius potentia ad omnia se extendat; sed potest usurpare alterius potestatem per sue potestatis abusum." Aug.Anc. *Summa* 20,6 (ed. Rome, 1479), fol. 75rb.

[298] "Dicendum est <quod> de potestate clavium respectu pape quia cum talis potestas sit sibi a deo collata non potest in ipsa excedere neque errare vel ea male

to advocate a paradoxical position: an infallible pope who can err. To understand his doctrine of the fallibility and infallibility of the pope, we need to delve deeper into his understanding of the pope as such, and of the pope as the *caput ecclesie*. Augustinus' *Summa* was intended to explicate the extent and the limits of ecclesiastical sovereignty, which are both present and encapsulated in his treatment of papal infallibility: the pope is infallible and his power is infinite, yet it is an infinity within a finite realm, which is determined by, among other things, the pope's capacity to err. What seem to be paradoxical positions in the *Summa*, are often resolved by unravelling the complexity of his understanding of the pope, or rather, of the papacy, and consequently of the Church's sovereignty and of Christ's reign. Whereas up to now we have focused on the extent of ecclesiastical power, it is time to turn to its boundaries and limits, in hope of revealing Augustinus' doctrine of the fallible, infallible pope.

One must not lose sight of what Augustinus was doing. He was writing a treatise on ecclesiastical power for Pope John XXII. He was not composing a work compiled of theoretical lectures in a classroom. He was trying to instruct, and to advise, pushing issues to extremes, to see how far one could go, and to find out just where the limits were. His position that the pope can make dispensation regarding the degrees of consanguinity for legitimate marriage except for that between parents and their children, is a case in point. Though he did not bring up the consequences of his position in this case, in effect he makes for the marriage of a brother and sister, or of an uncle and niece, or aunt and nephew, not only to be non-incestuous, but even sacramental. This is not to imply, however, that this was a position Augustinus was advocating, but it was a theoretical possibility. The same holds true regarding his position that the pope's power of jurisdiction can be completely separate from his power of ordination, and thus someone, even a layman, could be

---

uti per se et formaliter quia omnis usus clavis potentie rectus et iustus est cum ab illo sit derivata qui iustus est et rectum iudicium eius. Similiter omnis usus clavis scientie verus et rationabilis est cum sit derivata ab illo qui est via, veritas, et vita. Sed per accidens et materialiter papa et in clave potentie potest excedere et in clave scientie potest errare ... ergo est dicendum quod in potentia pape que est infinita non potest esse excessus quantum ad rectum usum iustitie et equitatis. Similiter clavis scientie nunquam obliquatur utendo ipsa secundum rationabilem usum veritatis." Aug.Anc. *Summa* 20,6 (ed. Rome, 1479), fol. 75[rb].

pope, and would truly be pope, even though he would not be the bishop of Rome, divorcing the papacy from the Roman church. That indeed is a theoretical possibility for Augustinus, as is brother-sister marriage. It is not, however, a position that Augustinus puts forth as the basis for his view of papal sovereignty in the real world. As stated above, Augustinus argued that only in Rome, or at least in Italy, can the pope exercise his full powers of jurisdiction, whereas if the pope were to reside anywhere else, he would be liable to capitulate to the prince.[299] For all the theoretical aspects of the *Summa*, it is intended as a practical guide. John XXII, after all, was in Avignon. Augustinus had to be able to account for that, yet Rome was where the pope belonged, and Augustinus wanted to be sure that John got the message.

In question twenty-one, article one, Augustinus addressed the issue of whether the pope is obligated to reside in Rome. He first gave three arguments for the position that the pope certainly is not bound to Rome. First, the pope can do all things, and therefore he can darn well choose where he wants to live with his curia. Second, the pope is the bishop of the universal Church, and therefore can make any church his residence. And third, the pope is not restricted by time, whereby he could do more at one given time than at another, and thus neither is he restricted by place.[300] Then comes the argument *contra*, which asserts that were the pope to abandon Rome, it would be as a man leaving his wife and thus involving her in adultery.[301] Finally, Augustinus makes his case.

He resolves the question by making the distinction between necessity (*de necessario*), and suitability or practicality (*de congruo*). By necessity the pope is not obligated to reside in Rome. With regard, however, to what is suitable, it is far more fitting that the pope indeed customarily make Rome his place of residence than any other

---

[299] See note 111 above.
[300] "Videtur enim quod papa non teneatur semper Rome residere cum sua curia, quia papa omnia potest. Ergo ubi placet, ibi potest residentiam facere. Preterea papa est episcopus universalis ecclesie, ut supra dictum est. Ergo in qualibet ecclesia potest residere. Preterea papa non artatur tempore, ut magis possit uno tempore quam alio. Ergo non debet artari loco, ut magis teneatur in uno loco residere quam in alio." Aug.Anc. *Summa* 21,1 (ed. Rome, 1479), fol. 75va.
[301] "In contrarium est quia papa singulariter est Romanus episcopus; sed sicut vir non debet adulterari suam uxorem, ita nec episcopus ecclesiam suam, ut illam dimittat." Aug.Anc. *Summa* 21,1 (ed. Rome, 1479), fol. 75va.

location.[302] Augustinus then put forth three reasons why Rome is optimal. Rome is where the bodies of Peter and Paul are buried, which gives it a certain preeminence. Moreover, Rome has a singular excellence as the place where the apostles were martyred, and was given special status by Paul, since whereas Rome had once been the teacher of errors, she had become the student of truth. The third reason for Rome's special relationship with the pope is her unique suitability, and here Augustinus argued as mentioned above that only in Rome could the pope fully exercise his authority and best serve the Christian people.[303] Yet he goes even further.

In his replies to the arguments set forth at the beginning, we find that Augustinus, in very strong terms, bound the pope to residency in Rome. He agrees, or admits, that theoretically the pope is not by necessity bound to Rome, for indeed the pope can do all things. Yet the pope *is* bound by truth and justice. Moreover, what is not explicitly commanded or forbidden by the scriptures, is subject to the justice of worthy custom. The customs and traditions of God's

---

[302] "Respondendo dicendum <est> quod vel queritur de necessario vel congruo. Si de necessario papa non necessitatur residere in aliquo determinato loco, quia vicarius est illius cuius *sedes celum* est, *et terra scabellum* pedum eius, ut scribitur Isaie sexagesimo sexto [Is. 66:1]. *Implet* enim *celum et terram* sua potestate et iurisdictione, ut scribitur Hieremie tertio decimo [sic; Jer. 23:24]. Sed si queritur de congruo, multum conveniens est ut Rome papa communiter suam residentiam faciat." Aug.Anc. *Summa* 21,1 (ed. Rome, 1479), fol. 75va.

[303] "Primo <habet> beatorum Petri et Pauli apostolorum corporalem presentiam. Unde scribitur in capitulis Ephesini concilii . . . quod in urbe Romana Petrus et Paulus martyrium detulerunt, que principatum et caput obtinebat nationum, ut ubi erat caput superstitionis, illic caput quiesceret sanctitatis, et ubi gentilium principes habitabant, illic ecclesiarum principes morarentur. Secundo habet singularem excellentiam. Unde dicitur in eisdem capitulis quod non sine causa factum esse putamus quod sancti apostoli passi sunt una die et in uno loco atque sub uno persecutore, quia dies datus est eis pro merito, locus pro gloria et persecutor decretus est eis pro virtute, et super illo verbo ad Romanos primo: *Omnibus qui sunt Rome* salutem [Rm. 1:7], dicit glossa quod Paulus singulariter Romam nominat quia licet quondam fuerit magistra erroris, per predicationem tamen apostolorum facta fuit disciplina veritatis. Tertio habet singularem convenientiam, in nulla enim patria papa potest uti tanta libertate et tanta iurisdictionis potestate, nec tantam pro populo christiano facere utilitatem sicut Rome et in patrimonio beati Petri; residendo enim in alia patria supponit se sub dominio regum et principum et sic vel timore vel amore non libere potest uti iustitia et equitate, sed cogitur ab ipsa deviare. Sed cum presit Rome papa et in partibus Italie per immediatam administrationem temporalibus et spiritualibus in nulla patria potest uti suo dominio universaliter sicut ibi, nec tantam utilitatem pro populo christiano facere, cum sit patria maioris affluentie et maioris convenientie pro convenientibus ad eius curiam quam aliqua alia." Aug.Anc. *Summa* 21,2 (Rome, 1479), fol. 75^{va-b}.

people have the force of law (*mos populi dei vel instituta maiorum pro lege tenenda sunt*), and if one were to dispute such law based on the customs and traditions of another people, one would cause wanton conflict in the Church. Further, even though the pope is indeed the bishop of the universal Church, he has the responsibility for the immediate administration of the temporal and spiritual realms of the Roman church as her bishop, and therefore Rome needs the pope more than any other church. And finally, though "by necessity the pope is not constrained by place, he is by suitability, *and even by necessity* with respect to his subjects, because his subjects, having no other temporal lord, are exposed to many dangers, rebellions, and damaging wars due to the absence of the pope, as experience teaches."[304]

Augustinus separated the pope's power of jurisdiction from his power of ordination, the office of the pope from the Roman church, as a theoretical reality, not as a *modus operandi*. The fight was for Rome, and for the bishop of Rome as the temporal and spiritual ruler of St. Peter's patrimony. The problem was that the bishop of Rome was in Avignon, and war was plaguing the papal states: theoretically by Marsilius of Padua's *Defensor Pacis* and Louis of Bavaria's *Sachsenhausen Appeal*, as well as practically by Louis' troops and those of his supporters, which Augustinus' immediate temporal lord, Robert d'Anjou, was trying to combat. The term *experientia docet* was a standard scholastic argument, the appeal to experience, common sense and common knowledge, that which everyone knew. It was common place, and certainly was convenient when other arguments could not be devised. Yet as so often, here with Augustinus it is most

---

[304] "Ad primum ergo est dicendum quod licet papa omnia possit, hoc tamen debet velle et posse quod iustitia requirit et laudabilis consuetudo. *Non enim possumus aliquid* contra *veritatem sed pro veritate*, ut dicebat apostolus secunde ad Corinthios tertio <decimo> [II Cor. 13:8], et Augustinus in libro de ieiunio diei sabbati [*cf.* Aug. ieiun. 7.9 (237,241–253)], quod in his rebus de quibus nihil certum statuit scriptura divina, mos populi dei vel instituta maiorum pro lege tenenda sunt, de quibus si disputare voluerimus et ex consuetudine aliorum, alios improbare, oriretur indeterminata luctatio in ecclesia dei. Ad secundum est dicendum quod papa est episcopus universalis ecclesie, per universalem iurisdictionem; sed episcopus Romanus est per spiritualium et temporalium immediatam administrationem. Ideo magis indiget presentia sua quam aliqua alia ecclesia. Ad tertium est dicendum quod papa non artatur loco per necessitatem, sed artatur per congruitatem, *et etiam quantum ad necessitatem* ex parte subditorum, quia subditi eius non habentes alium dominum in temporalibus nisi eum multis periculis et multis rebellionibus atque multis bellicis discriminibus exponuntur, per ipsius pape presentie carentiam, sicut experientia docet." Aug.Anc. *Summa* 21,2 (ed. Rome, 1479), fol. 75va–76ra; (emphasis added).

telling and revealing. "Experience teaches," was based on the given assumption of what that experience was. It was a rhetorical strategy of argumentation based on the lived reality of the audience addressed, as the scholastic counterpart to the *exempla* of sermons. And the lived reality of Augustinus, as much as that of his contemporaries, was that when the pope did not reside in Rome, the Roman church suffered terribly, and by consequence, so did the Church universal. Dangers, rebellions, wars: these were the results of the non-residency of the Roman bishop, and that was clear to all in 1326. Italy was being torn apart by factional warfare, and the pope was in Avignon. One might legitimately question whether John XXII could have done all that much anyway had he indeed been in residency, but the point was that he wasn't, even though John was doing his best. The papal states were without their leader, their sovereign, their lord, and the people were paying for it. Augustinus knew this well and knew it on an intimate level. War there was, and it was in no way simply a war of words.

Julius II (1502–1513), a close friend of the Augustinian General Giles of Viterbo, has the reputation for having been the "Warrior Pope," but John XXII is as deserving of the title. John was "one of the most important popes in the history of the crusades against Christian rulers,"[305] and beginning in 1321 until the end of his reign in 1334, he spent almost two-thirds of his entire income on his Italian wars, primarily against the Visconti and Louis IV.[306] He himself, however, did not take up the sword, but left that to his legate in northern Italy, the cardinal-bishop of Ostia, Bertrand du Poujet, and to the forces of his vicar, Robert d'Anjou.[307] John's crusading zeal was no idle threat, and for the promise of a plenary indulgence, people took up the cross for the cause. Both Louis of Bavaria and Marsilius of Padua fiercely attacked John's bellicose policy in the *Sachsenhausen Appeal* and the *Defensor Pacis* respectively.[308] Augustinus defended it,[309] for after all, one of the primary functions of the pope was to be a king fighting against tyrants. Rome must not fall.[310] Louis

---

[305] Housley, *The Italian Crusades*, 10.
[306] Ibid., 250–151.
[307] Ibid., passim.
[308] Ibid., 37, 41, 61.
[309] Ibid., 36–37.
[310] Ibid., 45–50.

and Marsilius, as well as the Visconti, were not only political and military adversaries of the pope, but were also, as if a distinction can be made, heretics, and thus enemies of the Church,[311] as had been Ezzelino of Romano, against whom Pope Alexander IV had waged perhaps the most successful Italian crusade during the years 1255–1260,[312] precisely as the Augustinian Order was being founded. Sicily too had for a long while been a major sphere of papal military operations. Even after the Treaty of Caltabellota of 1302, which recognized the Aragonese occupation of Sicily—finally settling matters after the Treaty of Tarascon had fallen apart upon the death of Alfonso of Aragon, the treaty that Benedict Caetani had orchestrated in 1291—relations were still strained and Robert d'Anjou never lost his designs on regaining the other part of his kingdom. He hoped his alliance with the pope would help.

This was all part of Augustinus' experience, his common knowledge. It was also the experience and common knowlege of Augustinus' entire Order, whose existence and privilege were dependent upon the support of the pope. Beginning in April of 1317, John XXII wrote to a number of bishops and archbishops in Italy, France, and Germany confirming the Augustinians' privileges to preach and hear confessions, as well as all the other privileges that had been granted them by the Holy See. The Augustinians had petitioned the pope that such privileges were being infringed upon. Local prelates, priests, and unspecified others were preventing the Augustinians from preaching and hearing confessions. John instructed his bishops that they were responsible for making sure that the Augustinians' rights were upheld and honored. It fell to the Roman pontiff to protect and defend those religious directly under his authority, as the Augustinians had been since the Bull *Sacer ordo vester* of Boniface VIII; thus John's admonitions to his bishops defending the rights of the Augustinians.[313] Shortly thereafter, all hell broke loose.

The General Chapter of the Augustinians meeting at Montepessulano in June of 1324 under the Prior General Alexander of San Elpidio began by stating baldly:

---

[311] *Ibid.*, 54–55.
[312] *Ibid.*, 158–161, 167–170.
[313] *Bullae Iohannis Papae XXII, AAug.* 4 (1911), 1–2. The text of the Bull regarding the Roman Province is given, with an example of the analogous Bulls regarding the French Province; the other recipients of similar Bulls are detailed in the first note.

In the first place, since the status of our Order depends in all ways on the favor of the highest pontiff, we declare and affirm with this present article that all the brothers of our Order, of all ranks and conditions, are diligently to observe and uphold with all solicitude the commands and mandates of the pope as well as those of papal legates.[314]

The Chapter continued by imposing a prison sentence of six months upon any member of the Order who was caught supporting those rebellious to the Church, thus causing confusion and scandal for the Order.[315] This was in 1324, as Alexander was completing his *De ecclesiastica potestate*, dedicated to John XXII. Two years later, the General Chapter met in Florence and reaffirmed this stipulation as the first order of business. It then commanded, in the strongest terms possible, all brothers, clerical or lay, who were residing in areas rebellious to the Church to return to their own provinces. Those not adhering to this directive were to be considered as rebels against the Order, sentenced to be bound in chains in perpetual incarceration, as were those who might support or take part in the rebellion against the Church.[316] And Augustinus was completing his *Summa*.

---

[314] "In primis cum status nostri ordinis a favore summi pontificis omnino dependeat, diffinimus et presenti diffinitione firmamus, omnibus fratribus cuiuscumque status vel conditionis existant mandantes quatenus cum omni sollicitudine et reverentia mandata summi pontificis et dominorum sedis apostolice legatorum inviolabiliter studeant observare." Esteban, *AAug.* 3 (1910), 466.

[315] "Rebellibus autem et inobedientibus ipsius sancte Matris ecclesie verbo vel facto, occulte vel publice, sollicite studeant obviare, ac eorum ambasciatas servitia et favores tamquam ipsius ecclesie rebellium debeant respuere ac eorum conversationem et familiaritatem penitus evitare. Quod si quis ita immemor sue salutis extiterit quod rebellibus sancte Matris ecclesie favores, ambasciatas vel servitia, per se vel per alium, modo aliquo prebere presumpserit, illum vel illos, cuiuscumque conditionis existant, presenti diffinitione pene carceris per sex menses adiudicamus, ut confusionem et scandalum quod ordini inferandum procurabant, in humilitatis spiritu disciplinam ordinis recognoscant." Esteban, *AAug.* 3 (1910), 466.

[316] "In primis confirmamus et approbamus diffinitionem primam factam in capitulo Montis Pessulani, que sic incipit: Cum status nostri ordinis etc. diffinimus et ordinamus etc. Item presenti diffinitione citamus ac etiam revocamus fratres singulos nostri ordinis, clericos sive laicos, commorantes in civitatibus vel in castris rebellium sancte matris ecclesie, ac etiam precipimus quantum possumus in meritum obedientie salutaris quod sine mora, statim cum aures ipsorum presens mandatum pervenerit, recedant ab huiusmodi civitatibus vel castris et provincialibus sue provincie se presentent, servatis solummodo tot fratribus laicis vel conversis, quot ad custodiam loci possunt sufficere. Si qui vero sue salutis immemores, presens mandatum neglexerint vel contempserint adimplere, precipimus quam districtius possumus singulis prioribus provincialibus nostri ordinis quatenus contra tales fratres in sua provincia huiusmodi nostra monita non servantes sicut contra rebelles nostri ordinis procedant cum ordinis disciplina perpetuo carceri ipsos in ferramentis et vinculis

And John was still waging war, as he had been since 1321. Crusades against Christian rulers seemed to many to be abominable, especially when the recovery of the Holy Land should be of primary importance. Moreover, how could the pope advocate the killing of Christians? Such a war could not be holy. Yet opposition to John's Italian campaigns came most often from the camp of those he was fighting. Nevertheless, the prestige of the papacy was being damaged, but was not so much based on the principle itself as on the fact the John was not making all that much headway; if the pope could not take care of his own, then perhaps the pope was not privy to the obedience and honor he was claiming.[317]

In addition to the forces of Robert d'Anjou, the primary method that John had at his disposal for recruiting troops for the fight for Rome, aside from employing pure mercenaries, which he did as well, was the preaching of the crusade, which offered those signing up a plenary indulgence. The appeal of time off in purgatory was most persuasive, and many succumbed and took up the cross in defense of the Church.[318] Augustinus was a big defender of indulgences and argued that the pope could free all from purgatory, except those not under his immediate jurisdiction, namely, those who had never been members of the *ecclesia militans* but due to the grace of God were members of the *ecclesia triumphans*.[319] This was good news for John XXII and his endeavor to mobilize his forces. Yet in Augustinus' treatment of indulgences, we also come upon the limits to which the pope can go.

Augustinus went beyond the theoretical to ask whether indeed the pope could in fact empty purgatory. He first confirmed that by his universal jurisdiction this was something the pope could do. However, whether he *should* do so is another matter. Moreover, if he did do so by granting such indulgences, whether God would accept such indulgences as satisfaction for the sins of those who had been so freed was most uncertain, and Augustinus admitted that he just did not know the answer—and neither could the pope. The pope's power

---

mancipantes. Et eidem pene adiudicamus quoscumque nostri ordinis fratres qui locum aliquem in rebellione tenuerint vel favorem et causam talibus ministraverint." Esteban, *AAug.* 4 (1911), 3–4.

[317] Housley, *The Italian Crusades*, 45, 252–257.
[318] *Ibid.*, 111–144.
[319] See note 230 above, and 320 below.

is infinite, but that itself limits the realm of its legitimate use. To use power rightly, one must know what one is doing and then do so with the right intent. The proper use of power is based on justice and the proper will. Since the pope exercises his power as the expression of God's will and equity, and since God's will and equity cannot be completely known by any human being, neither can the actual extent of the proper use of the pope's power. Were the pope to empty purgatory, Augustinus asserts, he would err in terms of exceeding the boundaries of both the key of knowledge and the key of power.[320] In other words, it would not be the use of his power, but its abuse, and the pope would have erred *per accidens et materialiter*.[321]

John XXII surely had no intent of emptying purgatory; it was, after all, most useful, but he was throwing the offer of plenary indulgences around rather indiscriminately, even as Augustinus cautioned against the pope using military force except in the case of extreme

---

[320] "Sequitur ergo quantum ad omnes predictos quod papa possit purgatorium spoliare. Loquendo ergo de potestate pape primo modo quantum ad absolutam eius iurisdictionem, videtur esse dicendum quod papa possit purgatorium spoliare, quantum ad omnes istos qui subiiciuntur iurisdictioni sue. Loquendo vero secundo modo de tali potestate quantum ad eius ordinatam executionem, puto quod papa non possit nec debet et illud probatur tribus rationibus ... Papa illud potest recto usu clavium ordinaria et legitima potestate quod facit potestate non excedente et clave scientie non errante, sed si totum purgatorium spoliaret esset excessus potestatis et error scientie, quia non esset iusta et rationabilis causa ut dictum est. Ergo legitima et rationabili potestate illud non potest nec debet ... Legitima et rationabili potestate thesaurus eccles non est aperiendus nisi militibus ecclesie et illud dumtaxat pro utilitate rei publice, quia sicut videmus quod thesaurus corporalis non dispensatur nisi militibus pro republica laborantibus, sic thesaurus spiritualis aperiri non debet nisi pro utilitate ecclesie, sed multi sunt in purgatorio qui non fuerunt milites ecclesie militantis secundum universalem legem et secundum gratiam communem sacramentalem. Multi sunt similiter qui carent illis qui faciunt pro eis pertinentia ad utilitatem ecclesie pro qua ordinatum est indulgentias valere. Ergo potestate legitma et ordinaria talibus thesaurus ecclesie aperiendus non est. Sed loquendo tertio modo quantum ad divinam acceptionem ut si papa illud faceret quod applicaret intentionem suam indulgentiam communicando omnibus qui sunt in purgatorio volendo predictum locum expoliare, an deus haberet acceptum, dico quod ignotum est mihi et puto quod ignotum sit cuilibet creature et ipsi papemet. Nec credo quod papa possit scire totum quod potest facere per potentiam suam et potissime quod potest facere per communicationem thesauri ecclesie. Et istud similiter probatur tribus rationibus quarum prima est talis. Illa potentia est homini ignota que est in virtute voluntatis et equitatis sibi ignota. Sed papa agit in virtute et equitate dei que sibi est ignota, similiter posse pape est ignotum ... Cum ergo talis satisfactio consistit in dei acceptatione sicut acceptatio dei est ignota pape et cuilibet creature, ita ut et talis satisfactio que fit per communicationem indulgentie ignota est sibi." Aug.Anc. *Summa* 32,3 (ed. Rome, 1479), fol. 113[ra–va].

[321] *Cf.* Horst, "Die Lehrautorität," 296–297.

need.³²² Here, in his treatment of indulgences, Augustinus further sought to make clear that the granting of indulgences was based on the proper use of the pope's will as an expression of the justice and will of God. The pope's power was infinite, but that did not mean that the pope could do whatever he liked. Augustinus expressly argued that the pope cannot grant indulgences simply based on his own will, at least not without good reason. Indulgences were based on the treasury of merit, and as such were to be used for the good of the Church. The pope was bound to use his power for that end.³²³ Any other use was not use, but abuse. And the pope, while he theoretically could live wherever he chose, was nevertheless bound to Rome.

By pushing issues to the extreme, Augustinus was circumscribing papal power. The pope was fallible, and that must be taken into account. Thus he noted as well seven types of excommunication that the faithful were not held to honor or fear. Six concerned cases when excommunication had been imposed by a prelate without the jurisdiction or authority to do so. The seventh dealt with papal excommunications. When a papal sentence of excommunication contains an intollerable error, a mortal sin, or anything else contrary to the faith, it is not to be observed.³²⁴ The pope could err indeed, even in the imposition of excommunication. But the question was, for Augustinus no less than for John XXII and his opponents, had he?

Augustinus gave no direct answer. This does not mean, though, that he was side-stepping the issue. For Augustinus such a question simply could not be answered. It was not for subjects to judge their superiors, and moreover, it was not the point anyway. Obedience

---

[322] See above, note 131.

[323] "Indulgentia datur mediante usu clavium, quarum virtute remittitur culpa et solvitur pena ... per has enim claves thesaurus ecclesie de quo stipendiantur milites Christi aperitur filiis ecclesie. Unde sicut ad dispensationem talis thesauri requiritur in papa rectus usus clavis potentie, ne talem thesaurum dispenset quibus non potest, ita ad dispensationem dicti thesauri requiritur rectus usus clavis discretionis et scientie, ne sic careat ratione et discretione ut pro sola voluntate sine rationabili causa indulgentiam faciat. Non enim potest papa adversus veritatem sed pro veritate ... Unde pro sola voluntate si subest probabilis ratio vel generalis ecclesie vel specialis alicuius persone potest indulgentiam facere aliter non." Aug.Anc. *Summa* 30,5 (ed. Rome, 1479), fol. 107vb.

[324] Aug.Anc. *Summa* 27,1–10 (ed. Rome, 1479), fol. 94va–98vb; "Septimus est si sententia contineat intollerabilem errorem, puta contineat peccatum mortale vel aliquod quod sit contra fidem. Planum est autem quod nullo istorum modorum excepto ultimo excommunicatio papalis contempnenda." Aug.Anc. *Summa* 27,3 (ed. Rome, 1479), fol. 95^{va-b}.

lay at the heart of the conflict, and Louis was being impudent. Sure there could be bad popes, erring popes, sinful popes, popes who misused their power, as Augustinus admitted right from the very beginning, in the second article of his first question.[325] Yet as long as the pope remained pope, he was to be honored, respected, and obeyed.[326]

As long as the pope remained pope: Louis actually did not have a bad case. Louis, together with his Franciscan co-author, had accused

---

[325] "Ad secundum sic proceditur. Videtur enim quod potestas cuiuslibet pape non sit a deo quia dei perfecta sunt opera. Si ergo omnis potestas pape sit a deo, omnis talis potestas erit perfecta, cuius contrarium videmus ad sensum. Preterea illorum potestas est a deo qui vocantur a deo tanquam Aaron, quia dicente apostolo, nullus debet sibi assumere honorem pontificatus nisi qui vocatur a deo tanquam Aaron. Sed multi pape non vocantur a deo sed magis industria et sagacitate hominum; ergo potestas talium non erit a deo. Preterea illius potestas non est a deo cuius usus est contra deum; sed multi pape utuntur potestate papali contra deum et precepta et mandata eius; ergo talium potestas non est a deo." Aug.Anc. *Summa* 1,2 (ed. Rome, 1479), fol. 4^{va-b}. Augustinus continued by arguing that all power was indeed from God, and thus so is the power of the pope. The divine order is good and from God, even if the use thereof is not: "Dicendum <est> quod in quolibet principatu et in qualibet potestate tria possumus considerare secundum que omnis talis principatus et omnis talis potestas est a deo. Et tria alia possumus considerare secundum que principatus et potestas non est a deo sed potius malitia a pravitate hominum... Nam in quolibet principatu est ordo quidam superioris ad inferiorem et inferioris ad superiorem. Et quantumcumque superiores vel inferiores sint mali, ipse tamen ordo de se habet rationes boni, quia etiam ipsa mala bene ordinata et suo loco posita laudabiliora sunt et eminentius commendant bona et semper ex tali ordine consurgit aliquod bonum propter quod etiam ex principatu malorum, ratione ordinis et ratione divine ordinationis insurgit aliquod bonum... Sunt enim aliqui, qui ipsum principatum et ipsam prelationem prave adipiscuntur quia vel per simoniam vel per minas... aliqui vero sunt, qui principatum et prelationem adeptam prave execuntur, qui non utuntur principatu et tali prelatione ad vindictam malefactorum et laudem bonorum sed potius econtrario... aliqui... sunt in principatu et prelatione adepta prave intentione illa agunt, ut propter sue glorie famationem magis quam propter iustitie observationem, et que exterius demonstrant, interius non habent... dicendum quod opera immediate a deo facta perfecta sunt, sed in operibus, que fiunt a deo mediante creatura potest defectus et imperfectio esse ratione actionis creature, qui defectibilis est... licet potestas boni pontificis et mali sit a deo, abusus tamen tali potestatis a deo non est." Aug.Anc. *Summa* 1,2 (ed. Rome, 1479), fol. 4vb–5rb.

[326] "Dicendum <est> quod pape aperte malo moribus vel vita obediendum est... nam potestas prelationis est donum gratie gratis date non donum gratie gratis facientis. Sed tale donum gratie gratis date non tollitur in papa per aliquod peccatum nisi solum per unum, puta pro crimine heresis... per tale enim peccatum solum papa desinit esse papa, sed per cetera alia peccata potestas prelationis in eo non tollitur, quia cum sit donum gratie gratis date non tollitur per peccatum sicut peccato directe non opponitur... est dicendum quod per que peccat aliquis, per illa debet punire quando istud potest fieri sine detrimento alterius; sed si pape aperte malo non obediretur, non posset fieri sine detrimento ecclesie, et ideo de hoc non debet puniri." Aug.Anc. *Summa* 5,8 (ed. Rome, 1479), fol. 34vb–35rb; "Videtur enim

John of heresy, and of notorious heresy, and thus called for a general council of the Church to depose the pretender to the see of Peter. In practice, according to Augustinus, a general council of the Church, together with the theologians, was indeed the instrument that was empowered to remove a pope from office, even if the theory was obtuse.[327] Theoretically no one can depose a pope, not a council, and certainly not an emperor. Only a pope can depose a pope, meaning, only the pope can depose himself. The pope is to be judged by God alone, not by any human institution. The pope is the vicar of Christ, the head of the Church, and as such is the source of life for all the body's members. Faith is the issue. Faith flows from Christ through the pope to the faithful. Without faith, it is impossible to please God and faith is the foundation of all hope:

---

quod pape aperte malo non debeatur honor, quia pape non debetur honor nisi propter Christum, cuius vicarius existit; sed Christum non honorat malos contemnentes ipsum ... papa ergo aperte malus est contemnendus non honorandus ... Dupliciter ergo potest exhiberi honor ipsi pape: primo in testimonium virtutis sue et gratia sue bonitatis et sanctitatis; secundo in testimonium virtutis Christi et gratia Christi cuius vicarius existit ... quamdiu ergo est vicarius Christi et quamdiu non desinit esse papa dato quod sit aperte malus honor papalis sibi subtrahendus non est ... est dicendum quod honor debetur aliquando ratione meriti, aliquando ratione officii. Primo modo deus non honorat malos; sed secundo modo tamdiu eos honorat, quamdiu eos tollerat in officio. Et isto modo papa aperte malus a fidelibus est honorandus quamdiu a deo tolleratur in papatu et quamdiu non desinit esse papa, quia non exhibetur alicui honor ille in testimonium virtutis sue sed alieni." Aug.Anc. *Summa* 9,6, (ed. Rome, 1479), fol. 46vb–47ra.

[327] "Videtur enim quod ad concilium non spectet papam in heresim deprehensum condemnare vel sententiare, quia per illud concilium potest damnari quod non potest sine eius auctoritate congregari; sed absque auctoritate Romani pontificis concilium congregari non debet ... ergo per concilium non potest sententiari. Preterea concilium non habet auctoritatem nisi papa approbante ... Dicendum <est> quod dupliciter potest ostendi in casu heresis depositionem pape ad concilium spectare. Primo quidem sicut papa mortuo potestas eius remanet in collegio cardinalium vel in collegio universalis ecclesie ... sic papa in heresi deprehenso statim ipso facto potestas eius remanet in ecclesia quia solum per tale crimen papa desinit esse papa; per talem igitur potestatem ecclesia posset illum damnare sicut per talem potestsatem potest alium sibi preficere. Secundo quia magis est periculosa heresis capitis quam membrorum ... <igitur> ad tollendam et damnandam heresim in capite ecclesie insurgentem statim universitas fidelium congregari deberet ... ergo est dicendum quod dum papa est papa concilium congregari non debet nisi auctoritate eius, sed per crimen heresis ut dictum est papa desinit esse papa; ideo in tali casu eius auctoritas non requireretur sed sufficeret auctoritas collegii et aliorum episcoporum ac doctorum sacre scripture ... similiter est dicendum licet enim in questionibus terminandis auctoritas pape dum est papa sit necessaria, cum tamen desinit esse papa per crimen heresis auctoritas illa remanet in ecclesia sicut ipso mortuo." Aug.Anc. *Summa* 5,6 (ed. Rome, 1479), fol. 34^{ra-va}.

If, therefore a pope deviates from the faith, he is dead in terms of spiritual life and consequently is not able to be the conduit of life for others. Wherefore, just as a dead man is not a human being, so a pope having fallen into heresy is not a pope, and on this account, is by the very fact deposed.[328]

An heretical pope was a contradiction in terms. This was the basis for Augustinus' position that it fell to a council to depose a pope, since an heretical pope posed the same case as a dead pope, and Louis was calling for a council.

Whether Louis, however, had justification for doing so was another matter, or even whether he had the right to do so. In question twenty-two Augustinus addressed the issue of the obedience to the pope required of Christians. He first set forth three arguments for the position that Christians are without exception, always to obey the pope, the second of which claimed that since subjects are not able to judge their superiors, and since everyone is subject to the pope, no one can judge the pope and thus the pope must be obeyed universally and absolutely. In his reply, Augustinus implicitly made a distinction between judgement and obedience. He first established that Christians are not always, without exception, to obey the pope. If the pope were to command something opposed to divine or natural law, the pope was to be resisted forcefully. Thus, should the pope command one to commit fornication, or to kill an innocent victim, or to worship other gods, he is in no way to be obeyed. Yet Augustinus agreed that subjects cannot judge their superiors. In response to the second argument, he asserted that it is not for subjects to determine when the pope is to be obeyed, as long as the pope does not command anything contrary to divine law and accepted custom. If, however, the pope were to do so, he has in fact judged himself, just as an heretical pope is no longer pope.[329]

---

[328] "Dicendum <est> quod papa eligitur in caput totius ecclesie ... Capitis autem est influere vitam omnibus membris. Principium autem vite spiritualis est ipsa fides, quia sine fide est impossibile placere deo. Unde apostolus ad Hebreos decimo uno: fidem dicit esse *substantiam*, id est fundamentum, omnium *sperandarum rerum* [*cf.* Hbr. 11:1]. Si ergo papa devius a fide, mortuus est ipse vita spirituali et per consequens aliis influere vitam non potest. Unde sicut homo mortuus non est homo, ita papa deprehensus in heresi non est papa, propter quod ipso facto est depositus." Aug.Anc. *Summa* 5,1 (ed. Rome, 1479), fol. 31vb–32ra.

[329] "Videtur enim quod pape christiani in omnibus teneantur obedire ... Preterea inferior non debet de superior iudicare, quia maiores a minoribus iudicari non possunt ... Respondendo dicendum <est> quod illa que papa precipit vel clauduntur

By distinguishing between judgement and obedience, Augustinus upheld the accepted principle that a superior authority cannot be judged or punished by an inferior, thus avoiding having to place the emperor, or council, above the pope as judge, while opening the door to forceful disobedience against a pope who has judged himself by contravening divine or natural law. A heretical pope has certainly done so, and thus Louis' compaign against John could very well be defended based on Augustinus' own principles, or so it might seem.

Had John commanded or acted against the dictates of divine law, Louis was justified. Yet heresy was the only point of Louis' charges that theoretically could be viable. All civil law, all human law, derives from the pope and thus, even if the pope errs in terms of human, positive law, it is not a case of heresy or for deposition, and the pope must simply be obeyed, including in cases of erroneous sentences of excommunication. An erring, fallible pope remains pope, remains Christ's vicar, and thus all honor and obedience are due. The *Sachsenhausen Appeal*, however, put forth the charge of heresy based on John's condemnation of Franciscan poverty, and his overturning the position of Nicholas III's Bull *Exiit*, which had become a doctrine of faith. John XXII had argued in *Cum inter nonnullos* that the Franciscan position contradicted scripture, and thus he could correct the position of his predecessor.[330] Augustinus was in com-

---

sub iure naturali vel sub iure divino vel sub iure positivo. Si clauduntur sub iure divino, non est obediendum pape. Si mandaret aliquid contra illa, puta si preciperet quod creatura aliqua honore latrie adoraretur vel quod nomen dei in vanum assumeretur, aut quod tempus deditum ad cultum dei sibi subtraheretur; sibi non esset obediendum, immo fortiter resistendum. Si autem clauduntur sub iure naturali et papa mandaret aliquid contra illa fieri, ut fornicari, furari vel innocentem occidere vel quod homo non commederet, similitur in talibus sibi obediendum non est. Sed si illa que precipit clauduntur sub iure positivo, cum omne ius positivum ab ipso dependet, vel per immediatam editionem ut ius canonicum, vel per confirmationem et approbationem, ut ius civile, tunc sicut eius et omnia precepta iuris positivi condere et confirmare seu interpretari, ita eius est omnia tollere in toto orbe, vel in parte. Unde in talibus si aliquid mandat contra ipsa, vel aliter interpretaretur quam scripta sint, sibi obediendum est... Ad secundum est dicendum quod subditus non debet iudicare vel discernere an debeat obedire pape si precipiat illa que sunt secundum deum et secundum illa que consueta sunt observari in religione christiana consona iuri divino et iuri naturali. Sed si notabiliter preciperentur inconsueta et dissona a preceptis dei et preceptis legis nature, cum papa sic precipiendo esset in infidelis, seipsum iudicaret, quia qui non recte credit, iam iudicatus est." Aug.Anc. *Summa* 22,1 (ed. Rome, 1479), fol. 77[va–b].

[330] Tierney, *Origins*, 181.

plete agreement, and he was clear not only that a pope is not bound by the pronouncements of his predecessors, since they are part of canon law, which is still positive law for Augustinus, but also, as seen above, that the pope is the final arbitor of scripture and its interpretation. Even for the crime of simony, Augustinus argued, the pope cannot be deposed.[331] Louis' charge of John's heresy did not have any basis for bringing into question the authority of the pope, and moreover, Louis was opposing divine order by his disobedience. He was a rebel against the Church.

An erring, fallible pope is still Christ's vicar and as such is worthy of all obedience and honor. And that is the point. Augustinus' *Summa* of ecclesiastical power is not the final stage in turning the papacy into a universal monarchy, but the first stage towards establishing the theocracy of Christ's kingdom. The pope is infallible and his power is infinite because he rules in Christ's place. Yet it is still a human being who sits on the throne.

Such an observation was not one that Augustinus made explicit when he put forth all his distinctions regarding the pope, which can be geometrically sketched as a three-by-three structure: a threefold understanding within a threefold distinction. 'The pope' is for Augustinus a highly composite term. The pope is pope as the administrator of Christ's temporal reign, exercising his power of jurisdiction, and to this extent, the pope is the vicar of Christ and instrumentally (*instrumentaliter*) the head of the Church (*caput ecclesie*). Yet within the conception of the pope as pope is the further threefold understanding of the prefiguration of the pope; the pope as person, that is, as the eternal person; and the office of the pope. The second aspect of the pope is that whereby he exercises his power of ordination as the bishop of Rome. The pope as the bishop of Rome is still the pope, though he is not the pope as pope, but the pope as the bishop of Rome. The third then, implicit throughout Augustinus' treatment, is the pope as human being. The pope as the papacy, the embodiment of the institution, is always composed of these three

---

[331] Aug.Anc.*Summa* 5,3 (ed. Rome, 1479), fol. 32va–33ra; *cf.* notes 362 and 363 below. "Doctrina ecclesie et summorum pontificum est doctrina Christi... dicendum <est> quod dicta doctorum comprobata sunt per summos pontifices, que ideo semper probata tenentur quia pertinent ad expositionem sacre scripture. Dicta unius pontificis contingit per alium revocari quia ut in pluribus sunt de actibus hominum, quod sicut contingit multipliciter variari, sic pro causarum et temporum congruitate contingit ipsa mutari." Aug.Anc. *Summa* 100 (ed. Rome, 1479), fol. 276vb–277ra.

elements: the pope as pope, the pope as the bishop of Rome, and the pope as human being.

To unravel the apparent paradox of the fallible, infallible pope, the "composite pope" is the point of departure. One might be tempted to explain Augustinus' position of the pope's fallibility and infallibility based on the distinction Augustine used for dealing with the Donatists, namely, that between the office and the person, whereby the office is holy, even if the incumbent is not.[332] Such a distinction is to the point, yet does not capture the entire picture. Augustinus himself made the distinction between the office and the person of the pope, but he did so in terms of the pope as pope, whereby the person of the pope is the eternal person, which is scarcely to be distinguished from Christ himself as the true *caput ecclesie*. The office of the pope as pope is the means through which the eternal person of the pope exercises his jurisdiction. The pope's office is not as such equated with the papacy, or the pope as institution, which always remains a composite that includes the pope as a human being, who is, nevertheless, as such, still the pope.

The office/person distinction does not account for Augustinus' position that the pope is infallible *per se et formaliter* whereas he is fallible *per accidens et materialiter*. It is not that the imperfect human being as such is equated with all error in the pope, disassociating the individual from the dignity. Though Augustinus does not use the Aristotelian fourfold causal analysis of the pope, if he had, the Church, not the pope as human being, would have been the material cause of the papacy, with the pope as human being as the efficient cause, Christ's reign as the formal cause, and the glory of God and salvation as the final cause. The pope as human being as such is not the reason that the pope is fallible *per accidens et materialiter*. The composite pope errs.

Augustinus explained his distinction with reference to Augustine's *De libero arbitrio*, noting that there can be no excess of virtue, nor can virtue be used wrongly *per se* because it is *per se* good. One does not err by having "too much" love, or patience, or hope, or prudence. However, *per accidens* is another matter. Augustinus gives the illustration that just as warm water more quickly condenses when placed in the wind than does cool water, since warm water is more

---

[332] *Cf.* Horst, "Lehrautorität," 296–298; Wilks, 503–504.

124 CHAPTER ONE

porous and rarefied, thereby allowing the cold in more quickly, so if the virtues are exposed in the wind, the "cold" can more easily enter, whereby one, because of one's virtues, becomes proud and vainglorious. Such is the wrong use of the virtues *per accidens*. *Per accidens* refers to a possible consequence resulting from the nature of the virtues themselves, but that is not an attribute of the virtues *per se*, just as *per se* water is neither warm nor cool. When one becomes proud, having become strong with an abundance of virtue, and then if based on such pride, one would commit acts contrary to justice, one would misuse, or abuse, the virtues, and thus one would err *materialiter*.[333] "Similarly," Augustinus explains,

> all use of the key of knowledge is true and reasonable, since it is derived from him who is the way, the truth, and the life. But *per accidens* and materially, the pope is able both to use the key of power excessively and to err in his use of the key of knowledge, in the same way as explained regarding the virtues.[334]

Augustinus then turned to responding to the arguments for papal infallibility with which he had begun, clarifying that the pope cannot err with respect to the keys of knowledge and power so long as

---

[333] "Dicendum quod sic est loquendum de potestate clavium sicut loquimur de virtutibus. Secundum autem Augustinum circa finem in libro <secundo> *De libero arbitrio*, in virtutibus non potest fieri excessus nec eis homo potest male uti, quod est verum per se et formaliter. Per se quidem <quia> omnis usus virtutis est bonus. Formaliter vero quia cum ipsa virtus sit quedam qualitas formaliter bona iuxta illud Augustini. Virtus est bona qualitas mentis, qua recte vivitur, qua nemo male utitur... Sicut a forma caloris non procedit nisi calor formaliter, sic a forma virtutis non procedit nisi bonum formaliter et opus virtuosum... Per accidens tamen et materialiter virtutibus homo potest male uti. Per accidens quidem quia sicut si aqua calefacta ponatur ad ventum, citius congelatur quam si ponatur ibi aqua fridiga, eo quod aqua calefacta est magis rarefacta et aperta in poris et eo magis subintrat frigus per aperturas illas ad congelandum ipsam, sic si virtutes exponantur vento, ut homo velit de eis vanam gloriam habere, male utitur eis... Materialiter vero ut si quis polleat magnitudine virtutum et exinde accipiat materiam superbiendi et violentiam contra iustitiam faciendi, virtutibus talis male utitur materialiter. Sicut ergo dictum est de virtutibus, ita quoque dicendum est de potestate clavium respectu pape, quia cum talis potestas sit sibi a deo collata non potest in ipsa excedere neque errare vel ea male uti per se et formaliter, quia omnis usus clavis potentie rectus et iustus est, cum ab illo sit derivata, qui iustus est et rectum iudicium eius." Aug.Anc. *Summa* 20,6 (ed. Rome, 1479), fol.75^{ra-b}; *cf.* Aug. lib.arb. II.18,50,190 (270,85–271,92).

[334] "Similiter omnis usus clavis scientie verus et rationabilis est, cum sit derivata ab illo, qui est via, veritas, et vita. Sed per accidens et materialiter papa et in clave potentie potest excedere et in clave scientie potest errare modo quo dictum est supra de virtutibus." Aug.Anc. *Summa* 20,6 (ed. Rome, 1479), fol. 75rb.

they are used in keeping with justice and equity, and with the understanding and reason upon which they are based. Any misuse is not use, but abuse, and such abuse is possible precisely because the pope's power is indeed infinite. As long as the keys are used properly, the Church is not able to err, and even if the entire Church did fall into error by abuse, so long as there was only one faithful catholic remaining, that faithful catholic would be the Church.[335]

The pope's power is truly infinite. Augustinus never gives any indication that the pope's power is anything else. It is infinite because Christ's power is infinite and Christ has conferred his infinite power on the pope through the eternal person of the pope, beginning with Peter. Yet as seen above in Augustinus' treatment of the question as to whether the pope could empty purgatory, infinite power entails a realm of ignorance, a realm that cannot be known, for the infinite cannot be known. Just and reasonable action must be based on knowledge and understanding. The pope is bound to use his infinite power in keeping with the justice, equity, knowledge, and understanding upon which his reign is based, namely, that of the reign of Christ, that of divine law. If the pope contravenes divine law, which he can do based on his infinite power, he errs. Indeed, the pope could lead the entire Church into error, but if he did so, the Church would cease to be the Church, in the same way that the pope ceases to be pope if he falls into heresy. The errant Church is as much a contradiction in terms as is an heretical pope. The Church is indeed infallible, for if only one faithful remained, that faithful Christian would be the Church, for Christ will never abandon his Church, his own mystical body, for which the universe was created and the son of God crucified. The reign of Christ will not fail, even if that of the pope does. Christ remains the *caput ecclesie* and the lord of the world, from whom all justice, power, law, authority, and jurisdiction derive, and it was against such that Louis was rebelling.

---

[335] "Ad primum ergo est dicendum quod in potentia pape, que est infinita, non potest esse excessus quantum ad rectum usum iustitie et equitatis. Similiter clavis scientie nunquam obliquatur utendo ipsa secundum rationabilem usum veritatis. Ad secundum est dicendum quod papa non potest usurpare potestatem alterius per sue potestatis usum, cum eius potentia ad omnia se extendat; sed potest usurpare alterius potestatem per sue potestatis abusum. Ad tertium est dicendum quod ecclesia non potest errare, quia si unus solus catholicus remaneret, ille esset ecclesia; vel ecclesia non potest errare utendo clave scientie secundum rationabilem usum et secundum intellectum quo inspirata est." Aug.Anc. *Summa* 20,6 (ed. Rome, 1479), fol. 75rb.

Wilks argued that Augustinus' position of the Church potentially residing in a single individual, combined with the possibility of a lay pope, based on the separation of the pope's power of ordination from his power of jurisdiction, was, together with the political theories of Ockham, the first step toward atomism, whereby "all political obligation is at an end. When everyone has authority over everybody else, there is logically no authority at all."[336] Wilks saw Augustinus as espousing a paradox indeed, whereby on the one hand his *Summa* represents the highest development of papal monarchy, while on the other, it advocates a theory that would soon be developed by Ockham and the conciliarists. Wilks even claimed that in his *Tractatus de potestate collegii mortuo papa* Augustinus advocated "the complete supremacy of the College [of Cardinals] over the pope," which is in "stark contrast" to his *Summa*.[337] Once again, however, the apparent paradoxes are resolved by seeing the broader nature of Augustinus' theory, and placing it in its historical, rather than strictly theoretical context.

The *De potestate collegii* is dated according to Wilks, following Ministeri, to c. 1315, as is Augustinus' *Tractatus de duplici potestate praelatorum et laicorum*. These two works were originally part of a *Quodlibet* held in Paris, where Augustinus ascended to the *magisterium* in either 1313 or 1315. Wilks sees in these two treatises the beginnings of Augustinus' mature political thought, and with good reason.[338] This

---

[336] Wilks, *The Problem of Sovereignty*, 514–523;521. Wilks also included as a major point in his argument Augustinus' position that a single faithful catholic can condemn a heretical pope. Yet Wilks gave this position of Augustinus an import and meaning not intended, or even purported; Augustinus was clear that many witnesses within a General Council of the Church were needed to condemn the pope; Aug.Anc. *Summa* 5,5 (ed. Rome, 1479), fol. 33va–34ra. His position *quilibet catholicum... contra eum sententiare posset* (Wilks, 520), is posed in the theoretical sense, as the lay pope or the entire Church remaining in one faithful individual, not in the actual juridical sense, and was in any case traditional canonistic teaching from the time of Gratian, namely, that a faithful Christian was superior to an heretical pope; Tierney, *Foundations*, 62.

[337] Wilks, *The Problem of Sovereignty*, 480.

[338] *Ibid.*, 5–6. Wilks phrases it as "He [Augustinus] became a master of theology at Paris in 1313–1315." *Ibid.*, 5, whereas Ministeri is clear in his reconstruction of Augustinus' biography that his promotion occurred in either 1313 or 1315, based on whether he read the *Sentences* at Paris in 1304–1306, or 1302–1304, though Ministeri leaned toward the later date; Ministeri, "De Vita et Operibus," 46–47, which would have placed Augustinus' promotion in 1315. However, it was customary that once having promoted, the new master of theology would hold the chair for two years while the next candidate for the *magisterium* incepted, and thus,

was not a particularly peaceful time in Paris, nor was the scene playing itself out on the stage of European politics a calm pastorale. Emperor Henry VII died on 24 August 1313, right in the midst of his attempts to behead King Robert d'Anjou. As mentioned above, Robert had already written to Pope Clement V, advising him that after Henry there should not be another emperor, or if an election could not be avoided, at least the candidate should have to come to Rome to be confirmed by the pope. Now there was a chance to see if the policy could be put into effect. Unfortunately, however, the opportunity was missed, since Clement himself went to meet his maker on 20 April 1314. An imperial election thus took place the following October, but it was not really very satisfying. On 19 October Frederick, Duke of Austria, was elected emperor, but the following day, Louis, Duke of Bavaria, was elected as well by an opposing faction.[339] The conflict could not be resolved and the two emperors-elect were left to figure things out, and this just as famine started to ravage northern Europe. Yet the College of Cardinals were not having any better time of it than were the imperial electors, and indeed worse: the electors had at least come up with two emperors, but the College could not even elect one pope. Having been split between the Italian cardinals and the French, the College just could not reach an agreement. Moreover, Rome was falling apart, and desperately needed a pope. Nothing, however, seemed to help, even though Philip IV, still King of France, as well as Edward II of England, both gave it their best shot.[340] Even before the imperial election, in the summer of 1314 Cardinal Napoleon Ursini wrote to Philip IV an urgent and passionate letter of lament for the state of the headless Church. Efforts to elect a new pope had proved fruitless, and consequently the Church was being subjected to ruin by the hand of God. All Italy was in complete shambles. Unless a new pope could be elected, the Church would be lost, as would the blood of all souls. The pope, as the vicar of Christ, provided the stability for Rome, for the Roman Church, and for the Christian faith, all of which were in jeopardy of dissipation and destruction.[341]

---

had Augustinus promoted in 1313, he most likely would still have been in Paris in 1315. Thus the *Quodlibet* in question was most likely held between 1313 and 1317, and hence c. 1315.

[339] Müller, *Der Kampf Ludwigs des Baiern*, 1–12.
[340] *Ibid.*, 12–22.
[341] Neap.Ur. *Ep.* (237–241).

The following September, Philip sent a letter to all the cardinals emploring them for the merciful wounds of Christ (*per viscera misericordie Iesu Christi*) to come to accord and elect a pope.[342] Philip offered what assistance he could, but two months later, on 29 November 1314, he himself made his exist from the world of the living. And it was just at this time that Augustinus, as the regent master of theology of his Order's *studium* in Paris, held his public disputation that has come down to us in part in two treatises.[343] It is probable that the rector of the university from December 1312 to March 1313 was at that time still in Paris. Thus it is not impossible, and perhaps even likely, that he was present at the disputation. Augustinus, in fact, may very well have known him, or at least have known of him, especially if Augustinus had begun his regency in 1313. The rector for those four months was an Italian master of arts from the city of Padua, who bore the Christian name of Marsilius.[344]

This was the historical context of Augustinus' *Quodlibet* and the development of his political thought. This was also at least the preparatory seedbed for Marsilius of Padua's *Defensor Pacis*. And it is the context for interpreting Augustinus' two early treatises, and indeed, expanded to include the coming decade, that for the entire *Summa*.

As noted above, Wilks argued that Augustinus' *De potestate collegii* subordinated the power of the pope to that of the College of Cardinals, but that is not quite the case. Augustinus wrote his treatise in the midst of a papal vacancy when the political stability of Europe was

---

[342] Phil.IV. *Ep.* (241–244).

[343] The papal vacancy offers the circumstantial evidence for dating Augustinus' *Quodlibet* and thus for dating Augustinus' promotion. That the two treatises, the *Tractatus de duplici potestate praelatorum et laicorum* and the *Tractatus de potestate collegii mortuo papa* belong together is supported by the latter's cross-reference to the former: "Primo ratio talis est. Nam, ut supra ostensum est..." Aug.Anc. *De pot.coll.* (501). The form of the treatises is that of a *determinatio*, which only a *magister* could give. If we can accept that the second treatise was composed after the death of Clement V, then that dates the *Quodlibet* to after 20 April 1314. If Augustinus began his regency in 1313, and was regent master of the Augustinian *studium* in Paris from 1313–1315, this places his *Quodlibet* precisely in the middle of his regency, as the issue of the papal vacancy was a major topic in the French capital. If Augustinus only became master of theology in 1315, then the *Quodlibet* would have had to have taken place after that date, and the new pope was elected on 7 August 1316. It is certainly possible that the *Quodlibet* was held sometime between 1315 and 7 August 1316, but it seems more likely that it was held between 20 April 1314 and 1315, when the papal vacancy was just becoming an issue.

[344] Marsilius *Def.pac.*, x; Gewirth, *Marsilius of Padua*, 21.

in turmoil. The issue the treatise addresses is not so much the relationship between pope and the College as it is the power and sovereignty of the Church, and what happens to it when there is no longer a vicar of Christ. The death of the pope was a unique case, and the power of the Church had to remain somewhere, and somehow. Otherwise, with the head gone, the body would die as well.[345] This was the problem Augustinus addressed, one very dire, immediate, and real.

Augustinus was clear that the pope is superior to the College of Cardinals, just as Christ is superior to the apostles, and as a teacher is superior to his students. The pope represents the person of Christ, whereas the College of Cardinals represents the apostles.[346] Upon the death of a pope, his power remains in the College as does the power of a tree's fallen branches; the branches flower and bring forth fruit, which is a power that should the branches be destroyed, remains in the tree's root or trunk.[347] Wilks referred to this metaphor as "root and branch conciliarism," based on the assumption that it entailed Christ having given his commission to the Church as such, or at least to all the apostles, where the power actually resides. The pope gets his power from the College as branches from the root. The power thus goes from Christ, to the apostles/College of Cardinals, and then to the pope, who finally is the administrator of the power for the rest of the body. When the pope dies, therefore, his authority reverts back to the College of Cardinals, since that was its source to begin with.[348]

---

[345] "Sed in corpore naturali ita videmus, quod mortuo corporis capite et destructo potestate capitis moriuntur et destruuntur membra et potestas ipsorum; immo cum membra omnia recipiunt influentiam a capite et virtus omnium membrorum vigeat in capite, videtur quod destructa virtute capitis, destruatur virtus omnium membrorum. Cum igitur papa sit caput in toto corpore mystico, quod est ecclesia, videtur quod destructa virtute et potestate pape tanquam capitis, non remaneat aliqua eius potestas in collegio vel in ecclesia, que est corpus eius." Aug.Anc. *De pot.coll.* (503–504).

[346] "Papa superior est collegio, sicut Christus superior apostolis et sicut magister superior discipulo." Aug.Anc. *De pot.coll.* (506); "Preterea collegium cardinalium representat collegium apostolorum, sicut papa representat personam Christi." Aug.Anc. *De pot.coll.* (507).

[347] "Videtur autem nobis, quantum ad presens potestatem papalem ipso papa mortuo remanere in collegio vel in ecclesia non in re, sed tamquam in radice... sicut potestas rami, que flores et fructum producit, remanet in radice ipso ramo destructo, sic, ut videtur, potestas papalis remanet in collegio vel in ecclesia, ipso papa mortuo." Aug.Anc. *De pot.coll.* (504–505).

[348] Wilks, *The Problem of Sovereignty*, 479–487.

Wilks, however, was misled by the "root-branch" analogy, which may indeed not have been all that felicitous for Augustinus to have made his point. Nevertheless, Augustinus used the metaphor not to show the relationship between the branches and the root, but to argue for the power of bringing forth flowers and fruit. That is the power of the branches and the purpose of the tree. Yet the question is, when the branches are gone, what happens to the tree's fecundity? Augustinus' answer was that it remains in the root, which does not have the power of the branches, but does have that to grow new branches. Upon the death of the pope, the College can "grow" a new pope, the same way the root grows new branches. The root cannot produce flowers or fruit of themselves, but only through the branches, the pope.[349] Indeed, Augustinus is clear that the power of the College is limited. The root power is that to defend and preserve the Church. It is not a true governing power except by default, so that in case of a papal vacancy, the College can do whatever is needed for running the Church, yet only the pope is the true *legislator*.[350]

The power of the pope is perpetual and eternal, for it is the power of Christ, who is the true head of the Church. For Augustinus the hierarchy is clear: power goes from Christ to the pope, who then is the source of all further power. During a papal vacancy Christ is still the head of the Church, and the papal power remains in the College of Cardinals as that of the branches remains in the root. It does not, however, *revert back* to the College, because it is a power

---

[349] "Radix ... potest secundo ipsum collegium in ramam producere quia potest eligere papam, et ex hoc potest tertio pullulare, quia per ramum et per ipsum papam productam potest florem et fructum producere." Aug.Anc. *De pot.coll.* (505–506).

[350] Aug.Anc. *De pot.coll.* (505–507); "Ulterius et in mandatis et statutis superioris quidquid non est permissum inferiori, videtur ei esse prohibitum, vel expresse datur intelligi, quod sit potentie superioris reservatum. Quidquid ergo per iura condita a papa et per statuta facta per ipsum non est collegio concessum, videtur, quod sit prohibitum ei, vel datur intelligi, quod sit pape potentie reservatum." Aug.Anc. *De pot.coll.* (506). Augustinus discusses the issue in terms of whether the College could annul laws made by the pope or his predecessor, and this is clearly not allowed to the College. He is though very careful and leaves the matter open: "Illa tamen, que diximus, utrum collegium posset mortuo papa, quod potest ipse vivens vel eo vivente, non dicimus veritatem determinando vel pertinaciter asserendo, sed magis conferendo, horum veritatem relinquendo superioribus et maioribus nobis dicere." Aug.Anc. *De pot.coll.* (507–508). He nevertheless considers the proposition that the College can do whatever a pope can do as a major question, if not doubtful: "forte est dubium." Aug.Anc. *De pot.coll.* (506).

that was never the cardinals' to begin with. As Augustinus affirmed, papal power remains in the College "not *in re*, but as if *in radice*."[351] On the same basis of hierarchical authority, and for the same reasons, Augustinus in his *Summa* took the argument one step further and claimed that even if the entire Church failed, the Church's power is perpetual because it is that of its head, Christ, and the Church would remain in a single faithful Christian.

Augustinus' *De potestate collegii* is not in stark contrast to his *Summa*, nor does it subordinate the power of the pope to the College of Cardinals. This becomes especially clear when it is read, as originally intended, together with the preceding treatise of the full lost *Quodlibet*, the *Tractatus de duplici potestate praelatorum et laicorum*. This work is misleadingly titled, for while Augustinus does indeed discuss the relationship between the power of prelates and that of the laity, he does so completely in terms of the power of the pope. And here, precisely as in the *Summa*, the pope is the single and only vicar of Christ, through whom all ecclesiastical power is derived, as well as all temporal jurisdiction. Thus the pope, as the *homo spiritualis* who judges all and can be judged by no one save God alone, can grant and revoke such authority as he sees fit.[352] Augustinus' treatment of papal power in the *Summa* is simply an elaboration and extension of

---

[351] "... omnino non esse simile de corpore et capite naturali et de corpore et capite mystico, quia membris corporis naturalis nulla virtus et nulla actio convenit sine virtute et influentia capitis, et ideo destructa tali virtute capitis, destruitur virtus omnium membrorum. Sed membris corporis mystici convenit aliqua virtus et aliqua actio sine virtute capitis... falsum esse, quod caput ecclesie simpliciter moriatur. Nam caput ecclesie simpliciter est ipse Christus... Moritur tamen hoc caput ecclesie vel illud, quia moritur iste papa vel ille. Sed caput ecclesie simpliciter est immortale, quia Christus, qui est caput ecclesie simpliciter, est pontifex sanctus in eternum secundum ordinem Melchisedech... et per consequens potestas pape est perpetua... Videtur autem nobis, quantum ad presens potestatem papalem ipso papa mortuo remanere in collegio vel in ecclesio non in re, sed tamquam in radice." Aug.Anc. *De pot.coll.* (504–505).

[352] "Sed spiritualis homo iudicat omnia et ipse a nemine iudicatur. Utramque ergo potestatem spiritualem et temporalem residere consequitur in summo pontifice... sed potestas spiritualis residet in ipso, quantum ad auctoritatem et ad executionem, sed temporalis, quantum ad auctoritatem, non autem quantum ad immediatam executionem, quia comittit executionem talis potestatis secularis regibus et principibus, qui debent organa et instrumenta eius... Secundum causam primariam, institutionem et auctoritatem universalem utraque potestas in romano pontifice residet et ab ipso, tamquam ab uno capite universalis ecclesie, in clericos et laicos debet derivari. Et per consequens omnes predicta potestate casu interveniente per Romanum pontificem possunt privari, quia sicut ab ipso potestas spiritualis et temporalis omnibus confertur, sic ab eis per eum auferri potest." Aug.Anc. *De dupl.pot.* (500).

that found already in his *De duplici potestate*, including his fundamental distinction between the pope's power of ordination and power of jurisdiction, and indeed, their separation, which Wilks saw as the final step to universal papal monarchy.

Augustinus' discussion of the pope's two powers is actually more clear and straightforward in the earlier work, and his definitions are the same as those found in the *Summa*. The pope's power of ordination is that by which he is the bishop of Rome and the highest priest; his power of jurisdiction, is that by which he exercises and administers his power of ordination.[353] He then continues to explain that these two powers are separate in *all ecclesiastical offices*, since the power of ordination is ordered in relationship to the power of jurisdiction.[354] With regard to the pope, Augustinus clarifies that:

> the power of jurisdiction is able to be bestowed on someone, on whom the power of ordination has not been, so that if a deacon or subdeacon were elected pope, having become pope all power of jurisdiction would be his, since there is no greater jurisdiction than that of the pope. Nevertheless, he would not have the power of ordination, unless he became ordained as priest and bishop.[355]

Augustinus did not go on to claim that even a lay person could be pope, but that is simply the logical consequence. In 1315 Augustinus had already separated theoretically the office of the pope from the bishopric of Rome; there could indeed be a pope, possessing all power of jurisdiction, who was not the Roman bishop. This was the point that Wilks saw as the final stage in the development of universal papal monarchy, and it was made in the same work, the original *Quodlibet*, that Wilks viewed as being in conflict with the *Summa* by Augustinus having placed the College of Cardinals above the pope in a "root and branch" form of conciliarism.

---

[353] "Sed potestas iurisdictionis est illa, per quam aliquis potest exequi vel executioni mandare primam potestatem, que est ordinis." Aug.Anc. *De dupl.pot.* (491).

[354] "Et sunt iste due potestates distincte et separate in omni prelatione ecclesiastica, quamvis una ordinetur ad aliam, quia potestas alicui competere potestas ordinis, cui non convenit aliqua potestas iurisdictionis et econtra." Aug.Anc. *De dupl. pot.* (491).

[355] "Similiter potest alicui convenire potestas iurisdictionis, cui non convenit potestas ordinis, ut si aliquis existens diaconus vel subdiaconus et fiat papa, facto papa sibi convenit omnis potestas jurisdictionis, cum supra iurisdictionem pape non sit iurisdictio maior, sibi tamen non competit potestas ordinis, nisi fiat sacerdos et episcopus." Aug.Anc. *De dupl.pot.* (491).

The theoretical can be misleading. The distinction and separation of the pope's power of ordination from his power of jurisdiction was also, and primarily, of highly practical import. Wilks seems to have forgotten that this was a position Augustinus put forth in his *Quodlibet* of c. 1315 during the papal vacancy after the death of Clement V. The problem was what happens to papal power upon the death of the pope? Augustinus considered his *De duplici potestate* as a given and as the point of departure for his *De potestate collegii*.[356] In the latter work, after already having theoretically separated the pope's two powers in the former, Augustinus explained that the power of ordination as a divine imprint inheres in the office, and thus a priest's power of ordination is not able to be or to remain in someone who has not been ordained. Neither is a bishop's power of ordination able to be or remain in someone who is not a bishop. Nor is such power able to be conferred on someone who is not respectively a priest or bishop. The power of jurisdiction, however, is different. The power of jurisdiction is not based upon a divine imprint, and thus the priest's and bishop's power of jurisdiction is able to remain in or to be conferred on someone who is neither a priest nor a bishop. And the same is true for that of the pope. The pope's power of jurisdiction is able to be conferred on, or to remain in, a "non-pope."[357] Were this not the case, given Augustinus' hierocratic theory of ecclesiastical and papal power, upon the death of a pope the Church would have a real problem on its hands, for how could the Church be administered when the power of jurisdiction had ceased to exist? Moreover, how could a new pope be elected, since there would be no body within the Church that would have the

---

[356] "Nam ut supra ostensum est..." Aug.Anc. *De pot.coll.* (501).

[357] "Sed est differentia inter potestatem ordinis et potestatem iurisdictionis, quia potestas ordinis non potest esse nec potest remanere in non ordinato, ut potestas sacerdotis nec potest esse nec potest remanere in non sacerdote et potestas episcopi nec esse potest nec potest remanere in non episcopo, nec per commissionem, quia potestas sacerdotis non potest committi non sacerdoti, et potestas episcopalis non potest committi non episcopo. Et dicemus potestatem sacerdotis non posse committi ei, qui non est sacerdos, ut in sacerdote est potestas ordinis, que est caracteris sacerdotalis impressio. Similiter dicimus potestatem epsicopi esse potestatem ordinis, que est caracteris perfectio, sed potestas jurisdictionis sacerdotis aliquando potest esse et potest remanere in non sacerdote, et potestas iurisdictionis episcopi esse potest et remanere potest in non episcopo. Similiter ergo erit de potestate pape, quia sua potestas, ut est iurisdictionis, potest remanere in non papa." Aug.Anc. *De pot.coll.* (501–502).

authority or jurisdiction to elect a pope? The head would in fact be cut off from the body and the body would thus be deprived of its vital force, and would die. But Christ is the head of the Church, and the pope's power of jurisdiction remains, even in a non-pope, by conferral, such as the non-pope that was the College of Cardinals. Augustinus' *De potestate collegii* did not subordinate the power of the pope to that of the College, but explored the extent to which the pope's power of jurisdiction remained within, or could be conferred upon, the College upon the death of a pope, a pope such as Clement V, whose passing was causing such havoc in Rome and in Italy. The Church was in danger of disintegration, as Cardinal Ursini wrote to Philip IV. Augustinus' separation of the pope's power of ordination from his power of jurisdiction, was not divorcing the office of the papacy from the bishopric of Rome in any way except purely theoretically. It was a practical distinction, responding to a present dilemma; it was a necessity that was required for preserving the headship of Christ through Christ's vicar when the individual occupying the office was no longer living, or, theoretically as seen above, had fallen into heresy and thus was no longer pope by his own self-judgement. Augustinus held the same position regarding papal power and ecclesiastical supremacy in 1315 as he did in 1326, and his *Quodlibet* in Paris in which these views were expressed, was one that Marsilius of Padua may very well have heard. It is a small world.

It is a small world indeed, and at times it becomes even smaller. The College of Cardinals had still not elected a pope by the summer of 1316, even after several attempts. Philip IV was dead and gone, and his successor, Louis X, died as well on 5 June 1316. Edward II's efforts to sow fertile seeds in the process fell on sterile ground, and thus Robert d'Anjou stepped in to try to get something achieved. Robert suggested his own candidate to the College, the Bishop of Avignon, who had been Robert's tutor while a youth, appointed in 1290 by Robert's father, King Charles II. When Robert ascended the throne in 1309, he appointed his tutor as royal chancellor, and only in 1310 did Robert's chancellor leave court to assume the bishopric of Avignon. It was a ploy that worked, and on 7 August 1316, Robert's former tutor and royal chancellor, Jacques Duèse from Cahors, was elected pope and took the name of John XXII.[358]

---

[358] Müller, *Der Kampf Ludwigs des Baiern*, 21–22.

Five years later, in 1321, John XXII announced his first crusade against the Lombard city states, and Augustinus received his call to Naples.

Augustinus completed his *Summa* in the tenth year of John's reign as a guide for understanding the boundaries of papal power and authority. There could indeed be bad popes, for the pope is a most fallible, limited human being. This too Augustinus wanted John to know. The pope must be humble, and make sure that his external apparatus not become the cause of scandal. The pope must guard against error, into which it is ever so easy to slip. The pope can err in his use of the key of knowledge, and can use the key of power to excess. And when he does so, the entire composite pope errs.

The pope was triune. Though Augustinus did not use the following analogy for his discussions and distinctions of the papacy, it helps to clarify his position: the composite pope consists of a double trinity, the three-by-three structure, whereby the distinctions can be made internally; yet as in trinitarian theology, the external works of the pope, the exercising of the pope's office, are those of the composite pope, just as the external acts of the divine Trinity (*ad extra*) cannot be divided up into those of the divine persons (*indivisa*). The entire Trinity is operative in the world. The trinitarian character of Augustinus' theory of the pope accounts for most of the seeming paradoxes that remain after one realizes the historical and practical nature of Augustinus' pushing issues to their limits: they are apparent due to the composite pope, who is *per se et formaliter* infallible, since the substantive form of the pope is that of Christ's reign. Nevertheless, *per accidens et materialiter* the pope can err in his use of both keys, since materially the Church is comprised of all the faithful, one of whom serves instrumentally as its head (*caput ecclesie instrumentaliter*), while Christ remains the principal ruler of his kingdom (*caput ecclesie principaliter*).

The fallibility of the infallible pope is not a paradox. It enters *per accidens* with regard to the instrumental nature of the office, the pope as the *caput ecclesie*.[359] The pope is bound by divine law, but he has infinite power. Augustinus argued that the pope cannot be deposed

---

[359] "Dicendum quod preceptum pape personaliter et instrumentaliter mutabile est et fallibile; sed auctoritative et principaliter immutabile est et infallibile, quia auctoritas divina cui innititur immutabilis et infallibilis est." Aug.Anc. *Summa* 63,1 (ed. Rome, 1479), fol. 183vb.

for simony because the pope cannot legally commit simony. The pope is above all law, he is free from the law, and indeed, his *will* has the force of law.[360] Augustinus introduced the formulation of Ulpian, found in the text *Princeps* of Justinian's *Digest*, to describe the pope's power: what pleases the prince has the force of law.[361] The will of the pope is at issue. With the right will, the right intent, and for the public good, the pope can accept money that would be sinful for a lesser prelate to accept.[362] Moreover, even if it might appear that the pope had done so for the wrong reasons, he cannot therefore be deposed, because the pope cannot be deposed for a wrong conscience, nor for a wrong intent. God alone judges the pope. The pope can only be deposed for public heresy.[363] In effect, whatever the pope can do with the right intent, he can do with the wrong intent and cannot be judged by any one save God, and cannot be deposed. John XXII could have had the wrong intent in his granting of indulgences, and he could have used the money collected for a crusade to the Holy Land to finance his Italian wars,[364] and he could have excommunicated the Visconti, the Lombard cities, and even Louis, as heretics for purely political motives, and he still could not be judged by any earthly authority because he could have also done all these things with the proper intent and for the public good, in keeping with right reason and the will of God. An errant pope, a pope clearly bad, nevertheless must still be obeyed. A bad pope is not an heretical pope. The pope can, since his power is infinite,

---

[360] "Dicendum quod certum est summum pontificem canonicam simoniam a iure positivo prohibitam non posse committere quia ipse est supra ius et eum iura positiva non ligant. Si enim imperator non ligatur iure, quia princeps legibus solutus est, ut dicit iurisconsultus in principio Digestorum, multo fortius papa nulla iure ligari potest, sed quod sibi placet legis vigorem habet." Aug.Anc. *Summa* 5,3 (ed. Rome, 1479), fol. 32vb.

[361] Pennigton, *The Prince and the Law*, 206.

[362] "Certum est similiter quod summus pontifex pro bono publico ab episcopis et aliis prelatis accipere potest summum pecunie prout secundum deum et rationem videtur sibi expedire, quod alii inferiores prelati facere sine peccato non possunt... Ideo recta intentio excusans summum pontificem alios prelatos inferiores excusare non potest." Aug.Anc. *Summa* 5,3 (ed. Rome, 1479), fol. 32vb.

[363] "Cum ergo papa non sit deponendus pro recta vel non recta conscientia, et pro simonia secundum quod est contra legem iuris naturalis, quia de talibus potest ipse dicere: 'quia autem iudicat me dominus est,' sed solum pro his, que aguntur in exteriori iudicio et que foris apparent. Cum isto modo simoniam prohibitam non possit committere, pro ea non est deponendus." Aug.Anc. *Summa* 5,3 (ed. Rome, 1479), fol. 32vb.

[364] Housley, *The Italian Crusades*, 173.

contravene all positive law, all canon law, all the customs and traditions of the Christian people, and can even set up his residency outside Rome, and no one, not even the emperor, can do anything about it.

Yet the pope can only act above the law without falling into error if he has good reason and the right intent for doing so, and if such is lacking, he will have to answer before the judgement seat of God. The pope's own eternal salvation is at stake when he errs, not that of his flock. His flock's eternal salvation is only endangered by his public heresy, when the pope has, in fact, become no pope at all. This too Augustinus wanted John to consider well. An errant pope would have to answer to God, but was still to be obeyed. Only when his flock's salvation was endangered was the pope to be fiercely resisted. The pope's will is the determining factor. The papal will has the force of law, and that is where the errancy and fallibility enter.

In true Augustinian fashion, with appeal to *De libero arbitrio*, Augustinus saw the pope's will, his intent, as the key to the keys. The use of the keys of knowledge and power, whether it was infallible or an abuse, was determined by the pope's will. There is no contradiction and no paradox. As Adam and Eve in paradise, the trinitarian, composite pope was perpetually in a state of being able to err or not to err based on his will; he was simultaneously fallible and infallible, simultaneously the vicar of Christ, the eternal person of the pope, and a sinful human being, a *viator*. His will was free indeed, for it had at its disposal the infinite power of Christ's reign. The fallible, infallible pope was also the infallible, fallible pope. Only the pope's will and divine law formed the boundaries of the proper use of ecclesiastical power.

Augustinus never lost perspective. His pope is not some semi-divine being, half-god and half-human, who rules by fiat. Nor is his *Summa* an abstract, out-of-touch theoretical construct of an absolute, universal entity. It is a practical treatise, composed in a given historical situation, written for the pope in Avignon, responding to the political needs, and fears, of Augustinus' immediate environment, the kingdom of Naples in the second decade of the fourteenth century. As Christ's vicar, the pope is subject to the lordship of Christ, the true head of the Church; the pope is bound by Christ's law and by Christ's faith. Moreover, the triune, composite pope is more bound than not to uphold justice, and to reside in Rome. If he contravenes Christ's law, he errs and will be sentenced in God's heavenly court.

The divine law of the Christian faith sets the limits to which the pope can go. If he exceeds those limits, he is by that very fact, no longer pope, but only an openly heretical pope can be deposed. In such a circumstance, Christ remains the head of his Church, even if the Church remains only in a single faithful catholic. Christ had entrusted his kingdom to Peter, rendering the person of Peter an eternal person, through whom Christ governs, and does so infallibly. The power of the pope is the power of the Church, the power of Christ, the theme of Augustinus' *Summa*. Christ's reign, Christ's power, Christ's kingdom is what Augustinus explicates, and this was a kingdom that was present on earth, existing in the world, even though not of the world. It was a kingdom that was the Church, body and soul, a kingdom that was Christendom, and wars raged for its possession. Augustinus did not establish a theory of papal monarchy. He constructed a comprehensive, universal theocracy, yet one that had a very real, earthly Rome as its capital: the Rome of Cicero and Vergil, of Caesar and Augustus, of Peter and Paul, of Constantine and Sylvester, no less than the Rome of the Annabaldi and the Colonna, or of Louis and John, the Rome of Augustinus and of the Augustinians, with all its grazing animals and stench, the eternal city, that before Augustinus' eyes was being besieged, and was crumbling.

III. The Augustinian High Way

It was not, to be proverbial, a pretty sight. For all the efforts made, from Giles of Rome to Augustinus of Ancona, for all the attempts to establish definitively the sovereignty of the Church, the Church was still suffering, was still being attacked, and was still caught in the grips of papal-imperial warfare. Theory is just theory, after all, and more is needed to bring it into effect than simply pen and parchment. Yet words were weapons, and carried a force beyond that of the purely grammatical. Words, moreover, provided both the battle plan and its motivation. Excommunication, jurisdiction, heretic, crusade, *hoc est corpus meum, ego te absolvo*: these were powerful words, words that distinguished heaven from hell. The splitting apart of the empire, the secession of churches from the Church universal, the rise of heretics, the falling away from the faith, the reign of Gog and Magog, the last days, the coming of the Antichrist: ominous words, portentous images, that Augustinus used for his exposition of Christ's kingdom on a cosmic scale. The earthly political conflicts were not left behind, but Augustinus placed them, at least in part, within a universal vision of the history of salvation. The last days were not yet at hand, but the final countdown had begun, and one could almost feel on the back of one's neck the hot breath of the panting apocalyptic horses beginning to gallop.[365] The Church was in a state of war, and one that surpassed even that of Louis and John. As long as such a battle continued, a proper military order was essential, with a single commander-in-chief. Only when the end

---

[365] "Quod ante antichristi adventum erit triplex in mundo dissensio, quia primo erit omnium hominum separatio a Romano imperio. Secundo erit multorum christianorum dissensio a fide catholica. Tertio erit separatio multarum ecclesiarum a Romana pontifice... Bestia quarta regnum quartum erit in terra, quod est maius omnibus regnis et devorabit universam terram... In capite bestie decem reges erunt, quod regnum maius est omnibus regnum Romanorum; per decem vero cornua intelliguntur decem regna, in que dividetur Romanum imperium tempore antichristi. Quia tempore divisionis predicti regni et de ipsis regnis in que dividetur orietur antichristus. De secunda vero divisione aliquis dissensione a fide catholica... Illo enim tempore... particulares ecclesie undique per orbem diffuse subtrahent se ab obedientia Romani pontificis, ita ut pauci sibi obediant et papa tunc temporis circa partes Romanas se recludet cum paucis aliis ab eius obedientia subtractis... antichristus per demonum ministerium et suos ministros procurabit ecclesie desolationem ubique terrarum... <sed> ecclesia non deficiet universaliter. Expugnabitur quidem, sed non desolabitur multa etiam membra ecclesie, que ex persecutione antichristi recedent a fide, ipso interfecto, ad fidem convertentur." Aug.Anc. *Summa* 21,4 (ed. Rome, 1479), fol. 77[ra-rb]; Aug.Anc. *Summa* 42,1–2 (ed. Rome, 1479), fol. 137[ra]–138[rb]; "Cum consumati fuerint mille anni solvetur Sathanas de carcere suo, quia priorem potestatem recipiet et exhibet et seducet gentes que sunt super quatuor angulos terre Gog et Magog et congregabit eos in prelium quorum numerus est sicut arena maria.... has duas gentes tectas et absconsas diabolus primo decipiet et per eas procedet ad seductionem et persecutionem fidelium ita quod antichristus per has duas gentes tectas et absconsas in angulis terre quroum numerus est sicut arena maris persequetur ecclesiam dei. Nam Gog et Magog idem est quod tectum de tecto, ut sit sensus quod tecte et absconse gentes debeant exire de tectis et absconsis locis ex imperio antichristi ad persecutionem ecclesie et si sic erit quod imperium ad tales gentes sit transferendum, cum clarum sit huiusmodi gentes nunquam fuisse nec esse sub Romano imperio, sequitur quod Romanum imperium usque in finem seculi duraturum non sit... Sed tunc tempore antichristi exibit tanquam tectus de tecto, quia detecta et occulta exibit in manifestam et apertam persecutionem, qui iam ante per multa mala et varia seducet multos. Sed tunc imminente finali iudicio universa civitas Christi in toto orbe terrarum ab universa civitate diaboli quantacunque erit utraque super terram apertam et manifestam persecutionem patietur. Unde secundum hoc dicendum est Romanum imperium usque ad finem mundi esse duraturum... Romanum imperium concessum ecclesie per Constantinum usque ad finem seculi durabit, quantum ad iurisdictionem, sed non quantum <ad> integrationem et actualem administrationem, vel quantum ad ipsorum subditorum subiectionem, quia antichristi tempore multi subtrahent se ante illud tempus a

had been reached, when the Church returned to eternal communion with God, when all had been played out, only then would there no longer be a need for any dominion, temporal jurisdiction, or power.[366] But that lay in the future as Augustinus was composing his *Summa*, even if not all that far off.

A few years later, the conflict escalated. In 1332, the Franciscan William of Ockham, from his base at the emperor's court in Munich, began his all-out attack on John XXII.[367] In the same year, if not before, the Augustinian Hermann of Schildesche opened his treatise, *Against the Heretics Denying the Immunity and Jurisdiction of the Holy Church*, with the verse from 1 John 2:18: *You were told that Antichrist was to come, and now many antichrists have appeared*, dedicated and sent to John XXII. All those, Hermann argued, who do not believe in the Holy Church, and place it in subjection to temporal rulers, are to be considered antichrists.[368] The last battle was beginning, and Augustine was the standard his hermit friars lifted high.

Throughout Hermann's treatise, Augustine was the overwhelming authority. Hermann cited his Order's founder 143 times, with Gratian

---

Romano imperio et ab ecclesiastico dominio . . . in novissimis temporibus discedent quidem a fide attendentes spiritibus erroris et doctrinis demoniorum." Aug.Anc. *Summa* 42,1 (ed. Rome, 1479), fol. 137^{rb-vb}; ". . . ante adventum antichristi illa triplex discessio erit, non tamen sic apperta et manifesta ad ecclesie impugnationem, sicut tunc erit scilicet tempore antichristi, multi enim sunt nunc secundum Augustinum sub dominio ecclesie et sub Romano imperio corpore non tamen animo et voluntate . . . Romanum imperium ante erit divisum in multas regna, sed tunc visio illa manifestabitur quantum ad impugnationem ecclesie, eo quod antichristi multos seducet et per illos seductos robustos Israhel interficiet. Et persequetur manifeste ecclesiam dei." Aug.Anc. *Summa* 42,2 (ed. Rome, 1479), fol. 138rb; cf. Wilks, *The Problem of Sovereignty*, 434–436.

[366] "Nam quamdiu sumus in hoc mundo, sumus in via et sumus in quodam bello. In bello autem necessario sunt aliqui principantes et aliqui subservientes. Et ideo quamdiu sumus bellatores et sumus in exercitu, tamdiu angeli dominabuntur angelis et homines hominibus, quia tota ecclesia militaris est terribilis ut catrorum acies ordinata. Sed cum pervenerimus ad deum tanquam ad terminum et finem felicitatis nostre, non erimus amplius bellatores, nec erit amplius necessaria dominatio vel prelatio . . . tunc erit finis, quia tunc evacuatus erit omnis principatus et omnis potestas." Aug.Anc. *Summa* 1,2 (ed. Rome, 1479), fol. 5ra; cf. Aeg.Rom. *De pot.eccl.*, note 62 above.

[367] Tierney, *Origins*, 206–237; Miethke, *De Potestate Papae*, 248–295.

[368] "*Audistis, quod antichristus venit, et ecce nunc antichristi facti sunt multi*, prima epistola Joannis secundo capitulo [I Io. 2:18]. Omnis enim, qui non credit in Jesum Christum, filium Dei, hic antichristus et seductor est . . . Quidam autem heretici nefarii et insani asserentes sanctam Ecclesiam sponsam Dei immaculatam subiectam esse debere temporali principi, non videntur credere in sanctam Ecclesiam . . . Quapropter omnes tales seductores et antichristi sunt censendi." Herm.Schild. *cont.neg.* 1,1 (5,5–6,14).

coming in second with 33 references, followed by Aristotle with 21 and Bernard with 5. In 1334 Hermann preached an extensive sermon on Augustine in Paris, praising Augustine as the father of his sons, the Hermits.[369] Twenty years later, Hermann's confrere and former colleague in Erfurt, Jordan of Quedlinburg, would use this sermon as a source for his *Liber Vitasfratrum*, the most extensive handbook of the Augustinian life in the Middle Ages.[370] In 1334 Hermann was on solid ground. The Order's mythic origins and religious identity had already, by and large, been created, even if they had not yet received their final form.[371] After what must have been nearly two hours of preaching, Hermann finally closed his sermon with the hymn *Magnus pater Augustinus*: "Oh devoted and honest shepherd/ sweet and true father/look upon your flock/have mercy on your sons/pastor us, guard us/make us see the good/in this land of the living."[372] Augustine was the Order's founder and father; he was the source of his sons' religious life. Augustinus too had called on the authority of Augustine far more often than any other, and when Augustinus died in 1328, he left unfinished a project that would become, upon its completion fifteen years later by the Augustinian Bartholomew of Urbino, the highpoint of Augustine scholarship in the later Middle Ages: the *Milleloquium Sancti Augustini*.[373] The high

---

[369] Zumkeller, *Schriftum und Lehre des Hermann von Schildesche*, 117–128.
[370] *Ibid.*, 123–125.
[371] See Chapter Two below.
[372] "Pie pastor et sincere/Pater dulcis, pater vere/Tuum gregem intuere/Filiorum miserere/Tu nos pasce, nos tuere/Tu nos bona fac videre/In terra viventium." As quoted by Zumkeller, *Schriftum und Lehre*, 127.
[373] The authorship of the *Milleloquium*, however, is not completely certain. Ministeri listed the *Milleloquium* as one of the authenticated works of Augustinus; Ministeri, "De Vita et Operibus," 223–224. Arbesmann, however, denied Augustinus' authorship, pointing to the fact that Bartholomew of Urbino makes no mention whatsoever of Augustinus, or of having completed a previously unfinished work. The tradition of Augustinus' authorship, Arbesmann showed, stemmed from Jordan of Quedlinburg's *Liber Vitasfratrum*, which has been repeated without further evidence or proof ever since; Arbesmann, "The Question of the Authorship of the *Milleloquium Veritatis S. Augustini*," *AAug.* 43 (1980), 163–185. Arbesmann, nevertheless, suggested that Augustinus could very well have been the author of the *Flores Beati Augustini*, found in Florence, Biblioteca Laurenziana, cod. Plut. 13.15, which seems to be the "workaday copy of a scholar." (*Ibid.*, 173) The *Flores*, if they are indeed genuinely the work of Augustinus, could have been the origin of the tradition that Augustinus began work on the *Milleloquium*. Eckermann accepts as an authentic work of Augustinus what he lists as *Flores beati Augustini seu Milleloquium ex scriptis Augustini*; Eckermann, "Augustinus Triumphus," *TRE* 4:742–744; 743. Miethke too accepts the Augustinus origin of the *Milleloquium*; Miethke, *De Potestate Papae*, 173–174. What can be said

way to heaven the Augustinians created was based on the appropriation of the life and works of their father, Augustine, who was needed as no other in the conflicts of the 1320s that extended into the 1330s and beyond. Augustine was unique. He was the Church's outstanding theologian and political architect; he was a hermit, and the founder of religious Orders. Yet Augustine was even more, which gave his sons, who were to be his imitators, a particular view of things. Unlike Francis and Dominic, the founding fathers of the two Orders that were the Augustinians' greatest competitors, Augustine had been a bishop.

Augustine had been a bishop. That is not a fact that was lost on the Augustinians, and certainly not on Augustinus. The father of the Order of Hermits was a bishop. It bears pondering. Augustine was a hermit, to be sure, a *servus dei*, and a sort of holy man, but he was most of all a theologian and episcopal pastor. He had a status within the Church hierarchy that no other founder of a religious Order in the west could claim. While Francis of Assisi was running around having stripped himself naked, preaching to birds and receiving the stigmata, Augustine had been defending orthodoxy, writing theological tracts against the Manicheans, Donatists, and Pelagians, preaching to his congregation from the cathedra, and administering his diocese. This was an image and heritage the Order adopted as their own, to the extent that Augustinus of Ancona could speak of the "episcopacy of Christ," which was the pinnacle of the ecclesiastical hierarchy, from which all bishops and all orders of Church prelates were derived.[374] Augustinus did not write a work on the power of the pope, but on ecclesiastical power, and the bishops had primacy of place. The pope was the unquestioned head of Church, yet the bishops were the successors and bearers of the apostolic life. For all the papal pavement, the Augustinian high way to heaven was fundamentally an episcopal road.

"Make us see the good in this land of the living." That was as much Augustinus' endeavor as were his warnings of the impending

---

for sure is that Bartholomew of Urbino was the author of the *Milleloquium*, though which very early on within the Order came to be seen as a project that Augustinus had begun, which may very well have been the case. See also E.L. Saak, "*Milleloquium Sancti Augustini*," in *Augustine Through the Ages*, 563.

[374] "Totius autem status episcopalis et ecclesiastice hierarchie caput est episcopatus Christi ad quem omnes episcopatus et prelationes omnes ecclesiastici ordinis reducuntur." Aug.Anc. *Summa* 88,1 (ed. Rome, 1479), fol. 248va.

apocalypse. While living in the world, all that was good, just, and loving, was to be found in the Church and its state of perfection in embodying the apostolic life. In the third part of his *Summa*, the longest of the work, Augustinus explicated the Church's state of perfection (*status perfectionis*) and how it was present in Christ, the apostles, the early Church, and the Church of his day, from the pope, to bishops, priests, members of religious Orders, theologians, preachers, medical doctors, notaries, lawyers, and judges.[375] Here Augustinus was being no more and no less polemical than he had been in the first two parts, which dealt with the power of the pope *per se*, and how it related to the pope's administration of his office.[376] The *Summa* is not a piece of papal propaganda, but the contemporary conflicts and debates are never far from Augustinus' mind. The *Sachsenhausen Appeal* and the *Defensor Pacis* had both undermined the very structure of the Church, which Augustinus sought to establish definitively. Bishops were the key, for they were the ones who represented the episcopacy of Christ, and the bishop *par excellence* for Augustinus was the

---

[375] The third part of the *Summa* begins with questio 76, and continues to questio 112. Augustinus first treats Christ, the apostles, and the early Church, and then in questiones 101–112 turns to the Church of his own times: "Visum est quomodo status perfectio in Christo fuit exemplariter demonstrata, et quomodo ab eo in eius apostolos fuit derivata et qualiter in primitiva ecclesia existit observata. Nunc videndum quomodo in viris ecclesiasticis presentis temporis est representata, accipiendo ecclesiasticos viros non solum illos qui assumuntur sed eos qui idoneitatem habent, ut ad gradum ecclesiasticum assumi possint. Circa quod duodecim consideranda occurrunt: Primo qualiter status perfectio representatur in papa; Secundo quomodo in cardinalibus; Tertio qualiter in episcopis; Quarto quomodo in curatis et presbyteris; Quinto quomodo in religiosis mendicantibus; Sexto quomodo in religiosis in communi possessiones habentibus; Septimo quomodo in sacre scripture predicatoribus; Octavo quomodo in magistris et doctoribus; Nono quomodo in medicis; Decimo quomodo in notariis; Undecimo quomodo in advocatis; Duodecimo qualiter in iudicibus et rectoribus." Aug.Anc. *Summa* 101,1, Pref. (ed. Rome, 1479), fol. 279^{rb-va}. Augustinus' ecclesiological vision is very intricate and detailed. A separate study would be needed to explicate comprehensively Augustinus' treatment of the *status perfectionis*. For present purposes, I focus only on the main lines in keeping with the scope and argument of the present chapter, trying to resist the urge to include here an entire book on Augustinus, which, however, is most needed, and for which there is ample material that at times offers delightful insights to Augustinus' world, such as his arguments regarding in what circumstances a lawyer is required to reimburse his clients after having lost their case. His treatment of medical doctors, lawyers, notaries, and judges turns primarily on the extent to which religious can perform such functions, rather than on the state of perfection of these professions themselves.

[376] For a complete list of questions as they are divided into the three parts, see Appendix C.

founding father of his Order: there was no religious rule more perfect than Augustine's, which was simply the rule of the apostles, and there was no religion more perfect, than the religion of bishops.[377]

It was a battle for religion. Both Louis of Bavaria and Marsilius of Padua had used the ideal of apostolic poverty to undermine ecclesiastical power: Louis and his Franciscan supporters held up against John XXII the Franciscan way of life as an infallible doctrine of the faith; Marsilius equally took the Franciscan ideal as the model, used to deny the temporal jurisdiction of the Church in general. Ulrich Horst placed Augustinus' *Summa* in the context of the debates over Franciscan poverty, yet noted that Augustinus did not address the conflict as such, citing neither Nicholas III's Bull *Exiit*, nor John XXII's *Cum inter nonnullas*.[378] Horst claimed that Augustinus adopted a Thomistic position on apostolic poverty, which John XXII would have been pleased to receive.[379] Though there may be Thomistic parallels, Augustinus was espousing his own Order's teaching on apostolic poverty, which had been established in Augustine's *Rule* and confirmed in the Order's Bull of foundation, *Licet ecclesiae catholicae*.[380] Moreover, Augustinus had a far broader vision than simply the details of *Cum inter nonnullas*. The Franciscan front was as much a threat to the status of the Augustinian Order as it was to that of the pope. Within a decade of Augustinus having completed his *Summa*, his confreres had tried to turn Francis himself into an Augustinian hermit in their arguments for the priority of the OESA.[381] Conflicts with the Franciscans over property and privileges had been an instrumental factor in the Augustinians having been taken under direct papal protection by Boniface VIII, which John XXII reaffirmed in 1317. And now these same Franciscans, or some of them anyway, were calling Pope John a heretic because he had denied the special

---

[377] "Communiter enim tenet ecclesia religionem episcoporum perfectiorem esse omni alia religione ... sicut nulla regula potest esse perfectior regula apostolorum, sic nulla regula potest esse perfectior regula beati Augustini, que non aliud essentialiter continet quam apostolorum documenta." Aug.Anc. *Summa* 97,5 (ed. Rome, 1479), fol. 270^{ra-b}.

[378] Horst, "Die Armut Christi," 475–476.

[379] *Ibid.*, 493–494.

[380] For the Augustinian teaching on poverty, see Fulgence Mathes, "The Poverty Movement and the Augustinian Hermits," *AAug.* 31 (1968), 5–154; *AAug.* 32 (1969), 5–116.

[381] See Chapter Two below.

status of their Order as that closest to the life of Christ and the apostles. The entire existence and status of the Augustinian Order depended upon the protection, goodwill, and favor of the holy pontiff, as Alexander of San Elpidio affirmed at the Order's General Chapter at Florence in 1324 and explicated in his *De ecclesiastica potestate*. Augustinus wanted to set the matter straight. His *Summa* is a forceful case not only for the primacy of the pope, but also for the superiority of Augustine's religion over the religion of St. Francis.

Religion is the worship of God. It is established for the good of the Church, and for leading one to perfect love.[382] All those, therefore, who worship God, can be called religious (*religiosi*), but in a more precise sense of the term, the religious are those who dedicate their entire lives to divine worship, removing themselves from the cares of the world by their official profession and wearing the habit of their chosen religious Order, devoted either to contemplation, teaching, or performing good works, all for advancing the Church and pursuing their own path to perfection.[383] In responding to the argument that the establishment of religion comes from the founders of particular religions, such as the religion of blessed Benedict, the religion of blessed Augustine, that of St. Francis, or St. Dominic, Augustinus countered by asserting that the entire Christian religion is established by Christ, and therefore it falls to the pope as Christ's vicar to establish and designate all religion.[384] Moreover, those religions, or religious practices, that are not approved and confirmed by the Church, are to be considered more as superstition than religion.[385] The pope, as Christ's vicar, establishes and confirms all particular religions, whether that of Augustine or of Francis, and should

---

[382] "In religione tria considerantur. Primo ex parte ecclesie promotio, nam quelibet religio ordinari debet principaliter ad cultum dei et ad promotionem ecclesie. Secundo ex parte religionem intrantium consideratur caritatis perfectio, quia quelibet religio est quedam via tenendi in perfectionem caritatis. Tertio ex parte divini cultus ad quem religio instituitur, consideratur debita ordinatio." Aug.Anc. *Summa* 71,3 (ed. Rome, 1479), fol. 212^{ra-b}.

[383] "Communiter omnes qui deum colunt, religiosi possunt appellari. Unde quia soli Iudei ad cultum unius dei dediti erant, religiosi nominati sunt. Proprie tamen religiosi dicuntur qui totam vitam eorum divino cultui dedicant et a mundanis negotiis se abstrahentes per professionem et habitus protestationem vel divine contemplationi vel animarum instructioni vel alicui fructuoso operi ad eorum perfectionis exercitationem et ecclesie promotionem insistunt." Aug.Anc. *Summa* 71,3 (ed. Rome, 1479), fol. 212rb.

[384] *Cf.* Appendix A.3.

[385] "Videtur enim quod non solum ad papam spectat ordinatio religionum...

a particular religion or religious practice go against the institution confirmed by the Church, it is superstitious, such as, perhaps, adhering to the doctrine of the absolute poverty of Christ and the apostles. Augustinus certainly does not say so as such, but his treatment of religion is a direct assault on the Franciscan ideal as espoused in the *Sachsenhausen Appeal* and Marsilius' *Defensor Pacis*.[386]

Religion, for Augustinus, in the strict sense, refers to the religious state (*status religiosorum*). As such, as the dedication of oneself to the worship of God, religion forms the final cause of the Church's state of perfection (*status perfectionis*). The religious vows themselves are the efficient cause; love of God and neighbor is the formal cause; and the material cause is either the blessing of the monastic habit upon one's completion of the period of probation, in other words, when one becomes a full member of a religious Order and receives the blessed habit of that Order, or, the consecration of a bishop. The monastic life and the episcopal life are the two pillars of the Church's state of perfection. There is, however, a fifth element of the state of perfection: the abdication of all temporal possessions, which is the instrumental cause. Religious poverty, however it is defined, is central to the state of perfection as one of the three religious vows, but as a principle in and of itself, it is only an instrumental cause of the state of perfection, and not central thereto; it is not, *pace* the Franciscans, the efficient, material, formal, or final cause of Christian perfection.[387]

<nam> religio nominatur ab ordinatione illius a quo religio fundatur, sicut religio beati Benedicti, religio beati Augustini, sancti Francisci, sancti Dominici. Non nominatur autem aliqua religio a papa; ergo non solum ad ipsum spectat religionum ordinatio ... est dicendum quod tota religio christiana a papa nominatur quia nominatur a Christo, cuius vicarius ipse existit. Religiones alie particulares quamvis ab eorum fundatoribus specialibus nominentur, religiones tamen dici non debent nisi quatenus sunt per ordinationem ecclesie approbate et confirmate ... Unde qui cultum deo exhibet contra modum divina auctoritate ab ecclesia institutum magis superstitiosus quam religiosus est dicendus." Aug.Anc. *Summa* 71,3 (ed. Rome, 1479), fol. 212[ra-va].

[386] For a concise treatment of Augustinus' view of poverty as such, see Horst, "Die Armut Christi." Augustinus treated the state of perfection first in Christ, then in the apostles, with regard to all three monastic vows. His treatment of poverty is found throughout Part III of the *Summa* and is as intricate and detailed as are his views of the religious life.

[387] "Respondendo <est> dicendum quod ad perfectionis statum quinque quantum ad presens requiruntur: Primo perpetua voti obligatio; Secundo dei et proximi dilectio; Tertio ad cultum dei oblatio et dedicatio; Quarto habitus benedictio vel persone consecratio; Quinto omnium temporalium abdicatio perpetua. Namque voti obligatio est causa efficiens perfectionis status ... Causa vero formalis perfectionis

There are, moreover, distinctions to be made within the realm of religion, whereby some religions are more perfect than others, and here, in question ninety-seven, was where Augustinus, for the first time since the Order's foundation, asserted the *Rule* of Augustine as that closest to the apostolic life. At issue was the argument that the more rigorous, ascetic, and difficult way of life was the more perfect way of life.[388] This Augustinus denied. He argued that no one can doubt that the religion of John the Baptist was harsher, more rigorous and more ascetic than any other religion or rule, or that the religion of Christ was more perfect than any other. Yet whereas John the Baptist wore a camel hair cloak, and ate nothing but wild locusts and honey, Christ came eating everything and drinking wine. Therefore, Augustinus concluded, the religion of Christ was less ascetic than that of John the Baptist, but Christ's religion was more perfect.[389] Augustinus then gave further examples of this principle. The religion of bishops, he asserted, is more perfect than any other religion. Yet any monk leads a more ascetic life than does a bishop.

---

status est dilectio dei et proximi. Nullum enim opus ponit hominem in perfectionis statu formaliter in vita spirituali nisi caritas. Unde <ad> Colossenses tertio enumeratis multis virtutibus que faciunt ad statum perfectionis, concludit apostolus: *super omnia autem hec caritatem* habere que *est vinculum perfectionis* [Col. 3:14]. Causa vero finalis status perfectionis est dedicare se et sua ad cultum dei ... Unde dedicatio persone ad cultum dei secundum tria vota est causa finalis perfectionis status. Causa autem materialis est benedictio habitus sicut fit in religiosis completo probationis termino vel episcopalis consecratio in qua emittit votum de cura habenda suarum ovium. Sed causa instrumentalis est abdicatio ipsorum temporalium. Ista ergo quinque per ordinem requiruntur ad perfectionis statum et secundum quod magis et minus ista in aliquibus reperiuntur sic magis et minus in statu perfectionis esse dicuntur ... relinquere omnia temporalia perfectorum est non quia hoc faciat ad perfectionis statum effective, formaliter, finaliter sive materialiter. Nam Socrates et multi alii temporalia dimiserunt qui non fuerunt in perfectionis statu. Sed facit ad perfectionem instrumentaliter ... propter quod per ipsarum abdicationem animus redditur magis liber ad diligendum deum et omnia propter ipsum." Aug.Anc. *Summa* 77,1 (ed. Rome, 1479), fol. 224^{ra-b}.

[388] "Videtur enim quod monachorum vita quanto sit artior, tanto fuerit perfectior." Aug.Anc. *Summa* 97,5 (ed. Rome, 1479), fol. 269va.

[389] "Nulli namque christiano debet venire in dubium quod ulla regula vel religio artior esse potest religione Johannis Baptiste, de quo scribitur Mathei tertio quod *vestimentum* eius erat *de pilis camelorum* ... *esca autem eius locuste et mel silvestre* [Mt. 3:4], super quo verbo dicit Hieronimus quod mirum erat in humano corpore tantam asperitatem vite conspicere; nec quod aliqua religio fuit perfectior religione Christi. Unde Mathei undecimo dixit: *Venit Johannes* Baptista *non manducans et bibes et di*xistis *quia demonium habet; venit filius hominis manducans et bibens et di*xistis*: 'Ecce, homo vorax et potator vini'* [Mt. 11:18–19] ... Religio ergo Christi fuit minus arta et maioris perfectionis." Aug.Anc. *Summa* 97,5 (ed. Rome, 1479), fol. 269vb.

Thus the more rigorous religious life is not equated with a greater degree of perfection.[390] The same applies to the various monastic rules. The mendicants live a more perfect life than do the monks,[391] and the habit, that distinguishing and defining mark of the state of perfection, signified the differentiation.[392] While a monk can receive dispensation to transfer from a less rigorous to a more rigorous Order, such as from the Augustinian Hermits to the Benedictines, this does not imply that the more rigorous rule is the more perfect. The Augustinian *Rule* is the most perfect *Rule* of the apostolic life, even if it is not the most rigorous,[393] in the same way that the religion of Christ was more perfect, though less rigorous, than the religion of John the Baptist.

Augustinus made his point almost as an aside. One could easily read over his comment, not pausing to be astounded by its implicit import. Yet the nonchalant manner in which Augustinus used his statement as an example of a larger principle is itself telling of his presuppositions. It is as though he just assumes his position is a given, generally accepted and clear to all, a subtle strategy for the persuasion of John XXII, in whose mind Augustinus wanted to plant

---

[390] "Communiter enim tenet ecclesia religionem episcoporum perfectiorem esse omni alia religione tam monachorum quam aliorum, et tamen experimentum docet quod quelibet religio artioris vite est quam religio episcoporum. Non ergo se concomitantur ista quod religio quanto artior, tanto perfectior. Potest enim maior perfectio cum minori artitudine et maior artitudo cum minori perfectione." Aug.Anc. *Summa* 97,5 (ed. Rome, 1479), fol. 270ra.

[391] "Quantum ad modi vivendi Christi et apostolorum imitationem, religiosi mendicantes magis illum modum vivendi sequuntur quam alii . . ." Aug.Anc. *Summa* 106,2 (ed. Rome, 1479), fol. 299va. Augustinus goes into great detail regarding the religious life, regarding the extent to which monks and friars exist in the state of perfection as such, as well as with respect to the contemplative and active lives. His treatment certainly impinges on the relationship he sees between the Franciscans and the Augustinians, and would need to be treated in depth in a separate study on his views of the religious life.

[392] "Apparet enim distinctio unius religionis ab alia potissime per habitum. Unde cum quis religiosus ad prelationem assumitur, eius habitum deserere non debet." Aug.Anc. *Summa* 106,4 (ed. Rome, 1479), fol. 300va.

[393] "Sicut nulla regula potest esse perfectior regula apostolorum, sic nulla regula potest esse perfectior regula beati Augustini, que non aliud essentialiter content quam apostolorum documenta. Profitentibus ergo regulam beati Augustini non conceditur licentia transvolandi ad regulam beati Benedicti tamquam ad perfectiorem simpliciter, sed tamquam ad exercitatiorem et perfectiorem huic eo enim ipso quod artior est in esu carnium et in aliis observantiis potest esse instrumentaliter magis via exercitandi se ut perveniat ad perfectionis statum. Corporalis tamen exercitatio non facit ad perfectionem simpliciter, quia ad modicum utilis est." Aug.Anc. *Summa* 106,4 (ed. Rome, 1479), fol. 270rb.

a seed. The entire crux of the debate raging when Augustinus composed his *Summa* was whether the Franciscan doctrine of apostolic poverty was that most representative of the life of Christ and the apostles. Had Augustinus entered the fray directly, meeting his opponents head-on, his treatise would have assumed the nature of just another polemical tract, rather than being an explication of traditional, accepted Church doctrine, repeated and explicated to combat the novelties that were flying around. When Augustinus made his statement about the Augustinian *Rule*, he had already argued that the doctrine of apostolic poverty in and of itself was at best only an instrumental cause of the Church's state of perfection, as well as having pointed out that only those religious rules and practices that had been approved and confirmed by the Church were indeed worthy of being considered religion. The *Rule* of St. Francis had been confirmed by the Church, and that was no problem for Augustinus. What he wanted to make clear was that such a *Rule*, based on poverty, was only an instrumental cause of perfection, not attaining to the real substance, the efficient, formal, material, and final cause. Moreover, should anyone try to make more of the Franciscan *Rule* than it being an instrumental cause of perfection, it would be a case of superstition, not religion. *Esssentialiter*, the *Rule* of St. Augustine was that of the apostles. A subtle strategy it may have been, but Augustinus' argument was one that exploded the Franciscan position as it was being used to damn John XXII and to undermine the power and authority of the institutional Church.

Bishops and monks, *episcopi* and *religiosi*: two ways of fulfilling the state of perfection, and for Augustinus, bishops were both. There were four states that pertained in ascending order to the state of perfection, all of which were established by Christ: the married state (*status coniugatorum*), the clerical state (*status clericorum*), the religious state (*status religiosorum*), and the state of prelates (*status prelatorum*).[394]

---

[394] "Respondendo dicendum <est> quod non intendimus hic loqui de statu secundum ethymologiam nominis, nec secundum quod ex diversis etatibus est variatus nec prout ex humana conditione vel terrena potestate per prospera et adversa interdum variatur, sed magis secundum quod ex potestate ecclesiastica vel ex aliquo sacramento in vita spirituali homo constituitur et ad cultum dei ordinatur. Perfectum namque proprie dicitur illud quod potest attingere proprie virtuti et proprio fini... Possumus ergo dicere quod in vita spirituali aliquis acquirit statum cum perpetua obligatione, et iste est status coniugatorum. Aliquis vero acquirit statum cum divinis cultus administratione, et iste est status clericorum. Aliquis autem statum acquirit

150   CHAPTER ONE

Bishops were the successors of the apostles, and the apostles were called both to the religious state and to the state of prelates. Christ first called the apostles to the religious state, the vows of poverty, chastity, and obedience, and only thereafter, were they called to the state of prelates. The apostles lived according to their vows, which had been established by Christ as the essence of the religious life. The religious life was not founded by any human being, such as Benedict or Augustine. It was instituted by Christ himself. The human founders of particular religions are so only accidentally, not substantively. The apostles lived the religious life as instituted by Christ, although they received their power of jurisdiction from Peter, who is the head of the apostles and the head of the Church. The fundamental point is that the apostles were called to be both religious and bishops, and thus so were their successors.[395]

---

cum operum perfectione et supererogatione, et iste est status religiosorum. Sed aliquis acquirit statum cum animarum perpetua instructione, et iste est status prelatorum. Statum ergo coniugatorum Christus rectificavit, Mathei quinto quando dixit: *dictum est quicumque dimiserit uxorem suam det illi libellum repudii. Ego autem dico vobis quod omnis qui dimiserit uxorem suam ... facit eam mechari* [Mt. 5:31–32]. Statum vero clericorum complevit Christus et terminavit, Mathei quinto quando ait: *Nisi habundaverit iustitia vestra plus quam scribarum et phariseorum non intrabitis in regnum celorum* [Mt. 5:20] ... Statum autem religiosorum Christus specificavit Mathei undevicesimo, ubi adolescenti querenti quid sibi deesset in vita spirituali, respondit: *Si vis perfectus esse, vade et vende omnia que habes et da pauperibus ... et veni sequere me* [Mt. 19:21] Sed statum prelatorum caritatis trina confessione Christus firmavit unde super illo verbo Johannis ultimo: *Simon Johannis amas me ... pasce oves meas* [Io. 21:17], dicit glosa quod trine negationi trina confessio redditur ne minus amori lingua serviat quam timori et ideo tertio interrogat et tertio iniungit sibi ovium curam, ostendens per hoc quantum ipse apprecietur prelationem ovium quoniam hoc est maxime eius amoris signum. Omnis ergo status perfectio et rectificatio a Christo est effective inchoata ... matrimonium secundum quod habet spiritualem perfectionem annexam consequitur ex eo quod est sacramentum ecclesie; tale autem sacramentum completum est in Christi incarnatione quia tunc Christus humanitatem sibi copulando nuptie celebrate sunt inter eum et ecclesiam ... Unde non solum statum matrimonii Christus perfecit rectificando verum etiam sacramentaliter implendo ... status prelatorum precedentium Christi adventum magis fuit firmatus timore quam amore quod patet de principibus sacerdotum in Christi adventum qui sibiipsis consulebant ne Romani venirent et tollerent locum eorum et gentem. Sed status prelatorum, quos Christus instituit, firmavit amore non timore ... donis gratiarum perfectio status acquiritur formaliter, effective tamen in fide Christi ante eius adventum et post eius adventum dona gratiarum ab ipso derivata sunt, *quia sicut lex per Moysen data est, sic gratia et veritas per Iesum Christum facta est,* Johannis primo [Io. 1:17]." Aug.Anc. *Summa* 76,1 (ed. Rome, 1479), fol. 221va–222ra; "... <qui> existentes in statu coniugali possunt quidem perfectionem habere et perfectionis opera facere; non tamen sunt in statu perfectionis quia obligatio qua unus coniugum obligatur alteri non est ad perfectionis opera, non est enim ad operationem spiritualem sed potius carnalem." Aug.Anc. *Summa* 77,1 (ed. Rome, 1479), fol. 224rb.

[395] "Videtur enim quod apostoli non prius fuerint vocati ad statum religionis quam

Though bishops partook of the religious state as well as the state of prelates, the state of prelates was more perfect than the religious, just as the religious state was more perfect than the clerical, and the clerical than the married. Augustinus explicitly addressed the issue and argued that in four aspects, prelates existed on a higher plane than the religious: the state of prelates was more perfect, more worthy and honorable, more useful, and more difficult. A bishop was more perfect than a religious because of him was required a greater degree of love, since prelates, stemming from Christ's charge to Peter to feed his sheep, were responsible for the care of the Church. The

---

prelationis... Preterea status religionum videtur esse institutus a puro homine puta a Benedicto vel Augustino vel ab aliis qui religiones aliquas instituerunt non ergo a Christo qui fuit deus et homo. Preterea Petrus fuit caput omnium apostolorum et prelatus totius ecclesie. Sed statim cum Christus vocavit eum Johannis primo dixit: *Tu vocaberis Cephas* [Io. 1:42], ergo statim ad prelationis statum vocatus est. In contrarium est quia via naturaliter precedit terminum; sed perfectio religionis est sicut via; perfectio vero prelationis est sicut terminum, nam prelatio presupponit iam hominem perfectum. Respondendo dicendum <est> quod perfectio religionum in tribus essentialiter consistit. Primo in spirituali paupertate per abdicationem mundialis substantie. Secundo in corporis et mentis castitate per abdicationem omnis carnalis concupiscentie. Tertio in obedientia per abdicationem omnis elationis superbie relinquendo proprie voluntatis motum. Ista autem tria vota facto et exemplo apostoli professi sunt in ipsa eorum prima vocatione quando Mathei quarto vocati a Christo, statim relictis omnibus secuti sunt eum... Si ergo apostoli in prima eorum vocatione... tria vota essentialia promiserunt, planum est tunc quod ad statum religionis sunt vocati. In prelatione autem eorum tria possumus considerare. Primo potestatis iurisdictionem que confertur in electione. Secundo spiritualem consecrationem que confertur in ordinatione. Tertio executionem que cum requirat divine scientie infusionem non potest fieri nisi per spiritus sancti missionem. Ad statum ergo prelationis apostoli quantum ad eorum iurisdictionem vocati sunt Mathei sexto decimo ubi dictum est Petro, a quo aliis potestatis iurisdictio erat taxanda: *Tibi dabo claves regni celorum* [Mt. 16:19]. Quantum vero ad eorum ordinationem vocati sunt ad prelationis statum Johannis vicesimo quando dictum est eis: *Accipite spiritum sanctum quorum remiseritis peccata remittuntur eis* [Io. 20:22–23], tunc enim facti sunt sacerdotes et episcopi. Sed quantum ad executionem vocati sunt ad prelationis statum Marci ultimo ubi postquam repleti sunt spiritu sancto, *predicaverunt ubique domino cooperante et sermone confirmante sequentibus signis* [Mc. 16:20]. Prius ergo apostoli vocati sunt ad statum religionis quam prelationis... dicendum <est> quod religiones non sunt institute a puro homine quantum ad vota essentialia in quibus consistit omnis religionis perfectio. Sed presupponuntur illa vota instituta a Christo in ipsa apostolorum vocatione, sed solum quantum ad quedam accidentalia puta quantum ad habitum et ordinationem regule vel constitutionum que nec sic firmitatem habent, nisi cum approbatione ecclesie... quantum ad Christi electionem, Petrus et alii apostoli eternaliter vocati sunt ad statum religionis et ad statum prelationis iuxta illud ad Ephesios primo: *Elegit nos in ipso ante mundi constitutionem ut essemus sancti et immaculati in conspectu eius in caritate* [Eph. 1:4], sed in operis executione prius facta est eorum vocatio ad statum religionis quam ad statum prelationis ut dictum est." Aug.Anc. *Summa* 84,1 (ed. Rome, 1479), fol. 238vb–239rb.

apostles, in so far as they were in the religious state, *imitated* Christ, but in so far as they were in the state of prelates, they *represented* Christ. Bishops are more useful than the religious, since they are to govern the divine cult, and to care for the flock. Being a bishop is, furthermore, more difficult than being a monk or friar because as a bishop one must administer one's temporal and spiritual office, rather than being concerned only with one's own spiritual progress.[396] These four characteristics are then explicitly named as those of bishops, which religious, as such, lack.[397] Moreover, the apostles received from Christ the powerful staff of temporal governance, the keys of administering the sacraments, the infusion of the holy spirit for the remission of sins, and the responsibility for preaching the Gospel, which requires great love. These four aspects only bishops receive as the true successors of the apostles.[398] They thus embody a greater

---

[396] "Respondendo dicendum <est> quod sicut supradictum est, apostoli fuerunt vocati ad statum religionis et ad statum prelationis. Si ergo fiat comparatio de statu uno respectu alterius, possumus dicere quod status prelationis in eis respectu status religionis fuit perfectior, fuit dignior, fuit utilior, et fuit difficilior. Perfectior quidem propter habundantiorem dilectionem. Unde habundantem dilectionem Christus expetivit a Petro quando sibi oves regendas commisit... Dignior vero propter persone representationem. Existentes enim apostoli in statu religionis Christum imitabantur, sed existentes in statu prelationis Christum representabant et eius vicem gerebant... Utilior autem propter proximorum exhortationem. Tenentur enim prelati non solum seipsos immo suos subditos in his que sunt fidei illuminare et ad divinum cultum ordinare. Unde prime ad Timotheum quarto Paulus scribens Timotheo dicit: *Esto fidelibus exemplum in conversatione, in verbo, in caritate... et dum venio attende lectioni exhortationi et doctrine* [I Tim. 4:12–13]. Sed difficilior propter temporalium et spiritualium administrationem, quorum administratio magni laboris et difficultatis est propter diversitatem et interdum pravitatem illorum quibus ministrantur, quos nisi prelatos dispositos videant et paratos magnis cruciatibus affliguntur, sicut de illos sancto Loth scribitur secunde Petri secundo: *Apectu enim et auditu iustus erat habitans inter eos qui de die in diem animam iustam iniquis operibus cruciabant* [II Pt. 2:8]. Excessit ergo status prelationis in apostolis eorummet statum religionis in perfectione, in dignitate, in utilitate, et difficultate." Aug.Anc. *Summa* 88,2 (ed. Rome, 1479), fol. 248vb–249ra.

[397] "Dicendum <est> quod status episcopalis quatuor includit quibus caret religio: primo habet episcopalis prelatio coniunctam honoris reverentiam; secundo presupponit in suscipiente caritatis habundantiam; tertio habet in administratione temporalium affluentiam; quarto exponitur ad periculorum imminentiam. Non est enim aliud potestas culminis nisi tempestas mentis in qua cogitationum semper procellis vani cordis quatitur huncque illuc incessanter." Aug.Anc. *Summa* 103,2 (ed. Rome, 1479), fol. 287vb. Augustinus treated the state of perfection of bishops in question 103; see Aug.Anc. *Summa* 103,1–5 (ed. Rome, 1479), fol. 287ra–289vb.

[398] "Fuerunt autem quatuor apostolis collata a Christo que perfectionem ostendebant, in quibus episcopi sunt eorum successores: primo virga potestativa in susceptione temporalium stipendiorum... Secundo claves in administrationis iurisdictione sacramentorum... Tertio inflatio spiritus sancti in remissionem pecccatorum...

degree of love than any religious, and no amount of Franciscan argument can change that. The Franciscan ideal was at best only an instrumental cause of the perfect life of Christ and the apostles, which substantially and essentially was continued in the most perfect religion of the bishops, based on love, and was preserved in the most perfect *Rule* of St. Augustine.

The issue was one of perfection. Augustinus built his *Summa* upon ascending degrees of perfection, based upon the apostolic life. The Church was the mystical body of Christ, which administered the true body of Christ, present on the altar. In keeping with his universal theocracy, Augustinus argued that the parish priest existed in a higher degree of perfection than did even the emperor, because the priest consecrated the host; the priest made present Christ's true body, and possessed both temporal and spiritual power with respect to his power of ordination, a power no lay person could claim.[399] Bishops shared

---

Quarto dispertio linguarum in predicatione evangeliorum... Intelligamus intus corda eorum sacra esse flammantia in dilectione dei et proximi, quia qui charitatem dei et proximi non habent, evangelii predicationem nullatenus assumere debent... In istis autem quatuor soli episcopi apostolorum perfectionis statum representant, non autem religiosi." Aug.Anc. *Summa* 103,1 (ed. Rome, 1479), fol. 287[rb]; *cf.* Ballweg, *Ordensreform*, 48–50.

[399] "Sacerdotes in regiminis cura preferuntur regibus quantum ad presens in quatuor: primo in temporis diuturnitate; secundo in operis qualitate; tertio in honoris dignitate; et quarto in iurisdictionis potestate. Fuit enim regimen sacerdotale prius regimine regali in cuius figura tribus Levi qui fuit genitus ante Iudam de quo reges sunt electi. Fuit electa ad ministerium sacerdotii, signanter tamen tertius filius Iacob, qui fuit Levi ad sacerdotium est electus, magis quam primus vel secundus... In operis vero qualitate preferuntur eis quia cura regiminis regum extendit se solum ad temporalia; regiminis autem cura sacerdotum respicit spirituale bonum, et illa que sunt perfectionis opera. Dicuntur enim sacerdotes quasi sacra dantes vel sacra recipientes vel sacra administrantes. Quod vero in honoris dignitate eis preferantur... duo sunt quippe, honor fratre et sublimitas episcopalis vel sacerdotalis, nullis poterit comparationibus adequari, si regum fulgori compares et principum diademati, longe erit inferius quam si plumbi metallum ad auri fulgorem compares. In iurisdictionis etiam potestate planum est quod eis preferuntur, cum iurisdictio regum solum sit super temporalia; sacerdotium vero potestas ad temporalia et spiritualia se extendit, quibus enim pretiose anime traduntur eorum potestate indigentibus bona temporalia dispensantur... Ergo est dicendum quod bonum commune prefertur bono privato in eodem genere operis, bonum enim matrimoniale et magis publicum et commune quam bonum continentie virginalis et tamen istud non prefertur illi cum illud sit consilii et supererogationis opus, nec tamen est verum quod regimen regale sit magis commune quam sacerdotale immo illud universalius est cum ad temporalia et spiritualia se extendat ut supra dictum est... reges inunguntur in cure regalis regiminis susceptione sicut episcopi inunguntur in susceptione cure pastoralis, non tamen reges dicuntur esse in pefectionis statu sicut episcopi, quia illorum cura respicit solum temporalia, istorum autem super his que

the divine imprint of ordination with the simple priest, but by their consecration as bishops, perfected that state and exist as the successors of the apostles. A bishop was a perfect, or rather, a perfected, priest, and as such, regarding the power of ordination, was equal to the pope and all other bishops.[400]

Yet in every state, Augustinus affirmed, there must be a head. Indeed, the unity is found in the head, for without a single head, it would not be a state of being, but dissolution. Therefore, there is one head of the state of prelates, and that is Peter, to whom Christ gave the power of jurisdiction, from whom then all other bishops receive their own power of jurisdiction.[401] Bishops are indeed in a state of perfection as having been already perfected, whereas the religious and all others, are in a state of becoming perfect. There is, however, still only one, the pope, who possesses the *highest* degree of

---

sunt perfectionis opera. Sacerdotes vero inunguntur ad consecrandum corpus Christi quorum unctio semper manet quia semper manent sacerdotes, non tamen inunguntur in cure parrochialis susceptione quia curam illam non recipiunt cum obligationis voto sicut episcopi ... quamvis alie tribus de quibus fuerunt reges priores fuerunt tempore tribu Levitica de qua electi sunt sacerdotes, eo quod Simeon fuit genitus ante Levi, non tamen ex hoc regimen regale fuit ante sacerdotale, quia ... omnes primogeniti a Noe usque ad Aaron fuerunt pontifices et omnes maiores natu induti veste sacerdotali cum benedictione patris decimas deo velut pontifices offerebant, ita quod iste due dignitates coniuncte erant ad invicem propter suam excellentiam ut qui erat sacerdos esset rex et econverso." Aug.Anc. *Summa* 104,3 (ed. Rome, 1479), fol. 290[rb]–291[vb].

[400] "Omnis potestas ordinis vel respicit caracteris impressionem vel respicit caracteris perfectionem. Nam caracteris impressio fit in septem ordinibus, quia in quolibet ordine imprimatur caracter. In episcopatu vero licet non imprimatur caracter, perficitur tamen caracter iam impressus, ut per talem perfectionem possit episcopus, qui est perfectus sacerdos, sibi similes generare. Sed omnes episcopi habent caracteris impressionem et caracteris perfectionem. Ergo omnes episcopi sunt equales pape in potestate ordinis." Aug.Anc. *Summa* 1,4 (ed. Rome, 1479), fol. 6[rb].

[401] "Respondendo <est> dicendum quod omnis status reducitur ad unum caput aliter non esset dicendum status sed casus. Ubicunque autem est capitis unitas, ibi est status. Ubicumque autem pluralitas casus est non status. Totius autem status episcopalis et ecclesiastice hierarchie caput est episcopatus Christi ad quem omnes episcopatus et prelationes omnes ecclesiastici ordinis reducuntur ... ergo est dicendum quod verum est in illa sufflatione spiritus sancti apostolos esse factos a Christo sacerdotes et episcopos et in sacerdotio receperunt potestatem ordinis respicientem Christi corpus verum et in episcopatu receperunt potestatem ordinis respicientem Christi corpus mysticum. Unde totam potestatem ordinis immediate a Christo recipiunt. Verumtamen potestatem iurisdictionem qua possent potestatem ordinis exequi in tanta vel in tali materia non receperunt nisi a Petro post missionem spiritus sancti ... planum est autem quod post missionem spiritus sancti solus Petrus fuit caput apostolorum et omnium populorum remansit ... predicare evangelium pertinet ad potestatem clavium; soli autem Petro potestas clavium commissa est." Aug.Anc. *Summa* 88,1 (ed. Rome, 1479), fol. 248[va–b].

perfection. Thus the bishops together with the pope, represent Christ and the apostles as no other. The religious, nevertheless, are in one way closer to the life of Christ and the apostles. In terms of imitation, as distinct from succession, the pope and his bishops essentially imitate Christ and the apostles more closely than do the religious, but the religious live a higher level of apostolic life in terms of the instrumental imitation of Christ, that which leads to the acquisition of perfection, a perfection that bishops and the pope already have.[402]

There was not much room left for Franciscan claims. And then the final knockout: with regard to the instrumental acquisition of perfection, Augustinus had already affirmed that the most perfect path thereto was that of Augustine's *Rule*, the *Rule* of a bishop, and Augustine, as a bishop, followed the most perfect religion. Augustine's religion was the most perfect form of the apostolic life. In opposition to the ecclesiological implications of the Franciscan ideal, as it was being used by Marsilius and Louis of Bavaria, Augustinus championed the hierarchical, episcopal Church, led by the pope, who was the vicar of Christ, from whom all jurisdiction and authority, all perfection, and all religion flowed, and who must be obeyed, even if he errs, for the pope gives life to Christ's mystical body as the

---

[402] "Videtur enim quod papa perfectionis statum Christi et apostolorum non perfectiori modo representet quam religiosi... dicendum <est> quod representare Christi et apostolorum perfectionis statum potest intelligi dupliciter: primo per eorum iam perfectorum successionem; secundo per ipsorum apostolorum quasi perficiendorum imitationem. Primo modo religiosi non representant Christi et apostolorum perfectionis statum sed solum papa et episcopi. Solus enim summus pontifex... representatione est sacerdos magnus, princeps apostolorum, primatu Abel, gubernatu Noe, patriarchatu Abraham, ordine Melchisedech, dignitate Aaron, auctoritate Moyses, iudicatu Samuel, potestate Petrus, unctione Christus. Sed secundo modo quantum ad illa que faciunt ad acquirendum perfectionis statum essentialiter adhuc papa magis representat Christi et apostolorum pefectionis statum quam aliquis religiosorum. Obligat enim se voto pro ovibus et pastoribus animam ponere, ultra quem gradum caritas que est perfectionis vinculum non se extendit. Sed quantum ad illa que faciunt ad acquirendum perfectionis statum instrumentaliter sicut est temporalium abdicatio in ieiuniis et vigiliis exercitatio, magis imitantur apostolorum vestigia religiosi quam papa vel episcopi. Sed hoc non est representare apostolorum statum iam perfectorum, sed magis perficiendorum. Dicebatur enim supra quod Christus prius vocavit apostolos ad statum religionis tamquam perficiendos, quam ad statum prelationis tamquam iam perfectos. Papa autem non est in statu perficiendorum, sed in statu perfectorum supremum gradum tenet." Aug.Anc. *Summa* 101,2 (ed. Rome, 1479), fol. 279[rb]; *cf.* Horst, "Die Armut Christi," 488–491. Augustinus dedicated a question explicitly to the state of perfection of the pope; see Aug.Anc. *Summa* 101,1–8 (ed. Rome, 1479), fol. 279[rb]–284[ra].

faithful make their way back to union with God. It was an Augustinian model, and an Augustinian vision. It was a high way indeed.

There were no winners. And it would be fallacious as well as erroneous to look for some. There was gain and loss on all sides. Augustinus' *Summa* did not stave off continued attacks on John XXII, nor on the hierarchical Church. In 1330 Louis of Bavaria returned to Germany for good, but that did not prevent him from waging his compaign: Marsilius and Ockham were at his court. The Franciscans too survived without horrendous damage, and continued to grow and flourish throughout the later Middle Ages. Compared to the schism that began fifty years after Augustinus' death, the Church was not shaken nearly as badly in the first decades of the fourteenth century as it was in the last. The body of Christ remained on the altar, and the power remained in the ideas.

The Augustinians were never, by anyone other than themselves, considered truly to embody the highest form of religious life, yet they emerged from the conflict in better shape than the other participants, whose reputations had at least been tarnished. The emperor, pope, and Franciscans limped along, essentially without much change in outlook or claims, but these are stories all well known.[403] That of the Augustinians has been forgotten, relegated merely to isolated political theorists bellowing impotently an abstract political theory, with their corporate identity erased, as they sat around in their

---

[403] See Ballweg, *Ordensreform*. Ballweg points out though that "Benedikt XII. äußert sich selber sehr wenig zum päpstlichen Jurisdiktionsprimat, vielleicht weil er wußte, wie wenig die Päpste seit Bonifaz VIII. damit erreicht hatten." *Ibid.*, 314. Ballweg comes to a rather negative conclusion, arguing that the fourteenth century was a "Phase spiritueller Erschlaffung und institutioneller Verkrustung, als der Kurialismus des 13. Jahrhunderts bürokratisch expandierte und die Inquisition gerade charismatische Formen von Religiosität bedrängte. Erst im Konziliarismus des ausgehenden 14. und frühen 15. Jahrhunderts trat die Kirchenreform in eine neue Phase." *Ibid.*, 315. While such an evaluation, which is essentially the old decline thesis, may fit the papacy of Benedict XII, I would argue that it does not apply as a whole, nor in the way Ballweg portrays it. The hierocratic theory, despite how one might view it, was certainly not an institutional encrustation, nor a simple bureaucratic expansion of 13th-century curialism, and was based upon a vibrant spiritual creativeness, especially when one actually reads an author such as Augustinus of Ancona in his historical context, rather than lifting individual positions out of his work for an abstract portrayal of the history of institutional ideas. Papal reform efforts may have indeed fit Ballweg's conclusion, but that should not obscure the vital reform efforts and programs within the Orders themselves, as I will be arguing throughout this study with regard to the OESA; see especially Chapter Three below.

lounges, unaware of the bodies being bloodied outside, sipping tea. The Augustinians were not the winners, nor the losers, but they were also not insignificant participants and players.

Giles of Rome had gotten the ball rolling, setting the Order on its path in 1292: the common life, regular observance, theology schools, and his own political accumen in his support of Boniface VIII. The Order prospered. Body and soul, heaven and hell, head and members, a theology and dominion of grace, a universal, hierarchical order, a vision, a commitment to the Order and to the Order's founder: these Giles imparted; this was his legacy. It was a path that was developed and followed by James of Viterbo, Augustinus of Ancona, Alexander of San Elpidio, William of Cremona, and Hermann of Schildesche, and it was a path the Order continued to follow and forge.

The Augustinians did not create the myth of Christendom, but they gave it its fullest ecclesiological expression, the theocracy of Christ, and that of his vicar, and they gave it an Augustinian stamp. By the mid-1320s, the Augustinians had not only met challenges to their existence and gained privileges and protection from the pope, but they had also formulated a world view that exalted the Order as the most perfect expression of the Christian life, based on the model of their founding father, the Bishop of Hippo. They had also begun establishing a network of theological schools throughout Europe,[404] and had initiated a programmatic endeavor to base their arguments, theories, and positions on the works not just of Giles of Rome, but on those of Augustine himself. Before the issue of the "modern Pelagians" ever raised its ugly head,[405] the Augustinians had already begun to mine the works of Augustine as the source of their theological teaching, and they had done so in the midst of fierce political conflict. The "Augustinianism" the Augustinians espoused, from Giles of Rome on, was inherently political: it was an integral component of the Order's platform that was beginning to emerge as a result of the power politics that were required for the Order's survival.[406] The existence and status of the Order was dependent on the goodwill and favor of the pope, which had made the

---

[404] See Chapter Four.
[405] For the issue of the modern Pelagians and the origins of late medieval Augustinianism, see Appendix A.1.
[406] The term "political Augustinianism" was formulated by Henri-Xavier Arquillière,

Order to begin with, with some help from Cardinal Riccardo Annabaldi. The OESA was a political creation, and it remained so. It would be wrong, however, to see it as merely a political institution; as wrong as viewing either Louis of Bavaria or John XXII as merely political opportunists, or Boniface VIII for that matter. The appropriation of Augustine by the Order became its heart and soul, and Augustine was both a spiritual leader and a theologian, a hermit and a bishop. Yet the power politics of the papal-princely conflicts between Boniface VIII and Philip IV, and between John XXII and Louis of Bavaria, made for the development of the Augustinian platform. The myth of Christendom received its highest expression in the works of the Augustinians, who incorporated that myth within their own programs and ideals as they strove to create their Order's identity. It was, moreover, not the Order's only myth. In 1326, the OESA was no longer a neophyte religious Order. It had accomplished much. And John XXII was as grateful as had been Boniface VIII. On 18 February 1326, John appointed Alexander of San Elpidio to the bishopric of Melfi in the kingdom of Naples.[407] On 20 December 1326, John wrote to Augustinus of Ancona in Naples, acknowledg-

---

L'Augustinisme politique (Paris, 1934), based largely on early medieval sources. See also his later defense of his position in his article "L'Essence de l'Augustinisme politique," in *Augustinus Magister*, Congrès International Augustinien, Études Augustiniennes, 3 vols. (Paris, 1955), 2:991–1001. De Lubac has questioned the validity of the term, arguing that it has nothing to do with Augustine himself; see Henri de Lubac, *Théologies d'occasion* (Paris, 1984), 255–308. In treating Giles of Rome and his school, de Lubac asserts: "Bref, l'augustinisme ici en question n'est pas le fait de saint Augustin: il serait plutôt l'inverse de l'augustinisme véritable." *Ibid.*, 261. De Lubac approaches "political Augustinianism" in the same fashion as most scholars have treated "Late Medieval Augustinianism" (see Appendix A.1), namely from a theological perspective based on the interpretation of Augustine's works themselves. On one level this approach has merit, yet it obscures the historical phenomena. Giles' works, together with those of his confreres, may very well have been an "inversion of the true Augustine," but more likely the case is that their Augustine is an inversion of de Lubac's Augustine. It is as likely too that Gile's "Averroism" as well as that of Augustinus of Ancona, as de Lubac views it, was also an inversion of the true Averroes, and therefore de Lubac's labels are themselves invalid, since he is willing to label Giles and Augustinus as 'Averroists' but not as 'Augustinians'; *ibid.*, 299. Troeltsch was certainly right: Augustine had no followers. But to dismiss the reception of Augustine and the impact of that reception, based on a theological interpretation of the "true Augustine" is to ignore the historical influence and power of Augustine and of his followers who saw themselves as being Augustine's true heirs, disciples, and sons.

[407] Miethke, *De Potestate Papae*, 106. Miethke cautions that we cannot know for sure whether this appointment was directly related to Alexander's *De potestate ecclesiastica*.

ing the receipt of his *Summa*, and sent him as well one hundred gold florins, together with an annual gift of ten gold ounces, *pro scribendis libris*.[408] But William of Cremona received the biggest prize of all. On 20 January 1327, John granted William's petition for the Augustinian Hermits to gain custody of Augustine's body.

---

[408] Ministeri, "De Vita et Operibus," 238–239, nrs. 4–7, which are the documents Ministeri prints from the Vatican Archive; see also Gutiérrez, *Geschichte*, I/1, 95, and Miethke, *De Potestate Papae* 172–173.

CHAPTER TWO

CREATING RELIGIOUS IDENTITY: THE MYTH OF AUGUSTINE

Reality may or may not be stranger than fiction, but it is from reality that myth is created. In 1327, reality descended on the Augustinian Order of Hermits. In the Bull *Veneranda sanctorum*, dated 20 January 1327, Pope John XXII recognized the special relationship between the Hermits and St. Augustine, referring to Augustine as the Order's teacher, father, leader, and head.[1] The pope gave the Order permission to build a monastery adjoining the basilica of San Pietro in Ciel d'Oro in Pavia large enough to house twenty-five to thirty friars, and to share religious services with the Augustinian Canons.[2] For the next four years there was considerable conflict between the two branches of Augustine's paternity regarding the practical implications of the papal privilege granted the Hermits. A dispute between two religious orders it may have been, but, what might not come as a surprise, it was one conducted in the midst of contemporary papal-imperial politics.

---

[1] "... pia devotione recolimus et profunda meditatione pensamus, dignum arbitramur et congruum, ut ubi tanti doctoris corpus et presulis tumulatum quiescere dicitur, ibi ultra id, quod sibi honoris et laudis ab universali exhibetur Ecclesia, singulari quadam reverentia a vobis et fratribus Ordinis vestri, qui sub eiusdem patris regula degitis et sancta observatione militatis, quique divinis insistitis laudibus, vacatis orationi, intenditis exhortationi, insudatis studio et animarum saluti propensius vigilatis, specialiter honoretur: quatenus inibi tanquam membra suo capiti, filii patri, magistro discipuli, duci milites, coherentes Deo et ipsi Sancto, auctoritate fulti apostolica, precordialius iubiletis, ubi et Preceptoris vestri, Patris, Ducis, et Capitis Augustini noveritis reliquias fore sepultas." John XXII, *Venerada sanctorum*, 20 January 1327, *CDP* 7 (14–15).

[2] "Eapropter ... auctoritate apostolica statuimus, ac etiam ordinamus, quod fratres vestri Ordinis presit prior secundum observantiam ipsius Ordinis Eremitarum, iuxta ecclesiam monasterii S. Petri in Celo aureo papiensis, cui preest abbas et conventus Canonicorum Regularium Ordinis B. Augustini predicti, degant inibi, sub eodem, etiam si ad Romanam Ecclesiam nullo pertineant mediante, ubi sacrum corpus eiusdem B. Augustini esse dicitur solemniter tumulatum, mediate vel immediate, prout eisdem priori et fratribus videbitur expedire et commode fieri poterit, usque ad vigesimum quintum, vel tricenum numerum ad minus, iuxta subscriptam formam debeant insimul, perpetuis futuris temporibus, habitare." *CDP* 7 (15).

In the cacophony of catastrophe that was the fourteenth century, the political struggles between pope and emperor threatened to negate the claims for a unified Christian society as much in theory as in practice. Yet such conflict had very little relevance for the majority of the European population. On the local level, the level of micro-history, for the individuals of Italy and France, of Germany and Britain, not to mention those of Scandinavia or the East, the Italian campaigns of pope and emperor did not mean all that much when on the home front people were struggling to scrape together an evening meal, or rose up against their archbishop or parish priest due to the exploitation of the flock the men of the Church were supposed to shepherd. When one is plowing a field in the cold and the wind, when one's ox is being stubborn, and the job has to be done if one's family is to have food the coming year, when agonizing in childbirth to bring forth a new soul who, one knows, may or may not survive the first year, when caring for the household in daily drudgery, the issues of who ruled Christendom are not on the forefront of one's mind; when one is living in the midst of crisis, personal and local, threatening one's only reality, one's immediate surroundings and day to day life, one's family and friends, leading one to question how to get up in the morning to face yet another day of labor and pain and sorrow, and how to prevent the starvation of one's self and one's loved ones, the pope and the emperor were Tweedledee and Tweedledum, less present and of less importance than the fleas and the ticks in one's bed—except when their troops passed through, with all the dignity and delight the military has a way of bestowing on what otherwise would be considered pure rape, pillage, and plunder.

Crisis is such an over-used word, lacking any real content or explanatory value, except for the realization that for individuals in crisis, pointing to the general trend of crises, explaining that everyone is in crisis and always has been, does little to assuage the anxiety of present, individual perception and reality. The crisis of the fourteenth century was real, as real as was its myth of a unified Christendom.[3] It is no help to historical understanding to adopt a position of historical distance and patronizingly report that civilization

---

[3] On the late medieval crisis, see Hartmut Boockmann, *Stauferzeit und spätes Mittelalter. Deutschland 1125–1517* (Berlin, 1987), ch. 6: *Spätmittelalterliche Krisen*, 228–246; Frantisek Graus, *Pest-Geissler-Judenmorde. Das 14. Jahrhundert als Krisenzeit* (Göttingen, 1987).

has always been in crisis and thus dismiss the depth of the prognosis. After the horrors of early modern and modern Europe, from the wars of religion of the sixteenth to the holocaust of the previous century, it is easy to relativize the crisis of the fourteenth century. It is difficult for the secular, contemporary mind to give much credence to the crisis stemming from the experience of the pope residing in Avignon, and then the shock of the Schism; or the fear of not knowing who would succumb to the plague during the night: mother, brother, father, sister, child, or neighbor; or from the anxiety of knowing for sure whether one's sins were really forgiven in the confessional, since if they were not, or inadequately so, one was destined for the tortures of hell; or the related insecurity arising from all of Europe being excommunicated by one of two competing popes. Yet crisis there was.

A crisis of identity was at play throughout the fourteenth century, which lay behind the pogroms and pyres. In such a situation, identity was found in groups, for groups provided the security for living day to day, whether the group was the family, the commune, the city, the cultural or political territory, the parish, a confraternity, or a religious order. Groups provided the demarcation between those who belonged, and the "other," the outsider, whether Jew or Turk, fellow citizen, foreigner, heretic, emperor, or pope. Christendom provided the myth for the European identity, but that, on the local level, was in itself insufficient given the circumstances. The fourteenth century was in search of identity, and myth provided the means of surviving the crisis, of achieving identity, when all around reality screamed for its absence.

In the early 1330s one such mythic identity was created: the Augustinian identity, formulated in the midst of crisis in attempt to carve a place for a religious order within the myth of Christendom.[4] In the general overarching melee of crisis of what it meant to be a Christian in such a society, in such a world, there emerged the Augustinain platform of the high way to heaven, based not only on the construction of a political vision of Christ's sovereignty in combating Franciscan religio-political claims, but also on the appropriation of a remembered past that never was. Myth creates meaning,

---

[4] *Cf.* Kaspar Elm, "Die Bedeutung historischer Legitimation für Entstehung, Funktion und Bestand des mittelalterlichen Ordenswesens," in *Herkunft und Ursprung. Historische und mythische Formen der Legitimation*, ed. Peter Wunderli (Sigmaringen, 1994), 71–90.

and meaning is reality. Theory, papal or imperial, was nothing more than a legitimizing myth, but one that had serious consequences and tentacles. Group identity, of city, of commune, of Guelf or Ghibelline, enabled individuals to deal with the crisis and gave them a firm foundation. Such was the Augustinian myth. Whereas the Augustinians from Giles of Rome to Augustinus of Ancona had developed their papal-Augustinian, episcopal ecclesiology in competition with the Order of Friars Minor, the Augustinian myth was created in a conflict closer to home, so to speak: the contentious disputes between the Augustinian Hermits and the Augustinian Regular Canons. Yet the myth of Augustine, as all myths perhaps, was a myth that for a long time after its creation, transformed the reality upon which it was based, for the group itself and for the society in which it functioned.

I. From Reality to Myth: The Politics of Augustine's Body

In the early fourteenth century, Pavia was not the city it once had been. In Carolingian times, Pavia was the capital of the Italian Kingdom, but began its decline with the Ottonians. In the eleventh century, Emperor Conrad II moved the imperial residency from the palace within the city's walls, to the monastery of San Pietro in Ciel d'Oro just outside,[5] the church, as tradition had it, that in the eighth century Luitbrand, the King of the Lombards, had built to house the body of St. Augustine.[6] By 1300 Pavia was ruled by the *signoria* of the Langosco, and was firmly in control of the Della Torre of Milan. In 1311 Pavia ranked tenth on the list of the richest Lombard cities, being assessed a tax of 9,020 gold florins by the Emperor Henry VII, as compared to the richest city, Genoa's 40,000, or Padua's 20,000, the third highest assessment.[7] It has been estimated that whereas the populations of Milan, Venice, Genoa, and Florence in the early fourteenth century were each in the neighborhood of 100,000 inhabitants, Pavia, together with Padua, Messina, and Pisa, only counted somewhat over 25,000 souls.[8] And it was amongst these souls that in 1327 scandal had arisen.

---

[5] See J.K. Hyde, *Society and Politics in Medieval Italy. The Evolution of the Civil Life, 1000–1300* (London/New York, 1973), 45–48.
[6] For a description of San Pietro in Ciel d'Oro and its history, including the tradition of Luitbrand bringing Augustine's body there, see *CDP*, ix–lii.
[7] Hyde, *Society and Politics*, Map 4, xxi–xxii.
[8] Roland Pauler, *Die Deutschen Könige und Italien im 14. Jahrhundert. Von Heinrich VII.*

On 13 April 1327, the Commune of Pavia wrote to Pope John XXII contesting the privilege granted to the Augustinian Hermits three months earlier regarding their right to share with the Augustinian Canons the religious services conducted in San Pietro in Ciel d'Oro.[9] A novelty, as the letter of the Commune called it, a useless *novitas*, was threatening to cause scandal and serious unrest amongst the population, leading itself to disgrace and danger for the Order of Hermits.[10] This was the result of John's Bull *Veneranda sanctorum* for the people of Pavia. And a novelty it was indeed. After all, the Hermits already had a house in Pavia, Santa Mustiola, which the bishop of Pavia, together with a number of ecclesiastical and civic dignitaries of the Commune, had placed in the hands of the Hermits for its reform on 2 April 1277.[11] Even Jordan of Quedlinburg, who viewed the reunion of the Order's father Augustine with his true sons as a sign of divine inspiration and guidance, recognized that such a grant seemed to have been made "completely beyond the boundaries of customary legal and rational channels."[12] A week after the Commune of Pavia wrote to the pope, John XXII replied on 20 April by writing to the abbot and convent of San Pietro to reaffirm his grant to the Hermits. John exhorted the Canons to receive the Hermits with good will and honesty, and requested in no uncertain terms that the Hermits even be allowed to share the

---

bis Karl IV (Darmstadt, 1997), 29; *cf.* Hyde, *Society and Politics*, Map 5, xxiii, which lists Pavia having a population of between 20,000 and 40,000.

[9] *CDP* 11 (26–28).

[10] "Per nostram civitatem diebus istis exierunt sermones in vulgus non modicae novitatis, videlicet quod religiosi viri magister generalis et fratres Ordinis Eremitarum, in monasterio S. Petri in Coelo Aureo Papiensi Canonicorum Regularium Ordinis S. Augustini... quodam callido forte praetextu, in vestro sanctissimo consistorio, quaedam in praeiudicium dicti monasterii, abbatis et conventus eiusdem, subreptitie, virtutum fratrum et conventus veritate tactita, et vitiorum falsitate expressa, a sanctissimo in Christo patre nostro de domino Summo Pontifice noviter impetrarunt, propter quae fratres conventus Eremitarum ipsorum Papiensium in rumoris populi fere periculum incurrerunt... Quapropter paternitati ac sanctitati vestrae, flexis genibus devotissime supplicamus, quatenus ob Dei et vestri reverentiam, ne forte, in damnum et periculum ipsorum fratrum Eremitarum, in populo tumultus oriatur et scandalum, sic dignemini agere, quod novitas huiusmodi penitus omittatur et maxime quia in huiusmodi novitate evidens utilitas non apparet." *CDP* 11 (26–28).

[11] *CDP* 3 (6–8); 4 (9–10); 5 (10); and 6 (11–12).

[12] "Nec mirum, si tam in donatione impetranda quam in possessione adipiscenda grandis admodum difficultas fuerit, cum hoc factum praeter solitum cursum iuris et rationis prorsus prima facie videretur." *VF* 1,18 (74–76). For Jordan's view of the importance of the Hermits gaining custody of Augustine's body, see Chapter Three below.

monastery itself with the Canons until the Hermits were able to build their own facilities adjoining the Church.[13]

It is difficult to know from the extant documents what really was going on in Pavia between the Hermits and the Canons. That there was conflict is no doubt, and little wonder. Pope John XXII's grant to the Hermits was truly a cause for controversy since it divided the rights and responsibilities for Augustine's tomb and for the religious services and benefits of San Pietro between the Canons and the Hermits. Much of the dispute it seems was over the practical details, but details that went to the very heart of both Orders. Who had the right to say mass on St. Augustine's feast day, August 28? Which Order was to receive the offerings given to San Pietro, and which offerings? Who would be hearing the parishioners' confessions, and when? Which Order would receive the income from donations to the Church regarding Augustine's relics? Which Order would have primacy of place in civic processions? Which Order would be responsible for burying deceased parishioners? Through which door would each Order enter San Pietro for celebrating the divine office? These were issues that were continuously bones of contention between the Hermits and the Canons, even though *Veneranda sanctorum* addressed many of them explicitly. Thus John XXII was clear that due to the temporal priority of the Canons, their abbot had the right to say mass and to preach on the major feast days, if he so desired, including Christmas, Epiphany, Palm Sunday, The feasts of the Resurrection and Ascension, Pentecost, the Birth of John the Baptist, all the feasts concerning the Blessed Virgin, the feast of St. Augustine, All Saints, and all other feast days when "a multitude of the faithful are accustomed to gather in the church of San Pietro."[14] Indeed, *Veneranda*

---

[13] *CDP* 12 (28–29); "Discretionem igitur vestram attente requirimus, monemus, rogamus et hortamur in domino, per apostolica vobis scripta mandantes, quantenus pro divina et apostolice sedis ac nostra reverentia, de huiusmodi nostrorum interventione rogaminum, fratres dicti Ordinis Eremitarum, qui iuxta premissam ordinationem nostram inibi fuerint deputati, benigne recipientes et honeste tractantes, in aliqua parte competenti dictarum habitationum vestrarum ipsius monasterii recipiatis, eosdem et sincera in domino charitate tractetis ac ipsos concedatis in parte huiusmodi habitare, donec ipsi de habitatione congrua iuxta eandem ecclesiam, ut supra dicitur, sibi duxerint providendum." *CDP* 12 (29).

[14] "... et quia idem abbas antiquior in loco, et dignitate maior existit, abbas, qui est, et pro tempore fuerit, in celebrationibus missarum, et predicationibus in Natalis Domini et Epiphanie, Dominice in Ramis palmarum, Resurrectionis et Ascensionis Dominice, Pentecostes, Nativitatis beati Iohannis Baptiste, in omnibus

sanctorum was very protective of the rights and privileges of the Canons, and was explicitly so regarding many of the practical consequences foreseen resulting from the shared residency.[15] The Hermits, in fact, were clearly given second place regarding the rights to celebrate mass, to hear confessions, to preach, and all the other religious services provided to the parish, though the abbot could certainly concede to the Hermits particular rights and privileges that were by decree and tradition those of the Canons.[16] When it came to offerings, however, the two Orders were to split all receipts, unless explicitly designated as given to one or the other Order.[17] Yet even given the stipulations, controversy there was, and it was a serious matter.

The conflict seems to have begun a month after John XXII issued *Veneranda sanctorum*. On 23 February 1327 there was a showdown in the Cathedral of Pavia. On one side stood the archdeacon of Pavia, Bergondius de Tortis, together with a number of canons of the Cathedral; Frater Philip, the abbot of the monastery of San Pietro in Ciel d'Oro; six additional canons of the monastery, and other ecclesiastical dignitaries. On the other side, stood the vicar general of the Lombard congregation of Augustinian Hermits, Girard; lector and Frater Albertus; and Frater Rufinus, prior of the Augustinian Hermits of Santa Mustiola in Pavia. Abbot Philip asked the Hermit delegation whether they had an official copy of the papal letter stating their granted privileges, for if they had, they, the Canons, would certainly abide by the dictates and wishes of the pope since their monastery, after all, was under direct papal jurisdiction. Girard responded for the Hermits that actually they had no such document in their possession, but they did have a letter from their prior general telling them of the papal grant. The abbot replied that that may all be well and good, but until he could be shown proof of the papal document itself, he was not willing to concede, but should

---

et singulis sanctorum Petri et Pauli Apostolorum, Assumptionis, et omnibus aliis B. Virginis, S. Augustini, omnium Sanctorum, Consecrationis seu Dedicationis Ecclesie dicti monasterii, et in omnibus Sanctorum solemnioribus eiusdem monasterii festivitatibus, quibus specialiter consuevit multitudo fidelium convenire in ecclesia dicti monasterii, preferatur, ut missam solemniorem celebrandam diebus huiusmodi celebret, et in solemniori predicatione ipsis etiam diebus predicet, si hoc voluerit idem abbas." *CDP* 7 (16).

[15] *CDP* 7 (17–18).
[16] *CDP* 7 (17–18).
[17] *CDP* 7 (18).

such proof be offered, he was most willing to adhere to the holy pontiff's wishes. Thus, there was stalemate.[18] The official documentation of this event, testifying to the protest of the ecclesiastical dignitaries of Pavia against the decree of the pope, was written and confirmed by the eye-witness Augustinus Panizarius, a notary by imperial authority.[19] By imperial authority: there was more going on in Pavia in 1327 than a squabble between two religious Orders.

Money was at stake. The economic basis of the Canons was being cut in half by having to share the income from San Pietro's and Augustine's tomb with the Hermits. Moreover, all of a sudden the pastoral responsibilities of the Canons were jeopardized by the assertions of the Hermits, as well as their prestige and patronage. It was a conflict over the control of sacred space. Which Order would say mass when, which Order would bury deceased parishioners, in what manner would each Order enter San Pietro to celebrate divine office, and through which door, and which Order would precede which in civic processions, these and all the other issues that stood central to the dispute may seem to modern ears to be much ado about nothing, or, to be reduced to the lowest level of sibling rivalry. Yet this was what it was about: the ritual life of a parish and of two religious Orders. This was reality, the reality of each Order's daily life, and the daily life of the parishioners of Pavia. Practical, down to earth, and economic squabbles over privileges there were indeed, but at issue was the administration of the sacred.

On 25 March 1327, Prior General William of Cremona wrote a letter to Lanfranc of Milan, the new Augustinian provincial prior of the Lombard Congregation, and to Frater Gerard of Bergamo, an Augustinian bachelor in theology who was very much involved in the dispute, to inform them of a concord reached between William and Abbot Philipp of the Canons.[20] Most of the issues had been settled, according to William, and William too was very concerned to ensure the rights and privileges of the Canons. Indeed, should it come about that any of the Hermits, in San Pietro itself or even throughout the region, misappropriated property of the Canons, or if the rights of the Canons were exceeded in any fashion, not only

---

[18] *CDP* 9 (20–21).
[19] *CDP* 9 (21).
[20] *CDP* 10 (21–26).

Lanfranc himself, but also the conventual priors of the Augustinian congregations geographically from Novara to Genoa would be held responsible and placed under excommunication.[21] Yet even with William's stern measures in attempt to convince the Canons that the Hermits would do them no harm, the conflict continued, and on 19 June 1327 Pope John XXII appointed Cardinal Bertrand del Poggetto as special envoy to ensure the execution and implementation of *Veneranda sanctorum*.[22]

The Canons of San Pietro, together with the Cathedral canons and numerous other Pavian ecclesiastical dignitaries who had made the protest in February, were holding out for sure proof of the papal grant. The document must be produced. It finally was, on 5 June 1331. Augustinus Panizarius, the imperial notary, attested to the presentation of the Bull that Lanfranc of Milan, the provincial prior of the OESA, and Frater Rainaldus, made to the abbot and Canons of San Pietro, noting that upon receipt of the Bull, there was a kiss of peace and the Canons accepted and received the Hermits.[23] On 8 June 1331, Fulconus and Ricardus de Duce sold land to the Hermits for the purpose of constructing their own monastery.[24] Almost four years later, Pope Benedict XII granted the Hermits the right to celebrate the feast of St. Augustine in San Pietro,[25] and on 27 March 1338, the Commune of Pavia granted the Hermits the privilege to divert civic water for the purpose of irrigating their gardens,

---

[21] "Item si contingerit fratres predicti Ordinis Eremitarum modo aliquo de iure vel de facto uti impetratis vel concessis, invadendo vel intrando ad possidendum aliquid, quod pertineret ad dictum monasterium, faciendo contra ea que superius sunt expressa, ipso facto et iure prior provincialis Lombardie nec non et priores conventuales civitatum Papie, Mediolani, Laude, Cumarum, Novarum, Vercellarum, Alexandrie, Ianue, Ast, Terdone et Placentie, sint etiam maioris excomunicationis vinculo innodati, et loca seu conventus dictarum civitatum dicti Ordinis Eremitarum sint supposita ecclesiastico interdicto, taliter etiam quod ad requisitionem vel monitionem abbatis dicti monasterii qui est vel pro tempore erit, seu ad requisitionem cuiuscumque legitimi procuratoris vel sindici eorum, teneantur et debeant archiepiscopi, episcopi et eorum vicarii nec non et aliarum ecclesiarum rectores dictarum civitatum, totiens quotiens contrarium factum fuerit per predictos fratres Eremitas, vel alium eorum nomine, publice excomunicatos eosdem denunciare et dicta loca predictorum fratrum Eremitarum esse supposita ecclesiastico interdicto." *CDP* 10 (22–23).

[22] *CDP* 14 (31–33).
[23] *CDP* 17 (40–41); see also 18, 19, and 20 (42–50).
[24] *CDP* 22 (54–56); see also 23 (57–58).
[25] *CDP* 27 (63).

an act written and notarized by Bernard Muricula, the civic notary.[26] In Pavia, the Hermits had won the day, or so it seemed.

If the Hermits emerged the victorious party, it was not an easy fight. The extant documents would seem to imply that the major issue involved was simply that the abbot of San Pietro wanted sure proof and documentation that Pope John XXII had really granted the privileges to the Hermits that they were claiming, which was not an unreasonable request. Yet it is hard to imagine how such holding out for evidence was the cause of scandal and unrest (*scandalum et tumultus*) among the populace. Implications of improper actions on the part of the Hermits, unjust appropriation and even thievery can be seen in the letter of protest of the Commune to John XXII as well as in William of Cremona's exhortations to the Lombard Province. We cannot know for sure, but the conflict apparently went beyond the request for an official copy of the papal Bull. And surely it would have, since the issue viscerally affected the regulation of the religious life of the parish of San Pietro, and that of the religious and economic life of the Canons of the monastery there. Moreover, what the Hermits were claiming were the privileges granted them, namely, a shared residency and custodianship, seemed to be so unusual that simply to take their word for it would have been imprudent. The tensions between the Augustinian Canons and Augustinian Hermits in Pavia transcended the bantering and maneuvering between two religious groups for prestige, privilege, and power; at the base thereof were the fundamentals of the religious life of the parish and Commune, as well as those of the two Orders. This was no abstract debate. If there was mud-slinging, and there certainly was, there was good cause: at stake was the daily life of parishioners, and the economic and political life of two international religious organizations. And yet, there was even more.

In his treatment of John XXII's grant of custody of St. Augustine's body to the Hermits in his *Liber Vitasfratrum*, Jordan of Quedlinburg noted that the Hermits had considerable difficulties at first, but were finally able to take up residence there thanks to the help of King John of Bohemia, who was at that time ruling in Pavia.[27] When

---

[26] *CDP* 32 (71–73).
[27] "Et quidem licet in principio haud modica resistentia fuerit, demum tamen opitulatione illustrissimi domini Johannis regis Bohemiae, tunc in Papia dominantis, fratres possessionem pacificam sunt adepti." *VF* 1,18 (64,71–73).

Veneranda sanctorum was issued, Pavia, a Ghibelline commune, was under the rule of the Visconti, who for the past ten years had been in a bitter battle with the papacy. Galeazzo Visconti was Duke of Milan and politically, at least for the time being, was able to thumb his nose at John XXII's attempts to cower the Lombard cities into obedience by imposing the interdict on Milan on 23 January 1322. Matteo Visconti had already been excommunicated as early as December 1317. The Visconti were maneuvering between political alliances against the pope with the French and the Emperor Louis of Bavaria, though they were by no means ready simply to fall in behind the German.[28] Three weeks after the showdown between the Canons and Hermits in the Cathedral at Pavia, Louis of Bavaria, who was already encamped in northern Italy at this time, left Trent and entered Milan, before proceeding on to Rome, where he was crowned emperor on 17 January 1328.[29] On May 12, Louis named the Franciscan Pietro da Corbara as Pope Nicholas V, and pronounced John XXII excommunicated and deposed, a sentence that John XXII had already lain on Louis four years previously, on 23 March 1324.

The situation was anything but clear and simple. As the Hermits were trying to take up residency in San Pietro's in Pavia, they were doing so with the emperor having been excommunicated, declared a heretic, and having a crusade called for against him, while the pope had also been excommunicated and deposed by the emperor and his anti-pope. Pavia itself was under the interdict that had been imposed upon the Visconti, and John XXII was calling on the aid of Robert d'Anjou to combat Louis' attempts to form a Ghibelline league in Lombardy under his own leadership. Louis was making friends with no one, and having returned from Rome to the North where he ran into conflict with the Visconti, had based himself in Pavia from where he was trying to gather together the military and financial resources for his fight against the papacy. His legitimacy for doing so, as well as his legitimacy for his entire Italian campaign, was based on the political theory of a member of his court who had accompanied him to Italy, Marsilius of Padua and his *Defensor Pacis*,

---

[28] For the complex political developments in Lombardy at this time, see Mollat, *The Popes at Avignon*, 76–110; and Pauler, *Die deutschen Könige*, 144–164. The account that here follows is drawn from these two works.

[29] Mollat, *The Popes at Avignon*, 206.

a treatise, as we saw in the previous chapter, that had been condemned by John XXII based on the fierce rebuttal offered by the architects of the papal political theory, namely, the Augustinian Hermits William of Cremona and Augustinus of Ancona. Both the emperor and the pope fought with more than finances, armies, and political allies: they both fought a war of words and ideas in justifying their positions as the rightful head of Christendom. Shortly after William of Cremona sent his refutation of *Defensor Pacis* to John XXII, the Pope granted William's petition for the Hermits to have custody of Augustine's body with the Bull *Veneranda sanctorum*, a proposal the Canons and Commune of Pavia found scandalous, causing tumult among the Ghibelline population which was at the time under interdict. There was little chance for the Hermits to be able to effect their newly gained privileges, especially when Louis came to town to set up camp, and expelled the Canons from the monastery of San Pietro to appropriate it for his own use in re-establishing the ancient imperial residency of the Saxon emperors in the Kingdom of Lombardy.

Louis' attempts to establish imperial hegemony in Northern Italy, much less over the papal states and Christendom as such, failed. Little would we have known, however, of his taking over the monastery of San Pietro in Pavia had it not been for Jordan's note regarding King John of Bohemia. We find the clarification in the autobiography of the reigning emperor when Jordan completed his *Liber Vitasfratrum*, Charles IV. In referring to the period of Louis' Italian campaign, Charles wrote that at that time he had been residing in the monastery of the Augustinians in Pavia, from which Louis expelled the abbot and Canons. Later, Charles recalled them to the very monastery that John XXII had handed over to the Hermits during the time when his father, King John of Bohemia, ruled Pavia, who himself had restored the monastery to the Hermits' possession.[30] King

---

[30] "Ego autem manebam illo tempore in monasterio S. Augustini, ubi corpus suum iacet in Papia, de quo monasterio expulerat Ludovicus de Bavaria Abbatem et Canonicos Regulares illius monasterii, quod ego revocans in praedictum monasterium introduxi; quod monasterium post obitum illorum fratrum papa Johannis Augustinianis, quorum Ordo hodie possidet, contulit, dominante patre meo, quibus pater meus possessionem tradidit." *Commentarius de vita Caroli Bohemiae regis et postea imperatoris IV, ab ipso Carolo conscriptus, Rerum Bohemicarum antiqui scriptores aliquot insignes...* Ex bibliotheca Marquardi Freheri (Hannoviae, 1602), 90, as cited in *VF*, 455, n. 25; cf. *CDP*, xxxix, n. 2.

John was following a political strategy of trying to secure his own interests by playing both to Louis and to the pope, though both sides were wary. His opportunity came in 1330, when Louis' desired Ghibelline alliance fell apart, the year that Mollat saw as:

> a decisive one in the history of the Italian peninsula: the threat from the Empire which had hung over Italy for so long finally disappeared under the concerted attacks from the Guelphs, Robert of Anjou and the Church... From this time, the names Guelph and Ghibelline ceased to have any real meaning, and Italy was only to witness the conflict of regional interests between cities or tyrants desiring to extend their domination over their neighbours.[31]

Galeazzo Visconti had died in 1328, and his successor in Milan, his son Azzo had had about enough of Louis. Azzo reconciled with the Pope, who in turn lifted the interdict. Louis' prospects thus worsened, and in February of 1330, he gave up and returned across the Alps to Germany, where at least he could rule as sole emperor, his rival, Frederick of Austria having just died on 13 January.[32]

Eight months later, Brescia was being besieged by Mastino della Scala, the tyrant of Verona. The Brescians had asked Robert d'Anjou for help, but to no avail, and thus, with Louis safely back on German soil, they turned to the descendent of Emperor Henry VII, King John of Bohemia, who entered Brescia on Christmas Eve. By that time the Bohemian King's intrigues had been sufficiently successful that he had been granted the *signoria* not only of Brescia, but also of Bergamo, Mantua, Como, Vercelli, Novara, Lucca, Parma, Modena, Reggio, Bobbio, and—Pavia.[33] On 5 June 1331, William of Cremona was finally able to produce the Bull *Veneranda sanctorum* and present it to the abbot and Canons of San Pietro in Ciel d'Oro in Pavia, whereupon the Hermits were received into the monastery, even with a kiss of peace. The conflict was settled, thanks to the intervention of King John, and much more.

This was the story of the Hermits gaining possession of Augustine's body: novelty, scandal, political intrigue, scheming and shamming, and just plain power politics, papal interdicts and excommunications, imperial assertions and force, armies and florins, from the Visconti

---

[31] Mollat, *The Popes at Avignon*, 102.
[32] See Müller, *Der Kampf Ludwigs des Baiern*, 244–246.
[33] Pauler, *Die deutschen Könige*, 165.

in the North to King Robert d'Anjou in the South with Pope John XXII in the middle, imperial pretensions of universal empire, and papal declarations of universal sovereignty, a masterful political *quid pro quo*, a battle of money, a battle of armies, a battle of traditional rights and privileges, a battle for civic independence and dominance, a battle of tyrants, a battle of ideas, ideals, and political theory, and a fight for the religious identity of a parish, a community, and a religious Order. This was the reality. Yet this was only the beginning.

The kiss of peace in the summer of 1331 between Lanfranc and the abbot of San Pietro's may have initiated a harmonious common life for both the Canons and Hermits of St. Augustine in Pavia, but the dispute regarding which Order actually had the right to be called the Order of St. Augustine, and thus to have rightful, legitimate custody of Augustine's tomb was just heating up. The debate between the Hermits and Canons continued long after the issue had been officially settled legally, becoming a late medieval *cause célèbre*, extending all the way to the eve of the Reformation.[34] Already in the early 1330s a Canon wrote a treatise against the privileged state of the Hermits, brashly stating his intent to demonstrate that:

> ... blessed Augustine is neither the unique father nor patron of the aforesaid brother Hermits, nor are the hermits the special sons of blessed Augustine in any sense other than are the Friar Preachers or any other religious whatsoever who are bound by the *Rule* of blessed Augustine, such as the Regular Canons. In short, the Hermits were founded neither uniquely nor especially by blessed Augustine. Further, I will show that blessed Augustine never wore the habit of the hermits, nor that he wrote their *Rule* or gave them their way of life, nor that he lived with them personally, but rather, he lived with the Regular Canons, for whom he principally and uniquely handed down a way of life and wrote a *Rule* based on their living together, from which the Regular Canons get their name.[35]

---

[34] Kaspar Elm, "*Augustinus Canonicus-Augustinus Eremita*: A Quattrocentro *Cause Célèbre*," in *Christianity and the Renaissance. Image and Religious Imagination in the Quattrocentro*, ed. Timothy Verdon and John Henderson (Syracuse, 1990): 83–107; see also volume two, *The Failed Reformation*.

[35] "Intendo in hoc opusculo clare ac lucide demonstrare... quod beatus Augustinus non est praedictorum fratrum heremitarum singularis pater nec patronus, nec ipsi fratres heremitae ipsius beati Augustini filii speciales nec singulares aliter quam sunt fratres praedicatores vel alii religiosi quicumque, qui regula beati Augustini innituntur, alii tamen a canonicis regularibus. Ita quod, breviter, ab ipso beato Augustino nec specialiter nec singulariter sunt instituti. Item quod ipse beatus Augustinus habitum istorum fratrum heremitarum numquam detulit nec portavit nec eorum regulam

This anonymous Canon may already have been responding to assertions of the Hermits. Virtually simultaneous with the reality of the debate between the Hermits and Canons in Pavia was a literary battle that brought the controversy to a higher level, from that of political maneuvering, to the creation of religious myth. The legitimacy of the Order was at stake, and the Hermits met the challenge in providing the Order with its myth of origins, and consequently, with its identity. *Veneranda sanctorum* was not the only document the Hermits produced.

In moving to an analysis of the texts authored by Augustinian Hermits in the late 1320s and early 1330s in which one finds the creation of the Augustinian myth, it is important to keep in mind the context of their composition: the religio-political reality of early fourteenth-century Pavia. The situation the Order faced was one that threatened its legitimacy and indeed, its very existence. In this context, Augustinians appealed to the mythic origins of the OESA when Augustine re-established order from the chaos of his dispersed heirs. The Augustinian myth provided the meaning and foundation for the reality of the Order's way of life; it was its guide, model, and identity.[36] The early fourteenth-century hermits constructed a biography of Augustine that gave historical proof of their Order's historical primacy, and formed the foundation for the Order's platform as the true sons of their father Augustine. The literary endeavor to establish the Hermits as the only original Order of Augustine was as detailed and masterful as were the Order's political machinations.

---

nec modum vividendi eis tradidit nec conscripsit nec cum eis personaliter convixit, sed potius cum regularibus canonicis, quibus principaliter et singulariter convivendo certum vivendi modum et certum regulam, a qua regulares canonici nuncupantur, tradidit et conscripsit." Vat. Bib. Apost., MS Vat. Reg. 565, fol. 1ᵛ, as quoted by Arbesmann, "Henry of Friemar's 'Treatise on the Origin and Development of the Order of the Hermit Friars and its True and Real Title,'" *Aug(L)* 6 (1956), 37–145; 59. Arbesmann notes that "the manuscript [itself] was written in 1354 by the Canon Regular Durandus de Aln (Ahlen in Westphalia?)." *Ibid.*, 58, n. 57.

[36] See Saak, "The Creation of Augustinian Identity," 113–114. As Mircea Eliade has argued, "It is the irruption of the sacred into the world, an irruption narrated in the myths, that establishes the world as a reality... To tell how things came into existence is to explain them and at the same time indirectly to answer another question: why did they come into existence? The why is always implied in the how—for the simple reason that to tell how a thing was born is to reveal an irruption of the sacred into the world, and the sacred is the ultimate cause of all real existence." Eliade, *The Sacred and the Profane*, (New York, 1957), 97.

To perceive how the Hermits went about creating their myth of Augustine from the reality of early fourteenth-century papal-imperial politics, we first need to turn to the medieval literary tradition of Augustine's biography, which provides the requisite background to the Hermits' ideological achievement.

II. The Medieval Augustine

The Middle Ages were not lacking for eulogies to Augustine. Long before the controversy between the Hermits and Canons broke out, Peter Comestor had already in the twelfth century claimed that by his expositing holy scriptures and by his being the wise architect of the apostolic life in providing his *Rule*, Augustine became an Abraham, the father of many.[37] When in the early fourteenth century members of the OESA wrote Augustine's biography anew, they had ample material upon which to draw that lauded Augustine's life, teaching, and influence. The biographies of Augustine written by Possidius, Philip of Harvengt, and Jacobus de Voragine formed the base upon which the late medieval Augustinians built their own mythic accounts. Two elements of Augustine's *curriculum vitae* were of particular importance: first, when and where he first established a monastery; and second, when he composed his *Rule*, and for whom. Minute alterations of the details could have enormous consequences for representations of Augustine as having originally been the father of the Hermits, or the founder of the Regular Canons. To perceive the importance of the shifts in emplotments central to the emergence of

---

[37] Comestor *Serm.* 32 (198,1707). Sermo 32 presents a lengthy analogy between Augustine and Abraham. The typology of Augustine as an *alter Abraham* continued, as we find in a sermon of the Bishop of Avignon, Fernandus de Hispania, preached in 1352: "... [Augustinus est] gloriosus Christi confessor velut alter Abraham...". This sermon is embedded in Jor. *OD* (ed. Strassburg, 1484; unpaginated), sermo 150. It appears in the midst of a series of Jordan's sermons on Augustine (*sermones* 129–151). The rubric reads: "Sermo de sancto Augustino, factus a magistro Fernando de Hispania persona saeculari et episcopo in Avinione, praesentibus omnibus cardinalibus, anno domini Mccclii." Josef Kürzinger has also pointed to a manuscript of this sermon, Munich, BStB MS Clm. 18223, which gives the same rubric on fol. 233ᵛ; see J. Kürzinger, *Alfonsus Vargas Toletanus und seine theologische Einleitungslehre*, BGPhThMA 29 (Münster, 1930), 98–99. *Cf.* "Sancti Augustini commendationes diversorum doctorum: Augustinus est alter magnus Abraham..." Simon de Bruna, OESA (d. 1448), *Collectanea*, Brünn, UB, MS A. 87 (IV. Z. e. 11), fol. 24ᵛ; as cited by Zumkeller *MSS* nr. 776 (357).

the Hermits' account, one must have the traditional rendering of the "Medieval Augustine" clearly in mind, the textual substratum for the later medieval re-inscription of Augustine's life.

A. *Possidius*

The foundational account of Augustine's biography for the Middle Ages was the *Vita Sancti Aurelii Augustini* of Possidius (d. c. 437), the bishop of Calamo, who had spent many years as Augustine's companion. Possidius set out to present the origin, development, and final end of his hero Augustine, based on his own personal experience.[38]

In Possidius' *Vita*, the overwhelming image of Augustine that emerges is that of the Church Father. Possidius first treated the period from Augustine's conversion to his ordination and founding a monastery in Hippo. He then turned to Augustine's campaign against the Manicheans, Donatists, Arians, and Pelagians. Augustine's daily life as bishop follows, and Possidius continued by relating Augustine's last days, from the writing of the *Retractationes* to his death and burial. The theme stressed is the triumph of the Church effected by Augustine; day by day the unity of peace and the brotherly love of God's Church increased, achieved by Augustine's work.[39]

In comparison with later *vitae*, the space given to Augustine's early life by Possidius is notably meager. Augustine's birth, early education, and conversion are all treated by Possidius in the first chapter, which is not of exceptional length. In chapter two Possidius presented a brief discussion of Augustine abandoning his position as *rhetor* and his decision to become a *servus dei* at the age of thirty.[40] Chapter three continues with Augustine's return to Africa and in chapter four, Possidius recounts how Augustine was made presbyter by acclamation, orchestrated by Valerius, the bishop of Hippo.[41] Then follows what would become the central issue for the Augustinian myth: Augustine's establishment of a monastery. "Directly upon being made presbyter," chapter five begins,

---

[38] Possid. vita Aug. Praef. (38,22–26; *PL* 32,33). Possidius' *Vita* also formed the basis for miscellaneous anonymous *Vitae Sancti Augustini* in medieval collections of saints lives, such as the *Vitae Sancti Augustini* contained in Paris, BnF MS lat. 11750, fol. 148^r–151^v (11th cent.); Paris, BnF MS lat. 11753, fol. 122vb–128rb (12th cent.); and Paris, BnF MS lat 11758, fol. 163va–188ra (13th cent.).

[39] Possid. vita Aug. 13 (82,1–6; *PL* 32,44).

[40] Possid. vita Aug. 2 (44,1–46,4; *PL* 32,34–36).

[41] Possid. vita Aug. 3–4 (48,1–52,25; *PL* 32,36–37).

... Augustine founded a monastery within the church compound, and began to live with the servants of God according to the custom and way of life established by the holy apostles: essentially, that no one in that society would possess anything of their own, but everything would be held in common, and that [goods] would be distributed to each on the basis of need; which he had previously done when he returned from across the sea to his homeland.[42]

Possidius continued to emphasize Augustine's monasticism and its influence on the growth of the Church. Augustine having been made bishop, and with the progress of true doctrine increasingly winning out over heresy, "serving God in the monastery under and with St. Augustine, clergy of the church of Hippo began to be ordained... From that monastery, which began and grew through that memorable man, the peace and unity of the Church first asked with great desire and then received clergy and bishops, which continued thereafter."[43] Possidius himself knew of at least ten monks whom Augustine sent forth to various churches, and these in turn founded monasteries. Thus Augustine's influence, way of life, and teaching spread throughout Africa and beyond.[44]

Possidius gave a detailed description of Augustine's daily life as a monk, including information on his dress, eating habits—noting especially his view on the healthiness of drinking wine in moderation[45]—and admonitions against associations with women, all of which became standard in later medieval accounts. Yet on two points Possidius gave less than clear cut answers, which opened the door to imagination, manipulation, and creation when these two issues became the center of heated controversy: the foundation of Augustine's *first* monastery and the composition of his *Rule*. As mentioned above, Possidius expressly tells of Augustine founding a monastery upon becoming

---

[42] "Factus ergo presbyter monasterium intra ecclesiam mox instituit et cum Dei servis vivere coepit secundum modum et regulam sub sanctis apostolis constitutam: maxime ut nemo quicquam proprium in illa societate haberet, sed eis essent omnia communia, et distribueretur unicuique sicut opus est, quod iam ipse prior fecerat, dum de transmarinis ad sua remeasset." Possid. vita Aug. 5 (52,1–8; *PL* 32,37).

[43] "Proficiente porro doctrina divina, sub sancto et cum sancto Augustino in monasterio Deo servientes ecclesiae Hipponensi clerici ordinari coeperunt... ex monasterio quod per illum memorabilem virum et esse et crescere coeperat magno desiderio poscere atque accipere episcopos et clericos pax Ecclesiae atque unitas et coepit primo et postea consecuta est." Possid. vita Aug. 11 (72,1–11; *PL* 32,42).

[44] Possid. vita Aug. 11 (74,12–26; *PL* 32,42).

[45] Possid. vita Aug. 22 (120,8–11; *PL* 32,51–52).

presbyter. He does not, however, indicate that this was Augustine's first such foundation. Although he writes that in this monastery Augustine, "began to live with the servants of God according to the custom and way of life established by the holy apostles," the verb 'began' is ambiguous, since after expositing just what such a life entailed based on Acts 4:32–35, Possidius adds the phrase, "which he had previously done when he returned from across the sea to his homeland."[46] Such a formulation gave later authors the leeway to claim, at least implicitly, that Augustine had previously lived as a monk, if not having already established a monastery himself well before having been ordained a priest.[47] Such ambiguity could have been avoided had Possidius mentioned Augustine's authorship of a monastic rule, which was to become the second major pillar in the later debates. Indeed, Possidius' silence on this issue has contributed to the controversies surrounding the authenticity of the Augustinian *Rule* to the present day.[48]

Much of the late medieval controversy between the Augustinian Canons and Augustinian Hermits over which Order was most authentically Augustine's true heir, revolved around the issue of which Order was the first to have received the *Rule* from Augustine. Had Possidius been explicit on this point, perhaps by the fourteenth century it would have been moot. Yet nowhere in his *Vita* did Possidius even allude to the *Regula Sancti Augustini*. There is, perhaps, an indirect reference. The passage in question is Possidius' explication of Augustine having lived "according to the custom and way of life established by the holy apostles." Possidius takes his exposition from Acts 4:32–35, which is also to be found in the *Rule*. Luc Verheijen has pointed out that the particular sequence of Acts 4:32 and 4:35 is found only twice in all patristic literature: in Possidius' *Vita* and in the *Regula Sancti Augustini*.[49] This is at least suggestive evidence that Possidius knew the *Rule*, even though he did not explicitly attribute such a work to Augustine. In any event, later authors were not content to leave the matter as seemingly open as did Possidius. Although basing their accounts to a large extent on Possidius, both Augustinian

---

[46] Possid. vita Aug. 5 (52,7–8; *PL* 32,37).
[47] For discussion on the importance of this phrase in later accounts, see B. Rano, "San Agustín y los orígenes de su Orden," 679–710.
[48] See above, Introduction, n. 29.
[49] L. Verheijen, *Règle*, 2:89–95.

Canons and Hermits went considerably beyond their source regarding the details of Augustine's early monastic experience, while at the same time taking over from Possidius the centrality of the monastic life to Augustine's biography and paternity.

B. *Philip of Harvengt*

In the mid twelfth century, the Premonstratensian abbot of the monastery of Bonne Espérance near Cambrai, Philip of Harvengt (d. c. 1182), composed his *Vita Sancti Augustini*, which Jordan of Quedlinburg would later refer to as the *Legenda famosa*. The Premonstratensians, according to Jacques de Vitry, himself an Augustinian canon at Oignies beginning in 1211, had been founded by Norbert of Xanten as a reform of the Regular Canons living under the Augustinian *Rule*.[50] That Philip was deeply concerned with fostering the truly religious life is evidenced by his treatise *De institutione clericorum*, which, although written for clerics in general, "is nevertheless a discussion of the clerical and cloistered life which is addressed by a regular canon to members of his own order."[51] According to Carolyn Bynum, the canonical movement of the twelfth century, to which the Premonstratensians belonged, in its renewed search for following the apostolic life represents "a fundamental turning point in the history of Christianity, a change perhaps as deep and as lasting as the fragmentation of the church in the sixteenth century or the spread of Christianity in the second to fourth centuries A.D."[52] The defining characteristic of the new spirituality was the emphasis on teaching and edifying within the context of the "mixed life," whereby the *vita activa* is given equal weight with the *vita contemplativa*, signified by the exhortation "to teach by word and example" (*docere verbo et exemplo*, and its equivalents). In summing up the different orientations of monks and canons, Bynum notes that "canonical authors see regular canons as teachers and learners, whereas monastic authors see monks only as learners."[53] In his sermons on St. Augustine, Peter Comestor, an Augustinian Canon in the abbey of Saint-Loup at

---

[50] Jac.V. *HO* 22 (133,3–12).
[51] Caroline Walker Bynum, *Docere verbo et exemplo. An Aspect of Twelfth-Century Spirituality*, Harvard Theological Studies 31 (Missoula, Montana, 1979), 13.
[52] *Ibid.*, 1.
[53] *Ibid.*, 35.

Troyes as early as 1135/36, who later retired to St. Victor, was clear that Augustine was more than just the giver of the *Rule*: Augustine was the renewer of the apostolic life, providing the Canons with their lives' simplicity, chastity, and humility, leading them from his own table to that of Christ. Augustine served as a new Abraham.[54] In this context, Philip of Harvengt wrote his life of Augustine, who was, in Philip's words, "the perfect imitator of the apostles."[55]

Philip's life of Augustine differs from that of Possidius most notably in the former's attention to Augustine's early life. Of the thirty-three chapters comprising Philip's biography, the first fourteen cover the period from Augustine's birth to his baptism, as compared with the single chapter devoted to the same material in Possidius' *Vita*.[56] Philip drew his material from the *Confessions*, including the account of Augustine's conversion experience, omitted by Possidius. Philip then narrated Augustine's decision to become a *servus dei*, his return to Africa and becoming presbyter, before recounting his election to the episcopacy and daily life as bishop. Augustine's old age follows, including the election of Augustine's successor, Heraclius, the invasion of the Vandals and Goths into Africa, and the miracles Augustine performed before his death, expanding those related by Possidius.[57] Philip followed the same procedure for his treatment of Augustine's death and burial, before turning in his final chapter to the translations of Augustine's body, the first being from Hippo to Sardinia, which Philip simply relates with the comment that how this occurred, when it occurred, or by whom, he could not say, since he was not able to find a source.[58] Philip does, however, give a rather lengthy account of the *translatio secunda*, brought about by Luitbrandus, king of the Lombards, who brought Augustine's body back to Pavia and built San Pietro in Ciel d'Oro to house the relics, for which Philip expresses his deep admiration and envy.[59] Augustine, for Philip, was not simply the legislator of the Augustinian Canons, but was their

---

[54] Comestor *Serm.* 30 (1790–1792), and note 37 above.
[55] ". . . [Augustinus] qui perfectus fuit imitator eorum [*scil.* apostolorum] . . ." Phil. vita Aug. 33 (1234).
[56] Phil. vita Aug. 1–14 (1205–1215); *cf.* Possid. vita Aug. 1 (42–44; *PL* 32,34–35).
[57] Phil. vita Aug. 30 (1227–1228); *cf.* Possid. vita Aug. 29 (156,11–158,30; *PL* 32,39).
[58] Phil. vita Aug. 33 (1230–1231).
[59] Phil. vita Aug. 33 (1234).

model and teacher: Augustine "is the splendor and embodiment of our profession, he is the mirror and measure of our religion."[60]

After Augustine renounced his position as *rhetor* and was baptized by Ambrose, he returned to Africa and first came to Carthage, where he enjoyed the hospitality of Innocentius.[61] He then returned to Thagaste, where he lived as a layman for a period of three years together with his friends, passing his time with study, teaching, and writing.[62] When Augustine visited Hippo, he was conscripted by the congregation and Bishop Valerius for their new priest, which he accepted, as both Possidius and Philip relate, only with tears for having to leave his contemplative life. Most aware of Augustine's disposition to the monastic life, Valerius gave him a garden in which he could establish a monastery, and live in community according to the rule of the apostles, "as he had already done," Philip affirms, "when he had returned from across the sea to his homeland."[63] Here Philip simply borrowed from Possidius, often word for word, except for the addition of Valerius' donation of a garden for Augustine's first monastery. This is Philip's first mention of Augustine's formal foundation of a monastery, although, as Possidius, he seems to imply that Augustine had lived a monastic life already in Thagaste with his repetition of the phrase, *which he had previously done when he returned from across the sea to his homeland*. Like Possidius, Philip did not mention here Augustine having composed a monastic *Rule* for his monastery. Three chapters later, however, Philip relates Augustine's election to the episcopacy, followed by his battle against heresy, and, having been made bishop, his founding a monastery in the episcopal residency, where he lived in common with his priests. From this monastery,

---

[60] "... non mediocriter arguendus est culpae qui se clericum profitetur, nisi Augustinum praeceptorem suum tenere diligat, devote recolat, sedulo veneretur. Ipse quippe est decus et forma hujus nostrae professionis, ipse speculum et regula nostrae religionis." Phil. vita Aug. 31 (1229).

[61] Phil. vita Aug. 17 (1217).

[62] Phil. vita Aug. 18 (1218).

[63] "Tandem flentem et frustra renitentem B. Valerius de turba segregavit, et, licet invitum presbyterum ordinavit. Sciens vero desiderium ejus propositum, quod scilicet cum clericis nihil habentibus, nihil habens optabat vivere, dedit hortum in quo mox aedificato monasterio coepit ejusdem propositi fratres colligere, et cum eis secundum modum et regulam sanctorum vivere apostolorum, ut omnia scilicet essent eis communia et nullus diceret sibi aliquid proprium, et distribueretur unicuique quod esset necessarium. Quod quidem ipse prior jam feceret, quando de transmarini ad sua redierat." Phil. vita Aug. 18 (1219).

Philip, echoing Possidius, claimed that the apostolic life spread and flourished throughout Africa and overseas, following the canonical model as instituted by Augustine.[64] After describing Augustine's daily life as bishop rather briefly, Philip explicitly tells of Augustine's authorship of a monastic *Rule*. Bringing together the servants of God into a regulated community, Augustine taught his brothers the way of living in poverty, chastity, and obedience, so that his group of clerics might truly live a common life. Yet to provide for the continuation of such a life in perpetuity, Augustine composed a monastic *Rule*, which proclaimed the obligations of an inferior in the community, a superior, and the community as a whole. To ensure that such regulations be well-known and followed, he prescribed the reading of the *Rule* each week, and he himself lived by its precepts as an example.[65] Thus whereas Possidius had been silent, Philip was explicit that Augustine founded his first monastery in the garden given him by Valerius, and then a second monastery within the bishop's residence. Only thereafter as bishop did he compose a *Rule* for his clergy, with whom he lived a common life. In Philip's account, Augustine composed his *Rule* for his Canons, and was indeed, the founder of the canonical life, for which he was the mirror and measure. For the twelfth-century Canons, there was no question: the Bishop of Hippo was their founding father.

The canonical tone of Philip's *Vita* is evident not only from his chronology of Augustine's monastic foundations and composing his *Rule*. Philip rewrites Possidius' narrative, giving it a definite canonical color and gloss, whereby it becomes clear that Augustine's episcopal monastery was the beginning of the Regular Canons.[66] Even when Augustine was living a contemplative life in Thagaste before his ordination as presbyter, he fulfilled the office of Mary and Martha,[67] an image not found in Possidius. Moreover, Philip referred to Augustine as teaching *verbo et exemplo*, the hallmark of the canonical ideal.[68] Augustine, for Philip, was not only the great Church Father and legislator of the Regular Canons; he was also their teacher and

---

[64] Phil. vita Aug. 22 (1221).
[65] Phil. vita Aug. 27 (1225).
[66] For the textual comparison of Philip's and Possidius' *vitae*, see Saak, "Augustinian Identity," 122–123.
[67] Phil. vita Aug. 18 (1218).
[68] Saak, "Augustinian Identity," 119.

exemplar, who taught as much by his outward deeds, as by his spoken and written words—*in vultu et habitu, in sermone et moribus*.[69] If Possidius' biography of Augustine idealized Augustine the Bishop, Philip presented a narrative representing Augustine as the founding father of the Regular Canons. Yet just as Philip "rewrote" Possidius, so in the early fourteenth century would Jordan of Quedlinburg and his fellow Augustinians "rewrite" Philip, using his *legenda famosa* as a major source for a new emplotment wherein Augustine was first and foremost the founder and father of the hermits.

C. *The* Legenda Aurea

The third major source contributing to the image of the historical Augustine in the later Middle Ages was the life of Augustine included in Jacobus de Voragine's *Legenda Aurea*. Born c. 1229, Jacobus entered the Dominican Order in 1244, and having studied in Bologna and Genoa, became subprior in Genoa and later prior in Como. After fulfilling various other offices within the Order, Jacobus was named archbishop of Genoa in 1292, an office he held until his death six years later. He is best known as the author, or compiler, of the *Legenda Aurea*, completed during the years 1252–1260.

The *Legenda Aurea* was one of the most widely spread texts in the Middle Ages, extant in various forms in more than 900 manuscripts.[70] The critical edition of the collection consists of 178 chapters, which provided the Order of Preachers with substantial material for its pastoral mission. Chapter 120 is *De Sancto Augustino*.[71] Jacobus' account begins with a general introduction, praising Augustine as excelling all other doctors of the Church, just as the Roman Augustus surpasses all other kings, and thus Augustine alone is worthy of comparison

---

[69] Phil. vita Aug. 24 (1222).

[70] See Barbara Fleith, *Studien zur Überlieferungsgeschichte der Lateinischen Legenda Aurea*, Subsidia Hagiographica, n. 72. Société des Bollandistes (Bruxelles, 1991), 9–16; and idem, "The Patristic Sources of the *Legenda Aurea*. A Research Report," in *The Reception of the Church Fathers in the West*, ed. Irena Backus, 2 vols. (Leiden, 1997): 1:231–287; *cf.* Sherry L. Reames, *The* Legenda aurea. *A Reexamination of Its Paradoxical History* (Madison, WI, 1985), 135–163.

[71] For the use of the *Legenda Aurea* as a handbook for preachers, see Fleith, *Studien*, 37–42. The *Legenda Aurea* also played a role in the Dominican educational system; see *ibid.*, 406–413. For the *Legenda Aurea*'s function in building the Dominican corporate identity, see Füser, "Vom *exemplum Christi*," 36–57.

with the sun.[72] Jacobus then traced Augustine's life, beginning with his birth to Monica and Patricius. As Philip of Harvengt, Jacobus recounted from the *Confessions* Augustine's own recollections of his youth, from his involvement with the Manichees, to his conversion to philosophy, becoming a *rhetor* in Milan, and his increasing adherence to Ambrose.[73] Jacobus then treated Augustine's conversion at some length, drawing from the *Confessions* the major events leading up to the *tolle, lege* scene.[74] The *Vita* continues with Augustine's baptism, immediately after which Ambrose and Augustine together composed the hymn, *Te Deum Laudamus*,[75] followed by his return to Africa with Nebridius and Evodius. In Thagaste Augustine began living a communal life, based on fasting, prayer, study, and teaching, though Jacobus does not claim that Augustine and his community became *servi dei*.[76] Nevertheless, from that community Augustine's fame spread and he was soon made presbyter in Hippo by Valerius, whereupon he founded a monastery of clerics.[77] Jacobus' account continues with brief descriptions of Augustine's service to the Church and elevation to the episcopacy, his daily life and household, and his campaigns against heretics, before relating his last days and death while the Vandals were ravaging Africa, in the year 440, according to Jacobus.[78] The final third of Jacobus' biography is devoted to praises of Augustine by Jerome, Ambrose, Gregory the Great, Prosper, Remigius and Bernard, to the two translations described as well by Philip of Harvengt, and to twelve distinct accounts of the miracles Augustine performed after his death.[79] Jacobus concluded by emphasizing Augustine's ascetic life of shunning riches and honors, and recounting the works he composed.[80]

Jacobus' *Legenda de Sancto Augustino* draws from the *Vitae* of Possidius and Philip of Harvengt, but is markedly different from the two primary biographies. Although throughout the Middle Ages biography and hagiography were closely related genres and often

---

[72] *LA* 120 (841,3).
[73] *LA* 120 (842,22–844,49).
[74] *LA* 120 (844,51–847,100).
[75] *LA* 120 (847,101–104).
[76] *LA* 120 (848,121).
[77] *LA* 120 (848,123–849,129).
[78] *LA* 120 (849,130–856,230).
[79] *LA* 120 (857,254–866,396).
[80] *LA* 120 (866,397–872,521).

indistinguishable, Jacobus' treatment fits more squarely within the latter genre than the former. If Possidius' Augustine was the celebrated bishop of Hippo, and Philip's Augustine's was the exemplary founder of the canonical life, Jacobus' Augustine was the outstanding catholic saint. Whereas both Possidius and Philip introduced their *Vitae* with personal statements of humility before the task of trying to portray the life of such a man of God,[81] Jacobus began directly by singing Augustine's praises, noting how Augustine "was magnificent in his life, famous in his teaching, blessed (*felix*) in his glory."[82] Not only did Jacobus compare Augustine with the Roman Augustus, but also analyzed the etymology of Augustine's name, claiming that it derived from *augeo* and *astin*, which means 'city', and *ana*, which is that which is above (*sursum*). Thus, Augustine is as a heavenly city, the city of God.[83]

In this light, it may not be surprising that Jacobus did not devote much space to the details of Augustine's life, aside from his conversion and death. His purpose was not so much to recount the historical Augustine as it was to reveal the Church's saint.[84] Yet it is noteworthy that in Jacobus' account, Augustine's life is stripped of its monastic components. As mentioned above, Jacobus did not apply the appellation *servus dei* to Augustine when telling of his return to Thagaste, a term that carried monastic connotations, even if somewhat vague, and one that both Possidius and Philip of Harvengt used for Augustine and his followers at that time. Moreover, Jacobus nowhere mentioned Augustine having composed a *Rule*. Even though Jacobus' own Order followed the *Regula Sancti Augustini*,[85] the only reference or allusion to Augustine's monastic life in Jacobus' account, aside from lauding Augustine's ascetic daily life albeit not placed in a monastic setting, is the narrative of Augustine's founding a monastery of clerics upon being ordained presbyter. Immediately upon becoming presbyter, Jacobus writes, Augustine "founded a monastery of clerics and began to live according to the way of life (*regulam*) established

---

[81] Possid. vita Aug. Praef. (38,19–40,42; *PL* 32,33–34); Phil. vita Aug. Prol. (1205).

[82] "... Augustinus dicitur magnificus, felix, praeclarus. Fuit enim magnificus in vita, praeclarus in doctrina, felix in gloria." *LA* 120 (842,19–20).

[83] *LA* 120 (841,10–14).

[84] Reames writes: "The saint's involvement in the ecclesiastical affairs of his day ... goes almost unmentioned in the *Legenda*. Nor does Jacobus preserve many glimpses of Augustine's care for his own flock." Reames, *The Legenda Aurea*, 150–151.

[85] *Cf.* Rano, "San Agustín y los orígenes de su Orden," 670–673.

by the holy apostles; from this monastery approximately ten monks became bishops."[86] Jacobus, however, omitted the qualifying phrase found both in Possidius' and Philip's *Vitae*, namely, *which he had previously done when he returned from across the sea to his homeland.* Jacobus' text gives no basis whatsoever, even for pure speculation, to assert that Augustine had lived a monastic life, even in a non-technical sense, at any time before he became a priest. One cannot explain this omission away by suggesting that perhaps Jacobus was unaware of the earlier treatments. Not only does he explicitly mention Possidius' *Vita* in the introduction to his *Legenda*,[87] but this very account is drawn from Possidius, as is evidenced by the number of monks who became bishops. Possidius mentioned that he personally knew of approximately ten holy, venerable, continent, and learned servants of God, whom Augustine sent out to other churches when asked. Philip of Harvengt gave no such number. Yet Jacobus' truncated account of Possidius is not limited to the omission of the phrase, *which he had previously done when he returned from across the sea to his homeland.* The account of Augustine's monks being sent out from his monastery to serve other churches, thereby spreading Augustine's doctrine throughout Africa and beyond, is found in the *Vitae* of both Possidius and Philip when they narrate Augustine's founding of his *second* monastery, namely, the one he established upon being elevated to the episcopate. Based on the relationship between Jacobus' text and that of Possidius, whereby Jacobus' phrase, . . . *from which monastery about ten bishops were chosen* . . . (. . . *de cujus monasterio fere decem episcopi sunt electi* . . .), echoes Possidius' . . . *for at least ten monks that I knew of . . . blessed Augustine gave to various churches when asked* . . . (. . . *nam ferme decem, quos ipse novi . . . beatus Augustinus diversis ecclesiis . . . rogatus dedit* . . .),[88] Jacobus compressed Augustine's presbyterial and episcopal monastic foundations into a single event, and divested that institution of its importance to the African Church and Augustine's influence attributed to it by Possidius and Philip of Harvengt. In sum, whereas for Possidius and Philip Augustine's true miracle was his life as a monk-bishop, for Jacobus, Augustine's monasticism was

---

[86] "Qui statim monasterium clericorum instituit et coepit vivere secundum regulam a sanctis apostolis constitutam, de cujus monasterio fere X episcopi sunt electi." *LA* 120 (849,128–129).

[87] *LA* 120 (842,21).

[88] *LA* 120 (849,120); *cf.* Possid. vita Aug. 11 (74,12–15; *PL* 32,42).

incidental at best; Augustine's saintly life was witnessed most of all by the miracles he performed long after his earthly existence. With Jacobus, Augustine's life itself became translated from the genre of hagiographical biography, to biographical hagiography. The biographical and hagiographical components of the "medieval" Augustine, would in the early fourteenth century be combined anew by the Augustinian Hermits in their attempt to recover and reconstruct the "historical" Augustine, conscripted for their own Order's foundation and legitimization, its program and platform.

III. The Creation of the Augustinian Myth

In his *Sermones de sanctis*, composed after 1365, Jordan of Quedlinburg gave a preeminent place to Augustine.[89] Whereas all other doctors of the Church could be compared to stars, Jordan eulogized, echoing Jacobus de Voragine's *Legenda Aurea*, only Augustine was worthy of comparison with the sun.[90] Jordan's estimation of Augustine was so great that he claimed: "... blessed Augustine can be called the city of God ... just as whatever is necessary for life can be had in a city, so in blessed Augustine can be found whatever is necessary for salvation."[91] Jordan even went so far as to assert that Augustine's teaching held such weight, "that nothing in divine scriptures is secure that is not confirmed by his authority."[92] Augustine was the lord and

---

[89] Jordan devoted sermons 129–151 of the 271 sermons of the *Opus Dan* to Augustine; in addition, sermons 59 and 185 are *De translatione Sancti Augustini*.

[90] "... [Augustinus] ceteros ecclesie doctores tam ingenio quam scientia vicit incomparabiliter. Unde cum aliis doctores assimilentur stellis, ipse soli comparatur." Jor. *OD* (ed. Strassburg, 1484), sermo 59D. This image Jordan quoted from *LA* 120 (841,3–4). Jordan did not, however, simply repeat previous praise. For Jordan, Augustine had renewed the apostolic life after the time of the apostles, see *VF* 3,2 (326ff); and he displayed the same perfections as St. Paul: "Et he sex perfectiones accipiuntur penes sex que contigerunt circa apostolum Paulum cum esset in via versus Damascum, que etiam invenimus in beato Augustino. Prima perfectio est divine gratie preveniens illustratio. Secunda est suiipsius omnimodo deiectio. Tertio est divini nutus inspiratio. Quarta est voluntatis in deum totalis transformatio. Quinta est mentis in seipsa ascensio. Sexta est naturalium virium relictio." Jor. *OD* (ed. Strassburg, 1484), sermo 135A.

[91] "... beatus Augustinus civitas dei dici potest ... sicut reperitur in civitate quicquid est necessarium vite, sic in beato Augustino quicquid est necessarium saluti invenitur." Jor. *OD* (ed. Strassburg, 1484), sermo 130B.

[92] "Tante enim autoritatis est eius doctrina, ut nihil in divinis scripturis sit solidum quod non sit eius autoritate confirmatum." Jor. *OD* (ed. Strassburg, 1484), sermo 131A.

head of all doctors of the church; he was the *sapiens architector ecclesie*, having restored the foundation of the apostolic life after the time of the apostles.[93] Augustine was the city on the hill, letting his light shine on all people.[94] As such, Augustine founded his Order of hermits, his true heirs and sons, who were to be the *imitatores Patris nostri Augustini*; as Jordan insisted in his *Liber Vitasfratrum*, the hermits were to follow Augustine as "the exemplar and rule of all our actions."[95] Thus, as Augustine, so was his Order to be the "city of God."[96]

Jordan's praise of his Order's founder was echoed by Augustine's sons throughout the later Middle Ages. The late fourteenth-century Augustinian, Augustinus Novellus de Padua, extolled Augustine's works as exceeding those of all other authors in richness, order, and eloquence.[97] A contemporary, Simon of Cremona (d. after 1390)—the *recollector Hugolini*[98]—uniformly began each of his sermons with a quotation from Augustine, the *lux doctorum*.[99] And the later fifteenth-century general of the Order, Ambrosius de Cora (d. 1485), not only repeated and expanded Jordan's arguments for the primacy of the

---

[93] "Beatissimus Augustinus dominus et caput est omnium doctorum. Nam sicut lux inter corpora habet locum primum, sic et hic inter omnes doctores obtinet principatum. Hic est sanctissimus Augustinus, qui tam sapiens architector ecclesie fundamentum post sanctissimos apostolos construxit et reparavit." Jor. *OD* (ed. Strassburg, 1484), sermo 130A; *cf. VF* 3,3 (330,3–332,54).

[94] "... beatus Augustinus fuit civitas non abscondita sed manifesta cunctibus gentibus." Jor. *OD* (ed. Strassburg, 1484), sermo 130B; "Nam sicut sol est fontale principium luminis ipsam lunam et stellas illustrans et ad omnem partem suos radios diffundens, sic beatus Augustinus lumen sue sapientie in omnes alios diffundens, quia revera hodie omnes doctores palpitarent in tenebris ignorantie nisi haurirent de fonte sapientie ... alii doctores comparantur stellis, Augustinus autem soli, quia sicut sol illuminat totum mundum, sic Augustinus totam ecclesiam perfudit lumine sue sapientie et doctrine." Jor. *OD* (ed. Strassburg, 1484), sermo 185C.

[95] "... beatissimus Pater noster Augustinus, qui debet esse omnis nostrae actionis exemplar et regula..." *VF* 1,11 (36,32–33).

[96] *Cf. LA* 120 (841,12–15).

[97] "... [Augustinus] omnes formae scriptores, qui de rebus sanctis sive in ipsis gentilium sive in nostris litteris ediderint, ubertate, ordine et elegantia superavit." Aug.Nov. *Sermo*, fol. 223[r].

[98] See D. Trapp, "Augustinian Theology of the Fourteenth Century. Notes on Editions, Marginalia, Opinions and Booklore." *Aug(L)* 6 (1956), 146–274; 255–263.

[99] Sim.C. *OEp*.: "... quia ut ait lux doctorum Augustinus de trinitate...," fol. 1[r]; "... doctorum lux Augustinus libro de sancta virginitate capitulo 42..." fol. 7[r]; "... lux doctorum Augustinus in sermone..." fol. 211[v]; "... lux doctorum Augustinus libro de oratione dominica..." fol. 222[r]. Simon's sermons are extant in thirty-two manuscripts and were printed in Reutlingen in 1484; see Zumkeller *MSS* nr. 787 (366–368). Zumkeller gives the title as *Sermones super epistolas dominicales*; in the

OESA as the only true heirs of the historical Augustine, but also claimed that the hermits were the first *fratres* to have preached the Gospel to the people.[100] Singing Augustine's praises was certainly not unique to members of the *Ordo Eremitarum Sancti Augustini*. Yet such hyperbole assumed additional shades of meaning in the writings of the friars. It was not just Augustine who was lauded, but Augustine as the historical founder of the Order.

The creation of the Augustinian myth can be detected and illustrated in five texts, all written between 1322 and 1343. The first is an anonymous *Vita* of Augustine; the second, an anonymous treatise on the origins of the OESA; the third, is Nicholas of Alessandria's *Sermo de Beato Augustino*; the fourth is Henry of Friemar's *Tractatus de origine et progressu ordinis fratrum heremitarum et vero ac proprio titulo eiusdem*; and the fifth, is Jordan of Quedlinburg's *Vita Sancti Augustini*. When read in light of the "Medieval Augustine," these texts evidence the creation of the mythic Augustine, the appropriation of Augustine for the OESA.[101]

A. *The* Vita Aurelii Augustini Hipponensis Episcopi

Manuscript Plut. 90 sup. 48 of the Biblioteca Laurenziana in Florence begins with an anonymous *Vita Aurelii Augustini Hipponensis Episcopi*.[102] Though the manuscript was written in 1470, the *Vita* was originally

---

Tübingen MS Simon refers to his work as "... opus epistolarum dominicalium totius anni...," fol. 1ʳ. The appellation of Augustine as the *lux doctorum* is seen already in a hymn on Augustine from the later thirteenth century: "Salve lux et dux doctorum/malleus haereticorum/conterens perfidiam." F.J. Mone, *Lateinische Hymnen des Mittelalters aus Handschriften herausgegeben und erklärt*, 3 vols. (Freiburg, 1853–1855), 3:205, nr. 815.

[100] "Ubi nota, quod primi fratres, qui praedicaverunt evangelium populo, fuerunt fratres heremitarum Sancti Augustini." Ambr.C. *Chron.* (ed. Rome, 1481), 742; Ambr.C. *Def.* (ed. Rome, 1481), 499–616; see also Balbino Rano, "San Agustín y su Orden en Algunos Sermones de Agustinos del Primer Siglo (1244–1344)," *AAug.* 53 (1990), 7–93.

[101] For the entire discussion that follows, *cf.* Rano, "San Agustín y los orígenes de su Orden." For my interpretation of the historical narratives here discussed, I have drawn from Arthur C. Danto, *Narration and Knowledge* (New York, 1985); Adam Zachary Newton, *Narrative Ethics* (Cambridge, MA, 1995); Paul Ricoeur, *Time and Narrative*, esp. vol. 3 (Chicago, 1988); Gabrielle M. Spiegel, *The Past as Text. The Theory and Practice of Medieval Historiography* (Baltimore, 1997); and Hayden White, *The Content of the Form. Narrative Discourse and Historical Representation* (Baltimore, 1987).

[102] For a description of the manuscript, and for an analysis of the *Vita*, see R. Arbesmann, "The 'Vita Aurelii Augustini Hipponensis Episcopi' in Cod. Laurent. Plut. 90 Sup. 48." *Traditio* 18 (1962), 319–355.

composed between 1322 and 1331.[103] The codex contains a number of saints' lives, as well as the treatise on the origins of the Order and the *Sermo* to be discussed below. The author of the *Vita* was the prior of Santo Spirito, the Augustinian house in Florence. In the later thirteenth century Santo Spirito flourished, benefiting from the commercial growth of the city, becoming, as Arbesmann states, "the religious and cultural center of the *Oltrarno*. As a matter of fact, soon the whole urban district across the Arno was called after Santo Spirito."[104] From 1287, Santo Spirito was also the site of the Order's *studium generale in Curia Romana*.[105] Thus Arbesmann concludes that the author of the *Vita* "was a man of administrative skill, experienced in the spiritual guidance of a religious community, and possessed of a keen sense for the needs of the time."[106] The manuscript as such is an "organic whole," whereby the anonymous compiler put together a "long line of holy ancestors the Augustinian Hermits of his day could claim for their institute."[107] The Life of Augustine,

> ... may well be called the cornerstone of the entire series. For, in it, Augustine is pictured as the great successor of the two founders and fathers of eremitical monasticism, St. Anthony and St. Paul the first Hermit. The *Vitae* that follow tell us about the virtues and miracles of holy men who distinguished themselves by their common devotion to the eremitical mode of monastic life which St. Augustine is said to have first organized in the western Church.[108]

The author of the *Vita*, which is rather brief, strung together portions of texts from Augustine's *Confessions*, though Arbesmann posits an older *Vita*, no longer extant, that served as the direct source.[109] For present purposes the three interpolations Arbesmann identifies as providing an "eremitical gloss" on the text are of greatest importance. The first is the account of Augustine's baptism. Repeating the inherited lore that after his baptism Augustine and Ambrose composed the hymn *Te deum laudamus* spontaneously in alternating phrases, the *Vita* proceeds to claim that Ambrose then invested Augustine in

---

[103] Arbesmann, "Vita," 331–332.
[104] *Ibid.*, 326–327.
[105] *Ibid.*, 328.
[106] *Ibid.*, 329.
[107] *Ibid.*, 322. For a listing of the contents of the ms. see *ibid.*, 320–321.
[108] *Ibid.*, 322.
[109] *Ibid.*, 336ff.

the habit of a hermit, based on the pseudo-Ambrosian *Sermo de baptismo et conversione S. Augustini*.[110] The second interpolation in the *Vita* Arbesmann points to is the account of Augustine, together with Alipius, Nebridius and Adeodatus, seeking a suitable place for living the monastic life. Finding a group of hermits in Tuscany following the traditions of Paul, the first Hermit, and St. Anthony, Augustine stayed with the Tuscan hermits for some time, and, quoting the *Vita*, "gave to them a way of life (*modus vivendi*), which later he widely established among the clerics and hermits in Africa."[111] The third piece of evidence Arbesmann brings forth is the account drawn from Possidius of Augustine's foundation of a monastery within the Church compound after having been made presbyter. Noting that Augustine had been granted both the permission and land for doing so by Bishop Valerius, the author of the *Vita* then comments as follows: "Likewise he established other monasteries in deserted and wooded places."[112] Taken together, Arbesmann claims:

> The aetiological character of the three interpolations we have discussed is obvious. In the first place, they serve to explain the Order's full title: 'ordo fratrum *heremitarum* sancti Augustini.' Moreover, in our author's time most of the information available concerning the origin of the Order overwhelmingly pointed to Tuscany and the Tuscan Hermits of the thirteenth century. The three legends provided the connecting links between St. Augustine and the Order of the Hermit Friars of St. Augustine as recognized by the popes in the course of that century. They soon became a fixed part in the Order's tradition.[113]

Though the author of the *Vita* gives Augustine's biography an eremitical flavor, he is still rather vague regarding the connections between Augustine's eremiticism, and that of the OESA. In the story of Ambrose investing Augustine in a habit upon his baptism, not found in the previous lives of Augustine, the phrase included in the *Vita* does not describe the habit Augustine assumed as the habit of the Order.[114] The second interpolation is inconclusive as well. While

---

[110] *Ibid.*, 340.

[111] "Cum quibus Augustinus aliquo tempore habitans modum vivendi, quem latius postea in Africa clericis et eremitis constituit, eis dedit." Anon. *Vita*, fol. 7ʳ; as quoted by Arbesmann, "Vita," 341.

[112] "Sic ipse alia monasteria construxit in locis desertis et nemorosis." Anon. *Vita*, fol. 8ʳ; as quoted by Arbesmann, "Vita," 348.

[113] Arbesmann, "Vita," 349.

[114] "... Ambrosio eum cucullam induente et habitum servorum dei..." Anon. *Vita*, fol. 7ʳ.

emphasizing the eremitical desires of Augustine and his associates realized, according to the *Vita*, in Tuscany among the group of hermits following Paul and Anthony, there is no explicit connection between the *modus vivendi* Augustine provided for the group, and the *Regula Sancti Augustini*;[115] the *Vita* only confirms that Augustine gave the Tuscan hermits the same *modus vivendi* that he later established among the clerics and hermits in Africa.[116] The same ambiguity applies to the account of Augustine's establishing a monastery within the church compound after his ordination. Arbesmann seemingly tries to make more of the passage than perhaps is warranted, when he states that after the story found in Possidius, the author of the *Vita* "then rather abruptly adds (fol. 8ʳ): 'Sic ipse alia monasteria construxit in locis desertis et nemorosis.'" Arbesmann then presents the lengthier account of Augustine's monastic foundations as present in the treatise on the Order's origins, using the fuller version to explain the one line of the *Vita*. The line in question, however, does not appear as abrupt when read as the conclusion of the passage and in parallel with Possidius.[117] The line, *Likewise he established other monasteries in deserted and wooded places* (*Sic ipse alia monasteria construxit in locis desertis et nemorosis*) of the *Vita*, interprets Possidius' *which he had previously done when he returned from across the sea to his homeland* (*quod iam ipse prior fecerat, dum de transmarinis ad sua remeasset*), yet in so doing leaves the temporal sequence ambiguous: the author does not specify whether Augustine had established "other monasteries" before or after the monastery he founded as presbyter, whereas Possidius' account is clear regarding Augustine's prior monastic life. Though the phrase *in locis desertis et nemorosis* puts an eremitical spin on the account, the *Vita*, in its rewriting of Possidius, refrains from suggesting an unambiguous relationship between Augustine's early monastic life and the OESA.

---

[115] In analyzing Possidius' statement that Augustine upon being made presbyter *cum dei servis vivere coepit secundum modum et regulam sub sanctis apostolis constitutam*, Verheijen dismisses the association of the terms *modus* and *regula* with a monastic *Rule* in a technical sense: "Mais dans la séquence *secundum modum et regulam*, le terme de *regula* ne peut pas avoir le sens technique de 'règle monastique.' Il doit être plus ou moins identique à celui de *modus*, si bien qu'il faut comprendre selon la facon de vivre..." Verheijen, *Règle*, 2:183.

[116] See Arbesmann, "Vita," 341.

[117] See Saak, "Augustinian Identity," 132–133.

The clearest association of Augustine's eremiticism with that of the OESA is found in a section which Arbesmann considers to be appendices to the *Vita*,[118] the third of which,

> ... is a brief note on the religious Orders which follow the Augustinian *Rule* (fol. 11ᵛ–12ʳ). It reflects the beginning of a long-drawn dispute between the Augustinian Hermits and Canons, both claiming for themselves the privilege of being the first religious Order founded by St. Augustine. Showing himself not averse to scholastic reasoning, our author makes the following subtle distinction. The *ordo fratrum heremitarum sancti Augustini* professes the Augustinian *Rule ex institutione*, that is, on the basis of its foundation by St. Augustine, their institute 'having proceeded from those who had received the said *Rule* from the same father Augustine and had carried his venerable body to Italy.' The *ordo canonicorum regularium*, on the other hand, professes the Augustinian *Rule ex devotione* only, its beginning dating no further back than 'to St. Ruf, bishop in a region of France about the year 1104 from the Incarnation of Our Lord.' Apparently satisfied with having disposed of the difficulty by his clever argument, the author quickly concludes the note with a short reference to the Order of St. Dominic 'and many other Orders of men as well as women.'[119]

There is, however, nothing in the text that states that Augustine *founded* the OESA. In the manuscript, the section of text in question is given the title: *Instituit regulam canonicis*. The text begins by affirming that Augustine "rewrote" the canonical rule which had been handed down by the apostles after Christ's ascension, but had been neglected for a long time. A multitude of religious follow this rule and it is avowed by the church of God.[120] The author then proceeds to mention the Orders that follow the rule:

> From its institution: the Order which is now called [the Order] of hermit brothers of Saint Augustine, which came about from those having received the said *Rule* from the same Father Augustine, and from

---

[118] Arbesmann considers the *Vita* to have three appendices, the first consisting of verses in praise of Augustine, the second, an account of the two translations of Augustine's body, and the third, a discussion of the Orders which follow the Augustinian *Rule*. See Arbesmann, "Vita," 349–353.

[119] Arbesmann, "Vita," 351–352. Arbesmann does not cite the manuscript for his discussion quoted here, though he translates passages therefrom. For the attribution of St. Ruf as the founder of the Canons, see Arbesmann, "Vita," 352.

[120] "*Instituit regulam canonicis*. Hic denique canonicam regulam ab apostolis post ascensionem domini primo traditam, sed longo tempore post neglectam, luculento sermone rescripsit, quam innumerabilis perfecta sequitur multitudo religiosorum et dei ecclesia multiplici illustrantium virtute profitetur." Anon. *Vita*, fol. 11ᵛ–12ʳ.

those having carried his venerable body to Italy. From devotion: the Order of Regular Canons, which was begun by Rufus, bishop in a region of France in the year of our Lord's Incarnation 1110; and the Order of Friar Preachers, which was begun by blessed Dominic in the region of Toulouse approximately in the year of our Lord's Incarnation 1200; and many other Orders of men as well as of women.[121]

There is no question that the OESA is given a special status, following the *Rule ex institutione* whereas all others follow the *Rule ex devotione*. Yet though the OESA arose from those who received the *Rule* from Augustine himself, Augustine did not explicitly write his *Rule* for the hermits. Earlier in the *Vita*, as noted above, the author claimed that Augustine provided the Tuscan hermits with a *modus vivendi*, without, however, explicitly designating such as the *Rule*. Nor is there explicit mention of the *Rule* in the author's discussion of Augustine's written works.[122] Leaving no doubt that the OESA has a special status following the *Rule ex institutione*, and providing an eremitical gloss to Augustine's biography not to be found in previous accounts, the author of the *Vita* is indeterminate with regard both to the composition of the *Rule* and to Augustine's monastic foundations. Moreover, he distances the OESA from Augustine's original group of hermits by referring to Augustine's Order as that Order "which is *now* called the [Order] of Hermits of Saint Augustine [emphasis mine]."[123] The relationship between Augustine's eremiticism and the OESA had not been firmly established. That would be the accomplishment of the prior of Santo Spirito's contemporaries.

B. *The* Initium sive Processus Ordinis Heremitarum Sancti Augustini

The same manuscript that contains the anonymous *Vita* includes as well a treatise on the origins of the OESA with the title *Initium sive Processus Ordinis Heremitarum Sancti Augustini*.[124] The author of the *Initium*,

---

[121] "Ex institutione ordo qui nunc fratrum heremitarum sancti Augustini nuncupatur, qui ex recipientibus ab eodem patro Augustino dictam regulam ac portantibus Italiam eius venerabile corpus evenit. Ex devotione ordo canonicorum regularium, qui ordo Rufo episcopo in partibus Gallie orta annos dominice incarnationis M.CX. [*sic*] incepit. Et ordo fratrum predicatorum, qui a beato Dominico in partibus Tolosanis circa annos dominice incarnationis M.CC. initium habuit. Multique alii ordines tam marium quam mulierum." Anon. *Vita*, fol. 12[r].
[122] Anon. *Vita*, fol. 9[v]
[123] See note 121 above.
[124] Anon. *Vita*, fols. 57[v]–62[v].

as the *Vita*, is not known, though the two works originated in the same general circles. Balbino Rano, the editor of the *Initium*, dates the work approximately to 1330.[125]

The *Initium* places the origins of the OESA within the historical development of western monasticism, with a special focus on the eremitical traditions. Taking Jerome's *Vita sancti Pauli primi eremitae* as his point of departure, the author argues that from the early anchorites, namely, Elias, John the Baptist, Anthony, and Paul the first Hermit, "every Order and religion of the modern religious takes its origin and beginning."[126] Following these first hermits, Basil and Pachomius established the apostolic life in the East,[127] whereas Augustine then did so in the West. After treating Augustine's monastic foundations, the author proceeds to discuss briefly the origins of the other religions, namely, the Benedictines, the Cistercians, the Regular Canons, the Carthusians, the Franciscans, and the Dominicans.[128] He then turns to listing the general priors and the papal approbations of the OESA, beginning in the later twelfth century, and culminating in the Great Union under Alexander IV. His desire to emphasize the antiquity of his Order is clear, when, for example, he begins his discussion of the OESA, having first treated the other Orders, with the phrase, *Ante quorum tempora*.[129] Moreover, he portrays the OESA as the genuine inheritors of the ancient eremitical tradition when he concludes that not only the OESA, "but virtually all religions have their beginning and origin from our ancient fathers."[130] The *Initium* continues with a mystical interpretation of the founders of religious Orders, associating them with Old Testament Fathers. Thus Basil is interpreted as the "ante diluvian" Enoch, and Augustine is equated with Noah, for Noah "entered the Ark of the Lord so that humankind might be saved," and Augustine "entering the Church of God, freed

---

[125] "Debío de ser en un tiempo no posterior aproximadamente al ano 1330." Balbino Rano, "Los dos Primeras Obras Conocidassobre el Origen de la Orden Agustiniana," *AAug*. 45 (1982), 331–376; 335.

[126] "Ab istis namque anachoritis omnis Ordo et religio modernorum religiosorum sumpsit exordium et principium." *Initium* (337).

[127] *Initium* (337).

[128] *Initium* (341). For the treatment of the origins of the other religions, see *Initium* (341–343).

[129] *Initium* (344).

[130] ". . . non tantum nos, sed fere omnes religiones a nostris patribus antiquis initium et principium habuerunt." *Initium* (345).

human kind from heretics."[131] Noah's three sons, Shem, Ham, and Japheth, are then interpreted as the three branches of religious that follow Augustine: "For Shem is interpreted as the Regular Canons, who fight under Augustine's *Rule*. Ham is understood as those who follow Augustine's *Rule* and life out of love. But Japheth is interpreted as those brother hermits, who, since they came to their country, having multiplied, grasp the world with the example of their holy life and the clarity of knowledge."[132] The entire treatise is designed to prove the temporal and qualitative priority of OESA within the religious life of the Church, based on the example of Augustine, who was "not only the father of hermits, but even lived himself as a hermit."[133]

Whereas Augustine's eremiticism and its relationship to the OESA in the *Vita* was indistinct, it is explicit in the emplotment of the *Initium*. Based on the *Confessions* and Possidius, the *Initium* goes far beyond the anonymous *Vita* in reconstructing an account of Augustine's early monastic life and offers conclusive evidence for Augustine's composition of the *Rule* for his first group of hermits, who were the forebears of the OESA.[134]

From the comparison of the *Initium* with the *Vita* and Possidius, a number of observations can be made.[135] Possidius makes no mention of Augustine's composition of a monastic *Rule*, but simply notes his foundation of a monastery upon being made presbyter, though Possidius comments that Augustine had previously lived a monastic life. As discussed above, the *Vita* includes this passage from Possidius, yet "summarizes" the ending of Possidius' account without giving any temporal indication of when Augustine had founded the other

---

[131] "Per patres enim sanctos ante diluvium, quorum Enoch adhuc vivit, patres omnium heremitarum, monachorum, servorum Dei omnium qui ultra mare fuerunt intelligitur beatus Basilius, qui floruit anno CCCLXX, cuius vita et regula usque in presens quam plures vivunt. Per Noë, qui archam Domini, ut salveretur genus humanum, intravit, beatus Augustinus intelligitur, qui intrans Dei Ecclesiam, humanum genus ab hereticis liberavit." *Initium* (345).

[132] "Per quos triplex genus Augustinum sequentium designatur. Nam per Sen intelliguntur canonici regulares, qui sub eius regulam militant. Per Cam, qui ex amoris calore vitam et regulam Augustini sequuntur. Sed per Iaphet, fratres isti heremite, qui ex quo ad terras venerunt exemplo sancte vite et scientie claritate multiplicati mundum comprehendunt." *Initium* (345–346).

[133] "Et multa alia dicit, que manifestissime ostendunt eum non tantum heremitarum patrem, verum etiam ipsum heremitam fuisse." *Initium* (340).

[134] Saak, "Augustinian Identity," 137.

[135] For a comparison of the texts, see *ibid.*

monasteries. The *Vita*, then, in an appendix, includes a discussion of Augustine composing his *Rule*, an account not found in Possidius, nor the other medieval *Vitae*. The *Initium* includes these two passages of text from the *Vita*, but inverts the order. The account of Augustine having composed the *Rule* comes first in the *Initium*, and does so in words very similar to the *Vita*. The comment that Augustine "eloquently put together in writing the apostolic rule handed down by the apostles after the Lord's ascension, but for a long time neglected," appears only in the *Vita* and the *Initium*, which suggests either that one text borrowed from the other, or that both had a common source. Given the textual variations of the phrase between the *Vita* and the *Initium*, it is unlikely that the author of the *Vita* drew from the *Initium*; the text in the *Initium* is far more explicit with regard to Augustine's active composition of the rule and its relationship to the OESA. Whereas the *Vita* gives this account to begin the appendix dealing with Augustine's institution of the rule, referring to Augustine simply in the third person, leaving him unnamed in the text (*Hic denique canonicam regulam . . . rescripsit*),[136] the *Initium* designates Augustine as *beatus pater Augustinus et doctor*. Further, whereas the *Vita* has Augustine "writing again" the canonical rule handed down by the apostles, the *Initium* distances the rule from all canonical connotations, and gives Augustine a far more active role in claiming that blessed father and doctor Augustine "put the apostolic rule together in writing" (*regulam apostolicam . . . conscripsit*).

The *Initium* then continues by discussing the various possible locations for Augustine's first eremitical community. Whereas the *Vita* was vague concerning the chronotopic account of Augustine's monasticism, the *Initium* is explicit: "first in Italy, then in Africa."[137] The precise location of Augustine's first hermitage, however, is left indeterminate; the author of the *Initium* mentions the possibility of Milan, Mons Pisanus, and Centumcellae, but notes that a decisive answer cannot be given due to the length of time ago that this occurred in the past, and to the scarcity of sources (*ex longitudine temporis quam ex pigritia scriptorum*). It could even have been, the author suggests, in several places where this took place. Nevertheless, it was most certainly in Italy, and for that first community, Augustine wrote his

---

[136] Anon. *Vita*, fol. 11ᵛ.
[137] ". . . in Italia primo, deinde in Affrica . . ." *Initium* (338).

Rule.[138] The author continues with a brief discussion of Monica's death, and then includes the passage from Possidius, affirming that upon being ordained presbyter by bishop Valerius, Augustine founded a monastery and lived according to the apostolic rule, "which he had previously done when he returned from across the sea to his homeland."[139] Whereas the *Vita* summarized this line from Possidius with the nebulous reference to "other monasteries in desert and wooded places," the *Initium* used Possidius' testimony as proof of the Italian origins of Augustine's eremiticism: "All these things show no doubt that [Augustine] instituted his own *Rule* in Italy, and even more so, that he himself lived as an anchorite in Italy after his conversion."[140] In contrast to the narratives of the medieval tradition, as well as that of the Florentine *Vita*, which employed Possidius' remark *which he had previously done when he returned from across the sea to his homeland*, as a vague conclusion, or even afterthought, to the account of Augustine's establishing a monastery after having been made presbyter, the *Initium* gives the phrase content by having first established Augustine's composition of the *Rule* for his first eremitical community in Italy, to which then Possidius' phrase, ... *which he had previously done* ... (*iam ipse prior fecerat*) refers back in the emplotment of the *Initium*. As if to leave no doubt, the author of the *Initium* changed Possidius' "[Augustine] began to live ... according to the custom and way of life established by the holy apostles," simply repeated by the author of the *Vita*, to "[Augustine] began to live according to the apostolic rule," whereby in place of the somewhat vague "according to the custom and way of life constituted by the apostles," (*secundum modum et regulam sub sanctis apostolis constitutam*), the author of the *Initium* referred back to the apostolic rule (*regulam apostolicam*) which "blessed father and doctor Augustine put together in writing," (*beatus pater Augustinus et doctor ... conscripsit*).

The author of the *Initium* did not stop here with his rewriting of Possidius. Having sufficiently dealt with Augustine's eremitical origins in Italy, the author then turned to Africa. Whereas Possidius simply reported Augustine establishing a monastery within the church

---

[138] *Initium* (338–339).
[139] *Initium* (339–340).
[140] "Que omnia [probant] nedum quod ipsam regulam in Italia instituerit, immo quod ipse anacorita, dum fuit in Italia post suam conversionem, extiterit." *Initium* (340).

compound after having been made presbyter, the *Initium* claimed that Augustine lived an eremitical life, "according to the apostolic rule," with blessed Valerius in a villa.[141] For this passage the author might have been taking his inspiration from Philip of Harvengt's *Vita*, rather than from Possidius. As seen above, Philip claimed that Valerius gave Augustine a garden in which to establish a monastery after having ordained him as presbyter, which seems more closely related to a villa than does Possidius' wording, *intra ecclesiam*. The point to be made is that the *Initium* is clear that Augustine's second eremitical community was that in Hippo, together with Valerius. After his ordination as bishop, the author continued, Augustine then "founded many monasteries in solitary places, in which he stayed, as the father of many, teaching, correcting and regulating his very own anchoritic sons, so that they might serve God worthily in keeping with the apostolic rule."[142] Taken all together, the author concluded, it is manifestly clear that Augustine "was not only the father of the hermits, but even was himself a hermit."[143]

Such a statement was not without political implications in 1330. It was made precisely when the OESA was in negotiations with the Regular Canons concerning custody of Augustine's tomb in San Pietro in Ciel d'Oro in Pavia. The *Initium* was not written simply for the edification of members of the OESA. After asserting Augustine's eremitical foundations and life, the author then launched a frontal attack against his opponents:

> Nor does it matter that the Regular Canons say that they received the *Rule* from blessed Augustine in Africa, whereby they call themselves Canons of St. Augustine. Wherefore they would have cause, some say, because in Africa Augustine gave his *Rule* and founded monasteries as much to and for the Canons as to and for hermits, and that we did not come about from the said hermits. This does not

---

[141] "In Affrica vero, ut ipse dicit in *sermone de vita clericorum*, quod cum beato Valentino [*sic*] in villa habitabat, et secundum regulam apostolicam vivebant." *Initium* (340).

[142] "Et postquam episcopus fuit yponensis, quam plurima monasteria in solitudine construxit, in quibus sicut pater plurimum morabatur, ipsos suos filios anacoritas instruendo, corrigendo et ordinando, ut Deo digne et secundum regulam apostolicam servirent." *Initium* (340).

[143] After citing an apocryphal phrase from Augustine's *In Iohannis Evangelium*, and from the pseudo-Augustinian *sermo de passione Domini Nostri Iesu Christi*, the author concludes: "Et multa alia dicit, que manifestissime ostendunt eum non tantum heremitarum patrem, verum etiam ipsum heremitam fuisse." *Initium* (340).

seem to be true with regard to the Canons, since Abbot Ioachim said that the Regular Canons had their beginning from blessed Rufus, bishop in parts of France.[144]

The author established both the antiquity of the OESA and its continuity with Augustine's original eremitical communities by then briefly discussing the origins of the various religious Orders, and the manifestation and approbation of the OESA in the context of that development.[145] Under the papacies of Alexander III, Innocent III, Gregory IX, and Alexander IV, the prior generals of the Order received special privileges. Alexander IV, however, played a special role:

> Pope Alexander, from his love of blessed Augustine, [who] appeared to him in a vision with a large head, but small body, in the first year of his pontificate increased the Order as much in members as in privileges, bringing together into this Order the Brictinenses, the Brethren of Favali, the followers of Friar John Bonus, and the Williamites, granting the Order privileges as never before to any other religion.[146]

This is the earliest account of Alexander's vision of Augustine in association with the Great Union. As we will see, it would be repeated by Nicholas of Alessandria, Henry of Friemar, and Jordan of Quedlinburg.[147] Already in the 1240s both the Franciscans and Dominicans had created mythical visions of their founding fathers to Pope Innocent III.[148] Now finally the OESA was on equal footing. With this account, the *Initium* established a connection between Augustine's original foundation of hermits in Italy, and his role in Alexander's establishing the OESA in the Great Union. There is a continuity

---

[144] "Nec obstat quod canonici regulares dicunt quod a beato Augustino in Affrica regulam receperint, ex quo dicunt se canonicos beati Augustini. Unde motivum habuerint, quidam dicunt, quod tam canonicis quam ipsis heremitis in Africa regulam dedit et monasteria construxit, et a dictis heremitis non evenimus. De canonicis non videtur verum, quoniam abbas Iohachyn dicit quod canonici regulares initium habuerunt a beato Rufo episcopo in partibus Galliae." *Initium* (341).

[145] *Initium* (341). For the discussion of the origins of the various Orders, see *Initium* (342–343).

[146] "... predictus papa Alexander ab amore beati Augustini, ei in visione magnus capite et parvus membris apparens, primo anno sui pontificatus predictum Ordinem tam in personis quam in gratiis augmentavit, huic Ordini brictones, fabarios, iambonitas, atque guglielmitas iungendo, gratias numquam similes alicui religioni traditas [condonando] ..." *Initium* (345).

[147] Arbesmann argued that Henry's account of the vision in his *Tractatus* was the first Augustinian mention of the vision; see Arbesmann, "Henry of Friemar's Treatise," 131. Henry's and Jordan's treatments of the vision will be discussed below.

[148] See Füser, "Vom *exemplum Christi*," 46–57; Wesjohann, "*Simplicitas*," 162–165.

between Augustine's eremiticism, and the eremiticism of the Augustinian Order, emphasized by the *Initium*'s concluding by returning to Jerome's discussion of the early desert fathers, to which Augustine and his hermits are added.[149] With the *Initium*, Augustine was not simply the historical bishop of Hippo and author of the apostolic rule: he had written his *Rule* for the OESA, of which he had become *pater noster*.

C. *Nicholas of Alessandria's* Sermo de beato Augustino

The third text in the Laurenziana manuscript that pertains to the creation of the Augustinian myth is a sermon on Augustine, preached in Paris in 1332 by Nicholas of Alessandria, edited together with the *Initium* by Rano. Nicholas of Alessandria became master of theology at Paris in 1333, and attended the General Chapter at Grasse in 1335, where the negotiations with the Regular Canons over the custody of Augustine's tomb were confirmed. Three years later he was also present in Siena at the General Chapter which renewed affirmation of the agreement. He was surely the same "Nicolas de Alessandria" designated as lector in the Curia on 19 May 1327, who together with the Prior General William of Cremona entered negotiations with the Canons and the Commune of Pavia regarding Augustine's tomb.[150] His *Sermo de beato Augustino* clearly testifies to his commitment to, and skill in, presenting the Hermits' case.

The sermon is divided into two distinct parts. The first consists of praises of Augustine's learning, character, and service to the Church, taking the pericope from 1 Macchabes 2:17: *You are great in this city, resplendent with brothers and sons* (*Magnus es in hac civitate et ornatus fratribus et filiis*). In part two, Nicholas turned to the history and development of western monasticism, beginning with Paul the first Hermit and Anthony. He continued by tracing the dispersals of the earliest eremitical groups, some of whom settled in Italy. Nicholas then treated Augustine's conversion and early monastic experiences, his composition of the *Rule* for the Tuscan Hermits, his return to Africa and his establishment of monasteries there. Virtually skipping over Augustine's life after his monastic foundations, Nicholas moved

---

[149] *Initium* (349).
[150] Rano, "Las Dos Primeras Obras Conocidas," 353–354; *CDP* 13 (29).

rather quickly to a brief mention of Augustine's death and the translations of his body, before finally arriving at the development of the Augustinian Hermits, placed chronologically well before the origins of the other Orders, namely, the Regular Canons, the Franciscans, and the Dominicans. He proceeded with his account by listing the earliest known priors general of the Order, pointing to the papal privileges they received, and the papal approbations of the Order culminating in Alexander IV's Great Union, concluding with a list of the priors general of the Order through William of Cremona and the OESA assuming custody of Augustine's tomb. The sermon closes with what could be seen as a third section, though which functions as a final *determinatio* of the matter at hand: Nicholas offered eight arguments and three proofs from authority to establish once and for all that Augustine was not only the founder of the Hermits, but also lived himself as one, thereby authenticating the historical continuity between Augustine's eremitical life and that of the OESA.

In Nicholas' sermon the representation is intensified in three respects: first, the detail given regarding Augustine's composition of the *Rule* and foundation of monasteries; second, the argument against the Canons; and third, the mythic elements of the historical account.

With Nicholas' historical reconstruction there is no longer a question regarding Augustine's composition of the *Rule* for his first eremitical community in Italy, nor where that first community was located. As stated above, the second part of the sermon begins with an account of the origins of eremitical monasticism with Paul the first Hermit and Anthony. From these origins, the eremitical life had three branches, founded by Basil and Pachomius in the East, and by Augustine in the West.[151] The followers of Paul and Anthony were dispersed by a combination of persecutions and divine providence. As a result, some of these early hermits came to Italy. There, they heard of a group of hermits living between Rome and Viterbo, who had originated from two groups: one around a hermit named Anthony, who lived on Mons Pisanus, and the other, the group of hermits led by blessed Mamilianus, who lived near Sardinia.[152] The

---

[151] Nic.Al. *Sermo* (353–364); cf. *Initium* (337–338).
[152] Nic.Al. *Sermo* (364). In the Laurenziana manuscript a short *Vita* of Mamilianus follows directly that of Augustine; Florence, Biblioteca Laurenziana, MS Plut. 90 Sup. 48, fol. 13r–15v.

new arrivals joined the group in the hermitage between Rome and Viterbo, and there the community grew and prospered, and built one hundred cells, in the place called Centumcellae. The inhabitants of the region built a church dedicated to the Holy Trinity for the hermits, and there, Nicholas affirmed, "in the course of time, was the first location of the Order of Hermits of Saint Augustine."[153] The reason for this Nicholas gave a little later on in the sermon. Turning to Augustine's conversion and baptism, Nicholas repeated the story of Augustine and Ambrose composing the *Te deum laudamus*. He then relates how for more than a year Augustine lived in the hermitage of Ambrose and Simplicianus outside Milan to be taught by his two seniors, who had been so instrumental in his conversion. Augustine did not at that time compose his *Rule*, since, Nicholas affirmed, he lived with Ambrose and Simplicianus as their student, not as their master.[154] During this period Augustine was persuaded by his mother to return to Africa, and on their way, they came upon the community of hermits in Centumcellae and stayed with them for a period of approximately two years. Asked by the community, Augustine composed his *Rule* for the group, "and from that time on they were called the hermit brothers of Augustine by reason of the *Rule* given to them, whereas previously they were only called hermits."[155] Moreover, Nicholas also gives a precise date for the *Rule*'s composition. In the first section of the sermon, in praising Augustine's administrative abilities, Nicholas used Augustine providing a *Rule* as an example, which "he composed," Nicholas affirmed, "940 years

---

[153] "Dicti autem heremite in prefata heremo inter Romam et Viterbium in tantum numero et merito satis cito creverunt, quod ibidem C cellas construxerunt iuxta locum qui Centum cellis dicitur et habitatores illius regionis in dicta heremo ecclesiam in honorem Sancte Trinitatis ipsis fratribus edificarunt et ibi in processu temporis fuit primus locus Ordinis heremitarum sancti Augustini . . ." Nic.Al. *Sermo* (365).

[154] Nic.Al. *Sermo* (366–367).

[155] "Instigante autem pia matre que affectabat eodem sepulcro cum viro suo in propria civitate recondi, ut ipse dicit 9 *Confessionum* ad Afficram . . . remeabat querens cottidie locum sibi aptum ad serviendum Deo. Cum vero ad introitum Tussie percinxit, plures servos Dei heremiticam vitam ducentes tam in monte Pisano quam in locis aliis ad predictam vitam aptis in dicta provincia invenit, et tandem ad locum Centumcellarum applicuit. Cum quibus fratribus diu commoratus, rogatus ab eis ut regulam et normam vivendi [traderet], ipsis composuit in loco sancte Trinitatis de Centumcellis. Et ex tunc vocati sunt fratres heremite Augustini ratione regule date qui prius heremite tantummodo dicebantur." Nic.Al. *Sermo* (367). Nicolas continues by noting the aptness of Augustine composing the *Rule* for the hermits in the church of the Holy Trinity; *ibid*.

ago."[156] Since the sermon is explicitly dated 1332,[157] Nicholas assigned the composition of the *Regula Sancti Augustini* to the year 392.[158]

Nicholas continued to build an argument from biographical details. At the time of his baptism Augustine was thirty years old and he was thirty-three when Monica died at Ostia. Thus, Nicholas argued, he spent approximately two years with the Tuscan hermits and one in the hermitage at Milan.[159] Nicholas then brought in Possidius as proof, citing the passage: "having been ordained presbyter, Augustine established a monastery and began to live with the servants of God according to the custom and way of life established by the holy apostles."[160] This clinched the argument for Nicholas: "From this it is perfectly clear that Augustine instituted and lived by the said *Rule* first in Italy."[161] Above I have stressed the ambiguity to which this phrase in Possidius gave rise. Even the author of the *Initium* was vague regarding the precise location of Augustine's first eremitical community for which he composed the *Rule*, affirming only, and using this line of Possidius as proof, that it was first in Italy. With Nicholas clarity was achieved. Possidius' *which he had previously done when he returned from across the sea to his homeland*, refers to Augustine composing the *Rule* in 392 for the Tuscan hermits in Centumcellae, which was the first location of the *Ordo Eremitarum Sancti Augustini*.

Nicholas was just as precise with regard to Augustine's monastic foundations. The first was that in Centumcellae. Nicholas then

---

[156] "Tertio, requiritur in prelato bono regularitas familie. Opus enim laudat opificem. Qualis enim est rex talis lex et talis grex. Quomodo autem beatus Augustinus regularem familiam statuerit patet satis ex ordinatissima regula sua, sub qua quasi infiniti regulariter et sancte vivunt et vixerunt. Iam iam sunt anni 940 quam composuit modo qui in fine narrabitur." Nic.Al. *Sermo* (361).

[157] The sermon explicitly states: "Hec Magister Nicolaus de Allexandria, anno Domini M CCC XXXII, Parisiis." Nic.Al. *Sermo* (376).

[158] For contemporary scholarship's dating of the *Rule*, see Lawless, *Augustine of Hippo and his Monastic Rule*, 148–154; Lawless reviews the various scholarly opinions and then concludes: "Barring more convincing evidence to the contrary, c. 397 seems to be a more likely time of composition for Augustine's *Rule*." *Ibid.*, 153. Nicholas seems not to have recognized the problem his dating posed for his argument, since at least by contemporary reconstructions, Augustine was ordained presbyter in 391.

[159] Nic.Al. *Sermo* (367–368).

[160] "... factus presbyter instituit monasterium et cepit vivere secundum regulam sub sanctis apostolis constitutam, quod ipse [*scripsi*; ipsum ed. Rano] prior fecerat, cum a transmarinis ad propria remeasset." Nic.Al. *Sermo* (368).

[161] "Ex quo manifeste patet quod dictam regulam instituit et servavit primo in Ytalia." Nic.Al. *Sermo* (368).

proceeded to Augustine's arrival in Africa, where together with his friends, he was received by Bishop Valerius. Regarding the African theater of Augustine's monastic operations, in the *Initium* only explicit mention is made of the villa which Valerius gave to Augustine, together with the further comment that Augustine founded many monasteries after he was ordained bishop, though the author of the *Initium* used Possidius' account of Augustine's monastic foundation upon being made presbyter as proof of the Italian priority of Augustine's eremiticism.[162] In comparison, Nicholas restored the proper order, as well as having combined Philip of Harvengt's garden with the *Initium*'s villa: after Augustine was received by Valerius, "Valerius gave him a certain garden in a certain wooded villa, so that together with his associates who followed him, they could live an eremitical and solitary life."[163] Thereafter, having been ordained presbyter, Augustine founded another monastery adjoined to the church in Hippo, repeating the account of Possidius.[164] Finally as bishop, Augustine founded many monasteries and hermitages "in which the servants of God, in keeping with the way of life and habit which he had seen in Italy, might live according to the *Rule* which he had composed."[165] Nicholas thus clearly distinguished four stages of Augustine's monastic foundations. The first was in Centumcellae; the second was in Valerius' garden/villa; the third was in the church compound in Hippo after having been made presbyter; and the fourth was multiple foundations after having been ordained bishop. Such clarity was called for in 1332 precisely due to the on-going debates having been initiated over whether Augustine originally wrote his *Rule* for the Canons or for the Hermits. Nicholas left no doubt.

With his precision of detail and dating concerning the development of Augustine's eremiticism, Nicholas was clear that Augustine *first* founded his Order of Hermits. Moreover, in Nicholas' representation

---

[162] See notes 141 and 142 above.

[163] "Defuncta igitur matre Augustini apud Hostia tyberina, in Affricam cum sociis profectus est, quem sanctus Valerius yponensis episcopus paterne suscepit et ei quemdam hortulum in quadam villa silvestri dedit, ut ibidem cum sociis qui ei adherebant solitariam et solitam agerent vitam." Nic.Al. *Sermo* (368).

[164] Nic.Al. *Sermo* (368).

[165] "Quando autem fuit in dicta ecclesia yponensis episcopus ordinatus, quam plura monasteria solitaria et heremitica construxit, in quibus servi Dei iuxta morem et habitum quem in Ytalia viderat regulam ab eo conditam servabant..." Nic.Al. *Sermo* (369).

a new argument for the OESA's priority over against the Regular Canons is advanced: the Order's habit. Augustinus of Ancona had claimed the monastic habit as the primary distinguishing factor of the *religiosi*, and Nicholas made the point his own. After delineating the four stages of Augustine's monastic foundations, Nicholas then argued:

> Some however believe that the friars, because they were hermit friars only lived in the said place and in other similar places outside the city, and in Augustine's monastery adjoined to the church in Hippo, lived the Regular Canons. But if truth be known this was not the case, as much because all religious overseas are clothed with a black tunic girded with a belt, as the friars of St. Basil, as because at that time no one in that region had seen such a habit as that which the Regular Canons now wear, and because Abbot Joachim in his *Exposition on the Apocalypse* clearly said that the Regular Canons had their origin from blessed Rufus, bishop in parts of France, approximately in the year of our Lord 1090. The Canons were called the Canons of St. Augustine, because Rufus gave them Augustine's *Rule*. From these Canons in time came blessed Dominic.[166]

Nicholas had previously concluded the first part of his sermon with the same argument, placed in context of his exposition of the pericope, making the distinction between Augustine's brothers (*fratres*) and sons (*filii*). Augustine's brothers are all those who founded Orders based on his *Rule*, such as the Regular Canons, founded by Rufus, the Order of Preachers, founded by Dominic, and many others.[167] "But we," Nicholas continued,

> are Augustine's sons, born immediately from him, and therefore we clearly carry his sign, namely the habit which he used directly after

---

[166] "Quidam autem quod fratres credunt quod fratres heremite solum in dicto loco et similibus extra civitatem habitarent et in illo monasterio, iuxta ecclesiam Canonici regulares, sed, salva veritate, hoc non videtur, tum quia omnes religiosi ultramarini tunica nigra desuper cincta zona induuntur, ut fratres sancti Basilii, tum quia illo tempore nullus ibi talem habitum vidit qualem nunc portant Canonici regulares, tum quia abbas Joachim in *expositione super apokalisim* [sic] expresse dicit quod Canonici regulares ortum habuerunt a beato Rufo episcopo in partibus Gallie circa annos Domini M°XC. Dicuntur tamen Canonici sancti Augustini, quia beatus Rufus eis regulam beati Augustini dedit. Ex quibus Canonicis in processu temporis fuit beatus Dominicus." Nic.Al. *Sermo* (369–370). Nicholas' dating of the founding of the Canons to 1090, whereas the anonymous *Vita* gives the date 1110, is a simple inversion, reading MXC or MCX; where Arbesmann came up with c. 1104 is unclear; see note 119 above.

[167] Nic.Al. *Sermo* (363).

his baptism. For never overseas had such a habit been seen as that which the Regular Canons wear, but all religious were clothed in black, and girded with a belt over the tunic.[168]

According to Nicholas, the habit itself differentiated Augustine's true sons from the Regular Canons. It was a sign of the primacy of Augustine's foundation. The habit of the OESA was that of Augustine himself, from the time of his baptism, and was one that only his true sons and heirs were entitled to share. It is only in light of the force of his argument that Nicholas can then make such conciliatory comments as the one with which he concluded his proof of the Hermits' priority: "The issue, however, is not to be greatly disputed, especially because if Augustine founded that Order and ours, it all goes to the praise of that glorious father, how very many sons in Christ he bore."[169]

Nicholas' historical evidence and arguments were designed to present convincing proof of Augustine's original foundation of the OESA. Embedded within the fictive narrative of the historical facts, however, were mythic elements. As the author of the *Initium*, Nicholas included the account of Augustine appearing to Alexander IV as catalyst for the Great Union.[170] In the *Initium*, Alexander is moved by his own love for Augustine, who then appeared to him with a large head but small body, whereupon Alexander effected the Union. With Nicholas there is a change, which can be seen as an intensification of the mythic. Nicholas nowhere mentions Alexander's love for Augustine. Augustine assumes a more active role with Nicholas, whereby based on Augustine's appearing to Alexander, Alexander was moved to act, whereas in the *Initium*, Alexander's love for Augustine preceded the vision, which then prompted his action. The author of the *Initium* makes Alexander the subject of the verb, performing the activity, adding the vision in a dependent clause—*Alexander . . . augmentavit*—whereas Nicholas places the verbal action with Augustine—*Augustinus . . . apparuit*—attributing to Alexander a

---

[168] "Sed nos sumus filii immediate ab eo geniti, ideo plene portamus signum ipsius, scilicet habitum quo usus fuit statim post conversionem. Nunquam enim ultra mare talis habitus visus est qualem portant Canonici regulares, sed omnes religiosi induuntur de nigro et super latam tunicam corrigia cinguntur." Nic.Al. *Sermo* (363).

[169] "Non est autem in hoc disputandum, maxime quia, et si illum Ordinem et nostrum instituit, totum ad laudem ipsius gloriosi patris cedit quanto plures filios in Christo genuit." Nic.Al. *Sermo* (370).

[170] See Saak, "Augustinian Identity," 147–148.

passive role—*ex quo motus fuit... unire.*[171] Such re-emplotment would then later become even more definite in Jordan of Quedlinburg's narration in his *Liber Vitasfratrum*, when Jordan claimed that Augustine appeared to Alexander, as a divine oracle, wanting to end the dispersion of his own religion.[172] There is a marked shift in the attribution of the initiative for the Great Union from Alexander to Augustine.[173] Nicholas goes even further when he then associates for the first time the foundation of the OESA in the Great Union with the *novus ordo* prophesied by Joachim.

All the evidence taken together, Nicholas claimed, proves that "blessed Augustine was the leader, teacher, head, and father of the hermits."[174] Nicholas concluded by arguing that the Church's approbation of the Order did not occur by chance, but that the Church declared the OESA to be the true sons of Augustine with good reason, and had from ancient times. Thus the Order merits its unique title, even if other orders as well follow Augustine's *Rule*.[175] Nicholas' intensifications of the historical details combined with mythic elements and his campaign against the Regular Canons, heightened as well the security of his co-religious listening to his sermon in Paris in 1332; as the true sons of Augustine they and they alone were entitled to call Augustine *pater noster*. The same essential argumentation and strategy would two years later be formulated anew in the first treatise explicitly written in defense of the Order, the *Tractatus* of Henry of Friemar.

---

[171] Nicolas continued with a list of the Order's prior generals, extending to and including William of Cremona; see Nic.Al. *Sermo* (372–373).

[172] *VF* 1,14 (47,80–85).

[173] The shift is from the *Initium*'s *Alexander ab amore beati Augustini, ei in visione... apparens... augmentavit...*; to Nicholas' *beatus Augustinus dicto pape Allexandro in visione apparuit... ex quo motus fuit dicto nostro Ordini unire...*; and then to Jordan's *beatus Augustinus, volens dispersionem suae Religionis congregari... in visione apparuit... ex qua visione velut divino oraculo papa commonitus unionem... consummavit*. See also Rano, "San Agustín y los orígenes de su Orden," 658–667; and esp. 658–659, where Rano also presents these three versions, together with Henry of Friemar's, in chronological succession, without, however, commenting on the relationship between them or on the construction of the myth.

[174] "Sic ergo apparet quod beatus Augustinus dux, magister, caput et pater fuit heremitarum." Nic.Al. *Sermo* (373).

[175] Nic.Al. *Sermo* (375–376).

D. *Henry of Friemar's* Tractatus

In 1334, as he was nearing the end of his career, Henry of Friemar composed his *Tractatus de origine et progressu ordinis fratrum heremitarum et vero ac proprio titulo eiusdem*. Henry began his treatise with a statement of purpose:

> Because some, being ignorant of the path of conversion and comportment of the most glorious doctor, blessed Augustine, our unique father and patron, are able to question by what reason the brothers of our religion are especially said to be the brothers of the Order of Hermits of St. Augustine in comparison with the other religious professing his *Rule*, the above stated truth, namely, wherefore justly and rationally such a title is attributed especially to us by the holy Roman Church, is therefore able to be made know in three ways.[176]

Henry then notes that such a truth is evident from Augustine's conversion, from his comportment, and from various statements and deeds concerning the Order's approbation.[177] These he treated in chapters one through three respectively, before summarizing the evidence in chapter four. Chapter five then continues with an enumeration of the priors general of the Order, both before and after the Great Union. The treatise concludes with a short chapter highlighting the Order's brothers of famous sanctity. Throughout Henry was clear that his purpose was to offer conclusive proof that only the OESA had the right to be called the true sons of Augustine, whose origins can be traced from the time of Augustine himself. In so doing, Henry also contributed to the creation of the Augustinian myth.

In chapter one Henry addressed Augustine's conversion and baptism. The catalysts for his baptism were divine inspiration, and the erudition of St. Ambrose. Yet in conjunction with these, was the influence of Simplicianus. According to Henry, Simplicianus was a hermit, "who first in Rome served God most devoutly from his youth,

---

[176] "Quia nonnulli ignorantes modum conversionis et actum conversationis gloriosissimi doctoris beati Augustini, singularis patris nostri et patroni, possent dubitare, ex qua ratione fratres nostrae religionis prae ceteris religiosis suam regulam profitentibus fratres ordinis eremitarum sancti Augustini specialiter dicerentur: ideo praedicta veritas, quare videlicet iuste et rationabiliter nobis per sanctam Romanam ecclesiam sit talis titulus specialiter attributus, potest via triplici declarari." Hen. *Tract.* 1 (90,1–8). I have translated *actus conversationis* as comportment, to distinguish this term from *modus vivendi*.

[177] Hen. *Tract.* 1 (90,9–11).

following the example of Paul, the first Hermit, and blessed Anthony, and afterwards, coming to Milan, fervently led a solitary and eremitical life with many associates."[178] Augustine visited Simplicianus, confessing to him the errors of his life, whereupon Simplicianus read him the lives of blessed Anthony and other desert fathers, and told him of the example of Victorinus, who publicly confessed his faith. Upon hearing such accounts, Augustine was set on fire for the catholic faith, leading eventually to his conversion and baptism.[179] Though Arbesmann claimed that Henry was the first Augustinian to have made Simplicianus into a hermit,[180] the first mention of Simplicianus as a hermit is actually found in the *Sermo de beato Augustino* of Nicholas of Alessandria.[181] Furthermore, the close parallels between this passage in the texts of Henry and Nicholas, suggest that either they had a common source, or that Henry used Nicholas' *Sermo*. Henry mentions that he drew from *antiquae legendae non abbreviatae*, yet such sources are no longer extent, if they ever were. As Arbesmann notes, Jordan of Quedlinburg referred to Philip of Harvengt's *Vita Sancti Augustini* as *legenda famosa, solemnis et antiqua*, which should caution against giving too much weight to the adjective *antiqua*.[182] If such legends were common knowledge to the members of the Order, it does cause one to question why earlier texts such as the anonymous Florentine *Vita* and the *Initium* were completely silent in this regard. In any case, Henry did not restrict his account to that given by Nicholas. Henry attributed to Simplicianus the story in the *Confessions* of Ponticianus having read Augustine the *Vita* of Anthony, which served as a major stimulus for his continued path toward conversion.[183] In Henry's account, after his encounter with Simplicianus, Augustine became a catechumen and together "with Alipius and Adeodatus began to live with blessed Simplicianus and his associates

---

[178] "Nam licet primarium motivum suae conversionis habuerit per divinam inspirationem et per beati Ambrosii salutarem eruditionem, complementum tamen suae conversionis habuit per beatum Simplicianum eremitam, qui primo Romae exemplo Pauli primi eremitae et beati Antonii a sua iuventute deo devotissime serviebat et postmodum veniens Mediolanum vitam solitarium et eremiticam cum multis sociis ferventissime duxit." Hen. *Tract.* 1 (90,12–19).
[179] Hen. *Tract.* 1 (90,19–91,29).
[180] Arbesmann, "Henry of Friemar's Treatise," 45–49.
[181] See Saak, "Augustinian Identity," 151.
[182] See Arbesmann, "Henry of Friemar's Treatise," 51ff.
[183] *Ibid.*

according to the way of life of those friars, by whose examples he was converted to the catholic faith."[184] Henry continued by repeating the story of Augustine's baptism and his composition together with Ambrose of the *Te deum laudamus*, leaving Augustine's investment with the monastic habit to the following chapter. Making sure that no one would miss the import, Henry concluded the first chapter by arguing:

> From these things it is evidently clear, that since blessed Augustine, from the example of the hermit saints, who were the first founders of our religion, was ultimately converted to the faith of Christ by blessed Simplicianus and for a certain time stayed with him and his associates [dressed] in their habit and afterwards handed down the *Rule* of living to our brothers following this eremitical life (as will be discussed below), that justly and reasonably the holy Roman Church called our brothers the friars of the Order of hermits of St. Augustine; for even though our brothers before being given the *Rule* by blessed Augustine were simply called hermits, nevertheless, based on the *Rule* given them by blessed Augustine that title for the Order was approved by the Roman Church, and from that time on they were appropriately called the friars of the Order of hermits of St. Augustine, whose unique and true father was Augustine, not only through his taking on the habit, but even from his living with them for a long time and his giving of the *Rule*, as will clearly be seen below.[185]

In chapter two Henry then begins with Augustine's baptism and assuming the habit of a hermit, given him by Ambrose and Simplicianus, together with an explication of the symbolic meaning

---

[184] "Et ex tunc beatus Augustinus, factus catechumenus a beato Ambrosio, cum Alipio et puero Adeodato coepit vivere cum beato Simpliciano et sociis eius secundum modum illorum fratrum, quorum exemplis est conversus ad fidem catholicam." Hen. *Tract.* 1 (91,36–39).

[185] "Ex quibus evidenter patet, quod cum beatus Augustinus exemplo sanctorum eremitarum, qui fuerunt primarii nostrae religionis fundatores, per beatus Simplicianus ad fidem Christi ultimate conversus fuerit et cum eodem et sociis suis in ipsorum habitu per tempus aliquod steterit et postea fratribus nostris hanc vitam eremiticam sectantibus regulam vivendi per se ipsum tradiderit (ut infra dicetur): quod iuste et rationabiliter sancta Romana ecclesia nostros fratres ordinis eremitarum sancti Augustini appellavit; licet enim fratres nostri prius ante dationem regulae per beatum Augustinum dicerentur simpliciter eremitae, ex regula tamen ipsis per beatum Augustinum tradita per Romanam ecclesiam iste titulus ordini approbatus fuit, ut ex tunc appropriate dicerentur fratres ordinis eremitarum sancti Augustini, quorum singulis et verus pater esset non tantum per habitus assumptionem sed etiam per suum diuturnum convictum et regulae dationem, ut infra clarius apparebit." Hen. *Tract.* 1 (92,53–68).

of the habit.[186] He then turns to Augustine's journey back to Africa. On the way, Augustine happened upon the hermits in Centumcellae, and stayed with them for a period of two years. For these he composed his *Rule*, and the hermitage in Centumcellae became the first location of the Order.[187] Finally arriving in Africa, Augustine was received by bishop Valerius. Knowing of Augustine's monastic desires, Valerius gave him a garden in a wooded villa where he could devote himself to contemplation, prayer and study.[188] Henry then brought in Possidius, to prove that Augustine's first monastery was that in the garden of Valerius: "In which place, as Possidius said, having directly built a monastery, he began to gather brothers of the same mind and with them to live according to the way of life and *Rule* of the holy apostles, which he had already done even earlier when he returned from across the sea to his homeland."[189] Henry apparently here inverted the temporal sequence, because he continued with Augustine's ordination as presbyter,[190] emphasizing that his first monastery was that in Valerius' garden. Possidius' phrase *which he had previously done when he returned from across the sea to his homeland*, is used as evidence of Augustine's early monastic foundations, before having been ordained. In chapter three Henry mentioned Augustine's monastery in Valerius' garden as proof of Augustine's eremitical life, again citing Possidius as evidence, and then a final time in chapter four, summarizing the points made in the first three chapters. In the last reference, Possidius' emplotment is restored, whereby Augustine founded a monastery upon his ordination as presbyter, used as conclusive proof of Augustine's early foundations.[191] What had been a vague reference, for Henry, as for Nicholas, was explicit evidence of Augustine's early eremitical life.

---

[186] Hen. *Tract.* 2 (92,1–95,67).

[187] Hen. *Tract.* 2 (95,68–96,90); *cf.* Nic.Al. *Sermo* (365–367). The textual parallels between Nicholas' *sermo* and Henry's *Tractatus* again are suggestive of Henry's knowledge of Nicholas' text; whereas the author of the *Initium* claimed it most uncertain precisely where Augustine's first eremitical community in Italy had been, Nicholas is then clear that it was Centumcellae, which Henry was as well.

[188] Hen. *Tract.* 2 (97,110–117); *cf.* Nic.Al. *Sermo* (368).

[189] "In quo loco, ut dicit Possidius, mox aedificato monasterio coepit eiusdem propositi fratres colligere et cum eis vivere secundum modum et regulam sanctorum apostolorum, quod etiam ipse pridem iam fecerat, quando trans mare ad sua redierat." Hen. *Tract.* 2 (97,117–121).

[190] Hen. *Tract.* 2 (97,121–127).

[191] Saak, "Augustinian Identity," 154–155.

Henry only treats Augustine's early monasticism, omitting discussion of Augustine's monastic foundations after having been ordained bishop. For Henry, the point to be made is that Augustine first lived as a hermit, and founded his Order accordingly; the rest is inconsequential. Thus in chapter three, Henry continued his argument "that blessed Augustine assumed the monastic habit of our fathers and held to an eremitical life with them from the time of his own conversion and also gave them a *Rule* and way of life," by bringing forth authorities, both of words and deeds.[192] Henry first mentioned Ambrose and the pseudo-Ambrosian *Sermo de baptismo et conversione sancti Augustini*, which he had cited previously in chapter two. The second proof-text offered is the pseudo-Augustinian *Sermo de Passione*, from which Henry then quotes.[193] He then claimed as his third point his overall theme, which he repeatedly hammers home, namely, that the members of the Order of Hermits of Saint Augustine "are the true and proper sons of blessed Augustine and he is their true father, which is clear because he wore their habit in their hermitage and gave them the *Rule* of living."[194] After citing canon law which pertained to the privileges of the OESA, Henry concluded that only the OESA has the right to be called by its title, even though other Orders might be called by Augustine's name and live according to his *Rule*; only the OESA is the original and true Order of Augustine and therefore "that title, *ordo eremitarum sancti Augustini* belongs only to our Order and to no other."[195] He then repeats the three pieces of evidence to prove that Augustine lived as a hermit, namely, his living as such with Simplicianus, his stay with the Tuscan hermits at Centumcellae, and finally, his establishing a monastery in Valerius' garden, citing Possidius as proof. Directly following, Henry claimed that this was confirmed by Pope John XXII in public consistory,

---

[192] "Nam quod beatus Augustinus habitum monasticum nostrorum patrum assumpserit ct vitam eremiticam cum eis in principio suae conversionis tenuerit ac etiam regulam et modum vivendi eis tradiderit, hoc ex variis auctoritatum dictis et etiam ex variis factis ostendi potest." Hen. *Tract.* 3 (98,1–5).

[193] Hen. *Tract.* 3 (98,6–99,28).

[194] "Tertio, hoc idem patet sic. Quod enim ordo fratrum eremitarum sancti Augustini et fratres illius ordinis sint veri et proprii filii beati Augustini et ipse sit eorum verus pater, ex hoc patet, quod eorum habitum in eremo portavit et eis regulam vivendi tradidit, ut patet ex supradictis." Hen. *Tract.* 3 (99,29–33).

[195] "Ex quo patet, quod iste titulus *ordo eremitarum sancti Augustini* est solum proprius nostro ordini et nulli alii." Hen. *Tract.* 3 (100,64–66); see *ibid.* (100,56–101,80) for Henry's discussion of the title.

which he, Henry, had heard from a reliable witness. Shortly thereafter, in the same chapter, in summarizing his arguments, Henry again mentioned the same approbation.

This begs the question of who this reliable witness might have been. Above I noted the textual parallels between Henry's *Tractatus* and Nicholas of Alessandria's *Sermo*. Though not absolutely conclusive, the *quidam vir authenticus*, from whom Henry had heard this tale, seems to have been Nicholas, since Nicholas included such a discussion in his *Sermo*.[196] Henry did not cite the text of *Veneranda sanctorum* verbatim; Nicholas' text is much closer to that of John XXII, though not without its own interpolations.[197] It thus seems highly unlikely that Henry was using a text of the Bull itself for his source. Moreover, Henry first stated that he had heard this account from a witness, rather than that he had read it, or had been present at the consistory himself. Nicholas' sermon would have served exceedingly well as his source, and Nicholas may indeed have been the witness from whom he heard the account. Further, Henry quoted the same passage from Joachim to argue that the OESA should be identified with the *novus ordo* as did Nicholas.[198] Though this last example in itself does not go far to suggest Henry's knowledge of Nicholas' *Sermo*, two other parallels are more difficult to dismiss. Arbesmann considered Henry to have been the first Augustinian to have made the claim that "before founding his own Order, St. Francis of Assisi had been a member of the Augustinian hermitage of St. James of Aquaviva near Pisa."[199] The same account, however, is found in Nicholas' *Sermo*, word for word.[200] Yet, *pace* Arbesmann, neither Henry, nor Nicholas, was the first to make the connection between Francis and the Augustinian hermits in Italy. In his discussion of the religious Orders that arose after the early Augustinian hermits, the author of the *Initium* then returned to the early groups of Tuscan anchorites

---

[196] Saak, "Augustinian Identity," 156–158.

[197] For the text of the Bull as cited by Henry, see Arbesmann's notes to Hen. *Tract.* 3 (104,164–105,174; 133–134).

[198] Hen. *Tract.* 4 (108,83–109,97); *cf.* Nic.Al. *Sermo* (372). For Joachimist influences in the OESA, see Marjorie Reeves, "Joachimist Expectations in the Order of Augustinian Hermits," *RThAM* 25 (1958), 111–141; *cf.* A. Zumkeller, "Joachim von Fiore und sein angeblicher Einfluss auf den Augustiner-Eremitenorden (Kritische Bemerkungen zu einer Untersuchung M. Reeves)," *Augustinianum* 3 (1963), 382–388.

[199] Arbesmann, "Henry of Friemar's Treatise," 62–63.

[200] Saak, "Augustinin Identity," 158.

and hermits, from whom the OESA originated. Among these the author mentioned blessed William and blessed Galganus.[201] He then commented: "Blessed Francis, visiting those said hermits, filled with the grace of the Holy Spirit in the year of our Lord 1206 began the perfect Order of Friars Minor."[202] If the version whereby Francis not only visited the Augustinian hermits in Tuscany, but also lived with them and perhaps was even one of them, had been commonly known within the Order in 1330, the author of the *Initium* surely would have reported the fact; yet he limited his account to Francis' visit to the Tuscan hermits. Only then with Nicholas do we find the account of Francis, as some say, having been a member of the Augustinian hermits in the hermitage of St. James of Aquaviva, near Pisa, which Henry copied verbatim. The author of the *Initium*, Nicholas, and Henry all composed their works within approximately four years of each other, 1330, 1332, and 1334 respectively. If the story of Francis' Augustinian origins had been common knowledge, it seems strange that the author of the *Initium* would have toned down the story to a mere visit, and have omitted the precise location thereof. It could be that both Nicholas and Henry used the same source, which perhaps was also their common source for their parallel representations of Simplicianus as a hermit, not found in the *Initium* or the earlier Florentine *Vita*. Yet even if not completely conclusive, taken together the evidence strongly suggests that Henry knew Nicholas' *Sermo*, and used it as a major source for his *Tractatus*. Moreover, Henry claimed that Valerius had given Augustine a garden in a wooded villa where he could establish his monastery. Nicholas was the first to place Valerius' garden in a wooded villa. Either Henry took this over from Nicholas, or happened to come up with the same rather odd presentation independently, which seems highly unlikely. Henry was present in Paris in 1329 for the General Chapter, at which the negotiations with the Canons were again discussed,[203] and as mentioned above, Nicholas had been involved with the negotiations from the very beginning. It is thus certainly possible that the two had met in Paris, or at least that they had known each other,

---

[201] *Initium* (343).
[202] "Beatus autem Franciscus dictos heremitas visitans, Sancti Spiritus gratia aff[l]atus, anno Domini MCCVI° perfectum Ordinem fratrum minorum incepit." *Initium* (343).
[203] Arbesmann, "Henry of Friemar's Treatise," 43.

given their respective positions in the Order. It should also be noted that Henry embellished the accounts found in Nicholas. I have already discussed this with regard to Henry's portrayal of Simplicianus. With the Francis account, in some of the manuscripts of the *Tractatus* there are additional interpolations. Arbesmann included these in his edition by printing them in smaller font and marking them as particular to a given manuscript, without having discussed the possibility of redaction.[204] Yet if Henry was "rewriting" Nicholas, it could very well have been that he first included a more straight-forward account drawn from Nicholas and then later re-worked his source, thus yielding the interpolations in the other manuscripts.

Henry's rewriting of Nicholas can also be seen in the third story that Arbesmann saw as originating with Henry, namely, the vision of Alexander IV.[205] Above I have pointed to the development in the representations of the vision, which first appears in the *Initium*, where we find as well the first mention of a connection between Francis and the Hermits. Henry's version is far closer to Nicholas' than to that of the *Initium*, which again, in light of the evidence presented here suggests that Henry had Nicholas' *Sermo* on his desk.[206] Two points are to be noted in this regard. First, Henry followed the version of the vision as found in Nicholas more closely than he did that in the *Initium*, and thus what I said above concerning the variations between the *Initium* and Nicholas applies as well to Henry's account, namely, an emphasis on the active role given to Augustine. Second, Henry did not simply copy Nicholas' version. As he did with the story of Simplicianus, Henry embellished the text as found in his source. There are two aspects of Henry's emplotment that merit special mention. First, he increased the active role of Augustine even further by being the first to refer to Augustine's appearance to Alexander as a divine oracle. As mentioned above and as to be discussed in more detail below, Jordan would take this over from Henry, while then adding his own contribution of attributing the instigation

---

[204] Hen. *Tract.* 5 (111–112); *cf.* Arbesmann, "Henry of Friemar's Treatise," 81–88.

[205] In his notes to Henry's presentation of the vision, Arbesmann refers the reader to the note in *VF* (450, note 9), concerning Jordan's version of the vision, in which Arbesmann and Hümpfner state that Henry was the first Augustinian to have included the vision, and note the parallel with the Franciscan tradition regarding Francis appearing to Innocent III in a vision, but do not mention the Dominican tradition.

[206] Saak, "Augustinian Identity," 160–161.

of the Union completely to Augustine's will (*volens dispersionem suae Religionis congregari*). If Nicholas' version represents an intensification of the story as given in the *Initium*, Henry's interpolation is an intensification of Nicholas. Second, Henry went beyond the mere repetition of the mythical account. To this vision, Henry joined the mission statement of the OESA: Alexander charging the Order with teaching and preaching, sending the hermits into the cities.

> For in the time of Pope Alexander IV, as he himself testified, blessed Augustine appeared to him in a vision with a large head, but small body. From this vision, as if from a divine oracle, the Pope was moved to unite with the hermit friars of St. Augustine many other Orders living similarly in hermitages, commanding them that their members capable of doing so were to bring forth fruits among the people by teaching the divine word, because they were to live in the cities and to nourish the people of God by their exemplary life, their salutary teaching, and by hearing confessions.[207]

The distinction in the Order's history drawn by Alexander commissioning the sons of Augustine to teach and preach in the cities supplies proof of the OESA's antiquity and continuity. As Henry affirmed, the OESA was much older than either the Franciscan or the Dominican Order with regard to its institution by Augustine himself, although in terms of its missionary, pastoral endeavor received from Alexander, it followed the other two mendicant Orders. Thus Henry was able to meet challenges regarding the OESA's recent origins. The Order itself can be traced back to Augustine, yet its missionary presence in the cities is dated to the time after the Great Union. Henry provided a defense for the ecclesiastical and papal confirmation of the Order's legitimacy in light of Lateran IV's ban on new religious Orders, repeated at the Second Council of Lyon.[208] This distinction Jordan would later designate as that between the *status antiquus* and *status modernus*.

---

[207] "Nam tempore Alexandri papae IV, ut ipsemet testatus est, beatus Augustinus eidem in visione apparuit grandis quidem capite sed membris exilis. Ex qua visione tamquam divino oraculo ipse papa commonitus univit fratribus eremitis sancti Augustini plures alios ordines similiter in eremis habitantes, mandans ipsis ut, quicumque ex eis essent idonei ad fructificandum in populo per doctrinam verbi divini, quod illi deberent in civitatibus habitare et exemplari vita ac salutari doctrina simulque confessione provida dei populum irrigare..." Hen. *Tract.* 3 (103, 120–128).

[208] Hen. *Tract.* 4 (109,98–105).

In his exposition of Augustine's vision to Alexander, Henry affirmed the Order's pastoral mission to bear fruit among the people. In his vision to Alexander, Augustine appeared with a large head but small body, which then was in need of "filling out." As Henry explicitly stated, the members of the Order were the members of Augustine's body: "holy mother Church recognized for our Order the most holy Augustine for our true father and unique head, and consequently the friars of this Order ought to be called his true sons and his own members."[209] The OESA was to be the embodiment of Augustine. When the Augustinian myth was put in service of a programmatic mission, myth gave birth to identity. This identity was still in its embryonic stage in Henry's *Tractatus*; Jordan would textually bring it to term in his *Collectanea Augustiniana*.

E. Jordan's *Collectanea Augustiniana*

Manuscript 251 of the Bibliothèque de l'Arsenal in Paris is the autograph copy of Jordan of Quedlinburg's *Collectanea Augustiniana*. As the ascribed title suggests, this manuscript contains a miscellany of writings dealing with Augustine.[210] In his prologue, Jordan mentions that he gathered together into one volume a number of sermons of Augustine, together with other works, including the *Vitae* of Augustine and Monica.[211] These Jordan presented to the Order's *studium* in Paris in 1343.[212] With the *Collectanea*, Jordan brought the discussion of the Order's origins to a new level. He based his narrative of Augustine's biography on a previously unused collection of sources: the sermons of Augustine himself. These sermons, which Jordan used as the major proof-texts for his *Vita Sancti Augustini*, offered hard evidence of Augustine's eremiticism for these were the *Sermones ad fratres*

---

[209] "... quod sancta mater ecclesia sanctissimum Augustinum nostro ordini pro vero patre et singulari capite recognoscit et per consequens fratres huius ordinis eius veri filii et eius membra propria dici debent." Hen. *Tract.* 3 (105,174–177).

[210] For a description of the manuscript, see Appendix D.

[211] The title is given by Hümpfner. Jordan does not give a title to the work as such. In his prologue he writes: "... quosdam sermones beatissimi patris nostri ac doctoris eximii Augustini, cum quibusdam aliis tractatibus, seu opusculis, vel legendis, de vita et gestis eiusdem sancti patris, ac sue pie matris sancte Monice atque de translationibus eorundem ... in unum volumen colleg ..." Jor. *Coll.*, fol. 1ʳ; *cf.* Hümpfner, intro., xxiv–xxv.

[212] It is reasonable to assume with Hümpfner that Jordan prepared this work to present to his brothers in Paris when he made his visitation of the French Province; Hümpfner, intro. xxv.

suos in eremo. No longer was there need to debate the details, offering creative reconstructions of Augustine's early monastic life in Italy and in Africa; the evidence was at hand. Thus in the prologue to his *Vita*, Jordan stated that he "resolved to insert nothing in this work that was not confirmed by Augustine's own words or by other authenticated sources."[213]

Hümpfner considered Jordan's acceptance of the *Sermones ad fratres in eremo* as authentic works of Augustine "regrettable," much in the same fashion as Arbesmann viewed Henry of Friemar's lack of historiographical acumen. Referring to Jordan's use of these pseudo-Augustinian sermons for his *Liber Vitasfratrum*, Hümpfner commented:

> In view of the manner of historical writing of this time, Jordanus deserves much credit for his critical attitude and his sincere efforts both to report only ascertained facts and to understand their background and interrelations ... In view of this evident striving for a critical and objective attitude towards matters of tradition, the failure of Jordanus to recognize the false attribution of the *Sermones ad fratres in eremo* is all the more regrettable. An additional cause was the confused and confusing controversy between the Augustinian Hermits and Regular Canons.[214]

The debate between the Hermits and the Canons was certainly a factor, even though Arbesmann argued that Jordan deplored the controversy, preferring to focus on religious obedience, rather than historical priority.[215] After all, even accepting the authenticity of the myth, routinely following the *Rule* did not, as such, make one truly an Augustinian; the habit, as Jordan affirmed, did not make the monk.[216] One must live the life established by the bishop of Hippo himself. This certainly was the Augustinian Gerard of Bergamo's argument in his quodlibetic question, *De praestantia religionis sancti Augustini*, debated in Paris in 1333. As already mentioned, Gerard had been involved in the negotiations with the Canons in Pavia from the very beginning, yet he refrained from appealing to any of the historico-mythic elements that were so important for the authors

---

[213] "... nichil huic operi inserendum censui, quod non ipsius propriis dictis, aut aliorum authenticis scriptis confirmetur." Jor., *Coll.* Prol., fol. 54rb.

[214] Hümpfner, intro. lxxiv–lxxv; *cf.* Arbesmann, "Henry of Friemar's Treatise," 45 and 66.

[215] Arbesmann, "Henry of Friemar's Treatise," 59–60; *cf. VF* 2,14 (165,3–179,412).

[216] "... quia habitus non facit monachum, sed professio et observantia regularis...," *VF* 1,20 (72); *cf.* Saak, "The *Figurae Bibliorum* of Antonius Rampegolus," 34.

treated above, and for Jordan to be treated forthwith and in the following chapter. Gerard formed his argument for the legitimacy of the OESA on the basis of its legitimately adhering and conforming to the way of life expressed in Augustine's *Rule*.[217] Jordan would have heartily agreed. To be an Augustinian, one had above all to live as an Augustinian, whether as a Canon or as a Hermit. The question was simply whether one could in fact do so as a Canon. Though Jordan indeed makes very conciliatory statements regarding the Canons and their coexistence with the Hermits as custodians of Augustine's tomb both to close his *Collectanea* and in his later *Opus Dan*,[218] his "deploring" the issue should be read in the broader context of his arguments for the priority of the Hermits.

The polemical nature of Jordan's *Collectanea*, as well as that of his *Liber Vitasfratrum*, is called into question by Hümpfner's argument that Jordan had conceived of the *Liber Vitasfratrum* already as a student in Bologna and Paris, using the *Collectanea* as preparatory material.[219] In the prologue to the *Collectanea*, Jordan states that he collected into one volume material which he had received from Paris, Rome, and other established monasteries.[220] On this basis, together with

---

[217] See Kaspar Elm, "*De praestantia religionis S. Augustini*: Eine als verloren geltende Quaestio quodlibetica des Augustiner-Eremiten Gerhard von Bergamo (d. 1355)," in *Mittelalterliche Texte. Überlieferung—Befund—Deutungen*, Kolloquium der Zentraldirektion der Monumenta Germaniae Historica am 28./29. Juni 1996, *MGH.SS* 42, ed. Rudolf Schieffer (Hannover, 1996), 155–172. Elm suggests Jordan's dependence on Gerhard's *Questio* ("*De praestantia*," 170–171), though I have found no such evidence.

[218] "Quod quidem festum reconditionis eiusdem sacratissimi corporis ibidem tam a canonicis regularibus quam a fratribus eremitarum ordinis in eadem basilica sancti Petri in celo aureo deo et eidem beatissimo patri utriusque ordinis eorum institutori pariter famulantibus condigna honorificentia peragitur et usque in hodiernum diem annis singulis sollemniter celebratur. Regnante domino nostro Iesu Christo cui est honor et gloria in secula seculorum, Amen." *Legenda Sancti Augustini*, Jor. *Coll.*, fol. 104[ra]. In his sermon *De translatione Sancti Augustini* of his *Opus Dan*, Jordan showed no signs of contention: "Unde pro maiori veneratione tanti Patris, iuxta ecclesiam sancti Petri in caelo aureo in qua requiescit, duo monasteria duorum ordinum quos idem pater seipsum instituisse legitur existunt constituta; unum videlicet canonicarum regularium et aliud fratrum heremitarum, qui diebus et noctibus in eadem ecclesia convenientes ad honorem et laudem dei et beati Patris Augustini divinis officiis invigilant incessanter." Jor. *OD* (ed. Strassburg, 1484), sermo 59F.

[219] Hümpfner, intro., l–li.

[220] ". . . quosdam sermones beatissimi patris nostri ac doctoris exemii Augustini . . . prout ad me fide digna assertione ac fideli communicatione undequaque exemplaria devenerunt, quibusdam quidem de Parisiis, quibusdam vero de Curia Romana, nonnullis quoque de antiquis et approbatis monasteriis ad me perductis, in unum volumen collegi . . ." Jor. *Coll.*, fol. 1[v]; *cf.* Hümpfner, intro., xxiv–xxv.

Jordan's self-reference as "least among the scholars of Paris," Hümpfner claimed that "the material was mainly collected in Paris,"[221] which he assumed Jordan himself had begun doing already in 1319–1322, at least five years previous to the onset of the controversy with the Canons.[222]

There is, however, no firm evidence for such an early origin for Jordan's conception of writing the history of his Order. Moreover one must question whether this was even possible, at least with regard to the *Sermones ad fratres in eremo*. The origins of these sermons remain in a fog of uncertainty and only a separate, thorough study of all the relevant material might shed new light on the matter. For now it must suffice to say that Hümpfner considered the *Sermones ad fratres in eremo* to have been compiled by a Benedictine monk long before Jordan's time.[223] Jordan's collection of the sermons nevertheless is the first such collection, and his manuscript was used by the Maurists and subsequently Migne for their editions, albeit containing a much expanded number of sermons. Hümpfner pointed to the *Sermones beatissimi patris Augustini ad heremitas fratres suos* collected by the Chancellor of the University of Paris, Robert de Bardis.[224] Two manuscripts containing de Bardis' collection claim that the sermons were "found in Paris" by de Bardis. The collection, and the order of the sermons thereof, is parallel to that of Jordan, leading Hümpfner to posit that de Bardis either copied from Jordan or from the same sources as Jordan.[225]

Robert de Bardis was chancellor from 1336 to 1349, a friend of Petrarch's, and a respected scholar of Augustine. Katherine Walsh has noted Hümpfner's claim regarding the relationship between Jordan's collection and that of de Bardis, though Walsh argues that the copying process must have gone in the reverse.[226] Hümpfner had mentioned that the relationship between de Bardis' collection and

---

[221] Hümpfner, intro. xxv.
[222] *Ibid.*, xxiv.
[223] *Ibid.*, xxix.
[224] *Ibid.*, xxvii.
[225] *Ibid.*
[226] Katherine Walsh, "Wie ein Bettelorden zu (s)einem Gründer kam. Fingierte Traditionen um die Entstehung der Augustiner-Eremiten," in *Fälschungen im Mittelalter*. Internationaler Kongress der Monumenta Germaniae Historica, München, 16.–19. September 1986, Teil V: *Fingierte Briefe, Frömmigkeit und Fälschung. Realienfälschungen*, *MGH.SS* 33/V (Hannover, 1988), 585–610; 599.

Jordan's could only be established by comparing the Vatican and Parisian manuscripts of Robert's collection, a task he was prevented from carrying out due to World War II. The Vatican manuscript, however, rather than stemming from the early fifteenth century as Hümpfner supposed based on the printed catalogue, actually dates from the first half of the fourteenth century; the manuscript, according to Walsh, is a typical example of Parisian book-production of the second third of the fourteenth century, and was de Bardis' personal copy.[227] The sermons contained in this collection, however, are not given the title *Sermones ad fratres in eremo*, and thus Walsh argues that Jordan, though not having been responsible for the collection as such, was the one to give the collection its name.[228] In this light, it seems highly unlikely that de Bardis used Jordan's *Collectanea* as his model, but it is most suggestive that Jordan's collection was made based on that of de Bardis; in other words, that Jordan came across the sermons only sometime after 1336. Moreover, Balbino Rano argues that the compiler/author of the *Sermones ad fratres in eremo*, whoever that might have been, used the historical works of Henry of Friemar, Nicholas of Alessandria, and the Anonymous Florentine, thus pointing as well to the origins of the sermons as dating from after 1334.[229] If the *Sermones ad fratres in eremo* did not exist before the mid 1330s, then Jordan could not have begun his literary work on the *Collectanea* already in 1319–1322 in Paris, aside from in a most rudimentary form. This would further imply that Jordan himself was most likely not the one who found the sermons, since he was at this time lector in Magdeburg. Yet had he made his desire of collecting material on Augustine known—and Hümpfner claimed that by 1338 at the General Chapter in Siena, knowledge of Jordan's project was already wide-spread in the Order[230]—his co-religious in Paris could very well have sent him the *sermones*, perhaps as copied from de Bardis, which would then also coincide with Jordan's statement in his prologue that he gathered together into one volume sources he had received.

Hümpfner argued that while Jordan was still in Bologna he developed the inspiration for his *Liber Vitasfratrum* having been influenced

---

[227] *Ibid.*
[228] *Ibid.*, 600.
[229] See Balbino Rano, "San Agustín y los orígenes de su Orden," 710–720.
[230] Hümpfner, intro. xxx.

by the Dominican *Vitasfratrum* and the *Libellus de principiis Ordinis Praedicatorum* of that Order's second General, the blessed Jordan of Saxony (d. 1237).[231] It may have been natural for our Jordan to have longed for such a book while a student at Bologna as the one he eventually wrote, yet the evidence suggests another course of progression. From 1322 to c. 1333 Jordan was lector in Erfurt, working very closely with Henry of Friemar. Henry exercised a considerable influence on Jordan. When Jordan assumed his position in Erfurt Henry was already an old man, having been born in 1245. Jordan himself testifies to Henry's age in his *Liber Vitasfratrum*. In his list of the outstanding scholars of the Order, Jordan includes Henry and praises his studiousness. Even in his old age, as a septuagenarian and beyond, Jordan relates, Henry studied night and day, and would remain in his study, even though "some young, new lector" might insist on daily academic disputations. There can be little doubt that the *lector recens aliquis* was Jordan himself, who would have arrived in Erfurt when Henry was seventy-seven years old. There was much affection between the two, and Jordan reveals his having often heard from Henry that although his head never hurt from studying, sometimes his backparts did (... *nonnumquam dorsum suum ex incubitu studii doluisse confessus est*)![232] And as seen above, during the years at least from 1329 to 1334, Henry was viscerally engrossed in the debates with the Canons over custody of Augustine's tomb in Pavia, and thus over the two Orders' respective claims to historical priority. His involvement in this issue might also have been the reason why in 1331 he delegated the responsibility of adjudicating the case of the archbishop of Magdeburg's murder to Jordan.[233] It is most plausible to assume that Jordan likewise became rapt with the Order's case during this time. Whereas coming to Erfurt eager for scholarly disputations in public forum, working closely with Henry, Jordan may very well have redirected his efforts, especially after his experience in 1327, two months before the Order received permission to establish a house adjoining San Pietro's in Pavia. As related in the *Liber Vitasfratrum*, William of Cremona was divinely moved to begin to consider the possibilities of regaining possession of Augustine's body.

---

[231] Hümpfner, intro. 1; for the Dominican *Liber Vitasfratrum*, see Füser, "Vom *exemplum Christi*," 78–94; and Schürer, "Die Dominikaner," *passim*.
[232] *VF* 2,22 (238,142–154).
[233] See Chapter Three below.

Even though, Jordan confesses, leaving aside all mention of the political maneuverings, such a suggestion seemed unthinkable and indeed impossible, William was nevertheless comforted by a divine oracle and began negotiations with the Papacy.[234] That William would be successful was indicated to a well-known brother of the Order in a vision. The *frater nominatus in Ordine* was surely none other than Jordan himself.[235] In the vision, the brother saw himself together with many other Augustinians, in a Church not of their Order, in which was a large tomb of a great bishop that had fallen into disrepair. As the brothers were gazing at the tomb, the image of the bishop on the tomb rose and went to the altar, and began to sing, "Come, come, come, my sons, and listen to me, and I will teach you the fear of the Lord." The brothers all sat before the bishop and he then gave them such exhortation as a father would give to his sons. On this basis, Jordan affirms, "that brother understood that he was spiritually in the presence of blessed Augustine." Augustine then gave each of the brothers drink from a glass, and when they had all drunk Augustine blessed them and returned to his tomb, whereupon the friars all began to weep, but Augustine comforted them saying in the words of Christ, "Do not weep, my sons, for I will be with you until the end of the world." Whereupon the brother woke, and still tasted the sweetness of the drink he had been given. From this vision, he was filled with wonder and praised God, hoping that the vision indicated that something beneficial for the Order was to come, and sure enough, within two months the documents arrived notifying the Order of the pope's decision to entrust the Hermits with Augustine's body.[236]

---

[234] *VF* 1,18 (62,22–63,31).
[235] Hümpfner, intro. li.
[236] "Porro ista diu affectata reunio, antequam facta esset, cuidam fratri nominato in Ordine per visum revalata fuit hoc modo. Videbatur enim ei, quod ipse cum multis fratribus et melioribus personis Ordinis esset in quadam ecclesia non nostri Ordinis, in qua erat quoddam sepulcrum elevatum unius magni sancti episcopi, sicut ex figura imaginis desuper sculptae ostendebatur. Quod quidem sepulcrum minus decenter a personis illius ecclesiae tenebatur. Nam pulpita et candelabra antiqua cum pulveribus irreverenter superiactata apparebant. Itaque fratribus in ecclesia stantibus et sepulcrum aspicientibus, ecce imago episcopi visa est se elevare et illas scorias super se iactatas indignanter reicere. Et sic surgens episcopus de tumulo pontificaliter indutus ivit stare ante altare et invitans ad se fratres cantare coepit: *Venite*, venite, venite, *filii, audite me: timorem Domini docebo vos* [Ps. 33:12]. Et cantavit haec verba in nota gradualis, sicut episcopi in inthronizationibus cantare solent. Quo expleto sedit ipse, et fratres omnes ante se per ordinem sedere iussit. Et tunc

While it might be tempting to view this account as having stemmed from Jordan having partaken a bit too much from the glass *cum potu valde claro et pulchro* before he had the vision, it can also be seen as a statement of his own realization of Augustine's paternity of the Order. And it could very well have been only as a result of such a vision that Jordan turned from seeking academic debate in the classroom to putting his energies into investigating the true sons of Augustine, their origins and their history and what it meant to be such in the first place. Working together then with Henry, he could have developed the conception for his project at that time, and began making known that he sought documentation of all sorts for the history of the Order, to extend on a grand scale the work that Henry in his very old age was sketching in his *Tractatus*. For such a project, in the years around 1327 and shortly thereafter, he would have known as well that a major issue in the debate with the Canons was the biography of Augustine with respect to his monastic foundations. Thus Jordan set to work, and began seeking information, which sometime in the mid 1330s resulted in his being sent the sermons of Augustine which Jordan recognized as having been addressed to Augustine's own hermits. In the later 1330s Jordan was busy writing the life of Augustine anew, from the ground up, so to speak, as well as working on his sermons, and fulfilling his teaching and administrative responsibilities. When in 1343 he was appointed to make the visitation of the Order's French Province, what better gift could he bring along than the first results he had achieved based on the

---

dulcem exhortationem velut pater suis filiis fecit. Ex quo iste frater intellexit in spiritu illum fore beatum Augustinum. Volens autem idem antistes fratribus amorem ostendere singularem, habebat quidem in manu sua vitrum mundum cum potu valde claro et pulchro, bibit ipse primo et postea per ordinem de manu singulis propinavit, intonans valde dulciter et cantans illud: *Aqua sapientiae salutaris potavit eos Dominus* [Sir. 15:3]. Et cum pervenisset episcopus ad fratrem istum, bibit et ipse, fuitque potus nobilis et dulcis, inusitatum saporem habens quasi claretum antiquum, ex quo potu frater iste totus exhilaratus fuit. Et cum bibissent omnes, episcopus benedixit eis, et sic ad sepulcrum suum redire coepit. Quod videntes fratres unanimiter fleverunt, dolentes de patris recessu. Ipse autem consolans eos paterne ait eis: 'Nolite flere, filii. *Ecce enim vobiscum ero usque ad consummationem saeculi*' [Mt. 28:20]. Hoc dicto frater iste evigilabit et invenit os suum, linguam et palatum de potu illo valde dulcoratum. Unde repletus stupore et gaudio gratias egit Deo, sperans illam visionem non esse otiosam, sed alicuius boni pro Ordine praesagam, sicut non multo post claruit in effectu. Nam infra duos menses vel circa venerunt litterae certae de Curia Romana nuntiantes nova, quomodo corpus beatissimi Patris Augustini esset Ordini redonatum. Per omnia benedictus Deus." *VF* 1,18 (65,98–67,135).

material that his brothers in Paris had procured for him, to gather it all together into one volume, to bring back to Paris the fruits of knowledge that had sprung from there in the first place, as he stated in the prologue to the *Collectanea*?[237]

Though such a portrayal is not based on concrete evidence, given the problems with dating the origins of the *Sermones ad fratres in eremo*, and given the context of Erfurt in the late 1320s and early 1330s, it seems as plausible, if not certainly more so, than Hümpfner's assumptions that Jordan conceived of his *Liber Vitasfratrum* while a student in Bologna, and then began preliminary work in Paris collecting material for his *Collectanea*, deploring all the while the controversy with the Canons. Jordan having joined Henry's campaign to defend the Order against the position of the Canons, continuing the work of his beloved teacher on a grand scale, seems more likely to account for the origins of Jordan's endeavor than his own piety in Bologna and Paris as a student. It also places both the *Collectanea* and the *Liber Vitasfratrum* within the context of the debates, which both texts clearly evidence. Hümpfner himself, after all, points to the final form of the *Collectanea* as taking shaping only after 1334. Despite what may seem on the surface as conciliatory remarks, much as those of Nicholas of Alessandria, Jordan's throwing bones to the Canons was possible only because in his eyes there was nothing in fact to debate; the Hermits were the only legitimate first-born sons of their father Augustine, the founder of the Order. And Jordan could prove such based on Augustine's words themselves, words preached to his own hermits, which offered the textual basis for Jordan's re-emplotment of Augustine's biography in the most extensive narrative since that of Philip of Harvengt. Jordan's *Vita Sancti Augustini* certainly evidences an ingenious reworking through the source material, the new as well as the old, and a reworking with the eye of a textual critic. Thereby, together with his *Liber Vitasfratrum*, Jordan gave new meaning and new foundations to his Order's mythic origins.[238]

---

[237] "Ipsumque ad locum parisiensem Mare utique copiosum, unde omnia scientiarum flumina exire dinoscuntur destinare sategi. Quatenus exinde fluat iterum per ordinem universum, obsecrans in visceribus caritatis, ut quicumque fratrum de studio conventus nostri parisiensis, cui hunc librum in libraria eiusdem conventus ad communem utilitatem ponendum pro munusculo caritatis donare decrevi, in eo legerit vel eum forsitan transcibi fecerit, oret pro donantis anima, ut Augustini meritis celi fruatur gaudiis. Amen." Jor. *Coll.*, fol. 1vb.

[238] For the text of Jordan's *Vita*, see Appendix D.

Jordan's *Vita Sancti Augustini* is based on a close reading of Augustine's *Confessions* and *Retractations*, together with the "Medieval Augustine," namely, the *Vitae Sancti Augustini* of Possidius, Philip of Harvengt, and Jacobus de Voragine's *Legenda Aurea*. Jordan supplemented this textual foundation with the sermons of Augustine collected in his *Collectanea*—and the *Sermones ad fratres in eremo* most of all—as well as with the *Chronica* of Datius, Bishop of Milan. In his *Annotatio temporum beati Augustini episcopi*, which follows the *Vita* in the *Collectanea*, Jordan reconstructed the basic outline of Augustine's life as extracted from the *Confessions*. In the *Annotatio* no mention is made of the *Sermones ad fratres in eremo*, and there it no evidence that they were used. Jordan only refers to Augustine's foundation of a monastery in Hippo before his ordination, which Jordan could have taken from Possidius' comment that Augustine founded a monastery upon being made presbyter, as he had previously done when he returned from overseas. It could be that the *Annotatio* represents Jordan's earliest work on his new project. Retracing Augustine's early years, Jordan argues that Augustine was thirty years of age when he was swayed by Ambrose's preaching, though not yet completely converted to the Christian faith. The following year, when he was thirty-one, Augustine visited Simplicianus. It was only thereafter when he was thirty-two that he was finally converted to Christ, and at Easter of his thirty-second year he was baptized. The following year, namely, his thirty-third, Monica died at Ostia and Augustine returned to Africa, remaining a layperson for a period of three years, which extended from the construction of his monastery outside of Hippo to his ordination as presbyter, the latter thus having occurred in his thirty-sixth year. Jordan expressly rejects the opinions of those who claim that Augustine was baptized when he was thirty years old, or when he was thirty-three.[239] This reconstruction thus negates speculations on Augustine having established his first monastery in Italy, writing the *Rule* for the Tuscan hermits of Centumcellae. Yet this does not imply that Jordan was immune from repeating the mythical aspects of the Order's origins. His *Vita Sancti Augustini* provided the historical proof for the Hermit's claims, including new evidence for the connections between Augustine's monasticism in Italy and Africa, which rendered the possible stay at Centumcellae irrelevant.

---

[239] For the text of Jordan's *Annotatio Temporum*, see Saak, "Augustinian Identity," 264, n. 35.

228   CHAPTER TWO

In Jordan's account, Simplicianus is given a role of even larger proportions than he already had in the representations of Nicholas of Alessandria and Henry of Friemar. God gave Augustine the idea, Jordan relates, to go to Simplicianus to confess the errors of his earlier life and to learn from him, since Simplicianus, a hermit, had served God most devoutly from his youth. This Augustine did, and Simplicianus exhorted him to follow the example of Victorinus, whose story Simplicianus told Augustine. Based on this example, Augustine was so moved that he desired only to serve God. Thus he was converted from the exhortation of the old saint Simplicianus and from the examples of Simplicianus' community of hermits, which Augustine desired to follow.[240] Having then been baptized by Ambrose, "Augustine received from that saint Simplicianus the habit of holy comportment and the form of living, which later he would spread everywhere in Africa."[241] When on the instigation of his mother, Augustine decided to return to Africa, "he went to St. Simplicianus asking him for some servants of God from his own group of brother hermits whom he could take along with him to Africa and with them to establish the Order there."[242] Simplicianus granted his request and gave to him twelve friars, the number of Christ's apostles, with whom Augustine returned to Africa, together with his friends Nebridius, Evodius,

---

[240] "Cum autem iam via Christi sibi placeret, sed per ipsam adhuc ire pigeret, misit dominus in mentem eius visumque est ei bonum pergere ad Simplicianum heremitam servum dei, audierat ei quod a iuventute sua devotissime deo servierat et vere sic erat. Iam vero senuerat et multa expertus, multa edoctus erat, et beatus Ambrosius vere eum ut patrem diligebat. Cui estus cordis et errorum circuitus manifestans, ipse scilicet Augustinus devote postulavit ut vir sanctus proferret ei quis esset aptus modus vivendi. Sic affecto ut ipse erat ad ambulandum in via dei, videbat enim plenam ecclesiam et alius sic ibat, alius autem sic displicebat quippe ei quidquid agebat in seculo pre dulcendine dei et decore domus eius quam dilexit. Simplicianus autem eum hortari cepit et ad humilitatem Christi precipue invitavit et inter invitandum Victorini Romani quondam rethoris conversionem in medium recitavit. Rome siquidem multis annis Victorinus ille magister fuerat, et ob insigne preclari magisterii statuam in Romano foro habere meruerat, qui tandem conversus loquacem scolam suam deserens in scola Christi humilis discipulus effectus est. Hoc exemplo commonitus Augustinus ad imitandum exarsit, et soli deo servire proposuit." Jor. *Vita* 4,1–3, fol. 57^{ra-b}.

[241] "Ab ipso sancto Simpliciano sancte conversationis habitum formamque vivendi accepit, quam postmodum in Africa exuberans redolevit." Jor. *Vita* 6,5, fol. 59vb.

[242] "Post hec autem cum instigante eius pia matre de Mediolano recedere et ad Africam remeare disponeret, adivit sanctum Simplicianum petens ut sibi aliquos de fratribus suis eremitis servos dei donaret, quos secum in Africam assumeret et cum eis ibi ordinem plantaret." Jor. *Vita* 7,1, fol. 60ra.

Alipius, and Pontianus, his mother, Monica, and son, Adeodatus. This information Jordan had from one of the *Sermones ad fratres in eremo*, which then also named the twelve, a passage that Jordan inserted into his *Vita* as proof.[243] Having returned to Africa, Jordan and his band of followers sought a place where they could live a life devoted to God, which they found outside Hippo, where bishop Valerius built for them a monastery. Here they began to live as a group according to the apostolic rule.[244] Jordan is very clear: this monastery was Augustine's first monastery, and there he gathered together dispersed hermits, giving them a form of living in keeping with the apostolic way of life and "thus Augustine instituted the Order of Hermits."[245]

This then was the first of Augustine's three principal monastic foundations. In the autograph each such foundation is given a separate rubricated heading. The second monastery Augustine founded was in Valerius' garden, after having been made presbyter. Though having been ordained a priest, Augustine still desired to live the monastic life. Being aware of this fact, and having often visited Augustine in his hermitage, Valerius gave him a garden in the city of Hippo where he could establish a second monastery and thus, even as priest, continue to live his monastic life following the apostolic rule, whereby no one would have private possessions, but everything would be held in common and distributed according to need, "which he had previously done," Jordan continued, "when he had

---

[243] "Cuius piis precibus pius ille pater Simplicianus annuens dedit ei duodecim fratres viros religiosos, cum quibus adiunctis sibi carissimis amicis suis qui diu secum fuerant, Nebridio, Evodio, Alipio, et Pontiano, cum matre et filio Adeodato, ad Africam proficiscendi iter arripuit. De hoc ipse in sermone de tribus generibus monachorum, qui incipit *Ut nobis per litteras declaravit sanctus pater Hieronimus*, loquens de genere et ordine heremitaru . . ." Jor. *Vita* 7,1, fol. 60ra. Jordan then quotes from sermon 21 of his own collection of the *sermones ad fratres in eremo*, Jor. *Coll.*, fol. 26^{ra-b}, which is also sermon 21 in the Migne edition, *PL* 40,1268–1269. The twelve hermits named are: Anastasius, Fabianus, Severus, Nicolaus, Dorotheus, Issac, Nicostratus, Paulus, Cyrillus, Stephanus, Iacobus, and Vitalus.

[244] "Itaque apud Hipponem in eremo segregata a gentibus locum aptum ad serviendum deo inveniens cum favore et subsidio sancti Valerii Hipponensis episcopi monasterium ibidem edificavit et in eo fratres eremitas quos undique per nemora conquisivit una cum amicis et fratribus prius eidem adherentibus collocavit et cum eis vivere cepit secundum regulam sub sanctis apostolis constitutam." Jor. *Vita* 9, fol. 61^{va-b}.

[245] "In prefato autem monasterio ipse Augustinus copiosum numerum fratrum congregavit, quibus et modum vivendi secundum formam vite apostolorum tradidit et sic ordinem eremitarum ipse instituit." Jor. *Vita* 9, fol. 62ra.

returned from across the seas to his homeland, as Possidius said."[246] Thus Jordan had made the bridge. There was no longer need to speculate on what this phrase in Possidius signified, creating differing accounts of Augustine's Italian monastic experience. With Jordan the case was closed. Possidius' statement referred to the monastery outside Hippo, which Augustine had first established upon returning from Italy. Yet the Italian origins of the Order were simultaneously established, since that first eremitical community was originally comprised of the *servi dei* from Simplicianus' hermitage whom Jordan had taken along with him from Milan. The eremitical way of life was thus transplanted from Simplicianus' Milan to Augustine's Africa, and it was the latter that served as the stock for all further growth, for it was there, Jordan confirms, that Augustine instituted the Order of Hermits. Moreover, Jordan had proved his point with the very words of Augustine. Yet Jordan did not stop here. Whereas Henry of Friemar linked the Order's charter to preach and teach in the cities with Augustine appearing to Alexander IV, Jordan explains that in his second monastery Augustine taught his friars monastic discipline and the observance of the *Rule*, as well as educating them in the study of holy Scriptures, "so that already they might not live only for themselves, but would also be able to be of benefit to others."[247] Augustine's hermits in his second monastery were to be hermits indeed, but living in the city, they were to study the scriptures in order to serve the populace. This ideal Augustine continued in his third monastic foundation, that which he established after

---

[246] "Reverso itaque Augustino ad monasterium suum, non enim sine monastica disciplina voluit vivere, placuit sancto seni Valerio ordinatori eius ipsum cum suis fratribus in eremo paterne visitare et eis ad tempus pro devotione commanere. Et tunc cognito proposito Augustini quod omnino cum fratribus suis nichil habentibus, nichil habens optabat vivere, monasterium autem istud in eremo nimium distabat a plebe, cuius curam ipse iam presbyter habebat gerere, dedit ei hortum civitati propinquum in quo mox monasterium edificavit et in eo de fratribus prioris monasterii quosdam secum locavit, colligens nichilominus et alios eiusdem propositi fratres clericos servientes et ibidem deo pariter et in communi viventes, secundum modum et regulam sub sanctis apostolis constitutam, maxime ut nemo quidquam proprium in illa sancta societate haberet, sed eis essent omnia communia et distribueretur unicuique sicut opus erat, quod iam ipse prior fecerat, dum de transmarinis ad sua remeasset, ut ait Possidonius." Jor. *Vita* 11,1, fol. 62vb.

[247] "Hos quoque fratres idem pater in omni disciplina et observantia regulari instruxit et nichilominus eos studio sacre scripture erudivit, ut iam non tantum sibi in simplicitate viverent sed et aliis prodesse valerent." Jor. *Vita* 11,1, fol. 63ra.

becoming bishop as a monastery of clerics within the episcopal residence.[248] There was no question: Augustine's Hermits were founded before his Canons, five years before, as Jordan calculated in his *Annotatio*.[249] In his first monastery outside Hippo Augustine had founded his Order of Hermits, which then continued in his second monastery in the city of Hippo, the members of which were to be preachers and teachers for the community. Only after having been ordained bishop did Augustine give a monastic *Rule* to his priests, the Canons. And again, Jordan established this *curriculum vitae* based on Augustine's own words, both those of the *Confessions*, and most of all those of his own sermons, which he had delivered both to his own hermits and to his own priests.[250] This was knowledge that Jordan's brothers in Paris could use very well indeed! It was also the basis for Jordan's comprehensive treatment of the Order, the *Liber Vitasfratrum*, which he completed fourteen years after donating his *Collectanea* to the *studium* in Paris.

The same fervor for the eremitical origins of the Order is present throughout Jordan's *Liber Vitasfratrum*. As he explained in the dedicatory letter to the lector in Avignon, John of Basel, the *Liber Vitasfratrum* was to enable one to determine whether one was a true

---

[248] "Videns autem beatus Augustinus quod necesse erat episcopum assiduam hospitalitatis humanitatem quibusque venientibus sive transeuntibus exhibere, quod in monasterio fratrum convenienter fieri non valebat, voluit in ipsa episcopali domo monasterium secum habere clericorum, ut qui presbyter in horto cum fratribus vixerat in episcopio nichilominus pauper cum pauperibus deo regulariter serviret." Jor. *Vita* 13,1, fol. 64rb.

[249] "Sic enim oportet dicere si volumus salvare calculationem Possidonii, qui dicit eum vixisse in clericatu annis ferme quadraginta et secundum hoc factus est clericus et presbyter anno suo tricesimo sexto. Stetit autem in presbyteratu antequam fieret episcopus per biennium, vel circa ut colligitur ex *Croncia* Eusebii, qui inter conversionem suam per beatum Ambrosium factam et episcopatum calculat octo annos. Quorum tres transegerat Mediolani et Rome, et apud Ostia Tibernia usque ad mortem matris, ut patet ex supradictis. Tres vero alios exegit morans apud agros proprios eo modo quo dictum est. Restat duo anni in presbyteratu, quod tempus videtur satis proportionatum considerata numerositate librorum quos ipse presbyter se scripsisse fatetur in primo libro *Retractationum*. Et secundum hoc non vixit in episcopatu nisi annis xxxviii. Obiit enim annorum lxxvi ut dicit Possidonius et idem in *Cronica* memorata. Et sic intelligendum quod ait Possidonius: Vixit, inquit, in clericatu vel episcopatu annis ferme quadraginta, ut duo anni referantur ad presbyteratum et residui ad episcopatum. Et sic totum tempus clericatus sui fuerunt anni quadraginta." *Annotatio temporum*, Jor. *Coll.*, fol. 72^{rb-va}.

[250] A number of the sermons Jordan includes in his *Collectanea* are designated as *sermones ad presbyteros suos*, which later became part of the larger corpus of the *sermones ad fratres in eremo*.

son of Augustine and thus a true member of Augustine's Order and Augustine's religion. For his *magnum opus*, Jordan re-narrated Augustine's biography in his treatment of the development of the Order, placed in context of the history of western monasticism. Jordan used his own *Vita Sancti Augustini* as a major source, inserting sections therefrom as needed. In his later work he also cited three additional *Sermones ad fratres in eremo* to those contained in the *Collectanea*. Yet while not leaving the controversy with the Canons behind completely, in his *Liber Vitasfratrum*, as we will see in the following chapter, Jordan assumed a far broader perspective and scope: the Augustinian religious identity itself.

These then are the texts of the Augustinian myth, produced within a span of at most twenty years. It is, however, certainly possible that the historical representations of the Order's origins had long been part of the Order's oral traditions, only achieving written form over a half century after the Great Union. Yet in the earliest texts narrating the Order's foundations, first by Augustine and then by Alexander IV—or rather, first by Augustine personally, and then later by Augustine supernaturally—the story does not emerge full-blown all at once. The author of the anonymous Florentine *Vita* may have been at work before he saw the dire need for the extensive account that his co-religious shortly thereafter gave, but certainly the author of the *Initium* sought to use whatever material he could come up with as evidence, even mentioning the lack of sources available for determining where Augustine had established his first monastery in Italy. Thus the *Initium* gives the first mention of St. Francis in connection with the Tuscan hermits, and the first textualization of Augustine appearing to Alexander IV in a vision. Approximately two years later, Nicholas of Alessandria offered embellished accounts of both these events, and turned Simplicianus himself into a hermit. Apparently drawing directly from Nicholas, Henry of Friemar then composed the first treatise explicitly as a defense of the Order, in which he too then rewrote what he found in his source. And Jordan wrote the first biography of Augustine based on clear proof, the words of Augustine himself, preached to his own hermits. The evidence and documentation had arrived; the Canons no longer had a case, for Jordan had Augustine's own *Sermones ad fratres in eremo*. The stories of Augustine's early monasticism may have all been "common knowledge," and they certainly would become so, but between 1330 and 1343, in Florence, Paris, and Erfurt, the accounts of the OESA's origins became increasingly mythicized as they became increasingly textualized.

It is tempting as well to see the embellishment of the myth progressing as it moved north. Having begun in Italy, most likely in Florence with the *Vita* and *Initium*, the myth of Augustine spread to Paris with Nicholas' *Sermo*, and then received its most flowery expression in the Erfurt of Henry, before achieving a historical veneer with Jordan. Such an *itinerarium* is especially compelling if I have been successful above in arguing for Henry's textual dependence on Nicholas' *Sermo*. Yet the fact remains that regardless of Henry's appeal to "ancient legends," and regardless of the *quidam dicunt*'s offered by Henry and Nicholas as rhetorical strategies for giving their accounts plausibility, unless new sources are discovered, the earliest texts extant representing the origins of the OESA are the ones I have treated above, and the ones in which we find a development of the story, the texts in which we find the creation and embellishment of the Augustinian myth. Nicholas' *Sermo* is the earliest extant text that explicitly names Centumcellae as the first location of the OESA, Augustine having lived with the hermits there for two years, and at their request, composed his *Rule*, which then he later established in Africa, once having returned to his homeland. If Nicholas' *Sermo* was also the earliest textual witness available, then recognizing a development of the account would be more tenuous, being the first textualization of an oral tradition. But the fact that the *Initium* leaves the precise details vague, arguing only, though forcefully, that Augustine's first hermitage was in Italy, and there he first wrote the *Rule*, suggests that the tradition of Centumcellae was not so firmly established in 1330 that it was simply accepted as fact. The generally known, accepted, and repeated account of Augustine's early eremitical life was created and established in the course of the 1330s when the author of the *Initium*, Nicholas, Henry, and Jordan created the Augustinian myth in answering the question of what made one an Augustinian, a question that was not simply existential, but one that demanded a clear answer in the political contest for custody of Augustine's relics and tomb. By 1332, within five years of John XXII's Bull *Veneranda sanctorum*, in the midst of the religio-political turmoil that contributed so strongly to the crises of the early fourteenth century, the Augustinian Order created its religious identity, and consequently, was transformed into a mythic community.[251]

Six years later, on 8 June 1338, the General Chapter of the Augustinians opened in Siena, with Prior General William of Cremona presiding. The first order of business was to reconfirm the agreement reached with the Canons.[252] Thereafter, William established 5 June as the Order's official feast day of the reunion of Augustine's body with its head, commemorating the day in 1331 when the evidence of John XXII's Bull was produced, and the Hermits were recognized and accepted in San Pietro in Ciel d'Oro with a kiss of peace.[253] Divine providence it may indeed have been. In attendance were a number of friars whose names we will easily recognize, either from the story thus far told, or soon to be so: in addition to William, and all the other representatives of the Order's provinces, gathered together in Siena were the doctors of theology Lanfranc of Milan, Gerard of Bergamo, and Nicholas of Alessandria; representing the Province of Romandiola was Frater Gregory of Rimini; and representing the Province of Saxony-Thuringia was Frater Jordan of Quedlinburg.[254]

---

[251] The term, 'mythic community' bears similarities to Brian Stock's 'textual communities'; see Stock, *The Implications of Literacy. Written Language and Models of Interpretation in the Eleventh and Twelfth Centuries* (Princeton, 1983); idem, *Listening For The Text. On the Uses of the Past* (Baltimore, 1990). The difference is that the center around which the community is formed is a particular myth rather than a particular text, though acknowledging the difficulties in defining a text as distinct from a myth. The Augustinian myth was certainly textual, but the text of the myth was not necessarily limited by any given written text. In this light, with a broad understanding of text, a mythic community can be considered to be a special type of textual community. To this extent, a mythic community also resembles Renaissance civic myths: see, for example, Donald Weinstein, *Savonarola and Florence. Prophecy and Patriotism in the Renaissance* (Princeton, 1970); Edward Muir, *Civic Ritual in Renaissance Venice* (Princeton, 1981); and Richard Trexler, *Public Life in Renaissance Florence* (New York, 1980). For the Franciscan and Dominican constructions of their mythic origins, see Füser, "Vom *exemplum Christi*," esp. 101–105; Wesjohann, "*Simplicitas*," 162–167.

[252] *CDP* 33 (74–75).
[253] Esteban, *AAug.* IV (1911), 177–178.
[254] *CDP* 33 (74); Esteban, *AAug.* IV (1911), 177.

CHAPTER THREE

PRECEPTS AND PRACTICE: JORDAN OF QUEDLINBURG
AND THE DEFINING OF AUGUSTINIAN LIFE

The Augustinians had their myth. By 1335 the Hermits had at least convinced themselves that they were Augustine's true sons and heirs. It would be ever so easy, so convenient, simply to accept their self-presentation as reflecting their lived reality. Listening to Nicholas of Alessandria and Henry of Friemar, one almost begins to believe that the issue was indeed one of historical priority and that the Hermits were much maligned by the false assertions of the Canons. One can almost forget King John of Bohemia, Louis of Bavaria, Pope John XXII, the Visconti in Milan, and the parishioners in Pavia. One can almost relegate the treatises of Giles of Rome, Augustinus of Ancona, and William of Cremona to the realm of pure political theory, overlooking their attempts to carve out a place for the Augustinians over against the Franciscans and the imperial ideology in the political and ideological battles of the early fourteenth century. One almost passes over unnoticed the Augustinian attempt to turn Francis himself into an Augustinian Hermit. One can almost ignore that the created Augustinian identity was one that was forged by striking the papal hammer against the Augustinian Canons, the Order of Friars Minor, and the emperor as well. One can almost remain peacefully oblivious to the fact that the Augustinian myth and the identity it produced were created in highly charged political contexts with power, prestige, privilege, and parishes at stake. One can almost fail to see that the Order's identity itself was one that was ever so fragile, requiring strenuous efforts to impose and enforce the created ideals by attempting to define and control the day to day experienced reality of the members themselves which ever threatened to shatter the image from inside—one can almost, but not quite. Ideals are like that, ever so seductive, until one actually begins to look beyond their facade.

Precepts and practice are not always at odds, but often they resonate only with dissonance. This was surely the case for the late medieval Augustinians, even at the height of their battle for identity and legitimacy. On 18 April 1328, Louis of Bavaria sat enthroned on the steps of St. Peter's in Rome, dressed in purple, with a crown on his head and scepter in his right hand. The Augustinian Hermit, Nicholas da Fabriano rose and cried out: "Is there any counsel willing to defend the priest Jacques de Cahors, styled John XXII?"[1] Almost a month later, the same Nicholas gave the opening sermon at the assembly that gathered on 12 May 1328 to elect the new pope. In his sermon Nicholas compared Louis of Bavaria with an angel of the Lord, and John XXII with Herod.[2] The choice was clear. The Franciscan Pietro de Corbara was elected as Pope Nicholas V. Nicholas' newly established episcopal hierarchy consisted of only sixteen bishops, chosen by preference from the Orders of Friars Minor and Augustinian Hermits, the two Orders, according to Mollat, that were the most enthusiastic supporters of the emperor's new pope.[3]

That the Augustinians themselves were aware of the tensions within their Order is clear. The Provincial Chapter of the Roman Province in 1328, reasserting the decrees of the General Chapters of 1324 and 1326, prohibited any brother, regardless of status within the Order, from traveling to a territory that was in rebellion against the Church, as well as from receiving or passing along letters or messages from anyone from a community or territory that was in rebellion, unless the benefit for the Church was sufficiently significant and evident. In such cases, special permission from the provincial prior could be granted. If anyone was found transgressing this statute, he would be sentenced to severe penance for a month for his first offense; a second offense carried the same penalty, though for a two-month period in addition to being prohibited from wearing the habit of the Order during that time; for a third offense, the culprit would be imprisoned for a month. Moreover, the same stipulations held for anyone found criticizing the Church, and especially for anyone at all who might dare to claim the anti-pope Pietro de Corbara as other than a heretic and schismatic.[4] This was serious business, and

---

[1] Mollat, *The Popes at Avignon*, 211; Müller, *Der Kampf Ludwigs des Baiern*, 183–184.
[2] Mollat, *The Popes at Avignon*, 212.
[3] *Ibid.*, 215.
[4] "Item quia ex accessu ad terras rebellium consueverunt scandala plurima evenire, cupientes scandalis supradictis salubri remedio obivare, ordinamus et presenti diffinitione mandamus quod nullus frater nostri ordinis, cuiuscumque status et conditionis existat, ad aliquam ire terram rebellem sancte matris ecclesie, nec litteras aliquas vel ambasciatam alicui dictorum rebellium vel communicati procurare debeat

the Augustinians wanted to make sure that their Order would not follow in the footsteps of the Franciscans in backing Louis and his campaign against Pope John XXII.

The extent of Augustinian support for Louis is uncertain, and there is no evidence of widespread defection. The Order, however, was well aware of the danger, and repeatedly stipulated prison sentences for anyone found supporting rebels to Mother Church.[5] Incarceration was no idle threat. The status of the Order was at stake. At the General Chapter meeting of Florence in 1324, Prior General Alexander of San Elpidio condemned as incorrigible Nicholas of Fabriano for having committed grave offenses both in the past and in the present, and sentenced him to be bound in chains for five years, after which he was to be expelled from the Order as a "diseased sheep." Apparently, however, Nicholas sensed the danger and had already fled, perhaps directly to Louis' camp in Pavia, for Alexander continued by commanding all the members of the Order to be on the lookout for Nicholas, and if possible to capture him so that he could be brought to justice.[6]

Alexander was a bit more successful, at least at first, with Frater Andreas of Recanati. At approximately the same time as Nicholas' sentence, Alexander had imprisoned Andreas in Todi for apparently similar reasons, and then transferred him to the Roman Province. This was Alexander's mistake. The prior provincial of the Roman Province, Jacob Sassi, took pity on Andreas, and Andreas became a trusted and respected member of the convent of San Triphone in Rome. He was chosen as one of only three brothers to be the

---

sine expressa licentia in scriptis habita prioris provincialis, quam sine magna et evidenti utilitate ecclesie concedere non presumat; quod si secus presumptum fuerit pro prima vice pene gravioris culpe per mensem transgressor debeat subiacere, pro secunda vero sine habitu continue dictam penam per duos mensem portare cogatur, pro tertia vero vice per mensem carceri mancipetur, cum gravaminibus que in nostris constitutionibus continentur; eidem pene per omnia adiudicamus obloquentes contra statum sancte matris ecclesie et omnes et singulos, qui fratrem Petrum [de Corbara, antipapa], scismaticum et haereticum, aliter quam sic presumpserit nominare." *Esteban, AAug.* 4 (1911/1912), 39.

[5] See above, Chapter One, ns. 314 and 315.

[6] "Item cum fr. Nicolaus qui dicitur monachus multa enormia commiserit de preterio ac etiam de presenti propter que eum merito incorrigibilem reputamus, diffinimus quod per V annos in compedibus teneatur et post penam tamquam ovis morbida de ordine expellatur. Mandamus insuper quod quilibet frater nostri ordinis, sive officialis sive non, ubi possibilitas adsit, ipsum capiat ut dicte pene valeat subiugari." *Esteban, AAug.* 4 (1911/1912), 471.

custodians of the treasures of San Triphone, including silver, books, and sacral vestments. Thus Andreas was privileged both to know where such treasures were kept hidden, and to have access to them. This came in handy for Andreas when Louis of Bavaria made his march on Rome, decimating the Roman clergy and religious who stood in his way, to the point that all the "good" Augustinians in Rome were either imprisoned, or fled. Andreas was one of the exceptions who remained. Coming once again out of the closet with his support for Louis, Andreas made off with the treasures of San Triphone, estimated to be worth a thousand florins, and handed the loot over to his confrere, Nicholas of Fabriano. For their support, Pope Nicholas V made Nicholas of Fabriano a cardinal, and Andreas the bishop of Recanati. Both Nicholas and Andreas, the only two Augustinians we have certain information about regarding their going over to Louis' camp, were from the March of Ancona, a "hot bed" of the Franciscan Spirituals, and both were from communes that John XXII had made objects of his crusades.[7]

[7] "Item anno Domini M CCC XXViij de mense Ianuarii in die Epiphanie supradictus Lodoycus de Bavaria intrauit Romam et venit per maritimam Tuscie, deinde transiens per montem altum venit Tuscanellam, et de Tuscanella Viterbium, et de Viterbio Romam, vbi stragie facta, tam clericorum quam religiosorum, ad tantam insaniam deuenerunt, ut adtentarent alium papam et alios cardinales facere, viuente sanctissimo papa Iohanne, qui fuerat in sede beati petri Xiij vel Xiiij annis. Et in adipapam [sic: antipapam] fecerunt fratrem Petrum de Corvaria, de ordine fratrum minorum. Et ipse cardinales aliquos fecit ad modum uere ecclesie Romane, per omnia eam scimiando [*simiae ad instar imitando*], inter quod fecit cardinalem fratrem Nicolaum, monachum, de Fabriano, qui fuerat de ordine nostro expulsus et ad carcerem perpetuo judicatus, secundum quod apparet in diffinitionibus capituli generalis Montispesulani celebrati et epsicopum fecit de Racaneto fratrem Andream de Racaneto, de provincia Marchie ambo; qui supradictus frater Andreas per magistrum Alexandrum, generealem, fuerat Tuderti positus in carcere et expulsus ad prouinciam Romanam, et veniens ad fratrem Iacobus Sassi, prouincialem, compatiendo sibi eum benigne recepit et caritative ipsum ad suam petitionem Romam pro conuentuali misit per iiij[or] uel V annos ante quam caderet in supradicto errore. Qui supradictus frater Andreas de Racaneto ita gratiosus extitit omnibus fratribus Romanis, ac si esset de terra propria, in tantum quod absente fratre Iacobo Sassi, provinciali, voluerunt fratres, qui erant tunc Rome, quod ipse frater Andreas esset unus de tribus fratribus Romanis, qui scirent ubi ascondebatur argentum, paramenta, libros et res alias conventus Sancti Triphonis, que omnia ascondebantur propter tyannidem maximam, quam supradictus Lodoycus de Bavaria exercebat in clericos et religiosos; propter quam tyrannidem omnis fratres de Roma boni recesserunt de Urbe. Nam aliqui capti, aliqui carcerati, aliqui verberati et expoliati, et nonnulli turpiter et cum multo timore fugati, aliqui usque ad ostium cabie leonis ducti [sunt]; propter que omnia loca de Roma fuerunt totaliter a fratribus Romanis relicta. Ipsa supradictus Andreas immediate dictis scismaticis excommunicatis adhesit, et totum thesaurum sacristiae Sancti Triphonis supradicto Nicolao, monacho de Fabriano,

In the case of Nicholas of Fabriano and Andreas of Recanati we see the practical application of the Augustinian platform. The very existence of the Order, as much in 1326 as in 1256, depended upon the support and good will of the pope. This is not to say, however, that the Order supported John XXII simply because he was willing to shower them with privileges and benefits. That there was a most desired symbiosis needs little comment, but there was more going on. As we saw in Chapter One, the Augustinians defended and supported the pope because they were Augustinians, not simply because the Order was created and maintained by the papacy. With legitimacy one could argue that the papacy in the later Middle Ages, at least theoretically, was created and maintained by the Augustinians, who did so based on their following in the footsteps of Augustine. If the foundation and model for the Franciscan way of life was the religious ideal of Christian perfection as embodied in the life of St. Francis, that of the Augustinians was the same ideal as embodied in St. Augustine, a body, moreover, that they obtained for themselves only with great effort. As his true sons never tired of repeating, Bishop Augustine had stated that he would not have believed the Gospel had it not been for the authority of the Church, even though at times we find indications, if not explicit statements, that the Augustinians, as themselves the embodiment of their founder and head, would not believe the Gospel, or the authority of the Church for that matter, were it not for the authority of Augustine. Two competing religious ideals, two competing religious identities defined the differences between the Franciscans and the Augustinians: the one could not adhere to a pope who had condemned as heretical the very foundation of its ideal, whereas the other's ideal itself entailed obedience to the pope as the point of departure. Yet tensions in both Orders there were. Not all Franciscans fled to Munich, either symbolically or actually, and at least two Augustinians did,[8] even

---

tradidit et capellam, quam frater Egydius, archiepiscopus bituricensis, conventui Sancti Triphonis dimiserat, acceperunt, que ascendebant ad valorem bene mille florenorum." *De ad.* (69).

[8] In addition to these two cases, the Augustinian prior of the convent in Bruges, William de Gravelgem, was in 1326 disobeying the interdict that had been placed on Flanders by Clement V as a result of the conflict between Philip IV and Robert, Count of Flanders. On 13 April 1326, John XXII wrote to the deacon of Tournai and to Bernardus de Albia, canon at Tournai, regarding the continued interdict. He then noted that he was especially disturbed by the disobedience of Prior William

after John XXII had recognized the Hermits as the true sons and heirs of their father, teacher, leader, and founder. Throughout the later Middle Ages the Augustinians were engaged in a continuous fight for their identity, both internally and externally, a conflagration that was all the more urgent in an Order with so few members.

There are no reliable statistics on the population of Augustinian Hermits in the later Middle Ages. We are better informed with respect to the number of provinces and their geographical distribution. In the early fourteenth century, the OESA numbered twenty-four provinces: eleven in Italy, four in Germany (with Belgium, The Netherlands, and Poland belonging to the Province of Cologne), four in France, two in Spain (which included Portugal), and then one in England, Hungary, and the Holy Land respectively.[9] By the early sixteenth century there were twenty-six or twenty-seven provinces, with most likely the additional number being Dalmatia and Greece.[10] The addition of two provinces over the course of two centuries does little to indicate the growth of the Order itself. As mentioned above, the numbers are simply lacking. The estimates that have been given are not all that convincing, and are rather varied as well. Gutiérrez claimed that in 1256 the Order numbered between 150 and 200 houses.[11] This number grew to at least 500 houses by 1356.[12] Gutiérrez used the conservative number of 12 members on average per house, which would put the pre-plague population of the OESA at approximately 6,000 members. He further claimed that during the Black Death the Order lost approximately 1,000 members,[13] dismissing as exaggeration the number of 5,084 Augustinians who died during the plague found in the *Chronica* of Ambrosius de Cora. Indeed, Gutiérrez argued that by 1512 the Order counted only some 800 houses, and

---

de Gravelgem, since he had at first indeed observed the restriction on ecclesiastical services, but now had been celebrating mass and burying parishioners; Joh. XXII *Let.* 1718 (2:30–32).

[9] Gutiérrez, *Geschichte*, I/1, 50–52.

[10] Gutiérrez gives twenty-four as the number of provinces in 1360, and twenty-seven in 1512, without, however, mentioning where the new provinces were founded; Gutiérrez, *History*, I/2, 46. Martin counts twenty-six, with thirteen for Italy, Dalmatia, and Greece; Martin, *Friar, Reformer, Renaissance Scholar*, 93. Gutiérrez does not mention Dalmatia or Greece in his list. Martin, on the other hand, does not mention the Holy Land, and attributes one province to Portugal.

[11] Gutiérrez, *Geschichte*, I/1, 51.

[12] *Ibid.*, 53.

[13] *Ibid.*, 54.

he then used the figure of 10 friars on average per house, "a generous figure," to come up with a total estimated population of the OESA in the early sixteenth century of 8,000.[14]

Even given the lack of certainty regarding precise population statistics for the OESA, constant growth of the Order is clear,[15] and such expansion took place when the general population of Europe was relatively stagnant until c. 1450, when it slowly began to recover and surpass its pre-plague level.[16] Nevertheless, the estimates do point to the low numbers of Augustinians in comparison to Franciscans and Dominicans, which were three to four times as large, each having a pre-plague population of c. 25,000.[17] In short, the only thing

---

[14] Gutiérrez, *History*, I/2, 96. Gutiérrez concluded: "How does this figure correspond with the estimate of 30,000 members 'before the Lutheran controversy,' a figure that is still contained in some reference works? There is no evidence for it and it was the creation of the Augustinian Battista degli Aloysi and the humanist Marco Antonio Sabellico who in fact tripled the membership of the Order for the years 1490–1510. The fact that the Franciscans and Dominicans had very large memberships offers no proof that the Augustinians approached 30,000. At that time the Dominicans and Franciscans in particular were the largest of the mendicant Orders. Since today there is not even agreement among historians of these Orders regarding membership data, it is clear that even these estimates lack a firm foundation." *Ibid.*

[15] Martin, however, claimed that by the early sixteenth century the OESA counted some 22,000 members in 1,000 friaries, thus yielding an average of 22 friars per convent; Martin, *Friar, Reformer, and Renaissance Scholar*, 93. The discrepancy between the figures of Martin and Gutiérrez is lowest concerning the number of houses, namely, Martin claiming 1,000 and Gutiérrez 800 by the early sixteenth century. If we average the figures of Martin and Gutiérrez we would have approximately 900 houses of the OESA with 16 members per house, thus yielding a total population of 14,400 Augustinians by 1512. Assuming the number of friars per house remained constant, and assuming Gutiérrez's figures are low by the 12.5% resulting from averaging the number of houses he gives and that of Martin for the early sixteenth century (i.e., an increase of 12.5% of the 800 houses is needed to reach the average 900), the pre-plague population of the OESA could have been 7,492 friars in 562 houses. Using these averages, the OESA increased in population by 91.7% between 1346 and 1512 (from 7,492 to 14,400), or, according to Gutiérrez's figures themselves, by 60% during the same period (accounting for the decrease of 1,000 friars lost to the plague, an increase from 5,000 to 8,000).

[16] For the European population in late medieval Europe, see Jan de Vries, "Population," in *Handbook of European History, 1400–1600. Late Middle Ages, Renaissance, and Reformation*, ed. Thomas A. Brady Jr., Heiko A. Oberman, and James D. Tracy (Leiden, 1994; hereafter cited as *Handbook*), 2 vols., 1:1–50; Bartolomé Yun, "Economic Cycles and Structural Changes," in *Handbook* 1:113–146; Carlo M. Cipolla, *Before the Industrial Revolution. European Society and Economy, 1000–1700* (New York, 1976), 3–5, 214–219.

[17] We also lack detailed statistics for the OFM and OP in the later Middle Ages. Moorman mentioned that by 1517 the Franciscan Order worldwide, including the Poor Clares, consisted of approximately 4,500 houses; John Moorman, *Medieval*

we can say with some degree of certainty given the lack of demographical information, is that in the later Middle Ages the OESA was a small religious Order, but one that was growing and expanding at a rate significantly surpassing the stagnation of the European population, but not as fast and not as much as its major competitors, the OFM and the OP. Moreover, it was a dispersed group, with small numbers spread over a wide geographical area, the whole of Europe. This in itself would have caused problems for centralized administration, and attempts to enforce religious observance. The tensions between the Order's precepts and practice were perhaps unavoidable. Yet the Order kept trying. From Giles of Rome

---

Franciscan Houses, Franciscan Institute Publications, History Series, n. 4 (St. Bonaventure, N.Y., 1983), ix. Though Moorman's *Medieval Franciscan Houses* is an invaluable catalogue of Franciscan priories, it does not give any information regarding population. In 1316, according to Moorman, there were only 1,408 male friaries, a numbers which by 1385 had only increased to 1,641; John Moorman, *A History of the Franciscan Order, From its Origins to the Year 1517* (Oxford, 1968), 350. Thus the pre-plague population of the OFM can be estimated at 25,000 Franciscans in 1,500 houses; *Ibid.*, 351. Using these figures, we can then estimate the total population of Franciscan friars in the early sixteenth century as approaching 60,000 members. This number is reached by using Moorman's figure of 17 friars per house, multiplied by 3,500 houses. The figure of 3,500 male Franciscan houses was reached by calculating from Moorman's estimation of approximately 4,500 houses worldwide of the friars and Poor Claires. Using Moorman's *Medieval Franciscan Houses* as the base, if we estimate that there are 7 houses listed per page, there are 530 pages listing male houses, and 151 pages female, we have a total of 3,710 male houses and 1,057 female houses, for a combined total of 4,767, which is near Moorman's estimate of 4,500 houses. Using then 3,500 as a rough figure for the number of male houses in the early sixteenth century, multiplied by the figure of 17 friars per house, we arrive at a total population of 59,500. The Dominicans, according to Hinnebusch, had a comparable population to the OFM, with an approximate total pre-plague population of 25,240; William A. Hinnebusch, O.P., *The History of the Dominican Order. Origins and Growth to 1500*, 2 vols. (New York, 1966), 262–263. Hinnebusch does not give any numbers for estimating the population of the OP in the early sixteenth century. It also should be noted that such estimates are even more tenuous for the OP because the Dominicans favored large houses. In the early fourteenth century, Hinnebusch lists 10 priories that counted 100 or more friars each, and Paris, he claimed, had a population of 250–300 friars. Of the 51 houses in England in 1300, Hinnebusch claimed that 28 had populations of 30–50 friars, 4 houses of 50–100, and at least 1, London, of over 100; Hinnebusch, *History*, 280. In 1358 there were only 631 houses (*Ibid.*, 262–263) of the Order, and thus, taking 40 as an average, we arrive at 25,240 total members, though such an average says very little about the actual population of the OP given the large variation in population per house, but it is most likely not far off, at least for our present purposes. Moreover, if these numbers are at least representative, then the Franciscan Order, in any case, experienced a far greater rate of growth than did the Augustinians, which itself was impressive when compared to the European population as a whole (i.e., from 25,000 to 60,000).

to Giles of Viterbo, the priors general of the Augustinians sought to reform the lack of obedience and uniformity they saw infesting their Order. For the Augustinians of the fourteenth century, no less than for those of the fifteenth and sixteenth, reform was needed, reform was essential. The basis for reform was returning to the precepts laid out in the *Rule* and *Constitutions*, and the internalization of the foundation myth and identity of the Order as the true sons of their father, teacher, leader, and head, Augustine of Hippo. Perhaps no other Augustinian friar did as much to contribute to the defining of those ideals as did Jordan of Quedlinburg, whose life itself was a microcosm of the universe that formed the Augustinian platform in the later Middle Ages.

I. Frater Jordanus

Jordan of Quedlinburg is not a name that instantly rings a bell in the minds of historians. It does not have the grandeur of such illustrious figures as Thomas Aquinas, Bonaventure, Marsilius of Padua, Jean Gerson or John Wycliff. The fact that Jordan also went by the more general appellation of Jordan of Saxony is not of great help in evoking recognition; it simply necessitates the footnote that he should not be confused with the more widely known thirteenth-century Dominican of the same name. When one stops to reflect on the noteworthy Augustinians of the later Middle Ages the likes of Giles of Rome and Gregory of Rimini are easily recalled. Jordan has been forgotten. He has remained an obscure friar from a relatively obscure place of origin: in the medieval *Who's Who* one rarely finds the designation "of Quedlinburg."

Jordan is one of many late medieval Augustinians about whom we know far too little.[18] He left no letters, no diary, no autobiography, and no confessions. He is a stranger to us, and must largely

---

[18] For Jordan's biography, I am following Hümpfner, intro.; A. Kunzelmann, *Geschichte der deutschen Augustiner-Eremiten*, vol. 5: *Die Sächsisch-Thüringische Provinz und die Sächsische Reformkongregation bis zum Untergang der Beiden* (Würzburg, 1974); and A. Zumkeller, "Jordan von Quedlinburg (Jordanus de Saxonia)," *VerLex* 4:853–861. See also A. Zumkeller, "Jourdain de Saxe ou de Quedlinburg, ermite de Saint-Augustin, vers 1300–1380 (1370?)," *DSp* 8:1423–1430; *idem*, "Jordan(us) von Quedlinburg (von Sachsen). Augustiner-Eremit, geistlicher und homiletischer Schriftsteller, c. 1300–1380," *NDB* 10:597–598; David Gutiérrez, O.S.A., *History* I/2; Arbesmann,

remain so. Yet Frater Jordanus tells of his world in ways that the more famous figures never could. He was an "average" Augustinian, but as such, he brings us closer to the center, nearer to the heart of the matter than do the remarkable exceptions. Viewing the Augustinian landscape in the later Middle Ages through the lens of Jordan's life and works offers a perspective for perceiving rarely seen shades, colors, and contours. Thus in what follows I strive to go beyond the mere glance and glimpse, to grasp what it meant to claim for oneself Augustine's paternity.

What we are able to discover about the details of Jordan's life must be gleaned from a variety of sources. Even so, we are left with such a paucity of information, tantalizing glimpses here and there, that it is impossible to compose a complete biography. Nevertheless, the historical record is not blank, even if vague and obscure. If, as a member of the Augustinian Hermits, Jordan's progress followed a normal course, he would have entered the Order perhaps as early as the thirteenth year of the fourteenth century, probably in his hometown where an Augustinian cloister had been established in 1295, which, as seen in Chapter One, was soon to become the source of conflict between the Augustinians and the Franciscans, when the latter tried to tear it down.[19] We know nothing of Jordan's family or childhood, or why he entered the religious life. We can assume, however, that once he had joined the Order, after a year of probation, his scholarly skills were noted, for Jordan was chosen to be sent to the Order's general *studium* at Bologna where he studied under Prosper of Regio and Albert of Padua.[20]

Jordan's tenure at Bologna was short-lived, from 1317–1319, at which time he was sent north and became "the very least among the scholars of Paris."[21] Paris had long been the theological Mecca

---

"Vita S. Augustini,"; and F. Rennhofer, "Jordan v. Quedlinburg (J.v. Sachsen)," *LThk* 5:1120. Jordan has been the subject of only a single monograph; Robrecht Lievens, *Jordanus van Quedlinburg in de Nederlanden. Een Onderzoek van de Handschriften* (Gent, 1958).

[19] A. Kunzelmann, *Geschichte*, 1:82; see above Chapter One, n. 39.

[20] Lievens claimed that Jordan first studied in Erfurt before being sent to Bologna; Lievens, *Jordanus van Quedlinburg*, 1. This is an assumption that has then been taken as fact; see *Middeleeuwse Handschriften en Oude Drukken in de Collectie Emmanuelshuizen te Zwolle*, Jos.M.M. Hermans and Aafje Lem (Zwolle, 1989), 36. There is, however, no evidence for placing Jordan's early studies in Erfurt.

[21] ". . . ego frater Jordanus de Saxonia dictus de Quedelingburg inter scolares Parisiensis minimus . . .," Jor. *Coll.*, fol. 1[vb].

of Europe, and the Augustinians venerated their first Parisian *magister*, Giles of Rome, more than saints Thomas and Bonaventure. Jordan hailed Giles as the first (*primus doctor*) of the Order's theological professors after Augustine.[22] In this tradition Jordan studied theology at Paris and obtained the "degree" of lector in 1322.[23]

A. *The Pleasures of Paris*

The Paris to which Jordan came in 1319 was about as different from Quedlinburg as is today Los Angeles from Gary, Indiana. Jordan had sampled city life in Bologna, but whether his two short years in the Italian capital of law adequately prepared him for the streets of Paris is hard to say. We do not mean to imply that Quedlinburg was any purer than Paris. Vice is rampant in small towns as well as in large; sometimes one must simply look more diligently for it. Yet in Paris Jordan could dine on delicacies not often found in a remote Saxon town; in the city of Abelard and Heloise, of the fabliaux and Jean de Meun, he learned far more than what was contained in the required books and lectures, or at least he had the opportunity to do so. He was there but three years. Nevertheless, Paris was, and is, a city that upon departure leaves a taste in one's mouth. Six years after Jordan had completed his Parisian tour of duty, the Order's prior general, William of Cremona, prohibited brothers residing in the cloister from riding horses through the city, without special permission.[24] No matter: to see at least some of the pleasures of Paris Jordan had no need for equestrian transportation. He simply had to open his eyes.

The Augustinian friars in Paris were a rowdy bunch. This, however, certainly does not describe them all, and perhaps not even the

---

[22] *VF* 2,22 (235,69–236,72). 'Primus' here can rightfully be interpreted both as quantitative chronological development and as qualitative esteem. Aegidius was the first Augustinian to hold a chair at Paris, and the primary theological authority for the Augustinians. Jordan refers to Aegidius as *doctor solemnis et famosus, VF* 2,22 (236,90).

[23] 'Lector' was not a university degree, but was a 'degree' and office within the educational system of the OESA. See Eelcko Ypma, *La formation des professeurs chez les ermites de saint-Augustin de 1256 à 1354. Un nouvel ordre à ses débuts théologiques* (Paris, 1956), and Chapter Four below.

[24] "Item, precipimus omnibus et singulis fratribus, tam presentibus quam futuris, quatenus nullus frater recedendo a loco isto, per civitatem Parysiensem, sub pena inobedientie nostre, audeat equitare." Letter of William of Cremona, *Pro Ordinatione Conventus Parisiensis*, dated 14 April 1328, *AAug.* 4 (1911/1912), 61.

majority. Living in the Parisian cloister were both conventuals, those brothers for whom Paris was home, and students coming to Paris from various provinces of the Order throughout Europe. It was some of these students who were singled out by General William as "ingrates," causing disturbances within the cloister, and worst of all, "when they are in Chapter, when they ought to be listening to the warnings of salvation and considering humbly their own guilt, they shamelessly stir up commotions with senseless chatter and moving their hands or feet . . . with their depraved morals and examples . . . they could care less that by their pernicious exploits they disturb the peace of the convent and *studium*."[25] William wrote this in a letter to the cloister at Paris dated 14 April 1328, when the conflict with the Canons was at its height. William intended to effect a reformation of all aspects of the Order's religious life in the city.[26] We cannot say for certain that this accurately represents the state of affairs six years previous, when Jordan was finishing his studies, but William's chastisements give us a peek inside the closets containing the Augustinians' skeletons, and here I am not referring to the charnel house. Just two years earlier William had written a general letter to the entire Order in which he lamented that religious life was completely dilapidated, and that indeed it had collapsed.[27] This was, perhaps, a reason why William initiated negotiations with John XXII regard-

---

[25] "Item, cum per plurium fidedignorum vive vocis oraculum, nosque etiam ipsi didicerimus, quod nonnulli in nostro Parysiensi Studio, qui in sola superficie studentium glorientur, tanquam Ordinis beneficiorum ingrati, eorum maligna conversatione non desistunt perturbare Studium et conventum, in tantum quod et ad observantias regulares, qui debent esse quasi religiosorum finis, in nullo videntur velle advertere et, quod detestabilius est, dum sunt in Capitulo, ubi debent monita salutis audire, et suas culpas humiliter recognoscere, ipsi labiorum sibilatione et pedum seu manuum commotione, non vereantur excitare tumultum, quidamque dicantur aliis discoli, qui suis pravis moribus et exemplis, pudicitiam videlicet odientes, non vereantur perniciosis ausibus pacem conventus et studii perturbare." *Ibid.*

[26] "Item, priori strice precipimus per obedientiam salutarem quatenus omnia puncta circa reformationem officii divini, sacristie, librorum chori, circa reformationem negociorum refectorii et coquine, circa etiam reformationem dormitorium et cellarum, circa etiam reformationem aliorum negociorum ad extra, prout sibi in scriptis relinquimus, cordi habeat diligenter et quod circa illa ita sit sollicitus et attentus et ita prompte studeat executioni mandare, quod de negligentia predictorum ipsum reprehendere non possimus." *Ibid.*, 65.

[27] "Quum sicut proborum virorum relatione comperimus et nos etiam ipsi oculata fide perspeximus sacra et veneranda nostra Religio, que tertia columpna in Dei edificio existere comprobatur, sit spiritualiter et collapsa et ab omni observantia paternarum traditionum et sacrarum constitutionum deficit." *AAug.* 4 (1911/1912), 29.

ing the possibility of the Hermits gaining custody of Augustine's tomb in Pavia. The Order needed a "shot in the arm." This was only four years after Jordan had left Paris. What he observed during his three-year sojourn might not have been as bad as William later portrayed it, but it is doubtful that the Paris Jordan experienced was the model of religious life oozing with piety and virtue. The best we can say is that from 1319 to 1322, Paris, no less than in 1328, offered ample opportunity for the heroics of piety; as Jordan later affirmed in his *Liber Vitasfratrum*, the greater the battle against temptation, the greater the virtue of victory.[28] He was speaking particularly of the battle for chastity. At Paris there were certainly some who racked up the merits; there were also those of depraved morals and pernicious exploits. What kind of "exploits" one might wonder?

William's letter does not go into the juicy details, nor do we find these in the Acts of the General and Provincial Chapters. The closest we can come to an inside view of Parisian depravity among the Augustinians remains in the realm of suggestion—but the evidence is very suggestive. Among the reform measures for which William called was the prohibition of "covered cells." Apparently the practice was common, since William notes that his predecessors had faced the same problem. Brothers, some brothers anyway, had been covering the windows, key holes, or any opening there might be that allowed someone outside the cell to see what was going on inside. This was cause for suspicion, for it cast the cell in darkness; only those who are up to no good are afraid of the light, William rebuked. The cells were to be kept sufficiently bright and unobstructed so that someone outside could easily see the interior.[29]

---

[28] "Ubi enim durior pugna, ibi gloriosior erit victoria et corona." *VF* 2,29 (275,147).

[29] "Item, cum alias per plures venerabiles predecessores nostros prudenter in isto conventu Parysiensi ordinatum extiterit quod celle fratrum nullatenus velarentur, quinymo ab extrinsecis per huiusmodi cellas posset clare et lucide intueri, cum talis velatio quandoque suspicionem non careat violenta, nam scriptum est quod qui male agit odit lucem, Volentes huic morbo, in quantum nobis ex officio incumbit, de oportuno remedio providere, ordinamus, et ex certa scientia ab omnibus fratribus quibuscumque inviolabiliter observari stricte precipimus et mandamus, quantenus in ostio cuiuscumque fratris sint et fiant tot foramina et tam magna aperta quod per totam cellam lucide possit et clare ab extrinsecis intueri, ita quod infra huiusmodi cellam nullum aliud velamen apponatur per quod huiusmodi aspectus quoquo modo valeat impediri." *AAug.* 4 (1911/1912), 62–63. A similar stipulation, though not as elaborate, and with somewhat differing conotations and far milder language with no mention of scandal, was made already at the General Chapter of Florence in

It could be that the brothers simply wanted privacy for their contemplation, and thus covered their windows, or kept their cells in darkness. Yet there are other possibilities. In his *Institutes of the Fathers*, John Cassian associated 'covering', or *velamen*—the word also used by William—with the veil of passion and carnal desire.[30] Jordan repeated Cassian's warning in the *Liber Vitasfratrum*.[31] If this connotation lay behind William's prohibition, he had reason for suspicion indeed. The suspicion is also ours, especially given other reform measures of William's letter. It seems that some of the friars had a different understanding of "brotherly love" than that intended by the *Rule* and *Constitutions*.

From William's letter we learn that some brothers had the habit of visiting other cells. Hence, he proscribed any brother from "daring to enter the cell of another, either during the day or at night without the special permission of the prior ... which should only be granted in cases of necessity."[32] This practice had been going on for quite a while, because William had mentioned the same issue two years previously, and did so as a recurring problem.[33] The punishment for nightly visitations was double that of daily, but in any case, upon the third offense, the culprit was either to be returned to his home province, if a student, or transferred out of France if he were a conventual.[34]

1287: "Concedimus ut in cellis fratrum nostrorum fieri possint ostia cancellata, et sic clara adeo et patentia, ut quicquid in cellis illis fiet, possit a stantibus de foris bene et aperte videri," *AAug.* 2 (1908), 277.

[30] "... monachum scripturarum notitiam pertingere cupientem nequaquam debere labores suos erga commentatorum libros impendere, sed potius omnem mentis industriam et intentionem cordis erga emundationem vitiorum carnalium detinere, quibus expulsis confestim cordis oculi sublato velamine passionum sacramenta scripturarum naturaliter contemplarentur." Cassian. inst. 5,34 (107,5–11).

[31] *VF* 2,23 (242,13–243,18).

[32] "... quod nullus frater ingredi audeat cellam alterius fratris, nec de die nec de nocte, sine sui prioris licentia speciali pro qualibet vice petita et obtenta, quam licentiam prior nullatenus concedat nisi in necessitatis articulo." *AAug.* 4 (1911/1912), 58.

[33] William used the same words in 1326; see *AAug.* 4 (1911/1912), 31. William prefaced his prohibition with the following: "Item volumus et mandamus quod observetur mandatum factum olim per generalibilem patrem priorem generalem predecessorem nostrum de ingressu cellarum ..." *Ibid.*

[34] "... volumus quod cellam alterius intrans, si de die fuerit, pro prima vice quinque dies in pane et aqua sedendo in terra sine dispensatione aliqua ieiunare cogatur, de nocte vero instrans pro prima vice penam supradictam sustineat duplicatam; pro secunda vero vice, qua quis huiusmodi cellam alterius aliter quam supradictum est intrare presumpserit, quindecim dies sedendo in terra panem solum et aquam manducet, si vero de nocte secundario intraverit penam etiam huiusmodi

Brothers "visiting" brothers, however, was not the only case of entering that was prohibited. In a seemingly unrelated stipulation, or one at least that William judiciously placed later on in his letter, he ordered that "no brother of whatever degree should dare or presume to bring some scribe or secular boy into his cell or into the cell of another for any reason."[35] Yet all hope was not lost, because with the prior's permission, if need be, "worthy and honorable men" could be so introduced.[36] Men were O.K., boys were to be avoided. Just be sure that others can see from outside what you are doing with those "worthy men."

It must have been such men who were given permission to sleep with a certain friar, whose case Jordan related in the *Liber Vitasfratrum*. This poor friar was mercilessly pestered by the devil at night. The devil would elevate him and move him around to various places in the cloister, so that he could not have a good night's sleep. Such disturbances, however, did not occur when he slept with others. Thus he obtained permission to have one or two brothers sleep in his cell.[37] This, for Jordan, was an example of the greater security the cenobitic life offered as compared to that of the anchoritic. There is strength in numbers, and perhaps other benefits too.

---

xv dierum sustineat duplicatam; pro tertia vice huiusmodi intrans cellam alterius tanquam inobediens, protervus et rebellis mandatis Ordinis per Priorem Parisiensem sine mora absque homore aliquo a Parysiensi Studio expellatur; si vero conventualis extiterit, si de die per unum mensem, si autem de nocte per duos penam supradictam portabit, et nihilominus peracta penitentia, statim de conventu amoveatur et provinciali Francie tra[n]smittatur in alio loco provincie collocandus." *AAug.* 4 (1911/1912), 58.

[35] ". . . precipimus et mandamus quatenus nullus frater cuiuscumque conditionis existat aliquem scriptorem seu iuvenem secularem ad suam cellam seu alterius cellam quacumque de causa introducere audeat vel presumat." *AAug.* 4 (1911/1912), 64.

[36] "Concedimus tamen quod valentes et honorabiles viri, de expressa prioris licentia pro qualibet vice petita et obtenta, ad cellas fratrum, si necesse fuerit, valeant introduci." *AAug.* 4 (1911/1912), 64.

[37] "Frater quidam nostri temporis a saevissimo hoste multas pertulit molestias, ita quod ubicumque saltem in nocte eum solum repperit, multa taedia absque tamen gravi laesione corporis ei intulit. Nimirum, quia sanctos viros ille malignus spiritus non ultra laedere praevalet quam ei divina permissione licuerit, sicut patet in sancto Job. Nam aliquando fratrem istum ille spiritus de lecto suo levavit et ad trabem vel ad tignum domus eum locavit, aliquando eum in lecto iacentem cum lecto elevavit, et sic eum sursum et deorusm vibrando agitavit. Nonnumquam vero ipsum de stratu suo traxit et in medio pavimenti domus ipsum iacere permisit. Quandocumque vero idem frater iacuit aliis sociatus, spiritus ille non fuit ausus eum tangere, sed tamen aliquibus signis suam presentiam designavit. Unde frater ille, quandocumque voluit habere pacem de nocte, unum vel duos fratres rogavit de licentia Prioris sui, ut apud se in cella sua dormirent." *VF* 1,5 (20,66–79).

If worthy, honorable men were permissible and admissible, boys, especially in a darkened, covered cell, were dangerous indeed. A decade after William wrote to the house in Paris, the General Chapter in Siena (1338), the one at which Jordan was present that established 5 June as the feast of the reunion of Augustine's head and body, proscribed the teaching of secular boys within the cloisters "since we have learned from experience that from this practice in some places scandals have arisen."[38] It is difficult to believe that the Order became the object of scandal as a result of their secular students, boys, being equipped with a thorough knowledge of Donatus and Peter of Spain. Certainly there is nothing conclusive in this definition that proves homosexual activity, but there is much that is suggestive, if not of the fact, at least of the suspicion, especially in light of William's letter of 1328. Almost two decades after the Chapter meeting in Siena, on 21 October 1357, Prior General Gregory of Rimini sent Frater Johannes Bindus to Pisa to investigate the case of a lay brother of the Order, Thomas de Aretio, who had, apparently, "violated one of the local boys."[39] Such accusations could have been simply that—accusations. I am not claiming widespread homosexuality amongst the Augustinians, and such stipulations of the General Chapters and priors general could also simply be warnings, attempts to keep control on the Order's morals with no implications of actual misconduct. But where there is smoke. . . .

There is very little information to be had regarding the brothers and their boys. Indeed, the other gender is met more frequently. Two minor rules made by the Provincial Chapter meeting in Viterbo in 1335 are evidence that young males were not the only object of temptation: no brother was to remain in the church with a woman

---

[38] ". . . prohibemus ne quis frater in domo Ordinis debeat docere pueros seculares in grammatica vel in scribendo et in huiusmodi puerilibus, cum experimento didicerimus ex hoc in nonnullis locis scandala Ordini provenisse." *AAug.* 4 (1911/1912), 181.

[39] "Item die XXI commissimus fratri Iohanni Bindi nostro vicario provincie Senensis . . . quod Thome converso de Aretio indiceret canonicam purgationem de violenti suspitione quam habemus contra eum, quod unum puerorum Pisiss violavit, si deficeret, vel confiteretur, ipsum carceraret, assumpto tamen secum venerabili magistro Angelo de Cortanio in hoc casu." Greg. *Reg.* 44 (48–49); *cf.* below, section III. For lay brothers, or *conversi*, in the Middle Ages, and their relationship to the established orders, see Kaspar Elm, ed., *Ordensstudien I: Beiträge zur Geschichte der Konversen im Mittelalter*, Berliner Historische Studien 2 (Berlin, 1980).

while the other brothers were eating;[40] in addition, no brother was to bring a woman into the cloister, nor have a woman take care of him when he was sick, although at point of death, a woman could visit.[41] Violators of these stipulations were subject to serious punishment. It is clear that the Order was well aware of the trials a brother faced in remaining chaste.

Augustine, Jordan told his brothers in the *Liber Vitasfratrum*, forbade "all illicit use of our genital members."[42] Jordan thus offered a lengthy list of ways to preserve one's chastity.[43] Castigation of the flesh was one of the best. One brother he had known, having been tempted by a girl, burned his genitals, "intending thus to extinguish the fire with fire, and this he did."[44] Another was so tempted by the devil when a woman was given shelter for the night that he stuck his finger in the flame of his lamp. The lust, however, did not go away. Persisting in his "cure," by morning he had burned all his fingers, but had remained pure.[45] An early version of the "cold shower" was also recommended, for the fifth guard of chastity that Jordan listed was "immersion in cold water."[46]

Jordan never mentioned lust for boys in his *Liber Vitasfratrum*; the *exemplum* of the friar needing a good night's sleep is as close as we get to homosexuality in Jordan's work. With lust, however, he was well acquainted, at least from others. When Jordan was a young

---

[40] "Item, diffinimus quod nullus frater remaneat in ecclesia cum aliqua muliere dum comedunt fratres; quod si quis contrafecerit pene gravioris culpe subiaceat per mensem pro qualibet vice." *AAug.* 4 (1911/1912), 158.

[41] "Item, diffinimus quod nulla mulier serviat alicui fratri infirmo infra domum, possit tamen ire ad videndum in ultima et periculo mortis; et quicumque frater introduxerit aliquam mulierem incurrat penam gravioris culpe per mensem." *AAug.* 4 (1911/1912), 159.

[42] ". . . omnis illicitus usus membrorum genitalium prohibetur secundum Augustinum." *VF* 2,28 (267,28–29).

[43] *VF* 2,30 (278ff).

[44] "Item novi fratrem, qui aliquando stimulo temptatus de quadam puella eum ad concubitum incitante secessit in partem et excusso igne de lapide cremium argens posuit super membrum genitale, intendens sic ignem igne exstinguere, quod et fecit." *VF* 2,30 (284,185–188).

[45] ". . . cum quaedam mulier hospitata esset de nocte et diabolus stimularet cor eius in eam, ipse accensa lucerna mittebat digitum suum in lucernam. Quem cum accendisset, ardorem non sentiebat propter nimiam flammam concupiscentie carnalis. Et ita usque mane faciens incedit omnes digitos suos et sic mansit immaculatus de ea." *VF* 2,30 (284,179–184); this is an *exemplum* Jordan borrowed from *VP* 5,37 (883f).

[46] *VF* 2,30 (286,233ff).

friar, he and some friends, apparently, asked an old friar, over a hundred, whether he still was bothered with lust. "I am still a man," he responded. Thus, Jordan concluded, "the defect of age does not exclude carnal desire, but rather even more so, with the defect of age carnal desire grows, at least in the heart."[47] It is unclear whether he was speaking as well from personal experience. Jordan had lived nearly sixty years himself when he recounted this story. Yet when he was young, perhaps when he was in Paris, Jordan learned that one's entire life as a friar was a battle to maintain one's chastity. It was a question that interested him. He had seen its results first-hand during his student days in Paris, when some friars brought boys and worthy men into their rooms, and others simply visited their neighbors making sure all the windows and keyholes were covered. Paris was a good training ground for our future teacher of the virtues and vices. Jordan would be a moralist. He returned to France in 1343 as the vicar of the prior general and presided over the Provincial Chapter at Barfleur. Only four definitions from this meeting have come down to us: two reaffirm regulations made in previous General Chapters, and two deal with means of incarceration.[48]

If there were pleasures to be had in Paris, there was austerity as well. Thus, in his same letter of 1328 William called for the destruction of furnaces within the cells. In light of his other restrictions perhaps he felt there was enough "heat" being generated already, and we have already met the benefits of cold Jordan saw, at least in its liquid form. In any case, the brothers were to be without the comfort of warm cells. The venerable masters and bachelors of Paris, however, were exempt from this decree; they simply were to be careful not to cause disturbance thereby.[49] As we will see in the follow-

---

[47] "Simile audivi ego a quodam fratre sene plus quam centenario. Hic interrogatus a nobis tunc iuvenibus, an ipse adhuc carnales concupiscentias sentiret respondit: 'Ego adhuc sum homo.' Defectus ergo aetatis non excludit concupiscentiam carnis, immo plerumque cum defectu aetatis crescit carnalis concupiscentia saltem cordis." *VF* 2,31 (315,150–154).

[48] See *Esteban, AAug.* 4 (1911/1912), 252–253.

[49] "Item, ordinamus quod omnes camini cellarum fratrum ubicumque sint destruantur, exceptis dumtaxat caminis illis qui sunt in cellis venerabilium magistrorum et bachelariorum. Ipsos tamen monemus et qua possumus affectione hortamur, quod quando propter ipsorum consolationem eos in eisdem cellis facere ignem contigerit, caveant ne ibidem societates teneant et tumultus faciant ipsorum honestati et Ordinis repugnantes; non enim sustinemus talia, si de hoc ad nostras aures rationabilis querimonia perveniret." *AAug.* 4 (1911/1912), 63.

ing chapter, the special status of bachelors and masters within the Order went beyond heated rooms. The General Chapter of Florence in 1326 had stated that "the stature and honor of our religion arises and is maintained especially by the reverend masters of theology, as if from the most important members of the Order."[50] Not comfort or pleasure, but to learn the wisdom of the Scriptures from these privileged and venerable scholars led Jordan to Paris in the first place in 1319. He was committed and diligent, and after listening to lectures during the day in addition to singing all the canonical hours, he returned to his room to study. Being among the "least of the scholars of Paris," he was not one of the privileged; his room was cold—or was supposed to be.

B. *The Making of a Lector*

To become a lector in the Augustinian Order required a minimum of five years of study.[51] When Jordan received the title lector in 1322 he had fulfilled this requirement, having studied for two years in Bologna and three in Paris. The precise curriculum Jordan pursued, however, is less than certain, though it is clear that Jordan did not receive his education during the heyday of the Order's scholarly prowess. The definitive form of the course of studies leading to the lectorate was not achieved until the later fourteenth century.[52] Until that time there were continual revisions of the stipulations; the gradual reform of the Augustinian educational system was slow in coming.[53] The year before Jordan was sent to Paris, the General Chapter meeting in Rimini (1318) acknowledged that due to the paucity of masters in Paris, the honor and fame of the Order had been damaged. Therefore, the Chapter decreed that from that time forward two masters of theology were always to be in residence at Paris.[54]

---

[50] "Item cum a Reverendis Magistris in theologia tamquam a principalibus membris ordinis nostre religionis singulariter oriatur pariter et conservetur..." Esteban, *AAug.* 4 (1911/1912), 10.

[51] Ypma, *La Formation des Professeurs*, 10, 39. For the course of study for the English Augustinians, see William J. Courtenay, *Schools and Scholars in Fourteenth Century England* (Princeton, 1987), 72–77.

[52] E. Ypma, "La Promotion au lectorat chez les Augustins et le *De lectorie gradu* d'Ambroise de Cora," *Aug(L)* 13 (1963), 401f.

[53] Ypma, *La Formation des Professeurs*, 2–3.

[54] Esteban, *AAug.* 3 (1909/10), 223–224. That the Order continued to have problems with the absenteeism at Paris is testified by the letters of the Prior General, Gregory of Rimini; see Greg. *Reg.* 88 (66), 257 (143), and 258 (143–144).

Before an Augustinian friar could assume the title lector, he would have been required to pass examinations in logic, philosophy, and theology. Yet even this definition was not codified until the General Chapter of Florence (1326), four years after Jordan had already finished his studies.[55] The General Chapter meeting at Padua in 1315 mentioned only the need for one year of philosophical study, although making an exception for students at Paris.[56] The *Constitutions* of the Order simply stated the need for examinations without delineating the content, although they did require the teaching of the three chief subjects.[57] With good reason Ypma, the leading scholar of the Augustinian educational system, called the requirements for the office of lector in the late thirteenth and early fourteenth centuries vague.[58]

We can assume, nevertheless, that Jordan studied these three subjects in Bologna and Paris, having already achieved a sufficient knowledge of Latin.[59] We only have indications of what these areas of instruction included from the time when Jordan was already teaching in Erfurt and Magdeburg. For logic, the Chapter of Siena of 1338 required the new and old logic,[60] which was modified by Thomas of Strassburg's *Additiones* to the Regensburg *Constitutions* (1290), ratified a decade later at the General Chapter in Pavia in 1348. Thomas stated that a candidate for the lectorate could either study one book of the new logic, or the entire old logic.[61] Aristotle held the day as

---

[55] *Esteban, AAug.* 4 (1911/12), 6. See also, Ypma, "La Promotion au Lectorat," 400.

[56] *Esteban, AAug.* 3 (1909/10), 176–177.

[57] *Const. Ratis.* 36.335 and 36.340 (112–113). *Cf.* Acts of General Chapter of Siena, 1295, *Esteban, AAug.* 2 (1907/08), 370.

[58] Ypma, "La Promotion au Lectorat," 394.

[59] The Acts of the General Chapters had stipulated since as early as the Chapter meeting in Siena in 1295 that no one was to be admitted to a *studium* unless he could read the divine office; *Esteban, AAug.* 2 (1907/08), 369; also cited by Ypma, *La Formation des Professeurs*, 147 (Ypma incorrectly cites page 370). *Cf.* The Chapter of Venice in 1332, *Esteban, AAug.* 4 (1911/12), 110 (also by Ypma, *La Formation des Professeurs*, 149).

[60] *Esteban, AAug.* 4 (1911/12), 178.

[61] Thom.Arg. *Add.* 36 (117). The new logic consisted of Aristotle's *Analytica priora*, *Analytica posteriora*, *Topica*, or *De sophisticis elenchis*, while the old logic was comprised of Porphory's *Isagoge*, Aristotle's *Categoriae* and *De interpretatione*, Boethius' *Liber divisionum* and *Liber Topicorum*, and Gilbert de la Porrée's *Liber sex principium*; see Alfonso Maierù, "Regulations Governing Teaching and Academic Exercises in Mendicant *Studia*," in Maierù, *University Training in Medieval Europe*, trans. and ed. D.N. Pryds, Education and Society in the Middle Ages and Renaissance 3 (Leiden, 1993), 1–35; 11.

well for the philosophy texts since either one of Aristotle's *Physics, Metaphysics, Politics, Ethics,* or *Rhetorics* was prescribed, or, *The Short Physical Treatises*.[62] Lombard's *Sentences* and the Bible were the theological texts. According to the *Constitutions*, before one could become the principal lector of a *studium generale* one had to have lectured on the *Sentences* for at least three years.[63] The General Chapter of 1335 determined that in every *studium generale* two books of the *Sentences* were to be taught each year, so that the entire work would be covered within a two-year period, a requirement repeated by Thomas of Strassburg in his *Additiones*.[64] The same two-year period was required for the Bible. The Chapter at Florence mandated that the bachelors lecturing on the Bible at Paris were to cover the entire text within two years, beginning with the Pentateuch, Joshua, Judges, Judith, Kings, Job, and the Sapiential books, all of which were to be presented in one year. The remaining books of the Old Testament and those of the New followed, the order of which was left to the bachelor's discretion.[65]

Although these stipulations postdate Jordan's stay at Paris, it is likely that after his three years there, together with the two he spent in Bologna, Jordan would have heard lectures on the entire Bible, all four books of the *Sentences*, and a good deal of Aristotle as well. The course of study for the lectorate was not simply elementary education preceding theological study at Paris or Oxford; it was a rigorous program leading to the "degree"—the license to teach as a lector within any school of the Order except for those associated with a university—that for most Augustinian students was the high point in their academic careers.[66] Jordan may have been among the "least of the scholars of Paris," but his training was anything but meager.[67]

Why Jordan never continued his studies by pursuing the degrees of bachelor and then master of theology is not known. Perhaps he was not selected to continue; advancement within the Order was not

---

[62] Thom.Arg. *Add.* 36 (117). See also Maierù, "Regulations," 17; Courtenay, *Schools and Scholars*, 30–36.
[63] *Const. Ratis.* 36.344 (113). Every *studium generale* was required to have two lectors; *Const. Ratis.* 36.340 (113).
[64] Esteban, *AAug.* 4 (1911/12), 140; *cf.* Thom.Arg. *Add.* 36 (119).
[65] Esteban, *AAug.* 4 (1911/12), 12.
[66] Courtenay, *Schools and Scholars*, 75.
[67] See Chapter Four below.

determined by one's own ambition, at least not entirely. Perhaps he did not choose to go on, following the example of his prior in Bologna, Johannes de Lana. Johannes, Jordan related in the *Liber Vitasfratrum*, was a bachelor of theology, but declined the opportunity to pursue the *magisterium* so that he could better serve his Order in a more humble position.[68] Jordan perhaps followed suit.

When Jordan left Paris, he also left behind the early phase of his career and his life. For the next three decades he was constantly busy with his teaching responsibilities and administrative duties within the Order. These were primarily concerned with his home province of Saxony-Thuringia, to which he returned in 1322 to assume the office of lector in the Order's *studium* at Erfurt. During his time at Erfurt, Jordan not only had the opportunity to work closely with and learn from Henry of Friemar, and for at least two years with Hermann of Schildesche, but also to become intimately involved in the realities of being a religious in late medieval Germany. The Augustinians were a contemplative Order, but this did not mean that they remained with their heads buried in spiritual sand. Jordan surely learned much in Paris, but little did he know that he was soon to play a central role in a major legal case thoroughly entwined with civic-ecclesiastical politics, and one that, moreover, came to involve both the Emperor Louis of Bavaria and Pope John XXII: the murder of Archbishop Burchard of Magdeburg.

C. *Murder and the Cathedral: The Realities of Religious Life*

The Erfurt to which Jordan came in 1322, fresh from the pleasures of Paris as a new lector, was a city in turmoil. Populated by pagan peasants in the eighth century (*olim urbs paganorum rusticorum*),[69] it became known by the mid-thirteenth century as a "Thuringian Rome."[70] Yet soon thereafter the bonds between the ecclesiastical establishment and the civic authority began to break under the pressure of power struggles that pitted the clergy, the citizens, and the nobility against one another, each claiming superiority. Tensions reached the boiling point in 1324, when the citizens accused a priest

---

[68] *VF* 2,8 (121,75–82). For Johannes, see Zumkeller, *AS*, 205–206.
[69] *UkStErf* nr. 1 (1).
[70] Ulmann Weiss, *Die frommen Bürger von Erfurt. Die Stadt und ihre Kirche im Spätmittelalter und in der Reformationszeit* (Weimar, 1988), 13.

of theft. Not waiting for the proper judicial procedures, the citizens took justice into their own hands and carried out their sentence: death by hanging. This outraged the clergy who immediately ceased all sacramental services, placing the city under the ban. The city had suffered interdict before and no longer were the citizens going to allow the clergy to interfere with religious life in this fashion.[71] Thus broke out "great discord between the clergy and the citizens of Erfurt," a *magna discordia* as the chronicler called it, which is perhaps more accurately labeled a genuine *Pfaffenkrieg*. It took the arrival of the Archbishop of Mainz to restore peace.[72] Yet this was only a foretaste of the urban pastorate for the newly arrived Augustinian lector, though it well illustrates the social tensions Jordan faced in his first years in Erfurt. Perhaps it prepared him somewhat for what was to follow.

On 21 September 1325, a group of citizens of Magdeburg brutally murdered their archbishop. Archbishop Burchard had been held captive in the episcopal palace for three weeks before being led from the palace to a place where ruffians and criminals were often held, and there clubbed to death. Thus, the chronicler hoped, he was made a martyr of Christ.[73]

---

[71] *Ibid.*, 17ff.

[72] *Cron.Erf.* (354–355). The date of this incident is somewhat unclear. In this chronicle it is listed as "Eodem anno" under a previous entry dated 1324. The editor, however, places 1322 in the margin as a possible date. *Cron.Eng.* (803) gives the date of 1323. *Cron.Cont.* (479–480), however, places the event in 1324. Weiss, who refers to the incident as a *Pfaffenkrieg* (21), follows Holder-Egger's suggestion that it took place in 1322 without discussing the other reports from other chronicles. For an excellent overview of the strained relationship between the Church and 'state' (i.e., both regional territory or city, as well as empire) in the fourteenth century, though one that focuses on the reign of Charles IV, see Johanna Naendrup-Reimann, "Territorien und Kirche im 14. Jahrhunder," in *Der Deutsche Territorialstaat im. 14 Jahrhundert*, Vorträge und Forschungen 13 (Munich, 1970), 117–174.

[73] *Gest.Mag.* (431). One could see this case as an early, and rather extreme, example of the *Episcopus Exclusus*; see J. Jeffery Tyler, *Lord of the Sacred City. The 'Episcopus Exclusus' in Late Medieval and Early Modern Germany*, SMRT 72 (Leiden, 1999); cf. Thomas A. Brady, Jr., "The Holy Roman Empire's Bishops on the Eve of the Reformation," in *Continuity and Change. The Harvest of Late Medieval and Reformation History*, Essays presented to Heiko A. Oberman on his 70th Birthday, ed. Robert J. Bast and Andrew C. Gow (Leiden, 2000), 20–47. The episcopal residence of Magdeburg was not relocated until the sixteenth century; Tyler, *Lord of the Sacred City*, 18. As we will see shortly, the case of Burchard's murder was soon to involve both Emperor Louis IV and Pope John XXII, whose conflict was central for other episcopal cities as well, such as Constance; *ibid.*, 47f. Tyler focused on the episcopal cities of Constance and Augsburg, and thus does not mention Burchard's murder, but he does briefly address the issue of episcopal murder; see *ibid.*, 15–17.

For Burchard's murder, the city was placed under interdict. It was not until 1331 that the citizens of Magdeburg arranged a solution with the pope. They were to build one chapel and six altars in Burchard's memory and give homage to the current Archbishop, Otto. As a result, they were to be absolved from excommunication and re-instated by the papal appointees Conrad, from the Monastery of the Blessed Virgin in Magdeburg, and Henry of Friemar, the prior of the Saxon Province of the Order of Augustinian Hermits.[74] We do not know the reason, but Henry delegated the responsibility for the case to Jordan, who was by this time an experienced lector of the Order's *studium* in Erfurt.[75] Although hindered from completing their mission for four months by the new archbishop and the cathedral chapter—who felt that far more should be required of the citizens—Jordan and Conrad were able to reconcile the two parties and restore peace.[76] In 1333 the citizens faithfully swore allegiance to Archbishop Otto,[77] and by 1349 they had completed the construction of the mandated chapel and altars, whereupon they were fully absolved.[78] The case of Burchard was finally settled.

As one of the adjudicators, Jordan would certainly have been aware of the complexities. Burchard's murder was not a simple, random act of violence. The chronicle telling of the event reports only the testimony of a single culprit who claimed that Burchard "... had impoverished him and taken all his goods, wherefore when the opportunity was presented, he was only too glad to avenge himself."[79] The conflict between Burchard and the burghers of Magdeburg, however, had been long-standing, dating back at least to 1309, when on 24 November, Archbishop Burchard and the city of Magdeburg

---

[74] *Gest. Mag.* (433–434).

[75] *Gest. Mag.* (434); *cf. UkLF* nr. 187 (171); *UrkM* nr. 339 (205–209); nr. 340 (209); nr. 348 (213–215). Henry's involvement in his Order's conflict with the Augustinian Canons was, however, a most likely explanation for his having delegated the case of Burchard to Jordan; see Chapter Two.

[76] *Gest.Mag.* (434); *cf. UrkM* nr. 350 (215–216).

[77] *UkLF* nr. 192 (dated April 24, 1333), 174.

[78] *UkLF* nr. 201 (dated June 26, 1349), 183; *cf. UrkM* nr. 404 (250). There was, however, also a financial aspect to the settlement. In 1331 and 1332 Magdeburg paid 9,000 florins to the papal *camera* as a fine for Burchard's murder; see *Die Einnahmen der apostolischen Kammer unter Johann XXII.*, ed. E. Göller, Vatikanische Quellen zur Geschichte der päpstlichen Hof-u. Finanzverwaltung, 1316–1378 (Paderborn, 1910), 1:524, as cited by Housley, *The Italian Crusades*, 186.

[79] "... eum depauperaverat et omnia bona sua sibi abstulerat, idcirco nacta oportunitate se de eo posse vindicare gaudebat." *Gest.Mag.* (432).

signed a treaty settling the points of contention between them. This treaty is the first mention of Burchard as archbishop that we find in the *Urkunden*,[80] indicating that Magdeburg and Burchard had a conflicted relationship from the very beginning. Nor was the fall of 1325 the first time that Burchard had been taken prisoner. Trouble in Magdeburg had been brewing for many years.

The central issues involved were economic and legal rights: disputed property, taxes and tithes, rights of jurisdiction. Such local, "mundane" concerns, however, soon became embroiled in papal-imperial politics. The conflict began to surpass the immediate local boundaries already in 1313, when the Magdeburg city council arranged with the bishop of Brandenburg and Markgrave Waldemar of Brandenburg to act as intermediaries between the two parties.[81] Such intercession did not prove very successful, for later in the year Burchard was captured by a group of citizens and held in the city's court house. To obtain his freedom he promised peace and friendship, and swore on the body of Christ to be faithful to the citizens. He was released and led to his palace with honor.[82] On 18 December 1314, Burchard and the burghers of Magdeburg signed a treaty resolving the problems that had led to Burchard's imprisonment, negotiated by Markgrave Waldemar.[83] Four months later, on 4 April 1315, Burchard himself concluded a treaty with the city in which he confirmed the agreements already made, and thus lifted the ban that he had placed on Magdeburg as a result of his capture.[84] In 1317, Pope John XXII wrote to Bertold Ronebiz, Arnold von Haldensleben, Ernst Hunger, Johann Weseke, Bruno Berndes, and Peter unter dem Ufer, burghers of Magdeburg, granting their request that they and their fellow citizens be released from the excommunication resulting from the conflict with their archbishop, based on the fact that they had presented sufficient evidence that the issues had been resolved and that Burchard was in complete agreement.[85] There was, finally, apparent peace. But, not for long, and it was no longer simply a local or regional matter.

---

[80] *UrkM* nr. 251 (133–136).
[81] *UrkM* nr. 265 (145–147).
[82] *Gest.Mag.* (430); cf. *UrkM* nr. 266 (147–148); nr. 270 (151–156).
[83] *UrkM* nr. 269 (149–151).
[84] *UrkM* nr. 270 (151–156).
[85] *UrkM* nr. 283 (164–165); cf. nr. 281 (163).

On 8 March 1324, just two weeks before he excommunicated Louis of Bavaria, Pope John XXII wrote to the deacon of St. Andreas in Hildesheim and the Provost of St. Serverus in Cologne, requesting their help to ensure peace between the two parties: the Church and archbishop on one side, and the citizens of Magdeburg on the other. The situation was precarious. Louis, in John's eyes still just the Duke of Bavaria, but "who calls himself the elected King of the Romans" (*qui se dixit in regem Romanorum electum*), had incited the citizens of Magdeburg against their archbishop, under the pretext that Burchard had refused to re-infeud the lands of Waldemar, the Markgrave of Brandenburg, immediately upon his death, the same Waldemar who had acted as peacemaker ten years earlier. These were lands that Waldemar held as a fief of the church of Magdeburg. Thus Louis was fomenting rebellion among the citizens against Burchard, even though the citizens of Magdeburg were under the temporal as well as the spiritual jurisdiction of the archbishop. The burghers of Magdeburg, the pope reported, were a difficult bunch, which he knew from experience, and now were trying to remove themselves from being subjects of the Church. They had entered into a pact with Louis and were conspiring, as the sons of Belial, against the Church and archbishop, plotting their ruin, despoiling ecclesiastical property, and imprisoning ecclesiastics, despite the efforts of Archbishop Burchard to maintain peace.[86] The conflict had reached boiling point. It was now the sons of Belial, the burghers of Magdeburg, spurred on by the Duke of Bavaria, who was styling himself as the King of the Romans, set in opposition to the pope and his faithful servant, Archbishop Burchard.

Pope John had cause for concern. On 1 August 1323, Louis of Bavaria had, as the King of the Romans, secured all the rights, privileges, and liberties of the city of Magdeburg that had ever been conceded to it by his predecessors, and assured the burghers that no one would impinge upon their rights, privileges, and liberties without incurring the consequences of imperial protection. He did so based on the request of the burghers themselves.[87] Four days later, Louis further affirmed his commitment to support Magdeburg, and to defend the city and its inhabitants from all its enemies.[88] On 9

---

[86] *UrkM* nr. 306 (176–178).
[87] *UrkM* nr. 299 (172).
[88] *UrkM* nr. 300 (172–173).

August, the burghers of Magdeburg reciprocated by affirming their defense of Louis against any and all who would challenge his authority, placing themselves under the emperor's protection as his faithful servants.[89] They now had secured imperial backing in their dispute with their archbishop. It was no longer a local affair, but one that pitted the emperor against the pope. On 24 August of the following year, John XXII wrote directly to the citizens of Magdeburg, imploring them to be obedient to Burchard.[90] Such exhortations fell on deaf ears. During the period from 13 October 1324 to 16 July 1325, the archbishop tried to ameliorate the situation diplomatically by signing treaties with Count Busso of Mansfeld, the cities of Magdeburg, Halle, Calbe, and Salze, with which Magdeburg had aligned itself, as well as with a number of nobles in the region.[91] It was not enough. In late August or early September of 1325, Burchard was once again captured and imprisoned, and finally on 21 September, he was clubbed to death.

These were all events of the recent past when Jordan became involved in the case in 1331. Moreover, the burghers of Magdeburg already on 1 September 1327 had been absolved from the guilt of the murder by the new Archbishop Otto (*a ea culpa eos absolvimus*).[92] Yet Jordan would have been fully informed of the history and details of the case, had he not known them already, in order to adjudicate as papal appointee. He also would have been aware of the papal-imperial conflict, especially since it continued with regard both to absolution, and to the resolution of the conflict. Archbishop Otto had absolved Magdeburg from the guilt of the deed, but not from the required penance. Eight months later, on 21 May 1328, Louis of Bavaria absolved the burghers of Magdeburg from all guilt and punishment regarding the murder.[93] Calling himself emperor of the Romans by the grace of God (*dei gratia Romanorum imperator*), and claiming that the dignity of the Roman Empire had its origins in the font of piety (*Dignitas Romani imperii, que a fonte pietatis sumsit originem*), Louis asserted that

> ... some citizens and persons, from our city and diocese of Magdeburg, who are beloved faithful servants of our holy empire, were not able

---
[89] *UrkM* nr. 302 (173).
[90] *UrkM* nr. 308 (179).
[91] *UrkM* nr. 309–316 (179–186).
[92] *UrkM* nr. 326 (193–194).
[93] *UrkM* nr. 331 (197–199).

to bear the genuine burdens and the most weighty personal injuries imposed on their necks by a certain Burchard by his depraved and evil actions and his unjust and perverse deeds—the latter of whom, if he can legitimately be referred to as the archbishop of our above named city and jealous rival of our empire, is more adequately called a thief and usurper—led by their zeal for justice, conspired to murder the same Burchard, having before the eyes of their hearts the divine eloquence that you are not to permit wickedness to live on earth.[94]

Louis acknowledged that the citizens had incurred punishment for their deed, which was, in his words, done in the cause of equity and rectitude (*rectitudinis et equitatis causa*), and thus rather than necessitating punishment, it should be the cause of great merit (*sed potius ad meritorum cumulum*). Therefore Louis absolved the citizens of Magdeburg and their descendants from all penalties resulting from the murder, whether arising from secular or ecclesiastical judgment.[95]

Two years later, on 30 June 1331, Pope John XXII followed suit and announced his absolution of the citizens of Magdeburg.[96] As one might expect, John XXII's representation of the case differed considerably from that of Louis. For John, the deed committed was a most painful memory of a horrible and wicked crime (*dolorosa memoria horribilis et nephandi facinoris*), committed against a most honorable member of the Holy Church; it was a sacrilege, and a serious offense to divine majesty, perpetrated in clear contempt of the Church; it was an inconceivable exasperation. The language John used was as strong as it could be, as damning as it could be: the citizens' act was an atrocity, a patricide, an abomination.[97] Nevertheless, since the citizens of Magdeburg were penitent, and had received their new

---

[94] "... quod nonnulli cives et populus Magdeburgensium civitatis et diocesis nostri et sacri imperii fideles dilecti non valentes sustinere onera realia et personalia gravia, imo gravissima, collis eorum imposita per Burchardum quondam, si dicere licet, archiepiscopum civitatis prefate nostrum et imperii emulum, quem potius usurpatorem et raptorem dicere deberemus, suis pravis et iniquiis actibus et operibus iniustis et perversis zelo iustitie ducti in ipsius Burchardi necem conspiraverunt, habentes pre oculis cordis illus divinum eloquium, maleficum non permittas vivere super terram..." *UrkM* nr. 331 (198).

[95] *UrkM* nr. 331 (198–199).

[96] *UrkM* nr. 339 (205–209).

[97] "Nos igitur, quamvis cedes eiusdem antistitis mentem nostram horrendi criminis atrocitate commoverit, dum inauditum sit facinus proprium necare pastorem, patricidale committere crimen in presulem et funestam perniciem in antistitem proprium, ministrantem subditis verbum fidei christiane, tam nequiter exercere..." *UrkM* nr. 339 (206).

Archbishop Otto, who had seen fit to absolve them, the pope was prepared to do so as well, with the stipulation of the required restitution and penance imposed, namely, the construction of the chapel and altars.[98] John then appointed Conrad, the provost from the cloister of the Blessed Virgin Mary in Magdeburg, and the provincial prior of the Saxon-Thuringian Province of the Augustinian Hermits as the official papal representatives in charge of the case and its final solution. This was on 30 June 1331.[99] The Augustinian provincial prior, Henry of Friemar, then delegated this responsibility to Jordan. It had only been twenty-five days before that the Hermits had presented the Augustinian Canons in Pavia with a copy of John XXII's Bull *Veneranda sanctorum*, and had thus been received in San Pietro's in Pavia. Perhaps there is thus little wonder why the pope chose Henry of Friemar to adjudicate the case of Burchard's murder, or Provost Conrad, for that matter: Sancta Maria Virginis in Magdeburg was the church of the Premonstratensians, a reformed, monastic branch of the Augustinian Canons.

A few years later (c. 1335), while Jordan was still busy with the case of Archbishop Burchard's murder and with reconciling the citizens of Magdeburg with their new archbishop and the pope, he left Erfurt to became lector in his Order's *studium* in Magdeburg, and was also at work on his *Collectanea Augustiniana* and *Liber Vitasfratrum*. It was, however, seemingly not smooth sailing. Though the burghers of Magdeburg were compliant, their relationship with their archbishop remained tense, sufficiently so that on 10 April 1344 Archbishop Otto allied himself by treaty with the Cathedral Chapter for mutual defense and aid against the violence committed against the church of Magdeburg by its citizens.[100] Nevertheless, five years later, Jordan, now himself the provincial prior of the Saxon-Thuringian Province, and Peter, the provost of Sancta Maria Virginis in Magdeburg, peacefully announced the completion of the St. Matthew's chapel and the five [*sic!*] altars, so that the case of Burchard could finally be put to rest.[101]

---

[98] *UrkM* nr. 339 (205–209); *cf.* note 78 above.
[99] See note 78 above.
[100] *UrkM* nr. 388 (238–240).
[101] *UrkM* nr. 404 (250); *cf. UrkM* nr. 402 (247–250).

D. *Theologian, Preacher, Administrator*

Such was the life of an Augustinian hermit in late medieval Germany. The case of the troubled relationship between the city of Magdeburg and its archbishop, and Jordan's role therein, witnesses to the social role of religion and of the religious in the later Middle Ages. As is often the case with late medieval anticlericalism, the realms of the sacred and the profane are entwined in ways that disallow attempts to separate distinctly the worldliness of the laity from the holiness of the clergy.[102] The consecrated eucharist in 1313 served as the symbol of fidelity for the citizens who later would murder their archbishop. The archbishop's exploitation of his flock led to the citizens' appropriation of episcopal sacred space. Moreover, a monk and a friar were the ones to act as intermediaries between the conflicting parties. Henry of Friemar and Jordan of Quedlinburg are usually classified as spiritual writers or as mystical theologians, when they are considered at all. Yet both Augustinian hermits were acutely involved in their social world, bringing their theology to bear on the practical problems of the day. And both were intimately involved not only with defending their Order's rights and traditions as the legitimate heir of Augustine of Hippo, but also in governing the Order itself. When Jordan served as negotiator between the citizens of Magdeburg and the archbishop, he acted in keeping with his religious identity as a son of Augustine. While he was handling the case of Burchard, Jordan was simultaneously writing theological works, a new biography of Augustine, and an extensive handbook on the Augustinian life, defining what it meant to be an Augustinian. He had personal experience. Jordan knew what most modern scholars of the tradition unfortunately have forgotten, namely, that Augustine's heritage cannot be limited to a body of systematic theological statements forming together an abstract entity labeled 'late medieval Augustinianism'. The Augustinian theological literature of the later Middle Ages was produced in an historical environment wherein theology and spirituality were part and parcel of religious devotion and social reality. The theological program of Augustine's late medieval heritage was developing in the early decades of the fourteenth-century, in cities such as Erfurt and Magdeburg, cities in turmoil,

---

[102] See *Anticlericalism in Late Medieval and Early Modern Europe*, ed. Peter A. Dykema and Heiko A. Oberman, *SMRT* 51 (Leiden, 1993).

and cities ministered to by mystics and theologians, some of whom were sons of Augustine.

After having returned from Paris to Erfurt in 1322, before becoming embroiled in the case of Burchard, Jordan began lecturing on the Gospel of Matthew. His students found his exegesis of Matthew 6:9–13 so engaging that they urged him to publish it separately as an exposition of the *Pater Noster*.[103] Jordan was now one of his Order's theologians, though only as a lector. He was to become its most outstanding preacher of the later Middle Ages. He was also soon to be a respected administrator.

Jordan's experiences in Erfurt and Magdeburg had served him well. In 1336, when the case of Archbishop Burchard's murder was still running its course, Jordan was in addition appointed papal Inquisitor in the case of a group of Waldensians in the Brandenburg city of Angermünde, and in 1350 he presided at the trial of Constantine of Erfurt.[104] Jordan's legal talents were soon widely extolled and he was often conscripted for the Order's governance. As we have already seen, he attended the General Chapter at Siena in 1338 as the elected representative of the Saxon-Thuringian Province. In 1343 he was present at the General Chapter of Milan.[105] In the same year he was charged with making the visitation of the French Augustinians, and officially represented the prior general at the Provincial Chapter in Barfleur as the *vicarius prioris generalis*.[106] Two years later he was elected prior provincial of the Saxon-Thuringian Province, an office he held until 1351.[107]

---

[103] See Chapter Four below.

[104] *Gest.Mag.* 42 (434–435); *cf.* Robert E. Lerner, *The Heresy of the Free Spirit in the Later Middle Ages* (Berkeley, 1972), 28, 128–130, 151. For the position of inquisitor in Germany during this time, see Richard Kieckhefer, *Repression of Heresy in Medieval Germany* (Pennsylvania, 1979). In 1965 Romana Guarnieri edited a small selection from sermons—seven pages in modern print—which concern the heresy of the 'Free Spirit' from Jordan's *Opus Postillarum* and *Opus Jor*; see Romana Guarnieri, "Il movimento del Libero Spirito," in *Archivio Italiano per la storia della pietà* IV (1965), 351–708; 444–450.

[105] Esteban, *AAug.* 4 (1911/12), 232.

[106] Esteban, *AAug.* 4 (1911/12), 252f. See also, Hümpfner, intro., xv, and Kunzelmann, *Geschichte*, 5:39. For the office of *vicarius*, and for the government of the Order, see Rudolph Arbesmann, "Some Notes on the Fourteenth-Century History of the Augustinian Order," *AAug.* 40 (1977), 62–78.

[107] It is most likely that Jordan had previously been the prior provincial of his home province from 1340–1343, but there is no concrete evidence for this. The assumption is based on Jordan's account of the death of Henry of Friemar in his *Liber Vitasfratrum*. Jordan records that the prior provincial was present at Henry's

After 1351 we lose the trail. Jordan's whereabouts and activities recede into the unrecorded past.[108] His later years, however, were his most productive as an author. From his pen came the *Liber Vitasfratrum*, completed by 1357, the *Meditationes de Passione Christi*, and his three major collections of sermons: the *Opus Postillarum*, *Opus Jor*, and *Opus Dan*.[109] Of Jordan, only texts remain, yet texts in which we can catch glimpses every now and then, if we look hard enough, of a fourteenth-century Augustinian friar, his cares and concerns, his experiences, his world, and the Augustinian platform which he did so much to construct.

If the members of the Order were truly to be the sons and heirs of their father Augustine, they needed some way of knowing what that entailed. Moreover, the Order's administration was in desperate need of enforcing obedience, and of establishing for itself what following in Augustine's footsteps meant. The lived reality of the Order's members could not be so easily regulated as the Order's hierarchy might wish, as was evident from the problems the Order had with defectors to the camp of Louis of Bavaria. The Order by the mid-fourteenth century had its theoretical justification and legitimization, it had its myth, its foundational lore, and its created identity. Yet despite the interpretation given to the Great Union of 1256, the Order of Hermits of St. Augustine was still a rather dispersed group in 1356, and a rather small group at that. Everywhere he looked, the new prior general of the Order, Gregory of Rimini, wrote in a letter to all the Provinces of the Order on 18 July 1357, brothers accumulated their own money and sought worldly honors, preferring the way of the seculars, and thus, echoing the admonitions of William of Cremona thirty years previously, "the path of religion

---

death bed; see *VF* 2,13 (154). Hümpfner argued that Jordan, "... himself was probably the Provincial who visited the sick friar... and gave him general absolution." Hümpfner, intro., xv. Jordan's personal account of Henry's last words seems to imply that Jordan was indeed the prior provincial in attendence.

[108] Jordan was, however, involved in the debate over the *Sachsenspiegel* with Johannes Klenkok in 1365, as Klenkok attests in his *Decadicon*, though this is known only through Klenkok; see Chistopher Ocker, *Johannes Klenkok: A Friar's Life, c. 1310–1374*, Transactions of the American Philosophical Society, vol. 38, part 5 (Philadelphia, 1993), 58–60.

[109] See Hümpfner, intro., xxxi–xxxiv, xxxix–xliii; and Zumkeller *MSS* nrs. 641–643, 648–648b. Zumkeller also lists a *Quadragesimale* (nr. 650) and *Sermones diversi* (nr. 653). These, however, were never printed, and it remains to be shown whether they contain sermons not in the other collections.

is deserted (*sicque religiositatis deserta semita*)."[110] There had to be some way to translate the Order's precepts into the Order's actual practice. There needed to be some "mirror" for the Order, much as Giles of Rome had written his *De regimine principum* for Philip IV. The *Constitutions* were fine, but somehow something more was needed. This "something more" Jordan provided with his *Liber Vitasfratrum*, completed by 1357 and sent to Gregory for approval. Official acceptance by Gregory never came, or has not in any case come down to us, but Jordan's *Liber Vitasfratrum* remains the most comprehensive explication of the Augustinian way of life in the later Middle Ages.

When he submitted his work to the prior general, Jordan had already had much experience as an administrator, theologian, and preacher of his Order. He knew what he was talking about. And he knew that the Augustinian life was not one that could be lived hidden away in contemplation in one's own cell. The Augustinian Hermits were there to serve the Church, and thus were charged with taking an active part in their social world. Jordan had done so himself. Yet they must also know their heritage, their foundational principles, the do's and the don'ts; they must know how to translate the precepts into the practice of being an Augustinian. This was the task Jordan set for himself: to provide an answer to the question of what it meant to be a son of Augustine. This was Jordan's *Liber Vitasfratrum*.

II. Living as a Son of Augustine: The *Liber Vitasfratrum*

Jordan's *Liber Vitasfratrum* is an extensive commentary on the Order's *Rule* and *Constitutions*. In his letter of dedication to the Augustinian lector in Avignon, John of Basel, Jordan followed the salutation with the *Rule*'s central dictum: "to have one heart and soul in God."[111] The entire work should be seen as an exposition of this precept. John had sought Jordan's advice on who is "a true son of our most blessed father Augustine."[112] Jordan offered his work as a mirror, so

---

[110] Greg.*Reg.* 1 (4); *AAug.* 4 (1911/1912), 372–376.
[111] "... cor unum et animam unam habere in Deo." *VF* Epist. (1).
[112] "Mirae caritatis virtus ex profluo pectoris vestri emanans fonte de quibusdam quaestionibus dudum conscientiam vestram, ut scripsistis, perurgentibus, utpote qui beatissimi Patris nostri Augustini verus filius existere..." *VF* Epist. (1,5–8).

that by reading it, "any brother will be able to know based on his own life, whether he is a true son of our most holy father Augustine, and thereby a true brother of his Order."[113] In the prologue Jordan stated that he collected accounts of the notable lives and deeds of the fathers and brothers of the Order[114] "... lest the examples of holy religion from the fathers and the brothers of times past fade into a cloud of oblivion."[115] These served as examples of the true *religio Augustini*, instituted by St. Augustine himself.

A. *Origins, Context, and Structure*

Jordan opened chapter one of the *Vitasfratrum* by recalling the life of the first Christian community: "The whole body of believers was united in heart and soul. No one claimed any of his possessions as his own, but everything was held in common, distributed to any who stood in need," (Acts 4:32f).[116] He then commented: "Augustine, the most blessed father and sower of our holy religion, intending to renew the apostolic life, based his entire vision on these words."[117] The common life was the most fundamental principle of Augustine's Order. According to Jordan, it was comprised of four parts: the communion of living together in a given place, the communion of spiritual union, the communion of worldly possessions, and the communion of distributing goods according to need.[118] On these four pillars of the *vita communis* Augustine based his *Rule*, and Jordan organized his *Vitasfratrum* accordingly, treating each in respective parts.[119]

In Part One Jordan narrated the origins of the Order within the broader context of the history of western monasticism. He discussed the Order's habit, title, move to the cities, papal confirmation, and

---

[113] "... tum quia eius lectione frater quilibet, an sit verus filius Patris nostri sanctissimi Augustini ac per hoc verus frater Ordinis sui, ex vita propria sua cognoscere valebit..." *VF* Epist. (2,21–23).

[114] *VF* Prol. (3,11–13).

[115] "... ne exempla sanctae Religionis a patribus et praecedentium temporum fratribus in oblivionis nublium deducantur..." *VF* Prol. (3,8–10).

[116] Acts 4:32–34; as cited in *VF* 1,1 (7,3–8).

[117] "Beatissimus Pater et sacrae nostrae Religionis plantator Augustinus, intendens vitam apostolicam renovare, super praelibatis verbis totam suam intentionem fundavit." *VF* 1,1 (7,9–11).

[118] The four parts are: communio localis cohabitationis; communio spiritualis unionis; communio temporalis possessionis; and communio proportionalis distributionis. See *VF* 1,1 (7–9).

[119] See *VF* 1,1 (9,60–65).

stipulations for living the combined *vita activa* and *vita contemplativa*. In Part Two he proceeded to expound the meaning of the *Rule*'s principle "to have one heart and one soul in God" as expressed in the ideals of humility, charity, chastity, obedience, singing the canonical hours, and prayer. In Part Three, apostolic poverty as exemplified in the Acts of the Apostles and renewed by St. Augustine's *Rule* becomes the focus. The final section of the work is devoted to the principle of "different but equal," whereby all brothers are aptly provided for according to their need, and not by hard-and-fast norms.

Throughout, Jordan illustrated his commentary with *exempla* from the Fathers, many of which are taken from the *Vitaspatrum*, and from exemplary brothers of "modern times." Jordan concluded each part of the *Vitasfratrum* with a chapter on how the *Constitutions* of the Order pertain to the doctrine first expounded. His overall purpose was to give his brothers a handbook of Augustine's religion, to provide them with the goals, ideals, and examples of what it meant to be a member of Augustine's Order.

When Jordan completed his *Liber Vitasfratrum* in 1357, the debate with the Canons over the true heirs of St. Augustine may not have been the controversy foremost on his mind. On 5 July 1350, Richard FitzRalph, the Bishop of Armagh, attacked mendicant privileges in his *Proposicio*, preached before Clement VI in full consistory.[120] His central thesis was not primarily the doctrine of apostolic poverty *per se*, as has traditionally been asserted, but rather, as Katherine Walsh has shown, the illegitimacy of mendicant privileges, namely, the rights of the friars to "preach, hear confessions, and bury the laity in their churches while retaining their privileged position of exemption from ordinary diocesan jurisdiction."[121] In FitzRalph's mind, the friars interfered with the *cura animarum* and thus they were corrupters of the Church's pastoral mission. According to the Bull of Boniface VIII, *Super cathedram* (1300), which Clement VI reiterated in 1349,[122] friars had the right to preach freely as long as they did not interfere with the preaching of the *prelati*.[123] FitzRalph pounced on the

---

[120] Katherine Walsh, *Richard FitzRalph in Oxford, Avignon and Armagh. A Fourteenth-Century Scholar and Primate* (Oxford, 1981), 350.
[121] *Ibid.*, 353.
[122] *Ibid.*, 359.
[123] *Ibid.*, 368.

meaning of the term *prelati* and argued that the term included not simply the bishops, but all those holding ecclesiastical offices.[124]

FitzRalph saw in the friars a contradiction between their involvement in society and their vow of poverty. By obtaining privileges, acting as confessors to kings and princes, and—in the case of the Franciscans—denying that they held *dominium* of their property,[125] the friars proved themselves to be hypocrites, even heretics. In his *De Pauperie Salvatoris* of 1356, FitzRalph went one step further than he had in his *Proposicio* and presented a detailed plea for the abolition not only of mendicant privileges, but also of the Orders themselves.

After the publication of FitzRalph's *De Pauperie Salvatoris* the mendicant controversy became a much debated issue both in Oxford and in Avignon. A papal commission was appointed to investigate the matter, but the *status quo* was preserved when the cause died inconclusively with FitzRalph himself in 1360.[126]

Jordan must have been aware of this debate when finishing his *Liber Vitasfratrum*. Indeed, it has been argued that Jordan's primary intent was to defend his Order's position on apostolic poverty.[127] Jordan did devote ample space to the discussion of the Augustinian view of poverty in his *Liber Vitasfratrum*.[128] Yet the doctrine of poverty *per se* was not the primary bone of contention for FitzRalph. Rather, the mendicant privileges of preaching and hearing confessions formed the basis for his attacks.[129] Jordan discussed the papal sanctions of the OESA's right to preach and hear confessions in his chapter concerning the introduction of the Order into the cities,[130] but his treatment is brief; it forms a stage in the much more encompassing exposition of the origins and development of the Order and gives no indication that it was intended as a defense against a formida-

---

[124] *Ibid.*, 369.
[125] *Ibid.*, 375.
[126] *Ibid.*, 447. FitzRalph's attack on mendicant privilege elicited response from the friars, and in the OESA particularly from Geoffrey Hardeby, whose *Liber de vita evangelica* was the only treatise that directly answered FitzRalph's *De Pauperie Salvatoris*; see Walsh, *Richard FitzRalph*, 394 and 413f; cf. Mathes, "The Poverty Movement," 5–78.
[127] Mathes, "The Poverty Movement," 79–110.
[128] See *VF*, Part 3.
[129] Walsh, *Richard FitzRalph*, 401. FitzRalph's doctrine of the dominion of grace, however, has been seen to reflect the "proto-type" as later adopted by Wycliff; cf. *ibid.*, 385.
[130] *VF* 1,16 (57–59).

ble challenge. Jordan, having served as an inquisitor and having written a treatise, now lost, against the heresy of the "Free Spirit,"[131] was no stranger to asserting orthodoxy against those whom he judged had distorted Church doctrine. It is likely that if he had envisioned his *Liber Vitasfratrum* as a reply to FitzRalph, he would have given some indication of this intent. In his lengthy treatment of poverty, the language is in the mode of explication and explanation, not of exoneration. There is no firm evidence, aside from temporal proximity, to claim that Jordan composed his *Liber Vitasfratrum* in the heat of the mendicant controversy. This is not to say that he was unaware of the matter, and it is not unlikely that when he submitted his work to Prior General Gregory of Rimini, he did so with hopes of contributing to the affirmation of his Order's religion.

While Hümpfner supposed the early origin of the *Vitasfratrum*, he did argue that the mendicant controversy brought the work to fruition. As evidence of Jordan's urgency to offer his solution to the problem, Hümpfner pointed to a passage in which Jordan announced a *Tractatus specialis in fine libri* concerning the miracles of St. Nicholas of Tolentino.[132] This treatise is to be found neither at the end of the *Vitasfratrum*, nor anywhere else in Jordan's works. Thus Hümpfner claimed that Jordan did not have time to compose this treatise; the mendicant controversy prompted his haste in sending his *Vitasfratrum* to the General.

There is, however, absolutely no connection between this passage and the issue of poverty or of mendicant privileges. Jordan announced a *Tractatus specialis* in the chapter concerning the care of sick brothers[133] In fact, the very same passage could be used with more validity to argue for an early date of composition. Jordan was discussing the miracles of Nicholas of Tolentino; he had heard many, but could not remember them in detail (*distincte non recolo*).[134] His intention of writing a special treatise dealing with the miracles of Nicholas could have been inspired by a decree of the General Chapter at Paris in 1329, which asked for all miracles of Augustinians to be collected and reported to the next General Chapter.[135] Those of Nicholas

---

[131] See R. Lerner, *The Heresy of the Free Spirit*, 130, n. 13, and Hümpfner, intro., xlv.
[132] Hümpfner, intro., lvi.
[133] *VF* 2,11 (136–142).
[134] *VF* 2,11 (142,149–150).
[135] Esteban, *AAug.* 4 (1911/12), 87; as quoted by Hümpfner, intro., li.

would have had special importance since in 1325 John XXII set in motion the process for Nicholas' canonization.[136] Though the Acts of the General Chapter at Venice in 1332 are silent regarding the success of this decree,[137] these circumstances provide a more likely context for interpreting Jordan's declaration of a future *Tractatus specialis* concerning Nicholas than does the mendicant controversy.

When we return to the debate with the Canons, we are on firm ground, since Jordan explicitly mentioned the issue. The very crux of the debate (*totum pondus questionis*) was how one made one's profession. The Canons, the flesh and blood behind Jordan's anonymous *alii*, vowed obedience to a prelate, rather than vowing obedience to the *Rule* itself.[138] The Hermits profess obedience "to live until death without possessions and in chastity according to the *Rule* of blessed Augustine," first to God, then to the Virgin Mary, and finally to the prior general and his successors. Their vow is not only obedience to the *Rule* or to a prelate, but to follow these three basic components of religion: obedience to God, to Mary, and to the general of the Order.[139]

As previously mentioned, Arbesmann argued that Jordan deplored the controversy with the Canons, preferring to focus on religious obedience rather than historical priority.[140] The extent of Jordan's antipathy towards the issue needs to be determined within the broader context of the treatise. In Arbesmann's proof text, Jordan included not only the OESA and the Canons, but all Orders that follow St. Augustine's *Rule*, namely, the Dominicans, Praemonstratensians, and

---

[136] Although the canonization process was begun by John XXII in 1325, Nicholas was not canonized until 1446. For the initial testimony concerning Nicholas' canonization, see *Il Processo per la Canonizzazione di S. Nicola da Tolentino*, ed. Nicola Occhioni, OSA (Rome, 1984). However, the decree from the Paris General Chapter does not specifically refer to Nicholas. Rather, it continues, after the passage cited by Hümpfner, by expressing a special interest in Giles of Rome; Esteban, *AAug.* 4 (1911/12), 87.

[137] Hümpfner, intro., li. However, an anonymous Augustinian from Pisa wrote a *Vita brevis aliquorum fratrum heremitarum*; see R. Arbesmann, "A Legendary of Early Augustinian Saints," *AAug.* 29 (1966), 5–58. Michael Goodich places this treatise, as well as both Henry of Friemar's *Tractatus* and Jordan's *Liber Vitasfratrum* in the context of the Paris mandate; Michael Goodich, *Vita Perfecta: The Ideal of Sainthood in the Thirteenth Century*, Monographien zur Geschichte des Mittelalters 25 (Stuttgart, 1982), 54; *cf.* Hümpfner, intro., li.

[138] *VF* 2,14 (177,336–347).

[139] *VF* 2,14 (177,348–356).

[140] Arbesmann, "Henry of Friemar's Treatise," 59–60.

"many others."[141] Jordan's strategy was not one of historical priority *per se*.[142] Rather, as Nicholas of Alessandria and Henry of Friemar, Jordan focused on establishing the "true sons" of St. Augustine. He admitted that many Orders say that they are the Order of St. Augustine, and many others are hermits, but only the OESA can properly claim to be called "The Order of Hermits of St. Augustine."[143] In fact, Jordan argued, neither the Regular Canons nor the Dominicans, both of whom follow St. Augustine's *Rule*, bear the appellation "Order of St. Augustine" in their title.[144] Even if not the first to receive Augustine's *Rule*, the Hermits are the true Order of St. Augustine by reason of 1) their original, primordial, institution (by Augustine the Order was *primordialiter propagatus*); 2) by reason of following the *Rule*; 3) by reason of their papal affirmation and approbation as the true Order of St. Augustine; and 4) by reason of their possessing St. Augustine's most holy body.[145] These four reasons can be applied to no other Order, thus confirming the fact that the Order of Hermits of St. Augustine is the true, original, and only Order of St. Augustine.[146] If Jordan deplored the dispute with the Canons, he did so because he saw it as completely unnecessary. The Hermits had gained custody of Augustine's body, which Jordan saw as proof of the Order's original institution. Yet if the Canons somehow could prove that they were the first to receive Augustine's *Rule*, all was not lost. Jordan, using the words taken from Hermann of Schildesche's *Sermo de Sancto Augustino*, affirmed that he would prefer to be a member of the Order that most faithfully represented the *religio Augustini*. In his mind, there was no question: it was the Hermits.[147]

Nevertheless, Jordan did not refrain from putting forward a claim to the historical priority of the Hermits. Based on the reconstruction of Augustine's biography in his *Vita Sancti Augustini*, Jordan explicitly stated: ". . . [Augustine] gave the *Rule* to the brothers, and not

---

[141] *VF* 2,14 (173,225–229).
[142] As Hümpfner noted, Jordan omitted the legend that Augustine provided the hermits in Tuscany with a *Rule*; Hümpfner, intro., lxxiv.
[143] *VF* 1,17 (59,9–60,23).
[144] *VF* 2,17 (60,35–37).
[145] *VF* 1,17 (61,63–70).
[146] *VF* 1,17 (61,70–72).
[147] *VF* 2,14 (173,229–237); *cf.* Hermann of Schildesche's *Sermo de beato Augustino*, which Hermann gave in Paris in 1334; see Zumkeller, *Schrifttum*, 117–128.

to the Canons."[148] His reasoning was that Augustine composed his *Rule* before he became a bishop and consequently he did not have the legal right to give his *Rule* to the Canons, since they were not under his authority.[149] Augustine, Jordan explained, wrote two *Rules*, or rather, wrote the same *Rule* twice for different recipients: one for the friars and one for the Canons, although the latter did not exclude the friars.[150] Yet the priority clearly lies with the friars and their original institution by Augustine.[151] When Jordan deplored the continued debate between the Canons and the Hermits, he did so because for him there was in fact nothing to debate.

Whereas in 1334 Henry of Friemar had already given the Order its first historical legitimization with his *Tractatus*, Jordan offered a comprehensive exposition of the Augustinian way of life, valid and continuous from its founder to his own time. There are sufficient parallels between the works of Henry and Jordan to intimate that Jordan derived the concept of his *Vitasfratrum* from Henry's *Tractatus*. As Henry's title states, his subject was the origin and development of the Order, and Jordan adopted this two-fold plan accordingly when in his prologue he explained that he would gather his material, "around the origin and development" of the Order (*circa hoc originem progressumque eiusdem Ordinis*).[152] Further, according to Henry, the original principle of the Order stemmed from the most holy fathers.[153] He opened chapter six of his treatise, which contains *exempla* from outstanding brothers, by claiming: "... but because some holy seeds were fruitfully germinated from the roots of such holiness of this Order's first fathers, I, therefore, was eager to put down in writing what I could find out about the famous fathers of our Order whose sanctity was well known."[154] And finally, Henry referred to

---

[148] "... istam Regulam fratribus dederit et non canonicis..." *VF* 2,14 (167,62).
[149] *VF* 1,14 (167,62–64).
[150] *VF* 2,14 (169,133–138). For Jordan's discussion of the tradition of the *Rule*, see this entire section. There are two manuscript traditions of this chapter. Hümpfner states that they represent Jordan's change of mind regarding the authenticity of the *Decretum*; see Hümpfner, intro., lxxvii; cf. *VF* 2,14 (169,139 col. A-170,164 col. A) and *VF* 2,14 (170,156–166 col. B).
[151] *VF* 2,14 (172,194–195).
[152] *VF* Prol. (7,13–14).
[153] Hen. *Tract.* 4 (106,34–35).
[154] "... verum quia a radice tantae sanctitatis primorum patrum huius ordinis nonnisi sancta germina decuit propagari, ideo sub compendio pro aedificatione fratrum fratres famosae et notoriae sanctitatis huius nostri ordinis, de quibus compertum habui, studui annotare." Hen. *Tract.* 6 (18,1–5).

the Order as "the holy progeny of the said fathers" (*illa sancta propago praedictorum patrum*).[155]

This sentiment and terminology were taken over by Jordan, who based his work on the principle that "the life of the brothers derived from the life of the fathers."[156] In Part One he traced Augustine's progeny (*illa sancta propago sancti Augustini*)[157] from the earliest desert fathers to the Great Union. Furthermore, Jordan incorporated entire sections of Henry's treatise.[158] Noting that in his *Tractatus* Henry sought to discuss the foundation, approbation, and confirmation by *exempla* of the Order, one should not fail to recognize the similarity to Jordan's overall scheme. Taken all together, the evidence currently available strongly suggests that Jordan conceived of his work in the later 1320s and early 1330s working together with Henry in Erfurt, precisely as the controversy with the Canons was foremost in Henry's mind, and was an issue raging throughout the Order, challenging the Order's religious identity.

Jordan began his work with a statement of purpose. Because the memorable deeds of the outstanding members of the Order should never be forgotten, Jordan affirmed, echoing Henry, ". . . I was desirous to gather together the life and deeds of the fathers and brothers of our Order . . . so that the examples of holy religion from the fathers and brothers of times past might not fade into a cloud of oblivion, but be stored away in eternal memory."[159] Although the *Liber Vitasfratrum* is not a work of history *per se*, it is eminently historical. Jordan was intent on presenting only what he knew to be true: ". . . truth is obtained most of all in fact; the facts that are able to be known from the particular deeds of devout persons are actually few with respect to those things that God secretly works in individual holy men . . . Therefore, I put down those few accounts that are known to me in some way."[160] For Jordan, history was based

---

[155] Hen. *Tract.* 4 (110).
[156] ". . . ex vita patrum formatur vita fratrum." *VF* Prol. (5,58–59).
[157] *VF* 1,14 (46,41).
[158] See *VF* 1,7 (22ff).
[159] ". . . ne exempla sanctae Religionis a patribus et praecedentium temporum fratribus in oblivionis nubilum deducantur, sed potius in aeterna memoria recondantur, idcirco studui patrum ac fratrum singularium gestorum et notabilium meritorum eiusdem Ordinis vitam gestaque . . ." *VF* Prol. (3,8–12).
[160] "Quod maxime veritatem obtinet in his, quae in facto consistunt; qualia sunt huiusmodi, quae de gestis particularibus personarum devotarum sciri possunt, quae revera pauca sunt respectu eorum, quae Deus occulte operatur in singulis viris sanctis . . . Perpauca igitur utcumque mihi cognita conscripsi." *VF* Prol. (3,21–4,27).

on fact. Accordingly, whereas Henry of Friemar had claimed for the Augustinians the title of the Joachite *novus ordo* and solidified his argument for the historical primacy of the Order with Augustine's two-year sojourn at Centumcellae, Jordan, as already seen in his work on the *Collectanea*, recognized that the chronology of Augustine's biography could not support more than a brief visit to the hermits at Centumcellae, and he makes no reference to the *novus ordo*. In addition, as mentioned above, Jordan based his case against the Canons on a historical analysis of Augustine's *Rule*; Augustine could not have given his *Rule* to the Canons first because he was not yet a bishop and therefore he did not have the jurisdiction to do so. The Hermits were the ones who truly lived the apostolic life, which Augustine had re-established in his *Rule*.

B. *The Genuine* Vita Apostolica

Jordan began his work by describing the character of the apostolic life initiated by Christ, who gave the apostles the example and rule for living.[161] The apostolic community grew over time, and gave birth to three generations of offspring. The first (*prima propago*), was the apostles themselves, who maintained the communal life after the Lord's resurrection, as narrated in the Acts of the Apostles.[162] Yet in time, the fervor of that first faith waned and became lax.[163] A group that remembered the pristine perfection of the apostolic community withdrew from the city and from association with those who were negligent in order to renew the apostolic institution in secret; thus the second generation.[164] The third generation resulted once again from a "cooling off" of devotion, and this time the move was by individuals who carried the apostolic fervor, but unable to live accordingly, left their parents and friends and chose a solitary life. For this reason, "they were called monks and on account of their common life, they were called cenobites."[165] This third form of the apostolic community lasted for many years, up until the time of the first hermits, St. Paul and St. Anthony.[166]

---

[161] *VF* 1,2 (10,25–26).
[162] *VF* 1,2 (10,26–32).
[163] *VF* 1,2 (11,63–69).
[164] *VF* 1,2 (11,69–12,76).
[165] "Qui propter solitariae vitae districtionem monachi nominati sunt et ex communione consortii coenobitae dicti sunt." *VF* 1,2 (12,81–86).
[166] *VF* 1,2 (12,87–90).

Jordan then proceeded to discuss the three types of monks.[167] Among the desert fathers were the anchorites, who live entirely alone, cenobites, who live in communities, and the sarabaites. These last were "detrimental and execrable," only pretending to live holy lives, like Ananias and Saphira; even if they appear as angels, in reality—if one could see their inner selves—they are wolves.[168] This type of monk should be avoided at all costs.[169]

Having brought the development of monasticism thus far, Jordan then entered into a rather lengthy discussion of the comparative values and dangers of the anchoritic and the cenobitic lives. The anchoritic form of monasticism provides the individual with the opportunity of pursuing his own perfection and in this sense the anchorite is the more perfect type of monk.[170] The anchorite's life, however, is so harsh and difficult that before entering upon such a vow, "one should be thoroughly practiced in all righteousness and virtue, and filled with the Holy Spirit."[171] Not only will one have to be content living alone in the desert on whatever bread and water can be found, but even greater danger, Jordan cautioned, will come from the devil; as Jerome told of Paul, "no one knows what great temptations of Satan he bore."[172] The serpent came to Eve in paradise when she was alone—and prevailed. It is certain, Jordan warned, "that the Tempter goes for solitude. Wherefore it is necessary that the solitary man be well armed against the enemy."[173]

For these reasons, the cenobitic life is safer.[174] Community is not to be shunned but cultivated, for Christ himself promised that where two or three are congregated in his name he would be among them.

---

[167] *VF* 1,3 (13,3–5). Jordan could have drawn on a number of sources for his discussion of the different types of monks, *e.g.* Cassian. coll. pat. 18 (1089–1124), or Ps.Aug. erem. 21 (Jor. *Coll.*, fol. 26ra–27vb; *PL* 40,1268f).

[168] *VF* 1,3 (14,30–40).

[169] *VF* 1,3 (13,3–5).

[170] *VF* 1,4 (16).

[171] "... volentes transire ad vitam eremiticam debent prius esse omni iustitia et virtute praeexercitati atque Spiritu Sancto repleti..." *VF* 1,4 (16,17–19).

[172] "Unde etiam de isto sancto Paulo dicit Hieronymus, quod quantas ipse temptationes Satanae pertulerit, nulli hominum cognitum habetur..." *VF* 1,4 (17,57–59).

[173] "Serpens etiam ille in paradiso, volens temptare matrem generis nostri Evam, solitariam eam aggressus est. Ex quibus omnibus convincitur, quod temptator solitudinem amat. Quare oportet hominem solitarium bene esse armatum contra hostem." *VF* 1,4 (17,60–63).

[174] *VF* 1,5 (18,3).

This would apply all the more when many are gathered.[175] Indeed, "it is better to say the canonical hours together with the brothers in church than alone in your cell."[176] Therefore, Jordan concluded, "the cenobitic life is more secure and is more conducive to acquiring perfection, whereas the anchoritic life is suitable for those already perfect."[177] Thus, the most perfect form of monastic life would be to combine the anchoritic and the cenobitic lives,[178] and this was the accomplishment of St. Augustine.

There is no doubt, Jordan claimed, that Augustine was a cenobite.[179] Nowhere is it read that Augustine was ever an anchorite.[180] Yet although he was a bishop, he desired solitude. Jordan interpreted this solitude as that of an anchorite, although he admitted that Augustine never actually lived as an anchorite.[181] Nevertheless, "although Augustine was never an anchorite in the strict sense, as has been shown, it is not subject to doubt that he often partook of an anchoritic life."[182]

This dual form of life was possible because of a distinction regarding the meaning of the term 'hermit'. Both anchorites and cenobites could dwell in a hermitage, that is, a solitary anchorite could live *in eremo*. This is also possible, on the other hand, for cenobites. Removed from the crowd and commotion of secular life, yet living in community, cenobites could also be *in eremo*. Whereas anchorite and cenobite refer to the type of life, hermit signifies the place of dwelling. Therefore, there are anchoritic hermits and cenobitic hermits (*eremitae anachoritae et eremitae coenobitae*),[183] and Augustine, from his time with Simplicianus, including both his stay with the hermits of Tuscany and his return to North Africa, lived as an eremetical cenobite.[184]

---

[175] *VF* 1,5 (19,35–37).

[176] "... quod melius est dicere horas canonicas in congregatione fratrum in ecclesia quam seorsum in cella..." *VF* 1,5 (19,42–43).

[177] "... vita cenobitica securior est et aptior ad perfectionem acquirendam, vita vero anachoritica competit iam perfectis." *VF* 1,5 (20,84–86).

[178] *VF* 1,6 (21,3–4).

[179] *VF* 1,7 (22,8–9).

[180] *VF* 1,7 (22,16–17).

[181] *VF* 1,7 (26,103–111).

[182] "Verum licet Augustinus numquam fuerit anachorita ex statu, ut ostensum est, sed actum anachoritarum non est dubium eum saepius habuisse." *VF* 1,7 (27,123–125).

[183] *VF* 1,7 (22,10–15); *cf. VF* 1,2 (12,90–96).

[184] *VF* 1,7 (23–26).

Augustine combined the "best of both worlds" and on this basis, founded his Order.

After the death of Augustine, the brothers who lived under the saint's guidance were dispersed due to the increasing hostility of the Vandals, who desecrated their monasteries and profaned their rituals. This did not, however, result in the loss of Augustine's heritage. Some of the brothers fled Africa and came to Tuscany, and there regrouped,

> ... some in solitary cells, and others in eremetical communities, serving the Lord, just as the Lord inspired them. And thus, that holy community, instituted by blessed Augustine and, as it is said, always guarded by him, was in no way broken asunder or abolished, but remained preserved in some good fathers, until in most recent times God deemed it worthy to call together that dispersion, just as He once congregated the dispersion of the Israelites.[185]

Even before this eventually occurred, the Church, beginning with Pope Innocent III, recognized the dispersed Order of Hermits of St. Augustine and granted them privileges. Thus the OESA preceded both the Franciscans and Dominicans, who were of more recent origin.[186] In addition, Jordan claimed, because they were hermits, the fathers of the OESA lived in more simplicity than even St. Francis, thus preserving the Augustinian origins of the apostolic life by focusing on religious devotion, as had Gerardo of Bergamo, without straining the historical record whereby Francis first lived as an Augustinian.[187]

According to Jordan, at the Fourth Lateran Council, Innocent III stopped just shy of officially confirming the Order, having avoided the issue with the word 'acceptance'. After such recognition, the gradual reunification continued apace.[188] In 1243 Innocent IV, recognizing the considerable fruits that the Dominicans and Franciscans were bringing the Church, desired to increase their benefit. Thus, he brought the diverse groups of Augustinian hermits living in Tuscany

---

[185] "... nonnulli eorum in cellis solitarie, alii in coenobiis eremiticis se receperunt, servientes Domino sicut cuique Dominus inspiravit. Et sic illa sancta communio per beatum Augustinum instituta et per eum semper, ut dictum est, observata non omnino dirupta fuit et abolita, sed in aliquibus bonis patribus extitit conservata, donec novissimis temporibus illam dispersionem Deus dignatus est congregare, sicut olim dispersiones Israelis congregavit." *VF* 1,14 (45,15–22).
[186] *VF* 1,14 (46,47–48).
[187] *VF* 1,14 (45,34–36).
[188] *VF* 1,14 (46,44–50).

into a single Order, and assigned to them a cardinal protector (Riccardo Annabaldi).[189] There were still, however, many other faithful heirs of St. Augustine who yet remained scattered. "At which time," Jordan explained recounting the myth of the Order's foundation,

> blessed Augustine, wanting to end the dispersion of his own religion, appeared in a vision with a large head but small body, to Innocent's successor to the apostolic see, Pope Alexander IV. On account of this vision, as if by a divine oracle, the Pope was moved to complete the union that had been begun by his predecessor, Pope Innocent.[190]

Whereas Augustine had originally founded his Order of Hermits in the monastery outside of Hippo, he "re-founded" them by appearing in a vision to Alexander. Jordan's account of this vision is the most developed version, and only with Jordan do we find Augustine's appearance motivated by Augustine's will to reunite the dispersed members of his own religion.

Thus began the *status modernus* of the Order, whose father was St. Augustine, by means of his foundation, and whose mother was the Church, through its approbation. Jordan distinguished the *status modernus* from the *status antiquus* just as he did the *patres* from the *fratres*. He did not view the *status antiquus* and the *status modernus* as "two conditions" in succession,[191] but rather as two stages in the single *status religionis* of Augustine's Order. The continuity, not the diversity, is stressed. *Status* was a legal term and in this case refers to the way of life established by Augustine; the adjective *antiquus* or *modernus* signified the periods pre- and post-union, respectively.[192] Jordan was not setting forth a theory of history, but presented historical evidence to establish that the OESA and the original hermits gathered

---

[189] *VF* 1,14 (46,62–47,79).

[190] "Unde beatus Augustinus, volens dispersionem suae Religionis congregari, succedenti ei in Sede apostolica, scilicet domino Alexandro papae IV, in visione apparuit, grandis quidem capite, sed membris exilis. Ex qua visione velut divino oraculo papa commonitus unionem per praedecessorem suum dominum Innocentium inchoatam consummavit." *VF* 1,14 (47,80–85).

[191] *Cf.* K. Elm, "*Augustinus Canonicus-Augustinus Eremita*," 93, and *idem*, "Elias, Paulus von Theben und Augustinus als Ordensgründer. Ein Beitrag zur Geschichtsschreibung und Geschichtsdeutung der Eremiten-und Bettelorden des 13. Jahrhunderts," in *Geschichtsschreibung und Geschichtsbewusstsein im späten Mittelalter*, ed. Hans Patze, Vorträge und Forschungen 31 (Sigmaringen, 1987), 371–397; 387.

[192] The unity of the term *status* as employed by Jordan can be seen in his analysis of the two different meanings of the term *religiosi*; see *VF* 2,25 (252,28–40); *cf.* Hen. *Tract.* 4 (109,98–102).

around Augustine were of one and the same stock. The apostolic life of the apostles—true evangelical poverty, the same as that practiced by Christ and the apostles—was renewed by Augustine's *Rule* and accepted by the Church.[193] Both the *patres* and the *fratres* followed the same *Rule*, the same way of life, in short, the same *status religionis*.

If Jordan can be said to have a theory of history, it is not one of successive *status*, but of continuous cycles of decline and renewal. This is seen in his discussion of the three *propagationes*, which eventually led to that holy community of St. Augustine's offspring, and in Jordan's treatment of the stages of development of apostolic poverty. Holding possessions in common, which even the pagan philosophers affirmed as a component of natural law,[194] was originally the principle of all Christians in the first apostolic community. In time, as the Church grew in members and in societal influence, the doctrine of apostolic poverty was gradually relaxed, becoming increasingly restricted to the *religiosi*, until finally restored to its pristine form by the *Rule*—and Order—of St. Augustine,[195] whose members, as the apostles, live with "one heart and soul in God":

> Therefore, this religion's holy community is able to be that city, that is, a union of cities, about which it is said in the psalm, *Glorious things are said of you, City of God*. Glorious things, I say, are told about your origin (*de propagatione tua*) which you once had from your father, namely blessed Augustine; even more glorious things, however, are said about your confirmation (*de institutione tua*), which you have from your mother, that is, the holy universal church.[196]

The Augustinian Order was truly the "city of God," a beacon in a dark sea with waves of decline and renewal. Jordan was certainly aware of Augustine's *De Civitate Dei*. It is, however, the differences that should be stressed between Jordan's use of the image 'the city

---

[193] *VF* 3,1 (320,8–16); *VF* 3,3 (330,3–9).
[194] *VF* 3,1 (322,63–75).
[195] *VF* 3,2 (326ff).
[196] "Haec igitur sancta communio huius Religionis potest esse illa civitas, id est civium unio, de qua dicitur in psalmo: Gloriosa dicta sunt de te, civitas Dei. Gloriosa, inquam, dicta sunt de propagatione tua, quam olim habuisti a Patre, scilicet beato Augustino; gloriosiora vero dicta sunt de institutione tua, quam habes a matre, scilicet sancta universali Ecclesia." *VF* 1,20 (70,76–81). This is the only place I have found where Jordan refers to the institution of the Order as derived from the Church. Usually, the foundation and institution of the Order is explicitly attributed to Augustine, with the Church's affirmation, and confirmation. See *VF* 1,14 (45f).

of God' in his *Vitasfratrum*, and Augustine's *magnum opus et arduum*. For the Bishop of Hippo, the account of the city of God was the history of salvation; it began with the separation of the light from darkness and reached its final end in the beatitude of eternal, heavenly peace. There is indeed a historical dimension to Augustine's city of God, but the historical is always in a dialectical relationship with the transhistorical.[197] For Jordan, the Order as the city of God is completely historical. It enjoys divine protection and guidance, but it functions as a historical example. Jordan never equated membership as such in this city of God with beatitude. Jordan's city of God, namely the exemplary function of the Order, is the model of the most perfect Christian life. Yet the Order as the city of God occupies a special place in the history of Christianity. To see more precisely how this was so for Jordan, we must look back to the Order's founder himself, St. Augustine.

Augustine harmonized the anchoritic and the cenobitic lives, and he established his Order on this principle. In his person and in his Order Augustine united the active with the contemplative life. For Jordan the contemplative life did not consist in meditation alone, but included the cure of souls and spiritual growth in all forms, carried out by preaching, guiding, and teaching. The active life pertained to physical necessity, of oneself or of a neighbor.[198] All aspects of the spiritual life were part of the contemplative life.[199] Augustine instituted his Order as a contemplative Order, but one that was to minister and preach to the people. Because of this original institution, the Church "directed the 'little brother hermits' of St. Augustine to the cities."[200] Just as St. Augustine, who frequently sought the solitude of contemplation, so the brothers of the Order lead an eremitical life of meditation and contemplation, but are eager to impart

---

[197] For Augustine's view of history and the city of God, see R.A. Markus, *Saeculum: History and Society in the Theology of St. Augustine* (Cambridge, 1970) and Sigurd Böhm, *La Temporalité dans l'Anthropologie Augustinienne* (Paris, 1984).

[198] *VF* 1,10 (33,6–9); *cf.* "Tertia conclusio est quod utraque vita simul est perfectissima ... opera vite active ea que fiunt ad subventionem proximi corporalem; contemplative vero ea que fiunt ad lucrum et profectum spiritualem, ut predicare et huiusmodi." Jor. *OD* (ed. Strassburg, 1484), sermo 39B.

[199] See Saak, "Saints in Society," 322.

[200] "Sane hunc modum primariae institutionis Ordinis attendens sacrosancta mater Ecclesia fratres eremicolas sancti Augustini ad civitates direxit..." *VF* 1,11 (35,23–25).

their spiritual goods to others by their works and their doctrine, teaching equally by example and word.[201]

For Jordan, the harmony of the anchoritic and cenobitic lives, together with the union of the active and contemplative lives, form not merely a perfect life, but the most perfect life, and this was the unique accomplishment of Augustine. In his *Rule* and institution, Augustine taught the most perfect life to his Order, which, as no other, is therefore able to be the city of God. The true sons of Augustine hold a special place within the history of Christianity as the embodiment of the *vita perfectissima*, the genuine *religio Augustini*.[202] Based on Christ's example when he spent forty days in the desert before beginning his preaching, the *vita perfectissima*, Jordan clarified, is "for a time to rest in contemplation in solitude with God alone, and for a time to go forth, through contemplation, to regurgitate from deep inside the spiritual wellsprings to others, for the purpose of winning souls."[203] The combination of the *vita activa* and the *vita contemplativa*, the harmonizing of the cenobitic and the anchoritic lives, was the unique accomplishment of Augustine, who founded his Order, and religion, accordingly.

Augustine's religion was defined by Augustine's life. Augustine, Jordan reminded his brothers, "is to be the exemplar and rule of all our actions."[204] As much as they were able, the Augustinian Hermits were to be 'the imitators of our Father Augustine' (*imitatores Patris nostri Augustini*).[205] Following Augustine as model for the religious life was in no way distinct from preaching and teaching. Jordan radically redefined the *vita contemplativa* whereby the contemplation of the Augustinians' most perfect life included all aspects pertaining to the soul, including teaching, preaching, and pastoral care, whereas the *vita activa* concerned the physical needs of oneself, the cloister,

---

[201] *VF* 1,11 (35,25–36,33). *Cf.* Caroline Walker Bynum, "The Canonical Concern with Edification Verbo et Exemplo," in *idem, Jesus as Mother. Studies in the Spirituality of the High Middle Ages* (Berkeley, 1982), 36–40.

[202] See Appendix A.3.

[203] "... hanc esse vitam perfectissimam nunc in solitudine soli Deo in contemplatione vacare et nunc exire per contemplationem hausta ad lucra animarum reportanda aliis eructare." *VF* 1,11 (35,8–11).

[204] "... qui [Augustine] debet esse omnis nostrae actionis exemplar et regula..." *VF* 1,11 (36).

[205] *VF* 2,21 (226,2–3).

or one's neighbor.[206] It was thus that the heirs of the historical Augustine were able to be both in the city and yet the city on the hill.

Jordan opened Part Two of the *Liber Vitasfratrum* with a discussion of what is meant by the *Rule*'s "one heart and one soul." Although these terms have been interpreted variously by theologians, Jordan explained that,

> ... in our present concern I plan to follow the intention of blessed Augustine in all things. Wherefore, it is evident that according to Augustine, 'one heart' should be understood as the unity of the will; by 'one soul' [is meant] the uniformity of life, or a single way of living according to that which Father Augustine himself approved.[207]

The unity of will and way of life form the unity of the common life. In such a life, there is no room for diversity of opinion or customs; division or multiplicity, "... is not the apostolic life, but Babylonian confusion; not Augustine's *Rule*, but inordinate abuse; not order, but horror!"[208]

Therefore, upon entering the religious life, the new friar must strip himself of his worldly possessions, as well as his internal affections,[209] and thus "naked and poor, follow the naked and poor Christ crucified."[210] Those brothers who do not live according to this precept, who retain for themselves either worldly goods or their own wills, are the followers of Ananias and Judas. If only there were no such types in his day, Jordan lamented.[211] Such deception and fraud undermines the unity of the *vita communis*,[212] which is to be a life of worship and prayer.[213] In singing the divine office, Jordan warned, one must always be careful to be intent on pleasing God, and not those who can hear, "for God is more concerned with devotion and purity

---

[206] E.L. Saak, "Saints in Society," 322–323.

[207] "... in praesenti negotio intentionem beati Augustini per omnia prosequi intendo, quantum apparet ex intentione Augustini, per cor unum intelligitur unanimitas voluntatis, per animam unam uniformitas vitae seu una forma vivendi secundum quod ipse Pater Augustinus innuit..." *VF* 2,1 (76,41–45).

[208] "Non est haec vita apostolica, sed confusio babylonica, non Augustini Regula, sed abusio anomala, non ordo, sed horror." *VF* 2,2 (78,87–89); *cf.* "... ubi non est ordo, ibi non est pulchritudo: sed horror et confusio." Aeg.Rom. 2 *Sent.*, Prol. (ed. Venice, 1581), fol. 2rb.

[209] *VF* 3,11 (359,32–35).

[210] "... nudus et pauper secutus nudum et pauperem Christum crucifixum." *VF* 3,11 (360,56–57).

[211] *VF* 3,15 (382,2–15).

[212] *VF* 3,17 (389f).

[213] *VF* 2,15 (180,2–8).

of heart than with the quality of voice."[214] Even if a brother does not know how to sing, or is unable to do so, as are the illiterate (*sicut idiotae et illiterati*), he is not prevented from participating in the divine office. These brothers, in place of singing, should say a *Pater Noster*, which Augustine himself advised.[215]

The chief goal of singing and praying the divine hours is complete inner devotion. Concentration and earnestness in prayer are prerequisites, because it is during prayer that the devil makes his sally. Thus, Jordan concluded, "amongst all good works, praying is the most difficult."[216] The Augustinians' entire life should be one of continuous prayer, and this is possible because there are three types of prayer: vocal prayer, mental prayer, and active prayer, or the prayer of works.[217] Whether one is singing the canonical hours, studying sacred scripture, or working for the maintenance of the cloister, the Augustinian should be in prayer.

Jordan illustrated the necessity of continuous prayer in the chapter treating the efficacy of intercessory prayer to the saints. This section is more personal than any other in the treatise, an indication of the importance of prayer for the Augustinians. Every *exemplum* he brought was drawn from his own experience; as he put it, "I will refer to certain stories of my own misfortune."[218] Here we learn that during his visitation of the French Province, Jordan was cured of a serious fever by St. Martin.[219] Jordan further reveals that he was not embarrassed to admit his negligence in fulfilling a vow to St. Peter. During the Black Death, Jordan was prior provincial of the Saxon-Thuringian Province. Because of the severity of the plague, many brothers wanted to flee to Rome to obtain a jubilee indulgence. If all who desired were to receive permission, Jordan realized, the convents would be left virtually empty.[220] Thus, Jordan exhorted his

---

[214] "In modo etiam cantandi semper plus quaerat frater placere Deo quam auditoribus. Qui enim studet Deo placere in cantando, quanto purius et simplicius cantaverit, tanto magis Deo placebit; plus enim attendit Deus devotionem et puritatem cordis quam modulationem vocis." *VF* 2,15 (181,46–50).
[215] *VF* 2,15 (184,123–125).
[216] "... quod inter omnia bona opera orare est difficillimum." *VF* 2,16 (189,110–111); *cf.* *VF* 2,16 (188,74–94).
[217] *VF* 2,19 (214,118–122).
[218] "Referam quasdam infelicitatis meae historias." *VF* 2,20 (218,7).
[219] *VF* 2,20 (225,199–216).
[220] *VF* 2,20, (223,158–162).

brothers to remain in their cloisters and tried to persuade them, as best he could, that they could make a spiritual pilgrimage with works of devotion to God and to St. Peter. To set an example, Jordan himself made such a vow.[221] After the plague subsided, however, and after Jordan completed his term of office, he forgot to fulfill his vow. Soon thereafter an elderly friar, Jordan's former confessor, was praying for Jordan before the altar when "the blessed apostle Peter appeared as if standing before him in effigy, just as he had seen his image in Rome, holding the two keys, and formally spoke these words: 'Tell brother Jordan that he has done nothing at all to fulfill his promise to me.' Having said these words, he disappeared."[222] The elderly brother told Jordan what had happened, whereupon Jordan carried out what he had promised St. Peter and the Lord the first chance he had.[223]

The Augustinian life of prayer was none other than the one founded by St. Augustine: an eremitical-cenobitic life, based on the first apostolic community in Jerusalem, and confirmed by Mother Church; a contemplative life of prayer, the true *religio Augustini*. Contemplation, for the hermits, included teaching and preaching, all aspects of the spiritual life, one's own and that of one's neighbor, and, as Augustine showed by his example, one's neighbor lived on both sides of the cloister's walls. The most perfect life was to rest in solitude with God alone, and then, through contemplation, to bring spiritual riches to the people. This charge—to contemplate God and act accordingly—formed the core of Augustine's religion.

C. *De-Sexing Augustine*

Of the four parts comprising the *Liber Vitasfratrum*, Part Two, concerning the spiritual union of having one heart and soul in God, is by far the longest, over three times longer than any other part of the work.[224] This should cause no surprise, for having one heart and

---

[221] *VF* 2,20 (223,162–224,171).

[222] "Et ecce apparuit ei beatus petrus apostolus quasi stans coram eo in effigie, sicut imaginem eius Romae viderat, habens in manu dextra duas claves dicensque ei formaliter haec verba: 'Dic fratri Jordano lectori, quod sponsionem mihi factam minime servavit.' Quibus verbis dictis disparuit." *VF* 2,20 (224,182–186).

[223] *VF* 2,20 (223,158–225,194).

[224] In the edition of Hümpfner and Arbesmann, Part Two extends over 244 pages (from page 75 to page 319); Part One has only 68 pages (7–74); Part Three, 72 (pages 320–391); and Part Four, 50 (pages 392–442).

soul in God was the central dictum of Augustine's *Rule*. Moreover, Jordan interpreted the heart as referring to the will, "for just as the bodily heart is the principle of all bodily movement, so is the will the principle of all spiritual movement."[225] Jordan then further exposited the soul as referring to a unified form of life (*una vivendi forma*).[226] Thus he organized the second part of his work according to the "heart" and the "soul," each of which had an associated virtue. That of the heart was obedience, which he treated in the first part of Part Two; that of the soul was chastity. "To repeat," Jordan wrote in chapter twenty-eight of Part Two, "just as obedience is the virtue that is the regulative force of the superior appetite, namely, of the will, which is understood by 'heart', as was stated above, so is chastity the regulative force of the inferior appetite, which is interpreted as 'soul'."[227]

In the first part of Part Two, on the virtue of obedience, or the *cor unum*, Jordan treated a variety of topics, everything from the virtue of obedience as such, to the relationship of the Order's prelates to their subjects, brotherly love, how to deal with disputes among the brothers, humility, patience, spiritual pride, brotherly correction, care and patience for the sick, preparation for death, the *Rule* and *Constitutions* of the Order, prayer, celebrating mass, theological studies, daily work, and the vice of lethargy. When he turned to the second part of Part Two, that dealing with the *anima una*, the lower appetite and its virtue chastity, chastity was the only topic he dealt with. Indeed, chapter 30 of Part Two, which treats the various ways and means a brother can use to preserve his chastity (*De cautelis castitatis*), is twice as long as any other single chapter in the entire work, consisting of 860 lines of text in the modern edition, as compared to the 412 lines given to his treatment of the Order's *Rule* and *Constitutions*. Chapters 28 through 31 of Part Two deal exclusively with the issue

---

[225] "Quod autem convenienter per cor voluntas accipiatur, patet. Nam sicut cor corporale est principium omnium motuum corporalium, ita et voluntas est principium omnium motuum spiritualium." *VF* 2,1 (77,52–54).

[226] *VF* 2,1 (77,71–74).

[227] "Rursus sicut oboedientia est virtus cohibitiva appetitus superioris, scilicet voluntatis, qui per cor intelligitur, ut supra dictum est, sic castitas est virtus cohibitiva appetitus inferioris, qui per animam intelligitur... Sicut ergo ex eo, quod nobis est cor unum, gignitur et nutritur virtus oboedientiae, sic ex eo, quod nobis est anima una, pro quanto anima casta se continet et non resolvitur in appetitu inferiori, generatur et nutritur virtus castitas." *VF* 2,28 (267,13–22).

of chastity (with the final chapter 32, as in each of the four parts of the *Liber Vitasfratrum*, detailing the corresponding regulations found in the *Rule* and *Constitutions*). Jordan essentially equated chastity with the Order's *una forma vivendi*. The issue of chastity was one of preponderant importance. And it was so, if for no other reason, because it had been as well for Augustine himself.

Chastity, for Augustine, was his one great obstacle. His lust was the last chain that bound him, and it did so as affecting his will, the lower part of his will, his libido. Book eight of the *Confessions* is an account of Augustine's struggle with his own demon, his lust, and his final victory over it. In book eight, chapter five, Augustine admitted that chastity

> was just what I longed for myself, but I was held back, and I was held back not by fetters put on me by someone else, but by the iron bondage of my own will. The enemy held my will and made a chain out of it and bound me with it. From a perverse will came lust, and slavery to lust became a habit, and the habit being constantly yielded to, became a necessity.[228]

Two chapters later he confessed:

> But I, wretched young man that I was, even more wretched at the beginning of my youth, had begged you for chastity and had said: 'Make me chaste and continent, but not yet.' I was afraid that you might hear me too soon and cure me too soon from the disease of a lust which I preferred to be satisfied than extinguished.[229]

Augustine's lust was almost legendary, and had produced a son, Adeodatus. Yet nowhere in the medieval *Vitae* of Augustine was his sexuality and his battles therewith ever mentioned. Adeodatus scarcely makes an appearance. Concupiscence for Augustine was the major obstacle preventing his conversion, and yet it is nowhere spoken of

---

[228] "Cui rei ego suspirabam ligatus non ferro alieno, sed mea ferrea voluntate. Velle meum tenebat inimicus et inde mihi catenam fecerat et constrinxerat me. Quippe voluntate perserva facta est libido, et dum servitur libidini, facta est consuetudo, et dum consuetudini non resistitur, facta est necessitas." Aug. *Conf.* 8.5,10 (119,8–12; trans. 168).

[229] "At ego adulescens miser valde, miserior in exordio ipsius adulescentiae, etiam petieram a te castitatem et dixeram: 'da mihi castitatem et continentiam, sed noli modo.' Timebam enim, ne me cito exaudires et cito sanares a morbo concupiscentiae, quem malebam expleri quam exstingui." Aug. *Conf.* 8,7,17 (124,20–24; trans. 173–174). For Augustine, see Peter Brown, *The Body and Society. Men, Women and Sexual Renunciation in Early Christianity* (New York, 1988), 387–427.

in the representations of his biography from Possidius to Jordan. No one mentions that Augustine's son was born of his concubine, a common-law wife, whom his mother made him dismiss to further his career, but whom Augustine loved deeply. No one mentions that before his conversion he loved sex and partook of it as often as possible, that he burned with desire. No one mentions that for him it was a major issue throughout his *Confessions*.[230] No one deals with the fruit of his lust, Adeodatus, whom Augustine so loved and admired, aside from the brief mention that he was baptized together with his father, and listing him as one of Augustine's companions whom he brought with him to Africa to establish his Order of Hermits. In the emplotments of Augustine's life, Augustine is not a sexual being at all, it is not an issue; his sexuality is erased, Augustine is de-sexed.

The Hermits were not the ones who effected the de-sexing of Augustine; that was long part of the tradition they inherited. And how could it have been otherwise? Augustine was, after all, one of the Church Fathers, and especially with the increasing enforcement of clerical celibacy from the eleventh century on,[231] how could a Church Father himself be a father? As a model for imitation, as a model of holiness, and as a representative of the Church, Augustine *had* to be "sexless." Whether as a bishop and founder of the Order of Canons, or as a *servus dei* and founder of an Order of Hermits, Augustine's battles with sex were not the most propitious part of his character for emulation, or even recitation. Even as an example of victory the record is silent: nowhere in the *Vitae* of Augustine, nor even in Jordan's *Liber Vitasfratrum*, is Augustine ever held up as the model of one who had overcome the temptations of the flesh, as one who had fought fiercely against lust, and had finally won. Yet the Hermits went even further in their de-sexing of Augustine not only by erasing his sexuality, but also by appropriating his fatherhood for themselves as his spiritual sons, and thus, they became the very embodiment of their own father.

That Augustine knew what it meant to be a father is clear from his *Confessions*, which the Hermits from Nicholas of Alessandria to

---

[230] See Margaret R. Miles, "Desire and Delight: A New Reading of Augustine's *Confessions*," in *Broken and Whole. Essays on Religion and the Body*, ed. Maureen A. Tilley and Susan A. Ross, College Theological Society 39 (London, 1993), 3–16.

[231] See Michael Frassetto, ed., *Medieval Purity and Piety. Essays on Medieval Clerical Celibacy and Religious Reform* (New York, 1998), and note 238 below.

Jordan knew backwards and forwards. Augustine speaks with such pride of Adeodatus, whom he considered to have been purely a gift of God; a product of his own sin, surely, but for Augustine that was unavoidable in all human procreation, and even so, Adeodatus was appropriately named. In book nine, chapter six of the *Confessions* we find Augustine's most detailed comments on his son.[232] Adeodatus for Augustine was a wonder, he was awe-inspiring, and he and his father were baptized together by Bishop Ambrose, which must have been an emotional experience for father and son alike. It is also in this chapter that Augustine tells that God took the life of Adeodatus in his sixteenth year. He continues by noting that for a life of such purity there was no reason why anyone should fear for him and his passing. Augustine continued by relating that during this time he himself spent his days meditating upon God's salvation of the human race and shedding tears in the singing of hymns, though tears of joy.[233] The next time Augustine mentions having wept is towards the end of book nine when he tells of the death of his mother, Monica. And then too Adeodatus was present, and wept. Augustine admits that he was led to the brink of tears upon hearing Adeodatus weeping for the death of his grandmother, but he held back. Augustine was not one to cry freely, or to tell of his weeping.[234] Only later, alone in his room, did he finally allow himself the needed release.[235] Such reticence surely was present as well six chapters earlier when Augustine mentioned his son having died such an early death, which Augustine continued forthwith by telling of the tears he shed in his meditations, meditations upon God's plan of salvation, for humankind, and, surely, for his own son. Augustine was a proud and loving father before he ever was turned into the spiritual father of his hermit sons, who usurped the place of Adeodatus in their representations of their own patrimony. Augustine was de-sexed not only as a lustful youth burning with passion and desire, but also as a hermit himself, a hermit who was truly a loving father. If Augustine's sexuality had not been silenced and erased, if Augustine had not been de-sexed, he never could have become the father of his late medieval sons.

---

[232] Aug. conf. 9,6,14 (140,1–141,27).
[233] Aug. conf. 9,6,14 (141,21–25).
[234] Aug. conf. 9,12,29 (150,1–13); Aug. conf. 9,12,32 (151,42–50).
[235] Aug. conf. 9,12,33 (152,67–79).

The spiritual sons of Augustine in the later Middle Ages, who had been propagated without the taint of human procreation, de-sexed the sexuality of their father, covering it up, almost as the sons of Noah; they brushed it under the table, shunned and suppressed, though they knew it well. They were, after all, products of the same heritage; with lust and concupiscence, and the battle for chastity, they were well acquainted, even if they refused to attribute such to the founder of their religion. If one can judge the importance of an issue based on the attention given to it, then chastity was the single most important topic facing the Order of Hermits of St. Augustine in the later Middle Ages, at least according to Jordan.

To point to the fact that chastity was a major theme for the Augustinian Hermits is perhaps stating the obvious. Clerical celibacy had been on the table of ecclesiastical concerns for quite a while, and there is nothing new to claim that the vow of chastity was a cornerstone of the religious life. Chastity was the main demarcation between the clerical estate and the lay, or at least between the holy and the "run of the mill."[236] As continent beings, the clergy existed on a higher level than those who decided to marry rather than burn. Indeed, in his letter to the Order of 1318, Prior General Alexander of San Elpidio confirmed that any religious, cleric in holy orders, or nun who contracted a marriage was *ipso facto* excommunicated.[237] Jordan, however, had a slightly different take on the matter. For Jordan, contracting a marriage, as well as the other religious vows, was not in and of itself contradictory to the clerical state, but it was for the religious.[238] The religious thus by definition existed on a

---

[236] See Brown, *The Body and Society*; Susanna Elm, *'Virgins of God'. The Making of Asceticism in Late Antiquity* (Oxford, 1994); Jacque Le Goff, *The Medieval Imagination*, translated by Arthur Goldhammer (Chicago, 1988), 83–103.

[237] "Item si quis Religiosus vel quicumque clericus in sacris ordinibus, vel quecumque Monialis contraxerit matrimonium ipso facto est excommunicatus." *AAug*. 3 (1909/1910), 229.

[238] "Religiosi autem continent totam perfectionem clericorum... Sunt autem illa tria continentia, obedientia et paupertas voluntaria. Etsi hec tria aliquo modo etiam clericis gerant, non tamen ita substantialiter inseparabiliter. Non enim repugnat sacerdoti, ut sacerdos est, contrahere matrimoniam, non sub esse proprio episcopo, et habere proprium, unde in istis etiam posset dispensare; sed hoc repugnat religios ut religiosus est." Jor. *OJ*, sermo 111, fol. 188^{ra-b}. Jordan is here either echoing early views on the admissibility of clerical marriage, or simply recognizing the fact thereof and legitimizing it to some degree by placing then the *religiosi* on a higher level. The campaign against clerical marriage began with force with the Gregorian reforms of the eleventh century, but by the late thirteen and early

higher plane than the secular clergy. Giles of Rome had already defined the human being as an animal who marries by nature, claiming that the continent lived above the human condition, as if in another realm, one closer to the angels.[239] Certainly that was the state of Augustine's Hermits, or at least was supposed to be. Yet as we have already seen, chastity was at times more likely a goal to be striven for in precept, than it was actually followed in practice: the members of the Order in Paris and Pisa bear witness. No wonder Jordan devoted so much attention and effort to treating the issue.

The importance of maintaining chastity for the Augustinian friar no less than for the parish priest, was one that, moreover, had practical consequences. Jordan's colleague at Erfurt for at least two years, Hermann of Schildesche, composed his *Speculum Manuale Sacerdotum* at approximately the same time as Jordan was finishing his *Liber Vitasfratrum*. Hermann's manual was to become one of the most popular handbooks for the parish clergy in the later Middle Ages, and it was one in which the theoretical discussions of chastity and clerical celibacy were brought to a most pertinent level.[240]

Hermann's *Speculum* highlights the practical problems that priests faced in their struggle to remain sexually pure. According to Hermann, if a priest had a wet dream the night before he was supposed to say mass, he was to refrain from celebrating, and this was just the beginning. If a priest had committed fornication before being scheduled to say mass, he was to abstain from celebrating for three days, and the same applied if he had voluntarily caused his nocturnal pollution. If, however, he was the recipient of a wet dream, through no fault of his own, and against his will, this did not entail the need for abstention.[241] Furthermore, the priest was cautioned against seduc-

---

fourteenth centuries, clerical marriage, or at least clerical concubinage was still common. See James Brundage, *Law, Sex, and Christian Society in Medieval Europe* (Chicago, 1987), 150–152, 214–225, 474–477; Morris, *The Papal Monarchy*, 103–105; Dyan Elliott, *Fallen Bodies. Pollution, Sexuality, and Demonology in the Middle Ages* (Philadelphia, 1999).

[239] "... homo est animal naturaliter coniugale..." Aeg. *Reg.* II,1,7; as cited by Zumkeller, "De Doctrina Sociali Scholae Augustinianae Aevi Medii," *AAug.* 22 (1951/52), 57–84; 59.

[240] For Hermann's *Speculum* and its manuscript and early printed edition history, see Chapter Four below.

[241] "Item cavendum est sibi, si habuit in somnis pollutionem ex sua culpa ne illo die celebret, et multomagis si fornicatus est, abstineat per triduum. Idem crederem si pollutus est voluntarie vigilando. De pollutione tamen que sine omni cupla sua in somnis accidit cum renisu voluntatis somniantis aliud credo quod proptera a

ing women in the confessional, and if he seduced a woman of his own parish, he was sentenced to do penance for ten years; if he seduced a woman he himself had baptized, he was to be defrocked.[242] Maintaining chastity had serious consequences, and if a priest was going to fornicate, he at least should do so with someone from another parish. From nocturnal emissions to sex in the confessional, the parish priest had to guard his chastity. And what applied to the parish priest applied as well to the Augustinian Hermits, who themselves were responsible for saying masses for their civic communities and hearing their parishioners' confessions, such as the two masses for the deceased relatives of Konrad Mach, burgher of Magdeburg, which the Augustinians in Magdeburg agreed to celebrate for his donation to the monastery in 1328 precisely as the Hermits were trying to gain entry to San Pietro's in Pavia and custody of Augustine's chaste body, and precisely as the case of Burchard's murder was in full swing.[243] There had to be at least one priest who had been free of wet dreams and fornication who thus would be available to say the required masses promised the citizens. The problem of maintaining chastity for the Augustinians, and by no means for the Augustinians alone, was one that was central not only to the individual souls of individual friars, but one that had consequences for the communities in and for which they lived and worked. Jordan's *Liber Vitasfratrum* was intended to help.

The contemporary reader, and interpreter, of Jordan's treatment of chastity is faced with the dilemma of how to deal with ideas and representations that are repugnant to modern sensitivities, and indeed, are simply repugnant in and of themselves. Yet Jordan's misogyny, as well as that of his Order and his society, cannot simply be condemned and dismissed out of hand lest we choose to overlook a central historical reality. It is, however, not my intent here to analyze the issues of sexuality, chastity, clerical celibacy, representations of

---

celebratione non oporteat abstinere." Herm.Sch. *Spec.*, fol. 13ʳ. Herman's reference to fornication here is most likely, though surely not exclusively, with respect to the priest having had sex with his concubine or wife; see note 238 above.

[242] "Item ne intendat per viam confessionis aliquam feminam procari vel sollicitare ad malum quia sic sub specie magne fidelitatis traderet eam ad mortem eternam, quod esset pessimum omnium peccatorum... Item sacerdos qui cognoscit filiam confessionis sue decem annis peniteat cum maximam traditionem fecerit, ut supra dictum est. Item si sacerdos cognoscit illam quam baptisavit, deponendus est." Herm.Sch. *Spec.*, fol. 18ᵛ–20ʳ.

[243] *UrkM* nr. 328 (194–196).

women, and misogyny in the later Middle Ages as such. The point is that preserving one's chastity and the struggle that it was, and the lengths to which one could go to do so, were matters of utmost seriousness and importance for Jordan and the late medieval Augustinians on a daily basis. The precarious situation of the contemporary historian, of the contemporary male historian, is one caught between the Scylla of adopting the role of judge or prosecuting attorney and pronouncing his sentence without having sufficiently come to terms with the historical understanding, and the Charybis of entering the realm of the voyeur or plain pervert. The challenge of presenting an empathetic interpretation with neither sympathy nor antipathy must be held as the goal independent from the personal perspectives of the one doing the interpreting, with the consciousness of the fact that as we look into the abyss, of in this case Jordan's and the Augustinians' fear of women and sexuality, the abyss, as Neitzsche put it, also looks into us.[244]

It would be easy to pyschologize Jordan's treatment of chastity, and even easier perhaps to psychologize it away. It was, after all, a most traditional suppression by the Order's institutionalized superego of the drives and passions of the members' egos and libidos. It was a degradation of women as the object of male desire combined with an exaltation of Mary and Mother Church, and a de-sexing, if not a symbolic castration, of the father figure Augustine. Little doubt that Oedipus stood behind the Augustinians' pure ideals.[245] And a psychologizing it was, for the virtue of chastity was the basis of the Augustinians' uniform way of life, which related to their goal of having one soul, *anima una*, one *psyche* in God. If in a general sense the vow of poverty was the defining ideal of the Franciscan Order, and that of obedience of the Dominican, the vow of chastity was that of the Order of Augustine's Hermits. The Augustinians had de-sexed their founding father, but as their myth made clear, they themselves were Augustine's embodiment and as such were compelled to strive to keep that body chaste as well.

---

[244] "Whoever fights monsters should see to it that in the process he does not become a monster. And when you look long into an abyss, the abyss also looks into you." Friedrich Nietzsche, *Beyond Good and Evil. Prelude to a Philosophy of the Future*, translated by Walter Kaufmann (New York, 1966), 89, nr. 143.

[245] Eugen Drewermann, *Kleriker. Psychogramm eines Ideals* (Munich, 1991), esp. 480–629; Janine Chasseguet-Smirgel, *Sexuality and Mind. The Role of the Father and the Mother in the Psyche* (New York, 1986); Paul Ricoeur, *Freud and Philosophy: An Essay on Interpretation*, trans. Denis Savage (New Haven, 1970), esp. 210–338.

In treating the castration of the heart as a means of guarding one's chastity,[246] Jordan tells his brothers that although one cannot avoid all thoughts of all kinds, it is within one's rational powers to think of the same object in several ways. Wherefore, he continues, "when the thought of some woman comes to you, it is in the power of your reason to view her as beautiful, desirable, and fit for the use of your carnal pleasure, or, to view her as a sack of shit, a net of the devil, and as deadly venom for your soul."[247] Jordan later tells a story from the *Vitae Patrum* of a brother living as a hermit in the Scythian desert who was bothered by his thoughts of a beautiful woman he knew. Once a brother from Egypt came to visit and informed him that his beloved had died. The first brother, upon hearing the news, went at night to her grave, opened it, and wiped his cloak in her rotting flesh; returning to his cell, he placed the stench before his eyes and said to himself: 'Look! Here is the object of your desire, satisfy yourself with this.'[248] This is the story as found in Jordan's source. Jordan abbreviated the account a bit, and with an important change. In Jordan's version, when the brother heard that the woman had died, "he took part of her body, and when his thoughts would turn to her, he placed her rotting flesh before his nose and eyes saying: 'Look! Here is the object of your desire. Satisfy yourself with this.'"[249] In the *Vitae Patrum* the story is a specific

---

[246] *VF* 2,30 (296,489–301,625); "Tredecima cautela est castratio cordis, ut videlicet homo ferro conaminis sui abscidat caput pessimarum cogitationum." *VF* 2,30 (296,489–490).

[247] "Unde cum tibi incidit cogitatio de aliqua muliere, in potestate rationis est eam apprehendere ut pulchram, delicatam et usui carnalis voluptatis aptam vel apprehendere eam ut saccum stercorum, rete diaboli, venenum pestiferum animae."*VF* 2,30 (296,505–297,508).

[248] "Erat quidam frater in eremo Scythiae promptus et alacer in opus Dei, et spiritali conversatione. Huic autem inimicus generis humani diabolus immisit cogitationes, ut recordaretur cuiusdam notae sibi mulieris pulchritudinem, et conturbaretur in cogitationibus suis vehementer. Contigit autem, ex dispensatione Domini Jesu, ut alius quidam frater de Aegypto veniret ad visitandum eum in charitate Christi. Et dum inter se loquebatuntur, evenit sermo ut diceret ille frater de Aegypto: Quia mortua est illa mulier. Ipsa autem erat, in cuius amore impugnabatur supradictus frater. Haec cum audisset ille, post paucos dies abiit ad locum illum ubi positum erat corpus illius defunctae mulieris, et aperuit noctu sepulcrum eius, et cum pallio suo tersit saniem putredinis eius et reversus est ad cellulam suam, ponebatque fetorem in conspectu suo, et dicebat cogitationibus suis: Ecce habetis desiderium quod quaerebatis, satiate vos ex eo, et ita in illo fetore cruciabat semetipsum, usquequo cessaret ab eo sordidissima impugnatio." *VP* 3,11 (744C–D); 5,22 (878D–879A).

[249] "Quemadmodum legitur de quodam, qui affligebatur cogitationibus de quadam muliere; quam cum audisset mortuam, tulit de cadavere suo, et cum invaderet

account, an *exemplum*, a one time event. For Jordan, it was an ongoing cure, which thus perhaps necessitated a part of the body, rather than simply a soiled cloak. He continued by noting that this was a deed that "although one might be horrified to copy literally, one nevertheless should not be reluctant to imitate in intention, namely, so that one might consider the person who is the object of one's fantasy as if she were dead and immediately changed into a rotting corpse. Even more so, if anyone considers sufficiently the rottenness and uncleanliness of a living woman, certainly he should be horrified not only actually to have sex with her crudely, but also even to ponder the matter in his heart."[250]

The exhortation to consider women as sacks of shit and as putrid, rotting corpses was a strategy, not a description. Jordan was trying to offer help to his brothers as they struggled with temptation. As already mentioned, for Jordan the greater the temptation, the greater the victory. Analogously we can say, the greater the temptation, the greater the need for a counterweight. Jordan's degradation of women here is thus itself a testimony to the fact that this was not his view of women as such, though I am by no means suggesting that Jordan's opinion of the female gender was laudatory, except perhaps, for his view of Mary, which itself calls into question taking his admonitions here as presenting his views of actual women. Mary, naturally, is an exception, but the contrast is not without import. Jordan, in keeping with his Order's fierce defense of the Immaculate Conception, considered Mary to have exalted feminine nature to such an extent that it was more powerful than the most powerful males singularly elected by God. Although by nature women are weak, unstable, and inclined to concupiscence, Mary completely removed all these weaknesses from the female sex thus elevating the feminine above all humans.[251] Moreover, Mary indeed marked the limits of God's omni-

---

cogitatio, posuit putredinem illam ante nares et oculos dicens: Ecce habes desiderium tuum. Satiare de eo.'" *VF* 2,30 (308,843–309,846).

[250] "Quod factum etsi quis sequi materialiter horreat, non tamen pigeat intentionaliter imitari, ut videlicet recogitet personam illam, circa quam cogitatione versatur, esse morituram et cito in cadaver putridum convertendam. Immo si quis etiam mulieris vivae putredinem et immunidtiam bene consideraret, horreret utique non solum ei turpiter commisceri, sed etiam abhorreret vel corde de ea tractare."*VF* 2,30 (309,847–852).

[251] "Ita ipsa [Maria] lapsum Eve per suam constantiam reparavit et totam naturam femineam super omnes homines nobilitavit, reddens eam fortiorem viris fortissimis a deo singulariter electis. Quod patet per hoc quod natura feminea est per

potence, for God could create a greater world and a greater heaven, but God could not create a greater mother than Mary, the mother of God.[252] Jordan's praise and estimation of Mary was not limited to Mary herself; Mary had, by her own virtue to be sure, ennobled her entire gender. Women, feminine nature, the female sex, not just Mary, had been raised by Mary to a position above even the most powerful, divinely favored males. And this was the female sex, the particular instantiations of which Jordan exhorted his confreres to view as unclean, putrid rotting corpses, as sacks of shit.

Such a disjunction is clarified somewhat by Jordan's distinctions between the soul and the flesh, and between nature, male or female, and actual living beings. Unregenerate human nature, as we will see in the following chapter, was for Jordan the realm of the flesh and as such, existed in the kingdom of the devil. The spirit was the subject of salvation and thus, of elevation. Humans, male and female, were held down by the weight of the flesh, all the while the spirit strove to return to its true nature, union with God. The individual progressed on her or his spiritual journey by subduing the affections of the flesh to the greatest extent possible. Only a foretaste of the soul's eventual reunion with the divine could be had in this life, in this world, which was always a battle, a battle between the flesh and the spirit, and a battle between God and the devil. In this context, created female nature was weak, but had, by the work of Mary, been elevated above even the most potent male nature, as an added attribute to the work of Christ, who had redeemed fallen human nature as such. Yet this was all in the realm of theory, or of potential being. Actual living beings were different, though bearing a relationship to their potential being. And this recognition brings us back down to earth for treating Jordan's view of women and chastity.

Feminine nature, the female sex, was more powerful than the most powerful masculine nature of the male sex. In his *Liber Vitasfratrum*, Jordan was addressing his male brothers, the *weaker* sex. This position, this theoretical position, had little if anything to do with the

---

naturam fluida et instabilis; est ad concupiscendum declivis; et est in sensu prudentie exilis et debilis. Sed istas tres conditiones beata virgo a sexu femineo totaliter removit et ideo ipsam mirabiliter super omnes homines nobilitavit." Jor. *OJ*, sermo 137, fol. 225[vb].

[252] "... quia deus sua omnipotentia maiorem vel digniorem [matrem] facere non posset; posset facere maiorem mundum, maius celum, maiorem matrem quam matrem dei non posset facere deus." Jor. *OJ.*, sermo 41, fol. 83[ra].

actual place of men and women in society. Husbands were still to rule over their wives. In the realm of daily life, in the real world of social and political action, Jordan did not differ from the norms of his society, norms that were at the time unabashedly and unapologetically patriarchal and misogynistic. As Dyan Elliott noted, "medieval sexual theory is undoubtedly one area in which two streams can coexist without any danger of either's drying up."[253] In his treatment of chastity in the *Liber Vitasfratrum* Jordan is only tangentially dealing with the real world; he is explicating measures for the health of the soul, the *anima una* that formed the Augustinians' *forma vivendi*. He was addressing weak male friars, the sons of their father Augustine, who as such knew that chastity was the key, chastity was the bridge from living in the world of the flesh to existing in the realm of the spirit. In beginning his discussion of chastity, Jordan not only pointed to the fact that one of the benefits of the battles between the spirit and the flesh was that it compelled one to recognize one's own weakness and that one was completely dependent on the grace of God,[254] but he also informed his brothers that "to the extent that a man is increasingly spiritual, that is, to the extent that he increasingly lives according to the spirit, to an even greater extent does the enemy sharpen his weapons against him. Wherefore the devil rages more fiercely against the religious than against others, and rejoices more from his victory over a single religious than he does from his victory over many others."[255] It may not be simple coincidence that the word 'enemy' in Latin, *hostis*, is a feminine noun, for in this battle with the devil, the weak, male friars faced their enemies indeed;[256]

---

[253] Dyan Elliott, *Spiritual Marriage. Sexual Abstinence in Medieval Wedlock* (Princeton, 1993), 137.

[254] "Tertia est [scil. *utilitas collucationis carnis et spiritus*], quia ad recognitionem infirmitatis nostrae nos impellit, ut non nostris viribus castitatem attribuere praesumamus. Et coincidit quodammodo cum praecedente, nisi quia illa attenditur penes superbiam mentis, ista vero penes infirmitatem naturae nostrae absque auxilio divinae gratiae." *VF* 2,29 (272,59–63). *Cf.*: "Secunda est secundum eundem, quia superbiam nostram reprimit. Nam cum quis longo tempore nullis incentivis carnalibus impugnatur et ex hoc et aliis spiritualibus profectibus extollitur, tunc caro suis incentivis hominem colaphizat ac per hoc humiliat." *VF* 2,29 (271,30–33*)*.

[255] Et quanto homo magis fuerit spiritualis, id est secundum spiritum vivens, tanto fortius arma sua hostis acuit contra eum. Et inde est, quod diabolus plus est infestus Religiosis quam aliis et plus gaudet de victoria sua contra unum Religiosum quam de multis aliis." *VF* 2,29 (276,166–170).

[256] Equating *hostis* with *mulier* was not lost on the classical authors, though usually in the sense of *mulier* as *uxor*: "ut, quo die captam hostem vidisset, eodem matrimonio junctam acciperet." Liv. 30,14,2; L&S 868B, IIA.

if not the feminine nature, or the female sex as such, females were dangerous for the souls of the sons of Augustine.

Jordan offered his brothers sixteen ways to guard one's chastity. The first is simply to avoid looking at women.[257] The very sight of a woman could well do its damage. This is not to say that Jordan was purporting that every time a friar happened to see a woman his chastity would be in danger; it is not the simple ocular vision, but the fixed stare that was rarely possible without arousing concupiscence.[258] The danger lay in the contemporary theory of vision, which applied to all images. The external vision produced images within the soul which thus could damage the condition of the soul,[259] especially when the images were of women. And this was what lay behind Jordan's exhortation for friars to view women as sacks of shit and putrid flesh. He was referring to the ability of the friars to control what sort of image was to enter their souls. Either the friar could see a woman as beautiful and desirable, or in quite another way. Attraction, desire, and pleasure were the dangers. At the base of Jordan's treatment of chastity was not so much an attitude towards women as women, and far less an explication of the nature of women, which he treated more directly in his discussion of Mary, but rather, a fear of male sexuality. As the weaker sex, the male friars were in danger due to the power of their own lust.

Controlling one's gaze was, fortunately, only the first of numerous ways to help suppress male desire. Avoiding association with women was another sure method, as was fasting, for after all, if one was sufficiently weakened from lack of food, the sexual drive would

---

[257] *VF* 2,30 (278,4–25).

[258] "Non igitur prohibetur aspectus feminae, sed aspectus fixus, qui raro potest esse sine concupiscentia." *VF* 2,28 (268,48–49). Jordan had touched on the dangers of looking at women in his very first chapter dealing with chastity, to which he refers his reader when in chapter 30 he turned directly to the various ways of guarding one's chastity: "Prima cautela est custodia oculorum, ne in feminam figantur, ut dictum est ex doctrina sancti Augustini supra, capitulo anteproximo, ubi etiam de hoc habes exempla." *VF* 2,30 (278,4–6).

[259] "Et dato, quod quis in ipsa hora aspectus contineat, species tamen formae... semel cordi per oculos illigata, manet et vix magni luctaminis manu solvitur; et sicut ait Chrysostomus, quando visa muliere flamma semel accensa fuerit et postea absente ea format quis apud se imagines turpium actionum, multotiens proceditur ad opus... quia per exteriorem visum interior corrumpitur animus, prohibet nos fixe aspicere quod non licet appetere." *VF* 2,28 (53–77). See also Elliott, *Fallen Bodies*, and Chapter Five below, where I treat Jordan's view of vision and images at length with respect to images of the Passion.

be diminished.[260] From fasting one could then proceed to actual corporal castigation, disciplining the flesh with rough clothing and a hard bed, leading even to whipping and beating oneself.[261] Among the examples of chastising one's flesh, Jordan told of the brother who burned his genitals as mentioned above, as well as the story of another brother he had heard. Wanting to drive away his burning lust with suffering, he took up a knife and circumcised himself, or as Jordan put it, taking a knife, "he amputated the end of his foreskin according to the custom of the Jews." As a result of the wound, he was not bothered by lust for many days. Jordan, however, was quick to add that he would not recommend such a cure and even felt that the brother should be heavily reprimanded. "Nevertheless," Jordan affirmed, "I praise his zeal for chastity."[262] If circumcision was not a recommended practice, even more objectionable was castration. Jordan himself had known two brothers who had castrated themselves, but they erred, according to Jordan, because chastity is to be sought in religion, not gained by the sword.[263]

A degradation of the body is at issue here, the male body as well as the female. Although Jordan did not advocate self-circumcision or self-castration, he gave no reprimand or warning to the brother who burned his genitals as a means of burning away his burning lust. The body, or the flesh, had to be controlled. Antonius Rampegolus, an Augustinian who may have entered the Order just when Jordan completed his *Liber Vitasfratrum*, composed a handbook of practical exegesis for his students in the *studium* at Naples.[264] His *Figurae Bibliorum*, published by 1384, is an alphabetical treatment of themes and does not include a separate chapter on 'chastity' as such.

---

[260] Cautelae 2 and 3, *VF* 2,30 (279,26–283,136).

[261] "Quarta cautela est corporis castigatio, videlicet non solum ieiuniis et vigiliis, sed etiam dsciplinis et laesionibus corporalibus, puta per asperitatem vestitus, duritiam strati, per plagas verberum et huiusmodi." *VF* 2,30 (283,138–140).

[262] "Item ab alio fratre audivi, quomodo ipse quadam vice dum incendio libidinis inflammatus esset, volens per dolorem concupiscentias abigere, arrepto cultello summitatem praeputii ad modum Judaeorum sibi ipsi amputavit; de quo vulnere sic laesus fuit, quod stimulus pluribus diebus quievit. Sed istum remedium non commendo, immo de hoc multum reprehendi fratrem illum; laudo tamen in eo zelum castitatis." *VF* 2,30 (285 (190–196).

[263] "Item novi duos fratres, qui sibi ipsis zelo castitatis virilia absciderunt credentes obsequium se praestare Deo. Sed erraverunt; non enim ferro, sed religione quaerenda est castitas." *VF* 2,30 (300, 608–610).

[264] On Rampegolus, see Chapters Five and Six below; for a discussion of the dating and textual tradition of his *Figure Bibliorum*, see Chapter Five, n. 229.

The work begins, however, with 'Abstinence' and the verse from Corinthians *Castigo corpus meum* (I Cor. 9:27). It also includes a long chapter on human flesh, maintaining the distinction between 'body' (*corpus*) and 'flesh' (*caro*), but only with blurred boundaries: "human flesh [*caro*] is the receptacle of the devil."[265] The bodily senses are the traitors of the spirit, handing it over to the devil.[266] Indeed, "nothing is viler than the human body [*corpus*]."[267] The female body may have been one that the Augustinian friars were exhorted to view as a rotting corpse and a stinking sack of shit, but it was their own male bodies that were to be whipped, beaten, and burned to suppress and control their own desires, lusts, and fantasies.

Such measures were extreme to be sure, and most of the advice Jordan offered was far less violent. As already mentioned, avoiding women, avoiding gazing upon them and talking with them was the first way to preserve one's chastity. Moreover, the Augustinian friar should avoid touching a woman, even for medical reasons, for that could have serious consequences. Jordan gave an *exemplum* of a brother he knew, one of great reputation, who was called to treat a sick woman. When he took her pulse, and examined with his hands the place of her suffering, which Jordan did not further define, he was so overcome with lust for her that afterwards, not only were his thoughts impure, but he was also driven to trying to seduce her whenever the opportunity presented itself, as if led beyond the boundaries of reason and discipline. Wherefore, Jordan concluded, regardless how pure and chaste he was at first, from that time on, until his death, the disease of his lust never left him.[268] Praying, meditating, and especially meditation on the Passion of Christ, devotion to a particular saint, manual labor, and, of course, the "cold shower,"

---

[265] "Receptaculum diaboli est caro humana." Ant.Ramp. *FB*, fol. 1va.

[266] "... quia continue adversarius noster diabolus tanquam leo rugiens circuit quaerens quem devoret, oportet enim quomodo ei resistere et temptationibus suis; sed primo oportet reprimere domesticos adversarios scilicet corporales sensus, qui sunt spiritus proditores." Ant.Ramp. *FB*, fol. 15ra.

[267] "... nichil putridius humano corpore." Ant.Ramp. *FB*, fol. 17va.

[268] "Item exemplum de quodam fratre magnae reputationis, viro mihi noto, qui cum vocatus fuisset ad quandam mulierem infirmam, ex tactu pulsus et loci doloris eius tanta concupiscentia ad eam exarsit, quod postea semper non solum impudicis cogitationibus, sed et illecebrosis gestis ad eam fuit permotus et quasi extra frenum rationis et camum disciplinae deductus, quandocumque opportunitas locum dabat. Et quamvis prius fuisset vir castae vitae et mundae, ex illo tempore pestis illa usque ad mortem eum non dimisit." *VF* 2,30 (281,79–86); *cf. VF* 2,30 (281,87–103).

were all means of keeping chaste, which, Jordan affirmed, as a gift of God to begin with was completely dependent on God's grace.

If controlling the body by various means of castigations and asceticism could be achieved, this did not in and of itself render the friar free from danger. Thoughts too must be controlled. Taking literally Jesus' intensification of the Law in the Sermon on the Mount, it was not only acting on one's lust, desires, and fantasies that was a problem, but the thoughts themselves. Jordan tells of a vision that a certain devoted person had of a brother, whom he, Jordan, had known, a brother of outstanding life who had great status in the Order. Most likely this "devoted person" was Jordan himself.[269] To this "devoted person" appeared one night the saintly Augustinian friar on the very day that he had died the previous year. Though he had been of great devotion, the friar told "Jordan," he had been suffering the atrocious punishments of hell. "Jordan" wondered how this was possible for someone who had led such a holy life, and asked the ghost why this was so. The ghost responded that it was because of his depraved thoughts, by which he was often afflicted in his heart; since he had not sufficiently done penance for them while he lived, he had to make compensation for a year after his death, even though he had been preserved from actually committing the deeds.[270]

Controlling one's thoughts, one's fantasies, one's deeds, and actions, avoiding women, avoiding talking with them, seeing them, gazing upon them, touching them, castigating one's flesh, whipping oneself into conformity, into obedience, disciplining one's desires, one's impulses, one's fantasies with fasts, hair shirts, hard beds, vigils, prayers, and meditations, this is what made for the chaste Augustinian, the Augustinian whose lust burned within him. Chastity was not, for the

---

[269] Jordan on several occasions refers to himself as a "certain friar," such as the *frater nominatus in ordine* who had the vision regarding the Hermits gaining custody of Augustine's tomb, or as the prior provincial who was present at Henry of Friemar's deathbed; see above n. 107.

[270] "Fuit quidam frater olim mihi notus, singularis vitae et magni status in Ordine, qui ad unum annum post mortem suam apparuit in visione cuidam devotae personae, dicens hucusque se fuisse in atrocissimis poenis, sed nunc Dei miseratione se fore liberatum et caelesti familiae associatum. Admirans autem ista persona, quod vir tantae sanctitatis, qualis ipse fuit ab hominibus reputatus, tanto tempore poenas gehennales sustinuisset, interrogavit eum, propter quam causam tanto tempore tantas poenas luisset. At ille respondit: 'Propter cogitationes pravas, quibus saepe in corde inquinabar, quas hic per paenitentiam non dilui, licet a foedis actibus divina propitiatio me custodierit." *VF* 2,30 (298,559–299,569).

Augustinians, an object of repression. Suppression yes, but the sons of Augustine met their lusts and their desires head-on. It was the lust of the weak males that was at issue, lust that could be aroused by the most innocuous sight or touch. Women were dangerous, but they were so because men were so susceptible. The male friars feared their own passion and desires. Male sexuality was the culprit, not female seduction. Nowhere does Jordan give the guilt to women. Male desire had to be suppressed in order for the Augustinians to live a life closer to the angels. Male sexuality, male fantasy, male titillation had to be suppressed, but it was definitely not repressed, not sublimated except in the most rare of cases: it always was just below the surface, as waves of desire just waiting to break spewing on the shore.

The senses were the points of contention. As we will see in a following chapter, one had to guard one's senses if one wished to remain chaste, to remain pure. Sight, touch, imagination: these were the dangers. The late medieval Augustinians were most definitely the sons of their father. Lust and concupiscence were never far from their sensuality. In 1456, a disputation was held in Strassburg between the Augustinians and the Franciscans, hosted by the Friars Minor. The Augustinian lector Henricus Rietmüller was pitted against his Franciscan foes, and he did his best to uphold the position of the Augustinians' *pater noster*. At issue were a number of theses as put forward in the *Prior* and *Posterior Analytics* of Aristotle. Yet after such weighty issues were debated, the event turned to lighter matters, simple "problems" (*problemata*) to be solved rather than questions (*questiones*) to be determined. One of the problems concerned the hierarchy of the human senses, based on Aristotelian principles. The quandary, as Heinrich formulated it, was "whether the most sweet lovers of refined young girls are more titillated by seeing their beloved, or by fondling her breasts."[271] His answer was that if it was an issue of frequency, or of having been deprived of the pleasure, then the lover was more excited by the mere sight of his beloved, as is proved by reference to the first book of Aristotle's *Metaphysics*; if, on the other hand, it is a question of intensity, then one is more intensely aroused by fondling the breasts of one's beloved than by merely gazing upon

---

[271] "Utrum perpolitarum dulcissimi amatores puellarum in visione earum magis delectentur vel tactu mammillarum?" Hen.Riet. *Quest.*, fol. 239ᵛ.

her, as is shown, he affirms, from the second book of Aristotle's *De anima*, and, as "experience teaches."[272] One immediately has the image of a group of horny monks sitting around and discussing the issue, the issue of whether one is more excited sexually by seeing a woman, or by fondling her breasts. One can only wonder how many erections ensued; one can only wonder how many friars then went and burned their genitalia; and this in an academic debate.

Male sexuality was the demon, male lust and male desire. If it could be projected onto an unreal woman, a fictional woman, an image, a creation, a woman who too had already been de-sexed, a perfect woman, the Virgin Mary, that was then permissible, and if not Mary, then Mother Church. Mother Church and Mother Mary were the only acceptable objects of the aim-inhibited love of male desire for the Augustinians, and as their father Augustine had so exalted his own mother Monica, so the Augustinian Hermits exalted their Mother in their attempt to return to the cosmic maternal womb to be reborn as spiritual beings. To do so, their own bodies must remain chaste, and their thoughts too, if at all possible, for they were the embodiment of their Father. Augustine's body had been de-sexed, and thus so were the bodies of his sons, at least in theory, at least as a goal to be striven for as an ideal, as a precept, even when the practice included the enticements of fondling breasts and bringing boys into one's darkened cell. To have one heart and soul in God necessitated keeping one's bodily members from entering any other human body, and keeping one's thoughts pure while doing so. Otherwise, one could not live as the angels, and one might be in danger of not being able to say mass, one could not be a part of Augustine's chaste body, and one hindered one's own return to God,

---

[272] "Utrum perpolitarum dulcissimi amatores puellarum in visione earum magis delectentur vel tactu mammilarum? Dico quod si ly magis denotat citius vel privorum et frequentius, tunc magis dilectantur in visione quam in tactu quia sensus visus plures rerum differentias nobis ostendit, ut habetur ex primo Metaphysice et quia etiam prior aliis sensibus, ut patet ex secundo De Anima. Si autem ly magis denotat illud quod intensius, tunc magis delectantur in tactu mammillarum, quia tactum certiorem habet homo aliis ut patet ex secundo De Anima et experientia docet." Hen.Riet. *Quest.*, fol. 239^v. Admittedly Henricus here was technically saying that one knows from experience that touch is the more certain sense, rather than that one is more aroused by fondling breasts than by sight, but the association was surely not lost on his audience, and he could have very well used another example to make his point concerning the "experience" of touch's intensity.

for chastity for the Augustinians was not only a high road, but the highest road to heaven.[273]

Spirit and flesh were at war. That is the point. Once such a determination is made, the rest follows naturally, just as does the emperor's subordination to the pope once one equates the emperor and temporal rule with the body and the pope with the soul. The lust and desires of the flesh were opposed to the desire and will of the spirit. The senses were the battlefield; the body, the victim. And yet, Jordan claims, while one "cannot live in the present life without temptations, since *the life of man on earth is a battle* (Job 7:1), the temptation of the flesh is less toxic than certain other vices, though one must still prudently resist."[274] This was Jordan's introductory statement leading into the longest chapter of his *Liber Vitasfratrum*, twice as long as any other: the chapter on how to preserve one's chastity. Other vices may indeed have been more pernicious, but Jordan does not treat them as such. There is a denial of male sexuality, or at least an attempt to view it as more limp than it was, while at the same time there is the most explicit condemnation of the male friar's lust and desire, of male pleasure, leading the soul to damnation. By claiming that the temptations of the flesh, that lust, that male sexuality, was not the most dangerous of vices, Jordan had de-sexed Augustine all over again, and for the last time. Augustine had known so viscerally and intimately that for him, in any case, lust was the last chain that bound him, the last hindrance to his leading a life for God. The other vices had fallen by the wayside already, but Augustine's lust remained. For Jordan, lust is less dangerous than other vices, which he does not delineate, but then he continues with a discussion that can only be seen mocking his attempted deflection. By denying the seriousness of lust, of male desire, and of male sexuality, Jordan ridiculed Augustine's own penetrating analysis of the importance and weight thereof. Augustine was not a sexual being, and neither were his sons, in theory. Yet Jordan's treatment itself gives lie to the precept. Only with diligence and superhuman effort

---

[273] The Augustinians formed a "chaste family," the "de-sexed family" of Mother, Father, and sons, based on the "interpenetration of the deployment of alliance and that of sexuality in the form of the family." See Michel Foucault, *The History of Sexuality*, vol. 1: *An Introduction* (New York, 1978), 103–114; 108.

[274] "Cum enim vita praesens sine temptationibus non ducatur, quia *militia est vita hominis super terram*, temptatio carnis minus noxia est quibusdam aliis vitiis, dum tamen homo prudenter relectetur." *VF* 2,29 (277, 193–196).

could the Augustinian friar maintain his pure mind and pure body, the mind and body of the weaker sex, in his battle to chastise and keep chaste the body of his father as he strove to return to the womb of his Mother, traveling along a high way to heaven, built from the bodies of the sons of Augustine. The de-sexing of Augustine was the point of departure of the Augustinian platform. So much for precepts. And so much for practice. And so much for the loves and desires, the pleasures and fantasies of the dispersed, disembodied friars: *Eros* and *Ananke* even before Freud,[275] the daily life of the Augustinian.

D. *Compelling Observance*

Taboos are compelling; the forbidden, seductive. Women, and boys, and fellow friars, may well have been proscribed for the sons of Augustine, but the taboo was desire, fantasy, and lust. Forbidden fruit is all the more delectable because of the prohibition. Women, and boys, and "worthy men" were the titillating temptations eliciting the taboo from its supposed silent slumber. The level of required suppression is directly proportional to the level of desire for that which one is denied. The solution: suppress, redirect, reinterpret, and reproduce a new meaning. Taboos are taboos after all; thank God we have them. Otherwise ... otherwise, we would have to create them, infusing them with new meaning in a new mythic universe. Taboos after all are the boundaries of institutionalized power, a corporate structure with its own modes of meaning, penetrating to the very foundations of the structures of emotions and thought,[276] which themselves develop the mechanisms for establishing conformity with the created identity and for compelling obedience to the ideals of the unified body, the body of a de-sexed founding father.

Establishing the taboos was a primary task for Jordan in his *Liber Vitasfratrum*, in which he used the foundational myth of the OESA to unite the *fratres* with the *patres*, the *status modernus* with the *status antiquus*. The overarching theme of the entire work is the exhorta-

---

[275] See Sigmund Freud, *Civilization and Its Discontents*, The Standard Edition (New York, 1989).

[276] See George Lakoff and Mark Johnson, *Philosophy in the Flesh. The Embodied Mind and Its Challenge to Western Thought* (New York, 1999); Arnold Cornelis, *Logica van het Gevoel. Filiosofie van de Stabiliteitslagen in de Cultuur als Nesteling der Emoties* (Amsterdam, 1998).

tion to imitate the life of Augustine, which Jordan had narrated in his *Vita Sancti Augustini*. The phenomenon of mythic imitation provided the link between the friars of Jordan's day and their Order's founder. For the Augustinians, Augustine's primordial foundation (*primordialiter propagatus*) was the archetype which they strove to imitate in their daily lives.[277] The imitation of Augustine gave the Augustinians their legitimacy, their unity, and their memory: it gave them their religious identity. As a mythic community,[278] the OESA was centered around the most perfect life established by Augustine, of which the *fratres* of the later Middle Ages were both the heirs and the imitators. While the historical argument of Jordan's text provided the members of the Order with the narrative of what made an Augustinian an Augustinian, the Augustinian myth itself equipped the Order with its self-understanding, to which members were compelled to conform.

The institutionalized Order provided the structure for discerning whether one was or was not a true son of Augustine. The Order of Augustinian Hermits from a sociological perspective was not only a group pursuing the most perfect life. It was simultaneously a religious organization in society. It was a "corporate body," a *corpus mysticum particulare*. As a social system, the Order's structuring of its religious life gave meaning to the designation 'Augustinian' independent from modern scholars' interpretations of the term's theological or philosophical content.[279] The Augustinian myth was the symbolic expression that identified an Augustinian as an Augustinian by negating all other possibilities of following Augustine, such as that of the Canons. This is seen in the Augustinian understanding of poverty as well, when Jordan differentiated the observance of poverty of Augustine's sons from that of the Franciscan and Dominican Orders.[280] In wearing the habit, singing the canonical hours, teaching, and preaching, the Augustinians were distinguished from all

---

[277] Cf. Eliade, *The Sacred and The Profane*, 101 and 105, and *idem*, *The Myth of Eternal Return* (New York, 1954). For the importance of the imitation not only of Augustine, but also the *imitatio Christi*, see Chapter Five.

[278] See Chapter Two, n. 251.

[279] On the issue of structuration, see Anthony Giddens, *The Constitution of Society. Outline of the Theory of Structuration* (Berkeley, 1984). For the sociological concept of meaning, and for the understanding of social systems, I have also drawn from the works of Niklas Luhmann, particularly, *Soziologische Aufklärung* I–IV (Opladen, 1970–1987); *Soziale Systeme. Grundriss einer allgemeinen Theorie* (Frankfurt, 1984); and *Die Wissenschaft der Gesellschaft* (Frankfurt, 1990).

[280] *VF* 3,4 (332f) and *VF* 3,8 (345ff).

others engaged in similar acts. This differentiation was the means by which the Augustinians ascribed meaning to their life. As a social system, the Augustinian Order itself gave meaning to the term 'Augustinian'. In the later Middle Ages, "being an Augustinian" had a social definition, the definition Jordan strove to explain in his *Liber Vitasfratrum*. The theology of the Order was taught and preached within the social system of the Order. To be an Augustinian theologian, one first had to be an Augustinian. Such definition may not satisfy continued attempts of historical theology to discover, uncover, or undress a late medieval Augustinianism, but it does come closer to a historical understanding. According to Jordan one entered the structures of meaning the term 'Augustinian' signified when one made one's profession, when one became an Augustinian as a member and follower of Augustine's religion.[281]

Jordan explicitly stated that he intended his *Liber Vitasfratrum* as a means by which any brother of the Order could know, based on his own life, whether he was a true son and heir of Augustine. Every brother was to read the text and compare it with his own life. The *Liber Vitasfratrum* provided a mirror for the Order as well as a handbook. It was designed to promote a common and unified understanding of the Augustinians' religious life.[282]

By expounding on the central dictum of the *Rule* throughout his treatise, Jordan attempted to promote a common conception of living with "one heart and soul in God" among all members of the Order. This was not merely a physical cohabitation. It was a spiritual union,[283] a unanimity of will and a unanimity of the form of living, based on obedience and chastity.[284] The strategies Jordan employed to stimulate conformity with the Augustinian myth reveal the intended function of the text, surpassing its mere cognitive explication.[285] To ensure the social bonds of the Order,[286] Jordan set forth

---

[281] *Cf.* the distinction between primary doctrines and governing doctrines of a religious community drawn by William A. Christian, Sr., *Doctrines of Religious Communities. A Philosophical Study* (New Haven/London, 1987).

[282] *Cf.* Thomas Scheff, *Microsociology. Discourse, Emotion and Social Structure* (Chicago, 1990), 31 and 103.

[283] *VF* 2,1 (75,9–11).

[284] *VF* 2,1 (76,36–44).

[285] *Cf.* Scheff, *Microsociology*, 74.

[286] On social bonds, see Scheff, *Microsociology*, 4–19 and *passim*, and Elias, *What is Sociology?* (New York, 1978), 134–157.

the means by which a negligent brother was to be kept in line, drawing from the exhortations in the Gospel of Matthew (Mt. 18:15–17). The responsibility for maintaining discipline lay not only with the superiors of the Order, but with every individual member.[287] When a member of the Order was recognized as derelict, the brother who took notice was to approach the brother in need of correction privately and make his error known to him. If he admitted his fault and sought to reform the matter went no further.[288] If, however, he remained unmoved by such private admonition, the next step was for the brother who had spoken with him to take the matter to the father confessor in the house, who would then approach the brother needing discipline, once again in private, and seek to lead him to repentance.[289] If he still remained obstinate the next course of action was to accuse him publicly in chapter.[290] After public declaration of the brother's fault, if he still persisted in his error, the process of expulsion began, again in three stages. The first consisted of social ostracism, by which no brother was to speak or associate with him.[291] The second step was incarceration, and only if all previous means were unsuccessful was the brother finally expelled completely from the Order.[292]

These procedures were instituted to preserve the uniformity of will and way of life within the Order. Every brother was responsible not only for himself, but also for his confreres. On the cognitive level the members were made aware of their responsibilities and the course of action to be taken should they recognize someone deviating from the established unity. On the emotional level such measures were based on the maintenance of social bonds.

By pointing to the realm of emotions I do not mean to imply that we can discern the feelings of late medieval Augustinians, at least not directly.[293] Nevertheless, Jordan's account reveals a level of coercion that surpasses the purely cognitive. Jordan was sensitive to the

---

[287] *VF* 2,4 (91ff) and *VF* 2,5 (99,2–5).
[288] *VF* 2,10 (131,38–40).
[289] *VF* 2,10 (131,40–43).
[290] *VF* 2,10 (132,53–59).
[291] *VF* 2,10 (133,84–87).
[292] *VF* 2,10 (133,89–94).
[293] In this context I follow Clifford Geertz, "'From the Native's Point of View': On the Nature of Anthropological Understanding," in Geertz, *Local Knowledge. Further Essays in Interpretive Anthropology* (New York, 1983), 58; cf. Gadamer, *Truth and Method*, 292.

emotional aspects of maintaining discipline by demarcating the degrees of the steps to be taken. A brother was first to be reprimanded in private. If private admonition was ineffective, public coercion was employed. Increasing peer pressure was the instrument used to enforce conformity. Jordan called for the emotional force that the Order could bring to bear on an incorrigible brother. If public pressure was insufficient, the social bonds uniting the brother to the group were severed by ostracism—and finally expulsion. In effect, the brother was shamed into obedience. Jordan never used the word shame directly for exhortation or admonition, but a hidden shame is implied in his exposition.[294]

The factor of hidden shame was not limited to a textual role in the *Liber Vitasfratrum*. To ensure conformity amongst the members, the *Liber Vitasfratrum* called for the omnipresent self-evaluation and reflection between the ideal as expressed in Jordan's text and the reality of the lived lives of the Order's members, thereby rendering hidden shame operative in the construction of the Augustinian religious individual. The *exempla* Jordan brought to illustrate his enunciation of the *religio Augustini* were not high ideals that formed the goals for which the individual brother was to strive as much as they were normative lessons according to which every member was to live. By continuous interaction between observation and imagination, or in other words, self-reflection and examination, the Augustinian was able to measure his life by the given standards. Jordan's *exempla* are not simply cognitive explications of the *Rule* and *Constitutions*, but are instruments to establish and maintain obedience to and conformity with the community's religious identity.

In his discussion of obedience, the primary virtue regarding the *cor unum*,[295] Jordan first described the proper understanding of the virtue in accordance with the *Rule* and Canon Law. He then added a number of *exempla*, in which the use of shame can be detected. Jordan related a story that he had heard himself second hand of a brother who was taken by a certain spirit to the place where the

---

[294] Norbert Elias described the importance of shame for society in *The Civilizing Process*. 2 vols. (New York, 1978). Going beyond Elias and drawing on the work of the research psychologist, Helen B. Lewis, Thomas Scheff has analyzed the concept of shame in greater detail than did Elias, and has emphasized "hidden shame"; see *Microsociology*, esp. chs. 5–7.

[295] *VF* 2,2 (78f).

damned were tortured. There he saw a woman who was more excruciatingly afflicted than all the others. When he asked the woman why this was so, she responded that she was being punished so severely because she was disobedient to her confessor, preferring to follow her own will. Thus, Jordan concluded, such will the be fate of all those brothers who want to follow their own will rather than to obey the Order's prelates.[296]

In this *exemplum*, Jordan's message was clear. Any brother reading this was, upon reflection, not only to understand the consequences of disobedience, but also to recognize the extent to which he was headed in this direction. If a reader realized that he had not been sufficiently obedient, this story was to instill fear for his fate. The cognitive understanding of obedience was joined to the emotional dimension to enforce uniformity of life.

Jordan did not leave matters here. He continued with another *exemplum* about a brother who often deceived his prior in order to win permission to leave the cloister and visit the city. One day as he was "sight seeing," he came upon a man possessed by a demon, who asked for exorcism. The brother was not able to refuse the request and thus commanded the demon in virtue of holy obedience to leave the man. The demon, however, responded: "Why do you think you can command me to be obedient when you yourself have never been truly obedient?" Upon hearing such a response, the brother turned away, disturbed and ashamed. Jordan affirmed that if that brother had been obedient to his superior, he surely would have been able to cast out the demon.[297] He did not explicitly say that a disobedient brother should be ashamed of his disobedience, but rather used a hidden shame, whereby the point is made indirectly. The reader was to evaluate his own obedience by the model presented in the story. If he had not been obedient, he should identify with the brother who not only could not cast out the demon, but who was also subject to the demon's reprimand. Shame was the result.

Throughout the *Liber Vitasfratrum* we find an analogous method employed, such as the *exemplum* cited above concerning Jordan's own failure to fulfill his vow to St. Peter. Jordan confessed that he was not embarrassed to relate the account, implying that there was a

---

[296] *VF* 2,2 (82,94–109).
[297] *VF* 2,2 (83,125–143).

degree of shame involved, particularly when his negligence was originally made known by St. Peter himself. The function of Jordan's treatise presupposes that the reader was to evaluate his own life in accordance with the principles and *exempla* given, and if his did not match up, he should be shamed into doing so. Yet this self-reflective understanding of the *religio Augustini* was not merely directed at individual *fratres*. It provided the basis for the intersubjective understanding for which every member was responsible. Every individual brother was intimately connected by social bonding based on hidden shame. The emotional as well as the cognitive must be considered for discerning more perspicuously the relationship between the individual and the OESA social system. Based on the Augustinian myth, hidden shame was an essential aspect of the ties that bound the Augustinian Order together in the late Middle Ages. The social bonds of Augustine's religion united the members of the Order as they individually and corporately related themselves to transcendence.

The *Liber Vitasfratrum* was Jordan's work, but it was not his creation alone.[298] For many years he had gathered materials for his treatise, which points to the social configuration in which the text took form,[299] and within the social system of the OESA his book resonated long after it was completed.[300] Although he was a cloistered friar, Jordan was not a *homo clausus*. When interpreting such a work as the *Liber Vitasfratrum* one must take into account the author in society.[301] In this context it was not simply Jordan's self-understanding that is voiced in the text, but an intersubjective understanding of the Augustinian identity.

The Augustinian Order in the later Middle Ages was a mythic community into which new members were assimilated through a socialization process, imbuing them with the Order's social knowledge and initiating them into a new subculture, the Order itself.[302] It was a process every brother underwent, even those who eventually were to become the Order's theologians. It is this dimension of

---

[298] See Luhmann, *Die Wissenschaft der Gesellschaft*, 159.
[299] On the concept of social configuration, see Elias *What is Sociology?*, 71–103.
[300] See Ralph Weinbrenner, *Klosterreform im 15. Jahrhundert zwischen Ideal und Praxis*, SuR.NR 7 (Tübingen, 1996), 115–116; *cf.* Hümpfner, intro., lxxii.
[301] See Elias, *The Society of Individuals* (Oxford, 1991), esp., 22 and 153–237.
[302] See Peter L. Berger and Thomas Luckmann, *The Social Construction of Reality. A Treatise in the Sociology of Knowledge* (New York, 1966), 45ff and 85ff; *cf.* Gurevich, *The Origins of European Individualism*, 14 and 89–90.

late medieval Augustinianism that historical research has not sufficiently taken into account. Most often the theological writings of the Augustinians are interpreted in terms of the university social system. Yet before a brother could adopt a historico-critical attitude in theology, which has been seen to characterize the *schola Augustiniana moderna*, he would have been inculcated with the historico-mythic attitude of the Order. If the Augustinian theologians sought to return to the theology of the original Augustine, they did so only after having returned to the original *religio Augustini*. Though it is not as such incorrect to choose the university as the context for interpreting late medieval Augustinianism, one must be aware that one is making such a choice. When one asks the question, however, of what made an Augustinian an Augustinian, or of what it meant to be an Augustinian in the later Middle Ages, the Augustinian social system is the only legitimate system of reference. This is not to say that a theologian who was not a member of the Order could not view himself as an 'Augustinian'. Rather, it is to claim that if he did so, he did so outside the historical structuration that gave meaning to the term. The Order itself provided the identity for the academic and pastoral theology that can be labeled Augustinian. During the century that separated the Great Union from Jordan's *Liber Vitasfratrum*, the OESA had developed from a conglomerate of various eremitical groups each following Augustine's *Rule*, to the saint's true sons and heirs. Contemporary historians and theologians may point to non-Augustinian Augustinians, but for the historical Austin Friar, it was only within the socio-religious bonds of the Order that one could claim the Bishop of Hippo as *Pater Noster*.

Jordan's *Liber Vitasfratrum* is the most comprehensive expression of the Order's identity in the later Middle Ages. It is a handbook for teaching how one was to be an Augustinian, complete with examples. Whereas in the course of the 1330s the Augustinian myth was created by the Anonymous Florentine, Nicholas of Alessandria, and Henry of Friemar in context of the Order's debate with the Canons over which was most authentically Augustine's true heirs, Jordan, who most likely conceived of his plan in the same context, textualized the myth on a grand scale, diffusing it throughout all aspects of the Order's life. The members of Augustine's religion were to imitate Augustine in all ways; he was their rule and exemplar for life within the Order. When Henry of Friemar recounted Augustine's appearance to Alexander IV, Henry turned the vision into that of a divine oracle. Jordan repeated Henry's insight, and added his own contribution by making the initiative for the Great Union that of Augustine himself, and Augustine's desire to reunite the dispersed members of his own *religio*. And whereas Henry associated the Order's charge to preach, teach, and hear confessions among the people in the cities with Alexander's approbation of the newly reunited Order, Jordan laid the foundation thereof in his *Vita Sancti Augustini* by showing how Augustine instituted his second monastery and taught its members the holy scriptures so that they would live not only for themselves, but also minister to the populace. This then became his *cantus firmus* for the entire *Liber Vitasfratrum*, for such a life comprised the combination of the anchoritic and cenobitic that Augustine had accomplished and passed along to his sons as the *vita perfectissima*. Imitating Augustine, the de-sexed Augustine, offered the model and measure of identity for being an Augustinian.

The complex of factors that comprised the Order's *vita contemplativa* was based on the created image of Augustine, which the Order supported and defended as uniquely its own. Only the members of Augustine's religion could legitimately call Augustine *Pater noster*, as the author of the *Initium*, Nicholas of Alessandria, Henry, and Jordan all made clear time and time again. It was not just an ideal that the sons of Augustine were following; it was a programmatic mission of perpetuating Augustine's heritage. By being Augustinians the hermits were filling out the chaste body of Augustine which was so diminished as it appeared to Alexander IV. The myth of Augustine started to flow as blood through the veins of Augustine's body throughout all facets of the Order, giving it life and form. Jordan's *Liber Vitasfratrum* is a textual witness, and was intended to be read as a mirror of the lives of the true sons of father Augustine. Augustine's little hermit friars were to serve the Church, not simply seek their own salvation. And to do so, they needed more than humility and piety. They needed training and education.

Following Augustine as model for the religious life was in no way distinct from preaching and teaching; as Jordan made clear, the *vita contemplativa* of the Augustinians' most perfect life included all aspects pertaining to the soul. Jordan had dedicated his *Collectanea* to the Order's Parisian house of studies. He had based his work on a return to the sources, an intensive reworking through Augustine's works. In the same year that Jordan brought his *Collectanea* to Paris, Bartholomew of Urbino was completing what would become the most ambitious piece of Augustinian scholarship in the later Middle Ages, the *Milleloquium Sancti Augustini*.[303] And in Paris, in 1343, the Augustinian Gregory of Rimini was lecturing on the *Sentences* of Peter Lombard, offering an academic, theological Augustinianism previously unparalleled. Jordan had surely met Gregory five years earlier at the General Chapter in Siena, where both were present, and Gregory might have learned of Jordan's work at that time. He most likely would have seen Jordan again in Paris in 1343 when Jordan delivered his *Collectanea* to the Parisian *studium* and its library. Fourteen years later, Jordan submitted his *Liber Vitasfratrum* to Gregory, who was then prior general of the Order, complete with the letter of dedication to John of Basel, whose works would become perhaps the culmination of what has been called the *schola Augustiniana moderna*. For the late medieval sons of Augustine, the Augustinian life could not be divided into separate departments of theology, history, political science, and religion, with evening extension courses on spirituality. The Order had been given a charge. And the Order had been given the rules and examples for carrying it out. Yet even so, the Order's precepts were not always reflected in the Order's practice, as the Order's highly esteemed theologian Gregory of Rimini was soon to find out. The lives of the *fratres* were not always exemplary.

III. Regulating Daily Life: The Generalate of Gregory of Rimini

Not all the Augustinians in the mid-fourteenth century were dealing in pigs. But some were, and in goats as well.[304] The new prior general of the Order had his work cut out for him. On 13 February 1358, Gregory of Rimini, who had only been in office for eight months, wrote to Frater John of Monterodono of the Province of Naples. Gregory did so to absolve John, who had been prior of the Augustinian house in Monterodono, from "the unspeakable act and most revolting crime" with which he had been charged both during the official visitation of the province as well as previously to Master Dionysius of Nursia, the general's vicar in Naples. Exactly

---

[303] See above, Chapter One, n. 373.
[304] See below, note 311.

what the allegations were we do not know for certain, but supposedly John, as prior, had committed an *actum indicibilem et scelus turpissimum* with some boy and friar Cobello Carociali of Naples. When the visitation was made, a trial was already in progress and witnesses were testifying. John's defense was to claim that his accusers were his enemies and were trying to sully his good reputation, which they had indeed. No sure evidence was brought forth, which Gregory saw as no real surprise since it was "virtually impossible to prove directly" a crime such as that of which John was being accused. Nevertheless, to clear his name, John had sufficiently purged himself, as the more respected brothers of the Order in Naples as well as other provincial priors had attested. Thus Gregory, "being more prone to absolve than to condemn," cleared John from all charges.[305]

Gregory, however, was not so lenient, or gullible, with lay brother Thomas of Aretio, who, as mentioned above, had been accused of violating one of the local boys in Pisa. Four and a half months after the case had first come to Gregory's attention nothing had happened in terms of judgment and punishment. Thus Gregory wrote to master Angelo of Cortonio on 5 March 1358 giving him the responsibility to see that Thomas was brought to Pisa and dealt with

---

[305] "Quia coram nobis in nostro visitatione seu inquisitione facta Neapoli denunciatus fuisti, te cum quodam puero <et> fratre Cobello Carociali de Neapoli, cum eras prior dicti conventus, actum indicibilem et scelus turpissimum commisisse, non sine gravi scandalo et infamia ex hoc apud fratres etiam subsecuta, nam alias de dicto peccato tunc temporis cum dicto fratre comisso fuisti similiter denunctiatus venerabili magistro Dyonisio de Nursia, tunc in dicta provincia vicario generalis, et inquisitio contra te etiam iam formata, propter quod recensentes acta inquisitionis magistri Dyonisii predicti, et examinantes testes etiam tunc in dicto facto productos, quamvis non directe actus iste probaretur ab eis, qui quodammodo est impossibile ut directe probetur, ipsosque testes ut inimicos tuos legitime in iudicio replueris coram nobis, nichilominus te probabiliter suspectum de crimine supradicto, maxime adhuc infamia remanente, que tuam famam bonam multipliciter denigrabat, et ideo ne contra Apostolum infirmorum corda de mala fama percutiantur eadem et ne vituperetur ministerium nostrum, neve securiores reliqui existentes in peccato licentius prolabantur, et ut tuam famam purgando monstrares, purgationem canonicam cum tertia manu tui ordinis tibi duximus iniungendam. Et quia per fratres notabiliores in provincia sepedicta, qui vitam tuam tam preteritam noverant, quam modernam, legitime te purgasti, secundum formam a sacris canonibus institutam, nos, qui in odore bone fame fratrum nostrorum potius quam super infamiam delectamur, et ad absolvendum sumus quam ad condempnandum etiam proniores, te auctoritate presentium absolvimus a crimine supradicto, et absolutum et purgatum esse decernimus per presentes, cassantes omnes processus et inquisitiones contra te habitas vel formatos ex causa predicta tam per nos, quam per alium officialem ordinis supradicti, ab eis et instantia iudicii nichilominus absolvendo." Greg. *Reg.* 236 (132–133).

accordingly, which entailed, if he was found guilty, imprisonment.[306] "Weakness of the flesh," as Gregory referred to sexual misconduct, indeed merited a prison sentence, as Frater John de Civita de Boiano of the Province of Lavoro discovered. John had been imprisoned *propter lapsum carnis* without further specification, though he was finally cleared by Gregory on 5 December 1357.[307] Frater John of Lucino in the Province of Milan was not so lucky. On 8 November 1357 Gregory sentenced John as an incurable apostate to a perpetual prison sentence since, among other crimes, John had committed multiple acts of adultery.[308] A prison sentence was also waiting lay brother Walter, from the Province of Spoleto, who had left the Order and had moved in with a woman, with whom he had a number of children, before realizing that perhaps his life in the Order was better after all and petitioned to return. As Gregory wrote to the prior provincial of Spoleto on 14 March 1358, Walter could be reinstated, but he would have to submit to the Order's system of discipline, starting off with doing time, and doing time until Gregory would give further notice.[309]

Such were the issues, or some of them, facing Gregory as prior general of the Augustinian Order. One might wonder how well his training in Paris had prepared the reverend master of theology Gregory for the job of dealing with the sins and excesses of his fellow brothers. Sexual misconduct, as that mentioned above, as well as one brother who abducted a nun,[310] fist-fights, drinking in taverns, horse-trading, gambling, and dealing in pigs and goats:[311] this

---

[306] Greg. *Reg.* 260 (145); *cf.*, Greg. *Reg.* 44 (48–49).

[307] Greg. *Reg.* 127 (80–81).

[308] "... nobis constat dictum fratrem Iohannem crimen falsi diversimode commisisse, reatum adulterii pluries perpetrasse, apostasie notam incurisse et nonnulla alia enormia flagicia et mala similiter atentasse ... ideo dictum fratrem Iohannem adiudicavimus et tenore presencium iudicamus perpetuo carceri mancipandum..." Greg. *Reg.* 114 (74–76; 75). John's case was an exceptionally nasty one, involving the vice-count of Milan as well as the papal inquisitor, and was not, certainly, limited to sex crimes; see also Greg. *Reg.* 13 (73–74).

[309] "... [frater Gualterius] moram ducens extra ordinem prelibatum cum quadam muliere de facto [matriomonium] contraxit et ex ea filios procreavit, propter quod excommunicationem incurrerat ... nunc ut coram nobis proposuit ad ordinem nostrum sit redire paratus ... [qui] ad ordinem recipi debeat salva ordinis disiciplina, videlicet, quod eum carceri mancipabis [*scil.* prior provincialis Vallis Spoleti] et tanto tempore in carcere retinebis inclusum, donec a nobis aliud receperis in mandatis." Greg. *Reg.* 265 (148–149).

[310] Greg. *Reg.* 409 (228).

[311] "Item die XXI commissimus fratri Iohanni Bindi nostro vicario provincie

is what Gregory had to deal with as prior general, a far cry from fighting the modern Pelagians, or proving that God by his absolute power could indeed undo the past, taking on his worthy opponents in a battle of words and ideas in the lecture halls of Paris. Perhaps in Gregory's view Frater John de Castello de Mutina simply lacked the *auxilium speciale dei*, one of Gregory's theological doctrines needed for every good work, when he, John, who had already spent five years in prison for theft, threw a stick, or perhaps even an arrow (*casu proiectionis arundinis*), at a fellow brother, making him bleed, for which he was once again imprisoned, for approximately another five years. After having served his time, however, John had lived a clean life and thus Gregory restored him to good standing in the Order.[312] Or maybe Frater John had just finally received God's special help of grace after all, which enabled him to live an honorable life, and thus Gregory should acknowledge as much and clear his name. It could be, but a prison sentence helps in any case, and Gregory never mentioned theological issues in his register. He was very practical and very detailed. He knew his Order's members. And he worked indefatigably to reform their way of life, to reform the Order, to bring the members back to living the true Augustinian life in upholding the *vita communis* and in adhering to regular observance.

Senensis ut contra fratres Cechum de Massa, Bartholomeum Ciatini, Galvanum et Guillelmum, quod invenimus habere soccidam porcorum et caprarum, diligenter visitaret et iustitie faceret complementum. Item quod visitaret contra fratrem Ugolinum de Massa, qui percussit fratrem Michaelem de sancta Flora cum effusione sanguinis... Item eidem commisimus quod fratres Bartholomeum Andree, Bartholomeum Francisci, Thomam de sancta Flora, Guillelmum de Rosia, Leonardum Petri et Bartholomeum de Stagia, nobis in visitatione Senensi denuntiatos de ludo taxillorum in Monte Ciano, quod frater Philippus Leonardi sponte in iudicio est confessus, propter quod eum debet carcerare, ad se vocaret et examinaret; et si confiterentur eos carceraret, si non, eos artaret ad confitendum." Senia, 21 Oct. 1357, Greg. *Reg.* 44 (48–49); "Item cum ex eo quod aliqui fratres supradicte provincie (*scil.* Vallis Spoleti), tenent equos proprios, palafredos et destrarios, venduntque et emunt velud negotiatores et mercatores equorum, multum religionis denigretur honestas, turbatio et scandalum generentur in mentibus plurimorum, huic labi cupientes obsistere, presenti constitutione mandamus, ut nullus frater nostri ordinis in predicta provincia cuiuscunque status, dignitatis vel conditionis existat, emat, vendat, permutet, donet, locet, habeat, vel teneat, per se vel per alium, colore quocunque quesito, causa, iure vel titulo destrarium aliquem, palafredum, roncinum, mulum, vel aliquod quodcunque animal proprium pertinens ad equitandum..." Perusii 1 May 1358, Greg. *Reg.* 7 (30); "Inhibemus etiam insuper ut nullus frater ordinis nostri ad tabernas ad bibendum presumat accedere..." Neapoli, 27 January 1358, Greg. *Reg.* 6 (22).

[312] Greg. *Reg.* 640 (328–329).

Gregory's register is the first extant source we have that offers an intimate, detailed portrait of the Order's daily life, and one as well of the tasks and challenges of a prior general. Gregory was elected prior general at the General Chapter of Montpellier on 24 May of 1357, following the death of his predecessor, Thomas of Strassburg, another Augustinian theologian who would become famous as such. The first entry of Gregory's register is undated, but can be placed in late June or early July of 1357. It is a general letter to the entire Order regarding reform.[313] It was an auspicious beginning.

Seventeen months: that was the extent of Gregory's generalate. He made the most of his time. There are 739 entries in Gregory's register. Many of these are naturally very short, granting a given brother the privilege of traveling to Rome, or giving permission for a member of the Order to become a student in a given *studium*. Many others, however, are far more substantial, covering the entire range of issues regarding the Order's administration, finances, and daily life. Given the epistolary nature of the entries it is difficult to categorize them in any fixed fashion since often when writing to a provincial prior Gregory addressed more than a single topic. Keeping this in mind, we can nevertheless, for illustrative purposes, group the entries in four general categories: Administrative, Financial, Reform and Discipline, and Pastoral Care and Education. Of the 739 entries, approximately 32.3% (239) are of a predominantly administrative nature; 26.6% (196) treat financial issues; 21.1% (156) concern reform and disciplinary measures, including absolutions and reinstatements of lapsed brothers; and 20% (148) of the entries deal with pastoral care and education.

As these figures show, Gregory was intimately involved in all aspects of governing the Order. Moreover, no issue or detail was too small or unimportant for Gregory to let pass. On 26 May 1358, for example, Gregory decreed that since Frater Angelus, prior of the Augustinian house in Cassiano, had unjustly deprived Frater Antonius of his annual provision, the prior was given until 1 November to make the required restitution of the one florin owed to Frater Antonius, or else it would be deducted from Frater Angelus' own account.[314]

---

[313] For the text of Gregory's circular letter to the Order, which he referred to as his *Ordinationes*, see Appendix E.

[314] "Cum frater Angelus olim dicti loci prior privaverit fratrem Antonium de sancta Anatolia sua annuali provisione iniuste, ideo tenore presentium tibi precipimus,

On 3 October 1358 Gregory released Frater Remigius of Florence, upon his own request, from the duties of saying mass because of Frater Remigius' blindness, stating as well that no one should try to force him to celebrate.[315] Two weeks later Gregory granted dispensation to eighty-year-old Frater Michael of Placentia giving him the privilege, due to his age and physical debilities, to sleep on a feather bed, which was, Gregory noted, entirely against the Order's stipulations in general, but given the case, Gregory was willing to make an exception for the elderly brother.[316] In each of these three cases Gregory had been petitioned. He was responding to a request. He otherwise might never have known of the injustice done to Frater Antonius, or of Frater Remigius' blindness, or of Frater Michael's need for comfort. Yet these were the types of issues that came across his desk, seeking his response. And respond he did. He was by no means a distant General, remaining in Rome concerned only with ecclesiastical politics or questions of theology, though he dealt as well with such issues, and was vitally concerned with the attacks Richard FitzRalph had made against the mendicants, so concerned in fact that he levied a tax of ten florins on all provinces to cover the expenses of combating FitzRalph at the Curia.[317]

Gregory knew his friars, and knew them well; he visited them, and lived with them. He governed his Order not only with letters, but also with personal presence. During his generalate, Gregory spent only a little over a month in Rome, from 22 February 1358 to 28 March of the same year;[318] he had been in Avignon, the seat of the Curia, for his election in the summer of 1357, but by 7 September he was already in Florence. He would never see Avignon again.

---

quatenus dicto fratri Antonio usque ad festum Omnium Sanctorum unum florenum solvere debeas integraliter cum effectu a receptione presentium; quod si nostrum mandatum adimplere contempseris de bonis tibi ab ordine appropriatis solvere tenearis eidem." Greg. *Reg.* 383 (215).

[315] Greg. *Reg.* 672 (344–345).
[316] Greg. *Reg.* 693 (355).
[317] Greg. *Reg.* 733 (373); 734 (374).
[318] Gregory's itinerary, here and in what follows, is based upon the entries in his register, which are dated with the location stipulated, at least for the entries uniformly following the first two, with the exceptions of numbers 10 through 23. Thus we cannot say with certainty that Gregory was in a given place exclusively for the time when we have register entries, and the time required for travel must certainly be taken into consideration, but we can say with certainty that he was in a given place for a given time, based on the entries in his register.

Indeed, he ventured north of the Alps only once, at the end of his generalate, never to return to Italy.

After having spent September of 1357 in Florence, Gregory moved on to Siena, where he stayed from 8–21 October. By 26 October, Gregory was already in Perugia, where he stayed for ten days, until 4 November. These were very productive days for Gregory, during which he issued forty-six entries in his register,[319] including sending his general letter of reform to the Provinces of Spoleto, the March of Treviso, Pisa, Apulia, Rome, and Romandiole, with special stipulations for the March of Ancona.[320] Among the provisions sent especially to the March of Ancona, Gregory included the prohibition of any brother from holding his own property, or even the usufruct thereof, and ordered the province within three months of receiving his letter to build a prison in every location suitable for and secure enough to hold delinquent brothers, including shackles with which to bind them, so that they could be kept in prison, allowed to leave only to satisfy the "necessities of nature."[321] For whatever reason, in Perugia Gregory was extra earnest about having secure prisons, for the following May, when he was once again in the city, he sent a similar letter to the Province of Spoleto.[322] Or perhaps it was simply a result of his travels that he saw the urgent need for strong discipline. Leaving Perugia on 4 November 1357, Gregory stopped over at Foligno on 5 May, from where he sent out letters comprising nine entries in his register,[323] before arriving in Nursia on 8 November and then on to Aquila on 11 November. Continuing south, Gregory reached Naples by 6 December 1357. He was to stay in Naples for a longer period than in any other single location during his generalate, until 15 February 1358, the only exception being the summer of 1358, which he spent in his home town of Rimini. From Naples,

---

[319] Greg. *Reg.* 8 (33–37), and 59 (54)–103 (... 71).
[320] Greg. *Reg.* 8 (33–37).
[321] "... mandaverimus fratribus universis dicte provincie, ne proprium aliquod, aut usufructum alicuius rei mobilis vel immobilis tenere vel possidere presumerent.... ordinamus priori provinciali dicte provincie mandantes per obedientiam salutarem, ut in quolibet loco sue provincie, in quo possibilitas fuerit, faciat infra spatium trium mensium a publicatione presenti fieri carcerem unum firmum et securum, cum compedibus et aliis munimentis, quibus carcerandi fratres tute custodiri valeant et teneri, ne fugere valeant ordinis disciplinam... ut nunquam eis exire liceat, nisi forsan ad necessaria facienda nature..." Greg. *Reg.* 8 (34–35).
[322] Greg. *Reg.* 7 (26–33;31).
[323] Greg. *Reg.* 104 (71)–112 (73).

Gregory moved back north to Rome, his only visit to the eternal city, before heading on to Viterbo, where he stayed from 30 March 1358 to 8 April. He then returned to Perugia, staying a couple of weeks (15 April–1 May), before he moved on to San Elpidio, where he spent the month of May. After a brief stop at Recanati (only one letter was registered, dated 28 May 1358),[324] Gregory returned to Rimini for the summer.

Gregory arrived in Rimini by 3 June, and was to stay until the end of August. He may have extended his time in Rimini due to his health. On 10 July Gregory wrote to Angelo de Cortonio in an unusually personal tone, referring to Angelo as "dearest master" (*Carissime magister*), and expressing his hope that Angelo would be "a light of the greatest clarity and a mirror of regular observance" for the convent in Siena. Gregory further apologized for not being able to respond to the details of Angelo's letters since he was disabled by sickness.[325] A week later, on 16 July, Gregory was still ill. In writing to Fratres Augustino de Penna and Philippo de Mantua, whom Gregory had appointed as visitors to the Hungarian Province, Gregory expressed his desire that they would be able to restore peace to the province and lead it back to regular observance, especially since he was unable to do so personally as he was sick.[326] Despite his illness, Gregory remained at work, issuing twenty-six documents during the week of 10–16 July,[327] including a harsh rebuke to the Province of Hungary for imprisoning Frater Nicholas de Sarvar, Gregory's officially appointed visitor. Gregory took this as an offense against his own office as prior general and a challenge to his authority, for only he

---

[324] Greg. *Reg.* 400 (224).

[325] "Carissime magister, contentari debetis esse in Sienensi convenu prout alii magistri ordinis alibi suas cathedras regere dignoscuntur, quia necdum aliquem ex magistris vicarium fecimus, quorum presentia, sicut et vestra esse potest inconventibus singulare lumen maxime claritatis et speculum observantie regularis, quod speramus presentia magistrali, cum non videamus adhuc oportunam fore aliquid agere novitiatis. Ceterum, quia infirmitate gravati fuimus etiam adhuc debiles, singulis in vestris litteris ennaratis non possumus respondere, sed de vicario Sienensis provincie et aliis oportunis, Dominio cooperante, providebimus ut decebit." Greg. *Reg.* 467 (260).

[326] "... providimus per vos, vice nostra, qui ad presens corporis debilitate et infirmitate gravati id personaliter ut voluntas aderat exequi non valemus, dictam provinciam ad statum pacificum et tranquillum, odorem fame et observantiam regularem reduci et in integrum restitui plenarie cum effectu." Greg. *Reg.* 492 (267–269; 268).

[327] Greg. *Reg.* 467 (260)–492(269).

had the right to judge one of his own officials and to administer punishment if required. Therefore, in no uncertain terms Gregory made clear, without expressing any indication of his own illness, that all the priors of the local convents in the Province of Hungary were held responsible and that under threat of their own imprisonment, were to make sure that the prior of the convent where Frater Nicholas was being held was to release him and allow him to take refuge in the place of his own choosing. Gregory, nevertheless, did not refrain from suggesting, among others, that Nicholas could stay with Frater Arnold, the personal physician of the King of Hungary.[328]

Nor did Gregory's sickness prevent him from attending to the more mundane aspects of his office. On 13 July, Gregory wrote to the convents of Ripa and Matelica, both in the March of Ancona, instructing the priors there to make over the yearly provisions of three florins to Fratres Angelo and Augustino respectively;[329] on the same day he wrote to Frater John, the prior provincial of the March of Ancona, giving him a list of nineteen individual friars who were competent and thereby authorized to hear the confessions of the local population;[330] so too he wrote to the convent and prior of the Augustinians in Vienna, authorizing Frater Henry of Cambia and Frater Nicholas Clavo to preach the word of God to the people of Vienna, even though they had both served prison sentences;[331] and on the same 13 July, Gregory further granted the following: to Frater Leonard de Vilaco in the Province of Bavaria permission to study in Paris; to Frater Nicholas de Frusten from the Province of Hungary

---

[328] "Scripsimus universis prioribus locorum et conventum vel eorum vicem gerentibus in provincia Ungarie in hac forma. Sicut vera relatione percepimus, frater Nicolaus de Sarvar, visitator et officialis noster in dicta provincia specialiter deputatus, de facto extitit carceri mancipatus et adhuc in carcere retinetur in nostri officii vituperium et gravamen. Propter quod non valentes tantam offensam sic conniventibus oculis pertransire, quia a nemine alio quam a nobis iudicari valuit vel puniri officialis noster prefatus... vobis et cuilibet vestrum precipimus per obedientiam salutarem et sub pena carceris, quam ipso facto contra veniendo vel nostris mandatis non parendo vos noveritis incursuros, quantenus statim visis presentibus quilibet vestrum, in cuius conventu dictus frater Nicolaus visitator noster est carceri mancipatus, ipsum teneatur restituere pristine libertati et associari facere ad locum sibi magis securum et tutum, liberum et solutum, sive Strigonum, sive ad fratrem Valentinum, sive ad fratrem Arnoldum phisicum domini regis Ungarie, vel alterum ad quem elegerit se conduci..." Greg. *Reg.* 479 (263–264).
[329] Greg. *Reg.* 471 (262), 472 (262).
[330] Greg. *Reg.* 473 (262).
[331] Greg. *Reg.* 474 (263).

permission to remain in the convent in Vienna until the time of the appointed visitation; and finally to Frater Valentino de Crisio from Hungary permission to lodge with Frater Arnold of Regensburg, the same royal physician whom Gregory had suggested as a protector for Nicholas de Sarvar, Gregory's official imprisoned in Hungary.[332] Gregory may have been ill, but his sickness did not prevent him from working. His time in Rimini was no summer vacation. There are 198 entries in his register during the time spent in his hometown in the summer of 1358;[333] from Rimini were sent almost 27% of all the entries for his entire generalate, in only approximately 18% of the time (3 of 17 months). Gregory may have been sick, but he continued working at a feverish pace, and was well enough by the end of the summer anyway to resume his travels. He left Rimini in the first days of September. By 6 September he was in Florence. He then began his trek north. It would be his last tour of duty.

Gregory is remembered as one of the outstanding theologians of the later Middle Ages. He surely would be pleased. Yet his work and his legacy as prior general of the Order was the culmination of his career, a career that did not end with the finishing touches on his *Sentences* commentary. His generalate was his crowning achievement, his unceasing efforts to define for his Order what it meant to be an Augustinian on a day to day basis, in the same vein as Jordan had provided his *Liber Vitasfratrum*. To bring about the reformation of the Order, to bring the Order back to its ideals of the common life, to bring the Order truly to regular observance, to ensure that every brother would truly live the Augustinian life: these were the terms, ideals, and goals of Gregory's reform endeavors. And doing so started not from a theological doctrine, but with the daily life of the brothers. This Gregory knew, and this was the approach he followed. His challenge was great, for Gregory was general during the nadir of the Order's religious life in the aftermath of the Black Death. Reform had to begin with the individual, it had to begin on the local level. And Gregory did much in his seventeen months to get the ball rolling, to start the Order's reformation, even if he did not live long enough to see it come to fruition.

If he can be faulted, his weakness was not a lack of effort, or an overscrupulous sternness; it was an inordinate amount of attention

---

[332] Greg. *Reg.* 475 (263)–467 (263).
[333] Greg. *Reg.* 402 (224)–599 (318).

given to the Italian provinces, or rather, a lack of attention given to the north. His itinerary itself indicates as much. Gregory traveled throughout Italy. The northern provinces were known to him only by reports. Of the 739 entries in his register, only 16.78% (122) were addressed to provinces or individuals north of the Alps. Of these, 46 went to Germany, 30 to France, 16 to Hungary, 9 to Spain, 6 to Bohemia, 6 as well to England, and 1 to Jerusalem.[334] Most of Gregory's successors as prior general throughout the later Middle Ages and on into the sixteenth century were as Italocentric as was Gregory. He himself was, after all, an Italian, and even the Latin of his registers bears a distinctive Italian flavor. Yet Gregory's concentrated efforts render him the unacknowledged father of the Augustinian Observant Movement.[335] His Italocentrism was part of his legacy. One might wonder how the history of the Order might have been different had Gregory lived longer and continued his travels, and his reform, in the north; one might wonder how history itself might have been different had Gregory shifted his sphere of influence and thus that of his office. Yet one can only wonder. Gregory left his Order the heritage of reform from above, led by the general, but a reform program and battle front that focused on the Order's Italian theater of operations.

It was not, however, that Gregory lacked concern for his brothers in the north. Quite the opposite is indicated by his letters that have come down to us. The first letter Gregory wrote after having finally reached Vienna, dated 16 November 1358, was to Frater John de Machelinea, professor of theology and prior provincial of the Province of Cologne. Gregory's nuncio to the Bavarian Province had brought Gregory letters from John dating from the previous August. Things were not well in Cologne: "Having read your letters, we grieve with you in the depths of our heart for the affliction of your province, which has suffered such a great loss of brothers. Yet we think that in such matters we ought patiently to accept the divine

---

[334] These figures add up to 114 entries. Eight entries were addresses to multiple provinces north of the Alps, together with two general letters addressed to all provinces of the Order. Jerusalem is naturally not a northern province, but since there is only one instance of an entry addressed to Jerusalem, Greg. *Reg.* 110 (73), which simply registers that Gregory had written to frater Winrico, master at the general hospital of St. Mary of the Germans in Jerusalem without further content, I included this non-Italian entry with the other transalpine provinces.

[335] See my forthcoming volume, *The Failed Reformation*.

will, for divine judgment is always just, even if we cannot see it."[336] The return of the plague was surely that to which Gregory was referring that had so damaged the Province of Cologne and was the cause of such commiseration. By 1357 the endemic plague had indeed returned to Germany,[337] as Gregory was certainly aware. On 23 March 1358 Gregory wrote to master Conrad, the prior provincial of the Rhenish Province, asking for a report on conditions and explicitly mentioned the plague, "which we have heard is now raging in Germany."[338] And yet, Gregory took some of the responsibility for the conditions in Cologne upon his own shoulders: "Nevertheless, we consider that the province has been injured due to the lack both of our letters sent to you and of our stipulations for the province."[339]

Gregory's register is not only a precious historical source. It was also a valuable instrument for his own administration, which is why it was kept in the first place. Gregory noted that he had sent a letter to Frater John of Foligno dated 5 November 1357, confirming him in his office as provincial prior of the Cologne Province and granting him privileges. This letter, however, had never arrived, as Gregory knew from reports from the prior of the Augustinian house in Bruges. He therefore was taking special measures, enlisting a special envoy to make sure that his present letter, which would repeat the provisions of his previous epistle, would arrive safely. The original letter, dated 5 November 1357, is still present in Gregory's register.[340] With all his other problems, Gregory certainly did not need

---

[336] "Recepimus die quintadecima mensis novembris in Vienna provincie Bavarie nunctium provincie vestre cum litteris datis infra octavas patris nostri beatissimi Augustini. Quibus perlectis compatimur ex intimis cordis nostri afflictioni provincie vestre, que in tali et tanto numero fratrum dispendiosam sustinuit lesionem, sed divinam pensamur in talibus voluntatem patienter ferre debemus, divina iudicia semper iusta etsi nobis occulta." Greg. *Reg.* 732 (371).

[337] Christiane Klapisch-Zuber, "Plague and Family Life," in *The New Cambridge Medieval History*, vol. VI: c. 1300–c. 1415, ed. Michael Jones (Cambridge, 2000), 124–154; 133.

[338] "Volumus insuper ut nobis quam citius poteris notificare curetis, si pax est in provincia Reni et securus accessus et transitus per eam maxime versus Parisius, et si in partibus illis viget mortalitas, quam audivimus in Alamania nunc vigere, ita quod de conditionibus patrie nos plenius informetis." Greg. *Reg.* 278 (156).

[339] ". . . necnon discrimini quod provincia est perpessa predicta ex carentia nostrarum litterarum vobis et dicte provincie directarum." Greg. *Reg.* 732 (371).

[340] "Super quo moveritis, quod dum fuimus Fulginii anno Domini MCCCLVII die V mensis novembris vobis venerabilis magister, litteras nostras actis vestris capituli responsivas direximus per nunctium vestrum proprium, qui nobis acta dicte provincie fideliter aportavit . . . Misimus et vobis tunc, sicut et nunc per vestrum

the mail exasperating matters. Yet the case of Cologne was not an isolated incident. On 11 August 1358 Gregory wrote to Frater Robert of Pisa instructing him, under the threat of imprisonment, to produce the letter he claimed to possess from Gregory exempting him from all prelates of the Order other than Gregory. Robert had apparently shown this letter to the Order's procurator general at the Roman Curia in Avignon.[341] Two weeks later Gregory wrote to the procurator general himself, Bernard of Manso, about this issue, claiming that he, Gregory, had not found any such letter in his register, nor did he remember having written such a letter.[342] Gregory, therefore, wanted to see a copy of the letter, and thus instructed Bernard to make sure that Frater Robert present Gregory with the original document.[343] We have no further information regarding the outcome of this case, but it testifies to the importance of Gregory's register for his own administration. And Gregory was not the only prior general who faced such problems. Already at the General Chapter of Padua in 1315 one of the definitions made was the prohibition of any brother forging the seal of the prior general, or a letter from the prior general, since such action posed the greatest danger to the Order.[344] The case of Frater Robert is clear testimony that such forgery was taking place, and Gregory's register could prove it.

It was hard being the prior general. One not only had to put up with brothers committing scandalous deeds with other brothers, or with local boys, or with nuns, or with local women, as well as with brothers fighting, drinking, gambling, and horse-trading, but also with instances of one's own letters and seal being forged for individual gain. It must have been exasperating. And then, the "postal system" was anything but reliable, which again is perhaps due to Gregory's

---

transmittimus nuntium specialem, litteras ordinationum nostrarum, comissionem domini summi penitentiarii, ac litteras vicariatus vestri capituli celebrandi. Et quia postea ex litteris receptis a priore Brugensi cognovimus nostras litteras ad dictam provinciam non venisse, nec presentatas fuisse, iterum in bono animo eas refici fecimus et magistro Iohanni de Placentia duximus destinandas, per cuius sollicitudinem vobis e vestigio mitterentur, sicut nobis idem prior per suas litteras destinavit, qui in hoc facto fuit diligens et sollicitus, nec negligens vel remissus in quantum nobis aparet et constat." Greg. *Reg.* 732 (371–372); *cf.* Greg. *Reg.* 106 (72).

[341] Greg. *Reg.* 546 (296).
[342] ". . . nos vero satis perquirentes in nostris registris talis sententiam littere invenire nequimus, nec nos etiam unquam fecisse meminimus." Greg. *Reg.* 584 (313), dated 29 Augustus 1358.
[343] Greg. *Reg.* 584 (313).
[344] *AAug.* 3 (1909/1910), 178.

predominantly Italian sphere of action; still today the Vatican operates its own post, which is generally acknowledged as far more reliable than that offered by the regular Italian "service." In any case, clogged lines of communication made Gregory's job all the more difficult, and interfered with his reform efforts. Gregory could not have staved off the plague from Cologne, but he could have perhaps been of more help had his letters and directives actually arrived at their intended destination.

Cologne, however, was not the only province of the Order north of the Alps that needed, or captured, Gregory's attention. On 21 June 1358, while Gregory was in Rimini, he sent a lengthy letter to master Gagliardus de Tolosa and to Frater Arnald de Conbello from the Province of Toulouse, appointing them as his official visitors to the Augustinian convents in Avignon and Carpentras. The case was serious. Something was rotten in the state of France. "We, indeed, have received many indications," Gregory lamented,

> and, my God, scathing reports, that in the convent at the Roman Curia, as well as in that of nearby Carpentras, where above all others all the grace mentioned above should be prominent, only the enemy of peace and the sower of maliciousness flourish, that in these houses reign dissensions and hate, seditions and schisms, quarrels and disputes, where the respect for religion is lost and the violation of the *Rule*'s mandates is common knowledge, offenses and injustices are not far behind, resulting in both serious disgrace and in an excessive, horrible conglomeration of scandals.[345]

True religion was the grace Gregory meant that should have been overflowing in Avignon. The lack thereof, he saw as the responsibility of his own office:

> It falls to our office to guard with all diligence and incessantly to be concerned to ensure that true religion, the responsibility for which God has entrusted us, everywhere might flourish in regular observance, might be vigorous in sanctity, might glimmer with respectability, might

---

[345] "Sane multiplici signficatione et famosa prohdolor relatione percepimus, quod in conventu Romane curie, ubi pre ceteris oporteret omnem antefatam gratiam eminere, et in conventu etiam Paternarum vicinio, tantum valuit emulus pacis et sator malitie, quod in illis dissensiones et odia, seditiones et scismata, lites et iurgia regnaverunt, periit religionis honestas et publica facta est regularium prevaricatio mandatorum, offensiones et iniurie subsecute sunt, ex quibus et gravis infamia et horrenda nimis copia scandalorum." Greg. *Reg.* 444 (247–250; 244).

rejoice in the tranquillity of peace, and might always serve the Lord, clinging to Him in the bond of charity.[346]

Avignon was obviously falling short, though other houses of the Order were by no means models of piety. The Province of Hungary was in a state of shambles, and Siena and the March of Ancona closer to home gave Gregory many headaches. But this was Avignon, after all. Something had to be done. Gregory gave his newly appointed emissaries wide powers and authority: they were to seek out all irregularities and deviations from the Order's *Rule* and *Constitutions*, as well as from the ordinances Gregory had sent to the provinces of the Order at the beginning of his generalate, with the rigor of justice, keeping the honor of God and the good state of the Order always before their eyes, working to effect the reformation of the province. Master Gagliardus and Frater Arnald could investigate, adjudicate, castigate, exculpate, incarcerate, repudiate, and excommunicate as they saw fit. And they had two months to do so. Gregory even gave them a lengthy list of names of brothers to interrogate and to settle their cases once and for all, including the name of Robert of Pisa, who was soon to forge a letter exempting him from the authority of all the Order's prelates aside from Gregory. Avignon needed a spanking, and Master Gagliardus and Frater Arnald were the ones to give it to them.[347]

Little wonder that the previous year or so Frater John, a student at the Order's *studium* in Avignon, was confused. By the time the visitors arrived in Avignon, Frater John had luckily already left and was teaching in Strassburg, having obtained the lectorate.[348] Yet he may have still been in Avignon, finishing up, when in September of 1357 the letter of the new prior general addressed specifically to Avignon arrived, complete with a set of regulations which began by stating that everywhere he looked, the path of true religion had been completely abandoned and friars everywhere were following the way of seculars, accumulating money, enjoying worldly delights, eager for

---

[346] "Officii nostri debitum exigit nos iugi sollicitudine vigilare et indesinenti satagere studio, ut religio ipsa, cuius nobis cura divina permissione commissa est, ubilibet regulari observantia vigeat, sanctitate polleat, honestate refulgeat, pacis tranquillitate gaudeat et semper vinculo caritatis innexa Domino famuletur." Greg. *Reg.* 444 (247).

[347] Greg. *Reg.* 444 (248–250); *cf.* Greg. *Reg.* 445 (251–252).

[348] For the office of lector, see Chapter Four below.

pomp and prestige.³⁴⁹ The new general, Gregory, then went on to detail how life was to be lived. Everyone, even priors and masters of theology, were diligently to say the divine hours, and if they were negligent in doing so, they would be forced to sit on the floor in the middle of the refectory during meals as an example of their delinquency, though a prior or a lector could sit at the table, but would have to sit with an empty plate.³⁵⁰ Moreover, no more feather beds, or linen sheets. No more pocket money, aside from the allotted provisions. And for Avignon, the masters of theology in residence would have to preach, in the vernacular, to the people, and they could only have two friars serving them at table, or keeping them company, and, if caught breaking these stipulations, one would pay a hefty penalty: forfeiting one's entire yearly provisions. Further, no women could be brought into the cloister. And at least in Avignon, one could only eat meat three times a week. What was the world coming to? And this new prior general threatened all over the place to inflict fines, or even prison sentences on those who didn't shape up and conform to the new regulations.³⁵¹ What was going on? Frater John had reason to be confused.

But John was confused even before Gregory's letter arrived. He was confused as to what it really meant to be a member of the Order. He was confused by what he saw going on in Avignon. It was much different where he came from. John, after all, was from Basel, and John wanted some questions answered. Gregory might not yet have even been in office when John wrote to the well-known and well-respected Frater Jordan, asking him what it meant to be a true son of Augustine and how one was to know if one was one in the first place. Frater Jordan replied with his *Liber Vitasfratrum*.

Defining the Augustinian life: that was what was needed. That was what Jordan tried to do with his answer to John of Basel. That was what Gregory tried to do in his generalate. And the word had to get out. "Ignorance," Gregory wrote to the Province of Lavoro

---

[349] "Super nostre religionis specula licet inmeriti constituti, dum plurimos immo fere omnes aspicimus ad divina desides, solicitos ad mundana, contra eorum professionem et statum proprias cumulare pecunias, perfrui deliciis, pompis seculi gloriari sicque religiositatis deserta semita vias potius incedere seculares, terret nos plurimum illa divina sententia, qua de manu negligentis speculatoris comminatur Dominus sanguinem requirere morientis." Greg. *Reg.* 1 (4); *cf.* Greg. *Reg.* 2 (8–12).
[350] Greg. *Reg.* 1 (4); see Appendix E for the text of Gregory's *Ordinationes*.
[351] Greg. *Reg.* 2 (8–12).

on 1 February 1358, "is the mother of all errors."[352] Therefore, Gregory was sending the province his ordinances, which, as he had explained to the Provinces of Aragon and Hungary on 3 November 1357, were intended "for the reformation of the morals and behavior of the brothers of our Order," and thus were to be strictly observed.[353] To the prior provincial of the Province of Lavoro, Gregory further stipulated that all the local priors of the Augustinian houses in the province were within six months to have their own parchment copies for their convents of the Order's *Constitutions*, together with the *Additiones* made thereto by Gregory's predecessor, Thomas of Strassburg, and if they were found not to have such central documents of the Order within the given time, they would be dismissed from their office as prior. Gregory held the prior provincial responsible for enforcing the regulation.[354]

The reform program as outlined in Gregory's *Ordinationes* was rather rudimentary. Katherine Walsh referred to Gregory's first registered act as prior general as the sending of "a severe letter to every province of the Order, painting a grim picture of the decline of the regular observance and the *vita communis*."[355] No doubt that the picture Gregory painted was grim, but only by rather low standards can his stipulations be considered as severe. The severity came, if at all, in his vigorous insistence that his orders be followed, with mandated punishments for negligence. He wanted to be clear that he meant business. He therefore stipulated that his *Ordinationes* be read publicly each month in every house of the Order.[356] His *Ordinationes*, his

---

[352] ". . . ignorantia est mater cunctorum errorum . . ." Greg. *Reg.* 5 (18).

[353] "Misimus etiam tibi litteras ordinationum nostrarum ad reformationem morum et actuum fratrum ordinis sepedicti, quas per fratres tuos facies et curabis inviolabiliter custodiri." Greg. *Reg.* 88 (65–66; 66), To Frater Bonanato, prior provincial of the Province of Aragon; "Mittimus insuper tibi litteras ordinatioum nostrarum per nos factarum ad reformationem morum et actuum fratrum ordinis sepedicti, quas in tua provincia firmiter precipimus observari." Greg. *Reg.* 89 (66–67; 67), To Frater Nicolaus de Waradino, prior provincial of the Province of Hungary.

[354] ". . . ideo presentium tenore mandamus omnibus et singulis prioribus vel eorum loca tenentibus dicte provincie, quatenus infra sex menses a publicatione presentium computandos in suis conventibus constitutiones et additiones ordinis nostri in pergameno proprias cuiuscumque conventus debeant habere conscriptas, sub pena absolutionis ab officio prioratus, ad quam tu prior provincialis contra hac facere negligentes procedere tenearis." Greg. *Reg.* 5 (18).

[355] Katherine Walsh, "Papal Policy and Local Reform: A) The Beginning of the Augustinian Observance in Tuscany," *Romische Historische Mitteilungen* 21 (1979), 35–57; 38.

[356] See Appendix E.

first registered act as prior general, were to be the basis for his reforming efforts throughout his generalate.

Gregory addressed four primary points. First, the divine hours must be kept diligently by all. Those neglecting to do so were, if they were priors or students, to sit in refectory with an empty plate (*ad mensam nudam*); brothers of other status were required to sit on the floor in the middle of the refectory. Lectors and masters, should they fail to attend Matins, were financially punished; lectors were to be deprived of their weekly provisions, and masters, half of theirs, unless the reason for their absence was due to their having to preach that day or take part in official academic exercises. The second was the common table. Eating outside the cloister was frowned upon and was seen as undermining the common life. Thus one was allowed to miss only three common meals a week, without the special permission of the prior, and those more often absent incurred the same punishment as those missing the divine office. The third bone of contention for Gregory was luxury. It seems that it had become rather common practice for Augustinians to sleep on feather mattresses. This was too much comfort. Thus Gregory ordered that all the feather mattresses in every convent of the Order be sold, except for a number reserved for the use of the sick. From the proceeds of the sale, straw mattresses were to be purchased and used throughout the Order. The local priors had three months to comply, on the threat of being removed from their office. Yearly visitations of the brothers' cells were to be made and if a feather mattress was found, the guilty party would lose his vote in chapter and be deprived of his yearly provisions. The fourth major issue for Gregory was a problem indeed: money and property. This he addressed in four subpoints. First, all friars were allowed to have two florins in their possession for their daily needs and expenses, which Gregory did not further explain. Any money beyond this amount was to be appropriated by the convent and placed in a common chest that was to be doubly locked, with the prior having one key and the convent's procurator another. Second, friars were strictly forbidden to lend money. Third, no friar was to possess or use silverware in the broadest sense: no silver plates, silver cups, goblets, spoons, or anything else. If such items were found in the convent, they were to be confiscated and sold, with the profits deposited in the common chest. Violators of this decree were subject to excommunication. And finally, no brother was to own property; doing so could land one in prison.

These are the points of reform that were Gregory's greatest concern: the divine office, the common table, straw mattresses, and private possessions and wealth. These were the issues that undermined the Order's *vita communis*, and were absolutely necessary to be followed and enforced to ensure regular observance, which Giles of Rome had already asserted as the central issue for the Order in 1292. There was, however, an underlying fifth major concern expressed implicitly in Gregory's *Ordinationes*, which was perhaps the most important of all: obedience. Obedience was mandatory, and Gregory was prepared to inflict what punishments were needed to insure his mandates had force. Behind Gregory's stipulations, the driving motivation of his *Ordinationes*, was the ideal of the common life, regular observance, and the vows of obedience, poverty—and chastity.

Chastity he only mentioned once directly in his *Ordinationes*, simply stating that the abdication of private possessions was as much a part of regular observance as was maintaining one's chastity. Yet as we have seen, the lack of chastity within the Order was a problem Gregory faced throughout his generalate. Though Augustine as founding father had been de-sexed, some of his body's members still preferred to have the thirst of their lust quenched in the sense of being satisfied, rather than extinguished. All the more reason for secure prisons. If Gregory did not explicitly address maintaining one's chastity in his *Ordinationes*, he certainly did his best with his letters of direction that he sent along with his reform program to various provinces. To Avignon, he wrote that no woman was to be brought into the cloister, and no secular person was to eat in the convent's refectory, except with good reason and in the presence of all, and no secular person was to be brought into a brother's cell. These prohibitions were to preserve the honor of the Order.[357] To the convent in Florence, he prohibited under the threat of excommunication any brother of whatever status, for whatever reason from visiting the nunneries in the city and diocese.[358] The same prohibition was sent

---

[357] "Item, propter honestatem ordinis conservandam, volumus et mandamus per priorem inviolabiliter observari ut omnem diligentiam adhibeat, quod nulla mulier ad puteum nostrum accedat, et quod nullus secularis in refectorio commedat, nisi aliquando ex rationabili causa cum toto conventu reficeretur ibidem. Nullus etiam fratrum secularem ad cellam aliquam introducat." Greg. *Reg.* 2 (11).

[358] "Et quoniam secundum Apostolum non solum a malo sed ab omni specie mala sit penitus abstinendum, monemus omnes et singulos fratres ordinis antedicti cuiuscumque status et conditionis existant, eis nichilominus sub excommunicationis

to the convent in Naples, with the penalty for transgression being a month in prison, and the further prohibition of friars bringing women into the cloister.[359] A prison sentence was likewise prescribed for brothers in the Province of Spoleto who would dare to visit a nunnery for any reason without the explicit permission of the prior since such was the cause for public scandal and damaged the Order's reputation.[360] And on it went. Gregory knew the dangers. Preserving the chastity of the Order's members was not a concern he ignored. Poverty, chastity, and obedience, the *vita communis*, and the *observantia regularis*: these were the foundations of Gregory's reform platform, for these were the foundations of the Augustinian life, as they had been from the very beginning, which Gregory was still earnestly striving to instill, enforce, and define.

Judging by his register, one could easily come to the conclusion that Gregory failed in his attempts to whip his Order into religious shape. The numerous instances of derelict friars, only some of which I have mentioned above, testify to the fact that the Augustinians in the mid-fourteenth century did not always conform to Jordan's image of the Order as the city of God, a shining example set on the hill, or even as the genuine imitators of their founding father, at least of their founding father once one reaches book nine of the *Confessions*. We must keep in mind, however, the nature of the source. Evaluating the level of religious observance within the Order based on Gregory's register would almost be like judging the level of discipline and order in an elementary school based on reports of visits to the principal's office. What is preserved in his register are Gregory's responses to trouble, and trouble there certainly was, but that is not the whole picture. There were still pious, obedient friars among the 5,000 or so left after the plague, such as old brother Michael, who did petition the prior general to ask permission to sleep on a feather mattress due to his infirmity and age. And Gregory granted the indulgence. He did not indiscriminately impose prison sentences and fines at will

---

pena mandantes ne aliquo modo aut causa aut titulo aut alio colore quesito ad monasteria sanctimonialium in civitate Florentina et eius diocesi constituta, cuiuscumque ordinis aut professionis vel conditionis existant, accedant, visitent aut frequentent." Greg. *Reg.* 3 (13). Gregory did, however, allow, with special permission, brothers to go to nunneries when invited to say mass or hear confessions, with the special permission of the prior.

[359] Greg. *Reg.* 6 (20–21, 25).
[360] Greg. *Reg.* 7 (32).

wherever he felt improvement could be made. He also realized that once having set the hardline, discretion was at times the greater part of valor, or at least offered a greater chance for eventual transformation. It is only the exceptional cases that we hear about, the blatant abuses. It was, after all, the good of the Order, its health and its vitality, as well as its reputation and influence, that he had at heart, and thus leniency at times was called for. When Gregory granted permission for lay brother Walter to return to the Order after having married, for all practical purposes, including that of procreation, he did so with the good of the Order in mind. Walter could return, if he submitted to discipline. Gregory obviously was not considering what would happen to Walter's common-law wife and children, but he was thinking of how best to bring back into the fold one of the Order's lost sheep. He can be damned for his callousness and myopia in this case, but not for his severity in terms of the Order itself. Even in the cases of money and property, Gregory could almost look the other way at times, once having set the standard. And issues over money and property were one of the most common points of contention that he had to deal with.

On 28 August 1358, Gregory granted permission to the provincial prior of the Province of Spoleto to allow Frater Gabriel de Cantiana to sell off part of his dowry that he had brought with him to the monastery in order to provide financial resources for his mother. Gregory admitted that he did not know much about the case, but if it proved valid, without fraud, ulterior motives, or damage to the local convent, then he saw no problem with allowing friar Gabriel to provide for his mother's needs from the property comprising the dowry he had brought to the monastery.[361] Three days later, Gregory wrote again to Matthew of Amelia, the prior provincial of Spoleto, with regard to a similar request. Frater Angelucio of the convent in Todi had already been given permission by Gregory to sell some of his possessions in Tosci for the purpose of meeting

---

[361] "Supplicavit nobis frater Gabriel de Cantiana et dum fuimus Perusii et nunc nobis per suas litteras intimavit, ut de nostra licentia matri sue reficere dotes suas posset, eidem concedere dignaremur. Nos vero in facto ipso non habentes notitiam pleniores, tenore predictarum fratrem oportet facere supradictum. Et si inveneris nullum ex hoc ordinis preiudicium generari, sed sine fraude vel dolo vel fictione dotes huiusmodi esse reficiendas ut petit, ex indulto nostro alias tibi facto, vendendi possessiones loci licentiam concedendi, eidem fratri Gabrieli concedere valeatis, ut dictas dotes reficere possit, tibi concedimus facultatem." Greg. *Reg.* 583 (312).

the debts of his father, and now it became clear that his mother was also in need of assistance. Thus Gregory instructed the prior provincial to look into the matter, and if he found reasonable cause, then Gregory would grant his permission to use the property of Angelucio to meet the debts of his mother.[362]

The properties in question in both of these cases were technically in the possession of the said monasteries, and thus were properties held in common. However, the line between private ownership and communal was rather thin. Gregory granted permission to the convents to sell property for the private use of the two mothers of the friars involved, based on the fact that these were properties that they had at least originally possessed as dowries, and therefore could be disposed with to meet private needs. Pope Alexander IV might have questioned the extent to which such transactions violated the precept of holding no property as one's own, but only in common, as stated in his privileges granted the Augustinians, which Gregory quoted verbatim in his *Ordinationes*,[363] but Gregory apparently saw no real problem.

Neither did Gregory refuse the three florins for yearly provisions to Frater Angelo and Frater Augustino from the March of Ancona, whose case I mentioned above, even though he had already stipulated that only two florins were allowed. When Master Bartholomew from Siena received far more than the allotted amount to cover the expenses of his inception to the *magisterium*, Gregory kept the matter quiet. Both Frater Bartholomew and Frater Angelus from Siena were allotted 100 florins for their festivities, but Frater Bartholomew took in from the province and other convents a total of more than 350 florins. This amount was certainly excessive, but the only sentence Gregory imposed was one of silence.[364] Yet Gregory had a soft

---

[362] "Ut conventus sancte Praxedis de Tuderto quandam possessionem Tosci, fratri Angelucio filio suo in testamento legatam, vendere posset et quedam debita per dictum Toscum patrem supradicti fratris Angelucii in dicta possessione relicta ex pretio satisfacere, licentiam libere concessimus. Sed quia nobis exponitur quod mater supradicti fratris Angelucii quedam alia debita supradicta possessione contraxit, unde petit ex pretio satisfieri eiusdem, idcirco mandamus tibi per obedientiam salutarem, quatenus cum supradictum conventum visitaveris diligenter de supradictis inquiras, et si inveneris quod mater supradicti fratris de iure aliquid in dicta possessione debeat recipere, prefatum conventum de pretio possessionis sepedicte solvere cogas cum effectu." Greg. *Reg.* 597 (317).

[363] Greg. *Reg.* 1 (7–8); see also Appendix E.

[364] "Ex cuius informatione distincte et clare nobis transmissa, quod magister

spot in his heart for scholars. Thus on 25 May 1358 he instructed the convent of Firmano to sell certain parcels of land in order to cover the expenses incurred by Frater Andreas during his studies in Paris, including the purchase of books. If the received price for the land exceeded the expenses of Frater Andreas, the remaining sum was to be deposited in the common chest. The debt that Andreas had incurred, which he himself could not meet, totaled thirty-four florins, thirty of which were for books, including selections from the *Milleloquium Sancti Augustini* compiled by Bartholomew of Urbino, and Augustine's *Sermones ad fratres in eremo*, which had not long previously been assembled by Frater Jordan. Fifteen years after Jordan had donated his *Collectanea* to the *studium* in Paris, the *Sermones ad fratres in eremo* were bringing in a hefty price. Andreas had spent sixteen florins for the extracts from the *Milleloquium*, together with the *Sermones ad fratres in eremo* and other *Sermones* of Augustine, perhaps also copied originally from Jordan's *Collectanea*. The *Soliloquia* of Augustine together with the *Meditationes* of St. Bernard carried the price of only two florins. Moreover, these books, as well as the others Andreas acquired in Paris, were to be in effect his private property until his death. Technically this surely was not so, since he would not be allowed to resell them or give them away, and after his death, they were to revert to the convent's library. Yet in effect, these were Andreas' private possessions, until his death, with the only stipulation being that he had to keep them as such. Moreover, convent property was to be sold to pay the costs, albeit property that had originally been in Andreas' family, much as the dowry of brother Gabriel.[365] In effect, whatever property a friar brought with him into the monastery became the communal property of the monastery, yet could be used for the private needs and expenses of the friar. Technically the friar had neither *dominium* nor *usufructus* of his dowry, yet the property bestowed on the monastery could be used, and sold, for the debts incurred by the friar or by his family.

Bartholomeus tam a provincia, quam a conventibus aliis recepit pro dicto subsidio ultra CCCL. Propter quod quoad ipsum dictam diffinitionem de C florenis dandis eidem cessamus presentium in tenore, cum secundum consuetudines nostras excessivam provisionem de quantitate receperit supradictam; unde nec vigore dicte diffinitionis, nec alio quocumque colore quesito, volumus quod de cetero aliquid a dicta provincia magister Bartholomeus percipiat pro subsidio magisteriis sui prestando, sibi super hoc perpetuum silentium imponentes." Greg. *Reg.* 262 (146).

[365] Greg. *Reg.* 376 (212).

Brothers' possessions were a sticky issue, and even if legally freed from falling under the category of private ownership, they often were treated as such. Friars' possessions upon their death were property in limbo, much as the no-man's-land between east and west Germany after the fall of the Berlin wall; they were possessions there to be claimed, or simply to be taken. At least that is how Frater Antonius de Iaquinto from Naples saw things. Gregory wrote to the prior of the Augustinians in Naples telling him that he, Gregory, knew of Frater Antonius from the reports of his visitors. Frater Antonius had broken into the cell of a friar recently deceased and made off with the friar's goods—an instance of plain theft. Yet the ambiguous nature of such goods certainly was a factor, and the breaking-in charge was simply that, a charge. Nevertheless, Frater Antonius was sentenced to three months in prison, bound in chains.[366]

Selling property, however, was not simply a transaction to cover the debts of brothers or their families. Most of the entries in Gregory's register dealing with finances are grants to individual convents or provinces of permission to sell property in order to use the proceeds for greater good, including building projects and the like. Books were also goods for trade. Yet books too, especially for Gregory, were precious assets. However, one did not need multiple copies, and thus Gregory often stipulates that duplicate books in a convent's library, or books of less value, could be sold either for building purposes, or to acquire more valuable or useful books. On 25 January 1358, in such a privilege granted to the convent of Trano, Gregory also gave a couple of examples of books *minus utiles*: the *Decretum* and Innocent IV's *Apparatus super quinque libros Decretalium*.[367] These works, however, could have been duplicates, though they are not mentioned as such, since on 7 June Gregory instructed the convent of Siena to sell a sufficient number of unchained books to reach the amount of 100 florins, 24 florins of which were to be used to purchase the *Decretum*, the *Decretales*, the *Sextus* and the *Clementines* for Frater Nisio de Arcochis. Much like Frater Andreas, Nisio was permitted to keep such books for his own use until his death, when they would revert to the convent of Siena, with the only condition being that he could not resell or give away his books.[368] Were such private libraries private prop-

---

[366] Greg. *Reg.* 218 (121).
[367] Greg. *Reg.* 183 (110).
[368] Greg. *Reg.* 419 (232–233).

erty? Technically no, but again, as with the dowries, the lines seem a bit fuzzy. If the rigorous reformer Gregory had a problem with such arrangements, there is certainly no indication thereof. The Augustinians were to be poor beggars, vowing complete individual poverty, yet as such they still could have at least two, or three, florins in their pockets for daily expenses, and masters could count on far larger sums to cover the costs of their festivities. Students and scholars could have their debts met by the convent though from sources they had originally donated, which still, however, were accounted towards their use; and students and scholars could have in their own private possession, until their death, their own books, without ever having to lay them at the feet of the apostles, except, naturally, at first, upon entering the Order to begin with. Gregory was scholastically trained after all, and such distinctions and casuistry seemed natural to him. It surely was to his benefit. One could only excommunicate or throw brothers in prison for so much, and whether the actual amount of the provisions was two florins or three did not matter as much as the principle behind Gregory's strict limitations. Based on his register, financial regulations seem to have been followed better than other requirements. We find more often cases of Gregory having to enforce the payment of provisions than we do of their excess or abuse. Discretion was indeed perhaps the approach to take.

The March of Ancona was not one of the more observant provinces. On 27 May 1358 Gregory sent a scathing letter to the prior provincial, imposing fines and penalties on numerous individual priors and brothers for multiple infractions.[369] In the province the local priors were not observing the Order's liturgical calendar, brothers were still sleeping on feather mattresses, brothers were lending money to various local citizens, and brothers were physically attacking other brothers and fist-fighting. Frater Thomasuctius from the convent of St. Victoria maliciously pushed Frater Matthew, of the same convent, from the monastery's walls, nearly causing Matthew's death (*dictus frater Matheus confractus fuit usque ad articulum mortis*); Frater Nicholas from St. Mary's in Georgia had run off with a widow of ill-repute, with whom he had two daughters; and Frater Stephanus de Pulverisio was a notorious gambler. Gregory ended his letter simply with the

---

[369] For the text of this letter, see Appendix E.

exhortation, and his expression of hope, that the prior provincial would attend to these matters and proceed according to the Order's mandates and regulations, dishing out the canonical punishments as needed.[370] No wonder Gregory focused his attention on Italy: there was so much in Italy to focus on.

In his chastising letter to the March of Ancona we see the exact same issues resurfacing that Gregory had originally addressed in his *Ordinationes* and accompanying letter to the March of Ancona of 30 October 1357. In that letter, Gregory had also instructed the prior provincial to make sure there were secure prisons throughout the province for derelict friars.[371] Only seven months later it was painfully obvious that such prisons were in dire need. Even one renegade Augustinian, going around visiting nunneries, organizing games of dice, dealing in pigs or trading horses, siring offspring with local women, or beating up on fellow brothers, not to mention committing other unspeakable acts with them, was one Augustinian too many. Such a false friar could seriously damage the Order's reputation, which was ever so important to an Order of so few, trying to reform, trying to establish its influence in the local communities and in the Church at large. That one brother had to be stopped. Thus Gregory's stern measures. Thus Gregory's imploring the Bishop of Tropea for help in hunting down, capturing, and bringing to justice Fratres Bartholomew Brancasolus and Robin Archamonus of Naples.[372] The issue was not about the soul of a single brother, though Gregory could be intimately concerned about that too; the issue was one of the entire Order. Gregory's reform measures, including all the prison sentences, all the fines, and all the discipline, were not repressive; they were strategically necessary steps for defending the Order. And they were aimed at the individual friar as well. Poverty, chastity, obedience, the common life, and regular observance: these were what defined the Augustinian life, and if they were not followed, what did that mean for the Order's self-understanding, or for that matter for its self-presentation? Not once in Gregory's register do we find the motto of his Order's founding father with respect to the Donatists, *compelle intrare*, but it was never far behind his reforming endeavors. Yet Gregory combined his stern-

---

[370] Greg. *Reg.* 319 (218–220).
[371] Greg. *Reg.* 8 (33–37).
[372] Greg. *Reg.* 197 (113–114); *cf.* Greg. *Reg.* 189 (111–112); 229 (125); 360 (203–205).

ness and harshness with a compassion and warmth completely in keeping with his Augustinian position as stated in his *Sentences* commentary, that the entire law, all the prophets, as well as the Gospels and the apostolic teachings, are directed toward and lead to love.[373] It was genuine concern and care, and deep love, that drove Gregory on, a love, care, and concern for each and every brother of his Order, as well as for the Order itself. With his ideals, hopes, and aspirations, together with his *Ordinationes* and reform program, Gregory finally left Rimini in the first days of September of 1357 and headed north, to bring his reformation beyond Italy, to the Order at large, as he had previously tried to do, and would continue trying to do on his way, by means of his letters and visitors sent out to all corners of Europe, wherever Augustinian communities could be found. Yet personal presence too was needed. Thus Gregory left the seaside and returned to Florence as the point of departure for embarking on his mission beyond the Alps.

We can trace the General's march north from his register, which indicates that he did not stay long in any one place. He was in Florence 6–7 September 1358, then moved on to Bologna, where he took a bit more time, remaining there from 13 September to 6 October. From 7–13 October he was in Ferarra; then on to Venice from 13–18 October. Thereafter, he picked up his pace. On 21–22 October he was in Treviso, before crossing the Alps, arriving at Volchmarch in the Province of Bavaria by 4 November. By 14 November he was in Baden, and he finally reached Vienna the following day, 15 November 1358. And in Vienna, his journey ended. The last entry of Gregory's register is dated 20 November 1358. It was addressed to the Rhenish Province of the Order, requesting them to cover the costs for the entombment of his predecessor Thomas, who had been buried in Vienna. The local convent had born the expense, fifteen golden florins. This amount Gregory asked the province to provide, thus reimbursing the house at Vienna, where Gregory was staying.[374] A strange feeling comes over one today when reading this last entry. Gregory's register is complete. His last act was to make financial arrangements for his predecessor's tomb.

---

[373] "Ecce quod tota lex et omnes prophetae et evangelia et apostolicae doctrinae et per consequens tota theologia ad caritatem ordinantur et virtualiter nos inducunt." Greg. 1 *Sent.* Prol. 5,4 (I.182,15–17).
[374] Greg. *Reg.* 739 (376).

Gregory never left Vienna. Little could he have known, perhaps, that not long thereafter, he himself would be buried, in Vienna, in the same tomb with his confrere Thomas.[375] Divine judgment is always just, even if it we cannot see it.

Gregory the reformer, Gregory the theologian: the two images we have of Gregory of Rimini, even though the first has scarcely been acknowledged. Two images that if not contradictory, seem at least to have little to do with each other. Neither was the image Gregory would have chosen as a self-portrait. They both are too limited, too focused, adequately to capture a human personality with the dreams, hopes, ideals, aspirations, sorrows, struggles, and achievements of this prior general. Yet they harmonize when placed together within the wider perspective that encapsulates his career and person to form a new image, and one that Gregory would have been more likely to recognize; a new image, and yet an old image, a historical image, of Gregory, the Augustinian.

Ad reformationem ordinis, "For the reformation of the Order": that should have been Gregory's epitaph. The reformation of the Order was the goal Gregory worked so intensely and intensively to achieve throughout his career, living truly as a shining example of what it meant to be a son of Augustine. Gregory expressed his hope that Frater Angelo would be such for the convent in Siena. Gregory was for his entire Order. Gregory had claimed that the Order's venerable masters of theology should by their life and character be held up as examples for the rest of their brothers.[376] He strove to imprint his own example throughout the Order of Augustine's hermits, or at least that example which he held up for himself as well. He did so with his tireless correspondence, with his vicars and visitors, with his goals and ideals and regulations, and with his personal presence, which was the most important of all. Only his inability to visit personally all the provinces of the Order necessitated the appointment of visitors and vicars, as he wrote to Fratres John de Monte Rodono and Cicho de Aversa in his letter naming them as his visitors to the Province of Apulia. Gregory simply could not physically visit all the provinces, even in Italy, even as he desired and as he felt he should.

---

[375] Damasus Trapp, "La tomba bisoma di Tommaso da Strasburgo e di Gregorio da Rimini," *Augustinianum* 6 (1966), 5–17.

[376] Greg. *Reg.* 1 (5); see also Appendix E.

Yet this lack should not deprive the provinces of the "needed reformation in head and members"—thus his visitors and their visitations, sent out to announce, establish, and enforce Gregory's platform for reform.[377] This was necessary, for ignorance was indeed the mother of all errors. The word had to be spread, and ignorance combated, corrected, and only if incorrigible, weeded out. Gregory's *re-formatio* was to be the *e-ducatio* of his entrusted flock from the kingdom of ignorance: education and reformation were scarcely distinguished. Priests who could not say mass correctly were to be banned from doing so, for such was unacceptable in the Order, as he angrily announced to the convent of Feraria in the March of Treviso on 13 October 1358 in decreeing that Frater Ulrich of Trent was never to celebrate mass again under the penalty of imprisonment because Ulrich could neither read the Missal nor pronounce the words of the Canon correctly.[378] Priests were to be examined before being permitted to say mass or hear confessions. The standards had to be maintained, both internally for the Order itself as well as externally for the Order's pastoral mission.[379] The brothers had to be taught. The life of the Order was at stake. How else could some of them be adequately prepared to preach, to teach, to hear confessions, to serve princes as chaplains, or to deal with a group of citizens who had murdered their archbishop? Masters of theology had to be produced to serve as the models and standards for the Order, and to defend the Order against such horrendous attacks as those launched by Richard FitzRalph. Being an Augustinian in the later Middle Ages meant devoutly celebrating the divine office, sleeping on straw mattresses, neither eating meat nor missing a common meal more than three times a week, renouncing private property and carnal desire, truly living the common life and adhering to regular observance, preaching and teaching the people and hearing their confessions. Not all were up to the task. Yet some were, and went even further, working diligently to become preachers and teachers, lectors and masters, in continuing to define that religious life, that religion, that had been established by father Augustine. This too was part of Gregory's heritage. And this too was part of the heritage left by his

---

[377] Greg. *Reg.* 658 (335); see also Appendix E.
[378] Greg. *Reg.* 685 (349).
[379] Greg. *Reg.* 165 (98); 336 (187–188); 338 (189–190).

contemporary, who had taken upon himself the challenge of writing a book on what it meant to be an Augustinian, who had become his Order's outstanding preacher, and who had been a lector in Erfurt and a student in Paris. *Ad reformationem ordinis*: that could have been the epitaph of Frater Jordan of Quedlinburg.

CHAPTER FOUR

ETHICS AND ERUDITION: THE THEOLOGICAL ENDEAVOR OF THE AUGUSTINIAN *STUDIA*

In their song "Cathedral," the folk group Crosby, Stills, and Nash gave a critique of Christianity that Christianity ignores only to its peril: "Too many people have lied in the name of Christ for anyone to heed the call. So many people have died in the name of Christ that I can't believe at all." If the Church is going to be of relevance to contemporary individuals, meeting their needs, addressing their fears, their hopes, their dreams, healing their hearts and their lives, it must take these two points very seriously and provide an answer. Yet the Church has never been all that open to critique, except in limited, controlled ways by which it can show its willingness to be reformed, just so long as the issues do not get too hot, too central, or too sensitive: witness Eugen Drewermann, witness Hans Küng, witness the splintering and "sectification" of American Protestantism. God may not yet be dead, we cannot, after all, know for certain, but theology soon will be if theology cannot meet the challenges posed by the dilemmas and anxieties of our post-modern, post-Christian society and culture.

While modern and contemporary theologians such as, among others, Paul Tillich, Rosemary Radford Reuther, David Tracy, Elizabeth Schüssler Fiorenza, Küng, and Drewermann, have met these questions head-on, the extent to which academic theology has penetrated to the level of pastoral theology and the minds, hearts, and faith of the "common church-goer," if she or he still exists, is one that bears considerable reflection. Drewermann, after all, was condemned, at least in part, because he was "popular."[1] Yet it would also be in

---

[1] In an interview with *Der Spiegel* on 16 March 1992, Archbishop Degenhardt, who had been the one to impose the ban on Drewerman, replied to the interviewer's comment that with respect to the virgin birth of Mary, virtually all evangelical as well as catholic New Testament scholars agree with Drewermann's position, with the following: "Ganz allgemein würde ich sagen, daß es einem großen Unterschied macht, ob jemand in einem Fachbuch die Möglichkeit erörtert, es habe keine Jungfrauengeburt gegeben, oder dies provokativ vor einem Millionenpublikum als

error to view the contemporary academic theological discussion as existing in a realm of utter irrelevance, with no implications for the Church at large. The problem is the disjunction between academic and pastoral theology, and how they correlate. The crisis is how can apologetics retain, or regain, an intellectual legitimacy beyond the realm of dogmatics, without sequestering itself within a safely defined and closed hermeneutic, in order to serve as the source of a reinvigorated pastoral theology that can respond to the accusations of both critical and erroneous interpretations?

This dilemma, the tensions between academic and pastoral theology, has been one that the Church has struggled with for millennia, and is precisely the issue involved in treatments of late medieval Augustinianism. Church historians have approached the late medieval Augustinian tradition from the perspective of academic theology, maintaining the 'ivory tower' nature of the debates. Social historians, on the other hand, have dismissed both the importance and the impact of theology on late medieval society. Consequently, 'late medieval Augustinianism,' as a descriptive term of the late medieval Augustinian tradition, has been given a markedly theological character, with little need to be taken seriously when one delves beyond the realms of the history of theology.[2] As a result, the late medieval Augustinian platform, which included both pastoral and academic theology, has gone unnoticed, unrecognized, and unmourned: consequently, so has its impact on the society and culture of the later Middle Ages. If we endeavor to understand the complexities of late medieval culture, the theological endeavor of the Augustinian platform can no longer be rendered mute, relegated to the ethereal realm of ideas, which, as Platonic forms, had no real bearing on the lives of individuals. Theology, contemporary or historical, only loses its relevancy as an irreducible historical factor when no one listens, or when theology itself withdraws and encloisters itself in its own world of speculation and theoretical debate. Neither was the case

---

felsenfeste Erkenntnis verkündet." Printed in *Drewermann und die Folgen. Vom Kleriker zum Ketzer? Stationen eines Konflikts* (Munich, 1992), 165–180; 176. While Degenhardt's point is well taken, nevertheless, it comes down to being the same as saying that Drewermann's position was condemned because he was popular, which is the general impression one receives with regard to far more than his views on the virgin birth.

[2] For a discussion of the historiography dealing with "late medieval Augustinianism," see Appendix A.1.

for late medieval culture, which could still accept the level of lies and deaths that already had been perpetrated in the "name of Christ."

I. Augustinian Pastoral Theology

The mendicant Orders were established in the thirteenth century as pastoral "storm troops" for the Church. They were, as Kaspar Elm has stated, "artificial constructs, which were conceived and placed in the world by the Curia for special service."[3] As such, they were theological organizations,[4] which exerted enormous influence on the social and cultural life of late medieval Europe. Yet in the realm of historical research, there has been a bifurcation of interpretation, whereby the theology of the mendicants has been factored out of the equation for measuring their impact on the piety (*Frömmigkeit*) of late medieval religious culture. There are certainly legitimate reasons for doing so. To understand how a lay population was affected by the preaching of the mendicants, the theological question of whether God by his absolute power could undo the past, or the precise relationship between prevenient and cooperative grace is of no concern. The issue is one of "supply" and "demand" in the late medieval economy of the sacred. To interpret a religious text, a sermon text for example, or a catechetical treatise, from the perspective of "demand," or reception, the historian is not obliged to analyze the "supply-side" as well, the theological factors that lay behind the text, and that often produced the text in the first place. The fallacy enters however when the "demand-side" is seen as the only legitimate historical dimension, relegating the "supply-side" to the realm of a pure history of theology. If "demand" drove "supply" in a mono-directional late medieval economy of the sacred, there might be good reasons for leaving the "supply-side theology" to the theologians. If, however, as I will argue in this and the following chapter, the relationship between supply and demand was that of a mutually reinforcing "feed-back loop," then to understand the historical phenomena

---

[3] "Orden ... entstanden, um mit dem Blick auf das 13. Jahrhundert einige Beispiele zu nennen, wie der Augustiner-Eremitenorden, als artifizielle Gebilde, die von der Kurie für spezielle Dienste konzipiert und in die Welt gesetzt wurden." Elm, "Die Bedeutung," 72.

[4] *Ibid.*, 71–72.

of late medieval religious culture the supply is ignored only to the detriment of historical understanding. The pastoral mission of the mendicants was itself a historical phenomenon that was based upon Order-specific, mendicant theologies.

The German terms *Frömmigkeit* and *Frömmigkeitstheologie*, which can only loosely be translated as "piety" and "pastoral theology," have become established in the secondary literature concerning the endeavor to shape late medieval religious culture. Using these concepts in analyzing the late medieval Augustinian tradition, Berndt Hamm, who coined the term *Frömmigkeitstheologie*, denied the existence of an Order-specific Augustinian school.[5] Focusing on the late fifteenth-century Augustinian, Johannes von Paltz, Hamm argued that the theology of the Augustinian Order in the later Middle Ages was representative of a general pastoral theology (*Frömmigkeitstheologie*) stemming from the influence of Jean Gerson. Such a theology stressed the importance of Christian life, evidenced in the practical goal of theology, rather than philosophical or theological teaching in obedience to a theological school.[6] Pastoral theology was half-academic, but learned theology, originating from the Gersonian impulses for reform, based on the combination of a practical mysticism and nominalism.[7] It was "*the* reform theology of the fifteenth century."[8] Hamm concluded that the Augustinianism of Paltz "can only be asserted in a broad sense of the term whereby one is correct to speak of an Augustinianism of late medieval pastoral theology in general. Augustine was attractive in a completely unspecified way as a teacher of the religious

---

[5] "*Die* Augustinerschule des Mittelalters gibt es nicht." Hamm, *Frömmigkeitstheologie am Anfang des 16. Jahrhunderts. Studien zu Johannes von Paltz und seinem Umkreis*, BhTh 65 (Tübingen, 1982), 330. See also Hamm's more recent work on the theme: Hamm, "Normative Centering in the Fifteenth and Sixteenth Centuries: Observations on Religiosity, Theology, and Iconology," *JEMH* 3 (1999), 307–354; "Wollen und Nicht-Können als Thema der spätmittelalterlicher Bußseelsorge," in *Spätmittelalterliche Frömmigkeit zwischen Ideal und Praxis*, ed. Berndt Hamm and Thomas Lentes, SuRNR 15 (Tübingen, 2001), 111–146. Also noteworthy in this excellent volume is Christoph Burger, "Direkte Zuwendung zu den 'Laien' und Rückgriff auf Vermittler in spätmittelalterlicher katechetische Literatur," *ibid.*, 85–110.

[6] Hamm, *Frömmigkeitstheologie*, 5. Hamm detailed his conception of *Frömmigkeitstheologie* in his article, "Frömmigkeit als Gegenstand theologiegeschichtlicher Forschung. Methodisch-historische Überlegungen am Beispiel von Spätmittelalter und Reformation," *ZThK* 74 (1977), 464–497; *cf.*: *Frömmigkeitstheologie*, 132ff.

[7] *Frömmigkeitstheologie*, 136f; *cf.* Hamm, "Frömmigkeit als Gegenstand theologiegeschichtlicher Forschung," 479–491.

[8] Hamm, *Frömmigkeitstheologie*, 138.

life, even as the three other great western Church Fathers and Bernard of Clairvaux."[9]

Yet the practical, affective nature of theology characterized not only a general pastoral theology originating under Gersonian influence, but also the theology of the Augustinian Order itself in the later Middle Ages. As we will see, the inseparability of life and knowledge, of ethics and erudition, was not the unique contribution of Gerson, merely imitated by the likes of Paltz and Staupitz: it was the very foundation of the Augustinians' educational endeavor, and had been since 1292. The Augustinians' mendicant theology was designed to bring the fruits of the contemplative life to others by teaching and preaching so that the brothers might live not only for themselves, but also to serve the Church. If pastoral theology can be considered a genre of late medieval theology, then to a large degree the theology of the Augustinian Order throughout the fourteenth and fifteenth centuries was pastoral theology. Paltz and Staupitz may have been representatives of a pastoral theology influenced by Gerson, but they can also be seen as representatives of their Order's pastoral theology that had been pursued long before the Chancellor of Paris put pen to paper.

Hamm does not take his own definition and argument far enough. After having delineated a general pastoral theology in the later Middle Ages, and this for Hamm is above all the fifteenth and early sixteenth century, he did not pursue the question of various forms within the genre. "Decisive for the concept of piety (*Frömmigkeit*)," Hamm explained, "is the mediate (theory of piety) or immediate (practice of piety) reference to a specific way of life, whether it is to the form of the inner life or the external life."[10] It is this "specific way of life" (*bestimmte Lebensgestaltung*) that is key here. In his study of Paltz and in his critique of the hypothesis of an Augustinian school,

---

[9] "Zusammenfassend kommen wir zu dem Ergebnis, daß man bei Dorsten und Paltz einen Augustinismus nur in dem weiten Sinne feststellen kann, in dem man von einem Augustinismus der spätmittelalterlichen Frömmigkeitstheologie überhaupt zu sprechen berechtigt ist. Augustin wird auf eine ganz unspezifische Weise als Lehrer des frommen Lebens herangezogen, ebenso wie die drei anderen großen abendländischen Kirchenlehrer und Bernhard von Clairvaux." *Ibid.*, 330. For a different reading of Paltz, see my forthcoming, *The Failed Reformation*.

[10] "Entscheidend für den Begriff der Frömmigkeit ist der mittelbare (Frömmigkeitstheorie) oder unmittelbare (Frömmigkeitspraxis) Bezug zu einer bestimmten Lebensgestaltung, sei es zur Gestaltung des inneren oder zu der des äußeren Lebens." Hamm, "Frömmigkeit als Gegenstand theologiegeschichtlicher Forschung," 466.

Hamm left undetermined the possible factors comprising a "specific way of life." In an earlier article, Hamm clarified that piety "thus consists not primarily in exceptional and certainly not in original, personal spiritual predecessors, but rather manifests itself structurally as a supra-individual mentality, which can be characteristic of a religious community (for example, of a religious order or a fraternity), an occupational group, an economic class, or of a comprehensive political unity such as a city or a territory."[11] If piety (*Frömmigkeit*) is a distinctive way of life, manifested as a mentality within structures of, for example, a religious order, then the piety of a particular way of life can be expressed theologically in a pastoral theology (*Frömmigkeitstheologie*). Hamm denied the existence of the Augustinian school based on his characterization of a general pastoral theology of the later Middle Ages without investigating the question as to the theological expression of the way of life manifested structurally within the mentality of the Augustinian Order.

It is, however, precisely at this level of analysis that the Augustinian school, as the self-understanding of the Augustinian theologians, is to be found. As Elm affirmed, the founding fathers of the mendicants passed on to their orders the desire to follow in their footsteps and to realize their intentions, functioning as their source for "adapting themselves to new situations, not only to renew themselves, but also to change themselves, and thus not only to confirm their existence, but also in a time in which the new was seen as suspect, to make possible their legitimacy by innovation."[12] In this light, rather than being either an abstract label employed by scholars to describe particular aspects and/or characteristics of selected texts of selected Augustinian theologians, or dismissed out of hand, being dissolved into a general late medieval pastoral theology, 'late medieval Augus-

---

[11] "Sie [Frömmigkeit] besteht dann nicht primär in exzeptionellen und erst recht nicht in originell-persönlichen Seelenvorgängernen, sondern erweist sich eher strukturell als überindividuell-prägende Mentalität, die typisch sein kann für eine religiöse Lebensgemeinschaft (z.B. einen Orden oder eine Bruderschaft), eine Berufsgruppe, eine Einkommensschicht oder für eine umfassende politische Einheit wie eine Stadt oder ein Territorium." *Ibid.*, 468.

[12] "Die Gründer und Gründungsväter, die Absicht, sie zu verstehen, und der Wille, ihre Intentionen zu verwirklichen, erwiesen sich nicht selten als Kräfte, die es erlaubten, sich nicht nur zu behaupten, sondern auch neuen Situationen anzupassen, sich nicht nur zu erneuern, sondern auch zu verändern, also nicht nur den Bestand zu sichern, sondern in einer Zeit, in der das Neue als suspekt empfunden wurde, die Legitimation von Innovationen zu ermöglichen." Elm, "Die Bedeutung," 90.

tinianism' signifies the historical phenomena that *produced* the texts of the tradition. Late medieval Augustinianism was the ideology of the Order's religious identity that effected the textualization of Augustine's heritage, providing in turn the pre-text, the pre-understanding, of the Order's textual production.[13] The endeavor to imitate Augustine in all aspects of the religious life, to follow Augustine's religion, yielded the new Augustine scholarship as a by-product of the Augustinian platform. As a historical phenomenon, late medieval Augustinianism was the "cultural ethic" of Augustine's religion.

The texts authored by Augustinian Hermits in the later Middle Ages attest to their pastoral endeavor and to their own pursuit of an Augustinian *Frömmigkeitstheologie*. Commentaries on Aristotle or Lombard comprise only a small portion of the Augustinian literary achievement.[14] Biblical commentaries and exegetical handbooks, sermon collections, treatises on spiritual life, catechetical works focusing on the Ten Commandments, the Lord's Prayer, the articles of faith, the Ave Maria, and the Creed, and works of practical theology form the largest portion of the Order's textual production. Moreover, many of these works are extant in numerous manuscripts and early printed editions, found in libraries of all the mendicant Orders, as well as those of the Carthusian, Benedictines and secular clergy.

Particularly noteworthy is the triumvirate of Augustinians at Erfurt in the early fourteenth century, names we have already met, namely, Jordan and his two colleagues, Henry of Friemar and Hermann of Schildesche. Henry of Friemar (the Elder) was prior provincial of the German province from 1296 to 1299, before he went to Paris to read the *Sentences* in 1300. Having completed his studies, Henry was regent master in Paris from 1305 to 1312, and then moved to Erfurt to assume the same position at the Order's *studium generale* there, where Jordan was named associate lecturer (*lector secundarius*) in 1322. Henry, best known as an ascetic and mystical author, served as Jordan's mentor, exercising a considerable influence on his younger colleague. As we have already seen, Henry's *Tractatus de origine et progressu ordinis fratrum eremitarum sancti Augustini* was a major source for Jordan's *Liber Vitasfratrum*, and in his *Expositio Orationis Dominice* Jordan

---

[13] See Appendix A.1.
[14] See Saak, "The Reception of Augustine," 369–370.

took over large sections *in toto* from Henry's work of the same title.[15] As with Jordan, Henry's extensive writings, including numerous sermons, philosophical, and theological treatises, are still largely unknown. This is especially true for his *Tractatus de decem preceptis*, one of the most widely circulated commentaries on the Ten Commandments of the later Middle Ages, extant in 259 manuscripts and eight incunabula editions, and translated into low German and early Dutch.[16]

Joining Henry in Erfurt during Jordan's early years there was Hermann of Schildesche. Born c. 1290, Hermann was lector in Erfurt from 1324 to 1326, and then in Cologne from 1328 to 1329, having previously served in the same office at Magdeburg. Hermann thereafter was sent to Paris, where in 1330–31 or 1331–32 he read the *Sentences* and received the doctorate in theology in 1334.[17] As seen in Chapter One, Hermann's *Tractatus contra haereticos*, dedicated to John XXII, was formed by the works of Augustine, and shortly thereafter, in the year of his promotion to the *magisterium*, Hermann preached an extensive sermon on his Order's *pater noster*. After serving as prior provincial of the Saxon-Thuringian province of the OESA, Hermann spent the last seventeen years of his life working as general vicar and regent master of theology for the bishop of Würzburg. Hermann's most widely circulated work, the *Speculum manuale sacerdotum*, has never been the focus of separate study.[18] Yet

---

[15] On Henry see Cl. Stroick, *Heinrich von Friemar: Leben, Werke, philosophisch-theologische Stellung in der Scholastik*, FTS 58 (Freiburg i. Br., 1954); Zumkeller, "Die Augustinerschule des Mittelalters: Vertreter und Philosophisch-Theologische Lehre," *AAug.* 27 (1964), 167–262; 200–201.

[16] See Zumkeller *MSS* nr. 325 (144–152). Henry's treatise was often published as the *Praeceptorium* of Nicolaus of Lyra. Henry's ethical and moral teaching, which include his *Commentaria in decem libros Ethicorum*, given as lectures in the Paris *studium* in 1310, form the core of his much larger *oeuvre*, consisting of sermons and smaller treatises, such as his *Sermones de tempore*, which he explicitly mentions he composed *ad eruditionem iuvenum fratrum*, his *Sermones super epistolas et evangelia dominicalia*, his *Tractatus de vitiis*, and his *Expositio Passionis Dominice*, known as well by the title, *Passio Domini litteraliter et moraliter explanata*, and his widely circulated and already edited *Tractatus de quatuor instinctibus*: A. Zumkeller and Robert G. Aarnock eds., *Traktat Heinrichs von Friemar über die Unterscheidung der Geister. Lateinsch-mittelhochdeutsche Textausgabe mit Untersuchungen* (Würzburg, 1977).

[17] See Kunzelmann, *Geschichte*, 5:26ff; Zumkeller, *Hermann v. Schildesche O.E.S.A. (d. 8 Juli 1357), zur 600. Wiederkehr seines Todestages*, Cassiciacum 14 (Würzburg, 1957); idem, *Schrifttum*; idem, "Die Augustinerschule," 210f; idem, "Hermann von Schildesche," in *VerLex* 3: 1107–1112.

[18] For the genre of pastoral manuals, see the excellent study by Peter Dykema, *Conflicting Expectations: Parish Priests in Late Medieval Germany*, Unpublished Ph.D. dissertation, University of Arizona, 1998. I would like to thank Dr. Dykema for

this treatise was one of the most popular educational handbooks for the clergy in the later Middle Ages. Written for the common parish priest, and focusing on the sacraments of baptism, the eucharist, and confession, Hermann's *Speculum* was printed nine times before 1500 and is extant in more than 160 manuscripts, with ten separate dedications.[19] Moreover, among his numerous works, of special note is his *Claustrum Animae*, composed between 1347 and 1349, which is a comprehensive explication of the religious life that had its origins in a series of German sermons he gave in Erfurt in 1324–1326, dedicated to Countess Elizabeth of Rabenswald, whose father confessor Hermann had been.[20] Hermann's *Claustrum Animae* bears close similarity in content, structure, and purpose, to the *Liber de vita monastica* of the fifteenth-century Augustinian Conrad of Zenn, which has been seen as the exemplary work of observant spirituality, and thus lacked an Order-specific character.[21] Equally of significance is Hermann's *Introductorium Iuris*, extent in forty-one manuscripts,[22] completed by 1334 and dedicated to Count Eberhard von der Mark, provost of Huy and canon of Cologne and Lüttick.[23]

Jordan himself contributed substantially to this Augustinian pastoral endeavor, beginning with his first teaching position in Erfurt. Given his extensive sermon collections, it is all the more unfortunate that Jordan remains virtually unknown to modern scholars of late medieval religion, theology, and piety.[24] This is particularly the case with regard to his *Expositio Orationis Dominice* and his *Meditationes de Passione Christi*. Though no general treatment of late medieval

---

providing me with a copy of his dissertation. In this work, Dykema focuses on fifteenth century texts, and thus Hermann is not discussed. In a recent article Dykema has taken his work further into the sixteenth century; see Dykema, "Handbooks for Pastors: Late Medieval Manuals for Parish Priests and Conrad Porta's *Pastorale Lutheri* (1582)," in *Continuity and Change*, 143–162.

[19] Zumkeller *MSS* nr. 319 (187–193). Zumkeller lists 148 manuscripts in his catalogue, yet in his biographical entry in *VerLex*, he mentions that Hermann's treatise "... liegt in mehr als 160 Hss. und 10 inkunabeldrucken vor." Zumkeller, "Hermann von Schildesche," *VerLex* 3:1111; *cf.* Zumkeller, *Schrifttum*, 47.

[20] Zumkeller, *Schrifttum und Lehre*, 67–78.

[21] See Hellmut Zschoch, *Klosterreform und monastische Spiritualität im 15. Jahrhundert. Conrad von Zenn OESA (d. 1460) und sein Liber de vita monastica*, BhTh 75 (Tübingen, 1988); *cf.* Weinbrenner, *Klosterreform*; and A. Zumkeller, "Der 'Liber de Vita Monastica' des Conradus de Zenn O.E.S.A. (d. 1460) und die Spiritualität der spätmittelalterlichen 'Observantia Regularis'," *Revista Agustiniana* 33 (1992), 921–938.

[22] Zumkeller *MSS* nr. 385 (183–184).

[23] Zumkeller, *Schrifttum und Lehre*, 88–95.

[24] See E.L. Saak, *Religio Augustini*, 13–41.

Passion literature or Passion devotion gives a central place to Jordan, the *Meditationes* are extant in 104 manuscripts of the Latin text (all but two of which date from the fifteenth century), thirty-seven manuscripts of German and Dutch translations, nine incunabula editions,[25] and as incorporated within his *Opus Postillarum* as *sermones* 189–254, there are at least an additional thirty-seven manuscripts.[26] In short,

---

[25] Zumkeller *MSS* nr. 646–646c (293–301).

[26] Zumkeller lists 153 manuscripts that contain at least part of Jordan's *Opus Postillarum*. The *Meditationes*, as sermones 189–254, were part of the *prima tertiae partis* of the four parts of the work. Based on Zumkeller's list, there are at least 37 manuscripts containing the *prima tertiae partis*, although a definitive and analytical listing of the manuscripts of Jordan's *Opus Postillarum* remains to be done. For the early Dutch translations, see Lievens, *Jordanus van Quedlinburg*; J.M. Willeumier-Schalij, "De LXV Artkelen van de Passie van Jordanus van Quedlinburg in Middelnederlandse handschriften," *OGE* 53 (1979), 15–35, which includes an edition of the Dutch translations of the prayers of the sixty-five articles (23–35); and Philip E. Weber, "Varieties of Popular Piety Suggested by Netherlandic *Vita Christi* Prayer Cycles," *OGE* 64 (1990), 195–226. There is also evidence that Jordan's *Meditationes* influenced later medieval British devotional literature; see J.T. Rhodes, "Prayers of the Passion: From Jordanus of Quedlinburg to John Fewterer of Syon," in *Durham University Journal* LXXXV #1; n.s. LIV #1 (1993), 27–38. Based on early printed editions and late fifteenth-century manuscripts, Rhodes claims that a distinction is to be made between the work that circulated under the title *Meditationes Jordani*, which may have been the compilation of an early printer, and Jordan's genuine *Articuli passionis*. Rhodes comments: "The title *Meditationes de Passione Christi* had been attached rather indiscriminately to what are, in fact, two different works." (27) From the fourteenth- and earlier fifteenth-century manuscript tradition, however, there is no question that Jordan was the author of the *Meditationes de Passione Christi*. It seems probable that what Rhodes views as two distinct works was actually the result of the wide distribution and diffusion of Jordan's one work. This is certainly the case for the Dutch tradition, which, as Lievens has shown, consisted both of the complete treatise, as well as independently circulated excerpts compiled therefrom; see Lievens, *Jordanus van Quedlinburg*, 37–51. Only the critical edition of Jordan's *Meditationes de Passione Christi*, however, will clarify the highly complex manuscript and early printed traditions of this most influential work. Given the manuscript tradition, it is thus all the more surprising that Jordan appears as a mere name dropped in the most recent works on Passion literature: see *Die Passion Christi in Literatur und Kunst des Spätmittelalters*, ed. Walter Haug and Burghart Wachinger (Tübingen, 1993); Giles Constable, *Three Studies in Medieval Religious and Social Thought* (Cambridge, 1995); Thomas H. Bestul, *Texts of the Passion. Latin Devotional Literature and Medieval Society* (Philadelphia, 1996); and *The Broken Body. Passion Devotion in Late Medieval Culture*, eds. A.A. MacDonald, H.N.B. Ridderbos, and R.M. Schlusemann (Groningen, 1998). Bestul gives exemplary evidence for how little Jordan is known when he writes: "The fourteenth-century *Meditationes de Passione Christi* of Jordan of Quedlinburg has left little manuscript evidence, but the work was printed at least six times before 1500 and thus seems to have been popular into the fifteenth century. The meditations, comparatively restrained in emotional fervor, begin with a discussion of the twelve fruits of meditation on the Passion, and continue with a series of prayers organized around the sixty-five articles." Bestul, *Texts*, 60; *cf. ibid.*, 191. Bestul seems unaware of the extensive manuscript tradition, the earliest manuscripts of which

Jordan's *Meditationes* was the most widely disseminated work on the Passion written by an Augustinian in the later Middle Ages.[27]

The works of Jordan, Hermann, and Henry, together with those of their confreres, were all directed toward forming and shaping the religious life of their co-religious as well as that of their society. In short, they comprised the endeavor of the Augustinian *Frömmigkeitstheologie* even before the reform campaign of Jean Gerson. Moreover, their works were being copied and printed repeatedly throughout the later Middle Ages, which indicates that they were also being read and used. Yet this itself raises the problem of interpretation. To what extent can we say that such works were the products of a general pastoral endeavor, and to what extent were they the products of the Augustinian platform? My argument is that they were both. To place the Augustinians' texts in the former category in order to negate the influence of the latter, is either to base such a determination on a theological, rather than on a historical understanding of 'Augustinianism,' or, is to dismiss as historically irrelevant the historical ideology that produced the texts in the first place. *Frömmigkeitstheologie* is a useful construct, but it must not be allowed to obscure the Order-specific theological platforms inherent in the production of the texts themselves, a platform that for the Augustinians, as we will see, was based upon the cultivation of "spiritual knowledge."

Henry, Hermann, and Jordan, wrote their works for all Christians. They were viscerally engaged in their Order's campaign to "Christianize" their world, a campaign that was fundamental to the Augustinian platform itself based on the model of Augustine. To interpret their achievements—Henry's exposition of the Ten Commandments, Jordan's exposition of the Lord's Prayer, or his meditations on the Passion of Christ, Hermann's handbook for parish priests—as examples of a general pastoral theology that had nothing to do with 'Augustinianism,' simply because a theological analysis of such works yields little if anything that is specifically 'Augustinian' in a

---

include no mention whatsoever of the fruits of the Passion, as well as of the possibility that Jordan was the originator of the sixty-five articles, or at least together with Ludolph of Saxony, was the major source for the sixty-five articles in the later Middle Ages. A.A. MacDonald, however, does recognize Jordan's importance; MacDonald, "Passion Devotion in Late-Medieval Scotland," in *The Broken Body*, 109–131; 128; see also Chapter Five below, and Appendix F.

[27] See Chapter Five below, and Appendix F. Jordan's *Expositio Orationis Dominice* forms the core of the present chapter.

technical, academic theological sense, is myopic, and is blind to the endeavor. Moreover, to find such a pastoral theological program originating only with Gerson that then flourished in the fifteenth century, is to ignore the historical record. The religious identity of Augustine's hermits demanded that they live their lives and their theology to serve the Church. The verbal nature must not be missed. The platform was to be pursued. The theological endeavor of the Augustinians was not restricted to producing masters of theology, or even preachers and teachers for the Order. It was designed to educate every member of Christendom, for Augustine was not only the Order's father, he was also the wise architect of the Church. As such, he was uniquely the teacher of his Order of hermit friars, whose theological endeavor was the vivification of the image of Augustine as the Augustinians' *preceptor*.

II. Spiritual Knowledge: The Augustinian Theological Core

"Blessed Augustine," Jordan explained in the *Liber Vitasfratrum*, "is our teacher for the religious life. Hence in this work I often refer to him as our teacher."[28] If it were not for the analogy Jordan used to illustrate what he meant by Augustine as teacher, one might easily pass over this comment as just another expression of admiration for his Order's mythic founder. Augustine was the Order's teacher neither as a wise spiritual director, nor as the master of apprentices. The equation Jordan gave for the meaning of *preceptor* in the phrase *preceptor noster* is one of professor and students: "Just as scholastic doctors and masters (*doctores et magistri*) are called teachers... so even is blessed Augustine our teacher..."[29] In his *Opus Postillarum* Jordan listed teaching among the spiritual alms,[30] and in the *Liber Vitasfratrum* he warned of the danger a solitary anchorite faced: without teaching the anchorite could easily slip into doctrinal error regarding the articles of faith and the holy scriptures.[31] Moreover, for the Augustinians

---

[28] "... beatus Augustinus est praeceptor noster in disciplina regulari. Unde et in hoc opere frequenter ipsum praeceptorem nostrum appellavi." *VF* 2,14 (178,369–371).

[29] "Unde doctores et magistri scholastici dicuntur praeceptores... Sic etiam beatus Augustinus est praeceptor noster..." *VF* 2,14 (178,364–369).

[30] Jor. *OP* sermo 439E (ed. Strassburg, 1483); see note 71 below.

[31] *VF* 1,5 (18,6–10).

teaching was part and parcel of the contemplative life.[32] It was in this sense of teaching that Jordan referred to Augustine as "our teacher." Augustine's precepts were to be understood *doctrinaliter*.[33] To follow in the footsteps of Augustine required more than merely living according to his *Rule*. If "to be an Augustinian" entailed accepting Augustine as teacher, Augustine's doctrine must be taught.

The Augustinians propagated the image of Augustine as the teacher of his hermits beginning in the early fourteenth century.[34] As Nicholas of Alessandria preached in 1332 in Paris, Augustine was the "leader, teacher, head, and father of the Hermits,"[35] the same list of attributes that John XXII listed in his Bull *Veneranda sanctorum* granting the OESA custody of Augustine's body. Augustine as the Order's teacher was an image that received its earliest expressions in the literary tradition, and then was expressed visually in manuscript miniatures and Church frescos.[36] Augustine as teacher was integral to the Order's identity, and yielded an Augustinian mendicant theology, whereby in the endeavor to maintain the Order's social bonds, the Order sought to inculcate its members with the doctrine of Augustine from the very first day a novice entered the Order. The emerging Augustinian platform institutionalized the Augustinian myth based on the image of Augustine as *pater et preceptor noster*. This enterprise was carried out by the theological program of the Augustinian *studia*.

---

[32] See E.L. Saak, "Saints in Society," 322–323.

[33] *VF* 2,14 (178,362–364).

[34] Concluding his study of thirteenth- and early fourteenth-century sermons on Augustine by Augustinian Hermits, Balbino Rano affirmed: "Los *Sermones sobre S. Augustín* de los citados Agustinos del primer siglo de la existencia de la Orden nos presentan bien a S. Agustín como Maestro de los miembros de la Orden." B. Rano, "San Agustín y su Orden en algunos Sermones de Agustinos del primer siglo (1244–1344)," *AAug.* 53 (1990), 7–93; 92.

[35] "Sic ergo apparet quod beatus Augustinus dux, magister, caput et pater fuit heremitarum." Nic.Al. *Sermo* (373).

[36] Dorothee Hansen has studied the artistic representations of Augustine as the Order's teacher; Dorothee Hansen, *Das Bild des Ordenslehrers und die Allegorie des Wissens. Ein gemaltes Programm der Augustiner* (Berlin, 1995). Hansen claims: "Das Bild des Ordenslehrers und die Allegorie des Wissens entstand... in den 40er Jahren des 14. Jh. Ihr Thema ist nicht der fromme Mönch und Regelstifter, sondern der Intellektuelle Augustinus, der *praeceptor* der Gelehrsamkeit des Ordens. Dieser Aspekt interessierte die frühen Ordenshistoriker Heinrich v. Friemar und Jordan v. Sachsen noch wenig." (39). Reconstructing the earlier representational program from the frescos in the Augustinian church of St. Andrea in Ferrara and the Augustinian Cortelleri Chapel in Padua, together with manuscript miniatures, Hansen argues that the image of Augustine as teacher of the Order was the creation of the Augustinian Hermits. The similar depiction of St. Thomas, found in the Spanish Chapel

In 1292, when the Augustinian Order was struggling to achieve recognition, Giles of Rome set the Hermits on their path, calling for the creation of theological schools, together with regular observance, as the two pillars of the Order that would make for its growth and establishment. Thirty years later, when Jordan of Quedlinburg left Paris to assume the office of lector in his home province, the Order was still facing difficult times, and was soon to become embroiled in the papal-imperial conflict that led to the creation of the Order's identity. Upon the conclusion of the General Chapter in Florence of 1326, which had issued such strong warnings against possible defection from the Order in support of those rebellious against the Church, Prior General William of Cremona, as he was completing his *Reprobatio* of the six articles drawn from the *Defensor Pacis*, wrote a letter to all provinces of the Order in which he set forth measures to combat what he saw as the ruin of the religious life.[37] "Our holy and venerable religion," William lamented, "is spiritually collapsed and has fallen away from all observance of its heritage and holy *Constitutions*."[38] Such conditions resulted most of all from the negligence of the Order's prelates, who wore the habit in vain, living as seculars rather than as examples of the Christian life.[39] Therefore, William declared, before a friar assumed an office of leadership, a thorough investigation was to be conducted to assure that the candidate was worthy of the position. This was necessary because incapable and evil prelates were the chief cause of the Order's dilapidated state.[40]

---

of Santa Maria Novella in Florence, was derived from the original Augustinian image (*ibid.*, 3). The textual representation then followed the pictorial, the latter being taken up in the Order's historiography only in the early fifteenth century with humanist influence (*ibid.*, 39). Hansen's work is of central importance for establishing the priority of the Augustinian image of Augustine as the Order's *preceptor*, especially in comparison to the similar Dominican depiction. Yet she underestimates the role of the literary tradition in the creation of the representation. Contrary to Hansen's claim that Henry of Friemar and Jordan had little interest in Augustine as *preceptor* of the Order, the textual evidence from the works of Jordan, Henry, and other early fourteenth-century Augustinians testify to the fact that the portrayal of Augustine not only as the founder of the Order, but also as the Order's teacher was prominent, and indeed, preceded the artistic representations by a decade.

[37] *AAug.* 4 (1911/12), 29; *cf.* William's letter of 14 April 1328 to the convent at Paris, *AAug.* 4 (1911/12), 57–65.

[38] "... sacra et veneranda nostra Religio ... sit spiritualiter et collapsa et ab omni observantia paternarum traditionum et sacrarum constitutionum defecit ..." *AAug.* 4 (1911/1912), 29.

[39] *AAug.* 4 (1911/12), 29.

[40] *AAug.* 4 (1911/12), 29–30.

Second on William's list was the need to maintain faithful celebration of the canonical hours. No brother was exempt, except for those seriously ill, lectors with teaching responsibilities, and brothers who were necessarily absent. Worship (*cultus divinus*) was the primary duty of the Christian. The onus of enforcing proper and devoted performance of the divine office lay with the prior, who was to reprimand and correct the negligence of the brothers under his care as diligently as he was his own.[41]

With this letter, William reaffirmed the definitions of the General Chapter at Florence. At Florence the Chapter had mandated that provincial priors were responsible for punishing and correcting the errors of the brothers within their province, with love for the individual but hate for the vice. Visitations were to be conducted and any negligence that could not be ameliorated effectively was to be dealt with publicly in the next Provincial Chapter.[42] Just as William called for examinations to approve a candidate for promotion to office, so had the Chapter at Florence strictly ordered that no brother should be promoted to the office of lector unless he was sufficiently learned in logic, philosophy, and theology.[43] Indeed, regulating theological studies was one of the leading issues for the definitions of the entire Chapter. Yet if this endeavor to assure the level of prerequisite instruction for the degree of lector seems here to be combined artificially with William's intent for the priors to enforce proper worship, it was not so in the eyes of the new lector in Erfurt. In Jordan's mind, theological studies were part and parcel of the divine cult.

For Jordan, as for William and Gregory of Rimini, the foundation of the religious life was worship. The *cultus divinus* was the life of prayer; "but because the brothers are not able to pray all the time," he instructed, "they ought, therefore, to spend certain hours in study."[44] Jordan cited Hugh of St. Victor's commentary on the *Rule* to affirm that the combination of prayer and study was the means to conquer the devil and attain eternal blessedness,[45] and

---

[41] *AAug.* 4 (1911/12), 30.
[42] Esteban, *AAug.* 4 (1911/12), 8–9; cf. Esteban, *AAug.* 3 (1909/10), 245.
[43] Esteban, *AAug.* 4 (1911/12), 6; cf. the decree of the General Chapter at Viterbo in 1312, Esteban, *AAug.* 3 (1909/10), 153.
[44] "Quia vero non semper fratres possunt actualiter orare, debent ergo certis horis etiam legere." *VF* 2,22 (233,2–3).
[45] *VF* 2,22 (234,23–33); cf. Hug.SV. *Reg.* 9 (912).

Augustine was the model. Augustine had prescribed study in his *Rule*, and when he himself was not observing the canonical hours or providing for the needs of the Church, he spent his time studying the Holy Scriptures.[46] Augustine was the first of the Order's professors (*huius religionis professores*); all subsequent followed in his footsteps.[47]

In the chapter on the study of scripture in the *Liber Vitasfratrum*, Jordan gave a list of the outstanding theologians of the Augustinian Order, complete with an enumeration of their works, from Giles of Rome, the first of the Order's theologians after Augustine, to Hermann of Schildesche. He then began the following chapter by claiming: "But beyond these types of knowledge, which are acquired by [listening to] the words of teachers and study, is another type of knowledge, namely, spiritual knowledge, which is not attained except through divine illumination."[48] Prerequisite to the gift of spiritual knowledge (*scientia spiritualis*), Jordan claimed, calling explicitly upon the tradition stemming from John Cassian, were the following four attributes: purity of heart, humility of mind, piety of prayer, and fecundity of works.[49] Cassian divided *scientia* into practical and theoretical knowledge, whereby the former concerned ethics, and the latter consisted in knowledge of the divine received in contemplation.[50] He continued by further dividing theoretical knowledge into the historical and spiritual senses of scripture; knowledge of the spiritual senses was equated with spiritual knowledge. The pure, ethical life grounded in practical knowledge was the foundation for progressing to spiritual knowledge: "For it is impossible," he wrote, "that an impure mind can acquire the gift of spiritual knowledge."[51] The scholar, in short, must also be pious, "for we attain to the revelation of [divine] secrets," Jordan explained in his *Opus Jor*, "more by the devotion of prayer than by rational investigation."[52] Of these

---

[46] *VF* 2,22 (233,3–5) and *VF* 2,22 (235,64–66).
[47] *VF* 2,22 (235,69–236,72).
[48] "Sed praeter has scientias, quae docentium verbis et studio lectionis acquiruntur, est alia scientia, scilicet spiritualis, quae non nisi per illuminationem divinam attingitur." *VF* 2,23 (242,2–4).
[49] *VF* 2,23 (242,4–245,80).
[50] Cassian. coll.pat. 14,1 (954B–955A). For a discussion of Cassian, see B. McGinn, *The Foundations of Mysticism. Origins to the Fifth Century* (New York, 1994), 218–227.
[51] "Impossibile namque est immundam mentem donum scientiae spiritalis adipisci." Cassian. coll.pat. 14,10 (970A); *cf.* Cassian. coll.pat. 14,8 (962B) and 14,9 (966B).
[52] "Magis enim proficimus ad secretorum revelationem orationis devotione quam a rationis investigatione..." Jor. *OJ* sermo 197, fol. 307vb.

four prerequisites for spiritual knowledge, humility reigned supreme: "the more one humbles oneself in prayer before God, the more God illumines him."[53] Humility was so important because it counteracts the effects of the fall, "for just as pride was the reason the angels were expelled from heaven and humans from paradise, so contrarily is humility the way we are led back to paradise."[54] Thus Jordan's characterization of spiritual knowledge, combined with his explicit reference to Cassian, places this term squarely in the context of Jordan's monastic spirituality.

This does not imply, however, that such knowledge was confined to the contemplative retreat of the brothers in their cells. The contrast made is not between knowledge and wisdom; Jordan was not setting in opposition the knowledge of the schools and the wisdom of the cloisters. The distinction is between knowledge that is spiritual and knowledge that is not; "book learning" can only take one so far. There is a continuum: study leads to illumination, which in turn yields spiritual knowledge. Jordan was no stranger to the schools. In his lectures on Matthew held in the *studium* at Erfurt in 1327, Jordan equated this spiritual knowledge with the Holy Spirit's gift of knowledge (*donum scientie*), associated with the fifth petition of the *Pater Noster*, "forgive us our debts." The gift of knowledge was prerequisite to justice and righteousness.[55] In this light, just as his chapter *De spirituali scientia* followed directly his treatment of his Order's university theologians, Jordan's spiritual knowledge should not itself be cloistered behind the walls of monastic spirituality; it is to be interpreted in the context of mendicant education within the Augustinian *studia*. One could penetrate the innermost core of holy scripture only with a knowledge that was spiritual, and the teaching and

---

[53] "... et quanto quis in oratione se coram deo plus humiliat, tanto dominus illum magis illuminat." Jor. *OJ* sermo 197, fol. 307vb.

[54] "Sicut enim superbia fuit in via, qua angelis de celo et homo de paradiso expulsus fuit, sic per contrarium humilitas est via, qua ad paradisum reducimur." Jor. *OJ* sermo 198, fol. 309ra; cf. *VF* 2,7 (114,75–117,184).

[55] "De donis introducitur hic scientia, quia dicit *Glossa* super Mattheum: Cum dicimus *dimitte nobis debita nostra*, spiritum scientie rogamus, quo delicta intelligimus que sine spiritu sancto non intelliguntur. Unde propheta in psalmo querit: *delicta quis intelligit?* [Ps. 18:13], quasi dicat, nullus nisi cui tu donum scientie dederis. Et ideo statim subdit *ab occultis meis munda me, domine* [Ps. 18:13]. Nec etiam possumus esse iusti nisi reddamus cuique debitum suum, sed quid sit illud debitum quod tenemur cuique nescimus nisi per donum scientie." Jor. *Exp.* 7, fol. 84ra; cf. *Glos.ord.* ad Matth. 6:12 (ed. Strassburg, 1480/1), IV.25B; (ed. Venice, 1588), V.25E.

interpretation of scripture was the fundamental goal of the theological endeavor.

Most often medieval theology has been distinguished by the division between monastic and scholastic theology, or partitioned by the veil running between scholastic theology and spirituality, the latter of which can include ascetic or mystical theology.[56] The distinction between a monastic and a scholastic theology appears to break down, however, when one considers, for example, the works of the anonymous Benedictine at Oxford known simply as the Monachus Niger, or the Cistercian Peter Ceffons at Paris.[57] In addition, the rise of the mendicants introduces another piece in the puzzle, for these cloistered religious, neither seculars nor monks in the strict sense, quickly became the leading theologians of the universities. If the terms 'monastic theology' and 'scholastic theology' are to be descriptive of the historical record, rather than abstract labels signifying genres of theology independent from historical theologians, a third approach to theology must be recognized: mendicant theology. 'Mendicant theology' is introduced to signify the theology that stood between monastic and scholastic theology. It was a theology thoroughly integrated within the universities, yet one that found its source in the religious life of the mendicant cloister and pastoral endeavor.

"Few areas of late medieval life," wrote a leading scholar of the late medieval universities, "seem as removed from spirituality as the university classrooms of late scholasticism. The highly abstract, rational, logic-oriented theology of the late Middle Ages... seem[s] to contrast markedly with the deeply emotional religious commitment associated with monastic spirituality or the various forms of lay piety."[58] William Courtenay continued by pointing to the religious

---

[56] See Jean Leclercq, "Monastic and Scholastic Theology in the Reformers of the Fourteenth to Sixteenth Century," in *From Cloister to Classroom. Monastic and Scholastic Approaches to Truth*, ed. E. Rozanne Elder (Kalamazoo, Michigan, 1986), 178–201; 194, and Ulrich Köpf, "Monastische Theologie im 15. Jahrhundert," in *Rottenburger Jahrbuch für Kirchengeschichte* 11 (1992), 117–135. *Cf.* John H. Van Engen, *Rupert of Deutz* (Berkeley, 1983), 367f.

[57] For Monachus Niger see W.J. Courtenay, "The 'Sentences'-Commentary of Stukle: A New Source for Oxford Theology in the Fourteenth Century," *Traditio* 34 (1978), 435–438; Paul A. Streveler, "Gregory of Rimini and the Black Monk on Sense and Reference: An Example of Fourteenth Century Philosophical Analysis," *Vivarium* 18 (1980), 67–78; and W.J. Courtenay, *Schools and Scholars, passim*; for Ceffons, see Trapp, "Peter Ceffons of Clairvaux," *RThAM* 24 (1957), 101–154.

[58] William J. Courtenay, "Spirituality and Late Scholasticism," in *Christian Spirituality. High Middle Ages and Reformation*, ed. Jill Raitt (London, 1987), 109–120; 109.

life of the universities and the place of the Bible in the curriculum in attempt to shed light on the relationship of the seemingly separate. The disparity between the actual importance of Biblical study and the "amount of time devoted to it"[59] in the late medieval universities highlights the seeming distinction between theology and spirituality. Yet upon further investigation this apparent disharmony might itself prove unseemly, for it was the study of holy scripture that was "the end of all knowledge," and "if [holy scripture] will enter your heart with wisdom and please your soul with knowledge, [divine] council will uphold you and prudence will guide you so that you might be snatched away from the path of evil." Thus wrote the fourteenth-century Augustinian Alphonsus Vargas in the prologue to his commentary on the first book of Lombard.[60] This was his point of departure, his "launch pad" into the realm of "highly abstract," "logic-oriented" theology. Behind the scholastic theology of the mendicants, indeed informing their distinctions and questions, definitions and resolutions, was an "emotional religious commitment associated with monastic spirituality."[61] It was indeed their prologue, that which came first and established the parameters for what followed, placing the frame around their abstract portrait of the theological landscape. Historians have interpreted the individual lines and forms of these masterpieces, but the overall schemes and purposes have often been missed. Single cubes of these late medieval Piccaso's have been analyzed without recognition of the intended impression. Thus the seeming disparity between theology and spirituality.

Within mendicant theology such distinctions are untenable. Another schema must be found, one that fathoms the spirituality *of* theology, one that strives not to sever the head from the heart of the late medieval theologian. Thus I turn to the Augustinians themselves to seek a characterization of theology that historically and descriptively gives a place to the Order's mendicant theology. For the late medieval Augustinians, theology was not a science of speculative abstraction, but was one of affections and praxis.

---

[59] *Ibid.*, 111.

[60] "... quia si intraverit sapientia cor tuum et scientia anime tue placuerit, consilium custodiet te et prudentia diriget te ut eruaris de via mala... Est igitur sacra scriptura omnium scientiarum finis." Alfon. *Sent.* Prol. (ed. Venice, 1490), 1,42–44; 2,23–24.

[61] Courtenay, "Spirituality and Late Scholasticism," 109.

In 1335, when Jordan was leaving Erfurt for Magdeburg, as the case of Archbishop Burchard's murder was still running its course, his confrere Thomas of Strassburg began his lectures on the *Sentences* in Paris. For Thomas the traditional distinction between speculative knowledge (*scientia speculativa*) and practical knowledge (*scientia practica*) was insufficient for theology.[62] The goal of theology, its most noble object and end, was not cognitive speculation of the divine essence, but love of the creator and redeemer.[63] Thus there was another type of knowledge above the speculative and practical, about which the ancient philosophers knew nothing: affective knowledge (*scientia affectiva*). "The philosophers," Thomas explained, "did not know another love that would be more noble than speculative [knowledge], which would be the end in itself of speculation."[64] This is not, however, a condemnation of philosophy. Philosophy cannot be blamed for its ignorance; it was simply unaware of Christian love. "For if," as Thomas continued, "the philosophers had known such love, or had been able [to know such love], they necessarily would have posited an affective knowledge, whose end in itself would have been such love because they would have directed the speculation of knowledge towards this type of love."[65] By and large the Dominicans under the influence of Thomas Aquinas focused on the speculative nature of theology, and the Franciscans, in the wake of Bonaventure, on the practical. Theology

---

[62] On this distinction, drawn from the third book of Aristotle's *Nicomachean Ethics*, see Ulrich Köpf, *Die Anfänge der theologischen Wissenschaftstheorie im 13. Jahrhundert* (Tübingen, 1974), esp. 198ff. Albert the Great was the first to treat the question explicitly; *ibid.*, 201.

[63] "... divisio illa est insufficiens: quia sacra theologia non attingit suum objectum per solam cognitionem; nec per practicam directionem: sed principaliter, et nobilissime attingit ipsum per supernam dilectionem ... illa divisio similiter est insufficiens: quia finis theologie, nec est cognitio veritatis etc., sed est ipsa caritas." Thom.Arg. *Sent.* Prol. 4 (ed. Venice, 1564), fol. 17ra.

[64] "... philosophi non cognoverunt aliquam dilectionem, quae esset nobilior speculativa: et quae esset finis per se speculationis." Thom.Arg. *Sent.* Prol. 4 (ed. Venice, 1564), fol. 17ra.

[65] "... si enim philosophi talem dilectionem cognovissent, et posuissent, necessario habuissent ponere scientiam affectivam, cuius per se finis fuisset talis dilectio, quia speculationem illius scientie ordinassent ad huiusmodi dilectionem." Thom.Arg., *Sent.* Prol. 4 (ed. Venice, 1564), fol. 17ra. Albert the Great had defined theology as *scientia affectiva* and he was followed in this by members of the so-called Old Franciscan School, such as Alexander of Hales, Odo Rigaldi, Wilhelm of Melitona, and Bonaventure; see Köpf, *Die Anfänge*, 200–203. In his *Summa* Albert shifted positions by claiming theology no longer as "affective knowledge," but as *scientia practica; ibid.*, 204.

as affective knowledge, a knowledge of the heart, rather than of the mind, became a hall-mark of Augustinian theology. "Theology," Giles of Rome affirmed, "cannot properly be said to be speculative or practical; rather it is affective."[66] When the Augustinian friar left his cell and ascended the lectern, he brought his affections with him. Theology of the classroom and of the cloister was directed and guided by its end. Or as Alphonsus Vargas put it, "the chief end intended in the theology of the *viator* is not 'to believe', but 'to love', because faith is in the end directed towards the love of God ... love, not faith, is the principal end of theology."[67] And here we have entered a different world from that of faith extending and completing reason, leading to the divine.

Theology for the Augustinians was most fundamentally an affective knowledge grounded in the love of God and love of neighbor,[68] which brings us to an essential ingredient for understanding late medieval Augustinianism: levels and purposes of theological knowledge. In the very first question of the prologue to his *Sentences* commentary, Gregory of Rimini discussed whether the theologian possessed a greater knowledge than the simple believer. He argued a negative conclusion: "a great theologian does not have a greater knowledge than the simple believer, neither certainly a greater faith." However, the theologian has an additional knowledge than the implicit faith of the believer, a knowledge directed towards proving and defending the faith.[69] Theology, for Gregory, as practical knowledge, served

---

[66] "... theologia nec speculativa nec practica proprie dici debet: sed affectiva." Aeg.Rom. *Sent.* Prol. 4 (ed. Venice, 1521), fol. 8rb. See also Martijn Schrama, "*Theologia Affectiva*. Traces of Monastic Theology in the Theological Prolegomena of Giles of Rome," *Bijdragen. Tijdschrift voor filosofie en theologie* 57 (1996), 381–404.

[67] "... quod finis principaliter intentus in theologia viatoris non est credere, sed diligere, quia fides ad dilectionem dei finaliter ordinatur ... dilectio igitur erit finis principalis theologie non fides." Alfon. *Sent.*, Prol. 4 (ed. Venice, 1490), 126,61–67.

[68] Even though Gregory of Rimini did not discuss theology as *notitia affectiva*, love was theology's end; see Greg. *Sent.* Prol. 5,4 (I.182,15–17); *cf.* Greg. *Sent.* Prol. 5,4 (I.180,22–181,10; 185,8–15). On the practical nature of Gregory's theology, see also Michael Shank, '*Unless You Believe, You Shall Not Understand*'. *Logic, University, and Society in Late Medieval Vienna* (Princeton, 1988), 82–85. *Cf.* Hug. *Sent.* Prol. 5,1 and 3 (I.145,342–146,359; 153,111–154,144); for Hugolino, see also Martijn Schrama, "*Studere debemus eam viriliter et humiliter*. Theologia Affectiva bei Hugolin von Orvieto (d. 1373)," *Bijdragen. Tijdschrift voor filosofie en theologie* 53 (1992), 135–151.

[69] "... quod magnus theologus non habet maiorem notitiam quam simplex fidelis, nec forte etiam maiorem fidem, saltem non est necessarium quod ita sit de his, scilicet quae simplex fidelis explicite credit, nihilominus tamen habet aliam notitiam, quam non habet fidelis, scilicet probandi et defendendi etc...." Greg. *Sent.* Prol.

to defend the doctrines of faith. In short, two levels of theological knowledge are discerned here: the knowledge of the simple believer, and the knowledge of the theologian. The faith is the same; the knowledge, on one level, is the same. The theologian's purpose and function, however, require an additional type of knowledge; theology, academic, university theology, functioned to defend the simple faith of the believer, the faith of the Church.[70]

Two tiers, two levels—theology and simple belief; this causes no surprise. These two strata have most often formed the basis for historical analysis and when it comes to investigations of late medieval Augustinianism, the first has taken priority. The academic theology of the Augustinians has been described, characterized, and "schooled," by attempts to squeeze it into predetermined holes within the late medieval theological grid. This has obscured a third level of theological knowledge, the middle level existing between the simple faith of the simple believer and the formulations of the theological champions. This middle level, which can loosely be called the pastoral theology of the Augustinians, has not played a decisive role in interpretations of Augustine's theological heritage.

A theology of love was the Augustinians' theology from Giles of Rome and Thomas of Strassburg to Gregory of Rimini and Hugolino of Orvieto. It was also the theology of Jordan. Love was expressed by acts of love, kindness, and mercy. Acts of mercy, the giving of alms, were love made concrete and real. There were, Jordan tells us in the *Opus Postillarum*, two types of alms: corporal and spiritual. Corporal, or physical alms, consisted in what usually comes to mind when one thinks of giving alms: works of mercy, such as feeding the hungry and clothing the naked. Spiritual alms, however, must not be ignored and these Jordan listed as teaching the ignorant, counseling those in doubt, consoling the suffering, correcting sinners, forgiving those committing offenses, bearing heavy burdens and praying for all.[71] These spiritual alms, teaching, preaching, counseling, praying, were carried out on a level of theological knowledge above that

---

1,4 (I.56,24–28); *cf.*: "... quanto quis habet maiorem sive perfectiorem fidem acquisitam modo superius dicto, tanto perfectiorem habet habitum theologie revelate; sed simplex vetula non habet isto modo maiorem fidem quam unus magnus theologus..." Alfon. *Sent.* Prol. 3,3 (ed. Venice, 1490), 59.

[70] Greg. *Sent.* Prol. 1,4 (56,12–57,21).

[71] "Et diffinitur sic: elemosina est opus quo datur aliquid indigenti ex compassione propter deum. Et habet multas species scilicet septem corporales et septem

of the simple believer, but below that of the academic proving and defending the faith. The teaching and preaching of the Order, this middle strata of theology, were part and parcel of Augustine's religion.

We are, therefore, working with three levels of theological knowledge: defending the faith, teaching and preaching, and simply believing. The university theologians were first trained in the middle level before they proceeded to Paris or Oxford, and it was not a lesson they left behind. In his *Sentences* commentary Gregory of Rimini extolled the function of preaching,[72] and defined theology as practical knowledge, directed toward the love of God and love of neighbor, the love of Jordan's spiritual alms. The university theology and the *studia* theology combined and harmonized within the Order's mendicant theology. Both were needed; they simply served different functions. Teaching and preaching, or proving and defending, the Augustinians promoted a theology of love, a theology of their founder, inseparable from the Order's spirituality.

The Augustinians' theology of love, combining ethics and erudition (*vita et scientia*), governed the ideal of the Order's educational endeavor. This ideal Jordan commemorated in the outstanding theologians of the Order. After Augustine and Giles of Rome, the Hermits were blessed with such luminaries as James of Viterbo, Henry of Friemar, Augustine of Ancona, Bartholomew of Urbino, Albert of Padua, and Hermann of Schildesche. These Jordan named as examples of outstanding members of Augustine's religion.[73] In other words, Jordan's chosen context for ascribing meaning to the Augustinian *magistri* was not the university, but the Order. Giles was a renowned theologian held in high esteem, but his primary concern was for the Order.[74] He was not alone. As Boniface VIII and John XXII both recognized, the Augustinians counted many very learned theologians. Jordan praised the Augustinian masters, as had Boniface, not just for their learning, but also for the quality of their lives; an exemplary

---

spirituales. Elemosynae corporales, quae vocantur communiter opera misericordiae, continentur in hoc versu: visito, potu, cibo, redimo, tego, colligo, condo. Quae quia sunt satis communia, ideo eorum declarationi non insisto. Elemosynae vero spirituales sunt hae: docere ignorantem, consulere dubitanti, consolari tristem, corrigere peccantem, remittere offendenti, portare onerosos et graves, et pro omnibus orare." Jor. *OP* sermo 439E (ed. Strassburg, 1483).

[72] See Greg. 2 *Sent.* 26–28,1 (VI.76).
[73] *VF* 2,22 (236–241).
[74] *VF* 2,22 (237,105–108).

life and knowledge went hand in hand. Theological studies were inseparable from the *religio Augustini*; the masters to be venerated as models were those following in the tradition of Augustine, those "in the same religion" (*in religione eadem*).[75] The study and teaching of the holy scriptures was a fundamental component of Augustinian worship. It was the combination, or even the identity, of study and worship— not the opposition of a "monastic" and a "scholastic" theology—that Jordan advocated for his Order and pursued himself as lector in the *studium* at Erfurt, and this in imitation of Augustine, the Order's *preceptor*.

III. THE AUGUSTINIAN EDUCATIONAL SYSTEM

Augustine was the Order's teacher, but the Augustinian educational system provided the classrooms for the inculcation of the Order's theological core.[76] Scholars who have investigated mendicant education have focused on the relationship between the mendicant *studia* and the universities, treating the earlier phases most often only as steps along the way. Yet the *studia* not associated with the universities trained the preachers and teachers of the Orders. These *studia*

---

[75] *VF* 2,23 (242,238–243).
[76] The educational system of the Augustinians was not unique. Each of the mendicant Orders developed structures for training prospective theologians. For the Augustinians, see E. Ypma, *La Formation des Professeurs*; for the Dominican *studia*, see Michele Mulchahey, *Dominican Education and the Dominican Ministry in the Thirteenth and Fourteenth Centuries: fra Jacopo Passavanti and the Florentine Convent of Santa Maria Novella*, unpublished Ph.D. dissertation, University of Toronto, 1988; *idem*, "The Dominican *Studium* System and the Universities of Europe in the thirteenth Century," in *Manuels, Programmes de Cours et Techniques d'Enseignement dans les Universités Médiévales*, ed. J. Hamesse (Louvain-la-Neuve, 1994), 277–324; *idem*, *"First the Bow is Bent in Study..." Dominican Education Before 1350*, Pontifical Institute of Medieval Studies: Studies and Texts 132 (Toronto, 1998); for the Franciscans, Bert Roest, *Reading the Book of History. Intellectual Contexts and Educational Functions of Franciscan Historiography, 1226–ca. 1350* (Groningen, 1996), esp. 128–151; *idem*, *A History of Franciscan Education (c. 1210–1517)*, ESMAR 11 (Leiden, 2000); and for the Carmelites, Franz-Bernard Lickteig, *The German Carmelites at the Medieval Universities* (Rome, 1981). For more general and comparative treatments of mendicant education, see D. Berg, *Armut und Wissenschaft. Beiträge zur Geschichte des Studienwesens der Bettelorden im 13. Jahrhundert* (Düsseldorf, 1977); K. Elm, "Mendikantenstudium,"; *idem*, "Studium und Studienwesen der Bettelorden. Die 'andere' Universität?" in *Stätten des Geistes. Große Universitäten Europas von der Antike bis zur Gegenwart*, ed. Alexander Demandt (Cologne/Weimar/Vienna, 1999), 111–126; William J. Courtenay, *Schools and Scholars*; and Isnard Frank, *Die Bettelordensstudia im Gefüge des spätmittelalterlichen Universitätswesens* (Stuttgart, 1988).

produced the theological literature that from an internal perspective formed an Order-specific theology. To comprehend the Augustinian theological production in the later Middle Ages the non-university *studia* cannot be ignored. Although not novel as such, the Order's indoctrination program stamped its students with the distinctive ideals combining ethics and erudition that identified a theologian as an Augustinian.

A. *The Least of Scholars*

If Jordan advocated humility as essential to the acquisition of knowledge, he did so as a practitioner himself. He called himself the "least of the scholars of Paris," and later referred to himself as "prior provincial of the Saxon-Thuringian Province, although unworthy."[77] In the *Liber Vitasfratrum* one finds once again the diminutive; in dedicating the book to John of Basel, Jordan christened himself as "the least of the Order's lectors," (*inter eiusdem Ordinis lectores minimus*).[78] Such self-denigration could have been mere literary formula, not worthy of attention.[79] Yet Jordan's brief comment that he was the least among the Order's lectors reveals more than the rhetorical politeness of a salutation. In Jordan's minimal approach one discerns

---

[77] "... ego Jordanus, prior provincialis quamvis inmeritus provincie Thuringie et Saxonie ordinis...." *UkErf* nr. 79 (2:61). This is one of two times Jordan's name appears among the *Urkunden* published by Overmann. The document, dated 24 July 1350, confirms Henry of Friemar's (the Younger) grant to the Erfurt cloister of twenty pounds, for which he was to receive a yearly rent of two pounds. There is no mention of common possessions here! The other time Jordan's name appears is his letter of July 7 to the Erfurt cloister after his visitation in 1346 concerning care for the library. Here the document contains no diminutive: "Frater Iordanus, prior provincialis provincie Thuringie et Saxonie ordinis Fratrum Heremitarum sancti Augustini...," *UkErf* nr. 63 (2:50).

[78] *VF* Ep. (1,1–3).

[79] The second reference, namely Jordan calling himself the prior provincial of the Saxon-Thuringian province though *indignus*, does seem to have been formulaic; Gregory of Rimini used the same designation for himself as prior general: "Fr. Gregorius, prior generalis ordinis fratrum heremitarum sancti Augustini licet indignus." *Greg. Reg.* 1 (4); *AAug.* 4 (1911/12), 372. For the same formulation, see also *AAug.* 4 (1911/12), 423 (letter from Gregory to cloister in Avignon); *cf.* Greg. *Reg.* 2 (8); and *AAug.* 4 (1911/12), 443 (letter from Gregory to cloister in Florence); *cf.* Greg. *Reg.* 3 (13). The self-designation *minimus*, however, was not only a genuine statement of Jordan's humility, but also carried Pauline overtones. In a sermon on Paul's conversion in the *Opus Dan*, Jordan wrote: "Quantum autem ipse [Paul] in humiliatione sui descenderit, apparet in eo quod ipse dicit se *minimum apostolorum* et *non esse dignum vocari apostolus* [I Cor. 15:9]." Jor. *OD* sermo 50B (ed. Strassburg, 1484).

much about his position and the Order's educational hierarchy. Rhetoric it may have been, but it calls for further investigation.

Jordan was a lector, and I have already discussed what such a degree entailed.[80] The lectorate was the first stage in the Order's educational system leading eventually to the bachelor of theology and finally to the *magisterium*. Lectors were the teachers in the Order's schools not associated with a university. At times, however, the individual filling the office of lector was already a master. Thus, after having completed his studies in Paris, Gregory of Rimini was appointed as the principal lector in the *studium generale* of Rimini.[81] Jordan never progressed beyond the office of lector. In this light he had good reason to refer to himself as *minimus* amongst the Order's theologians; with respect to the level of education, Jordan was indeed among the least when compared to Gregory, or to Jordan's own teacher in Bologna, Prosper of Regio, or to his close associate at Erfurt, Henry of Friemar—all lectors who were also masters. In short, the designation 'lector' referred both to the office of lector, and to the title lector; lectors, bachelors, or masters could serve in the office of lector. As lector by title and by office, Jordan was clear on where he stood within the Order's educational hierarchy.

The distinction between lectors, bachelors, and masters was evident not merely by the official academic degree. In the Acts of the General Chapters there was never confusion between the office and title. When Gregory was appointed lector in Rimini it was clear: he was the "reverend master" Gregory.[82] Even as lector, *magister Gregorius* enjoyed special privileges. The Order's masters and bachelors were a group apart. As noted above, in 1328 William of Cremona called for the destruction of furnaces in the cells of the friars at Paris, yet made an exception for the venerable bachelors and masters.[83] In addition, the General Chapter of Florence (1326) decreed that the average Augustinian friar was not to have the luxury of linen sheets,

---

[80] See Chapter Three.

[81] See Ypma, *La Formation des Professeurs*, 70–71.

[82] The same held for lectors who were masters appointed to other types of schools; the Chapter of the Roman Province in 1326 appointed Master John of Rome as lector in their school for logic, *Esteban, AAug.* 4 (1911/12), 34; and the same Chapter made clear that the appointed lector in their school for philosophy was a lector by title as well, *Esteban, AAug.* 4 (1911/12), 34. One also finds the distinction made between bachelors who were lectors, and lectors, who were lectors; *e.g., Esteban, AAug.* 2 (1907/08), 481.

[83] *AAug.* 4 (1911/12), 63.

nor was he to have separate sleeping quarters, but was to remain in the common dormitory. The reverend masters and bachelors of theology, however, were exempt.[84] The pecking order was set. The General Chapter meeting in Genoa in 1308 had declared that no bachelor should dare to dispute in public if a master were present, nor should a lector if a bachelor were on hand, without the special permission of the higher-ranking scholar.[85] Such privilege was not limited to prestige. The Chapter at Rimini (1318) stipulated that in every general *studium* a master of theology was to receive six florins for his clothing needs, a bachelor five, and a lector four;[86] in 1329 the Chapter at Paris conceded twice as much to the masters for their weekly needs as to bachelors, and three times what lectors received.[87] The perquisites as well as the title distinguished the academic degrees within the Order. The system itself counted Jordan among the least of the privileged scholarly class, a lector in office and name.

Jordan may have played the role of the humble friar as the least of the Order's lectors, and he may have had reasons to consider himself as such, but here one must be on guard. Jordan's self-deprecation must not be allowed to affect one's perspective on the lector's title and office. The lectorate was indeed the lowest of the academic hierarchy, but it should not be viewed as only a holding pattern for future scholars until they were given the clearance to blast off for the higher orbits of the reverend bachelors and masters. Nor was it a consolation prize for those industrious brothers who were just not quite good enough to continue, but deserved some form of recognition, some sort of title, for their five plus years of diligent study. If the Order can be compared to a military organization, as it was in the Order's foundation charter,[88] then the general of the Order was a Major General; the masters also held the general rank, bearing, however, a lesser number of stars; the bachelors were the majors and captains; but the lectors were the lieutenants and field commanders. The higher ranks are certainly necessary,

---

[84] *Esteban, AAug.* 4 (1911/12), 7.
[85] *Esteban, AAug.* 3 (1909/10), 81; *cf.* General Chapter at Naples, 1300, *Esteban, AAug.* 3 (1909/10), 16; cited also by Ypma, *La Formation des Professeurs*, 150.
[86] *Esteban, AAug.* 3 (1909/10), 225.
[87] *Esteban, AAug.* 4 (1911/12), 84–85.
[88] *LEC* (11,6–7).

and most impressive, but as every student of military affairs knows, without lieutenants and field commanders few battles can be fought, much less won. We must not ignore the lieutenants. Yet before turning directly to the actual functions of the lectors, the organizational flow chart of the Order's system of education needs explication.

The Augustinians' program of education began from the moment a new brother donned the garb of the novice. It could continue, theoretically, until one achieved the doctorate in theology. There were four levels of the system in the first decades of the fourteenth century: the novitiate; the specialized or provincial schools (*studia particularia* or *studia provincialia*); the general schools (*studia generalia*); and the universities, namely Paris and Oxford. To pass through them all required much time and effort.

The Order did not delay initiating its indoctrination. The *Constitutions* mandated that "one learned and honest brother, approved and zealous for the Order" act as master of novices. This *magister* was to teach the neophytes the *Rule*, *Constitutions*, and way of life. In short, he was responsible for inculcating all that was necessary for living as one of Augustine's own.[89] In 1326, the prior general extended this initial period of close supervision and guidance until the young friars reached the age of twenty. William of Cremona viewed the inadequate indoctrination of novices and young friars as one of the causes that had lead to "the confusion of our religion." He therefore stipulated that after the novitiate, the young Augustinians were to be handed over to the care of an older friar who was to be obeyed just as the master of novices.[90] It may not technically be precise to list such indoctrination, the inculcation of the Order's social stock of knowledge, as part of the educational system, but in the eyes of William, such instruction was vital to the well-being of the Order. The novices may not have sat in classrooms every morning, but they most certainly were schooled by a teacher, or even by two: their *magister*, and their *preceptor*, Augustine.

Among the subjects to be taught listed in the *Constitutions*, singing was mentioned along with grammar, philosophy, and theology.[91] The friars were to sing, or chant, seven times a day at the appointed

---

[89] *Const. Ratis.* 17,111 (59).
[90] *AAug.* 4 (1911/12), 31. William repeated these stipulations two years later in his letter to the house in Paris; see, *AAug.* 4 (1911/12), 59.
[91] *Const. Ratis.* 17,111 (59).

canonical hours. It was not so much the quality of voice they learned as it was simply to carry the tunes of the chants; at least this was Jordan's opinion on the matter, when in the *Liber Vitasfratrum* he cautioned brothers against being concerned with the beauty of their voices when they should be intent on pleasing God.[92] In any case, the Order deemed learning to sing important for the novices, in keeping with the focus on the divine cult. Thus the *Constitutions* also stipulated that young friars were to be taught to sing in the summers, or perhaps I should say, they were to be "schooled" in singing, for this regulation appears in chapter 36 of the *Constitutions*, the chapter treating the form of studies.[93] 'Schooled' is indeed the proper term, for the General Chapter at Padua decreed in 1315 that every province of the Order was to have two schools to teach singing.[94]

The *studia in cantu* bring us from the first level of the Order's educational system to the second: the schools of chant were specialized schools, among which we find as well schools for grammar, logic, and philosophy. The Acts of the General Chapters employed both the designation *studia particularia* and *studia provincialia* to refer to provincial schools for chant, grammar, logic, and philosophy.[95] Basic instruction in grammar came first. The *Constitutions* mandated the establishment of schools in every province to teach logic for the elementary instruction of unlearned brothers.[96] The Chapter meeting in Siena just five years after the *Constitutions* were adopted in Regensburg (1290) prohibited any brother from being sent to any *studium*, unless he could say the divine office distinctly,[97] and the Chapter at Venice in 1332 required a knowledge of grammar and a speaking knowledge of Latin before one could proceed to a school for logic or a general *studium*.[98] Even Jordan preached the need to study grammar before moving on to dialectic and the subtle and difficult questions of natural philosophy. Grammar was the foundation of all knowledge,[99] and the

---

[92] *VF* 2,15 (181,46–50).
[93] *Const. Ratis.* 36,364 (116).
[94] Esteban, *AAug.* 3 (1909/10), 177; *cf.* Esteban, *AAug.* 4 (1911/12), 8.
[95] See *e.g.* Esteban, *AAug.* 4 (1911/12), 6 and 178.
[96] *Const. Ratis.* 36,363 (116); see also *Const. Ratis.* 36,329 and 341 (110, 113).
[97] Esteban, *AAug.* 2 (1907/08), 369.
[98] Esteban, *AAug.* 4 (1912/11), 110.
[99] "Primo ergo doceantur regulae Grammaticae ... quae sunt scientiarum omnium fundamenta, assumantur materiae ad versificandum, et sic de aliis. Non debent statim transire ad Dialecticam et antequam etiam fundentur in Dialectica, quidam volare volunt ad subtiles et difficiles quaestiones naturales. Icarus dum elatus iuvenili

Chapter at Padua (1315) ordered every province to have two grammar schools,[100] in addition to the two schools for chant.

After having acquired a sufficient knowledge of Latin grammar, the young Augustinian scholar could begin studying logic and natural philosophy at one of the specialized schools of his province. The General Chapter at Florence (1326) recommended that every province set aside two locations for schools, one of which would teach logic and the other natural philosophy. The lector of philosophy was to complete Aristotle's natural philosophy within three years, while the logic teacher also had three years to lecture on the entire logic (old and new).[101] If, however, two separate locations could not be found, one was sufficient, providing the *studium* had two lectors, one for philosophy and one for logic.[102] This three-year course in logic and natural philosophy provided the required education before a brother could be sent to a *studium generale*. In other words, before an Augustinian could begin the five-year course leading to the lectorate, he had to spend three years in a provincial school. In 1338 the General Chapter at Siena mandated that in order to maintain the level of instruction worthy of the general *studia*, no brother was to be admitted to such a school unless he had first completed the three-year course in the provincial schools, at least with respect to logic.[103] Only after such preliminary education had been completed in grammar, logic, and philosophy could an Augustinian begin his studies at a general school.

The *studia generalia* formed the third level within the Order's educational system and the core of the Augustinian program of indoctrination. By 1354 there were thirty-two such *studia*, designed "to create a large, well trained corps of teachers."[104] The *Constitutions* mandated at least four general *studia* in Italy, exhorting other provinces to follow suit,[105] and the General Chapter at Treviso (1321) required every province to maintain a general school to teach the Scriptures,

---

aetate fertur in coelum volando fluctibus marinis immergitur. Et dum se in artibus elevant, cadunt." Jor. *OS* sermo 270 (ed. Paris, 1521), fol. 434ᵛ.

[100] Esteban, *AAug.* 3 (1909/10), 177.
[101] Esteban, *AAug.* 4 (1911/12), 6.
[102] *Ibid.*
[103] Esteban, *AAug.* 4 (1911/12), 178; *cf.* Thom.Arg. *Add.* 36 (118).
[104] "Le but de tout cela était de créer un corps de professeurs, nombreux et bien instruits." Ypma, *La Formation des Professeurs*, 23; *cf. ibid.*, 47.
[105] *Const. Ratis.* 36,340 (113).

the *Sentences*, and logic to students from the province.[106] "One student from every province," the *Constitutions* declared, "sufficiently learned in grammar and logic, should be sent to [one of] the general schools of the province and after having studied in such a school for five years, if found worthy, attain to the office of lector."[107] The general schools were vital to the Order because they provided the basic theological training required for the priests and preachers of the Order; the prerequisite instruction in theology for admission to a university; and produced the Order's "learned corps of teachers," the lectors.[108]

Among the Order's *studia generalia*, one in particular held primacy of place: Paris. On the one hand Paris was no different from any other *studium generale*.[109] Yet on the other, the Augustinian *studium* at Paris was unique indeed for it was closely associated with the University, beginning in 1285 when Giles of Rome became the first Augustinian to be granted a chair in Theology.[110]

---

[106] Esteban, *AAug*. 3 (1909/10), 247. The *Constitutiones* required the teaching of the Bible, the *Sentences*, logic and philosophy; *Const. Ratis*. 36,340 (113).

[107] "Et ad praedicta quidem Studia de qualibet Provincia mittatur unus Studens, in Grammaticalibus et Logicalibus ita sufficienter instructus, quod postquam in tali Studio per quinquennium steterit, inveniatur idoneus officio Lectoriae." *Const.Ratis*. 36,341 (113); cf. *Const.Ratis*. 36,342 (113).

[108] For the requirements for the "degree" of lector, see Chapter Three. The promotion of unqualified lectors was a constant concern for the General Chapters; see Esteban, *AAug*. 3 (1909/10), 153; Ypma, *La Formation des Professeurs*, 28ff and the texts given in Ypma's appendix, 150–155, among which is also this decree from Viterbo (150/51); cf. Ypma, "La Promotion au Lectorat chez les Augustins," 395ff. The priests and clerics of the Order were exhorted to attend the theological lectures of the schools in their region; *Const.Ratis*. 36,358 (115).

[109] See Ypma, *La Formation des Professeurs*, 38–39. We do find a differentiation in *studia generalia* between those designed as *totius ordinis* and those *provincie*. This distinction is not, however, between "lower" and "higher" levels of general schools, or between *studia generalia* and universities; the *studia generalia* established by the General Chapter in 1303 for the Bavarian Province, the Rhenisch Province, the Cologne Province and at Montepulciano were designated as *studia generalia totius ordinis*; Esteban, *AAug*. 3 (1909/10), 54–55. The distinction indicates that students from all provinces of the Order could attend a *studium generale totius ordinis*, whereas *studia generalia provincie* were limited to students from the same province; see Ypma, *La Formation Professeurs*, 47, 54–60. The provincial *studia generalia* took the pressure off Paris; cf. Esteban, *AAug*. 3 (1909/10), 468 and Thom.Arg. Add. 36 (116).

[110] The special attention given to the *studium* at Paris was due to its special status. William of Cremona was vitally concerned to reform the house at Paris, and between 1345 and 1348 Prior General Thomas of Strassburg issued special "statutes" for Paris; see Ypma, "Le *Mare Magnum*: Un code médiéval du couvent augustinien de Paris," *Aug(L)* 6 (1956), 275–321.

The Augustinian *studium* at Paris was part of the Order's educational system, not, in and of itself, an institution of the university. As an Augustinian, one could study at the *studium* at Paris, without studying at the University of Paris. The reverse, however, did not hold; if, as an Augustinian, one studied at the University of Paris, one did so in the Order's *studium generale* at Paris. The point of connection was the chair in Theology. For an Augustinian friar to study at the University of Paris, he had to be accepted by the Augustinian master. As a university student, the friar's studies were governed by university regulations. The requirements for the university degrees of bachelor and master were determined by the university, not by the Order. Thus there are no stipulations regarding the requirements for university *degrees* in the Acts of the General Chapter, but only regulations for university *study*, concerning how one got there in the first place, and who was able to stay and continue. It was only when the Augustinians gained a university chair in Theology that the relationship between the *studium* and university was firmly established. In other words, the Order's *studium* and the university were different educational systems, linked by the master.[111]

The course of study leading to the bachelor's degree and finally to the doctorate in theology was long and grueling.[112] Only after the future theologian had spent three years in a *studium provinciale*, and five in a *studium generale*, was he then eligible, having been made a lector, to be sent to the university for yet another five years required of members of religious Orders in order to achieve the first bachelor's degree, the *baccalaureus biblicus*. After two further years of lecturing on the *Sentences* as *baccalaureus Sententiarum*, the bachelor could become "formed" as a *baccalaureus formatus*. It would only be four more years, however, and numerous disputations later that he could be presented to the chancellor of the university to become a *magister*.[113]

It took eleven years as a university student for an Augustinian to reach the pinnacle of the career that had begun the day he entered the Order. When this is added to the eight years of preliminary edu-

---

[111] See Ypma, *La Formation des Professeurs*, 84ff.

[112] See Venicio Marcolino, "Der Augustinertheologe an der Universität Paris," in *Gregor von Rimini. Werk und Wirkung*, 127–194; *cf.* Ypma, *La Formation des Professeurs*, 81–123. For the Augustinians at Oxford, and the program of studies for the English Augustinians in general, see Courtenay, *Schools and Scholars*, 72ff.

[113] See Marcolino, "Der Augustinertheologe," 183–194; Ypma, *La Formation des Professeurs*, 91, 109, and 120.

cation required before one began at the university, the result is nineteen years, as a minimum.[114] Two decades were needed before the Augustinian theologian could become one of the privileged few, a reverend master of theology.

The Augustinian masters of theology may have been the most esteemed, the most decorated members of the militia brought together in 1256 as the Order of Augustine's Hermits, and they have certainly been the most studied. Surveying the Order's four-tiered educational system, however, one begins to realize that the "reverend bachelors and masters" were merely the top echelon of a far deeper and more extensive system. The Order may have venerated the bachelors and masters more than the others, and I have already pointed to the fringe benefits accompanying these degrees, but the lectors in the *studia generalia* were the work horses of the Augustinians' educational endeavor. Efforts to ensure the production of lectors, to create an educated corps of teachers, fill the pages of the Acts of the General Chapters. Though the lectorate was not a university degree, the Order-licensed lectors were the teachers of the Order's doctrines and the propagators of the Order's theology, yet they remain overlooked in portrayals of late medieval Augustinianism as only a stage on the way to more lofty goals.

Three considerations must be kept in mind when analyzing the office of lector. First is the distinction between the office of lector and the title lector. Second, the lectorate was a stage within the Order's educational system through which all future bachelors and masters would have passed. Third, the lectorate was not simply a preliminary stage, but was a specific office within the Order, with its own duties and functions. I have already discussed the first two; the third now calls for special attention.

The lectors performed central functions for the Order. They were the framers of the decrees at Chapter meetings, examiners of

---

[114] According to the acts of the General Chapters, a friar could only stay in Paris for five years. After that time he had to return to his home province to teach for a number of years, before being eligible to be sent back to Paris for further study; see *Esteban, AAug.* 2 (1907/08), 293 and *AAug.* 4 (1911/12), 178. The *cursor* within the Augustinian educational system was not a *bachalareus biblicus* who read the text of the Bible *cusorie*, but rather the cursorate for the Augustinians was a year of student teaching before one recieved the title lector, mandated for the candidates for the lectorate, or before one advanced to Paris in the first place. See Ypma, "Les *cursores* chez les Augustins," *RThAM* 26 (1959), 137–144.

preachers, served as inquisitors and visitors, and most importantly worked as preachers and teachers. As stated by the *Constitutions*, a lector was to be the "lover and teacher of the divine law" (*tanquam divinae legis amator et instructor*) and the model for others to follow.[115] In short, they were the "theological watchdogs" of the Order. Aside from their teaching responsibilities, the documents do not delineate the specific duties accompanying the office of lector. Yet the actual functions lectors performed can be extracted from the Acts of the General and Provincial Chapters where the various roles lectors assumed are mentioned.

The most common function fulfilled by lectors was that of the officially elected provincial representatives who were responsible for drawing up and voting on the stipulations of the Chapter (*diffinitores*).[116] Thus, the recorded Acts usually begin in a similar fashion to that of the Chapter of 1287: "These are the decisions recorded during the General Chapter of the Order of Hermits of Saint Augustine, celebrated at Florence in the year of our Lord 1287 in the month of May, on the day of holy Pentecost, by brother Clement, Prior General, and by the representatives (*diffinitores*) of the Order's provinces, officially gathered."[117] Not infrequently the names of the representatives are given, and most often they are lectors.[118] The office of lector carried great responsibility and could not be given to just anyone. Thus, on account of confusion arising from unqualified brothers seeking a vote in chapter by aspiring to the lectorate, the General Chapter at Montpellier (1324), presided over by Prior General Alexander of San Elpidio, who was finishing his *De ecclesiastica potestate* and was going after brother Nicholas of Fabriano, restricted the

---

[115] *Const.Ratis.* 36,350 (114). The lectors were exhorted to observe the divine hours as examples for others; *Const.Ratis.* 36,353 (115); *cf.* Greg. *Reg.* 1 (4–8; esp. 4–5); *AAug.* 4 (1911/12), 373.

[116] See *Const.Ratis.* 32 (93ff).

[117] "Iste sunt Diffinitiones facte in Capitulo Generali ordinis Fratrum Heremitarum Sancti Augustini Florentie celebrato. Anno domini Millesimo CCLXXXVII. Mense Madii. In die Sancto Pentecostes per fratrem Clementem, Priorem Generalem, et per Diffinitores provinciarum eiusdem ordinis sollempniter congregatos." Esteban, *AAug.* 2 (1907–08), 274.

[118] At the Chapter of the Roman Province in 1316, for example, the *diffinitores* were brothers Bartholus de Viterbio, Sabas de Roma, Iohannes de Urbeveteri, and Andreas de Perusio, lectors; Esteban, *AAug.* 3 (1909/10), 175. Twice the designation lector was added to the official record in later notes, implying the importance of the office; see Esteban, *AAug.* 3 (1909/10), 297, 318.

right to vote in provincial Chapters to previous representatives, provincial priors, and lectors actually teaching.[119] As official representatives of the provinces, lectors took an active role in governing the Order; they were not only to be lovers of divine law, but also the Order's legislative backbone.[120]

Two further roles that lectors often filled were visitors and inquisitors. The *Constitutions* stipulated that the General Chapters were to choose as visitors brothers who were "prudent and discrete, zealots of righteousness and religiosity who were never tainted with any notable vice."[121] These visitors were to correct and reform any errors in religious observance and were to report their findings to the prior general and the legislators (*diffinitores*) of the General Chapter.[122] The brothers most often selected for this office were designated as lectors.[123]

In close connection with the office of visitor was that of inquisitor. There was no specific office of inquisitor within the Order, but

---

[119] *Esteban, AAug.* 3 (1909/10), 466; *cf.* Thom.Arg. *Add.* 36 (120).

[120] Lectors were not the only ones named as *diffinitores*, even though they were the ones appointed as such most often. The Roman Province, for example, in 1296 named four *diffinitores*: "Item tum electi fuerunt quatuor diffinitores, videlicet, frater Franciscus de Roma, Baccellarius in studio Romane Curie; frater Symon, lector de Viterbio; frater Domincus, lector de Castroplebis; et frater Augustinus de Urbeveteri, Predicator." *Esteban, AAug.* 2 (1907/08), 390. Here we see the clear distinction between lectors, bachelors, and simple friars or preachers. The following year we find four *diffinitores* once again, but this time two are lectors and two are preachers, *ibid.*, 394, whereas in 1300 three of the four *diffinitores* were lectors, *Esteban, AAug.* 3 (1909/10), 35. The General Chapter at Padua (1315), gave masters equal rights to *diffinitores*, *ibid.*, 179, though lectors fulfilled the role of *diffinitor* most often. Thus in the Provincial Chapter of the Roman Province in 1319 we find once again three of the four *diffinitores* named as lectors; *ibid.*, 249. The title lector, however, was not always provided. Thus, in the General Chapter at Siena in 1338 the names of the participants were given with the masters and bachelors designated as such, including those who served also as *diffinitores*, but, Jordan, who attended as a *diffinitor* of the Saxon-Thuringian Province, was only listed as "Jordanus de Madaborch diffinitore provincie Turingie et Saxonie," although he was at that time lector in Magdeburg; see *Esteban, AAug.* 4 (1911/12), 177, n. 2.

[121] "In generali Capitulo, quod debet de triennio in triennium celebrari, Generalis Prior et Definitores ipsius Capituli eligant plures Fratres providos et discretos, iustitiae et religiositatis non modicum zelatores et qui numquam in Ordine de aliquo vitio notabili fuerint notati." *Const.Ratis.* 41,439 (141).

[122] *Const.Ratis.* 41,443 (141–142).

[123] See, for example, *Esteban, AAug.* 2 (1907/08), 396; *AAug.* 3 (1909/10), 250; and *AAug.* 4 (1911/12), 35; *cf. Esteban, AAug.* 3 (1909/10), 248, and 320. Visitors did not have to be lectors, but it is clear the majority of visitors were lectors. The importance of visitations was stressed in 1340 in the French provincial chapter; see *Esteban, AAug.* 4 (1911/12), 187.

we do find a report of an inquisition into a specific problem. In 1325 the Roman Province instructed Franciscus of Viterbo and Dyonisius of Viterbo to investigate a scandal caused by brother Petrus of Viterbo. They were to report their findings speedily to the provincial prior. Both Franciscus and Dyonisius were specified as lectors.[124]

As inquisitors and visitors, lectors appear as those especially charged with ensuring correct observance of the Order's religious life. They were also specifically commissioned to preach. This is not to imply that bachelors and masters did not preach. Preaching was an essential part of the academic responsibilities at the universities,[125] and extensive sermon collections are extant from Augustinian *magistri* such as Albert of Padua and Henry of Friemar. Nevertheless the lectors were singled out especially as charged to preach. The *Constitutions* required lectors to teach, sermonize, and preach,[126] and the Provincial Chapter of Rome in 1325 named "all lectors and all others who are accustomed to preach" to the office of preacher.[127] Though bachelors and masters and other brothers preached, only the lectors were given a special mandate to do so. Indeed, Thomas of Strassburg affirmed in the *Additiones* that no one should be sent to Paris or be licensed as lector unless he had first proved sufficiently learned in logic and philosophy and had given at least one sermon either in a Provincial Chapter or in a general *studium*.[128]

---

[124] *Esteban, AAug.* 3 (1909/10), 298. Franciscus and Dyonisius were at this time anyway not the visitators. It thus appears that in such cases "inquisitors" were appointed. However, in 1297 the Roman Provincial Chapter simply instructed the prior provincial himself to investigate accusations made against Symon de Viterbio and Alexandrus de Viterbio, both of whom were lectors; *Esteban, AAug.* 2 (1907/08), 396.

[125] See Maierù, "Regulations,"; David d'Avray, *The Preaching of the Friars. Sermons diffused from Paris before 1300* (Oxford, 1985); and Beryl Smalley, "Oxford University Sermons, 1290–1293," in *Medieval Learning and Literature. Essays Presented to Richard William Hunt*, ed. J.J.G. Alexander and M.T. Gibson (Oxford, 1976), 307–327.

[126] "Lector sane a consueto principio Studii usque ad festum sancti Petri continue legat, et sermocinetur et praedicet tempore opportuno." *Const.Ratis.* 36,350 (114).

[127] "Item eligimus ad officium predicationis omnes lectores et omnes alios qui praedicare consueverunt." *Esteban, AAug.* 3 (1909/10), 296. In 1328 the Roman Provincial Chapter once again conscripted lectors as preachers; *Esteban, AAug.* 4 (1911/12), 39. This had been a long-standing concern, since the Roman province stipulated already in 1294 that lectors were to preach; *Esteban, AAug.* 2 (1907/08), 363.

[128] *Thom.Arg. Add.* 36 (117). In 1365 at the General Chapter in Siena, candidates for the lectorate were to have preached at least ten times *coram populo* in the vernacular; *Esteban, AAug.* 4 (1911/12), 450; as cited by Ypma, "La Promotion au Lectorat," 403. The need for preaching in the vernacular had previously been stressed by Gregory of Rimini; see Greg. *Reg.* 2 (9); *AAug.* 4 (1911/12), 423.

Closely associated with the lectors' role as preachers was their function as examiners of those other brothers who desired to preach. The *Constitutions* asserted that the Word of God was not to be preached except by qualified preachers who were sufficiently learned. Thus, two lectors, chosen by the provincial prior and the provincial representatives (*diffinitores*), were to examine potential preachers. Only those found qualified to preach were granted permission to do so.[129]

Yet it was not only potential preachers who were to be examined by lectors. Lectors were also responsible for examining candidates to be sent to Paris,[130] and participated in the examinations of candidates for the lectorate itself. In the previous chapter, I addressed the prerequisites for the office of lector, namely, sufficient knowledge of logic, philosophy, and theology, and noted the required examination. One part of the exam, however, I omitted. Not only was the candidate scrutinized on how much Aristotle, Lombard, and scripture he had learned in his three years in provincial schools and five in general schools, but also on his moral character. The quality of the future lector's life was as fundamental to his promotion as was the quantity of his knowledge. To be sent to Paris the budding theologian was not only to be sufficiently learned in grammar and logic, but also to have led a laudable life;[131] or as the *Constitutions* phrased it, he was to be examined as much for his knowledge as for his life, (*tam de scientia quam de vita*).[132] The same applied to the office of lector; the candidates were to be examined on their life, morals, and knowledge, (*super vita, moribus, atque scientia*).[133] The Augustinian theologians of all levels, masters, bachelors, and lectors, were to combine an exemplary life with academic achievement; or as Jordan would put it, "book learning" was not enough. The knowledge gained from lectures and books was insufficient without the spiritual knowledge of illumination, the knowledge stemming from a pure heart, a humble mind, a pious prayer life, and fruitful works: the combination of ethics and erudition in imitation of Augustine. The task to

---

[129] *Const.Ratis.* 36,360 (115–116); *cf.* Esteban, *AAug.* 2 (1907/08), 395 and *AAug.* 4 (1911/12), 180.
[130] See Esteban, *AAug.* 2 (1907/08), 252; *cf. Const.Ratis.* 36,330 (110).
[131] Esteban, *AAug.* 2 (1907/08), 252.
[132] *Const.Ratis.* 36,330 (110); *cf.* Esteban, *AAug.* 3 (1909/10), 321.
[133] Esteban, *AAug.* 4 (1911/12), 256; *cf.* Thom.Arg. *Add.* 36 (117). See also Ypma, *La Formation des Professeurs*, 29.

ensure such harmony of life and knowledge, of morals and study, was incumbent upon all members of the Order, but most of all upon the lectors, the "watchdogs" of the Order, who examined and preached, made inquisitions and visitations, and who legislated the *religio Augustini*.

The lectorate was the first stage in the Augustinians' educational system on the way towards the *magisterium*, but it was also much more. The lectorate formed future theologians. This preliminary education has been overlooked all too frequently in turning immediately to *Sentences* commentaries to create the definitions of the '-ism' adjoined to the adjective Augustinian. Before one could partake of the privileges granted to brothers holding university degrees, one had served one's time, and had had one's morals and knowledge rigorously examined. The lectorate was not only a stepping stone to higher degrees. It was an office in its own right, with its own responsibilities and functions.

In addition to being legislators, visitors, examiners, and preachers, lectors were first and foremost teachers. They were the ones who taught the courses in grammar, logic, philosophy, and theology in the provincial and general schools of the Order. It was their theological lectures that trained the Order's preachers and provided the theological foundation for all further study. They were the ones making the decisions on the selection of brothers to be sent to Paris or Oxford. And they were the ones who together with the provincial priors were to make sure the general schools were up to par.[134]

There were three universities in the first half of the fourteenth century to which Augustinians could be sent: first Paris, and after 1318, Oxford and Cambridge.[135] There were thirty-two *studia generalia* and an equal or even greater number of provincial schools. All these trained preachers and lectors, all of whom were taught by lectors and were examined by lectors. Numbers alone testify that the theology of the Order was not restricted to the theology of the Order's university-trained theologians. The teaching of the lectors to a greater extent than that of the masters comprised the Order's mendicant theology,[136] the theology of Augustine's religion, though this is a theology still largely unknown.

---

[134] *Esteban, AAug.* 3 (1909/10), 177.
[135] Ypma, *La Formation des Professeurs*, 122–123.
[136] Elm, for example, has mentioned that of the more than 200 known names

B. *Theology in the* Studia: *Jordan's Lectures in Erfurt*

When the focal point for interpreting Augustinian theology in the later Middle Ages shifts from the universities to the *studia*, an additional problem is encountered. When one wants to know what the Order's theologians at Paris or Oxford had to say about faith and reason, or God's omnipotence, or angels and demons, one has ample material: the *Sentences* commentaries of Giles of Rome, Thomas of Strassburg, Gregory of Rimini, Hugolino of Orvieto, or John Klenkok come to mind. When one seeks the theology taught in the *studia generalia* in Cologne, Nürnberg, or Erfurt, one runs into a dark abyss. Sources for analyzing the theology of the lectors are not readily apparent. Prosper of Regio's *Compendium* of theological questions discussed at Paris in the early fourteenth century comes close. Prosper's text is an invaluable source for early Parisian theology, but does not represent actual lectures in the Order's *studium* in Bologna.[137] At first sight one could be tempted to turn to John of Basel's *Decem Responsiones*. These he prepared for his bachelor exams. They indeed represent a different level within the Augustinian system of education than is presented in commentaries on Lombard, but they are at least one step removed from what was required of a lector.[138] Hugolino of Orvieto's *Physics* commentary is also a possibility, at least for the philosophy the young scholars might have learned, but we cannot be sure.[139] We do know that the *Sentences* were read in the non-university

---

of Augustinians belonging to the cloisters in Osnabrück, Herford and Lippstadt between the thirteenth and sixteenth centuries, sixty were designated as lectors and only sixteen as masters or doctors. Elm, "Mendikantenstudium," 595.

[137] Prosper's *In Libros Sententiarum* is extent in Vat., Bib. Apost., MS Vat. lat. 1086. The work is a compilation of questions discussed at Paris in the early fourteenth century, containing forty-six questions on the prologue alone. See A. Pelzer, "Prosper de Reggio Emilia des Ermites de Saint-Augustin et le manuscrit latin 1086 de la Bibilothèque Vaticane." *Revue néo-scholastique* 30 (1928), 316–351, and *idem*, *Codices Vaticani Latini* II.1 (Vatican City, 1931), 654–683; Zumkeller, "Die Augustinerschule," 203–205.

[138] John's *Decem Responsiones* have not yet been published. They are ten questions he determined in preparation for his bachelor's degree, dealing with such varied topics as Christology, poverty, cognition, and the Christian life. Twice he cited Jordan's *Opus Postillarum*; Vienna, NB, MS 4319, fol. 19ʳ and fol. 33ʳ. For John's theology, see A. Zumkeller, "Der Augustinertheologe Johannes Hiltalingen von Basel (d. 1392) Über Urstand, Erbsünde, Gnade und Verdienst," *AAug.* 43 (1980), 57–162.

[139] See Hug. *Phys.*, 7. Whether Hugolin's teaching is representative of the lectures held in the provincial schools for philosophy is a question that cannot be answered until further evidence is discovered. For Hugolino, see also Willigis Eckermann and Bernd Ulrich Hurcker, eds., *Hugolin von Orvieto. Ein Spätmittelalterlicher*

studia. We do not know, however, *how* the *Sentences* were read. There are no extant lectures on the *Sentences* given in the non-university *studia* to be compared with those of the *magistri* in order to characterize the Order's mendicant theology at this level.[140] There is, nevertheless, a precious source that reveals the theological instruction given in the Augustinian *studia*: Jordan of Quedlinburg's *Expositio Orationis Dominice*.

Augustinertheologe in seiner Zeit (Cloppenburg, 1992); and Willigis Eckermann, ed., *Schwerpunkte und Wirkungen des Sentenzenkommentars Hugolino von Orvieto, OESA* (Würzburg, 1990).

[140] There is, however, some indication, slight though it may be, of how the *Sentences* were read in the mendicant *studia* not associated with a university. Such is the widely circulated *Conclusiones in libros Sententiarum* of the Franciscan Johannes de Fonte (13th/14th century; see *LThK* 5:1033). The text is direct and straightforward, without commentary or explanations, and is extant in 86 manuscripts; see F. Stegmüller, *Repertorium Commentariorum in Sententias Petri Lombardi*, 2 vols. (Würzburg, 1947), I: 217–218; nr. 446, and P.V. Doucet, *Commentaires sur les Sentences. Supplement au Repertoire de M. Frédéric Stegmüller* (Quaracchi, 1954), 50; *cf. Bibliographie Annuelle du Moyen Age Tardif. Auteurs et texts latins* 5 (1995), 258 nrs. 2098–2100. Zumkeller noted that the Augustinian Dionysius de Florentina (d. after 1443) used Johannes' work as the model for his own *Summa libri Sententiarum*; Zumkeller *MSS* nr. 235 (110). Dionysius' work is very short and extant in only two manuscripts: Wolfenbüttel, Herzog-August Bibl. MS Helmst. 269, fol. 52^v–53^v, and Bamberg, StB MS Theol. 209, fol. 199^r–201^r (which begins with the fourth book, distinction 34, c. 4), whereas Johannes' *Compendium*, is substantially longer (e.g.: Bamberg, StB MS Theol. 209, fol. 1^r–48^r). Similar to the work of Dionysius and Johannes are the registers of the *Sentences*, such as that of Theobaldus Coci de Miltenberg, OESA (d.c. 1480), extant in a single manuscript, Tübingen, UB MS Mc 327, fol. 3^r–21^r; Zumkeller, *MSS*, nr. 799 (371). Theobaldus offered an alphabetical register of topics dealt with in the *Sentences*, though on fol. 21^v a new compendium begins: *Registrum compedii theologicae iuridicae*, which also proceeds alphabetically and topically, but the references are to canon law. In addition, Theobaldus offered a list of Lombard's doctrines rejected by theologians (*Hec sunt opiniones magistri, que non tenentur a doctoribus*) fol. 20^v–21^r. There is also a *Tabula brevis et utilis super quatuor libros Sententiarum* ascribed by an 18th-century hand to Petrus de Brunniquello, OESA (d. 1328), although it is questionable whether this is genuinely a work of Petrus or even if it can be dated to the 14th century; the only extant manuscript is dated 1460 (München, BStB MS Clm. 26702, fol. 89va–94va); see Zumkeller, *MSS*, nr. 750 (348). For the process of composition of *Sentences* commentaries in general, see Marcolino, "Der Augustinertheologe," 168–183; *idem*, Greg.1 *Sent*., "Einleitung," xciii–xcvii; Trapp, "Dreistufiger Editionsprozess und dreiartige Zitationsweise bei den Augustinertheologen des 14. Jahrhunderts?" *Aug(L)* 25 (1975), 283–292; *idem*, "Gregory of Rimini Manuscripts, Editions, and Additions," *Aug(L)* 8 (1958), 425–443, esp. 425f; and William J. Courtenay, "Conrad of Megenberg: The Parisian Years," *Vivarium* 35 (1997), 102–124. Perhaps the best indication of the reading of the *Sentences* in the non-university *studia* can be seen in the *Abbreviatio in I Sententiarum* of James of Viterbo, which was composed before James went to Paris to read the *Sentences*; see E. Ypma, "Recherches sur la productivité littéraire de Jacques de Viterbe jusqu'a 1300," *Aug(L)* 25 (1975), 230–249; *idem*, "Jacques de Viterbe témoin valable?" *RThAM* 52 (1985), 232–234.

In 1327, Jordan lectured *ordinarie* on the Gospel of Matthew in the Augustinian *studium* at Erfurt, just as the Order had been granted custody of Augustine's body in Pavia. At the request of his students, he published 10 lectures on the sixth chapter, verses 9–13. These formed his *Exposition of the Lord's Prayer* and this treatise is all that remains of Jordan's lecture course.[141] He later incorporated his commentary on the *Pater Noster* into his first major sermon collection. Fifty-seven manuscripts of Jordan's *Expositio* have survived as an independent treatise, and possibly as many as another thirty-seven as part of his *Opus Postillarum*.[142]

At first sight, Jordan's *Expositio* is one treatise dealing with the Lord's Prayer among many in the Middle Ages, offering nothing of special import. Yet the reason this text merits our attention is not its uniqueness. Indeed, no less a scholar than Erasmus of Rotterdam

---

[141] Lectures given *ordinarie* were reserved for the regent master or lector, in which philosophical and theological questions were expected to be treated rather than a "cursory" reading of the text. See Ypma, *La Formation des Professeurs*, 36.

[142] The number of extant manuscripts of Jordan's *Expositio* has been derived from Zumkeller *MSS* nr. 647 (301); M. Bloomfield *et al.* eds., *Incipits of Latin Works on the Virtues and Vices, 1100–1500 A.D., Including a Section of Incipits of Works on the Pater Noster*. The Medieval Academy of America. (Cambridge, 1979), nr. 8440 (608); F. Stegmüller, *Repertorium Biblicum Medii Aevi*, 11 vols. (Madrid, 1949–1980), nr. 5138–5139 (3:465–466); and the *Bibliographie Annuelle du Moyen Age Tardif. Auteurs et textes latins* (Turnhout, 1991–). For a discussion of the textual tradition of Jordan's work, see the Introduction to my forthcoming edition, *Jordani de Quedlinburg Expositio Orationis Dominice. Introduction, Critical Edition, Translation, and Commentary*. The number of extant manuscripts of the *Opus Postillarum* containing Jordan's *Expositio* has not yet been determined. Many of the manuscripts listed in manuscript catalogues do not indicate that often many sermons were omitted. Among the manuscripts of Jordan's *Opus Postillarum* extant in the Netherlands, for example, sermons 289–298 are seemingly systematically omitted in all but two. Yet the evidence is clear that Jordan's work was widely received in the later Middle Ages, and by no means only among the Augustinians; manuscripts are extant from Benedictine, Carthusian, Franciscan, and Dominican libraries, as well as from those of the Brothers and Sisters of the Common Life and secular clergy. For the text of the *Expositio* presented in the notes for the remainder of this study, I have followed the reading of Berlin, StB, MS theol. fol. qu. 175, fols. 73ra–89vb. All further references to Jordan's *Expositio* are to this manuscript, cited as: Jor. *Exp.*, followed by *lectio* number, and the foliation of the Berlin manuscript, *B*. I have collated the text of *B* with that of the other mid fourteenth-century manuscript: *M*: Munich, BStB, MS Clm. 8151, fols. 85^r–106^r, as well as with *S*: the text of the *Expositio* as present in the 1483 Strassburg edition of Jordan's *Opus Postillarum*. When I have emended the reading of *B* based on *M*, I present the variant reading of *B* in square brackets [ ] in the text; when there are omissions of text in *B* that I have supplied from *M*, the text of *M* is then printed within brackets {}; when I have emended the reading of *B* on other bases, most often based on *S*, I include the emendation within brackets <>. I have standardized the orthography based on *B*.

entered Jordan on a list of preachers, "now fortunately rendered obsolete," who provided negative examples of the art of preaching, composing sermons perhaps useful to impress their audience, but devoid of learning.[143] If, however, one accepted the judgment of Erasmus, one would lose the opportunity to learn what this single text has to teach. I am not concerned here with the *ars praedicandi*. It is not even as an exposition of the *Pater Noster* that Jordan's exposition evokes attention. Its uniqueness is rather to be found in the fact that Jordan's ten lectures on Matthew 6:9–13 offer access to the level of instruction within the Augustinian *studia* not associated with a university; they were lectures by a lector who never became a master or even a bachelor.

This is precisely why Jordan's *Expositio Orationis Dominice* is of such importance. While Biblical commentaries from other Augustinian theologians that originated as lectures in non-university *studia* are extant, Jordan's lectures on the *Pater Noster* provide the first evidence of theological lectures in a non-university *studium* given by a lector who was not already a *magister*.[144] As such they reveal the level of theological training within the Augustinian *studia* as few other sources. Jordan's theology was thoroughly Augustinian and represents a theology more pervasive within the Order than that of the *Sentences* commentaries of the Augustinian *magistri*. As a product of the Order's educational system, Jordan's theology reveals the extent to which the Order's mendicant theology formed the theological program of the Augustinian *studia*, whereby ethics and erudition were inseparable from living the religious life.

---

[143] Eras. *Eccl.* 2 (268,475–480). I would like to thank my colleague Pete Dykema for bringing this reference to my attention. Not all contemporaries of Erasmus agreed with his judgment. In 1521 Jordan's *Opus Dan* (*Sermones de sanctis*) was published for the sixth and last time, the third edition issued by Parisian printers. In the dedicatory epistle we read: "... implerisque copiose abundantius tamen et excellentius in hisce Iordani Sermonibus invenias: ut eorum lectione sic recreetur anima tua quasi biberis de fontibus Salvatoris." Jor. *OS* Ep. (ed. Paris, 1521), fol. Aii^v.

[144] Such are the lectures on Matthew of Augustine of Ancona which he held in the *studium* at Venice in 1321. As noted in Chapter One, Augustine of Ancona received the *magisterium* at Paris in either 1313 or 1315; see Chapter One, ns. 338 and 343; *cf.* Zumkeller, "Die Augustinerschule," 201f. For Augustine's *Lectura in Evangelium Matthaei*, see Zumkeller *MSS* nr. 133 (73), extant in 40 manuscripts. For Augustine's, *Lectura in epistolas canonicas*, Zumkeller *MSS* nr. 124 (69), also extant in 40 manuscripts; and regarding his *Lectura in epistolas Pauli*, nr. 140 (77).

IV. The Mendicant Theology of the Augustinian *Studia*

Augustine of Hippo was not a systematic theologian. Constructing an Augustinian theological system, therefore, is theologically questionable and historically dubious. Augustine's works defy concretization in tightly defined categorical propositions. Throughout the western tradition, various shades and colors of Augustine's thought have been emphasized. Yet the hallmark of Augustine's "Augustinian theology" is generally agreed to have been his doctrine of grace and love. Though scholars can debate the extent to which the stridently anti-Pelagian Augustine was the most authentic Augustine, Augustine's influence as the teacher of grace (*Doctor Gratiae*) has been truly amazing.

In the fourteenth century a renewed anti-Pelagian Augustinian theology can be documented beginning in the works of Thomas Bradwardine and Gregory of Rimini. A thoroughly Augustinian theology of grace, however, was not limited to theological polemics against neo-Pelagians. With Augustine as the Order's *preceptor*, the Augustinian theological program exhibited a multi-dimensional Augustinian theology on all levels, as Jordan's *Expositio Orationis Dominice* witnesses. Jordan was not a systematic theologian, but the Augustinian nature of his theology is manifest.

Jordan's *Expositio Orationis Dominice* is first and foremost an exposition of Matthew 6:9–13. The questions Jordan raised were not designed to treat points of doctrine in systematic fashion, as was the case with *Sentences* commentaries. In addition, Jordan did not enter into debate with fellow theologians. On the occasions when one finds such references as *alii dicunt* the point at issue is scriptural interpretation, not argument for or against a given theological position. In the context of the *studium* at Erfurt there were no *socii* with whom Jordan would have to take issue.[145]

---

[145] There is, however, evidence that lectors took part in disputations in other mendicant houses; in 1456 Henricus Riettmüller de Liechtstal (d. 1478), held three quodlibetic questions, two in the Dominican house in Strassburg, and one in the Strassburg Franciscan house; see Zumkeller, *MSS*, nr. 356–358 (171–172). In the previous year he also held a disputation in the Carmelite house; *ibid.*, nr. 354 (171): "... de domo et scola fratrum beate Marie de monte Carmeli..." Hen.Riet. *Quest.*, fol. 161ʳ. In these disputations Henry directly took on his opponents; he was explicit that he directed one of his conclusions, "... contra quamdam conclusionem, quam pater meus cursor de domo et schola fratrum predictorum posuit in suo rutilanti principio, que talis fui..." Hen.Riet. *Quest.*, fol. 159ᵛ. We find similar statements

Although Jordan did not present a systematic treatment of theological doctrine in his *Expositio*, central themes of his theology can be extracted from his lectures. In this and the following chapter, the theological issues contained in his commentary on the Lord's Prayer will be elaborated with the aid of Jordan's sermons. The *Opus Postillarum* and *Opus Jor* in particular are rich sources for Jordan's theology, though it is not Jordan's theology *per se* that is the focus of my analysis; the *Expositio* will remain central as the lectures given in the Erfurt *studium*. Nevertheless, the *Opus Postillarum* is a theological biblical commentary as much as it is a collection of model sermons,[146] and Jordan incorporated his *Expositio* into his *Opus Postillarum*. Thus these two works should be seen as representative of the same level of theology as is found in the *Expositio*, and, together with the *Opus Dan*, allow for a more complete explication of the theology contained in Jordan's lectures than would otherwise be possible.

A. *Divine Dialectic*

The theological point of departure in Jordan's *Expositio* was the doctrine of God. Jordan did not, however, deal with the traditional scholastic questions on the theme. There is no discussion of God's existence, being, or knowledge. Nor is God's sovereignty stressed, as it was by Jordan's English contemporary Thomas Bradwardine.[147] Rather, the central idea for Jordan's doctrine of God is God as humans' end (*finis*), and as such, He is to be desired.[148] Yet the

---

in his *Principium et Collatio* of 1456: "Corrolarium primum: Natura non nata deum beatifice intueri sine contradictione non potest ei ypostatice uniri, quod corrolarium opponitur cuidam correlario patris mei bacalarii..." Hen.Riet *Quest.*, fol. 145ʳ; "... quod quidem corrolarium videtur directe obviare cuidam corrolario, quod pater meus bacalarius posuit in suo eleganti principio, quod tale fuit informa." Hen.Riet. *Quest.*, fol. 146ᵛ; "... sed verum est quod pater meus cursor suam maiorem tali defendebat medio primo pro prima parte... sed nego sibi minorem..." Hen.Riet. *Quest.*, fol. 147ᵛ.

[146] Jordan began his *Opus Postillarum* by stating his intent to exposit the scriptures. The readings of the Church year provide the structure and form of his exposition: "*Jordanis ripas alvei sui tempore messis impleverat.* Josue tertio [Ios. 3:15]... Intendens igitur Christo duce, secundum mee tenuitatis modulum, ad exponendum sequentias Evangeliorum dominicalium prout leguntur in ecclesia stilum arripere pro ingressu eiusmodi negotii ad commendationem evangeliorum apicum verba premissa assumpsi *Jordanis ripas* etc." Jor. *OP* sermo 1A (ed. Strassburg, 1484).

[147] Oberman, *Archbishop Thomas Bradwardine*, 49–64.

[148] "{Omnia enim que hic petuntur eo ordine} desideranda sunt que ponitur. Primo autem cadit in desiderio finis, deinde ea que sunt ad finem. Finis autem nos-

majesty and power of God are indeed acknowledged and have a central role, for God always reigns in his kingdom and His will is always carried out, even without the petitions of Christians.[149] It is not the hidden God that Jordan presented in his lectures. Nor is there reference to the two realms of God's powers (*potentia dei absoluta/ordinata*).[150] Jordan explicated the revealed triune God, who is immanently present, for with respect to God's work in creation (*opera ad extra*) the entire Trinity is involved.[151] This is not to imply that Jordan left the persons of the Trinity undistinguished, as his first two lectures demonstrate.

Jordan treated the first phrase of the prayer as a prologue, which functions as a *captatio benevolentie* whereby trust in God's ability to grant what is asked is aroused.[152] If someone lacks this confidence it is the result of the belief that God either cannot grant what one

---

ter deus est, in quem noster affectus tendit dupliciter: uno quidem modo prout volumus gloriam deo; alio modo prout volumus frui gloria eius. Quorum primum pertinet ad dilectionem, qua deum in seipso diligimus; secundum vero pertinet ad dilectionem qua diligimus nos in deo." Jor. *Exp*. 3, fol. 76[ra]. Here and throughout this chapter I am using the masculine pronoun for the deity based on Jordan's use, not on any theological or personal assumptions or opinions as to the gender of the divine.

[149] In his fourth lecture, treating *Adveniat regnum tuum*, Jordan answers the dubia of whether or not it is in vain that we pray this petition by responding that God indeed reigns independently of our asking, but that we ask for his kingdom to come to us: "Dicendum quod non est intelligendum quod hic petamus ut regnum deo adveniat, quasi ipse iam non regnet, sed quod nobis adveniat." Jor. *Exp*. 4, fol. 77[vb]. A similar answer is given in the following lectio regarding God's will: "Nec putet aliquis nos hic petere ut deus faciet voluntatem suam, quia hoc potest et facit absque nostra petitione. Sed petimus ut sua voluntas a nobis fiat et impleatur." Jor. *Exp*. 5, fol. 79[ra].

[150] On this distinction, see, William J. Courtenay, *Capacity and Volition*. In his *Opus Postillarum* Jordan did employ the distinction once. In discussing the question of God's entering the soul of sinners, Jordan explained: "Unde de potentia absoluta deus etiam posset salvare diabolum, sed non potest, id est, non vult de potentia ordinata in animam intrare nisi volentem." Jor. *OP* sermo 267G (ed. Strassburg, 1484). The distinction, however, did not play a role in Jordan's theology. Rather than the dialectic of God's power, for Jordan the divine dialectic was that of God's justice and mercy.

[151] "Vel potest dici, quod hoc nomen 'pater' non accipitur hic personaliter, sed essentialiter prout omnibus personis simul convenit. Omnia enim illa tria esse in nobis tota trinitas operatur et dat, cum opera trinitatis ad extra sint indivisa." Jor. *Exp*. 1, fol. 74[ra].

[152] "Dividitur autem hec oratio in exordium, tractatum et conclusionem. In exordio benevolentia captatur cum dicitur *Pater noster, qui es in celis*... captatio benevolentie non premittitur propter deum, ut ipse flectatur, sed propter nos, ut fiducia petendi in nobisipsis excitetur." Jor. *Exp*. 1, fol. 73[va].

asks, or is not willing to do so.[153] The very opening of the prayer, *Our Father, who is in heaven*, sufficiently responds to this doubt. The first part of the phrase, 'Our Father', indicates that God is the loving Father, while 'who is in heaven' signifies His power and majesty. Therefore, the words 'who is in heaven', Jordan explained, more properly refer to God because this phrase does so with respect to God himself, whereas 'Our Father' names God in relation to humans.[154] Yet 'Our Father' and 'who is in heaven' remain together, and thus even though the majesty and power of God are always recognized, they are not separated from the love of God.

There are three aspects of God's power which are common to all three persons of the Trinity: God's infinity, God's eternity, and God's majesty.[155] Jordan did not thoroughly analyze God's infinity, eternity, or majesty. Nor does one find a discussion of the relationship between God and time, as one might expect based on contemporary scholastic treatments of the issue. Jordan simply noted that 'who' (*qui*) is grammatically a term that signifies infinity whereas 'is' (*es*) signifies eternity. These two terms, however, in effect name God who cannot be named, and Jordan cited the response given to Moses in Exodus 3 as proof: "I am who I am."[156]

---

[153] "Igitur quod aliquis non habeat fiduciam petendi aliquem, contingit ex duobus: aut quia presumit illum dare nolle, aut dare non posse." Jor. *Exp*. 1, fol. 73va.

[154] "Econtrario, fiducia petendi excitatur aut considerando eius quem petimus erga nos dilectionem qua bonum nostrum vult, aut considerando eius potentiam et maiestatem qua id quod petimus dare potest. Et hec duo in hoc exordio consideranda proponuntur: ratione primi dicimus *Pater noster*; ratione secundi *qui es in celis*." Jor. *Exp*. 1, fol. 73va; "Propter quod istis verbis *qui es in celis* magis proprie nominamus deum quam predictis scilicet *pater noster*, quia cum dicimus *pater noster* nominamus eum per comparationem ad nos; cum vero dicimus *qui es in celis* nominamus eum per considerationem in se." Jor. *Exp*. 2, fol. 74rb.

[155] "Tanguntur autem hic tria que ad potentiam pertinent et excellentiam videlicet infinitas, eternitas et maiestas. Que tria sunt omnibus tribus personis communia, nec alicui alteri a deo attribui possiblia." Jor. *Exp*. 2, fol. 74rb.

[156] "Infinitas tangitur in eo quod dicitur *qui*, quod secundum grammaticos est nomen infinitum. Eternitas notatur cum dicitur *es*, quod secundum grammaticos est verbum substantivum [sonantium *B*] significatione, presens consignificatione, primum resolutione, quia in ipsum omnia alia verba resoluntur. Que tria eternitati congruunt. Illud enim est vere eternum, quod per seipsum subsistit a nullo dependens, quod semper presens incommunicabiliter persistit et quo nichil prius existit. Maiestas notatur cum additur *in celis*, que sunt corpora virtute et potentissima. De primis duobus simul—et est sciendum quod iste due dictiones, *qui es* simul accepte congruentissime deo—conveniunt in tantum quod per eas deus, qui innominabilis est, quasi proprio nomine explicatur. Unde Exodi <tertio> [tertio decimo *B*], cum Moyses quereret de nomine dei: Si querunt, inquit, *quod est nomen eius qui misit te, quid dicam?* [Ex. 3:13] Respondit dominus: *sic*, inquit, *dices filiis Israel, qui est misit me*

Jordan's exposition of 'in heaven' (*in celis*), which corresponds to God's majesty, presents his doctrine of God in encapsulated form. The God of majesty is God enthroned, and one must never lose sight of this aspect of God. The term 'in heaven' signifies the heavenly king. The divine majesty, however, is only one of five reasons God is said to be 'in heaven'.[157] The second reason one says 'in heaven', which is still referring to God's power and majesty *per se*, is on account of the unlearned (*rudes homines*). In the next three reasons Jordan's own "dialectic of God's omnipotence" becomes evident, a dialectic between God's majesty and God's love. While ever aware of the divine majesty, God is said to be 'in heaven' so that humans might recognize that the heavenly father wants to have heavenly sons; so that one might pray for heavenly things; and finally so that Christians might seek their inheritance in heaven.[158]

God, however, is not only humans' end. He is also their beginning, and indeed their very being. Drawing upon Thomas Aquinas without acknowledgment, Jordan explained that God is called 'Our Father' because of the three-fold being (*esse*) humans receive from Him: the being of nature, of grace, and of glory. In creation God gave humans their nature (*esse nature*); in recreation or redemption, God gives His grace (*esse gratie*); and in imparting His kingdom, humans will receive glory (*esse glorie*). Thus God is praise-worthy in His creation; lovable in His redemption; and desirable in granting His Kingdom.[159]

[Ex. 3:14], et congruentissime, ut ipse, qui est infinite essentie et eterne subsistentie nomine infinito et verbo substantivo [sonativo *B*] explicetur." Jor. *Exp.* 2, fol. 74rb–74va. *Cf.* Prisc. gramm. (3:20,21–30; 2:414,13–16).

[157] "Dicitur tamen potius esse in celis quam in aliis locis propter quinque rationes. Primo, quia in eis magis relucet divine operationis." Jor. *Exp.* 2, fol. 74vb.

[158] "Secundo propter rudes homines, quia secundum Augustinum convenit ut omnium sensibus, tam magnorum quam parvulorum bene sentiatur de eo [Aug.de serm.dom. 2,5,18 (108,389–396)]. Et ideo qui nondum possunt aliquid incorporeum cogitare, tolerabilior est eorum opinio, si deum in celis potius esse credant quam in terra. Tertio ut innuat quod celestis pater celestes vult habere filios. Unde dicit Chrysostomus: erubescant se terrenis rebus substernere, qui patrem habent in celis. [Ps.Chrysost. in Matth. 14 (711)] Quarto ut orantes celestia petamus. Unde Chrysostomus in homelia in celis deum esse dicit non illic eum concludens sed a terra abducens mentem orantis et celestibus affigens. [Chrysost. hom.in Matth. 19 (278)] Quinto ut hereditatem nostram in celis queramus. Unde Cassianus in *Collationibus Patrum*: ad illam, inquit, regionem in quam patrem nostrum morari fatemur, summo desiderio properemus [Cassian. coll.pat. 19,18 (789A)]." Jor. *Exp.* 2, fol. 74vb; *cf.* Thom.Aq. *CA* ad Matth. 6:9 (103b).

[159] "Est autem notandum, quod ipse deus dicitur *pater noster* tripliciter, secundum

It might seem that this three-fold exposition would lead Jordan to associate each with a specific person of the Trinity. He used this very opportunity, however, to stress the unity of the three persons. Jordan posed the question of why the prayer is not directed to Christ since the being of the second person of the Trinity is most closely related to human nature: Christ also had natural being (*esse naturae*). Jordan responded that the Son is from the Father and received from the Father whatever he had, and therefore he always attributed honor to the Father. Further, humans are indeed most closely joined to Christ and in Christ they are redeemed. Christians are redeemed by Christ, but whatever Christ received, he received from the Father and thus human redemption originates from the Father, "who, in order to redeem us, sent his son into the world." Therefore, when one says 'Our Father' one adores all three persons of the Trinity with a single adoration. The terms do not refer to the persons, but to the essence of the Godhead. Because the works of the Trinity in creation (*ad extra*) are not distinguished according to persons, the entire Trinity gives and effects in humans the three-fold being received from God.[160]

triplex esse quod ab eo accepimus scilicet nature, gratie, et glorie. Esse nature dedit nobis in creatione; esse gratie in recreatione sive redemptione; et esse glorie dabit in regni communicatione... Hoc triplex esse quod a deo recepimus, correspondet triplicibus beneficiis que filius carnalis accepit a patre. Primum beneficium est generationis, quo in esse nature producitur quantum ad primum. Secundum est beneficium educationis, quo nutritur et alitur quantum ad secundum. Tertium beneficium hereditationis, quo vite solacium ducitur quo ad tertium. Et hec tria comprehenduntur in illo dicto poetico, quod assumit Paulus Actuum 17: *in ipso*, scilicet deo, *vivimus, movemur, et sumus* [Act. 17:28]. Sumus, inquam, in natura; movemur in gratia; vivimus in gloria. Ratione primi, deus est a nobis summe laudabilis; ratione secundi, valde amabilis; ratione tertii, maxime desiderabilis." Jor. *Exp.* 1, fol. 73^{va-b}. *Cf.* Thom.Aq., *STh* II/II, 1, 8, resp.

[160] "Cadunt autem super hec particularia tres dubitationes. Prima est, quare Christus non docuit nos dirigere orationem ad se, ut diceremus, 'Christe, fili dei, qui es in celis etc.,' vel aliquid huiusmodi, quod tamen videretur esse conveniens cum persona filii sit <nobis> magis familiariter coniuncta per susceptionem nature, quare etc. Ad hoc dicendum quod quia filius est a patre et quidquid habet nascendo accepit, ut Augustinus dicit, ideo patri honorem semper attribuit, iuxta illud Johannis octavo: *Ego gloriam meam {non quero}, sed honorifico patrem meum* etc. [Io. 8:49] Nec obstat quod filius magis coniunctus est {nobis}, et quod in ipso redempti sumus, quia nostra redemptio originaliter a patre fuit, qui ut nos redimeret, filium suum in mundum misit, etiam omnes tres persone simul una adoratione adorantur, et ideo non refert. Principaliter tamen oratio dirigitur ad patrem propter causam iam dictam. Vel potest dici, quod hoc nomen 'pater' non accipitur hic personaliter, sed essentialiter prout omnibus personis simul convenit. Omnia enim illa tria esse in nobis tota trinitas operatur et dat, cum opera trinitatis ad extra sint indivisa." Jor. *Exp.* 1, fol. 73vb–74ra.

In a similar manner, the words 'who is' are also directed to all three persons, corresponding both to the Trinity as a whole and to the individual persons. Jordan argued that in the first place there is no real distinction in the divine essence, and the words 'who is' refer to the divine essence. Second, each person exists *per se* and therefore does not depend on any other being, though the second and third persons of the Trinity are 'from' something other than themselves. Here Jordan made a distinction between 'depending on another' and 'being from another'. Dependence implies imperfection, whereas 'being from another' signifies origin. To clarify Jordan further differentiated 'previous' (*prius*) from 'priority' (*prior*). There is nothing previous to the second and third persons of the Trinity, but there is something prior in terms of priority, namely the Father. This priority is not a priority of temporal duration and thus takes nothing away from the eternity of all three persons. It is a priority of origin, which can be understood in the sense of "placed before," rather than "existing" before.[161]

Jordan's doctrine of God is not based on the "Being of God," but on the works of the Trinity. There is no juridical interplay whereby the Son makes propitiation to the Father for human sin. The entire Trinity works human salvation. The entire Trinity is the object of the prayer, through which one recognizes not only the majesty and power of God, but also the love of God. God is the Christian's end and beginning, the Christian's desire and being.

Jordan's Trinitarian theology is present throughout his exposition. In his discussion of the various interpretations of 'our daily bread', not only do we find Christ in the bread of the eucharist, but also the present face of God in its pure divinity. The wheat bread of the

---

[161] "Dicendum quod hoc nomen *qui es* convenit omnibus tribus personis simul generaliter et singule persone singulariter. Primum patet quod cum in essentia divina nulla sit distinctio realis et hoc nomen significet essentiam quod de se patet, planum est quod convenit simul omnibus tribus. Secundum etiam patet, nam <cum> quelibet persona per seipsum subsistit, quia dicitur Iohannis quinto: *Sicut enim pater habet vitam in semetipso, sic dedit et filio vitam habere in semetipso* [Io. 5:26], et similiter de spiritu sancto. Et sicut de vita, ita eadem ratione est de esse. Quelibet ergo persona habet esse in seipsa et per seipsam. Unde nulla earum dependet ab alia, licet una sit ab alia. Aliud est enim 'dependere ab alio' et aliud <est> 'esse ab alio', quia 'dependere' dicit imperfectionem; 'esse' autem ab alio notat originis nomen. Nulla quidem personarum habet aliud prius se, licet bene habeat alium priorem se. Et nec illa est prioritas durationis qualis derogat eternitati, sed est prioritas originis, que non repugnat coeternis et coevis." Jor. *Exp.* 2, fol. 74[va–b].

sacrament is thus truly 'our daily bread' because "we are not able to survive a single moment without it."[162] God's power and majesty ensure that the prayer is efficacious and the Christian must never forget that God is the heavenly king who always reigns 'in heaven'. Yet it is precisely this heavenly king who is also the loving Father. The dialectic of God's majesty and God's love formed the nucleus of Jordan's exposition of the Lord's Prayer, and, I might add, of his entire theology. The heavens are God's habitation, but "so that the soul might become ever increasingly capable of receiving God, it is fitting that it is extended and broadened through grace and love." In effect, the human soul is expanded in order to contain the heavens which God has extended to the soul, as Jordan affirmed by citing Psalm 103:2: "[God] extending heaven just as a tent."[163] And this 'extension' of the heavens and expansion of the soul provides the transition from Jordan's doctrine of God, to his doctrine of grace.

B. *The* Lector Gratie

Considering the common categories used to describe a work such as Jordan's, it may be surprising that I have named grace as one of its leading theological themes. The Trier manuscript of the *Expositio* notes that it is *valde solemnis*.[164] On first sight Jordan's commentary on the Lord's Prayer appears as a work of monastic piety. If it can be considered a theological work at all, rather than one of practical spirituality, it surely should be placed within the genre of pastoral theology (*Frömmigkeitstheologie*), which, at least in the later fifteenth century, was "semi-Pelagian."[165] Jordan's emphasis on the virtues and

---

[162] "Est propterea panis triticeus, in quantum ipsos reficit nude divinitatis ostentatione, quam in ipso clare et nude feliciter contemplantur. Et sic sive ingrediantur per divinitatis contemplationem, sive egrediantur per humanitatis intuitionem semper pascua invenient per nove dulcedinis degustationem. De quibus pascuis dicit Gregorius: Que sunt illa pascua nisi interna semper virentis paradisi gaudia? [Greg.M. in evang. 14,5 (1130A)] Pascua namque electorum sunt presens vultus dei, qui dum sine defectu conspicitur, sine fine mens cibo satiatur. Iste igitur glorisosus panis dicitur supersubstantialis, quia super omnes substantias est et omnes superat creaturas. Dicitur etiam cottidianus, quia cottidie, id est eternaliter, ipso reficiemur et nec uno momento sine ipso subsistere possumus." Jor. *Exp*. 6, fol. 81vb.

[163] "Ut autem anima semper magis et magis sit capax dei, oportet eam per gratiam et caritatem extendi et dilatari, dicente Apostolo 2 Corinthiorum 5 dilatamini in caritate [*cf*. II Cor. 6:1–13]. De hac dilectione et extensione dicitur in psalmo: *extendens celum sicut pellem* [Ps. 103:2]." Jor. *Exp*. 2, fol. 75ra.

[164] Trier StB, MS 69/1053. As cited by Hümpfner, intro. xxx.

[165] Hamm, *Frömmigkeitstheologie*, 253ff.

vices, moreover, provides preliminary evidence to claim that Jordan is a preacher of moral perfection, far more than a teacher of grace. Indeed, in his explication of what leads humans to their end directly and principally Jordan named the merit "by which we merit blessedness by obeying God."[166] Further, it is not grace that enables one to merit blessedness, but peace. Peace is the cause of redemption, Jordan explained, "to the extent that through peace we earn the right (*meremur*) to be participants of redemption, and such peace the impious do not have."[167] If, however, one reads Jordan's text through the lens of such statements as these, his theology of grace remains hidden from view. From a theological standpoint we must begin with the beginning, and this for Jordan was, as I have already noted, the extension of God's kingdom to the soul, expanded through love and grace. The other side of the issue is therefore what is the role of human initiative? This question provides the point of departure for discerning Jordan's theology of grace.[168] In his lectures on Matthew, Jordan exhibited such a strong theology of grace that it is fitting to christen him the *Lector Gratie*, who clearly stood in the tradition of the *Doctor Gratie*, St. Augustine.

Uncovering Jordan's theology of grace is difficult because he did not directly address the precise relationship between grace and merit. The traditional scholastic terms used for explicating how humans achieve salvation are not to be found in Jordan's lectures. He did not employ the distinction between 'half merit' (*meritum de congruo*) and 'full merit' (*meritum de condigno*), nor that between the general grace of God, or 'grace given gratuitously' (*gratia gratis data*) and 'sanctifying grace' (*gratia gratum faciens*).[169] Nevertheless, the relationship

---

[166] "Ad finem autem predictum ordinat nos aliquid dupliciter: uno modo per se; alio modo per accidens. Per se quidem bonum quod est utile in finem. Est autem aliquid utile in finem beatitudinis dupliciter: uno modo directe et principaliter, secundum meritum quo beatitudinem meremur deo obediendo, et quantum ad hoc ponitur *fiat voluntas tua*; alio modo instrumentaliter, et quasi coadiuvans nos ad merendum, et ad hoc pertinet quod dicitur *panem nostrem cottidianum*. Per accidens autem ordinamur in beatitudinem per remotionem prohibentis." Jor. *Exp.* 3, fol. 76^{ra-b}.

[167] "Pax est effectus nostre redemptionis in quantum per redemptionem sumus in pace positi. Aliter: pax potest esse causa redemptionis in quantum per pacem meremur esse participes redemptionis, et talem pacem non habent impii." Jor. *Exp.* 3, fol. 77va.

[168] Schulze has noted that this was the decisive question for Gregory of Rimini; see Schulze, "*Via Gregorii*," 80.

[169] On the various definitions, distinctions, and functions of grace in scholastic theology, see A.M. Landgraf, *Dogmengeschichte der Frühscholastik*. Vol. 1/1, *Die Gnadenlehre*

between God's grace and human initiative is clearly spelled out. Though Jordan did not explicitly use the scholastic term 'in the state of nature' (*ex puris naturalibus*), when it comes to what humans can do on their own without grace he is emphatic: "we do not have the ability (*non valemus*) to carry out God's will with our own powers... therefore we ask this of God so that He might give grace to us."[170]

In his *Expositio* Jordan did not address the consequences of the fall. For the effects of Adam's sin one must turn to the *Opus Postillarum*. Here Jordan gave a detailed account of the wondrous attributes humans enjoyed in paradise.[171] The state of innocence entailed humans living in the untarnished image of God and in complete obedience to God, which is Jordan's definition of original righteousness (*iustitia originalis*). The will was completely free to follow God. All this harmony was lost in the fall. Nevertheless, both the image of God and free will remained. As a consequence of sin, however, the image of God in humans is harmed and spoiled, and the free will is held captive to sin. Jordan echoed Augustine's definition of the effects of the fall on free will:

> Free will certainly remains [after the fall] but it is depraved and rotten because with sin came the difficulty to do good and the propensity to do evil. With his free will before the fall, man was able to sin and able not to sin, but after the fall man was able to sin and not able not to sin. The image of God in the soul also remained after the fall but afterwards it is a deformed image.[172]

(Regensburg, 1952); and for late medieval theological terms, see Heiko A. Oberman, *The Harvest of Medieval Theology. Gabriel Biel and Late Medieval Nominalism* (Cambridge, 1963; reprint: Durham, N.C., 1983), 459–476.

[170] "Et quia voluntatem dei nostris viribus perficere non valemus... ideo hoc petimus a deo quatinus ipse det nobis gratiam." Jor. *Exp.* 5, fol. 79ra.

[171] Jordan states that there were twelve conditions humans enjoyed in paradise: "... duodecim nobiles et praeclaras conditiones, in quibus homo conditus fuit, quarum sex accipiuntur penes corpus et sex aliae penes animam. Prima fuit propagationis castitas... Secunda, complexionis sanitas... Tertia, iustitiae originalis integritas... Quarta, corporis et animae impassibilitas... Quinta fuit immortalitas... Sexta, loci tranquilitas... Septima fuit peccati immunitas... Octava, cognitionis perspicacitas... Nona fuit virtutum serenitas... Decima, beatitudinis securitas... Undecima, arbitrii libertas... Duodecima fuit divinae imaginis dignitas." Jor. *OP* sermo 7B (ed. Strassburg, 1483).

[172] "Duobus solum lineis ultimis adhuc vix superextantibus scilicet liberi arbitrii dotatione et divine imaginis insignitione, que duo velut due linee adhuc remanserant secundum essentiam; vulnerata tamen quo ad naturalia et spoliata quo ad gratuita. Remansit quippe liberum arbitrium sed depravatum et imminutum, quia per peccatum difficultatem recipit ad bonum et pronitatem ad malum. Prius enim homo

In his seventh lecture on the Our Father Jordan stated that "someone lives in God when they live without sin."[173] He had previously clarified in his first lecture when explicating Acts 17:28, "in God we live, we are moved, and we are," that 'to live in God' refers to the state of glory (*esse glorie*), that is, to when one is living with God in heaven.[174] Thus directly after stating that humans live in God when they live without sin, Jordan is quick to affirm that everyone needs to pray 'forgive us our debts' because "no man is free from sin."[175] Humans left to their own powers do not even have the smallest kernel of the bread they need daily unless God gives it to them.[176]

Jordan's picture of the human condition is not pretty. The sinful soul, he affirmed in the *Opus Jor*, is a daughter of Babylon, throwing the entire divine order into chaos. The sinner, in and of himself (*quantum in se est*), causes bedlam in all of nature; he is the molester of all creation, of the scriptures and of all grace.[177] Humans are captive to sin and on their own can only ask for God's grace. "By ourselves we are weak and fragile," Jordan lamented in his *Meditationes de Passione Christi*, "and devoid of all good, unless we are held by the right hand of God."[178] Never certain of his own righteousness, one must "never think himself to be safe from the devil... man is wretched and fragile, certain of nothing except the death of Christ alone."[179]

---

per liberum arbitrium poterat peccare et non peccare, sed post potuit peccare et non potuit non peccare. Imago etiam dei remansit in anima post peccatum, sed quasi deformata." Jor. *OP* sermo 7B (ed. Strassburg, 1483); *cf.* Aug. corrept. 12 (936) and Aug. civ. 22,30 (863,52–864,73). Landgraf attributed the formula *posse peccare, non posse non peccare*, to Hugh of St. Victor; Landgraf, *Die Gnadenlehre*, 102.

[173] "In deo autem aliquis vivit quando sine peccato vivit." Jor. *Exp.* 7, fol. 82va.

[174] See note 159 above.

[175] "Et ex hoc elicitur quod quia omnes ad dicendum istam orationem tenentur nullum hominem a peccato esse immunem." Jor. *Exp.* 7, fol. 82^{va-b}.

[176] "... per hoc quod dicitur *da*, quasi dicat quod nec minimum granum ex nobis habere possumus nisi tu des." Jor. *Exp.* 6, fol. 80va.

[177] "Significanter autem anima peccatrix dicitur filia babilonis et confusionis, quia ipsa est eterna confusione digna, qui totum ordinem divine dispositionis deordinavit. Peccator enim quantum in se est deordinatio est omnium naturarum. Est enim abusor omnium creaturarum, omnium scripturarum, omnium gratiarum, contemnit etiam per peccatum consortium divinarum personarum et ideo omnium deordinator ex verbis merito filia babilonis, id est, confusionis appellatur." Jor. *OJ* sermo 84, fol. 152rb.

[178] "nos ex nobis esse infirmos et fragiles, ac omni bono vacuos, nisi dextera dei nos manu teneat." Jor. *Med.* art. 34, fol. 23va.

[179] "nunquam... se puteat securus de diabolo... homo miser et fragilis, certe de nullo nisi solum de morte Christi." Jor. *Med.* art. 62, fol. 39vb; *cf.* "... quia enim

The flesh is the "ass of the soul," as Jordan defined it in the *Opus Postillarum*,[180] and human nature is beastly: "for just as certain men are as beasts and are extraordinarily evil, namely falling below the level of humanity (*citra modum hominum*), so even are other men as divine beings and live beyond the human condition (*super hominem*)."[181] For Jordan, unless one lives "beyond oneself" one is truly beastly for on one's own one lives according to the "ass of the soul." What enables humans to live beyond themselves, what enables them to do something other than wallow in sin, is God expanding the soul and extending the heavens through love and grace. It is only by grace that humans have their being in the first place for grace is an expression of God's love for humans. Grace is not something earned; left on one's own, one can only sin. Thus, one must ask again, what is Jordan's understanding of 'grace'? How does it 'work'?

C. *Grace Given Gratuitously*

In his penultimate lecture Jordan defined grace. Drawing from Thomas Aquinas, Jordan explained that grace "is a habit perfecting the essence of the soul by purging the sickness of guilt and by elevating the soul

---

pena, quam peccator debet sustinere, excedit vires eius, ideo ordinavit deus ex magna misericordia ut pro eo et cum eo primo satisfaciat meritum passionis Christi, qui per suam passionem non solum mundum redemit sed etiam suum meritum pro peccatoribus satisfacit." Jor. *OJ* sermo 104, fol. 180rb; ". . . ut videlicet petamus eruari a potestate diaboli quia expellatur ab anima nostra . . . petamus non confidentes de meritis nostris, sed de sola misericordia dei." Jor. *OJ*, sermo 97, fol. 171ra.

[180] "Nam in nostro corpore idem sunt asinus et servus. Caro siquidem nostra quid est aliud quam asina animae?" Jor. *OP* sermo 437A (ed. Strassburg, 1483).

[181] "Nam sicut quidam homines sunt quasi bestie et supermali videlicet citra modum hominum, sic etiam aliqui homines sunt quasi divini et super hominem." Jor. *OP* sermo 439G (ed. Strassburg, 1483). Jordan clarified that such a "super virtue" is such: ". . . non quod sit supra potestatem humanam, sed quia est supra id, quod communiter in hominibus invenitur." *Ibid*. In the *OP-B* some of the material comprising Jordan's *Tractatus de virtutibus et vitiis*, i.e., sermones 439–441 of *OP* (ed. Strassburg, 1483), was placed within sermones 437 and 438. Sermones 439–441 were omitted from *OP-B*, which breaks off at sermo 438 (*OP-B*, fol. 186vb; fol. 187^{r}–217 contain a seemingly random collection of various material, which remains to be determined whether it came from Jordan's pen), which actually is from the section *De Iustitia* of the *Tractatus de virtutibus et vitiis*, *OP*, sermo 440 (ed. Strassburg, 1483). *OP-B* reads slightly differently: "Nam sicut quidem homines sunt quasi bestie et semper mali videlicet circa modum hominum, sic aliquis homines sunt quasi divini et semper boni ultra modum humanum." Jor. *OP-B* sermo 437, fol. 184ra. This distinction between the *bestie* and the *mali* Jordan took from Giles of Rome's *De Regimine Principum*: "Nam sicut aliqui homines sunt sicut bestiae, et sunt mali ultra modum hominum, sic aliqui sunt quasi divini, et sunt boni supra modum

to a certain supernatural state of being."[182] As such, grace, for Jordan, is infused in the soul by God. In traditional scholastic terminology this infused grace was sanctifying grace (*gratia gratum faciens*). In his commentary on the *Sentences* of Lombard, Jordan's confrere Thomas of Strassburg distinguished the general grace of God (*gratia gratis data*) from sanctifying grace (*gratia gratum faciens*) precisely in this manner. Sanctifying grace is infused, sacramental grace.[183] Echoing Jordan, Thomas clarified that sanctifying grace "perfects the essence of the soul."[184] That Jordan was referring to infused sacramental grace in his definition, or at least that he intended to encompass such grace, is seen in his sixth lecture. In discussing the various interpretations of 'our daily bread', he first explained that the 'daily bread' of the Lucan version (*panem cottidianum*) is identical with the 'added bread of substance' (*panem supersubstantialem*) of Matthew.[185] He then proceeded to interpret 'our daily bread' as doctrinal bread, sacramental bread, and celestial bread. Doctrinal bread, or the 'bread of understanding' (*panis doctrinalis vel sit panis intelligentie*) is called 'supersubstantial' "because it is a special addition added to the substance of our soul, informing it with noble habits, namely, with holy virtues and spiritual gifts."[186] Further, by partaking of the eucharistic bread

---

<humanum>, propter quod tales supervirtuosi dici possunt." Aeg.Rom. *Reg.Princ.* I,2,4 (57). The same statement is found in Aeg.Rom. *Reg.Princ.* I,2,32 (146), and II,1,7 (240). *Cf.* Antonius Rampegolus' view of the *religiosi*; Saak, "The *Figurae Bibliorum* of Antonius Rampegolus," 35f.

[182] "Gratia est enim habitus perficiens essentiam anime purgando egritudinem culpe et ad quoddam esse supernaturale animam elevando." Jor. *Exp.* 9, fol. 87rb; see also J. Aertsen, *Nature and Creature. Thomas Aquinas's Way of Thought*, STGMA 21 (Leiden, 1988), 370; and Landgraf, *Die Gnadenlehre*, 158.

[183] ". . . quod prout communiter distinguitur duplex est gratia. Una, que dicitur gratum faciens; alia non gratum faciens, quamvis sit gratis data. De prima procedit praesens inquisitio, quia tam gratia sacramentorum, quam gratia virtutum, loquendo de infusis virtutibus, est gratia gratum faciens." Thom.Arg. 4 *Sent.* 2,2 (ed. Venice, 1564), fol. 66va.

[184] "Et haec, scilicet gratia gratum faciens potest dupliciter considerari. Uno modo secundum suam essentiam. Alio modo secundum redundantiam. Primo modo, perficit essentiam animae. Secundo modo, perficit potentias animae." Thom.Arg. 4 *Sent.* 2,2 (ed. Venice, 1564), fol. 66va.

[185] "Ubi autem Mattheus dicit supersubstantialem, Lucas dicit cottidianum, et refertur ad idem." Jor. *Exp.* 6, fol. 80va.

[186] "Alio modo hec petitio potest exponi de pane mystico et spirituali, et sic exponendo possumus dicere quod est triplex panis: panis doctrinalis, sacramentalis, et celestis, vel sic: panis intelligentie, eucharistie, glorie. Primus repellit famen erroris. Secundus est in nutrimentum amoris. Tertius prebet delectamentum saporis. De primo pane dicitur Ecclesiastici quinto decimo: *Cibavit illum panem vite et intellectus*

one is united with God, wherefore "it is called the sacrament of unity." The 'heavenly bread' is the bread of glory received in beatitude.[187] These three 'breads' are thus related to the three-fold being humans receive from God and at least the first two are virtually identical with Jordan's definition of grace: grace perfects the soul by the infusion of virtues, which leads to union with God in a supernatural state of being. Given Jordan's only explicit definition of grace, therefore, it would seem that essentially all grace is infused (*gratia infusa*), which was traditionally considered to be sanctifying grace (*gratia gratum faciens*).

When we turn to Jordan's *Opus Postillarum* we find further clarification, or at least, additional information. In discussing the goods of grace (*de bonis gratie*) that humans receive from God, Jordan explained that:

> some are acquired, such as knowledge, prudence, justice, fortitude, temperance, and the other moral virtues, which, although they are acquired through human effort, nevertheless are not acquired without grace, for what do you have that you have not received? Other goods of grace are infused, such as faith, hope, love, and grace given gratuitously (*gratie gratis date*).[188]

[Sir. 15:3], et Matthei quarto: *non in solo pane vivit homo* etc. [Mt. 4:4]. Iste panis dicitur supersubstantialis quia superadditur substantie anime nostre informans ipsam habitibus nobilibus, puta scientiis, virtutibus et spiritualibus carismatibus." Jor. *Exp.* 6, fol. 81ra. Jordan took this passage virtually verbatim from Hen. *Exp.*, fol. 187r.

[187] "De secundo pane, scilicet eucharistie, dicitur Johannis sexto: *Ego sum panis vivus*, etc. [Io. 6:45] . . . Et revera iste benedictus panis est summe egregius et nobis maxime peculiaris. Non enim est tam grandis natio quam habeat deos appropinquantes sibi sicut adest nobis dominus deus noster. Ex eo videlicet quod manducamus istum sanctissimum panem, quo deo unimur, propter quod dicitur esse sacramentum unitatis. Unde dicitur Iohannis sexto: *Qui manducat meam carnem* etc., *in me manet et ego in eo* [Io. 6:57]. Dicitur etiam panis cottidianus, quia cottidie, id est omni die, sumendus est. . . . De tertio pane scilicet celesti sive glorie dicitur Luce quarto decimo: *Beatus qui manducat panem in regno dei* [Lc. 14:15]. Et bene illa beata fruitio dicitur panis, quia sicut panis corporalis satiat appetitum edentis, sic fruitio illa satiat desiderium contemplantis, psalmo: *Satiabor cum apparuerit gloria tua* [Ps. 16:15]. Reficimur autem ibi non solum visione divinitatis, sed et pascimur deliciosa contemplatione humanitatis in Christo." Jor. *Exp.* 6, fol. 81rb-va. Once again Jordan took his exposition from Hen. *Exp.*, fol. 187r-v.

[188] "De bonis gratiae . . . quaedam sunt acquisita sicut scientia, prudentia, iusticia, fortitudo, temperantia et ceterae virtutes morales, quae quamvis sint humano studio acquisita, nequaquam tamen absque dei gratia acquiruntur: *quid enim habes quod non accepisti?* prime ad Corinthios quarto [I Cor. 4:7]; quaedam infunduntur a deo, ut fides, spes, caritas, et gratiae gratis datae." Jor. *OP* sermo 436C (ed. Strassburg, 1483).

For Jordan, infused grace is not sanctifying grace (*gratia gratum faciens*), but rather the general grace of God given gratuitously (*gratia gratis data*).

In this same sermon Jordan equated the goods humans receive from God with the feudal relationship between a lord and vassal. One's goods are not one's own possessions (*propria*); humans are simply administrators who must make good use of the goods they hold for their Lord:

> We owe stewardship of those goods conceded to us, for God did not give us those goods which we have from Him on account of our merits, or so to say, on account of our beautiful hair, but on account of His own goodness and for His service. For example: princes and lords concede some goods to their men in the feudal pact so that their men might be able to do some services for them or might pay a certain debt from them. Therefore, the goods which we hold from God are not to be considered given to us from God as our own, but rather for our use so that we might be administrators and stewards of them, rather than our own lords.[189]

All the goods one possesses, even those infused in the soul, cannot be called one's own. Christians are merely administrators of the goods given *gratis*.[190] For Jordan all grace is gratuitously given.

---

[189] "... debemus pensionem deo de bonis nobis concessis. Non enim deus dedit nobis bona illa, quae habemus ab eo, propter nostra merita vel secundum modum loquendi, propter nostros pulchros capillos, sed propter suam bonitatem et ad suum servitium. Exemplum de principibus et dominis qui hominibus <suis> concedunt alia bona in foedum ut de ipsis faciant ei cetera servitia vel certam pensionem de eis solvant. Igitur bona, quae tenemus a deo, non reputemus nobis data <a deo> ut propria sed tamquam ad usum concessa ut eorum simus administratores et dispensatores potius quam domini." Jor. *OP* sermo 436A (ed. Strassburg, 1483). The emendations were made based on *OP-B*, fol. 178[ra-b]. Similar statements were made by the Augustinians Hermann of Schildesche, Johannes Zachariae, and Johannes von Dorsten. See Zumkeller, *Erbsünde*, 289, 378.

[190] In the *Opus Jor* Jordan presents a hymn of sorts to the goods God has given humans: "Vide admirabilem providentiam dei nostri. Dederat enim homini visum, auditum, gustum, odoratum et tactum etc. Attende ergo quod genera colorum nunc alborum nunc nigrorum nunc mediorum tibi dederit per visum. Vide quod consonantias vocum, quod voces omnium modulantium, quod genera musicorum instrumentorum, quod etiam genera cantilenarum tibi dederit propter auditum. Vide quod genera odorum, quod genera herbarum et florum et genera specierum et aliorum odorabilium corporum tibi dederit propter olefactum. Vide quod genera saporum, quod genera carnium, quod genera piscium, quod genera fructuum, quod genera blandorum, quod genera vinorum, quod genera olerum tibi dedit propter gustum. Vide genera liquidorum et aridorum, quod genera calidorum et frigidorum, quod genera vestimentorum tibi data sunt propter tactum. Si enim ista et alia plurima, que dimitto, diligenter considerantur, valde admirabilis dominus noster.... Tertio,

Jordan's view of grace as the gifts Christians hold from their Lord is the theological expression of the *usus pauper*.[191] As an Augustinian, Jordan did not hold to the Franciscan understanding of "poor use." Yet there is an *usus pauper* of sort in the Augustinians' view of poverty regarding the relationship between the prior and the *fratres*. Upon entering the Order, the friar was to remit all his worldly possessions to the prior. The prior could then concede to the friar the use of goods according to his needs.[192] The prior played the role of the lord in distributing to the brothers the needed goods for their use.[193] This is an elaboration of the *Rule*, where Augustine affirms that when

---

o homo, si tibi non sufficiunt quod tibi paravit bona nature et fortune, saltem attende quia tibi paravit bona gratie ex quo a te valde est diligendus quia hoc bonum non est bonum ventris sed mentis. Dederat enim deus humane anime potentiam cognitivam, qua posset universam cognoscere; dederat potentiam amativam, qua posset per amorem suo precipio adherere; dederat enim et operativam, qua posset regi servire. Attende igitur, o homo, quod genera dederit scientiarum, contemplativarum, activarum sive naturalium et moralium propter intellectivam. Attende quod genera tibi dederit gratiarum virtutum et donorum beatitudinum et fructuum spiritualium propter potentiam affectivam. Attende nihilominus homo quod genera dederit preceptorum, consiliorum et exemplorum, promissionum et comminationum propter operativam; et si ista tibi pauca videntur, attende qualem gratiam tibi fecit dominus dum se ipsum in pretium tibi dedit in patibulo cruci et in cibum tibi se tradidit in sacramento altaris.... Attende ergo ex parte corporis, quod tibi dona paravit. Nam ibi visus, qui nunc pascitur coloribus vanis, illam regionem luminosam videbit, que ex parte lucis consistit. Si sol unus sic mundum illuminat, cogita quam luminosa est illa regio, que ex sua natura ex luce purissima, ubi in mirabilia corpora supra solem splendientia, ubi Christus, humanitate illuminatius universa, et ubi insuper divina essentia super hec omnia radiat in virtute. Si ergo propter hoc ultimum oculus super omnia iam dicta intuebitur, item si cantus avium, si cantilene homini nunc dilectant auditum, quid erit omnium sanctorum audire contentum deum laudandum? Quid olefactum ibi erit, ubi odor inestimabilis, quid gustu dulcedinis dulcius summe delectabili, quid tactui ubi summa mollicies erit, quid toto corpore cuius erit tanta claritas ut supra solem resplendeat, tanta agilitas ut in modico totum mundum pertranseat et ubicumque volet se statim inveniet, tanta virtuositas sive subtilitas ut omne corpus quantumcumque solidum penetrare valeat, tanta etiam impassibilitas ut nulli passione subiaceant?... Ad hec igitur bona, ab eterna homini preparata, invitabit deus in die ultima quando dicet Matthei vicesimo quinto: *Venite ecce ab omni malo separato benedicti patris mei* [Mt. 25:34]. Ecce summum horum collatio, quod nobis paratum est ab origine mundi. Ecce eterna predestinatio, que nihil aliud est quam preparatio gratie in presenti et glorie in futuro.... Ergo, carissimi, qui vult effugere mala pene, studeat deum agnoscere ex bonis nature, studeat cognoscere et admirari ex bonis fortune, studeat cognoscere et adimitari et amare ex bonis gratie, ut per hoc possit in fine pertingere ad bona glorie." Jor. *OJ* sermo 240, fol. 373ra–374va.

[191] On the *usus pauper*, see David Burr, *Olivi and Franciscan Poverty. The Origin of the 'Usus Pauper' Controversy* (Philadelphia, 1989).
[192] *VF* 3,9 (352,58–64).
[193] *VF* 3,13 (376,140–145).

one recognizes the observance of the *Rule* one should give thanks to God, who is the "giver of all goods."[194] Moreover, Jordan's view of grace is completely in keeping with his Order's emphasis on a dominion of grace, as we have seen advocated by Giles of Rome, William of Cremona, and Augustinus of Ancona. God is the lord of all goods, the possessor of all good, and only in union with God's grace can one possess goods justly. The economy of grace in the Augustinian cloister became translated by Jordan into his theology of grace, whereby the Christian receives goods from the Lord to be used for serving the Lord. All the Christian possesses he or she possesses not as property, but in terms of a "poor use"; God retains the title, but concedes the use of the goods and graces that He gives by means of grace given gratuitously (*gratia gratis data*).

Why Jordan interpreted all grace as God's general grace (*gratia gratis data*) is impossible to say for certain. It could be that he simply did not understand the distinction between the general grace of God and sanctifying grace, if he was even aware of it. Though if he did grasp the distinction knowingly, he either might have chosen to ignore it, or he consciously reinterpreted sanctifying grace as grace given gratuitously.

Given Jordan's training it is unlikely that he was unfamiliar with the two types of grace. Further, Jordan was giving lectures on Matthew in the Augustinian *studium* in Erfurt. These lectures were prerequisite to university study and thus were intended to inculcate basic theological instruction. This included reading the *Sentences*. Sanctifying grace (*gratia gratum faciens*) is not found in the text of Lombard. In book two, distinctions 26 and 27, Lombard discussed grace and here one does find grace given gratuitously (*gratia gratis data*).[195] It is most plausible that Jordan desired not to introduce terms in his Biblical lectures not found in the *Sentences*, and thus avoided the distinction between the general grace of God given gratuitously and sanctifying grace.

It also should be noted that Giles of Rome defined sanctifying grace not in distinction to the general grace of God, but as an additional mode of grace. Sanctifying grace is indeed also grace given

---

[194] "Et ubi uos inueneritis ea quae scripta sunt facientes, agite gratias domino bonorum omnium largitori." *Regula* 8,2 (437,242–243). See also, Zumkeller, "The Spirituality of the Augustinians," 64.

[195] Lombardus 2 *Sent.* 26,7–8 (477–478).

gratuitously.[196] Giles distinguished three ways of understanding grace: in a general sense, in a narrower general sense, and in a special sense. Sanctifying grace is this special sense.[197] The narrower general sense of grace, as the most general sense, is grace given gratuitously (*gratia gratis data*). This narrower general sense includes not only those things necessary for salvation, but also those things necessary to what is necessary for salvation.[198] This includes, for example, preaching to and prayers for both the *boni* and the *mali*. In other words, those graces that serve the Church are graces given gratuitously.[199]

Jordan's lectures were intended not only for future theologians of the Order who would have time to debate the finer distinctions between the various understandings of grace, but also for the Order's preachers. Given Giles' discussion of the grace for the Church as gratuitously given, it is certainly plausible that Jordan had this definition in mind. His lectures had the practical purpose of teach-

---

[196] "Gratia ergo gratum faciens condividitur contra gratiam gratis datam. Non quod huiusmodi gratia non sit gratis data: sed quia ultra hoc, quod est gratis data, est etiam gratum faciens... Malos ergo non habentes gratiam gratum facientem: dato quod habeant multas gratias gratis datas, diligit deus secundum quod ista bona commutabilia sunt bona secundum quid: sed habentes gratiam gratum facientem, dicit deus diligere simpliciter, qui tales sunt digni deo, qui non est bonum secundum quid, sed simpliciter. Dividitur ergo gratia gratum faciens a gratiis gratis datis sicut simpliciter dividitur a secundum quid, quia omnia alia bona sunt, sunt secundum quid: sed habentes gratiam gratum facientem sunt digni deo, qui est bonum simpliciter, respectu cuius omnia alia sunt secundum quid." Aeg.Rom. 2 *Sent.* 26, 2,2 (ed. Venice, 1581), 328Ib–d.

[197] "Propter primum sciendum quod gratia tripliciter potest accipi, vel omnino generaliter, vel minus generaliter, vel omnino specialiter... Tertio modo potest accipi gratia omnino specialiter: et sic sola gratia gratum faciens dicitur huiusmodi gratia." Aeg.Rom. 2 *Sent.* 26, 2,2 (ed. Venice, 1581), 327Ia–IId. Gabriel Biel posited the same three-fold understanding of grace, in which Oberman saw a "lack of clarity"; see, Oberman, *Harvest*, 136f.

[198] "Possunt etiam accipi huiusmodi gratiae non solum, quia sunt in rebus salvandis, vel ordinatis ad salutem, sed etiam ex ordine huiusmodi rerum." Aeg.Rom. 2 *Sent.* 26,2,2 (ed. Venice, 1581), 327IIb.

[199] "Ordinavit enim deus propter salutem nostram praedicationes bonis, et malis. Praecepit etiam, ut oramus non solum pro amicis, sed pro inimicis nostris, quae omnia sunt quaedam gratiae, quas deus ordinavit ad salutem nostram. Omnia ergo huiusmodi sunt gratiae gratis datae, cum fiant praedicationes bonis et malis, et fiant orationes pro utrisque, et fiant multa alia, secundum quod ordinavit deus ad utilitatem ecclesiae... Hoc ergo modo gratia est accepta minus generaliter, quam prius. Nam secundum primum modum ipsa naturalia dicebantur quaedam gratiae, sed secundum hunc modum solum ea, quae sunt superaddita naturae, et ad quae non possumus per naturam, dicuntur gratiae." Aeg.Rom. 2 *Sent.* 26, 2,2 (ed. Venice, 1581), 327IIb–c.

ing the doctrine of grace that would be appropriate and applicable for his audience and this, following Giles, was grace, all grace, as gratuitously given by God.

Further, the question to which Giles devotes as much or even greater attention than that concerning the distinction between the general grace of God and sanctifying grace, is the distinction between 'operating grace' (*gratia operans*) and 'cooperating grace' (*gratia cooperans*), which is also found in Lombard. Lombard defined operating grace as the grace that "prepares the will of man so that it might will the good." Cooperating grace is 'helping' grace that aids the will so that it does not will the good in vain.[200] These two graces, however, are actually one grace that both operates and cooperates. They are distinguished by their effects, not as different types of grace.[201]

Giles distinguished between operating and cooperating grace by how they function. Works of grace come from God and from humans, and yet all grace comes from God. In a certain way (*aliquo modo*) works of grace are from God, and in another way (*aliquo modo*) they are from individuals.[202] Giles then proceeded to explain this 'other way' by making the distinction between prior (*prius*) and posterior (*posterius*). This is needed because Scripture states both that God first converts humans before they convert to God, and that humans must first convert in order for God to convert to them.[203] Giles solved this dilemma by interpreting prior and posterior in two ways. First, that which is prior can be seen as imperfect whereas that which is posterior is perfect; thus in nature there is always the progression from

---

[200] "Haec est gratia operans et cooperans; operans enim gratia praeparat hominis voluntatem, ut velit bonum; gratia cooperans adiuvat, ne frustra velit." Lombardus 2 *Sent.* 26,1 (470,3–5).

[201] Lombardus 2 *Sent.* 26,8,2 (478,9–15).

[202] "Propter quod sciendum, quod opera gratiae dici possunt esse a nobis, et a Deo; et dici possunt esse totaliter a Deo, cum omnia sint a Deo; et possumus dicere, quod aliquo modo sunt a Deo, et aliquo modo a nobis." Aeg.Rom. 2 *Sent.* 26,2,3 (ed. Venice, 1581), 329Ib.

[203] "Omnibus enim his modis utitur scriptura sacra. Nam quod a deo sint secundum prioritatem: a nobis autem secundum posteritatem, habetur Trenorum ultimo ubi dicitur: *Converte nos Domine ad te, et convertemur ad te* [Lam. 5:21]. Prius ergo deus nos convertit ad se et postea nos convertimur ad ipsum: sed contrarium videtur quod dicitur Iacobi primo: *Convertimini ad me* ait Dominus exercituum, *et convertar ad vos*, dicit Dominus [Iac. 4:8]. Hoc enim videtur dicere scriptura, quod prius nos convertimur ad dominum, et postea ipse convertitur ad nos, convertendo nos." Aeg.Rom. 2 *Sent.* 26,2,3 (ed. Venice, 1581), 329Ib.

the imperfect to the perfect. In this light, the priority of works that comes from humans is indeed prior but it is also therefore imperfect. That which is posterior is the perfection of the works and this comes from God.[204] Second, priority can be interpreted as that which is principal and works principally, whereas posteriority is instrumental. Works, therefore, are principally attributed to God, and instrumentally attributed to individuals.[205] And this is the distinction between operating and cooperating grace,[206] as it was for Augustinus of Ancona regarding Christ as the *caput ecclesie* and the pope as the head of the Church.[207]

In light of Giles' treatment, one recognizes that Jordan acknowledged an operating and cooperating grace. In addition, this distinction may be the key for understanding his statement that we merit blessedness. In his third lecture Jordan claimed that what leads humans to their end directly and *principally* is the merit by which one merits blessedness by being obedient to God. Yet this is only one way to understand how humans are led to their end. The other way, Jordan explained, is that humans are led to their end *instrumentally*, "as if being helped to merit."[208] What cooperates with humans to merit (*coadiuvans nos ad merendum*) does so instrumentally, which was

---

[204] "Ad quod dici potest, quod prius et posterius in opere dupliciter considerari possunt, quia aliquando prioritas dicit imperfectionem: posterioritas, perfectionem; quia res naturaliter vadunt de imperfecto ad perfectum. Et secundum hoc potest continere, quod prioritas operis propter imperfectionem attribuatur nobis: posterioritas vero propter perfectionem attribuatur deo." Aeg.Rom. 2 *Sent.* 26,2,3 (ed. Venice, 1581), 329Ic.

[205] "Aliquando vero prioritas dicit principalitatem, vel dicit agere principaliter: posterioritas vero dicit agere instrumentaliter. Et secundum hunc modum prioritas boni operis propter principalitatem attribuetur deo: posterioritas vero, quod est agere instrumentaliter, poterit attribui nobis, quia coadiutores dei sumus, et instrumenta eius in agendo. Secundum hunc etiam modum totum aliquod opus principium, et finis poterit attribui nobis instrumentaliter, et totum deo principaliter." Aeg.Rom. 2 *Sent.* 26,2,3 (ed. Venice, 1581), 329Id.

[206] "Potest dici, quod nos inchoamus illud opus operando instrumentaliter et imperfecte: et deus cooperatur perficiendo illud opus principaliter et perfecte. Et quia quod nos inchoemus opus pertinens ad salutem nostram, habemus hoc a deo, refertur totum ad deum. Erit ergo inchoatio operis gratia operans et consummatio, gratia cooperans." Aeg.Rom. 2 *Sent.* 26,2,3 (ed. Venice, 1581), 329IIc.

[207] See Chapter One.

[208] "Est autem aliquid utile in finem beatitudinis dupliciter: uno modo directe et principaliter, secundum meritum quo beatitudinem meremur deo obediendo, et quantum ad hoc ponitur *fiat voluntas tua*; alio modo instrumentaliter, et quasi coadiuvans nos ad merendum, et ad hoc pertinet quod dicitur *panem nostrem cottidianum*. Per accidens autem ordinamur in beatitudinem per remotionem prohibentis." Jor. *Exp.* 3, fol. 76rb.

Giles' definition of cooperating grace. The merit by which one merits blessedness, is that which leads one to one's end directly and principally (*principaliter*), which Giles defined as operating grace. In other words, the merit of blessedness, is actually operative grace, which is in keeping with Jordan's emphasis that humans possess no good works of their own, but that they hold them of their Lord. Jordan's merit is the work of operative grace, which is attributed to God alone.[209]

If Giles' discussion of operative and cooperative grace lay behind Jordan's distinction between merit principally and instrumentally, and

---

[209] *Cf.*: "Hic cadunt due questiones. Prima, utrum homo possit se preparare ad gratiam sine gratia. Secunda, utrum ex neccessitate detur gratia se preparanti ad gratiam. Ad primam respondeo, quod gratia dicitur duplex: uno modo, ipsum habituale donum infusum anime a deo; secundo modo dicitur gratia auxilium dei moventis animam ad bonum. Primo modo accipiendo gratiam preexigitur aliqua preparatio ad eam, quia nulla forma introduci potest nisi in materia disposita. Et hec preparatio paulative, quandoque fit subito, quia ut dicitur Ecclesiastici 1<1>: *facile est in oculis dei honestare pauperem* [Sir. 11:23]. Et in hanc preparationem non potest homo sine gratia, secundo modo dicta. Sed ad istam secundo modo dictam non requiritur aliqua preparatio ex parte hominis quasi preveniens divinum auxilium, scilicet potius quecumque preparatio in homine esse potest, est ex auxilio dei moventis animam ad bonum. Dicitur ergo homo se preparare ad gratiam, scilicet habitualem in quantum movetur eius liberum arbitrium a deo per gratiam prevenientem, que non dicitur donum sed dei auxilium movens animam ad hec preparatoria... Ad secundam questionem respondeo: quod preparatio hominis ad gratiam potest considerari dupliciter. Uno modo ut a libero arbitrio et sic nullam necessitatem habet ad gratie consecutionem, quia donum gratie excedit omnem preparationem virtutis humane. Alio modo potest considerari secundum quod est a deo movente et tunc habet necessitatem ad illud ad quod ordinatur a deo, non quidem coactionis sed infallibilitatis, quia intentio dei deficere non potest. Unde Johannis sexto: *Qui audit a patre meo et didicit, venit ad me* [Io. 6:45]. Sequitur secundum scilicet motus divina per gratiam; hoc significatur per angelum qui movebat aquam. Hic motus dicitur fuisse vel propter sacrificia, que in illa piscina abluebantur vel propter lignum crucis quod in ea dicitur iacuisse a tempore Salomonis usque ad tempus Christi et tunc incepit super nature; sed certum est quod angelus fecit talem motum et ex illa aqua vim sanativam habuerit. Signat autem iste motus aque motum illum, quo deus movet liberum arbitrium per gratiam. Unde sicut aqua ille ex se non habet vim illam sed ex motu angeli, sic actus liberi arbitrii ex se vim merendi non habet, sed movente per gratiam ut dictum est." Jor. *OJ* sermo 99, fol. 173rb–174ra; "Sed an ista preparatoria preveniant gratiam et an ista possumus sine gratia, dicendum quod gratia dicitur dupliciter. Uno modo dicitur habituale donum, quod est principium operis meritorii. Alio modo dicitur gratia auxilium gratuitum dei interius animam moventis sine bonum propositum inspirantis. Primo modo non oportet presupponere aliquod aliud donum habitale in anima quia sic procederetur in infinitum. Secundo autem modo gratia procedit tale habituale donum, nam sine divino auxilio, quo movetur liberum arbitrium ad bonum, non possumus nos preparare ad gratiam." Jor. *OJ* sermo 247, fol. 382vb.

we do know that Jordan had at least seen Giles' commentary,[210] not only can we understand his statement that one merits blessedness in light of his clear emphasis on the complete dependency on God, but we also see that with the distinction between cooperating and operating grace Jordan did not need to distinguish between sanctifying grace and grace gratuitously given, because according to Lombard operating grace and cooperating grace were the same grace, with different effects.[211] There were sufficient theological reasons for Jordan not to have employed the term 'sanctifying grace' (*gratia gratum faciens*) that one cannot conclude that he simply did not know, or did not understand, the various scholastic distinctions of grace. On the contrary, it seems most probable that Jordan was indeed aware of the various graces and either chose not to introduce such terminology into his lectures, or purposefully redefined all sanctifying grace (*gratia gratum faciens*) as grace gratuitously given (*gratia gratis data*).

D. *The Direction of Grace*

Since Jordan did not use the term 'sanctifying grace' it may not be entirely appropriate to claim that he reinterpreted the concept. Traditionally 'sanctifying grace' was seen as infused grace and this Jordan considered to be grace given gratuitously. The explicit reinterpretation of sanctifying grace was given, as David Steinmetz has shown, over a century later by Jordan's fellow Augustinian, Johannes von Staupitz. For Staupitz, sanctifying grace was not the grace that made humans acceptable to God, but rather the reverse: sanctifying grace was the grace that made God acceptable to humans.[212] Heiko A. Oberman pointed to the possibility that the earlier fifteenth-century Augustinian Augustinus Favaroni may have been a "forerunner" of Staupitz in this regard, or at least that he provides evidence that Staupitz's reinterpretation may not have come *ex nihilo*. In this

---

[210] In the *Liber Vitasfratrum* Jordan lists *Super Sententiarum tres libros* among the works of Giles "inter quae sunt quae ego vidi." *VF* 2,22 (236,90ff). One must also not forget that General Chapter at Florence in 1287 decreed that all lectors and students follow Giles' teaching; Esteban, *AAug.* 2 (1907/08), 275.

[211] See note 200 above. Jordan may indeed have had Giles in mind, though his direct literary source for this passage was not Giles, but Thomas Aquinas, from whom Jordan borrowed word for word. See Thom.Aq. *STh* II/II 83,9 resp. (1848b,47–1849a,53).

[212] D. Steinmetz, *Misericordia Dei. The Theology of Johannes von Staupitz in its Late Medieval Setting*, SMRT 4 (Leiden, 1968), 84–85.

context Oberman also mentioned Jordan, who closed the prologue to his *Meditationes de Passione Christi* by affirming that "all that Christ suffered ought to be accepted by and pleasing to man, as if Christ suffered such things for humans' salvation alone."[213] This seems to hint at the reversal of the understanding of sanctifying grace over a hundred years before Staupitz.

It is in this context that I have used the term 'reinterpretation'. Jordan did not technically "reinterpret" sanctifying grace; he did not even use the term.[214] Yet his understanding of grace is based on the

---

[213] Jor. *Med.* Prol., fol. 2vb. Oberman pointed to this phrase as providing "a key to Staupitz's seemingly unprecedented campaign against the scholastic *gratia gratum faciens*. Whereas Staupitz wants to reinterpret *gratia gratum faciens* not as the grace which makes us acceptable to God but vice versa as the grace which makes God acceptable to us, we read with Jordan: 'Omnia quae Christus passus est, ita debent homini esse accepta et grata, ac si pro ipsius solummodo salute ea sit passus.' [Jor. *Med.*, fol. 2vb] Out of this tradition emerges, finally, that aspect of the first of Luther's Ninety-five Theses according to which penance is a lasting mark of the Christian life." "Headwaters of the Reformation," in *idem*, *The Dawn of the Reformation* (Edinburgh, 1986), 72. Oberman cited Jordan from the article of Martin Elze, "Das Verständnis der Passion Jesu im ausgehenden Mittelalter und bei Luther," in *Geist und Geschichte der Reformation. Festgabe Hanns Rückert zum 65. Geburtstag*, ed. K. Scholder (Berlin, 1966), 127–151. Elze argued that Jordan's Prologue, with the emphasis on Christ as the *exemplar*, is "repräsentativ für die ganze spätmittelalterliche Passionsbetrachtung." (134) Although Elze acknowledged Jordan's *pro nobis* (130), he claimed that Jordan's treatment of the Passion, "ist in die Lebensform des mönchischen Standes; daß also der satisfaktorische Charakter des 'pro nobis' hier nicht zur Diskussion steht, weil er doch immer schon in bestimmten Sinne vorausgesetzt ist." (130) Yet though the *exemplum* aspect of Christ's death is certainly central for Jordan (see Chapter Five), this should not be taken as deemphasizing the salvific nature of Jordan's *theologia crucis*.

[214] We do, however, find the term at least twice, once in the *Opus Postillarum* and once in the *Opus Jor*. In the former the term is used to refer to the grace or graces Adam enjoyed before the Fall: "Et quia primus homo acceperat etiam gratiam tam gratis datam quam gratum facientem, ideo dicitur quod istud semen natum quidem fuit, id est, germinavit, sed natum adveniente escu temptationis diabolicae, aruit per amissionem gratiae, quia non habebat humorem, utpote gratia sibi subtracta." Jor. *OP* sermo 137J (ed. Strassburg, 1483). In the *OJ* Jordan referred to *gratia gratum faciens* as the smallest form of grace, which was not able to remain with even the slightest amount of sin: : "... imaginari debemus quod nec minimus gradus gratie, scilicet gratum facientis spiritus sancti potest stare cum minimo gradu culpe mortalis..." Jor. *OJ* sermo 216, fol. 336va. Even though Jordan did not employ the distinction between *gratia gratis data* and *gratia gratum faciens* in any consistant fashion, to the point that it is accurate to say that it does not have a part in his doctrine of grace, his reference to *gratia gratum faciens* as the *minimus gradus gratie* stands in contrast to the common scholastic understanding of *gratia gratum faciens* as infused sacramental grace. Thus, in discussing Gabriel Biel's understanding of justification, Oberman explained: "While as we saw, the *gratia gratis data* does not seriously enter the discussion on justification and when mentioned either connotes a special charisma for the use of the Church at large or more generally a gift of

concept that God first comes to humans and that it is human love and devotion that must be stimulated. This is the function of meditation on the Passion. When one considers all that Christ suffered for humankind, God essentially becomes pleasing to the meditant, and devotion is the result. The same position is found in Jordan's *Expositio*. God is the heavenly king, who is also the loving Father. Thus one prays "Our Father, who is in heaven," as a *captatio benevolentie*, not in attempt to gain God's good will, but rather on our account so that one might have the trust to ask God for the things one needs. Jordan cited Augustine to affirm that "God is always prepared to give us His own light, but we are not always prepared to receive it. Thus a stimulus to devotion is require on our part, which is a certain capture of divine good will."[215] In other words, God must become pleasing to humans.

Jordan reverses the "direction," so to speak. Sanctifying grace was the infused grace that enabled humans to become acceptable to God. The direction here is from what is "in" humans, albeit certainly not without grace coming from God first, towards God's acceptance. Sanctifying grace is what makes it possible to move towards God. For Jordan, on the other hand, left on one's own one can only wallow in sin. Humans cannot raise themselves from sin;[216] all that one does on one's own, without God's aid, "is nothing and is sin."[217] Therefore, we do not pray that we might come to the kingdom of God, but rather that the kingdom might come to us.[218] Similarly,

---

God—in the same sense in which the natural powers of man are gifts of God—the *gratia gratum faciens*, habitual sanctifying grace, is seen as a power that directs the will to produce meritorious acts." *Harvest*, 164.

[215] "Ad quod dicendum quod captatio benevolentie non premittitur propter deum, ut ipse flectatur, sed propter nos, ut fiducia petendi in nobis ipsis excitetur, quia secundum Augustinum: Deus semper paratus est nobis dare suam lucem, sed nos non semper sumus parati accipere [Aug. de serm.dom. 2,3,14 (104,286–288)]. Unde ex parte nostri requiritur devotionis excitatio, que est quedam divine benevolentie captatio." Jor. *Exp.* 1, fol. 73va.

[216] "... homo enim per se labi in peccatum potest, sed per se surgere non potest sine auxilio gratie dei...," Jor. *OJ* sermo 131, fol. 215rb.

[217] "... considerandum est quod omne, quod quis facit ex se ipso non ex deo motus, peccatum est et nichil." Jor. *OJ* sermo 103, fol. 179rb.

[218] "Sed hic incidit duplex dubitatio. Prima est quia vanum videtur petere advenire regnum eius, qui semper regnat; sed regnum dei semper est, quare etc. Dicendum <est> quod non est intelligendum quod hic petamus ut regnum deo adveniat, quasi ipse iam non regnet, sed quod nobis adveniat. Unde Augustinus *Ad Probam*: regnum dei adveniat sive velimus sive nolimus, sed desiderium nostrum ad illud excitamus, ut nobis veniat atque in eo regnemus [Aug. epist. 130,11,21 (63,11–12)]. Est

when one prays that God's will be done, it is not that there is a possibility that God's will would not be done. Christians pray that God's will might be done by them, even though humans do not have the ability to do God's will. Thus they pray for the grace needed.[219] And this grace is, once again, grace gratuitously given. The "direction" is God coming toward humans, which humans must then recognize and accept. The heavens have been extended through God's love and grace. The Christian is to realize this fact and to allow one's soul to be expanded in turn, in order to become increasingly *capax dei*. In short, humans are to know that God is their loving Father, and as such God is to become pleasing to humans, because humans are already pleasing to God through his love and grace.

Technically Jordan may not have reinterpreted sanctifying grace, but with his understanding of infused grace as grace gratuitously given, and with his "directional" emphasis on God coming to humans, in the early fourteenth century in the Augustinian *studium* at Erfurt a doctrine of grace was propounded that paralleled Staupitz's "re"-interpretation of sanctifying grace as the grace that makes God pleasing to us.

Jordan's doctrine of grace was thoroughly Augustinian. This is not to imply, however, that Jordan was a Gregory of Rimini on a lower academic level. The centrality of grace to the Augustinian school has never been questioned. What Jordan as the *Lector Gratie* indicates is that the centrality of grace in the theological teaching of the Augustinian Order was operative both in the universities and in the *studia*. The Order's mendicant theology as such was based on an

---

ergo sensus *adveniat* id est, ad nos veniat regnum tuum. Secunda dubitatio est quare non dicit, 'veniamus ad regnum tuum', quod tamen videretur convenientius, quia potius nos venimus {ad regnum} quam regnum ad nos? Ad hoc dicendum <est> quod nos ad deum venire non possumus nisi prius deus veniat ad nos, secundum illud Iohannis: *Nemo venit ad me nisi pater meus traxerit illum* [Io. 6:44]. Et ideo quia venire ad regnum non est in nostra potestate sed ex divina gratia et voluntate; ideo potius petimus regnum dei venire ad nos quam nos venire ad regnum <dei>." Jor. *Exp.* 4, fol. 77[vb].

[219] "Et quia voluntatem dei nostris viribus perficere non valemus, dicente Apostolo Romanorum septimo: *velle quidem adiacet michi, perficere autem non invenio bonum* [Rm. 7:18], ideo hoc petimus a deo quatinus ipse det nobis gratiam, ut sicut voluntas sua perfecte fit ab angelis et sanctis in celo, ita fiat a nobis qui sumus in terra. Nec putet aliquis nos hic petere ut deus faciet voluntatem suam, quia hoc potest et facit absque nostra petitione. Sed petimus ut sua voluntas a nobis fiat et impleatur." Jor. *Exp.* 5, fol. 79[ra].

Augustinian theology of grace, yet one that was not disharmonious with a pastoral theology emphasizing moral perfection. But here I have run ahead of myself. In order to show how Jordan's theology of grace synthesized with his call for moral growth, I first need to treat his doctrine of sanctification, the means by which Christians become saints. If Jordan's doctrine of God was the theological nucleus of his *Expositio*, his doctrine of sanctification was the atom itself.

E. *Becoming Saints*

If all grace is gratuitously given, it would seem that a doctrine of predestination is required. Jordan did not discuss the question of predestination in his *Expositio*. In his eighth lecture he included the beatitude of meekness to which corresponds the possession of the earth. This possession, he noted, is both that the blessed possess God, and that God possesses them. Jordan seemed to espouse a doctrine of election when he continued by citing Augustine to affirm that "God will be the possession of no one whom he has not first possessed."[220] Previously Jordan had mentioned the elect as those who see the face of God in its purity,[221] yet he never addressed the doctrine of election explicitly in his lectures.

Rather than predestination and election, Jordan emphasized a doctrine of adoption. It is through the blood of Christ that Christians

---

[220] "Mitis enim est qui nec patitur nec deducitur... Unde mititas, prout est beatitudo, est quidam [quedam *B*] status iam purgati animi, quando scilicet homo post multarum temptationum frequentem victoriam quasi victor divina gratia in quietudine mentis ponitur, et quantum possibile est in hac vita temptationum impulsibus amplius non quassatur. Ex quo satis patet convenientia istius beatitudinis ad hanc petitionem, quantum ad omnia genera temptationum predictarum. Huic autem beatitudini respondet pro premio possessio terre. Conveniens enim est ut qui pacifice sedatis temptationum tumultibus possidentur a deo et ipsi possideant deum, qui est beata habitatio viventium, quia secundum Augustinum, nullius erit deus possessio nisi eius, quem ipse prius possiderit [*cf.* Aug. in psalm. 145,11 (2113,17–31)]. Hec autem posessio dei hic inchoatur, et in futuro perficitur." Jor. *Exp.* 8, fol. 85^{va-b}.

[221] "Est propterea panis triticeus, in quantum ipsos reficit nude divinitatis ostentatione, quam in ipso clare et nude feliciter contemplantur. Et sic sive ingrediantur per divinitatis contemplationem, sive egrediantur per humanitatis intuitionem semper pascua invenient per nove dulcedinis degustationem. De quibus pascuis dicit Gregorius: Que sunt illa pascua nisi interna semper virentis paradisi gaudia? [Greg.M. in evang. 14,5 (1130A)]. Pascua namque electorum sunt presens vultus dei, qui dum sine defectu conspicitur, sine fine mens cibo satiatur. Iste igitur glorisosus panis dicitur supersubstantialis, quia super omnes substantias est et omnes superat creaturas. Dicitur etiam cottidianus, quia cottidie, id est eternaliter, ipso reficiemur et nec uno momento sine ipso subsistere possumus." Jor. *Exp.* 6, fol. 81vb.

are made sons of God and thereby can confidently cry *Abba, father*, which enables them to pray, *Pater noster*.[222] The adoption of humans as the sons of God by grace is evident in praying "Our Father." It was Christ and Christ alone, Jordan explained, who could say, "My father."[223] As adopted sons of God, Christians pray for the name of God to be sanctified in themselves, so that they might "feel" their redemption, and thus might truly be saints, as if having been washed by the blood of Christ. By adoption Christians are called sons of God and therefore saints, not just in name, but in reality.[224]

"Becoming saints" is not achieved through merit or works, but rather through faith. Faith for Jordan is the first of the theological virtues, which are supernaturally infused in the soul.[225] It is

---

[222] "Nos igitur per sanguinem Iesu Christi adoptionis filii effecti confidenter clamamus *Abba, pater*, secundum Apostolum ad Galatas quarto [Gal. 4:6]. Audenter ergo dicere possumus *pater noster*." Jor. *Exp*. 1, fol. 73va.

[223] "Tertia dubitatio est quare non dixit 'meus' sed 'noster', quod tamen videretur congruum cum simus persone private quibus pluraliter locutio videtur sonare in pompam? Ad quod dicendum hic dicit 'noster' primo ad designandum differentiam filiationis Christi et nostre. Christus enim filius dei est per naturam, quod sibi est singulare et ideo sibi competit dicere, 'pater meus'. Nos autem sumus filii dei per adoptionis gratiam, quod est commune. Hanc filiationis differentiam signavit ipse Christus tum dixit Iohannis vicesimo: *ascendo ad patrem meum et patrem vestrum* [Io. 20:17]; 'meum' inquam per naturam singulariter, 'vestrum' autem per gratiam communiter." Jor. *Exp*. 1, fol. 74ra.

[224] "Hoc nomen in nobis sanctificari petimus, ut fructum redemptionis in nobis sentiamus, ut sic vere simus sancti, quasi sanguine tincti. Quales sunt illi de quibus dicitur Apocalypsis septimo: *Isti sunt qui venerunt ex magna tribulatione et laverunt stolas suas in sanguine agni* [Apc. 7:14]. Et Apocalypsis primo: *Lavit nos in sanguine suo a peccatis nostris*. Et sic est sensus *sanctificetur nomen tuum* [Apc. 1:5], id est, fructificet in nobis redemptio tua. Secundo modo 'nomen dei' dicitur privilegium filialis adoptionis, et in hoc sensu specialiter accipitur hic. Istud nomen tunc sanctificatur in nobis, quoniam sicut nomine dicimur filii dei, ita sumus et re." Jor. *Exp*. 3, fol. 76va. Jordan also treated the theme of Christians becoming sons of God in sermons 50–52 of the *OJ*, which is designated in the Vatican manuscript as a *Tractatus de filiatione divina*, Jor. *OJ*, fol. 97rb–106ra.

[225] "Introducitur autem per hanc petitionem de virtutibus fides, que est prima virtus theologica. Habet enim fides tres effectus correspondentes sanctificationi triplicis nominis dei predicti. Per fidem enim in sanguine Christi abluimur, quantum ad primum; vere filii dei efficimur, quantum ad secundum; gloriam dei prosequimur, quantum ad tertium." Jor. *Exp*. 3, fol. 77ra; "Sciendum autem quod quinque sunt que consequenter se habent ad animam perficiendam videlicet gratia, virtus, donum, beatitudo, et fructus. Gratia est enim habitus perficiens essentiam anime purgando egritudinem culpe et ad quodam esse supernaturale animam elevando. Virtus vero et donum perficiunt potentiam sed differenter, quia virtus perficit potentiam purgando eius defectum et habilitando ipsam ad operandum sive naturaliter, si sit virtus acquisita, sive supernaturaliter, si sit virtus infusa." Jor. *Exp*. 9, fol. 87^{rb-va}.

associated with the clear vision that God works in the blessed.[226] Through faith "we are washed in the blood of Christ, are made true sons of God, and progress to the glory of God."[227] In short, the Christian is saved, or sanctified through faith. In the lecture treating the petition, 'Hallowed be thy name', Jordan placed not only the virtue faith, but also faith as the fruit of the Holy Spirit.[228] The saints are saints through faith. In this light it is not incorrect to speak of a doctrine of *sola fide* in Jordan's theology, even though it is a term he does not use. Faith was the ontological doorway between the state of grace (*esse gratie*) and the state of glory (*esse glorie*). Yet Jordan's *sola fide* is placed in terms of his doctrine of sanctification, rather than in those of justification. Through faith as the infused virtue, humans become children of God and experience the "delicious delight" resulting therefrom.[229] This is essentially all Jordan had to say about faith in his *Expositio*. As little as this may be quantitatively, qualitatively faith is the basis for the sanctification of the Christian.

In turning to the *Opus Postillarum* we find more information regarding Jordan's understanding of faith. In the *Tractatus de virtutibus et vitiis* (sermons 439–441) Jordan presented thirteen different meanings of the term 'faith', which renders the common division between what is believed (*fides quae*) and belief (*fides qua*) less than adequate. Faith can be interpreted as promise, as security, as a legal fidelity, as a simplicity or innocence, as equity, as conscience, as belief, as chastity, as the sacrament of baptism, as the articles of the catholic faith, as the act of faith, as informing faith, and finally as the theological virtue, which is faith supernaturally infused and is that faith

---

[226] "Sunt enim tres precipue perfectiones beatorum: visio inobfuscabilis, que succedit fidei et perficit rationalem; tentio inamissibilis, que succedit spei et perficit irascibilem; fruitio infastidibilis, que respondet caritati et satiat concupiscientialem." Jor. *Exp.* 2, fol. 75va.

[227] "Habet enim fides tres effectus correspondentes sanctificationi triplicis nominis dei predicti. Per fidem enim in sanguine Christi abluimur, quantum ad primum; vere filii dei efficimur, quantum ad secundum; gloriam dei prosequimur, quantum ad tertium." Jor. *Exp.* 3, fol. 77ra.

[228] "Introducuntur propterea per hanc petitionem duo fructus, scilicet fides et pax, quorum adaptatio patet ex dictis." Jor. *Exp.* 3, fol. 77va.

[229] "Beatitudo vero est operatio doni et sic ... perfecta virtus appellatur donum. Fructus autem est deliciosa delectatio consurgens ex predicta operatione." Jor. *Exp.* 9, fol. 87va; *cf.* note 187 above.

that is informed by love (*fides caritate informata*).[230] Jordan did not continue with an explanation of this love informed faith, but turned directly to an enumeration of the twelve articles of faith.[231]

Faith leads humans to their end, for through faith one comes to know the truth, which is the object of faith.[232] Fear (*timor*) and the purification of the heart are the effects of faith, for through faith one comes to fear separation from God, who is the highest good (*summum bonum*); one's heart is purified by faith, which directs one to one's end.[233]

---

[230] "Fides multipliciter accipitur. Quandoque enim fides dicitur sponsio... Quandoque fides sumitur pro conventionali securitate, quae etiam hosti servanda est... Quandoque pro legalitate seu fidelitate... Quandoque pro simplicitate bona seu innocentia... Quandoque pro aequitate et exuberantia actionum, sicut in iure dicitur quod quaedam sunt actiones bonae fidei, quaedam stricti iuris. Quandoque pro conscientia... Quandoque pro credulitate... Quandoque pro castitate... Quandoque pro sacramento baptismi... Quandoque pro credito et collectione creditorum scilicet articulorum... Quandoque sumitur fides pro actu fidei... Quandoque pro fide informi... Ultimo sumitur pro habitu infuso supernaturaliter, et haec est fides viva puta caritate informata." Jor. *OP* sermo 439A (ed. Strassburg, 1483).

[231] Jor. *OP* sermo 439A (ed. Strassburg, 1483). Jordan also related the articles of faith to the twelve disciples, which he later did as well in his *Tractatus de articulis fidei*, Jor. *OD* sermo 102 (ed. Strassburg, 1484). It should be noted that Hümpfner referred to Jordan's *Tractatus de articulis fidei* as sermo 52 of the *Opus Dan*, (Hümpfner, intro., xliii), an identification that was then followed by Zumkeller *MSS* nr. 642 (292). Hümpfner's text, however, is obviously problematic regarding numbering since after making sermo 52 of the *Opus Dan* Jordan's treatise, he then states: "It is 'sermo quartus' in a sequence of *Sermones* and *Subsermones*, beginning with *Sermo* No. 197, on the subject, *De divisione apostolorum*." Hümpfner, intro., xliii. The *Tractatus de articulis fidei* is indeed noted by Jordan as the fourth primary sermon in a series which, however, began with sermo 97, *In divisione apostolorum*. In the treatise, each apostle is accorded with having contributed one of the twelve articles of faith, drawn from the Apostles' Creed. In addition, to each apostle and article Jordan ascribed a fruit of the Holy Spirit. Thus, for example: "Tertius articulus est, 'Qui conceptus est de spirito sanctu, natus ex Maria Virgine... hunc articulum posuit Iohannes, qui fuit Virgini custos... per hanc articulum introducitur pax...'" Jor. *OD* sermo 102C (ed. Strassburg, 1484).

[232] "Explicatis fidei articulis perspiciamus ad alia ad fidem pertinentia, quae sunt tria ad praesens. Primum est veritas; veritas prima, quae est fidei obiectum. Et hoc secundum formalem rationem obiecti, non enim per fidem assentimus alicui nisi quia prima veritate revelatum..." Jor. *OP* sermo 439C (ed. Strassburg, 1483).

[233] "Alia duo sunt timor et cordis purificatio, quae sunt fidei effectus. Timor quidem tam servilis, quo quis timet a deo puniri, quam filialis, quo quis timet a deo separari. Per fidem enim apprehendimus poenas, quae secundum divinum iudicium inferuntur. Item per fidem aestimationem habeamus de deo, quod ipse sit summum bonum, a quo separari est pessimum. Quod etiam purificatio cordis sit effectus fidei patet quia cor purificatur ex hoc quod tendit in deum sicut econtrario ex hoc quod per amorem temporalibus se subiicit, redditur impurum. Primum autem per quod in deum tenditur est fides." Jor. *OP* sermo 439C (ed. Strassburg, 1483).

Although Jordan did not enter into a lengthy explication of faith in either his *Expositio* or *Opus Postillarum*, faith occupied a place of central importance to his theology as the linchpin connecting the state of grace (*esse gratie*) with the state of glory (*esse glorie*). Yet faith was not isolated in this function: faith stood together with hope, love, and the Church, in a theological cooperative union held together by grace.

Jordan's strong assertion that through grace and faith Christians become adopted sons of God and thus saints *in re*, does not mean that humans become "saintly." His emphasis on the lack of human goodness remains. It is only by faith and grace, through the Passion of Christ, that individuals are saints. In his *Opus Postillarum* Jordan was crystal clear that one can never be certain of one's salvation. In keeping with his Order's tradition on the insufficiency of works,[234] and echoing his teacher Albert of Padua, Jordan affirmed that the presumption of one's own righteousness is indeed a sin. No one is able to know for sure whether his works are really true, for a false righteousness deceives many. No human work is ever pure; works are always contaminated with sin. Indeed, "there has never been a righteous person or a saint who was free from sin."[235]

---

[234] See Zumkeller, "Das Ungenügen der menschlichen Werke," *ZKTh* 81 (1959), 265–305.

[235] Enumerating the defects of works stemming from pride, Jordan wrote: "Secundus defectus illorum fuit de sua iustitia presumptio. Et quantum ad hoc dicit 'tamquam iusti'. Circa quod considerandum quod nullus [homo], quantumcumque magni meriti, de suis iustitiis presumere debet... nullus enim scire potest pro certo an opera sua vera sint an iusta; falsa enim iusticia multos decepit... nostrae iustitiae purae non sunt sed semper habent aliquid <peccati> macule annexum Isaie 64: *facti sumus ut immundi omnes nos et quasi pannus menstruate universe iusticie nostre* [Is. 64:6] ... Nemo est absque peccato, nec infans cuius est unius diei vita super terram. Item nec quicumque iusti et sancti sunt sine peccato..." Jor. *OP* sermo 374B (ed. Strassburg, 1483); Jor. *OP-B*, fol. 90rb–90va. Jordan drew from Albert of Padua virtually word for word. See Albert's sermon on Luke 18:9–14 for the tenth Sunday after Pentecost, Albert. *Exp.*, fol. S-2ra–b. See also Zumkeller, "Das Ungenügen der menschlichen Werke," 276, where this passage is quoted, and Zumkeller, "The Spirituality of the Augustinians," 66–67, for a brief English translation of the major points. Zumkeller used this passage, among others, to argue for the general insufficiency of works in the later Middle Ages, and especially among the Augustinian preachers. Heiko A. Oberman expressed caution regarding Zumkeller's argument by pointing to the fact that Zumkeller drew heavily from sermons on this text, *i.e.* Luke 18:9–14, the parable of the Pharisee and the Publican; H. Oberman, *Harvest*, 181f, n. 112. In Jordan's case the evidence is overwhelming that human works are not that by which one gains God's favor, or that by which one earns a reward.

Jordan concluded his tirade against security in one's own works with a statement that seems to go beyond his Order's tradition: "And this is the argument, that a humble sinner is better than someone just but proud, because by the very fact that a sinner humbles himself, he is already no longer a sinner, and the just person, by the very fact that he is proud, is already no longer just."[236] Bearing echoes of Augustinus of Ancona's argument that an heretical pope is by that fact no longer pope, Jordan claimed not only that the prideful just individual is by that fact alone no longer just, but also that the humble sinner, the sinner who confesses himself as such, is truly a saint, the adopted son of God through grace given *gratis*. And here we have a fourteenth-century version of Luther's *simul iustus et peccator*!

Before I become carried away and claim to have found the true origins of Reformation theology, I should reemphasize my last statement: this is a *fourteenth-century* version of the Christian being simultaneously a sinner and justified. For Jordan this was used to drive home the inability of knowing for certain whether one's works were meritorious. For Luther, on the other hand, this doctrine was the very basis for the certitude of salvation. For Jordan the *simul iustus et peccator* was used to emphasize human reliance on God's grace. The sinner could take no confidence in his works, because all his works were not his own, they were merely for his use. All good works come from God's grace given gratuitously, which flows from God's love in extending the heavens and expanding the soul through His grace and love. For Luther, the *simul iustus et peccator* was the central encapsulation of his doctrine of justification *sola fide* and *sola gratia*. For Jordan, grace and justification were separate issues.

F. *Attaining the Blessed End*

The Christian is redeemed in Christ. That is the central message of Jordan's lectures. Through faith in Christ one is washed in the blood

---

[236] "Et hic est argumentum: quod melior est peccator humilis quam iustus superbus; quia eo ipso quod peccator se humiliat, iam non est peccator; et iustus eo ipso quod superbit, iam non est iustus." Jor. *OP* sermo 376A (ed. Strassburg, 1483); *cf*.: "In hoc evangelio [Lc. 18:9–14] commendatur virtus orationis et ostenditur quia in qua consistat summa totius humane perfectionis. Et introducuntur hic duo homines, unus iustus et alter peccator. Iustus, quia nescivit orare, fuit reprobatus; sed peccator, qui scivit orare, fuit iustificatus." Jor. *OJ* sermo 256, fol. 396[rb-va]. See also Saak, "Saints in Society," 331–333.

of Christ, made a true son of God, and attains to the glory of God.[237] This corresponds to the three-fold name of God that one prays to be sanctified internally (*in nobis*): the name of God is the mystery of redemption, the privilege of filial adoption, and the announcement of God's glorification.[238] Indeed, it is Christ who makes it at all possible that one can pray, "Our Father," because, Jordan exclaimed, who would have dared to pray for God's kingdom or to call God, "his Father" under the old law?[239] God has granted the state of grace (*esse gratie*), which is humans' redemption, equated with the kingdom of grace (*regnum gratie*) in human souls.[240] This kingdom is given *gratis*, for "we are not able to come to God unless God first comes to us... and therefore because to come to the kingdom is not in our power, but comes from divine grace and will, we therefore pray for the Kingdom of God to come to us rather than that we might come to the kingdom."[241] Christians have been adopted as God's children through grace;[242] their redemption has already been given, it is a done deal.

Yet one still prays for God's kingdom to come, for His will to be done, and that Christians might become saints. And one still prays the Lord's Prayer so that one might attain the blessed end (*ut pertingamus ad finem*): God himself. For the Christian, redemption has been given, but it has not been completely realized. Nevertheless, humans know what God's will is, as Jordan explained in his fifth lecture. Spiritually understood, God wants three things with respect

---

[237] "Introducitur autem per hanc petitionem de virtutibus fides, que est prima theologica. Habet enim fides tres effectus correspondentes sanctificationi triplicis nominis dei predicti. Per fidem enim in sanguine Christi abluimur, quantum ad primum; vere filii dei efficimur, quantum ad secundum; gloriam dei prosequimur, quantum ad tertium." Jor. *Exp*. 3, fol. 77ra.

[238] "Dicamus ergo *sanctificetur nomen tuum*: quod est mysterium nostre redemptionis; privilegium filialis adoptionis; preconium tue glorificationis." Jor. *Exp*. 3, fol. 76vb.

[239] "O quanta fiducia et fiducialis audacia quod futura factorem servus dominum hoc deum patrem suum audeat nuncupare et regnum eius postulare. Quis umquam ausus est in veteri lege talia presumere? Nemo utique." Jor. *Exp*. 1, fol. 73rb.

[240] "Esse nature dedit nobis in creatione; esse gratie in recreatione sive redemptione." Jor. *Exp*. 1, fol. 73vb; "Notandum autem quod regnum dei triplex est. Primum regnum dicitur esse ecclesia militans... secundum regnum dei est in anima, quod est regnum gratie... tertium regnum dei est in vita eterna." Jor. *Exp*. 4, fol. 77vb.

[241] "... nos ad deum venire non possumus nisi prius deus veniat ad nos... et ideo quia venire ad regnum non est in nostra potestate sed ex divina gratia et voluntate, ideo potius petimus regnum dei venire ad nos quam {nos} venire ad regnum." Jor. *Exp*. 4, fol. 77vb.

[242] "Nos autem sumus filii dei per adoptionis gratiam." Jor. *Exp*. 1, fol. 74ra.

to humans: the conversion of sinners, the sanctification of the converted, and the glorification of the sanctified. God desires the salvation of all.[243] This is God's will, and this is the Christian's end.

This general will of salvation, combined with Jordan's doctrine of grace, once again begs the question regarding Jordan's doctrine of election and predestination. If God desires the salvation of all, and if God gives His grace *gratis* to all, and if redemption has already been "completed," then why do not all humans achieve their end? In other words, what is the relationship between Jordan's doctrine of redemption and the justification of the sinner?

I have already pointed to the hints Jordan gave regarding election, and these are only hints. For now it suffices to state that Jordan seems to have held a doctrine of election of some sort. He did not espouse a doctrine of justification in his *Expositio*, or rather, he did not espouse a doctrine of justification in the sense of what justifies the sinner before God. Yet as I will argue shortly, Jordan did have a doctrine of justification. Jordan was not as concerned with justification as that which justifies the sinner to be admitted into heaven, as he was with the process by which the sinner becomes just. In other words, Jordan subordinated justification to sanctification. It is ontological states that Jordan explicated in his lectures on the Lord's Prayer rather than what renders one justified before the heavenly judge. Thus before I seek to unfold Jordan's doctrine of justification, I begin with his understanding of sanctification, which is the central theme of his exposition. Christians are to become saints, adopted sons of God, by realizing the redemption effected and offered by Christ, and thus to attain the end, to complete the "homeward journey" to eternal blessedness with God. One may ask of Jordan what the basis is for justification before God, that which effects the final step between the states of grace (*esse gratie*) and glory (*esse glorie*), but to do so is to ask Jordan to give an answer to a question he does not treat. Jordan is not in search of a righteous God; he already knows the loving Father who has offered humans redemption through the cross of Christ.

---

[243] "Notandum autem quod voluntas dei fit a nobis generaliter in mandatorum suorum observatione... Specialiter tamen dei voluntas circa nos est triplex, secundum quod ipse specialiter a nobis vult tria. Vult enim deus: peccatorum conversionem; conversorum sanctificationem; sanctificatorum glorificationem." Jor. *Exp.* 5, fol. 79^{ra-b}.

As Jordan stated at the very outset of his exposition, the Lord's Prayer contains all that is necessary for salvation: it is the summary of the commandments and leads to eternal blessedness.[244] He is also very clear in what this blessedness entails. "There are," Jordan explained, "three chief perfections of the blessed: clear vision, which goes with faith and perfects the rational powers of the soul; ever present possession, which accompanies hope and perfects the emotional powers of the soul; and an unyielding fruition, which corresponds with love and satisfies all the soul's desire."[245] This blessedness is the result of God's operation within the saints, for "in the saints God illumines the intellect by removing errors, regulates the affections by directing their love, and cares for their progress by administering strength."[246]

---

[244] "Huic dominice orationi beatus Gregorius premittit prefationem sive prologum in officio misse, que talis est: Preceptis salutaribus moniti, et divina institutione formati audemus dicere [Greg.M. sacr. 4,83 (28C)]... Dignitas autem cuiuslibet rei ex suis causis tollitur, et tanguntur in hoc prologo quatuor cause istius orationis. Materialis <causa> in hoc quod dicit *preceptis salutaribus*. Nam omnes iste petitiones sunt de preceptis, utpote de hiis que sunt de necessitate salutis. Unde Cyprianus in libro *De Dominica Oratione* dicit istam orationem esse compendium preceptorum divinorum [Cypr. domin.orat. 28 (107,519–524)]... Finalis <causa> tangitur in hoc quod dicit *moniti*. Monitio enim fit vel ut adipiscamur finem vel ne decidamus a fine. In hac autem oratione utrumque monemur petere: et ut pertingamus ad finem beatitudinis eterne et ut removeantur impeditiva ipsius finis... Efficiens <causa> innuitur cum dicitur *divina institutione*. Hec enim oratio divinitus est instituta puta ab ipso Christo dictata, ut patet Matthei sexto et Luce undecimo. Propter quod dominica oratio nuncupatur et ob hoc ista oratio merito efficacissima est et maxime exaudibilis... Unde impossibile est ceteris paribus aliquam orationem esse uberiorem et magis exaudibilem quam istam, immo nec eque. Sciendum ergo quod hec sanctissima oratio specialiter super omnem orationem triplicem habet effectum seu efficientiam. Est enim hec oratio pre omnibus exaudibilis et impetrativa... Est <enim> secundo <hec oratio> mentis sursum provectiva... Est enim <hec oratio> peccatorum venialium expulsiva, propter quod Augustinus et alii doctores sancti dicunt ipsam valere ad expiationem venialium peccatorum. Nec dubium quantoplures alios effectus salubres licet nos latentes habeant, quos divina clementia secundum uniuscuiusque orantis devotionem et affectum misericorditer influit et dispensat. Formalis vero causa tangitur in eo quod dicit *formati*. Hec enim oratio est nobis forma orandi et quantum ad res petendas, et quantum ad ordinem petendorum; propter quod ipsa est totius nostri affectus informativa." Jor. *Exp.* 1, fol. 73^{ra-b}.

[245] "Sunt enim tres precipue perfectiones beatorum: visio inobfuscabilis, que succedit fidei et perficit rationalem; tentio inamissibilis, que succedit spei et perficit irascibilem; fruitio infastidibilis, que respondet caritati et satiat concupiscientialem." Jor. *Exp.* 2, fol. 75va.

[246] "Habent enim celi: in lumine claritatem; in motu regularitatem; in virtute caliditatem. Hiis correspondent in sanctis: deus <enim> illuminat intellectum, removendo errorem; regulat affectum, ordinando amorem; attendit {ad} profectum [affectum *B*], ministrando vigorem." Jor. *Exp.* 2, fol. 75rb.

ETHICS AND ERUDITION   421

The term to be noted here is 'affections', which is only a slightly better translation of the Latin *affectus* than is 'emotions'. For Jordan blessedness was the harmony of the affections with the will of God. Rather than a Thomistic intellectual union, theology for Jordan aimed at an affective union with God, which places his theology squarely within the Augustinian tradition.[247] Indeed, the reign of grace (*regnum gratie*) is realized "when all the powers and motions in man are obedient to divine governance."[248] Jordan did not ignore the intellective powers of the soul, and as just mentioned, illumination of the intellect is one of the works that God operates in the blessed. The affective powers, however, reign supreme. Even the gift of understanding (*donum intellectus*) not only illumines the intellect, but also purifies the affections, and Jordan cited Augustine as his proof text.[249] When the affections are in proper order, one is truly blessed, for then one is at peace. Peace, Jordan affirmed, "is delight in God without the contradiction of the flesh, the world, or the devil," and thus "peace redeems the soul, brings about the sons of God, and pays honor to God." Peace redeems the soul in that it "is the effect of our redemption to the extent that by redemption we are placed in peace."[250] The saints, therefore, are those who are in peace, whose

---

[247] See K. Zur Mühlen, "Affekt II," *TRE* 1:600–605. Jordan's view of the affects being brought into harmony with God's will is also seen in his discussion of the *donum sapientie*, which, as the *donum scientie*, is clearly defined as *scientia spiritualis*: "Introducitur etiam per hanc petitionem donum sapientie, quia dicit *Glossa* super Mattheum, dicendo *sanctificetur nomen tuum*, spiritum sapientie postulamus ne a sanctificatione nominis <tui> in aliquo discrepemus, sed patris nomen in nobis tamquam in filiis vita et moribus ostendamus [*Glos.ord.* ad Matth. 6:9 (ed. Strassburg, 1480/81), IV.25A]. Est autem sapientia proprie ut pro dono sumitur cognitio suavitatis divine per experientiam habita. Unde dicta est sapientia, quasi sapida scientia, cognitio autem et experientia suavitatis divine habetur ex sanctificatione triplicis nominis predicti. Surgit enim mentis suavitas in nobis adpresens ex tribus: ex passionis Christi devota meditatione; ex dilectionis dei erga nos memoratione; ex divine laudis iugi modulatione." Jor. *Exp.* 3, fol. 77^{ra-b}.

[248] "Secundum regnum dei est in anima, quod est regnum gratie ... Et hoc est quando omnes vires et motus in homine divine gubernationi obediunt." Jor. *Exp.* 4, fol. 77vb.

[249] "Donum siquidem intellectus non solum illustrat intellectum, sed etiam depurat affectum, ut dicit Augustinus in quodam sermone de timore <dei>: Sextus, inquit, gradus est intellectus ubi ab omni falsitate carnalis, vanitatis corda mundantur, ut pura intentio dirigatur in deum [Aug. serm. 347,3 (1526)]." Jor. *Exp.* 4, fol. 78vb.

[250] "Introducitur nichilominus <hic> beatitudo pacis de qua dicitur Matthei 5: *Beati pacifici* [Mt. 5:9], que secundum Augustinum adaptatur dono sapientie [Aug. de serm.dom. 1,4,11 (10,217*sqq*); *ibid.*, 2,11,38 (129,862–863)]. Dicit enim quendam

422   CHAPTER FOUR

affections are completely in harmony with God's will, which is the purpose and effect of the entire Lord's prayer: to direct and "inform" all human affections.[251] For Jordan, as for his Order's university theologians, theology was affective.

G. *Divine Geography*

Thus far I have left undifferentiated the distinction between the blessed and the saints, and I have done so because there is gray area in Jordan's treatment. On closer examination Jordan distinguished between the *beati* and the *sancti*. While explicating the various ways to understand how God is in heaven, Jordan stated that we can understand 'in heaven' as referring to celestial bodies, celestial spirits, or the heavens of eternal blessedness.[252] He then proceeded to explain that 'in heaven' is not to be taken as a spatial

---

statum virtutis, in quo est delectatio in deo sine contradictione carnis, mundi et diaboli, vel si est aliqua, inefficax est in hoc statu quietis et sine repugnantia nomen dei in nobis sanctificatur. Includit enim hec beatitudo triplicem significationem triplicis nominis dei, secundum tres eius effectus. Pax enim animam redimit; filios dei efficit; honorem deo tribuit. Primo, inquam, animam redimit vel potius redemptam ostendit. Unde psalmus: *Redimet* in pace *animam meam* [Ps. 48:16; *cf.* Ps. 114:7–8], et sic pax est effectus nostre redemptionis in quantum per redemptionem sumus in pace positi. Aliter pax potest esse causa redemptionis in quantum per pacem meremur esse participes redemptionis, et talem pacem non habent impii, iuxta illud Isaie 47: *non est pax impiis dicit dominus* [Is. 48:22]. Secundo etiam pax filios dei efficit, Matthei 5: *Beati pacifici, quoniam filii dei vocabuntur* [Mt. 5:9]. Et <hoc> merito quia faciunt officium filii dei, qui ad hoc venit in mundum ut pacem faceret inter deum et hominem, quod officium gerunt pacifici in seipsis et aliis pacem facientes. Tertio pax gloriam deo tribuit. Unde dicit Apostolus Colossensium 3: *et pax dei exultet in cordibus vestris* [Col. 3:15], et sequitur ad propositum, *commonentes nosmetipsos in psalmis et hymnis et canticis spiritualibus in gratia cantantes in cordibus vestris deo* [Col. 3:16]. Jor. *Exp*. 3, fol. 77[va]. Two things are to be noted here. First, the peace that Jordan is discussing is the peace of beatitude, *Beati pacifici*, which corresponds with the petition *sanctificetur nomen tuum*. Second, Giles defined *gratia gratum faciens* as that grace that the *mali* do not have: "Gratia gratum faciens non dividitur contra gratias gratis datas, quin ipsa sit gratis data: sed quia ultra hoc, quod est gratis data, est etiam gratum faciens, aliae autem gratiae secundum se, non sunt gratum facientes, cum possint haberi a malis, qui non sint deo grati... Malos ergo non habentes gratiam gratum facientem: dato quod habeant multas gratias gratis datas..." Aeg.Rom. 2 *Sent*. 26,2,2 (ed. Venice, 1581), 328Ib–c. For Jordan the *impii*, or the *mali* do not lack *gratia gratum faciens*, but rather *beatitudo* and *pax*. 'Merit' in this context for Jordan is not something one earns; rather it is something one gains or acquires through the *gratia gratis data*.

[251] "Hec enim oratio est nobis forma orandi et quantum ad res petendas et quantum ad ordinem petendorum, propter quod ipsa est totius nostri affectus informativa." Jor. *Exp*. 1, fol. 73[rb].

[252] "Possumus autem hic per 'celos' intelligere vel celos corporales, corpora scil-

dimension, and he states the five reasons we say that God is in heaven mentioned above. Regarding the second interpretation of 'in heaven', Jordan included the *sancti*, who are such on account of the beauty and splendor of their spiritual ornamentation, because of the purity of their heavenly comportment, and on account of the dignity and sanctity of their divine habitation.[253] It is in these saints that God illumines the intellect, regulates the affections, and cares for their progress. Yet this heavenly habitation is not physically in heaven, for Jordan continued by explaining that the regulation of the affections is that regulation by which "those things that are to be loved are loved, and are loved in the proper order, and thus all the motions of our affections are placed in sync."[254] Thus the heavenly saints can, at least in part, include humans. The third interpretation of 'in heaven' refers to the heaven of eternal blessedness, which stimulates the mind to prayer most of all,[255] and in these heavens are the *beati*, who enjoy the three perfections of the blessed.

The lines of demarcation, however, become somewhat blurred because Jordan included a beatitude that corresponds to each of the petitions, which at least gives the impression that some degree of beatitude is attainable in this life.[256] The *sancti* are comprised not only of those humans who are spiritually saints, but also of the saints already in heaven. In explicating the second petition, "Your will be done, on earth as it is in heaven," Jordan explained that 'in heaven' can be interpreted as "the angels and saints in heaven" whereas 'on earth', refers to "humans passing their time on earth." Thus, Jordan

---

icet supercelestia, vel celos spirituales, animas scilicet sanctas, vel etiam celos eterne beatitudinis." Jor. *Exp.* 2, fol. 74vb.

[253] "Dicuntur autem veri sancti celi propter tria: propter spiritualis ornatus pulchritudinem et sponsitatem; propter celestis conversationis celsitudinem et puritatem; propter divine inhabitationis sanctitudinem et dignitatem." Jor. *Exp.* 2, fol. 75ra.

[254] "De secundo Canticorum 2: *Ordinavit in me caritatem* [Ct. 2:4], que quidem ordinatio in hoc attenditur ut diligantur diligenda, et eo ordine, quo diligenda sunt. Et per hoc omnes motus affectionum nostrarum regulariter ordinantur." Jor. *Exp.* 2, fol. 75rb.

[255] "Tertio hic potest exponi de celis beatitudinis eterne, ex quorum consideratione maxime mens ad orandum excitatur." Jor. *Exp.* 2, fol. 75va.

[256] Jordan defined beatitudo in his ninth lecture: "Beatitudo vero est operatio doni ... ex quibus patet quod beatitudo et fructus non dicunt novos habitus alios a virtutibus et donis, sed sunt earum actus, qui quidem actus reponunt hominem in quodam perfectionis statu. Et hinc est quod beatitudines et fructus quidam status appellantur. Dicitur enim beatitudo status et perfectio iam purgati animi." Jor. *Exp.* 9, fol. 87va.

continued, "just as your will is done by the angels and blessed in heaven, who are perfectly conformed to your will, so even may it be done by us humans on earth, so that we might thus do your will here and hence might perfectly conform ourselves to your will in glory."[257] Humans passing their time on earth are saints as adopted sons of God and receive "beatitudes" from God, and yet there are also those *sancti et beati* who are truly in heaven. The distinctions are made, but there seems to be rather fine lines dividing the *sancti* who to some degree can become *beati* here on earth, and the *sancti* and *beati* already in heaven.

To gain a better grasp of Jordan's doctrine of sanctification I suggest two possible backgrounds: the second distinction of the second book of Lombard's *Sentences*, specifically as explicated by Giles of Rome, and Augustine's *De Civitate Dei*. I may indeed be entering the realm of pure speculation here, but such an exercise will help to read between the lines of Jordan's text as far as is possible. In doing so, it should be kept in mind that I am discussing the ontological relation between the state of grace and the state of glory, both of which, according to Jordan, are gifts of God.

In distinctions two through eleven of the second book of the *Sentences*, Lombard treated the nature and being of the angels. In the second distinction, he discussed the question of where the angels were created, and gave the answer that they were created and are in heaven, but not the heaven that is understood to have been the firmament created on the second day. They are in the *celum empyreum*, which is as fire from its splendor, created on the first day.[258] Giles further clarified that the *celum empyreum* is as flames, and that after the resurrection of the body the saints will be shining just as the sun, in that they will be shining with their own light, rather than as the planets and stars which shine with light from the sun. They will shine not as the sun is now, but how it will be then, in that it

---

[257] "Tertio modo potest exponi ut per celum intelligantur angeli et sancti in celo, per terram vero homines degentes in terra. Et hec expositio <cor>respondet tertie voluntati dei et <ut sic> est sensus: sicut voluntas tua fit in angelis et beatis in celo, qui perfecti sunt voluntati tue conformati, ita et in nobis hominibus in terra, ut <scilicet> ita voluntatem tuam hic faciamus quod et nos in gloria tue voluntati perfecte conformemur." Jor. *Exp*. 5, fol. 79rb-va.

[258] Lombardus 2 *Sent*. 2,4,2 (339,17–21); *cf*. "... prima die fuit creatum coelum, quod vocatur empyreum, id est igneum, non a calore, sed a splendore ..." Aeg.Rom. 2 *Sent*. 2,2,2 (ed. Venice, 1581), 138IId.

will be seven times as bright. Thus is the splendor and flames of the *celum empyreum*.[259]

Jordan had claimed that the *sancti* are said to be in heaven because of their spiritual ornateness, which he likened to the heavens being decorated by the sun, moon, and stars. It is somewhat unclear, however, precisely where these saints are. On the one hand, Jordan was discussing the spiritual heavens (*de celis spiritualibus*), which could be interpreted as a spiritual state of being, but on the other hand, these saints are also said to be in heaven on account of the sanctity and dignity of the divine habitation.[260] The latter could indeed be referring as well to a spiritual mode of existence, but the locational connotations suggest other possibilities. It could be that Jordan was referring to the saints of the *celum empyreum*. This indeed seems the case when he interpreted 'on earth as it is in heaven' as referring to the angels and saints in heaven regarding the former and humans passing their time on earth regarding the latter. And as we have already seen, for Giles and Lombard the angels are in the *celum empyreum*, which is also where Jordan placed them in his *Opus Jor.*[261]

If Jordan was indeed referring to the *celum empyreum* the demarcations between the *sancti* and *beati* come into sharper focus. Going

---

[259] "Sic ergo imaginabimur, quod totum coelum empyreum non ratione caloris, sed ratione splendoris est quasi quaedam flamma. Ibi ergo post resurrectionem corpora Sanctorum existentia, quae lucebunt sicut Sol, non sicut Sol nunc, sed sicut Sol tunc, qui erit in luciditate septuplus, quia tunc lux solis erit sicut lux 7 dierum." Aeg.Rom. 2 *Sent.* 2,2,2 (ed. Venice, 1581), 145Ic. Giles had shortly before explained that: ". . . . distinctio reperitur in coelis, quia sunt ibi aliqua spissa, non pervia, sed lucentia et resplendentia: non per lucem, quam habeant a se, sed per eam, quam habent a Sole. Et huiusmodi sunt omnes stellae, sive sint planetae, sive sint stellae fixae." Aeg.Rom. 2 *Sent.* 2,2,2 (ed. Venice, 1581), 144IIb.

[260] See note 253 above.

[261] Jordan stated that God gave a natural place to all creation; he then gave examples, among which are the angels: "Sicut patet de angelis, qui omnes sunt in celo empyreo; et de stellis, que omnes sunt in firmamento; et de piscibus, qui omnes sunt in aqua; et de plantis, que omnes sunt in terra." Jor. *OJ* sermo 68, fol. 127rb; *cf.*: "Sicut autem triplices sunt celi, tripliciter differentie in motus quia quidem celis moventur motu proprio et motu raptus, sicut omnes orbes septem planetarum; octava sphera movetur solum motu proprio et non motu raptus. Celum autem empyreum est penitus immobili in quo sunt deus et spiritus beatorum. . . . Tertius actus contemplativorum, cognitio dei quantum possibile est in seipso absque omni meditatione creaturarum et absque omni iudicio de creaturis; et in isto modo anima contemplativa fit quodammodo immobilis, ad modum celi empyrei, quia in unico bono divine dulcedinis immobiliter conquiescit." Jor. *OJ* sermo 208, fol. 326ra–326rb. For the *celum empyreum* in medieval cosmology, see Edward Grant, "Cosmology," in *Science in the Middle Ages*, ed. David C. Lindberg (Chicago, 1978), 265–302; 275ff; and *idem*, *Planets, Stars, and Orbs. The Medieval Cosmos, 1200–1687* (Cambridge, 1994).

beyond Lombard, Giles explained that the *celum empyreum* can be interpreted both as corporal and as spiritual.[262] It should not be doubted that the *celum empyreum* is indeed corporal; it is so as the place of the angels' contemplation, and was created on the first day.[263] Giles placed the *beati* as well in the *celum empyreum*; the *celum empyreum* is where the separated souls of the blessed go after they leave their bodies. After the death of the individual, the individual's soul, if it is blessed, is taken to the *celum empyreum* to await the resurrection of the body.[264] Yet the *celum empyreum*, as the place of contemplation, can be understood in a spiritual sense; it is the third heaven into which Paul was taken up. In this sense the *celum empyreum* is that without which there can be no *beati*, because beatitude is the vision of God, which is spiritual. If, Giles argued, we say that some souls by divine virtue experience the sense of damnation without actually going to a corporal place, this is to be understood in a spiritual sense; likewise the blessedness of the *celum empyreum* can be experienced spiritually.[265]

For angels in medieval thought, see Peter van der Eerden, "Engelen en demonen," in *De middeleeuwse ideeënwereld, 1000–1300*, ed. Manuel Stoffers (Hilversum, 1994), 117–143, and Marcia Colish, "Early Scholastic Angelology," *RThAM* 62 (1995), 80–109.

[262] Aeg.Rom. 2 *Sent.* 2,2,1 (ed. Venice, 1581), 137IIc *sqq.*

[263] "Sed si loquamur quantum ad congruitatem, sic coelum, quod est locus contemplationis angelorum, dicitur summum coelum corporale, quia prima die fuit creatum coelum, quod vocatur empyreum, id est igneum: non a calore, sed a splendore..." Aeg.Rom. 2 *Sent.* 2,2,1 (ed. Venice, 1581), 138IId.

[264] "Dicendum, quod per coelum empyreum intelligimus locum aliquem, in quo sunt angeli, et ad quem vadunt animae beatorum... congruum est, quod ipsae substantiae spirituales, id est, angeli beati, quae sunt suprema pars universi, sint in supremo corpore, id est, in celo empyreo. Esset enim universum dissolutum, si spiritualia et corporalia non essent coniuncta. Congruum est etiam, quod ibi sint animae beatae exuatae a corpore: cum sint spirituales substantiae, et cum erunt post resurrectionem coniunctae cum corporibus: congruum erit, quod simul cum corporibus sint ibi in coelo empyreo: ubi erunt angeli..." Aeg.Rom. 2 *Sent.* 2,2,1 (ed. Venice, 1581), 137Iib; 139Ib–c.

[265] "Uno modo, ut dicatur huiusmodi coelum illud, quod est ipsa beatitudo angelorum vel animarum: vel illud, sine quo nec angeli nec animae possunt esse beati. Et sic tale coelum non est quid corporale, sed quid spirituale. Deus enim ipse, vel visio eius, vel dilectio illa summa, quam habebimus in patria, potest dici huiusmodi coelum. Ipse enim deus est illa regio, in qua optime est animae nam ad ipsum facti sumus et inquietum est cor nostrum donec requiescamus in ipso, ut vult Augustinus circa principium libri Confessionum. Istud autem est tertium coelum ad quod raptus fuit Paulus ad visionem, scilicet dei apertam, quae non fit per corpus, neque per similitudinem corporis, sed per ipsam divinam essentiam. Et sicut coelum, vel regio superior, in qua sunt angeli, vel animae beatae, potest nobis dicere quid spirituale, non corporale, sic et infernus vel locus inferior, ad quem feruntur animae

For Giles the *celum empyreum* was the habitation of the angels and blessed souls, but it was also a spiritual location to which the blessed in this life can spiritually be taken. In this light, Jordan's description of the heavens takes on added dimensions. Jordan offered three interpretations of the heavens: the heaven of the celestial bodies, the heaven of the true saints, and the heaven of eternal blessedness. If the *celum empyreum* stood behind his exposition, then we come to see that the problematic 'heaven of the true saints', is the spiritual understanding of the *celum empyreum*, to which Christians have access, albeit most limited, through contemplation. The *beati* are those separated souls who are truly in heaven, whereas the *sancti* are both the *beati* residing with the angels and the saints here on earth, the saints who by grace are similar to the angels.[266]

The spiritual understanding of the *celum empyreum* is of utmost importance for interpreting not only Jordan's understanding of 'in heaven', but also for grasping his doctrine of sanctification, and, perhaps unexpectedly, for gaining insight into his view of his Order. In expositing 'in heaven' as the saints, Jordan declared that the human soul is expanded by grace and love to become increasingly capable of containing God, and thus God extended the heavens, as a tent,

---

damnatae, potest dicere quid spirituale, non corporale, nam poena animarum damnatorum est duplex: una poena damni. Et alia sensus; et prima debet reputari maior quam secunda: plus enim debent dolere animae damnatae de poena damni, quia carent tanto bono: sicut est visio dei, quam de poena sensus, ut quia sentiunt sic cruciatum acerbum; feruntur ergo animae damnatae ad infernum, id est, ad aliquid triste, ut ad poenam damnandi, vel ad poenam sensus. Si ergo per huiusmodi triste intelligatur poena damni, certum est quod huiusmodi triste est quid spirituale: sed si per huiusmodi triste intelligatur poena sensus, non oportet quod nominet locum corporalem; possunt enim animae virtute divina habere huiusmodi poenam, absque eo, quod sint in loco illo inferior. Coelum ergo empyreum, id est igneum, in quo sunt angeli beati, et sine quo beati esse non possunt: debet dici quid spirituale." Aeg.Rom. 2 *Sent.* 2,2,1 (ed. Venice, 1581), 138Ic–IIa.

[266] "... nostra conversatio est in celis ... vivendo et intelligendo similes sumus angelis; hoc efficit gratia." Jor. *OJ* sermo 30, fol. 64ra. Expositing the phrase *in celis* as referring in part to the *celum empyreum* became incorporated within the exegetical tradition. Thus the rector of the schools in Ulm, Johannes Müntzinger (d. 1417), explained: "... nota quod triplex est celum scilicet celum supra nos, quod dicitur celum divinum et empireum, et stelle illius celi sunt angeli; secundum celum est intra nos et est anima nostra, et huius stelle sunt virtutes; tertium celum est iuxta nos, et hoc celum est ecclesia, cuius stelle sunt Christifideles. Et ergo dicimus *Qui es in celis* in plurali numero et non in singulari numero." Müntzinger *Exp.*, fol. 61[v]. We find a similar interpretation in the catechetical expositions of the 'Our Father'; see the fifteenth-century treatise, *Unser aller liebster her Ihesus*, edited by Bernd Adam in his, *Katechetische Vaterunserauslegungen. Texte und Untersuchungen zu deutschsprachigen Auslegungen des. 14. und 15. Jahrhunderts* (Munich, 1976), 109–110.

to fill the expanded souls. In light of the above analysis, the heaven that has been extended appears as the spiritual *celum empyreum*. As an "extended heaven" it is theoretically open not only to those like Paul who was taken up into the third heaven, but also to each contemplative soul. And it is in these souls, these saints, that God illumines the intellect by removing errors, regulates the affections by ordering love, and cares for their progress by administering strength. Jordan compared these saints to the heavenly bodies, which greatly shine with the majesty of God. In expositing Psalm 67:9, "For the heavens drip forth from the face of the God of Sinai, from the face of the God of Israel," Jordan explained that those heavens are the saints, "who drip forth by pouring out works of charity." To drip forth, Jordan continued, "is to pour forth drops, drop by drop," and these drops are the key to spiritual growth: it is by pouring out drops of one's virtues through works that one merits and grows. This merit and growth, however, have their source in the God of Sinai, which Jordan interpreted as obedience to God's commandments, or the active life, and the God of Israel, or seeing God, which is the contemplative life.[267]

---

[267] "Ut autem anima semper magis et magis sit capax dei, oportet eam per gratiam et caritatem extendi et dilatari, dicente Apostolo secunde Corinthiorum quinto: dilatamini in caritate [*cf.* II Cor. 6:1–13]. De hac dilectione et extensione dicitur in psalmo: *extendens celum sicut pellem* [Ps. 103:2] ... sic anima misericordia dei ungitur et gratia dilatatur, dilatatur autem non in substantia, sed in virtute quo etiam modo *crescit in templum sanctum in domino*, Ephesiorum secundo [Eph. 2:21]. In istis celis, scilicet sanctis animabus, deus tria operatur. Accepta sunt tria, que videmus in celis corporalibus, in quibus maxime maiestas divine operationis relucet. Habent enim celi: in lumine claritatem; in motu regularitatem; in virtute caliditatem. Hiis correspondent in sanctis <tria que operatur deus in eis>: deus <enim> illuminat intellectum, removendo errorem; regulat affectum, ordinando amorem; attendit {ad} profectum [affectum *B*], ministrando vigorem. De primo psalmo: *Quoniam tu illuminat lumen* [*cf.* Ps. 135:5–7; Ps. 35:10], id est intellectum meum, domine etc. De secundo Canticorum secundo: *Ordinavit in me caritatem* [Ct. 2:4], que quidem ordinatio in hoc attenditur ut diligantur diligenda, et eo ordine, quo diligenda sunt. Et per hoc omnes motus affectionum nostrarum regulariter ordinantur. De tertio psalmo: *Et enim celi distillaverunt a facie dei Synai; a facie dei Israel* [Ps. 67:9]. Isti celi sunt sancti, qui distillant diffundando opera caritatis, que quidem diffusio convenienter dicitur distillatio. 'Distillare' enim est guttatim stillas diffundere. Sic est in profectu spirituali, quo paulatim et quasi guttatim de una virtute ad aliam proceditur. Nemo enim repente fit summus et cum quis omnes virtutes quasi iam perfectus habuerit, diffundat stillam cuiuslibet virtutis per operis exercitium secundum oportunitatem temporis, ut nunc distillat murram amaritudinis per carnis mortificationem, secundum illud Canticorum quinto: *Manus mee distillaverunt murram* [Ct. 5:5], nunc distillant favum dulcedinis per doctrinam et contemplationem, iuxta illud Canticorum quarto: *favus distillans labia tua* [Ct. 4:11]. Et sic discurrendo per singulas virtutes

Several points are to be noted here. First, merit stems from God, or rather, flows from God; it is not a human acquisition by which individuals progress towards God. Second, and most importantly, this is Jordan's summation of sanctification. Here, in his exposition of the heavenly saints, he spelled out the progress of the sanctified life. The saints are saints by pouring forth works of charity, drop by drop, in both the active and the contemplative lives. The saints are not holy individuals but the springs of love, virtue, and divine splendor. The saints are those who keep God's commandments and those who see God. Third, Jordan's summation of sanctification here is the theological explication of Augustine's religion. As already seen, the *vita perfectissima* according to Jordan, was to rest in God and then to bring the fruits of contemplation to others.[268] This is echoed here not only by the emphasis on the active and contemplative lives, but also when Jordan listed among what is poured out by the saints, "... the honeycomb of sweetness through doctrine and contemplation,"[269] which is both the resting in God and the going out to others of the *vita perfectissima*. The brothers of the Order were not only to be imitators of Augustine, but also heavenly saints. Finally, even though Jordan's doctrine of sanctification as here expressed was inseparable from his understanding of his Order, sanctification was not limited to the members of the OESA. All Christians are saints by keeping God's commandments in conforming themselves to God's will.[270] The saints reflect the splendor of divine majesty, and as Jordan confirmed in a sermon specifically addressed to the cloistered, "the religious, indeed every Christian ought to be bright and shining."[271] The true saints are not only the *fratres Augustini*, nor even the

---

quelibet virtus stillam sui actus suo tempore diffundat. Hec autem distillatio est a facie dei Synai et Israel. Synai interpretatur 'mandatum meum' et significat act vam vitam, que consistit in mandatorum dei observationem; Israel, quod interpretatur 'videns deum', significat contemplativam vitam; utraque enim vita a facie dei est, a qua omnis nostra distillatio sumit meritum et profectum." Jor. *Exp.* 2, fol. 75ra-b.

[268] *VF* 1,11 (35,9–11).

[269] "... distillant [sancti] favum dulcedinis per doctrinam et contemplationem..." Jor. *Exp.* 2, fol. 75rb.

[270] "... voluntas dei fit a nobis generaliter in mandatorum suorum observatione." Jor. *Exp.* 5, fol. 79ra.

[271] "Sic debent homo religiosus et quilibet christianus esse clarus et luminosus." Jor. *OS* sermo 256 (ed. Paris, 1521), fol. 412v. The same emphasis is seen in Jor. *Med.*, which he composed for his fellow religious and for the laity; see Chapter Five.

religiosi. The true saints are the *Christiani*. Every Christian, *quilibet Christianus*, is to be a saint.[272]

H. *The City of God in Exile*

This brings me to my second interpretative lens, Augustine's *De Civitate Dei*. I turn to Augustine not to highlight textual parallels between Jordan's *Expositio* and the Bishop of Hippo's *magnum opus et arduum*; Jordan indeed cited the work but once. Yet Augustine's doctrine of the two cities casts light on Jordan's doctrine of sanctification that reveals shades which might otherwise be overlooked.

To begin I should mention that Giles explicitly appealed to Augustine's *civitas Dei* as referring to the community of the blessed and angels in the *celum empyreum*: "now the angels and blessed humans comprise the one city of God; then [i.e., after the resurrection of the body] the *celum empyreum* will be one city of God, whose citizens will be the angels and the blessed humans. Likewise at that time that hellish place far below will be one city of the devil, whose citizens will be the demons and the damned."[273] Jordan, on the other hand, did not explicitly refer to the *sancti* and *beati* as the citizens of the city of God. Nevertheless, the parallels to Augustine's two cities are striking.

For Augustine the two cities had their origins when God separated the light from the darkness, and from this time onwards they steadily proceed through the historical drama towards their merited ends (*debiti fines*). The two cities are defined most succinctly as two loves; the dwellers in the heavenly city love God whereas those in the other city love themselves. The inhabitants of the heavenly city are destined towards eternal blessedness in heaven, whereas the citizens from hell are truly hell bent. In this life the cities are mixed, a *corpus permixtum*, in the sense that individuals do not carry passports issued by their respective eternal governments. Yet the citizens of the heavenly city are forced to dwell in time, and thus they are resident aliens on earth, *peregrini*, who are separated from their home-

---

[272] See E.L. Saak, "Saints in Society," 317–338.
[273] Referring to Aug. civ. 12, 1, Giles writes: ". . . nunc angeli et homines beati facient unam civitatem Dei: erit tunc caelum empyreum una civitas dei; cuius cives erunt angeli et homines beati: et tunc infernus locus ille profundus inferior erit una civitas diaboli, cuius cives erunt daemones et homines damnati." Aeg.Rom. 2 *Sent.* 2,2,1 (ed. Venice, 1581), 139Ic.

land. The *pondus anime*, the weight of historical existence renders the heavenly citizens estranged. There is an ontological yearning for blessedness, which they await in hope, manifested in their inquietude. The citizens of the heavenly city will only obtain peace when they reach their home and their end.[274]

This crystallizes Jordan's doctrine of sanctification. As I have already noted, Jordan cited *De Civitate Dei* only once in his *Expositio*, though this single reference reveals the hidden importance of this work for Jordan. Jordan concluded his exposition of the prologue of the prayer by setting forth the three chief perfections of the blessed. Even here we see the indeterminacy between the *sancti* and the *beati* because the ever present possession (*tentio inamissibilia*) which the *beati* enjoy is related to hope, and perfects the emotional powers of the soul, rather than a state of being in heaven. "But," Jordan clarified, "so that we might have future blessedness present here and now, we need the kingdom of glory (*regnum glorie*)."[275] This is the context in which Jordan placed the 'ever present possession' of the blessed. Christians are saints awaiting future blessedness and as long as they are in this life, they await with hope. And this is where *De Civitate Dei* entered Jordan's text. In explicating the three chief perfections of the *beati* to conclude the prologue in which he set up the entire context of the prayer, with respect to the first, 'clear vision' (*visio inobfuscabilis*), Jordan simply cited Job, Exodus, and Psalms. When it

---

[274] *Cf.* R.A. Markus, *Saeculum*; Isabelle Bochet, *Saint Augustin et Le Desir de Dieu* (Paris, 1982); S. Böhm, *La Temporalité*; and Johannes van Oort, *Jerusalem and Babylon. A Study into Augustine's 'City of God' and the Sources of his Doctrine of the Two Cities*, Supplements to Vigiliae Christianae 14 (Leiden, 1991). For an excellent study of Augustine's doctrine of the two cities as they relate to socio-political life, see Miikka Ruokanen, *Theology of Social Life in Augustine's* De Civitate Dei, Forschung zur Kirchen- und Dogmengeschichte 53 (Göttingen, 1993).

[275] "Introducitur autem per hanc petitionem de virtutibus spes, per quam regnum exspectamus. Describitur enim spes a magistro *Sententiarum* libro 3, distinctione 26: "Spes est certa exspectatio future beatitudinis, veniens ex dei gratia et ex meritis precedentibus [Lombardus 3 *Sent.* 26,1 (2:159,17–18)]." In qua descriptione ponitur tria correspondentia triplici regno dei predicto, nam quod dicit 'certa exspectatio' respicit regnum ecclesie, quod in fidei firmitate consistit. Unde certitudo spei certitudini fidei innititur, *spes enim que videtur non est spes*, Romanorum 8 [Rm. 8:24]. Quod autem dicit 'future beatitudinis', respicit regnum glorie. Quod vero addit 'ex dei gratia etc.,' respicit regnum gratie et patet. Ut igitur exspectatio sit certa, indigemus regno ecclesie; ut autem talis exspectatio ex gratia dei et nostris meritis proveniat, opus est regno gratie; ut vero futuram beatitudinem presentialiter habeamus, requiritur regnum glorie. Sic ergo per hoc quod petimus regnum dei, introducitur spes." Jor. *Exp.* 4, fol. 78$^{\text{rb-va}}$.

came to the second, however, the 'ever present possession' that is related to hope, he first cited Exodus 15: "Lead them and plant them in the mountain of your heredity." The "Lead them," he explained, is in the present tense and relates to hope, which is of the future; "plant them," signifies the ever present possession that is firm and secure. To drive the point home, Jordan brought in *De Civitate Dei*: "Wherefore Augustine in the last book of *The City of God*: 'There we will rest and see, we will see and love, we will love and praise. Behold what will be in the end without end, for what else is our end but to come to the kingdom which has no end?'"[276] To describe humankind's end, to which the entire *Pater Noster* is directed and which Christians must await in hope, Jordan appealed to *De Civitate Dei*.[277]

Hope is the Moses of the *sancti* and *beati*, which leads them out of the land of Egypt and plants them in the promised land. It was the link between the state of grace (*esse gratie*) and the state of glory (*esse glorie*), or perhaps more accurately, between the kingdom of grace (*regnum gratie*) and the eternal kingdom (*regnum glorie*). As such it occupied a place of central importance in Jordan's theology. Faith makes one a saint in a strict sense, but while the saints remain in this life,

---

[276] "Sunt enim tres precipue perfectiones beatorum: visio inobfuscabilis, que succedit fidei et perficit rationalem; tentio inamissibilis, que succedit spei et perficit irascibilem; fruitio infastidibilis, que respondet caritati et satiat concupiscientialem. De primo Iob 23: *Quis michi det ut cognoscam et inveniam illum et veniam usque ad solium eius?* [Iob 23:3] Hanc etiam perfectionem petiit Moyses cum dicebat, Deuteronomii 33: *Ostende michi gloriam tuam*, cui *respondit* dominus: *Ego ostendam tibi omne bonum* [Ex. 33:18–19]. Hec est perfectio rationalis, psalmo: *sicut audivimus, sic vidimus* etc. [Ps. 47:9]. De secundo Exodi 15: *Introduces eos et plantabis in monte hereditatis tue* etc. [Ex. 15:17] 'Introduces' inquam presentialiter, quantum ad spei successionem, que est futurorum, et 'plantabis' inamissabiliter quantum ad firmam et securam tentionem. Unde Augustinus ultimo *De Civitate Dei*: Ibi vacabimus et videbimus, videbimus et amabimus, amabimus et laudabimus. Ecce quod erit in fine sine fine, nam quis alius noster est finis nisi venire ad regnum eius nullus est finis? [Aug. civ. 22,30 (866,145–148)]." Jor. *Exp.* 2, fol. 75va.

[277] The importance of this text to Jordan's thought is testified to not only by its inclusion within the *Expositio Orationis Dominice*, but also by the fact that Jordan selected this same passage to conclude his *Opus Postillarum*. After discussing the need for both the active and the contemplative lives, the Augustinian *vita perfectissima*, Jordan summarized: "Ibant inquam ad actionem et revertebantur ad contemplationem, et vice versa. Quam etiam desiderabilem vicissitudinem et nos continuare studeamus donec ad illam celestem montem perveniamus, ubi, secundum Augustinum libro De civitate dei, vacabimus et videbimus, videbimus et amabimus, amabimus et laudabimus. Ecce quod erit in fine sine fine. Quo nos perducere digneretur deus deorum, qui vivit et regnat per infinita saecula saeculorum, Amen." Jor. *OP* sermo 460 (ed. Strassburg, 1483).

hope offers them the foretaste of eternal blessedness, leading them towards their end. Faith ontologically makes one a saint, providing the bridge between the state of grace and the state of glory, but hope experientially makes one a saint, securing the promise within the kingdom of grace of the kingdom of glory.

In his fourth lecture Jordan introduced the theological virtue, hope, defined as that "by which we await the kingdom." He then cited Lombard's definition of hope as the "certain expectation of future blessedness, coming from God's grace and from [our] preceding merits." The 'certain expectation', Jordan clarified, refers to the Church (*regnum ecclesie*), "which consists in the firmness of faith," and therefore "the certitude of hope relies on the certitude of faith." Yet since Lombard mentioned future blessedness, the kingdom of glory is also involved. This expectation comes from God's grace, and corresponds to the reign of grace (*regnum gratie*), but hope brings the eternal kingdom (*regnum glorie*) to the saints here and now. Having been made a saint by faith, the saint awaits his or her final end in hope, which allows for an experience of that end for those saints "doing their time on earth" (*degentes in terra*). Whereas faith is that by which God's name is sanctified in the sinner, hope brings about the coming of God's kingdom and offers the certitude of future blessedness, which is needed to conduct the war with the devil.[278]

The promised land, the Christian's merited end, is the goal of the saint's journey, and yet even now one can catch glimpses. In explicating the third chief perfection of the *beati*, unyielding delight (*fruitio infastidibilis*), Jordan once again drew on Augustine, but this time from *De Libero Arbitrio*: "So great is the joy of the eternal light that

---

[278] In the *Tractatus de virtutibus et vitiis*, Jordan presented a short treatment of hope that parallels his exposition in his lecture on Matthew: "Secunda virtus theologica est spes. Spes autem in sacra scriptura accipitur multis modis. Sumitur enim quandoque pro re, quam speramus, ut ad Titum secundo: *exspectantes beatam spem* [Tit. 2:13]. Quandoque pro certitudine gloriae futurae, Romanos quinto: *probatio vero spem* [Rm. 5:4]; gloria id est certitudinem futurae gloriae. Quandoque pro virtute, ut prime Corinthiorum tertio <decimo>, *Nunc autem manent fides, spes et caritas* [I Cor. 13:13]. Quandoque pro motu virtutis, et sic describit eam magister Sententiarum libro tertio 3, distinctione 26: *Spes est certa expectatio beatitudinis futurae veniens ex dei gratia et ex meritis precedentibus*, secundum eundem etiam describitur sic: *spes est appetitus excellentis boni cum fiducia obtinende*. Sed prout est virtus sic describitur: spes est virtus, qua spiritualia et aeterna bona sperantur, id est cum fiducia exspectantur. Et sic accipitur hic huius virtutis communiter non assignantur aliquae species sive partes; obiectum autem eius proprium est beatitudo aeterna, quam proprie et principaliter a deo sperare debemus." Jor. *OP* sermo 439D (ed. Strassburg, 1483).

even though it is not possible to remain in it for more than a brief time of a single day, on account of this alone innumerable days of this life are filled with delight, and the ebb and flow of temporal goods are rightly disparaged."[279] It is in this context that the *sancti* are the *beati*, who can experience a foretaste of the *celum empyreum* as they make their way "home." For Jordan, as for Augustine, the saints are citizens of the heavenly city, who must await their return in hope. It is this tension, this ontological tension, that the city of God experiences as resident aliens in this life; it is the ontological tension between the state of grace and that of glory that the saints experience as they make their way from this life to their blessed end.[280]

This end, however, is not something that humans achieve in the present life. The *Pater Noster* is the prayer that leads one to "stretch towards" one's end, or to "extend towards" the end (*ut pertingamus ad finem*).[281] Thus one must have patience (*longanimitas*), because the kingdom of glory is not immediate, but rather it is put off to the future. Thus in the meantime Christians await and expect the future delight with patience.[282] In doing so they must conform themselves to God's will. They must direct their affections toward heaven, for the distinction between the righteous and the sinners, Jordan clarified in echoes of Augustine, is based on diverse affections: those of the just are directed toward heaven while those of sinners are concerned with earthly matters.[283] Two separate affections, two separate loves

---

[279] "De tertio psalmo: *Satiabor cum apparuerit gloria tua* [Ps. 16:15]. Hec satietas est infastidibilis, quia ut dicit Augustinus tertio libro *De Libero Arbitrio*, capitulo 42: Tanta est iocunditas lucis eterne, ut si etiam non liceret in ea amplius manere quam unius diei mora, propter hoc solum innumerabiles huius vite dies pleni deliciis et circumfluentia temporalium bonorum recte meritoque contemnerentur. [Aug. lib.arb. 3,25,77 (321,63–68)]." Jor. *Exp.* 2, fol. 75^(va–b).

[280] *Cf.*: "... nostra conversatio in celis est, videmus enim quod peregrinus non libenter contrahit in terra peregrinationis precipue si terra sit ignorabilis, sed redit ad locum nativitatis. Ita apostolus volens conubium facere congruens sue nobilitati dicebat: non habemus hic manentem civitatem sed futuram inquirimus." Jor. *OJ* sermo 66, fol. 125^(rb).

[281] "In hac autem oratione utrumque monemur petere: et ut pertingamus ad finem beatitudinis eterne et ut removeantur impeditiva ipsius finis." Jor. *Exp.* 1, fol. 73^(ra).

[282] "Longanimitas etiam quia non statim ut postulatur regnum possidetur, sed plerumque differtur maxime regnum glorie. Et ideo opus est longanimitate, qua mens interim delectata exspectet. Est enim longanimitas diuturna exspectatio boni desiderati cum delectatione spei certitudinem consequente." Jor. *Exp.* 4, fol. 79^(ra).

[283] "Secundum patet per Augustinum in libro de sermone domini in monte ubi

distinguish the sinners from the saints. Yet even the saints are weighed down by the flesh. It is not, however, so much the *pondus anime* that Jordan explicates, as the *asinus anime*;[284] the flesh and the spirit are in opposition and must be brought into harmony. Hence one prays for God's will to be done "on earth as it is in heaven," at least in part, for 'heaven' here refers to the soul, and 'earth,' to the flesh. The spirit of the righteous (*spiritus iustorum*) resists the flesh, which must be made obedient to and brought in harmony with the spirit, otherwise it is in rebellion and can prevent sanctification.[285] Sanctification is indeed living as if not of this world, *quasi sine terra*, and to be saints Christians must live without worldly or earthly affections.[286] Yet to do so in this life is not within human power. One prays for God's will to be done in the spirit as in the flesh, but this can only be achieved imperfectly in this life, although it will be brought to perfection in eternal life. Thus one prays that it might

---

dicit quod tantum spiritualiter interesse videtur inter iustos et peccatores, quantum corporaliter inter celum et terram [Aug. de serm.dom. 2,5,17 (107,379–381)]. Et hoc accidit ex diversitate affectuum, nam affectus iusti erat circa celestia, iuxta illud Philippiensium tertio: *Nostra conversatio in celis est* [Phil. 3:20]; peccatorum autem affectus circa terrena versatur, de quibus dicitur in psalmo: *oculos suos statuerunt declinare in terram* [Ps. 16:11]." Jor. *Exp.* 2, fol. 75ra.

[284] The term *asinus anime* is not found in Jor. *Exp.*, but in Jor. *OP*, where Jordan also speaks of the 'weight' the soul bears due to the flesh: "gravamur nexibus carnis." Jor. *OP* sermo 5D (ed. Strassburg, 1483).

[285] "Alio modo ut per celum intelligatur vel accipiatur spiritus, per terram caro. Et sic respondet secunde voluntati dei, ut sit sensus: sicut voluntas tua fit in spiritu, quod non resistit tibi, ita et in corpore, ut non resistat spiritui et per consequens nec tibi. Spiritus enim iustorum deo non resistit {sed caro}, quia dicit Apostolus Romanorum septimo: *mente*, inquit, *servio legi dei, carne autem legi peccati* [Rm. 7:25], et iterum: *condelector enim legi dei secundum interiorem hominem, video autem aliam legem in membris meis* etc. [Rm. 7:22–23]. Et secundum hoc, hic petimus ut caro non resistat spiritui, vel si resistat et rebellet, quod non prevaleat quod pertinet ad sanctificationem hominis conversi." Jor. *Exp.* 5, fol. 79rb; *cf.*: "Secundum regnum dei est in anima, quod est regnum gratie, de quo Luce septimo decimo: *Regnum dei intra vos est* [Lc. 17:21; *cf.* Lc. 10:9]. Et hoc est quando omnes vires et motus in homine divine gubernationi obediunt, secus quando ibi est rebellio." Jor. *Exp.* 4, fol. 77vb.

[286] "Secundo modo 'nomen dei' dicitur privilegium filialis adoptionis et in hoc sensu specialiter accipitur hic. Istud nomen tunc sanctificatur in nobis, quoniam sicut nomine dicimur filii {dei}, ita sumus et re. Et sic dicimur 'sancti', quasi sine terra, id est, terrenis affectibus exuti. 'Sanctus' enim Latine, 'agios' dicitur Grece, quod dicitur ab 'a', quod est 'sine', et 'geos', terra, quasi sine terra. Et hoc {est} proprium filiorum dei, ut qui patrem habent in celis affectu non ambulent in terris. Et hoc est quod dicit dominus per prophetam: *Sancti estote quoniam ego sanctus sum* [Lv. 11:44]. Et hoc modo est sensus *sanctificetur nomen tuum*, id est, immaculata conservetur in nobis filiatio tua, ut vere simus filii tui, quorum tu pater esse dignaris." Jor. *Exp.* 3, fol. 76va.

be given one to do God's will to the extent possible for humans in this life, which is valid as well with regard to the sanctification of God's name and the coming of his Kingdom.[287] It is only in eternal life that the Christian will have perfect blessedness, when the affections will be in perfect obedience to God's will, when the saints will delight in God without contradictions of the flesh, the world, or the devil, for then they will be in perfect peace, then they will be "home," *in patria*,[288] then, they will have reached their end.

For Jordan the saints were defined by the direction of their affections, which distinguish them from the sinners. Their home, their end, is in heaven, which they await with patience and hope. They live as if not of this world, as if they are citizens of another city, the city that is their blessed end in which they will find perfect peace.[289] Even though Jordan only cited *De Civitate Dei* once, albeit in a place of central importance to the text, we pick up the scent of his overall scheme of sanctification only when we recognize the implicit presence of the two cities.

I. *Election and Predestination*

With the *celum empyreum* and Augustine's *De Civitate Dei* as background, the gray area between the saints and blessed begins to take on dis-

---

[287] "Notandum autem... quod hec clausula *sicut in celo et in terra* referri debet super omnes tres petitiones premissas, verbi gratia: sanctificetur nomen tuum, sicut in celo et in terra; adveniat regnum tuum, sicut in celo et in terra; fiat voluntas tua, sicut in celo et in terra, ad designandum quod he tres petitiones perfecte complebuntur in vita futura, sed in hac vita complentur imperfecte, secundum modum nobis possibilem. Petimus ergo in istis tribus petitionibus ut illa, que in eis petimus, et hic secundum modum possibilem nobis donentur, et illuc perveniamus ubi perfecte compleantur." Jor. *Exp.* 5, fol. 79va.

[288] "Est autem munditia cordis duplex: una est depuratio mentis ab erroribus ut ea, que de deo proponuntur, sane et pure capiantur, quod pertinet ad donum intellectus, ut dictum est. Et in hac munditia consistit regnum ecclesie. Alia est depuratio affectus ab inordinatis affectionibus, quod etiam pertinet ad donum intellectus. Et in hac munditia consistit regnum gratie. <Et> [est *B*] quoniam hec duplex munditia hic habetur imperfecte, perficietur autem in patria. Hinc est quod in tali perfectione et consumatione consistit regnum glorie. Ex quibus etiam patet quod convenienter huic beatitudini respondet pro premio visio dei, que si perfecta sit, secundum quod videtur deus per essentiam, pertinet ad donum intellectus et munditiam cordis consumatam; si vero sit imperfecta, pertinet ad ea prout habentur in via, et sic semper visio munditiam coexigit." Jor. *Exp.* 4, fol. 78vb–79ra.

[289] *Cf.*: "... mundus non convenit nostre quieti, quia nullus in hoc mundo quietus est, eo quod mundus semper sit in motu; videmus enim quod quidquid est in remota semper movetur, ut qui vadit in navi. Unde Augustinus: fecisti nos domine a te ut inquietum est cor meum donec requiescat in te." Jor. *OJ* sermo 66, fol. 125rb–125va.

tinct color and form. The *sancti* and *beati*, those already in the *celum empyreum* as well as those on earth, together comprise the city of God. This places the question of election and predestination in Jordan's theology in more direct light. Jordan was not addressing the individual who is concerned about how he or she can obtain grace; rather he addressed the saints who are saints by adoption as God's sons through grace. The grace has already been given, the redemption has already been effected. The question Jordan strove to answer was not the means by which the individual finds a "righteous God," which was to be the chief theological question of the later fifteenth century,[290] but rather after one has already been redeemed, after one has already been given gifts, after one is already a saint, after one knows that God is the loving Father—now what? This is the question: how are Christians, as saints by adoption, to be good administrators of God's gifts? How do they go about, as saints, pouring forth works of love? It is in this context that Jordan spoke of merit: one merits blessedness by being a good administrator after one has already been adopted by God.

Jordan was explicit in the *Opus Postillarum* regarding the steps, or stages of grace and merit. There is, he explained, a three-fold image of God in humans. First, there is the image of God given at creation; second, the reformed, or recreated image after the fall; and third, the image of likeness to God.[291] The first image was formed by God according to nature.[292] This image, however, was deformed by sin.[293] Thus, the second image of God in humans is the recreated image, reformed by the grace of God. The third image, the similitude to the Trinity, is accomplished by the grace of God and by human habits and works.[294] Human cooperation only has its place

---

[290] See Hamm, *Frömmigkeitstheologie*, 261f.

[291] "... imago hominis interior triplex est scilicet imago creationis, imago recreationis et imago similitudinis." Jor. *OP* sermo 445A (ed. Strassburg, 1483).

[292] "Prima imago est a deo secundum naturam formata." Jor. *OP* sermo 445A (ed. Strassburg, 1483).

[293] "Haec autem imago creata per peccatum hominis deformata est." Jor. *OP* sermo 445B (ed. Strassburg, 1483).

[294] "Secunda est a deo per gratiam reformata. Sed tertia est a deo et ab homine habitibus et actibus informata... Prima est imago in qua homo creatus est scilicet ratio; secunda est per quam reformatur imago creata scilicet dei gratia, quae menti reparandae infunditur. Tertia est imago ad quam factus est homo scilicet ad imaginem et similitudinem ipsius trinitatis." Jor. *OP* sermo 445A (ed. Strassburg, 1483). The image of God is central for Jordan, for this image separates the elect from the reprobate. In commenting on Mc. 12:15–17, Jordan clarified: "... deus

once the deformed image has been recreated and reformed by the infusion of God's grace. The order is clear: human merit does not precede, but follows the infusion of grace.

Merit for Jordan was not a *quid pro quo*.[295] If one can speak of merit, one can do so only based on what humans do with the grace bestowed on them to begin with, and all merit is dependent upon God's acceptance.[296] Human free will does not have the ability to merit.[297] All the meritorious works of humans are not their own, but are worked in them. Individuals only perform meritorious works when the Holy Spirit moves their free will to do so, "just as a boy

---

in extremo iudicio hanc quaestionem proponit exigendo a quolibet rationem quomodo imaginem suam in se custodierit et veneratus fuerit. Nam secundum dispositionem imaginis in quolibet ad conformitatem vel difformitatem Christi iudicabuntur. Et secundum hoc electi a reprobis discernentur." Jor. *OP* sermo 446C (ed. Strassburg, 1483). By conforming oneself to the image of Christ one returns to God.

[295] *Cf.*: "... quantumcumque quis sit perfectus, semper se debet reputare servum inutilem propter tres rationes. Prima est, quia bona, que fecimus, non sunt nostra... Secunda ratio est, quia nulla est compensatio earum ad finem beatitudinis. Illud enim dicitur inutile quod nullatenus attinget finem suum... Tertia ratio est ex humilitate; sic Maria: *ecce ancilla dominum* [Lc. 1:38]." Jor. *OJ* sermo 33, fol. 69ra.

[296] "... nulla enim virtus sufficiens est perducere ad deum, faciendo scilicet hominem meritorie dignum vite eterne nisi supposita acceptatione divina, quod sit per gratiam." Jor. *OJ* sermo 57, fol. 111^{ra-b}; "... et ideo quod homo convertatur ad deum, hoc non potest esse nisi deo ipsum convertente. Hec autem est preparare se ad gratiam, quasi ad deum converti sicut ille qui habet oculum aversum a sole per hoc se preparat ad recipiendum lumen solis quod oculos suos convertit versus solem; et hoc est quod dicitur Trenorum 5: *Converte nos domine ad te et convertimur* [Lam. 5:21]. Et si dicitur *hominis est preparare animam* etc, ut scribitur Proverbiorum 16 [Prv. 16:1]. Dicendum quod hoc facit per liberum arbitrium, sed cum hoc non facit sine auxilio dei moventis liberum arbitrium et ad se hominem trahentis, Unde Iohannis 7: *nemo venit ad me nisi pater meus qui misit me traxerit illum* [Io. 6:44]. Dico ergo quod predicta preparatoria facere non possumus sine gratia. Secundo modo dicta possumus cum ea sine habituali dono saltem initiative et imperfecte; perfecte autem et meritorie ea non possumus sine gratia, que est donum habituale." Jor. *OJ* sermo 247, fol. 383ra. Meritorious works clearly follow the initial infusion of grace; one does not merit grace, but can only perform meritorious works after having received grace. Jordan does not employ the distinction between *meritum de congruo* and *meritum de condigno*, although we do find the terms on occasion. *Meritum de congruo* for Jordan is not that by which we merit grace, but rather that by which someone already just can merit first grace for someone else: "... notandum quod omnis oratio nostra tendere debet ad salutem eternam tam pro nobis quam pro aliis, pro quibus oramus. Quilibet enim iustus orando pro peccatore potest sibi mereri primam gratiam de congruo. Exemplum de beato Stephano qui meruit Paulo primam gratiam." Jor. *OJ* sermo 206, fol. 321vb. *Meritum de congruo* is also used to refer to the disposition required for grace: "... motus detestationis peccati, que est dispositio vel meritum de congruo..." Jor. *OJ* sermo 111, fol. 186rb.

[297] "... actus liberi arbitrii ex se vim merendi non habet..." Jor. *OJ* sermo 99, fol. 174ra.

cannot write with a pen, unless his hand is led by the hand of a teacher."[298]

The *Opus Postillarum* offers additional evidence that Jordan did indeed hold a doctrine of election and reprobation. Jordan discussed the three advents of Christ, the advent in the flesh (*adventus in carnem*), and advent in the believer (*adventus in mentem*), and the advent in judgment (*adventus in iudicium*).[299] Regarding the last Jordan affirmed that Christ will come to judge the world in human form: first in order to judge in human form those who had condemned him in human form; second, to confuse the Jews in so far as they will see themselves being judged by someone they did not want to believe in; and third, both for the punishment of the reprobate, finding themselves judged not by an angel, but by a man, and for the glory of the elect, recognizing the excellence of human nature.[300] God will give the morning star as the crown to the works of the elect, in reference to the second chapter of the Apocalypse.[301] Yet as the morning stars, the works of the elect "never last until the evening, but are always in the morning, as if they begin from a new origin... further, just as the stars, which are immense even though they appear to be small, so are our virtuous works. However great and excellent they may be, they ought to appear small in our eyes."[302]

---

[298] "Augmentum autem caritatis et gratie... non potest esse nisi ex spirituali assistentia spiritus sancti animam in opus meritorium dirigentem... Opus enim meritorium est anime in proportionatum sicut penna in manu pueri; ideo anima nisi spiritu sancto ducatur in opus meritorium non exibit, sicut puer non scribit penna nisi ducatur sibi manus per magistrum..." Jor. *OJ* sermo 222, fol. 346rb.

[299] Jordan took this scheme most likely from Hen. *In mentem, passim*.

[300] "Notandum etiam quod dominus iudicabit mundum in forma humanae naturae propter tria. Primo quia sicut venire in forma humana hominem redimere, qui scilicet homo ipsum Christum in eadem forma condempnavit iniuste, ita ipse Christus in eadem forma eum iuste iudicet.... Secundo ad confusionem iudeorum, quatinus videntes se iudicari ab homine, in quem credere noluerunt, confundantur... Tertio ad poenam reproborum videntium se iudicari non ab angelo sed ab homine et ad gloriam electorum videntium in iudice humanam naturam excellentissime exaltatam." Jor. *OP* sermo 4B (ed. Strassburg, 1483). Jordan took this exposition word for word from his teacher, Albert. *Exp.*, fol. A3^{ra}.

[301] "In stellis, id est operibus electis, debet esse signum victoriae et supererogationis. Apocalypsis secundo: *qui vicerit et custodierit opera mea, dabo illi stellam matutinam* [Apc. 2:26–28], id est, premium correspondens merito, merito operum electorum." Jor. *OP* sermo 3H (ed. Strassburg, 1483).

[302] "Haec stella, id est luminositas, bonorum operum nunquam tendit ad occasum, sed semper erit in mane quasi de novo oriri incipiat... Item sicut stella cum magna sit, apparet parva, sic opera nostra virtuosa quantumcumque magna sint et excellentia, debent in oculis nostris apparere parva." Jor. *OP* sermo 3H (ed. Strassburg, 1483).

440   CHAPTER FOUR

Jordan's doctrine of the elect is further clarified in his exposition of the parable of the sower (Mt. 13:4–8). Christ is the farmer sowing his seeds in the field, some of which fall on the stones, some on the path, some fall among the thorns, while others land in good soil.[303] The seed is his Word, sowed by the preacher. It is hopeless, however, to preach to the incorrigible because stones cannot become earth, neither can the thorns be other than thorns, nor the path other than the path. The stones, path, and thorns, it appears, signify the reprobate, since Jordan refers to them as hardened, unteachable fools. Yet for rational creatures, it *is* possible for stones to become earth, and for the path not to be trod underfoot, and for thorns to be weeded. Thus it is not in vain, but most useful indeed for the preacher to preach to sinners, regardless of how evil they may be.[304] In Jordan's view the stones, path, and thorns were the reprobate, referring to them as hardened, unteachable fools. The sinners, or the rational creatures, therefore, comprise the *corpus permixtum* in this life, and one should not forget that for Jordan the saint was a sinner. To these sinners, who certainly could become part of the damned, the word of God must be preached for they can be converted, or are, perhaps, already part of the elect.

In this light, Jordan's understanding of the general will of God for the salvation of sinners needs to be refined. Jordan did not say that God wills the salvation of all. God does not will the conversion, sanctification, and glorification of all universally; God wills the conversion of sinners, among whom are included the members of the elect who are just not "there" yet. In the *Opus Jor*, Jordan first affirmed God's general will of salvation: Christ died not just for the Jews, but for all. This "for all," however, was not unequivocally "all," but referred to all the sons of God: that is, our preacher clarified, the eternally predestined.[305] "In the beginning," Jordan explained

---

[303] Jordan devotes all of sermo 137 to the exposition of this parable. See Jor. *OP* sermo 137A–K (ed. Strassburg, 1483).

[304] "Sic et praedicator non intendit praedicare indocibilibus et ineptis, sed ipse facit quod in se est praedicando, sed si verbum recipitur sic vel sic, hoc est ex parte auditorum ... increpandus esset agricola qui super sensibiles spinas vel petram vel viam seminaret. Non est possibile petram terram fieri, nec viam non esse viam, nec spinas non esse spinas. In rationalibus vero secus est; possibile est enim petram converti in terram pinguem, et viam non conculcari, et spinas dissipari. Unde non est vanum, immo valde utile praedicare peccatoribus, quamcumque malis." Jor. *OP* sermo 137F (ed. Strassburg, 1483).

[305] ". . . . Christus enim non solum mori voluit pro salute populi iudaici, quibus

calling on Augustine's *De Civitate Dei*, "two cities were established from men and angels; one was comprised of the good men and angels, and the other from the evil."[306] Many are called by God, but few are chosen.[307] These few are few indeed with respect to the number of the damned.[308] They are the beloved of Christ, and to them Jordan spoke:

> ... [Christ] always loved us, for from eternity he chose and predestined us, and within the realm of time, when we were nothing, he gave us our being, and he stamped it with his own image, which we have desecrated with sin; moreover, he restored us with his own blood, and so that he might always make known his plentiful love, he completely nourishes us with the food of his own body.[309]

The good and the just, the saints, are such by grace, and therefore they "ought to give Christ the greatest thanks because they were called by Christ out of the entire degenerate mob and chosen by grace from the number of the damned."[310]

Thus Jordan did have a doctrine of election and predestination after all, and here he based it explicitly on Augustine's two cities.

---

non solum in lege promissum fuerat, sed et pro salute totius generis et hoc innuit evangelica cum subdit, *Et non solum pro gente*, scilicet iudaica, *sed ut filios dei* eternaliter scilicet predestinatos a deo in omnibus gentibus [haberet]. [Io. 11:52]" Jor. *OJ* sermo 143, fol. 233vb.

[306] "... beati Augustini 11 de civitate dei in principio ex angelis et hominibus due constituuntur civitates; una ex angelis et hominibus bonis, alter ex angelis et hominibus malis ... [*cf.* Aug. civ. 11,1–22 (321–341)]" Jor. *OJ*, sermo 125, fol. 208ra.

[307] "*Multi sunt vocati, pauci vero electi*, Mt. 13 [Mt. 20:16]. In verbis istis duo notantur. Primum est divina vocatio generalis ibi multi sunt vocati; secundum est divina electio singularis, ibi pauci vero electi." Jor. *OJ* sermo 76, fol. 136rb–136va.

[308] "... non totum genus humanum damnatur sed aliqui eliguntur ad salutem qui valde pauci sunt respectu multitudinis damnatorum." Jor. *OJ* sermo 248, fol. 385ra.

[309] "... semper nos dilexit quia patet ab eterno enim in seipso nos elegit et predestinavit et in tempore cum nichil essemus, nobis esse nature contulit, quod etiam propria imagine insignavit, quam cum per peccatum fedissemus, nos iterum proprio sanguine restauravit et nobis plenius suam dilectionem ostenderet nos insuper alimento sui corporis satiavit ..." Jor. *OJ* sermo 159, fol. 251rb–251va; *cf.*: "... Christus valde dulciter captat nostram benevolentiam cum dicit: 'venite filii', quasi dicens, filii quos eternaliter predestinavi, quos temporaliter glorificavi, quos sacramentaliter proprio corpore pavi, quos spiritualiter meo sanguine lavi, venite acquiescendo firmiter mee resurrectionis articulo congaudendo titulo." Jor. *OJ* sermo 188, fol. 292ra.

[310] "... ut iusti plurimum deo regratientur quia quod boni sunt non habent a natura sed a divina gratia ... debent ergo iusti Christo plurimas gratias agere quod de massa tota corrupta vocati sunt a Christo et electi per gratiam de numero pereuntium." Jor. *OJ* sermo 72, fol. 133rb.

Jordan indeed was uncompromising: "God the Father rules the elect in this world, just as a *paterfamilias* governs his subjects in his own house."[311] Moreover, if Gregory of Rimini merited the title, *tortor infantium*, for adhering to a strict Augustinian doctrine of predestination, it was one he could have shared with Jordan. Unbaptized children were associated with the damned and condemned to hell.[312] Following closely on their heels, however, were mothers who killed their infants before baptism. In doing so they deprived the angels of great good and sent the souls of their children straight to hell: "Oh God, how greatly they will be tortured," Jordan lamented.[313] And finally, as he explained in the *Opus Dan* with strong echoes of Augustine, the elect are to replace the fallen angels; they are to fill the heavenly mansions the fallen angels had vacated.[314] It thus becomes clear. The elect inhabit the heavenly mansions of the angels, the bright and shining mansions within the *celum empyreum*, which was where Jordan placed the angels. These elect are the saints, who have one foot in that heaven, but are held down by their other foot firmly planted on earth. With the help of his sermons, we begin to recognize that Jordan addressed his *Expositio* to the saints to serve as a guide for the elect's journey homeward to their heavenly city.

Jordan never discussed the precise origins of the reprobate and elect, in that he never explicitly broached the question of the relationship between predestination and God's foreknowledge. Nevertheless, as repeatedly seen, Jordan was crystal clear regarding the source of the initiative.[315] When Christ comes in judgment, the reprobate, those

---

[311] "... paterfamilias est deus pater qui electos regit in mundo sicut paterfamilias subditos in domo." Jor. *OJ* sermo 73, fol. 133vb.

[312] In discussing the effects of Christ's passion, Jordan lists one as freeing the patriarchs, among others, from Limbo, but, he then adds: "Damnati autem et pueri non baptizati huius meriti capaces non fuerunt. Ideo tales non liberavit sed in statu suo reliquit." Jor. *OJ* sermo 143, fol. 234rb.

[313] "Infelices mulieres, que partum impediunt vel suffocant sine baptismate... quantum bonum angelis aufferant... et quantum maledictionem incurrunt... O deus quantum cruciabitur, qui puerum non baptizatum interficit et animam ad infernum mittat." Jor. *OJ* sermo 65, fol. 124^{ra-b}.

[314] "Et secundum illa [Io.14:2] sumuntur diversae mansiones, quas mansiones omnium electorum sumere possumus secundum choros angelorum, ad quorum ruinam restaurandam homo est creatus. Quia enim de singulis choris aliqui angeli ceciderunt et in tanto numero quod unum chorum per se fecissent; ideo dicitur decimus chorus cecidisse iuxta parabolam de decem dragmis. Et ideo ruina cuiuslibet chori debet per electos homines reparari." Jor. *OD* sermo 70E (ed. Strassburg, 1484).

[315] *Cf*.: "Ad hec igitur bona ab eterna homini preparata invitabit deus in die

seemingly already reprobate rather than those awaiting their sentencing to damnation, will be additionally punished by being judged by a human, while the elect will delight in the glory of human nature and their works will receive the crown of the morning star. The works of the just, however, are to appear small in the eyes of the elect, and this is the context of Jordan's *simul iustus et peccator*: the elect, the saints, perform works of charity and thus contribute to their own perfection, but they must realize that all their works are contaminated by sin because of their imperfection. It is only at the end that the elect can glory in their own election. Until then, they are starting ever anew with works, working towards their perfection which is only possible because of their adoption and election. The elect are the saints, but they are the saints who are in this life awaiting their glory, caught in the ontological tension between the state of grace and the state of glory. Jordan's *simul iustus et peccator* is not a doctrine of justification, but a description of the saints' state of being. Thus Jordan could say that the saints' redemption is still approaching, that it is to be expected, for as long as Christians are weighed down by the flesh (*gravamur nexibus carnis*) the effects of their redemption lie in the future.[316]

---

ultima quando dicet Matthei 25: *Venite* ecce ab omni malo separati *benedicti Patris mei* [Mt. 25:34]. Ecce summum horum collatio, quod nobis paratum est ab origine mundi. Ecce eterna predestinatio, que nichil aliud est quam preparatio gratie in presenti et glorie in futuro [Aug. persev. (1014)]." Jor. *OJ* sermo 240, fol. 374rb. Jordan's model for human preparation for grace was Paul, and Paul, according to Jordan, was converted by God 'violently'. After stating that some are called by gifts, some by castigations, and some by compulsion, Jordan gives Paul's conversion as an example of the latter, together with the conversions of the Germans by Charlemagne: "*Multi sunt vocati, pauci vero electi.* Matthei 13 [Mt. 20:16]. In verbis istis duo notantur. Primum est divina vocatio generalis ibi multi sunt vocati; secundum est divina electio singularis, ibi pauci vero electi. Quantum ad primum est sciendum quod aliqui vocantur a deo tribus modis. Primo donatione, secundo castigatione, tertio, coactione. . . . deus potest ergo quidquid vult. Aliquando ergo aliquos malos, quos non potest per dona vel per castigationes vacare, vocat cum violentia. Exemplum in Paulo, quem vocavit violenter et omnes veteros Alamanos, quos rex Carolus coegit fieri Christianos et modo sunt boni Christiani. Unde completum est illud evangelicum Luce nono: *compelle intrare* [Lc. 14:23], quia ipse Carolus compulit eos intrare, id est, fidem acceptare, ut impleretur domus, et hoc quantum ad primum." Jor. *OJ* sermo 76, fol. 136rb–vb. Jordan may not have been explicit regarding predestination *ante* or *post previsa merita*, but he was clear regarding the initiative: predestination stems from God's will and is not based on God's promise to reward foreseen good works.

[316] In responding to the question of why we say that our redemption approaches when it has already been given by Christ, Jordan answers: "dicendum quod virtute passionis Christi facta quidem est redemptio, sed nondum eiusdem redemptionis

To grasp Jordan's understanding of election, grace, and merit, terms placed in an order of which he would have approved, one must remind oneself that he was not writing a theological defense of an Augustinian doctrine of grace against the threat of the "modern Pelagians." Rather, his preaching predestination was a theological call to arms. Election was the fife and drum as the soldiers of Christ marched into battle. The foundation of Jordan's doctrine of sanctification was election, predestination, and adoption. The problem he faced was that one does not know, one cannot know precisely who the saints are. Hence he directed his exposition of the "Our Father" to the community of the saints existing within the *corpus permixtum*, who as saints are to be good administrators of the gifts they have received, not for their merits or beautiful hair, but purely from God's love and grace; they are to pour forth works of charity as they make their way in hope and patience to their merited end. They must recognize the gifts they have received from God and in response fulfill the office of sainthood by conforming themselves to the will of their Lord, who possessed them before He ever became their possession. Only in this context, as humble administrators and servants, are the saints also the just.

With this last statement I have returned to the theme of justification. Justification, for Jordan, was subsumed within his doctrine of sanctification. It was part of his answer to the "and now what?" question. The saint in this life must also be just. Being just, however, was not according to Jordan first and foremost that which justifies the sinner before God. Being just is upholding justice, or in other words, paying what one owes: *Redde quod debes*.[317] And in this light, Jordan's doctrines of grace and justification are separate issues. Jordan's doctrine of sanctification and grace explains the relationship between the state of grace and that of glory, whereas his understanding of justification, or rather, of justice, pertains to his conception of the Christian life.

---

effectus plenarie consecuti sunt, adhuc ergo gravamur nexibus carnis quamdiu enim sumus in isto habitaculo corporis ingemuimus gravati." Jor. *OP* sermo 5D (ed. Strassburg, 1483); *cf.*: "Nota quod virtute passionis Christi redemptio electorum facta est, sed eiusdem redemptionis effectum nondum plenarie consecuti sunt. Adhuc enim gravamur nexibus corporis." Albert. *Exp.*, fol. A3[va].

[317] "Introducitur autem hic virtus iustitie cuius est reddere unicuique debitum suum." Jor. *Exp.* 7, fol. 84[ra].

J. Between God and the Devil

When one moves from the heavenly life of the saints to the earthly existence of the Christian, the focus shifts regarding the ontological level of Jordan's theology from the relationship between the states of grace and glory, to that between the state of nature (*esse nature*) and the state of grace (*esse gratie*). In this context it is not the *simul iustus et peccator* that takes precedence, but rather the call for spiritual progression.

In the *Opus Postillarum* Jordan referred to God as the primary mover (*primus motor*),

> from whom the motive power in the soul is derived, just as from a certain primal font, from which grace flows into the soul, by which God moves the free will to love Him and to virtuous acts. This motion of God in the soul is three-fold according to the three-fold state of humans: He moves those beginning [in the spiritual life] (*incipientes*) to the recognition of their guilt and to the sorrowful recollection of their sins; those who have achieved an intermediate level of spiritual perfection (*proficientes*) God moves to continuous spiritual growth and progress; but the contemplatives (*contemplativi*) He moves to the internal taste of divine sweetness.[318]

This passage is reflected in Jordan's *Expositio* when he rhapsodized that the faithful exist in God, are moved by God, and live in God.[319] Christians are moved by God's grace to progress from beginners in

---

[318] "... deus est sicut motor primus, a quo virtus motiva derivatur in animam, sicut a quodam fonte paterno, a quo fluit gratia in animam per quam deus movet liberum arbitrium ad se amandum et virtuose operandum. Hec autem motio dei in anima triplex est secundum triplicem statum: incipientes movet ad culpe compunctionem et peccatorum dolorosam rememorationem; proficientes movet ad profectus spiritualis continuam progressionem; sed contemplativos movet ad divine dulcedinis internum degustationem." Jor. *OP* sermo 11A (ed. Strassburg, 1483). This three-fold scheme stems from Ps.Dionysius' *De ecclesiastica hierarchia* (*PG* 3, 369–584), yet Jordan most likely took his description of the three-fold stages of the Christian's progress from either Thom.Aq., *STh* II/II q. 186, art. 1, ad 3; Giles of Rome, *Tractatus de laudibus divine sapientie*, (ed. Rome, 1555; reprint: Aegidius Romanus, *Opuscula* I, Frankfurt, 1968), fol. 31va; or Henry of Friemar, *Tractatus de adventu verbi in mentem*. Markus Wriedt has pointed to this well-known schema in the works of Johann von Staupitz, which Wriedt traces back to Hugh of St. Cher, Johannes Gerson, Dionysius the Carthusian, and Augustinus Favaroni; M. Wriedt, *Gnade und Erwählung*, 223. This three-fold progression is also present in 10th–11th century Sufism; see M. Eliade, *A History of Religious Ideas*, vol. 3: *From Muhammad to the Age of Reforms* (Chicago, 1985), 131.

[319] "Hoc triplex esse quod a deo recepimus, correspondet triplicibus beneficiis que filius carnalis accepit a patre. Primum beneficium est generationis, quo in esse nature producitur quantum ad primum. Secundum est beneficium educationis, quo nutritur

the spiritual life, to an intermediate level of proficiency, and finally to the level of the contemplatives, or truly to living in God and God's glory. The motion comes from God's grace, primarily and principally; but the exercise of virtue cooperates with God's grace instrumentally as the Christian progresses in spiritual development.

The Christian life for Jordan was not conducted in a laboratory where God injects grace into the specimen and leaves it to the theologians to figure out how the grace works when it works, and why it does not work when it does not. The Christian finds him or herself on the battlefield where the kingdom of the devil is assaulting the kingdom of God. To be sure, this battle will only last as long as God allows,[320] until He comes in judgment with his army of patriarchs, prophets, apostles, martyrs, and all the elect and saints.[321] The situation the Christian faces in this life is not repose in which she or he can work on spiritual development. Christian life is a battle between God and the devil. Only in this context can one properly understand Jordan's moral exhortation regarding the virtues and vices.

In his *Expositio* Jordan contrasted the three-fold kingdom of God—the kingdom of the Church, of grace, and of glory—with the three-fold kingdom of the devil. In opposition to the ecclesiastical realm (*regnum ecclesie*) stands the devil's synagogue of Satan (*synagoga Satane*). Just as the Church is the congregation of the faithful (*congregatio Christifidelium*), so is the synagogue of Satan the congregation of the devil (*congregatio diaboli*). The second kingdom of the devil is the kingdom of sin (*regnum peccati*), which stands opposed to the kingdom of

et alitur quantum ad secundum. Tertium beneficium hereditationis, quo vite solacium ducitur quo ad tertium. Et hec tria comprehenduntur in illo dicto poetico, quod assumit Paulus Actuum 17: *in ipso,* scilicet deo, *vivimus, movemur, et sumus* [Act. 17:28]. Sumus, inquam, in natura; movemur in gratia; vivimus in gloria. Ratione primi, deus est a nobis summe laudabilis; ratione secundi, valde amabilis; ratione tertii, maxime desiderabilis." Jor. *Exp.* 1, fol. 73vb.

[320] "Iste angelus [*scil.* quintus angelus Apocalypsis] est filius dei, qui est magni consilii angelus; bestia est diabolus, cuius sedes est infernus; fiala super bestia et eius sedem effusa, est sententia divine iustitie, puta damnationis extreme. Fiala enim habet orificium artum et longum, sed ventrem largum, propter quod est magne capacitatis sed tarde effusionis. Sic deus diu tollerat et exspectat in effundendo iram suam et sententiam extremam, sed finaliter eam plene effundit." Jor. *Exp.* 4, fol. 78ra.

[321] "Et nota quod maiestas Christi apparebit in homine concomitantium scilicet in multitudine caelestium spirituum, patriarcharum, prophetarum, apostolorum, martirum et omnium electorum, iuxta illud Zachariae 1<4>: *Ecce dominus veniet et omnes sancti eius cum eo,* etc. [Za. 14:5]" Jor. *OP* sermo 4C (ed. Strassburg, 1483).

grace (*regnum gratie*). Just as God reigns in the soul through grace, so does the devil reign in the soul through sin. The third kingdom of the devil is the kingdom of misery and eternal damnation, which is the counterpart to the kingdom of glory.[322]

The situation in which the Christian finds himself is one caught between the kingdom of God and the kingdom of the devil. Thus when one prays, 'Thy Kingdom come', one is praying for the three-fold kingdom of God to destroy the three-fold kingdom of the devil. Yet it is not for the destruction of the devil himself that one prays. The devil is to remain to reign over all the damned. Christians pray that they might not be ruled by the devil and find themselves in his kingdom. The kingdom of darkness is eternal.[323]

In this battle, however, Christians are not left to themselves. God is on their side and gives them the grace of His gifts with which they fight. Thus, as Jordan trumpeted in the *Opus Jor*, works are as the king's standard leading Christians as they march to battle against the devil.[324] Indeed, works of love, the works of the saints, are the Christian's most powerful weapons, for good works, Jordan confirmed in the *Opus Postillarum*, are contrary to the devil; the devil fears nothing more than love.[325] Love appears in Jordan's *Expositio* as the third

---

[322] "Huic autem triplici regno dei opponitur triplex regnum diaboli. Primum est regnum synagoge Satane, quod opponitur regno ecclesie. De hoc regno dicitur Apocalypsis secundo de quibusdam quod sunt synagoga Satane. Sicut enim ecclesia est congregatio Christifidelium in bono, sic synagoga Satane est congregatio diaboli in malo et suorum. Secundum est regnum peccati, de quo Romanorum sexto: *Non regnet peccatum in vestro mortali corpore* [Rm. 6:12]. Et istud opponitur regno gratie, nam sicut deus in anima regnat per gratiam, sic diabolus per peccatum. Unde Romanorum quinto dicit Apostolus: *sicut regnavit peccatum in mortem, ita et gratia regnet per iustitiam* [Rm. 5:21]. Tertium regnum diaboli est regnum miserie et damnationis eterne, quod opponitur regno glorie. De hoc regno dicitur Apocalypsis sexto decimo: *Quintus angelus effudit fialam suam super sedem bestie et factum est regnum eius tenebrosum* [Apc. 16:10]." Jor. *Exp.* 4, fol. 77vb–78ra.

[323] "Cum ergo dicimus *Adveniat regnum tuum*, petimus ut adveniat triplex regnum dei et per oppositum destruatur triplex regnum diaboli ... Dicamus ergo *Adveniat regnum tuum* ecclesie; gratie; <et> glorie; ut destruatur regnum synagoge Satane; peccati et malitie; tenebrarum et miserie. Et sciendum quod in hac ultima combinatione, non petimus ita destrui regnum tenebrarum ne diabolus ibi sit, sed ne ipse ibi habeat regnare super nos, id est, ne nos illuc veniamus in regnum suum. Ipse enim regnat super omnes damnatos, iuxta illud Iob 41: *Ipse est rex super omnes filios superbie* [Iob 41:25]." Jor. *Exp.* 4, fol. 78^{ra-b}.

[324] "... diabolus ... fidem, spem, caritatem et bona opera laborat auferre, sed debet quilibet resistere de fide scutum facere, de spe galeam, de caritate lanceam, opera autem debet ponere super omnia arma tamquam regis insignia." Jor. *OJ* sermo 114, fol. 191va.

[325] "Impugnamus autem eum [*i.e.* diabolum] per bona opera, quae sibi sunt a

theological virtue, accompanying the petition 'Thy will be done'. Through love Christians are conformed to the divine will, for love draws one to God in conversion, unites one with God in sanctification, and crowns one by God in glory.[326]

Each petition of the *Pater Noster* is designed to introduce a particular virtue, and to exclude a particular vice. It is not only a prayer that leads one to one's end in a positive sense, or as Jordan said, *per se*, but also *per accidens* by removing the impediments to the attainment of the end. Individuals are kept from moving toward their end by sin, temptation, and the present sufferings of this life.[327] The final cause (*causa finalis*) of the prayer, Jordan stated at the outset, is the exhortation that we stretch towards our end, and that we do not fall away from our end.[328] Virtues are not merely means by which one grows towards spiritual perfection: they are the Christian's weapons in the fight against the devil.

---

tota specie contraria et maxime per caritatem, quia ut dicit Hugo in *Expositione Regulae*, 'nihil est quod ipse diabolus tantum timeat quantum caritatis unitatem' [Hug.SV. *Reg.* 1 (883C)]." Jor. *OP*, sermo 437B (ed. Strassburg, 1483).

[326] "Unde ipsa [*scil.* caritas] . . . transformat amantem in amatum, quod intelligendum est secundum conformitatem affectuum et voluntatum. Impletur autem voluntas dei in nobis per caritatem specialiter quantum ad triplicem voluntatem dei predictam. Per caritatem enim ad deum trahimur in conversione; deo unimur in sanctificatione; <et> a deo coronamur in glorificatione. Jor. *Exp.* 5, fol. 79vb–80ra; *cf.* Jor. *OP* sermo 439E (ed. Strassburg, 1483).

[327] "Ad finem autem predictum ordinat nos aliquid dupliciter: uno modo per se; alio modo per accidens. Per se quidem bonum quod est utile in finem. Est autem aliquid utile in finem beatitudinis dupliciter: uno modo directe et principaliter, secundum meritum quo beatitudinem meremur deo obediendo, et quantum ad hoc ponitur *fiat voluntas tua*; alio modo instrumentaliter, et quasi coadiuvans nos ad merendum, et ad hoc pertinet quod dicitur *panem nostrum cottidianum*. Per accidens autem ordinamur in beatitudinem per remotionem prohibentis. Tria autem sunt que nos a beatitudine prohibent. Primo quidem peccatum quod directe nos prohibet et ad hoc pertinet quod dicitur *dimitte nobis debita nostra*. Secundo temptatio que nos impedit ab observantia divine voluntatis et ad hoc pertinet quod dicitur *et ne nos inducas in temptationem*. Tertio penalitas presens que impedit sufficientiam vite et quantum ad hoc dicitur <*sed*> *libera nos a malo*. Ex hiis patet ordinis congruentia et petitionum sufficientia et nichilominus totalis divisio harum petitionum in suas partes." Jor. *Exp.* 3, fol. 76^{ra-b}.

[328] "Finalis <causa> tangitur in hoc quod dicit *moniti*. Monitio enim fit vel ut adipiscamur finem vel ne decidamus a fine. In hac autem oratione utrumque monemur petere: et ut pertingamus ad finem beatitudinis eterne et ut removeantur impeditiva ipsius finis, ut patet infra in lectione tertia." Jor. *Exp.* 1, fol. 73ra.

K. *The Law Old and New*

From Jordan's perspective, the sinners of his day followed the devil more often than they followed God.[329] Vice was rampant, and our moralist lashed out against the excess: "in this day and age men are accustomed to drink excessively. From morning till evening they are eager for libations." Drunkenness is contrary to the soul; it obscures the reason, and leads to the loss of salvation.[330] Yet if Jordan's contemporaries were prone to drunkenness, they were no better with gluttony. The glutton truly lay in the gutter; not bothering to praise God, he was headed for hell. Gluttony worked against nature; it was precisely to prevent gluttony that humans were created with two eyes, two nostrils, two hands, and two feet, but only one mouth.[331]

But food and drink alone were not the single object of Jordan's censures. Another vice had arisen that was dangerous indeed: song and dance. Groups of dancers and singers were sheer vanity and Jordan was afraid: "I greatly fear," he preached, "that . . . today God is angered by the many vain things they sing, among which are found lies, filth, and extravagance."[332] Such dances are a waste of

---

[329] "Sed heu, peccatores hodie magis secuntur diabolum quam deum." Jor. *OJ* sermo 241, fol. 375vb.

[330] ". . . homines hoc tempore solent nimis potare a mane usque ad vesperam, student potationibus, Isaiae 5: *Ve qui consurgitis mane ad ebrietatem sectandum et potandum usque ad vesperam ut vino escuetis* [Is. 5:11]; magna fatuitas quod homo se cottidie ingurgitat et quod tamen bibit quod usum rationis omittit, Ps.: *Anima eorum in malis tabescebat* [Ps. 106:26] usque *sapientia eorum devorata est* [Ps. 106:27]. Tunc homo in malis tabescit, id est, deficit, quando ebrietatem, quae contraria est anime, querit; tunc omnis sapientia devoratur quando homo ita inebriabitur quod beneficiorum dei et homini, que ad salutem anime spectant, obliviscitur." Jor. *OJ* sermo 83, fol. 149vb; *cf.*: "Ebriosus confundit naturam, amittit gratiam et perdit gloriam, et incurrit damnationem eternam." Jor. *OD* sermo 31C (ed. Strassburg, 1483).

[331] "Audi, O gulose, tu ventrem tuum imples et a laude dei taces; tu habundas superfluis et pauper eget necessariis . . . qui epulabatur cottidie splendide et pauperem Lazarum nolebat in aliquo respicere post ea ductus ad infernum ad tantam devenit inopiam quod ardens inflammis guttam aque habere non potuit. Noli ergo sequi gulam . . . Noli avidus esse in omnium epulatione et non te offendas super omnem escam, in multis enim escis erit infirmitas et sequitur propter crapulam multi perierunt; qui autem abstinens est, adiciet vitam. Unde inter animalia magnorum corporum nulli dedit natura ita parvum os sicut homini. Et hoc ideo ut homo parce commedat . . . Item propter eandem rationem natura dedit homini duos oculos, duas nares, duas manus, duos pedes, unum os tamen dedit ne homo nimis commedat." Jor. *OJ* sermo 83, fol. 149rb–149vb.

[332] ". . . homines solent in hoc tempore vana cantare, nam hoc tempore in singulis civitatibus et villis et castris per totam diem vana cantantur; talis fuit cantus filiorum Israel, de quo Exodi 32 duxit Moyses vocem cantantium *ego audio. Cumque appropinquasset, vidit vitulum* [Ex. 32:18–19] et choreas iratus, que est nimis. Timeo

time and offer the occasion for all kinds of sin, and most of all the sin of pride.[333] Yet even worse, the dancers mock the Passion of Christ:

> for [whereas] Christ on the cross extended his hands in great punishment, you on the other hand, open your arms with great vanity. Likewise, [whereas] Christ bowed his head on the cross, you, however, hold your head up proudly in the dances. Further, Christ's feet were nailed to the cross so that he could not move them, but you move not only your feet, but also your entire body dancing and singing in circles... Christ hung naked [on the cross], but you dress up for your dances... In short, [the difference between] Christ on the cross and you in your dances [is easily summarized]: Christ prayed, you mock; Christ wept, you laugh; Christ called out for you, you against Christ; Christ had a crown of thorns, you [wear a crown] of flowers; Christ died, you never think of death.[334]

---

valde, quod eodem modo irascitur deus hodie multis, que vana cantant, in quibus continentur mendacia, turpia, luxuriosa etc." Jor. *OJ* sermo 83, fol. 150ᵛᵃ.

[333] "Nota quod choree detestabiles sunt propter multa mala, que mihi provenit. Primo, in chorea est temporis amissio, quando tempus illud, quod datum est nobis pro premia, acquirenda et salute expendimus in vanitate, secunde Corinthiorum sexto: *Ecce nunc tempus acceptabile* etc. [II Cor. 6:2]. In choreis de salute nichil cogitamus et ideo tempus amittimus. Augustinus: tempus in quo de deo nihil cogitas, puta te perdidisse. Secundo, in choreis, que ut frequentius fiunt, diebus sacris et sabbati violatio contra illud preceptum divinum, Exodi undevicesimo: *memento ut diem sabbati sanctifices* [Ex. 20:8] diebus enim sacris non debent homines facere labores serviles ut heu multi per totam septimanam non laborant tamen neccessaria conquerendo sicut laborant diebus sacris vanas choreas ducendo, Augustinus: Melius est diebus sacris arare vel federe quam choreas ducere, cuius ratio est quia in primo est necessitas; in secundo, vanitas et superfluitas. Tertio, in choreis est multorum peccatorum occasio, scilicet superbie, quia unus vult alii se preferre in cantando incedendo invidie quia unus invidet a se melius incedat vel si meliorem ornatum habeat. Ibi provenit luxuria ex contactu et ex propinquo aspectu, ex familiari colloquio. Si enim David videns a remotis mulierem statim concupivit, quanto magis qui appropinquo et manu tenent audient mulieres, qui se ad hoc ornant ut choreas ducant compositio gradu incedant. Ut aliis placeant et nutibus oculorum animas illaqueant, quid dicatur eis Isaie tertio, pro eo quod *elevate sunt filie Sion et ambulaverunt extento collo et nutibus oculorum ibant et plaudebant, ambulabant pedibus suis et composito gradu incedebant* [Is. 3:16]. Ecce quam plane et plane describitur modum chorizandi decalvabit dominus virtutem filiorum Sion hoc erit in sepulchro, quando capillos, de quibus modo mulieres superbiunt, fluent de capite. Sequitur: *in die illa auferet dominus ornamentum calciamentorum* etc. [Is. 3:18]; vere emeriat plura ornamenta quibus mulieres solent se ornare, que omnia auferentur illo tempore, quo corpus mulieris operietur vili panniculo et vermibus devorandum proicietur in sepulchro." Jor. *OJ* sermo 83, fol. 150ᵛᵇ–151ʳᵇ.

[334] "... in choreis est derisio passionis Christi. Christus enim in cruce expandit manus cum magna penalitate; tu vero in chorea expandis cum magna vanitate. Item, Christus inclinavit caput in cruce; tu vero pre superbia in choreis erigis caput. Item, Christus habuit pedes confixos crucique movere non poterat et tu moves pedes

Christ's Passion was the perfect counterpart to all vice, and Jordan held up this model before the eyes of all, the dancers and the drunkards.[335] It was not merely the Augustinian in his cell, but the Christian in society who should always keep the Passion before the mind's eyes.[336] As such, the Passion could act as the prick of the conscience, since the conscience functioned in a way as a sour stomach: "For there are some people," Jordan explained, "in whom stomach pains do not cease until they vomit up whatever it was [causing the problem], as if spitting out the foulness. In the same way the sinner's conscience does not leave him in peace until he vomits up the foulness of sin through confession and penance."[337]

Fortunately God has given not only the grace and the gifts with which to fight the battle against vice, sin, and the devil, but also the battle plan. "If we are sons of God," Jordan argued in the *Opus Postillarum*, "it is therefore fitting that we imitate God in works of mercy."[338] The Christian imitates God by imitating Christ and by following His will. God's will, as Jordan explained in the *Expositio* is done when one observes God's commandments. It makes sense that one completely conforms oneself to the will of him, whose kingdom one seeks. Thus, praying for God's kingdom, one asks in the following petition to be able to do God's will.[339] This indeed is the

---

et totum corpus et re tamen in circuitu saltando. Unde Ps.: *In circuitu impii ambulant* [Ps. 11:9]. Item Christus pependit nudus, tu in choreis incedis ornatus. Ps.: *filie eorum composite* etc. [Ps. 143:12]. Et ut breviter includam Christus, in cruce tu in choreis: Christus oravit, tu insultas; Christus flevit, tu rides; Christus clamavit pro te, tu contra Christum; Christus habuit coronam de spinis, tu de floribus; Christus moriebatur, tu de morte numquam cogitas." Jor. *OJ* sermo 83, fol. 151rb.

[335] "O si velles cogitare sitim quam Christus pro te sustinuit, certus sum quod numquam peccares per ebrietatem; pro te sitivit, quando fatigatus ex itinere sedit supra fontem et pro uno hausto aque instanter petivit; pro te sitivit, quando pendens in cruce dicit, *sitio* [Io. 19:28]. Nec tamen poterat habere haustum aque, sed oblatum est ei vinum cum mirra et felle mixtum, quod cum gustasset noluit bibere ista [*cf.* Io. 19:29]. O homo, debes cogitare et te a superfluis potationibus cohibere." Jor. *OJ* sermo 83, fol. 149vb–150ra.

[336] See Chapter Five.

[337] "Sunt enim quidam ... in quibus dolor stomachi non cessant quousque evomant quedam quod est sicut accetum bulliens. Sic peccatoris conscientia non quiescit quousque per penitentiam et per confessionem evomat accetum peccati ..." Jor. *OJ* sermo 86, fol. 156ra; *cf.* Aug. conf. 10,14.

[338] "Si ergo filii dei sumus, oportet nos ipsum in operibus misericordiae imitari." Jor. *OP* sermo 324A (ed. Strassburg, 1483).

[339] "*Fiat voluntas tua sicut in celo et in terra.* Hec tertia petitio rationabiliter sequitur secundam, quia ... postquam dominus docuit concupiscere celestia dicendo *adveniat regnum tuum*, antequam ad celum perveniatur in ipsa terra docet fieri celum per hoc

function of the *Pater Noster* since it is the summary of the commandments.[340] Obedience to God's commandments is part of the very definition of what makes a saint. By obeying the commandments, one conforms oneself to God's will, becomes a saint, and fights the devil. There is no "easier way" (*via securior*) for Jordan as there was to be over a century and a half later for his fellow Augustinian Johannes von Paltz.[341] The Christian life is a battle.

In his emphasis on keeping the commandments, not only does the moral direction of Jordan's theology come to light, but also the importance of the old law. The law is God's will most perfectly revealed. Indeed, it is only through Christ that one can fulfill the law in so far as one recognizes in the law the loving Father. The law of the Old Testament nevertheless continues to provide the guidelines for the Christian life. Just as God gathered together the scattered tribes of Israel, so did He gather together the various groups of Augustinian hermits to unite them into a single Order; and just as Moses led the Israelites out of the land of Egypt and into the promised land, so does hope lead the saints to their promised land in heaven. And on the way to that promised land, as Christians wander through the desert, they are guided by the God of Sinai and the God of Israel, the active and contemplative lives; they are lead by the vision of God, and by keeping God's law. If the city of God was one model for Jordan's theology, particularly with regard to his doctrine of sanctification, the children of Israel wandering in the desert was the model for his doctrine of the Christian life.[342]

---

quod dicit *fiat voluntas tua*. Est etiam congruum ut a quo regnum postulamus eius voluntati totaliter nos conformemus. Ideo rationabiliter hec petitio sequitur premissam. Et quia voluntatem dei nostris viribus perficere non valemus, dicente Apostolo Romanorum septimo: *velle quidem adiacet michi, perficere autem non invenio bonum* [Rm. 7:18], ideo hoc petimus a deo quatinus ipse det nobis gratiam, ut sicut voluntas sua perfecte fit ab angelis et sanctis in celo, ita fiat a nobis qui sumus in terra. Nec putet aliquis nos hic petere ut deus faciet voluntatem suam, quia hoc potest et facit absque nostra petitione. Sed petimus ut sua voluntas a nobis fiat et impleatur.... Notandum autem quod voluntas dei fit a nobis generaliter in mandatorum suorum observatione." Jor. *Exp.* 5, fol. 79ra.

[340] "Nam omnes iste petitiones sunt de preceptis, utpote de hiis que sunt de necessitate salutis. Unde Cyprianus in libro de dominica oratione dicit istam orationem esse compendium preceptorum divinorum [Cypr. domin.orat. 28 (107,519–524) ..." Jor. *Exp.* 1, fol. 73ra.

[341] See Hamm, *Frömmigkeitstheologie*, esp. 247ff.

[342] *Cf.*: "... quando per iniquiorum tribulationes tangitur homo, probatur per ipsius patientiam, si ipse sit filius dei stimulando, ut electi in via huius exilii segnes non efficiantur, sed festinent ad patriam suam, sicut figuratur Exodi septimo urge-

As Jordan explained in the *Opus Postillarum*, Christ the farmer goes out to sow his seed. He has sown five types. First is the seed of the natural law, which is sown in the minds of all men, and is identical to the "Golden Rule." Second is the written law of the two tables of the Ten Commandments. Third is the evangelical law, which Christ has sown in the Church for all the faithful. Fourth is the law of perfection given to the religious as the counsels of poverty, chastity, patience, and obedience. Fifth is the good seed of virtues and gifts in human souls.[343]

When he proceeded to interpret the harvest of this sowing, he gave preeminence to the old law. In the parable in Matthew, some of the seeds that fell in the good soil brought forth a yield of a hundred-fold, others sixty-fold, while others thirty-fold. Jordan presented three interpretations of the various yields. The first was most traditional: the hundred-fold can be seen as the virgins, the sixty-fold as the continent, and the thirty-fold as the married. When he continued, however, he set conventional exegesis on its head: the hundred-fold yield, according to Jordan, could refer to the doctors, the sixty-fold to the martyrs and the thirty-fold to the apostles. In other words, as far as the harvest is concerned, the doctors yield more than the martyrs or apostles! Yet the third interpretation is especially at issue here: the hundred-fold yield, Jordan explained, is the observance of the old law; the sixty-fold is the observance of the new law; and the thirty-fold is the observance of the counsels.[344] Not only has he placed

---

bat Egyptii populum exire de terra velociter." Jor. *OJ* sermo 72, fol. 133[va-b]; *cf.* "Et sic per hunc Iordanem aperta est via populis christianis, vere israelitis, qua transire possunt ad terram promissionis vitae aeternae." Jor. *OD* sermo 50A (ed. Strassburg, 1483).

[343] "Seminavit autem quinque <genera> seminum. Primo, seminavit legem naturalem in mente cuiuslibet hominis, sicut est quid tibi non vis fieri, aliis ne feceris et quid tibi vis, aliis feceris. Secundo, seminavit legem scriptam, decem scilicet praecepta in duabus tabulis. Tertio, seminavit legem evangelicam in ecclesia omnibus fidelibus. Quarto, seminavit legem perfectionis, scilicet consilia paupertatis, castitatis et patientiae obedientiae in religionibus. Quinto, secundum Theophylum, non cessat dei filius semper in nostris animabus seminare non solum cum dedicet, sed etiam cum creat in nostris animabus semina bona virtutum scilicet et donorum." Jor. *OP* sermo 137C (ed. Strassburg, 1483); *cf.*: "Quatuor autem genera seminum seminavit. Seminavit enim legem naturalem in mente cuiuslibet, scilicet quid tibi non vis, aliis ne feceris et quid tibi vis fieri, aliis feceris. Item aliis seminavit legem scriptam, scilicet praecepta legis in duabus tabulis. Item seminavit evangelicam legem in ecclesia. Item seminavit perfecta conscilia paupertatis, castitatis et obedientiae in religionibus." Albert. *Exp.*, fol. I-1[vb].

[344] "Notandum autem quod Matthei tertio decimo [Mt. 13:18–23] magis explicite

454

CHAPTER FOUR

the monastic counsels in last place, bearing the smallest yield of fruit, but he has also elevated the observance of the old law above that of the new. It is the old law most of all, and chiefly the Ten Commandments, that Jordan equated with God's will, and consequently with following Christ, for he continued by clarifying his exposition with reference to Matthew 19:29 where those who leave everything and follow Christ receive a hundred-fold.[345] The old law as expressed in the Ten Commandments reveals God's will and is to be followed by every Christian. To this will, each and every Christian must strive to conform her or himself in the on-going battle between God and the devil.

In the *Expositio* Jordan offered a summary of the law. Not only are God's commandments contained in the *Pater Noster*, but they are summarized, or reduced to the words of Michah: "do justice, love mercy, and walk humbly before your God."[346] For the summary of the law Jordan turned not to Christ's words in the Gospel (Mt. 22:36–40), but rather to an Old Testament prophet. This is what God requires of the Christian, and the Christian is helped in this because he knows what doing justice is: it is being just by doing works of justice,[347] and by paying what one owes.[348] Christians are

---

agitur de huiusmodi fructibus ubi dicitur quod alius centesimus, alius sexagesimus, alius tricesimus. Primus est virginum; secundus continentium; tertius coniugatorum. Vel primus est doctorum; secundus martirum; tertius apostolorum. Vel primus datur per observantiam legis veteris; secundus per observantiam legis nove; tertius per observantiam consiliorum." Jor. *OP* sermo 137G (ed. Strassburg, 1483). Jordan's emphasis on the importance of the old law stands out even further when compared to Albert of Padua's treatment of the same passage. Jordan, who closely followed Albert in this sermon, reversed the order: "Nota quod triplex ponitur fructus istius seminis, scilicet tricesimus, sexagesimus et centesimus. Primus est coniugatorum; secundus, continentium; tertius, virginum: vel primus est doctorum, secundus est martirum, tertius apostolorum: vel primus datur propter observantiam antique legis; secundum propter observantiam nove; tertius propter observantiam consiliorum." Albert. *Exp.*, fol. I-2rb.

[345] "Unde Matthei 19 dicitur: *vos qui reliquistis omnia et secuti estis me, centuplum accipietis* [Mt. 19:29]." Jor. *OP* sermo 137G (ed. Strassburg, 1483).

[346] "Notandum autem quod voluntas dei fit a nobis generaliter in mandatorum suorum observatione. Unde dicit propheta Michee sexto: *Indicabo tibi, o homo, quid sit bonum et quid dominus requirat a te: facere iudicium et diligere misericordiam et sollicitum ambulare coram deo tuo* [Mi. 6:8], ubi tria dicit ad que omnia mandata divina reducuntur si bene considerentur." Jor. *Exp.* 5, fol. 79^{ra-b}.

[347] "De beatitudinibus vero introducitur per hanc petitionem esuries iustitie... Est autem esuries et sitis hic vehemens desiderium boni... non satis est velle iustitiam nisi iustitie patiamur famem, ut sic sub hoc exemplo numquam nos satis iustos et semper esurire iustitie opera intelligamus... Et accipitur hic iustitia generaliter secundum quod ab ea dicitur homo iustus propter opera virtuosa." *Exp.* 6, fol. 82rb.

[348] "Introducitur autem hic virtus iustitie cuius est reddere unicuique debitum

the children of Israel who know they have a loving Father and therefore they are to conform themselves to God's will as He had revealed it to the patriarchs and prophets of old. Jordan's God was the loving Father, but He was also the God of the Old Testament who led His children out of the land of Egypt and towards the promised land. Christians are to obey this God and conform themselves to His will, *in order* to arrive in the promised land. God is a loving God, and has provided his justice as the guide through the desert. No one can accumulate enough merit to put God in one's debt. Nor has God promised to reward human works with grace. God has simply given humans His grace and gifts for their use. The question of justification for Jordan is not what has God promised to reward with the payment of eternal life, but rather what it is that Christians owe God. Christians are God's debtors and they always have a negative balance. And thus they must pray, "forgive us our debts."

L. *Paying What is Owed*

In the seventh lecture of his *Expositio* Jordan set forth a radical interpretation of justice, which he later expanded in his *Tractatus de virtutibus et vitiis*.[349] Justice, as noted above, in Jordan's eyes was paying what is owed. The problem is to know precisely what it is that one owes, for unless one is aware of what one owes, one cannot pay it.[350] Unpaid debts not only put the debtor further in the red, but further in the red with respect to the heavenly creditor. All debts include sin. Indeed, debt is a more encompassing category than is sin and for this reason one prays 'forgive us our debts', rather than 'forgive us our sins'.[351] This works the other way around as well: all

---

suum. Et hec est eius propria ratio prout describitur et a philosophis et a iurisperitis." Jor. *Exp.* 7, fol. 84ra.

[349] Jor. *OP* sermo 440A–F (ed. Strassburg, 1483).

[350] "Nec etiam possumus esse iusti nisi reddamus cuique debitum suum, sed quid sit illud debitum quod tenemur cuique nescimus nisi per donum scientie." Jor. *Exp.* 7, fol. 84ra.

[351] "Dicendum quod pro tanto dicuntur peccata debita quia inde peccata contraximus, quia debita non solvimus, id est, quia non fecimus quod debuimus et ob hoc iudici penam debemus. Sicut ergo qui non solvit pecuniam creditori statuto termino dupliciter incurrit debitum ultra debitum pecunie, puta debitum culpe, ex eo quod non solvit per quod offendit creditorem, et debitum pene, quam debet iudici ex eo quod contra iustitiam egit, sic in proposito ex eo quod non facimus debitum nostrum illis quibus debemus, contrahimus duo mala scilicet peccatum et reatum: peccatum quantum ad culpam; reatum quantum ad penam, que utraque

sin is debt. Sin is a legal term for Jordan which he equated with unfulfilled debts. To be just is to pay all one's debts.

There are three creditors to whom Christians owe, to whom Christians must pay their debts by giving them what is rightly theirs: God, themselves, and their neighbor. To God Christians owe religion; to themselves they owe governance; to their neighbor they owe love. Jordan viewed religion as a moral virtue, associated with justice, consisting of *latria*, namely, adoration, prayers, offerings, praise, vows, oaths, and other similar acts owed to God.[352] To themselves Christians owe the discipline of the flesh so that they might live according to the spirit; and to their neighbor they simply owe love.[353] This corresponds to Jordan's exegesis of the first phrase of the prayer when he explained that we pray 'Our Father' to signify that we are all brothers, regardless of our state; whether we are poor or rich,

---

nomine debiti intelliguntur. Ex quo patet quod potius et melius dicitur hic 'debita nostra' quam 'peccata <nostra>', quia plus petimus dicendo *dimitte nobis debita <nostra>*, quia per hoc petimus <nobis> dimissionem culpe et pene, quam si diceremus, 'dimitte nobis peccata nostra', quia nonnunquam dimittitur peccatum quantum ad culpam, remanente reatu quo ad penam. Ulterius quia dictum est quod inde peccata contrahimus quia debita nostra quibus debemus non solvimus, dubitaret aliquis quibus et que debita debeamus." Jor. *Exp.* 7, fol. 82vb.

[352] "Propter quod est sciendum quod aliquid debemus deo, aliquid nobisipsis, et aliquid proximis nostris: debemus <enim> deo religionem; nobisipsis debitam gubernationem; proximis <nostris> mutuam dilectionem. Debemus inquam deo religionem, Levitici 16: *affligetis animas vestras deo religione perpetua* [Lv. 16:31]. Est autem sciendum quod religio non accipitur hic pro statu religiosorum; sed est quedam virtus moralis, que est pars iustitie. Ad quam virtutem pertinet deo cultum exhibere et comprehendit sub se latriam. Et actus huius virtutis sunt adoratio, oratio, oblatio, laus, votum, iuramentum et cetera talia, que soli deo debentur." Jor. *Exp.* 7, fol. 82vb–83ra. Here Jordan was again following Hen. *Exp.*, fol. 188^{r-v}.

[353] "Debemus etiam nobisipsis debitam gubernationem. Quale autem sit debitum nostre gubernationis docet Apostolus Romanorum 8: *debitores*, inquid, *sumus non carni, ut secundum carnem vivamus, si enim secundum carnem vixeritis moriemini, si autem spiritu facta carnis mortificaveritis vivetis* [Rm. 8:12–13]. Ex quo patet quod debitores sumus non carni sed spiritui, ita quod spiritui ex debito servire debemus quod quidem facimus quando carnem spiritui subicimus et secundum spiritum vivimus. Et in hoc est debitum quod nobisipsis debemus. Debemus tertio proximis nostris mutuam dilectionem. De hoc debito dicit Apostolus Romanorum 13: *Nemini quidquam debeatis nisi ut invicem diligatis* [Rm. 13:8], ubi *Glossa*, id est, cetera ita solvite ut non debeatis aliquid, caritatem vero ita solvite ut semper debeatis. Sola enim caritas est que etiam reddita semper detinet debitorem [*cf. Glos.ord.* ad Rm. 13:8 (ed. Strassburg, 1480/81), IV.301B; (ed. Venice, 1588), V.28E]. Igitur quando hec debita non solvimus faciendo unicuique quod sibi debemus, sive deo, sive nobisipsis, sive <etiam> proximis nostris, ut dictum est, tunc debita, id est peccata, contrahimus pro quibus penam debemus. Hec ergo debita tam quoad culpam quam quoad penam dimitti nobis petimus dicendo *dimitte nobis debita nostra*. Debita inquam nostra quecumque commissimus: contra te; contra nosipsos; et contra proximos nostros." Jor. *Exp.* 7, fol. 83ra.

noble or common, we all pray the same prayer and we all have the same Lord and Savior.[354] As Jordan admonished in a sermon on the nobility (*De nobilibus*): "Those in a position of superiority and the nobles are not to despise their inferiors and the common folk since they are made from the same matter and are redeemed by the same price, are called to the same glory, and were created by the same God."[355]

Jordan advocated a single standard of justice. The individual is just before God in the same way as that by which she or he is just in society. From one perspective Jordan lowered the justice of God to the level of the just in society; or from another, he elevated the justice of society to the level of divine justice. The result from either vantage point is the same. Not to love one's neighbor is not to give him or her what is owed and this entails sin, the same sin one incurs when one does not render to God what is God's.

In the *Opus Postillarum* there is further clarification of what it is that one owes, and of what justice is. Jordan began his exposition of the words of Matthew, *redde quod debes* (Mt. 18:28), by stating that in the scriptures they are spoken parabolically, whereas they can also be understood as spoken by the supreme judge to every person at death, or in the last judgment.[356] For his own exposition, however, Jordan interpreted the same words as the admonition to the faithful by any preacher or doctor, or even confessor, to render what they owe faithfully.[357] Here Jordan's radical view of justice comes into view. Justice, as defined by rendering what is due, is the basis for the last judgment. When individuals stand before God in judgment He will ask them whether they have "paid their debts." The justice of God was Jordan's standard for all justice, or perhaps the legal understanding of justice provided Jordan with his model of divine

---

[354] "Ad quod dicendum hic dicit 'noster' ... tertio ad innuendum nos omnes esse fratres, tam pauperes quam divites, nobiles et ignobiles." Jor. *Exp*. 1, fol. 74rb.

[355] "... superiores et nobiles non debent inferiores et ignobiles contemnere, cum sunt de eadem materia facti, et de eadem pretio redempti, ad eandem gloriam vocati, ab uno deo creati." Jor. *OD* sermo 268A (ed. Strassburg, 1484).

[356] "*Redde quod debes*, Matthei 18 [Mt. 18:28]. Licet haec verba parabolice dicta fuerint a servo debitum a suo conservo atrociter extorquente, mystice autem haec verba possunt accipi ut dicenda a summo iudice ad quemlibet hominem in morte vel in iudicio extremo rationem ab ipso iudicialiter exigente." Jor. *OP* sermo 436A (ed. Strassburg, 1483).

[357] "... ad praesens tamen accipi possunt ut dicantur a quolibet praedicatore et doctore vel etiam confessore fideles ad redditionem sui debiti fideliter exhortante dicendo cuilibet, *redde quod debes*." *Ibid*.

justice. In either case, what is expected of the just citizen in this life is precisely the same as that which is expected of the just citizen for eternal life, for citizenship within the heavenly city of God—and vice versa. This is the God of the Old Testament, this is Jordan's God, and the God before whom every Christian will stand, not for one's souls to be weighed to determine how much grace is therein, but for one's account to be settled. The theology that is taught and preached in this life, as well as the justice of the confessional, is not a *via securior* by which the sinner can be assured of divine mercy; it is the foretaste of the final judgment before the divine judge. The justice of the confessional, the justice called for by the preacher, is the same justice as that exacted in the final judgment.[358]

The *Opus Postillarum* contains further explanation of what it is that Christians owe God: in addition to religion, humans owe God obedience to His commandments, reverence for the sacraments, stewardship of the goods He has loaned them, and satisfaction for their offenses.[359] It is here that Jordan equated the goods Christians receive from God with the goods a vassal receives from his Lord in the feudal contract, rather than as rewards for their merits, or for their beautiful hair.[360] Thus for all the Christian has, for all the Christian possesses, he or she is indebted to God. This included paying what is owed God with respect to all the powers of the soul, both internal and external. One's memory, will, and intellect one owes to God. Indeed, loving God before and above all else is not something that humans do naturally in order first to merit grace, as was debated in the universities, but is simply something owed.[361] For all humans have, their physical and mental goods, their worldly goods, their

---

[358] *Cf*.: "Ubi est diligenter advertendum quod istud triduum [i.e., Mt. 15 feeding the 5,000 or so who had been there for three days] significat tria tempora que precesserunt institutionem huius sacramenti, quarum primum est tempus legis nature; secundum legis scripture; tertium est tempus prophetie, in quo nobis Christus promittebatur in carne venturus. Post illud triduum verbum eternum in carnem misericorditer veniens pro spirituali refectione. Istud viaticum instituit ne deficeremus in via presentis exilii." *Opus Jor* sermo 230, fol. 357vb.

[359] "Debemus autem deo in genere loquendi quinque, videlicet, obedientiam in praeceptis, reverentiam in sacramentis, religionem in obsequiis, pensionem de bonis concessis, et satisfactionem de offensis." Jor. *OP* sermo 436A (ed. Strassburg, 1483).

[360] Jor. *OP-B* sermo 436, fol. 178^{ra-rb}.

[361] "Sunt autem huiusmodi bona, quae a deo accepimus in triplici genere; quia quaedam sunt bona naturae, quaedam bona fortunae, et quaedam bona gratiae. Bona naturae quaedam pertinent ad animam et quaedam ad corpus. Bona animae quantum ad partem rationalem sunt memoria, intellectus, et voluntas, quae sunt

individual fame, fortune, and honor, they owe to God, and therefore they are indebted to Him.[362] When they do not pay what they owe, when they do not render to those what is theirs, they not only incur debt, they also sin. This is Jordan's radicalization of justice. Justice is the justice of the divine judge as revealed in the Old Testament, who has given humans all they have. This is their debt, this is what they owe. And this is Jordan's doctrine of justification.

One might expect that with this radical view of justice Jordan would find some way out, some lessening of the debt one owed. Simply put, he did not. He stridently affirmed that therefore, all must pray the "Our Father," because "no man is free from sin."[363] Every individual is held to this strict understanding of justice. Because, however, humans cannot even begin to know what it is they owe,

---

partes imaginis de quibus pensum debemus deo, ut de memoria reddamus ei primitias omnium recordationum nostrarum; de intellectu pensum omnium cognitionum nostrarum; de voluntate reddamus censum amoris et omnium affectionum nostrarum. Unde cum primo de nocte evigilaverimus primum quod revoluimus in memoria, sit aliquid de deo; primum circa quod versatur intelligentia in cognitione sit de deo. Et primum circa quod afficitur voluntas per amorem et desiderium sit deus. Et deinde cetera omnia earundem virium exercitia referantur in deum. Hae sunt primitiae fructuum, quo deo debemus de parte rationali, de quibus potest exponi illud quod dicitur, Nehemiae X: offeramus *primitias frumenti vini et olei in domo domini Dei nostri* [II Esr. 10:38–39]. Haec domus domini est mens rationalis, de qua psalmo.: *Domum tuam domine decet sanctitudo* [Ps. 92:5]. In hac domo debemus offere deo primitias frumenti, id est primum fructum memoriae, quae multa grana recolligit, pro refectione spiritus, psalmus.: *adipe frumenti satiat te* [Ps. 147:14]. Item debemus offere primitias vini, id est, primum fructum intelligentiae. Canticorum 7: Guttur tuum vinum optimum, etc [*cf.* Ct. 7:5]. Item debemus offerre primitias olei, id est, primum fructum voluntatis in diligendo deum ante omnia et super omnia, sicut oleum supernatat, Canticorum 1: *oleum effusum nomen tuum* [Ct. 1:3]. Bona autem animae quantum ad partem sensitivam sunt vis cogitativa, irascibilis, concupiscibilis, sensus interiores [et exteriores *add.* OP-B], de quibus omnibus pensum deo offerre debemus... Et quando sic tota anima quantum ad omnes vires suas, tam interiores quam exteriores, debitum servitutis deo rediderit, tunc impleri videtur mandatum dilectionis, quo praecipitur *deus diligi ex toto corde, ex tota anima, ex tota mente*, ex tota virtute et fortitudine, et omnibus viribus. [Mt. 22:37]" Jor. *OP* sermo 436B (ed. Strassburg, 1483). This is where Jordan most clearly differentiated his understanding of justice from that of Thomas Aquinas; *cf.* Thom.Aq. *STh* II/II, 58, art. 8–9 (1724b–1726b).

[362] "Bona vero fortunae sunt divitiae, potestas, [familiaritas seu, *add.* OP-B] familiares, honores, amici, consanguinei, fama et gloria etc, de quibus omnibus debitum deo reddere tenemur, ut eis principaliter ad laudem et servitium dei utamur, et sicut ratio dispensaverit omnia in deum referamus, ut sic omnia flumina bonorum dei fluant in mare divinae magnificentiae ut iterum fluant, Ecclesiastici 1 [*cf.* Sir. 1:1–4]." Jor. *OP* sermo 436B (ed. Strassburg, 1483).

[363] "Et ex hoc elicitur quod quia omnes ad dicendum istam orationem tenentur nullum hominem a peccato esse immunem." Jor. *Exp.* 7, fol. 82^{va-b}.

connected with the petition, 'Forgive us our debts', is the gift of knowledge (*donum scientie*):

> We are not able to be just unless we render to each what is owed them, but what that debt is to which we are held we do not know unless by the gift of knowledge. Wherefore without the gift of knowledge we are not able to do just works.[364]

Here Jordan makes the connection between the Old Law and the New, between the majesty and justice of God and the love of God, for the gift of knowledge is an infused gift; indeed, it is due to Christ himself, and on account of *his* merit, that the Christian is given the gift of knowledge. Christ therefore, justifies humans in that he makes Christians just by teaching them what it is they owe, namely to God, to themselves, and to their neighbor. Nevertheless, humans still sin. The beatitude, therefore, associated with this petition is the blessedness of weeping. Since one sins even with the gift of knowledge, one weeps for one's sins and for the sins of others, and therefore one will be consoled by God, beginning in this life, but perfected in the life to come.[365]

---

[364] "Nec etiam possumus esse iusti nisi reddamus cuique debitum suum, sed quid sit illud debitum quod tenemur cuique nescimus nisi per donum scientie. Unde absque dono scientie opera iustitie facere non possumus." Jor. *Exp.* 7, fol. 84ra.

[365] "Unde absque dono scientie opera iustitie facere non possumus, propter quod dicit Isaie 53: *in scientia sua iustificavit multos* [Is. 53:11], et loquitur de Christo cui attribuuntur dona spiritus sancti in ratione meriti, quia propter meritum suum nobis dantur. Unde etiam ipse spiritus sanctus dicitur *spiritus filii*, ad Galatas 4 [Gal. 4:6]. Christus igitur in scientia sua, id est per donum scientie, iustificat, id est, iustos facit multos docendo videlicet eos quid cuique debeant, puta quid deo, quid sibiipsis et quid proximis; et nichilominus que debita peccando contraxerunt. Et quia hec omnia sine dono scientie scire non valemus, ideo in hac petitione spiritum scientie postulamus. Introducitur consequenter hic beatitudo luctus, que secundum Augustinum adaptatur dono scientie per quod scitur de quibus lugendum sit [Aug. de serm.dom. 2,11,38 (129,840–842)], cuius etiam convenientie signum est in natura que idem membrum ordinavit ad visum et ad luctum. Lugendum est autem pro delictis et peccatis tam que commisimus contra deum tam que contra nosmetipsos vel etiam contra proximos nostros. De hoc luctu dicit psalmo: *Quasi lugens et contristatus sic humiliabitur* [Ps. 34:14]. Non solum etiam lugendum est pro peccatis propriis, sed etiam pro alienis quod est maioris perfectionis... Lugere autem peccata est ipsa odire, itaque surgamus ad destructionem eorum. Est <autem> et alius luctus qui etiam ad hanc beatitudinem pertinet, scilicet lugere pro incolatu presentis miserie et pro dilatione <celestis> glorie. Hoc luctu luxit propheta cum dicebat: *heu michi quia incolatus meus prolongatus est*, etc. [Ps. 119:5]. Huic beatitudini respondet pro premio consolatio, que in hac vita inchoatur, perficitur autem in futura. Dignum est enim ut qui propter deum hic tristatur, ipse a deo consoletur." Jor. *Exp.* 7, fol. 84ra–b.

ETHICS AND ERUDITION   461

Jordan's divine dialectic is clearly in view here. The majesty and justice of God are intricately synthesized with His love. Humans cannot be just, even though they are held to being just.[366] It is a gift of God that one even knows what it is one owes in the first place, and thus recognizes just how short one falls. Thus Christians weep for their sins, and for the sins of others; they weep for the injustice done to God. And God will console this weeping. Not as a reward; humans have done nothing to deserve a reward. It is not that Christians weep for their sins and then God bestows His grace; rather He bestows His grace and Christians recognize what they have received and what they owe in return—and they weep. Christians are called to justice, they are held to being just, but they cannot be "justified." Humans are saints by adoption, through grace, and it is thus that Jordan espoused his *simul iustus et peccator*. It is only the sinner, who recognizes that he or she cannot be truly just, who is the adopted child of God, and is therefore a saint. Yet the saints must continue to strive for justice, for the absolute standard of justice remains; they aspire to good works lest God's grace be received in a vacuum. Christians do not merit grace; they only merit the loss of grace.[367] The divine dialectic is neither an either/or, nor a first/then, but is always a true dialectic: 'Our Father' is indeed the loving Father, but He is also the God of majesty and justice 'in heaven'.

With Jordan's view of justice, combined with his understanding of predestination, one might consider claiming that Jordan espoused a theology of justification that was simultaneously by grace alone (*sola gratia*) and by works alone (*solis operibus*), much the same as that of Gabriel Biel in the later fifteenth century.[368] It is actually, however, the differences between Jordan's theology and a theology such as

---

[366] "Primo igitur debemus deo obedientiam in preceptis, Levitici 2<0>: *Custodite precepta mea et facite ea* [Lv. 20:8]. Et istud est debitum necessitatis in tantum quod de eius plena solutione numquam nos esse tutos praesumere valeamus, iuxta istud Lucae 17: *Cum feceritis omnia, quae praecepta sunt vobis, dicite servi inutiles sumus, quod debuimus facere, fecimus* [Lc. 17:10]; quantumcumque enim homo praecepta dei impleat, semper videt sibi superesse quod timeat." Jor. *OP* sermo 436A (ed. Strassburg, 1483).

[367] "De quibus omnibus gratiis deo debemus servitium, propter quod sicut nobis collate. Ad quod exsolvendum hortatur nos apostolus secunde Corinthiorum sexto: *Exhortamur vos ne in vacuum gratiam dei recipiatis* [II Cor. 6:1] ... Gratiam dei in vacuum recipit, qui non post exercet se in operibus bonis, et talis propter vitium ingratitudinis meretur perdere gratiam." Jor. *OP* sermo 436C (ed. Strassburg, 1483).

[368] "... it is clear that Biel has a remarkable doctrine of justification: seen from different vantage points, justification is at once *sola gratia* and *solis operibus!*" Oberman, *Harvest*, 176.

Biel's that must be stressed. As Jordan, Biel too posited a dialectic between God's mercy and God's justice, but this dialectic was placed in the context of the dialectic between the absolute and ordained powers of God. God's mercy is evidenced by the former, whereas God's justice is operative within the latter; the merciful God bound himself to an ordained order of justice in which the Christian (*viator*) must do his very best in order to receive the promised infusion of grace. The ordained order "proves to be the 'dome' within which the actual life of the *viator* unfolds."[369]

The dialectic of God's absolute and ordained powers did not play a role in Jordan's theology. This fact emphasizes his radicalization of divine justice: the order to which God has bound Himself is the absolute standard of justice as revealed in the Old Testament. The relationship between God's justice and God's mercy in Jordan's theology was the inversion of that advocated by Biel. Whereas for Biel the "outer realm" signified God's mercy, within which God ordained the "dome" of justice, for Jordan the "outer realm" was equated with God's justice, within which God's mercy was operative for the elect: God's mercy was a subset of God's justice. Here again we see the Augustinian elements of Jordan's theology: the saints are those who have been chosen by God from the degenerate mob of the damned (*massa perditionis*).

God's mercy, however, does not circumvent His justice. Even the true saints are held to render to God what is God's. In addition, no one can be certain of one's election, and thus Jordan addressed his *Expositio* to the *corpus permixtum*, for the citizens of the city of God are hindered in their homeward journey by the constant battle with the devil. In this perspective one cannot rely on the personal certitude of election, for the true saint is one who confesses himself a sinner, but rather one must fight to maintain God's justice over against the kingdom of Satan and sin. Jordan's theology was not only an affirmation of God's merciful election: it was also a call to arms.

M. *Fighting the Devil*

In striving for justice the Christian combats the devil who is ever at work standing in opposition to the kingdom of God. The kingdom

---

[369] Oberman, *Harvest*, 186.

of sin sallies forth against the kingdom of grace to capture the soul of the sinner. This is the individual's personal battle, which is fought with works of love flowing from God's grace. Yet as long as Christians are in this life they find themselves also in a corporate battle, defending the militant Church from the synagogue of Satan. Jordan did not give much insight into his conception of the Church in his *Expositio* other than the Church as the *milites Christi* at war with the devil's minions. The Church appears as the congregation of lovers battling the devil. In describing Christ's advent in judgment in his *Opus Postillarum* Jordan stated, echoing Giles of Rome and Augustinus of Ancona, that "then all church offices [*prelatia*] will cease because there will be no need for them."[370] The Church is the means to the end, the point of departure for the saint's homeward journey.[371] Yet there is no salvation outside the Church,[372] which is the congregation of the faithful in battle with Satan as it makes its way to its final destination.

Thus in this life one must continue to work towards justice corporately and personally by performing works of love; one must continue to strive to fulfill God's will and to follow His commandments just as the angels and saints in heaven. But this goal is unattainable without God's grace, and therefore Christians pray that it might be given to them to do so *to the extent possible* for them in this life.[373]

---

[370] "... sed tunc omnis praelatio cessabit, quia necessarium non erit." Jor. *OP* sermo 3K (ed. Strassburg, 1483).

[371] "Regnum enim ecclesie militantis non est nisi quedam via, qua ad regnum glorie gradimur." Jor. *Exp*. 4, fol. 78va.

[372] "Omnis christianus qui a sacerdote excommunicatur, satane traditur, extra enim ecclesiam diabolus est..." Jor. *OJ* sermo 213, fol. 331va; *cf.*: "... sententias excommunicationis sic iniustas prelati nostri temporis fecerunt sepe et omni sententia sic iniusta est servanda et patienter ferenda. Tunc enim non nocet, sed prodest meretur enim talis et in hoc quod verecundiam sustinet... quando enim quis iuste excommunicatur, tunc illa sententia valde est timenda propter periculum damnum et obprobrium." Jor. *OJ* sermo 213, fol. 331^{rb-va}.

[373] "Ideo rationabiliter hec petitio sequitur premissam. Et quia voluntatem dei nostris viribus perficere non valemus, dicente Apostolo Romanorum septimo: *velle quidem adiacet michi, perficere autem non invenio bonum* [Rm. 7:18], ideo hoc petimus a deo quatinus ipse det nobis gratiam, ut sicut voluntas sua perfecte fit ab angelis et sanctis in celo, ita fiat a nobis qui sumus in terra. Nec putet aliquis nos hic petere ut deus faciet voluntatem suam, quia hoc potest et facit absque nostra petitione. Sed petimus ut sua voluntas a nobis fiat et impleatur. Unde dicit Cyprianus: "Non petimus ut deus faciet quod vult, sed ut nos facere possimus quod deus vult, quod ut fiat in nobis opus est dei voluntate, id est, opera eius et protectione, quia nemo suis viribus fortis est, sed dei misericordia tutus [Cypr. domin.orat. 14 (98,245–252)]." Jor. *Exp*. 5, fol. 79ra; "Notandum autem secundum Chrysostomum, quod hec clausula,

They continue to strive for justice in the midst of the battle between God and the devil, when sin, temptation, and the present misery of life are constantly at work trying to divert them from their path home; when the flesh, the world, and the devil are constantly trying to keep humans from being just; when the synagogue of Satan and the kingdom of sin are at war with the kingdom of God's Church and God's grace. In this context, in the midst of this war, not only do humans owe religion, obedience, and justice to God and love to their neighbor, but they also must give the devil his due.

In the *Opus Postillarum* Jordan included an additional creditor to whom Christians are indebted.[374] Satan is on the Christian's list of creditors as well, and to Satan is owed hostility, resistance, and battle.[375] This is where good works have their role most of all. Good works, and particularly love, are contrary to Satan. Indeed Satan greatly fears humans being joined in love, for it was this union of love that he had despised in heaven.[376] Good works are not that by which Christians merit God's grace, but the arms infused with the grace already given employed to fight Satan. By works of virtue one excludes the impediments to reaching one's end, and progresses from a beginner in the spiritual life, to the final stage of contemplation in which one sees God. In doing so, Christians follow the God of

---

sicut in celo et in terra, referri debet super omnes tres petitiones premissas, verbi gratia: sanctificetur nomen tuum, sicut in celo et in terra; adveniat regnum tuum, sicut in celo et in terra; fiat voluntas tua, sicut in celo et in terra [Ps.Chrysost. in Matth. 14 (712); Thom.Aq. *CA* ad Matth. 6:10 (105a)], ad designandum quod he tres petitiones perfecte complebuntur in vita futura, sed in hac vita complentur imperfecte, secundum modum nobis possibilem. Petimus ergo in istis tribus petitionibus ut illa, que in eis petimus, et hic secundum modum possibilem nobis donentur, et illuc perveniamus ubi perfecte compleantur. Unde secundum Augustinum, he tres petitiones complentur in vita futura, quatuor vero sequentes <petitiones> pertinent ad necessitatem vite presentis [Aug. de serm.dom. 2,10,36–37 (127,795–801)]." Jor. *Exp.* 5, fol. 79va.

[374] "... sciendum quod quaedam debemus deo supra nos, quaedem nobisipsis intra nos, quaedam vero proximis nostris iuxta nos, quaedam etiam diabolo, qui est infra nos." Jor. *OP* sermo 436A (ed. Strassburg, 1483).

[375] "Postremo videndum quid debeamus diabolo, qui infra nos est, ipse et satellites eius scilicet peccata et vitia. Et ... debemus ei tria scilicet inimicitiam, resistentiam et pugnam." Jor. *OP* sermo 437B (ed. Strassburg, 1483).

[376] "Impugnamus autem eum [*i.e.* diabolum] per bona opera, quae sibi sunt a tota specie contraria et maxime per caritatem, quia ut dicit Hugo in *Expositione Regulae*, 'nihil est quod ipse diabolus tantum timeat quam caritatis unitatem.' [Hug.SV. *Reg.* 1 (883C)] Si enim caritate coniungimur, inde vehementer expavescit, quia hoc tenemus in terra quod ipse in caelo servare contempsit." Jor. *OP* sermo 437B (ed. Strassburg, 1483).

Sinai and the God of Israel, the active and the contemplative lives, by which one conforms oneself to God's will and keeps His commandments—to the extent possible in this life. The devil is always at work and humans must be on guard; the temptations of the flesh, the world, and the devil are omnipresent, but Christians are not left alone. Whereas the world cries out, "I will forsake you," and the flesh cries out, "I will corrupt you," and the devil cries out, "I will deceive you," Christ cries out, "I will restore you!"[377] Christ is the Christian's redemption and stands with all those progressing in the Christian life from beginners to contemplatives in their battle with the devil, for through faith in Christ humans are made sons of God. The battle continues, but it is Christ who leads his elect from this life, to the blessedness of the life to come, to one's home, and one's end. *Hec Jordanus*.

N. *In the Trenches*

Jordan's theology was intimately entwined with the ideals of his Order. It was a theology, however, designed not simply for the brother in his cell, but for the Christian making his or her way back to God, the heavenly judge and the loving Father. It was a moral theology that exhorted the believer to fight fiercely the forces of Satan. The etymological unity of 'vice' and 'vicious' sharply reveals the lines of battle, which easily disappear in a moralized fog of "virtues and vices." The devil was a vicious enemy.

Whether an accident of history, or of historians, the virtues and vices have not played a central role in portrayals of late medieval academic theology.[378] Questions of epistemology, soteriology, and ecclesiology have dominated the field. Yet Thomas of Strassburg published his commentary on the third book of Lombard's *Sentences*, the book in which the virtues were placed center stage. Like Jordan, Thomas followed Augustine in combining the seven virtues with the gifts of the Holy Spirit, the beatitudes, and the fruits of the Holy Spirit, placed in opposition to the seven vices: pride, avarice, gluttony, luxury, sloth, envy, and anger (*superbia, avaritia, gula, luxuria, acedia,*

---

[377] "Mundus clamat: ego deficiam; caro: ego inficiam; diabolus: ego decipiam; Christus vero dicit: ego reficiam." Jor. *Exp.* 8, fol. 85ra.

[378] *Cf.* R. Newhauser, *The Treatise on Vices and Virtues in Latin and the Vernacular*, Typologie des sources du Moyen Age occidental, fasc. 68 (Turnhout, 1993).

invidia, ira).[379] One can assume that the virtues and vices were not ignored in the universities; we know this to have been the case in the classrooms of the other *studia* of the Augustinian school. Jordan's *Expositio* stands as witness.[380]

Jordan's theology was a practical, mendicant theology. Theology in the Augustinian Order was affective knowledge, leading towards the love of God and neighbor. Jordan followed suit. As an intermediate level of theology, Jordan's lectures on Matthew provide an indispensable link between the lectern and the pulpit. They were not simply intended to prepare future theologians for the rigors of university training; they were not only a step, or stage within the Augustinians' educational system. They represent the Order's theology *par excellence*. Before a young *sententiarius* would have taken on all challengers in debate over such intricacies as whether God generates God, or whether theoretically God could accept one to salvation without the habit of love or faith, or whether God's entering the soul after having stood at the door and knocked should be attributed to God's grace, or to human merit, he would have already learned what being a saint means in the context of the battle with Satan in a *studium* other than Paris or Oxford, a *studium* such as Erfurt, from lectures such as Jordan's. For the majority of Augustinians absolving the sins of Europe's sinners and preaching sanctification of divine militarization from pulpits and street corners, Jordan's theology was all they knew. It was not inconsiderable; it should not remain unconsidered.

---

[379] Thom.Arg. 3 *Sent.* 34–35 (ed. Venice, 1564), fol. 49rb–55rb; *cf.* Thom.Arg. 2 *Sent.* 42 (ed. Venice, 1564), fol. 199vb; Zumkeller, "De Doctrina Sociali," 57–84.

[380] See also E.L. Saak, "Pelagian/Anti-Pelagian Preaching: Predestination, Grace, and Good Works in the Sermons of Jordan of Quedlinburg," forthcoming in *Aug(L)*.

CHAPTER FIVE

PASSION AND PIETY: CATECHESIS AND THE POWER OF
IMAGES IN THE LATER MIDDLE AGES

Crucifixion was not a pleasant death. It was cruel, slow torture. It was reserved only for the lowest dregs of society, those who did not deserve a more honorable, comfortable execution. One can scarcely imagine a more excruciating exhibition of violent inhumanity. Yet, the crucified God became the image, the symbol, the event that defines the Christian religion. Christian identity was and still is to be found in the cross, serving as a constant corrective to all forms of Christian triumphalism.[1]

For the medieval theologian no less than for us today, it is a contradiction in terms: a crucified savior. The reality of Jesus hanging on the cross is not one that sits easily with the sensibilities of contemporary civic religion, which uses Christ's victory over the cross as a comfort and support for a satisfied sense of sanctity and sensibility, not considering the extent to which the cross points to the fact that it was the established religion that had put Jesus there in the first place. So much preaching and believing in the crucified has been and continues to be perpetuated by the same sort of individuals who were the crucifiers: the moral, upright, good, religious, God-fearing middle class, terrified of being unsettled, of becoming unclean, of losing their privilege, being challenged to the very foundation of their view of reality and existence by such a figure, by such an outcast, a non-conformist, idealistic radical who threatened a revolution more sinister and dangerous than one with arms. Such an individual could not be permitted to live. Thank God we are no longer nailing humans to trees. We prefer more antiseptic treatments, less graphic even if as gruesome, being bothered by images published in magazines and broadcast on television of human beings dying of hunger, famine, disease, cold, war, and violence, especially when they are ever so close to home, living and dying on our streets

---

[1] See Jürgen Moltmann, *Der Gekreuzigte Gott. Das Kreuz Christi als Grund und Kritik Christlicher Theologie* (Munich, 1972), 23–29, and *passim*.

right before our eyes. Something should be done about them. The cross has been forgotten: *Crux, crux, et non est crux.*

The bleeding, broken body hanging on the cross: that is what defines Christianity and always has: that, and one's response. There is no resurrection without the cross, no victory without defeat, no joy without suffering, no divinity without the human, no infinity without the finite, and no life without death. That is the paradox. How easily we forget. All the altar pieces, crucifixes, and panels portraying the blood-drenched Jesus with the crown of thorns dug deeply into his skull, having been whipped and beaten, spat upon and mocked, appear ever so distant and foreign to anesthetized contemporary Christianity. Life under the cross—thank God we no longer have to suffer such. Thank God we have now all become respectable publicans and can distance ourselves from the sinners. And thank God too that it is not too late to remember, let us hope, a time when the cross and Christ's suffering was still central, defining Christian life and Christian being, when the point of departure for living the Christian life was not Easter morning, but the despair of calling out *My God, my God, why have you forsaken me?*

The Augustinian platform was constructed not only upon political theory and pastoral theology. It was built on the Passion of Christ, which formed the basis for the theory as well as for the theology. For the Augustinians, the exhortation to imitate Christ was drawn directly from the Order upholding Augustine as the exemplar of its religious life. In one of the sermons Jordan of Quedlinburg included in his *Collectanea*, Augustine instructed his followers in the words of Paul "to be my imitators, just as I am the imitator of Christ,"[2] which was given pictorial expression in the fifteenth-century *Historia Augustini*. Directly after representing Augustine's foundation of a monastery and the composition of his *Rule*, the *Historia Augustini* continues with four scenes depicting Augustine's graphic vision of and devotion to the Passion, followed then by Augustine writing letters in service to the Church, and his teaching his hermit friars.[3] The Passion is portrayed as the source of Augustine's pastoral mission, which then was

---

[2] "*Imitatores mei estote sicut et ego Christi* [I Cor. 11:1]," Jor. *Coll.* sermo 27, fol. 33ra.

[3] J. Courcelle and P. Courcelle, *Iconographie de Saint Augustin. Les Cycles du XVe Siècle* (Paris, 1969), plates 17 and 18; see the discussion of this work on pages 29–64, and the reproduction of all 123 scenes in plates II–XXXV. The *Historia Augustini* was composed in southern Germany between 1430 and 1440.

to be imitated by his followers. Just as the Augustinians propagated the image of Augustine as the paradigm for living the most perfect life of Augustine's religion, so did they propagate the exemplar of Christ's Passion as the source of identity, the norm of action, for following the Christian religion. As Henry of Friemar put it in his *Tractatus de quattuor instinctibus*, which originated as sermons given to the Augustinians in Erfurt and was later widely received, "anyone [*quilibet homo*] who rightly considers the bitterness of Christ's Passion, ought not only to suffer patiently, but even willingly and rejoicingly for Christ."[4] The Passion was the expression of perfect religion, and thus functioned catechetically. This held as true for the Augustinians, and indeed for all the *religiosi*, as it did for all Christians. The Augustinians worked for the sanctification of society by teaching the people the basic doctrines of the Christian religion and what it was that humans owed God. They did so by composing catechetical treatises, which included sermons on the Passion, in their pursuit of a transformational sanctity.[5] They followed their religion's platform of imitating Augustine not only as their *pater* and *preceptor*, but also as the *sapiens architector ecclesie*, whose light shone more brightly than that of all other doctors of the Church, as Jordan of Quedlinburg eulogized in his *Opus Dan*.[6] The Augustinian high way to heaven was, at the core, the lowly way of the cross.

To grasp the place of the Passion in the culture of the late medieval Augustinians and their society, we must turn to another Christianity than that of our own, that of the twelfth to the early sixteenth centuries, when the Passion of Christ was lived and breathed as perhaps never since. It is an age gone by, existing only in the past, in texts and in art, in word and in memory, leaving us only an image of what was. Yet then as now, this was an image that determined Christian identity, even if in ways the savior himself would have disavowed. Knowledge is never pure, even knowledge of the divine, even knowledge of the cross.[7]

---

[4] "... quod quilibet homo, qui recte amaritudinem passionis Christi considerat, non solum patienter, sed etiam voluntarie et gaudenter pro Christo pati debet" Hen. *Inst.* 4 (230,447–449). Henry's treatise is extant in over 150 manuscripts of the Latin text and at least 20 manuscripts of German and Dutch translations.

[5] See Saak, "Saints in Society," 320–321, 336–338.

[6] *Ibid.*, 321–322.

[7] For a discussion of "Passion discourse" as I will be treating it in this chapter, see Appendix F.

I. Passion for the Passion

Johannes von Paltz can legitimately lay claim to having been the Billy Graham of the late fifteenth century. On 15 March 1502, Wolfgang Schenck in Erfurt published the first edition of a treatise by this Erfurt Augustinian Professor of Theology, which has become the point of departure for describing late medieval 'revival' theology (*Frömmigkeitstheologie*). Paltz's *Coelifodina* was a Latin translation and expansion of his vernacular work, *Die himmlische Fundgrube*, published in 1490.[8] In both works the focus is on penance, and both works use the Passion of Christ as the exemplary instrument to lead the sinner to the confessional. The Latin version also gives detailed instruction to the preacher of penance regarding how Christ's Passion should be presented to achieve the maximum effect. And behind both works was the recommendation of indulgences, appearing on the crest of the wave of preaching in the wake of the Jubilee Indulgence (1489/90; 1501–1503),[9] which had first been established by Boniface VIII in 1300.

Yet Paltz' *Coelifodina* is far more than a strategy for indulgence hawkers. It is an explication of how to live the Christian life, with the Passion of Christ as the center piece. Indeed, after having gone through in detail the various ways and means for making the Passion a part of one's very being as a Christian, achieved through meditation, Paltz then turned in the second part of his treatise to ways of controlling mental images.[10] Images were central, and were the very basis of meditating on the Passion. Only the likes of the Jews, Paltz asserted, fall into the error "of thinking that one does not sin based on one's thoughts. I say, therefore, that one can sin in one's thoughts alone, and on this basis one can be sentenced to eternal damnation."[11] Paltz left no territory uncovered. In the second part of his treatise dealing with controlling one's thoughts and mental

---

[8] Hamm, *Frömmigkeitstheologie*, 110f. For the phenomenon of translations into Latin of works originally composed in the vernacular, see Burger, "Direkte Zuwendung," esp. 91–105.

[9] Paltz, *Coel.*, vi.

[10] See the introductory paragraph of the second principal part; Paltz, *Coel.* 2 (139,3–9).

[11] "Illa quaestio non sine causa movetur, quia multi putant quod cogitationibus non possint peccare, sed tantum opere. In illo errore erant Iudei, qui putabant in cogitationibus non esse peccatum. Dico ergo, quod homo peccare potest solis cogitationibus et sic aeternaliter damnari." Paltz, *Coel.* 2 (139,12–16).

images, we find Paltz condemning 'French kissing' (*libidinosa osculatio*). The 'lustful kiss' is in the vernacular called 'tasty' (*lecker*), and is so from the act of 'licking' or 'tonguing'. Moreover, such palatable kisses can lead even further: to fornication, adultery, sacrilege, incest, or God forbid, sodomy.[12] And it all starts with thoughts and images in the mind—and then with a kiss. As Jordan of Quedlinburg told his confreres almost 150 years before Paltz composed his work, controlling mental images, one's thoughts, and one's fantasies, not just one's deeds, was central to maintaining one's chastity, and the failure to do so, would cost one time in purgatory. Paltz would have said a loud *Amen*. And for both Jordan and Paltz, meditating on Christ's Passion was the best way to do so. In the later Middle Ages, passion and piety joined together in intimate intercourse in union with the Passion of Christ.[13]

Seventeen years after Paltz first published his *Coelifodina*, and only four years after its last printing in Leipzig, Paltz's younger confrere, who had begun his career as an Augustinian in Erfurt, preached to the Wittenberg Augustinians:

> ... the singular, natural work of Christ's Passion is that it makes humans resemble Christ, for how Christ was terribly martyred in body

---

[12] Paltz's comments are found in a rather detailed section *De decensu cogitationum in deterium*; Paltz, *Coel.* 2 (147,31–160,6). The first level of the second level of degradation is the 'fixed gaze,' which we also saw was central for Jordan: "Primus igitur gradus istius ruinae [secundae] est illicita visus fixio." Paltz, *Coel.* 2, (151,1). He then goes on to cite Augustine's *Regula* and sermo 31 of the *Sermones ad fratres in heremo*; Paltz, *Coel.* 2 (151,2–4; 151,12–152,4). This sermo is not found in Jordan's *Collectanea*, or cited in his *Liber Vitasfratrum*. The fourth level of the second level of degradation is the *libidinosa osculatio*, the third genre of which is the *osculum detestabile*: "Tertium osculum detestabile dicitur libidinis, et est quod fit propter inducere se vel alium in actum libidinosum extra matriomoniam vel in consensum delectationis talis actus. Et est semper mortale..." Paltz, *Coel.* 2 (156,21–24). The fifth level is when one actually commits further acts, the *turpis operatio*: "Quintus gradus est turpis operatio, id est turpe factum, quod secundum diversitatem generum peccatorum diversas sortitur species. Si fuerit cum soluta, dicitur fornicatio; si cum legitima, adulterium; si cum cognata, stuprum, et tanto gravius, quanto propinquior; si cum persona spirituali, sacrilegium, et tanto nequium, quanto sacratior persona; si in eadem sexu, sodomiticum et contra naturam, quod secundum beatum Augustinum est gravius stupro cum propria matre." Paltz, *Coel.* 2 (157,5–11). Thus for Paltz, it seems, incest is better than homosexuality. In the following level of degradation, the third, we find further discussion of the *libidinosa osculatio*: "Ex quarto gradu [tertiae ruinae], videlicet osculo libidinoso, dicuntur vulgariter 'lecker' a lingendo. Ex quinto gradu, scilicet operis perpetratione, dictuntur fornicatores, adulteri, sacrilegi, Sodomitae." Paltz, *Coel.* 2 (159,20–22).

[13] For a thorough treatment of Paltz, see Hamm, *Frömmigkeitstheologie*; I will be dealing with Paltz extensively in my forthcoming, *The Failed Reformation*.

and soul for our sins, must we likewise thus be martyred for him in our consciousness of our sins. This though has nothing to do with words, but with deep meditation... And that is the correct consideration of Christ's Passion, that are the fruits of his Passion and who thus practices himself herein, does better than were he to hear all Passions or read all masses. This is not to say that masses are not good, but that they do not help with such meditation and practice. This also means that the true Christian is he who takes for himself Christ's name and life, as Saint Paul said, for he who thus belongs to Christ, has his flesh with all its desires crucified with Christ. Thus Christ's Passion must be treated not with words and appearances, but truly with life.[14]

With such an exhortation Frater Martin Luther was perpetuating a long tradition of preaching the Passion of Christ as the model for living the Christian life. For there are many fruits of Christ's Passion, Luther preached the previous year, and meditation upon the Passion

---

[14] "... das eygene naturlich werck des leydens Christi ist, das es yhm den menschen gleychformig mache, das wie Christus am leyb unnd seel jamerlich in unsern sunden gemartet wirt, mussen wir auch ym nach also gemartert werden im gewissen von unsernn sunden. Es geht auch hie nit zu mit vielen worten, sondern mit tieffen gedancken... Und das ist recht Christus leyden bedacht, das seynd die frucht seyns leydens, und wer also sich darynnen ubet, der thut besser dan das er alle passion hœret adder alle messe lesse. Nit das die messen nit gutt seyn, sundern das sie an solche bedencken und ubung nichts helffen. Das heyssen auch rechte Christen, die Christus leben und namen also yn yhr leben zyhen, wie S. Paulus sagt: Die do Christo zuu gehœren, die haben yhr fleysch mit allennen synen begirden gecreutziget mit Christo [Gal. 5:24]. Dan Christus leyden muß nit mit worten und scheyn, sondern mit dem leben und warhafftig gehandeldt werden." Luther, *Ein Sermon von der Betrachtung des heiligen Leidens Christi*, WA 2.138,19–142,1; *cf.*: "Ideo qui vult fructuose passionem Christi audire, meditari, legere, oportet eum induere affectum talis compassionis, ac si sociatus Christo in passione, quicquid audit Christum sustinere, se quoque fingat vel putet sustinere iuxta eum, ut, si Christus audit alapis caedi, vinculis ligari, se pone eum alapis similiter caedi et vinculis ligari, et quando sibi videbitur dolere, ita incomparabiliter magis credat et sciat Christum in eodem dolore, et se quidem iuste, Christum autem pro se et aliis hominibus. Hanc compassionem optime novit latro in cruce. Deinde discat sic cognitionem ex Christo, ut magis ploret.... Quae cognitio si in nobis obtineret et nostrum defectum praevaleret, facile esset nos mittes, patientes, humiles, viles, clementes, mundi contemptores fieri et exemplum passionis Christi imitari... Nam passio Christi, ut sanctus pater Augustinus dicit, non solum nobis exemplum est, ut sequamur eius vestigia et in nobis membra terrena crucifigamus, sed etiam est sacramentum et mysterium, Christum per suam temporalem et corporalem passionem nostram spiritualem perpetuam passionem veteris hominis vicisse et crucifixisse. Itaque passionem Christi utiliter vel auditurus vel lecturus vel consideraturus talem concipias necesse est affectum, tamquam ipse eandem passionem in et cum Christo patereris." Luther, *Duo sermones de passione Christi*, 1518, WA 1.336,26–339,24.

is often more efficacious than prayers or works.[15] In doing so, Luther, as Paltz, was following his Order's platform stemming from the teaching in the Augustinian *studia*.

By the early sixteenth century, the Augustinian theological program had already for nearly two centuries been turning out preachers, teachers, and scholars, who wrote treatises dedicated to edifying and educating the Christian flock. As we saw in the previous chapter, since at least the early fourteenth century, Augustinian lectors, bachelors, and masters of theology had been composing works on all facets on the religious life, their own, as well as that of Christians in general. This scholarly production included works aimed for the simple clergy, such as Hermann of Schildesche's *Speculum Manuale Sacerdotum*, which gave instructions not only on what a priest was or was not to do when he had a wet dream, but also on how to baptize Siamese twins.[16] Such instruction was needed by the parish priest who was not even sure how to pronounce the words that made the sacraments effective;[17] and such instruction as that found in Paltz's

---

[15] "Nam sicut multi sunt fructus Christi passionem meditandi, sine dubio per contrarium erunt damna opposita obliviscentium eam. Tales fructus vide alibi, in Roseto et aliis. Notandum tamen, quod prae omnibus Scriptura nos monet caritatem attendere in ista passione. Nam incarnatio et passio Christi licet ad omnem affectum et intellectus eruditionem nobis commendentur inspicienda, maxime tamen ad caritatem Dei inspiciendam cognoscendamque erga nos per Scripturam nobis exhibentur contemplanda.... Tales meditationes saepe utiliores sunt quam orations et operationes. Ratio est, quia magis perficiunt affectum..." Luther, *Duo sermones de passione Christi*, 1518 WA 1.341,34–342,10.

[16] "Si nascatur puer cum duobus capitibus qui habet duo colla et duo pectora distincta, presumitur quod ibi sint duo corda et due anime. Ergo ut duo homines singillatim baptizandi sunt. Si tamen dubitetur an sint duo homines, illa pars in qua maior vivacitas apparet primo baptisetur <simpliciter et absolute; deinde baptizetur> aliud caput et alia pars cum conditione." Herm.Sch. *Spec.*, fol. 11^r; text within <> supplied from the Mainz, 1480 edition. Baptizing conditionally Hermann explained earlier on in his treatise, is to be used in cases of doubt concerning any aspect of the sacrament. The formulation is: "Si es baptisatus, non te baptiso; sed si non es baptisatus, ego baptiso te in nomine patris, et filii, et spiritus sancti." Herm.Sch. *Spec.*, fol. 8^v.

[17] "Ista sunt cavenda circa hanc formam: ne dicat 'lavo' vel 'balneo', vel 'in nomine genitoris et geniti et flaminis almi', vel 'in nomine trinitatis' vel 'dei' vel 'Iesu Cristi'. Item ne fiat aliqua additio maxime erronea, ut fuit additio Arrii, qui baptisabat 'in nomine patris maioris et filii minoris'. Cavenda est etiam omnis alia additio, scilicet ne dicatur: 'in nomine patris et filii et spiritus sancti et beate virginis et sancti Nycolai', licet quidam dicunt talem additionem non obesse, nisi tunc sine tali additione baptisans non crederet posse baptismum fieri. Cavenda est etiam omnis diminutio vel corruptio maxime circa principium dictionis, scilicet ne quis dicat: 'atris' vel 'matris' pro 'patris' et sic de similibus, non enim fieret baptismus

Coelifodina was needed for the pious laity regarding how to keep their passions under control. Human passion was to be absorbed in the Passion of Christ. Providing such instruction for the Church at large, for Paltz and Luther no less than for Henry, Hermann, and Jordan, was an integral part of being an Augustinian. In imitation of their father, the sons of Augustine, from the time of his second monastery in Hippo, were not to live only for themselves, but also to abet the Church, and they did so by preaching and teaching in their Order's schools, in the universities, and in their churches in their communities. As prior general, Gregory of Rimini had directed the Order's theologians in Avignon to preach to the people in the vernacular to win them for their congregation (... *ut populus istius civitatis eo numerosior et fervencior ad ecclesiam nostram conveniat*...),[18] and in 1365, the General Chapter at Siena made preaching in the vernacular *coram populo*—at least ten times!—a requirement for the lectorate.[19] In a world caught between God and the devil, the Gospel was to be spread, and it was to be spread to win souls for God. The symbols of Augustine as *pater noster, preceptor noster* and *sapiens architector ecclesie* were fused in the creation of the Order's religious identity and epitomized in the Augustinians' most perfect life. The internal, group-specific identity, entailed going beyond the boundaries of the group itself, thus forming the Order's social platform: the theological imperative to sanctify society. In pursuing this platform, Augustine's hermits entered their socio-cultural world and became major contributors to the late medieval catechetical endeavor.

Christian indoctrination was an on-going concern of the church from the very beginnings of Christianity. Catechetical literature designed to instruct the laity on the basic doctrines of the faith emerged in the Middle Ages as a distinct genre,[20] beginning with

---

sic dicendo, quia sublatum esset significatum dictionis. Si tamen ex simplicitate et sine omni malitia fieret diminutio vel corruptio circa finem dictionis alicuius non obesset. Verbi gratia: Si quis diceret 'patri' vel 'patrias' aut 'filias' ex ignorantia vel simplicitate non noceret." Herm.Sch. *Spec.*, fol. 9ʳ. Hermann gives similar instructions regarding each sacrament he treats, namely, baptism as here, the eucharist, and confession.

[18] Greg. *Reg.* 2 (9); *AAug.* 4 (1911/12), 423.

[19] Esteban, *AAug.* 4 (1911/12), 450; *cf.* Ypma, "La Promotion au Lectorat," 403.

[20] On the various genres of medieval catechetical literature, see Dieter Harmening, "Katechismusliteratur. Grundlagen religiöser Laienbildung im Spätmittelalter," in *Wissenorganisierende und wissensvermittelnde Literatur im Mittelalter. Perspektiven ihrer Erforschung, Kolloquium 5.–7. Dezember 1985*, ed. Norbert Richard Wolf (Wiesbaden, 1987), 91–102.

the pastoral literature of the twelfth century,[21] and then, according to Egino Weidenhiller, taking off as never before rather suddenly from 1370 onwards.[22] The Augustinians contributed to this renewed catechetical endeavor with model sermon collections, treatises on the Ten Commandments, expositions of the Lord's Prayer, treatises on the virtues and vices, on the Ave Maria, and on the articles of faith. Based on the extant manuscripts, the proliferation of such Augustinian texts moreover coincides with the explosion of catechetical literature. Yet identifying a marked increase of interest in catechesis in the later Middle Ages does not account for the causes thereof. While it may be tempting to see the catechetical renewal stemming from a general "crisis mentality" having resulted from a variety of social, economic, political, and ecclesiastical factors,[23] such recognition is in itself insufficient for an understanding of the catechetical program, being either too broad, offered as an explanation for virtually all cultural products of the fourteenth through the sixteenth centuries, or too narrow, conceived as a specific late medieval cultural phenomenon that itself is in need of analysis and interpretation rather than serving as the cause of other *explananda*. While an ever renewed sense of urgency and crisis was no doubt an influence, a crisis mentality itself was not the engine driving the late medieval catechetical machine. That, as I will argue, was the religious platforms of the various religions within Christendom. These micro-religions, the *religiolae in religione*, brought their group-specific ideals and programs to the Church at large in the ongoing endeavor to Christianize society.[24]

The underlying argument of the present chapter is four-fold. First, if 'catechesis' is taken as synonymous with Christian indoctrination, then that which is considered catechetical cannot be restricted to those literary genres and forms that eventually amalgamated into the early modern catechism. Second, treatises that have often been seen

---

[21] See J. Goering, *William de Montibus (c. 1140–1213): The Schools and the Literature of Pastoral Care* (Toronto, 1992).

[22] P. Egino Weidenhiller, *Untersuchungen zur deutschsprachigen katechetischen Literatur des späten Mittelalters* (München, 1965), 206–212. See also *Faire Croire. Modalités de la diffusion et de la réception des messages religieux du XIIe au XVe siècle*. Table Ronde organisée par l'Ecole francaise de Rome, en collaboration avec l'Institut d'histoire médiévale de l'Université de Padoue, Rome, 22–23 juin 1979 (Rome, 1981); and Robert J. Bast, *Honor Your Fathers: Catechisms and the Emergence of a Patriarchal Ideology in Germany, c. 1400–1600*, SMRT 63 (Leiden, 1997).

[23] Bast, *Honor Your Fathers*, 32–45.

[24] For the concept of the 'micro-religions,' see Appendix A.3.

as representatives of a broadly based, generic pastoral theology (*Frömmigkeitstheologie*), and/or as generic devotional or catechetical works aimed at the laity, often had very group-specific theological origins and content. Third, the nature of late medieval catechesis was twofold: first, there was the endeavor to indoctrinate society at large with the basic principles of Christian life, in keeping with religion defined as the moral virtue consisting of all things owed to God; and second, there was the endeavor to indoctrinate the members of one's own specific religion with the basic principles of that religion, in keeping with religion defined as being *in statu religionis*, or more broadly, with being a *religiosus* or *religiosa*.[25] The pastoral mission of the micro-religions was the major factor involved in the late medieval wave of catechesis as the micro-religions sought to relate themselves to the broader understanding of religion incumbent upon every believer, which for the Augustinians, then, was inherent in and symbolized by their imitation of Augustine as the *sapiens architector ecclesie*. And fourth, the catechetical program of the Augustinians in the later Middle Ages was the implementation of the theological imperative of the Order's mendicant theology as created by and disseminated from the Augustinian *studia*, in the attempt to vivify late medieval religious life with spiritual knowledge. Thus here I take a far broader perspective in placing the theological production of the Augustinian *studia* in the context of late medieval religious culture, with special emphasis given to the catechetical nature of treatments of Christ's Passion. I begin with the *Meditationes de Passione Christi* of Jordan of Quedlinburg.

II. Jordan of Quedlinburg's *Meditationes de Passione Christi*

Late Medieval cultural life in general, Huizinga, explained, "was an out-flowing of thought which became bogged down in images. The entire content of mental life was expressed in images."[26] Perhaps no other religious image is as indicative of this trend Huizinga pointed to than representations of the Passion. As Huizinga himself put it,

---

[25] See Appendix A.3.
[26] "... het is als een uitvloeien, een verzanden van de gedachten in het beeld. De ganse inhoud van het gedachtenleven wil uitgedrukt worden in verbeeldingen." J. Huizinga, *Herfsttij der middeleeuwen* (1919; Amsterdam, 1997²²), 159; *cf. ibid.*, 211.

"Ever since the sweet, lyrical mysticism of Saint Bernard had initiated the fugue of the crescendoing endearment towards the Passion of Christ, the medieval soul was increasingly filled in expanding capacity with swooning emotion over the Passion; it was thoroughly saturated with the concepts of Christ and the cross."[27]

Jordan's of Quedlinburg's highly influential *Meditationes de Passione Christi* would seem to support Huizinga's view.[28] In his prologue

---

[27] "Van de tijd af, dat de zoet-lyrische mystiek van Bernard van Clairvaux in de twaalfde eeuw de fuga geopend had van bloeiende vertedering over het lijden Christi, was de geest in steeds stijgende mate vervuld van de smeltende aandoening over de passie; hij was doortrokken en verzadigd geworden van Christus en het kruis." *Ibid.*, 197; *cf.* Richard Kieckhefer, "Major Currents in Late Medieval Devotion," in *Christian Spirituality II: High Middle Ages and Reformation*, ed. Jill Rait, in collaboration with Bernard McGinn and John Meyendorff, *World Spirituality: An Encyclopedic History of the Religious Quest* 17 (New York, 1988), 75–108; 83. For an excellent study of late medieval Passion theology, see Petra Seegets, *Passionstheologie und Passionsfrömmigkeit im ausgehenden Mittelalter. Der Nürnberger Franziskaner Stephan Fridolin (gest. 1498) zwischen Kloster und Stadt*, SuR.NR 10 (Tübingen, 1998). For a discussion of the distinctions in terminology regarding Passion literature that I have employed in this chapter, see Appendix F.

[28] For the manuscripts of Jordan's *Meditationes*, see above Chapter Four, n. 26. Though Jordan's *Meditationes de Passione Christi* was one of the most influential works on the Passion in the later Middle Ages, Walter Baier's monumental three-volume study of Ludolph of Saxony's *Vita Christi* still offers the most thorough treatment of this work to date; Walter Baier, *Untersuchungen zu den Passionsbetrachtungen in der 'Vita Christi' des Ludolf von Sachsen. Ein quellenkritischer Beitrag zu Leben und Werk Ludolfs und zur Geschichte der Passionstheologie*, 3 vols. Analecta Cartusiana 44. Institut für Englische Sprache und Literatur, Universität Salzburg (Salzburg, 1977). Baier challenges two previously held assumptions: first, that for his own account of the Passion Ludolph simply copied from Jordan's *Meditationes*; and second, that Jordan incorporated his *Meditationes* into his *Opus postillarum*. Baier points to article 64 of the *Meditationes* in which Jordan cites his own sermon 81 of the *Opus postillarum*; Baier, 2.3.13.1 (312f). The oldest manuscripts of the *Meditationes* include this reference which gives weightier evidence to Baier's position than Hümpfner's argument based on the 1483 edition of the *Opus Postillarum*; see Hümpfner, intro. xxxviii; *cf.* Baier, 2.3.13.1 (312f). Baier thus persuasively—if not conclusively—argues that the *Meditationes* originated with Jordan's sermons and should be dated c. 1364, which consequently places the relationship between Jordan's *Meditationes* and Ludolph's *Vita Christi* in different light. Baier argues that Ludolph is not dependent on Jordan since the *Vita Christi* was composed no later than 1368 and perhaps as early as 1348; Baier, 2.3.13.2 (315). Neither, however, was Jordan dependent on Ludolph, but rather, both drew on a common source or sources. Since these two authors were stylistically exceptional in dividing their works on the passion into articles, Baier postulates an otherwise unknown source which he designates the *Articulus-Quelle*; Baier, 2.1.13.2 (320f). In his *Coelifodina* Johannes von Paltz referred anonymously to Ludolph and Jordan when in the section *Divisio passionis dominicae* he wrote: "... hic posset dividere eam cum Guilhelmo Parisiensi vel aliter in valde multos articulos iuxta textus exigentiam." Paltz, *Coel.* 1 (12,17–18); though he shortly thereafter mentioned them by name; Paltz, *Coel.* 1 (13,2–5). Only the critical edition of Jordan's *Meditationes* and *Opus Postillarum*, as well as that of Ludolph's *Vita Christi*, will firmly settle the

478   CHAPTER FIVE

Jordan began with the exhortation from Exodus, which informs his entire work: "Behold, and act according to the exemplar," (Ex. 25:40) the two parts of which he explained as being first "what is to be diligently perceived by the eye of the heart," and second, "what is to be efficaciously imitated in act. Therefore in the entire unfolding of that most blessed Passion, our consideration focuses on these two aspects."[29] Jordan was clear as to what the 'Behold' entailed: the creation of mental images, to be held before the eyes of the heart and those of the mind. It is well known that images were the means of educating the illiterate, a tradition stemming back at least to Gregory the Great.[30] Yet more is at issue here: "we can only understand the role of the visual in popular piety," Bob Scribner explained, "in relationship to a people's entire perception of truth (*Wahrnehmungsfähigkeit*)."[31] For medieval society, visual imagery, which functioned

---

question as to the relationship between the two. A similar textual relationship exists between Jordan's *Expositio Psalterii* and Ludolph's *Enarratio in Psalmos*. Erfurt Stadtbibliothek (MS Amploniana F. 75) contains what Hümpfner called, "... a fairly extensive expositio" on the Psalms, dated c. 1378 (Hümpfner, intro., xliv). The prologue of the text explicitly attributes it to Jordan, although this has never been confirmed by thorough study; Hümpfner, intro., xliv; see also, Zumkeller *MSS* nr. 649 (313). There are many similarities between the works of Jordan and Ludolph, and both drew from a common source, the *Expositio Alani*, composed by Alan of Lille or one of his students; Baier, 1.3.1.1 (86–97). Baier argues that Jordan's *Expositio* should be dated after 1365 based on the date of the single Erfurt manuscript. He admits that the work has never been studied previously but does not question whether it could actually stem from Jordan's early teaching career and gives no textual evidence in support of the later date; Baier, 1.3.1.1 (93). Although Baier devotes far more space to Jordan's *Meditationes*, his brief treatment of Jordan's *Expositio* is the only scholarship on this work. Baier's focus is Ludolph, not Jordan, and therefore Baier only discusses the latter as he related to the former. Nevertheless, Baier has made a substantial contribution to our knowledge of Jordan, and his work serves as a stimulus for further research. This is especially true with regard to the dating of Jordan's *Meditationes* and the controversial textual relationship to Ludolph. Referring to Baier's argument, Zumkeller retorts: "Aber das bleibt ohne Nachweis der Quelle eine blosse These." Zumkeller, "Jordan von Quedlinburg," *VerLex* 4:857; *cf.* Willeumier-Schalij, "De LXV Artikelen van de Passie van Jordanus van Quedlinburg," 22, who echoes Zumkeller's reservations and offers counter arguments to Baier's thesis. I will be presenting new evidence of Ludolph's dependence on Jordan in my forthcoming work, *Jordani de Quedlinburg Opera Selecta*, vol. 1: *Jordani de Quedlinburg Expositio Orationis Dominice. Introduction, Critical Text, Translation, and Commentary*.

[29] "*Inspice et fac secundum exemplar quod tibi in monte monstratum est*... Ecce primum quod est diligenter cordis oculo inspiciendum ... ecce secundum quod est efficaciter in facto imittandum. Igitur circa hec duo versabitur nostra consideratio in toto processu istius beate passionis." Jor. *Med.* Prol., fol. 1ra.

[30] See David Freedberg, *The Power of Images. Studies in the History and Theory of Response* (Chicago, 1989), 163f.

[31] "Die Rolle des Visuellen in der Volksfrömmigkeit können wir nur im Verhältnis

mediatorily between a text and its audience, was central to the perception of reality.[32]

In the *Meditationes* Jordan paints a visual image of Christ's sufferings. It is the *Christus illusus* that Christians should have before their eyes.[33] Calling on Augustine, Jordan instructed his readers that: "When some foul thought pesters me, I go back to the wounds of Christ. When my flesh weighs on me, I take strength in the memory of the wounds of my Lord. When the devil tries to ensnare me, I flee to the entrails (*viscera*) of my Lord and the devil leaves me... In all my adversities, I find no cure so potent as the wounds of Christ."[34] For Jordan, a vivid image of Christ's Passion was fundamental to Christian life.

Jordan divided his *Meditationes* into sixty-five articles, each of which treats a specific stage of the Passion at which "Christ suffered something notably."[35] The articles begin with a prayer

---

zur ganzen Wahrnehmungsfähigkeit des Menschen verstehen." Bob Scribner, "Das Visuelle in der Volksfrömmigkeit," in *Bilder und Bildersturm im Spätmittelalter und in der frühen Neuzeit*, ed. Bob Scribner, Wolfenbütteler Forschungen 46 (Wiesbaden, 1990), 9–20; 13; see also *idem*, "Popular Piety and Modes of Visual Perception in Late Medieval and Reformation Germany," in R.W. Scribner, *Religion and Culture in Germany (1400–1800)*, ed. Lyndal Roper, SMRT 81 (Leiden, 2001), 104–128.

[32] See above all Horst Wenzel, *Hören und Sehen, Schrift und Bild. Kultur und Gedächtnis im Mittelalter* (München, 1995).

[33] "... quod nos Christum illusum ante mentis nostre oculos habeamus..." Jor. *Med.* art. 39, fol. 25ra.

[34] "Cum me pulsat aliqua turpis cogitatio, recurro ad vulnera Christi. Cum me premit caro mea, recordatione vulnerum Domini mei resurgo. Cum diabolus parat michi insidias, fugio ad viscera Domini mei et recedit a me... In omnibus adversitatibus meis, non invenio tam efficax remedium quam vulnera Christi." Jor. *Med.* art. 48, fol. 31rb. Jordan cited Ps.Aug. man. 22 (960D–961A), which he believed to be the authentic voice of the *Doctor gratiae*; *cf.* VF 2,29 (276,166–170) and 2,30 (291,368–375).

[35] "Nec est intentionis mee circa singula gesta historie passionis immorari, sed circa illa precipue puncta, in quibus singulis Christus aliquid notabiliter passus fuit." Jor. *Med.* Prol., fol. 1va. He divided the Passion according to the canonical hours, drawing on the tradition stemming from Ps.Beda. Matins as the first part of Jordan's work contains scenes of the Passion from Christ beginning to suffer in Gethsemane and extends to his being mockingly asked to prophesy before Caiphas. The first part of the *Meditationes* contains twenty articles. Then follow eight articles concerning Christ's presentation to both Pilate and Herod, and his return to Pilate, which constitute the second part and Prime. The third part, *de hora tertia*, treats in twelve articles the Jews' choice of Barabbas over Christ up to their cry *Crucifige!* Jesus is led to the tribunal, condemned to death, crucified and mocked by the thief on the cross in the fourth section of Jordan's work, which concludes with an appeal to join in suffering with Mary. This part, *de hora sexta*, is the second longest of the *Meditationes*, containing eighteen articles. The ninth hour, and the fifth part, opens

(*theorema*),³⁶ followed by an explication of the particular scene of the Passion (*articulus*), lessons derived therefrom (*documenta*), and conclude with suggestions on how to conform oneself to the theme being discussed (*conformatio*). The entire work is designed to give instruction concerning the Passion itself, and to show what should be the proper response. Thus, in article fifteen, treating Christ's condemnation to death, Jordan warns that by persisting in mortal sin, sinners themselves speak the words of the Jews: "He deserves to die," (*Reus est mortis*).³⁷ He then adds the *conformatio*: "In order to conform ourselves to this article, one should consider how often one is deserving of death because of one's own sins, but that God's mercy has thus far persevered for his own emendation."³⁸

---

with article fifty-nine: Christ's abandonment by God on the cross. Four articles later, Christ has died, and the Roman soldier Longinus has pierced his side. This leads to the last two articles, each of which comprises a separate part of the treatise and a separate hour. The deposition is the subject for Vespers as the sixth part, and the canonical day ends with Compline and Christ's burial. In the fourteenth century hymns were written commemorating the Passion and divided into stanzas according to the canonical hours. See, for example, the hymn *Horae canonicae salvatoris*, in *Lateinische Hymnen des Mittelalters*, ed. Franz Joseph Mone (Freiburg im Breisgau 1853; reprint ed. Aalen 1964), nrs. 82–83, 87. This hymn is found in several fourteenth-century manuscripts of Breviaries (107). Jordan dividing his work according to the canonical hours is congruent with both the meditative and the liturgical traditions of his society.

³⁶ Jordan's *theoremata* bear a close formulaic similarity to fifteenth-century sequences or tropes "de passione Christi"; see *Lateinische Sequenzen des Mittelalters*, ed. Joseph Kehrein (Mainz, 1873; reprint: Hildesheim, 1969). In one sequence (nr. 45) we read: "Ave Iesu Christe, qui ab impiis Iudaeis reprobari et a Iuda osculo tradi voluisti..." (*Sequenzen*, 54); *cf.* Jordan's *theoremata* preceding article 5: "Iesu, qui a iudeis capi et teneri voluisti..." Jor. *Med.* Art. 5, fol. 7ᵃ. The vocative 'Iesu', combined with a subordinate passive clause, is both the formula for the sequence and for Jordan's *theoremata*, which then include a supplication (*da mihi*...). The close relationship between Jordan's *Meditationes de Passione Christi* and the liturgical life of the church for both the *religiosi* and the *laici* must not be overlooked when interpreting this treatise.

³⁷ "Ex hoc articulo habemus duo documenta. Primum est, ut caveamus ne umquam illa vox iudeorum, *Reus est mortis* [Mt. 26:66], que Christi auribus innocenter insonuit, nostris mentalibus auribus insonet. Nam de quocumque exeunte in mortali peccato, verum est dicere: *Reus est mortis*." Jor. *Med.* art. 15, fol. 14ᵛᵃ; *cf.*: "Quamdiu enim peccator in peccatis est, Christum in cruce distentum quantum in se est vinculat et crucifigit, peccata enim nostra sunt in causa quod Christus crucifixus est." Jor. *Med.* art. 64, fol. 42ᵛᵃ. Here Jordan echoes one of Ps.Aug.'s sermons *ad populum* which Jordan had included in his *Collectanea*: "O iudei deo semper rebelles, O ceci, O obstinati, cur non consideratis mirabilia que deus operatur in medio terre vestre? Cur Christum non queritis? Cur deum et hominem non agnoscatis? Cur eum ut verum dei filium non adoratis? O fratres non solum iudei sed mali Christiani hodie Christum occidere querunt." Jor. *Coll.* sermo 31, fol. 41ᵛᵇ–42ʳᵃ.

³⁸ "Ad conformandum nos isti articulo, recogitet homo qualiter ipse sepe propter

The *conformationes* are not guides to mystical contemplation, or to ascetical imitation. Most often they simply consist of the exhortation to consider intently (*recogite*) what Christ suffered and the degree to which Christians are the cause of his suffering. Jordan's *Meditationes* are devotional, intended to instruct the meditant about the Passion, and to evoke love for what Christ did *pro nobis*.[39]

The function of meditating on the Passion was not solely to ignite emotion. For Jordan, meditation was fundamental to the process of salvation by cooperating with grace to restore the *imago Dei*. Following Augustine, Jordan stated that the image of God is reflected in the tripartite division of the soul into memory, understanding, and love. These three faculties reflect the similarity to the Father, Son, and Holy Spirit respectively. The image of God in humans is violated by sin. Thus even if someone remembers and understands something about God, but persists in mortal sin, the image is broken asunder because love is not present. The ability to restore the complete Trinitarian *imago Dei* comes not from one's own endeavor, but is the result of grace. Grace enables the believer to preserve the memory of God, the understanding of God, and the love for God in habit and in act.[40]

---

demerita sua reum mortis se fecerit, sed dei misericordia sit hactenus conservatus pro sua emendatione." Jor. *Med.* art. 15, fol. 14[va].

[39] This is again in keeping with Augustine's exhortations as presented in the *Collectanea*: "Iste est qui natus est nuper de Maria virgine et homo factus est, ut nos deos faceret factus est homo. Iste est qui esurivit, ut nos reficeret; qui sitivit, ut nobis vite pocula ministraret. Iste est qui pro nobis temptatur, ut nos a temptationibus liberaret; qui pro nobis ligatur, ut nos absolveret; qui pro nobis humiliatur, ut nos exaltaret; qui pro nobis exspoliatur, ut nos tegeret; qui pro nobis coronatur, ut nos coronaret; qui felle et aceto potatur, ut nobis fontes mellifluos appariret; <qui> mortem suscepit, ut nobis eternam vitam donaret; <qui> sepultus est, ut sepulturum suorum benediceret; <qui> ascendit in celum, ut nobis portas celorum appariret; <qui> sedet ad dexteram patris, ut credentium preces et vota exaudiret. Ecce ergo ad quid natus est Christus, ecce propter quid ad nos descendit Christus." Jor. *Coll.*, sermo 31, fol. 42[ra-b]. On the function of meditating on images, see Freedberg, *The Power of Images*, 161–191.

[40] "Ad cuius evidentiam est sciendum, quod imago dei in mente habet tres conditiones nobilissimas. Primo, habet puritatem, nam imago in mente in omnimoda puritate creata est, et menti impressa. Et hec puritas maculatur sordibus peccatorum tamquam sputis sordidissimis, quibus facies Christi conspuitur, ut in articulo precedenti. Secundo, habet imago dei, que per Christi faciem intelligitur integritatem, quia non solum patrem vel solum filium nec solum spiritum sanctum, sed omnes tres personas assimulat. Ipsa per memoriam similis est patri; per intelligentiam filio; per amorem spiritu sancto. Et hec integritas imaginis violatur et offenditur per peccatum. Nam homo existens in peccato mortali etsi memoretur vel intelligat aliquid de deo, non tamen amat deum. Et sic violata est integritas imaginis quia

Jordan's *Meditationes* were to stimulate the act of memory, understanding, and love for Christ, designed to teach the sinner about Christ's Passion, calling for the need to keep ever in mind what Jesus suffered for us: "... [Christ] wanted his face to be spat on, so that he might clean his image polluted in us; he willingly let his face be slapped, so that he might make whole his image broken in us; he allowed his face to be covered, so that he might uncover and make shine his image veiled and obscured in us."[41] By practicing the *Meditationes*, the devout person begins to create a habit of remembering, understanding, and loving the Passion of Christ. By his suffering and crucifixion, Jesus made whole the image of God in humans, which is torn and broken by sin. Meditating on the Passion was not meant to lead to a mystical union with Christ, nor did it promote an ascetical imitation of Christ's sufferings. Meditation was to stimulate the faculties of the memory, intellect, and love, in restoring the *imago Dei*.

In discussing the *Meditationes*, Hümpfner stated that Jordan "stands in the middle of the current of German mysticism."[42] Jordan him-

---

deest tertia persona. Rursus, si memoretur et enim intelligat nec amet, violata est imago quem ad duas potentias. Et maxime hoc vera ponendo veritatem imaginis non secundum naturalem aptitudinem ad memoriam, intelligendum et amandum sed secundum quod homo actu vel habitu deum meminit, intelligit et amat, quod hec esse per conformitatem gratie, secundum hoc enim magis proprie attenditur ratio imaginis secundum Augustinum." Jor. *Med*. art. 18, fol. 16[ra].

[41] "Igitur Christus voluit faciem suam sputis conspui, ut imaginem suam in nobis pollutam lavaret; voluit in faciem suam percuti, ut imaginem suam in nobis lesam reintegraret; voluit faciem suam velari, ut imaginem suam in nobis velatam et obscuratam detegeret et illustraret." Jor. *Med*. art. 18, fol. 16rb.

[42] Hümpfner, intro. xxxix. This is an estimate that can be traced at least to the seventeenth-century historian of the Augustinian Order, F. Milensius, who saw in the *Meditationes* proof that Jordan "fuit... valde contemplativus." F. Milensius, *Alphabetum de monachis et monasteriis Germaniae et Sarmatiae citerioris Ordinis Eremitarum S. Augustini* (Prague, 1614), 69; as cited by Hümpfner, intro., xxxix. Jordan was involved as well with Meister Eckhardt and knew his commentary on the Gospel of John, though he was critical of Eckhardt's unorthodox teachings. See Jeremiah Hackett, "The Use of a text quotation from Meister Eckhart by Jordan of Quedlinburg OSA," in *Proceedings of the Patristic-Medieval and Renaissance Conference* 2. Villanova, 1977, 97–102; idem, "Verbum mentalis conceptio in Meister Eckhart and Jordanus of Quedlinburg. A Text Study," in *Sprache und Erkenntnis im Mittelalter*, Akten des VI. Internationalen Kongresses für mittelalterliche Philosophie der Societe internationale pour l'Étude de la Philosophie Médiévale, 29 August–3 September 1977, 2 vols. (Berlin-New York, 1979), 2:1003–1011; idem, "Augustinian Mysticism in Fourteenth-Century Germany: Henry of Friemar and Jordanus of Quedlinburg," in *Augustine: Mystic and Mystagogue*, ed. Frederick van Fleteren, Joseph C. Schnaubelt, OSA, Joseph Reino *et al*. (New York, 1994), 439–456.

self attests to this when in his *Opus Dan (Sermones de sanctis)* in a sermon addressed to the religious, he sets forth the "nine steps by which the contemplative soul is drawn to God."[43] It is not until the seventh step that the contemplative achieves "the foretaste of divine sweetness," finding one's consciousness "in the midst of the choir of angels."[44] The final level of this mystical ascent, is "the union of the bride and bridegroom, begun here in this life, but joyously consummated in the future life."[45] Yet there is nothing of this *itinerarium mentis* in Jordan's *Meditationes*. The *Meditationes* are inseparable from Jordan's preaching endeavor, and the charge, based on the example of Augustine himself, to bring the riches of the soul to the people. Meditation for Jordan is neither mystical nor ascetical; it calls for neither a spiritual union with the heavenly Christ, nor a literal imitation of the Man of Sorrows. Meditation is a method, as it was for St. Augustine,[46] designed to lead to the knowledge of God and of self. By meditating on the sufferings of Christ, the meditant comes to realize both the complete implications of the Passion, and the extent to which he or she causes Christ to suffer continually. As Jordan explained in his *Tractatus de virtutibus et vitiis*, meditation, as part of devotion, is the means by which an individual recognizes what has been revealed to him by God from the consideration of divine goodness, resulting in love, combined with the realization of one's own insufficiency.[47]

Jordan was indeed a contemplative and a mystic. In his sermon concerning the nine steps of the soul to God, Jordan attests to his

---

[43] "... quod animae contemplativae novem gradus preponuntur quibus in Deum tenditur." Jor. *OS* (ed. Paris, 1521), fol. 410^v.

[44] "Septimus gradus, aliis nobilior, est praegustatio divinae dulcedinis; si non corporis tamen mentis cognitione et fruitione angelorum choris interesse..." Jor. *OS* (ed. Paris, 1521), fol. 411^v.

[45] "Nonus gradus est sponsi et sponsae unio. Hec in ista vita inchoatur, sed in futura vita foeliciter consummatur." Jor. *OS* (ed. Paris, 1521), fol. 412^r.

[46] Klara Erdei, *Auf dem Wege zu sich selbst: Die Meditation im 16. Jahrhundert. Eine Funktionsanalytische Gattungsbeschreibung* (Wiesbaden, 1990), 22; Brian Stock, *Augustine the Reader. Meditation, Self-Knowledge, and the Ethics of Interpretation* (Cambridge, MA, 1996). For an overview of the meaning of meditation in the Middle Ages, in addition to Erdei, see Martin Nicol, *Meditation bei Luther* (Göttingen, 1984), 14–20, and above all Bernard McGinn, *The Growth of Mysticism, passim*.

[47] "... devotionis autem causa est meditatio... in quantum scilicet per meditationem homo concipit quod se tradat divino obsequi, quod fit ex consideratione divine bonitatis. Unde excitatur dilectio, et ex consideratione nostri defectus, unde excluditur presumptio." Jor. *OP-B*, fol. 185vb.

experience in the spiritual realm beyond the senses. This sermon, however, was specifically addressed to his fellow religious. The *Meditationes*, on the other hand, are completely silent about supernatural spiritual practice. They do not reveal direct evidence for evaluating Jordan's own mystical temperament. Rather, they speak of Jordan's pastoral mission: his attempt to offer spiritual guidance to clergy and laity alike.

Jordan instructs his readers to form for themselves the image of Christ in their minds, in order to conform themselves to Christ's suffering.[48] It is by creating the image that believers recognize how far they fall short of the image. Nevertheless, one should strive to conform oneself to the image. Conformation is not union; it is not seeing Christ "face to face" (*facies ad faciem*). By creating an image on one's own initiative, one thereby forcefully recognizes what Christ has done: "For if our Lord and Savior himself deemed it worthy to be unjustly despised and sold for a meager price for us, why should we, who are genuinely despicable because we are utterly worthless, if we wish to consider the misery of our condition, not suffer to be despised—even more so—to be considered as nothing at all for Christ?"[49]

This image formation is possible for any Christian. The *conformationes* are not strenuous spiritual exercises that can only be performed by "spiritual athletes." When Jordan treats Christ's sweating blood in Gethsemane (art. 2), for the *conformatio* he exhorts the meditant to lie face down on the ground and pray intently. Yet one should be aware of the angelic presence that comforts us in present and future anguish. Jordan further instructs the meditant to try his or her best to shed tears for all the sufferings and love of Christ. If someone cannot actually cry, Jordan reassures that "tears of the heart" suffice.[50] For conforming oneself to the sufferings of Christ,

---

[48] "Ad conformandum se huic articulo, formet homo in mente sua Christum tam horribiliter sputis in facie decrepatum et regratietur sibi pro magna gloria nostra." Jor. *Med.* art. 17, fol. 15va; "Ad conformandum se isti articulo, formet se homo imaginem Christi..." Jor. *Med.* art. 12, fol. 13rb.

[49] "Si enim ipse Dominus et Salvator noster pro nobis dignatus est exiguo pretio vendi et vilipendi iniuste, nos, qui iuste vilipensibiles sumus, quia veraciter viles existimus si conditionis nostre miseriam aspicere volumus, cur non pro Christo vilipendi immo nichilipendi patiamur?" Jor. *Med.* art. 3, fol. 6va.

[50] "In recolendo istum articulum, procidat homo in faciem in terra orando intente, et cogite angelicam presentiam sibi tunc adesse, recogitet etiam agonem suum futurum, et conetur quantum potest habere lacrimas ex tota passione et amore Christi, quas si habere non valeat per oculos, fundat lacrimas saltem cordis." Jor. *Med.* art. 2, fol. 5vb.

the intent is as potent as the performance. The *conformationes* are aides for recreating the various scenes of the Passion in one's mind. It is thus by meditation, not through contemplation or mystical union, that the Christian can fulfill Jordan's directive with which he began his treatise and that informs his entire work: "Behold, and act according to the exemplar," (*Inspice et fac secundum exemplar*).[51]

Jordan's treatise is intended as an instrument to guide the meditant in the formation of mental images before the mind's eye. The sixty-five articles portray the various scenes of the Passion as independent, but connected episodes, rather than presenting a continuous narrative of the Passion story. The Passion forms the narrative substance of Jordan's treatise which yields a "picturalization" of the Passion text. As Frank Ankersmit has argued, if there is a narrative aspect of the picture, there is even more so a pictorial aspect of the text, whereby "... the text assumes the form of a 'picture' of the past,"[52] which is indeed the case for Jordan's *Meditationes*.

To stimulate the creation of a visual image, Jordan did not refrain from graphically portraying Christ's sufferings, going far beyond the Passion text of the Gospels.[53] The meditant must see the various scenes of the Passion; when one sees, one is moved to compassion. Thus we learn that Christ was bound three times: first, by his captors in Gethsemane; then as he was led from Annas to Caiphas; and finally before Pilate, Jesus was bound to a column and whipped.[54] Likewise, after having been interrogated by Caiphas, Christ was spat

---

[51] Jor. *Med.* Prol., fol. 1ra; cf. Eliade, *The Myth of Eternal Return* (New York, 1954; 9th ed. New York, 1991), 6–7.

[52] F. Ankersmit, "Statements, Texts and Pictures," in *A New Philosophy of History*, ed. Frank Ankersmit and Hans Kellner (Chicago, 1995), 212–240; 214; cf. F.R. Ankersmit, *De navel van de geschiedenis. Over interpretatie, representatie en historische realiteit* (Groningen, 1990).

[53] See F.P. Pickering, *Literatur und darstellende Kunst im Mittelalter* (Berlin, 1966); idem, "The Gothic image of Christ. The sources of medieval representations of the crucifixion," in Pickering, *Essays on Medieval German Literature and Iconography* (Cambridge, 1980); James H. Marrow, *Passion Iconography in Northern European Art of the Late Middle Ages and Early Renaissance. A Study of the Transformation of Sacred Metaphor into Descriptive Narrative* (Kortrijk, Belgium, 1979).

[54] "Et nota quod tria legitur dominus ligatus in evangelia. Primo statim cum captus esset Iohannis 18: *comprehenderunt Iesum et ligaverunt eum et adduxerunt eum ad Annam primum* [Io. 18:12–13]. Secundo, cum de Anna duceretur ad Caipham ... Tertio, cum duceretur ante Pilatum ... Et continue tenuerunt eum vinctum ab hora captionis usque ad crucifixionem ubi etiam ipsum clavis vinxerunt. Et sic semper vinctus fuisset usque ad depositionem de cruce ... Quarto potest addi, quod etiam ligatus fuit cum flagellaretur, licet homo in evangelio non exprimatur, creditur tamen tunc fuisse ligatus ad columnam." Jor. *Med.* art. 6, fol. 8vb.

on and beaten by Caiphas' soldiers so that he appeared "as a leper," an image drawn from Isaiah 53.[55] Further, his face was so beaten that "blood flowed from his nose and his mouth," although Jordan notes that this is not mentioned by the Evangelists.[56] Jordan devotes an entire article (art. 46) to the explication of psalm 21:18: "they take reckoning of all my bones (*Dinumeraverunt omnia ossa mea*)," as it relates to Christ hanging on the cross,[57] and tells of the two competing theories regarding the actual crucifixion, namely, that Christ was first nailed to the cross on the ground and then lifted into place, or, that the cross was first erected, so that Christ had to ascend a ladder before he was nailed.[58] We further learn that after Jesus' death on the cross, the blind Roman soldier Longinus pierced Christ's side with a lance. The blood from the wound fell on Longinus' eyes, whereupon he was immediately able to see.[59]

All these images were current in the Passion literature of the High and Later Middle Ages.[60] Yet Jordan never used such imagery for mere sensationalism. He employed images for pedagogical and homiletical purposes, always directing his enhancements toward stimulating meditation. Jordan's *Meditationes* were part of this pastoral mission. That Jordan's work was not intended for religious alone is indicated

---

[55] "Et sic illa facies benedicta facta est ita abhorriabilis quasi esset leprosa exputis et verberibus, que ei in faciem dederunt, ut sequitur, unde ad impletus est in eo illud Isaie 53: *Et nos reputavimus eum quasi leprosum, percussum a deo et humiliatum* [Is. 53:4]." Jor. *Med.* art.17, fol. 15ra.

[56] "In facie enim sunt omnes sensus et sunt ibi membra tenera, facile lesibilia. Unde verisimile est quod ex tali percussione fluxerit sanguis per nares et per os, licet hoc ab evangelistis non exprimatur. O quam horrendum scelus impiissimorum iudeorum, quod faciem tam formosam tam crudeliter verberibus affecerunt!" Jor. *Med.* art. 18, fol. 15^{va-vb}.

[57] Jor. *Med.* art. 46, fol. 29vb–30rb.

[58] "Quinquagesimus secundus articulus est in cruce levatio. Nam secundum quosdam crucifixio facta fuit cruce iacente in terra et postea eo affixo levaverunt eum cum cruce... Ista autem levatio non dubium quin maximum doloris fuerit eo quod ex ponderositate corporis tunc lacerabantur vulnera manuum et pedum, quod sine magno dolore nequaquam esse potuit. Secundum alios autem et est communior existimatio, crux prius erecta fuit et terre infixa et postea fecerunt eum ascendere forte per scalam et sic applicantes eum cruci affixerunt eum. Et si sic, tunc articulus ille deberet precedere sex immediate premissos. Nec illa crucis ascensio et applicatio potuit sine singulari pena. Unde qualitercumque accipiatur, planum est quod levatio in cruce vel ascensio et applicatio ad crucem fuit penalis, quare non immerito facit articulum specialem." Jor. *Med.* art. 52, fol. 32^{rb-va}.

[59] "Et ille miles dicitur fuisse Longinus, cuius oculi caligaverant, et cum casu vel nutu divino sicut et lanceavit licet nesciens sanguine Christi defluente per lanceam oculos tangeret clare vidit." Jor. *Med.* art. 63, fol. 40va.

[60] See Marrow, *Passion Iconography*.

when he mentions such themes as the efficacy of relics, pilgrimages, processions, and the virtue of the nobility.[61] Yet he goes even further when he compares the horror of Judas' kiss of betrayal to kissing someone with "sickening breath," a direct opposite of Paltz' *osculum libidinosum*: "For if it is sickening for anyone to receive a kiss from someone with disgusting breath (*os fetidum*), how much greater was it a punishment for Christ to receive a kiss from a mouth of such foulness?"[62] Jordan shows his awareness of human relationships when he exhorts his readers that when they are abandoned by friends and neighbors in times of need, they should calmly bear in mind that Christ was abandoned by his own apostles.[63] Such references suggest that the *Meditationes* were not written by a cloistered monk out of contact with society: this work was not intended for Jordan's co-religious alone.

Jordan certainly had his fellow friars in mind when he stated that just as Christ was shorn on Calvary (*decalvatus fuit*) for us, "so are we shaven when we strip ourselves of all our temporal possessions through the vow of voluntary poverty."[64] He had harsh words for *religiosi* who do not reveal and surrender to their prelate their entire will, because Christ did as much by completely entrusting his spirit to the Father on the cross. Those *religiosi* who retain some of their own will are *mali religiosi*: "they are liars and they hinder the resurrection," since Christ's resurrection would not have occurred if he had not committed everything to God, "and therefore they are antichrists."[65]

---

[61] For the virtue of the nobility, see Jor. *Med.* art. 37, fol. 24ra; reference to the efficacy of relics is found in Jor. *Med.* art. 54, fol. 33vb; for pilgrimages, see art.44, fol. 29ra; and for processions, also see art. 44, fol. 29ra.

[62] "Si enim nauseabile est cuique homini suscipere osculum ab aliquo habente os fetidum, quanto magis Christo fuit penale suscipere osculum ab ore tante feditatis..." Jor. *Med.* art. 4, fol. 7ra. Jordan is drawing from Hier. adv.Iovin. 1,27 (287).

[63] "... quod si interdum hi, qui videntur amici nostri et proximi recedant a nobis tempore necessitatis vel adversitatis, equanimiter hoc feramus memores quod et apostoli in necessitate recesserunt a Christo." Jor. *Med.* art. 7, fol. 10ra.

[64] "Sic et nos decalvamur quando per paupertatem voluntariam ab omni proprietate temporalium denudamur." Jor. *Med.* art. 44, fol. 29rb.

[65] "Tertium documentum specialiter pro religiosis, qui moriuntur mundo in religionis ingressu vel saltem in professione, est. Quod ipsi debent spiritum, id est voluntatem et sensum suum, tradere in manus patris spiritualis, scilicet prelati, quod amplius non resumant usque ad diem resurrectionis, exemplo Christi, qui spiritum suum moriens in manus patris commendaverat ulterius non resumsit nisi in resurrectione sua. Mali ergo religiosi, qui nunquam deposuerunt spiritum suum puta qui

At times Jordan explicitly states that a particular lesson is *pro religiosis*.[66] By specifically designating occasional *documenta* as *pro religiosis*, Jordan intended the majority of the lessons for the laity. Thus he notes that even though the *religiosi* are especially to be the imitators of Christ,[67] "all those who desire to live devoutly according to the 'new man' are ridiculed by those who live according to the 'old man'."[68] All true Christians must tolerate derision from the wicked and strive to be an example; as Jordan exhorted in the *Opus Dan*, every Christian is to be bright and shining.[69] The reason for this, as he told in his *Meditationes*, calling on his blessed father Augustine, is that "the entire life of any Christian, if he lives according to the Gospel, is some type of cross, or even martyrdom."[70] Jordan composed his *Meditationes* as a way of bringing the monastic imitation of Christ to the people at large. The importance of the *quilibet christianus* should not be underestimated.[71] The *Meditationes* may not have originated from the people, but they were intended for the people.[72] Jordan's *Meditationes* must not be cloistered from the broad sense of *religio* in the later Middle Ages.

In light of the above, a historical analysis of Jordan's *Meditationes* must ask not only what Jordan is saying, but to whom he is saying it as well. This raises the issue of his cognitive style. A semiotic analysis of Jordan's *imago passionis*, which he vividly presented "before the eyes of our mind," requires taking into account his culture's *imago*

---

volunt facere secundum voluntatem suam et sequi sensum suum, mendaces sunt et preveniunt resurrectionem, et ideo antichristi sunt." Jor. *Med*. art. 62, fol. 39vb.

[66] See for example note 65 above, and Jor. *Med*. art. 62, fol. 39vb.

[67] "Ex hoc articulo est documentum, quod religiosi, qui specialiter debet esse immitatores Christi . . ." Jor. *Med*. art. 22, fol. 19ra.

[68] ". . . omnes qui pie volunt vivere secundum novum hominem illuduntur ab hiis, qui vivunt secundum veterem hominem." Jor. *Med*. art. 27, fol. 20ra.

[69] "Sic debent homo religiosus et quilibet christianus esse clarus et luminosus." Jor. *OS*, sermo 256, fol. 412^{v}.

[70] ". . . tota vita cuiuslibet christiani hominis, si secundum evangelium vivat, quedam crux atque martyrium sit." Jor. *Med*. Prol., fol. 1rb. This statement is repeated in Jor. *Med*. art. 43, fol. 28rb. Jordan quotes the same passage in Jor. *OD* Prol. sermo 1A (ed. Strassburg, 1484).

[71] See Saak, "Saints and Society."

[72] Alan E. Bernstein has made this distinction in his article, "Theology between Heresy and Folklore: William of Auvergne on Punishment after Death," in *Studies in Medieval and Renaissance History* 5 (1982), 41; *cf*. J.C. Schmitt, "Religion populaire et culture folklorique. A propos d'une réédition: 'La pieté populaire au Moyen Age,'" *Annales E.S.C.* 31:5 (1976), 942.

passionis.⁷³ Such an analysis is lacking when his *Meditationes* are approached from the vantage point of theology or spirituality alone.

Throughout his work, Jordan graphically portrayed the scenes of the passion. Christ abandoned by God on the cross (*Christus derelictus*) is the central image of imitation; the crucified Christ calling out from the cross, *My God, my God, why have you forsaken me?*, forms the very climax of the Passion narrative (*articulus articulorum passionis Christi*). Without this, Jordan avowed, Christ would not have truly suffered.⁷⁴ Here Christ's divinity ceased to support his humanity, and yet the *corpus domini* remains God.⁷⁵ When the soldiers pierced the dead Christ's side, Christ did not suffer since he was already dead, but true blood and water—the signs of life—poured forth from his side.⁷⁶ The ambivalence of the dead but active Christ, artistically represented in the later Middle Ages by the *imago pietatis*,⁷⁷ becomes the sinner's access route to Christ. Jordan exhorted the imitator to enter into Christ's body through the wound in his side—*per amorem*—and there be united with Christ's heart.⁷⁸ He closed his *Meditationes* with

---

⁷³ For a definition of 'cognitive style' and the social aspects thereof, see Michael Baxandall, *Painting and Experience*, esp. 39–40; *cf.* Clifford Geertz, "Art as a Cultural System," in *Local Knowledge. Further Essays in Interpretive Anthropology* (New York, 1983), 94–120; and Wenzel, *Hören und Sehen*, 340. To interpret such a work as Jordan's *Meditationes* historically, one must follow a synchronous approach to texts; see Aron Gurevich, *Medieval Popular Culture. Problems of Belief and Perception*, trans. Janos M. Bak and Paul A. Hollingsworth (Cambridge, 1988), 111.

⁷⁴ "... ipse videns divinitatem in nullo suffragari sensualiti sue in alleviatione penarum bene conqueri potuit se a deo derelictum. Et hec pena derelictionis fuit maior omnibus penis suis, immo sine hac, nulla ei fuisset pena. Unde iste articulus potest dici articulus articulorum passionis Christi, quanto sine eo nulla ei fuisset passio." Jor. *Med.* art. 59, fol. 37ra. *Cf.* Moltmann, *Der Gekreuzigte Gott*, 146.

⁷⁵ See Jor. *Med.* art. 59, fol. 36va–37ra; "... corpus illud fuit verus deus..." Jor. *Med.* art. 63, fol. 40va.

⁷⁶ "... istud vulnus lateris Christus non senserit cum fuerit mortuum corpus..." Jor. *Med.* art. 63, fol. 40rb: "Et iste sanguis erat verum et purus sanguis, et aqua vera et pura... et hoc fuit miraculosum, eo modo ut dictum est supra articulo secundo [art. 2, fol. 4va–b]." Jor. *Med.* art. 63, fol. 40va–b.

⁷⁷ See Hans Belting, *The Image and Its Public in the Middle Ages. Form and Function of Early Paintings of the Passion*, trans. Mark Bartusis and Raymond Meyer (New York, 1990); originally published under the title *Das Bild und sein Publikum im Mittelalter: Form und Funktion früher Bildtafeln der Passion* (Berlin, 1981), esp. 32–33; *cf.* Anne Derbes, *Picturing the Passion in Late Medieval Italy. Narrative Painting, Franciscan Ideologies, and the Levant* (Cambridge, 1996); and Bernhard Ridderbos, "The Man of Sorrows: Pictorial Images and Metaphorical Statements," in *The Broken Body*, 145–181.

⁷⁸ "... nos omnem voluntatem nostram conformare debemus voluntati divine, etiam quod voluntas dei in omnibus et super omnia sic nobis accepta eo quod cor Christi vulneratum est amoris vulnere propter nos, quatenus nos per amorem recipertitum intrare possimus per ostium lateris ad cor eius, et ibi omnem amorem

an analogous, but opposite image when he referred to the heart of the meditant as the *sepulcrum Christi*.[79] The meditant's heart becomes the tomb of Christ. Jordan made the *imago passionis* an intimately personal image. Whereas relics of the Lord's tomb were among the most popular of those relics relating to the Passion of Christ in fourteenth-century Erfurt, for Jordan, the true relic of the tomb is the heart of the imitator who must guard the dead, but life-giving Christ, which Jordan portrayed as a visual bodily image.[80]

The active nature of the images can further be seen in the event that took place in Erfurt in 1324, just two years after Jordan's arrival, introduced above in Chapter Three. Conflict arose between the citizens and the clergy when the citizens hanged a priest accused of theft. The clergy responded by withholding the sacraments, whereupon the citizens attacked them and Church property. The Archbishop of Mainz came to Erfurt and restored peace[81]—but not for long. Later that year a "motley crowd" lead by a man named Zcinke rose up against an unnamed cleric and despoiled a chapel and its altar. A poem was written commemorating this event and telling of its resolution: because the chapel had been attacked, the *corpus de virgine natum* not only set things straight, but also defused the power of Herr Zcinke, which, the poet tells us, was artificial, and protected the said cleric henceforth: *hic et in evum!*[82] The power of the image was the true power, overcoming the false power of the perpetrator, Herr Zincke. For the popular mind, "... images ... had come alive."[83] This is true as well for Jordan's *imago passionis*.

Jordan's *imago passionis*, a visual image, exerted a power over the imitator by establishing a direct bond between image and imitator in the economy of the sacred, a bond discernible in Jordan's con-

---

nostrum ad suum divinum amorem counire, ut sicut ferrum candens cum igne in unum redigatur amorem..." Jor. *Med.* art. 63, fol. 41rb.

[79] "... imaginetur homo quasi cor suum sit Christi sepulcrum et in ibi ipsum venerabiliter recondat, reconditum lamentabiliter defleat et diligenter custodiat ne ipsum amittat." Jor. *Med.* art. 65, fol. 43vb.

[80] Of the thirty-seven relics relating to Christ listed in the *Chronicle of St. Peter's* in Erfurt, twenty-three directly concerned the Passion, and almost half of these date from the fourteenth century. Relics *de ligno domini* and *de sepulcro domini* were the most popular, and in the fourteenth century their numbers equalled that of the two preceding centuries combined; as compiled from *Cron.Erf.* (417ff).

[81] *Cron.Erf.* (354–355).

[82] *Cron.Erf.* (355).

[83] Carlos Eire, *War Against the Idols. The Reformation of Worship From Erasmus to Calvin* (Cambridge, 1986), 21. See especially Freedberg, *The Power of Images*, 283–316.

cept of imitation.[84] Yet the question of the visual image's potency for Jordan goes beyond the efficacy of ritualized, liminal imitation.[85] An analysis of Jordan's conception of the visual image and the mind's eye reveals his philosophical Augustinian presuppositions.

The terms 'the mind's eye', the 'eyes of the soul', or 'the eyes of the heart', all employed by Jordan, have a long history in the Christian tradition. The eyes were used to refer to the 'windows of the soul' by Gregory the Great, as the organs of spiritual vision by Ambrose, and, as the inner eyes of the mind or soul, were equated with the intellect by Augustine, and with *scientia* by Hildegard of Bingen.[86] On the literary level there is little question that these designations are metaphorical, including Jordan's use of the 'mind's eye'. Yet to perceive what lies behind the metaphor we must not stop at literary analysis. Why were the eyes used as such? Is there a level at which for Jordan the 'mind's eye' is not metaphorical? If the mind as well as the body has eyes, how did these eyes see?

When Jordan composed his *Meditationes*, scholars in the Christian west were by no means unified regarding a theory of vision. Nevertheless, a neo-Platonized Aristotelianism provided the point of departure for various interpretations.[87] In medieval *perspectiva* the theory of sensible species was dominant, whereby the object seen emitted images or species that were transported through the medium of light to the organ of vision, namely, the eyes. The debate came in the interpretation of the means by which the species reached the eyes, and the nature of the species themselves.[88] According to Roger Bacon, one of the most influential medieval scholars of vision, vision occurs when the eyes receive the sensible species emitted from the object seen and thus the recipient is transformed in keeping with the essence

---

[84] See R.W. Scribner, "Cosmic Order and Daily Life: Sacred and Secular in Pre-Industrial German Society," in *Popular Culture and Popular Movements in Reformation Germany* (London, 1987), 2–16; cf. R. Po-chia Hsia, *The Myth of Ritual Murder. Jews and Magic in Reformation Germany* (New Haven and London, 1988), 10; Michael Camille, *The Gothic Idol. Ideology and Image-Making in Medieval Art* (Cambridge, 1989); Wenzel, *Hören und Sehen.*

[85] See Victor W. Turner, *The Ritual Process. Structure and Anti-Structure* (Chicago, 1969).

[86] See Gudrun Schleusener-Eichholz's extensive study of the eyes in medieval literature, Gudrun Schleusener-Eichholz, *Das Auge im Mittelalter*, Münstersche Mittelalter-Schriften 35, 2 vols. (München, 1985), 2: 884.

[87] See Bacon *Mult.Spec.*, xlix.

[88] *Ibid.*, liii–lxxi.

of the seen object as effected by the received species. Yet once the sensible species are received by the eyes, the object seen is not ready for intellection. An additional step is needed. For intellection to take place, the intellect must first transform the sensible species into intelligible species by the process of abstraction conducted by the agent intellect. Once the agent intellect has created intelligible species, the object within the soul becomes the basis for further cognitive processes and is stored in memory. It is at this level that Aristotle claimed that the knower and the object known are one in so far as something is known.[89]

This highly attenuated account is not intended to represent the complexities and varieties of medieval theories of vision, but rather to give an indication of the physical and cognitive ideas concerning vision to which Jordan would have been exposed as a student at Bologna and Paris, where he would have heard lectures on Aristotle's natural philosophy as stipulated by his Order's statutes. In order to understand what lies behind Jordan's exhortation to keep the scenes of the Passion before the mind's eye, the epistemological, psychological, and ontological components of his cognitive model of vision come to the fore. Such image formation was far more than metaphorical, literary expressions of religious devotion.[90]

Jordan was indeed familiar with the theory of sensible species. In his *Opus Postillarum*, he explained that with regard to the sense of sight, our sense is completely passive, a mere receptacle of the images emitted from an object. The object is the active partner:

---

[89] Bacon explained: "Dicitur autem similitudo et ymago respectu generantis eam, cui assimilatur et quod imitatur. Dicitur autem species respectu sensus et intellectus secundum usum Aristotelis et naturalium, quia dicit secundo *De anima* quod sensus universaliter suscipit species sensibilium, et in tertio dicit quod intellectus est locus specierum." Bacon, *Mult.Spec.* 1,1 (4,42–46). Bacon's theory of species was part of his attempt to explain natural causation, and regarding vision, the object emitting sensible species provides the first effect: "Et ideo nulli dubium est quin species sit primus effectus. Quod vero iste primus effectus cuiuslibet agentis naturaliter similis sit ei in essentia specifica et natura et operatione manifestum est ex dicendis, quia agens intendit assimilare sibi patiens, eo quod patiens, ut vult Aristoteles *Libro de generatione*, universaliter est in potentia tale quale est agens in actu, sicut ibidem dicit." Bacon *Mult.Spec.* 1,1 (6,80–85). See also the discussion on this theme in Richard Sorabji, *Time, Creation and the Continuum. Theories in Antiquity and the Early Middle Ages* (New York, 1983), 144–149. On intelligible species, see Leen Spruit, '*Species Intelligibilis*'. *From Perception to Knowledge*, BSIH 48 (Leiden, 1994).

[90] For an analysis of the role of cognitive models, see George Lakoff, *Women, Fire, and Dangerous Things. What Categories Reveal about the Mind* (Chicago, 1987), *passim*, but esp. 68–135; *cf.* Scribner, "From the Sacred Image to the Sensual Gaze: Sense

> Three things occur together to bring about any vision, namely, an organ, species, and an object. The eyes are the organ of sight [working] with the intention of the will, and these concern the one who sees. A species is an image or similitude of the visible thing, impressed in the eyes, which is the vision itself and the formed sense. The object is that body which is seen, from which alone that informed sense is brought forth that is called vision.[91]

In his *Opus Jor*, discussing the various meanings of Paul's statement to the Corinthians that we "see in a mirror darkly" (I Cor. 13:12), Jordan explained that,

> ... to see something naturally with the eyes is three-fold: first, something is seen in its actual essence, such as when visible essence is joined to sight, as when the eyes see light; second, we see species (*per speciem*), namely, when the similitude of the thing itself, from the thing itself, is impressed in our sight, as when we see a rock; and third, we see through a mirror (*per speculum*), and this is when the similitude of a thing, by which it is known, comes into sight through a medium, not from the object seen itself, but from that in which the similitude of the thing is represented, such as when sensible objects appear in a mirror.[92]

Only in the third way of seeing, seeing in a mirror (*per speculum*), is fallen human nature able to see God in this life.[93]

Perceptions and the Visual in the Objectification of the Female Body in Sixteenth-Century Germany," ... in Scribner, *Religion and Culture*, 129–145.

[91] "... implicantur tria, quae ad quamlibet visionem concurrunt, videlicet, organum, species et objectum. Organum visus sunt oculi cum intentione voluntatis, et haec se tenent ex parte videntis. Species est imago vel similitudo rei visibilis impressa in oculo, quae est ipsa visio et sensus formatus. Objectum est ipsum corpus quod videtur, a quo solo fit illa informatio sensus, quae visio dicitur..." Jor. *OP* sermo 387A (Strassburg, 1483).

[92] "... est sciendum quod naturaliter aliquid videre tripliciter oculo corporali, uno modo, aliud videtur per essentiam suam, sicut quando essentia visibilis coniungitur visui, sicut oculus videt lucem. Alio modo per speciem, scilicet quando similitudo ipsius rei ab ipsa re imprimitur in visum sicut cum video lapidem. Tertio modo per speculum, et hic est quando similitudo rei per quam cognoscitur fit in visu in mediate non ab ipsa re, sed ab eo in quo similitudo rei representatur, sicut in speculo resultat sensibiles sensibilium." Jor. *OJ* sermo 81, fol. 147[ra]. For an excellent analysis of the place of sensible species within late medieval epistemology and theories of vision, see Katherine Tachau, *Vision and Certitude in the Age of Ockham. Optics, Epistemology and The Foundations of Semantics, 1250–1345*, STGMA 22 (Leiden, 1988).

[93] "Ex quibus patet quod imperfectio nostra in hoc consistit, quod videre deum non possumus nisi videndo speculum, in speculo et per speculum." Jor. *OJ* sermo 81, fol. 147[va].

The point to be made here is that the mind receives images of perceptible objects, either directly from the species themselves (*per speciem*), or indirectly as in a mirror (*per speculum*). Based on the received images, the mind creates mental images, or as Jordan put it, the soul receives the images received from external sources and creates images internally: "For when the senses are allowed to go out to perceive the external delights of the world, their images are generated internally within the soul."[94] Jordan seems here to be referring to the agent intellect, though he does not say so explicitly at this point. In his *Tractatus de filiatione divina*, sermons 50–52 of his *Opus Jor*, Jordan refutes those positions regarding the agent intellect he deems erroneous and dangerous to the Catholic faith precisely because they impinge upon the manner in which humans are created in the image of God, and how *that* image is known. In rejecting the view that the agent intellect is a separate intelligence, or, a power of the soul, Jordan argues that "... the agent intellect does not itself understand, but is a certain intelligible light, in which the soul, by means of the intellect, comprehends intelligible truth... Wherefore, just as corporeal light does not see but is the basis of the eye's vision, so the light of the agent intellect does not itself understand, but is the basis of the possible intellect's understanding."[95] He then continues by arguing that the agent intellect does not have an anthropological role in the *imago dei* in humans, putting forth in opposition the Augustinian tripartite division of the soul into memory, understanding, and will. Yet Jordan's understanding of the agent intellect as that by which the intellect knows seems to be the catalyst for the creation of internal images within the soul, or in more strictly technical terms, the faculty that abstracts intelligible species from sensible species. Once the process of abstraction has

---

[94] "Nam quando sensus permittuntur ad exteriora mundi delectabilia, tunc intrinsecus generant in anima imagines eorum ..." Jor. *OJ* sermo 91, fol. 161rb; cf. Hug. *Phys.* 1, q. 2, art. 2 (73,62–64).

[95] "Intellectus agens non intelligit sed est lumen quedam intelligibile in quo anima per intellectum possibilem veritatem intelligibilem comprehendit, et ratio huius est secundum omnes philosophos quia intelligere nostrum est passio quedam et perficitur recipiendo similitudinem obiecti. Sed intellectus possibilis est que recipit non autem intellectus agens quia contra naturam agentis est recipere sed solum agens habet agere et influere in quantum huiusmodi. Unde sicut lumen corporale non videt sed est oculo ratio videndi, ita lumen intellectus agentis non intelligit sed est intellctum possibile rato intelligendi." Jor. *OJ* sermo 50, fol. 99vb; cf. Hug. *Phys.* 1, q. 2, art. 2 (83,408–414).

taken place, namely, in Jordan's terms, once within the soul internal images are created from the received external images, the internal images function on the same psychological level whether they were received as sensible species *per speciem* or *per speculum*. In Jordan's theory of vision, and correspondingly his theory of images, his epistemology, psychology, and ontology were intimately and intricately entwined, a matrix into which I need to enter yet a bit further in attempt to discern with more depth what lay behind Jordan's conception of the eyes of the mind.

Jordan's epistemological point of departure was derived from an Aristotelian anthropology.[96] The human organism requires forty-five days gestation; the soul is infused in the body only at the very end.[97] At the time of "animation," the soul is a *tabula rasa*, impressed with neither knowledge nor virtues.[98] Yet Jordan betrayed his neo-Platonic hand when interpreting the daughters of Zion in the Song of Songs (Ct. 3:5-11) he claimed:

> Zion is a mirror, and signifies the height of divine wisdom. The daughters of Zion are the faithful souls begotten and elected by God to the contemplation of divine wisdom. They are thus rightly called daughters, because they were created by God at the same time as the eternal word according to the ideal reason... Thus, in keeping with this ideal reason, they can be called predestined daughters, betrothed to Christ in eternity.[99]

---

[96] What follows is not intended to be a complete analysis or portrayal of Jordan's epistemology and its place and function within his theology, or within the history of cognitive theory. I am trying to bring to the fore fundamental aspects of his view of cognition necessary to illumine his view of images. A comprehensive treatment of Jordan's epistemology within the context of his thought would require a separate study. The treatment here, however, fills a gap in the understanding of images' power as discussed by Freedberg. Freedberg did not delve into the epistemological, physiological, and ontological process by which images were seen, focusing on the cognitive and emotional response to viewing images.

[97] "... per philosophum in de Animalibus et per beatum Augustinum in libro 83 quaestionum, corpus humanum formatio 45 diebus perficitur, quia 6 diebus est sub forma lactis; postea 9 diebus sub forma sanguinis; 12 aliis diebus solidatur in carne, et ex tunc in 18 diebus sequentibus organizatur, et tunc demum anima infunditur..." Jor. *OP* sermo 7A (ed. Strassburg, 1483).

[98] "Secundo propter anime perfectionem. Anima enim infunditur corpori sicut tabula rasa, in qua nichil est depictum, neque scientia neque virtutes." Jor. *OJ* sermo 106, fol. 181rb.

[99] "Sion interpretatur specula, et significat altitudinem divine sapientie, cuius filie sunt anime fideles ad divine sapientie contemplationem a deo procreate et electe, que bene dicuntur filie, quia a deo patre simul cum verbo eterno secundum rationem idealem producte... Quantum ad illam rationem possunt dici filie in eternitate

Although the soul at birth is a blank slate, it is a fallen blank slate; the blankness in no way implies an original perfection. The two chief faculties of the soul, the will and the reason, are hindered by the effects of the fall, even though the image of God remains. In short, the human soul at birth is both an empty soul and a deformed image of God.[100]

Jordan compared the soul to a kingdom. In this kingdom three things were necessary: a king to rule the kingdom, counselors to give advice, and servants to serve the king. The king of the human soul is the will, the counselor, the reason, and the senses are the servants. The reason is to consult the eternal laws and keep its sights on the higher things, for in this way it will be illumined and able to give wise counsel. The faculty that performs this function is the higher part of the reason (*superior portio*). If, however, the reason turns away from what is eternal to what is inferior, it will only be able to give wicked counsel; and this is the lower part of the reason (*inferior portio*). The senses provide information to the reason, since, Jordan affirmed citing Aristotle, "nothing is in the intellect that was not first in the senses." If the senses are not on their guard and devolve into sensuality, they could win over the inferior part of the reason, which could then convince the superior part of the reason, which in turn could persuade the king, the will, and thus the individual will fall

---

predestinate et Christo desponsate." Jor. *OD* sermo 19A (ed. Strassburg, 1484). On the role of ideas in medieval epistemology, see M.J.F.M. Hoenen, *Marsilius of Inghen. Divine Knowledge in Late Medieval Thought*, SHCT 50 (Leiden, 1993); Jan Aertsen, *Nature and Creature*, 311; Joseph Owens, C.SS.R., "Faith, ideas, illumination, and experience," in *Cambridge History of Later Medieval Philosophy*, ed. Norman Kretzmann, Anthony Kenny, and Jan Pinborg, assist. ed., Eleonore Stump (Cambridge, 1982), 440–459.

[100] ". . . liberi arbitrii dotatione et divinae imaginis insignatione, quae duo velut duo lineae adhuc remanserant secundum essentiam, vulnerata tamen quo ad naturalia et spoliata quo ad gratuita. Remansit quippe liberum arbitrium, sed depravatum et immunitum, quia peccatum recepit difficultatem ad bonum et pronitatem ad malum. Prius enim homo per liberum arbitrium poterat peccare et non peccare, sed post potuit peccare et non potuit non peccare. Imago etiam dei remansit in anima post peccatum, sed quasi deformata." Jor. *OP* sermo 7B (ed. Strassburg, 1483). Jordan seems to come close to having adopted a Gnostic or Manichean position when he wrote: "Anima enim pueri carni recenter infusa contrahit ex carnis corruptione caliginem ignorantie in intellectu, putredinem concupiscientie in affectu." Jor. *OD* sermo 270A (ed. Strassburg, 1484). The Augustinian position of a flesh/spirit dichotomy is virtually surpassed by Jordan not only by his adopting the sinfulness of the flesh, but the sinfulness of creation as well by claiming the soul is corrupted at infusion, or closely thereafter. Such a determinination, however, must await a comprehensive study of Jordan's theology.

into sin. "Therefore," Jordan warned, "if you want to find Jesus, you ought to be a wise king, namely, one who rules your household well, that is, one who keeps watch on one's senses."[101]

Two points are to be noted here. First, we find an emphasis on sight and particularly, the sight of the reason. The reason should keep its sights on the higher things and the eternal laws: *ratio... aspicit superiora*. By doing so, the sight, or gaze, of the reason is illumined: *per hunc aspectum illuminatur*. Thus in the fourth of his lectures on the *Pater Noster*, Jordan associated the eyes with the intellect.[102] The object of the eyes and the reason influences the reason itself. The second point follows the first. Just as the reason is to an extent determined by its object, so are the senses. A sinful act begins in the senses, and for Jordan, as for the Middle Ages in general, the primary sense was the sense of sight.[103]

---

[101] "Vita enim hominis comparatur regno, in quo constituit dominus tria regno necessaria, scilicet, regem regnum regentem; consiliarium consilia tribuentem; servos regi servientes. Rex autem huius regni est ipsa voluntas sive liberum arbitrium quod pro tanto dicitur liberum, quia ab omni coactione liberum est; dicitur autem voluntas rex in hoc regno quia sicut ad regem pertinet omnia disponere in regno et ei omnia sunt subdita, sic ipsi voluntati omnia sunt subdit quae sunt in vita hominis, sensus et omnes vires... Consiliarius huius regis est ipsa ratio, quae quandoque aspicit superiora et consulit leges aeternas et per hunc aspectum illuminatur et confortatur... et haec vocatur superior portio rationis. Quandoque etiam eadem ratio aspicit ad istam inferiora et per conversionem ad inferiora emollitur et excecatur et secundum hoc damnosa consilia tribuit voluntati; et haec vocatur inferior portio rationis. Tertio huiusmodi regno sunt quinque sensus seu sensualitas, quorum servicio in bene vivendo non potest homo carere, sicut ergo peccatum consummatum fuit in primis parentibus, sic adhuc secundum Augustinum consummatur in quolibet homine peccante, serpens suadit, mulier commedit, vir consensit; sic sensualitas suadet portioni inferiori, quia secundum philosophum in De Anima, Nihil est in intellectu, nisi prius fuerit in sensu. Tunc ulterius inferior portio offert superiori portioni; si tunc superior portio consentit vel non cohibet vel non refrenat, peccatum committitur et sibi imputatur. Si ergo cupis Iesum invenire, oportet te esse sapientem regem, scilicet, ut familiam tuam bene regas, id est sensus tuos bene custodias." Jor. *OD* sermo 36A (ed. Strassburg, 1484); *cf*.: "... hostium scilicet mentis quia angustum est et ferreum optime custodiri potest. Potens enim est ratio dirigere et ordinare omnes vires inferiores. Per hanc portam qua intratur in cubiculum, nihil intrare permittitur nisi quod ratio bonum esse iudicaverit. Et habet haec porta tres custodes, scilicet sinderesim, rationem et voluntatem. Sinderesis semper clamat nullum malum esse admittendum...." Jor. *OP* sermo 265F (ed. Strassburg, 1483).

[102] "Quia etiam donum intellectus est quoddam iuvamentum promovens et dirigens opera nostra in finem cognitum et intentum, ideo... intellectus assimulatur oculo..." Jor. *Exp.* 4, fol. 78vb.

[103] See Aertsen, *Nature and Creature*, 7, 34; *cf.* Wenzel, *Hören und Sehen*, 388.

With regard to sight, the human sense is a passive receptacle of the images emitted from an object. The object is the active partner,[104] and here we have come to the crux of the matter. The soul is a *tabula rasa*, but one capable of receiving sensible species, or images, from the external world. The senses are the portholes through which the soul communicates with the external world and through which the external world enters the soul.[105] By entering the soul, the external images exert an influence on, or a power over the soul. The individual is bombarded with external images that enter the soul through the senses. Thus the individual must constantly be on guard to control what images he or she allows in, lest the senses turn to sensuality, and the inferior reason infects the superior reason which then gives wicked counsel to the king, the will, and the individual falls into sin: "If therefore," Jordan explained,

> we desire to preserve innocence, we should keep diligent control over our exterior senses, and most of all we must guard the sense of sight, so that we wish to see nothing except what we are permissibly able to desire... If, therefore, you want to maintain innocence, keep diligent control on your eyes, so that you only see what leads to your salvation... For we are as a castle under siege by a most powerful enemy with most subtle arrows. The windows of this castle are useful to an extent, but if they are not closely guarded they are extremely dangerous, because flaming arrows can often enter through them and thus destroy the entire castle. Thus our eyes, which are as the windows of our bodies, are continually and from all sides besieged by both the fiercest battle and the keenest enemies in the world—demons. If we do not guard our eyes with care and concern, pernicious images (*species*) will enter [our soul]... which will destroy the entire kingdom of our soul.[106]

---

[104] "... implicantur tria, quae ad quamlibet visionem concurrunt, videlicet, organum, species et objectum. Organum visus sunt oculi cum intentione voluntatis, et haec se tenent ex parte videntis. Species est imago vel similitudo rei visibilis impressa in oculo, quae est ipsa visio et sensus formatus. Objectum est ipsum corpus quod videtur, a quo solo fit illa informatio sensus, quae visio dicitur..." Jor. *OP* sermo 387A (ed. Strassburg, 1483).

[105] "Porte nostre sensus nostri sunt, scilicet visus auditus etc. Per hos enim sensus quasi per quidem ostiam anima ad exteriora exit et exteriora intrant ad eam." Jor. *OJ* sermo 185, fol. 287ra.

[106] "Si ergo volumus servare innocentiam, habeamus sensuum exteriorum diligentem custodiam. Et primo custodiamus diligenter sensum visus, ut nihil velimus videre nisi quid licite possumus appetere... Si vis ergo servare innocentiam, adhibeas oculis diligentem custodiam ut non videant nisi quid sit ad salutem tuam... Nam ita est de nobis sicut de uno castro a fortissimis adversariis et subtilissimis sagitariis obsesso, in quo, quamvis fenestrae utiles sint quantum ad aliquid, sunt tamen valde

External images exert an ontological power over the soul since they are able to enter it through the senses. The theory of sensible species was the generally accepted theory of vision. No less an academic than Marsilius of Inghen recounted the story of a women accused of adultery after having given birth to a beautiful baby, most dissimilar to its parents. She was acquitted because such a picture hung in her room, which impressed its image on her fetus. Likewise, another woman was cleared of such charges when it was discovered that the cause of her delivering a black baby was the image of an Ethiopian she had had in her mind at the time of conception; the power of the image was sufficient to change the color of the baby's skin.[107] Images in the later Middle Ages, for the popular mind as well as for the learned, were powerful indeed.

---

periculosae, nisi bene custodiantur, quia per eas frequenter intrant sagittae ignitae, quibus totum castrum dissipatur. Sic oculi, qui sunt tamquam fenestrae corporis nostri undique et continue obsessi et pugnatia fortissimis et sagacissimis hostibus in mundo, scilicet daemonibus, nisi attente et solicite custodiantur, intrant species periculosae ... quibus destruitur totum regnum animae." Jor. *OD* sermo 31C (ed. Strassburg, 1484); *cf.*: "Unde quando quis videt mulierem vel aliam speciem allectivam, si cor avertit ne de ea cogitet, tunc licet apertum fuerit hostium sensum, hostium tamen cordis manet clausum. Si autem homo aperit hostium cordis et permittit speciem illam intrare, periculosum est." Jor. *OP* sermo 265B (ed. Strassbureg, 1483). *Cf.* Hen. *In mentem* 2.3 (60,140–144).

[107] "Tertio notandum quod videtur probabile quod in statu ante peccatum fuerat in potestate parentum generare masculum vel feminam sola imaginatione et voluntate. Patet quia corpus omnimode videtur fuisse subiectum anime et erant in natura perfecta et ergo imaginando et volendo determinabant vel determinassent materiam ad sexum quem voluissent. Item imaginatio naturaliter imprimit figuram fetui; ergo hoc magis poterat in statu originali ... Item, recitat Hieronymus se legisse in libris Hypocratis quod quedam mulier fuisset suspecta de adulterio, eo quod filium pulcherrimum peperat, utrique parentum dissimilem. Et propter hoc punienda, nisi Hypocras movisset questionem ne forte talis imago esset in cubili eorum depicta. Qua inventa, mulier est a suspitione liberata, quod non fuisset nisi cogitatio de pulchritudine imaginis formam puero impressisset. Item, refert Hieronymus in libro hebraicis questionibus, quod hoc modo Quintilianus liberavit mulierem que peperat ethiopem, quia tempore conceptus, ethiopis habuit imaginationem. Hec ergo videntur facere quod cogitatio matris sive parentum imprimit figuram, colorem, et huiusmodi fetui, et hoc potissimum in statu integro, ubi corpus obediens fuerat voluntati." Mars.Ing. 2 *Sent.* 17,13,1 (ed. Strassburg, 1501), fol. 260vb. The stories Marsilius recounted stand in a tradition of similar tales which can be traced back to the third-century BCE and Heliodorus' Greek romance, *Aethiopian Tale about Theagenes and Charicleia*; in varied forms, similar accounts of the power of images on conception were still prevalent in the early 17th century, as seen in Guilio Mancini's *Considerazioni sulla pittura*; see Freedberg, *The Power of Images*, 2–8. The influence of mental images on conception was a standard part of medieval medicine; see *Sal.Quest.* B 46 (22–23) and W 7 (268–269).

We are now in a position to understand more completely the importance for Jordan of keeping the *imago passionis* before the mind's eye. Just as the sense of sight, so the sight of the mind functioned as a sense by which images entered the soul, as Jordan made explicit in his *Opus Postillarum*: "wherefore, just as in bodily vision three things come together—namely, the organ, object, and medium, whereby the organ is the eye seeing, the object is the thing which is seen, and the medium is light or illumined air—so in spiritual vision the eyes seeing are humans contemplating, the thing seen is the object of contemplation, and the medium is the light of grace or glory, unifying the species or even the object itself with the eye."[108] By always having the Passion, and especially Christ abandoned by God on the cross (*Christus derelictus*) as the object of the mind's eye, the efficacious and powerful image of the Passion enters the soul and directs the reason (*superior portio rationis*) towards higher things, enabling it to give wise counsel to the will.[109]

Such vision was not a natural power. Whereas the incorporation of evil images required no divine aid, we should recall that when the higher part of the reason (*superior portio rationis*) maintains its sight on the eternal law and the higher things it is illumined. Central to Jordan's epistemology was the Augustinian theory of divine illumination: "In the first place, the Holy Spirit gives life to the intellect," Jordan explained, "for the intellect without true cognition is as good as dead, for a thing deprived of its proper function is said to be dead. The proper function of the intellect, however, is true cognition, and this cognition of the true comes from the Holy Spirit . . . for although some truth is able to be known without the Holy Spirit, this is nevertheless not free from being mixed with falsehood."[110] In

---

[108] "Unde sicut in visione corporali tria concurrunt, organum, obiectum et medium deferens; organum est oculus videns, objectum est res, quae videri debet, medium est lumen vel aer illuminatus, sic in visione spirituali oculi videntes sunt viri contemplativi, res videnda est materia contemplandi, medium deferens vel uniens speciem vel etiam ipsum obiectum cum oculo est lumen gratiae vel gloriae." Jor. *OP* sermo 388A (ed. Strassburg, 1483).

[109] Freedberg mistakenly ascribed the importance of vision in meditation for controlling the imagination to the 17th century and Antonius Sucquet's *Road of Eternal Life*; Freedberg, *The Power of Images*, 184ff; *cf.* Hans Belting, *Likeness and Presence. A history of the Image before the Era of Art* (Chicago, 1994); originally published as, *Bild und Kult. Eine Geschichte des Bildes vor dem Zeitalter der Kunst* (Munich, 1990).

[110] "Primo enim spiritus sanctus dat vitam intellectui. Intellectus enim sine veri cognitione quasi mortuus est, res enim privata propria operatione dicitur mortua. Propria autem intellectus est cognitio veri et hec veri cognitio est ex spiritu sancto . . .

other words, "book learning" is not enough; one must proceed to the spiritual knowledge of divine illumination. In addition, such knowledge must be based on love. In keeping with the Augustinian tradition of theology as affective knowledge, Jordan claimed that, "just as undigested food yields bad humors and thus corrupts the body, so knowledge which is not digested by the ardor of love and transformed into good morals, leads to sin."[111] In this light, Jordan's *Meditationes de Passione Christi* were not a quasi-mystical treatise for the devout layperson and friar, but part and parcel of his understanding of the Augustinian *vita contemplativa*—the pursuit to bring the spiritual fruits of contemplation to the people at large through teaching and preaching. Jordan acted as a "power broker" for the images of the passion already extant in his society. He sought to channel the power of the Passion's images along the lines of the *religio Augustini*, and this on both sides of the cloister's walls.

To impress upon the imitator the sufferings of Christ, Jordan advocated a moderate flagellation.[112] The central image of imitation, however, is not the suffering Christ (*Christus patiens*), but the abandoned Christ (*Christus derelictus*). This contrasts markedly with the imitation of the flagellants who appeared at the gates of cities throughout Germany in 1349. Designated as a "most pernicious sect" by official religion,[113] Frantisek Graus considered the flagellants to be a lay movement.[114] The *Kreuzbrüder*, as related by the Magdeburg *Schöppenchronik*, advocated an imitation of the physically suffering Christ, and preached the efficacy of their processions as a way of cleaning oneself to prepare for God's complete forgiveness.[115] The flagellants, as an example of negative cult, formed a systematic asceticism that served to remove "the barriers which separate the sacred from the profane," thereby preparing for the positive cult.[116]

---

licet enim verum aliquod posset sciri sine spiritu sancto, hoc non est tamen sine falsitatis permixtione..." Jor. *OJ* sermo 222, fol. 346ra.

[111] "Nam sicut cibus indigestus malos humores generat et corpus corrumpit, sic scientia, quae non fuerit ardore caritatis digesta et in bonos mores transformata, peccatum inducit." Jor. *OD* sermo 7C (ed. Strassburg, 1484).

[112] "Ad conformandum se isti articulo, poterit homo sibiipsi dare alapam moderatam ad representandam alapam Christi..." Jor. *Med.* art. 11, fol. 12vb.

[113] See *Gest.Mag.* (437,1–12); cf. *Schp.chron.* (204ff).

[114] Frantisek Graus, *Pest-Geissler-Judenmorde. Das 14. Jahrhundert als Krisenzeit* (Göttingen, 1987), 56.

[115] See *Schp.chron.* (205,17–206,3).

[116] Emile Durkheim, *The Elementary Forms of Religious Life*, trans. Joseph Ward Swain, 2nd Edition (London, 1976), 299–325.

For Jordan, in contrast, imitation is not based on a cleansing process of the profane to prepare for the sacred, but focuses upon their simultaneous co-existence. Treating Christ's last words, "It is accomplished," (Io. 19:30) Jordan set up the familiar relationship between the first Adam, and the second Adam, Christ: "Wherefore in the very hour that the first Adam brought death into this world by sinning, the second Adam destroyed death by dying."[117] Imitation, for Jordan, is not works' righteousness, but is in keeping with his Augustinian theology of grace and his fourteenth-century theological doctrine of *simul iustus et peccator*.

The importance of this for what can be called the "theology of the imitator," is that the relationship between the imitator and Christ—or more precisely, between the imitator and the *imago passionis*—is one of analogy, an imitative rite, based on the principle of "like produces like": "We must die with the dying Christ... if we wish to live with Christ in eternal life."[118] With imitative rites as part of the positive cult, Jordan's concept of imitation thus had a different function from that of the flagellants: he moved the imitation of Christ from the negative cult to the positive.

The *imago passionis* exerts a power over the imitator by establishing, in the words of Bob Scribner, "a radically different order of being," namely, the discursive nature of the imitation: "To be raised to this order and at one with it represents 'salvation'."[119] For Jordan, the imitator remains a worldly sinner with Adam, but by imitating the image of the abandoned Christ (*Christus derelictus*)—"in union with the Passion of Christ, crying out these words in complete similarity to Christ, 'My God, My God, why have you forsaken me?'"[120]—he or she becomes simultaneously one with Christ. This simultaneity is

---

[117] "Item nota quod eadem hora, qua primus Adam peccavit, secundus exspiravit. Primus enim post meridiem quia mox ut peccavit, vocem domino ambulantis in paradiso ad auram post meridiem audivit. Et nunc circa horam nonam secundus Adam exspiravit. Unde, qua hora primus Adam peccando mortem huic mundo induxit, eadem hora secundus Adam mortem moriendo destruxit. Et qua hora illi paradisus est clausus, eadem hora ille paradisum apparuit." Jor. *Med.* art. 62, fol. 39rb.

[118] "Nos debemus commori Christo moriendo, videlicet mundo et peccatis, si cum Christo in eterna vita vivere voluerimus." Jor. *Med.* art. 62, fol. 39va.

[119] Scribner, "Cosmic Order and Daily Life," 2.

[120] "... in unione passionum Chisti, clamans in toto simile cum Christo verba hec: *Deus, Deus meus, respice in me ut quid dereliquisti me?* [Ps. 21:2; Mt. 27:46]" Jor. *Med.* art. 59, fol. 37rb–37va.

not only a corrective to the imitation of the flagellants, but is also the ambivalent co-existence of the sacred and profane.[121] Jordan transformed the objective *imago passionis* in Erfurt into a subjective image; the power of the image had not been changed, but channeled.

Jordan's *Meditationes* were indeed a product of Augustinian spirituality. Yet he did not compose his treatise in the solitude of his cell; it is neither a soliloquy nor a mystical vision. The *Meditationes* stemmed from the Augustinian platform to sanctify society. Whether one views the later Middle Ages as a period of spiritual saturation, as did Huizinga, or as contributing to the emergence of a collective guilt culture, as does Jean Delumeau,[122] fourteenth-century society cultivated a devotion to the Passion as never before, evident in art, literature, drama, and the celebrations of *corpus Christi*.[123] In this light, Jordan's *Meditationes* represent not only his Order's mendicant theology, but also a common Passion piety in late medieval culture.

What I have termed the 'theology of imitation' has most often been viewed as either an example of a 'Passion mysticism', or as an example of the late medieval piety against which the Reformation revolted.[124] By analyzing the symbolic meaning of Jordan's *imago passionis*, I have argued that neither portrayal completely characterizes the context of Jordan's *Meditationes*. The civic function of the *imago*, such as "resolving" the anticlericalism in Erfurt in 1324, is not sufficiently grasped by the former portrayal, and the *simul* nature of Jordan's *imitatio* has gone unrecognized by the latter.[125]

---

[121] According to Aron Gurevich, the ambivalent co-existence of the sacred and the profane are central to the medieval grotesque; see Gurevich, *Medieval Popular Culture*, 208.

[122] J. Delumeau, *Sin and Fear. The Emergence of a Western Guilt Culture, 13th–18th Centuries*, trans. Eric Nicholson (New York, 1990), 1–5 and *passim*.

[123] See Miri Rubin, *Corpus Christi. The Eucharist in Late Medieval Culture* (Cambridge, 1991), and the extensive study by B.A.M. Ramakers, *Spelen en Figuren. Toneelkunst en processiecultuur in Oudenaarde tussen Middeleeuwen en Moderne Tijd* (Amsterdam, 1996), esp. 167–247.

[124] See, Elze, "Das Verständnis der Passion Jesu im ausgehenden Mittelalter und bei Luther," in *Geist und Geschichte der Reformation. Festgabe Hanns Rückert zum 65. Geburtstag* (Berlin, 1966), 127–151; Berndt Hamm, *Frömmigkeitstheologie*; Bernd Moeller, "Luther und die Städte," in *Aus der Lutherforschung. Drei Vorträge*, ed. Die gemeinsame Kommision der Rheinisch-Westfälischen Akademie der Wissenschaften and the Gerda Henkel Stiftung, 1983, 9–26.

[125] It was Johannes von Paltz, writing in the context of the Jubilee Indulgence of 1490, and not Jordan, who argued that the fruits of meditating on Christ's Passion lead to contrition, confession, satisfaction, and sanctification. See Paltz *Coel*.

The symbolic meaning of the *corpus de virgine natum* in Erfurt was its peace-making and protective power, a power that Jordan's *Christus derelictus* exerts upon the meditant in the ambivalent simultaneity of the imitation, a mimesis significantly different from that of the flagellants. The *simul* nature of the theology of imitation is passed over when works such as Jordan's *Meditationes* are abstracted from their social context and interpreted as representing the "theology of the *viator*."

In sum, we must listen for Jordan's voice in the cultural text. The collective *imago passionis*, that of painters and of burghers, conditioned the reception of Jordan's contribution to that image. The synchronous approach to Jordan's text—namely, recognizing the non-canonical influences upon the creation of the text as well as the catechetical attempt to shape the *imago passionis* mimetically—reveals the richness of Jordan's *Meditationes de Passione Christi*. Jordan was both a propagator and a purgator of popular piety.

Based on the classic text of the Christian tradition, Jordan sought to make the historical Passion present historical knowledge by rendering it as "not passed" in the consciousness of the meditant performing the *Meditationes*.[126] Jordan's *Meditationes* functioned as a sophisticated and applied hermeneutical theology of imitation. As the received images, transformed into intelligible species by the mind's eye were imitations of the object itself, so the *imago dei* in humans is restored by the mimesis of humans' *exemplar*, namely, Christ's Passion. Jordan's text was designed to aide and instruct the meditant in creating mental images of the Passion, efficacious mental images that properly understood through divine illumination resulted in the ontological elevation of the soul's status on its return to God. Jordan's text itself functioned as a mirror; by reading the text, and by performing the text, the images of the Passion entered the soul *per speculum*.

Implicit within Jordan's *Meditationes*, as well as explicitly behind them, was an Augustinian ontology, epistemology, psychology, and theology as taught in the Augustinian *studia*, even if not always evident to the readers of his text. Jordan's *Meditationes de Passione Christi*

---

1 (98ff). Jordan's work is a practical guide to the religious life, a "popular christology," encouraging identification with the *Christus derelictus*, while making no mention of increasing steps to perfection, or the efficacy of the penitential system.

[126] See note 177 below.

were inseparable from his understanding of the Augustinian *vita contemplativa*, the pursuit to bring the spiritual fruits of contemplation to the people at large through teaching and preaching.

Here I have only been able to touch briefly on the intricacy and contexts of Jordan's thought, which still awaits comprehensive treatment, and his texts still await readers, interpreters, and editors. Jordan's works are representative of far more than general trends in medieval religion, whereby devotion and spirituality are seen as clearly distinct from theology and philosophy. Jordan may not have been on the cutting edge of his age's intellectual achievements, but his texts present a sophisticated grasp of his society and its religious thought in the broadest signification of the term, holding together genres and categories modern scholars have in their wisdom broken asunder. Jordan still possessed something we moderns have lost: a unified, albeit in no way uniform, view of reality. It is only by striving to grasp that view that we can understand Jordan's literary metaphor of the eyes of the mind. Huizinga may have been right regarding late medieval culture having been saturated with images, but Jordan would have interpreted the situation differently: the religious atmosphere of the later Middles ages was *insufficiently* saturated with images of the Passion, present before the mind's eye.

III. Reading the Passion: Exegesis, Catechesis, and Devotion to the Passion in the Later Middle Ages

Jordan's *Meditationes de Passione Christi* stood in a long and broad tradition of treatments of Christ's Passion. Authors in the later Middle Ages inherited their material from the twelfth and thirteenth centuries. During this time the general shift in medieval spirituality from the *Christus triumphans* to the *Christus patiens* was initiated and effected.[127]

---

[127] See, R.W. Southern, *The Making of the Middle Ages* (New Haven and London, 1953), 231ff; and Carl Richstaetter, *Christusfrömmigkeit in ihrer historischen Entfaltung: Ein quellenmässiger Beitrag zur Geschichte des Gebetes und des mystischen Innenlebens der Kirche* (Köln, 1949). Richard Kieckhefer has argued against the notion of shifts in late medieval devotion; see Kieckhefer, "Major Currents," 100. For treatments of the passion in general, see Kurt Ruh, "Zur Theologie des mittelalterlichen Passionstraktates," *Theologische Zeitschrift* 6 (1970), 17–39; R. Kieckhefer, *Unquiet Souls*, 89–121; and Ewert Cousins, "The Humanity and the Passion of Christ," in *Christian Spirituality*, 375–391. For artistic representations of the Passion, see James Marrow, *Passion*

The humanity and humility of Christ were stressed in the works of Bernard of Clairvaux and exemplified in the life and stigmatization of St. Francis. Both the art and the literature of the High Middle Ages began to portray the crucifix with the bleeding corpse, and not as the living, reigning Christ. The pseudonymous works of the twelfth and thirteenth centuries attributed to Bede, Anselm, and Bernard gave forceful expression to the efficacy of meditating on the suffering Christ. In these tracts we find the foundation of fourteenth-century treatments of the Passion: the detailed enumeration and exposition of Christ's individual wounds, from his capture in Gethsemane to the piercing of his side on the cross; deep compassion for Mary; and the division of the scenes of the Passion according to the canonical hours.[128]

Focusing on the *Meditationes Vitae Christi* previously attributed to Bonaventure, Robert Frank has pointed to the importance of imagination in treatises on the Passion. Although they later achieved popularity among secular clergy and laity, the *Meditationes*, according to Frank, were composed in the late thirteenth century for a member of the Poor Clares. Frank claimed that the *Meditationes* represent a watershed in medieval Passion literature by emphasizing the need to create an image of Jesus' sufferings in one's mind.[129] Rather than "the distance separating the sinful mortal from his God,"[130] which characterizes Passion literature preceding the *Meditationes*, Ps-Bonaventure, according to Frank, established "the radical reduction in distance between meditant and divinity." The *Meditationes* constitute "a revolutionary reinterpretation of the relationship between God and man."[131] The meditant need no longer fear a distant God, but rather embraces

---

Iconography; Hans Belting, *The Image and Its Public*; and Anne Derbes, *Picturing the Passion*.

[128] See Ps.Anselm. *Dial.*; Ps.Anselm. *Men.Cr.*; Ps.Beda *Med.*; Ps.Bern. *Lam.*; Ps.Bern. *Med.*; Ps.Bern. *Vit.Myst.*; see also K. Erdei, *Auf dem Wege*, 33.

[129] Frank, "The Logistics of Access to Divinity," 39–50. For the place of the imagination in late medieval religiosity in general, see Timothy Verdon, "Christianity, The Renaissance, and the Study of History: Environments of Experience and Imagination," in *Christianity and the Renaissance. Image and Religious Imagination in the Quattrocento*, ed. Timothy Verdon and John Henderson (Syracuse, N.Y., 1990): 1–37. For the Ps-Bonaventure, *Meditationes de Vita Christi*, see Isa Ragusa and Rosalie B. Green, *Meditations on the Life of Christ. An Illustrated Manuscript of the Fourteenth Century* (Princeton, 1961). Ragusa and Green translated the work of the Ps-Bonaventure from Paris, BnF, MS. Ital. 115, and provided commentary.

[130] Frank, "The Logistics of Access," 41.

[131] *Ibid.*, 40.

a loving God intimately present. The Passion is personalized by the meditant becoming a member of the "Passion Family," present at Calvary with the Virgin Mary and John.[132] The imagination becomes the means by which the meditant recognizes the Father's love, revealed through the Son on the cross.

Recent scholarship has conclusively attributed the *Meditationes Vitae Christi* to the Franciscan Johannes de Caulibus, and has dated the work between 1346 and 1364.[133] The *Meditationes* represent a particular strain of fourteenth-century Passion narratives that contrasts with contemporary treatments of the Passion constructed for other purposes, such as Ludolph of Saxony's *Vita Christi*, which, as Lawrence F. Hundersmarck has argued, "not only called its readers back to the past but also focused on the present.... For the Carthusian preacher, much more than for the Franciscan [author of the *Meditationes Vitae Christi*], piety is to be translated into action."[134] Ludolph's work is neither one of personal, mystical vision, nor strictly one directed toward monastic piety; rather it is intended to teach the believer how to live devoutly. Ludolph "sees the Passion as a textbook for the Christian life."[135]

Yet reading the Passion as offering instruction for how to live devoutly can be found long before the middle of the fourteenth century and Ludolph's *magnum opus*. It is not so much in the Passion literature in the strict sense, meaning meditations and treatises specifically on the theme, as it is in the earlier exegetical tradition that we find at least the beginnings of a reading of the Passion

---

[132] *Ibid.*, 44f.

[133] See *MVC*, esp. ix–xi. Thomas Bestul, however, without further comment, still follows the older position (Bestul, *Texts*, 48), as does Bert Roest, "A Meditative Spectacle: Christ's Bodily Passion in the *Satirica Ystoria*," in *The Broken Body*, 31–54; 33.

[134] Lawrence F. Hundersmarck, "Preaching the Passion: Late Medieval 'Lives of Christ' as Sermon Vehicles," in *De Ore Domini. Preacher and Word in the Middle Ages*, ed. Thomas L. Amos, Eugene A. Green, and Beverly Mayne Kienzle (Kalamazoo, 1989), 147–167; 162. Johannes de Caulibus wrote the *Meditationes* most likely for a Poor Clare, and thus focuses on the personal, individual benefits of meditating on the Passion, rather than on the pastoral nature. Discussing the *vita activa* and *vita contemplativa*, for which de Caulibus essentially simply cites Bernard of Clairvaux, de Caulibus explains: "... qualiter ad lucrum animarum et ad utilitatem proximi sit exeundum non intendo tractare, quia tuus status hoc non requirit. Sufficit tibi et in hoc totum studium tuum ponere, ut uiciis emendata ac uirtutibus imbuta per primam partem actiue Deo tuo, uacare possis per contemplacionem." *MVC* 47 (179,122–127); *cf.* Jordan's definition of the *vita perfectissima*, Chapter Three, n. 203.

[135] Hundersmarck, "Preaching the Passion," 162.

applied to the contemporary Christian as a model for living the Christian life. In his commentary on Matthew composed c. 1089, Bruno of Segni not infrequently exposited the text tropologically, even if not explicitly, by pointing to the exemplary nature of a given passage.[136] In treating Christ going alone to pray on the mount of Olives, Bruno commented that in this "he taught us what we ought to do in our prayers,"[137] and Bruno held up St. Peter's penance for having denied Christ as the example of Christian penance: "This is the form of penance: you have sinned? be still, sorrowful, and weep; and learn with the apostle to love to shed tears."[138] Furthermore, Bruno is very clear that the Church, as the body of Christ, is responsible for instructing the flock; the doctors of the Church, Bruno notes commenting on the empty tomb, "show us the place in which the Lord was placed; while expositing the *exempla* of the Holy Scripture, they teach us where Christ's birth, Passion, and resurrection is prophesied."[139] With commentaries such as Bruno's, together with the *Glossa Ordinaria* and Peter Comestor's *Historia Scholastica*, late medieval authors had a stock-pile of exegetical material on the Passion to apply in ways that exceeded the strictly exegetical.

The new trends in Passion piety in the high and later Middle Ages echo the exegetical tradition. In the ninth century, Rabanus Maurus commenting on Christ's calling out from the cross, *My God, my God, why have you forsaken me?*, affirmed that it was the human nature of Christ that God had abandoned, not the divine nature, and exposited this scene as showing "just how much those who sin ought to cry, when he who never sinned cried so."[140] In the late

---

[136] For Bruno, see Beryl Smalley, *The Gospels in the Schools c. 1100–c. 1280* (London, 1985), 46–47.

[137] "Separatus a discipulis pusillum progreditur, in faciem procidit: quatenus nos doceat quid in nostris orationibus agere debeamus." Bruno *In Matth.* 4,26 (293B–C).

[138] "Hic est poenitentiae modus: peccasti? quiesce, dole, et lacrymare; et disce cum apostolo flere amare." Bruno *In Matth.* 4,26 (299A).

[139] "Nam et Ecclesiae doctores saepe nobis locum ostendunt in quo Dominus positus fuerat, dum sanctarum exempla scripturarum exponentes, ubi ejus nativitas, passio et resurrectio sit prophetata, nos doceant." Bruno *In Matth.* 4,28 (311A).

[140] "Ipsa enim natura quam ille susceperat, derelicta fuerat a Patre, non Filius, qui una cum Patre est. Ostenditque quantum flere debeant qui peccant, quando sic flevit qui nunquam peccavit." R. Maur. *In Matth.* (1142C). For Rabanus in general, see Mayke de Jong, "Old Law and New-Found Power: Hrabanus Maurus and the Old Testament," in *Centers of Learning. Learning and Location in Pre-Modern Europe and the Near East*, ed. Jan Willem Drijvers and Alasdair A. MacDonald, *BSIH* 61 (Leiden, 1995), 161–176.

eleventh century, Bruno interpreted the same text by pointing out that "no one is abandoned by God, except he who sins, for as often as we sin, we are abandoned by God."[141] In the fourteenth century, as seen above, this scene of the Passion became for Jordan the *articulus articulorum passionis Christi*. And whereas Bruno held up Peter as the model of Christian penance, Jordan, in his *Tractatus de articulis fidei*, in which he divided the creed into twelve articles of faith, each being supplied by one of the apostles, claimed not Peter, but Judas as the model for Christian penance, associated with the communion of saints and the sacrament of matrimony, through which all who live in the world are saved and are able to live without mortal sin, made possible through the life and Passion of Christ.[142] Peter Comestor had drawn on Jerome's commentary on psalm 108 to emphasize that Judas offended God more by hanging himself than he had by betraying Christ. After betraying Jesus, Judas began to feel remorse for what he had done, Satan having left him having achieved his goal. Judas' remorse, however, offered Satan the opportunity to enter Judas once again, this time causing him to hang himself.[143] In his *De Concordia Evangelistarum*, composed c. 1140–1145, Zachary of

---

[141] "Homo est qui loquitur, et quis se derelictum dicit. Corpus suum, quod est Ecclesia, secundum quosdam a Deo derelictum: ipse enim secundum se nunquam a Deo derelinquitur: nemo enim derelinquitur a Deo, nisi ille qui peccat. Quoties enim peccamus, toties a Deo derelinquimur." Bruno *in Matth.* 4,27 (305C–306A).

[142] "Septimum sacramentum est matrimonium, in quo si munde vivitur, salvantur et possunt sine peccato mortali vivere. Per hec autem septem sacramenta consequimur remissionem peccatorum et ideo sequitur remissionem peccatorum per hoc datum est apostolis dimittere peccata. Et ideo credendum est quod ministri potestatem habeant absolvendi et quod in ecclesia sit plena potestas dimittendi peccata. Sciendum est preterea quod non solum meritum passionis Christi communicatur nobis, sed etiam meritum vite Christi et quidquid boni fecerunt sancti communicant his qui in caritate vivunt, quia omnes unus sunt... Ex premissis patent fructus huius articuli que consistunt in communione omnium sanctorum ecclesie. Hunc articulum pasuit Iudas, qui interpretatur confitens, quid convenit sacramento penitentie et consequenter omnibus aliis sacramentis." Jor. *OD* sermo 102L (ed. Strassburg, 1484). Such division of the creed into articles stems from 12th-century developments in exegesis; see Joseph Goering, "The Summa *Qui bene presunt* and Its Author," in *Literature and Religion in the Later Middle Ages. Philological Studies in Honor of Siegfried Wenzel*, ed. Richard G. Newhauser and John A. Alford, Medieval and Renaissance Texts and Studies 118 (New York, 1995), 143–159. Jordan's emphasis on life in the world as the state of penance, is echoed in his upholding Mary Magdalena as the means by which the apostles were converted to faith: "... nunc conversa est ad benedicendum deum et ad predicandum verbum dei. Unde ipsa doctrix et apostola etiam ipsorum apostolorum quos omnes in fide dubios in morte Christi ad fidem convertit." Jor. *OD* sermo 103A (ed. Strassburg, 1484).

[143] Comestor *HS* (1624D); *cf.* Hier. in psalm. 108,7 (212,101–106).

510 CHAPTER FIVE

Besançon claimed that Judas' penance was a false penance, and thus was an even worse sin.[144] Jordan, on the other hand, repeated Comestor's and Jerome's statement concerning Judas in his *Opus Ior*, but rather than offering Judas as a negative example explicitly, Jordan used Judas as the symbol of penance, to remind one of God's mercy. No sin is so great that it cannot be forgiven by the mercy of God, except for the sin of despair,[145] and thus Judas in Jordan's *Tractatus de articulis fidei* is associated with the penitential state, which is the condition of life in the world. In his *Meditationes*, however, Jordan employed the image of Judas differently. Here Jordan equated Judas with false Christians, who betray Christ by vocally proclaiming belief, but whose deeds prove otherwise;[146] an image used forcefully by Jean Gerson in his vernacular sermon *Ad deum vadit*, preached before the French Royal court in 1402.[147] When we seek to discern the various readings of the Passion in the later Middle Ages, the genres of exegetical, catechetical, homiletical, and devotional literature become blurred, or even cease to have meaning. This is especially so when we take into account, in the words of Michael Holly, "the post-text, the afterlife of the object as it continues to work at organizing its remembrance in the cultural histories that emplot it."[148]

The post-text of the Passion narrative could not be ignored, but was to be read ever a-new, for as the fourteenth-century monk of Farne, John Whitering, wrote, Christ "hanging on the cross is a

---

[144] Zach.Bes. *Con.Evang.* (561D–562A). See also Smalley, *Gospels*, 30–33. Zachary was here himself drawing on Hier. in psalm. 108,7 (212,101f).

[145] "Quarto in confessione vel in contritione debet esse spes venia inpetrandi... Si quis habet veram contritionem, necesse est ut habeat spem sine qua contritio vero esse non potest. Noli dicere cum Cain *maior est iniquitas mea* etc. Gen. 3 [Gn. 4:13]. Iudas desperans laqueo se suspendit et plus deum offendit desperando quam ante tradendo. Sed forte dicis multa sunt peccata mea et tam magna quod dominus nunquam remittet mihi, noli hoc dicere. Cogita quod misericordia dei semper maior cum sit infinita." Jor. *OJ* sermo 96, fol. 170rb–170va.

[146] "In se ipso etiam dominum osculo tradit qui ore dicit se nosse deum et credere in eum, factis autem negat." Jor. *Med.* art. 4, fol. 7rb. Jordan frequently equated the Jews with the *mali christiani*: "Sextus decimus articulus est colaphizatio, que est percussio in collo, de quo ait Evangelista, quod *colaphis eum cedebant* [Mt. 26:67; Mc.14:65] ... Ex hoc articulo tale habetur documentum, quod caveamus ne et nos aliquando Christum colaphizemus, quia ... colaphizant Christum omnes falsi christiani qui ore confitentur Christum, factis autem negant." Jor. *Med.* art. 16, fol. 14^{va-b}; *cf.* Zach.Bes. *Con.Evang.* (560C).

[147] Gerson *Ad deum* (56–60; see esp. 57.596–58.611).

[148] Michael Ann Holly, *Past Looking. Historical Imagination and the Rhetoric of the Image* (Ithaca, N.Y., 1996), 14–15.

book, open for your perusal... without knowledge of this book, both general and particular, it is impossible for you to be saved,"[149] or as Jordan phrased it in his *Opus Postillarum*, Jesus hanging on the cross offers himself as "the sign post of the path, the mirror of truth, [and] the book of life. Seek diligently in the book of the Lord and read."[150] Devotion to the Passion in the later Middle Ages can be seen as the ongoing attempt to interpret, exposit, and inculcate an adequate reading of the text of Christ's Passion.

A. *Passion and Devotion*

In the early fourteenth century, Sister Katharina compiled a book for her sisters in the Dominican house in Unterlinden. In telling of Sister Agnes von Bilzheim, Katherina wrote:

> For [Agnes] clearly saw in this said vision the Lord Jesus Christ, as it were, suffer again, seized by a crowd of Jews, cruelly bound, and most vilely treated. With terrible shouts and in tumultuous ways, they pulled him from one court of justice to another, mocking him, giving him a box on the ear and frequent blows; they spat into his face, crowned him with thorns, and scourged him with sharp instruments until blood flowed. Finally, after having been tortured [until he suffered] immeasurable pain and after he had become satiated with the disdain and mockery of the faithless, Christ was nailed most cruelly to the cross. The sister who saw all this also heard clearly with her bodily ears how the Lord's most sacred hands and feet were pierced with nails and driven in with frequent terrible hammer blows. After the vision, she remained lifeless and motionless because of her soul's pain for a long time. For the sword of the bitterest Passion of Christ, that she had seen in this vision with her spiritual eyes, had penetrated her entire soul with such pain of compassion that afterwards she could not live any longer.[151]

A similar experience was had by the Augustinian friar Hartmut de Gotha, which Jordan related in his *Liber Vitasfratrum*. Hartmut was so filled with devotion that he asked to see

---

[149] As quoted by Kieckhefer, *Unquiet Souls*, 103.

[150] "Exaltatus autem Iesus proponit tibi se signum vie, veritatis speculum, vite librum... Requirite diligenter in libro domini et legite." Jor. *OP* sermo 163B (ed. Strassburg, 1483).

[151] As cited and translated by Gertrud Jaron Lewis, *By Women, for Women, about Women: The Sister-Books of Fourteenth-Century Germany* (Toronto, 1996), 106–107. For a description of the Unterlinden Sister-book, see *ibid.*, 13–15; *cf.* Susanne Bürkle, *Literatur im Kloster. Historische Funktion und rhetorische Legitimation frauenmystischer Texte des 14. Jahrhunderts*, Bibliotheca Germanica 38 (Tübingen/Basel, 1999).

God's Son, Christ our Lord, on the cross just as he had once hung on it. This was given to him in a vision, by which his heart was so pierced by the spear of love that the sword of sorrow, in his sharing in the Passion, seemed to have penetrated his soul. Not long afterwards, on fire with love for heavenly desires, he sought from the Lord to be shown that glory and joy in which the Mother of the only begotten Son of God was taken up to Heaven, about which he had heard. O what unspeakable devotion! By his first prayer he saw Christ on the cross, just as John the Evangelist had once seen him; and by his second petition he saw the celebration and joy of the assumption of the Glorious Virgin. Just as his first vision was filled with love and suffering, so no one should doubt that his second vision brought him sweetness and delight. Both of these visions were so marvelous, that seeing himself previously as healthy and whole, afterwards he became weak and infirm, because no mortal body is able to sustain such wonderful visions. He confessed to his prior that he had committed a great sin, because as a miserable and unworthy sinner, he had sought to be shown such glorious things. After a few days, filled with his good works, he returned his spirit to God, whereupon he continued to shine with clear signs. One of these that is worth noting, was that a certain important individual, who was afflicted with leprosy, made a vow to visit Hartmut's grave, and he was instantly cured.[152]

These two visions represent one manifestation of experiencing the Passion in the later Middle Ages, namely, the visionary and more specifically, "participatory visions."[153] Participatory visions are the fifth of the seven categories of visions Elizabeth Petroff has described, and are preceded in the hierarchy by purgative visions, psychic

---

[152] "... ut sibi ostenderet filium suum Christum Dominum nostrum in cruce, sicut olim pependerat in illa; quod et sibi datum est. Ex qua visione cor eius ita amoris iaculo transfixum est, ut videretur animam ipsius compassivi doloris gladius pertransisse. Non multo post caelestium desideriorum ardore flagrans petivit a Domino sibi ostendi illam gloriam et laetitiam, in qua Mater unigeniti Filii Dei ad caelum assumpta fuerat; de quo etiam exauditus fuit. O virum ineffabilis devotionis! Quo petente vidit Christum in cruce, sicut olim eum viderat Johannes Evangelista; quo petente vidit festum et iocunditatem assumptionis Virginis gloriosae. Sicut armara et dolorosa sibi fuerat prima visio, sic nulli dubium, quin dulcis et laetabunda ei fuerit visio secunda. Utraque haec visio ita excellens fuit, quod aspiciens prius sanus, factus fuit ex visione infirmus, quia mortale corpus tam excellentissimas visiones ferre non potuit. Infirmatus itaque dixit culpam suam Priori suo, confitens se maximum peccatum perpetrasse in eo, quod petierit sibi misero et indigno talia ostendi. Et post paucos dies plenus bonis operibus spiritum Deo reddens signis evidentibus coruscavit. Inter quae unum memoriale fuit, quod quaedam magna persona lepra infecta, voto emisso de suo sepulcro visitando, in momento curata fuit." VF 2,19 (213,88–214,108). Cf. Hen. Tract. 6 (119,10–12).

[153] On participatory visions, see Elizabeth Alvilda Petroff, *Medieval Women's Visionary Literature* (Oxford, 1986), 3–20.

visions, doctrinal visions, and devotional visions, whereas the last two categories are unitive or erotic visions and visions of cosmic ordering.[154] If participatory visions are a "higher" form of mystical experience than devotional visions, then neither Agnes' nor Hartmut's vision can properly be considered as a form of Passion *devotion*; they have transcended the level of devotion, even if the visions remain of the Passion of Christ.

In taking Passion devotion as the object of analysis, the cultural historian is faced straight away with the problem of what constitutes both 'devotion' and 'Christ's Passion'. Richard Kieckhefer has claimed that "because it is so diffuse, devotional religion eludes precise definition,"[155] categorizing devotion as the intermediate phenomenon between liturgical exercises and contemplative piety. Medieval devotions, Kieckhefer explains, "are hard to pin down. Unlike liturgy and contemplation, devotions are defined more by their objects than by their form: a devotion is usually to a particular saint, or to the Virgin, or to the suffering Christ, or to the Eucharist, or to some other object. In any case, their importance in late medieval Christendom is paramount."[156] Kieckhefer allows for both personal and social devotions, but with the vagueness of the definition, it is rather easy to view devotion as simply a "warm fuzzy spiritual feeling" directed to a particular object.[157]

Medieval authors, on the other hand, did give definitions of devotion, and even if they remained somewhat amorphous, they nevertheless offer an instructive point of departure. In the *Secunda Secundae* of his *Summa Theologiae*, Thomas Aquinas treated devotion in question 82, which followed question 81, *De religione*. For Thomas, devotion "seems to be nothing other than a certain will to give oneself promptly to those things that pertain to the service of God."[158] Thomas continued by categorizing devotion as a "religious act" (*actus*

---

[154] *Ibid.*, 6.
[155] Kieckhefer, "Major Currents in Late Medieval Devotion," 76; *cf.* R.N. Swanson, "Passion and Practice: The Social and Ecclesiastical Implications of Passion Devotion in the Late Middle Ages," in *The Broken Body*, 1–30.
[156] *Ibid.*
[157] See also Henk van Os, *Gebed in Schoonheid. Schatten van privé-devotie in Europa, 1300–1500* (Amsterdam, 1994), 54 and 61.
[158] "Unde devotio nihil aliud esse videtur quam voluntas quaedam prompte tradendi se ad ea quae pertinent ad Dei famulatum." *STh* II/II q. 82, art. 1, resp. (1837b.2–5).

religionis),[159] caused by God primarily, but also stimulated by human action, aroused namely in meditation and contemplation,[160] leading to joy and love.[161] As a religious act, devotion was part of natural righteousness, for Thomas defined *religio* drawing on Cicero, Augustine, and Isidore of Seville, as a moral virtue, distinct from the theological or intellectual virtues,[162] which pertains to the worship of God.[163]

The *Secunda Secundae* circulated widely in the later Middle Ages,[164] and Jordan drew heavily upon Thomas for his *Tractatus de virtutibus et vitiis*, incorporated within his first major collection of sermons, the *Opus Postillarum*, completed after 1365. After defining *religio* as a moral virtue, that part of natural righteousness (*iustitia naturalis*) which pertains to the worship of God,[165] Jordan then entered into a discussion of the various religious acts, which he listed as devotion, prayer, supplication, sacrifice, offering, vows, oaths, swearing, and divine praise.[166] Jordan defined devotion as an act of religion:

> Devotion is our stimulus for doing those things that pertain to divine worship ... the cause, however, of devotion is meditation or contemplation, namely, to the extent that through meditation humans come to know that they give themselves to divine obedience, which stems from the consideration of divine goodness, wherefore love is aroused; and from the consideration of our defects, wherefore presumption is excluded. The effect of devotion, however, is spiritual joy, in so far as devotion proceeds from the consideration of divine goodness.[167]

Though still somewhat unclear on what precisely the phenomenon of devotion entails, Jordan's definition, which was by no means unique

---

[159] *STh* II/II q. 82, prol. (1837a.2–4); *cf. STh* II/II q. 82, art. 2, resp. (1838a.24–31).
[160] *STh* II/II q. 82, art. 3, resp. (1838b.48–1839a.13).
[161] *STh* II/II q. 82, art. 4, resp. (1839b.50–184031).
[162] *STh* II/II q. 81, art. 5, ad tertium (1834a.11–13).
[163] *STh* II/II q. 81 (1829a.45–1836b.41); see also Appendix A.3.
[164] See L.E. Boyle, O.P., "The *Summa Confessorum* of John of Freiburg and the Popularization of the Moral Teaching of St. Thomas and of some of his Contemporaries," in *St. Thomas Aquinas, 1274–1974. Commemorative Studies*, 2 vols., ed. Etienne Gilson et al. (Toronto, 1974), 2:245–286.
[165] Jor. *OP-B*, fol. 185[rb–va].
[166] Jordan lists the following, giving definitions of each: *devotio, oratio, obsecratio, sacrificia, oblatio, votum, iuramentum, adjuratio*, and *laus divina*. Jor. *OP-B*, fol. 185[va]–186[va].
[167] "Devotio est prompta nostra faciendi ea que ad divinum cultum pertinet... devotionis autem causa est meditatio vel contemplatio, in quantum scilicet per meditationem homo concipit quod se tradat divino obsequio, quod sit ex consideratione divine bonitatis, unde excitatur dilectio; et ex consideratione nostri defectus, unde excluditur presumptio. Effectus vero devotionis est spiritualis letitia, in quantum devotio ex consideratione divine bonitatis procedit." Jor. *OP-B*, fol. 185[v].

in the later Middle Ages, of devotion as a religious act associated with natural righteousness, consisting of the volitional attitude by which humans more promptly perform their duties pertaining to the worship of God, places devotion more squarely within medieval categories than modern definitions, and assumptions, of what devotion is or was, situating it somewhere on the scale between customary participation in the liturgy, and the extremes of contemplative piety. It is also of importance here to note that Jordan's definition of devotion as resulting from meditation or contemplation leads to the understanding of what humans owe God, which Jordan gave as a definition of *religio* in his *Expositio Orationis Dominice; religio* is that moral virtue that "pays back" to God what humans owe, namely worship. In the context of devotion, meditation reveals that which humans owe God, and results in the love of God.

Yet if devotion as a religious phenomenon is somewhat slippery, even using medieval definitions, the 'Passion of Christ' is as well when the two terms become linked. Meditation on the Passion narrative is perhaps the prototype for Passion devotion,[168] but the Passion of Christ, as the central event of the Christian religion, far exceeded the boundaries of the Passion text. The eucharist was the body of Christ continually being sacrificed by the Church, which itself was the mystical body of Christ. The distinction between eucharistic devotion and Passion devotion becomes increasingly blurred when we take into account the emphasis on the real presence throughout the high and later Middle Ages. Already in the mid-eleventh century, Lanfranc of Bec stridently defended the equation of Christ's body on the cross with Christ's body on the altar,[169] and in the later fifteenth century Gabriel Biel in his *Canonis Missae Expositio*, which consists of lectures to theology students at the University of Tübingen during the years 1484–1488, exhorted the faithful to meditate upon the Passion of Christ at the elevation of the host and especially on the elevation of Christ on the cross, hung between two thieves.[170] If

---

[168] For the concept of prototypes, see G. Lakoff, *Women, Fire and Dangerous Things*, 58–67, and *passim*.

[169] See Lanf. *Cor.* 15 (425B–C). For Lanfranc's place in biblical studies, see Jean Châtillon, "La Bible dans les écoles du XIIe siècle," in *Le Moyen Age et la Bible*, ed. Pierre Riché and Guy Lobrichon (Paris, 1984), 163–197.

[170] Biel *Exp.* 50M (2: 281). See also Eamon Duffy, *The Stripping of the Altars. Traditional Religion in England c. 1400–c. 1580* (New Haven, 1992), 91–130; and Zumkeller's discussion of Hermann of Schildesche's *Breviloquium de expositione missae*,

eucharistic devotion needs to be considered part of Passion devotion, then Passion devotion can be taken to include such "para-Passion" religious phenomena as the celebrations of *Corpus Christi*, devotion to the Holy Cross and indeed Marian devotion as well, for as the later fourteenth-century Augustinian Antonius Rampegolus explained in his *Figure Bibliorum*, Mary was the book in which the prophets first depicted the Passion of Christ.[171] Indeed, the Christian life itself was often interpreted as an imitation of Christ's Passion, and not only for those who desired a more literal *imitatio Christi*; in his *Hortulus rosarum* Thomas a Kempis wrote: "No one is found so good and devout, that some burden and weight does not fall on them. When, therefore, you are in tribulation and heaviness of heart, then you are with Christ on the cross;"[172] and in his *Meditationes de Passione Christi* Jordan repeated the frequently quoted statement attributed to Augustine, that "the entire life of any Christian, if he lives according to the Gospel, is a certain cross or martyrdom."[173] Indeed, as Kieckhefer put it: "Devotion to the passion was ubiquitous in late medieval piety."[174]

Passion discourse, whether found in accounts of visions, treatises on the life and Passion of Christ, meditations, sermons on the Passion, or expositions of the Mass, was polyvalent and cannot be reduced to a specific manifestation of late medieval religion. Devotion to the Passion was simultaneously as individualized and internalized as it was institutionalized and socialized.[175] The single unifying element among experiences and expressions of the Passion in the later Middle

---

in which Hermann portrayed the mass as offering daily contact with Christ's Passion; Zumkeller, *Schrifttum*, 15–16, and 154–155.

[171] "... fuit ibi Maria in qua scribitur tanquam in libro, quia beata virgo fuit liber in quo prius Prophete depinxerunt passionem Christi..." Ant.Ramp. *FB*, fol. 74vb.

[172] "Nemo inuenitur tam bonus et deuotus, cui non occurit aliquid oneris et grauitatis. Cum ergo fueris in tribulatione et cordis merore, tunc es cum Ihesu in cruce." Thom.Kemp. *Hort.* 7 (353,154–165); *cf.*: "Audi fili. Quando es in tribulatione et cordis merore, tunc es cum Ihesu in cruce et quando iterum consolaris in deuotione et delectaris in ymnis et canticis diuinis, tunc resurgis cum Ihesu *in nouitate spiritus* et quasi a mortuis suscitaris de sepulchro." Thom.Kemp. *Vall.*, 6,166–168 (395).

[173] "... tota vita cuiuslibet christiani hominis si secundum evangelium vivat quedam crux atque martyrium sit..." Jor. *Med.* Prol., fol. 1rb.

[174] Kieckhefer, "Major Currents," 83.

[175] *Cf.* Miri Rubin, *Corpus Christi*, 357–358; and Sarah Beckwith, *Christ's Body. Identity, Culture and Society in Late Medieval Writings* (London, 1993), 76.

Ages was the Passion text, which served as the basis for a variety of "Passion hermeneutics"; the account of Christ's Passion—not limited to the text of the Gospels—was the classic text of the Christian tradition, whereby "the classical epitomizes a general characteristic of historical being: preservation amid the ruins of time. The general nature of tradition is such that only the part of the past that is not past offers the possibility of historical knowledge."[176] Medieval authors and artists sought to make the Passion present reality by and in the performance of the Passion in representation and imitation,[177] thereby effecting a "normative centering" of late medieval religion.[178]

In the later Middle Ages, reading the Passion went far beyond the Passion text as related in the Gospels. Authors drew from Old Testament prophecy to provide exegetically the graphic details of Christ's Passion that the Gospels omitted; they turned to prophecy to describe what "must have happened," and to portray the scenes of the Passion more forcefully.[179] Thus the anonymous author of the mid-fourteenth century vernacular tract, *Christi Leiden in einer Vision geschaut* described one scene received in a vision as follows:

> Then they seized Christ with raving violent devilish gesticulations, one grasped his hair, a second his clothes, a third his beard. These three were as foul hounds as ever might cling to him... and so he was pulled away, with violent wild raving abandon, with fierce blows of mailed hands and fists upon his neck and between his shoulders, on his back, on his head, across his cheeks, on his throat, on his breast...

---

[176] Gadamer, *Truth and Method*, 2nd rev. ed., trans. Joel Weinsheimer and Donald G. Marshall (New York, 1993), 289; see also introduction to Appendix F.

[177] On the performance of texts, see Gadamer, *Truth and Method*, 399. Gadamer argued that representation and imitation "... are not merely a repetition, a copy, but knowledge of the essence. Because they are not merely repetition, but a 'bringing forth,' they imply a spectator as well. They contain in themselves an essential relation to everyone for whom the representation exists. Indeed, one can say even more: the presentation of the essence, far from being a mere imitation, is necessarily revelatory." Gadamer, *Truth and Method*, 114–115. See also Morrison, *The Mimetic Tradition*; Paul Ricoeur, *Time and Narrative*, v. 1, *passim*; and Michael Camille, "Mimetic Identification and Passion Devotion in the Later Middle Ages: A Double-sided Panel by Meister Franke," in *The Broken Body*, 183–210.

[178] For the concept of normative centering, see the important article by Berndt Hamm, "Normative Centering in the Fifteenth and Sixteenth Centuries: Observations on Religiosity, Theology, and Iconology," *JEMH* 3 (!999), 307–354.

[179] See F.P. Pickering, *Literatur und darstellende Kunst im Mittelalter* (Berlin, 1966); idem, "The Gothic image of Christ. The sources of medieval representations of the crucifixion," in Pickering, *Essays on Medieval German Literature and Iconography* (Cambridge, 1980); J. Marrow, *Passion Iconography*.

> They tore his hair from his head so that the locks lay strewn around on the ground; one pulled him one way by the hair, the other pulled him back by the beard ... So they dragged him down from the Mount ... And they hauled him to the gate of the town in such a way that he never set foot properly on the ground ... until they brought him into Annas' house.[180]

F. Pickering notes that in this treatise, "there are no pauses in the narrative account for prayers or compassionate outpourings, or for reflections on the significance for mankind of these sufferings."[181] Such a treatise causes one to ask what the function of such description might have been; it appears as graphic simply for the sake of impression and thus falls outside the realm of devotion as defined by Thomas and Jordan, as the disposition of the will to perform promptly those acts pertaining to the worship of God. It certainly falls within the realm of experiences and expressions of the Passion, but whether it is legitimately categorized in historical terms as 'devotional' is another question, much as the two visions recounted above, namely those of Agnes and Hartmut. The visions of Agnes and Hartmut may very well fall beyond the category of 'Passion devotion,' but even so, their comparison offers a useful corrective to viewing devotion to the Passion as signifying an increase in individualized, personal, lay piety.

The differences between Agnes' and Hartmut's visions are as striking as are the similarities. Agnes' vision gives a descriptive account of Christ's Passion, whereas Hartmut simply asked to see Christ on the cross as the historical event, without describing what he saw. Agnes' vision is only of the Passion, whereas Hartmut asked for a second vision of the Assumption. Agnes simply could not live any longer after her vision, whereas Hartmut repented of his sin in asking for such a vision, and then returned his spirit to God, but continued serving as an efficacious source of divine power. Hartmut, moreover, asked for his vision, whereas Agnes was granted hers. What is, however, the sharpest distinction between these two visions is one of function. In Jordan's account Hartmut confessed his *sin* in

---

[180] As quoted by Pickering, "The Gothic Image of Christ," 3. Pickering is following the edition and translation of Robert Priebsch, *Christi Leiden in einer Vision geschaut*, (Heidelberg 1936), 32f. Pickering himself published an edition of this work, *Christi Leiden in einer Vision geschaut ... A critical account of the published and unpublished manuscripts, with an edition based on the text of Ms. Bernkastel-Cues 115* (Manchester, 1952).

[181] Pickering, "The Gothic Image of Christ," 3.

having asked for such a vision. Hartmut, Jordan tells us, was a priest completely devoted to God.[182] He came to recognize and to confess that he had committed a great sin (*confitens se maximum peccatum perpetrasse*) in having asked for such visions, thus showing his devotion even more so by submitting to the institutionalized order. It should also be noted that Jordan used this *exemplum* not as a model for devotion, even though Jordan extolled Hartmut's devotion, nor for the imitation of the Passion. Jordan told of Hartmut as an example of the efficacy of prayer, and prayer was a specific religious act distinct from devotion according to Jordan's *Tractatus de virtutibus et vitiis*. The laudatory and exemplary aspect of Hartmut's vision was not his vision as such, but his trust in the promise of John 16:23: *Whatever you ask the Father in my name will be given to you*, as Jordan makes clear when he explained that the examples given illustrate "that whatever a devout man asks from God with persistence, he will eventually obtain with the desired effect, if, namely, it contributes to his salvation."[183] Whereas Sister Katherine reported Agnes' vision as an example of devotion for her community, Jordan used his narrative of Hartmut's vision to stress the efficacy of prayer placed in context of the established ecclesiastical structures. Jordan subordinated the power of the visionary to the power of penance. In his *Opus Jor*, Jordan claimed:

> If Mary would come to you in her very person and give you with her own hand the body of her most sweet son, which nevertheless would be beyond the form of all human consolation, I say to you, if you are a sinner, one good confession is worth more to you than all those benefits conferred by the Virgin Mary. Further I say, if you were to die in the bosom of mother Mary with mortal sin, nevertheless the power of all demons would prevail against you.[184]

Hartmut's devotion to the Passion had to be controlled by subjugating it to the institution of confession, and only if Judas had

---

[182] *VF* 2,19 (213,84–85).

[183] "Ex quibus exemplis patet, quod quidquid devotus homo cum instantia petit a Deo, finaliter obtinet cum desiderato effectu, si tamen est ad salutem." *VF* 2,19 (214,109–111).

[184] "Item, si Maria veniret ad te in persona propria ... te manu propria tibi daret corpus sui dulcissimi filii quod tamen esset utque supra modum omnium hominum solacium, dico tibi si peccator es plus valet tibi una bona confessio quam omnia illa beneficia inpensa a virgine Maria ... Item dico si morieris in sinu matris Marie cum peccata mortali, potestas tamen demonium omnium prevaleret in te ... " Jor. *OJ* sermo 90, fol. 160vb.

confessed and done penance for his sin, he would have been saved, for just as no sin is so great that it surpasses God's mercy, even the sin of betraying Christ, so is one mortal sin so great that Mary herself is of no avail. The Passion of Christ itself offers the form of penance for the Christian life.[185] The body of Christ broken on the altar was equated with the body of Christ as the Church, which offered the only means of salvation.

If the crucified Christ was an open book to be read, it was the task of the doctors and pastors of the Church to offer and enforce the proper interpretation, as Bruno of Segni made clear. Among the multifarious expression, experience, and exegesis of the Passion in the later Middle Ages, authors such as Jordan and Ludolph of Saxony strove to ensure that the Passion was appropriately understood, namely, as the source for and as the example of living the Christian life, consisting of rendering unto God what is God's, for as Ludolph put it, echoing Thomas Aquinas, imitating the Passion of Christ "is the highest and perfect religion of the perfect. This is the rule and exemplar of the perfection of all life and virtue, namely, to imitate Christ in his Passion and death."[186] To grasp the driving force of devotion to the Passion in the later Middle Ages, we must seek its source: the pastoral endeavor to inculcate the moral virtue of religion.

B. *Teaching and Preaching the Passion*

The ubiquity of Passion discourse in the later Middle Ages necessitates the attempt to discern the contours of devotion to the Passion as a specific function of such discourse when we define *devotio* in terms of the medieval categories of religious acts. Analyzing how Christ's Passion was taught and the function of the Passion within such teaching can help to demarcate devotion to the Passion as a distinct religious phenomenon of the polysemous expressions and

---

[185] "... nos cum Christo corporaliter mortuo debemus spiritualiter esse mortui peccato ... Et quia ista mortificatio habet fieri per penitentiam, ideo in morte Christi data est nobis et ostensa forma penitentie nostre." Jor. *OJ* sermo 179, fol. 280vb.

[186] "... nam imitatio Christi est summa et perfecta religio perfecti. Haec est regula et exemplar perfectionis omnis vitae et virtutis, scilicet Christum imitari in Passione, et in morte." *VC*, II.58.11 (IV, 465); "Perfectio religionis maxime consistit in imitatione Christi..." Thomas Aquinas, *STh* II/II q. 186, art. 5, s.c. (2362b,24–25); *cf.* Constable, *Three Studies*, 238.

representations of a "Passion-saturated" late medieval culture. Thus I turn to four case studies to illustrate the various ways in which the Passion of Christ was presented in the texts of late medieval pastoral theology, before turning to an analysis of late medieval Passion hermeneutics.

i. *Ons heren passie*
Manuscript Me.IV.3 in the University Library at Tübingen consists of three parts. Written in an Amsterdam dialect, the first consists of a rhymed version of the Gospel Passion account, which is given the title, *Ons heren passie*, together with a rhymed treatise on the Virgin Mary. The second part is a treatise on the last judgment, while the third is a short excerpt of Gregory the Great's *Moralia in Iob*. The first two parts of the manuscript were written around the mid-fifteenth century, while the third part was a sixteenth-century addition, written in the hand of a sister from the Saint Gertrude cloister in Amsterdam.[187] Saint Gertrude's was originally a cloister of the second Order of St. Francis, but between 1450 and 1456 became transferred to the Order of Regular Canonesses of St. Augustine.[188] The manuscript was in the possession of St. Gertrude's at least by the early sixteenth century, if not before, and therefore, the manuscript is known as the Tübingen Saint Gertrude Manuscript.[189]

Ons heren passie, which forms a textual and codicological unity with the treatises on Mary and the Last Judgment, follows the Passion narrative compiled from all four Evangelists. In the preface the author states that she or he is putting the Passion story into rhyme to teach the simple people, and because a previous attempt to have done so is less than satisfactory.[190] The "little book" is intended as a help, "for those who cannot understand Latin, and also for those who do not know the contents of the Gospels; for these I want to offer material for them to think about."[191] The goal is to learn the story by

---

[187] See *TSG* (9–42, 139–142).
[188] *TSG* (141).
[189] *TSG* (9 and 38).
[190] *TSG* (49,15–34). On the didactic function of rhyme, see Wenzel, *Hören und Sehen*, 89–94.
[191] "Alleen so set ic hier die zaec/Waer om dat ic dit boexken maec/Dat is dat het sel hulplic sijn/Die gheen die niet verstaen latijn/End oec dystori niet en wisten/Na inhout der ewangelisten/Dien wil ic hier materi scencken/Dat si wat hebben op te deyncken." *TSG* (50,55–62).

heart, especially for those who cannot read.[192] Although the manuscript was in the possession of St. Gertrude's in the early sixteenth century, the editors suggest that the originally intended audience was not monastic.[193] The *simpel luden* for whom the book was made were most likely lay citizens in or around Amsterdam.

Ons heren passie is not, however, only a rhymed version of the Gospels. It is designed to teach the reader, or the listener, the Passion narrative and to encourage the audience to consider well the pain Jesus suffered.[194] Thus the author interrupts the narrative account at times to offer special points of consideration, which in the margin of the manuscript are labeled 'glosses'. At five scenes of the Passion we find such glosses: the first appears with Jesus' sweating blood; the second, as Jesus arrived at Pilate's house, sent from Caiphas; the third is the *Ecce Homo* scene; the crucifixion itself is the fourth, which is also the longest of the glosses, and the last gloss treats the suffering of Mary as a witness to her son's Passion.[195] At each point in the narrative, the author offers pause and exhorts the audience to consider especially the given scene, and how it applies to themselves. Thus at the presentation of Christ, the author implores the audience to consider their sweet God, covered with slimy blood and gore,[196] and then rhetorically asks and instructs, "How can you hold back your tears gazing on this wretched spectacle? Consider well that you are a cause of this great tragedy!"[197] The audience is exhorted not only to learn the text of the Passion, but also to imagine the historical event, and the author's intent is to offer aide and instruction for such image formation, as is stated explicitly to begin the gloss on the crucifixion itself.[198] After finishing the Passion narrative, the author emphasizes the great love that Jesus showed in his Passion, leaving humans an example to follow: Christians are to learn to suffer with Christ so they might reign with Christ in heaven.[199]

---

[192] *TSG* (50,63–66).
[193] *TSG* (11).
[194] *TSG* (50,67–68).
[195] The glosses, which I have numbered 1 through 5, are found in the text as follows according to line numbers: 1.: 237–248; 2.: 413–424; 3.: 515–530; 4.: 623–698; 5.: 757–822.
[196] *TSG* (62,517–524).
[197] "Hoe moechstu nv dijn tranen houwen/In dit ontfermelic aenscouwen/ Ghedenc doch dattu bist een zaec/Van desen groten onghemaec." *TSG* (62,525–528).
[198] *TSG* (65,623–624).
[199] *TSG* (73,895–74,932).

The author of *Ons heren passie* self-consciously gave the Passion narrative a catechetical function of instructing the audience on the Passion plot while simultaneously constructing rhetorically an intimate bond between the events of the Passion and the contemporary audience. The Passion of Christ was to evoke love and compassion in response to the love Christ exhibited. Adopting the Passion as the exemplar for the Christian life did not, however, entail a literal *imitatio Christi*. By suffering with Christ in this life, by following his example, and by loving the Passion of Christ, while bearing in mind the extent to which human sin is the cause of Christ's sufferings, the audience of the text was offered the hope thereby of reigning with Christ in eternal life.

The function of the Passion is emphasized when *Ons heren passie* is read together as originally composed with the treatises on Mary and the Last Judgment. The Last Judgment is to serve as a constant reminder that no one knows how much time is left, as well as to invoke fear. Still written in rhyme, the treatise is of a more learned character and the author explicitly mentions that she or he will follow the teachings of Thomas Aquinas.[200] Textually, codicologically, and doctrinally, the treatise on Mary stands between the fear of the Last Judgment and the hope of salvation offered by the Passion; Mary's divinity is so endless that no sinner is so bad that he cannot find mercy with Mary, making Mary's divinity and mercy analogous to that of God the Father as portrayed by Jordan.[201] In short, the Tübingen St. Gertrude's Manuscript is a catechetical summation of the Christian life designed for the unlettered and unlearned laity. While the Passion is central, *Ons heren passie* can only be extracted artificially from the more intricate web of late medieval pastoral theology. Moreover, we find the same function of the Passion in late medieval *Pastoralia*, namely, homiletical and exegetical handbooks, which often derived from mendicant *studia*, designed to provide the 'raw material' for the preaching of the Passion to the laity.

ii. *Fasciculus Morum*

Shortly after 1300 an anonymous Franciscan composed a *summa* of the virtues and vices, known as the *Fasciculus Morum*.[202] The work is

---

[200] *TSG* (88,19–40). The editors do not identify any of the references.
[201] *TSG* (74,1–20); *cf.* note 145 above.
[202] See Siegfried Wenzel, *Verses in Sermons. "Fasciculus Morum" and Its Middle English Poems* (Cambridge, Mass., 1978).

extant in twenty-eight manuscripts, three of which date from the late fourteenth century, with the rest dated in the fifteenth. In the short prologue to the work, the author states that at the request of his co-religious, he had "collected from various treatises and woven together as well as I could a small and unpretentious bundle of vices and virtues, to comfort you and to help the unlettered."[203] He did so for the purpose of providing material for preaching, in keeping with the *Rule* of St. Francis.[204] Organized in seven parts according to the seven chief vices and their opposing virtues, the *Fasciculus Morum* served as an encyclopedia of moral, pastoral theology, which could be adapted to suit the individual needs of preachers, as is indicated by the four distinct redactions in which the text has survived.

In the third section, "On Envy" (*De Invidia*), there is a rather extensive treatment of Christ's Passion. Envy "is the most precious daughter of the devil because she follows his footsteps by hindering good and promoting evil."[205] The virtue set in opposition to envy is charity, since charity "in every respect opposes wicked Envy with its followers and goes against it. For as much as Envy delights in evil, so much does Charity delight in good. And thus it is a most valiant fighter against Envy and our ancient foes, whom it continually confronts, combats, overthrows, and defeats."[206] Charity, which "consists and is established in the love of God and the love of our neighbor, so that God is loved for his own sake and for our need, and our neighbor for the sake of God's love,"[207] is found in the love Christ showed in his incarnation and in his Passion. Christ's Passion, "which he suffered for us, will lead us back to perfect love,"[208] which was

---

[203] "... ad vestram peticionem fasciculum pauperculum viciorum et virtutum ad vestrum solacium et utilitatem simplicium e diversis tractatibus collegi et hic modulo meo inserui." *FM* Prol. (30,5–7; trans. Wenzel, 31).

[204] *FM* I.i.(32,1–3).

[205] "... de invidia, que filia diaboli est karissima sua vestigia imitando, scilicet bonum impediendo et malum promovendo." *FM* III.i. (148,1–3; trans. Wenzel, 149).

[206] "[N]unc ad virtutem caritatis est advertendum, que in omnibus pessime invidie cum suis sequacibus se obicit et contrariatur. Nam quantum invidia ista in malis, tantum ista caritas in bonis delectatur. Et ideo pugil fortissimus contra illam et hostes antiquos, quos constanter aggreditur, pugnat, prosternit, et devincit." *FM* III.vi. (174,1–5; trans. Wenzel, 175).

[207] "... caritas consistit et stabilitur in dileccione Dei et proximi, ita ut Deus ipse diligatur propter se et propter nostram necessitatem, et proximus propter amorem suum..." *FM* III.vii (176,1–3; trans. Wenzel, 177).

[208] "Ista ergo passio quam pro nobis sustinuit ad perfectam caritatem reducet." *FM* III.x (200,16–17; trans. Wenzel, 201).

the author's purpose in discussing the Passion, namely, to show how charity is to be recovered "when it has been driven away and is almost completely lost."[209] Therefore, the author explains, "I will treat of it as follows: first, why he shed his blood; second, on what day, how, and where he suffered; third, at what hour, what age, and what time; fourth, by whom he was accused and how much he was taunted; and fifth, of the mystery and power of his cross."[210] The treatment of envy concludes, after the discussion of the Passion, by expositing Christ's advent, life, death, resurrection, and ascension, followed by the sending of the Holy Spirit and the blessed Trinity.

According to the author of *Fasciculus Morum*, there are five reasons that Christ shed his blood for humans: first, as "a help to sinners and a remedy against our spiritual enemies and fleshly sins;"[211] second, to "draw us to his love and charity;"[212] third, to "call back the fugitives and exiles to the land of peace;"[213] fourth, to "wash us from the sickness of guilt;"[214] and finally to "exclude the devil from purchasing us."[215] Christ purchased the souls of the faithful "through his bitter and terrible death,"[216] and thus offered his body as a charter:

> As a result, we are his children and not the devil's. On that exchange he left a most reliable charter for us. Notice that a charter that is written in blood carries with it extreme reliability and produces much admiration. Just such a charter did Christ write for us on the cross when he ... stretched out his blessed body, as a parchment-maker can

---

[209] "[R]estat ergo iam quarto et ultimo videre quomodo hec caritas sic elongata et quasi deper<d>ita poterit inveniri et recuperari." *FM* III.x (200,1–2; trans. Wenzel, 201).

[210] "De qua sic intendo procedere, scilicet primo quare sanguinem suum fudit; secundo quo die passus est, et quomodo, et ubi; tercio qua hora, qua etate, et quo tempore; quarto de quibus accusabatur et quociens illusus; quinto de misterio et virtute crucis sue." *FM* III.x (200,17–20; trans. Wenzel, 201).

[211] "... primo sanguinem suum fudit ut esset peccatoribus in auxilium et remedium contra hostes spirituales et peccata temporalia carnalia." *FM* III.x (200,21–23; trans. Wenzel, 201).

[212] "Secundo, Christus passus est et sanguinem eius fudit pro nobis, ut nos ad eius amorem et caritatem alliceret." *FM* III.x (204,83–84; trans. Wenzel, 205).

[213] "Tercio ... ut profugos et exules ad terram pacis revocaret." *FM* III.x (206,128–129; trans. Wenzel, 207).

[214] "Quarto ... ut nos a morbo culpe lavaret." *FM* III.x (206,146; trans. Wenzel, 207).

[215] "Quinto ... ut diabolum ab empcione nostra excluderet." *FM* III.x (212,244–245; trans. Wenzel, 213).

[216] "... ut sic per suam mortem amaram et diram de dura et crudeli diaboli potestate nos liberaret." *FM* III.x (212,249–250).

526   CHAPTER FIVE

> be seen to spread a hide in the sun. In this way Christ, when his hands and feet were nailed to the cross, offered his body like a charter to be written on. The nails in his hands were used as a quill, and his precious blood as ink. And thus, with this charter he restored to us our heritage that we had lost...[217]

Hence, Christ shedding his blood in his Passion "leads the sinner to the sorrow of contrition, to the shame of confession, and to the labor of satisfaction."[218]

The *Fasciculus Morum* not only holds up Christ's Passion as a stimulus to love and compassion, and as the means by which sinners are freed from the snares of the devil, but also as an example to be followed. In the section on the hour, age, and time of Christ's Passion, the author notes that Christ chose the season of Lent in which to do so, when lust, in all animals, is raging. Thus,

> He ordained this season before any other for his Passion so that by his example we might resist our various natural desires through penance. For the Apostle says: "Every action of Christ serves for our instruction." Wherefore it is said in Exodus 25: "Look and do according to the pattern that was shown you on the mount." ... a faithful person should meditate in faith and loving memory on the shedding of Christ's blood and thereby become armed and stirred to do battle against the devil, the world, and the flesh.[219]

---

[217] "Et per consequens, sui sumus et non diaboli filii. Super quod cartam firmissimam nobis reliquit. Et nota quod carta conscripta sanguine vehementer solet importare securitatem et magnam <generare> admiracionem; set huiusmodi carta[m] scripsit nobis in cruce quando ... corpus suum benedictum extendit, sicut pergamenarius ad solem pergamenum explicare videtur. Sic Christus manibus et pedibus in cruce affixus corpus suum ad cartam scribendam exposuit; clav<o>s eciam in manibus habuit pro calamo, sanguinem preciosum pro encausto. Per hanc cartam hereditatem amissam nobis restituit..." *FM* III.x (212,251–259; trans. Wenzel, 213). For the image of Christ's Passion as a legal charter, see Rubin, *Corpus Christi*, 306–308.

[218] "Unde notandum quod maximum remedium est eius sanguinis effusio eo quod inducit peccatorem ad dolorem contricionis, ad pudorem confessionis, et ad laborem satisfactionis." *FM* III.x (200,23–25; trans. Wenzel, 201).

[219] "Circa vero tempus in quo Christus passus est, sciendum quod fuit in Quadragesima, in qua ut communiter omnia animalia ad suam voluptatem magis excitantur. Et ideo illud tempus magis ordinavit quam aliud pro sua passione, ut sic nos exemplo sui voluptatibus naturalibus et diversis per penitenciam resistamus. Dicit enim Apostolus: 'Omnis Christi actio nostra est instructio.' Et ideo dicitur Exodi 25: 'Inspice et fac secundum exemplar quod tibi in monte monstratum est.' ... sic fidel<i>s, considerata per fidem et amantem memoriam sanguinis Christi effusione, armari debet et acui in prelium contra diabolum, mundum, et carnem." *FM* III.xii (222,71–82; trans. Wenzel, 223).

The example Christ's Passion offers, however, is not one that is intended to inspire literal imitation. It is not a private, individualized devotion to the Passion that is called for: evoking the memory of all Christ suffered, the Passion is to function as a call to penance and as a call to arms, based on leading a moral life, defined most of all by following the Ten Commandments, which the believer is to copy down word for word on the tablets of the heart:

> In order to keep these commandments, follow Christ's teaching; Exodus 25: "Look and do according to the exemplar that was shown to you." An exemplar of these commandments has been literally shown. The first was shown to Moses on Mount Sinai, and it was written on stone tablets . . . But notice: We see that sometimes an exemplar is given to a scribe so that he may transfer its contents into another volume or piece of parchment, without adding or subtracting anything, for scribes are usually not sufficiently learned to correct books by adding or subtracting anything without making mistakes. And yet, in spite of this, a faulty scribe, when he is guided by the number of lines or points in his exemplar, still sometimes skips material; he hopes that his fault will not be detected, and once he has been paid, he cares but little if his fault is found out. Thus it happens often that such a scribe is not worth his pay but rather deserves punishment, for the parchment on which he has written is completely wasted . . . In spiritual terms: All Christians are said to be scribes who must transcribe God's commandments on the tablets of their hearts . . . But I fear that many are faulty scribes, to whom a reward is promised if they copy well, but they still try to cheat and skip in the most breathtaking way . . . Therefore, because of their cheating they do not deserve a reward but very much a punishment, because they ruin the codex in which they write, that is, their heart, so that it is of no further use; and perhaps they dare to do so because their work is not at once examined through eager love of God and fervent charity. But I advise them to beware. God will not be cheated. They should therefore copy all that is written in their exemplar carefully and faithfully . . .[220]

---

[220] "Unde pro istis preceptis servandis fac doctrinam Christi, Exodi 25: 'Inspice, inquit, et fac secundum exemplar quod tibi monstratum est.' Ad litteram autem exemplar istorum preceptorum ostensum est. Primo erat in monte Syna Moysi et in tabulis paideis conscriptum . . . Set adverte: Videmus enim quod aliquando datur scriptori exemplar, ut illa que in illo continentur in aliud volumen seu pergamenum transferat nichil addendo vel minuendo, quia ut communiter scriptores non sunt scioli ad libros corrigendos, addendo vel minuendo nisi errant. Et tamen hiis non obstantibus scriptor falsus quando conducitur secundum numerum linearum aut punctorum que sunt in exemplari, adhuc tamen aliquando transiliit, quia sperat quod sua falsitas non statim deprehendetur. Set postquam sibi fuerit satisfactum, non curat tunc nisi parum quamvis eius falsitas denudetur. . . . Spiritualiter loquendo:

528   CHAPTER FIVE

The exemplar Christ offers is his Passion, which serves to combat all vice. Thus we find reference to Christ's Passion throughout the *Fasciculus Morum*. In Part Five, for example, *De Accidia*, the author treats the methods of prayer and offers the canonical hours as the model, in which one recalls the various scenes of Christ's Passion;[221] in the section on avarice, the opposing virtue is contempt of the world, which "consists in three things: memory of the Lord's passion, meditation on the certainty of death, and love of voluntary poverty,"[222] while Christ's cross is also the model and teacher of perfect poverty.[223] Moreover, those who only pretend to confess their sins, but return to them "as a dog returns to his vomit," truly "crucify the Son of God a second time,"[224] and not confessing at all could have such consequences as once happened to one man, who did not want to confess, and to whom Christ himself came and "took blood from his wound, and threw it in his face."[225] And it is patience and peace that counter wrath, for through his patience and peace Christ provided the legal charter, confirming his purchasing the kingdom of heaven from the Father for sinners, written with Christ's own blood, read and published throughout the world: "Written, read, confirmed, and given to mankind on Good Friday on Mount Calvary, publicly and openly, to last forever, in the year 5232 after the Creation of the world."[226] Although the *Fasciculus Morum* treats the Passion of

---

Omnes Christiani dicuntur scriptores et debent mandata divina transcribere in tabulis cordis... Set timeo quod multi sunt falsi scriptores, quibus merces promittitur si bene scribant, set tamen credunt decipere, unde mirabiliter transiliunt... Unde propter falsitatem eorum non sunt digni premio set pena dignissimi, quia perdunt volumen in quo scribunt, scilicet cor suum, ita quod nulli usui est aptum, et forsan hoc facere audent, quia non statim opus eorum per diligentem amorem et ferventem caritatem non examinatur. Sed consulo quod caveant. Non enim vult Deus defraudari. Et ideo omnia que scripta sunt in exemplari, diligenter et fideliter transumant." *FM* III.vii (182,121–184.156; trans. Wenzel, 183–185).

[221] *FM* V.xix (518,1–39).
[222] "Set nota quod iste mundi contemptus avaricie extirpator in tribus consistit, videlicet in dominice passionis recordacione, in certe mortis consideracione, in voluntarie puapertatis dilectione." *FM* IV.xi (382,9–11; trans. Wenzel, 383).
[223] *FM* IV.xii (386,38–388.43).
[224] "Set rogo quid dicemus de talibus qui ficte confitentur in Quadragesima et statim post Pascha 'sicut canis ad vomitum' sic et ipsi redeunt ad peccatum? Revera, quantum in illis est iterum Filium Dei crucifigunt." *FM* V.xiii (482,24–26; trans. Wenzel, 483); *cf. FM* V.xiii (26–189).
[225] "Et hic nota narracionem de illo qui eciam noluit confiteri, et quomodo sibi Christus apparuit et extraxit sanguinem de vulnere et proiecit in faciem suam." *FM* V.xiii (490,177–179; trans. Wenzel, 491).
[226] "Scripta, lecta, confirmata, et generi humano tradita feria sexta Parasceves

Christ especially in the third part on envy, the Passion is present throughout as the intertext,[227] the memory of which is the exemplar of the Christian life, calling the believer to penance and love, leading to the moral life of keeping God's commandments.[228] It was the Passion as the exemplar of the moral life that believers as faithful scribes were to copy on the tablets of their hearts and that preachers were to teach to the people.

iii. *Antonius Rampegolus'* Figure Bibliorum

A very different work from the *Fasciculus Morum* is the *Figure Bibliorum* of the Augustinian friar Antonius Rampegolus. Composed by 1384, and perhaps as early as 1354, the *Figure Bibliorum* provides a wealth of material for preaching, and was written, as Rampegolus states in his prologue, at the request of his students in the Augustinian *studium* in Naples.[229] Arranged thematically and alphabetically, *Figure Bibliorum* is first and foremost a handbook for the exegesis of biblical passages

---

supra montem Calvarie, publice et aperte, in eternum duratura, anno a creacione mundi 5<2>32." *FM* II.vii (146,95–97; trans. Wenzel, 147). The text of the entire charter is given; see *FM* II.vii (146,84–98).

[227] On the relationship between text and intertext as I have used the terms here, see Michael Riffaterre, "The Mind's Eye: Memory and Textuality," in *The New Medievalism*, ed. Marina S. Brownlee, Kevin Brownlee, and Stephen G. Nichols (Baltimore, 1991), 29–45.

[228] A similar function of the passion can be seen in English religious lyrics; see Siegfried Wenzel, *Preachers, Poets, and the Early English Lyric* (Princeton, 1986), 142–144.

[229] See Saak, "The *Figurae Bibliorum* of Antonius Rampegolus," 19–41. The problem of dating the work, especially with regard to Rampegolus' biography, has not only not been resolved, but has become more complex and mysterious. Uppsala, UB MS C 162 is dated 1384 and is explicitly attributed to Rampegolus, but Uppsala, UB MS C 121, which is of the same work, is anonymous and dated 1373. See Saak, "The *Figurae Bibliorum* of Antonius Rampegolus," 20–24. The picture is all the more complex than I originally realized, since in an inventory of the library in the convent of Monticianensis in the province of Siena, contained in the archive of the Augustinian convent of the Holy Spirit in Florence, made by the visitation under Prior General Matthew of Ascoli dated to 1360 we find the entry: "Item figure Rampigolli in tabulis rubeis." See David Gutiérrez, O.E.S.A., "De Antiquis Ordinis Eremitarum Sancti Augustini Bibliothecis," *AAug.* 23 (1954), 154–372; 220. Further, on 22 October 1357 Gregory of Rimini wrote to Master Ricardus de Ianua, giving him permission to reinstate to good standing brothers Nicelosinus, Nicolinus, and Antonius de Ianua, since they had made progress and could now sufficiently read Latin. Greg. *Reg.* 53 (52). If this Antonius de Ianua, was the same Antonius de Ianua who was granted permission to celebrate mass in Genoa in 1384, though was so as a reconfirmation of such privilege (see Saak, "The *Figurae Bibliorum*," 23), it could have been the same as our Antonius Rampegolus de Ianua. Moreover, Den Haag, KB MS 71 G 57 contains a *Liber figurarum* attributed to Rampegolus, though not in the manuscript. The *Catalogus Codicum Manuscriptorum Bibliothecae Regiae*,

pertaining to the given themes, whereby for each theme Rampegolus offers a number of different *figurae* drawn from both the Old and New Testaments, together with their exegesis *spiritualiter*. Rampegolus himself was a popular preacher, and represented the city of Genoa at the Council of Constance, at which he earned distinction by

vol. 1: *Libri Theologici* (Den Haag, 1922), 121, nr. 467, notes that this manuscript was originally two separate manuscripts, bound together in the fifteenth century. The second part of the codex is a fifteenth-century copy of the *Constitutiones novae Constantini*. Zumkeller then took the fifteenth-century dating over; Zumkeller *MSS* nr. 117 (65). However, the first part of the codex containing the *Liber figurarum* is explicitly dated 1354: "Anno domini M ccc liiij completus est iste liber in die sancti Valentini proxima die post Epyphaniam. Explicit liber figurarum utilis et perfectus non omnino rudibus sed pro maiori suo ingenio profectis, habens insertas quatuor centum figuras ad misticum sensum realiter redactus. Tabula de singulis figuris quovismodo placuerit habetur in consequenti approbata." Den Haag, MS 71 G 57, fol. 114[vb]. The work, lacking the prologue, is organized alphabetically by topics, and the individual *figurae* are numbered, totalling 424. It presents a rudimentary form of the text, with *figurae* that later appear in the tradition not present in this early phase, and all of the *figurae* that are present, are so in shorter form than later. This manuscript could very well represent the earliest form of Rampegolus' *Figure Bibliorum*, which would then explain how it was listed in the 1360 Siena inventory. Nevertheless, if in 1357 Rampegolus had only recently learned Latin sufficiently, it seems unlikely that he could have composed a work such as *Figure Bibliorum* already by 1354, though not impossible, especially depending on what "sufficient" entailed for Gregory and for what purposes. The 1354 version of the text is most elementary, and could be the work of a student. If 1354 can be said to be the *terminus post quem* of the composition, then whereas chronologically this would place Rampegolus sufficiently to be indeed the same Antonius de Ianua mentioned in Gregory's *Register*, it would call into question his activities at Constance. If he were only eighteen in 1354 when he began work on what would become his *Figure Bibliorum*, then he would have been seventy-eight years old when the Council of Constance opened, and eighty-six at the time of his supposed death in 1422. In itself this is not impossible, yet 4 November 1389 is a confirmed date for Rampegolus being granted permission to take the examinations required for the decree of lector (see Saak, "The *Figurae Bibliorum*," 22), placing him at an age of fifty-four when he would have begun his official teaching career. In any case, we do know that Rampegolus continued working on and revising his *Figure Bibliorum*, including adding new *figurae*. In the Cologne 1505 edition there is printed an *Excusatio Auctoris*, in which Rampegolus, apparently, notes: "Correxi ergo opusculum a capite rescribendo et quasdam figuras occurrentes addendo a quibus gratia ut dixi domini nostri Ihesu christi, nec non sanctorum doctorum a quibus iam non de paleis spicas excussisse sed de archa me fateor recepisse frumentum." *FB* (ed. Cologne, 1505) fol. 18[rb]. In the Venice, 1500 edition there is likewise an *Excusatio Auctoris*, which is clearly written by the corrector, Frater Antonius Terre Senensis, who dedicated the work to master Paulus de Spoleto; *FB* (ed. Venice, 1500) fol. 12[va]. I am currently working on a separate study of Rampegolus and his *Figurae Bibliorum* which will detail the textual tradition. For present purposes, I have here and throughout the rest of this study, relied primarily on Uppsala, UB, MS C 162, collating it with Uppsala, UB MS C 121, the Cologne 1505 edition, and the Cologne 1609 edition, the first expurgated edition.

preaching fiercely against Hus. Though Rampegolus' own life was essentially restricted to activity in Italy, his *Figure Bibliorum* became widely known. There are at least thirty-eight extant manuscripts of the work, and twenty-two printed editions, eight of which are *incunabula*, ten sixteenth-century editions, three seventeenth-century editions, and the last edition was completed in Naples in 1848. There were five Parisian editions, five as well done in Venice, two each in Strassburg, Ulm, and Cologne, and then single editions appeared in Lyon, Augsburg, Nürnberg, Milan and Antwerp.[230] In short, *Figure Bibliorum* was a late medieval "best seller."[231]

In the section *De Passione Christi*, Rampegolus treats forty-one *figurae*, of which thirteen are taken from the Pentateuch, six each from the Prophets, Psalms, and Kings, one from Joshua, one from Ecclesiasticus, and then two from Matthew and six from the Gospel of John.[232] He calls on the authority of patristic and twelfth-century authors, without referring to a single work from the thirteenth or fourteenth century, with Augustine, Leo I, Origen, Anselm, Bernard and Peter Comestor being the most frequently cited. Rampegolus' treatment of Christ's Passion follows the section *De Oratione*, and begins with the *figura* drawn from 4 Kings 2: "The chariot and charioteer of Israel." Rampegolus exposits this passage by noting that a chariot, understood as the cross and Passion of Christ, is carried by the four wheels of the four most perfect virtues: "For the first two wheels bringing Christ to the cross were charity and obedience ... the second set of wheels were patience and humility."[233] Turning then to 3 Kings 18 and Elias' ordering Achab to hitch the chariot to the

---

[230] See E.L. Saak, "The *Figurae Bibliorum*," 21–24.

[231] To call Rampegolus' *Figure Bibliorum* a "best-seller" is stretching the matter a bit. It was popular, printed more often before 1500 than any Augustinian commentary on the *Sentences*, yet compared to the real "best-sellers" it cannot be so categorized. Michael Milway has produced a most insightful study of the late medieval "best-sellers"; Milway, "Forgotten Best-Sellers From the Dawn of the Reformation," in *Continuity and Change*, 113–140. Milway gives a list of the top fifty works as well as the top fifty authors. The *Lucidarius* of Honorius Augustodunensis is number 50, with 54 printings; Johannes Sulpitius Verulanus comes in as the fiftieth most popular author, with 73 printings; see Milway, "Best-Sellers," 141–142. Milway does though mention that Rampegolus' *Figure Bibliorum* was the last book printed that qualifies as an incunable, printed by Arrivabenus in Venice on 31 December 1500; *ibid.*, 122.

[232] This list is drawn only from the specific *figurae* he treats, and is not a listing of his citations of scripture.

[233] "Per currum qui trahitur quatuor rotis, subaudi crucem et passionem Christi, quas traxerunt quatuor perfectissime virtutes. Nam prime due virtutes trahentes

horses, Rampegolus notes that "being ordered by Christ, we therefore get into the chariot... carrying the cross we follow Christ... Let us not fall away from contemplating his Passion, from the very beginning all the way to the spilling of all his blood, for then we will be saved. For so great is the protection of this blood, that no one protected thereby is able to be injured."[234]

The cross for Rampegolus served as the source of salvation. In expositing Nebuchadnezzor's dream of the tree placed in the center of the earth, recounted in Daniel 4, Rampegolus equated the tree with the cross of Christ, as did the author of the *Fasciculus Morum*.[235] For Rampegolus, the cross of Christ offered nourishment to all, just as the branches of the tree,[236] and attacked hell, seriously injuring the devil, freeing the devil's prisoners.[237] This equation of the cross with the Passion illustrates the fusion of specific objects of devotion in the later Middle Ages when devotion to the cross is distinguished from devotion to the Passion, in so far as the cross itself became a devotional object with its own feast day, *de inventione sancte crucis*.[238] Yet the cross and Christ's Passion were inseparable, for as Rampegolus explained, Christ is a book to be expounded having been placed on the lectern of the cross.

Christum ad crucem fuerunt caritas et obedientia... due rote sequentes fuerunt patientia et humilitas." Ant.Ramp. *FB*, fol. 86[vb].

[234] "Ascendamus igitur iubente Christo currum... tollentes crucem sequamur Christum... Non deficiamur contemplando eius passionem a principio usque ad effusionem totius sanguinis ipsius, et tunc salvabimur. Tanta enim est protectio huius sanguinis, quod nemo ledi potest ab eodem protectus." Ant.Ramp. *FB*, fol. 86[vb]–87[ra].

[235] "Figura Danielis 12 [*sic*; Dn. 4:7–9] ubi narratur visio sub tali forma: 'Ecce arbor in medio terre...' Spiritualiter. Per hanc arborem subaudi crucem Christ... in medio terre quod etiam ad litteram sic fuit, quia crux Christi posita erat in medio mundi, ita quod sol existens in maxima declinatione ab equinoctiali versus polum articum perpendiculariter inclinat radium super illum locum." Ant.Ramp. *FB*, fol. 88[vb]–89[ra]; *cf*.: *FM* III.xiii (230.22–56), and Pinder, *SP* III, fol. 83[ra], which will be treated in the section that follows.

[236] "Esca universorum in ea, quia parvis et magnis, ac insipientibus et perfectis, ipsa subvenit omnibus volentibus se prebet. Ista arbor habet fructus salutiferos." Ant.Ramp. *FB*, fol. 89[ra]. In the previous *figura* on Matthew 7, *Arbor bona fructus bonos facit*, Rampegolus offered the spiritual interpretation: "Crux Christi arbor bona fuit magna, lata et frondosa, nobis fructus suavitatis et satietatis tribuens, atque omnes fideles ab incursibus ferarum, id est demonum securissime defendens." Ant.Ramp. *FB*, fol. 88vb.

[237] "Et tunc virga crucis apprehensa, percussit infernum et diabolum multipliciter vulneravit, captivos suos de carcere liberavit..." Ant.Ramp. *FB*, fol. 87va.

[238] See *LA* 68 (303–311); for the cross itself as an object of devotion, see Ulrich Köpf, "Kreuz IV. Mittelalter," in *TRE* 19: 732–761.

In interpreting the figure from Isaiah 8:1, *The Lord said to me, Take a large tablet (librum grandem) and write on it in common writing*, Rampegolus offered the following exegesis:

> Before a book is fully complete, seven ordered steps are required. For first, the book is written. Second, the written book is shown. Third, it is corrected. Fourth, it is bound. Fifth, it is presented. Sixth the miniatures are added. And seventh, it is opened widely on the lectern to be read to those standing around. Spiritual interpretation: Christ the son of God is the book of the Father containing all the predestined... First, therefore, that book was written in the mind of the Father, namely, that our savior and redeemer, predestined from eternity, would suffer for us... Second, that book was made known by the disciple who betrayed him... And third, that book was corrected by Pilate... Fourth, it was bound in his feet and hands having been affixed to the cross. Fifth, that book was presented, namely, when the guard opened his side with a lance. Sixth, it was illuminated, namely, when his body pouring forth his blood was thus dyed... Finally, that book thus written, bound etc., was exposited in public, opened wide on the wood of the cross, so that anyone might read it there.[239]

He continued by explaining that there is a three-fold reading of the book that is Christ. First, one reads therein the lamentations of the Virgin, as did Simeon. The second reading is songs of rejoicing, which the saints sing. And finally, the third reading of that book is of woe, the extinction of joy, which refers to the damned, and to the joy of the Jews having been extinguished by Christ's Passion.[240]

---

[239] "Antequam liber sit plene completus, septem per ordinem requiruntur. Primum namque scribitur. Secundo scriptus manifestatur. Tertio corrigitur. Quarto ligatur. Quinto presentatur. Sexto miniatur. Septimo super pulpitum extensus et legendus astantibus ponitur. Spiritualiter. Christus dei filius est liber patris continens omnes praedestinatos... Primo igitur iste liber fuit scriptus in mente patris, scilicet praedestinatus ab eterno salvator et redemptor noster, ut pro nobis pateretur... Secundo fuit manifestatus prodente ipsum discipulo... Tertio iste liber fuit correctus a Pilato... Quarto ipse fuit ligatus in pedibus et manibus cruci affixus est. Quinto fuit presentatus, quando miles lancea latus eius aperuit. Sexto, fuit luminatus, quando, scilicet corpus eius cruore perfusum undique tinctum erat... Ultimo, liber sic scriptus, ligatus etc., expositus est sic in publico, id est in ligno crucis extensus, ut quilibet legat ibi." Ant.Ramp. *FB*, fol. 92rb-va.

[240] "Triplex autem libri scriptura tria supradicta et diversis ibidem lecta significat. Nam scripte in eo erant lamentationes virginis matris dei, quas in eodem libro Syme<on> antiquus legerat, atque virgini praedixerat, Luce secundo: *Et tuam ipsius animam pertransibit gladius.* [Lc. 2:35] Secundo scriptura dicitur carmen, quod dicitur canticum letitie. Et istud fecerunt sancti in die illa psalmi: *Hec est dies quam fecit Dominus, exultemus et letemur in ea.* [Ps. 117:24] Tertia vero scriptura fuit <vae>, quod dicitur vel sonat extinctio omnis gaudii, quod recte de potentatibus infernalibus intelligi potest, ut expositum fuit supra. Posset etiam de iudaeorum perfidia non

"Therefore," Rampegolus concludes, "if we as good scholars read in this book preserving the writings of his memory, we will perceive there the memory of our salvation."[241]

The book of Christ's Passion, read correctly, offers the way to salvation by revealing the prophetic character of the Holy Scriptures.[242] It is not, however, just anyone indiscriminately who can exposit such a book. Rampegolus was clear. The Dominicans, Franciscans, and Augustinians were especially chosen by God, having been granted the gift of understanding the scriptures, namely, the understanding of the prophetic sense of the scriptures and the knowledge of how to harmonize the Old with the New Testament.[243] Thereby, they were able to lead the people on the path of salvation, distributing to their flock the spiritual food contained in the scriptures.[244]

Rampegolus' clerical, and indeed mendicant, appropriation of reading the Passion is further seen in his treatment of the eucharist. Whereas an emphasis on elevation and seeing the host became increasingly of importance in the later Middle Ages, Rampegolus advocated a fourteenth-century *fides ex auditu*.[245] Just as the words of

---

immerito exponi, cuius letitia totaliter extincta fuit, ut satis in superioribus patet." Ant.Ramp. *FB*, fol. 92^{va-b}.

[241] "Igitur si nos velut boni scolares [*scripsi*; seculares *cod.*] legerimus in hoc libro scripturas eius memorie commendantes, percipiemus ibi nostre salutis memoriam." Ant.Ramp. *FB*, fol. 92vb.

[242] "Liber iste Christus erat, ut dictum est, sed in eo quod dicitur manus Prophete missa librum continens debet intellegi quod prophetia divinitus revelata est prophete cuius intellectus continebat Christum passurum et moriturum pro nobis." Ant.Ramp. *FB*, fol. 92va.

[243] "Ex filiis Israel, id est ex populo Christiano, prepositus Christi, id est spiritus sanctus, elegit tres pueros, id est tres ordines, scilicet predicatorum, minorum et heremitarum sancti Augustini... ideo Dominus dedit illis donum intellectus sacre scripture, didicerunt enim linguam chaldaicam, id est sensum prophetarum et legis, ut sciant optime concordare antiqua novis, et populum viam docere salutis." Ant.Ramp. *FB*, fol. 108^{r-v}; *cf.* Saak, "The *Figurae Bibliorum*," 33.

[244] Saak, "The *Figurae Bibliorum*," 29–36.

[245] "Certitudo istius sacramenti pro statu vie solum fide habetur, que per auditum solum est et de experientia nichil habet, quia non habet fides meritum ubi humana ratio prebet experimentum. Unde in confessione huius sacramenti solum percipitur per auditum; omnes alii sensus a deceptione immunes non sunt. Cum enim dicitur *hoc est corpus meum*, hic non decipiuntur aures, quia audiuntur quod illud sit verum corpus Christi, sed bene decipiuntur oculi, gustus, tactus et odoratus." Ant.Ramp. *FB*, fol. 19vb. The term *fides ex auditu* is a formulation that is particularly associated with Luther and Reformation theology. See Ernst Bizer, *Fides ex auditu: Eine Untersuchung über die Entdeckung der Gerechtigkeit Gottes durch Martin Luther*, 3rd rev. ed. (Neukirchen-Vluyn, 1966); and Euan Cameron, *The European Reformation* (Oxford, 1991), 117–120. For the emphasis on sight, see Bynum, *Holy Feast and Holy*

the preacher were to exposit the book of Christ's Passion, so were the words of the priest the means by which the eucharist received its efficacy and was made known, which was to be consumed keeping ever in mind what Christ suffered *pro nobis*.[246] The body of Christ was the soul's food,[247] as well as the book, that when placed upon the lectern of the cross, provided the spiritual food that was to be distributed by the words of the preacher, offering nourishment simultaneously with calling sinners to penance and to arms in the fight against the devil.[248] The penitential state was a city of peace and justice, since "from penance man is justified."[249] And the Passion of Christ was the chariot of Israel, drawn by the four wheels of charity, obedience, patience, and humility. Interpreted correctly by the mendicant preachers, for whom Rampegolus composed his *Figure Bibliorum*, the book of Christ's Passion was the source for living the moral life.

iv. *Ulrich Pinder's* Speculum Passionis

In 1507 the Nürnberg *Stadtarzt*, Ulrich Pinder, published an extensive work on the Passion, compiled from numerous sources, to which he gave the title *Speculum Passionis*. Pinder had previously worked as a medical doctor in Nördlingen (1484–1489), and then as the court physician for Friedrich the Wise, Elector of Saxony, before accepting the position in Nürnberg in 1491. Pinder had close associations with the *Sodalitas Celtica* in Nürnberg, and from 1505 to 1513 published nine works with himself named as printer. The *Speculum Passionis* was reprinted in 1519 by Friedrich Peypus, who had taken over Pinder's publishing endeavors after having married his daughter in 1512, and by 1535 had published fifty works of Luther.[250] Pinder's

---

Fast. The Religious Significance of Food to Medieval Women (Berkeley, 1987), 54f; Rubin, *Corpus Christi, passim*.

[246] "... debet recipi paschalis agnus, scilicet corpus dominicum, cum lactatis agrestibus, id est, lacrimabili devotione vulnera sua benedicta, que pro nobis in corpore pertulit educando nos de Egypto inferni..." Ant.Ramp. *FB*, fol. 18va.

[247] "Nos sumus in continuo agone contra diabolum, mundum, peccatum et carnem, et vix aliquando labore resistimus, ideo libenter refici debemus cibo anime, a quo vires resumimus et fortitudinem... corpus Christi subaudi quod dulcius est super mel et fanum." Ant.Ramp. *FB*, fol. 19vb.

[248] Saak, "The *Figurae Bibliorum*," 29–37.

[249] "Status penitentie dicitur iustitie civitas quia ex penitentia iustificatur homo et peccatis de conscientia fugatis tranquille anima requiescit." Ant.Ramp. *FB*, fol. 101rb.

[250] Pinder *SbL*, comm. 1–11.

Speculum Passionis is a compilation of medieval Passion discourse, which, according to Helmar Junghans, resulted in a "three-part Handbook" bringing the learned piety of the cloister to the civic community.[251] The work was translated into German and published in Salzburg by Johann Baptist Mayr in 1663.

The *Speculum Passionis* is divided into three parts, which Pinder designated as an introduction, consisting of a fruitful meditation; an exposition, containing an extended explanation of the Passion; and a conclusion, in which the miracles of Christ's suffering and death would be treated.[252] Pinder begins by setting forth how the Passion should be read by Christians, calling on Bernard to affirm that "the Christian at least seven times a day should think [on the Passion] . . . the daily reading of a Christian should be nothing else than a meditation on the Passion of Christ."[253] The *Christus patiens* is to be received firstly in the understanding, then in the emotions, thirdly in works, fourthly in resignation, and finally in contempt.[254] Consideration of Christ's sufferings by the reason leads to an affective response, or as Pinder explained, one is moved from *cogitatio* to *affectus*.[255] The emotional response has two parts, a bitter and a sweet, whereby in considering Christ's Passion what was bitter is transformed into what is for the Christian sweet, leading then to efficacious

---

[251] Pinder *SbL*, comm. 22–23.

[252] "Divisio huius speculi. Hoc speculum passionis dominici dividitur in tres partes, scilicet in Prohemium, in executionem, et in conclusionem. Prohemium erit dominice passionis meditatio fructuosa. Executio erit dominice passionis declaratio sententiosa. Conclusio erit dominice passionis contestatio miraculosa." Pinder *SP* Prol. (ed. Nürnberg, 1507), fol. 1rb.

[253] "Occurrit nunc ut passionem domini nostri Iesu Christi quomodolibet exercitio tractemus, de qua ad minus sepcies in die recordari debet christianus iuxta sententiam beati Bernhardi dicentis: Cottidiana christiani hominis lectio debet esse dominice passionis recordatio, cum nihil sic cor humanum accendat quemadmodum sepe et sedula recogitata passio et humanitas salvatoris." Pinder *SP* I (ed. Nürnberg, 1507), fol. 2va.

[254] "Habet namque talis exercitatio gradus suos quibus meditantibus ad perfectionem omnis sanctitatis possumus pervenire. Debemus ergo ad Pauli ammonitionem passionem domini sentire in nobis. Primo in intellectu; secundo in affectu; tertio in efffectu; quarto in defectu; quinto per despectum." Pinder *SP* I (ed. Nürnberg, 1507), fol. 3ra.

[255] "Secundo passio domini que usque huc in intellectu est memoriter pertractata transit in affectum, ut non solum per intellectum cogetur sed ut meditantis devotio per affectum inflammetur, quia si fideliter agit intellectus in eo quo potest cito mutant in affectum, ut passio domini non solum in intellectu cogitetur sed affectus per pietatem et compossionem inflammetur." Pinder *SP* I (ed. Nürnberg, 1507), fol. 3rb.

works.[256] From efficacious works, the Christian is led to suffering all things in humility, renouncing all except what is necessary for life thereby making Christ's Passion a present reality,[257] and finally to contempt for all sin. The last step consists of the recognition that human sin is the cause of Christ's Passion, wherefore the Christian should confess in his or her heart, "I am guilty of Christ's death."[258] Such a process of reading instills in the Christian desire to follow Christ, which is the highest form of religious life and an example of all perfection of life and of truth, for Christ on the cross is as a book placed on a lectern, from which one should learn obedience, patience, humility, and love.[259] Thus in the prologue, Pinder had already explicated the two-fold nature of considering Christ's Passion, drawn from Exodus 25: Christ is the Christian's exemplar, which is to be beheld by the eyes of the heart, and then imitated efficaciously in works. The exemplar calls one to penance, for penance is pleasing to God, and to teach penance God "wanted to offer his son as a written book on the cross opened before the eyes of the entire world."[260] Christ's Passion is a call to penance, for the words of the

---

[256] "Sentitur autem hoc modo in corde dupliciter, scilicet per amarum affectum compassionis, cum tanta compassione meditatur christi passio ut amarissimas lachrymas eliciat devotio, ut dicere possit devotus homo illud Ecclesiastici 41: *O mors quam amara est memoria tua* [Sir. 41:1] Secundo sentitur in corde per dulcissimum affectum deuotionis, cum eandem domini passionem tam intimissime meditamur ut talis devotio dulcissimas lachrymas eliciat ... Tertio passio domini sentiri debet per effectum, ut videlicet de interiori affectu in exteriorem operis effectum procedat ut dum passio que intus hominem devotum afficit, exterius per exhi<bi>tionem operis declaretur." Pinder *SP* I (ed. Nürnberg, 1507), fol. 3[rb–va].

[257] "Quarto passio domini sentiri debet in defectu, ut videlicet in recompensam passionis eius omnem paupertatem et penuriam sufferamus, omne quod secundum hominem delectat vel unquam preter necessitatem tenuem admittentes." Pinder *SP* I (ed. Nürnberg, 1507), fol. 3va.

[258] "Quinto passio domini sentiri debet per despectum idest per profundam humilitatem nos incinerare debemus, dicentes semper in cordibus nostris et dicendo gementes: Ego sum reus mortis Christi." Pinder *SP* I (ed. Nürnberg, 1507), fol. 3vb.

[259] "Passio Christi primo considerari debet ad imitandum. Nam Christi imitatio summa et perfecta perfecti est religio, regula et exemplar perfectionis omnis vite et veritatis scilicet imitari in passione et in morte per morosam meditationem, affectuosam compassionem, et virtuosam operationem scilicet regula nostra et modus bene vivendi quo mereri contigit sit passio salvatoris. Cum ipse sit quasi liber positus in pulpito crucis ubi obedientiam, patientiam, humilitatem, et charitatem edocuit, que sola nos feliciter coronant." Pinder *SP* I (ed. Nürnberg, 1507), fol. 4ra.

[260] "... quam carum haberet celum quod nisi per mortem filii sui hominibus voluit aperire; quantum desiderat et amat penitentiam hominum, ad quam docendam filium suum quasi quendam librum suum scriptum in cruce coram oculis omnium expandi voluit." Pinder *SP* Prol. (ed. Nürnberg, 1507), fol. 1ra.

book that is Christ's Passion are an admonition to penance: "He called us to penance through his word and the Gospels, but still more so through his example: behold in this mirror the face of your savior, and act according to the example given you on the mount."[261] This is so because Christ's Passion "is the foundation of the entire Christian faith,"[262] which Pinder explicates by excerpting from the Augustinian Reinhard von Laudenburg's *Passio Domini*, published in Nürnberg in 1501, concerning the twenty fruits of the Passion.[263] Following Christ's Passion offers hope to the believer, and inflames love; the Passion contains all virtues, gifts and fruits, and by imitating the Passion the believer is brought in order, for the Passion also reveals God's commandments.[264] "In sum," Pinder affirmed, "we should consider well all that Christ suffered for us, and how he handled himself in his Passion, so that as much as possible we can conform ourselves to him, since without following and imitating the suffering Christ his Passion will not save us."[265]

In the second part of the work Pinder then turned to an exposition of the Passion, which he considered to be the core of his mirror, referring to it as the mirror's *Executio* or *Vollziehung*.[266] In the preface beginning Part Two, Pinder explicitly mentions the sources upon which he will draw: Jerome, Augustine, Bernard, Simon of

---

[261] "... quid enim dicunt lacryme, quid dolor, quid verecundia, quid vulnera, quid brachia extensa, quid verba eius dulcissima nisi nostre penitentie motiva? Vocavit nos ad penitentiam verbo, vocavit nos evangelio; sed multo magis vocavit nos exemplo. Inspice igitur in hoc speculum in faciem Christi tui et fac secundum exemplar quod tibi monstratum est in monte." Pinder *SP* Prol. (ed. Nürnberg, 1507), fol. 1ra.

[262] "Nam primum hec passio domini robur est et fundamentum totius fidei christiane." Pinder *SP* I (ed. Nürnberg, 1507), fol. 8ra.

[263] Pinder *SP* I (ed. Nürnberg, 1507), fol. 5rb–7rb. For Reinhard's treatise, see Zumkeller *MSS* nr. 764 (353); there are no extant manuscripts of Reinhard's *Passio Domini nostri Jesu Christi, per modum quadragesimalis predicata*.

[264] "In ea [*scil.* passione Christi] quoque relucet speculum sapientie et intellectus, consilii et fortitudinis, scientie et pietatis, atque timoris domini, de quibus infra dicemus propriis capitulis. Similiter et octo beatitudines, quorum fons est et origo allectivum et directivum exemplar. Item fructus illi suavissimi quos enarrat apostolus ad Galatas et omnia mandata dei." Pinder *SP* I (ed. Nürnberg, 1507), fol. 8rb.

[265] "Et in summa breviter consideremus que ipse pro nobis sustinuit, et in passionibus qualiter se habuit, ut eidem quantum possumus conformemur. Nam sine imitatione et aliquali conformatione ipsius Christi patientis passio eius non salvat." Pinder *SP* I (ed. Nürnberg, 1507), fol. 4rb.

[266] "Pars secunda speculi passionis dominice. Executio." Pinder *SP* II (ed. Nürnberg, 1507), fol. 21rb; Mayer translated this as follows: "Der andere Thail des Spiegels unsers herrn Christi Leydens. Executio oder die Vollziehung." Pinder, *SbL*, II (92).

Cascia, Reinhard of Laudenburg, and, most of all he notes, Ludolph of Saxony.[267] Yet the most important source for this second part, if not for the entire *Speculum*, remains unnamed by Pinder: Jordan's *Meditationes de Passione Christi*. The second part of the *Speculum* consists of sixty-five articles of the Passion, which follow those of Jordan's in form, content, and order, though Pinder at times adds material from his named sources, substituting them for parts of Jordan's text, or simply condenses the treatment found in Jordan.[268] Some of Jordan's text present anonymously in Pinder's *Speculum* can also be found in Ludolph's *Vita Christi*,[269] yet often the textual parallels between Pinder's work and Jordan's cannot be attributed to Pinder's gleaning

---

[267] "Executio huius speculi puta dominice passionis erit declaratio sententiosa a plerisque sacre scripture professoribus approbata; ut scilicet a Hieronimo, Augustino, Bernhardo, Simone de Cassia, Reinhardo de Laudenberg, et pro maiori parte Ludolpho Carthusiensi, iuxta traditionem evangelice professionis." Pinder *SP* II (ed. Nürnberg, 1507), fol. 21rb; Simone Fidati of Cassia's extensive *De Gestis Domini Salvatoris* is currently being edited by Willigis Eckermann. To date three large volumes have appeared, containing the first seven books of the work's eighteen: *Simonis Fidati de Cassia OESA De Gestis Domini Salvatoris*, CSA 7/1–3, ed. W. Eckermann (Rome, 1998–1999).

[268] Junghans in his commentary notes: "Unerwähnt bleibt der Augustinereremit Jordan von Sachsen mit seiner später *Meditationes de passione Christi* benannten Schrift. Er stellt ihr eine Evangelienharmonie voran und unterteilt die Meditation entsprechend den Stundengebeten, zu denen die Mönche und die Chorherren sich verpflichtet hatten. Gleichzeitig gliedert er den Stoff in 65 Artikeln auf, deren Benennung bei Pinder wortwörtlich wiederkehrt ... Für die Leidensgeschichte hat er [Ludophus] das Werk Jordans übernommen, ohne aber die Bezeichnung 'Artikel' zu verwenden oder sklavisch deren Benennung zu folgen. Er behält aber die Aufteilung auf die Stundengebete bei und fügt in sein Werk sogar Jordans Vorwort zur Betrachtung des Leidens Christi ein. Pinder hebt hervor, besonders aus seinem Werk geschöpft zu haben." Pinder *SbL*, comm., 18. Fritz Oskar Schuppisser gave both Pinder and Jordan a brief mention in his article, "Schauen mit den Augen des Herzens. Zur Methodik der spätmittelalterlichen Passionsmeditation, besonders in der Devotio Moderna und bei den Augustinern," in *Die Passion Christi in Literatur und Kunst des Spätmittelalters*, 169–210; Schuppisser writes: "Pinders Druck übernimmt dieses Layout für die gesamte Meditation der Passion nach den 65 Artikeln Jordans von Quedlinburg und verwendet zudem zusätzlich seitengrosse Holzschnitte zu den wichtigen Szenen der Passion." Schuppisser, "Schauen," 178. This is the only mention of Jordan in the article. Jordan is likewise given a mere mention, as is Pinder though without making a connection between the two, by Ulrich Köpf in his article in the same volume; see Köpf, "Die Passion Christi in der lateinischen religiösen und theologischen Literatur des Spätmittelalters," 21–41; 34. Both Köpf and Schuppisser use the reprint of the 1663 edition.

[269] Pinder's actual use of Jordan and Ludolph can only be determined once the relationship between Jordan's *Meditationes* and Ludolph's *Vita Christi* has been established, for which critical editions of both texts are prerequiste, neither of which, unfortunately, is to be expected in the near future.

from Ludolph. Ludolph did not give titles or numbers to the articles he treated, and thus the only way to distinguish the various articles is by the *documenta* sections, which begin formulaically, *ex hoc articulo*. The first such article Ludolph treats is Judas' selling of Christ (*Venditio*). This appears in the *Vita Christi*, Part II, chapter 52,[270] which follows the section of the work that parallels Jordan's prologue.[271] The next article treated by Ludolph is Christ's agony seven chapters later,[272] followed by Ludolph's chronological treatment of the events on the Mount of Olives which then include the third and fourth articles, Christ's sweating blood and capture respectively.[273] In other words, Ludolph's chapters do not correspond to the articles, but rather the articles appear within a chronological and thematic organization of chapters. Jordan, on the other hand, organized his work itself by the articles, which then Pinder followed explicitly, treating Christ's agony on the Mount of Olives as the first article, followed by his sweating blood, and then the selling of Christ and Christ's capture. Pinder could have rearranged and numbered Ludolph's text himself, but the parallels with Jordan are too close to be mere coincidence.

Moreover, Pinder began his *Speculum* with Jordan's prologue to his *Meditationes*, text which can be found as well in Ludolph, but again, Jordan seems the more probable source.[274] Pinder continued with text not to be found in Jordan or Ludolph, but in his preface to Part Two of his *Speculum*, after naming the sources upon which he will be drawing, Pinder returns to Jordan's prologue and its conclusion to conclude his own preface, and this text is not to be found in Ludolph.[275] Comparison between Pinder, Ludolph, and Jordan leaves no doubt that Pinder used the text of Jordan's *Meditationes* directly, rather than simply gleaning the material from Ludolph.

Why Pinder did not name Jordan is left to speculation. As mentioned above, Erasmus was not overly taken with Jordan's works, and if Erasmus' opinion was the common one among northern humanists it could be that given Pinder's association with humanist

---

[270] *VC* II.52 (III.380–384).
[271] *VC* II.51 (III.374ff).
[272] *VC* II.59,1–4 (IV.468–471).
[273] *VC* II.59,10–19 (IV.476–485).
[274] See Appendix F.1.
[275] See Appendix F.1.

circles he might not have wanted to have admitted his source that in so many ways offered him the model for his entire *Speculum*.[276] In any case, the point to be made is that Pinder used Jordan for what he considered to be the heart of his treatment of the Passion, his exposition and explanation of the Passion, and for his overall plan, whereby he organized his work, as did Jordan his *Meditationes*, according to the exhortation of Exodus 25: *Behold, and act according to the exemplar*. Though he followed Jordan verbatim, Pinder did not portray the second part of his work as meditations, which he had offered in the first part of his work as preparatory for his treatment of the Passion proper. It should also be pointed out that of the sources Pinder explicitly mentions upon which he drew for the second part of his treatise, though he cites them all throughout the *Speculum*, namely Jerome, Augustine, Bernard, Simon of Cascia, Reinhard of Laudenburg, and Ludolph, leaving aside the two patristic authorities, two of the four mentioned, Simon of Cascia and Reinhard of Laudenburg, were Augustinian hermits, and joined then with Jordan as the "ghost source" behind it all, the Augustinians appear as the major contributors to Pinder's *Speculum*.

Pinder's *Speculum Passionis* is a summary of Christian doctrine, for he himself portrayed the Passion as the exemplar of the Christian life. If one wants to know the Christian virtues, or God's commandments, one can find them most of all in the Passion of Christ. Imitating the Passion is not designed as ascetic practice, but simply as that which is required for the Christian, for the Passion calls one to penance, leads to remorse and contempt for one's sins, spurs one to virtue and obedience, and most of all, evokes love for what Christ suffered for humankind. In short, the cross of Christ was offered as a general example, or a mirror, for men and angels, showing the way that Christ ascended into heaven, having left behind his cross and Passion as the guide by which Christians could follow the same path.[277] All one had to be able to do was to read the Passion correctly, and thus efficaciously in thought and deed.

---

[276] See above Chapter Four, n. 143.

[277] ". . . crux est tanquam commune exemplum et speculum scilicet hominibus et angelis sanctis. Nam ipsa est via per qua Christus pervenit ad summum celorum, et hoc exemplum omnibus desiderantibus celum ascendere dereliquit." Pinder *SP* III (ed. Nürnberg, 1507), fol. 84ra.

The four texts that I have discussed above come from very different cultural milieus: a mid-fifteenth-century Dutch vernacular treatise, an early fourteenth-century English Franciscan *Summa* of the virtues and vices, a later fourteenth-century Italian Augustinian exegetical handbook, and an early sixteenth-century compilation of Passion texts constructed by a lay, German humanist physician. Yet what these works have in common is a view of the Passion as the summary of the Christian life. Christ's Passion was to evoke love for what Christ did for Christians, and thereby, in the recognition of the extent to which human sin continuously causes Christ's suffering, the Passion is a call to penance. Knowledge of the Passion, when one considered what Jesus actually experienced, and meditation on that experience, had a reflexive value. Although Pinder's text is the only one treated above that is explicitly titled a *Speculum*, each of these four works portrays the Passion as a mirror for Christian life.[278] If one imitates the Passion by following the suffering Christ, one then leads a life that encompasses all the virtues and the commandments as well. Though recognizing the Passion as the summary of the Christian life in late medieval Passion literature is certainly not novel,[279] the catechetical function of Passion discourse has not been given consideration. To teach the virtues, to teach the commandments, to teach what is required of the Christian, these treatises, which are far more representative than outstanding, used the Passion of Christ to do so.[280] The devotion to the Passion these authors sought to instill in their audiences was to inculcate the virtuous life, evoke love, and lead to penance. When Christian catechesis is taken as the endeavor to indoctrinate Christians with the fundamental precepts of the Christian religion, the ultimate late medieval catechetical endeavor was conducted by means of teaching and preaching the Passion of Christ. Within the polyvalent Passion discourse in the later Middle Ages, in addition to the more ascetic and mystical functions

---

[278] For the literary genre of such mirrors in context of their cultural and religious function, see P. Bange, *Spiegels der Christenen. Zelfreflectie en ideaalbeeld in laat-middeleeuwse moralistisch-didactische traktaten* (Nijmegen, 1986).

[279] "Others were inspired by the more internal and moral ideal set forth in the *Meditations on the life of Christi* and the various *Lives* of Christ and above all in *The Imitation of Christi*, from which suffering was not excluded but which present Christ as the exemplar of life for all Christians." Constable, *Three Studies*, 218; *cf.* Constable, *The Reformation of the Twelfth Century*, 257–295.

[280] *Cf. Epist.VPD* (89,21–92,106).

of the Passion, the catechetical function needs to be considered as well. To learn what it meant to be a Christian one only had to read the book of Christ's Passion. The book of Christ's Passion needed proper exegesis, and in this hermeneutical enterprise the catechetical function of Passion discourse comes into even clearer relief.

IV. Passion Hermeneutics

By portraying Christ's Passion as a book to be read, late medieval authors were drawing on a well established tradition.[281] Isidore of Seville had equated red ink with Christ's blood,[282] and Hugh of St. Victor claimed that "the entire scripture is one book, and that one book is Christ, because all divine scripture speaks about Christ and all divine scripture is fulfilled in Christ."[283] The book of Christ's Passion was the summary of the Christian life and as such required proper interpretation. As Antonius Rampegolus made clear, in his view only the mendicant theologians were capable of expositing the text accurately, a view expressed analogously already in the late eleventh century by Bruno of Segni.[284] Though much has been written about the rise of private devotion to the Passion in the later Middle Ages, for many authors the issue was one of providing correct interpretation, for the crucified Christ as the book, placed on the lectern of the cross, was an image that implied a teacher. The origins of lay Passion devotion stemming from the clergy, and most of all from the mendicants, has certainly been noted, resulting, as Bart Ramakers put it, in two general tendencies, one being an increasing interiorization of devotion and the other an overflowing of Passion piety in late medieval society.[285] The "demand side" of the equation has been predominantly the focus, leaving the "supply side" insufficiently analyzed, simply noting the producers and providers for

---

[281] For the metaphor of the book in medieval literature, see Ernst Robert Curtius, *European Literature and the Latin Middle Ages*, 7th printing with Afterword by Peter Godman (Princeton, 1990), 302–347.

[282] Curtius, *European Literature*, 313.

[283] "Omnis scriptura unus liber est, et ille unus liber Christus est quia omnis scriptura divina de Christo loquitur, et omnis scriptura divina in Christo impletur." Hug.SV. *Arc.Moral.* 2,9 (642D).

[284] See note 139 above.

[285] Ramakers, *Spelen en Figuren*, 197–199.

the lay consumers of Passion discourse. The meaning ascribed to the Passion in its textualization by the producers themselves calls for further investigation. It was not as though mendicant theologians composed treatises saturated with their own spirituality only then to give them over to the lay populace to interpret at will. The two lines of development Ramakers highlighted were more intertwined than parallel. Devotion to the Passion arose from meditation on the Passion text, but devotion was not strictly a personal, interior religious act. As Thomas Aquinas and Jordan emphasized, devotion was inseparable from worship. The internalization of devotion to the Passion functioned to extend pastoral control over the consciousness of believers, whereby the book of Christ's Passion exposited by the clergy, was to be read as a mirror of the moral life, leading to penance, confession, and obedience. As Ludolph stated, "in all virtues and good morals therefore always hold before you that most clear mirror and exemplar of all sanctity, namely, the life and character of the son of God, our Lord Jesus Christ, who was sent to us from heaven to lead us in the way of virtue and to give to us by his own example the law of life and of discipline."[286] The pastoral endeavor to ignite devotion, when devotion was defined as a stimulus for doing those things that pertain to divine worship, sought to link the private with the public, the individual with the social, and the personal with the institutional by regulating and shaping the reading of the Passion in the minds and hearts of the audience, exhorting one to a personal, private devotion, but one that was placed squarely in context of divine cult, leading directly to love, the acquisition of virtues, good works, obedience, and most of all, penance. The catechetical function of Passion discourse is seen when the focus of analysis shifts from the personal, individualized piety to the broader socio-cultural matrix in which the book of Christ's Passion was interpreted.

The ethical reading of the Passion emerged with the rise of devotion to the Passion in the reformation of the twelfth century.[287] This

---

[286] "In omnibus itaque virtutibus et bonis moribus, semper praepone tibi illud clarissimum speculum et totius sanctitatis exemplar, scilicet vitam et mores Filii Dei Domini nostri Jesu Christi, qui ad hoc de coelo nobis missus est, ut praeiret nos in via virtutum, et legem vitae ac disciplinae suo nobis daret exemplo..." *VC* Pro. 10 (I.7–8).

[287] See Constable, *The Reformation of the Twelfth Century; idem, Three Essays*. For the concept of ethical reading, see B. Stock, *Augustine the Reader*, and John Dagenais,

was a period, according to Giles Constable, that "was a watershed in the history of the church and of Christian society as well as of monasticism and religious life. It involved a passionate reexamination of what it meant to be a Christian in a world where the traditional links between people and between the individual and God were loosened, and where the boundaries between the sacred and the profane ... were redefined within the course of less than a long lifetime."[288] It was also the time when Christendom was emerging as an identifiable and self-conscious political entity,[289] and as a "persecuting society."[290] And the twelfth century saw a change in attitudes toward Christ, whereby Christ's humanity and Passion become paramount, reaching such emotional and graphic heights as found in Bernard, who, commenting on the Song of Songs, exclaimed that whatever he lacked he took for himself from the entrails of Christ, for through the openings in Christ's hands, feet, and side, ran rivers of honey, from which one was able "to taste and see how sweet is the Lord," (... *gustare et videre quoniam suavis est Dominus*).[291]

Getting a grasp on treatments of the Passion in the twelfth, no less than in the fourteenth and fifteenth centuries, is rather difficult. Christ's Passion was as ubiquitous in twelfth-century as in late medieval culture. The classic text of Christ's Passion served as the basis for a variety of Passion discourses, and a variety of functions of those discourses, emplotted within a variety of literary genres. In Biblical commentaries, and especially those on the Gospels, the Psalms, and the Song of Songs, in Meditations, in treatises, and in letters the Passion played, or could play, a central role. There was no genre of 'Passion Literature', though explications of the Passion can be found in a variety of genres, each with its own form, function, norms, and boundaries. And while I have referred to the 'classic text' of

---

The Ethics of Reading in Manuscript Culture. Glossing the Libro de Buen Amor (Princeton, 1994). My use of the term 'ethical reading' is intended to encompass both the Augustinian sense of reading as analyzed and described by Stock, and the modern critic's interpretation of medieval reading practices as defended by Dagenais.

[288] Constable, *The Reformation of the Twelfth Century*, 325.

[289] See Robert Bartlett, *The Making of Europe. Conquest, Colonization and Cultural Change 950–1350* (Princeton, 1993), esp. 250–268.

[290] See R.I. Moore, *The Formation of a Persecuting Society. Power and Deviance in Western Europe, 950–1250* (Oxford, 1987). For an erudite and insightful critique of Moore, especially with respect to violence against Jews, see David Nirenberg, *Communities of Violence. Persecution of Minorities in the Middle Ages* (Princeton, 1996).

[291] Bernardus, *Super Cant.* 61,4 (II.150,19–23).

the Passion, the Passion was not limited to the strictly textual; for believers, the Passion was a historical event, and one whose efficacy continued into the present, experienced directly and most of all daily in the mass. This extra-textual dimension to the Passion allowed for textualizations of the Passion that were not limited by textual traditions. Thus meditations could emplot the Passion, drawn from and based upon the Passion narratives as found in the Gospels, in ways that far transcended the texts of the narratives themselves. The relating of the extra-textual dimension of the Passion to the textual took place within specific socio-cultural conditions, conditions that Thomas Bestul claims render works on the Passion "especially effective in maintaining and advancing the dominant ideology,"[292] and conditions that I would prefer to view as the contexts for various Passion hermeneutics whereby the classic text of Christ's Passion served as the foundational 'document' for the emerging, self-defining and persecuting Christian society.

That the Passion had a role in Christian self-definition and persecution should not come as a surprise when we realize that parallel to the rise in Passion piety in the later eleventh and twelfth centuries was an analogous rise in anti-Judaism.[293] In 1010–1012 there were indications that attitudes toward the Jews in Europe were changing, when Jews in Limoges, Orléans, Rouen, and Mainz were attacked after the rumor spread that the Holy Sepulcher in Jerusalem had been sacked.[294] Such incidents occurred with increasing frequency in the eleventh century, culminating in the massacres of 1096 in the Rhine cities. Twelve years previous, in 1084, the first walled ghetto was established in Speyer on the instigation of Bishop Rudiger.[295]

---

[292] Bestul, *Texts*, 73; cf. ibid, 8–25. Bestul, however, never discusses what that ideology was that devotional works on the Passion both worked to subvert and to sustain; cf. Robert J. Bast, "Strategies of Communication: Late-Medieval Catechisms and the Passion Tradition," in *The Broken Body*, 133–144.

[293] On the rise of anti-Judaism, see Robert Chazan, *Medieval Stereotypes and Modern Antisemitism* (Berkeley, 1997); Bestul, *Texts*, 69–110; G. Langmuir, *History, Religion, and Antisemitism* (Berkeley, 1990); idem, *Toward a Definition of Antisemitism* (Berkeley, 1990); R.I. Moore, *The Formation of a Persecuting Society*, 27–45; D. Nirenberg, *Communities of Violence*, 200–230; Jeremy Cohen, *The Friars and the Jews. The Evolution of Medieval Anti-Judaism* (Ithaca, N.Y., 1982); Lester K. Little, *Religious Poverty and the Profit Economy in Medieval Europe* (London, 1978), 42–57; Heiko A. Oberman, "The Stubborn Jews: Timing the Escalation of Antisemitism in Late Medieval Europe," in idem, *The Impact of the Reformation* (Grand Rapids, MI, 1994), 122–140; and Miri Rubin, *Gentile Tales*.

[294] R.I. Moore, *The Formation of a Persecuting Society*, 29.

[295] Little, *Religious Poverty*, 43.

And 1148 saw the first documented case of ritual murder, the first of an increasing number in the later twelfth and on into the thirteenth century.[296] In referring to Eckbert of Schönau's *Stimulus amoris*, composed between 1155 and 1184,[297] Bestul suggests that Eckbert's work "is the earliest Passion treatise that we know of in which the role of the Jews is noticeably emphasized."[298] There can be little question that the Jews were increasingly demonized in literature dealing with the Passion as the perpetrators of Christ's violent death. Yet anti-Jewish polemic was endemic within the tradition from the very beginnings.[299] Already during the fourth and fifth centuries the legends of Helena finding the true cross and of the Veronica were given anti-Jewish twists, later to be repeated and codified in Jacob of Voragine's *Legenda Aurea*.[300] In the early twelfth century, Petrus Alfonsi, in his *Dialogi contra Iudeos* (c. 1110), was the first author to have claimed that the Jews killed Christ knowingly; whereas Judas betrayed Christ out of avarice, the Jews killed Christ out of envy, which then provides the reason why the author of the *Fasciculus Morum* treated the Passion especially in the section *De Invidia*.[301] Already in the late eleventh century we find not only an affective reading of Christ's Passion, but also harsh treatment of the Jews. Though the new emphasis on the humanity of the suffering Christ

---

[296] See R. Po-chia Hsia, *The Myth of Ritual Murder*, 2–13; and Rubin, *Gentile Tales*, *passim*.

[297] Bestul, *Texts*, 82.

[298] Bestul, *Texts*, 79. The Jewish connection is one of three contextual readings, together with gender and torture, Bestul offers in his attempt to provide "a cultural contextualization" for treatises he considers to be devotional works on the Passion, (see *ibid.*, 1).

[299] See H. Schreckenberg, *Die christlichen Adversus-Judeos-Texte und ihr literarisches und historisches Umfeld (1.–11. Jh.)* (Frankfurt am Main, 1982; 2nd rev. ed., 1990). For a very balanced account which penetrates behind the anti-Jewish rhetoric of the 'victorious' Christians, see J.G. Gager, *The Origins of Anti-Semitism. Attitudes toward Judaism in Pagan and Christian Antiquity* (Oxford, 1983); *cf.* Miriam S. Taylor, *Anti-Judaism and Early Christian Identity. A Critique of the Scholarly Consensus*, Studia Post-Biblica 46 (Leiden, 1995).

[300] *LA* 68 (303–311) for the former and *LA* 53 (233–235) for the latter. For the early development of the legend of finding the true cross, see Jan Willem Drijvers, *Helena Augusta. The Mother of Constantine the Great and the Legend of Her Finding the True Cross*, BSIH 27 (Leiden, 1992).

[301] On Petrus Alfonsi, see John Tolan, *Petrus Alfonsi and His Medieval Readers* (Gainesville, Florida 1993), esp. 19–22; *cf. LA* 53 (231). The association of avarice with Judas and envy with the Jews, however, is already present in Hier. in Matth. 4 (263,1480–1491; 266,1554); *cf.* Thom.Aq., *STh* III, q. 47, art. 3, ad 3 (2731a,4–6). Bestul certainly is aware of this literature, though he does not give it a place in his portrayals of the anti-Judaism in Passion treatises, see Bestul, *Texts*, 76.

is often attributed to Bernardine, Cistercian spirituality, adopted and adapted then by Francis and the Franciscan tradition, the Benedictines have often been overlooked in the development of affective piety. Yet as John Van Engen has shown, Rupert of Deutz advanced interpretations of Christ's life and Passion that are usually ascribed to a later origin,[302] and Rupert was frequently cited together with the likes of Bernard and Hugh of St. Victor as an authority in later medieval works. In this light, Rupert's fellow Benedictine, Bruno of Segni offers a representative counter-example to the high medieval developments in affective piety that are all too often simply given the label of 'Cistercian' or 'Franciscan'. Moreover, in his *Commentary on Matthew* (c. 1089), Bruno offered a Passion hermeneutic that provides needed perspective on the relationship between the demonization of the Jews, the Passion text, and the catechetical function of Passion discourse.

Bruno was bishop of Segni from 1079 to 1123, an office he held jointly from 1103 to 1112 with that of abbot of Montecassino. A firm supporter of Gregory VII and the reform movement, Bruno's Gospel commentaries, according to Beryl Smalley, "breathed new life into exegesis... Although they did not enter into the School tradition they deserve mention... both as a contrast to what went before and as a foretaste of what would follow."[303] Bruno's *Commentary on Matthew* is a running gloss on the Gospel text, in which Bruno brings in whatever material he feels pertinent for his explication. His treatment of Matthew is also his major exposition of the Passion. In his commentary on Luke, in treating Christ's sweating blood, Bruno notes that the bloody sweat poured forth from all over Christ's body, which he is quick to point out, signifies the Church, and then refers the reader for the rest of the Passion account to his commentary on Matthew.[304] Bruno also does not refrain from offering his own personal opinions at times. Thus in treating Pilate's wife's dream and exhortation to Pilate to have nothing to do with Jesus, Bruno notes: "Although evil people too foresee many things in visions, nevertheless I would believe that this woman had a good spirit,"[305] and in

---

[302] John Van Engen, *Rupert of Deutz*, 51 and 110ff.
[303] B. Smalley, *Gospels*, 46; see also the literature on Bruno there cited.
[304] Bruno *In Luc.* 2,23 (445C).
[305] "Quamvis enim et mali in visione multa praevideant; ego tamen hanc mulierem boni spiritus fuisse crediderim." Bruno *In Matth.* 4,27 (301A).

accounting for Christ's absence from the tomb after his resurrection, when Mary Magdalena could not find him, Bruno comments on the words *Non est hic*, by noting: "namely, the presence of his body, for the power of his divinity is everywhere. But where then do we believe him to have been? I certainly would find it easy to believe that then he was visiting his mother, who, having suffered more than the others, was expecting his resurrection. And so what if the Evangelists don't mention this, for as John said, not all of his deeds are written,"[306] a story that then was greatly expanded in later medieval accounts, such as Ludolph's *Vita Christi* and Pinder's *Speculum Passionis*.[307]

Basing much of his treatment on the exegesis of Jerome, Bruno intensified the anti-Jewish polemic found already in his source. Throughout his account of the Passion narrative Bruno harshly condemns the Jews for their part therein. Jesus had wanted the Jews to be saved.[308] Thus when he prayed on the Mount of Olives for the cup to be taken from him, if it be God's will, Bruno comments:

> No one should think that he prayed in the fear of death that the cup of the Passion be taken from him ... for he did not pray absolutely that the cup be taken from him, but *that* cup, because although he came to die for the salvation of the world, nevertheless if it were possible, he did not want to be killed by the Jews. But the Father on the other hand wanted him to be killed by the Jews, because the Jews were more evil than all others; wherefore they added this to the pile [of causes] of their own damnation, [for] the Jews in any case were to be damned even if they had not killed Christ ... If it is not possible, he said, that I not be killed by the Jews, then thus it is in your will, your will be done. The will therefore of the Father was that the Jews would kill Christ.[309]

---

[306] "*Non est hic*: videlicet praesentia corporis, qui ubique est potentia divinitatis. Sed ubi credimus tunc eum fuisse? Ego quidem facile crediderim cum tunc matrem visitasse, quae plus caeteris dolore afflicta, ejus resurrectionem exspectabat. Quid enim, si hoc evangelistae non dicant? Non enim, ut Joannes ait, omnia ejus facta scripta sunt." Bruno *In Matth.* 4,28 (310C–311A).

[307] See *VC* II.70.6 (IV.666–667); Pinder, *SP* III, fol. 70ra–b.

[308] Bruno *In Matth.* 4,26 (293A).

[309] "Nemo autem putet, timore mortis eum orare, ut calix passionis ab eo transferatur ... Non enim absolute orat, ut calix ab eo transferatur, sed calix iste; quia etsi pro salute mundi mori venerat, a Judaeis tamen, si fieri posset, occidi nolebat. Pater vero econtra ab illis eum occidi volebat, quia aliis omnibus nequiores erant; quatenus ad suae damnationis cumulum hoc addidissent, qui utique damnandi erant, etiamsi Christum non occidissent ... Si non potest, inquit, fieri, ut me Judaei non occidant, et sic in voluntate tua positum est, fiat voluntas tua. Voluntas igitur Patris fuit ut Christum Judaei interficerent." Bruno *In Matth.* 4,26 (293C–294C). *Cf.* Hier. in Matth. 4 (255,1249–1254).

Bruno continued by arguing:

> But what other people (*alia gens*) ought to have killed Christ except for the more malevolent who thirsted for his blood more than others? For God compels no one to sin, although he allows those to sin who vehemently desire to sin. God wanted, therefore, that such as these, whose entire will is turned to evil, would kill his own saints, to the extent that for them the punishment would grow greater and the glory for the saints would grow more abundant... And thus God the Father wanted the Jews to kill his own son, and because they were the most insidious, that they would carry out the greatest wickedness to the extent that they would have no excuse and would be subject to greater punishment.[310]

Thus Bruno asserts,

> The Jews killed their own Lord; they damned him and called for their own savior to be crucified; they chose Barrabas for themselves, who is interpreted as the *son of their master*. For their master is the devil, who taught them to cry out so and to make the choice they did, that they would choose the son of the devil for themselves and crucify the son of God ... for it was not by accusation, but by shouting out, not from judgment, but from violence that the Jews pursued their cause to kill Christ. Pilate asked them what evil he had done and to this the Jews responded with nothing, for they had nothing with which to respond. Therefore they cried out, and foamed, and raved...[311]

For Bruno, the maliciousness of the Jews was not restricted to the time of the crucifixion. Whereas Christ thirsted for faith, the Jews offered him the sour wine of their venomous and erroneous doctrine which was continuously being poured out by the Synagogue

---

[310] "Sed quae alia gens Christum occidere debuit, nisi illa quae iniquior erat, et quae plus caeteris ejus sanguinem sitiebat? Deus enim neminem cogit ad peccandum; eos tamen peccare permittit, qui vehementer peccare desiderant. Vult igitur Deus, ut hi tales, quorum tota voluntas prona est ad malum, sanctos suos interficiant, quatenus et his major poena, et illis adundantior gloria crescat... Ac per hoc vult Deus Pater, ut Filium suum Judaei interficerent; et quia iniquissimi erant, maximum scelus perpetrarent, quatenus nullam habeant excusationem, et majori poenae subjiciantur." Bruno *In Matth.* 4,26 (295A–B).

[311] "Occidunt Judaei Dominum suum; damnant, et crucifigi praecipiunt Salvatorem suum; petunt sibi Barraban, qui *filius magistri* eorum interpretatur. Magister namque eorum diabolus est, qui eos sic clamare, et hanc optionem facere docuit, ut filium diaboli sibi eligerent, et Dei Filium crucifigerent... Jam non accusatione, sed clamore; non judicio, sed violentia Christum Judaei occidere contendunt. Interrogat Pilatus quid mali fecerit: nihil huic interrogationi respondent, quoniam quid respondeant non habent. Clamant igitur, fremunt et insaniunt..." Bruno *In Matth.* 4,27 (301B–C).

against Christ.[312] The Jews of his day were as malevolent, vicious, and insidious as were their forefathers who killed Christ. The Jews were an evil people, a *gens iniquissima*, who deserved damnation and the harshest punishment, and as a people merited such *even if they had not killed Christ!* A half-century previous to when Bestul finds "the earliest Passion treatise that we know of in which the role of the Jews is noticeably emphasized,"[313] in the exegetical tradition we find a judgment on the Jews that teeters on the balance between "traditional" Christian anti-Judaism, and racial anti-Semitism.[314]

Yet by focusing on the representations themselves, the hermeneutic is easily lost. Why were the Jews so portrayed, and how did such representations function? These questions may not always have discernible answers but they must be posed nonetheless. In Bruno's case it could very well have been his personal animosity against the Jews, and against either his imagined Jews, or against the Jewish community in Segni. Though psychological and social factors are not to be dismissed, the textual function of his treatment of the Jews is of primary importance.

The representation of the Jews in Bruno's text is unquestionably negative. The Jews were just wretched, for not only did they sell Christ, handing him over to be crucified, but after the resurrection they also paid off the guards of the tomb to spread the story that Jesus' disciples had stolen the body during the night, and thus the Jews kill Christ again by denying his resurrection, and all for the love of money.[315] Bruno's *O miseri Judaei* echoes his earlier exclamation for Judas, *Infelix Judas!* and Judas had sinned not only by first selling Christ, but then, having recognized his sin, by trying to buy Christ back for the same meager price, and when he was not able to do so, he hung himself in despair. "Wretched Judas!" Bruno laments, "you began to return to the way of salvation, but the devil himself, who had spurred you to betraying your Lord and master, gave you the suggestion to kill yourself, and this alone would have

---

[312] Bruno *In Matth.* 4,27 (306B); *cf.* Hier. in Matth. 4 (275,1790–1793).

[313] Bestul, *Texts*, 79. The problem here is again Bestul's lack of definitions, not explicating precisely what is and is not a 'Passion treatise'.

[314] For a cogent discussion of the distinction between anti-Judaisim and anti-Semitism, as well as for a provocative account of the relationship between the two and the emergence of the latter from the former, see Heiko A. Oberman, *The Roots of Anti-Semitism in the Age of Renaissance and Reformation* (Philadelphia, 1984).

[315] Bruno *In Matth.* 4,28 (312B–C).

sufficed for your damnation, even if you had not handed over the Lord. How much better would it have been for you if you had humbled yourself at the feet of Christ and sought his indulgence, for Christ spurns no one coming to him."[316] Bruno's exegesis of Judas then parallels his earlier representation of the Jews whereby, because of their wickedness, they were to be damned anyway, even if they had not killed Christ. At the root of both passages Bruno places the love of money, which he then contrasts with penance. In expositing the Jews' response to Pilate, accepting the guilt for Christ's crucifixion, *May his blood be upon us and our sons*, Bruno explained that "the Jews passed along this hereditary malediction to their descendants, to which are subject all those who imitate the Jews, and those whom this deed of the Jews does not displease."[317]

Yet Bruno's anti-Judaism seems to be at odds with his portrayal of Christ. Above I mentioned that Bruno not infrequently interprets the text tropologically, applying the various scenes of the Passion to the contemporary Christian. Thus Peter's penance is the model for Christian penance, and through sin Christians are abandoned by God, as was Christ on the cross.[318] If Christians were to identify with Christ, or at least were to follow Christ, as Bruno explicitly stated in an Easter sermon,[319] then Christians would seek the salvation of the Jews, not their damnation, since Bruno took great pains to show that it was God the Father who willed his son to be killed by the Jews, whereas Christ prayed that it would not be so. The

---

[316] "Cognovit Judas se peccasse, argenteos reddit, quasi eodem pretio quo eum vendidit, Christum Dominum redimere possit... Infelix Judas! ad vitam salutis redire coepisti; sed diabolus, qui te ad tradendum magistrum et Dominum incitavit, ipse tibi ut te occideres consilium dedit: hoc enim solum sufficiebat tibi ad perditionem, etiamsi Dominum non tradidisses. Quanto tibi melius fuerat ut Christi pedibus te humiliares, et ab eo indulgentiam peteres, qui neminem ad se venientem repellit." Bruno *In Matth.* 4,27 (299B). This exposition was echoed by Gerhoch of Reichersberg, a mid-twelfth-century Augustinian Canon, who also was a fervent proponent of ecclesiastical reform along the Gregorian lines; see Gerhoch *In psalm.* 31 (18,20–29; 45,8–9). For Gerhoch, see Peter Classen, *Gerhoch von Reichersberg. Eine Biographie mit einem Anhang über die Quellen, ihre Handschriftliche Überlieferung und ihre Chronologie* (Wiesbaden, 1960), esp. 114–121 regarding Gerhoch's Psalms commentary.

[317] "*Et respondens universus populus dixit: Sanguis ejus super nos et super filios nostros*. Hanc enim haereditariam maledictionem in posteros suos Judaei transmiserunt; cui subjacent omnes qui illos imitantur, et quibus hoc illorum factum non displicet." Bruno *In Matth.* 4,27 (302B). *Cf.* Hier. in Matth. 4 (267,1595–1606).

[318] See notes 138 and 141 above.

[319] Bruno *Lib.Sent.* 4,10 (1007C).

apparent disjunction between Bruno's own Christian exegesis as an imitator of Christ, and his fierce polemic against the Jews, begs the question of the meaning given to the Jews in his representations. Were the Jews really the Jews?

A key for interpreting Bruno's portrayal of the Jews in his *Commentary on Matthew* is found in his *Responsio ad eam quaestionem: Cur corruptus tunc temporis ecclesiae status*. In keeping with Bruno's staunch support of the Gregorian reform program, this treatise is a harsh rebuke to simoniacs. In asking rhetorically whether simoniacs are worse than heretics such as the Arians, Novatians, Donatists, Nestorians, and Eutychians, Bruno answers that he does not know, but he is certain that "it is a great wickedness to sell or to buy the Holy Spirit. For if it was a great sin to sell or to buy Christ, it is also a great sin to sell or buy the Holy Spirit. For the Father, Son, and Holy Spirit are equal. It was Judas who sold, and the Jew who bought; and both, however, the sellers and the buyers, the Lord threw out of the temple."[320] In expositing Genesis 26:15 concerning the servants of Abraham digging wells, only to have them filled up by the Philistines in book six of his *Libri Sententiarum*, Bruno interpreted the Philistines as heretics, Jews, and philosophers "who not understanding or expositing the doctrine of the apostles and prophets always try to obstruct these waters."[321] Yet there is not all that much separating the Christians from the Jews and heretics when scripture is interpreted broadly,[322] Bruno affirms, without however giving too much ground: "and thus therefore we go to the well, if when heretics, Jews, and Gentiles want to make a deal with us, and we come to the Gospels, and all together at the same time drink from the one font, and hold to the one faith. They would receive the seven lambs from our hands, by which is signified the seven gifts of the Holy Spirit, which certainly no one else aside from Christians are able to give or to receive. In

---

[320] "Utrum Simoniaci peiores sint, nescio. Unum tamen scio, quia magnum scelus est vendere, vel emere Spiritum sanctum. Si enim magnum peccatum fuit vendere vel emere Christum, magnum utique peccatum est vendere vel emere Spiritum sanctum. Aequales enim sunt et Pater et Filius et Spiritus sanctus. Judas est, qui vendit; Judaeus est, qui emit; utrumque autem et vendentem, et ementem de templo Dominus ejecit." Bruno *Resp.* (1131B–C).

[321] "Philisthaei autem heretici sunt, Judaei quoque et philosophi, qui apostolorum et prophetarum doctrinam non intelligentes et exponentes, semper has aquas obstruere conantur." Bruno *Lib.Sent.* 4,3 (1054D–1055A).

[322] Bruno *Lib.Sent.* 4,3 (1055B).

no other way would a pact and concord between us and them be able to come about."[323]

In light of Bruno's reform program, the Jews are not only the Jews, but also those who imitate the Jews, the heretics, and most of all the simoniacs, who, for the love of money, buy and sell Christ, rather than repenting of their sin and throwing themselves on the mercy of Christ and of Christ's Church. The Church in its corrupt state is in need of a "wake-up call," as Bruno explicitly exposited the sleep of the disciples on the Mount of Olives waiting with Christ: "that sleep of the disciples signifies the sleep and laziness of the Church, which often falls into great temptations, unless it is shaken up by frequent visits of Christ."[324] And it is by no means the Jews alone who are damned, for in his commentary on the Song of Songs, Bruno affirmed that "therefore many monks and bishops will be damned, those who pour out goods from their lips and mouths, keeping their vices within."[325] If Bruno demonized the Jews, he was simultaneously demonizing simoniacs, heretics, and hypocrites. Such a tropological interpretation of the Passion narrative became a standard part of the exegetical tradition, as E. Ann Matter has shown for commentaries on the Song of Songs,[326] and was codified in the *Glossa Ordinaria*. Whereas in his exposition on Exodus Bruno had claimed that those who take the Lord's name in vain includes he who "makes an oath in the name of Christ and does not keep it, and he who in the name of Christ is called Christian, but does not keep the faith of Christ,"[327] in the *Glossa* false Christians are the ones

---

[323] "Sic igitur et nos, si quando haeretici, Judaei, gentiles nobiscum pactum facere volunt, ad puteum accedamus, ad Evangelia veniamus, simulque omnes de uno fonte bibamus, et unam fidem teneamus. Suscipiant septem agnas de manibus nostris, per quas septem gratiae Spiritus sancti significantur, quas quidem nulli alii praeter Christianos vel dare, vel accipere possunt. Nullo alio modo inter nos et illos pactum et concordiam fieri licet." Bruno *Lib.Sent.* 4,3 (1055D–1056A).

[324] "Somnus iste discipulorum, Ecclesiae somnum et torporem significabat, quae in magnis tentationibus saepe tabescit et deficit, nisi Christi frequenti visitatione excitetur." Bruno *In Matth.* 4,26 (295B).

[325] "Damnabuntur igitur multi monachi et episcopi, qui ex labiis oreque bona defluentes, interius vitia reservantes..." Bruno *In Cant.* (1273B); *cf.* Gerhoch *In psalm.* 31 (22,7–10); Hier. in Matth. 4 (281,1978–282,1987).

[326] E. Ann Matter, *The Voice of My Beloved. The Song of Songs in Western Medieval Christianity* (Philadelphia, 1990), esp. 106–111.

[327] "Nam uterque reus est, et ille qui in Christi nomine jurat, et non custodit, et ille qui in Christi nomine vocatur Christianus, et fidem Christi non observat." Bruno *In Ex.* 20 (278D).

who now are spitting in Christ's face, and giving Christ slaps.[328] In tropological readings of the Passion narrative, the Jews indeed become demonized, but they become demonized as instruments of programs other than anti-Judaism, in Bruno's case, the ecclesiastical political program of the late eleventh-century Gregorian reform.[329]

The ethical reading of the Passion narrative continued in the later Middle Ages in such treatises as Jordan's *Meditationes de Passione Christi* and Ludolph's *Vita Christi*.[330] The Jews may have been increasingly demonized, but they were demonized as a by-product of the increasing demonization of human sin. The intensification was made from Christ having suffered and died *for* human sin, to human sin having been and continuously being the *cause and agent* of Christ's continued Passion. It was not only the heretics who were likened to the Jews, but all human sin, the false Christians and the bad Christians, the *mali Christiani*, who by their sin, continuously betrayed Christ as did Judas, spat in Christ's face, bore the crown of thorns into his head, and cried out, *Crucify him, crucify him*. This is not to imply that the Jews were simply a literary tool, and that treatments of the Passion had no connections with nor evidence reciprocal influences of the social experience of the Jews in society during a period when literary polemic joined with a rising apocalypticism had its counterpart in physical persecution.[331] What it does suggest is the elements

---

[328] *Glos.Ord.*, ad Matth. 26:67 (ed. Strassburg, 1480/81), IV.82B; 85A; and *Glos.ord.* ad Luc. 22:64 (ed. Strassburg, 1480/81), IV.215B.

[329] The exposition of the Passion in the Gregorian reform, that of Bruno or that of Gerhoch, cannot sufficiently be treated as such without a comprehensive analysis of, *inter alia*, the Christological debates of the time and Biblical exegesis in general, particularly the Psalms, the Song of Songs, and the Apocalypse. For a fuller treatment of Gerhoch's context, see Classen, *Gerhoch von Reichersberg*.

[330] Though pointing very interestingly to Ludolph's use of the word *pestiferus* referring to the Jews spitting in Christ's face (Bestul, *Texts*, 107), Bestul relegates such readings to a mere comment in his notes, not taking them into account in his interpretation; see Bestul, *Texts*, 226, n. 148.

[331] See Andrew Colin Gow, *The Red Jews: Antisemitism in an Apocalyptic Age 1200–1600*, SMRT 55 (Leiden, 1995); Rubin, *Gentile Tales*, 48–57, and *passim*; Rubin writes: "Even when narratives and cultural stereotypes exist as a resource within the culture, and they always do, these must be mobilised from thought to action. Once violent intolerant language is about, increasingly heard, spoken with impunity, then violent action is almost sure to follow. Words are thus never 'only words'." Rubin, *Gentile Tales*, 194. Rubin gives a much more nuanced and sophisticated reading of such 'Passion literature' regarding the relationship between rhetoric and reality than does Thomas Bestuhl in his *Texts*. *Cf.* Oberman, "The Stubborn Jews," 134–140; and Bast, "Strategies," 142–143.

forming and contributing to the increasing violence against the Jews cannot be mono-causally interpreted, simply taking apparent literary evidence as reflecting and causing social conditions; as David Nirenberg has shown, violence against the Jews was a most complex phenomenon that cannot be reduced to slogans and representations of Jewish perfidy.[332] In this light the question that must be asked all the more is what program then did such a Passion hermeneutic serve? How do we account for the fact that the relating of the classic Passion text and the extra-textual dimensions of the Passion to textual forms as varied as the *Fasciculus Morum*—whose author claimed that those whose penance is false crucify the Son of God a second time—Jordan's *Meditationes*, Ludolph's *Vita Christi*, Jean Gerson's sermon *Ad deum vadit*, and Ulrich Pinder's *Speculum Passionis*, all included an identification of sinners, the *mali Christiani*, and of human sin with Judas and the Jews as the agents of Christ's Passion, itself portrayed in increasingly graphic detail?

An answer can be found in a general Passion hermeneutic, expressed in a wide variety of textual forms, that related doctrine to indoctrination. The Passion text was interpreted, as I have argued above, as the summary of the Christian life, containing all the virtues needed for fulfilling one's obligations to God, or in other words, for fulfilling the obligations incumbent upon all members of the Christian *religio*. Moreover, as the four texts discussed above show, the Passion was to evoke love, and lead to penance. If the doctrine that was to be indoctrinated consisted of the virtues as contrasted to the vices, and primarily the seven deadly ones, summarizing human sin, which was to be confessed, what better way to emphasize the severity of human sin than to intensify its diabolical, demonic character? By demonizing human sin in readings of the Passion by demonizing the Jews, who were then associated with human sin, indoctrination was brought to the level of the individual conscience.

The shift from doctrine to indoctrination, or from exegesis to catechesis, neither of which can be limited to particular literary genres, entailed the tactical accentuation of the graphic representation of Christ's Passion. Such an intensification demonized the Jewish role, which was then equated with the continued agency of such horrific violence done to the most beautiful, loving savior by con-

---

[332] Nirenberg, *Communities of Violence*, 229; cf. Gager, *The Origins of Antisemitism*.

tinued human sin. Works were composed that not only exposited the Passion narrative by offering a tropological reading of the classic Passion text, but also that were intended to teach the readers of such texts how the classic text should be read. When Jordan composed his *Meditationes*, he did so to teach the meditant how to read Christ's Passion. When Gerson preached to the royal court in 1402, he tried to make clear how his listeners should understand the Passion account he offered. The reflexive reading of the Passion, as seen explicitly in *Ons heren passie* and Pinder's *Speculum*, whereby the Passion functioned as a mirror, was a powerful strategy for inculcating the foundational text of the Christian religion by rhetorically equating the readers of the text with the text's antagonists, the Jews.

Meditating on the Passion, according to Jordan and to Thomas Aquinas, was to stimulate devotion. Yet devotion was to stimulate fulfilling the obligations of *religio*. Devotion to the Passion in the later Middle Ages, stemming from the developments in the reformation of the twelfth century, was increasingly individualized and privatized to be sure, but it was so in context of the later medieval catechetical endeavor to indoctrinate Christendom with the basic principles of the Christian faith, summarized in the classic text of Christ's Passion, with the overriding goal of such devotion as being the endeavor to evoke the desire for penance. Many of the texts dealing with the Passion in the later Middle Ages were indeed devotional, and private; but they were private in the same sense in which the confessional was private. As the renewed emphasis on the real presence, and as the renewed emphasis on confession, the renewed emphasis on Christ's Passion from the twelfth century all the way into the later fifteenth, functioned as an instrument of clerical control over the individual consciousness of believers by equating the Passion with the summary of the Christian life to be taught to the public at large by means of the general Passion hermeneutic.

Such a reading of the Passion is implicit in Jordan's *Meditationes*, as is illustrated by the seventeenth article which treats the spitting in Christ's face.[333] Jordan begins as he does each of the articles with a prayer preparing the reader for the article to follow. He then turns to his explication of the Passion scene, in which he also heightens the graphic portrayal of the horror of Christ's face having been spat

---

[333] See Appendix F.2.

upon, and the wickedness of the Jews for having committed such a foul act, which even according to their own law is vile. The reader is to be moved by the scene and outraged at what Christ suffered at the hands of the Jews.

Jordan thereafter moves to the lessons to be drawn. Here we find Jordan's rhetorical strategy for making the Passion effective for the contemporary reader. After having set the scene, Jordan turns to the reflexive reading by cautioning the reader to beware lest he or she ever spit in Christ's face as did the Jews. So that the reader might not dismiss such a warning as not applicable to him or herself, Jordan then carefully explains how such an act is continuously perpetrated by sinful Christians. Sordid thoughts and acts defile one's conscience, which is the image of God, and thus function analogously to the Jews having spat in Christ's face. Moreover, ridiculing the righteous is likewise spitting in Christ's face, as is literally, Jordan notes, taking communion unworthily, and disrespecting one's priest.

To drive the point home, Jordan exhorts the reader to keep the image of Christ having been spat upon clearly in mind. This image serves a dual function: first, it should remind one what Christ suffered for humans and thus evoke thanksgiving, but then one should consider how often one's sin causes the defilement of that image. The message was clear. The scrutiny of one's conscience was effected by a reflexive reading of the Passion in which the horridness of the Passion scene was made graphically evident, which then was caused not only by the Jews, but by sinful Christians who, in this case, received the host unworthily, which implies, not having sufficiently confessed before hand. Jordan's *Meditationes* were devotional indeed, as were many such treatises in the later Middle Ages; they were devotional in the sense that meditation was to evoke love of God by showing one what one owed God, thereby stimulating one's desire for divine worship. Such a text was meant for "private devotion" in so far as the reader was to perform the meditations in private. A private reading, however, was not to remain private, but was to lead the depths of one's conscience to the public institution of the Church and its confessional. The general Passion hermeneutic in the later Middle Ages, which Jordan's *Meditationes* witness, was one that offered a tropological, and a catechetical exegesis of the classic text of Christ's Passion.

By pointing to the late medieval general Passion hermeneutic, that by which the book of Christ's Passion was to be read, I do not mean to exclude various specific Passion hermeneutics. Relating the classic Passion text and the extra-textual dimensions of the Passion to various textual forms entailed various textualizations of the Passion in various socio-cultural contexts that cannot be limited to a single explication of what 'Passion literature' was or how it functioned, as we have seen in the four case studies presented above. Nor do I mean to imply that the devotional-catechetical function of the Passion was the only function of the Passion's textualization, or that the clergy had a monopoly on readings of the Passion, as the vision of Sister Agnes of Bilzheim and that of *Christi Leiden in einer Vision geschaut* testify. My argument is that when the focus of analysis is the production of the text, or the "supply side," rather than speculations on the use of the text, many treatises dealing with the Passion, even if not all, that have most often been seen as treatises intended for personal, private devotional reading, were by design catechetical treatises that sought to form, shape, and control how the Passion was read within a specific hermeneutical context, by means of the general Passion hermeneutic in linking the private and the individual with the public and social dimensions of the institutional Church.

The specific hermeneutical contexts for texts with devotional/catechetical functions further implies that such texts are to be interpreted within those contexts, as well as within that of the general hermeneutic. With the general hermeneutic as the tropological reading of Christ's Passion rhetorically using the classic text of the Passion to unite the depths of the individual conscience with the pastoral goals of the institutional Church, the specific hermeneutical contexts entailed various religion-specific readings to be implicitly, even if not explicitly, textualized.

Jordan's *Meditationes* sought to mold the images of the Passion current in his society in accordance with Augustine's religion. The general hermeneutic applied in so far as Jordan's *Meditationes* were catechetical, and the specific hermeneutic to the extent that they were Augustinian. To grasp the specific hermeneutic Jordan's Augustinian epistemology and ontology are prerequisite, whereas to perceive the general hermeneutic, one needs only to recognize the rhetorical strategies for linking the individual with the social by striving to determine how the Passion text was to be read. And for the Augustinians, the general and specific hermeneutic were held together by their imitation of Augustine as the *sapiens architector ecclesie*.

This double hermeneutic was operative as well within a far broader corpus of catechetical literature than works on the Passion. To demonstrate the extent to which this was the case, I return to Jordan's treatment of the *Pater Noster* and the *religio Augustini*. In so doing, I am by no means leaving the catechetical function of the Passion behind. It is reasonable to assume that some of the material in Jordan's *Meditationes* had its origins in his Erfurt lectures on Matthew.[334] Not only the Lord's Prayer, but also his Passion is found in that Gospel. In addition, the Lord's Prayer and Lord's Passion were intimately related. As Jordan argued in his *Expositio Orationis Dominice*, it is the Passion that binds Christians to Christ,[335] and it is through the Passion of Christ that believers are able to experience Christ's sweetness.[336] In the Prologue to the *Meditationes*, Jordan exhorted the meditant to say fifteen *Pater Noster*'s every day for an entire year. This exercise would result in one having said one *Pater Noster* for every wound Christ suffered.[337] Imitation of the Passion was the summary of the Christian life. The Christian must be crucified with

---

[334] A decisive answer to the question of the relationship between Jordan's *Meditationes* and his *Opus Postillarum* awaits the critical edition of these works, but for now we should not rule out categorically a possible early origin of Jordan's text.

[335] "Moraliter: lumbare illud quod absconditum erat *in foramine petre* iuxta Eufratem ubi computruerat [*cf.* Ier. 13:4–9], significat humanam naturam vel quemlibet hominem christianum, qui sicut lumbare lumbis, sic Christo per meritum passionis est coniunctus." Jor. *Exp.* 3, fol. 76vb–77ra.

[336] "Est autem sapientia proprie ut pro dono sumitur cognitio suavitatis divine per experientiam habita. Unde dicta est sapientia, quasi sapida scientia, cognitio autem et experientia suavitatis divine habetur ex sanctificatione triplicis nominis predicti. Surgit enim mentis suavitas in nobis adpresens ex tribus: ex passionis Christi devota meditatione; ex dilectionis dei erga nos memoratione; ex divine laudis iugi modulatione. De primo Ecclesiastici 24 dicit sapientia increata *quasi murra electa dedi suavitatem odoris* [Sir. 24:20]. Christus enim in passione comperatur murre, propter mortis amaritudinem et penarum acerbitatem. Et licet sibi passio fuerit amara, nobis tamen dat suavitatem odoris pro quanto mens spiritualibus delectationibus reficitur, que de ea devote meditatur." Jor. *Exp.* 3, fol. 77rb.

[337] "Accipiendo, videlicet, quamlibet plagam flagellationis pro uno vulnere, et puncturam cuiuslibet spine pro vulnere uno, unde quicumque cottidie dixerit quindecim Pater Noster in memoriam passionis Iesus Christi per unum annum continuum, hic completo anno cuilibet vulneri dixerit unum Pater Noster." Jor. *Med.* Prol., fol. 1va. Johannes von Paltz included excerpts from prayer cycles in the section "De modo legendi et meditandi quinque vulnera" of his *Coelifodina*, which prescribe saying a *Pater noster* for each wound; see Paltz, *Coel.* 1 (109ff). The editors noted: "Diese Gebetszyklen basieren auf einer Gebets- und Andachtstradition, die sich im Spätmittelalter zu weitgehend festen Gebetsformen verdichtet hat, wie sie sich in den Gebetbüchern des 15. u. 16. Jahrhunderts manifestieren." (108f, n. 19). Hümpfner pointed to suggestive evidence that Jordan's *Meditationes* influenced late medieval prayer book literature; see, Hümpfner, intro., xxxvii.

Christ, and is so by the nails of the commandments of righteousness.[338] Yet the Lord's Prayer is the summary of the commandments.[339] Moreover, the passage Jordan used as the point of departure for his *Expositio Arboris*, which he appended to his lectures on the *Pater Noster* as a summary for the "common folk," was Daniel 4:7–9, the tree of Nebuchadnezzor's dream, which the author of the *Fasciculus Morum*, Rampegolus, and Pinder all interpreted as the cross.[340] Christ's Prayer and Passion were two sides of the same coin: both were explications of the religious life within the cloister, and beyond.

V. Beyond the Walls: From Exegesis to Catechesis

"Spiritual and subtle things should be preached to the spiritual, simple and common things to the unlearned and general public."[341] Thus Jordan stated his opinion of the preacher's task in his *Opus Postillarum*. If one were to conduct a census of fourteenth-century Europe, going door to door, one would find that the majority of souls comprised the "simple" of Jordan's day, the *illiterati*, who were found in the garb of friar and farmer. These "simple souls" were not to be ignored. Although it is not known if the last section of his *Expositio Orationis Dominice* was first delivered in the classroom of Erfurt, when Jordan prepared his lectures for publication he did not set his quill aside having explicated the *Amen*: "so that the exclusion of the vices and the introduction of the virtues, gifts, beatitudes, and fruits corresponding to the individual petitions might be lucid and

---

[338] "Ex isto articulo trahitur documentum, quod et nos crucifigere debemus carnem nostram cum vitiis et concupiscentiis... In hac qualis cruce semper in hac vita pendere debet christianus, ut sic fixus clavis, id est, preceptis iustitie sicut Christus in cruce clavis confixus fuit." Jor. *Med.* art. 47, fol. 30^{va-b}.

[339] "Nam omnes iste petitiones sunt de preceptis, utpote de hiis que sunt de necessitate salutis. Unde Cyprianus in libro *De Dominica Oratione* dicit istam orationem esse compendium preceptorum divinorum [Cypr. domin.orat. 28 (107,519–524)]..." Jor. *Exp.* 1, fol. 73ra.

[340] See note 235 above.

[341] "Secundo, ponitur sermonis congruitas. Congruus enim modus predicandi est ut doctrina sit secundum exigentiam auditorum, ut spiritualibus spiritualia et subtilia; rudibus et popularibus simplicia et grossa predicentur." Jor. *OP* sermo 137B (ed. Strassburg, 1483); "... de retentione autem dicit aliquis se ob defectum memorie et ruditatem verbum dei se retinere non posse. Cui dicendum quod homines simplices non tenentur retinere singula verba predicationis, sed sufficit retinere virtutem sententie saltim in generali." Jor. *OJ* sermo 157, fol. 249va.

clear even to the common and simple (*rudibus et simplicibus*), I decided to summarize my entire exposition here around [the image of] a single tree."[342] With these lines Jordan began an additional treatise which in the Berlin manuscript is given the title *Expositio Arboris*.

There can be little doubt that Jordan's *Expositio Orationis Dominice* originated in the context of the Augustinian *studium* at Erfurt.[343] If we stopped our analysis here, however, we would be missing the point. Jordan's treatise was composed of academic lectures, yet lectures in which the catechetical nature of his work shines through. With such an exposition as the *Expositio Arboris*, Jordan sought not only to assure that the unschooled clerics in his audience would understand the proper interpretation of the Lord's Prayer, but also to provide an example of how that prayer could and should be accommodated to a common audience. Those hearing or reading the text could then learn the academic interpretation of the Lord's Prayer from the lector, and simultaneously be prepared to preach and teach the prayer to the people. Thus at the very top of the tree, above all else, one finds the radiant image of God the Father, from whom the prayer begins, to whom the prayer is directed, by

---

[342] "Ut autem exclusio vitiorum et introductio virtutum, donorum, beatitudinum et fructuum per singulas petitiones secundum adaptationes premissas lucide et oculatim etiam rudibus et simplicibus patefiant, omnia hec in unam arborem redigere decrevi." Jor. *Exp.* 10, fol. 88[ra-b]. For the text of Jordan's *Expositio Arboris*, see Appendix F.3.

[343] The ten lectures that comprise this treatise resemble in method and form Augustinus of Ancona's (d. 1328) magisterial lectures on Matthew given in the Order's *studium* at Naples. At the end of his prologue Augustinus spelled out his method: "Nunc igitur intentionis nostre textum evangelii beati Matthei de hac incarnatione principaliter tractantem ipsam breviter et succincte exponere et postremo aliqua per modum questionum et dubitationem summatim recolligere, ut facilius ab auditoribus capiatur, fructuosius queratur et fortius retineatur adiuvante ipso domino nostro Iesu Christo, cui semper honor et gloria in secula seculorum Amen." Aug.Anc. *Sup.Matth.*, fol. 2[va]. In turning to the *Pater Noster*, Augustinus explained: "Secundum hoc possunt esse quinque dubitationes. Prima, utrum oratio dominica sit excellentior omni alia oratione; secunda, utrum in hac oratione contineantur solum septem petitiones; tertia utrum licet oranti alia petere preter illa, que petenda sunt in hac oratione sine peccato; quarta utrum his septem petitionibus, que hic ponuntur, corresponderunt septem dona spiritus sancti; quinta, utrum his septem petitionibus correspondeant septem beatitudines. . . ." Aug.Anc. *Sup.Matth.*, fol. 81[rb]; Jordan devoted two lectures to the prologue of the prayer (*Pater Noster, qui es in celis*), one to each of the seven petitions, and a final one to the conclusion (*Amen*). His method of exposition was a combination of *distinctiones* and *questiones*; in each lecture he distinguished the various meanings of key terms as well as raised and solved *dubia*, some bearing striking similarities to those of Augustinus. In the Berlin manuscript the majority of the *lectiones* are noted.

whom it is carried out, and in whom it is delightedly fulfilled—and this, Jordan affirmed, regardless of whether the term *pater* is interpreted essentially or personally, as he had discussed previously. This tree is an image that everyone, even the unlearned, can grasp, learn, and remember.[344] Jordan offered material that was not only meant to be learned in the classroom, but that was also intended to be preached from the pulpit. Going "beyond the walls" of the cloister by preaching, teaching, and hearing confessions in attempt to sanctify society was the theological program of the Augustinian *studia*. What is spiritual for the spiritual, and common for the common.

Since the Carolingian age the *Pater Noster* had been the people's prayer.[345] In the later Middle Ages it was diffused throughout religious life, from the liturgy[346] and confessional,[347] to prayer books[348] and catechisms.[349] It was a prayer pregnant with meaning and sacrament, as an anonymous German exposition of the fifteenth century observed.[350] The "Our Father" was intimately intertwined with popular religion.[351] It assumed a power of its own that was used as a magic charm for protection of all types. In animals and humans alike, it warded off sickness and evil spirits.[352] It is not surprising, therefore, that we find a variety of late medieval works which sought to teach the proper interpretation of the *Pater Noster* to the laity, striving to act as intermediaries "between learned culture and lay piety."[353]

---

[344] See Appendix F.3; cf. Hen. *In mentem* 2.1 (39–40).

[345] B. Adam, *Katechetische Vaterunserauslegungen*, 7f.

[346] See J.A. Jungmann, S.J., *The Mass of the Roman Rite: Its Origins and Development*, 2 vols. (New York, 1951), 2:277ff.

[347] See Thomas N. Tentler, *Sin and Confession on the Eve of the Reformation* (Princeton, 1977), 84.

[348] See F. Haimerl, *Mittelalterliche Frömmigkeit im Spiegel der Gebetbuchliteratur Süddeutschlands* (München, 1952).

[349] See Adam, *Katechetische Vaterunserauslegungen*; for the importance of the *Pater Noster* to the tenth-century popular sectarian movement of the Bogomils, see Eliade, *From Muhammad to the Age of Reforms*, 181–185.

[350] *Unser aller liebster her Ihesus*, ed. by B. Adam, *Katechetische Vaterunserauslegungen*, 104.

[351] Concerning the definition of 'popular religion' as used here, see Peter Dinzelbacher, "Zur Erforschung der Geschichte der Volksreligion. Einführung und Bibliographie," in *Volksreligion im hohen und späten Mittelalter*, ed. Peter Dinzelbacher and Dieter R. Bauer (Paderborn, 1990), 9–27, and André Vauchez, "La pieté populaire au moyen âge. Etat des travaux et position des problèmes," in Vauchez, *Religion et societé dans l'occident mediéval* (Torino, 1980), 324–325.

[352] See, "Vaterunser," in *Handwörterbuch des deutschen Aberglauben*, ed. Hanns Bächtold-Stäubi, et al. (Berlin-New York, 1987), 8:1513–1515.

[353] "Het *Ridderboec* laat ... zien hoe de geestelijke elite kon optreden als inter-

Evidence that Jordan attempted to reach a popular audience is found not only by his explicit statement that his *Expositio Arboris* was specifically designated for the unlearned, but also by his choice of the tree as image. The tree image has a long history in ancient and medieval cultures. In the Minoan-Mycenaean civilization we find the

---

mediair tussen geleerdencultuur en lekenvroomheid." Geert Warnar, *Het Ridderboec. Over Middelnederlandse literatuur en lekenvroomheid* (Amsterdam, 1995), 170. For the *Pater Noster* exposition within the *Ridderboec*, see especially pages 58–71. It is rather astonishing to note that the *Pater Noster* has not been given the attention it deserves in studies of late medieval religion. This is especially so when one takes note of the abundant number of commentaries on the prayer listed by Morton Bloomfield: *Incipits of Latin Works on the Virtues and Vices, 1100–1500 A.D., Including a Section of Incipits of Works on the Pater Noster*, ed. Morton W. Bloomfield, *et al.*, The Medieval Academy of America (Cambridge, 1979). Yet In Hervé Martin's *Le métier de prédicateur à la fin du moyen âge, 1350–1500*, for example, there are only three references to the 'Our Father', two of which appear without further comment by Martin in fifteenth-century quotations he cites from the Franciscan Louis Peresi and the secular priest Robert Ciboule, and this in a chapter devoted to the catechetical function of sermons! See Martin, *Le métier de prédicateur à la fin du moyen âge, 1350–1520* (Paris, 1988): ch. ix: "Un Catechisme avant le Lettre," 296–297; 361. Martin by no means stands alone; the theme with which we are concerned here has not been treated by the very authors who have contributed most to our understanding of religion in the later Middle Ages. Discussions of the place and function of the *Pater Noster* in the treatments of late medieval religion are not to be found in: Caroline Walker Bynum, *Jesus as Mother. Studies in the Spirituality of the High Middle Ages* (Berkeley/Los Angeles/London, 1982); *idem*, *Holy Feast and Holy Fast*; and *idem*, *Fragmentation and Redemption. Essays on Gender and the Human Body in Medieval Religion* (New York, 1992); Herbert Grundmann, *Religiöse Bewegungen im Mittelalter* (Berlin, 1935; reprint: Hildesheim/Zürich/New York, 1977); A. Gurevich, *Medieval Popular Culture*; Raoul Manselli, *La religion populaire au moyen âge. Problemes de methode et d'histoire* (Paris, 1975); Francis Rapp, *L'Eglise et la vie religieuse en occident à la fin du moyen âge* (Paris, 1971); and André Vauchez, *Religion et societé dans l'occident médiéval* (Torino, 1980). This lacuna contrasts with the extensive literature dealing with the "Our Father" in Biblical scholarship; see Jean Carmignac, *Recherches sur le 'Notre Père'* (Paris, 1969), which includes a comprehensive bibliography. In this context scholars have focused on the origins of the prayer in the Hebrew and Greek traditions, and have sought to determine the primacy of the Matthean or the Lucan versions. This research was intensified after the discovery of the Dead Sea Scrolls to the point that, Carmignac has remarked: "Le but essentiel de ce travail est donc d'intégrer à l'exégèse du Notre Père l'apport des manuscrits de Qumran." *Recherches*, 5. Noteworthy for our concerns here is a particular line of research within biblical scholarship on the Lord's Prayer that has sought to decipher the 'Pater Noster cryptograms' found at Pompei and Budapest; see Henri Leclercq, "Croix et Crucifix," *DAChL* 3/2: 3045–3131; *idem*, "Oraison dominicale," *DAChL* 12: 2244–2255; *idem*, "Sator-Arepo," *DAChL* 15/1: 913–915; Jean Danielou, *Les symboles chrétiens primitifs* (Paris, 1961); J. Carmignac, *Recherches*, 446–468. This provides evidence for a symbolic conjunction of the *Pater Noster* and the cross, an association we meet in the relationship for Jordan between the Lord's Prayer and the Lord's Passion. For a most concise and cogent treatment of the 'Our Father' in terms of exegesis, see John P. Meier, *A Marginal Jew. Rethinking the Historical Jesus*, vol. 2: *Mentor, Message,*

cult of the sacred tree,[354] and the "world tree" was the common variant for the sacred "center of the world" in religious cultures as diverse as those of Shamanism, Vedic India, ancient China, and German mythology.[355] In medieval Kabbala, Moses de León portrayed the ten manifested attributes of God (*Sephiroth*) in the form of a tree in the *Zohar* (c. 1275),[356] and within Christian iconography the tree signified the "tree of life," the "tree of knowledge of good and evil," as well as the "tree of Calvary."[357] Moreover, Augustine compared the church to a tree,[358] and by the time Jordan composed his exposition, the tree of the virtues and vices was well established in religious literature, a tradition dating back to Cassian (d.c. 435).[359]

---

and Miracles (New York, 1994), 291–302. For historical treatments of the Lord's Prayer, see: P. Goebel, *Geschichte der Katechese im Abendlande vom Verfalle des Katechumenats bis zum Ende des Mittelalters* (Kempten, 1880); O. Dibelius, *Das Vaterunser. Umrisse zu einer Geschichte des Gebets in der alten und mittleren Kirche* (Giessen, 1903); Klaus Schnurr, *Hören und Handeln. Lateinische Auslegungen des Vaterunsers in der Alten Kirche bis zum 5. Jahrhundert*, FTS 132 (Freiburg, 1985); Maria-Barbara von Stritzky, *Studien zur Überlieferung und Interpretation des Vaterunsers in der frühchristlichen Literatur* (Münster, 1989); Roy Hammerling, *The History and Interpretation of the Lord's Prayer in the Latin West from the First to the Eighth Century* (unpublished Ph.D. Dissertation, University of Notre Dame, 1997); R. Rudolf, *Thomas Peuntners Betrachtungen über das Vater unser und das Ave Maria, nach österreichischen Handschriften hrsg. und untersucht* (Wien, 1953); F.M. Schwab, *David of Augsburg's 'Pater Noster' and the Authenticity of His German Works* (München, 1971); B. Adam, *Katechetische Vaterunserauslegungen*.

[354] See Sir Arthur Evans, *Mycenaean Tree and Pillar Cult* (London, 1901); and George Emmanuel Mylonas, "Religion in Prehistoric Greece," in *Ancient Religions*, ed. Vergilius Ferm (New York, 1950; first paper back ed. 1965): 147–167.

[355] Mircea Eliade, *Images and Symbols. Studies in Religious Symbolism* (Princeton, 1991; originally published as *Images et Symboles* (Paris, 1952), 44ff, 161ff; *idem*, "Shamanism," in *Ancient Religions*, 299–308; 302f; Murray Fowler, "Old Norse Religion," in *Ancient Religions*, 237–250; 242f; *cf.* Eliade, *From Muhammad to the Age of Reforms*, 7f; and *idem*, *Rites and Symbols of Initiation. The Mysteries of Birth and Rebirth*, trans. by Willard R. Trask, with a new Forward by Michael Meade (Dallas, 1994).

[356] Eliade, *From Muhammad to the Age of Reforms*, 169–171.

[357] See Liselotte Stauch and Walther Föhl, "Baum," in *Reallexikon zur Deutschen Kunstgeschichte*, ed. Otto Schmitt (Stuttgart, 1948), 2:63–90; J. Flemming, "Baum, Bäume," in *Lexikon der Christlichen Ikonographie*, ed. Engelbert Kirschbaum, S.J. *et al.* (Rome/Freiburg/Basel/Vienna 1968), 1:258–268; and Rab Hatfield, "The Tree of Life and the Holy Cross. Franciscan Spirituality in the Trecento and the Quattrocento," in *Christianity and the Renaissance*, 132–160. For a psychological interpretation of the tree of knowledge within the context of comparative religion, see Eugen Drewermann, *Strukturen des Bösen*. Vol. II: *Die jawistische Urgeschichte in pyschoanalytischer Sicht* (Paderborn, 1978; fifth edition, 1988), 52–69.

[358] Aug. serm. 44,1–3 (258–260).

[359] See Bloomfield, *The Seven Deadly Sins. An Introduction to the History of a Religious Concept, with Special Reference to Medieval English Literature* (Michigan, State College Press, 1952), 70 and *passim*; and Gerhart B. Ladner, *God, Cosmos, and Humankind. The World of Early Christian Symbolism*, trans. by Thomas Dunlap (Berkeley, 1992), 99–101, 124 and *passim*.

The tree Jordan chose as image, however, was not the tree of Genesis, nor that of the Gospels. Jordan based his *Expositio Arboris* on the tree of Nebuchadnezzar's dream, recounted in Daniel 4:7–9. Jordan's tree, a variation of the tree of the virtues and vices, was the tree of the Lord's Prayer which issued forth from the words of Christ, firmly rooted in his truth. It stood in the center of the world, which Jordan interpreted as the human heart.[360]

The trunk of the tree is formed by seven girls, each of whom holds a sheet inscribed with one of the seven petitions of the prayer. From each girl, as from a trunk, grows a branch containing the virtues, gifts, beatitudes and fruits corresponding to the individual petitions. Opposed to the branches of the virtues are corresponding branches of the vices. These branches, however, are not attached to the tree, but are being chewed in the mouths of seven beasts around the tree—the bull frog, the otter, the dog, the bear, the porcupine, the pig, and the ass—representing the seven principle vices. Driving away the beasts are seven angels, which represent the exclusion of the vices. The vices are further symbolized by seven birds residing in the branches of the vices: a peacock, jackdaw, vulture, raven, magpie, sparrow, and owl. These are opposed by seven doves in the branches of the virtues, which hold in their mouths leaves inscribed with the seven gifts of the Holy Spirit. Jordan closed his exposition of the *Pater Noster* tree by asserting that Christ had given the ability to understand the tree and to partake of its fruits.[361]

To interpret Jordan's *Expositio Arboris*, one must recognize that the image Jordan presented was not an allegory of the prayer in a strict sense. To make the prayer, and his exposition of it, clear and lucid, even to the unlearned, Jordan constructed a visual image; the tree was designed to make the meaning of the prayer "appear all the more evidently" (*evidentius appareat*). The summary of his academic lectures was not a literary moralization or allegory of the Lord's Prayer. It was an attempt to make the prayer efficacious and powerful for the unlearned by creating a visual image to be kept before

---

[360] See Appendix F.3. For the importance of the center in the history of religions, see, Eliade, *The Sacred and the Prophane*, 36–47; and *idem*, *Rites and Symbols of Initiation*, passim.

[361] See Appendix F.3. The image of the tree Jordan portrays bears resemblance to shamanic myth; see Eliade, *From Muhammad to the Age of Reforms*, 16; as well as having connotations of the symbolic kingdom of heaven related in Mt. 13:31–32.

the mind's eye as its object. To translate his lectures for the common folk, Jordan concretized his theological ideas; to make the prayer understandable to the unlearned, he constructed a visual image which could be understood clearly and easily by all.

In the discussion of Jordan's *Meditationes* above, I analyzed the epistemological and ontological background to his creation of visual images that were to be held before the eyes of the mind, showing that mental images functioned on the same psychological level as images received via the senses. As a visual image, the Tree of the Lord's Prayer worked analogously. The prayer exerted a power over the one praying it by emitting images into the soul, just as the *imago passionis* exerted a power over the meditant. This visual image, one that was to be more evidently perceived, was especially designed for the uneducated, but it was not for them alone. Jordan was clear that this was an image for all, the simple and learned alike.

With his *Expositio Arboris* Jordan sought to control the images of the *Pater Noster* that were current in his society in the same way he did with the *imago Passionis*. As a prayer of the people, pregnant with meaning, the Our Father was often used in ways that exceeded orthodox teaching.[362] Jordan sought to tap into the social power of the prayer by attempting to shape the images of the prayer. Just as he did with his *Meditationes*, so did Jordan strive to channel popular religion by ascribing to a "supply side" economics of the sacred. For "it should be noted," he clarified, "that the heart of man is so weak that we are scarcely able to say one *Pater Noster*."[363] By attempting to stimulate and control the images of the Our Father with his *Expositio Arboris*, Jordan could hope to regulate as well the power of the prayer as it entered the souls of believers. Not only the visual image of the Passion, but also that of the Lord's Prayer functioned sacramentally.[364]

---

[362] In 1472 the Carthusian Werner Rolevinck concluded his *De Regimine Rusticorum* with an exposition of the Lord's Prayer in which he sought to teach the ignorant and illiterate rural folk; see, Egidius Holzapfel, *Werner Rolevincks Bauernspiegel. Untersuchung und Neuherausgabe von 'De Regimine Rusticorum'*, FTS 76 (Freiburg, 1959), 142–145; *cf.* 136–137.

[363] "Notandum autem quod cor hominis est tam labile quod vix possumus dicere unum pater noster." Jor. *OJ* sermo 266, fol. 409vb.

[364] See B. Scribner, "Das Visuelle in der Volksfrömmigkeit," 17. In this light, particularly in context of Jordan's understanding of the *religio Augustini*, both his *Meditationes de passione Christi* and his *Expositio Orationis Dominice* (including the *Expositio Arboris*) can be seen as contributing to the phenomenon of monastic piety "breaking

The *Expositio Arboris* witnesses the levels of theological knowledge as discussed in Chapter Four. Whereas in his lectures in the Erfurt *studium* Jordan presented a discursive analysis and exposition of Matthew 6:9–13, his *Expositio Arboris* created a symbolic visual image. His "tree of the Our Father" was an attempt to teach and to preach, to pour forth spiritual alms, directed to the simple believer on the most fundamental level of theological knowledge. The distinction Jordan made between reaching his students headed for Paris and the simple and unlearned was cognitive; his translation of the "Our Father" was based on different approaches to perceptions of truth.[365]

This translation process should not be seen as pure accommodation for the uneducated; even the learned could benefit from the creation of the symbolic, visual image. The lectures Jordan gave in the *studium* were designed to yield "book knowledge" preparatory to university study, as well as the fundamental theological training for the Order's preachers and teachers. Although such knowledge could lead to *scientia spiritualis*, by creating the visual image Jordan thereby constructed a "power source" that used properly led to an improved ontological state of the soul by removing vices and introducing virtues effected by grace. The exclusion of the vices and the introduction of the virtues of which Jordan spoke were not a literary formula; they were statements of the power of visual images entering the soul. Thus, for Jordan the most basic level of theological knowledge, that of the simple believer, was simultaneously the highest, namely, that of *scientia spiritualis*.

The image of the tree itself, however, calls for further consideration. Jordan's tree, as previously mentioned, did not fit within the common categories of the tree of knowledge and the cross of Christ. What then did the image of the tree itself mean to Jordan? What was the religious function of Jordan's tree of the "Our Father" in addition to being a visual image?

In his sermons Jordan often employed the image of the tree. Here we find the tree likened to all the virtues: "In the first place, therefore, the soul, or the conscience, into which Christ ought to come, should be adorned with a variety of virtues; for just as plants and

---

out of the walls" of the cloister; see, Bernd Moeller, "Frömmigkeit in Deutschland um 1500," *ARG* 56 (1965), 15; such an image, however, was already put forth by Theodor Kolde, *Martin Luther*, 15–16.

[365] *Cf.* Wenzel, *Hören und Sehen*, 322.

trees in a garden, so are the diverse virtues in the soul, of which one tree is faith, another hope, another love, another justice, another prudence, another fortitude, another temperance, and on it goes. These trees are only planted and maintained by the ultimate gardener."[366] The virtues are rooted in the soul by Christ, just as trees in a garden. The planting is all important, for the roots determine the tree. Thus, Adam was the root of all humanity.[367] The roots are the source of the tree, and hence the virtues stem from the roots of love, for God's commandments stem from love "just as branches from the root, streams from a headwater, rays from the sun, and all heat from fire,"[368] employing an image that Giles of Rome and Augustinus of Ancona had used for the pope. The more firmly and deeply rooted, the higher the tree will be able to grow, and the same is true for humans, whom Jordan compared to a tree. Unless one is deeply rooted, one will dry up. A good tree can only bring forth good fruit, and a bad tree, only bad. Therefore, "every tree that does not bring forth good fruit should be cut down and cast into the fire," (Mt. 7:18–19).[369] Further, the tree is a symbol of unity. God loves unity and thus created unity out of diversity; "from many angels [God created] one heavenly city; from many stars, the firmament; from the multiplicity of elements, the world; from diverse members, the body; from many branches, one tree; from many monks, one monastery; and from many citizens, one city." It was to ensure this unity that Christ became incarnate. If one desires to receive the

---

[366] "Primo ergo anima sive conscientia in quam Christus debet venire, debet esse adornata varietate virtutum: sicut enim plante et arbores in orto ita diverse virtutes in anima, quarum una arbor est fides, alia spes, alia caritas, alia iustitia, alia prudentia, alia fortitudo, alia temperantia et sic de ceteris, que non plantantur vel servuntur nisi a summo agricola." Jor. *OJ* sermo 11, fol. 21rb.

[367] "Item patet de radice, que est totius vigoris in arbore principium, qua corrupta, corrumpitur arbor. Et de primo homine, qui fuit principium totius humane generationis." Jor. *OJ* sermo 106, fol. 181ra.

[368] "... nota quod omnia mandata dei ordinantur a caritate sicut rami a radice, rivuli a fonte, radii a sole, omnis calor ab igne." Jor. *OJ* sermo 120, fol. 201vb.

[369] "... neque potest arbor bona fructus malos facere, neque arbor mala fructus bonos facere. Omnis arbor que non facit fructum bonum excidetur et in ignem mittetur... homo comparatur arbori propter has propietates arborum. Primo quia quanto arbor profundius descendit, tanto altius ascendit... Secundo, quia quanto minus dilatatur in ramis inferius, tanto altius ascendit... Tertio quia quanto melius purgatur, tanto magis fructificat... Quarto, quia nisi in altum radices habeat, desiccatur et non fert fructum... Quinto, quia ab humore nutritur et ideo sine illo moritur..." Jor. *OJ* sermo 250, fol. 388vb–389ra.

Savior, one must bring all one's thoughts and affections into unity with him.[370]

Jordan's use of the tree as an image was not an allegorical image of the cross or of the tree of knowledge. It was an analogue drawn from nature. The *exempla* he used would have been readily understood by an audience attuned to the agricultural cycles of planting, growth, and harvest. The nature of which Jordan spoke was the nature created and immanently maintained by God, and this brings us back to Jordan's ontology. God's creation took place within the divine reason. There God created the ideas of all being, including the human soul, and from God all creation proceeded. Jordan thus distinguished sharply between the being of a creation and its existence. The being of a creation is its essential nature and is contained within a being's existence, albeit only potentially, "just as," Jordan explained, "the entire tree [is contained] within a simple seed, although it is dissimilar in so far as the tree is in the seed materially. When the form of the seed breaks down, the matter of the seed transforms into the tree." The difference between the seed/tree analogy and the emanation of the divine ideas, is that the existence of created being is not a part of God materially, or as Jordan put it, the relationship is not univocal, but equivocal; creation is not similar to God, but emanates from God.[371] The creation of the tree within the divine mind comes first; then the actual existence of the tree in nature, emanating from God. In nature the tree exists both within the seed and as a tree, but does so bearing an equivocal relationship to the essence of the tree within the divine mind: "For God, the wisest

---

[370] "Unde quicumque vult salvator ad se venire, debet in se habere unitatem, ut cogitationes et affectiones et omnes motus tendant in unum. Nam deus unitatem diligit et ideo ex multis fecit unum: sicut ex multis angelis unam celestem civitatem; ex multis stellis firmamentum; ex multis elementis mundum; ex multis membris corpus; ex multis ramis arborem; ex multis monachis monasterium; et ex multis civibus civitatem et sic multum diliget unitatem et ideo ut unitas esse perfecta, voluit incarnari in utero virginali." Jor. *OJ* sermo 132, fol. 216[va].

[371] "Et notandum quod aliud est esse in eius [*scil.* dei] essentia; aliud in eius notitia; aliud in eius visione. Nam in eius essentia esse est contineri in ea et in eius infinita simplicitate et simplici infinitate secundum rationes perfectionales. Et hoc secundum modum essentie in quantum in deo perfectiones omnium generum eminenter et unitive preexistunt. Sicut tota arbor in simplici grano, licet dissimile sit quo ad hoc quod arbor est in grano materialiter; et forma grani corrupta, transit materia grani in arborem, quod de deo nephas est dicere respectu creature; sicut in exemplari et virtute productiva non univoca et simili sed equivoca et eminenti." Jor. *OD* sermo 59A (ed. Strassburg, 1484); *cf.* K. Morrison, *The Mimetic Tradition*, 16.

craftsman, did not need something to be guided by an exemplar outside Himself, but all things are to be ordered and measured in Himself and in His wisdom or word."[372] The exemplar of the tree resides within God's reason while individual examples of trees exist in nature.

Here we have finally reached the root of the tree image. A tree in nature tends towards its exemplar within the divine mind; in other words, it tends towards its end. Similarly, the tree of the Lord's prayer tends towards its end. The *Pater Noster* tree was planted by God and germinates in Him; it proceeds from God and is perfected by God. By placing this tree in the heart of the believer, *in medio hominis*, Jordan firmly equated the tree with the soul. The entire purpose of the Lord's Prayer is to lead humans to their end. Just as the natural tree grows according to its exemplar in the divine mind, so does the human soul progress toward its end, its exemplar within the divine mind from whence it came.[373] Thus faithful souls become sons of God, when the created image is transformed into the uncreated image.[374]

Whereas the exemplar of the natural tree exists only in the mind of God, the exemplar of the human soul has been revealed: Christ is the exemplar, as the *Christus derelictus*. Jordan forcefully expressed this with the words opening his *Meditationes de Passione Christi*: "Behold, and act according to the exemplar shown to you on the mount." By imitating the Passion, the Christian soul restores the *imago dei*

---

[372] "Non enim indiget deus sapientissimus artifex ut aliquid extra se exemplari reguletur, sed in seipso et in sua sapientia vel verbo omnia ordinanda et disponenda." Jor. *OD* sermo 23B (ed. Strassburg, 1484).

[373] "Omne agens operatur secundum aliquod exemplar, quod patet in deo, natura et arte. Deus enim mundum produxit secundum exemplar quod habet in se ipso... ab exemplo natura, ut dicit Sapientie, Ex similibus simila producti sequens, scilicet exemplar divinum, id est, earum que primo producta sunt. Ars imitatur naturam, ut dicit philosophus, idem exemplar nature ut patet in pictore et sculptore, cuius signum vel scupltura melius indicatur quanto expressius representat ipsam rem naturalem puta equum et similia... una res exemplar est alterius quantum ad esse..." Jor. *OJ* sermo 86, fol. 154vb. Jordan is drawing on a neoplatonic metaphysics of exemplarism, readily available to him in the works of Augustine and Thomas Aquinas; see Aertsen, *Nature and Creature*, 157, 164, 171, 190.

[374] "Sciendum ergo quod nos nascimur filii dei quatuor modis. Uno modo per gratie sacramentalem regenerationem. Alio modo per ipsius dei obiectalem cognitionem. Tertio modo per voluntaris in deum totalem transformationem... Quatuor modo nascimur filii dei per imaginis create in imaginem increatam superformationem." Jor. *OJ* sermo 45, fol. 90ra; *cf.* Hen. *In mentem* 2,3 (56,34–58,93).

within itself and returns to its exemplar in God and consequently to God: "if we desire the heights of heaven," Jordan exhorted, "we ought to imitate the perfection that God has essentially so that we might have some of it by way of participation."[375] Just as the heart of the meditant becomes the tomb of Christ, so within the heart of the believer the tree of the Lord's Prayer is firmly planted, leading the soul back to its origin and end.

The theme of returning to God permeated Jordan's thought.[376] In the *Expositio Arboris* we find another image of the *Pater Noster* in addition to the tree. After affirming that the learned as well as the simple, indeed Christians of all stages, can partake of the fruit from the tree of the Lord's Prayer, Jordan continued by stating that the prayer "is like a river."[377] The river image for Jordan had special significance for he began his *Collectanea* and all three of his major collections of sermons with references to a river, and particularly the river Jordan.[378] The flow of the river Jordan represents the two advents of Christ[379] and separates the infidel from the faithful.[380] It also portrays the Christian life, signified by the conversions of Paul and Augustine, since the river Jordan takes a winding path and actually flows backwards (*retrorsum*).[381] Jordan further interpreted the love of God as a

---

[375] "... si volumus ... altitudinem caeli, imitari oportet quod de illa perfectione, quam habet deus essentialiter, habeamus nos aliquid participative." Jor. *OD* sermo 18B (ed. Strassburg, 1484); *cf.*: "... nam venire ad Christum nihil aliud est quam se eius vitae conformare." Jor. *OD* sermo 5C (ed. Strassburg, 1484).

[376] The return to God is the central theme of Jordan's theology, intimately connected to his understanding of the *adventus domini in mentem*, a doctrine Jordan adopted from Henry of Friemar, and hence I can only mention it here. It may not be overstating the issue, however, to claim Jordan's theology as well as much of the pastoral theology in the later Middle Ages, as a theology of theosis.

[377] See Appendix F.3.

[378] "Quia iuxta dictum sapientis ad locum unde ereunt flumina revertunt ut iterum fluant." Jor. *Coll.* Prol., fol. 1vb.

[379] "Et hic duplex adventus innuitur etiam in origine jordanis fluvii, qui ut dictum est oritur ex libano et secundum Hieronimum habet duos fontes, jor et dan. Prior, quod interpretatur fluvius vel rivus, designatur primus adventus ... Per dan, quod interpretatur iudicium, significatur secundus adventus." Jor. *OP* sermo 2C (ed. Strassburg, 1483).

[380] "Jordanis enim fluvius dividit iudeam et arabiam ... hoc est regionem fidelium puta iudearum a regione gentilium incredulorum separat. Et revera sacer fluvius evangelicus distinguit fideles ab infidelibus, quia sola fide evangelii fideles ab incredulis secernuntur, quemadmodum olim in veteri lege circumcisio populum illum ab aliis distinguebat." Jor. *OP* sermo 1B (ed. Strassburg, 1483).

[381] "... qualiter Paulus retrorsum conversus intelligitur? Nota quod iste terminus retrorsum aliquando in scriptura ponitur in malo, ut Hieremie septimo de quibusdam perversis dicitur, *Facti sunt retrorsum et non ante* [Ier. 7:24]. Aliquando vero

headwater with two streams, one flowing upwards towards God and one downwards toward one's neighbors.[382] Christ himself is a sort of river, for from Christ flow the gifts of wisdom, forming a "river" which flows back to Christ and eternal life.[383]

With this additional image of the *Pater Noster* as a river, Jordan reemphasized the ontological process by which the soul returns to its exemplar.[384] The human soul has its source in God, as a river in its headwaters. Like the river Jordan, the human soul at conversion shifts its course—*retrorsum*—and flows back towards its source.[385] Just as a seed must be deeply planted, watered, and nurtured to sprout and grow into a tree according to its exemplar in the divine mind, so the soul must be firmly and deeply rooted in Christ, the farmer of the soul,[386] in order to grow into its exemplar, by the imitation of Christ, in keeping with its original creation in the divine mind—*simul cum verbo eterno*. The soul is able to grow towards its exemplar ontologically by the infusion of virtues into the blank slate of the soul at birth. And here Jordan's epistemology and ontology meet:

---

in bono ponitur ut hic: *Iordanis conversus et retrorsum* [Ps. 113:3]. Propter quod sciendum quod meritum et demeritum nostrum consistit in conversione et aversione ... In hoc sensu Paulus, qui totus aversus erat a Christo serviendo in persecutione, conversus erat retrorsum ad Christum fide et dilectione. Sic etiam Augustinus conversus erat retrorsum, qui prius persequebatur ecclesiam et impugnabat sacram scripturam ... sed ipse conversus retrorsum vertendo faciem ad lumen clare illuminabatur et ex tunc propugnabat divinas scripturas, quas prius impugnaverat, recte sicut Paulus. Rogemus deum et peccatis nostris a se aversos convertat nos retrorsum ad se per gratiam." Jor. *OD* sermo 50D (ed. Strassburg, 1484).

[382] "Hec est enim caritas dei ut mandata eius custodiamus et mandata eius gravia non sunt. Nichil enim exigit ita deus a creatura rationalibi sicut amorem et hoc mandato nichil est brevius ad retinendum, manifestius ad intelligendum, facilius ad faciendum, delectabilius ad custodiendum, fructuosius ad premium recipiendum, inextasabilius ad puniendum. Iste autem amor fons est habens duos rivulos: unum tendentem sursum. Hec est amor dei. Unum deorsum, sed intendentem per planum, hec est amor proximi." Jor. *OJ* sermo 120, fol. 201vb–202ra.

[383] "*Qui biberit aquam, quam ego do, fiat in eo fons aque salientis in vitam eternam* [Io. 4:13–14]. Statim ergo ab ipsa et insilit in nos per ipsum et resilit in vitam eternam. In ipso et in ipsum plenus ergo sapientia, quoniam ex ipso et per ipsum et in ipso sunt omnia dona sapientie, quo ad effluxum, quo ad influxum, quo ad reflexum. Omnis ergo sapientia a Christo domino est, et cum illo fuit semper et est ante eum." Jor. *OJ* sermo 46, fol. 92va.

[384] *Cf.* Aertsen, *Nature and Creature*, 192.

[385] *Cf. ibid.*, 41f.

[386] "... ipse [Iesus] seminat omnem semen bonum in orto anime tue et in cordibus fidelium suorum; ipse omne bonum plantat et rigat manibus sanctorum ..." Jor. *OJ* sermo 189, fol. 298rb–298va; *cf.*: "Tunc enim ortus plantationum, id est, rationalis anima, quam ipse deus propria manu plantavit, irrigatur quando per influentiam divine gratie virtutum germine fecundatur." Jor. *OD* sermo 13D (ed. Strassburg, 1484).

the soul's *tabula rasa* is given ontological content by the infusion of virtues into the soul, which enter the soul through the eyes, or rather, through the sense of sight which includes the eyes of the body and of the mind. By keeping its sights on the higher things and on the eternal law, the intellect becomes illumined by the Holy Spirit and obtains its proper function, namely, the spiritual knowledge obtained by the true cognition of reality. Thereby the soul is elevated towards a higher level of being, making its way back towards its source and its final end,[387] the end to which the entire Lord's Prayer is directed.

We thus come to recognize ever more clearly the cyclical nature of Jordan's world view: the seasons of planting and harvest, the ebb and flow of rivers, ever new births and non-ceasing death. The agricultural cycles gave shape to Jordan's world and to the world of his audience, the simple folk of Erfurt and Magdeburg who would have had no trouble recognizing the image of the *Pater Noster* tree with its beasts and its birds. When Jordan incorporated his exposition of the Lord's Prayer into his *Opus Postillarum*, he chose the season of Easter to do so.[388] Spring in both agricultural and ecclesiastical time is the time of new growth, and Jordan seized the opportunity to expound the *Pater Noster* as a tree planted in the heart of believers that was to bring forth the fruits of the Holy Spirit.

As an Augustinian friar Jordan's own immediate world was also cyclically organized. Based on the charge to bring the spiritual fruits of the *vita contemplativa* to the people at large, the daily life of Augustine's religion offers an additional frame of reference for understanding the *Expositio Arboris*. In the *Liber Vitasfratrum* Jordan advised those brothers who did not know how to sing the canonical hours, or who were unable to do so, to pray the *Pater Noster*.[389] In the Order's *Constitutions* we find further instructions. All brothers begin each liturgical hour by praying the *Pater Noster* silently and crossing themselves facing the altar.[390] Lay brothers, that is the *illiterati*, do so as well. During Matins, rather than singing the office, they should say twenty five *Pater Noster's*, concluding each with an *Ave Maria*. For Lauds, ten *Pater Noster's* are

---

[387] *Cf.* Aertsen, *Nature and Creature*, 106, 331.

[388] Jordan's *Expositio Orationis Dominice*, together with the *Expositio Arboris*, are sermones 289–298 of the *Opus Postillarum*. These he included after three sermons designated for the fifth Sunday after Easter (*Dominica Quinta post Pasca*), based on Io. 16:23–30. Sermo 299 is *De eadem Dominica*. *Cf.* Eliade, *The Myth of Eternal Return*, 130.

[389] *VF* 2,15 (184,123–125).

[390] *Const.Ratis.* 1,7 (32).

prescribed as they are for Vespers. The other hours are to be performed with seven *Pater Noster's*.[391] In addition, whereas those ordained are to say three Masses for the deceased brothers, associates, and benefactors of the Order, lay brothers are to say fifty *Pater Noster's*, and for those living, another fifty, while the priests say another three Masses. Upon the death of a pope, a general of the Order, and any brother, every priest is to say three Masses and the lay brothers fifty *Pater Noster's*.[392] The liturgical life of the Order was demarcated by the level of education,[393] and the "Our Father" was specifically for the unlettered.

The distinction between learned and lay of the *Expositio Arboris* was ingrained in the Order's daily routine. The *Pater Noster* was certainly a prayer for all, but it had special importance for the *illiterati*, for whom it comprised the divine office. Jordan's accommodation of his theological exposition was his attempt to make known the efficacy of the prayer, even to the uneducated. He wanted to be clear: it is not in the mere repetition of words that the power of the prayer is to be found, but in the devotion of the mind.[394] His *Expositio Arboris* was the needed translation of the prayer's power for the simple and unlettered, and this translation process both simple priests and prospective theologians could learn. It was this translation that was needed to teach the lay brothers of the Order the importance of their divine office.

In providing the *Expositio Arboris* for his students Jordan not only took his Order as the model, but also his Order's founder. Augustine had taught the laity, the simple saints of the original Order, how they were to pray the Our Father.[395] As an imitator of the Bishop

---

[391] *Const.Ratis.* 1,7 (32).

[392] *Const.Ratis.* 6,38–43 (40–41).

[393] The lay brothers, for example, were prohibited from reading unless they clearly knew how; see *Const.Ratis.* 2,13 (34). The *Pater Noster* likewise served as the divine office for the illiterate members of confraternities; see Lawrence, *The Friars*, 113.

[394] See Appendix F.3.

[395] *VF* 2,2 (80,40–43); *cf.*: "Diximus enim primo ubi, quomodo psallere, orare et manibus laborare debeatis, quando neccesse fuerit et si vobis tempus super fuerit, *pater noster* dicere non differatis. Ipsa enim dominica oratio appellatur, in qua septem petitiones reperiuntur, in quibus omnis spes orationis comprehenditur, quibus deum interpellamus pro appetendis bonis, pro vitandis malum, ac pro delendis commissis. Tres enim prime petitiones pertinent ad eternitatem, reliqui vero quatuor ad hanc vitam temporalem pertinere videntur, quia et panis cottidianus scilicet spiritualis, licet sic sempiternus, ad hanc tamen vitam pertinent in quantum ministratur anime quibusdam signis dictis vel scriptis et ideo panis, quia laborando discitur et

of Hippo, Jordan followed suit. Augustine was *preceptor noster*, as well as the most blessed *plantator* of the Augustinians' religion.[396] The seeds of this religion Jordan strove to bring to fruition on both sides of the cloister's walls. The theology contained in Jordan's *Expositio Orationis Dominice* and *Meditationes de Passione Christi* was the theological expression of Augustine's religion.

VI. The Truly Religious

In his *Figure Bibliorum* Antonius Rampegolus expressed an often repeated monastic teaching: it is not the habit that makes the monk, but the internal disposition.[397] He did so in the section of his work devoted to the *religiosi*, in which he also made clear that he spoke not about all the religious uniformly, but only the "perfect," those who truly live the religious life. Rampegolus was not concerned with the external form of religious vocation, but rather with the actual

---

disserendo ita quasi manducando deglutitur. Nunc quoque peccata dimittuntur nobis et nos dimittimus aliis. Et nunc temptationes vitam infestant quia dei iustitia mortem incurrimus. Unde dei misericordia liberati sumus, que cum ita sint, ipsarum petitionum verba diligentius pertractanda sunt, ut intellecta maiorem generent cordis affectum et quod petitur ad velociorem perducatur effectum. Orate igitur fratres, dicentes *pater noster*, referentes gratias largitori omnium, qui dulcedo nostra est, vita et resurrexio nostra est, spes nostra et lumen oculorum nostrorum, baculus senectutis nostre, donans nobis sensum ut eum agnoscamus et secreta secretorum suorum intelligamus. Ipse enim dedit nobis efficaciam in opere, gratiam intellectionis, effectum in suis et suorum preceptis, solamen et constantiam in adversis, cautelam in prosperis et timorem et quocumque utimur sua grandis misericordia nos prevenit. O fratres mei non negligamus orare, non carnem domare, non vigilare et tamen quid ei retribuemus qui non permisit nos submergi cum in mari magno essemus? Ecce enim consumpti eramus et nos iberavit, errantes eramus in seculo cum reduxit nos ad viam, ignorantes eramus et docuit nos veritatem. Non igitur tedeat nos orare quia non familiam regere sed tantum debemus deo placere. Et ut bene psallere et orare possitis absque magno corporis impedimento de bonis episcopatus ecclesie Hipponensis centum et quadraginta vestimenta cum calciamentis vobis dilectis fratribus meis deportari precepi ut tempore frigoris quantum neccesse fuerit unusquisque recipiat, reponentes ea et custodientes in communi vestiario cum omni diligentia et caritate. Scientes quod vera caritas non querit que sua sunt, sed que dei. Sic autem facientes non deficiatis. Deus autem pacis qui eduxit de mortuis pastorem magnum ovium in sanguine testis et in dominum nostrum Iesum Christum, aptet vos in omni bono ut faciatis eius voluntatem, faciens autem vobis quod placeat coram se, per Christum Iesum, cui est honor et gloria in secula seculorum, Amen." Jor. *Coll.* sermo 22, fol. 28vb–29rb.

[396] *VF* 1,1 (7,9–10).
[397] Saak, "The *Figurae Bibliorum*," 34, n. 77.

experience of being a religious. To elucidate what that meant for his fellow friars was the major goal of his work. The distinction he made between the religious was the same for the figures of scripture; it was not the letter, but the spirit that carried the truth. Those religious who only followed the formal aspects of religion, opting for adhering to the letter without advancing to the spirit, Rampegolus equated with the *mali religiosi*. Entering the religious life was not sufficient for being a true religious. To be a true religious, one had to be thoroughly inculcated with religion.

In the course of the fourteenth century the Augustinian Order established a system of *studia* for indoctrinating its members with the foundational doctrines of Augustine's religion. As the *imitatores Sancti Augustini*, the members of the Order were instructed in what following Augustine entailed. Yet the teaching the members of the Order were to receive was the explication of Christian doctrine accommodated to a given member's capacity for learning. Thus Jordan constructed his *Expositio Arboris* as a summary of his *Expositio Orationis Dominice* for those members of the Order who were not sufficiently learned to grasp his discursive presentation. Jordan further composed his *Meditationes de Passione Christi*, and indeed his three major collections of sermons, for the instruction of his fellow religious. As he wrote in the prologue to his *Opus Jor*, Jordan was desirous to offer his sermons for the benefit of his Order's studious brothers,[398] echoing the prologue of Henry of Friemar's *Sermones de tempore*, in which Henry stated that he produced his work "for the teaching of the young friars."[399] Teaching Christian doctrine within the framework of the Order's religion, was fundamental to the Order's theological program of following Augustine as *preceptor noster*. When catechesis is taken to refer to the indoctrination of a given religion's fundamental doctrines, the educational endeavor of the OESA appears as catechetical through and through, from the first day a novice donned the habit.[400] In this light, we come to recognize not only the

---

[398] "... studerem colligere pro studiosorum fratrum exercitio et profectu..." Jor. *OJ* Prol., fol. 1ra.

[399] "... istud opusculum sermonum contraxi ad eruditionem iuvenum fratrum..." Henry of Friemar, *Sermones de tempore*, as quoted by Zumkeller *MSS* nr. 331 (158).

[400] Catechesis in the broad definition of teaching, or indoctrinating, was used by Ephraem Syrus to refer to monastic discipline; see G.W.H. Lampe, *A Patristic Greek Lexicon*, (Oxford, 1991; first published 1961), 733; *cf.* Thes.LL. III.599,9–24; 43–600,5; DuCange II.237f.

"external" attempt to catechize society at large, but also the "internal" attempt to catechize the members of one's own micro-religion. This catechetical program, the endeavor to instill the spiritual knowledge of the Christian religion on both sides of the cloister's walls, was the purpose of the theology of the Augustinian *studia*.

The goal, however, was not to make everyone into an Augustinian Hermit, even if that might have been an unexpressed desire. Not everyone could lead the most perfect life. Moreover, the imitation of Augustine called for bringing the Order's own ideals of the religious life to Christian society as such. If the foundational event and history of the most perfect life could not be applicable to each and every Christian, the Augustinians could at least offer something of their way of life to the common Christian, and something of their insight into what the foundational event and history for the common Christian actually was. The Augustinians could not make everyone an Augustinian by religion, but their platform entailed preaching their views of what being a religious in society meant, for as Jordan asserted in his *Opus Dan*, not only the *religiosi*, but "each Christian whatsoever (*quilibet christianus*) ought to be bright and shining, so that he might show forth the light of God's grace, received from Christ, the true sun, in exterior good works."[401] The Augustinian theological program dictated the vying to shape, form, and create the religious ideas of late medieval society.

The foundational event of the Christian religion in the broad sense of the term was the Passion of Christ. The religious and the monks, Jordan explained in his *Meditationes de Passione Christi*, were especially to be the imitators of Christ and to hold the *Christus illusus* always before their eyes.[402] Nevertheless, each and every Christian leads a life of martyrdom under a certain cross if he or she lives according to the Gospels.[403] Whereas following Augustine as the exemplar and rule of all actions entailed following the *vita perfectissima* of the

---

[401] "Sic debent homo religiosus et quilibet christianus esse clarus et luminosus ut lumen gratie dei a Christo vero sole acceptum ostendat in bono opere exteriori." Jor. *OD* sermo 256A (ed. Strassburg, 1484); *cf.* Saak, "Quilibet Christianus."

[402] "... nos Christum illusum ante mentis nostre oculos habeamus, et in vestitu et in exteriori apparatu non vane gloriemur quoniam dominus noster in vestitu illusus est. Ex maxime in hoc sequi Christum debent religiosi et monachi, qui Christum illusum in habitu, tonsura et ferulis representant." Jor. *Med.* art. 39, fol. 25ra; *cf.* Weinbrenner, *Klosterreform*, 181–197.

[403] "... cum etiam tota vita cuiuslibet christiani hominis si secundum evangelium vivat, quedam crux atque martyrium sit..." Jor. *Med.* Prol., fol. 1rb.

Augustinians' religion, following Christ as the exemplar and rule for all one's actions formed the foundation for the Christian life. The Passion of Christ offered the standard for what it meant to be a Christian. At every mass the Passion was re-enacted. Christians, as members of the Church, were to be the body of Christ, as analogously the Augustinian Hermits were to be the embodiment of Augustine.

Whereas the created image of Augustine was the model for determining one's identity as an Augustinian, the Passion of Christ offered the model for one's identity as a Christian. As Christ suffered on the cross for human sin, so then should Christians, as Christ's body, be willing to suffer for Christ. The Augustinians were by no means the only religious Order that sought to Christianize society based on their own Order's religious ideals.[404] As Augustinians from Giles of Rome to Gregory of Rimini viscerally knew, and as Richard FitzRalph was fearfully aware, the various religious Orders were in fierce competition for the souls of Europe's Christians, and in competition amongst themselves as well as with the secular parish clergy. In this light it is not all that misleading to view the various *religiones* in the later Middle Ages as "religious corporations" competing for their share of the religious economy.[405] With the Passion of Christ as Christianity's foundational event, repeated daily in the mass, if the Christian *religio* was to be inculcated, and inculcated in forms extending beyond those of the individual *religiones*, what better way for the members of the *religiones* to do so than to preach and teach the Passion of Christ, which was the foundation of their own religious life above and beyond their adherence to a specific *religio*? Is it mere coincidence that between 1340 and 1370 the Augustinian Simone Fidati of Cascia composed his *De Gestis Domini Salvatoris*, Jordan his *Meditationes*, the Franciscan Johannes de Caulibus the *Meditationes Vitae Christi*, and the Carthusian Ludolph his *Vita Christi*?[406] The teaching

---

[404] As Anne Derbes has shown, the Franciscan ideology had already by the mid-thirteenth century effected a transformation of narrative paintings of the Passion. This should not imply, however, that all spirituality associated with the suffering Christ was Franciscan in origin or character, giving the label Franciscan to virtually all 'affective piety' of the Passion. There is no historical, descriptive, explanatory or didactic value in referring, for example, to Jordan's *Meditationes* as an example of 'Franciscan spirituality'. See Derbes, *Picturing the Passion*, 17.

[405] See W. Bainbridge and R. Stark, *A Theory of Religion* (New York, 1987).

[406] For Simone Fidati of Cascia, see M.G. McNiel, *Simone Fidati and his 'De Gestis Domini Salvatoris'* (Washington, 1950), 50–64; for the dating of Jordan's *Meditationes*

of religion, based on the religious teaching of the micro-religions, reached beyond the indoctrination of the specific micro-religions to include the teaching of the Christian religion itself. Or in other words, the catechetical endeavor to indoctrinate the members of one's own micro-religion became identified with the endeavor of the *studia* to catechize all members of Christendom. Christ's Passion offered a mark of identity, a standard by which one could measure the extent to which one was "one of us" or was "one of them"—the *mali Christiani*, the heretics, and the Jews. During the course of the eleventh to the fourteenth century, Christian identity received its content by identification with the human suffering Jesus, whose followers became his body by membership in the Church, by psychological confederation, and by ritual cannibalism in their ingesting their crucified God in the eucharist.[407] Those who would not partake of the body and blood of Christ were outside the realm of the Church, and outside the realm of the Empire, for they were outside the realm of God as the *massa perditionis*. And those feigned Christians, who are called Christian by name, but do not keep the faith, crucify the savior ever anew. Conformity was to be enforced, for membership in Christendom had its costs as well as its benefits, the costs of having to pay one's debts, and to render unto God what was rightfully his: worship, and

---

and Ludolph's *Vita Christi*, see above, note 28; for Johannes de Caulibus and the *Meditationes Vitae Christi*, see above note 133. Simone Fidati's *Vita cristiana*, which has been seen as a preparatory treatise to his *De gestis Salvatoris*, has been called "the first Italian catechism,"; see McNiel, 50.

[407] See Peggy Reeves Sandy, *Divine Hunger. Cannibalism as a Cultural System* (Cambridge, 1986). In discussing Aztec practices, Sandy writes: "The Aztec, not only in human sacrifice but generally, cast their most comprehensive ideas of the way things are and the way humans should therefore act, into physical symbols and acts focused on the body. The fusion, and thereby the regeneration, of the individual, social, and divine was more than a matter of mere belief. What occurred in the mind at the level of belief was concretely enacted in the sacrifice of the hearts of humans. The gods ate offered hearts and drank human blood. Humans ate parts of the offered victims . . . and donned their skins in order to become the god represented by the victim, for in these sacrifices only gods could be offered to gods. Thus, the divine was brought to earth and the human raised to the divine in bloody and fetid . . . transubstantiation." Sandy, 172. In the thirteenth century Christians accused Jews of ritual cannibalism; see Langmuir, *History, Religion and Antisemitism*, 299–300. The intensified emphasis on the real presence of Christ in the Host, combined with the increasingly graphic portrayals of the Passion, and the parallel rise in Christian accusations of the Jews for practicing ritual cannibalism, crucifixion, and murder, in light of the cultural function of cannibalism in archaic societies is a complex of issues that I in no way pretend to even begin to unravel, though feel it of import to note.

praise, love and prayer, sacrifice, devotion and penance. The Passion of Christ was the instrument by which one came to know not only what one owed, but also how far short one fell from the exemplar. Antonius Rampegolus' exhortations to his confreres regarding the need to distinguish between the *mali* and the *veri* or *boni* could easily be multiplied in numerous medieval sources, including Jordan's *Liber Vitasfratrum*.[408] Yet the same applied to each and every Christian. The Christian life was not conceived as simply formal. Once a Christian, one had to be continuously Christianized. Or in other words, once a religious, whether a member of a legally established religious order, or a religious in terms of following the Christian religion, one had to be continuously "religionized." The on-going, secondary Christianization campaign conducted by the mendicant *studia* was the catechetical enterprise to inculcate correct doctrine among believers, spawning a parallel development to the rise in catechetical literature: an escalation in the generation of micro-religions. Part and parcel of late medieval catechesis, therefore, was a general and a specific program of "religionization."[409]

Religionization, the application of the religious life to each and every Christian, was a development within the general upsurge in catechesis. The concept of religionization is introduced to recapture the verbal aspects of the medieval understanding of *religio*: that of being a religious, of fulfilling one's duties to God, of paying back to God what one owed, namely worship. When one no longer simply lived according to the evangelical *regula* under the supreme abbot Christ, but chose a particular *religio* in which to do so, one then assumed consciously or not that religion's identity for one's self-understanding of "being religious." A religious identity provided the structures for the verbal nature of being a religious in a given *religio*. Religion as a *status* was no longer sufficient. Being a religious was dynamic, as Jordan made clear in his discussion of sanctification and the three levels thereof, the *incipientes*, *proficientes*, and the *perfecti*. One could not simply put on the habit of the OESA and call oneself an Augustinian. The internal disposition was as important if not more so than the exterior form. To make sure his fellow friars, the friars of his religion, understood what it meant to be a follower of Augustine,

---

[408] See E.L. Saak, "The *Figurae Bibliorum*," 34, n. 77.
[409] See Appendix A.4.

Jordan composed his mirror for the Order, the *Liber Vitasfratrum*. To teach his brothers and all others, each and every Christian, what it meant to be a follower of the Christian religion, Jordan composed his *Expositio Orationis Dominice*, explicating the Lord's Prayer as the summary of God's commandants, and his *Meditationes de Passione Christi*, showing in the mirror of Christ's Passion what it was that Christians owed God. Such a mirror was to evoke love for what Christ suffered *pro nobis*, which would lead one to penance and good works, works of love that were the most potent weapons in the fight against the devil and his vicious forces of evil. And Jordan by no means stood alone. Before the emergence of the catechism, there was an intense effort to catechize society based on the inculcation of the moral virtue of religion, and the endeavor to religionize oneself, one's co-religious, and one's community at large.

When catechetical literature is seen not as the literary precursor to the early modern catechism as such, but as literature that sought to indoctrinate Christendom with the basic teachings of the Christian *religio*, then the "explosion" of catechetical literature dated to c. 1370 needs to be placed in the broader development of late medieval religionization, for which works treating the Passion of Christ were central. In this light, the renewed emphasis on the *Pater Noster* and the Ten Commandments appears as an extension and continuation of the on-going catechetical program based on the Passion of Christ, which had its origins in the twelfth and thirteenth centuries, but continued through the end of the Middle Ages and beyond, as Pinder's *Speculum Passionis* testifies. Pinder's work, moreover, was by no means an exception; the Passion of Christ remained the foundation of the *religio Christiana*, and as such, central to the catechetical endeavor. Yet to catechize society, as the late medieval Augustinians strove to do, one first had to catechize oneself; catechesis began at home, so to speak. Late medieval catechesis can only be grasped by recognizing its double character, whereby religion spawned religion. This was, however, not a natural process, a chemical reaction whereby an added agent caused a liquid that had been more or less stable to begin to boil and then to overflow its beaker, mixing and messing with everything with which it came into contact as it finally boiled out all over the laboratory floor. Monastic spirituality did not simply overflow the walls of the cloister to influence, infiltrate, or to infect lay society, nor did lay society use some sort of spiritual pipette to suck out the spirituality from the test-tubes of the monasteries.

Members of the micro-religions actively sought to inseminate society with the seeds of their own religion. This was a mission of cosmic proportions, for it entailed teaching what was owed God, and how to fend off the forces of Satan. A crisis mentality in the later Middle Ages may well have been a contributing factor, but the religionization platforms proceeding from the micro-religions' identities coalesced as the force instigating and propagating the late medieval catechetical program.

The Augustinian platform to sanctify the souls of society was conducted by the theological program of the Augustinian *studia*. It was the foundation of the Augustinians' religious life, the foundation of their religion. The Order's educational endeavor required the little brother Hermits, the true sons of Augustine, to bring Augustine's light to the Church, to win souls for Christ. It was their charter and command, for they and they alone lived the *vita perfectissima*, the most perfect life in imitation of Augustine, their father and teacher, the *sapiens architector ecclesie*, who as such first founded, and then re-founded his Order of Hermits to serve the Church by bringing the fruits of the contemplative life to society at large. Living according to Augustine's model, as the rule and exemplar of one's every action, whether it be preaching on the street corner, hearing confessions, teaching in the *studia*, or pouring out any other of the spiritual alms, gave one one's identity as a true heir of Augustine, a true follower of Augustine's religion. And this in the later Middle Ages was what made one an Augustinian. The religion of late medieval Augustinianism inherently entailed the Order's catechetical endeavor to religionize society. As a member of the Order, the Order's religious identity likewise dictated that one catechize oneself by conforming oneself to the Order's created image of Augustine. If that quest was sufficiently accomplished, the sons of Augustine could indeed fulfill their role as the denizens of the city on the hill, the city of God as the model for Christian life, letting their light shine, in passionate imitation of the powerful image of their founder, father, and teacher.

CHAPTER SIX

BETWEEN REFORM AND REFORMATION

The Augustinian platform had been established. By Jordan's death in 1380, the Augustinian high way to heaven had achieved a clear profile: to be the embodiment of Augustine, who was the standard and model for living the *vita perfectissima* in context of the common life of having one heart and soul in God, based on chastity and Christ's Passion, lived in the battle between God and the devil, and placed in service of the pope as Christ's vicar on earth in a theocratic vision of society; and thus to propagate Augustine's religion in preaching and teaching, bringing the fruits of the Order's spiritual knowledge to the Church and society at large in imitation of Augustine as *pater noster, preceptor noster*, and *sapiens architector ecclesie*. Moreover, the Order had developed institutions, structures, and programs for the platform's realization, which can be summarized in three general strategies: 1.) *Regulation*: the *Rule* and *Constitutions* formed the basis for the Order's government and general operation, which were enforced and applied to the daily life of the Order by the directives and leadership of the prior general and by the General and Provincial Chapters; 2.) *Indoctrination*: the Order's system of education extended from the instruction of novices to the promotion of new *magistri*, designed to create a "learned core" of theologians, preachers, and teachers; 3.) *Religionization*: the on-going catechetical endeavor based on preaching both from the pulpit and with the pen, the later of which included the composition of sermon collections, catechetical works, treatises on pastoral care and pastoral theology, and works on spiritual direction and spirituality. These three strategies worked together reciprocally for the Order *internally*, as the means to enforce conformity with the Order's religious ideals and identity in effecting the Order's platform; and *externally*, as the foundation of the Order's pastoral mission in Church and society.

Yet at the time of Jordan's passing, the Augustinian platform was beginning to face challenges of greater magnitude than it even had previously: how was the Order to maintain its religion and religious identity in the age of Schism, the age of Jean Gerson, Pierre d'Ailly,

Simon de Cramaud, and Emperor Sigismund; of the Ciompi in Florence (1378), the English Peasant revolt of 1381, the uprisings in Ghent and Bruges in 1380 and 1381; the age of Wycliff and Hus; the Councils of Constance and Basel; the danger of the splintering of the platform itself with the rise of the Observant movement and the onset of the *Fürstenreformation*, when the German Observant congregation "placed itself in the hands of the princes as their instrument" for reform;[1] the age of the Pragmatic Sanction of Bruges, Joan of Arc, and the *Malleus Maleficarum*? Whereas throughout most of the fourteenth century the Augustinian high way to heaven was struggling to create a religious identity, profile, and program, in the course of the fifteenth century it found itself in the midst of a battle for its very foundation.

In 1479, the Augustinian prior of Santa Maria del Popolo in Rome, Paul Lulmeus of Bergamo, edited and had printed a copy of Augustinus of Ancona's *Summa de ecclesiastica potestate*, a work Paul considered to be "a treasure chest filled with all doctrines." Paul sent this treasure to Prior General Ambrosius de Cora. Paul told his general that "among all the other doctors of our Augustinian religion, Augustinus of Ancona shines above the rest, in that his teaching of the ancient doctors and of canon law encompasses the testimonies and decrees of the Church Councils to the greatest extent."[2] Ambrosius perhaps should have been more attentive. Having been elected prior general in 1476, he was re-elected by order of Pope Sixtus IV in 1482, whereupon he took the initiative to remove Gaspar of Ovieto as the procurator of the Order, and replaced him with one of his cronies. Gaspar did not take kindly to this turn of events, and when

---

[1] "Die Kongregation gab sich dem Fürsten als Instrument in die Hand, um die Reform in den einzelnen Konventen auch über die Anfänge und die ständigen Gefährdungen hinwegtragen zu können." Manfred Schulze, *Fürsten und Reformation. Geistliche Reformpolitik weltlicher Fürsten vor der Reformation*, SuR.NR 2 (Tübingen, 1991), 88.

[2] "Reverendissimo in Christo patri frater Ambrosio de Cora Romano, sacrarum litterarum egregio interpreti, sacrique ordinis fratrum heremitarum beati Augustini priori generali dignissimo, suus frater Paulus Lulmeus Bergomensis eiusdem ordinis et voti, sancte Marie de populo in urbe prior, fidelem affectum. Augustinum Anconitanum clarissimum divine legis interpretatorem sacri ordinis heremitarm beati Augustini de ecclesiastica potestate, velut omnium doctrinarum plenum armarium, paternitati tue colendissime formis impressum et emendatum offero. Is equidem inter ceteros religionis nostre Augustiniane doctores in eo plurimum enituit quam eius doctrina veterum doctorum sacrique canonis testimonia ac conciliorum decreta ad plenum complexa est." Aug.Anc. *Summa* (ed. Roma, 1479), fol. 2ª. For Paulus Lulmeus, see Ministeri, "De Vita et Operibus," 151–152.

Sixtus' successor, Innocent VIII, took office on 29 August 1484, Gaspar presented the pope with evidence of Ambrosius having made defamatory statements against him. Innocent responded by imprisoning Ambrosius in Castel Sant'Angelo in January of 1485, where he was punished for a month, before being moved to St. Augustine's in Rome. He died in prison the end of May.[3]

We do not know for sure what statements Ambrosius made that were so offensive, or whether they actually were of his authorship. He was charged, nevertheless, with having commented that, "Innocent was created in darkness, lives in darkness, and will die in darkness,"[4] anything but a "politically correct" statement. Ambrosius may very well have adhered to a similar hierocratic theory as his early fourteenth-century predecessors, and he may still have realized that the Order's very existence and status depended on the pope's favor, but he was not able to work the pope politically to the Order's benefit to the same degree as Giles of Rome did Pope Boniface VIII, or William of Cremona Pope John XXII.

In the political, social, and religious turmoil of the post-Schism world, the Augustinian high way to heaven began to espouse a "highway to heaven" whereby ease and expediency served a "minimized" pastoral program as much as did the Order's ideals and ideology.[5] Whereas in the course of the fourteenth century the Augustinian platform was created as the foundation for reform, in the fifteenth century, with the shock of the Schism, the rise of the Observance, and the general political-ecclesiastical mess, the platform itself became the object of reform. Times were ominous, and the sons of Augustine were struggling to maintain their religious identity that they had fought so hard to create. It did not help matters that their task was made all the more difficult by the crumbling of medieval society and the "birthpangs" of the modern era,[6] which rendered the Augustinian

---

[3] Gutiérrez, *History*, I/II, 37. I will be treating Ambrosius at length in volume 2, *The Failed Reformation*.

[4] "[Innocent] in tenebris fuit creatum, in tenebris vivit, et in tenebris morietur." As cited by Gutiérrez, *ibid.*, 37, n. 18.

[5] See Hamm, *Frömmigkeitstheologie*, 247–303, which is an explication of Paltz's "Minimalprogramm"; *ibid.*, 259f.

[6] *Cf.* Heiko A. Oberman, "The Shape of Late Medieval Thought: The Birthpangs of the Modern Era," in *idem*, *The Dawn of the Reformation. Essays in Late Medieval and Early Reformation Thought* (Edinburgh, 1986), 18–38; originally published in *ARG* 64 (1973), 13–33.

platform, if not defunct, then frayed at the edges, caught in the tension between the endeavors to effect the Order's reformation that had been called for since the days of William of Cremona and Gregory of Rimini, and the new reform programs and movements that threatened to shatter the unity of the Order itself.

I. Apocalypse Now: The Origins of the Augustinian Observance

The year 1378 was a watershed for European history. On 20 September of that year, all the French cardinals, together with three Italian, elected Cardinal Robert of Geneva as Pope Clement VII. The new Pope enjoyed the support of the Francophone world, including Scotland, Spain, and Naples, but most of the rest of Europe remained obedient to Pope Urban VI, who had been elected in Rome on 8 April. Pope Clement settled comfortably in Avignon beginning on 20 June 1379, and the Great Schism had begun. It was to last for the next thirty-eight years, until 11 November 1417 with the election of Pope Martin V at the Council of Constance. Though the Schism was ended, the damage had been done, and Europe was never to be the same again.

So often the year 1517 has been seen at least symbolically as marking the beginnings of early modern Europe, and with good reason. But 1417 is perhaps the more historically accurate turning point. In working through the shock of the Schism, Europe was being transformed; forces were unleashed, as the four horses of the Apocalypse, which simply gathered momentum and speed. If 1417 was not the beginning of 'Early Modern Europe,' it should at least be acknowledged as the beginning of early, 'Early Modern Europe.'[7]

In the vast sweep of history, thirty-eight years is not much time, a mere drop in the bucket. But when we think of cultural change, of individual lives, of individual generations, of people and of nations,

---

[7] *Cf.*: "Die Ausbildung und Entwicklung der Fürstenmacht über die Kirche gehört ebenfalls zu den Merkmalen der frühneuzeitlichen Staatsentwicklung. Im Bereich der Kirchenpolitik beginnt die Neuzeit bereits im 15 Jahrhundert." Schulze, *Fürsten und Reformation*, 16; *cf.* Heinz Schilling, "*Vita religiosa* des Spätmittelalters und frühneuzeitliche Differenzierung der *christianitas*—Beobachtungen zu Wegen und Früchten eines Gesprächs zwischen Spätmittelalter- und Frühneuzeithistorikern," in *Vita Religiosa*, 785–796.

thirty-eight years is a long period indeed, almost an entire lifetime. The difference between American culture in 1963 and 2001 is enormous; thirty-eight years is nine and one half American presidential terms. It is the difference between the America of John F. Kennedy and the America of George Bush, Jr. And similar comparisons could be made with German culture, Russian culture, European culture.

Thirty-eight years: this was the time of the Great European Schism, the great transformation, a time when Europe was beginning to become early modern, a birth in which the Augustinian platform played a major role. Whereas for us today, the beginnings of early modern Europe signify liberty, freedom, progress, for the late medieval Augustinian Hermits, the beginnings of early modern Europe were the beginnings of the end of time, the last days, the advent of the Antichrist, and Christ's return to judgment. Thus the imperative urgency to reform, thus the imperative urgency to find the high way to heaven—before it was too late.

A. *Schism and the Antichrist*

Johannes Zachariae knew the Schism well. He had almost grown up with it. He was, in any case, no more than sixteen when the Schism began, and his entire adult life was spent either directly in a split Church and a bifurcated Europe, or in the debacle's aftermath. He died in 1428. The first mention we find in the sources of this eminent Augustinian friar is on 16 March 1384, when Johannes was sent to his Order's *studium generale* in Oxford.[8] Zachariae, unlike many of his successors, experienced the full range of the Augustinian educational system; he was finally promoted to the *magisterium* in Bologna in 1399,[9] fifteen years after having begun in Oxford, for which he would have been required first to have spent at least three years studying logic and philosophy in his Order's provincial schools. After having finally achieved the doctorate in theology, Zachariae returned to Erfurt, where he assumed his Order's chair in theology at the university.[10] After having given lectures on the four Gospels, Zachariae

---

[8] Adolar Zumkeller, *Leben, Schrifttum und Lehrrichtung des Erfurter Universitätsprofessors Johannes Zachariae O.S.A. (d. 1428)*, Cassiciacum 34 (Würzburg, 1984), 16–17.

[9] *Ibid.*, 32. For the decline of the Augustinians' educational system, and the length of time requried to achieve the doctorate in theology in the later fifteenth century, see Appendix A.1.

[10] See A. Kunzelmann, "Die Bedeutung des alten Erfurter Augustinerkloster," in

turned to the Apocalypse, beginning in 1405. He continued lecturing on this book for at least the following six years. His commentary was to become his masterpiece, though only his exposition of the first eleven chapters of the Apocalypse has survived.[11]

In the lecture hall in Erfurt, Zachariae explained to his students: "If we consider the four horses of the Apocalypse (Apc. 9:17) to be those today who are persecuting the Church with schism, then I say that those horsemen are sitting on the horses of the wantonness of the flesh and the authority of temporal power."[12] This was no rhetorical statement. For Zachariae, the schismatics and the *mali christiani*, who raged and raved against the true pope, Urban VI and his successor Boniface IX, were truly the sons of the devil. And yet, the true Church remains unblemished, the true Church remains unified, the true Church remains, for the schismatics supporting the anti-Pope, "are not members of our catholic Church," they are *membra diaboli*.[13] The last days were at hand. Echoing and intensifying Augustinus of Ancona's *Summa* of almost two centuries earlier, Zachariae explained that there are three secessions that preceded the last judgment. Based on Paul's second letter to the Thessalonians (II Th. 2:3), where Paul states that the Antichrist, the son of perdition, will not appear until the final rebellion against God, Zachariae clarified that such rebellion is a historical, temporal rebellion. The first stage thereof is

---

Scientia Augustiniana. Studien über Augustinus, den Augustinismus und den Augustinerorden, Festschrift P. Dr. theol. Dr. phil. Adolar Zumkeller OSA zum 60. Geburtstag, ed. Cornelius Petrus Mayer and Willigis Eckermann, Cassiciacum 30 (Würzburg, 1975), 609–629.

[11] Zumkeller, *Zachariae*, 96–97. Zachariae's *Expositio in Apocalypsim*, is extant is a single manuscript: Trier, SdtB MS 106/1086.

[12] "Si per equos et equestre volumus intelligere illos, qui nunc persequuntur Ecclesiam schismate, tunc dico, quod illi equestres sedent super equos, id est super libertatem carnis et dignitatem temporalis potestatis." As cited by Zumkeller, *Zachariae*, 53, n. 154.

[13] "Filii enim sunt non Dei, sed diaboli ... schismatici illi, qui tenent partem Clementis antipapae, sunt membra diaboli ... Notandum tamen, quod licet appareat schisma in Ecclesia Dei, non tamen proprie dicitur in Ecclesia. Schismatici enim, qui tenent partem antipapae, non sunt de nostra Eccelsia catholica ..." As quoted by Zumkeller, *Zachariae*, 50–51, n. 148; "... sub aperte malis christianis et schismaticis, quales nunc sunt antipapistae, scilicet qui dominum nostrum Urbanum sextum et suum successorem Bonifacium nonum, veros papas, spreverunt et spernunt et versus occidentem cum regibus et schismaticis se colligentes nostrum orientem id est Ecclesiam sanctam usque in hodiernum diem violenter et turbiter tribulant et impugnant." *Ibid.*, 51, n. 149.

... the secession (*discessio*) of the people from the Roman Empire; the second, is the breaking away (*discessio*) of particular churches from obedience to the Roman Church, and this precedes the day of the Lord; the third aspect of the final rebellion is the falling away (*discessio*) of Christians from the catholic faith, which will also be in the time directly before the final judgment. If these are true signs, then the last judgment is not far off. For the first secession of the people from the Roman Empire has already happened for the most part, because the empire has been divided in many parts, that of King Wenceslaus in Bohemia, King Sigismund in Hungary, and King Ruprecht in Bavaria. The second sign of the final rebellion has too already occurred, which is just so plainly clear, because so many individual churches have fallen away from obedience to the Roman Church that there are almost as many who have left as those who remain, though the latter are still in the majority. As for the third secession, it is already so common; in all parts of the world heretics have arisen, heretics who are falling away and have fallen away from the catholic faith. Therefore, with these signs as witness, we can expect the coming of the Lord in judgment.[14]

The dream of a unified Christendom, led by the pope with the emperor at his side was crushed. One of the foundational pillars of the Augustinian platform had crumbled. The end of the world was at hand. The Antichrist was coming as king and pope.[15] The true Church was being attacked by the devil's minions. The final judgment was imminent. And Johannes Zachariae was not alone.

Between 1392 and 1412, four Augustinians lectured on the Apocalypse: Augustinus Favaroni in Bologna from 1392–1394; Hermann

---

[14] "Discessio illa potest temporaliter fieri et intelligi ... primo modo de discessione gentium a Romano imperio ... secundo modo ... de discessione ecclesiarum particularium ab oboedientia Romanae Ecclesiae, quae discessio diem Domini praecedit; tertio modo de discessione quorundam christianorum a fide catholica, quae etiam circa ista tempora erit ... Haec si vera sunt significantia, tunc non multum debet dies extremi iudicii distare. Iam enim pro magna parte facta [est] prima discessio a Romano imperio, quod divisum est in plures partes: illud enim Bohemi, illud Ungari, illud Bouari obtinere nituntur. Facta etiam est, ut planissime patet, secunda discessio, quia multae ecclesiae particulares ab oboedientia Romanae Ecclesiae discesserunt et fere tot sunt discedentes quot remanentes, utinam non plures ab ea sint discessantes. Tertia est etiam discessio, est satis communi in omnibus mundi partibus, in quibus reperiuntur heretici, qui a fide catholica discedunt et discesserunt. Ergo adventus Domini ad iudicium praedictis signis de facto praevenitur." *Ibid.*, 53–54, n. 155; *cf.* Chapter One, n. 365 above.

[15] "Sed ista opinio (*scil.* regnaturum antichristum in imperio Romano) non est multum fundabilis in sacra Scriptura, nisi vellemus dicere, sicut probabiliter potest dici, quod antichristus erit rex et sacerdos, id est tenebit se pro imperatore simul et pro papa." *Ibid.*, 54, n. 156.

of Mindelheim in Prague in 1402; Zachariae in Erfurt; and Bertold Puchhauser of Regensburg in Vienna from 1404–1411.[16] Both Bertold and Zachariae were students of Favaroni in Bologna and had attended his lectures, and both were fervent defenders of the Roman obedience to Urban VI and his successors, in keeping with the direction of Prior General Bartholomew of Venice of 27 April 1386.[17] And both Bertold and Zachariae preached at the Council of Constance against Hus, in support of union and ending the Schism; and they were only two of sixteen Augustinians who were in attendance.[18] The Schism must be ended. Unity must be restored. Reform must be effected. The last days were at hand. The Schism, heresy, and political divisions were clear signs. Time was running out. The Church had been split by the sons of the devil, the harbingers of the Antichrist and the Last Judgment. The foundational principle of the Augustinian platform, the privilege and support of Christ's vicar on earth, the embodiment of the Church, the Order's Mother, had been shattered, and the Order itself had been split.

On 18 September 1379, Pope Clement VII of the Avignon obedience appointed John of Basel as the prior general of the Order of Hermits of St. Augustine. Bonaventure of Padua had been and remained the Order's general supporting Pope Urban VI.[19] John of

---

[16] Augustinus Favaroni, *Lectura in Apocalypsim*, extant in three manuscripts; see Zumkeller *MSS* nr. 154 (82). On Favaroni and his relationship to Zachariae, see Zumkeller, *Zachariae*, 164–173; Willigis Eckermann has discussed Favaroni's Apocalypse commentary in relationship to the ecclesiological and Christological doctrines of Wycliff; and the positions of Favaroni which were condemned by the Council of Basel; Eckermann, "Augustinus Favaroni von Rom und Johannes Wycliff. Der Ansatz ihrer Lehre über die Kirche," in *Scientia Augustiniana*, 323–348. Hermann of Mindelheim, *Lectura super Apocalypsim*, Ossegg, StiB MS 37, fol. 1–129; Zumkeller *MSS* nr. 375 (179); for Hermann's commentary, see also J. Kadlec, "Hermann Schwab von Mindelheim und sein Apokalypskommentar," in *Scientia Augustiniana*, 276–288. Bertold Puchhauser of Regensburg, *Lectura super Apocalypsim*, Munich, BStB MS Clm 26676, 200 fols.; and Clm 26910, 217 fols. Clm. 26676 contains 107 lectures given in Vienna over the years 1404–1409; Clm. 26910 contains another 107 lectures of the years 1409–1411; both manuscripts are Bertold's autograph; see Zumkeller *MSS* nr. 190 (93–94). A thorough analysis of these Augustinian Apocalypse commentaries would require a separate study, and will be pursued in volume two of the trilogy, *The Failed Reformation*.

[17] For Bartholomew's letter to the entire Order, see Francis Roth, "The Great Schism and the Augustinian Order," *Aug(L)* 8 (1958), 281–298; the letter is edited on pages 296–298.

[18] Gutiérrez, *History* I/II, 150–151. Gutiérrez mentions that sixteen Augustinians participated, though only the names of eight are known.

[19] Roth, "The Great Schism and the Augustinian Order," 282–288; see also

Basel had been lector in the Order's *studium generale* in Avignon, the *studium curiale*, before going to Paris to lecture on the *Sentences* (1365/66); he was promoted to the *magisterium* in 1371. While still in Avignon, as we have seen, John had asked Jordan of Quedlinburg how one was to know whether one was a true son of Augustine, and Jordan responded to his query by dedicating his *Liber Vitasfratrum* to John. John was well aware that Augustine was the Order's Father, and the Church, embodied in the pope, was its Mother. John knew what made one an Augustinian. Moreover, his *Sentences* commentary can legitimately be seen as the high point of late medieval Augustinian theology. Damasus Trapp claimed that John left ". . . a theological legacy which, without exaggeration, might be called a *Petit dictionnaire de la théologie du XIVe siècle*,"[20] referring to his *Sentences* commentary as the "gateway to research and study in Augustinian modern theology."[21] Though at the beginning of the Schism, John supported Urban VI, and previously had been appointed as the procurator general of the Order by Gregory IX, who also employed John for diplomatic missions, John soon made the difficult choice to switch camps, and advocated Clement VII as the true pope.[22] For the next forty years the Augustinian Order was divided between two popes and between two priors general, and the Augustinian theologians began to lecture on the Apocalypse.

The Augustinians had an imposing presence at Constance. In addition to their preaching, the Augustinians at Constance were host to the legate of Pope Gregory XII, Cardinal John Dominici, who resided in the Augustinian house at Constance together with the titular patriarch from the Eastern Church, John of Constantinople. Moreover,

---

Gutiérrez, *History* I/II, 147–152. Roth writes: "Bonaventure was so zealous in his support of Urban VI that St. Catherine of Siena procured his creation as Cardinal Priest of St. Cecilia in 1378 He continued to fill the office of General because it was impractical to hold a new election in the early days of the Great Schism: in 1385 he was murdered by a bowman attached to Francis Carrara, a leading nobleman of Pavia, who resented the vigor with which Badoer [i.e., Bonaventure Badoer of Padua] defended the Pope's rights." Roth, "The Great Schism," 283.

[20] Trapp, "Hiltalinger's Augustinian Quotations," in *Via Augustini*, 190.

[21] Trapp, "Augustinian Theology of the Fourteenth Century," 242. For John of Basel, see Trapp, Hitalinger's Augustinian Quotations," and A. Zumkeller, "Der Augustinertheologe Johannes Hiltalingen von Basel (d. 1392) über Urstand, Erbsünde, Gnade und Verdienst," *AAug.* 43 (1980), 57–162. John's works have never been edited; *cf.* Heiko A. Oberman, "Einleitung zur Reihe Spätmittelalter und Reformation. Texte und Untersuchungen," in Hug. *Phys.*, xvii–xxvi.

[22] Roth, "The Great Schism," 283–284.

also in residence with the Augustinians in Constance were the Bishops of Worms, Speyer, and Verdun, and in 1417 Emperor Sigismund himself moved in with the Augustinians and chose Frater John of Swabia as his court chaplain. On 21 November 1417, after having been crowned Pope, Martin V "went in solemn procession to the Augustinian church and there gave his discourse of thanksgiving."[23]

Yet the schism within the Order continued for nearly two more years. Martin V granted permission to both priors general to remain in charge of their respective regions and obediences until the next General Chapter, to meet at Asti in August of 1419. At the Chapter of Asti, both priors general, Jerome of Pistoia and Thomas Fabri, were to appear and to submit their resignations, whereupon the Chapter would elect a new head of the Order, restoring unity. Due to the unusual circumstances, Martin V appointed a president of the Chapter to preside over the proceedings and new election. His choice was an influential preacher at the Council of Constance, whose sermons Martin himself surely would have heard: the provincial prior of the Saxon-Thuringian Province, Johannes Zachariae. Both Jerome and Thomas did indeed abdicate their offices, and the Chapter moved on to the business at hand. The vote for the new prior general ended in a tie; consequently it fell to magister Johannes, the president of the Chapter by the appointment of the pope, to cast the deciding ballot. His choice was between Jerome of Pistoia, who had been the Prior General of the Roman obedience, and the Order's Professor of Theology in Florence, Augustinus Favaroni. Johannes named his former teacher in Bologna as the new prior general. The Order, as the Church, was finally united.[24]

The division within the Order may have been overcome, but the issue of reform burned ever so ardently. The bleeding caused by the Schism had stopped, but a festering wound remained. The new General Favaroni became a staunch supporter of the Augustinian Observance,[25] which itself had begun in the wake of the Schism. The monastery of Lecceto near Siena became the first center of the

---

[23] Gutiérrez, *History* I/II, 150.

[24] Roth, "The Great Schism," 295–296; Gutiérrez, *History* I/II, 31–32.

[25] See Katherine Walsh, "Papal Policy and Local Reform, a) The Beginnings of the Augustinian Observance in Tuscany, b) *Congregatio Ilicetana*: The Augustinian Observant Movement in Tuscany and the Humanist Ideal," *Römische Historische Mitteilungen* 21 (1979), 35–57; 22 (1980), 105–145; "*Congregatio Ilicetana*," 105–114.

Augustinian Observance in 1387, when the Prior General Bartholomew of Venice placed the hermitage under his direct jurisdiction, after having strongly admonished his Order to remain obedient to Urban.[26] Five years later Augustinus Favaroni began his lectures on the Apocalypse in Bologna. His students in Bologna, Johannes Zachariae and Bertold of Regensburg, also lectured on the Apocalypse and both were instrumental in establishing the Observance in the Provinces of Saxony-Thuringia and Bavaria respectively. The seed-bed for the Observance was not religious piety and devotion: it was the Schism and the apocalyptic it unleashed. And this was not limited to the Biblical lectures of Augustinian professors of theology. Joining Zachariae and Bertold at Constance, preaching for reform and unity, and against the heresy of Hus, was an Italian Augustinian representing the city of Genoa: Frater Antonius Rampegolus.

B. *Antonius Rampegolus and the Observant Mentality*

It is not as a preacher against Hus at Constance that Rampegolus grabs our attention. In this capacity he is indeed known only by reputation, though one that considered him to have been the leading preacher of his age.[27] Unfortunately no sermons of his are extant, or at least have not been found, upon which to evaluate the seventeenth- and eighteenth-century estimation of the Augustinian bibliographers. We can only say for certain that he was the author of two very influential works, both handbooks of practical biblical interpretation composed for his Order's preachers: the *Figure Bibliorum*

---

[26] Though the Augustinian convent at Pavia had been removed from the jurisdiction of the Lombard Provincial and placed directly under the Prior General in 1357, as Walsh has shown, "the decision of Bartolomeo da Venezia to set aside the hermitage of Lecceto as a special centre for reform, exempt from provincial jurisdiction and answerable to the prior general in person, was the first attempt to direct the reform from above by giving it privileges and protection." Walsh, "The Beginnings of the Augustinian Observance," 40.

[27] "... magnamque et sibi et Religioni nostrae in Concilio Constantiensi, cui nomine Reipublicae Genuensis interfuit, perperit laudem, strenue enim contra Hussitas decertavit." J.F. Ossinger, *Bibliotheca Augustinina* (Ingolstadt-Augsburg, 1768), 732–733; 732. I have, however, found no mention of Rampegolus in H. Finke, ed., *Acta Concilii Constantiensis*, 4 vols. (Münster, 1896–1928), volume 2 of which deals with the sermons preached at Constance, nor in Mansi's *Collectio Conciliorum*, vol. 27 (Graz reprint ed., 1961), nor in Giorgio Stella's *Annales Genuenses*, ed. Giovanna Petti Balbi, in Muratori, *Rerum Italicarum Scriptores*, N.S. (Bologna, 1975), XVII/2, 317, 323. See also Saak, "The *Figure Bibliorum*," 20.

and the *Biblia Aurea*, the latter of which is rather a shortened "rewrite" of his major *opus*. We have already met Rampegolus in the previous chapter concerning his treatment of Christ's Passion, as well as in Chapter Three regarding his view of the human body. We return to him here because his *Figure Bibliorum* is a precious, and perhaps unique, source for revealing the mentality of the early Augustinian Observance.[28]

Katherine Walsh has noted that we are limited in our understanding of the early Observance by administrative sources. We can trace when and where the Observance was introduced by the registers of the priors general, but we do not know why, or the circumstances leading thereto, much less the "grass-root" sentiments.[29] In Naples and Genoa, for example, the two major geographical spheres of Rampegolus' operations, the Observance was not introduced until after Rampegolus published his *Figure Bibliorum*.[30] In Naples, the earliest documentation we have of the Observance dates to 1419, the first year of Favaroni's Generalate;[31] for Genoa, comprising part of the Observantine Congregation of Lombardy, 1422 marks the beginnings, when Favaroni named Paul Vivaldi as the reformer of the hermitage of Santa Tecla.[32] Yet already in 1384, we have evidence of an Observantine mentality when Rampegolus dedicated his Biblical handbook to his "beloved students" in the *studium* at Naples.[33] In this work we find the urgency for reform necessitated by the devil's assault, the diabolical success in the Schism, the last days, and the call for the truly religious (*veri religiosi*) to be separated out as the last hope for the reform of the Church. And this, Rampegolus' *Figure Bibliorum*, was not an isolated treatise of one of

---

[28] See Saak, "The *Figure Bibliorum*," 34–37; with reference to Lecceto, Walsh writes: "Regrettably there is a dearth of information about the daily life of the community, or about what they felt to be their raison d'être, and this lack is to a remarkable degree characteristic of the early observants. They were not notably articulate, and there is virtually no surviving sermon literature or treatises on the spiritual life which might represent an apologia for this singularly conservative movement." Walsh, "Papal Policy and Local Reform: The Beginnings," 53.

[29] Walsh, "The Observance: Sources for a History of the Observant Reform Movement in the Order of Augustinian Friars in the Fourteenth and Fifteenth Centuries," *Rivista Di Storia Della Chiesa in Italia* 31 (1977), 40–67; 53.

[30] For the dating of the work, see Chapter Five, note 229.

[31] Gutiérrez, *History* I/II, 76.

[32] *Ibid.*, 79; see also Saak, "The *Figure Bibilorum*," 35, n. 82.

[33] See note 88 below.

the Order's university theologians. Rampegolus, as Jordan of Quedlinburg, was a simple lector, and his major work was composed even before he received the title.[34] Zachariae's Apocalypse commentary is extant in a single manuscript, as are those of Bertold of Regensburg and Hermann of Mindelheim; Favaroni's commentary has come down to us in only three manuscripts. None of these works were printed. Rampegolus' *Figure Bibliorum* is extant is at least thirty-eight manuscripts, and had received eight printed editions by 1500.[35] What we are dealing with here is a work of wide readership and significance, and one in which we can smell the origins of the Augustinian Observance.[36]

i. *Inimicus Crudelissimus*
The devil has launched his assault on the Church. That is the overriding message of the *Figure Bibliorum*. Among the opponents of the Church, the devil is the cruelest enemy of all, attacking the faithful without cease.[37] Woe to those who do not maintain the fight, who succumb to the devil's treachery and deceit, for they become the *filii diaboli*. For Rampegolus, as for Augustinus of Ancona and Jordan of Quedlinburg, the Christian life is a constant battle, a *pugna continua*, against the devil and the forces of Satan.

The human body is the devil's battleground; the human soul, his prize. And love is the determining factor: "Nothing is able to distinguish good Christians (*boni*) from evil (*mali*)," Rampegolus explained, "as does love (*caritas*). Thus Christ told his own sons in the thirteenth chapter of John: *if you are in concord with one another, then people will know that you are my disciples*; and this, the devil opposes, because among all the other goods, he hates love most of all, and therefore he does his best to extinguish it."[38] All that works against love is the

---

[34] See Saak, "The *Figure Bibliorum*," 22.
[35] See Chapter Five, n. 229; Zumkeller *MSS* nr. 117 (65); and Saak, "The *Figure Bibliorum*," 24.
[36] The following is not intended as a comprehensive treatment of Rampegolus' theology, which would require a separate study. *Figure Bibliorum* is in many ways a *loci communes*, addressing selected topics, arranged alphabetically, yet topics that Rampegolus chose. My analysis here seeks to portray the general tenor of the work, bringing to light its central perspective which informs the work throughout.
[37] "Diabolus est inimicus crudelissimus et pessimus dominus et pessimus servos suos tractans." Ant.Ramp. *FB* De diabolo, fol. 31ra; "Nos habemus proditorem scilicet diabolum, qui videns nos proficere in virtutibus die noctuque nos impugnare non cessat." Ant.Ramp. *FB* De diabolo, fol. 31rb.
[38] "Nulla talis potest reperiri differentia discernens bona a malis, qualis est chari-

work of the devil. Thus "back biters" spew forth their venom as the devil's farts.[39] Yet the flatterer is no better. In offering rosy words of false praise, the flatterer corrupts the mind more easily than anything else; the tongue of the flatterer is more damaging than the sword of the persecutor;[40] the flatterer is the devil's servant (*servus diaboli*).[41]

Virtues and vices: that is the issue. It would be easy to pass over Rampegolus as yet just another moralist advocating the virtues of faith, hope, love, fortitude, temperance, prudence, and justice,[42] and portraying the devil as the symbolized moralization of sin, defined by the corresponding seven vices: pride, greed, gluttony, luxury, sloth, envy and anger. And that he was. Rampegolus, as so many of his Order, was a moral theologian, advocating the absolute necessity of

---

tas: illa ergo est que distinguit filios Dei a filiis diaboli. Idcirco Christus de propriis filiis ait, Iohannis 13: *In hoc cognoscent homines quod discipuli mei eritis, si habueritis pacem ad invicem* [Io. 13: 35; *dilectionem ad invicem*], et in hoc sibi oppositus est diabolus, quia summe pre omnibus bonis odio habet charitatem, ideo plus ad ipsius extinctionem conatur." *FB*, De charitate (ed. Cologne, 1505), fol. 28ᵛ.

[39] "Lingua detractoris est sicut scorpio, quia in facie hominum aliqua premittit que ad laudem cadant, cedant eius cui vult detrahere ut non videatur illum odio habere, disponit enim per hoc et domulezauris [*sic*] audientium credendum et suscipiendum venenum quod paratum habet." *FB*, De detractione, fol. 29ᵛᵇ. *Cf*.: "Detractor blanditur ut scorpio, quia in facie et retro percutit, disponit etiam aures audientium aliqua virtuosa illius cui vult detrahere, ut inducat audientes ad credendum venenosa, que cupit proferre." *FB*, De detractione (ed. Cologne, 1505), 62ʳ; "Et subaudi per bestiam [*scil*. Apc. 16] diabolum, per cuius flatum detractores loquuntur." *FB*, De detractione, fol. 30ʳᵃ; the Cologne 1505 edition reads: ". . . per cuius flatum seu anhelitum . . ." (ed. Cologne, 1505), fol. 62ᵛ; *cf*. Heiko A. Oberman, "Teufelsdreck: Eschatology and Scatology in the 'Old' Luther," in Oberman, *The Impact of the Reformation*, 51–68.

[40] "Nihil est quod tam facile corrumpat mentem hominum ut adulatio. Plus enim nocet lingua adulatoris, quam gladius persecutoris." *FB*, De adulatione, fol. 2ᵛᵃ.

[41] ". . . [diabolus] in mundi prosperitatibus facit hominem per appetitum superbie ad alta saltaris et postmodum habet servos suos paratos scilicet adulatores, qui propinant sibi huiusmodi potum scilicet adulationis verba, qui velut cecus assumens coram omnibus qui vident hoc falsum vituperatur." *FB*, De adulatione, fol. 3ᵛᵃ; *cf*.: ". . . [diabolus] pulvere arrogantie excecat hominem et suum captivum facit, cogit eum saltare hincinde per mundi prospera et querere humanas laudes; et paratis servis diaboli, id est adulatoribus per eos ipse diabolus propinat potum confusionis et ignominie, qui assumens coram adstantibus vituperatur, qui laudes ipsius cognoscunt esse falsas." *FB*, De adulatione (ed. Cologne, 1505), fol. 6ʳ.

[42] "Ecclesia militans assimilatur stelle [*cf*. Sir. 43:10: *species caeli gloriosa stellarum*] supradicte immobili per firmitatem et constantiam fidei, quia nulla concussione quamvis gravi moveri poterit a fide que Christo totaliter est coniuncta . . . habet enim ecclesia circa se septem stelas, id est septem virtutes scilicet tres theologicas et quatuor cardinales, que voce predicatorum in ecclesie et nunquam ipsam deserunt." *FB*, De ecclesia, fol. 42ᵛᵃ⁻ᵇ.

moral theology, and as such, he was no mere moralist, and his theology was no mere morality. With his *Figure Bibliorum* and his moralizations, Rampegolus was fighting the final battle against the forces of hell, which had been unleashed on the Church and were attacking the faithful night and day: "Our life is a battle. Our enemy takes command of those whom he is not able to conquer with open evil, by invading our souls secretly so that he might snatch them away, for he prepares traps for us according to our desires, which he does not know how to bring to his consent openly."[43] Rampegolus' moralism was one that placed at issue not the "good" and the "bad," but heaven and hell. Those were the stakes. The present life was a most dangerous journey lived between God and the devil.[44]

The bodily senses are the betrayers of the soul,[45] for through the senses one is tempted. The devil has placed the human body in a mud hole of inebriation (*lutum crapule*) so that he might then be able more easily to subject it to the fires of lust.[46] *Avaritia* and *cupiditas* are the great enemies, comprising the kingdom of darkness, the realm of the devil, who sends out his sons to oversee the world as the harshest taskmasters, not allowing one any rest.[47] Human reason (*iudi-*

---

[43] "Vita nostra malitia est, superet inimicus noster quos aperto sceleris vincere nequit, occulte insidiatur, ut rapiat, insidias enim nobis parat iuxta appetitum nostrum quem novit apertum ad consensum." *FB*. De diabolo, fol. 34ᵛᵃ; *cf*.: "Nos sumus in continua pugna contra diabolum et peccata, et ubi non valet nos aperte superire, ipse nobis insidiatur occulte ut draco. Ideo semper debet esse in nobis lumen verbi Dei, a quo discamus et cogniscamus insidias et occultas eius tentationes." (ed. Cologne, 1505), fol. 70ʳ.

[44] "Via presentis vite scrupulosa et periculosa est valde et habet ab una parte altitudinem maximam, quia de celo, quia ad infernum; ad alia parte habet declinem quandam planitiem, quia vita corporalem que per affectiones inordinatas frequenter quasi prona deorsum in precipuum tendit." *FB*, De diabolo, fol. 35ʳᵇ⁻ᵛᵃ; *cf*.: "Nos sumus cuiusdam periculosi itineris viatores, scilicet vite presentis, et est maxima altitudo ex una parte, quia a celo usque ad infernum. Ideo qui cadit casu illo non potest amplius sublevari." *FB*, De diabolo (ed. Cologne, 1505), fol. 71ᵛ.

[45] "... continue adversarius noster diabolus, tanquam leo rugiens circuit querens quem devoret; oportet enim quomodo ei resistamus et temptationibus suis, sed primo oportet reprimere domesticos adversarios scilicet corporales sensus, qui sunt spiritus proditores." *FB*, De carne, fol. 15ʳᵃ.

[46] "Diabolus ponit corpus humanum in lutum crapule ut postmodum facilius ponat ipsum in fornacem luxurie, nam madefactum crapula libidinis incendium non perpendit, quod in statu abstinentie utique abhorreret." *FB*, De abstinentia, fol. 2ᵛᵇ; *cf*.: "Diabolus ponit corpus in lutum crapule ut facilius postmodum ponat illud in ignem seu fornacem libidinis. Nam madefactus ebrietate, libidinis incendia non perpendit, quae in statu abstinentiae abhorrebat." *FB*, De abstinentia (ed. Cologne, 1505), fol. 3ᵛ.

[47] "Pharao [*cf*. Ex. 1] denotat diabolum regem Egypti, scilicet tenebrarum, qui

cium rationis) is the leader of the resistance. The enemies of reason, namely, the devil, the world, and the bodily senses, constantly strive to overthrow reason in order to capture the soul.[48] Once the devil has been able to get a foothold in the soul, he sets to work to destroy it completely: he blinds the reason; extinguishes love; silences the word of God; deletes the sorrow and shame for sin, rendering the soul a harlot; obliterates prayers; perverts the heart and the eyes, eliminating the possibility of tears of contrition; and finally tears to shreds the cloak of innocence attained in baptism. Thus one becomes wretched, for whereas one had been the temple of God, one has become the devil's whorehouse, the receptacle for the demons of hell. Confession even can no longer help, for as soon as the devil takes control of the soul as of a city, he murders the princes of the soul, which are contrition, confession, and satisfaction, for otherwise the city would rebel. Thus all one's good works are obliterated, and being bounded in chains, the strongest chains made of one's own sins, one is then led blind into Babylon, the realm of confusion and ignorance, and there kept in the hands of the devil.[49]

---

cecitatis filios, id est avaros et cupidos, subdure cervicis servitute detinet, cogit eos dispergi per universam Egyptum ad colligendas divitias, que luto et paleis comparantur et ordinat super ipsos uxores et filios qui velut superstites urgent illos congregare pecuniam, nec permittunt eos aliqua anime saluti vacare." *FB*, De avaritia, fol. 9va.

[48] "Iudicium rationis quem est totius exercitus anime princeps et dux, expertus est nequitiam sensuum corporalium et calliditatem ipsorum contra se. Ideo nichilominus debet de ipsis confidere, sed eos taliter deicere et captivatos affligere, quod amplius non permittantur nec possint offendere." *FB*, De carne humana, fol. 15va; *cf.*: "Iudicium rationis dicitur esse princeps in nobis et ad ipsum spectat opprimere impugnationes hostiles, que interdum fiunt contra animam nedum a mundo et a diabolo, verum etiam a propriis corporalibus sensibus, qui omni conatu student animam captivare." *FB*, De carne humana (ed. Cologne, 1505), fol. 31^r.

[49] "Diabolus vincens animam nostram [*cf.* 4 Rg. 25], intrat templum cordis et mentis et primo extinguit candelabri lumen scilicet rationis. Secundo, altare aureum, per quod notatur caritas. Tertio, mensas propositionis, per quas notatur predicatio verbi domini que est anime cibum. Quarto, coronas faciei templi, per quas nota<tur> testimonium bone conscientie. Et vasa incensi, per que devota oratio designatur. Et vasa aque sacrificii, per que lacrimas devotas subaudi et vestes sacerdotales, per quas anime innocentiam nota<tur>. His igitur destructis et comminutis remanet anima brutalium cogitationum et omnium affectionum immundarum spelunca. Patet igitur qualiter diabolus istam dilaniat caritatem. Sed post hec in tanta mala populum ducit captivum in Babylonem, quia memoriam et intelligentiam et voluntatem, visum, auditum et ceteros sensus confundit et catenat vinculis gravissimis ac vinculatos multum prosterint vel nichil boni amplius agere possint vel cogitare."*FB*, De diabolo, fol. 32^{va-b}; *cf.*: "Diabolus vincens animam nostram, intrat templum cordis et mentis nostre et primo extinguit candelabrium lumen, id est, excecat iudicium

The devil is the Christian's cruelest enemy, and the cruelest tyrant. The entire Christian life is a constant battle against the vicious insidiousness of the devil. Yet even when the devil has won, when the devil has led the sinner bound into Babylon, when all one's merits and good works have been obliterated, all is not lost. After having set forth how one is bound by the chains of one's sins, Rampegolus quoted Augustine's *Confessions*, the same passage quoted above in Chapter Three concerning the chain of lust that bound Augustine. He did so by adding a line of his own with no further comment, a line not found in his immediate source:

> Thus Augustine in his *Confessions*: I sighed, having been bound, not by the fetters put on me by someone else, but by the iron bondage of my own will. The enemy held my will and made a chain out of it and bound me with it. From my will came lust, lust became habit, and the habit became necessity. Divine grace alone frees man.[50]

---

rationis. Secundo, surripit altare aureum, per quod charitas notatur. Tertio, mensas panis propositionis evertit ac destruit, per quas subaudi predicationes verbi Dei, quod dicitur panis spiritualis anime. Quarto, coronam faciei templi removet, quia delet de facie verecundiam et ruborem peccandi, ut anima efficiatur quasi meretrix sine fronte. Quinto, destruit vasa incensi per que notantur orationes devote. Sexto vasa aque sacrificii, quia pervertit cor et oculos, ne ibi inveniri possit lachrymarum contritio, per quam sit Deo acceptum sacrificium nostrum. Ultimo lacerat vestem sacerdotalem, scilicet innocentie pallium, quod nobis Christus acquisivit, et quod accepimus in baptismo. His igitur expoliatis, miser homo, qui erat templum Dei, efficitur diaboli prostibulum et receptaculum gentis Babylonis, id est, demonum infernalium." *FB*, De diabolo (ed. Cologne, 1505), fol. 66ᵛ–67ʳ; "Vite presentis affectio est terra inimicorum, ibi tres insidiantes inimicos habemus, scilicet carnem, mundum, et diabolum." *FB*, De inferno, fol. 62ʳᵃ; "Per Nabuchodonosor, regem Babylonie, [*cf.* Ier. 52:4–11] subaudi diabolum, capit enim regem Zedechiam in Ierusalem quia capit et flagellat iustum peccato mediante, nam Zedechias iustus interpreatione succendit Ierusalem id est visionem pacis, quando de quieto et tranquillo conscientie precipitat iustum in terrenam concupiscentiam, sed occidit principes Iuda scilicet confessionem, contritionem, et satisfactionem. Hii enim principes si viverent, utique regem cito liberarent. Ideo eos diabolus quanto citius potest occidit. Perdit etiam filios regis quia omnes fructus anime, omnia bona opera, que in statu penitentie vivebant, extinguit. Tunc excecatur rex, quia obtenebrat diabolus sibi rationis lumen et sic ducit eum in Babylonem id est ad confusionem et miseriam ac tristissiam sempiternam et ponitur in domo carceris, vinculis peccatorum ligatus, pro tanto usque ad diem mortis sue, quia in quantum in se est nunquam de manibus diaboli propria virtute potest amplius fugere. Facit igitur omnia hec diabolus peccatori." *FB*, De diabolo, fol. 33ʳᵃ.

[50] "Unde Augustinus in libro *Confessionum*: Suspirabam ligatus non alieno ferro, sed mea ferrea voluntate. Velle enim meum tenebat inimicus et de illo michi catenam fecerat et constrinxerat me, ex voluntate facta est libido, et ex libidine facta est consuetudo, ex consuetudine facta est necessitas, sed sola gratia divina liberat hominem." *FB*, De diabolo, fol. 33ʳᵃ⁻ᵇ; *cf.* Aug. conf. 8.5.10 (119,8–12).

Sola gratia liberat hominem: sola gratia was Rampegolus' last glimmer of hope he held out to the sinner bound by Satan. The heart of the sinner is God's temple, but even if that temple has become the devil's brothel, "if we turn our face to Christ through the affections of our heart, crying out with the prophet: *Save me Lord, for I am drowning,* Christ will reach out his hand from on high and free us from these depths and from the harshness of the storm."[51] Rampegolus thus affirmed that "not by seeing, but by believing, will you be born into the body of the Church."[52] The Church was the realm of salvation. Yet the war against the devil continued, for this was not simply an individual battle; it was also a corporate battle of ultimate magnitude. Once inside the Church, the sinner was not free from the forces of Satan, for Satan had preceded him. The devil was already at work within the Church herself.

ii. *Ecclesia Concussa*

The Church is being shaken to its foundations. This is the perspective of Rampegolus. He opened his section *De ecclesia* with a *figura* drawn from psalm 44:11:

> *Listen, my daughter, hear my words and consider them: forget your own people and your father's house*: Just as he is commonly thought to be blessed and entirely happy who has an honest, gentle, and good-willed wife, so is he always considered to be miserable who has an obstinate and angry wife, for he spends few, if any, good, carefree days. It is much better to live with snakes than with a real bitch.[53]

In interpreting this passage, Rampegolus related the belligerent wife with the Synagogue, who takes on other lovers, and follows idols

---

[51] "Templum vero est cor nostrum. Igitur facies versus Christum per cordis affectum ponamus, cum Propheta clamentes: *Salvum me fac deus, quoniam intraverunt aque usque ad animam meam*. Et ipse emittet manum suam [*scripsi*; tuam *cod.*] de alto eripere me et libera<t> me de aquis multis id est de profundo et amaritudine tempestatis vitiorum." *FB*, De gratia, fol. 53^(vb).

[52] "... in corpus ecclesie non videndo sed credendo te transtulisti." *FB*, De gratia, fol. 54^(ra); *cf.*: "... in corpore ecclesie non uniendo sed credendo te transtulisti." *FB*, De gratia (ed. Cologne, 1505), fol. 100^(v); "... in corpore ecclesie non vivendo sed credendo te transtulisti." *FB*, De gratia (ed. Cologne, 1609), 267.

[53] "*Audi filia et vide et inclina aurem tuam et obliviscere populum tuum in domum patris tui.* Ps. <44:11>. Sicut ille beatus a vulgo censetur et felix omnino qui habet uxorem benivolam, mansuetam, et honestam, ita est semper tristis censendus, qui habet uxorem obstinatam et obiragantem, paucos enim aut nullos ducit securos dies in bonis. Multo autem melius esset habitari inter serpentes quam cum muliere rixosa et in malitia obstinata." *FB*, De ecclesia, fol. 41^(va).

and gross sins, thus leaving her proper husband and lord.[54] Yet the Synagogue is only one of four plagues persecuting the Church. Taking the *figura* of Matthew 8:24, *the boat was overwhelmed by the waves*, Rampegolus interpreted the cause thereof as being the four winds, east, west, south, and north.[55] He then explained that these four winds were four groups inflicting great damage on the Church.[56] The first were the Jews, who raged against their own savior and his members.[57] The second were the pagans, who, distancing themselves from the warmth of love poured forth the blood of the saints as water.[58] The third were the Turks, who, perverting the scriptures by the farts of their deadly doctrines, cause a terrible storm.[59] The fourth, however, was the perversity of the *mali christiani*, which "began a long time ago through their divisions and belligerency, in the course of which the Church has been harshly attacked; or, we can say, that this fourth plague is that of the Turks; or even that this is the plague that will come in the time of the Antichrist, when the sun of the present life has already set."[60]

---

[54] "Synagoga ferrea semper fuit uxor prava et pestifera, que super proprium virum altos induxit turpissimos amatores, id est diversas spurcitias sive immundicias, idola et alia enorma peccata, post que in exultatione ibat, relicto proprio domino suo." *FB*, De ecclesia, fol. 41va.

[55] "*Navis operiebatur fluctibus*, Mt. 8<:24>. Nota quod quatuor sunt principales venti in mari, scilicet oriens, occidens, australis, et aquilo, quorum motione marina causatur pestis. Nam mare non fluctuat, nisi concussione ventorum." *FB*, De ecclesia, fol. 42vb.

[56] "Erga navem ecclesie per huius maris procellas navigantem, quatuor nationes pestem maximam induxerunt, nam ab ipsis cunabulis, ei non defuit persequatio." *FB*, De ecclesia, fol. 42vb–43ra.

[57] "Primo ut ita dicam concussa fuit a iudeorum collegio, tanquam ab originali plaga furente et fluctuante contra redemptorem proprium et ipsius membra." *FB*, De ecclesia, fol. 43ra.

[58] "Secundo, a populo gentilium, quorum insipientia frigidi et sicii, a vari solis lumine et caritatis calore distantes, funderunt sanguinem sanctorum tamquam aquam." *Ibid.*

[59] "Tertio, a secta saracenorum, qui australem fecunditatem sacre scripture pervertentes flatu sue mortifere doctrine pestilem procellam induxerunt." *Ibid.; cf.*: "Tertio a secta hereticorum, que australi fecunditate sacre scripture accipientes fructus, suo pestifero flatu convertebant fluctus." *FB*, De ecclesia (ed. Cologne, 1505), fol. 79^r.

[60] "Quarto dicere possumus quod fuit malorum christianorum perversitas, que a magno tempore incepit, per ipsorum divisiones et rixas inter quos ecclesia non modicum est concussa; vel possumus dicere, quod quarta ista plaga est saracenorum; vel etiam plaga, que ventura est tempore antichristi, iam occidente presentis vite sole." *FB*, De ecclesia, fol. 43ra; *cf.*: "Quarto possumus dicere, quod a falsis christianis, quorum divisio ecclesiam multo tempore non modicum conturbavit. Vel possumus dicere quod ista quarta concussio reservatur fienda tempore antichristi iam occidenti presentis vite luce." *FB*, De ecclesia (ed. Cologne, 1505), fol. 79^r.

Rampegolus then continued by relating these four plagues to the four beasts of Daniel 7:2–14. The first beast is once again that of the Synagogue,[61] and the second, that of the pagans.[62] The third, however, rather than the Turks, is the beast of the heretics, which, however dangerous, can be put to flight by the doctors of the Church.[63] And the fourth beast, is the beast that cannot be named. This terrible beast is the division of Christians, the division of Christendom, which cannot be named "because there is no reason why this fourth savageness should rise up amongst the people of God. This beast is truly said to be without name, because his names are clearly written on his hands by his works, or, on his forehead by his hate for his neighbors. Therefore, all his names will be deleted from the book of life and will be cast into the pool of God's anger."[64] This fourth beast is the Antichrist:

> ... what this beast does not slash up with his teeth, he tramples under his feet, because those who are not permitted to take up arms against Christians or their neighbors, kill them then in their wills and affections. But my God, the evil hearts of Christians rage, as if boiling up against the ship of the Church, so that among the sons for whom the inheritance is intended, the drowning of the sons of contention and discord might be openly seen in the waves, but those bastard sons who do not fulfill their vows, are to be cast out from God's kingdom and handed over to the eternal fires of hell together with their father, the devil, who apostasized from paradise... We can further understand this fourth beast as the Antichrist, who in his time raises great havoc among the faithful of the Church. If his days are not cut short, no one will be saved.[65]

---

[61] "Nam per leenam duas alas habentem synagoga notatur, de tota prophetia et lege quibus ad superna volare debebat pro sui creatoris meditatione sed cito hiis depositis cecidit in terram, et commixta est inter gentes per cupiditatem et nequitiam et opera eorum dedicit per idolatriam. Hec fecit illud nephandissimum seclus furens contra redemptorem suum, facta illi sicut leo in silva, Ier. 12. Et non solum in caput, sed etiam in membra deseviebat." *FB*, De ecclesia, fol. 43^{ra-b}.

[62] "Secunda bestia fuit gentilium natio, que triplici peccatorum gradu scilicet concupiscentia carnis, concupiscentia occulorum, et superbia vite regebatur." *FB*, De ecclesia, fol. 43rb.

[63] "Tertia vero bestia pardo similis fuit secta hereticorum, qui depicti et colorati diversorum errorum colore simplices incebantur decipere... sed hanc bestiam fugarunt sancti doctores a confinibus ecclesie." *Ibid*.

[64] "Quarta vero terribilis bestia hoc est divisio christianorum, que nullo nominatur nomine, quia nulla causa est quare feritas inter christianicolas dei vigeat. Et vere dicitur 'sine nomine', quia nomina eorum huius bestie characterem portant in manibus per opera vel in fronte per odium proximorum. Delebuntur de libro vite et proicientur in stanum ire dei." *Ibid*.

[65] "... sed quod hec bestia non lacerat dentibus, hoc pedibus conculcat, quia

The division of Christendom, brought about by the *mali christiani*, is the time of the Antichrist, when the bastard sons join their father the devil in hell, and if this division, if this time of the Antichrist, is not quickly ended, then all is lost. The Church has always had its opponents, the Jews, the pagans, the heretics, and Turks, and the *mali christiani*, but only these last, working within the Church, signify the coming of the Antichrist, when the Church has been divided for no reason. Rampegolus did not explicitly mention the Schism as such. But for him the *divisio christianorum* was the work of the devil and signified the reign of the Antichrist. For Jordan of Quedlinburg writing in 1365, the Antichrist had not yet made himself known.[66] Less than twenty years later, for Rampegolus, he had.

Rampegolus' view of the Antichrist is somewhat vague. On the one hand, the time of the Antichrist lies in the future, but on the other, it is marked by the division of Christendom. There is certainly an apocalyptic in Rampegolus' work, but one cannot find a developed apocalypticism. His is a "reform apocalyptic," calling Christians to mend their lives, to turn from their sins, and be united with the Church fighting against the devil.[67] Even in his section on the Last Judgment we do not find explicit statements of the imminent end, but only the stringent calls to think of one's death, and not to be caught off guard, for

---

quidam quibus non licitum arma suscipere contra christianos seu proximos, ipsos tunc voluntatibus et affectibus occidunt. Sed sic prochdolor, fluctuant prava corda christianorum quasi mare ferviens contra navem, ut operiri fluctibus videatur litis et discordie filiorum ymus inter filios quibus reservatur hereditas, sed spuriorum apostatarum qui abiciendi sunt a regno et tradendi igni eterno cum patre eorum diabolo, qui est apostata paradisi . . . Possumus tamen per quartam bestiam antichristum intelligere, qui tempore suo de fidelibus ecclesie magnam faciet stragem et nisi abreviarentur dies illius, non fieret salva omnis caro." *FB*, De ecclesia, fol. 43[va].

[66] "Si ergo a Vespasiano et Tito incipiunt computare qui fuerunt post nativitatem Christi anno lxxvi, tunc secundum eos antichristus deberet venire anno mccclxv, qui est presens annus quo ego iam scribo. Non tamen adhuc de antichristo per dei gratiam aliquid experimur." Jor. *OP*, sermo 455, as quoted by Hümpfner, intro., xix.

[67] For a sophisticated treatment of various types of apocalypticism, see Curtis V. Bostick, *The Antichrist and the Lollards. Apocalypticism in Late Medieval and Reformation England*, SMRT 70 (Leiden, 1998), esp. 12–18. Bostick categorizes 'reformist' apocalypticism as being Joachite; Bostick, *The Antichrist*, 15–16. Rampeoglus' apocalyptic is not Joachite, but is reformist. For Joachimism in the OESA, see Marjory Reeves, "Joachimist Expectations in the Order of Augustinian Hermits," *RThAM* 25 (1958), 111–141; *cf.* Adolar Zumkeller, "Joachim von Fiore und sein angeblicher Einfluß auf den Augustiner-Eremitenorden (kritische Bemerkungen zu einer Untersuchung M. Reeves')," *Augustinianum* 3 (1963), 382–388.

... how will we be able to make satisfaction to God when we are called suddenly to the final judgment, especially when we do not believe the hour has come? For that last day is great and most bitter, and this is certain: when that terrible last trumpet sounds beyond all expectation over all of those busy with mundane business and those dealing with concerns for wealth, who will be able to hide?[68]

Rampegolus did not really say anything more than what had already been said for ages. Petrarch, Rampegolus' fellow countryman, had viewed the pope as the Antichrist and the Avignon papacy as being the Babylonian Captivity of the Church.[69] Little wonder Rampegolus shared similar opinions. The origins of his work were in Naples, where Petrarch had served at the court of Robert d'Anjou, to whom Giles of Rome dedicated his commentary on the second book of the *Sentences*, where James of Viterbo had been the archbishop, where Augustinus of Ancona had been councilor and chaplain, and where the Augustinian Dionysius de Burgo, a close friend of Petrarch's, had also done duty. This was Naples, the realm of the papal vicar in Italy, and for Petrarch, the papacy had abandoned Italy for France. Yet when Rampegolus was teaching in Naples, the days of the wise and pious King Robert were no more;[70] the kingdom of Naples was in turmoil, and the Church and his Order were split between Rome and Avignon. It makes little difference that Rampegolus' view was not unique. For him, the devil was at work, the time of the Antichrist was at hand, the fourth beast with no name. Even if one could not say that the final judgment was just around the corner, or that the actual Antichrist had made his final appearance, he was coming; he was coming, and if his time of destruction could not be limited, all would be lost.

---

[68] "Unde possimus satisfacere domino quando nos subito ab eterno iudice vocamur, etiam hora qua non credimus? Novissimus enim ille dies magnus et amarissimus, et certus est, quando tonabit tonitruum illud terribile super omnes operatores terre ac dispensatores thesauri, excludens omnem expectationem, et quis poterit se abscondere?" *FB*, De iudicio, fol. 63^{rb-va}; *cf.*: "Unde possimus vocati a deo satisfacere, quoniam ab eterno iudice subito requiremur, et hora qua nos nescimus vocabit. Novissimus enim dies ille magnus et amarus, incertus est quando tonabit illud tonitruum terribile super omnes operatores terre et dispensatores divini thesauri, excludens omne expectationis tempus, et nullus poterit se abscondere." *FB*, De iudicio (ed. Cologne, 1505), fol. 118^v.

[69] For Petrarch, see Paul Piur, *Petrarcas 'Buch Ohne Namen' und die Päpstliche Kurie. Ein Beitrag zur Geistesgeschichte der Frührenaissance* (Halle, 1925).

[70] See above, Chapter One, note 115.

Rampegolus' analysis of the situation was in many ways very similar to that of Petrarch. Avarice and cupidity were the culprits, the devil's tools, which had infected the soul of Christendom. Avarice was a darkness that had fallen, as the darkness of the ninth plague God sent against Egypt:

> By darkness is signified avarice and cupidity, which today indeed have condemned every nation, both the temporal and the spiritual realms, because they are able to be taken in by apparent faith. Wherefore a brother does not acknowledge his own brother on account of money, neither a son his father, nor a friend his friend; so great is the antisocial behavior of human desire today, which tries to take over wherever it can.[71]

Avarice is the servant of the devil, and the avaricious are the sons of blindness, held in servitude to the devil and his kingdom.[72] This was a pestilence that infected almost everyone in Rampegolus' eyes, including Christians.[73] Yet even worse: avarice had even infected the very leaders of the Church, the *prelati*.

The prelates are the mediators between God and their subjects, the pillars of the Church.[74] They are the ones who are to steer the

---

[71] "Exodi 10 [*cf*. Ex. 10:21], ubi legitur quod octava plaga Egypti fuerunt tenebre palpabiles. Ita ut frater fratrem non videret, ut enim dictum est. Per tenebras notatur avaritiam et cupiditatem, que hodie adeo condemnate sunt erga omnem nationem et temporalem et spiritualem quod oculata fide tangi possunt. Unde frater ob pecuniam non cognoscit fratrem, nec filius patrem, nec amicus amicum. Tanta est enim insociabilitas hodie appetitus humani quod undecumque potest conatur capere." *FB*, De avaritia, fol 8vb–9ra; *cf*.: "Exodi 10, ubi legitur quod in nona plaga Egypti fuerunt super terram totam tenebre, que palpari poterant, ita ut frater fratrem non videret. Spiritualiter. Per tenebras subaudi, ut dictum est, avaritiam et cupiditatem, que adeo hodie mundum tinxerunt et corda hominum fedaverunt." *FB*, De avaritia (ed. Cologne, 1505), fol. 15^v.

[72] "Pharao denotat diabolum, regem Egypti scilicet tenebrarum, qui cecitatis filios, id est avaros et cupidos subdure cervicis servitute detinet." *FB*, De avaritia, fol. 9va.

[73] "Diabolus cognoscens hodie humanum appetitum ad simulachra et idola pecunie contemplandum atque ad exequendum in taberna sua id est in vita presenti depinxit hec simulachra scilicet auri et argenti seu cupiditatis et avaritie ad que ita libenter hodie declinant homines ... Nam sicut peccatores citius sunt in taberna quam in ecclesia, ita ferre omnes homines christiani potius avaritie quam divine meditationi vacant." *FB*, De avaritia, fol. 10rb; *cf*.: "Diabolus cognoscens humanum appetitum esse pronum ad simulachra et idololatriam, pecunia contemplanda et etiam exercenda seu colligenda in sua taberna, hoc est in mundo, depinxit statuas et imagines argenti et auri, ut cupidi et avari videntes declineat ad cellarium diaboli, id est ad pecuniam et usuram, furta et rapinam, quod fere omnes faciunt gentes hodie relictis Deo et animarum salute." *FB*, De avaritia (ed. Cologne, 1505), fol. 18^v.

[74] "Prelatus dicitur esse medius, sive mediator inter deum et subditos, ut sit

Church's ship, the *navis religionis*, through the tempests of this harsh and arduous life, bringing it with safety into the tranquil port of a good life.[75] Yet the prelates of Rampegolus' day were more concerned with money, office, power, and prestige than they were with shepherding their flocks. And it began with ambition. The cleric who aspires to higher office is a snake, spewing forth his venom while pretending to be holy and righteous if only he can achieve a bishopric.[76] Such a cleric is an "Absolon,"

> ... who always has bitterness in his mind until he is able to obtain his disgusting desires; such is said to commit fratricide, because by his own evil example, he kills his neighbors and brothers. With his hypocrisy he tries to give his electors and promoters a good impression with his virtuous words, deceitfully promising great and wonderful deeds, which he never intends to do ... but [having attained his desire] he becomes even worse than he was before, for he banishes his own father, that

transitus ad deum ab ipsis subditis, mediante prelato per vitam et doctrinam ipsius prelati." *FB*, De prelatione (ed. Cologne, 1505), fol. 207^v–208^r; "... [prelatus] locum dei inter subditos tenet." *FB*, De prelatione, fol. 106ra; "Prelati sunt membra principalia in tota ecclesie corpore." *FB*, De prelatione (ed. Cologne, 1505), fol. 218^r.

[75] "Per navem subaudi religio <intelligitur>, quia sicut navis de terra fertili terre sterili victum adducit, sic religio de habundantia sacre scripture celestibus hominibus celestia alimenta ministrat... Igitur primo debet elegi principalis nauta scilicet prelatus <non> in sorte carnis vel sanguinis scilicet nobilitatis, sed ille qui precellit scientia et bonitate cui omnes tamquam patri et pastori reverenter debent obedire et per ipsum ordinari ad officia pro quibus singuli apti sunt. Non enim haurienda est aqua cum soterularibus, sed etiam <non> debet poni idiota ad docendum nec pravus ad regendum, sed valentibus et scientibus debent imponi officia. Debet etiam unusquisque in loco sibi assignato quiescere, videmus enim quod in navi rusticus stat circa militem et aliquando super militem eo quod peritior sit in arte nautica, nec querendus talis locus est in navi que arca est, qualis queritur in terra que lata et spatiosa est. Sic in proposito qui veniunt ad sanctam religionis societatem ex deliciis et divitiis mundi non debent habere fastidio proximos suos qui ad illam ex paupertate venerunt. Nec debent dedignari subesse prelato seu rustico vili natione cui deus scientiam regiminis condonavit. Potius enim debent Christi humilitatis reminisci qui dum esset eterni regis filius non abhorruit induere formam servi et erat subditus Marie et Joseph. Nec talem debent in religione querere locum honoris et eminentis status qualem in mundo habuisset cum sit stricta et arta via que tendit ad gloriam, sed ipsi debent carius cor intentum ad considerandum premii magnitudinem ut terrena non querant. Si igitur sic navis religionis gubernetur, faciliter pertransibit huius furibundi maris procellas et perveniat ad bone vite tranquillitatem." *FB*, De religiosis, fol. 109$^{ra–b}$.

[76] "*Venenum aspidum sub labiis eorum.* Ps. 13<:3> ... Per aspidem, que fertur surda ad vocem incantantium, clericus elatus ad prelationem anhelans denotatur, qui surdum se prebet ad vocem Christi ... hic etiam dum cupit prelationi coniungi per simulatam equitatem, videtur venenum deponere, promittens et pretendens sanctitatem et iustitiam, si perducatur ad cathedram." *FB*, De prelatione (ed. Cologne 1505), fol. 207^r.

is Christ, and his teachings from his entire territory; he suppresses good men and promotes evil, he chooses money, and sells Church property, and he does nothing but evil.[77]

When a prelate sins, "he kills with his sin not only himself, but also his subjects."[78] Such was the state of the Church, for the entire world was burning with avarice, the work of the devil.[79]

Yet just as pernicious as evil prelates, are those who placed them in office. The electors of unworthy bishops, who have made their appointments based on money and nepotism, are thieves, and even worse than thieves because they murder their victims both physically and spiritually. They hand over the Church to the leporousness of unworthy prelates, and thus the Church, "which had been cloaked in golden saffron, is now covered with shit." The electors of unfit prelates "give honor to the devil, and mock Christ."[80] This abuse,

---

[77] "Absalon interpretatur amaricatio et bene denotat clericum toto affectu ad prelationem suspirantem, qui semper est in mentis amaritudine quousque valeat quod prave cupit obtinere. Fratricida pro tanto dicitur, quia suo malo exemplo proximos et fratres occidit. Hic ergo per artem hypocrisis conatur informare electores ac promotores verbis virtuosis, sub dolo promittens magna et mirabilia, que nequaquam exercere intendit... Sed adeptus deterior efficitur quam prius. Expellit enim patrem eius, scilicet Christum et doctrinam eius de finibus regni sui. Bonos deprimit, malos promovet, pecuniam elicit, sacra vendit, et omnia mala facit." *FB*, De prelatione (ed. Cologne, 1505), fol. 207^v.

[78] "Ergo prelatus dum peccat non se tantum, sed subditum etiam peccato occidit." *FB*, De prelatione (ed. Cologne, 1505), fol. 209^r; "prelatus malus, qui prave abutitur officio pastorali, proficiens honoribus, deficiensque moribus vertitur super ipsum totum pondus populi, quia sanguis populi pereuntis requireretur de manibus suis." *Ibid.*

[79] "Diabolus plenus iniquitie hodie undique ecclesiam Christi cupiditatis et avaritie igne circumdedit, ut recte illud quod scribitur psalmi sexto de talibus verificetur a propheta inquit usque ad sacerdotium omnes avaritie student. Nullus igitur evadendi aditus fidelibus remansit, nisi altitudo contemplationis celestium. Inde enim potest homo ab isto igne se excutere et inimicos ledere quia virtus illa superna caritas dei capitur qua percutitur et vincitur inimicus." *FB*, De avaritia, fol. 9va; *cf.*: "Totus mundus positus est maligno scilicet in malo igne cupiditatis et pauci valent fugere ignem hinc... A minimo usque ad maiorem, a propheta usque ad sacerdotem omnes avaritiae student. Nullum ergo facilius est remedium, quam per contemplationem ascendere ad divinorum bonorum, atque caelestium altitudinem. Tunc enim sordescunt haec inferiora, prae nimia supercaelestium dulcedine et assuctus in hac charitate accensus se ab omni incursu liberabit diaboli... [diabolus] conatur igitur accendere ecclesiam igne cupiditatis et avaritie, cuius summo desiderio, appetitu quam plures." (ed. Cologne, 1505), fol. 17^{r-v}.

[80] "Figura: 4 Regum 5, ubi legimus quod latrunculi Syrie duxerunt puellam ex Israel captivam et vendiderunt eam Naamam leproso, qui ipsam tradidit in obsequium uxori sue. Spiritualiter: Per latrunculos istos notandi sunt electores maligni quorum sacrilege manus, ut repleantur pecunia prompti sunt ponere quemcumque

the elevating of unworthy prelates and the suppressing of qualified candidates, had divided the Church.[81] The greed leading to the unjust appointment of prelates based on money and family ties, was the fourth beast afflicting the Church, the *mali christiani*, the beast with no name, the Antichrist.

The times were precarious, but there was still the possibility of amelioration. Discipline must establish the rule of law and justice, both in society and in religion. And those who were to enforce discipline were the worthy prelates, together with the secular judges. Church and society were to be reformed together. Yet the judges and prelates needed help, for Amalech had invaded.

In Exodus 17, Amalech was attacking Israel. Moses sent Joshua to lead the defense. Meanwhile, Moses and Aaron observed the

---

indignum in sedem cathedralem. Isti sunt deteriores latronibus, qui peregrinos expoliatos trucidant, quia illi corporaliter, isti utroque modo, scilicet spiritualiter et corporaliter occidunt. Ideo longe melius super furcas starent. Puella vero ex Israel religionem seu ecclesiam significat, que per scripture sancte notitiam deum videt. Dum hec ergo puella tam nobilibus orta natalibus, ex qua Christus multos adoptionis generat filios, transmigrat per latrunculos huiusmodi quid facient filii eius? . . . Traditur Naamam leproso, id est immundo et enormi prelato, qui hanc puellam servam tradidit proprie voluptati et liberos eius cibat prohibitis et immundis per male conversationis exempla. Et sic qui vestebantur in croceis, stercora amplexantur. Heu nefanda abusio honorant diabolum, et derident Christum." *FB*, De prelatione (ed. Cologne, 1505) fol. 209^v; "Non enim nobilitas sanguinis aut seculi divitie sive carnalis affectio homini sufficientiam prebent, sed scientie studium et vite approbate . . . Non debent ergo eligere in prelatum potestatem habentem super electione illum vel illos, quos mundus representat, quantumcunque affluant divitiis, potentiis vel nobilitate, quia deus eligendo tales non attendit; sed debet eligi ille qui vita et moribus alios dignoscitur excellere . . . discant electorum principes non eos qui consanguinitate iuncti sunt, neque carnis propinquitate sociantur testamento signare, neque in hereditate tradere ecclesie principatum, sed deferant ad iudicium dei, et non eligunt illum quem humanus commendat affectus." *FB*, De prelatione, fol. 105vb–106ra.

[81] "Sylvester falco [*cf.* Gn. 49:9] secularem predonem significat qui sufficientibus spoliis pro se congregatis, a preda quiescit et cessat. Sed domesticus falco denotat domesticum predonem, clericum vel religiosum per suum superiorem promotum. Hunc oportet preter sibi necessaria pro domino suo predari spolia subditorum, ut ingluviem domini sui promotoris contentet insatiabilem. Tali modo ac pacto ipsum prelationis culmen intrare oportuit. Plus enim petit promotor et vult pro labore promotionis interdum recipere a promoto quam sint reditus, quos promotor acquirit. Ideo efficitur falco domesticus predans et expolians subditos undique ut fauces domini sui possit replere qui aliter illum non promovisset. Hec detestanda perversitas figurata fuit 3 Regum 13, ubi legimus quod qui volebat implere marsupium Ieroboam fiebat sacerdos. Spiritualiter: Ieroboam interpretatur divisio populi, per quem notatur munerum amator et mercator matrimonii crucifixi. Ille enim adeo dividit populum suum indignos sublevando et exaltando, bonos vero deprimendo et concludando." *FB*, De prelatione (ed. Cologne, 1505), fol. 210^{r-v}.

battle from a hilltop. Moses had in his possession the Lord's staff, the same staff with which he made water flow from the rocks in the desert. When Moses held his staff high, the forces of Joshua put Amalech to flight, but when he lowered his staff, Amalech regained the upper hand. Moses' arms grew weary, and thus the Israelites were in danger. Aaron therefore supported Moses' arms, enabling the staff to remain raised and thus the Israelites won the day.

Rampegolus interpreted Amalech and his forces as a fierce and savage people, the sins and vices of pride, envy, and anger. Amalech's invasion of Israel was the invasion of sin in the Church, attacking the "faithful Christians in their camps, that is, in their cities, districts, and all other groupings lacking geographical boundaries, with the intent of destroying civic unity and religious observance."[82] Moses is the worthy prelate or judge, one who keeps himself from all depraved morals, who holds up the staff of correction, lest the discipline of justice fall in slumber and thus Amalech will put the people of Israel to flight.[83] Yet Moses needs help. He cannot keep his arms lifted indefinitely on his own. And support there is, "for there are two who sustain the hands of the prelate in both spheres, namely, the secular sphere and the religious: these are the secular power and the nobles, and if they do so, Amalech, that is sin and vice, is easily put to flight; if, however, they fail, then the devil conquers and exterminates all."[84] The enforcement of discipline, religious discipline as well as secular, the fight against vice and sin, is dependent on the

---

[82] "Per Amalech qui interpretetur gens bruta, subaudi vicia et peccata, per que homines potius brutales nuncupantur. Nam cum homo superbit, comperatur leoni; cum invidet, serpenti; cum irascitur, cani, et sic de aliis. Igitur Amalech invadit populum Israel quando peccata diversa invadunt filios sive fideles Christi in castris, id est, in civitatibus et regionibus et quibuscumque aliis collegiis sine locis, ita ut dissolvatur civium unitas et observatia regularis." *FB*, De iudicio, fol. 64[va–b]; *cf.*: "Igitur Amalech invadit populum Israel quando peccata diversa invadunt populum Christi in castris, id est, in civitatibus et religionibus, vel quibuscunque aliis collegiis ubi servatur civium unitas aut regularis observantia." *FB*, De iustitia (ed. Cologne, 1505), fol. 121[r].

[83] "Debet igitur Moyses, id est iudex aut rector vel prelatus, in monte medicinalis punitionis ascendere et virgam correctionis elevatam tenere, ut cum culpa exegerit delinquentibus non dormat iustitie disciplina, sic enim fugabit populum Amalech, id est mores pecudum brutales. Sed nota quod debet esse Moyses ille qui tenet virgam qui assumptus est de aquis, quia iudex et prelatus debet a moribus pravis et corruptus esse semotus." *FB*, De iudicio, fol. 64[vb].

[84] "Duo enim sunt qui manum sustentant prelati in utroque collegio, seculari videlicet et religioso, scilicet potestas secularis et nobiles populares, quod si sic fiat, leviter fugatur Amalech, id est vitia et peccata. Si autem econverso, tunc diabolus

prelate and judge being supported by the prince and nobles. If the secular rulers and nobles do not hold up the hands of the prelates, the devil will conquer all, and sin and vice will rule, and the Antichrist will reign with the sun of the present life having already set, and darkness will cover all. This was Rampegolus' apocalyptic. And this was an apocalyptic that saw the only hope for the Church to reside in a *Fürstenreformation*

Good and worthy prelates are vital, the support of the secular authorities is indispensable, but there are only a few who are willing to subject themselves to discipline.[85] There are only a few, who shun avarice, riches, and wealth, and truly follow a life of poverty, remaining truly within Christ's fold.[86] These are the *pauperes Christi*, who are the ones fighting on the front lines for the salvation of the Church against the devil's assaults; these are the knights, who "free us from the hands of the devil."[87] These few, these few following poverty leading a life of discipline, these few fighting against the forces of hell, these few holding off the coming of the Antichrist, are indeed the truly religious.

---

devincet et expugnat omnes." *FB*, De iudicio, fol. 65ra; *cf.*: "Duo enim <sunt> que debent sustentare manus prelati in utroque collegio. Nam manus potestatis secularis debent protegere nobiles et populares; manus vero prelati in religione protegere debent magistri et baccularii, quod si fiat, leviter fugatur Amalech et superantur vitia et peccata. Si autem econverso, diabolus vincit omnes." *FB*, De iustitia (ed. Cologne, 1505), fol. 121^v.

[85] ". . . sed pauci sunt qui se iustitie subdere volunt." *FB*, De iudicio, fol. 64vb.

[86] "Ita quod hodie totus populus christianus relictus [*scripsi*; relicta *cod.*] Ierusalem eterne meditationis adeo hos deos colit, quod nullus curat eos relinquere, sed prochdolor quod peius est: illi qui erant habitatores Ierusalem iuxta templum, descenderunt ad vitulos videlicet clerici, prelati, et religiosi." *FB*, De avaritia, fol. 10va; *cf.*: "Ideo populum suum praecipit hos vitulos adorare, asserens aurum et argentum esse deos qui homines educant ab Egyptiaca egestate, id est a confusione paupertatis. Curetis solum pecuniis, dicit diabolus de divitiarum congregatione templum dei penitus dimittentes. Et prodolor, quam bene obeditur ei quia non tantum quisquam de populo suo ascendit ad templum dei, sed quod detestibilius est, qui videbantur in templo dei esse et etiam ipsi ministri templi descenderunt ad vitulos: ita ut pauci cum vero rege Christo maneant. Patet ergo grande malum quod avaritia peperit in hoc mundo." *FB*, De avaritia (ed. Cologne, 1505), fol. 19^r.

[87] "Nos oportet frequenter esse in duro prelio cum sumus in vita presenti, que nobis militia est assidue. Ideo notitiam debemus habere cum militibus conducere nobis stipendio pugnatores, quibus sumus cari et amabiles, ut ipsi necessitatis tempore congregati nos ab inimicorum periculis defendant. Huiusmodi milites sunt Christi pauperes, quis si elemosinis conducimus et per compassionem cum ipsis reversando participes de illorum labora fuerimus, prebendo ipsis consolationem humanam ipsi tempore necessario de manibus diaboli nos eripient." *FB*, De elemoysina, fol 40vb.

iii. *Veri Religiosi*

"Greetings to the religious men, my students beloved in God, in the convent of Hermit friars of Saint Augustine in Naples, from Frater Antonius Rampegolus of Genoa, member of the same Order."[88] Thus Rampegolus began the prologue to his *Figure Bibliorum*. It was surely these same *viri religiosi*, at least in part, his students in the Order's *studium* in Naples, whom he had especially in mind when he composed the section *De religiosis* later on in his work, a chapter Rampegolus dedicated to making sure that the *viri religiosi* would know what it meant to be *veri religiosi*.

He opened his chapter on the religious by emphasizing the ponderous importance of studying the holy scripture. In expositing Genesis 6:4, *These are men of mercy* (*Hii sunt viri misericordie*),[89] Rampegolus explained that,

> Among all the things of the world, the most difficult to obtain by human capacity is the <understanding of the> holy scriptures, for the pinnacle of the human mind is not able to fathom the scriptures with its own resources. Yet when divinity flows into those keeping their own intellect captive in allegiance to Christ, leaving behind therefore those onerous, bodily concerns that by their own weight drag the spirit down to the lower regions, in its core the intellect becomes agile and empowered, so that it might rise to the heights of contemplation in grasping the holy scriptures. This is clear in the case of the truly religious, who, setting aside the pleasures of the flesh, follow true chastity; with greed pulsating, they follow voluntary poverty, and abandoning their own will, they hold to true obedience. These, therefore, are made strong and agile, drawing the wisdom of God from the bosom of divine contemplation.[90]

---

[88] "Religiosis viris in deo dilectis studentibus Neapolitani conventus fratrum Eremitarum Sancti Augustini, frater Antonius Rampegolus de Ianua, ordinis memorati, salutem." *FB*, Auctoris Prologus, fol. 1ra.

[89] The *viri misericordie*, as quoted by Rampegolus, seems to refer to *viri potentes* of Genesis 6:4, which are the Nephilim, the offspring of the sons of God who had intercourse with daughters of man. The Vulgate text reads: *Gigantes autem erant super terram in diebus illis; postquam enim ingressi sunt filii Dei ad filias hominum illaeque genuerunt. Isti sunt potentes a seculo viri famosi*; the New English Bible version reads: *In those days, when the sons of the gods had intercourse with the daughters of men and got children by them, the Nephilim were on earth. They were the heroes of old, men of renown*. Rampegolus ignores the context of the passage to use the lines *viri potentes* for his own purpose. The Cologne editions of 1505 and 1609 read: *Isti sunt viri potentes*, (ed. Cologne, 1505,) fol. 214r; (ed. Cologne, 1609), 576.

[90] "Inter omnia igitur mundi difficilia obtinenda ab humano ingenio est sacra scriptura, ad illam enim ex natura non potest attingere humane mentis acies, sed

This is what Rampegolus wanted his beloved students in Naples to know. He wanted to be sure they realized that one can only understand God's word in the scriptures when one follows true chastity, poverty, and obedience, which enables one to be illumined in contemplation. He wanted them to be part of the very few who are brought into the king's secrete chamber for intimate conversation, where they would learn of the king's prize treasures.[91] He wanted to impress upon them that the holy scriptures, the food of the soul,[92] can only be grasped with great difficulty, and only by the few, only by those who are truly religious.

While the intellect is certainly needed for the interpretation of scripture, faith is what allows one to crack the shell of obscurity.[93] The truth of the scriptures is cloaked in shadow, in *figure*, the understanding of which is only achieved by penetrating to the spiritual

---

divinitus infunditur captivantibus proprium intellectum in obsequium Christi, relictis ergo gravaminibus et certis corporalibus que suis ponderibus spiritum trahunt ad ima, intus fit agilis et potentior intellectus ut ascendat ad contemplationis altitudinem rapiendo illam. Et patet de veris religiosis, qui deponentes carnis voluptates, veram castitatem; pulsa cupiditate, paupertatem voluntariam sectantur; abnegantes voluntatem propriam, et veram tenent obedientiam. Hii igitur fortes facti et agiles de sinu divine contemplationis exhauriant dei sapientiam." *FB*, De religiosis, fol. 107[va-b]; "Bethlehem enim interpretatur domus panis, et sacra scriptura dicitur archa panis spiritualis scilicet qui de celo descendit. Tres viri fortissimi sunt virtutes iam dicte scilicet paupertas voluntaria, castitas, et obedientia. Unde queque fortissima est et difficilis ad servandum sed quia predicte tres virtutes hominem expoliant ab oneribus mundi faciliter perducunt ad sacre scripture sensum. Nec valet contradicere philisteorum exercitus, id est demonum, nam hiis pollens virtutibus, nichil habet quo a diabolo possit impediri." *Ibid.*, fol. 107[vb].

[91] "Ecclesia est domus optime ordinata, quia ibi est introitus magnus et latus per copiam indulgentie, et omni militanto intrare violentium largam inveniet benedictionem, sive sint infideles per baptismum intrantes, sive sint peccatores per lachrymas redeuntes. Secundo, habet atrium securum ubi conveniunt fideles aliqua cum rege suo Christo, per orationes devotas, ubi cum multa petierint, nequaquam dubitent exaudiri. Tertio est ibi thalamus secretior, id est contemplationis actus, in quo eternus rex cum paucioribus familiaribus loquitur, ibi sunt regis cariores thesauri." *FB*, De ecclesia, fol. 44[ra].

[92] "... sacram scripturam, que est anime sancte cibus." *Ibid.*, fol. 42[ra].

[93] "Nos omnes fideles in stadio currimus per spatium vite presentis et comprehendamus bravium eterne beatitudinis. Sed notandum quod duplici gressu currimus scilicet fide et intellectus, et licet per intellectum citius curramus, nihilominus oportet in hoc quin fidem necessario precedere intellectum... Igitur currunt ambo [*cf.* Io. 20: 4–8] scilicet fides et scientia ad intellectum sacre scripture. Et licet Iohanni scientia et intellectus acuties promptior ad intelligendum, non valet tamen prius fide intrare... Petrus siquidem est fidei symbolum, Iohannes significat intellectum; ac per hoc quoniam scriptum est: Nisi credideritis non intelligetis, necessario precedit fides in monumentum sacre scripture, demum sequens intrat intellectus cui per fidem preparatur aditus." *FB*, De sacra scriptura, fol 111[vb]–112[ra].

sense. The *sensus spiritualis* is hidden from the perfidy of the Jews and from those who in their laziness are content to satisfy their every desire and appetite, admiring only the beauty of the appearance of the soul's holy food. Understanding of the scriptures is given only to the "observant faithful."[94] These *fideles observantes* are the truly religious, to whom God has given all wisdom and all knowledge:

> Human reason marvels, because in such great adversities of the world, the good and the holy lead an angelic life, although they are men. For even though the entire world is wallowing in evil, that is, is placed in evil fire, the *religiosi* are not burned. And though this world is filled with the concupiscence of the eyes from its greed, the *religiosi* live a life of poverty. And when the world is overflowing with carnal lust through its vileness, the *religiosi* remain chaste. And when the world is infected with pride, the *religiosi* retain the humility of obedience. Therefore, God gave them all wisdom and all knowledge.[95]

The *veri religiosi*, however, were not to keep such knowledge to themselves: they were to preach and teach God's wisdom to the people, dispensing the spiritual food contained in the scriptures and calling the faithful to battle against the devil.[96]

Yet the *viri religiosi* in Naples, were not the only *veri religiosi* Rampegolus had in mind. Nor were the sons of Augustine as such for that matter. In expositing the first chapter of Daniel, Rampegolus explained that

> The present life is called the Babylonian Captivity, because in many ways in this life man is held captive and is confused, for in this life

---

[94] "Per manna [*cf.* Ex. 16] omnem saporem continens, subaudi sacrarum scripturarum intellectum continentem omnes spirituales dulcedines. Hoc enim est <datum> fidelibus observantibus dies resurrectionis dominice usque in finem mundi, usque ad illam sextam feriam, in qua Christus venerit mundum iudicare et nihilominus exclusus atque remotus est a perfidis Iudeis sabbatizantibus, et in umbra tantum morantibus seu figura, et non attendentibus ad dulcorem huius suavissimi cibi, qui sua pinguedine omnem desiderium et omnem appetitum reficit." *FB*, De sacra scriptura (ed. Cologne, 1505), fol. 225ᵛ–226ʳ; see also Saak, "The *Figure Bibliorum*," 29–30.

[95] "In non modicum admirationem potest induci humana cognitio quod inter tot mundi adversa loquendo de bonis et sancti ducant vitam angelicam, cum sint homines. Cum enim totus mundus sit in maligno positus [I Io. 5:19], id est in malo igne, ipsi tamen non igniuntur. Cum autem mundus iste plenus est concupiscentia occulorum per avaritiam, ipsi nichilominus servant paupertatem. Cum etiam mundus repletus sit concupiscentia carnis per immundiam, ipsi vero servant castitatem. Et cum mundus infectus sit per superbiam, ipsi servant obedientie humilitatem [*cf.* I Io. 2:16–17]. Ideo deus dedit illis omnem sapientiam et scientiam." *FB*, De religiosis, fol. 108ʳᵇ.

[96] Saak, "The *Figure Bibliorum*," 32–37.

the people of faith are held captive until they are freed from the chains of the body. From the sons of Israel, that is, from the Christian people, Christ's appointed administrator, namely, the Holy Spirit, has chosen three youths, that is, three Orders: the Dominicans, the Franciscans, and the Augustinian Hermits. These three live pure lives without stain, not being contaminated by the foods of Babylon, which are carnal desire, greed, and pride. Yet here I am speaking about the perfect and the good, who have truly made progress in their religion, not, however, about those who simply don't cut it. God, therefore, gave to them the understanding of Holy Scripture, for they learned the Chaldaic language, that is, the true meaning of the Law and Prophets, so that they might know best how to harmonize the Old Testament with the New, and would be able to teach people the way of salvation.[97]

The Dominicans, the Franciscans, and the Augustinians, these were the Orders that comprised the *veri religiosi*, or at least the Orders that contained them. The mendicants were the only ones who knew what the scriptures had to offer, for they were the only ones who truly lived the religious life. The *veri religiosi*, however, were a group apart, even among the mendicants themselves.

---

[97] "Vita presens dicitur captivitas Babylonis quia multipliciter in ipsa homo capitur et confunditur. In hac enim vita populus fidelium est captivus quousque a corporis vinculis liberentur. Ex fillis Israel, id est ex populo christiano, prepositus Christi, id est Spiritus Sanctus, elegit tres pueros, id est tres ordines scilicet predicatorum, minorum, et heremitarum sancti Augustini, qui puri et sine macula viventes, non sunt contaminati a cibis Babylonicis, qui sunt concupiscentia carnis, concupiscentia occulorum, et superbia vite. Loquor enim de perfectis et bonis, qui profecerunt in religione, non autem de hiis qui <de>fecerunt. Ideo Dominus dedit illis donum intellectus sacre scripture, dedicerunt enim linguam Chaldaicam, id est sensum prophetarum et legis, ut sciant optime concordare antiqua novis, et populum viam docere salutis." *FB*, De religiosis, fol. 108[rb-va]; *cf.* Uppsala, UB, MS C 121, fol. 126[va]; ed. Cologne, 1505, fol. 216[r]. Here we find already the "observant ideal" that focused on the religious life itself, rather than one's own Order, which was expressed most completely by Conrad of Zenn in his *Liber de vita monastica*; see Zschoch, *Klosterreform*, *passim*, and was codified in papal decrees following the Council of Basel; see *Stat.Con.* 1–2 (245–254). This should not, however, be seen as a denial of an Order-specific ideal. Johannes von Paltz still viewed Augustine as the founder of all religions, defending forcefully the priority of the OESA: "Sanctus Augustinus est pater et principium omnis solitudinis claustralis et per consequence omnis religionis, ubi vivitur in communi secundum vitam apostolicam." Paltz *Suppl.Coel.* (144,17–19). "Sumus enim de illo ordine, cuius pater, scilicet Augustinus, est auctor et quodammodo pater omnium ordinum in nova lege innovatione." Paltz *Suppl.Coel.* (272,25–27). Paltz based his arguments on Augustinus of Ancona and Ambrosius de Cora. It should also be noted that the pastoral emphasis on the religious life in general can already be found in the works of Henry of Friemar, Hermann of Schildesche, and Jordan of Quedlinburg; see Chapter Four, ns. 15–27. This is a theme I will be addressing extensively in volume two, *The Failed Reformation*.

616   CHAPTER SIX

In the section *De ecclesia*, Rampegolus equated the heavenly stars of Ecclesiasticus 43:10, *The brilliant stars are the beauty of the sky*,[98] with the immobile faith of the Church militant. As such, there are seven specific stars that surround the Church, the seven stars of the seven virtues, which because they are preached, never desert the Church.[99] When he turned to the religious, Rampegolus interpreted the *stelle celi* as the *religiosi*. There are, he noted, three types of stars: the fixed stars, the planets which move with an irregular motion in addition to that of their orbits, and then vapors, which at times appear as stars though they are not.[100] The *vere stelle* are the *veri religiosi*, who either live their lives in contemplation of the scriptures, teaching people God's commandments, or live their lives serving people. Both forms of life, namely, the *vita contemplativa* and the *vita activa*, as the stars, impact social life by performing works of mercy, building up the *bonum commune*. There are also those, however, who even though they appear as *religiosi*, are not so in fact; they wear a religious habit, but their hearts are turned completely to the pleasures of the flesh and the world. These *pseudoreligiosi* are fallen stars from heaven, who neither serve the Lord as Mary, nor serve their neighbors as Martha, but only serve themselves, as Judas. They betray their Lord, they betray their calling, they betray their religion, even though they aspire to be seen as religious.[101] Therefore, these *pseudoreligiosi*, the

---

[98] Sir. 43:10: *species celi gloriosa stellarum*.

[99] "*Species celi gloria stellarum*, Eccl. 44 ... ecclesia militans assimilatur stelle supradicte immobili per firmitatem et constantiam fidei, quia nulla concussione quamvis gravi moveri poterit a fide que Christo totaliter est coniuncta unio ... habet enim ecclesia circa se septem stellas, id est septem virtutes scilicet tres theologicas et quatuor cardinales, que voce predicatorum in ecclesia et nunquam ipsam deserunt." *FB*, De ecclesia, fol. 42^{va-b}.

[100] "*Multiplicato semen tuum sicut stellas*, Gen.17 [Gn. 22:17; *cf*. Gn. 16:10, Gn. 17:2,20]. Nota quod in celo sunt stelle fixe scilicet in firmamento. Sunt enim ut clavus in rota et non habent motum alium nisi motum suis orbis. Sunt et alie stelle que vocantur erratice ut sunt planete, qui alium motum habent preterquam motum proprii orbis. Et licet iste stelle sint mobile, habent tamen suam influentiam super terram, nec superflue moventur moto proprio. Sed verum est quod interdum videmus quedam motum vaporum, qui videntur stelle et non sunt, non enim sunt in aliqua celesti spera, sed infra speras activorum et passivorum quamquam apariant stelle cuius signum est quia in se mox evanescunt, ut patet in cometa. Stelle autem vere in perpetuum permanent." *FB*, De religiosis, fol. 108va.

[101] "Stelle celi donotant religiosos, quos <deus> in suis ordinibus quasi in speris suis multipliciter ordinavit et collocavit et ad pulchra et diversa distinxit officia. Aliquos ordinavit ad scripture sacre contemplationem, qui populum instruant et illos doceant divina mandata, de quibus Daniel: *Qui me elucidant, fulgebunt quasi stelle in firmamento*. Alii vero sunt qui licet moveantur celesti contemplatione, moventur tamen

"wicked and licentious" (*pravi et discoli*), lest they contaminate many with their diseased way of life are to be separated from the peaceful and devoted, the *veri religiosi*, and subjected to compulsory correction.[102] It is only the *veri religiosi*, the *vere stelle celi*, who serve the Church. The truly religious, the *pauci*, the *fideles observantes*, are to be kept separate from those lacking in observance; they must be kept

---

cum hoc necessario et utili actione scilicet visitando personas secularis in tribulationibus plurimis; prebendo consolationem afflictis; inferendo consilium deviis; et reducendo peccatores confessionibus suis; interdum etiam pro se et aliis victum et vestitum procurando et multas alias actiones necessarias exercendo. Hii igitur licet hunc motum habeant circa terrena, non tamen est superfluus quia necessaria est Martha ut Maria. Sunt enim vere stelle, id est veri religiosi, et habent influentia ad bonum commune multa misericordie opera prosequendo. Sed ut dicebatur sunt quidam vapores terrestres qui videntur esse stelle et non sunt quia quidam portant religionis habitum, religiosi tamen non sunt secundum cor et affectum, nec sunt in aliqua supercelesti spera per contemplationem, nec in aliis inferioribus speris per alicuius sancte operationis executionem, sed solum sunt infra speras activorum et passivorum, id est infra carnem et mundum, ubi nichil aliud invenitur quam actio malorum et passio penarum. Isti igitur nec ut Maria sunt in celo per divinam contemplationem, nec ut Martha in terra per piam et utilem activitatem. Isti vero tales non sunt, quia nec deo vacant contemplando ut Maria, nec procurant ut Martha, sed solum sibiipsis ut Iudas, et quia non sunt in aliquo celo fixi, cito inflati concupiscentie igne super terram cadunt et deficiunt in ea ... per has stellas cadentes subaudi pseudoreligiosos quos proicit deus, eo quod in religione nullam habent firmitatem confirmata eorum nequitia quam aliquali simulatione boni cooperiebant, cognoscuntur et reiciuntur, et sic cadentes in terram, celeste non capiunt premium sed fugit ab eis sicut liber involutus et clausus in quo numquam voluerunt legere et cum hoc perdunt bona temporalia quia comperta eorum nequitia despiciuntur eo quod cognoscuntur affectum possuisse circa terrena et per eorum gestus simulatos cupiunt reputari celestes, relinquunt divitias corpore sed non mente. Unde iusto dei iudicio eternis privabuntur divitiis et a vero pauperum premio ipsi penitus efficiuntur alieni." *FB*, De religiosis, fol. 108[va-b].

[102] "Per archam [*cf.* Gn. 6:14] diversis lignis fabricatam et conglutinatam bitumine subaudi religionem diversis coaduntam hominibus et conglutinatam glutio caritatis. Noe qui interpretatur requies, prelatum significat qui tam pro se quam pro subditis suis eternam debet requiem querere ac enim prius quesita omnia bona adiciuntur illi. Per homines vero superius commorrantes notantur viri vita et scientie bonitate precellentes. Per animalia vero mansueta intelliguntur simplices et pauperes qui de humili seculi paupertate ad religionem venerunt. Per ferocia vero animalia notantur divites et potentes qui de seculi magnitudine ad religionem descenderunt. Hii igitur debent et possunt se omnes mutuo sustinere. Nec debet pauperibus molestum esse si hiis qui ex moribus delicatioribus ad monasterium venerunt aliquid alimentorum vel vestimentorum prebetur. Nec debent divites de suis divitiis superbire magis illis in obsequio Christi relictis quam superbiret si eis in seculo frueretur. Sed nota quod animalia munda ab immundis segregantur, quia in religione debent pravi et discoli a pacificis et devotis fratribus separari, debunt enim deici et deprimi ponendo inferius per debitam correctionem ne sua contagione pestifera plurimos perdant." *FB*, De religiosis, fol. 109[rb].

apart to fulfill their rightful role, for the truly religious are truly the stars and the only hope for the embattled church militant.

Shortly after Rampegolus completed his *Figure Bibliorum*, the first Observant Congregation of Augustinians was established at Lecceto, exempted from the authority of the provincial prior and placed directly under the prior general. It was an administrative move: reform from above, from on high, yet one that had been prepared by the mentality expressed in Rampegolus' *Figure Bibliorum*, and by the reformation program of Gregory of Rimini. For Rampegolus, the *fideles observantes*, the *veri religiosi*, must be kept separate as the means for saving the Church from the destruction of the Antichrist. Fourteen years later, in 1419, the Schism in the Church was over, as was that in the Order. Yet the Observance was just beginning. And the Observance would bifurcate the Order on a more fundamental and profound level than had the bicephalicism of Rome and Avignon.[103] The Antichrist so looked for and so expected never came, and the Observance, for the time being, was left without an apocalyptic. Little, however, did Rampegolus, Zachariae, or Augustinus Favaroni, know that their predictions were not wrong, but only premature. The Antichrist had been there all along, just not recognized. He soon would be, revealed by another Augustinian Observant friar who was truly an apocalyptic prophet. For the Augustinian platform and its high way to heaven, 1520, far more than 1378, was indeed apocalypse now.

II. Beatus Vir

One holy, catholic, and apostolic church: thus Boniface VIII began his most famous Bull, *Unam Sanctam*. While Europe was becoming early modern, the Church may have remained holy, it may, in one sense, even have remained catholic and apostolic. But it would not

---

[103] See volume two, *The Failed Reformation*; for an overview of the Augustinian Observance, see Francis S. Martin, O.S.A., "The Augustinian Observance," in *Reformbemühungen und Observanzbestrebungen im spätmittelalterlichen Ordenswesen*, Berliner Historische Studien 14/Ordensstudien 6, ed. Kaspar Elm (Berlin, 1989), 325–345; *cf.* Gutiérrez, *History* I/2, 73–98, 222–223 and the literature cited there, and Weinbrenner, *Klosterreform*; for the Observant movement in general, see Elm, *Reformbemühungen*, which contains essays on all major aspects of the observance.

remain one. Shortly after he completed his treatise *On Monastic Vows*, Martin Luther could still sign his name as *Martinus Lutherus Augustinianus* and as *frater Martinus Lutherus*.[104] On 18 December 1521 Frater Martinus wrote from the Wartburg to his friend and confrere Wenzeslaus Link: "For I will remain in this habit and way of life unless the world should become another."[105] Three and a half years later Luther gave up the Augustinian habit and way of life and married the former nun Katherine von Bora. By 13 June 1525, the world had indeed "become another."

The brave new world Luther had entered, and one for which he himself had served as midwife, was not what had been expected, it was not that for which one had hoped. Luther powerfully stated his view of the conditions of the world in a letter of 26 March 1542, addressed to Jacob Propst, the former prior of the Augustinian convent in Antwerp, who became the Lutheran Bishop of Bremen:

> Although I do not have the leisure to write many things to you, my dear Jacob, for I am consumed by age and labor: "Old, cold, and miss-shapened" (as it is said), and yet I am not allowed to rest being harassed daily by all the reasons and occasions for writing, I know more than you about the fate of this age. The world is threatened with destruction, this is certain. Satan so rages and the world is so brutish that only this one relief stands firm: the last day is at hand. Germany is a thing of the past and will never again be what it was. The nobility is concerned for their own rule above everything else, cities plot against each other, (and on the basis of law). Thus a kingdom divided against itself must meet the army of mad demons, the Turks. Neither are we concerned at all whether we have the Lord's favor, or His wrath, but we would conquer and command the Turks, the demons, God, and everyone else, all by ourselves. Such is the most

---

[104] *WABr* 2.392,36–37; *WABr* 2.506,21.

[105] "... nam et ego in habitu et ritu isto manebo, nisi mundus alius fiat." *WABr* 2.415, 25–26. Luther's adherence, loyalty, and obedience to his Order, as the Order of St. Augustine, has been called into question by Scott Henrix. Hendrix has proposed a creative and insightful analysis of Luther's relationship to his father Hans, in comparison to his loyalty to the Order; Scott Hendrix, "Luther's Loyalties and the Augustinian Order," in Hendrix, *Tradition and Authority in the Reformation* (Variorum, Aldershot, 1996), 236–258. Hendrix takes as his point of departure Luther's letter to his father prefacing his *De Votis Monasticis*, arguing that in this treatise Luther rejected not only monastic vows, but also his life as a monk. While Hendrix's analysis offers insightful and fruitful material for further consideration, his assertions that Luther abadoned the monastic life in 1521 with this treatise is called into question by Luther's own assertions, as evidenced here in his letter to Link. Nevertheless, Hendrix's argument serves as a partner in dialogue for my very different analysis and interpretation here, and through the rest of this chapter.

insane trust and security of ruined Germany. What, however, are we to do? We complain in vain, we cry out in vain. It is only left for us to pray: *Thy will be done*, for the reign and for the sanctification of the name of God.[106]

In such a situation, there was only one thing left to do: pray the Lord's Prayer, the prayer that Jordan of Quedlinburg had taught in Erfurt two hundred and fifteen years earlier as the summary of God's commandments, as the epitome of Christian righteousness in the battle between God and the devil. Two hundred and fifteen years later, it still was.

Times had changed. The battle remained. Yet the field of combat had become of far greater dimensions. The stakes were the same, the salvation, or damnation, of souls, but the continuous battle, the *pugna continua*, was becoming a war. A year and a half prior to Luther's letter to his confrere Jacob Propst, Pope Paul III had officially recognized his "storm troops," the Jesuit Order; three years later, Luther wrote his fiercest attack yet: *Wider das Papsttum zu Rom, vom Teufel gestiftet*;[107] on 13 December 1545, as the Schmalkaldic League was preparing for conflict no less than were the imperial forces of Charles V, the long awaited Church Council opened in Trent; only nine weeks later, Luther was dead. The high way to heaven of the Augustinian platform lay shattered in rubble.

---

[106] "Quamquam non vacat multa scribere, mi Iacobe, Sum enim confectus aetate et laboribus: Alt, kaldt, ungestalt (ut dicitur), nec sic tamen quiescere permittor, tot causis et scribendi occupationibus quotidie vexatus, plura scio quam tu de huius saeculi fatalibus. Minatur mundus ruinam, hoc est certum, ita furit Satan, ita brutescit mundus, nisi quod unum hoc solatium restat, diem illum brevi instare... Germania fuit, et nunquam erit, quod fuit. Nobilitas cogitat regnum super omnia, civitates contra sibi consulunt (et iure). Ita regnum in sese divisum occurrere debet exercitui daemonum in Turcis furentium. Nec nos magnopere curamus, Dominumne propitium an iratum habeamus, per nos ipsos scilicet victuri et imperaturi Tucis, daemonibus, Deo et omnibus. Tanta est pereuntis Germaniae furentissima fiducia et securitas. Reliquum est, ut oremus: Fiat voluntas tua, pro regno, pro sanctificatione nominis Dei." *WABr* 10.23,3–19; *cf*.: "Primum et maximum est omnium sanctificatio nominis dei. Quod cum perfectum fuerit, omnia consummata sunt. Sed plene sanctificari non potest, nisi ista vita (quae sine peccato, idest nominis divini irreverentia non agitur) finita regnum dei adveniat. Ideo ne regnum dei propter nos ipsos cupiamus, primo praemittitur sanctificatio nominis dei, ut sic salvari petamus et regnum dei venire, non, ut nobis bene sit, sed ut nomen et gloria domini magnificetur. Ad cuius magnificationem statim se ipso sequitur, quod nobis bene sit. Verum nec regnum dei advenire potest, nisi fiat voluntas dei." Martinus Lutherus, *Eine kurze und gute Auslegung des Vaterunsers vor sich und hinter sich*, 1516, *WA* 59.23,7–15.

[107] Oberman, "Teufelsdreck," 61.

Yet Luther was not the only one who feared for the fate of the Church and society. He was not the only one who saw the devil at work. Between late September of 1531 and mid-June of the following year, the Augustinian Bartholomeus Arnoldi von Usingen composed his reply to Philip Melanchthon's *Apologia Confessionis Augustanae*. Usingen's *Responsio* is no curt polemical dismissal. It is an extensive and detailed counter-attack, fueled by the same passion and by the same fear that drove Luther, who had been Usingen's student in philosophy at Erfurt. The Church and the Empire were cataclysmically close to dissolution. Usingen took up his pen with such fervor in attempt to win the heretics and schismatics back to obedience, "so that they might leave behind their own opinions and return to catholic doctrine, lest they shatter the unity of the holy Church and throw the Empire into turmoil, a turmoil that would result in endangering the salvation of souls and in throwing away the whole of Christian society."[108] The apostates, the *Lutherani*, completely against Christian love, were concerned far more with their own pipe dreams (*merae nugae*) than they were with the truth.[109] "There is no doubt," Usingen lamented, "that Satan, Christ's enemy, has put you up to this, so that through his insidious agents and teachers of lies he might undermine the Gospel of Christ in infinite ways."[110] Moreover, the heretics were perverting the Gospel itself, turning "the Gospel of Christ into the Gospel of Satan."[111] With all their slanderous and scandalous "back biting"[112] the *Lutherani* were spewing forth "all the

---

[108] "Quos comperiens in multis a doctrina catholica deviare et a praxi Ecclesiae sanctae declinare coepit adiutorio piorum et eruditorum virorum illos clementer instruere et admonere suorum errorum, obnixe rogans, ut cederent suis opinionibus et cum catholica doctrina remanentes non scinderent unitatem Ecclesiae sanctae nec sic imperium turbarent, quae turbatio esset in periculum salutis animarum et in iacturam rerum totius rei publicae christianae." Barth.Arn. *Resp.* Prol. (3,18–25).

[109] "Adversarii nulla criminatione gravant vos, sed quod veritas est, dicunt decentia, qua decet. Si autem vos gravat veritas, signum est vos ex veritate non esse, quia non amatis illam, sed potius nugas vestras." Barth.Arn. *Resp.*. 2,5 (675,728–731); *cf. ibid.* (677,820–835).

[110] "Non est dubium satanam, Christi adversarium, ad hoc conari, ut per subdolos operarios et magistros mendaces deformet Evangelium Christi infinitis modis." Barth.Arn. *Resp.* 2, 5 (673,678–680). For Usingen, see Simoniti's introduction and the literature cited there, *ibid.*, xi–xxiv.

[111] "... de Evangelio Christi fit evangelium satanae..." Barth.Arn. *Resp.* 2, 5 (673,686–687).

[112] "Tu impie et scandalose nec non contra caritatem proximi et contra omnem veritatem absque rubore et erubescentia multa mentiris in monachos probos, quorum ceremoniae et observationes piae sunt et honestae, conducentes ad humilitatem

shit of all heretics," preaching and teaching doctrine more impure and rotten than had ever been preached since the very beginning of the Church.[113] And not only Germany had been infected, but England, France, Spain, and Italy as well.[114] "I am completely dumbfounded," Usingen confessed, "what sort of most haughty, egotistical devil has so possessed you that you are not able to tolerate that which is honest, humble, and devout."[115] Reconciliation, however, was still possible. The heretics must return to Mother Church. But that was the only hope left.

Usingen, unlike Luther, was not an apocalyptic. He did not view the situation as one heralding the Antichrist and the last days. Yet clearly the devil was at work, and if reconciliation could not be achieved, if the heretics would not return to the one, true, holy, and apostolic Church, and if the faithful Christians did not take it upon themselves to root out such wickedness, then God would vent his anger and send his scourge in punishment: either the Turk or some other tyrant, who would carry out the just judgment of God against such a great crime and against such great evil.[116] Church and society were at stake. Divine judgment is always just, even if one cannot see it.

---

et divni cultus ornatum. Tu autem linguae tuae virulentia et petulantia pervertere conaris et in peius interpretari omnia, quae apud illos pie aguntur, humiliter et devote... Et quis occidit bonos viros pia docentes? Tu occidere non erubescis bonos viros pia docentes virulentia linguae tuae, qua detrahis illis et nugis tuis impudentissimis infamas eos." Barth.Arn. *Resp.* 2, 5 (676,800–677,819).

[113] "... qui vos estis gloriantes coram populo vos pure et munde Evangelium praedicare et docere, cum ab initio nascentis Ecclesiae impurius et foedius praedicatum non sit, quam a Lutheranis concionatoribus praedicatur, qui hoc foedant et contaminant admixtione paene omnium stercorum hereticorum..." Barth.Arn. *Resp.* 2, 5 (673,680–685).

[114] Barth.Arn. *Resp.* 2, 5 (674,694–699).

[115] "Mirum, quis diabolus tam superbus te obsideat, ut nihil honestum, humile et devotum possis ferre." Barth.Arn. *Resp.* 2, 5 (677,806–807).

[116] "Non est saevitia aliqua apud nos. Si qui autem apud nos digna factis vel receperunt vel adhuc recipient, hoc iuri, non nobis habent tribuere. Quod ius etiam si in vos practicatum esset vel adhuc practicaretur, facile concordia fieret et pax rediret Ecclesiae, quamdiu autem hoc non fit, non habemus aliquam sperare pacem, quia non sinet Deus tantam impietatem et perfidiam, quam vos attulistis, diu inultam, et si hanc vindicare neglexerint christiani, mittet Deus virgam furoris sui, vel Turcam vel alium tyrannum, qui tantum facinus tandem tantumque malum iusto Dei iudicio expiabit." Barth.Arn. *Resp.* 2, 5 (679,904–913).

A. *Entering the Black Hole: The Reformation Discovery*

The high way to heaven: Luther knew it well. The first week of January, 1519, Luther wrote again to the most blessed father, Pope Leo X. He had done so just eight months before, prostrating himself at Leo's feet, seeking the Holy Father's judgment of his theses against indulgences as that of the voice of Christ.[117] In mid-November, the papal nuncio, Karl von Miltitz, left Rome for Germany. His mission was delicate: to deliver the "Golden Rose" to Frederick the Wise; to secure Saxony's support for the "Turkish Tax"; and to deal with the Luther issue. Over the course of two days, 5 and 6 January, Luther met with Miltitz in Spalatin's home in Altenburg.[118] The nuncio reported back to his boss that Luther had promised to keep quiet on indulgences and that the matter could well be settled. Luther himself wrote to the pope, but his letter may never have arrived.[119] On 29 March, Leo wrote to his "beloved son" Martin Luther, with no mention of having received his letter, expressing joy over the report he had from Miltitz, and "invited" Luther to Rome so that Leo himself could hear his recantation.[120]

Luther's letter to Leo has been called an apology.[121] It is, however, not an apology at all, nor an *apologia*: it is a desperate appeal. As a professor of theology, Luther had taken up the fight against indulgences in striving to preserve the honor of the Roman Church, but things had gotten out of hand.[122] The preachers of indulgences,

---

[117] See above, Introduction, n. 8.

[118] On Miltitz' mission, see Martin Brecht, *Martin Luther. His Road to Reformation, 1483–1521*, trans. James L. Schaaf (Philadelphia, 1985); originally published as: *Martin Luther: Sein Weg zur Reformation, 1483–1521* (Stuttgart, 1981).

[119] *WABr* 1.292–293. The editor, Otto Clemen, noted in comments prefacing this letter that due to the report of Miltitz, such a letter from Luther was not needed and "so ist anzunehmen, daß unser Brief gar nicht abgesandt wurde, sondern Entwurf blieb." *WABr* 1.291. Without giving further evidence or argument, Brecht stated: "The draft of Luther's letter of apology to the pope, which, however, was not sent, has been preserved." Brecht, *Road to Reformation*, 268.

[120] *WABr* 1.364–365.

[121] Brecht, *Road to Reformation*, 268. As the introductory comments note, the appellation 'apology' was added to the text by a later hand: "D. Luthers Entschuldigung an der Papst..." *WABr* 1.292

[122] "Fuit apud nos honestus hic vir Carolus Milditz, Beatitudinis tuae secretus cubicularius, gravissime causatus nomine Beatitudinis tuae apud Illustrissimum principem Fridricum de mea in Romanam Ecclesiam et Beatitudinem tuam et irreverentia et temeritate expostulans satisfactionem. Ego ista audiens plurimum dolui officiosissimum officium meum tam infelix esse, ut, quod pro tuendo honore Eccclesiae

whom he had been attacking, had turned things around and claimed that he, Luther, was irreverently undermining both the pope's authority, and that of the Church. Luther was exasperated.[123] And the most blessed father had to know what was going on. Luther wanted to be perfectly clear:

> Now, most blessed father, before God and with all his creation as my witness, I did not, nor do I want today, in any way to assault or pull down with any type of deceit, the sovereignty of the Roman Church or that of your holiness. Wherefore I confess as thoroughly as possible that the sovereignty of this Church is above every other authority, and nothing whatsoever in heaven or on earth is to be placed before it, aside from Jesus Christ, the one Lord of all. And your holiness should not believe any evil connivers who would fabricate any thing different about this Martin... for there is one thing alone that I seek: that our Mother, the Roman Church, might not be polluted with the filth of a foreign avarice, and that the people might not be seduced into error and learn to set indulgences before love. About everything else, I could not care less.[124]

Frater Martin wanted to do whatever he could to rectify the matter. He would be silent regarding indulgences, if his adversaries would just shut up as well.[125] And, he would recant. He would recant with-

---

Romanae susceperam, in irreverentiam etiam apud ipsum verticem eiusdem Ecclesiae ac plenam omnis mali suspitionem venerit." *WABr* 1.292,6–13.

[123] "Sed quid agam, Beatissime pater? Desunt mihi consilia prorsus, potestatem irae tuae ferre non possum, et quomodo eripiar, ignoro ... Illi, illi, heu pater, hanc Ecclesiae Romanae intulerunt iniuriam et pene infamiam apud nos, quibus ego restiti, idest qui insulsissimis suis sermonibus sub nomine Beatitudinis tuae non nisi teterrimam avaritiam coluerunt et opprobrio aegypti contaminatam et abominandam reddiderunt sanctificationem. Et quasi id non satis fuerit malorum, me, qui tantis eorum monstris occurri, authorem suae temeritatis apud Beatitudinem tuam inculpant." *WABr* 1.292,13–15, 26–30.

[124] "Nunc, Beatissime pater, coram deo et tota creatura sua testor me neque voluisse neque hodie velle Ecclesiae Romanae ac Beatitudinis tuae potestatem ullo modo tangere aut quacunque versutia demoliri. Quin plenissime confiteor huius Ecclesie potestatem esse super omnia nec ei praeferendum quicquam sive in caelo sive in terra praeter unum Ihesum Christum dominum omnium. Nec Beatitudo tua ullis malis dolis credat, qui aliter de Martino hoc machinantur... Nam id unicum a me quesitum est, ne avaritiae alienae feditate pollueretur Ecclesia Romana, mater noster, neve populi seducerentur in errorem et charitatem discerent posthabere indulgentiis. Caetera omnia, ut sunt neutralia, a me vilius aestimantur." *WABr* 1.292,31–293,37; 293,45–49.

[125] "Et quod unum in ista causa facere possum, promittam libentissime Beatitudini tuae istam de indulgentiis materiam me deinceps relicturum penitusque tactiturum, modo et illi suas vanas ampullas cohibeant." *WABr* 1.293,38–40.

out delay—if it would do any good.[126] But his theses on indulgences had spread so widely, more so than he had ever desired, and since it was his attackers who were the real threat, "if I want to honor the Roman Church, which I see as my greatest concern, I cannot in any way recant, for nothing would come out of it except that the Roman Church would increasingly be muddied and handed over to be accused by word of mouth."[127] His letter closes with his assuring the pope, "if there is even more that I can do, or learn, I am, no doubt, most prepared to do so."[128]

January 1519. By all counts, Luther wrote this letter to Leo *after* his so-called "Reformation breakthrough." His discovery of justification *sola fide* was made as an Augustinian Hermit, a son of Augustine, and such he remained even after his great insight. Luther's theological development through January 1519 was that of an Augustinian *magister*, following his Order's platform on the high way to heaven. Frater Martin had one concern: to protect the honor and dignity of Mother Church and of Christ's vicar, the pope, and to teach his flock Christian love. Nothing was higher than the sovereignty of St. Peter's primacy.[129] Luther's *Turmerlebnis* was not the turning point. Yet a turning point there was, and it was not far off. The catastrophe was coming.

---

[126] "Revocationem expostulor disputationis. Quae si id posset praestare, quod per eam quaeritur, sine mora ego praestarem eam." *WABr* 1.292,15–17.

[127] "Nunc autem, cum resistentibus et prementibus adversariis scripta mea latius vagentur, quam unquam speravi, simul profundius inhaeserint plurimorum animis, quam ut revocari possent? Quin cum Germania nostra hodie mire floreat ingeniis, eruditione, iudicio, si Ecclesiam Romanam volo honorare, id quam maxime mihi curandum video, ne quid ullo modo revocem, nam istum revocare nihil fieret nisi Ecclesiam Romanam magis ac magis fedare et in ora hominum accusandum tradere." *WABr* 1.292,17–24.

[128] "Si autem et plura facere potero aut cognovero, sine dubio paratissimus ero." *WABr* 1.293,49–50.

[129] The development of Luther's ecclesiological thought between the Diets, i.e., Augsburg 1518 and Worms 1520, is exceedingly complex. His *Resolutio Lutheriana super propositione sua decima tertia de potestate papae* of June 1519 (*WA* 2.183–240), seems to contradict much of what Luther says in his letter to Leo X, and even his *Doctor Martinus Luther Augustiners Unterricht auff etlich artickell, die im von seynen abgunnern auffgelegt und zu gemessen werden* (*WA* 2.69–73), published the end of February 1519, has a different tone. The question to a large degree turns on how his letter to Leo X is read. One can ignore or dismiss it as a rather disingenuous attempt to appease the Pope to buy time, or even to see it as a formulaically required response; or, one can view it as an expression of Luther's true position. If the latter, then it should be the interpretive lens through which to read his other work of the period, as well as his refusal to recant. Luther's letter to Leo is so powerful that to read it in any

626   CHAPTER SIX

24 February 1520. Everything changed. It was not without preparation, though, and Luther felt it coming. Ten days or so previously Luther wrote to Spalatin. He could see the "signs of the times" and they were grave; unless God would restrain Satan, war could not be avoided, and it would be holy war. No longer a *pugna continua*, this was the *bellum domini* for the cause of Christ, who had come with a sword, not to bring peace, and who had fought with his own blood, as did the martyrs after him.[130] And then came the shocking realization:

> Unaware, I have all along both taught and held all the doctrines of Johannes Hus, and so even has Johannes Staupitz. In short, we are all Hussites without knowing it. And then too, so are Paul and Augustine; Hussites to the letter. I implore you just to look at the horrific black whole into which we are entering, without a Bohemian leader or teacher. I am too dumbfounded to even know what to think seeing such a terrifying judgment of God among men that the true Gospel is considered worthy of being damned, having been torched so blatantly in public for over a hundred years, and that no one can admit it. It is the woe of the world! Vale. Martinus Lutherus.[131]

---

way other than as an expression of his deepest convictions would be *ipso facto* to accuse Luther of being a two-faced hypocrite trying to save his own skin by saying whatever he felt was needed. Luther's letter to Leo, is the genuine Luther. I will be treating Luther's ecclesiology in this period at length, as well as the relevant historiography, in the second volume of the trilogy, my forthcoming study, *The Failed Reformation*.

[130] "Data est mihi notio futurae alicuius insignis turbulae, nisi Deus Satanam prohibuerit. Vidi cogitationes eius artificiosissimas in malum et meum et multorum. Quid vis? Verbum pietatis nunquam sine turbine, tumultu, periculo tractari potuit. Verbum est infinitae maiestatis, magna operatur, et est mirabile in altis et sublimibus, ut Propheta dicit, pingues Israel occidit et electos eius impedit. Aut ergo desperandum est de pace et tranquillitate huius rei, aut verbum negandum est. Bellum Domini est, qui non venit pacem mittere. Tu ergo cave, ne speres Christum in terra promoveri cum pace et suavitate, quem vides proprio sanguine pugnasse, et post eum omnes martyres." *WABr* 2.41,12–42,22.

[131] "Ego imprudens hucusque omnia Iohannis Huss et docui et tenui. Docuit eadem imprudentia et Iohannes Staupitz. Breviter: sumus omnes Hussitae ignorantes. Denique Paulus et Augustinus ad verbum sunt Hussitae. Vide monstra, quaeso, in quae venimus sine duce et doctore Bohemico. Ego prae stupore nescio, quid cogitem, videns tam terribilia Dei iudicia in hominibus, quod veritas evangelica apertissima iam publice plus centum annis exusta, pro damnata habetur, nec licet hoc confiteri. Vae terrae! Vale Martinus Lutherus." *WABr* 2.42,22–30; *cf.* Heiko A. Oberman, "Hus and Luther: Prophets of a Radical Reformation," in *The Contentious Triangle: Church, State, and University. A Festschrift in Honor of Professor George Huntston Williams*, ed. Rodney L. Peterson and Calvin Augustine Pater, Sixteenth Century Essays & Studies 51 (Kirksville, MO, 1999), 135–166.

The only thing Luther could do, was to pray for God's mercy.[132]

Ten days later, on 24 February, Luther once again wrote to Spalatin. This letter Luther concluded in a completely different tone: "Nevertheless, I will do as much as I am able to do. Be well, and pray for me."[133] Luther had begun very matter-of-factly, reporting on the latest developments. He started a new paragraph, and the first line appears simply to continue in the style with which the letter had opened: "I have in my hands, from the printing house of Dominicus Schleupner, Lorenzo Valla's refutation of the *Donation of Constantine*, published by Hutten."[134] But then came the earth-shattering revelation that shook Luther to the very depths of his soul, the revelation that changed everything:

> Good God! You would be amazed how in God's judgment not only such impure, such crass and naked lies of such massive Roman darkness or Roman iniquity have lasted through the ages, but also how they have prevailed and been handed down in Canon Law, one following after the other, lest some sort of the most horrible beast imaginable be kept from infecting the articles of faith. I am so overwhelmingly horrified in the very depths of my being that I can scarcely doubt that the pope is that very Antichrist which, as commonly known, the world has expected, since it all fits, how he lives, what he does, what he says, and what he proclaims.[135]

The Antichrist had been revealed. And Luther was no longer only going to pray for God's mercy: he was going to do whatever he could. On 15 June, in the Bull *Exsurge Domine*, Luther was threatened with excommunication if he did not recant by Leo X, whom only a year previously Luther had addressed as "Most blessed father"; in August appeared Luther's *Address to the Christian Nobility of the German*

---

[132] "Unum possum, orare scilicet Dei misericordiam." *WABr* 2.41,12.

[133] "Agam tamen quantum possum. Vale et ora pro me." *WABr* 2.49,39–40.

[134] "Habeo in manibus officio Dominici Schleupner Donationem Constantini a Laurentio Vallensi confutatam per Huttenum editam." *WABr* 2.48,20–22.

[135] "Deus bone, quantae seu tenebrae seu nequitiae Romanensium et quod in Dei iudicio mireris per tot saecula non modo durasse, sed etiam prevaluisse ac inter decretales relata esse tam impura tam crassa tam impudentia mendacia inque fidei articulorum (nequid monstrosissimi monstri desit) vicem successisse. Ego sic angor, ut prope non dubitem papam esse proprie Antichristum illum, quem vulgata opinione expectat mundus, adeo conveniunt omnia: quae vivit, facit, loquitur, statuit." *WABr* 2.48,22–49,29. Luther then promised to make sure Spalatin had a copy of Valla's debunking, if he had not already seen it: "Sed haec magis coram. Si non vidisti, curabo ut legas." *WABr* 2.49,29, and then turned to matters of the University, *WABr* 2.49,30–39.

Nation; on 6 October, *The Babylonian Captivity of the Church* was published; in November, *The Freedom of the Christian*; on 10 December, Luther put to flames *Exsurge Domine* together with the *Corpus Iuris Canonici*, writings of Eck and Emser, and others, explaining his action in a treatise *Why the Books of the Pope and his Disciples were Burned by Doctor Martin Luther*, which appeared by the end of the month. Luther had mobilized and was engaging in the last battle, the war with the Antichrist. The Apocalypse was in progress.

Popes had been called the Antichrist before, and surely were believed to have been so. It was really not all that uncommon for claims to be made that the Antichrist was sitting upon the throne of St. Peter. For Luther, however, the Antichrist was not sitting upon Peter's throne—*but his own*. That was the shock. It was not the pope, but the papacy itself that was the Antichrist, and had been all along. It was a discovery that Luther could not have made had he not adhered to the hierocratic theory of his Order and its platform. As Giles of Rome and Augustinus of Ancona affirmed, there could certainly be bad popes, even heretical popes, but the pope as the vicar of Christ, as Peter's successor, was, on one level, the same pope as Peter himself. The pope was the embodiment of an eternal office, an eternal person. A distinction had to be made between the pope as bishop, priest, and fallible human, and the pope as pope. The pope as pope embodied the papacy. Luther knew well enough that popes had previously been seen as the Antichrist, even when he was making his impassioned appeal to Leo X, asserting as clearly and as strongly as he could his faith in the supremacy of the see of Peter. And he knew the distinction between the pope and 'The Pope'. The Pope had been Luther's faith and trust and only hope; and it was this very 'The Pope' that Luther finally saw revealed as Antichrist. The shock and horror was cataclysmic. Only recognizing Luther as an Augustinian, following the Order's platform on the high way to heaven, can we understand the depth and significance of Luther's discovery; and only understanding Luther as an Augustinian can we begin to grasp his words: *Deus bone . . . ego sic angor.* 24 February 1520: the day the Reformation began.

B. *The Black Satan: From Reformation to Reform*

Rome was not built in a day, and the Reformation was certainly not made by any one event. It is perhaps an unavoidable expediency that textbooks and university courses fence off historical development into nice, neat manageable chunks of time, bounded by significant events that serve as the required demarcations of human experience for it to be easily packaged and sold. Early Modern Europe: 1500–1789. We need our events.

Events, however, the "great events," the momentous, the prodigious, effected by privileged, western males, can so readily become tyrannical when we forget that they obscure and erase as much as they illumine and explain. Social history, micro-history, feminist history, cultural history, the history of *mentalité* and *la longue durée* have proven as much, and have forced a reconceptualization of what an 'event' is, or was, in the first place. Events are experiences, actions, thoughts, feelings, understandings that we lift up and imbue with significance and meaning in our attempts to come to grips with our own lives as much as with the those of history. Yet in doing so, we pass over other events, other happenings, either from suppression, repression, deceit, forgetfulness, political programs, or simply by choice, that might have been of far greater effect and of far greater meaning than we are willing to given them, or to admit.

Narratives of religious conversion are exemplary. From Augustine's *Confessions* on there has been a tradition of "sudden" conversion, *subito*, where the biographer, either of oneself or of another, points to a moment in time that changed everything, a single experience, a single event.[136] And sometimes it actually happens that way. In individual lives, there are those defining moments, the experiences and occurrences that affect us and change us once and for all, so that the person we were yesterday is not the same as the one we are today. We then extrapolate from individual experience to seek the events that supposedly functioned in the same way for historical movements, and historical periods. Yet even for the individual, no single event, no single breakthrough, ever stands alone; there are no isolated events. Events occur within a socio-psychological matrix that extends over time, from which we pick and choose particular points to emplot the texts of the story of our lives—and those of our histories.

Subito: it is not a word Luther used to describe his own conversion from papal monk to Protestant reformer.[137] Yet the search for that moment in time has been conducted with such passion and

---

[136] See Karl F. Morrison, *Understanding Conversion* (Charlottesville, VA, 1992).
[137] Luther's famous "autobiography," in which he recounts his discovery of the

energy that the total number of "scholar hours" devoted thereto threatens to approach that of the descendants of Abraham. All the while, scholars have passed over, if even mentioned, the event that marked that transition far more clearly, far more symbolically, and far more historically than can any number of highlighted lines in the *Weimar Ausgabe* picked out to encapsulate the theological demarcation: 9 October 1524, Luther's defrocking. That was an event, and the fact that it was a "self-defrocking" does not take away from its significance. To perceive the import of that act, its symbolic and historical meaning, we will need to enter our own "black hole," groping to reconstruct the socio-psychological matrix in which the event took place. Thus we begin at the beginning, long before the question of Luther's "Reformation breakthrough" can even be broached; a point in time when, not just for his interpreters, but also for Luther himself there was indeed a *subito*: "Help me saint Anne, I will become a monk."

i. *Misericordia dei*

The story is well known. On 2 July 1505, Martin Luther was returning to Erfurt after having visited his parents. It was a stormy day, and when a lightening bolt struck nearby, Martin was terrified and made his vow. Two weeks later, on 17 July, Luther rang at the gate of the Erfurt Augustinians.[138]

Entering a monastery was not like joining the Lion's Club. Becoming a member of a religious Order was to assume a completely new existence. What one did, what one wore, what and how one ate,

---

righteousness of God, is his preface to the Latin edition of his *Opera Omnia* of 1545. *Subito* is not a word he uses. See *WA* 54.179,2–187,7. The literature on Luther's "Reformation Discovery" is enormous. For the most perceptive treatment thereof, see Oberman, *Luther*, 159–184. For Luther's views on "conversion," especially as they relate to his own, see Marilyn J. Harran, *Luther on Conversion. The Early Years* (Ithaca, NY, 1983), esp. 174–188 for a discussion of the famous "tower experience." At the time of his death, Heiko Oberman was preparing a book for press, contracted with Yale University Press, *The Reformation. From the Last Days to the Beginning of the New World: Luther's Beachhead and the Shores of America*. Chapter Four of this work bears the title: " Martin Luther: Friar in the Lion's Den," and is a brilliant and breath-taking analysis of Luther's breakthrough with respect to his treatise *De Votis Monasticis*. Prof. Oberman had made a pre-publication version of this chapter available for my use. I cite the page numbers of the printout of that chapter. In this light, I could refer the reader to Oberman, "Friar in the Lion's Den," 1–11. Oberman's *The Reformation. From the Last Days to the Beginning of the New World* is planned to appear with Yale, edited by Donald Weinstein.

[138] See Brecht, *Road to Reformation*, 46–50.

how one walked, how one slept, how one lived were all prescribed by the Order in its attempt to enforce, inculcate, and unite one with the Order's order of being, the ritualized symbolic ontology of being a religious *in statu religionis*. As seen above, some remained impervious to such acculturation. Yet for those souls that were sufficiently sensitive and sincere to suck up the significance of the external observance, it became their very blood and marrow, transforming the person into a new being socially, sexually, physically, and psychologically. It became their religion, and their religious identity. The habit did not make the monk: that was known, and accepted as given, a dictum often employed to remind that the truly religious was so in so far as religion flowed through one's bones and one's veins. The habit did not make the monk: and yet paradoxically, it did.

When Luther stood at the gate and knocked on that July day in 1505, he would have been led to a guest room, where he would remain for an unspecified time, perhaps for several weeks.[139] This was a time of reflection and confirmation for both the community and the petitioner. Luther was sincere. When it was clear to his prior, Winand of Diedenhofen, that Luther indeed was certain of his intention, Prior Diedenhofen heard Luther's full confession, and at some point thereafter, Luther was received into the Order as a novice.

We know the details of Luther's initiatory rite. The vicar-general of the Saxon-Thurigian Congregation of Observant Augustinians, Johannes Staupitz, had published in 1504 new constitutions: the *Constitutions of the brother hermits of St. Augustine according to the form of apostolic privileges for the reformation of Germany*,[140] which applied the Rule to the specifics of the Order's daily life. Luther would have been led into either the chapter room or the church to make his official profession before the prior and the assembled community. The prior sat before the altar. Luther would have stood in the midst of the gathering and then knelt before the prior. Prior Winand asked: "What do you seek?" Luther responded: "God's mercy, and yours."[141] Luther

---

[139] *Ibid.*, 58. In the Order's *Constitutiones* no time is specified for this period of probation. Brecht makes the valid assumption that those seeking to join the Order would initially be received in the same fashion as all guests.

[140] Staupitz *Const.* (142/143).

[141] "Et in medio ante priorem ad gradus altaris sedentem stantes, prosternant se. Interrogante autem priore: 'Quid petitis?', respondeant: 'Misericordiam dei et vestram.'" Stauptiz *Const.* 15 (186,11–14).

was then told to rise, and questioned if he was married, indentured, in debt, or whether he had any physical defect or weakness that was not apparent. Having been assured of his worthy status, Prior Winand explained to Luther the Order's austerity: the abdication of one's will, course and sparse food, harsh clothing, nightly vigils, daily labor, castigation of the flesh, the disgrace of poverty, the embarrassment of begging, the fatigue of fasting, the weight and weariness of the cloister, and all the rest, inquiring if he was prepared to endure such. Luther responded, as stipulated, that he was ready, with God's help, insofar as human weakness was allowed, to preserve and maintain the Order's way of life.[142] Prior Winand responded: "May God, who has started the good work in you, bring it to completion"; the chapter: "Amen."[143] Then, having already been tonsured, while the chapter sang the hymn, "Oh great father Augustine," Luther removed his clothes; he undressed, and then redressed himself in the novice's habit, while the prior pronounced: "the Lord dresses you as the new man, who was created according to God in the righteousness and holiness of truth. Amen."[144] A series of antiphonal prayers and responses followed, as Luther knelt again, cloaked as the *novus homo* before the prior. These prayers invoked God's aid and mercy, as well as that of St. Augustine and the Virgin Mary.[145] Thereafter, Luther was led into the convent. Prior Winand approached; Luther again knelt and crossed himself. He was told: "Not those who begin, but those who persevere to the end will be saved." Prior Winand then gave Luther the kiss of peace, as did each member of the chapter,[146] before he was handed over to Frater Johannes Greffenstein, the master of novices.[147] And this was only the beginning.

---

[142] Staupitz *Const.* 15 (186,14–187,25).

[143] "Post hoc dicat ipsis prior: 'Deus qui incepit in vobis bonum opus, perficiat,' et conventus respondeat: 'Amen'." Staupitz *Const.* 15 (187,26–27).

[144] "Tunc cantor incipiat hymnum: 'Magne pater Augustine'. Qui dum cantatur, novitiandi, tonsis prius crinibus, vestibus saecularibus exuantur habituque religionis induantur, dicente priore cuilibet: 'Induat te dominus novum hominem, qui secundum deum creatus est in iustitia et sanctitate veritatis. Amen.'" Staupitz *Const.* 15 (187,28–32).

[145] Staupitz *Const.* 15 (187,32–188,77).

[146] "His expletis, ducantur ad conventum, primo a priore, postea ab aliis pacis osculum accepturi. Demum flexis genibus ante priorem audiant ab eo: 'Non qui inceperit, sed qui perseveraverit usque in finem, hic salvus erit.'" Staupitz *Const.* 15 (188,77–189,80).

[147] Staupitz *Const.* 15 (189,81–86); *cf.* Staupitz *Const.* 17 (193,4–194,44).

Luther's novitiate was to last a year and a day. During this time he lived his new identity, that of a lay brother, and was instructed by *magister* Greffenstein in the Order's *Rule, Constitutions*, liturgy, traditions, and way of life. He further would have studied Hugh of St. Victore's *Commentary on the Rule of St. Augustine*, and, the *Liber Vitasfratrum* of Jordan of Quedlinburg.[148] Luther was, after all, going through the same process as his forebears, saying the same words, praying the same prayers, living the same life, following the same religion as had Augustinians since at least the *Regensburg Constitutions* of 1290. The Order's ritual and common life unified the Order from Giles of Rome to Martin Luther. It was what made one an Augustinian. And as tradition had it, it is what unified the Order with its father himself, St. Augustine, and his original group of hermits. There was no doubt. The *novus homo* that the initiate became was the first step on the evolutionary path that would finally lead once again to one being proclaimed a *novus homo* in one's profession, when the *novus homo* had finally become *homo Augustiniensis*. During that first year, the year of probation, the novitiate could leave at any time. He had not taken any vows. Luther stayed. The following summer, the summer of 1506, he was ready for the final commitment.

We do not know exactly when Luther made his profession in the Order. Yet when he did, he was led once again into the church or the chapter room, this time cloaked as a novice, by *magister* Greffenstein.[149] As when he had entered the novitiate, all the members of the convent would have been present, and Prior Winand sat before the altar. *Magister* Greffenstein brought Luther to the Prior, and Luther knelt. Prior Winand then began:

> Dear brother, the time of your probation is complete, during which you have become acquainted with the austerity of our Order. You have lived with us, joining in all aspects of our life, just as one of us, except for the monastic counsels. Therefore, you now are to choose

---

[148] Brecht, *Road to Reformation*, 59. There is, however, no specific prescribed reading for novices given in the *Constitutiones* aside from the *Regula* and the *Constitutiones* themselves; Staupitz *Const.* 17 (193–194). Brecht gives no evidence that Jordan's *Liber Vitasfratrum* would have been required, or recommended reading. The detailed stipulations of what the novice was to be taught, however, follow very closely the topics treated by Jordan: the divine office, prayers, meals, silence, obedience, etc. The novices were, though, explicitly ordered to read and study scripture: "Sacram scripturam avide legat, devote audiat et ardenter addiscat." Staupitz *Const.* 17 (194,38–39).

[149] Staupitz *Const.* 18 (195,4–9).

634   CHAPTER SIX

one of two paths: either you leave us, or, you renounce this world and not only offer, but also truly give yourself completely to God, and then to our Order. After having given up such, thus offering yourself as a sacrifice, you will not be permitted for whatever reason to throw off from your neck the yoke of obedience, which with such serious consideration you freely accepted when you were still able to leave.[150]

Martin chose the latter. The habit of a professed Augustinian was then brought in and laid at the prior's feet. The prior blessed the new habit, speaking, not singing, the following, with Martin responding:

> P.: Our help is in the name of the Lord
> M.: Who created heaven and earth
> P.: Hear me oh Lord
> M.: For I cry to you
> P.: The Lord be with you
> M.: And with your spirit.
> P. Let us pray: Lord Jesus Christ, who deemed it worthy to take on the cloak of our mortality, we beseech the immense abundance of your generosity that you might thus see fitting to bless this form of dress which the holy fathers renouncing the world sanctified by wearing to symbolize humility and innocence, so that this your servant Martin, who will use these vestments, might be worthy to dress himself with you. God, the most faithful promisor and the most certain executor of eternal riches, who has promised the vestments of salvation and the clothing of joy to your faithful, we humbly implore your clemency, that you might fruitfully bless these clothes, which signify the humility of heart and the contempt for the world, by which your servant is visibly confirmed in his decision, so that the habit of holy renunciation which he receives hoping in you, might keep him safe being protected by you, and that you might desire to dress him with the vestments of a religion to be honored so that you might clothe him with eternal blessedness. Who lives and reigns with God the Father in the unity of the Holy Spirit, one God, for ever and ever, Amen[151]

---

[150] "Care frater, tempus probationis tuae completum est, in quo asperitatem ordinis nostri expertus es: Fuisti namque in omnibus nobiscum sicut unus ex nobis praeterquam in consiliis. Nunc ergo e duobus oportet te eligere unum: sive a nobis discedere, vel saeculo huic renuntiare teque totum deo primum et dehinc ordini nostro dedicare atque offere, adiecto quod, postquam sic te obtuleris, de subiungo oboedientiae collum tuum quacumque ex causa excutere non licebit, quod sub tam morosa deliberatione, cum recusare libere posses, sponte suscipere voluisti." Staupitz *Const.* 18 (195,11–19).

[151] "Qui, si responderit velle se sic deo et ordini offere, deferatur ad pedes prioris habitus professorum, qui benedicens ipsum hoc modo incipiat sine cantu: 'Adiutorium nostrum in nomine domini,' respondetur: 'Qui fecit coelum et terram,'

Then both the habit and brother Martin were anointed with incense and holy water.[152] While the chapter sang "Great father Augustine," Prior Winand himself this time undressed Luther, saying: "the Lord strips you of the man you used to be together with his acts. Amen." Then, Prior Winand re-dressed Luther in the blest habit of profession that had lain at his feet, the habit of the Order, saying: "The Lord clothes you as a new individual, who was created in the image of God in the righteousness and holiness of truth. Amen."[153] Frater Martin then crossed himself before the altar or choir, and Prior Winand. Prayers to Augustine and Christ followed, and then the antiphon, *Come Holy Spirit*.[154] After the prayers, hymn, and responses, prior Winand sat himself opposite Luther, who knelt and crossed himself. Prior Winand placed his hands on Luther's head, and Luther made his solemn profession, his solemn vows:

> I, Frater Martin Luther, make my profession, and promise obedience to God omnipotent, to blessed Mary, ever virgin, and to you, Frater Winand, prior of this convent, as the representative of the prior general of the Order of brother Hermits of Bishop Saint Augustine, and his successors canonically elected, to live without possessions and in chastity according to the *Rule* of the same blessed Augustine until the time of my death.[155]

---

versus: 'Domine, exaudi,' respondetur: 'et clamor'; 'Dominus vobiscum', respondetur: 'et cum spiritu.' Oremus: Domine Iesu Christi, qui tegumentum nostrae mortalitatis induere dignatus es, obsecramus immensam tuae largitatis abundantiam, ut hoc genus indumenti, quod sancti patres ad innocentiae et humilitatis indicium abrenuntiantes saeculo ferre sanxerunt, tu ita benedicere digneris, ut hic famulus tuus N., qui eo usus fuerit, te induere mereatur. Deus, aeternorum bonorum fidelissimus promissor et certissimus persolutor, qui vestimentum salutis et indumentum iucunditatis tuis fidelibus promisisti, clementiam tuam humiliter deposcimus, ut hoc indumentum, humilitatem cordis et contemptum mundi significans, quo famulus tuus est visibiliter firmandus in proposito, propitius benedicas, ut beatae abnegationis habitum, quem te aspirante suscepit, te protegente custodiat et, quem vestibus venerandae religionis induere voluisti, beata facias immortalitate vestiri. Qui vivis et regnas cum deo patre in unitate spiritus sancti, deus per omnia saecula saeculorum, Amen." Staupitz *Const.* 18 (195,20–196,39).

[152] Staupitz *Const.* 18 (196,40–41).

[153] "Deinde prior exuat novitium habitum novitialem dicendo hunc versum: 'Exuat te dominus veterem hominem cum actibus suis. Amen.' Consequenter induat eum veste professorum dicens: 'Induat te dominus novum hominem, qui secundum deum creatus est in iustitia et sanctitate veritatis. Amen.' Interim fratres cantent hymnum: 'Magne pater Augustine.'" Staupitz *Const.* 18 (196,41–46).

[154] Staupitz *Const.* 18 (196,46–197,57).

[155] "His expletis sedeat prior contra novitium. Et novitius acceptam regulam priori propinquans, iterum genibus flexis apertam deponat in genibus prioris sedentis eamque sic apertam recipientis, tenensque manus super eam, faciat professionem

A candle was then lit, and the prior said: "Let us pray, dearest brothers, that our new brother, having professed with words, might fulfill his vows happily and faithfully in his actions, with the help of our Lord, Jesus Christ, who with the Father and Holy Spirit, lives and reigns, one God, for ever and ever." "Amen," replied all.[156] More prayers to Augustine, Mary, and Christ followed, before Prior Winand raised Martin to his feet, and gave him the kiss of peace, telling Martin to give to God what he had vowed, by living chastely in mind and body, having no possessions, including his own will, and by being obedient to his superior, without grumbling or opposition, to live according to the way of life that he had learned during his novitiate, reminding Martin that during his novitiate he had lived the Augustinian life freely, but that now he had vowed to do so. Thereupon, all left the chapter room in peace.[157]

It was a ritualized re-birth, a rite of initiation into a new world, and a deeply solemn and impressive ritual. And his habit, in which the Lord himself had clothed him, to whom Frater Martin had vowed obedience first and foremost, was the symbol thereof. This was the habit of the Augustinians, the same habit worn by Augustine himself and his first community of hermits; the habit that symbolized Christ's Passion, and love for one's neighbor; the habit that distinguished the Augustinians from all other monastic Orders, and especially from the Canons; the habit of the true sons of father Augustine; the habit that symbolized the mercy of God, which Martin had sought when he had first knocked at the monastery's gate over a year before; the habit that made him a new individual, a *novus homo*,

---

sollemniter in tono lectionum hoc modo: 'Ego frater N facio professionem et promitto oboedientiam deo omnipotenti et beatae Mariae semper virgini et tibi fratri N, priori huius loci, nomine et vice generalis prioris ordinis fratrum Eremitarum sancti Augustini episcopi et successorum eius canonice intrantium, vivere sine proprio et in castitate secundum regulam eiusdem beati Augustini usque ad mortem.'" Staupitz *Const.* 18 (197,58–67).

[156] "Tunc detur sic professo candela accensa. Et prior dicat hanc orationem absolute: 'Oremus, fratres carissimi, ut, quod frater noster ore professus est, opere fidelissime feliciterque compleat, auxiliante domino nostro Iesu Christo, qui cum patre et spiritu sancto vivit et regnat, deus in saecula saeculorum,' respondetur: 'Amen.'" Staupitz *Const.* 18 (197,67–198,72).

[157] Staupitz *Const.* 18 (198,73–199,127). For Luther's entry into the Augustinians, in addition to Brecht, *Road to Reformation*, 46–59, see also the still insightful and informative account of Theodor Kolde, *Martin Luther. Eine Biographie* (Gotha, 1884), 46–55.

and the habit that gave him a new identity.[158] He was to wear it for eighteen years. Making a vow to God is not easily broken.

ii. *Pater et Preceptor*
The point of departure for understanding the significance of Luther's putting off his habit is the impact and meaning of his having put it on in the first place. By taking off his habit, Luther was breaking the vows he had made to God. He was iconoclastically denying the ritual and symbols that had made him a new being in Christ, and rejecting the world of meaning that had given him his identity for eighteen years. Little wonder he was reluctant.

Heiko Oberman insightfully encapsulated Luther's transformation from monk to reformer: "In the Reformation discovery, Luther's obedience to his Order became faith in Christ."[159] There are three components to this statement: 1.) the Reformation discovery; 2.) Luther's obedience to his Order; and 3.) faith in Christ. Oberman associated the third with the first component, placed in opposition to the second. This we need to analyze further.

By all accounts, the Reformation discovery occurred by 1518.[160] Yet still as late as 18 December 1521, Luther could write to Wenceslaus Link that he would stay in his habit and way of life unless the world were to become another,[161] as strong an affirmation of his vows and obedience as can be imagined. When the Reformation discovery, however that is defined, is found to have occurred in 1518, 1514, somewhere inbetween—or even in 1520!—it is then ever so easy to view Luther from that point on as "the Reformer," and not to take seriously such comments as the one he made to Link at the end of 1521, simply by-passing them as remnants of the "Pre-Protestant" Luther that do not have all that much significance. The "Reformation discovery" is the dividing line, the swinging door leading from popery to Protestantism. Perhaps Luther was just being stubborn, or nostalgic, and in his letter to Link had already put behind him his vow of obedience to his Order. But there is another possibility.

---

[158] See Jor. *VF* 1,15 (48,1–57,244); *cf.* Chapter One, n. 392 above.
[159] "In der reformatorischen Entdeckung ist der Ordensgehorsam zum Glauben an Christus geworden." Oberman, *Luther. Mensch Zwischen Gott und Teufel*, 153; *cf.* n. 105 above.
[160] See note 137 above.
[161] See note 105 above.

To solve the puzzle of Luther's letter to Link and the "Reformation breakthrough," the three components of Oberman's statement quoted above can remain, but the syntax needs to be rearranged, whereby the third is associated with the second, and placed before the first: 'In obedience to his Order and the faith in Christ it prescribed, Luther made his Reformation discovery.' In other words, Luther's Reformation discovery, the theological insight and all that entailed, was made as a faithful, obedient Augustinian friar, completely in keeping with his vows and the habit he wore. And even further: Luther's "Reformation discovery" was made while he was still concerned, above all else to defend the honor of the Roman Church and the holy father, the pope, as he wrote to Leo X in 1519; it was made by an obedient, faithful, sincere, and observant Augustinian friar, who, in keeping with his Order's high way to heaven and its platform, was also a devout "papist," as he himself stated on 18 March 1539: "in my time as a monk, I so reverently worshipped the pope, that I wanted to serve all the papists who ever were. I did not make my vows to fill my stomach, but to save my soul, and I kept our Order's *Rule* and *Constitutions* rigorously ... I took off my habit with difficulty and pain ... and only at last in 1523."[162] Whether

---

[162] "... in meo monachatu papam tam reverenter colui, das ich allen papisten wolde trotz bitten, qui fuerunt et sunt. Ego enim non ventris, sed salutis meae causa vovebam et rigidissime servabam nostra statuta. Item dicebat, quam aegre et difficulter deposuisset habitum ... Et tandem anno 1523 deposui habitum ..." *WAT* 4, nr. 4414; 303,14–30; 18 March 1539. Luther continued by explaining that he had taken off his habit "... in gloriam Dei et confusionem Sathanae." *WAT* 4, nr. 4414; 303,30; 18 March 1539. *Cf.* Oberman, "A Friar in the Lion's Den," 32–33 (as in note 137 above). The date of 1523 is that given by Luther in this *Tischreden* of 1539, and repeated by Brecht, *Road to Reformation*, 64, on this basis. Brecht later gives the date of 9 October 1524, commenting that this was the date that Luther "for the first time ... appeared in public in secular clothing. A week later he discarded the cowl permanently." Brecht, *Shaping and Defining the Reformation*, 95. The evidence for the 9 October 1524 date is given in the manuscript of Luther's sermon on that day. There is no mention there that Luther put the habit back on, only to discard it permanently a week later. The only evidence that Brecht cites that could be taken to infer such a schedule, is Luther's *Tischreden* from late Spring or early Summer 1540: "Ego semel deposui cappam, ut indicarem libertatem eius vestis, postea indui iterum." *WAT* 4, nr. 5034; 624,14–15. Here too it should be noted that Luther mentions only the *cappa*. Technically the *cappa* was the hood that went together with the *cucullus*, or the cowl, both of which were black. All the vestments together comprised the *habitus*; see Staupitz *Const.* 24 (215,6–216,13). The evidence to claim that Luther on 16 October 1524 discarded his habit for good is found in a report of Spalatin; *WABr* 3.301, n. 6; nr. 748. This together with the manuscript evidence for 9 October 1524 as being the first time Luther appeared in public, in any case, without the habit, is more secure evidence than is Luther's statement in his *Tischreden* of 1539 that he finally took off his habit in 1523.

we accept Luther's memory in 1539 that 1523 was the year he took off his habit, or the clear evidence giving 9 October 1524 as the date,[163] does not take away from the fact that Luther, by his own account, was wearing the habit as a faithful friar when his "Reformation breakthrough" was made. Further, his comments regarding his reverence for the papacy give support to the sincerity of his letter to Leo X of 1519, before his realization that the papacy was the throne of the Antichrist. In fact, as we have seen, there was nothing in his vows regarding obedience to the pope, or even to the Roman Church. He vowed obedience to God, then to Mary, and then to the prior general of the Order. Obedience to God came first, even as Luther told Pope Leo in 1519: there was nothing that should be placed above the sovereignty of the pope and the Church, except the one Lord, Jesus Christ, a position inherent in the Order's platform since at least the time of Augustinus of Ancona. When a year later, Luther realized the pope as Antichrist, he was not repudiating his vows. Rather, he followed his vows and went on in the only direction he could go: up. The authority, majesty, respect, and awe for the papacy had been overthrown; only Christ was left, Christ who had been there all along in the realm *supra papam* and *supra ecclesiam*, the same Christ who had dressed Frater Martin in the habit of the Augustinian Order and to whom the Order prayed that he, Christ, would bring to fruition the good work that he had begun in the new being that Luther had become, signified and symbolized in the habit. Luther's Reformation breakthrough, as well as his writings of 1520, were not those of the reformer, but of *Frater* Martin Luther, the observant Augustinian friar, being obedient to his vows and to his habit, as he followed the high way to heaven of his Order's platform.

Recognizing the extent to which Luther was an obedient friar is not only of central importance for placing his early career, including the Reformation breakthrough, in historical, rather than theological, perspective, but also for understanding that momentous event of 9 October 1524, when Luther took off his habit. In doing so, he was abandoning the very identity that had set him on his path. This was an identity, however, that was beginning to break apart. 9 October 1524 did not arrive without preparation. On 14 October 1518, Luther's vicar-general, Johannes Staupitz had already released Luther from his vow of obedience; on 3 January 1521 Luther was

---

[163] See note 162 above.

finally excommunicated; on 21 November 1521, Luther completed his treatise *On Monastic Vows*, though it was not printed until February;[164] yet all the while Luther remained an Augustinian friar.[165] He was in fierce combat with the Antichrist, fighting with all his might against the diabolical machinations of the Roman Church, the Roman Church which in 1519 he had still seen as "our Mother." But Luther himself remained a son of Augustine. There may have been some sarcasm in his comments to Spalatin on 1 September 1520, a little over six months after the great discovery, when Luther wrote: "See to it first of all, my good Spalatin, that you thank the Illustrious Prince for me, Frederick the Wise, who has fattened me up with wild game, since I am a monk."[166] Yet he still signed his name as *Frater Martinus Lutherus Augustinianus*; on 17 April 1522, writing to Gabriel Zwilling regarding providing an evangelical preacher for Altenburg, Luther, for the last time, referred to himself as a friar, signing his name as *Frater Martinus Lutherus*.[167] But he still wore his Order's habit. Luther was still an Augustinian.

Luther's observance of his vow of obedience is actually the key for interpreting his act of 9 October 1524. We can only do so, however, when we recognize what had brought Luther to that point. It was not his "Reformation discovery"; it was not his realization of the pope as Antichrist; it was not even his re-working through the theory and practice of the monastic vows themselves. It was more

---

[164] Brecht, *Shaping and Defining the Reformation*, 23.

[165] For the best interpretation of Luther's *De Votis Monasticis*, see Oberman, "Martin Luther: A Friar in the Lion's Den," (as in note 137 above). In his detailed tracing of Luther's relationship to the monastic life, Heinz-Meinholf Stamm concluded: "Die von der Lutherdeutung bis auf den heutigen Tag vorgetragene Interpretation, Luther habe das Ordenswesen als solches abgelehnt und ihm durch die Aufhebung der ewigen Bindung der Gelübde den Todesstoß versetzt, erweist sich somit als Fehlinterpretation. Das Gegenteil ist der Fall. Luther hat sich zeitlebens für ein echtes, Gott wohlgefälliges Ordensleben eingesetzt, im Geiste—wie er immer wieder betont hat—der Gerechtigkeit Gottes. In der evangelischen Freiheit erblickt er sogar eine Stärkung und Festigung der ewigen Verpflichtung der Gelübde." Stamm, *Luthers Stellung zum Ordensleben, VIEG* 101 (Wiesbaden, 1980), 162. Stamm's conclusions are further supported by the continuing existence throughout the sixteenth and on into the early seventeenth century of Lutheran, and Calvinist, female cloisters; see Lucia Koch, "'Eingezogenes Stilles Wesen'? Protestantische Damenstifte an der Wende zum 17. Jahrhundert," in *"In Christo ist weder Man noch Weyb" Frauen in der Zeit der Reformation und der katholischen Reform*, ed. Anne Conrad (Münster, 1999), 199–230.

[166] "Primum omnium vide, mi Spalatine, ut pro me gratias agas illustrissimo principi, qui me ferinis saginat, cum sim monachus." *WABr* 2.180,4–5.

[167] *WABr* 2.506,31.

personal. It was more intimate. It was more in keeping with the nature of his vows themselves. Luther did not take off his habit until another break was made, the break with the person to whom Luther applied the names traditionally given by his Order to Augustine, *pater et preceptor*; the break with his superior to whom he had vowed obedience, and who had composed the Order's *Constitutiones* in 1504, and who had set Luther on his path: Johannes Staupitz.

The relationship between Luther and Staupitz has long been a stumbling block for Reformation scholars.[168] That there was a very close, personal relationship no one questions: that between father and son, teacher and student, elder and younger brothers, and that, from 1512 on, between the vicar-general of the German Observant Augustinians, and a provincial prior.[169] On 17 September 1523 Luther wrote to Staupitz for the last time, and strongly affirmed that he, Staupitz, had been the one who had first brought the light of the Gospel. Seven months later, Staupitz replied, acknowledging his role as "forerunner," a statement that has been seen as a "theological time-bomb."[170] If Luther "hatched the egg that Hus had lain," Staupitz was his nest. Even though Jordan of Quedlinburg had already

---

[168] The first full treatment of Staupitz and his relationship to the Reformation was the still valuable study of Theodor Kolde, *Die Deutsche Augustiner-Kongregation und Johann von Staupitz. Ein Beitrag zur Ordens-und Reformationsgeschichte nach meist ungedruckten Quellen* (Gotha, 1879). A century later, David Steinmetz re-examined the relationship between Luther and Staupitz in his essay, *Luther and Staupitz. An Essay in the Intellectual Origins of the Protestant Reformation*, Duke Monographs in Medieval and Renaissance Studies 4 (Durham, N.C., 1980). For a broader perspective, see Lothar Graf zu Dohna, "Staupitz and Luther: Continuity and Breakthrough at the Beginning of the Reformation," in *Via Augustini*, 116–129. For Staupitz's theology, see Steinmetz, *Misericordia Dei. The Theology of Johann von Staupitz in its Late Medieval Setting*, SMRT 4 (Leiden, 1969), together with the more recent studies by Markus Wriedt, *Gnade und Erwählung. Eine Untersuchung zu Johann von Staupitz und Martin Luther*, VIEG 141 (Mainz, 1991), Adolar Zumkeller, *Johannes von Staupitz und Seine Christliche Heilslehre*, Cassiciacum 45 (Würzburg, 1994), and Heiko A. Oberman, "*Captivitas Babylonica*: Johann von Staupitz's Critical Ecclesiology," in Oberman, *The Impact of the Reformation*, 26–34, and idem, "*Duplex Misericordia*: The Devil and the Church in the Early Theology of Johann von Staupitz," ibid., 35–47. For the best overview of Staupitz to date, including his relationship to Luther, see Berndt Hamm, "Johann von Staupitz (ca. 1468–1524): spätmittelalterlicher Reformer und 'Vater' der Reformation," *ARG* 92 (2001), 6–41.

[169] For Luther's role as provincial prior of the Observant German Congregation of the Augustinians, see Wilhelm E. Winterhager, "Martin Luther und das Amt des Provinzialvikars in der Reformkongregation der deutschen Augustiner-Eremiten," in *Vita Religiosa im Mittelalter*, 707–738.

[170] Oberman, "*Duplex Misericordia*," 37.

reinterpreted the scholastic *gratia gratum faciens*, Luther had learned of the grace that makes God acceptable to humans, rather than the other way around, based on God's love and mercy from Staupitz, not Jordan. *Misericordia dei*, the hallmark of Staupitz's theology which had enabled the Gospel to shine once again, was something that Luther took to heart. Staupitz's understanding of God's mercy was one that allowed him "to combine the mercy of God with critique of the church in so seamless and complete a fashion that even at the end of his life he was able to hate the Babylonian Captivity of the church without declaring war on the pope as the antichrist."[171] It was with this understanding of mercy that Luther wrote to Spalatin—after the shock that Hus had been right all along and that he, Luther, together with Staupitz, as well as Paul and Augustine, were all Hussites—that the only thing left to do was to pray for the *misericordia dei*. But then came the horrible discovery of 24 February 1520: the pope was Antichrist. And where was Staupitz?

Attempts to reconstruct the development of the relationship between Luther and his vicar-general are hindered by the lack of complete documentary evidence. The extant correspondence between the two consists of only twelve letters, ten of which are those of Luther. We know from other comments Luther made that he had received more letters from Staupitz than the two preserved in the *Weimar Ausgabe*. Yet these sparse comments, together with the letters we do have, are the only sources we possess for detailing what became a most painful, and finally eventful, relationship.

Luther's early letters to Staupitz report on the latest developments in Wittenberg, they express his concerns, his fears, and his hopes. Thus we find him telling Staupitz in 1518 that he is reading the scholastic doctors, and doing so with a critical eye; it is not that he dismisses everything they say, but he tests everything they say against scripture, and if the Scotists and Gabriel Biel can disagree with the Thomists, and if the Thomists can disagree with the entire world, why is he not allowed to put his two-cents worth in as well?[172] We find him telling Staupitz, also in 1518, that Staupitz's interpretation of true penance was what led him to compose his thesis against indulgences, as well as his re-affirming his desire to honor the Roman

---

[171] *Ibid.*, 42.
[172] *WABr* 1.159–160; nr. 66; 31 March 1518.

Church.[173] We find him complaining to Staupitz about a dispute in the *studium* at Erfurt, expressing his dissatisfaction with how long such disobedience would continue.[174] But then, on 20 February 1519, there is an important change. Luther had last written only three months previous, but now, before he reported on his meeting with Miltitz in Altenburg, Luther launched a complaint, an appeal, with a tone of fear and despair that will reappear: Staupitz had been silent; Staupitz had abandoned the cause, and had abandoned Luther:

> Although you know much about what is going on here, you are both distant and holding your tongue, reverend father, and neither do you write any letters which we are sitting on the edge of our seats waiting to receive. Nevertheless, I am going to break the silence. We wish, everyone wishes, for you in some way to make yourself known in this assault on heaven. I believe that you have received my report on the Diet of Augsburg, that is, my anger and indignation at Rome. God has seized me, and is driving me, and even leading me on; I am not the one in control. I want to be at peace, but I am snatched up and placed in the middle of an uprising.[175]

The period of Staupitz's silence had not been that long. He had written to Luther in mid-December of 1518, expressing his support, and far more.[176] The world was so turned against the truth, that such was the hate that had once crucified Christ, and the cross of Christ was the only hope left.[177] Staupitz wanted to be by Luther's side: "I would wish, that you would leave Wittenberg at your convenience, and that you would join me, so that we might live and die together."[178] Then came a revealing and shocking statement: "Thus it should be: having abandoned the desert, let us follow Christ."[179] Two months earlier Staupitz had released Luther from

---

[173] *WA* 1.525–527; *WABr* 1.179; nr. 79; 30 May 1518; *WABr* 1.193,8; nr. 89; 1 September 1518.

[174] *WABr* 1.258,25–29; nr. 114; 25 November 1518.

[175] "Etsi tu multum nobis et distas et taces, Reverende Pater, nec exspectantibus exspectantissimas literas scribis, nos tamen rumpemus silentium. Optamus nos, optant omnes te in hac plaga coeli aliquando videri. Credo ad te pervenisse Acta mea, id est, iram et indignationem Romanam; Deus rapit, pellit, necdum ducit me; non sum compos mei, volo esse quietus, et rapior in medios tumultus." *WABr* 1.344,4–9; nr.152. Luther was referring to his *Acta Augustana* of December 1518; see *WA* 2.6–26.

[176] *WABr* 1.267,2–13; nr. 119; mid-December 1518.

[177] *WABr* 1.267,2–9; nr. 119.

[178] "Placet mihi, ut Wittembergam ad tempus deseras meque accedas, ut simul vivamus moriamurque." *WABr* 1.267,9–10; nr. 119.

[179] "Expedit ita fieri, quatenus deserti desertum, sequamur Christum." *WABr* 1.267,11–12; nr. 119.

his vow of obedience. But here, already by the end of 1518, Staupitz announced that *both* he *and* Luther had already left the desert, the desert of the Augustinian hermits. These were his parting words. It would take Staupitz almost two more years actually to do so; it would take Luther almost six. But in Staupitz's mind, it had already occurred. Two months later, Luther replied, complaining of Staupitz's silence. The silence continued, and on 13 April 1519 in a letter to Johannes Lang, Luther wrote: "Our Reverend Father Vicar is as good as dead to us, since he has not written a word."[180] It was a letter he signed: *Frater Martinus Lutherus Augustinianus*.

On 3 October 1519 Luther tried again. He wrote to Staupitz giving a full report, including mentioning that he had received a book by Hus, but had not read it yet.[181] The storm clouds had not completely broken, but they would soon. In the midst of his narration, Luther then abruptly interjects a personal outburst:

> Enough of all this. What do you want from me? You have completely abandoned me. The day that you left me in Augsburg I was devastated. I had hung onto you like a weaning child hangs onto its mother. Yet still I ask you to praise God in me, a sinner. I hate this terrible life. I fear death, and I am completely devoid of faith. I am filled with other gifts though, which Christ knows how much I don't want, except to serve him.[182]

Luther then continued with a report on the "Franciscan Debate" at Wittenberg, but came back to the personal to close his letter: "Last night I had a dream about you. You had left me, and I was crying and suffering most bitterly. But you told me in sign that if I would be quiet, you would come back to me. This certainly was true that day in Augsburg. But fine, be well and pray for me, wretched soul that I am."[183]

---

[180] "Reverendus Pater Vicarius oblitus est nostri, adeo nihil scribit." *WABr* 1.370,87; nr. 167.

[181] *WABr* 1.514,27–29; nr. 202.

[182] "Verum haec de aliis. De me quid vis? Nimis me derelinquis. Ego super te, *sicut ablactatus super matre sua* [Ps. 130:2] tristissimus hac die fui. Obsecro te, Dominum laudes in me etiam peccatore; vitam odi pessimam, mortem horreo, et fide vacuus sum, aliis donis plenus, quae scit Christus quam non desiderem, nisi ei serviam." *WABr* 1.514,49–53; nr. 202.

[183] "Hac nocte somnium de te habui, tanquam recessuro a me, amarissime me flente et dolente, verum te manu mota mihi dicente, quiescerem, te reversurum esse ad me; hoc certe verum factum est hoc ipso die. Sed iam vale et ora pro me miserrimo." *WABr* 1.515,75–78; nr. 202. Referring to this letter, Brecht writes: "The

Despair, abandonment, fear, combined with a whimpering hope: these are the emotions we read in Luther's later letters to Staupitz. There was an insoluble bond between the two, the vicar-general and his provincial prior, and Luther felt that he needed Staupitz, and needed him not only for his own personal reasons. The cause needed Staupitz, for he had been the one who had initiated it to begin with. Luther was carrying out Staupitz's program, Luther was being obedient. And Staupitz, Luther feared, was bailing out.

That the silence was broken we know only from Luther's letter to Johannes Lang of 18 December 1519, when Luther simply mentions that "the Reverend father vicar is healthy and honored in Salzburg."[184] The next we hear of Staupitz from Luther is on 5 May 1520. Luther had by this time made his two startling discoveries: he was a Hussite, and the Pope was Antichrist. If Luther was feeling down in the autumn of 1519, the new year did little to raise his spirits. What it did do, however, was to focus his energy for the last battle. Luther needed Staupitz more than ever, but indications of Staupitz's readiness were not hopeful. On 5 May 1520, Luther wrote to Spalatin letting him know that the vicar-general had planned the General Chapter of the Saxon-Thuringian Congregation of Observant Augustinian Hermits for the feast day of their founding father, 28 August 1520, to meet in Eisleben, and, rumor had it, that Pater Staupitz was going to resign.[185] That he did. Luther's reaction is not preserved, but he seems to have accepted Staupitz decision. He must have been worried however, especially, as he reported to Link, after Staupitz had requested him from Erfurt only a little over a week before the Chapter meeting to hold off publishing his "little book" until it could be emended. The work to which Luther referred was

---

dream ended happily, however, with Staupitz's promise to return." Brecht, *Road to Reformation*, 336. The context of Luther's letter however is clear; Staupitz had abandoned him. Brecht interprets Luther's *hoc certe verum factum est hoc ipso die* as referring to Staupitz's return to Luther, should he, Luther, remain quiet; I have interpreted these words as referring to the dream itself and Staupitz's leaving, even with his "promise" to return, and read the letter as ending on a note of despair, not of happiness, placing the dream account in context of Luther's earlier statement in the letter, *Nimis me derelinquis... hac die*, to which the *hoc ipso die* refers. Regarding Stauptiz' "abandonment" of Luther after Augsburg, see Brecht, *Road to Reformation*, 258, 336.

[184] "Reverendus Pater Vicarius Saltzburgae agit sanus et honoratus..." *WABr* 1.597,37; nr. 232.
[185] *WABr* 2.101,8–9; nr. 285.

his *On Christian Freedom.* He called it a "little book on being a Christian" (*libellus de statu christianorum*). He did not know why Staupitz had made the request, or who had accused his book of needing correction, but in any case, it was too late. It was already out.[186] Staupitz certainly had cause for concern. Luther had turned what for centuries past had been the *status religiosorum* into the *status christianorum.* He had not yet attacked monastic vows, but he was close. Yet he still signed his name *frater Martinus Lutherus Augustinianus.*[187] On 1 September Luther mentioned to Spalatin that the reverend father Staupitz had arrived in Wittenberg, together with his successor, *magister* Wenceslaus.[188] We do not know what Luther and Staupitz discussed during this, their last time together, but although Luther's affection for Staupitz remained, his anxiety was rising. Staupitz had resigned; Luther had discovered that the pope was Antichrist; Staupitz seemingly had requested him to "tone it down," and the beginning of the final break had begun.

"Having abandoned the desert, let us follow Christ." Staupitz's words came back to haunt him. The temptation for Luther to "turn Staupitzian" must have been great when Staupitz invited him to Salzburg to live and die with him. Luther had already once before gone against the explicit wishes of his father when he entered the monastery at Erfurt. He was to do so again. Luther had gone far, and he had done so precisely based on his vows of obedience to Staupitz and the vows he took in his profession: to be obedient to God above all else. His vows themselves, and the habit that symbolized them, prevented Luther from following his own will. He and Staupitz understood the vows differently, as was becoming painfully apparent, but the force of the vows as such remained. And Staupitz had been a part of it all. On 14 January 1521 Luther wrote to Staupitz for the first time after he had resigned as vicar-general. Luther did not pull any punches:

> When we were together in Augsburg, reverend father, among other things that we discussed concerning my case, you said to me: "Remember

---

[186] "Reverendus pater Vicarius heri ex Erffordia mihi scripsit, rogans, ne ederem libellum de statu christianorum emendando, nescio enim, quo nomine ei sit accusatus, sed tarde venit, iam edito libello." *WABr* 2.168,12–15; nr. 328.

[187] Luther signed his letter of 19 August 1520 to Link simply as *Tuus frater Martinus Lutherus,* but we find variants throughout, *Martinus Lutherus Augustinianus, Martinus Lutherus Augustiniensis; frater Martinus Lutherus Augustinianus*; see .e.g., *WABr* 2.170,16–17; nr.329; 180,18–19; nr. 335; 212,65; nr. 351.

[188] *WABr* 2.180,5–7; nr. 335.

well, brother, that you began all of this in the name of our Lord Jesus Christ." These words I took as having been said to me not by you, but through you. I have remembered them exceedingly well, and I have them etched in my mind. Now, therefore, I turn your own words back to you: You too remember well that you said this to me. Up until now, it has been a game, but it is time to get serious, and just as you said, unless God brings it about, it won't happen. But clearly, it is already so completely in the hands of God, that no one should think of denying it. Who is going to debate about it? What is one to think? The storm rages so furiously that I do not see how it is going to be calmed, except by the last day. Such is the fierceness of both sides.[189]

After having then detailed all the trials and tribulations he was facing, from Jerome Emser to Thomas Müntzer, Luther ended his letter with a plea, though not directly: "Be well, my dear Father, and pray for me and for the word of God; I am being snatched up and beaten around by all these waves."[190] A whimper for help of an abandoned child.

One month later, 9 February 1521, Luther wrote yet again to Staupitz. This time, Luther was not only fearful and worried, he was also mad. He addressed his letter: "To the reverend and best of men, Johannes Staupitz, Professor of Theology, Augustinian Hermit, and his own superior in the Lord, Greetings."[191] The intended rhetorical effect should not be missed, and it surely was not by Staupitz. Luther used Staupitz's most formal titles as if to remind him of his office: that of a Professor of Theology and an Augustinian Hermit. Luther was trying to call him back to the cause. Staupitz had already stepped down from his office as vicar-general, and had gone to Salzburg, were he had an endowed preaching post under Cardinal-Archbishop Matthäus Lang. As Luther had reminded Staupitz just

---

[189] "Cum Augustae essemus, reverendissime Pater, inter caetera, quae de hac mea causa tractabamus, dicebas ad me: 'Memor esto, frater, te ista in nomine Domini nostri Ihesu Christi incepisse.'; quod verbum non a te, sed per te mihi dictum accepi et memori valde mente repositum teneo. Tuo itaque nunc te verbo isto peto: 'Memor esto et tu, hoc te verbum ad me dixisse.' Hactenus lusum est in ista re, serius instat, et, sicut tu dixisti, nisi Deus hoc perficiat, impossibile est perfici; plane in manu Dei iam sunt ista potentissimi, ut negare nemo queat. Quis hic consulit? Quod cogitet homo? Tumultus egregie tumultuatur, ut nisi extremo die sedari mihi posse non videtur. Tantum est animi ex utraque parte." WABr 2.245,2-12; nr. 366.

[190] "Vale, mi Pater, pro verbo Dei ac me ora; ego fluctibus his rapior et volvor." WABr 2.245,31-32; nr. 366.

[191] "Reverendo et optimo viro, Iohanni Staupitio, S.T. Magistro, Augustinianae Eremitae, suo in Domino maiori, Salutem." WABr 2.263,1-3; nr. 376.

a month before of the words that he himself has spoken to Luther in Augsburg, he now wanted Staupitz to remember that he was still a professor of theology and still an Augustinian hermit. And that meant a great deal. It would not be the last time Luther used a salutation to Staupitz rhetorically packed with punch.

Luther put it straight. He had heard that Staupitz had caved in to Cardinal Lang and Pope Leo X and had denounced Luther's teachings. If he would not retract from having done so, Luther asserted that it was tantamount to his denying Luther completely and his entire cause. Even more so, it was to deny everything that Staupitz himself had taught about the mercy of God.[192] Luther's letter is an impassioned exhortation: "For it is not time to be a wimp, but to scream out, when our Lord Jesus Christ is being damned, burned, and blasphemed."[193] The *monstra* that Luther had foreseen the movement was entering after his discovery that they were all Hussites had become reality. It was a fight to the finish, with no holding back. After having appealed to Staupitz as an Augustinian Hermit at the beginning, Luther trespassed the boundaries imposed upon him by the habit he wore: "Wherefore just as much as you have exhorted me to humility, I urge you to pride, for you have too much humility, just as I have too much pride."[194] Whereas in December of 1518 Staupitz had already mentioned implicitly that the both of them, having left the desert of the Augustinian Hermits were to follow Christ, now Luther exhorts Staupitz to go beyond the humility espoused by the Order, the humility that the habit itself was supposed to symbolize. Christ himself was at stake. The vow of obedience to Christ must be followed even before the wearing of the habit and the identity that it entailed. The habit had come between Christ and the pope, between Christ and Antichrist, and this was precisely the position Luther feared Staupitz was taking: "I write these things to you most faithfully, because I am terribly afraid that you are trying to hold middle ground between Christ and the pope, which you nevertheless see are completely antagonistic antithe-

---

[192] *WABr* 2.263,13–50; nr. 376; see H.A. Oberman, "*Duplex Misericordia*," 41–42.
[193] "Non enim hic tempus timendi, sed clamandi, ubi Dominus noster Ihesus Christus damnatur, exuitur et blasphematur." *WABr* 2.263,23–25.
[194] "Unde, quantum tu me ad humilitatem exhortaris, tantum ego te ad superbiam exhortor. Tibi adest nimia humilitas, sicut mihi nimia superbia." *WABr* 2.263,24–26; nr. 376.

ses of each other."[195] As we will see shortly, this understanding was determinative for Luther's decision three years and eight months later to take off his habit. But Staupitz would in this too be Luther's "forerunner." Luther was right. Fourteen months after Luther wrote imploring that Staupitz join the fight, Staupitz received papal dispensation to leave the OESA and enter the Abbey of St. Peter's in Salzburg, a cloister of the Order of St. Benedict. The next time Luther wrote to his beloved father Staupitz, Luther had already heard rumors of what was to come, and he himself had in November of 1521 while in the Wartburg completed his treatise *On Monastic Vows*.

We come now to the last three extant letters of the correspondence. That there had been more we know from Luther's opening lines to his penultimate letter to Staupitz, dated 27 June 1522. The letter is addressed to "Dr. Johannes Staupitz, Ecclesiastic in Salzburg."[196] Rumors were everywhere that Staupitz had become abbot of the Benedictine cloister of St. Peters, and the reports were so consistent that Luther would have been forced to believe them had he not received letters from Staupitz setting him straight.[197] We do not know what Staupitz had written, but it certainly had its sobering affect. Luther tells Staupitz that surely just as he, Luther, had heard of Staupitz becoming abbot from false rumors, so Staupitz was hearing lies about what was going on in Wittenberg.[198] Yet Luther no longer tried to enlist Staupitz in the battle. Luther did, however, express his dismay and realized that Staupitz's abbacy was under consideration: "Although I do not want to stand in the way of God's will, nevertheless, with my unrefined mind, I just for the life of me cannot grasp how the will of God would be for you to become abbot, nor does it seem to me to be a well thought out decision. But I want to be neither the opponent nor the judge of your soul."[199]

---

[195] "Fidentius haec ad te scribo, quod valde timeo, ne inter Christum et papam medius haereas, quos vides tamen summa contentione contrarios esse." *WABr* 2.264,42–44; nr. 376.

[196] "D. Iohanni Staupitio, Ecclesiastici Salzburgensi." *WABr* 2.567,1; nr. 512.

[197] "Reverende et optime Pater, de abbatia tua non tam ex Prioris Norinbergensis literis, quam ex vulgata fama audivi, ita constanter asserente, ut, nisi tuas vidissem literas, credere coactus fuissem." *WABr* 2.567,2–5; nr. 512.

[198] *WABr* 2.567,5–6; nr. 512.

[199] "Et quamquam nec ego velim Dei voluntati subtrahi, tamen pro mea ruditate plane nondum capio, si voluntas Dei esse possit, ut abbas fieres, neque mihi consultum videtur; verum tuo spiritui neque reluctator neque iudex esse volo." *WABr* 2.567,6–9; nr. 512.

Rather than exhortation, acting as the divine whip for God's party, here Luther prays only for one thing: that Staupitz not believe the trash that was being said about Wittenberg, either with regard to Wenceslaus Link, or to himself.[200]

Though somber, sober, and restrained, Luther's letter is nevertheless rhetorically intricate, striving to get to Staupitz, both on the gut level, the personal level, and on the higher level of God's plan and will. When Luther prayed of Staupitz only one thing, he was asking for Staupitz's good will, and Luther did so, calling on the "open wounds of Christ," *per viscera Christi*. In 1519 Luther had preached on Christ's Passion and how best to meditate thereon. In keeping with his Order's tradition, Luther advocated meditating on Christ's wounds as a cure for temptation.[201] In his letter to Staupitz of 30 May 1518 prefacing his *Resolutiones Disputationum de induglentiarum virtute*, in which he had told Staupitz that it was Staupitz's own teaching on true penance that had led to his intensive dealing with indulgences, Luther then further related that he now saw that God's commandments are to be read not only in books, but also "in the most sweet wounds of our Savior."[202] The *viscera Christi* for the Augustinian Passion tradition referred to the very guts of Christ, revealed through his open wounds. It was appealing to this graphic image that Luther pleaded with Staupitz not to believe his detractors. Staupitz, who had taught him at the beginning of his journey that God's commandments were found in the wounds of Christ, was being reminded of his own origins, the origins of the movement that Staupitz had done so much himself to initiate and that now had taken on entirely new proportions. Luther continued his letter by asserting his own resolution to fight against the papacy. It was the cause of Christ, and it was in Christ's hands.[203] Then, having already put forth the image of the *viscera Christi*, Luther tried to jog Staupitz's memory: "Remember how at the beginning my cause was always seen by the world to be unbearable and horrible yet it nevertheless

---

[200] "Unum autem oro te per viscera Christi, ne facile credas delatoribus nostris, sive adversus Wenceslaum, sive erga me." *WABr* 2.567,9–10; nr. 512.

[201] *Sermon von der Betrachtung des heiligen Leidens Christi*, 1519; *WA* 2.136–142; 141,8–34; *cf.* Chapter Five above, notes 14 and 15.

[202] "Ita enim dulcescunt praecepta dei, quando non in libris tantum, sed in vulneribus dulcissimi Salvatoris legenda intelligimus." *WA* 1.525,21–23.

[203] *WABr* 2.567,11–25; nr. 512.

grew in strength day by day."²⁰⁴ He then informed Staupitz that three Augustinians in Antwerp had been arrested, and Luther assumed that the prior, Jacob, the future Lutheran bishop of Bremen, had already been burned.²⁰⁵ Luther then tried to move Staupitz's fatherly heartstrings further at the same time that he forcefully reasserted his position: "they have also schemed to burn me, but I am going to provoke Satan and his minions all the more so that the day when Christ will destroy the Antichrist might come as soon as possible."²⁰⁶ Staupitz may have been moved. He may have sympathized greatly. But he remained firm on his own path, and on 1 August he made his profession as a Benedictine. With the forceful "recommendation" of Cardinal Lang, Staupitz was the very next day elected as abbot of St. Peter's, assuming his new duties on 17 August 1522.²⁰⁷

Luther made one last attempt, one last appeal. It came on 17 September 1523. One senses in Luther's last letter to Staupitz an aura of resignation, of hopelessness, yet that did not prevent Luther from giving it his best shot. Perhaps, if only...

The irony and depth of the salutation itself reveals much of what was to follow. Luther addressed his final hope: "To the reverend Father in Christ, Dr. Johannes, Abbot of St. Peter's of the Order of Benedict at Salzburg, his own superior in the Lord, father and teacher, Grace and peace in Christ Jesus, Our Lord!"²⁰⁸ Staupitz would have seen it immediately. Luther had never addressed him in such a fashion before. His very first extant letter to Staupitz, dated 31 March 1518, Luther greeted Staupitz as "his own father and superior in Christ, Staupitz."²⁰⁹ For the next five letters thereafter, with some variation, Luther wrote to Staupitz as "Reverend Father Johannes Staupitz, vicar of the Augustinian Hermits, his own superior in Christ, Greetings." Then came the letter of 14 January 1521,

---

[204] "Memento, quam ab initio mea causa semper formidolosa et intolerabilis visa est mundo, et tamen de die in diem praevaluit." *WABr* 2,567,26–27; nr. 512.

[205] *WABr* 2.567,30–34; nr. 512.

[206] "De me quoque exurendo consultatur, at ego indies magis provoco Satanam et suas squamas, ut acceleretur dies ille Christi destructurus Antichristum istum." *WABr* 2.567,34–36; nr. 512.

[207] Zumkeller, *Staupitz*, 7.

[208] "Reverendo in Christo Patri, D. Iohanni, Abbati S. Petri Ordinis Benedictini Salisburgae, suo in Domino maiori, patri et praeceptori, Gratia et pax in Christo Iesu, Domino nostro!" *WABr* 3.155,1–3; nr. 659.

[209] "Suo in Christo Patri et Maiori Staupitio. Ihesus. Salutem." *WABr* 1.160,1–3; nr. 66.

when Luther began expressing his fear and anger. This letter simply began "Greetings."[210] The epistle of 9 February 1521 discussed above followed, and then that of 27 June, addressed to "Dr. Johannes Staupitz, Ecclesiastic in Salzburg."[211] Here, on 17 September 1523, Luther was making a point. Despite the formulaic formality, Luther addressed *Dr. Johannes*, the first time Luther called Staupitz by his first name alone, which on the one hand in such a formal address leaves an impression of disrespect, while at the same time, given their long standing relationship, indicates a new sense of familiarity. The irony was intended. Luther wrote much of the letter, not in the first person, but using the "royal we." This could indicate that Luther was writing to Staupitz for all the Wittenbergers, but more likely, the rhetorical tool was most conscious, especially when at the end of his letter, after having switched back briefly to the first person 'I', only then reverting again to the plural, and continuing to alternate, Luther virtually admitted as much: "You see, therefore, reverend father, how ambiguously I am writing."[212]

Abbot of St. Peter's of the Order of Benedict in Salzburg: this was the first time Luther had written to Staupitz after so strongly expressing his feelings that Staupitz becoming abbot was against God's will and the very Gospel itself. Here, Luther concedes, and recognizes Staupitz's new title at the same time that he refrains from referring to Benedict as saint. Staupitz had become a member of the OSB, the *Ordo Sancti Benedicti*, and Luther and Staupitz both knew it. Luther desacralized Staupitz's new profession.

But then came the biggest irony of all: Luther addressed Staupitz as his *pater et preceptor*. Luther, throughout their correspondence, explicitly named Staupitz as his father, and often in very personal, intimate terms, *mi pater*. Yet far more is going on here. Luther had begun by calling him "reverend father," and then he repeats the designation, together with that of his teacher. The combination *Pater et Preceptor* was the title the Augustinians had always, since the creation of their identity as the sons of Augustine, used for Augustine and Augustine alone, the founder of their Order, the Order's father and teacher. And this title, this designation, Luther transferred to

---

[210] *WABr* 2. 245,2; nr. 366.
[211] *WABr* 2.567,1; nr. 512.
[212] "Vides itaque, reverende Pater, quam ambigue scribam..." *WABr* 3.156,33; nr. 659.

Staupitz, and to Staupitz, the Benedictine abbot. But together with the sarcasm and irony, there was genuine sincerity. As Luther had tried to make clear before, Staupitz *was* his father and teacher and had been the one to have taught Luther the mercy and love of God in true penance which started the entire movement. The letter that followed is in so many ways simply an elaboration of the salutation, ending in similar fashion with Luther signing his name, as he had before, "Your son, Martin Luther."[213]

Luther began with a theme previously at issue after Staupitz had abandoned him at Augsburg in 1518, Staupitz's silence, and he did so with a frontal attack: "Reverend father in Christ! Your exceeding silence is unjust, which we should think would be very clear to you. But even though we have ceased being in your good graces or even good will, it is nevertheless not appropriate to be unmindful or even ungrateful to you, through whom the light of the Gospel first began to shine out of the darkness into our hearts."[214] He then makes an apparent concession: "Yet I also have to say this as well: it would have been more agreeable to us if you had not become abbot. But now that it is a done deal, we should consider the good of us both and allow each of us to flourish in his own way."[215] But then Luther gets to the real point:

> I, surely, together with your best friends carry such pain in our hearts not only because you are alienated from us, but also because you have become so close to that Cardinal of yours who is a well known monster, who does whatever he wants and can get away with, from which virtually the entire world suffers, but nevertheless you try to keep quiet and put up with such things. It is a wonder if you are not dangerously close to denying Christ. Consequently, we plead and beseech you to return to us, and make your escape from the prison of that tyranny, and we deeply hope that you will consider doing so. For as I have known you up until now, I am not able in any way to put together these two contradictions, namely, that if you are the same

---

[213] "Filius tuus, Martinus Lutherus." *WABr* 3.156,41.

[214] "Reverende in Christo! Iniustum est nimio silentium tuum, de quo ut nos cogitare debeamus, ipse facile perspicis. Sed nos certe etiamsi desivimus tibi grati ac placiti esse, tamen tui non decet esse immemores et ingratos, per quem primum coepit evangelii lux de tenebris splendescere in cordis nostris." *WABr* 3.155,3–156,8; nr. 659.

[215] "Sed hoc etiam verum esse fatear, nobis fuisse acceptius, te non esse factum Abbatem; nunc, cum factus sis, utrinque boni consulamus, unumquemque sensu suo abundare permittamus." *WABr* 3.156,8–10; nr. 659.

> person you used to be, how you can thus decide to stay where you
> are, or, if you are the same person, why you would not greatly prefer to get the hell out. Since however, we would like to esteem you
> highly and wish you the best before you take further action, for the
> time being we keep the faith, although your silence is beating on us
> very hard day by day.[216]

Luther probably realized that Staupitz was no more going to leave Salzburg and return to Wittenberg, than was Luther in 1518 going to leave Wittenberg and go to Salzburg to be with Staupitz. Yet he had to hope, though it was a hope that was his last.

After having asked Staupitz to help find provisions and care for Brother Achatio,[217] Luther returned to his hope and his fear. He wanted to think the best of Staupitz, but he was doubtful, and if he had indeed changed, Luther was not going to waste further words, but simply invoke the mercy of God, Staupitz's own *misericordia dei*, for Staupitz, "and for us all."[218] The letter ends with a final appeal, with a final attempt to change Staupitz's mind, to bring him back: "I clearly am not going to stop wishing and praying that you might alienate yourself from that Cardinal of yours and from the papacy, just as I am, and even more so, just as you used to be. May the Lord hear me and bring you to Himself, together with us, Amen."[219] Luther's last words to Staupitz.

---

[216] "Ego sane cum tuis optimis amicis non tam aegre ferimus, esse te alienum a nobis, quam quod monstro illi famoso, Cardinali tuo, proprius factus es, cui quae libeat ac liceat facere, orbis paene non fert, haec tamen tu ferre et tacere cogeris. Mirum, si non Christum negare periclitaris. Proinde nos oramus plane et optamus te nobis reddi, et redditum dari ex istius tyrannidis carcere, idque speramus et a te cogitari. Nam ego, ut hactenus te novi, non possum ullo modo duo ista pugnantia componere, nempe, ut idem sis, qui fueris, si sic manere statueris, aut si idem sis, non assidue moliaris discessum. Cum autem optima cogitemus et optemus tibi posterius, adhuc tenemus spe bona, licet diuturno tuo silentio satis fortiter pulsata." *WABr* 3.156,10–21; nr. 659. The editors have punctuated lines 19 and 20 as follows: "Cum autem optima cogitemus et optemus tibi, posterius adhuc tenemus spe bona . . .", and in note 7 suggest a possible better reading to be: "in posterum adhuc tenemur spe bona". I have interpreted 'posterius' in the sense of 'posterius dicere' as used by Plautus; see L&S 1405, *posterius*, col. B, IIA, 2b.

[217] *WABr* 3.156,22–28; nr. 659.

[218] "Et ego in dubio incertus, meliorem spem apprehendi et in hanc partem inclinavi, ut adhuc omnia optima de te praesumam. Sin autem mutatus es in alium virum erga nos, quod avertat Christus (libere loquar tecum), nolim plura verba perdere, sed misericordiam Dei super te et nos omnes invocare." *WABr* 3.156,29–33; nr. 156.

[219] "Ego plane non desinam optare et orare, quam ut alienus a Cardinale tuo et papatu fias, sicut ego sum, imo sicut et tu fuisti. Dominus autem exaudiat me et

Luther's final letter to his beloved father is a powerful and packed work of art. It is a desperate attempt to win Staupitz back, for Luther himself, and for Wittenberg. Luther reminds Staupitz, as he had as well in his previous letter, of Staupitz's origins, and how Staupitz had been the one who had first brought the Gospel to light. Luther still hoped to reach him, in some way, he still hoped that Staupitz had not changed into someone so close to the papacy and the wretched Cardinal Lang, but the hope was ever so fragile, and Luther knew it. Yet still he hoped to be able to hope, against hope. Six and a half months later, the silence was broken. Staupitz replied.

Tit for tat, one could view it such. And in some ways that is what it was. Staupitz's reply to Luther is as deeply moving, powerful, and touching, as was the letter which he was answering. It is dated 1 April 1524, and it too began with the salutation: "To Dr. Martin Luther, my greatest friend and servant of Christ, your brother and pupil, Johannes, a servant of Christ, sends his greetings."[220] Staupitz opened his letter with a *captatio benevolentiae*, a "confession of faith," though one not without hints that Staupitz himself was struggling. Whereas Staupitz replied to Luther questioning his commitment by affirming his constancy (*constantia*) in the faith, he then went on to declare his undying and unbroken love for Luther (*constantissimus . . . amor*):

> You are always writing, my good Martin, that you question my commitment. To this I respond: my faith in Christ and the Gospel remains pure, even though, I have my work cut out for me in my prayers as a Benedictine that Christ might help my unbelief and that I might become a despiser of things human and at least lukewarmly be able to embrace the church. For you my love is as firm and strong as possible, remaining unbroken, even above the love of women.[221]

---

assumat te sibi nobiscum, Amen." *WABr* 3.156,36–39; nr. 659. The *alienus a Cardinale tuo et papatu fias* echoes line 11 where Luther refers to Staupitz as *alienum a nobis*. *Alienus* has the connotations of being alienated, being foreign, apart from, outside of, and thus I have chosen in both cases to use the cognate which best captures the sense; *cf.* Oberman, "*Captivitas Babylonica*," 33.

[220] "D.M.L., amico summo et Christi servo, Frater et discipulus tuus Iohannes, Christi servus, Salutem." *WABr* 3.263,1–4; nr. 726.

[221] "Scribis totiens, optime Martine, et suspectam habes constantiam meam. Ad quod ego: fides mea in Christum et evangelium integra perseverat, tametsi oratione opus habeam, ut Christus adiuvet incredulitatem meam detesterque humana et ecclesiam tepide amplectar. In te constantissimus mihi amor est, etiam supra amorem mulierum, semper infractus." *WABr* 3.263,4–9; nr. 726. Luther would not have missed the play on words with Staupitz's *oratione opus*. The central task of the Benedictine Order was the *Opus Dei*, praying the divine hours.

Staupitz's openness about his own lack of faith and that he needed to work hard in prayer to be able to embrace the church even lukewarmly (*tepide amplectar*), is a telling indication that he himself was wrestling with his new life, as was Luther, as seen in the salutation of his last letter. By becoming a Benedictine, Staupitz had not only left the Augustinian Order, and had not only left Luther, but he may in fact have left the Order, even with papal dispensation, against the express dictates of the very *Constitutions* that he himself had written.[222] When Luther wrote to him that he, Luther, did not want to be the judge of his, Staupitz's soul, such a consideration could not have been a negligible factor. Yet Luther left it all to Christ, and Staupitz was doing the same, even if the two former Augustinian friars had different understandings as to what that really meant. They had started out together on the same path, but their trails diverged. For Staupitz they had together taken one fork in the road already in 1518, when he told Luther that they must follow Christ, having left the desert. But then, Staupitz took his own fork, when he resigned his office as vicar-general and left for Salzburg. No matter how parallel the two paths might have run, they were irreconcilable, and the twain were not to meet again.

Staupitz's letter is firm, respectful, grateful, tender, and affectionate. Yet we would misread it, if we failed to notice its wistful whimpers. Having admitted that he was struggling even lukewarmly to embrace the church, Staupitz confesses his indebtedness to Luther: "We owe you a lot, Martin. You were the one who brought us out from the pig sty and led us into the pastures of life, to the words of salvation. The Lord Jesus gives the increase ... but though the Spirit will blow where it will, we are grateful to you because you have planted and watered, serving the glory of God, to whom alone, we give the power of making sons of God."[223] God alone makes sons of God,

---

[222] See Staupitz *Const.* 50 (314,34–44). Staupitz had written that no Augustinian was to be granted permission to transfer to another Order, explicitly mentioning the *nigri monachi* and the *albi monachi*, the Benedictines and the Cistercians, unless the same regular observance and discipline flourished in the new convent as in the Augustinian: "Quod dicimus propter statutum Benedicti papae, qui statuit, quod religiosi mendicantes non possint transire ad nigros monachos vel ad albos, praecipientes districte, quod nullus deliberate petat aut det licentiam transeundi ad aliquod collegium quorumcumque religiosorum, ubi non viget de facto disciplina vel observantia regularis." Staupitz *Const.* 50 (314,38–43); *cf. ibid.* (314,20–28).

[223] "Debemus tibi, Martine, multa, qui nos a siliquis porcorum reduxisti ad pascua vitae, ad verba salutis. Dominus Ihesus tribuat incrementum ... Sed spiritus

but Martin had planted and irrigated, echoing the tradition of Augustine as the *plantator* of the Augustinians' religion. Staupitz ends his letter with his hope that his prayers for Luther and Wittenberg might be taken to heart, and then asserts as strongly as he affirms: "I, who was once your forerunner in teaching the holy Gospel, in the same way even today, still hate the Babylonian Captivity."[224] Heiko Oberman has most insightfully analyzed this statement of Staupitz, pointing to the significance of Staupitz as Luther's "forerunner." He has shown that for Staupitz the mercy of God, the *misericordia Dei*, even as early as his Tübingen sermons (1498), "allowed him, in the 1520s, to see the state of the church clearly and call it as he sees it—a Babylonian Captivity—and yet to remain in captivity and bear it patiently."[225] Oberman hit the nail on the head, but in doing so passes over Staupitz's comment at the beginning of his letter, that he prayed for Christ's help to be able even lukewarmly to embrace the Church. Staupitz firmly asserts his position to Luther, which Luther had not grasped, but even so, Staupitz was struggling with his own decision. There he was in Salzburg, after having received Luther's letter, for whom he had such deep affection, charging him with having abandoned the cause and having abandoned Christ, imploring him to leave and return to Wittenberg, and Staupitz stayed, even though he knew the score. The pathos must not be forgotten.

Yet neither should the core of his letter. Pointing to the impact of Staupitz's statement that he was Luther's forerunner must not obscure the central message. Staupitz's response to Luther was one that expressed his deep appreciation, admiration, respect, and affection, yet also took his former pupil to task, indicated from the salutation itself when he not only took up as a self-reference Luther's address to him as Dr. Johannes, but also ironically referred to himself as Luther's disciple, Luther's follower, Luther's student, only later to turn it back around and remind Luther of how it all started. From Luther, Staupitz had learned much, and he was most grateful. His

---

ubi vult spirat, vobis debemus gratias, quia plantastis et rigastis, Deo servantes gloriam, cui soli damus potestatem faciendi filios Dei." *WABr* 3.264,22–29; nr. 726.

[224] "Valeant apud vos preces meae indignae, qui olim praecusor extiti sanctae evangelicae doctrinae et quemadmodum etiam hodie exosam habui captivitatem babylonicam." *WABr* 3.264,34–36; nr. 726.

[225] Oberman, "*Duplex Misericordia*," 47, and *passim*; see also Oberman, "*Captivitas Babylonica*."

use of the "royal we" was not used for playful if deeply meaningful rhetorical affect. It was admitting that "we," all of Christendom, owed ever so much to Luther. Staupitz's concluding remarks rhetorically reply to and confirm Luther's assertion that Staupitz had been the one who had preceded him, whose movement it had been to begin with. This Staupitz acknowledges, and then turns it back to Luther, effectively saying, 'Yes, Martin, my faith is firm, my love for you untouchable, and agreed the situation is pretty bad and I am rather suffering and struggling myself, but, Martin, remember I was the one who started this, *and you have gone too far*.' Directly after having affirmed his steadfast love for Luther, Staupitz then continued: "But please excuse me, if at times due to the slowness of my capacities, I cannot grasp what you are doing, and thus I remain in silence."[226] Here Staupitz was responding to, and echoing, Luther's letter to him of 27 June 1522. Whereas Luther had written that he, Luther, in his simple mind could not understand how it was God's will that Staupitz would become abbot—*tamen pro mea ruditate plane nondum capio*—Staupitz responded by saying that he, Staupitz, did not understand due to his own limited abilities what Luther was about—*ob tarditatem ingenii mei tua non capio*.[227] But then he continued:

> You seem to me to damn many things that are entirely external, which have nothing to do with faith or righteousness, they are neutral, and in doing so you burden the conscience greatly in the faith of our Lord Jesus Christ. Why therefore do you throw into confusion the hearts of the simple? And what is it about the monk's habit that makes such a stench for your nose, the habit which many wear in the holy faith of Christ? Sad that it is, abuse enters into virtually every single human act, and they are rare indeed, who gather in the harvest in faith, nevertheless, there are some. The substance therefore of something is not to be repudiated on account of evil accidents, which are there. You throw away indiscriminately all vows, although in the minutest details, or perhaps even in only one, you have good reason to do so. I, therefore, pour out my prayers to you, most sweet friend, to remember the little ones, and not to disturb their fearful consciences. Those things that are neutral, and are able to remain with sincere faith, I pray you, do not condemn. But in those matters that oppose the faith, do not stop crying out at the top of your lungs.[228]

---

[226] "Sed parce mihi, si quandoque ob tarditatem ingenii mei tua non capio atque ita silentio pertranseo." *WABr* 3.263,9–10; nr. 726.
[227] *Cf.* Oberman, "*Duplex Misericordia*," 38–39.
[228] "Videmini mihi damnare multa prorsus externa, quae ad fidem et iustitiam

Staupitz then told Martin how much "we" owed him, and finally ended his letter, after reasserting his own role in the matter, by sending his greetings not only to Luther, but also to Philip Melanchthon, Nicolas Amsdorf, Jerome Schurf, and the rest of his friends.[229] Luther was not to hear from Staupitz again.

Staupitz's last letter to Luther is as powerful and packed as was Luther's last letter to his previous vicar-general. And it matched that of Luther as a work of art. Staupitz's major points were that Luther had gone too far. He should consider the weak, the small, those whose conscience was bothered by all the changes. The monastic vows and habit should not be so despised. Staupitz implored Luther to be more pastoral, and to recognize and distinguish the substance from the accidents, those issues that truly were contradictory to the faith from those matters that were neutral. Staupitz, in keeping with his view of a *duplex misericordia*,[230] was able to view the Church and all its evil as itself being held captive in Babylon, a captivity he hated, and yet the essence, the substance, remained. For Luther, the very substance was that of the Antichrist. Neither fully grasped the position of the other. Staupitz's major points were ones that Luther had heard before, and would hear again: the non-essentials, concern for the weak.

Almost nine months later, on 28 December 1524, Staupitz died. Luther never responded to his letter, and Staupitz never wrote again. On 23 January 1525 Luther wrote to Nicolas Amsdorf and mentioned Staupitz's death in passing;[231] on 7 February Luther wrote to Wenceslaus Link, telling him that he, Luther, was sending him a small book by Staupitz, which was "rather cold, just as it always was and not very passionate. Do with it what you will, it is not

---

nihil faciunt, neutra sunt, et in fide domini nostri Ihesu Christi facta minime conscientiam gravant. Cur igitur turbantur simplicium corda, et quid monachorum habitus naribus tuis odio fecit, quem plerique in sancta fide Christi gestant? Intervenit proh dolor fere in singulis humanis exercitiis abusus, et rari sunt, qui fide metantur omnia, sunt nihilominus aliqui, ideo non est rei substantia reprobanda propter accidens malum, quod in aliquibus est. Vota passim omnia abiicitis, in paucissimis, forte uno duntaxat, fundati. Effundo itaque ad te preces, dulcissime amice, recordare parvulorum et non inquietes pavidas conscientias. Quae neutra sunt et cum sincera fide stare possunt, ora ne damnes. In illis vero, quae fidei adversantur, clama, ne cesses." *WABr* 3.263,10–264,22; nr. 726.

[229] *WABr* 3.264,36–37; nr. 726.
[230] See Oberman, "*Duplex Misericordia.*"
[231] *WABr* 3.428,5; nr. 821.

unworthy of being published since today such wretched things are coming out and being sold."[232] For the rest, Luther remained silent, and did so for the next seven years.[233] The break had been made. It was final and complete.

Yet Luther did take one of Staupitz's exhortations to heart: he continued to yell at the top of his lungs against those matters that he saw contradicting the faith, the faith in Christ, to whom he had vowed obedience above all in the summer of 1506. And Luther did reply to Staupitz, and had done so even before his death. On the twentieth Sunday after Trinity Sunday, Luther ascended the pulpit in Wittenberg to preach on the Gospel of the day, Matthew 22:1–14. The date was 9 October 1524. The world had indeed become another, and Luther, for the first time, was not wearing the habit of the Augustinians.

iii. *Vestes Nuptiales*

> Indeed, in these years I have given enough consideration to the weak. Therefore, because they are hardened day by day, everything should be done and said most openly. For I too should finally start to cast aside even my cowl, which up till now I have kept on to support the weak and to ridicule the pope. Let the dead bury their dead; they are blind and are even the leaders of the blind.[234]

Thus wrote Luther to Wolfgang Capito on 25 May 1524. Luther had catered to the weak long enough. The verb Luther used here for the weak, *indurantur*, has a double connotation: to be strengthened, or to be intransigent. Luther meant them both. And the weak were becoming increasingly so. Some of the weak were becoming stronger by the day, while others were becoming ever more hardened, immovable, more intransigent. The latter are the ones who are dead, and are left to bury their dead; they are blind, leading

---

[232] "Remitto Staupitium; frigidulus est, sicut semper fuit, et parum vehemens. Fac, quod libet; indignus non est luce et publico libellus, cum tot monstra quotidie prodeant et vendantur." *WABr* 3.437,8–10; *cf.* Brecht, *Shaping and Defining the Reformation*, 97. Brecht only mentions Luther's letter to Amsdorf.

[233] Heiko Oberman, *Mensch zwischen Gott und Teufel*, 107.

[234] "Quin ego iam satis arbitror hi annis indultum infirmis. Deinceps, quia indurantur de die in diem, liberrime omnia sunt agenda et dicenda. Nam et ego incipiam tandem etiam cucullum reiicere, quem ad sustentationem infirmorum et ad ludibrium papae hactenus retinui. Sinamus mortuos sepelire mortuos suos, caeci sunt et duces caecorum." *WABr* 3.299,21–26; nr. 748.

the blind. As Heiko Oberman has poignantly made clear, Luther here has put himself with the weak.[235] But things were going to change. The weak had had their day, including Luther himself: "For I too should finally start to cast aside even my cowl...".[236]

Not long before Luther wrote to Capito, he had received Staupitz's last letter. He must have been shocked. It must have been clear to him that there was no more hope to win Staupitz back. And even more so, Staupitz had told him: 'Martin, you are going too far,' imploring Luther to be mindful of the simple, the weak. Luther and Staupitz had started out together, and Luther remained obedient to the program of his superior in the Order, the one who had essentially forced him to become a doctor of theology, and who had with his own teaching gotten the ball rolling in the first place. And now Staupitz had not only bailed out, but had also pulled back the reigns and had told Luther, stop, you are going too far, remember the weak. Luther responded in the only way he could, the same way General McAulif responded in the Battle of Bastogne: "Nuts." Luther had finally had enough of the weak, including his own weakness, as he so forcefully told Capito. And now, and only now, could he take the last step: *etiam cucullum*. Staupitz had proved himself intransigent. He continued to "sleep in the same bed" with "his" Cardinal Lang and the pope, not being able to see that this was not an issue of substance and accidents. The pope was the Antichrist, and if Staupitz could not see that... Let the dead bury their dead, they are blind, leading the blind.

On 9 October 1524 Luther finally did it. He took off his habit, and went in to preach on the parable of the wedding feast. For the first time, Luther had broken his vows. He had turned his back on the person that he had been, and on his own religious identity. He

---

[235] "Oberman, "A Friar in the Lion's Den," 33.
[236] "Nam et ego incipiam tandem etiam cucullum reiicere..." *WABr* 299,23–24. Oberman translates this phrase as: "Accordingly, even I finally start to stop wearing my cowl." Oberman, "A Friar in the Lion's Den," 33. Oberman has most perceptively pointed to the formulation *et ego... tandem* as indicating Luther including himself with the weak. However, Luther's words are even more packed. He is not saying "even I finally start to stop wearing my cowl." The *incipiam* is in the subjunctive, expressing the force of 'should'. Luther did not use the form *incipio*. As important as the *et ego... tandem*, is Luther's *incipiam... etiam cucullum reiicere*. Luther is saying that he *should* begin to get rid of *etiam cucullum*, even his cowl. The verbal mood is extremely important. It places the action in the future as something that should be done, not something that Luther is at that time presently doing.

was no longer an Augustinian friar. The *novus homo* of the *homo Augustiniensis* had to break free and evolve one step higher, to become the *homo Christianus*. The highly symbolic act of Luther casting aside his habit was furthermore only reinforced by the sermon he gave. It is a scathing attack on false Christians and those who pretend to have the Gospel, but do not live it. It represents a breakthrough indeed: it is Luther's "Nuts" to Staupitz.

The text is well known, and Luther had preached on it many times before. 'The kingdom of heaven is like the king, whose son was getting married. The King sent out his servants to extend invitations to the desired list of guests. Yet when they were invited, they all had reasons why they could not attend, and some even attacked the very servants who had delivered the invitations. The King was furious. He sent troops to punish those who had killed his servants, and then instructed others to go out to invite everyone they could find; the wedding feast was ready. That they did. When the hall was filled, the King entered and noticed that one of the guests had arrived without wearing the appropriate wedding attire. The King asked him why this was so, and the guest had no answer. Therefore, the King ordered the guest without the proper wedding clothes to be bound hand and foot, and cast out into the outer darkness, where there was wailing and the gnashing of teeth. For though many are invited, only a few are chosen.'

The parable itself is difficult enough. But what Luther did with the text most likely passed by most of his listeners, though surely not all. He had preached on the same Gospel many times previously, and we can notice continuity. God is the King, Jesus is the groom, and the Church is the bride. The wedding vestments are faith in Christ. On the first list, the invited guests are the Jews. The gentiles, or Christians, are then the second round of guests, and the guest without the proper attire who was cast out are the false Christians. When we compare Luther's sermons on this text for the years 1522 through 1524, these themes remain more or less the same, though with variations.[237] While the basic exegesis remains similar, it is the change and shift in tone, emphasis, and application that become striking. There are four themes in particular that stand

---

[237] *WA* 10/3.410,11–22; 412.,29–413,32 (1522); *WA* 12.668.3–11; 669.,30–40; 670.,24–30 (1523); *WA* 15.714,32–33; 715.22–24,31–32; 716,4–21 (1524).

out: the Kingdom of God; blindness; the Holy Spirit; and Satan, or the devil. None of these four played any role in his sermon on Matthew 22:1–14 in 1522.[238] The devil makes an entrance in 1523, which then is significantly heightened in 1524. The Kingdom of God, blindness, and the Holy Spirit only become issues in 1524.

In 1522 and 1523 Luther opened his sermon by focusing on the wedding itself and the guests who were invited. We do, nevertheless find a broader perspective in 1523. In 1522 Luther began by explaining that the Gospel text was a parable of a wedding, which has to be understood spiritually. He then clarified that the king of the story is God, the son, is Christ, the bride is the church, and the originally invited guests were the Jews.[239] In 1523, though the Jews and the Gentiles remain, Luther set a different tone from his very first words: "This Gospel puts before us in a parable the very essence of Christian belief from its beginning extending all the way to its very end, which concerns especially the Jews and the Gentiles."[240] In 1524, the Kingdom of God stands central: "This Gospel is about us, who hear the Gospel and think that we are Christians, and in this regard our judgment is very liberal. Yet Christ is the one who determines how the Gospel is actually being followed, how it is being served throughout the whole world, and in this light we see that there is the kingdom of heaven and the kingdom of the earth, light and darkness, or rather, two enemies."[241] This is the tone for the rest of the sermon. The Augustinian dichotomy, as embedded in the Order's tradition since Giles of Rome, is set: one belongs either to God or to the devil. One must choose. But such a choice, such a decision is not made by one's own free will. It is only the grace of Christ, the unmediated grace of Christ that places one in God's kingdom. Free will, or rather, the false assumption of free will, is one of the factors that comes between Christ and Satan, preached by those who

---

[238] In 1522 Luther does mention blindness once; *WA* 10/3.414,2, but it does not have the same weight or emphasis as in 1524: *cf. WA* 15.714,20–23.
[239] *WA* 10/3.410,2–6,13–22.
[240] "Hoc Evangelium proponit nobis in similitudine das ganz wesen Christianae professionis a principio usque zu seinem end, betrifft sonderlich Iudeos et gentiles." *WA* 12.668,3–5.
[241] "Hoc Evangelium ghet uns an, die audimus Evangelium et putamus Christianos, et hic nostrum iudicium est latum. Et Christus indicat, wie es dem Evangelio ghet, quomodo servetur in toto mundo, et hic videtur, quid regnum celorum et terrae, lumen et tenebrae: imo duo hostes." *WA* 15.713,3–6.

think they are Christians, who think they know the Gospel, but all the while it is Satan who is working in them. There is no middle ground between the kingdom of God and the kingdom of the devil, and the Gospel as such is not enough.[242] If one wants to know if one is truly a Christian, look at how one is living. The Gospel only goes so far. It is, certainly, a great work of grace for one to know the Gospel and to recognize the pope as the Antichrist, but more is needed: the working of the Holy Spirit. The Holy Spirit is what the Gospel brings and is what enables one to live a truly Christian life, not that of the false, pseudochristians.[243] There is no middle ground. There is no compromise. One is either a member of the kingdom of God or of the kingdom of Satan; one either has God as king or the devil,[244] and those who do not realize this, have been blinded by the devil.[245] True Christians are dressed in faith for the wedding feast, living life led by the Holy Spirit, for it is only the Holy Spirit, not free will, that enables one to say: I am Christ's and he is mine. Yet the only thing that will truly make this clear, that will

---

[242] "Interim dicunt: das tu hoc diabolo, quod spiritus sancti est? Nemo persuadet eos, ut verum sit, vel deus vel diabolus. Medium invenerunt statum. Putant et somniant diabolum esse in crassis et interim in eorum voluntate esse, quod possint venire vel ad deum vel diabolum. Evangelium hoc non potest efficere. Sed nos scimus non esse medium: aut deus aut diabolus. Si spiritum Christi non habes, es sub regno diaboli. Per hoc sequitur, ut sis eciam obnoxius ei, ut non habeas liberum arbitrium. Impellit te, ut fuereris; scortaris, et facis libere. Tu es der hengst, diabolus te equitat. Aut sub diabolo es aut spiritu sancto. Ideo non credunt, sed occidunt. Ita fecerunt Iudei, qui occiderunt prophetas." WA 15.714,24–33; "Ideo non facit liberum arbitrium Nisi posset homo per spiritum sanctum dicere: Ego Christi et ille meus." WA 15.716,29–30.

[243] "Vide in vitam tuam, tum videbis, an Christianus sis. Gratia magna est, quando scis Evangelium et Papam esse Antichristum . . . Si saltem sciret quis se liberum a Papa. Sed coram deo non sufficit, oportet habes veste de qua varie torserunt se. Sed pro fide vera expono, quae spiritus sanctus secum adfert. Hoc regnum non fert impios, oportet habeas spiritum . . . Evangelium praedicatur, ut adferat spiritum sanctum. Ibi est, oportet spiritus sanctus sit, ubi es fide praeditus. Et hoc est vestis nuptialis. Non est charitas . . . Ideo hoc Evangelium loquitur contra falsos Christianos, qui noverunt Evangelium et tamen non vivunt." WA 15.715,15–32.

[244] What Luther is doing in this sermon is in keeping with his "opening of the canon of scripture," that Heiko Oberman revealed as having occurred concurrently with Luther's "opening" of the monastic walls in his De Votis Monasticis, which has been erased by Luther scholarship; the "extra-curricular acts of God" provide the "marching orders" for the Church militant in the battle between God and the devil; Oberman, "Friar in the Lion's Den," 50–55.

[245] "Evangelium venit et dicit vos cecos et corda habere eorum in manu. Sicut ipse adfectus, ita et vos. Excecat magis per hoc quod vobis depingit pulchrum cultum." WA 15.714,21–23.

separate the true Christians from the false, is the last judgment, when the pseudochristians will be bound hand and foot and cast into the darkness. Then, we will see, says Luther, to close his sermon.[246]

The devil in this sermon of 1524 is far more present, emphasized, and demonized than just a year before. There is an intensification of the "Satan-factor" in 1524. Quantitative analysis makes the point: the frequency of use of the terms *Diabolus, Satan, Teufel, Antichristus,* and *demones* reveals a surprising result. In 1522, there is only one instance of any of these terms, and that is *demones*;[247] in 1523, Luther uses one of these terms fifteen times, or once every 6.8 lines of text; in 1524 there are a total of thirty-two instances of use, or once every 4.41 lines. This is combined with an increased emphasis on the Holy Spirit, a term not found in either the 1522 or the 1523 sermon on this Gospel, but in 1524 appears ten times. For some reason, Luther read this text differently in 1524 than he did even in 1523. The war between God and the devil was more intense, and more insidious, and the Holy Spirit was the distinguishing element.

That Luther had reasonable cause to pump up the "Satan-factor" in 1524 can scarcely be questioned. He was at this time viscerally busy with dealing with the radicals Thomas Müntzer and Andreas Karlstadt.[248] Already in 1523, Luther had explicitly named the *Schwärmer* as signified by the guest without the proper wedding clothes.[249] At the end of July of 1524, Luther had published his *Letter to the Princes of Saxony Concerning the Rebellious Spirit*, directed against Müntzer, and in the Fall he was working on his *Against the Heavenly Prophets in the Matter of Images and Sacraments*, which took on Karlstadt. Thus his dichotomizing of the Kingdom of God and the Kingdom of Satan in his sermon on 9 October should come as no surprise. Yet there was more.

Just as one cannot overlook the context of Luther's battle with his "false brethren" for interpreting his sermon of 1524 on Matthew 22:1–14, so must one not forget an additional frame of reference. This was, after all, the first time Luther preached without his cowl.

---

[246] "Ideo non facit liberum arbitrium, Nisi posset homo per spiritum sanctum dicere: Ego Christi et ille meus. In novissimo die videbimus. Si posset videre cor, prae gaudio rumperetur." *WA* 15.716,29–31.
[247] *WA* 10/3.415,4.
[248] See Brecht, *Shaping and Defining the Reformation*, 146–172.
[249] "Qui non habent vestem nuptialem, sunt die schwirmer, qui sciunt evangelium, reden darvon." *WA* 12.669,19–20.

And this was the first time that we find a new term created and employed, not just in his sermons, but in all of Luther's works, namely, not only Satan, but the 'Black Satan', the *niger Satan*. It appears when Luther is discussing false Christians. He had already launched his attack: "Look at your own life, for there you will see whether or not you are a Christian. It is a great grace when you know the Gospel and recognize the pope as the Antichrist... if at least you would know that you are free from the pope. But standing before God is not enough, you are to have your wedding vestments."[250] After explaining that the wedding garment is faith led by the Holy Spirit, not love,[251] Luther then asserts that "this Gospel is spoken against false Christians, who know the Gospel, yet nevertheless do not live it... they have their divine punishment, who had the word of the Holy Spirit, but lost it. They live as Christians, but they are of the devil."[252] Such Christians are the devil's tools, and through them, sects arise.[253] Then the black Satan makes his appearance:

> When the devil has this covering over Christ and the Gospel, underneath lies the black Satan, so that we might think: 'oh, he has the Gospel and he talks a good talk,' and in the mean time we do not see Satan. These are the most obstinate of all, to the point that they are never able to loose themselves, and finally can do nothing to free themselves.[254]

This is the black Satan, who is hiding under the Gospel, placing a covering between Christ and the soul, ensnaring the false Christians who cannot do anything to free themselves.

---

[250] "Vide in vitam tuam, tum videbis an Christianus sis. Gratia magna est, quando scis Evangelium et Papam esse Antichristum... si saltem sciret quis se liberum a Papa. Sed coram Deo non sufficit, oportet habeas veste." *WA* 15.715,15–19.

[251] "Sed pro fide expono, quae spiritus sanctus secum adfert. Hoc regnum non fert impios, oportet habeas spiritum... Evangelium praedicatur, ut adferat spiritum sanctum. Ibi est, oportet spiritus sanctus sit, ubi es fide praedictus. Et hoc est vestis nuptialis, Non est charitas."*WA* 15.715,19–24.

[252] "Ideo hoc Evangelium loquitur contra falsos Christianos, qui noverunt Evangelium et tamen non vivunt... Hi habent plagam, qui verbum habent spiritus sancti, sed illo carent. Sunt sub Christianis et tamen sunt sub diabolo." *WA* 15.715,31–35.

[253] "Attamen diabolus efficit per eum, ut sectae erigantur. Isti omnem pernitiem facient, qui Evangelium habent. Carnales persecutores non sic faciunt." *WA* 15.715, 36–38.

[254] "Quando diabolus hoc operculum habet Christum et Evangelium, sub quo lateat niger Satan, ut putemus: hic habet Evangelium et bene loquitur, interim non videmus Satan, hic sunt obstinatissimi ita ut nunquam hic solvi possint, et tandem nihil facere possent, quo liberentur." *WA* 15.,715,38–716,1.

Black Satan, *niger Satan*: why black? In his early works Luther used the adjective 'black' in a most common fashion. Black was the opposite of white,[255] black signified evil, especially in contrast with white representing purity,[256] it was the color of darkness, death, and the law.[257] Luther also used 'black' descriptively referring to the color itself, which he employed most often in terms of the black dress of the monks; thus he referred to the Carthusians as white and the Benedictines as black, both of which follow the traditions of their own sects, which even seculars imitate.[258]

These are the uses of the term 'black' in Luther's works before the appearance of the 'black Satan'. In his sermon of 14 May 1525 on John 16, Luther once again used the term 'black Satan' in so far as Satan was seen as black. There are, he explained,

> ... two types of groups that belong to Satan. The first are the openly evil, and there Satan is seen as being completely black. The other group is bright and shining, and there Satan is thought to be God. These two the world and human reason are not able to distinguish clearly since the world and human reason are purple and are the wedding garments of the devil. Thus is all sin, because the Holy Spirit is absent, and in sin Satan dresses himself up and death reigns. This Gospel is the new preaching from heaven, which the world does not understand. The reason says: this guy is innocent, because he is not a fornicator. Reason is not able to say: not to have God's Holy Spirit is sin, and is not to know Christ.[259]

This would seem to contradict Luther's use of the black Satan in his sermon of 1524, since there, the black Satan appears under the guise of the Gospel. But the devil is a tricky one. What appears to

---

[255] *WA* 1.42,30.
[256] "... et sic externe sum nigra, interne formosa." *WA* 5.456,37; *cf.* *WA* 3.409,30.
[257] "Niger color est tenebrarum et mortis..." *WA* 13.606,12; "Color albus promissio et Evangelium, color niger lex." *WA* 9.412,35.
[258] "Carthusianus, Benedictinus. Quisque suam sectam praefert alterius. Item seculares imitantur hoc: ille utitur nigra veste, ille die mercurii non vescitur carnibus" *WA* 14.216,15–17; *cf.* "... nec nigra nec alba cuculla..." *WA* 2.160,13.
[259] "Duplex populus est Satanae ut palam impii, ibi videtur Satan penitus niger, Alter hauff ornatus, et putatur ibi deus esse. Hos mundus et ratio non potest arguere, hi sunt purpura et vestis nuptialis diaboli, et omnia peccata, quia spiritus sanctus non adest, in quo Satan ornat se et regnat inter eos mors. Haec est nova praedicatio e coelis, quam mundus non intellexit. Ratio dicit: hic est inculpatus, quia non fornicatur, non potest dicere: spiritus sanctum dei non habere est peccatum et Christum non cognoscere." *WA* 17/1.245,3–10. For Luther's use of the word *hauff*, see Renate und Gustav Bebermeyer, *Wörterbuch zu Martin Luthers Deutschen Schriften, Härtiglich-Heilig* (Hildesheim/Zürich/New York, 1997), 219–227.

be "white and shining" but nevertheless is diabolical, though this can be termed the 'white devil', when it comes down to it, the black devil is there underneath. In his Galatians commentary of 1531, Luther makes this distinction, and whereas in his sermon on John 16 of 1525 we find the key term of the devil's wedding garment, in 1531 Luther used the same word as he did in 1524, *operculum*, to refer to the covering which the devil uses to blind sinners:

> No heretic presents himself under the title of error and of Satan, <but> as the white devil. But even more so it is the black devil, when he instigates open disgrace, <and> constructs an image or screen for the sinner: the murderer does not see the murder in his rage; he has his own screen. The adulterer has his own enjoyment and cloak. But when the devil comes in spiritual matters, then he first causes that one says that the devil's doctrine is actually that of grace, 'my word is from God.'[260]

The covering of the devil, the devil's 'screen', his *operculum*, makes the devil seem to be white and shining, when in reality, it is the *niger diabolus*, the black devil, which is the one at work. The *Schwämer*, coming under the guise of preaching the Gospel, are the false Christians, who at the last judgment are cast out into outer darkness. Yet underneath their schemes, lies the black devil, the *niger Satan*, who puts up a screen, even if of smoke, to seduce one into thinking that one has the Gospel truth. Human reason and the way of the world cannot grasp this, for the devil is cloaked in his own wedding garment, the screen, the covering, that renders one blind to the true Gospel and God's Holy Spirit. This was the *niger Satan* of Luther's sermon on 9 October 1524, which put his own vestments, his own wedding clothes, as a screen or covering for blinding the Gospel truth.

We must not forget that the first time we find the black Satan, who lies hidden under the cover that the devil has placed between the soul and Christ, is in a sermon that is dealing with what the proper wedding vestments are. The answer Luther gives is that the genuine, true wedding garment is faith led by the Holy Spirit, a ser-

---

[260] "Nullus hereticus venit sub titulo erroris et Satanae, ut diabolus praesertim albus. Imo diabolus niger, quando ad manifesta flagitia impellit, facit speciem peccatori: homicidia non videt homicidium in furore, habet suum operculum, Adulter habet suas blanditias et opercula. Sed quando venit in istis spiritualibus, da fort erst zu, dicit suam doctrinam esse gratiae: meum verbum est dei." *WA* 40/1.108,5–10.

mon that Luther gave for the first time without his own vestments, the black habit of the Augustinians. In his *Coelifodina*, Johannes von Paltz referred to the mendicants as the Lord's sheep dogs guarding the flock. There were four, and they were distinguished by their color. The dog of multi-color was the Dominicans; the gray dog, was the Franciscans; the white dog, the Carmelites; and the black dog, the *canis niger* was the Augustinians.[261] The Augustinians were the black friars, and on 9 October 1524 Luther created the image and preached about the black Satan, having finally taken off the black vestments of his Order, removing the covering that had existed between his soul and Christ. It was not only the sects, the *sectae* of the radicals, but also those whom the radicals imitated, the monks, who put up the false image of proper vestments. The black habit of the Augustinians had been the veil preventing Luther from truly and completely following the Holy Spirit revealed in God's Gospel. The true wedding garment was not the habit, but faith in Christ, led by the Spirit.

Yet this was not all. Those under the spell of the black Satan were those false Christians who had the Gospel, and then lost it. They were the obstinate, who could do nothing to free themselves. They were the ones who tried to hold the middle ground between Christ and the pope, and even if they could see that the pope was Antichrist, they were blind to be able to do anything about it, not being led by the Holy Spirit. They were obstinate, intransigent. They were the blind, leading the blind, putting charity before faith. And sad it truly was, as Luther later also defined the color black: black signifies *tristitia*.[262] Not only the *Schwärmer*, Karlstadt, and Müntzer, did Luther have in mind in his sermon on the wedding feast of 1524, and not only his own black cowl which he had been so reluctant to lay aside, but also ringing in his ears were the words of one whom Luther himself had accused of trying to hold the middle ground between Christ and Antichrist, who refused to free himself, who had told Luther: 'Martin, you are going too far,' and who still,

---

[261] "In hoc, quod commisit sibi oves, commisit sibi canes ovium, scilicet ordines mendicantes, qui positi sunt in angulis ovilis: in uno angulo canis diversi coloris, scilicet ordo Praedicatorum, in alio angulo canis griseus, scilicet ordo Minorum, in tertio angulo canis albus, scilicet ordo Carmelitarum, in quarto angulo canis niger, scilicet ordo fratrum Eremitarum sancti Augustini." Paltz *Coel.* 2 (326,21–26).

[262] "Nigredo tristitiam significat." *WA* 31/2.14,7.

unlike Luther for the first time, was clothed in black, the black habit of the *Ordo Sancti Benedicti*: Johannes Staupitz. The black monk Staupitz, as much as anyone else, signified for Luther the *niger Satan*. The black cowl, whether of the Augustinians or of the Benedictines, Luther finally saw as the screen preventing the workings of the Holy Spirit in faith, representing the wedding vestments of the devil rather than of the true Christian. The blind, the weak, had had their day. Luther's sermon, combined with the highly symbolical act of preaching it after finally having removed his habit, was Luther's answer to Staupitz's last letter. Luther's Reformation discovery was indeed transferring his obedience to his Order to his faith in Christ.

iv. *Frater Martinus*
There are no isolated events. There are no accurate mono-causal explanations of historical phenomena, especially of historical individuals. It would be as fallacious to claim that the Augustinian platform caused, and therefore explains, Martin Luther, as it would be to argue that Luther caused the Reformation. Yet the latter is inconceivable without the former. Reductionistic approaches are so appealing, but we must recognize our own "Black Satan" and guard against the "white and shining" appearance of over-simplified interpretations offering themselves as statements of truth, be they theological or historical. When Luther took off his habit on 9 October 1524, there had been a multiplicity of factors and developments leading thereto: theological insight and understanding that became conviction, a recognition of the pope as Antichrist, dilemma and struggles with the new-found freedom, slanders, threats, uncertainty, and hesitation. In the same letter to Link of 7 February 1525 that Luther commented on Staupitz's "rather cold" book that deserved to be published in any case, he also mentioned that he had responded to Karlstadt, that hell was breaking loose in Basel and Strassburg, and that the "Orlamunda peasants" had "purged" his little book, "thus Satan rages."[263] Even so one can almost hear behind Luther's comment on Staupitz's work a reference or hint that Staupitz himself was intended: *frigidulus, sicut semper fuit*. Luther's reluctance to take off his cowl was based on his own self understanding as an Augustinian

---

[263] "Respondi Carlstadio, sicut vides. Basilae subvertit multos, Oecolampadium, Pellicanum et alios, ita ut nos rideant tam securi de sua opinione. Orlamundenses rustici nates libello meo purgant, sic Satan furit." *WABr* 3.437,11–15; nr. 827.

friar, and all that the cowl symbolized. He himself was weak, and with good reason. Luther had stopped referring to himself as *frater Martinus* already in 1522, yet his cowl remained. Staupitz's last letter had reminded Luther to think of the weak, rebuking him for having gone "too far." Christ must be followed, above all else. Luther's last discovery: I too am weak, *Et ego*, and the final step was taken, was required: *etiam cucullum*. Luther finally stripped himself of the entire tradition that had given him his identity. Once again, it was symbolized with clothes, with vestments. Luther took off his habit, and became once again a *novus homo*, dressed this time only with his faith in Christ. Yet even this act, this event, cannot be understood isolated from the entire complex of phenomena, structures, and ideals that gave the event its significance and meaning, so much of which were embodied and symbolized by the one last thread to his past, his vicar-general, to whom he had vowed obedience, his father and teacher, Johannes Staupitz. Luther's act of 9 October 1524 marked the end of the Augustinian Reformation, a Reformation that had been in progress for almost two hundred years, from Gregory of Rimini and Jordan of Quedlinburg, to Johannes Staupitz and Martin Luther. It had come to an end, and thereafter, the Augustinian platform became an instrument of Roman Catholic reform.[264]

In 1513 Frater Martinus, Professor of Biblical Theology at the University of Wittenberg, and Augustinian Hermit, began lecturing on the psalms. He was certainly not the first Augustinian to have done so. The Book of Psalms was the monastic heartbeat, prophesying the coming of Christ and his Passion, the psalms of penitence, the songs of praise. Every Augustinian, every professed religious, knew the psalms backwards and forwards. The psalms were the pulse of the monastic life. Lecturing on such a book was not a task Luther took up voluntarily. The previous year, at Staupitz's insistence, Frater Martinus took his doctorate in theology. He did so only most reluctantly. Now he stood as lector of the Wittenberg *studium generale* at the appointment of the Order's prior general, Giles of Viterbo, and as professor of Wittenberg's University.[265] He began at the beginning, psalm 1:1: *Blessed is the man who does not follow the advice of the wicked, Beatus vir qui non abiit in consilio impiorum.*

---

[264] This theme will be treated in volume three of the trilogy, *The True Church*.
[265] See Brecht, *Road to Reformation*, 125–128.

672   CHAPTER SIX

In Luther's exposition of psalm 1:1 we find a text fragment, or at least what appears to be a text fragment given the condition of the Dresden manuscript of Luther's *Dictata*. The commentary begins on folio 2ª and continues until fol. 5ᵇ; folios 6 and 7 are missing; folios 8–11 are numbered, but are blank; the fragment then is found on folio 12ª; fol. 12ᵇ is blank; fol. 13 is missing; fol. 14ª is blank, and then on fol. 14ᵇ one finds the *praefatio* to Luther's commentary.[266] The fragment was most likely, as Erich Vogelsang suggested, an insert by Luther from one of his sermons, a lost *sermo de Sancto Augustino*.[267]

There are, Luther explained, three paths one must follow to heaven: not to follow the advice of the wicked; not to remain in the path of sinners; and not to teach evil. Each of these prohibitions, however, carried with it an opposite charge: to resist greatly and to flee from the advice of the wicked, and to follow the advice of the righteous; to subject oneself to the justice of God, through confession and self accusation, to justify God, giving thanks, for this is to stand with the saints; and finally to teach the good.[268] These three paths, Luther then explained, shine forth most clearly in St. Augustine, and are exemplified in his entire life. Therefore, the words *beatus vir* praise Augustine most uniquely (*Igitur singularissima laus est Augustini in hoc versiculo*).[269] Augustine is the *beatus vir* of psalm 1:1.

In Luther's sermon, we not only hear echoes of Jordan of Quedlinburg's summary of the Law based on Michah 6:8: "do justice, love mercy, and walk humbly before your God,"[270] but we also find something of even greater significance. This three-fold path to heaven that Luther explicated based on Augustine's life was *his* understanding of the Augustinian platform, it was his high way to heaven: to

---

[266] *WA* 3.26–27 and the notes given; see also *WA* 3.5–6.
[267] *Luthers Werke in Auswahl* 5, ed. Erich Vogelsang (Berlin, 1963³), 86–87; see also A. Hamel, *Der junge Luther und Augustin* (Gütersloh, 1934; reprint: Hildesheim/New York, 1980), 40–45.
[268] "Sed gradus tres oppositi et ad celum: Primus est non abire in consilium impiorum i.e. maxime resistere, refugere et ire in consilium piorum, declinare conventicula illorum de sanguinibus Idumeorum. Secundus: Non stare in via peccatorum i.e. non statuere suam iustitiam, subiici iustitie dei, induere confessionem: in principio accusare seipsum, iudicare se ipsum, iustificare deum, gratias agere, paratus audire et acquiescere: et sensui ac monenti alteri cedere. Hoc est stare in via sanctorum. Stant enim sancti: quia humilitate et confessione nituntur. Tercius est non docere malum, i.e. maxime docere bona." *WA* 3.26,19–28.
[269] *WA* 3.26,28–27,6.
[270] See above Chapter Four, note 346.

walk in the way of the righteous, to follow the path of the saints, and to teach the good. And it was so following Augustine as the *beatus vir*, his Order's *pater et preceptor*. The Augustinian lector in Wittenberg was pursuing a program and following a path that had been begun by Giles of Rome over two centuries previous. He was carrying out his Order's platform, and he was wearing his Order's habit. He was an obedient friar, following to the fullest his Order's traditions as expressed in his vows. It was a high calling. Little did he know, no more in 1512 or 1513 than in 1505 or even in 1519, where such a high way would lead. "Blessed is the man..."

III. The Sons of Augustine

Martin Luther was not the end. He was not the goal or the telos towards which the story tends from its very beginning. Luther was an Augustinian, a son of Augustine, and as such his was an important voice in telling of the Augustinian platform in the later Middle Ages. He reveals as much about the Augustinian high way to heaven as does the high way itself about him. Luther's story as such is important to retell, but it is another story than the one here narrated. If in doing so, new light is shed on Luther, all the better. Yet the point is not to explain Luther, but the Augustinian tradition and what it unleashed.

Luther was a climax, as were so many along the way: Giles of Rome, Augustinus of Ancona, Jordan of Quedlinburg, Gregory of Rimini. The story, however, has not been fully told. The last page has not yet been turned. What did it mean to follow Augustine? What did it mean to be an Augustinian? Even if we could answer such questions definitively, once and for all, we would be mistaken if we felt that we therefore could understand and explain each and every aspect of the unfolding plot. Luther was Luther, and as such was unique, an individual, who viewed his role differently than did all the rest, and all the rest, each and every one, viewed their roles differently from his, each and every one was unique: William of Cremona, John of Basel, Johannes Zachariae. To point to what was common, what they all shared, an ideal, an ideology, an identity, the striving to follow in the footsteps of Augustine as their *pater*, their *preceptor*, and as the *sapiens architector ecclesie*, is not intended to take away from their originality or from their individuality. Conformity and unity were sought, but the ideal did not disallow innovation, did not cover up or suppress creativity, or individual achievement. Martin Luther was not Gregory of Rimini, and Gregory of Rimini was not Giles of Rome, and Giles of Rome was not Jordan of Quedlinburg. Each was as unique and as special as the others, each had their own contribution to make. And each was a son of Augustine. Unity and conformity do not necessitate uniformity.

Creativity, development, change, insight: these are what made the Augustinian tradition dynamic, that which gave it its life and its force. Augustine himself remains an enigma, a figure impossible to confine by ready-made labels, a person, mind, and soul resisting categorization and final definition. And there is his lasting influence and power, his lasting relevance. We catch only glimpses here and there, and only every now and then, without ever exhausting the possibilities for new understandings. Like father, like son. It was an image, a myth, and one they themselves created, as do perhaps all sons that of their fathers, even to the extent of not seeing their fathers for who they actually were. Love is always blind.

It was an inheritance without genetics, an appropriated heritage, a politically created identity. Yet they wore on their bodies the mark of their lineage, the habit of Augustine's hermits, and they followed their father's dictates for life, his *Rule* for living, and they followed his religion. There was something that bound them together, even recognizing all the differences, something ephemeral, something intangible, a motivation, a goal, a platform. There was the unity. And what did it all mean? That was the question they were striving to answer. Regulation, religionization, indoctrination: to live with one heart and soul in God, to bring the riches of the contemplative life to society at large, to be the embodiment of Augustine himself, to live the most perfect life, to teach and to preach, to serve the Church: to face the challenges of the world they met and to do so as faithful sons of their father. It was a question that had to be answered anew in every new situation, which was every moment. To be truly religious meant to be truly an Augustinian, even if that entailed rebellion, even if that entailed following an antipope or seeing the papacy itself as Antichrist. They had to be faithful to their vows: obedience to God, to Mary, and to their Order, the Order's continuity.

Living between God and the devil, relying upon God's grace and God's love, viewing the human as will more than intellect, calling upon God's mercy, knowing the eternal fact of predestination, striving to be an example, striving to teach the way to heaven on the earthly journey back to union with God, recognizing that life is one of alienation, a following of Christ's Passion, a taking up of Christ's cross, something one must suffer and endure chastely and purely, and that one can only do so with God's saving power, praying for God's will to be done, and for God's name to be sanctified, and for the coming of God's kingdom: such was the unity of the sons of Augustine.

It was a constant struggle, a constant battle. Some fell by the wayside, some could not be brought back into the fold, some were incorrigible, and some led towards new directions, some had new insights. Reform and reformation, the constant endeavor to bring to reality Augustine's cultural ethic of brotherly love and living for God: there is the story. Political power and intrigue, moral exhortations, incarceration, theological speculation, impassioned preaching, striving for observance, coercion, persuasion, conviction: the sons of Augustine, from Giles of Rome to Martin Luther, were striving with all means to do whatever they could to make real in their daily lives the ideal and the hope that the members of the Order, and of all Christendom, from that of Boniface VIII and John XXII to Julius II and Leo X, in their common fight with the devil would finally indeed be changed and transformed by the holy. That it never came about, that it was never realized, was not for lack of effort. The reformation of the Order evolved into the reform of society precisely as society was being torn asunder by the very platform the Order had initiated and pursued. A battle for observance, a battle for religion, the impact of theology: Thy will be done, the last days were at hand, and were at hand as never before. The first martyrs of what we now call the Reformation, were Augustinian friars, burned at the stake in Brussels on 1 July 1523.[271] And where was the mercy of God? One could only pray for the coming of God's kingdom. *Veni Creator Spiritus, Magne Pater Augustine.* In the tensions between reform and reformation something had to give way. It did. The world had indeed become another, and the high way to heaven had unknowingly unleashed the horrors of hell.

---

[271] See Brad S. Gregory, "Late Medieval Religiosity and the Renaissance of Christian Martyrdom in the Reformation Era," in *Continuity and Change*, 379–399; 380–381. For a comprehensive view of martyrdom, see Gregory, *Salvation at Stake. Christian Martyrdom in Early Modern Europe*, Harvard Historical Studies 134 (Cambridge, MA, 1999).

> *The heart is the most deceitful of all things,*
> *desperately sick; who can fathom it?*
> Jer. 17:9
>
> *It is a wicked, godless generation that asks for a sign;*
> *and the only sign that will be given it is the sign*
> *of the prophet Jonah.*
> Mt. 12:39

EPILOGUE

We are all Hegelians. We pick through bones, and stones, looking for some glimpse of what was, scouring the scraps that have been left to us trying to sniff the smells, taste the tastes, and hear the sounds that exist only as distant echoes, wallowing through all the undisciplined squads of emotion, in hope of finding a meaning that can make it all make sense, in search of the *Zeitgeist*. The nun at the spinning wheel, the peasant plowing his field, slogging through all the mud and manure, the prostitute and her patrons, the lost, the forgotten, the mother and child crying in the cold of night, the murderer and the murdered, the thief, the beggar, the priest, they all speak to us as ghosts who no longer exist except to haunt our thirst to know them, which, we hope and believe on faith might somehow give us deeper knowledge and broader understanding not of them, our objects, but of ourselves. And then we explain and pontificate as if we know. They are not there to contradict. We too have our black Satan. And all the while what we are explicating as truth, as reality, as past society, turns out to be mere projection of our own values and ideals, which we hope to discover are not so unique after all in order to ease our conscience, or loneliness, in order, as the poet put it, "to recover what has been lost, and found, and lost again and again: and now under conditions that seem unpropitious."[1] And somehow, underneath all our intrigue, all our interest and care, all our seeking for the truth, lies denied a sublimated necrophilia. Let the dead bury the dead, and may they rest in peace,

---

[1] T.S. Eliot, *Four Quartets* 2: "East Coker," V, in T.S. Eliot, *The Complete Poems and Plays, 1909–1950* (New York, 1971), 128.

undisturbed by our sniffling attempts to pick through the remnants of their bodies and souls. It is a flawed endeavor. Yet the *Geist* remains in spite of the *Zeit*, and the *Da* is still finding its way into the *Sein*.

It is a story we tell. And the plot is so often that of our own making. But oh yes, there is time, there is time, for visions and revisions, and for versions and aversions. When it comes down to it, only the spirit remains, only the ideas that we appropriate and project, which we try to formulate into some sort of semblance of meaning. A skeleton is just a skeleton after all, and broken, shattered walls just piles of rubble, and manuscripts simply markings on the manufactured skin of a cow or sheep that gave its life to a so-called higher purpose than that of the lord's dinner table, only later to be shat out into the sewer. What we are really getting at, striving for, is the reconstitution not of castles and cities, bishoprics and battles, but of the broken pieces of the shattered dreams that they all represent, remaining as signs thereof, crying out of the silence, saying "Hear me too," doing so under the guise of "objectivity," pretending we are following something greater than the *Zeitgeist* of our specialties, our departments, and our societies. And yet citizens still clubbed to death their archbishop, and miners' sons still became monks, and we still write our books.

Ceasing to be is not nearly so horrifying as being thrown into existence in the first place. It is ever so easy to forget. Much more difficult is to remember, and there is the rub. Memory, will, and love: that dastardly trinity, compelling us on indiscriminently, forcing us to create something for which we can rejoice. And create we do, by breaking apart and destroying previous creations, to reform and to reshape, what was never there to begin with, and doing so all in our own image. We all take vows unaware.

It did not exist. There was no such 'thing' as the Augustinian platform, any more than there was a 'thing' that was called 'Augustinianism,' '*Frömmigkeitstheologie*', '*Semireligiosentum*', 'Religionization', or even 'The Reformation'. What did it 'mean' to 'be' 'Augustinian'? What does it mean to be German, or American, or Dutch, or Spanish, or Australian, or Chinese, or Korean, or Irish, or Bengalese, or Russian, or Vietnamese, or female, or male, or father, or mother, or Buddhist, or Christian? As the late medieval nominalists knew, words signify *ad placitum*, as desired, agreed upon, willed, the original social contract. There was and is no 'being' that corresponds to any such labels, nor to that of liberal, conservative, democrat, republican, gay, queer, fag, nigger, Jew, bitch, bastard, slut, or saint. All constructs, creations that we make ourselves and apply at will, in order to give meaning and significance to the reality we define according to our own pleasure, and according to our own purpose. Yet it is one thing to label others, and another to label ourselves, and in the latter is substance and meaning and understanding, as long as we recognize that every moment is a shocking valuation of all we have been. All such words, all such labels, all such descriptions, have years of encrustations clinging onto them, giving them connotations and meaning beyond what we might like or desire, or find as fitting with our own construction of reality. It is a good thing to be shocked, and shaken to the very foundation. There are no isolated events, and there are no isolated words. There is no breaking of the bonds of language, and thus we continue to strive to grasp the meaning we think we have found, the meaning we think we have, attributing significance beyond the realm of words, appealing to and searching for the realm of spirit. There are only isolated individuals.

We all have our myths, and no amount of even healthy demythification can take away completely the mystery, or debunk definitively what is the most fundamental level of social reality. Memory, will, and love remain, unbroken, untarnished, undiminished, even if obscured, even if forgotten, undesired, and hated. Hopes, goals, struggles, ideals, aspirations, emotions, and dreams: these are what made history, and are what make it still. The drives to eat, to procreate or fornicate, or to possess, have no force when not recognized, when not set in motion by mental structures and constructs which provide the means of the drives' fulfillment. Ideas and emotions are far more powerful and are far more determining than simple biological needs and appetites. Inseparable from the economics of materialism is the economics of the spirit, the economics of the heart, which no social history worthy of its own pretensions can ignore. Religion may have been and may still be an illusion, but if so, the illusion has proven of more historical influence than the mythic reality set in opposition. The holy remains holy, even when our own creation, even when ever so mundane and ever so materialistic.

Monks were men and nuns were women. They hungered, they ate, they slept, they urinated and defecated; monks ejaculated and nuns menstruated, and some of both genders even fornicated. They were sons and daughters, mothers and fathers, they were born, they struggled to live, they bled, they cried, they hurt, they rejoiced, and they died. They stole, they gambled, they traded, they worked, they sang, and they prayed. Some were saints, some were devils, some were politicians, some were theologians, and some were preachers and teachers. In so many ways they were not all that different from the burghers and peasants, or the lords and ladies from whose ranks they came. And in so many ways they were not all that different from we who tell their stories. We are all seeking something "out there," wherever that may be and wherever we may choose to look, whether food, shelter, financial success, scholarly prowess, admiration, love, attention, acknowledgment, influence, power or position, or the eternal salvation of our souls; we are all seeking our own sort of monastery, where we are safe and secure, our own sort of sanctification and justification; we are all seeking some sort of meaning and understanding of our lives beyond what can be touched and tasted and felt. We all hear voices. The only question is where are they leading us?

The sons of Augustine, the little hermit friars, have been silenced for too long. When heard in the past, their words have most often been used and abused for purposes other than they themselves had intended. Giles of Rome, Augustinus of Ancona, William of Cremona, Nicholas of Alessandria, Henry of Friemar, Hermann of Schildesche, Jordan of Quedlinburg, Gregory of Rimini, Antonius Rampegolus, Johannes Zachariae, Ambrosius de Cora, Johannes von Paltz, Johannes Staupitz, Giles of Viterbo, Martin Luther, to name just a few: names of bodies no longer present, names of a past hope and dream, a past spirit, names of Augustinians, and names of human beings seeking to find meaning in their lives and their worlds, names of individuals who all wore the black habit of Augustine's hermits, and followed Augustine's religion. They were all friars and all religious; they were all monks and all hermits; they were all human flesh and blood; they all did all those things that human beings do, which we so often forget, or do not like to think about. They all had human bodies, human hearts, and human minds, and they all followed an ideal, a hope, and a dream, following a high way to heaven in creating a platform and religious identity for themselves and their Order, for their brothers, for their family, and in doing so, they made and changed history. A hope, a dream, an idea, an ideal, an identity, a fantasy, an illusion; these they passed on, this was their heritage: to have one heart and one soul in God, whereby memory, love, and will are joined in the love that exists between the lover and the beloved. By listening to their voices, and those of their confreres, we begin to realize that we too are following their path, even if unrecognized and unrecognizable; we too are following hopes and dreams, ideas and ideals, fantasies and illusions, in attempt to create an identity and to find meaning. And we too love, and remember, and will, even if ever so imperfectly.

The sons of Augustine. What do they have to teach us? Why should we care? Why should we give a damn? Why should we try to hear the voices long since mute, the voices of brother Remigius or eighty-year old brother Michael? It was all an ideal, all an illusion. Oh the craziness of imitating Christ's Passion. Oh the craziness of living in poverty, chastity, and obedience. Or was it simply self service, seeking privilege: Giles of Rome, Augustinus of Ancona, William of Cremona, Jordan of Quedlinburg, Gregory of Rimini, Martin Luther? Politics and privilege there certainly were. What are souls after all? Both God and the devil we have dismissed, have done away with, no longer take seriously, relegated to past fantasies, to past childhood. Oh we enlightened ones! Memories, loves, and wills, long since overcome, long since forgotten, surpassed—and yet....

Perhaps, if we listen closely enough, there is something we can learn. It could be that we might begin to realize, as if for the first time, that like it or not, regardless of present, individual understanding and interpretation, regardless of creed or conviction, regardless of all our histories and of all our long-windedness parading the glory of our erect erudition, and so often completely unaware and even against our wills and our memories and our loves, that we humans always have been, and are still being, irreparably changed by the holy.

APPENDICES

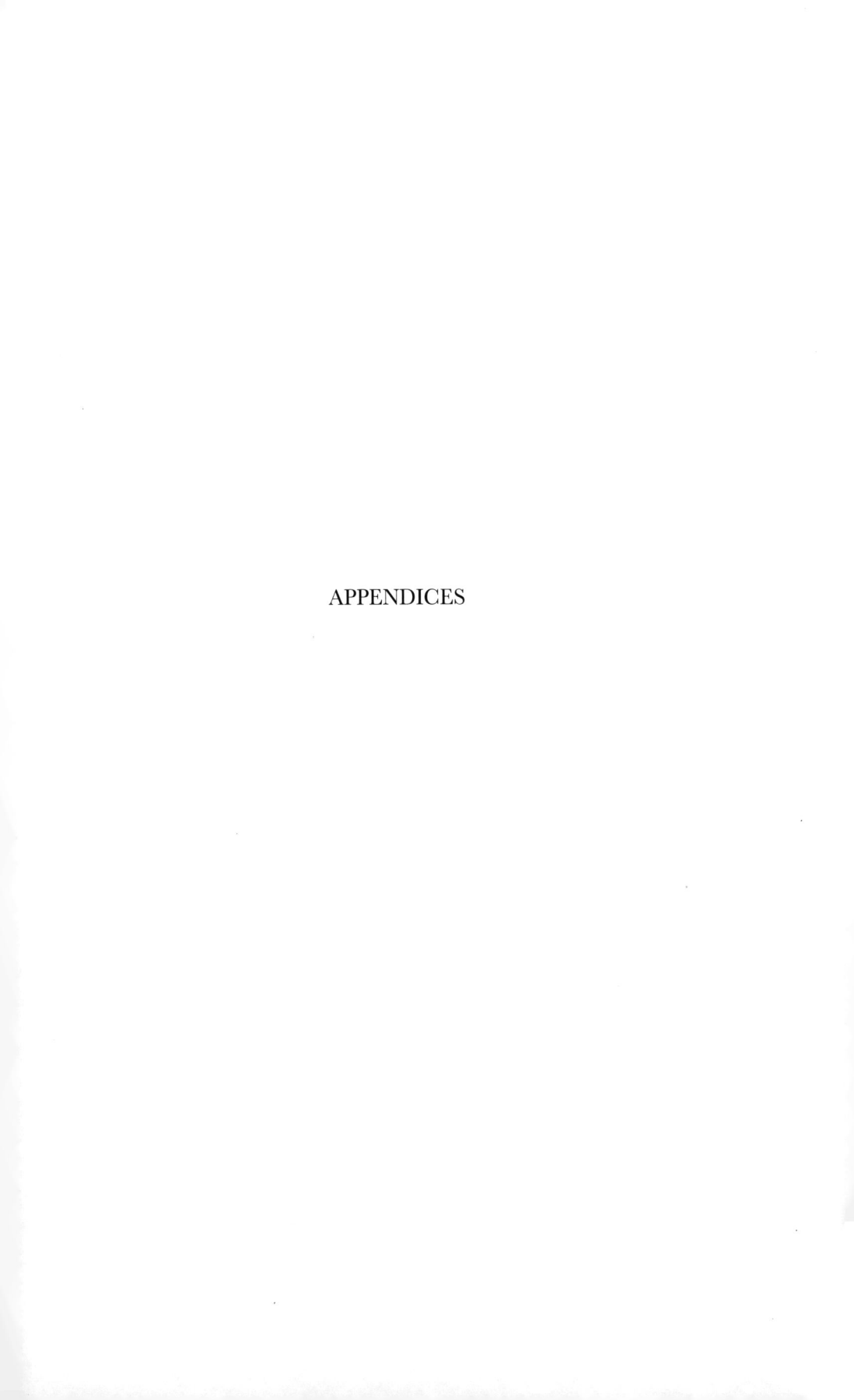

APPENDIX A

TERMS, CONCEPTS, AND DEFINITIONS

In the preceding study there are four major terms that are central to the overall conception: 1. Late medieval Augustinianism; 2. Ideology; 3. Religion/*religio*; and 4. Religionization. It was apparent, however, that lengthy discussions of these terms and how I use them, would have interrupted the text. Thus, I offer here descriptions of these key terms, which I hope will provide more concrete theoretical understanding of what I have tried to accomplish, and of my argument in general, than is evident from the text itself and the notes.

Late medieval Augustinianism is a historiographical concept, and thus I treat it here in a historiographical essay. Ideology is a term with as many definitions as it has uses, and thus I given an indication of how I have employed the term. Religion/*religio* is central to my presentation of Augustine's religion as being the historically accurate referent for 'late medieval Augustinianism'. Thus I detail the basis for my use and conception of *religio*. Religionization is a term I have coined to refer to the secondary, on-going catechetical process in the later Middle Ages. Here I present a more extensive sketch of the concept to serve as background to the text's argument. This is only a sketch, but one that I feel is illuminating, and by presenting it here, I at least give the reader the opportunity to see what ideas I have had in mind. These four terms, while distinct, are nevertheless inter-related. My definition of late medieval Augustinianism is based on the historical concept of *religio* as it pertained to the religion of the OESA, which was expressed in the Order's platform that can be described most comprehensively as the Order's institutionalized ideology, and when viewed as an on-going process, can be interpreted as a specific instance of religionization.

1. Late Medieval Augustinianism

Late Medieval Augustinianism is not a term with a clear definition. Though the past century of scholarship has produced seminal editions of texts and interpretive insights that have deepened and expanded the knowledge of Augustine's heritage in the later Middle Ages, modern research has yet to yield a consensus on how to characterize what can be categorized as 'Augustinian'. Was Augustinianism essentially a renaissance of Augustine's anti-Pelagianism, or a specific theological tradition in the Order? At stake in this debate is not only the shape of late medieval intellectual history, but also the relationship between late medieval Augustinianism and the emergence of Reformation theology. Much of the scholarship of the past century has been fueled by the question of Martin Luther's relationship to his Order, which has obscured the distinction between the existence of the late medieval Augustinian school and the renewed campaign against the "modern Pelagians."

A. *The Augustinian School*

In 1883 Karl Werner published the first monographic treatment of late medieval Augustinianism.[1] Werner traced the origins of fourteenth-century Augustinianism to the thirteenth-century reaction against Aristotelianism. He argued forcefully for an Order-specific Augustinianism: the Augustinian School is defined by the doctrines of Giles of Rome, according to which Augustinian theologians were required to teach, as formulated by the General Chapter of Florence in 1287.[2] Werner dedicated the first part of the work to explicating Giles' position on the major theological topics: epistemology, ontology and metaphysics, cosmology and anthropology, the doctrine of God, Christology, soteriology, the sacraments, and ethics.[3] When he came to Gregory of Rimini (d. 1358), Werner saw a major rift in the Augustinian School.[4] Whereas Giles viewed theology as affective knowledge, Gregory, having been strongly influenced by the works of the Franciscan theologian and philosopher William of Ockham (d. 1347), sought to combat the uncertainty of the speculative nature of Giles' theology by turning theology into scientific, practical knowledge.[5] Only by purifying the Order's theology of speculative Aristotelianism could a true Augustinianism come into being.[6] Yet it is here that Werner evidenced his own position. Gregory's Ockhamism was not much better than the determinism of the Oxford secular theologian Thomas Bradwardine (d. 1349), which Werner treated in the second part of his book. With the extremes of Gregory on the one hand and those of Bradwardine on the other, the Church was in dire need of a restora-

---

[1] Karl Werner, *Die Scholastik des späteren Mittelalters*, vol. 3: *Der Augustinismus in der Scholastik des späteren Mittelalters* (Wien, 1883). Werner has often been overlooked in the later historiography, appearing essentially only in the footnotes as a reference to someone who labeled Thomas Bradwardine a determinist—Heiko A. Oberman, for example, in his study, *Archbishop Thomas Bradwardine. A Fourteenth-Century Augustinian* (Utrecht, 1958), cites Werner some 11 times; although not always negatively (*e.g.*, page 75), Werner is nevertheless most often used as a negative example—or as the first to deal with the subject in monographic fashion (Schulze, "*Via Gregorii*," 3, n. 21; as in note 94 below). Werner is not mentioned by David Steinmetz in his overview of the scholarship; see Steinmetz, *Luther and Staupitz. An Essay in the Intellectual Origins of the Protestant Reformation*, Duke Monographs in Medieval and Renaissance Studies 4 (Durham, N.C., 1980), 16–27.

[2] Werner, *Der Augustinismus*, 13. As genuine followers of Giles, Werner listed James of Viterbo, Augustinus of Ancona, Gerard of Siena, Prosper of Reggio, Albert of Padua, Henry of Friemar, and Thomas of Strassburg; *ibid.*, 14f.

[3] These are treated in chap. 4–11.

[4] Werner, *Der Augustinismus*, 15.

[5] *Ibid.*, 26f.

[6] *Ibid.*, 26.

tion of the teachings of St. Thomas Aquinas, which only came about in the Council of Trent.[7]

Modern scholarship has corrected Werner's portrayal of Bradwardine and Gregory. Yet Werner's overarching thesis that there was an identifiable Augustinian School, founded on the doctrines of Giles, has remained controversial, although it has often been attributed to other scholars. Werner clearly distinguished between the Augustinian School and renewed anti-Pelagianism, treated in parts one and two of his monograph. For Werner, the Augustinian School and an Augustinian campaign against the modern Pelagians were two separate phenomena of the fourteenth century.

The diversity of positions within late medieval Augustinianism, and within late medieval theology in general, was stressed in 1925 by Franz Ehrle.[8] Focusing on the *Sentences* commentary of Peter of Candia (ca. 1378), Ehrle identified four distinct schools of thought Peter took into account in his commentary: the nominalist School, the Scotist School, the Thomistic School, and the Augustinian School. The nominalists themselves were a varied group, unified by terminist logic, rather than by theological positions.[9] Thus Peter numbered not only William of Ockham, but also Gregory of Rimini among the nominalists. Ehrle devoted far more space to the nominalist School than he did to the other three, in an attempt to prove that the theology of the University of Paris in the fourteenth and fifteenth centuries cannot be said to have been dominated by nominalism, or by any other theological school.[10]

Ehrle continued his study by tracing the influence of nominalism within the universities of Europe through the *Wegestreit* of the fifteenth century. It was not nominalism or humanism that caused the "death of scholasticism," but rather Lutheranism,[11] which for Ehrle, though lying beyond the boundaries of his study, was clearly "a-catholic."[12]

When he finally turned to brief treatments of the Scotist, Thomistic and Augustinian traditions, Ehrle distinguished two ways of understanding theological schools. The first, labeled as internal and objective, is characterized by the succession of theological doctrine. The second is the legislated mandate to teach in the tradition of a specific theologian. For the Dominicans, Thomas Aquinas was the Order's theologian, and for the Augustinians, it was Giles of Rome.[13]

Although Peter rarely cited Augustinians in his commentary, Ehrle identified a specific Augustinian School.[14] The Augustinian School was evidenced not

---

[7] *Ibid.*, 305–306.
[8] Franz Ehrle, S.J., *Der Sentenzenkommentar Peters von Candia, des Pisaner Papstes Alexanders V. Ein Beitrag zur Scheidung der Schulen in der Scholastik des vierzehnten Jahrhunderts und zur Geschichte des Wegestreites*, Franziskanische Studien, Beiheft 9 (Münster, 1925).
[9] *Ibid.*, 106.
[10] *Ibid.*, 138.
[11] *Ibid.*, 250.
[12] *Ibid.*, 251.
[13] *Ibid.*, 264f.
[14] *Ibid.*, 265f.

only by the official decree of the General Chapter, but also—in reality, Ehrle noted (*in Wirklichkeit*)—in the self-consciousness (*im Bewußtsein*) of the Order's theologians.[15] Thus Alphonsus Vargas cited Giles as *doctor noster* and other theologians of the Order as *quidam doctor noster*. Ehrle found convincing proof of the psychological adherence to a specific School of thought in the Augustinian John of Basel's (d. 1392) explicit reference to the *schola nostra*.[16] Ehrle was quick to point out that such references do not signify theological unity in all respects. Gregory of Rimini's theology was clearly distant from that of the conservative Augustinian Thomas of Strassburg (d. 1357). Ehrle then posited the question whether it was not so much theological doctrine that provided the unity of the Augustinian School, as it was a certain "group spirit" (*ein gewisser Korpsgeist*).[17] Although Ehrle did not go so far as to claim this group spirit as a third way of understanding a theological school, his treatment of the Augustinian School came very near doing so. He simply affirmed that before such a question could be answered, far more work in the manuscripts of the Augustinians must be done.[18] It was over a quarter of a century later that members of the Augustinian Order in particular set themselves the task of determining in far greater detail the contours of the Augustinian School, based on thorough study of the manuscripts.

In his pioneering, monographic article published in 1956, Damasus Trapp focused on the academic Augustinianism of the Order's theologians in the fourteenth century. The question Trapp sought to answer was not one of a "group spirit" or of the leading theological doctrines within the Order. Rather, Trapp turned to the question of how Augustine was appropriated by the Order's theologians. Based on extensive and detailed manuscript work, Trapp argued that the *schola Augustiniana moderna* was characterized by a historico-critical attitude toward the citation of sources, combined with an erudition regarding the entire corpus of St. Augustine's works.[19] Trapp pointed to a shift in late medieval Augustinianism from the older Augustinianism of Giles of Rome to the newer Augustinianism initiated by Gregory of Rimini. "Augustinianism of Giles," according to Trapp, ended with Thomas of Strassburg and was characterized by an epistemological focus on the common nature of things (*cognitio rei universalis*).[20] It did not emphasize the historical Augustine as much as did Gregory, the "best Augustine scholar of the Middle Ages."[21] The *schola Augustiniana moderna* gave epistemological priority to individual objects (*cognitio rei particularis*), which went

---

[15] *Ibid.*, 265.

[16] Ehrle also pointed to John of Basel's statement, *ex dictis doctorum nostrorum, faciunt doctores nostri*, as evidence for an Augustinian School; *ibid.*, 266.

[17] *Ibid.*

[18] *Ibid.*

[19] Damasus Trapp, "Augustinian Theology of the Fourteenth Century. Notes on Editions, Marginalia, Opinions and Booklore," *Aug(L)* 6 (1956), 146–274.

[20] *Ibid.*, 181; for Trapp's discussion of the shift in priority from the *cognitio rei universalis* to the *cognitio rei particularis*, see *ibid.*, 147–152.

[21] *Ibid.*, 181.

hand in hand with the pursuit of evidence.[22] The "happy quoters," as Trapp called the modern Augustinians,[23] were no longer satisfied with the anonymous *quidam* quotations, but went to the specific source to cite chapter, title, and author. The call *ad fontes* in the fourteenth century was not only central to Italian literary humanism, but was also a defining characteristic of the modern Augustinian School.[24] This rebirth of Augustinianism culminated, according to Trapp, in John of Basel, who read the *Sentences* at Paris in 1365/66, and later became the General of the Order under the Avignonese Pope Clement VII. Trapp claimed that John of Basel left ". . . a theological legacy which, without exaggeration, might be called a *Petit dictionnaire de la théologie du XIVe siècle*,"[25] referring to his *Sentences* commentary as the "gateway to research and study in Augustinian modern theology."[26]

Trapp decisively reoriented the debate about late medieval Augustinianism to the scholarly reception of Augustine's works. The modern Augustinians, following Gregory of Rimini, simply knew their Augustine better than did other theologians. Hence, the modern Augustinian School was a specific tradition within the Order of Augustinian Hermits. Yet the *schola Augustiniana moderna* was short-lived. It was founded by Gregory of Rimini and ended less than a half-century thereafter: "The death knell of the *Schola Modernorum*," Trapp proclaimed, "rang when the schism destroyed the scholastic standards of Paris by subordinating the academic world, its institutions and its magisterial dignities to political expediency."[27]

Three years after the appearance of Trapp's article, Agostino Trapè sought to broaden the definition of the Augustinian School to include both the Order's spirituality and its theology.[28] Whereas Trapp focused on the detailed manuscript work called for by Ehrle, Trapè turned to explicate the "group spirit" of the Augustinian theologians.

Trapè's point of departure was Giles of Rome's letter of 1292 to all the provinces of the Order, in which Giles exhorted his co-religious to pursue theological studies with the argument that the study of theology, together with the observance of the rule, was the means by which the Order would grow and flourish.[29] According to Trapè, the Order's spirituality and theology formed a grand system of doctrine, which incorporated historical, psychological, and affective dimensions regarding the relationship between

---

[22] See *ibid.*, 149–152, 182–190; *cf.* Trapp, "A Round-Table Discussion of a Parisian OCist-Team and OESA-Team about AD 1350," *RThAM* 51 (1984), 206–222; 215.

[23] Trapp, "Hiltalinger's Augustinian Quotations," *Aug(L)* 4 (1954), 412–449; 427; reprinted in *Via Augustini*, 189–220.

[24] For the relationship between late medieval Augustinianism and humanism, see Trapp, "Hiltalinger's Augustinian Quotations," and Rudolph Arbesmann, *Der Augustiner-Eremitenorden und der Beginn der humanistischen Bewegung* (Würzburg, 1965).

[25] Trapp, "Hiltalinger's Augustinian Quotations," 414.

[26] Trapp, "Augustinian Theology of the Fourteenth Century," 242.

[27] Trapp, "Hiltalinger's Augustinian Quotations," 424.

[28] A. Trapè, "Scuola Teologica e Spiritualia nell'Ordine Agostiniano," in *Sanctus Augustinus Vitae Spiritualis Magister*, 2 vols. (Rome, 1959), 2:5–75.

[29] *Ibid.*, 8f.

humans and the supernatural.[30] The Augustinian School in this sense can be characterized by three unifying factors: the primacy of love, the primacy of grace and the primacy of Christ.[31]

The primacy of love for Trapè was marked by a moderate voluntarism within the Order's theology.[32] From Giles of Rome to Thomas of Strassburg and Alphonsus Vargas (d. 1366), theologians emphasized the will above the intellect, arguing that the will is the more noble faculty.[33] The will was the basis of the innate human desire to see God.[34] Furthermore, the Augustinian theologians defined theology as affective knowledge. It was not the knowledge of the intellect, but that of the heart, leading to union with God, that formed the object of the Augustinians' theology.

Closely connected with the primacy of love was the primacy of grace. A common teaching in the Order regarding infralapsarian predestination and an emphasis on healing grace (*gratia sanans*) can be identified.[35] The fall and its consequences prevent humans from meriting grace without the prevenient grace of God, which yielded a common teaching on the infusion of grace before foreseen merits (*ante praevisa merita*). It was, however, the primacy of Christ that provided the spiritual theology of the Augustinian School with its foundation.[36]

These three characteristics of the Augustinian School were professed by the theologians of the Order precisely because they were emphases to be found in the writings of Augustine himself.[37] Trapè, however, did not ground his portrayal of the Augustinian School on its knowledge of Augustine. Apparently taking the Augustinian School as a given, perhaps in the second sense of theological schools given by Ehrle, Trapè argued that this School was also unified in its theological spirituality. Indeed, the Order's theology cannot be separated from its spirituality. Thus Trapè brought the illusive group spirit posited by Ehrle onto the center stage of discussions of the Augustinian School.

Since his programmatic article published in 1964, Adolar Zumkeller has been the major proponent for a clearly identifiable Augustinian School. Encompassing elements found in Werner, Ehrle, Trapp, and Trapè, Zumkeller emphasized the influence of Giles of Rome on the School's affective theology, and claimed that as a group the Augustinian theologians held to a primacy of love and a primacy of grace.[38] Focusing on the self-perception of the Order's theologians, Zumkeller echoed Ehrle in finding the unity of the school in the terms *doctores nostri* and *schola nostra*.[39] The *Augustinerschule*, which spanned the fourteenth and fifteenth centuries, was a concerted effort

---

[30] *Ibid.*, 9.
[31] *Ibid.*, 12.
[32] *Ibid.*, 13–18.
[33] *Ibid.*, 15.
[34] *Ibid.*, 19–22.
[35] *Ibid.*, 37–45.
[36] *Ibid.*, 48–62.
[37] *Ibid.*, 62–75.
[38] Zumkeller, "Die Augustinerschule," 194.
[39] *Ibid.*, 172f.

of the Augustinian *magistri* to adhere to an Augustinian theology in the tradition of Giles.[40]

Twenty years later, and after further detailed manuscript research on individual Augustinian theologians, focusing on their doctrines of original sin, grace, merit, and justification, Zumkeller refined his position. In his extensive study of the Augustinians at Erfurt, Zumkeller admitted that in his earlier article he over-emphasized the unity of the theological teaching in the Order.[41] Nevertheless, he insisted, the existence of the Augustinian School is not to be denied.[42] Rather than a particular unity of doctrine within the Order, Zumkeller defined the Augustinian School as the self-understanding of the Order's theologians.[43] Following the definitions of theological schools put forth by Ehrle and Karl Rahner,[44] Zumkeller points out that all Augustinian theologians were members of the Order of Saint Augustine and as such felt the responsibility to further his spiritual heritage.[45] The Augustinian School, as the Franciscan, Dominican, or Carmelite Schools, is defined as the sum of the theologians belonging to the Order of Augustinian Hermits who showed in their teaching a more or less strong spiritual relationship and often also a certain dependency on one another. Thus, for Zumkeller the group spirit of the Augustinians formed the foundation of the Augustinian School.[46]

The very thesis, however, of an Augustinian School has been called into question, and not only by the concept of a general late medieval *Frömmigkeitstheologie*.[47] Making a sharp distinction between members of the Order (*Ordensbrüder*) and the Order's teaching tradition (*Lehrrichtung*), William J. Courtenay has shown that such terms as *magistri nostri*, *doctores nostri*, *magister meus*, and the like cannot be used to delineate schools of thought.[48] Rather, such designations often were employed in the same fashion as scholars today refer to "my esteemed colleague."[49] Marsilius of Inghen, for example, referred to Gregory of Rimini as "our teacher" (*frater magister noster Gregorius*).[50] The same criticism is valid for *schola nostra*, which can be taken as reference to the academic context rather than to a specific theological school. Such

---

[40] *Ibid.*, 171 and *passim*.

[41] See, Zumkeller, *Erbsünde, Gnade, Rechtfertigung und Verdienst nach der Lehre der Erfurter Augustinertheologen des Spätmittelalters* (Würzburg, 1984), 437–439.

[42] *Ibid.*, 439.

[43] *Ibid.*, 439–440. Zumkeller had stated his revised position on the Augustinian school already in 1980; see Zumkeller, "Augustinerschule," in *LexMA* I:1222–1223.

[44] See Zumkeller, *Erbsünde*, 440.

[45] *Ibid.*, 441.

[46] *Ibid.*, 1.

[47] See above, Chapter Four.

[48] See William J. Courtenay, "Augustinianism at Oxford in the Fourteenth Century," *Aug(L)* 30 (1980), 58–70; see also Courtenay, *Schools and Scholars in Fourteenth Century England* (Princeton, 1987), 171ff.

[49] William J. Courtenay, "Marsilius von Inghen (d. 1396) als Heidelberger Theologe," *Heidelberger Jahrbücher* 32 (1988), 26–42; 28f.

[50] *Ibid.*, 29. Further, Courtenay identified the *Marsilius noster* cited by the Augustinian Angelus Dobelinus as Marsilius of Inghen, rather than Angelus' fellow Augustinian Luigi Marsili, as was posited by Damasus Trapp; *ibid.*, 33.

terms were academic formulas, not terms of theological demarcation. This is supported by the fact that the terms *magistri vestri* or *schola vestra* are not to be found.[51] Thus the existence of an Augustinian School cannot be based on John of Basel's reference to *schola nostra*. Courtenay calls for the clear distinction between the new Augustinianism—doctrinally understood, encompassing theology, philosophy and political theory—and the Augustinian School. The members of the Augustinian Order may or may not have been Augustinian, and there certainly were some theologians who unmistakably were Augustinian (such as Bradwardine) although they did not belong to the OESA.[52]

Courtenay's argument is persuasive and should caution against accepting every reference to a *doctor noster* or a *schola nostra* as conclusive evidence of a unified school. Nevertheless, even if such terms were academic formulas, it does not follow that they could not also be used as school associations, given Zumkeller's definition. When Marsilius of Inghen referred to Gregory of Rimini as "our teacher," the term very possibly had different connotations from the instances when Augustinians designated a fellow Augustinian as *magister noster*. Moreover, Thomas of Strassburg did use the term *doctor tuus*, albeit indirectly in quoting the Franciscan Peter Aureolus. According to Thomas, Aureolus referred to Giles as *doctor tuus*, whom Thomas then defended, designating Giles as *doctor noster*. Aureolus' argument against Giles was invalid because neither Giles nor his *discipuli* adhered to the position attributed to him by the Franciscan: Aureolus established nothing *contra nos*.[53] This case demonstrates that *doctor noster* could signify a self-conscious adherence to the Augustinian School when used by an Augustinian to refer to an Augustinian, and particularly to Giles.

If one takes the term Augustinian School as referring to a strict adherence to a unified theological teaching within the Order, one will look for it in vain. Scholarship of the past thirty years has demonstrated the diversity of late medieval thought. Just as one can no longer legitimately set the "nominalists" over against the "Augustinians,"[54] so one can no longer speak

---

[51] *Ibid.*, 30; see also Courtenay, *Schools and Scholars*, 171ff and 307–324.

[52] Courtenay, *Schools and Scholars*, 305–324; esp. 310–311. Courtenay asserts: "It would also be helpful if we did not use the term 'Augustinianism' to describe the thought of theologians who belonged to the mendicant order known as the Augustinian hermits or Austin Friars, as Adolar Zumkeller, Damasus Trapp, and others have done." *Ibid.*, 310. Courtenay is correct to list Zumkeller here, but Trapp never made such an association; in fact, he argued the opposite: "Augustinianism should not be looked at as belonging to the exclusive domain of any one group of scholars." Trapp, "A Round-Table Discussion," 208.

[53] Thom.Arg. 1 *Sent.* 20,1,1, fol. 78ʳ, as cited by Joseph L Shannon, *Good Works and Predestination According to Thomas of Strassburg, O.S.A.* (Baltimore, 1940), 16. The influence of Giles is also evidenced by Thomas' reference to *nostri iuniores Doctores, volentes salvare venerabilem Doctorem nostrum Aegidium*, Shannon, *Good Works*, 15.

[54] See William J. Courtenay, "Augustine and Nominalism," in *Saint Augustine and his Influence in the Middle Ages*, ed. Edward B. King and Jacqueline T. Schaefer (Sewanee, TN, 1988), 91–97.

of a unified theological Augustinianism inside—or outside—the Augustinian Order in the later Middle Ages. Continued research in tracing the transmission and influence of Giles and Gregory in the Augustinian Order as well as detailed analysis of the knowledge and reception of Augustine's works needs to be pursued, but the unity of late medieval Augustinianism will not be found by such endeavors. Late medieval Augustinianism as an identifiable, unified phenomenon is to be discerned in the realm of the Order's religious life, rather than in further refinements of the philosophy and theology of Augustinian theologians.

Closely related to the debates over the existence and characteristics of an Augustinian School has been a line of research focusing on the relationship between late medieval Augustinianism and Martin Luther. Indeed, these two historiographical traditions have often overlapped; they have been so closely intertwined that it is often difficult to separate the one from the other, as is clear in the case of Werner and Ehrle. Thus Zumkeller concluded his study of the Erfurt Augustinians by asserting that their theology cannot be labeled as Ockhamistic. This provided Zumkeller with evidence of the distance separating the Augustinian School from Luther.[55] Nevertheless, a distinction can be discerned between those scholars who have closely identified late medieval Augustinianism with the Augustinian School defined as the Order's theology, and those who have described late medieval Augustinianism as a revival of anti-Pelagianism. For the latter especially, the debate has turned on the degree to which anti-Pelagianism was transmitted to Luther by the theologians of his own Order.

B. *Luther and Late Medieval Augustinianism*

Four years before the appearance of Werner's monograph on late medieval Augustinianism, Theodor Kolde published a detailed study of Johannes von Staupitz and the German Augustinians.[56] As he clearly outlined in his introduction, Kolde's goal was to portray the theological and religious tradition in which Luther developed to combat Luther-scholars who lacked the courage to see Luther as other than a new phenomenon.[57]

Kolde argued that neither in the Augustinian Order in general, nor in the theology of Staupitz in particular, is an Augustinianism to be found. It

---

[55] Zumkeller, *Erbsünde*, 503–504. Zumkeller, however, does not deny that Luther was influenced by his Order, particularly with regard to the critique of Aristotle; see, *Erbsünde*, 461–502. Much of this discussion is a restatement of two earlier articles: "Die Augustinertheologen Simon Fidati von Cascia und Hugolin von Orvieto und Martin Luthers Kritik an Aristoteles," *ARG* 54 (1963), 15–37; and, "Martin Luther und sein Orden," *AAug.* 25 (1962), 254–290. In effect, one can summarize Zumkeller's position by saying that what was "good" in Luther, Luther received from the Order; what was "bad," is to be attributed to Luther himself.

[56] Th. Kolde, *Die deutsche Augustiner-Congregation und Johann von Staupitz. Ein Beitrag zur Ordens und Reformationsgeschichte* (Gotha, 1879).

[57] *Ibid.*, v.

was Staupitz's personal influence that contributed to Luther's development.[58] Yet the Augustinian Order contributed significantly to the spread of the Reformation. Indeed, the Order's preachers should be seen as the carriers of evangelical teaching, particularly in northern Germany.[59]

Kolde based his thesis on a distinction regarding the term Augustinian. On the one hand he pointed to an Augustinianism resulting from close adherence to the writings of Augustine, and therefore (sic!), to a clear evangelical doctrine of grace. In this light, there were no traces of Augustinianism in the theology of late medieval Augustinian theologians. On the other hand, the Order was genuinely Augustinian, when 'Augustinian' is understood as following the ecclesiology and pastoral concerns of the Order's founder.[60]

Two points are to be noted here. First, Kolde was explicit that Augustinianism was a theologically defined term based on an evangelical understanding of grace. Second, such a definition was not the only valid means of identifying Augustinianism. The Augustinianism of the Augustinian Order was a genuine Augustinianism, even though it was not an Augustinianism in the evangelical theological sense. Unfortunately, Kolde's distinction between the varied meanings of the term Augustinian became blurred and even lost in twentieth-century scholarship.

At the turn of the century Carl Stange published two articles in which he forcefully argued that Luther's membership in the Augustinian Order was of importance for his theological development.[61] Stange, as Werner, Ehrle, and Zumkeller, emphasized the importance of the Order's mandate for their theologians to teach according to the doctrines of Giles of Rome. In this light, he claimed that the theology of the later Middle Ages should be described as a theology of Orders.[62] Even though the Order's tradition stemming from Giles was interrupted by Gregory of Rimini—following Werner—Stange saw a resurgence of 'Aegidianism' (Giles of Rome = Aegidius Romanus) in the later fifteenth century. It was, however, the Gregorian tradition in the Order that was determining for Luther's development.[63]

Stange's thesis of late medieval theology as a theology of Orders was countered shortly thereafter by Heinrich Hermelink, who argued that the theology of the later Middle Ages is better described as a theology of universities.[64] Yet the position that Luther was indebted to the theology of his Order, and particularly to the Gregorian line, was energetically appropriated by the ex-Dominican, Alphons Victor Müller.[65] Müller, arguing in fierce polemic against Heinrich Denifle's position that Luther was simply

---

[58] *Ibid.*, 250f.
[59] *Ibid.*, 402.
[60] *Ibid.*, 36–38.
[61] Stange, "Über Luthers Beziehungen zur Theologie seines Ordens," *NKZ* 11 (1900), 574–595; 575; *idem*, "Luther über Gregor von Rimini," *NKZ* 13 (1902), 721–727; *cf.* Stange, *Studien zur Theologie Luthers* (Gütersloh, 1928).
[62] Stange, "Über Luthers Beziehungen zur Theologie seines Ordens," 575.
[63] *Ibid.*, 580–581.
[64] Hermelink, *Die theologische Fakultät in Tübingen vor der Reformation, 1477–1534* (Stuttgart, 1906); see especially, 95f.
[65] A.V. Müller, *Luthers theologische Quellen* (Giessen, 1912).

ignorant of the medieval theological tradition,[66] claimed to have identified a specific Augustinian—and early evangelical!—tradition within the Augustinian Order, represented not only by Gregory of Rimini, but also by Simon Fidati of Cascia, Hugolino of Orvieto, Augustinus Favaroni, Jacob Pérez of Valencia and Johannes Hoffmeister.

Müller's thesis was sharply attacked by Catholics and Protestants alike.[67] A part of his thesis was nevertheless adopted by Eduard Stakemeier, who argued that the late medieval Augustinian tradition continued not in Luther and the Reformation, but in Jerome Seripando and the Augustinian theologians at the Council of Trent.[68] Moreover, Heiko Oberman found in Müller's thesis poignant points of departure for further research, divorced from the overtly polemical overtones of the original.[69]

Oberman described a broad movement in late medieval thought, which he named the Augustinian Renaissance. Such a renaissance encompassed theologians of widely diverse orientations, from the realist Thomas Bradwardine to the nominalist Gregory of Rimini. For Oberman the campaign against the *pelagiani moderni* gave rise to a renewed emphasis on Augustine's doctrine of grace and predestination. The influence of this renaissance can be traced within the Augustinian Order through such theologians as Gregory of Rimini, Simon Fidati of Cascia, Hugolino of Orvieto, and Johannes von Staupitz. Outside the Order we find evidence of the Augustinian Renaissance in the works not only of the fourteenth-century secular theologian Bradwardine, but also in the later fifteenth century in the writings of Wendelin Steinbach, the student of Gabriel Biel, and in the works of Andreas Karlstadt in the early sixteenth century. Having instigated an intense academic interest in the writings of Augustine, and particularly the anti-Pelagian treatises, the Augustinian Renaissance culminated in the Amerbach edition of Augustine's works. There was no direct line, however, from the late medieval Augustinian Renaissance to Luther's Reformation theology. Nevertheless, the *schola Augustiniana moderna*, "initiated by Gregory of Rimini, reflected by Hugolin of Orvieto, apparently spiritually alive in the Erfurt Augustinian monastery, and transformed into a pastoral reform-theology by Staupitz," should be seen "as the *occasio proxima*—not *causa!*—for the inception of the *theologia vera* at Wittenberg."[70] In Oberman's thesis we hear echoes not only of Müller,

---

[66] See Heinrich Denifle, O.P., *Luther und Luthertum in der ersten Entwicklung*, 2 vols. (Mainz, 1904–1909).

[67] See Hubert Jedin, *A History of the Council of Trent. The First Sessions at Trent*, trans., Ernest Graf, O.S.A. (Edinburgh, 1961), 2:258; Gordon Rupp, *The Righteousness of God* (London, 1953), 140.

[68] Stakemeier, *Der Kampf um Augustin auf dem Tridentinum* (Paderborn, 1937).

[69] See Heiko A. Oberman, "Headwaters of the Reformation: Initia Lutheri—Initia Reformationis," in Heiko A. Oberman, *The Dawn of the Reformation. Essays in Late Medieval and Early Reformation Thought* (Edinburgh 1986), 39–83; 69ff.

[70] Oberman, "Headwaters," 82; *cf. idem, Werden und Wertung der Reformation. Vom Wegestreit zum Glaubenskampf* (Tübingen, 1977; 2nd ed. Tübingen, 1979), 82–140. Oberman's position regarding the lack of direct influence between a rebirth of Augustinianism in the later Middle Ages and the theology of Luther was already put forth in his dissertation, *Archbishop Thomas Bradwardine*, (as in note 1 above).

but also of Kolde and Trapp. In addition, the hues on Stange's canvas highlighting the importance of Gregory of Rimini for Luther's development are painted anew by Oberman in bright colors and with broad strokes in his emphasis on the significance of the *via Gregorii* at Wittenberg, according to which Luther was to teach by statute.[71] Yet at precisely this point Oberman met his fiercest challengers.

Leif Grane has denied the significance of late medieval Augustinianism, and of the *via Gregorii* in particular, for Luther's development. His argument is based on the fact that conclusive, hard evidence that Luther was acquainted with Gregory's works before the Leipzig Debate (1519) is lacking.[72] From a close reading of Luther's early writings, to explain genetically Luther's theology,[73] Grane has argued that it was not the Augustine of the Order, but rather it was Augustine as the Pauline exegete whom Luther found and understood in the anti-Pelagian writings, which he intensively and energetically studied beginning with his lectures on Romans.[74]

With Grane, the question of how late medieval Augustinianism should be defined has been left far behind; the central issue is Luther, or rather, Luther's theology. Yet at stake in this debate is far more than the problem of determining precisely when Luther became acquainted with Gregory of Rimini. As the continuation of the exchange between Grane and Oberman showed, the question of Luther and late medieval Augustinianism is inseparably bound with a much broader issue concerning the very nature of historical and of historical-theological research.

In 1977 Oberman published a programmatic article in which he responded to Grane's position in *Modus loquendi theologicus*.[75] According to Oberman, Grane's book was an example of the dangers of the theological Luther renaissance; it further entrenched traditional Luther scholarship by divorcing Luther from his historical context.[76]

---

[71] Oberman, *Werden und Wertung*, 90f.

[72] Grane, "Gregor von Rimini und Luthers Leipziger Disputation," *Studia Theologica* 22 (1968), 29–49; 30ff; see also *idem*, "Divus Paulus et S. Augustinus, Interpres eius fidelissimus. Über Luthers Verhältnis zu Augustin," in *Festschrift für Ernst Fuchs*, ed., G. Ebeling, E. Jüngel, and G. Schunack (Tübingen, 1973), 133–146; *idem, Modus loquendi theologicus. Luthers Kampf um die Erneuerung der Theologie (1515–1518)* (Leiden, 1975).

[73] Grane, *Modus Loquendi*, 12.

[74] Grane, *Modus loquendi*, 26. In this context, one can point to the work of A. Hamel, *Der junge Luther und Augustin*. Hamel thoroughly analyzed Luther's use of Augustine from his early marginalia on Lombard and Augustine through his Commentary on Hebrews of 1517/1518. His work provides the point of departure for all further research on Luther's knowledge and use of Augustine's works themselves. Hamel acknowledged the OESA as an important conduit of Augustine for Luther, but does not focus or treat the extent to which Luther was the heir of a 'late medieval Augustinianism' present within his Order, and therefore I have not treated him separately in this historiographical survey.

[75] Oberman, "Reformation: Epoche oder Episode," *ARG* 68 (1977), 56–109.

[76] The section of Oberman's article in which he attacked Grane's position was given the subtitle: "Lutherrenaissance als Gefährdung des historischen Luther," Oberman, "Reformation: Epoche oder Episode," 88–109.

Grane's rebuttal was published together with Oberman's article.[77] According to Grane, Oberman misunderstood his intentions. Grane was not trying to explain Luther and the entire Reformation; rather, he sought to describe Luther's internal theological development as it could be discerned from the texts themselves, on methodologically determined grounds.[78] He intended his work for theologians and claimed that he never denied the validity of other forms of research.[79] When it came to Gregory and Luther, Grane claimed to have left the question open; he simply stressed that no certain evidence can be brought forth as conclusive proof.[80] Thus the scholar must rely on what is certain, and that, for Grane, is Luther's texts. In appealing for his method of research not to be overlooked, Grane concluded by arguing that "Reformation research, as much as historical portrayals of the Reformation period, needs textual analysis *and* synthesis."[81] In contrast, Oberman concluded his article with the challenge to rehistoricize Luther research so that "theology will be taken into account as an irreducible *historical* factor."[82] Whereas Grane argued for the importance of traditional, historical-theological explication of Luther's texts, Oberman crusaded for giving the history of theology a historical importance beyond the circles of theologians.

The Oberman-Grane debate highlights two points of particular concern. First, the issue of Augustine's heritage has implications surpassing the characterization and definition of late medieval Augustinianism as a subdivision of late medieval intellectual history. Not only is it of primary importance for conceptions and interpretations of the Reformation, but it also carries implicit— and at times explicit—overtones of how history should be done in the first place. Second, the question of the contours and definition of late medieval Augustinianism has been inextricably connected with theological concerns. Grane is clear that his interest is the internal development of Luther's theology, whereby a late medieval Augustinian School would have importance only if concrete, conclusive evidence could be uncovered to prove its influence on Luther's texts; evidence that Grane finds lacking. Oberman fought a two-front battle. On the eastern front he combated traditional Luther scholars who are content to remain within the closed world of historical theology. On the western front, Oberman stood against historians who tend to marginalize theology to the realm of historical insignificance. He argued for the *historical* importance of theology to be sure, but likewise it is only the historical context that brings to light Luther's *theology*. Whereas Grane is a historical theologian, Oberman appears as a historian of theology in broad terms.

---

[77] Grane, "Kritische Berichte. Lutherforschung und Geistesgeschichte. Auseinandersetzung mit Heiko A. Oberman," *ARG* 68 (1977), 302–315.
[78] *Ibid.*, 303.
[79] *Ibid.*, 305–306.
[80] *Ibid.*, 310.
[81] "Sowohl die Reformations*forschung* als auch die Geschichts*schreibung* des Reformationszeitalters brauchen Textanalysen *und* Synthesen." *Ibid.*, 314.
[82] "... daß die Theologie berücksichtigt wird als irreduzibler *historischer* Faktor in dem *vielfältigen* Kräftespiel, das von Erich Hassinger bezeichnet wurde als 'das Werden des neuzeitlichen Europa.'" Oberman, "Reformation: Epoche oder Episode," 109.

The goal of both is to bring to light Luther's uniqueness: Grane, by ignoring Luther's predecessors, and Oberman by arguing that only in context of the preceding tradition does Luther's genuine, that is historical, uniqueness come into focus.[83] Finally, the Oberman-Grane debate has had repercussions extending beyond the original participants: the battle lines have been drawn.

In 1975 David Steinmetz supported Grane's position over against Oberman in an article echoed in his 1980 study of Luther and Staupitz.[84] Steinmetz detected five different meanings of how the term 'Augustinian' has been used. First, Augustinian can be used to describe the theology of the West in general; second, Augustinian can be applied to the theology of the Augustinian Order; third, a particular party within the Augustinian Order can be labeled Augustinian; fourth, Augustinian has been used to describe the "right wing" of late medieval theology; and fifth, Augustinian has appeared as the counter-position to Pelagianism.[85]

Steinmetz takes as his point of departure the thesis that Staupitz was the mediator of the *via Gregorii* to Luther.[86] He points out that although one can find similarities between Staupitz and Gregory, there are many differences as well. Thus Staupitz appears as "no disciple of Gregory of Rimini, though he would cite him if he knew him better."[87] In addition, Staupitz is more closely associated with the "older Augustinian School" than he is with the *schola Augustiniana moderna* of Gregory. It was not an Augustinian tradition within the Order that led Staupitz to his Augustinian theology, but rather a reading of Augustine's works themselves. If parallels can be found between Staupitz and the likes of Augustinus Favaroni, this does not prove influence, but simple similarity: it points to the fact that there was a common source. The Augustinian elements in Staupitz's theology can be accounted for by appealing to Augustine himself, rather than to a tradition within the Order. Staupitz certainly exerted a major influence on Luther's early development, but it was not one that included transmission of the *via Gregorii*.[88]

In his insistence that parallels do not prove influence, but simply point to similarities, Steinmetz followed Grane's method of focusing on the texts themselves without appealing to the historical context unless evidently merited. Concrete proof of the influence of the *via Gregorii* is lacking, and therefore another explanation of Luther's development is called for.

The year following Steinmetz's work on Luther and Staupitz, Manfred Schulze published the first thorough study of the *via Gregorii*.[89] Schulze com-

---

[83] As early as his *Forerunners of the Reformation* (1966; reprint: Philadelphia, 1981), 39, Oberman argued for a shift in research from a causal to a contextual reading of intellectual history.

[84] Steinmetz, "Luther and the Late Medieval Augustinians: Another Look," *CTM* 44 (1975), 245–260; idem, *Luther and Staupitz*, 13–27.

[85] Steinmetz, *Luther and Staupitz*, 13–16.

[86] Ibid., 27.

[87] Ibid., 28.

[88] Ibid., 27–34.

[89] Manfred Schulze, "Via Gregorii in Forschung und Quellen," in *Gregor von Rimini. Werk und Wirkung bis zur Reformation*, ed. H.A. Oberman, SuR 20 (Berlin/New York, 1981), 1–126.

prehensively surveyed both the sources pertinent to Luther's place within the *via Gregorii*, and the secondary literature on the subject. Based on the available evidence, Schulze argued that Steinmetz's reduction of the data to the categories of influence and similarities is insufficient. There is another category that particularly in the case of the *via Gregorii* must not be overlooked: environment.[90] "If Gregory of Rimini had proven to be a forgotten author in the fifteenth and early sixteenth centuries," Schulze summarized, "and if Augustinian theology had been ignored as long out of date by this time, then there would be no real cause to deal seriously with Gregory's importance for Wittenberg. The *via Gregorii* would in fact be a scribal error in the statutes."[91] Schulze finds Grane's and Steinmetz's solution that Augustine, rather than an Augustinian tradition, was the link between Gregory and Luther to be too simple.[92] The contextual evidence is too strong to ignore.

After Schulze's attempt to establish the *via Gregorii* contextually, Markus Wriedt countered by returning to a textual analysis, rejecting the influence of Gregory on Staupitz.[93] Wriedt analyzed the various passages of Staupitz's *Libellus de Exsecutione Aeternae Praedestinationis* where the editors noted parallels to Gregory of Rimini.[94] He came to the same conclusion as Steinmetz: parallels do not prove influence, but point to a common source or sources.[95] Wriedt argued that the traditional scholastic schools are insufficient for describing Staupitz's theology, and certainly cannot provide the answer to the transmission of an Augustinian tradition within the Order to Luther via Staupitz.[96] Staupitz should be considered as promoting a late medieval pastoral theology (*Frömmigkeitstheologie*; here Wriedt explicitly drew on Hamm)

---

[90] *Ibid.*, 125.
[91] "Wenn sich uns Gregor von Rimini im 15. und beginnenden 16. Jahrhundert als vergessener Autor erwiesen hätte und die Augustintheologie als längst überholt zu dieser Zeit übergegangen worden wäre, dann bestände in der Tat kein Anlass, ernsthaft mit Gregors Bedeutung für Wittenberg zu rechnen. Die *via Gregorii* wäre tatsächlich ein Schreibfehler in den Statuten." *Ibid.*, 125. It remains incomprehensible that Christopher Ocker, seemingly referring to this passage, could claim that Schulze "has shown that the *via Gregorii* had suffered a kind of chronological lapse. Gregory, at the end of the fifteenth century, was a rediscovered theologian. He had been forgotten." Ocker, "Augustinianism in Fourteenth-Century Theology," *Augustinian Studies* 18 (1987), 81–106; 84 and 84, n. 14 (endnote, found on page 98). *Cf.* "Der 'Doctor modernus' Gregor von Rimini wird noch im Jahre 1517 der Tübinger Schule zum herausfordernden Gegner." Schulze, *Via Gregorii*, 100.
[92] Schulze, *Via Gregorii*, 125–126.
[93] Markus Wriedt, "Via Guilelmi—Via Gregorii: Zur Frage einer Augustinerschule im Gefolge Gregors von Rimini under besonderer Berücksichtigung Johannes von Staupitz," in *Deutschland und Europa in der Neuzeit. Festschrift für Karl Otmar Freiherr von Aretin zum 65. Geburtstag*, ed. Ralph Melville, Claus Scharg, Martin Vogt, and Ulrich Wengenroth, VIEG 134 (Mainz, 1988), 111–131; idem, *Gnade und Erwählung. Eine Untersuchung zu Johann von Staupitz und Martin Luther*, VIEG 141 (Mainz, 1991).
[94] *Ibid.*, 217–221.
[95] *Ibid.*, 221.
[96] *Ibid.*, 224.

and thus should be approached as an eclectic.[97] For Wriedt, as for Steinmetz, Staupitz was not the conduit of the *via Gregorii* but the religious personality and advisor who influenced Luther, a position that has proven to be the view of the majority.

C. *Overview*

Reflecting on the preceding century of scholarship concerned with late medieval Augustinianism, four points come to light. First, during the course of the twentieth century the definition of late medieval Augustinianism became inextricably intertwined with theological Augustinianism. The distinctions drawn last century by both Kolde and Werner between two different definitions of 'Augustinian' in the former case and between the Augustinian School and a renewed anti-Pelagianism in the latter, became lost. This is clearly seen in Schulze's definition of the Augustinianism of the modern Augustinian School based exclusively on the anti-Pelagian Augustine.[98] The question here is not whether Gregory of Rimini viewed the anti-Pelagian Augustine as the authentic Augustine, but rather whether Gregory and the anti-Pelagian Augustine can be taken as the only genuine Augustinian representatives.

Second, research on late medieval Augustinianism must be conducted independently from the question of the relationship between late medieval Augustinianism and Martin Luther. For a century Luther has provided the catalyst for scholarship that has broadened and deepened the knowledge of Augustine's heritage. Yet conclusive proof of Luther's dependence on or independence from the tradition(s) of his Order has lain beyond the grasp of scholars working intensively on all aspects of the question. The extent to which Luther was influenced by the likes of Gregory of Rimini, Hugolino of Orvieto, or Simon Fidati of Cascia remains in the realm of speculation and theological debate.[99] This assertion, however, has a corollary: before the question of Luther and late medieval Augustinianism can be answered with greater probability than is now possible, we must first learn far more about late medieval Augustinianism.

Third, the attempt to chart the theology of late medieval Augustinianism has centered around the examination of *Sentences* commentaries of the Augustinian theologians at the universities. Little attention has been paid to the teaching in the other schools of the Order. Yet the instruction in the diverse schools of the Order should not be seen as only preparatory to higher degrees, or categorized simply as spiritual teaching. The *studia* trained the preachers and priests of the Order. Few friars reached the pinnacle of the Augustinian educational system. The theological teaching of the majority of the Order's preachers and teachers—those who did not become masters—conducted in the majority of the Order's schools, is more

---

[97] *Ibid.*, 224–227.
[98] *Ibid.*, 63.
[99] See Zumkeller, *Erbsünde*, 481f and 492–503.

representative of the Order's theology than are the doctrines of the relatively few masters of theology in Paris and Oxford.

And finally, the problem of definition has never been solved. Whereas Zumkeller, following in the tradition of Werner and Ehrle, has argued for the importance of the Augustinian School, the debate has most often centered around the degree to which an anti-Pelagian Augustinianism was communicated to Luther by his Order. The distinctions between the Augustinian School, the *schola Augustiniana moderna*, the Augustinian Renaissance, and the *via Gregorii* have not always been made and have often merged into a nebulous concept of Augustine's heritage. Steinmetz clearly delineated some of the various possible meanings of the term Augustinian, but the majority of the recent debate has focused primarily on his third and fifth senses, including Steinmetz's own contribution. The broader conception of late medieval Augustinianism, as it was still present in the perspectives of Werner and Kolde, has been increasingly narrowed, whereby those parts of the tradition that have not been brought into the discussion about the line leading to Luther have been marginalized, or even ignored. In this light, new conceptions are needed to reinvigorate the field of research that has become stale with theological debate.

This is all the more valid given the fact that the cohesion of Augustine's religion in the later Middle Ages, or the lack thereof, poses problems and challenges. Even if there was a religion-specific Augustinian platform in the fourteenth century formed by the Order's religious identity, and espousing an Order-specific theology, this can not be taken as proof that later members of the Order, such as Johannes von Paltz and Johannes Staupitz, consciously shared this identity and its theology. As Hamm has convincingly shown, Jean Gerson, not Jordan of Quedlinburg, was indeed the source for Paltz.[100] Moreover, Hamm has noted a rapid decline in each traditional type of scholastic question-literature in the later period.[101] Whereas in the fourteenth century, Thomas of Strassburg, Hugolino of Orvieto, Johannes Klenkok, John of Basel and Angelus Dobelinus produced surviving commentaries on all four books of the *Sentences*, from fifteenth-century Augustinians only Jacques le Grand and Augustinus Favaroni left extant works on all of Lombard. And whereas extensive commentaries on the first or first two books of Lombard have survived from Gregory of Rimini and Alphonsus Vargas, in the fifteenth century only William Becchi commented on Book One of the *Sentences*, although commentaries on Book Four are extant from Andreas de Saxonia, Gottschalk Hollen and a frater Nicholas. On the qualitative side this points to a shift in interests corresponding to Hamm's portrayal

---

[100] See Hamm, *Frömmigkeitstheologie*, 202; and volume two of the trilogy, *The Failed Reformation*.

[101] "So wurde in den letzten Jahrzehnten vor der Reformation kaum noch ein vollständiger Sentenzenkommentar ausgearbeitet. Und auch die Zeit der spekulativ-diskursiven Summen, Quodlibeta oder Quaestiones disputatae neigt sich ihrem Ende zu. Die Vertreter einer rein akademischen, streng scholastichen Theologie treten literarisch fast nicht mehr in Erscheinung..." Hamm, *Frömmigkeitstheologie*, 179.

of late medieval pastoral theology (*Frömmigkeitstheologie*) from epistemological and soteriological questions to issues concerning ecclesiology and the sacraments, suggested as well by the alternative title of Hollen's commentary: *Tractatus de sacramentis*. Based on the works that survive, Lombard's text was apparently of less importance for the fifteenth-century Augustinians than was the Apocalypse, on which there are extant commentaries from Augustinus Favaroni, Bertold of Regensburg, Hermanus de Mindelheim and Johannes Zacharie.[102] This bibliographical data indicates a shift of interests in the Order away from the traditional scholastic theological literature of the fourteenth century as the sons of Augustine entered the fifteenth.[103]

Furthermore, changes in the Order's educational system itself are evident. In the fourteenth century, nineteen years of study were required for an Augustinian to attain the doctorate in theology. In the fifteenth century, a different story is to be told. Johannes Dorsten, for example, began his theological studies in 1459 and received the doctorate six years later;[104] Paltz took only two years to be promoted to the *magisterium*;[105] and Martin Luther became a doctor of theology only six years after having entered the Order. Moreover, as Hamm has noted, all the leading Augustinian doctors of theology at Erfurt in the second half of the fifteenth and early sixteenth century entered the Order as masters of arts.[106] Their theological training began simultaneously with their becoming Augustinians. In other words, the Augustinian program of indoctrination had minimal influence on the intellectual formation of the very scholars who became its university theologians. The later medieval Augustinians at Erfurt had become theologians of the Order before they became seasoned members of the Order. Even if they exhibited dedication towards the Augustinian Observance, they were adopted sons of the Order who had been reared by other parents before becoming the heirs of the Order's venerable tradition at Erfurt. The earlier conscious effort to inculcate the brothers with the *religio Augustini* from the very beginning of their education played little or no part in the training of these later Augustinians.

Closely associated with the re-alignment of *Sentences* commentaries, the lessening of requirements and the quick promotion of "converts,"[107] was a depreciation in the office of lector itself. Ypma has noted that during the fifteenth century the designation of lector was no longer exclusively academic. There was a growing tendency to confer the lector's title as an honorary reward for service.[108] In the fourteenth century there is ample evidence for the importance of the office of lector. Bypassing the stringent requirements for, and control of, the title by granting the degree as an honorary appellation signifies a break-down in the Order's educational system analogous

---

[102] See Chapter Six.
[103] See Hamm, *Frömmigkeitstheologie*, 179f.
[104] *Ibid.*, 60f.
[105] *Ibid.*, 51f.
[106] *Ibid.*, 59.
[107] *Ibid.*
[108] Ypma, "La promotion au Lectorat," 412–414.

to the quick promotion of doctors. The lectors had been the theological "watch dogs" of the Order. What were the consequences when the "watch dogs" became "show dogs"? With the devaluation of the degree of lector, the masters had to "step down" to fill the gap, as seen in the shift of interests indicated by the extant theological literature and the lessening of requirements for the doctorate, thus abandoning their theological base.

What happened to the theology of the Augustinian *studia*? Did the spiritual knowledge cultivated and disseminated in the context of the Augustinian religious identity somehow dissipate with the rise of the Observant movement after the wide-spread shock of the Schism?[109] Or in the on-going attempt to religionize society did members of the Order lose sight of the need to religionize themselves? Was there a difference between the mendicant theology of the Order in the fourteenth century with its emphasis on the combination of ethics and erudition and the *Frömmigkeitstheologie* upholding a similar axiom on the eve of the Reformation?[110] What had happened to the three strategies for effecting the platform, namely, regulation, indoctrination, and religionization, combining to ensure conformity with the Order's religious identity? In the age of Schism, Observance, Conciliarism, decentralization, national Churches, papal pretensions, European wide political maneuvering, rising popular devotion, heresy, increasing anti-Judaism, provincialization, rising anti-clericalism, and increasing lay piety, what happened to the Augustinian platform when it was no longer only the base for, but also the object of, reform?[111] The answer to such questions are to be found in turning from the historigraphical to the historical definition of late medieval Augustinianism as the understanding of living the Augustinian life in imitation of Augustine.

D. *Perspectives and Points of Departure*

Pater Noster, Preceptor Noster, and *Sapiens Architechtor Ecclesie*: these were the three symbols that combined to form the ideological matrix of late medieval Augustinianism. Yet from the historical perspective there was no such 'thing' as 'late medieval Augustinianism'. Late medieval Augustinianism is a creation

---

[109] For the Augustinian Observance, including the emphasis on *religio*, see Ralph Weinbrenner, *Klosterreform*. *Cf.* Trapp's view of the end of the *schola Augustiniana Moderna* marked by the Schism; see Trapp, "Hiltalinger's Augustinian Quotations," in *Via Augustini*, 198–199.

[110] Referring to Andreas Proles and Paltz, Weinbrenner writes: "Das fromme Leben, das er [Proles] selbst führte, hatte zum größten Teil transitiven Charakter. Es war ein Leben für das fromme Leben seiner Gemeinschaft. An den würdigen Worten des Paltz ist bemerkenswert, daß der inoffizielle Doktorgrad, den 'viele' dem Lektor der heiligen Theologie zuerkennen möchten, nicht nur durch die wissenschaftlichen Fähigkeiten, sondern ebenso durch die Frömmigkeit und den *splendor eloquentiae* begründet wird. Tatsächlich sieht Paltz einen weitgehenden Zusammenhang zwischen akademischer Bildung und persönlichem Lebenswandel." Weinbrenner, *Klosterreform*, 65. As here formulated, the same could be said with equal validity for the educational endeavor of the Order in the early fourteenth century; see Chapter Four.

[111] These are questions I will be addressing explicitly in vol. 2, *The Failed Reformation*.

of scholars attempting to describe, define, and control St. Augustine's influence in the later Middle Ages. As seen detailed above, much of the debate concerning Augustine's late medieval heritage and its relationship to the emergence of Reformation theology has been determined by theological understandings of the term 'Augustinian'. When one approaches the extant texts of the later Middle Ages with a theologically determined conception of what is and what is not 'Augustinianism,' one can then rather easily apply the definition to the theology contained in particular texts as either fitting within or without the category. This holds true regardless of the *a priori* definition employed. The fallacy of equivocation, however, has marred the scholarly exchange. Based on giving a particular content to the 'X' in the formulation: "Late Medieval Augustinianism was X," scholars have then jumped into the historiographical debate, not taking into consideration whether the 'X' of their particular definition has been the same 'X' as employed by others. To take the three predominant definitions, late medieval Augustinianism has been defined as the *schola Augustiniana moderna*, as the *Augustinian School*, and as the Augustinian Renaissance. Based on any of these, or as is most often the case, based on some conglomeration, scholars can then affirm that there was no such Augustinian School in the later Middle Ages, whether taking into account or not the self-understanding of the members of the Augustinian Order. One can say that late Medieval Augustinianism was a close adherence to the writings of Augustine and especially to his anti-Pelagian writings since these reflect what was most genuinely and authentically Augustinian in the first place, and on that basis show that there is virtually no evidence in the later Middle Ages for the existence of such an Augustinianism among authors who were members of the OESA. Or one can say that since there is no conclusive evidence that Luther or Staupitz was influenced by the writings of Gregory of Rimini, that the *via Gregorii* at Wittenberg was simply a misnomer, with no historical relevance. Such approaches to the question, and the debates surrounding them, stem from the history of ideas, and from the history of ideas on a rather ethereal level, including, as they do, questions concerning Augustine himself and how his doctrine is to be characterized, as much as the presence or absence of that doctrine in the later Middle Ages. As useful as such scholarly exercises can be, such interpretations overlook the internal perspective of the Order's theologians themselves in attempt to render judgment from a "better informed" position. They are removed from the historical understanding of what it meant to be an Augustinian in the fourteen and fifteenth centuries as determined by fourteenth- and fifteenth-century authors. If late medieval Augustinianism is to be used as a descriptive term, the question that must be asked is what is being described: a theological position, or a historical phenomenon?

This brings us back to the issue that came to light in the context of the Oberman-Grane debate, namely, how history, or the history of theology in any case, is to be done in the first place. When Grane and Oberman published their articles in the 1970s, the difference between the two approaches can be described as that between historical theology based on textual analysis, and the history of theology placed in the intellectual context. Or one might claim using more current categories, that at least in the broader implications the debate was between the history of ideas and the social history of ideas.

While the addition of the qualifier 'social' to the history of ideas has the advantage of bringing the historian back to the ground from the ethereal flight in the realm of thought, it carries with it the danger of passing over ideas that seemingly have nothing social about them. In the economy of ideas, the social history of ideas has moved from the strictly "supply-side" economics of the history of ideas to the "demand-side." The traditional history of ideas, on the other hand, focuses only on what counts to progress the height of intellectual development. Both approaches have difficulties in dealing with the entire textual production of a given author. Yet Augustine's religion called both for contemplation and for bringing the fruits of contemplation to the Church at large. The combination of life and knowledge, of ethics and erudition, as pursued by the lectors in the Augustinian *studia*—and not simply as an ideal, but as a prescribed requirement in the Order's statutes—held together the Augustinian theologian's heart and head. The "head" of the *studia*'s theological program is lost sight of when the social history of ideas seeks only to see the impact of ideas on society, or the extent to which society impacted the creation of the ideas, and the "heart" of the program is lost by the history of ideas in its attempt to chart the evolution of cerebral emissions.

To interpret late medieval Augustinianism historically, another approach must be adopted, one that strives to take into account both the supply and the demand of late medieval theological production. The goal of such an approach is to uncover the historical understanding of the Augustinian theologians both in the *studia* and in the pulpit. What is called for is an intellectual history that seeks to uncover the history of *intellectus*, the history of understanding, which is by definition a social phenomenon.

This is not a plea for returning to a history of elites. Intellectual history, as the history of *intellectus*, encompasses all classes of society, from the *intellectus* of peasants to that of professors. The social history that has nothing to do with "intellectual history" is archeology, or the history of material culture. It is only half of the history to view the spiritual knowledge of the theology of the Augustinian Order's *studia* as residing in the realm of the history of ideas, or in the rarefied realm of "pure" intellectual history, when interpreted from the perspective of the clerical "elite," and as lay devotional literature having a social dimension when interpreted from the perspective of the audience. Jordan of Quedlinburg knew he was accommodating his theology to fit his audience, as did every late medieval preacher and pastoral theologian. To ignore or dismiss the supply-side of interpretation is to ignore or dismiss half of the history of understanding. To understand the historical *intellectus* of late medieval Augustinianism we are far better served by asking the authors of the texts themselves how, why, and to what extent they viewed themselves as Augustinians than we are by constructing *a priori* definitions of the term which can then be so eruditely applied to the historical evidence. Late medieval religious texts were produced within the context of particular religions, each with its own understanding of what that religion entailed.

As a specific micro-religion among the various *religiones* of *Christianitas*, the *religio Augustini* formed the most perfect life in its combination of anchoritic and cenobitic monasticism, consisting in the combination of *vita* and *scientia*, placed in the context of the contemplative life defined as concerning all endeavors that pertain to salvation. In the early decades of the fourteenth century, the Augustinian lectors Nicholas of Alessandria, Henry of Friemar, and Jordan of Quedlinburg, asserted emphatically that the members of the OESA were the true sons of Augustine. By imitating Augustine in all facets of their lives, the sons of Augustine filled out the body of Augustine as it appeared in the Order's foundation myth. The Order was the embodiment of Augustine, and as such, was charged to bring the spiritual fruits of contemplation to the Church at large, distributing the spiritual alms of the *vita perfectissima*'s contemplative life: teaching, preaching, and caring for souls. This entailed pursuing a theological program of religionization which sought to bring the *religio Augustini* to Christendom in the endeavor to sanctify the souls of late medieval society. For the late medieval sons of Augustine, Augustinian theology was the theological expression of Augustine's religion.

Augustinian theology was made affective and effective by its definition as spiritual knowledge. Spiritual knowledge was the goal of the Augustinian *studia*'s theological program. It was only acquired with divine illumination, being granted as the gift of knowledge to those with a pure heart, a humble mind, piety of prayer and fruitfulness of works, the combination of *vita* and *scientia*, of ethics and erudition, which was a prerequisite for those Augustinians with hopes of being sent to Paris. Spiritual knowledge, a knowledge of the heart as well as of the head, sought to communicate the true cognition of reality resulting from the illumination of the Holy Spirit to Christian society, in imitation of Augustine as the Order's founder and father.

The spiritual knowledge of the *studia* was explicated by the Order's university theologians as the affective knowledge that characterized the Order's academic theology. At the universities, the Augustinian *magistri* gave lectures on Aristotle, Lombard, and the Bible, defending the Augustinian theology of *scientia affectiva*, Jordan's *scientia spiritualis*, against opinions, positions, and assertions of theologians from other religions in the tournament for enunciating the faith of Christendom. The extant theological literature produced by the Augustinian masters of theology evidences a renewed endeavor to interpret the scriptures in keeping with the works of Augustine. This has been generally recognized. What has not been, however, is that when the Order's university theologians initiated a renaissance of Augustinian scholarship in the mid-fourteenth century, they did so only having been trained first in the religious Augustinianism of their Order, in which context masters, bachelors, and lectors lectured in the non-university *studia* on Aristotle, Lombard, and the Bible to produce the teachers and preachers of Augustine's religion.

The extant literary production of the Augustinian *studia*, moreover, far exceeds that of the universities. Treatises such as Jordan's *Expositio Orationis*

Dominice, Meditationes de Passione Christi, and his three major collection of sermons, point to the fact that the focus of the theological program of the *studia* was not only the internal formation of future theologians, but was also the programmatic endeavor to translate the spiritual knowledge acquired in the *studia* for the common Christian, and for the common Christian both within and without the Augustinian Order. What *Sentences* commentaries were to the university theology, sermon collections and *Postilla*, were to the *studia* theology. To interpret the literature produced by the sons of Augustine in the later Middle Ages historically, the double hermeneutic of religionization must be employed, whereby both the internal and the external contexts are taken into consideration, the specific and the general hermeneutic.[112]

This hermeneutic is discerned in the creation, dissemination, and reception of texts when scrutinized from the perspective that texts are social products. Authors of theological and devotional treatises composed their works as members of religious groups in society, groups that were defined in medieval terms as distinctive religions, one of which was the *religio Augustini*.

The question of how to define 'late medieval Augustinianism' is especially pertinent regarding the relationship between the late medieval Augustinian tradition and the emergence of Reformation theology. In October of 1516 Luther wrote to Spalatin: "I defend Augustine not because I am an Augustinian; before I began to deal with his writings, he did not mean anything to me."[113] Such a statement is unthinkable a hundred and fifty years earlier. Luther made this comment as lector in the Augustinian cloister in Wittenberg, as the Order's district vicar in charge of eleven Augustinian houses, including the cloister at Erfurt and its *studium*, and as the University's Professor of Biblical Theology, where he was required to teach according to the *via Gregorii*. Over a decade ago Jan Matsura published previously unknown marginals of Luther's, dating from his earliest period, on William of Ockham's *De Sacramento Altaris*, which give strong evidence of Luther's knowledge of Gregory of Rimini well before the Leipzig debate.[114] The search for Luther's

---

[112] See below, Appendix A.4.

[113] *WA Br* 1.70, 19–21; to Spalatin, 19 October 1516; as quoted by Oberman, *Luther*, 170; cf. Hamel, *Der junge Luther und Augustin*, 1–25.

[114] Jan Matsura, "Restbestände aus der Bibliothek des Erfurter Augustinerklosters zu Luthers Zeit und bisher unbekannte eigenhändige Notizen Luthers. Ein Bericht," In *Lutheriana. Zum 500. Geburtstag Martin Luthers von dem Mitarbeitern der Weimarer Ausgabe*, ed. Gerhard Hammer and Karl-Heinz zur Mühlen, AWA 5, (Köln 1984), 315–330. In his notes on chapter 4 of Ockham's seventh Quodlibet, *De Sacramento Altaris*, Luther wrote: "Gabrie lect.42 sup(er) canon Et dis.xvii:li.2. ibid(em) Gre: arym. tene(n)t q(uod) in vno co(m)posito sit vna t(antu)m forma con(tra) occam & scotu(m)." Matsura, "Restbestände," 330. This evidence may seem to be sufficient proof against Grane that Luther was acquainted with Gregory well before Leipzig. Such a conclusion, however, is not so readily achieved. In this note Luther first cited Gabriel Biel's *Canonis Misse Expositio*, lectio 42. In this lectio Biel himself cited Gregory's *Sentences* Commentary, bk. II, d. 16, q. 2, and gave Gregory's conclusion on substance and form in composite beings that Luther noted: "Consequenter notandum quod corpus accipitur tripliciter post Gregorium de arimino in ii Scripti, dist.xvi, quest ii. . . . Item genus predicatur de omnibus speciebus et individuis sub eo contentis. Sub corpore autem tanquam sub genere continentur omnes species specialissime et

adherence to the *via Gregorii*, however, must go beyond his knowledge and use of Gregory's texts to ask what was Luther's *understanding* of his teaching within the *via Gregorii*. Following a late medieval *via* was not the same

---

individua substantie, significantes res compositas, ut homo, asinus, ioannes, petrus, paulus, tales autem significant res totales per se in genere, et per consequens corpus non verificatur de eis si significaret rem partialem." Biel, *Exp.*, 2:128 C. Biel also refuted the position which he attributed to Scotus and Ockham, namely, that in man, in addition to the form of the intellect, there is also a form of the body; Biel, *Exp.*, 2:130, 131. He did so by using "Ockham's razor" against him, and by claiming that Gregory of Rimini sufficiently solved the problem of the plurality of forms: "Sed quia paucitas est semper ponenda ubi plura ponendi nulla est necessitas, cui tanquam principio phisico utrique Scotus et Ockham frequenter innituntur, nec aliqua necessitas cogens ad ponendum plures formas substantiales in eodem composito apparet, ideo secundo opinio que pluralitatem formarum vitat probabilior videtur. Nam omnes rationes quas alii contra hanc opinionem inducunt, tam phisicas quam theologicas, sufficienter solvit Gregorius de arimino in ii, dist. xvi, quest.ii." Biel, *Exp.*, 2:131 E. Hence, it would appear possible—if not probable—that Luther took his reference to Gregory directly from Biel. More likely, however, is that Luther did have first-hand knowledge of Gregory. It should be noted that Gregory of Rimini combined distinctions 16 and 17 and thus Luther citing dist. 17 and Biel citing dist. 16 refer to the same place in Gregory's text. This is evidence that Luther indeed had a first hand knowledge of Gregory! When making his marginals on Ockham's *De Sacramento Altaris*, Luther drew on two separate sources which applied to the problem rather than merely repeating what he had read in Biel. He further learned the great importance of Gregory from Biel and perhaps began studying for himself his order's *Doctor Authenticus*. In addition, in bk. II, d. 16 and 17, q. 3, Gregory discussed the problem of the plurality of forms in the context of the Trinity whereas Biel did not in lectio 42 of his *Expositio*. For Gregory, accepting the plurality of forms in a composite being would infringe upon the unity of the divine essence; Greg. 2 *Sent.* 16–17, 3 (V.369,20–31 to 370,1–16;373,1–5). Further, on the authority of Augustine, Gregory accepted the position that the divine essence and the divine persons can be distinguished by the acts of the divine essence; Greg. 2 *Sent.* 16–17,3 (V.372,17–35). This same argument, on the basis that a composite being, such as the Trinity, has only one substantive form, is also found in Luther's Christmas Day 1514 sermon on John 1:1. The Trinity is a composite being consisting of three persons, but it has only one substantive form, the divine essence; *WA* 1.21,31–35. As Gregory, so did Luther draw on St. Augustine's *De Trinitate* and used Aristotle's physics regarding potentiality and actuality as distinct from being itself to describe the relationship between the divine persons and the divine essence. When read in light of Gregory's position, Luther's discussion of the Trinity in this sermon suggests Luther's knowledge of Gregory. Yet the extent to which Luther consciously taught within a *via Gregorii* and the influence of such a *via* on the development of his thought is another question. Knowledge of Gregory's texts does not in and of itself indicate adherence to a coherent and definite *via Gregorii*. Moreover, as Heinz Scheible has shown, there is no evidence that lectures were ever held in Wittenberg according to the *via Gregorii*, so that even if the statutes of the university designated a *via Gregorii* in addition to the *viae* of the Thomists and Scotists, it does not appear to have had any actual part in the curriculum; see Heinz Scheible, "Aristoteles und die Witttenberg Universitätsreform. Zum Quellenwert von Lutherbriefen," in *Humanismus und Wittenberger Reformation. Festgabe anläßlich des 500. Geburtstages des Praeceptor Germaniae Philipp Melanchthon am 16. Februar 1997*, ed. Michael Beyer and Günter Wartenberg, with Hans-Peter Hasse (Leipzig, 1996), 123–144; 129–130.

as lecturing on the *Sentences* of Lombard *secundum alium*. As an important theologian and administrator for his Order, Luther seems not to have been imbued with his Order's religion, even if he did follow the *via Gregorii* and did so based on his knowledge of Gregory's texts. By limiting the question of the relationship between late medieval Augustinianism and Luther's theological development to the extent to which Luther was familiar with the texts and/or theology of Gregory of Rimini as a follower of the *via Gregorii* is again separating the head from the heart of the late medieval Augustinian.

The religious identity of the Augustinian Order provides the frame of reference for interpreting late medieval Augustinianism historically. A theological, Augustinian anti-Pelagianism can no longer be seen as the exclusive, or even as the primary catalyst for the renaissance of Augustine scholarship.[115] Theologians and philosophers can legitimately continue to debate the meaning of the term 'Augustinianism' and its appropriateness for designating their referents of choice, but for an understanding of the term's historical signification in the later Middle Ages, the sons of Augustine pursuing the spiritual knowledge of the Order's *studia* in following their father's religion uniquely claim 'Augustinianism' for themselves as their religious identity and its theological expression.

Rather than being an abstract label employed by scholars to describe particular aspects and/or characteristics of selected texts of selected Augustinian theologians, late medieval Augustinianism signifies the historical phenomena that *produced* the texts of the tradition. Late medieval Augustinianism was the ideology of the Order's religious identity that provided the pretext, the pre-understanding, of the Order's textual production, which effected the textualization of Augustine's heritage. As such, it cannot be limited to theological positions. The historical Augustinian renaissance of the later Middle Ages, as distinct from the theological, was fundamentally the renaissance of Augustine's cultural ethic, founded on the monastic life, the highest good, and brotherly love, in imitation of Augustine himself, as Ernst Troeltsch saw over almost a century ago, though whose position and insight has been ignored by the theological bantering.[116] The endeavor to imitate Augustine in all aspects of the religious life, to follow Augustine's religion, yielded the new Augustine scholarship as a by-product of the OESA's platform. As a historical phenomenon, late medieval Augustinianism was the textual condition of Augustine's religion.[117]

When the question of late medieval Augustinianism is redirected to the historical understanding of living as a son and heir of Augustine as a member of Augustine's religion, though the problem of definition might be solved, the enigma of the phenomenon is unmasked as far more mysterious and perplexing than even imagined. A myriad of previously ignored texts must be read and interpreted, and interpreted and read in light of the double hermeneutic of religionization which takes into account the

---

[115] See Saak, "The Reception of Augustine."
[116] See above, Introduction, ns. 20–22.
[117] See J. McGann, *The Textual Condition* (Princeton, 1991).

"social logic of the texts,"[118] the social history of the ideas, and the social contexts of understanding, without dismissing those texts, ideas, and understandings that seem on the surface to have nothing social about them. The academic, university theology of the Order and the pastoral teaching and preaching of the Order become far less distinct when the verbal nature of the Order's mendicant theology is taken into account: the endeavor to do theology and to be a theologian, and to be a son of Augustine. In imitation of Augustine, the late medieval Augustinian hermits produced a textual corpus, ranging from political theory and theology, to spirituality and catechesis, that played a major role in shaping the religious culture of the later Middle Ages. For understanding Augustine's heritage as it was embodied in the Order's religion and how that religion impacted society with its theological program emanating from the spiritual knowledge of the *studia*, Jordan of Quedlinburg, Gregory of Rimini, Johannes von Paltz, Johannes Staupitz, and Martin Luther were not Augustine's only sons in the later Middle Ages whose works still have much to reveal.

2. Ideology

In keeping with the attempt to re-historicize the late medieval Augustinian tradition, implicit within the argument of the preceding study is an approach to interpreting texts that largely derives from Augustine himself. As Robert Markus stated with regard to Augustine's theory of signs and their significations as explicated in *De Doctrine Christina*, the consequence of Augustine's theory is that, "a particular human group is defined by the boundaries of the system of signs in use among its members."[119] Trying to understand the "system of signs" used among members of the OESA in the later Middle Ages has been the endeavor I have pursued, striving to grasp what the members of the Order understood to have been the significance of their "being" Augustinians. Acknowledging the intricate interrelationship of history, literature, religion, and theology, I have tried to perceive the hermeneutical circle of late medieval Augustinianism. This has required reading theological texts historically and historical texts theologically in attempt to break through the disciplinary boundaries constraining the late medieval Augustinians' dynamic system of understanding to a systematic enunciation of theological doctrines. In other words, to interpret the texts of the Augustinian tradition historically one must seek to perceive the Augustinian ideology, whereby ideology, in the words of Hayed White, is seen "as a process by which different kinds of meaning are produced and reproduced by the establishment of a mental set towards the world in which certain sign sys-

---

[118] See Gabrielle M. Spiegel, *The Past as Text. The Theory and Practice of Medieval Historiography* (Baltimore, 1997).

[119] Robert Markus, "Sign, Communication, and Communities in Augustine's *De Doctrina Christiana*," in *De doctrina christiana. A Classic of Western Culture*, ed. Duane W.H. Arnold and Pamela Bright (Notre Dame, 1995), 97–108; 103.

tems are privileged as necessary, even natural, ways of recognizing a 'meaning' in things and others are suppressed, ignored or hidden in the very process of representing a world to consciousness."[120] Ideology is created by and discerned in the production of texts, from popular polemical pieces of propaganda to theoretically informed theological treatises;[121] ideology forms the hermeneutical circle in which texts were created and read. This hermeneutical circle then becomes the object of historical analysis, rather than specific texts, manuscripts, or events in themselves. The challenge of the historical endeavor is thus to uncover the various ways texts ascribed meaning within a given historical context.[122] The Augustinian ideology, therefore, refers to the textualization of the manifestations and representations of the Augustinian Order's ideals, that in turn formed and shaped the meaning of those ideals, which provided the perspective for members of the Order to form their views of their religious life and to act accordingly.

By using the term 'ideology' I do not intend to enter the theoretical fray over its descriptive value. Often ideology is used simply as an alternative for ideas, ideals, world-views, or mentalities in attempt to bridge the gap between mental processes and society or the mutual influence of text and context, remaining undistinguished from what Mannheim called "styles of thought," or Michael Baxandall, "cognitive style."[123] Yet it is precisely in the relationship between text and context, and/or that of the individual and the social that ideology is to be found, and is so to the extent that White claimed ideology as "the central problem of intellectual history because intellectual history has to do with meaning, its production, distribution, and consumption, so to speak, in different historical epochs,"[124] or as Michael Freeden put it, "ideology is thus located at the meeting point between meaning and form."[125] This has been how I have employed the term,

---

[120] Hayden White, *The Content of the Form. Narrative Discourse and Historical Representation* (Baltimore, 1987), 192.

[121] *Cf.* Michael Freeden, *Ideologies and Political Theory. A Conceptual Approach* (Oxford, 1996), 44–45.

[122] *Cf.* Gadamer, *Truth and Method*, 2nd rev. ed., trans. Joel Weinsheimer and Donald G. Marshall (New York, 1993), 292; *cf.* Anthony Giddens, *New Rules of Sociological Method. A Positive Critique of Interpretative Sociologies*, 2nd ed. (Stanford, 1993), 9–15 and 166.

[123] See K. Mannheim, "Conservative Thought," in K. Mannheim, *Essays on Sociology and Social Psychology*, ed. P. Kecskemeti (London, 1953), 74–164; 74–79; M. Baxandall, *Painting and Experience in Fifteenth-Century Italy* (Oxford, 1972). For a very concise explication of the distinctions between ideology and mentality, see Peter Burke, *History and Social Theory* (New York, 1992), 91–96; *cf.* Michel Vovelle, *Ideologies and Mentalities*, trans. Eamon O'Flaherty (Oxford, 1990).

[124] White, *The Content of the Form*, 190.

[125] M. Freeden, *Ideologies*, 54. For the development of the term 'ideology' and a number of its varied uses since the time of Destutt de Tracy, see the collection of readings with introductions by Terry Eagleton, *Ideology* (New York, 1994); *cf. idem*, *Ideology: An Introduction* (London, 1991), and D. La Capra, "Culture and Ideology: From Geertz to Marx," in La Capra, *Soundings in Critical Theory* (New York, 1989). For my own use of the term ideology in this case, I am following in a general sense the views of White and Freeden in the works here cited, and Paul Ricoeur, *Lectures on Ideology and Utopia*, edited by George H. Taylor (New York, 1986).

whereby the meeting point between meaning and form was evident in the system of signs used by the OESA, given expression in the Order's stated attempt to follow Augustine's religion.

3. Religion

"Religion," Jordan of Quedlinburg clarified for his students in the Augustinian *studium* at Erfurt in 1327, "is a certain moral virtue," consisting of all the ceremonies and acts that are owed to God,[126] a definition he would repeat over thirty years later in his *Opus Postillarum*.[127] In the *Liber Vitasfratrum* Jordan commented further. Religion, he explained, comes from the gerundive *religandus*, 'to be bound'.[128] To be a 'religious', therefore, is to be bound to God. There are two ways in which this term should be taken. The first refers to those who bind themselves to God by private vow, as were the monks of old, the contemporary Beghards, the followers of Raymond Lull, and the like.[129] These are not bound to a Rule, but lead their chosen life according to their own resolve (*ad libitum*).[130] The second meaning of religious is the 'state' of being a religious. Those who bind themselves to a *Rule* perpetually in solemn profession are properly said to be *in statu religionis*.[131] This second meaning of religion Jordan addressed in his *Liber Vitasfratrum*; for Jordan the type of religion he exhorted his fellow friars to follow, the friars "... of this holy Religion..."[132] was that advocated by the Bishop of Hippo, "our most blessed father Augustine, who ought to be

---

[126] "Est autem sciendum quod religio non accipitur hic pro statu religiosorum, sed est quedam virtus moralis, que est pars iustitie. Ad quam virtutem pertinet deo cultum exhibere et comprehendit sub se latriam. Et actus huius virtutis sunt adoratio, oratio, oblatio, laus, votum, iuramentum et cetera alia, que soli deo debentur." Jor. *Exp.*, 7, fol. 82vb–83ra.

[127] "Religio est virtus ad quam pertinet cultum deo exhibere." Jor. *OP* sermo 440C (ed. Strassburg, 1483).

[128] "Considerandum autem, quod cum Religiosi dicantur a religando..." *VF* 2,25 (252,28).

[129] "Uno modo, ut dicantur Religiosi, qui se religaverunt Deo obligatione privata, sicut fuerunt antiquitus aliqui monachi et sicut nunc sunt Beghardi vel Lullardi et consimiles..." *VF* 2,25 (252,29–32); *cf.* Jor. *OP* sermo 440C (ed. Strassburg, 1483).

[130] "... qui nullum Religionis Regulam profitentur, sed talem modum vivendi ad libitum assumunt." *VF* 2,25 (252,32–33).

[131] "Alio modo dicuntur Religiosi, qui se Deo obligaverunt Religione perpetua et solemni per professionem alicuius Regulae approbatae. Et isti habent statum Religionis. Secus illi. Status enim quandam immobilitatem importat; unde dicitur status a stando. Illi ergo, qui ordinantur ad Religionem cum hac duplici conditione, videlicet cum obligatione perpetua et cum solemnitate professionis, proprie dicuntur esse in statu Religionis; et ubi alterum deest, ibi est quis Religiosus, ita quod non est in statu Religionis." *Ibid.*, (252,33–40). Jordan most likely took this distinction from Hostiensis' *Summa aurea*, III, 1–3; see Constable, *The Reformation of the Twelfth Century* (Cambridge, 1996), 7–8.

[132] "... fratres huius sacrae Religionis..." *VF* 1,16 (57,2).

the exemplar and rule of our every action."[133] Jordan left no doubt. The religion of which he spoke was the religion of Augustine: "[Our] most blessed father Augustine, the progenitor of our holy Religion.... founded his... Religion...."[134]

In the opening paragraph of his study of religion in *Economy and Society*, Max Weber asserted: "To define 'religion', to say what it *is*, is not possible at the start of a presentation such as this. Definition can be attempted, if at all, only at the conclusion of the study."[135] A contemporary of Weber's, Emile Durkheim, shared this sentiment: "It is not," he affirmed in *The Elementary Forms of Religious Life*, "that we dream of arriving at once at the profound characteristics which really explain religion: these can be determined only at the end of our study."[136] With such caveats it is by no means my intent to offer a comprehensive definition of the *religio Augustini* here and now. Nevertheless, we must delve a bit deeper into the use of the term *religio* precisely because, adapting the words of Durkheim, "if we are going to look for" Augustine's religion, "it is necessary to begin by defining what is meant by a religion; for without this, we would run the risk of giving the name to a system of ideas and practices which has nothing at all religious about it, or else of leaving to one side many religious facts, without perceiving their true nature."[137]

Modern scholars of religion have often sought to define their object of study in the tradition of Rudolph Otto, whereby 'religion' is the experience of the 'holy', the *mysterium tremendum et fascinans*.[138] In this general vein can be placed the works of Joachim Wach, focusing on a sociological typology,[139] Mircea Eliade, who has striven to go beyond Otto by turning his attention to the "sacred in its entirety," as expressed in comparative myths, symbols and rituals,[140] and most recently John Hick, who defines religion as humans' belief in the transcendent.[141] Durkheim as well has been a major catalyst for much research approaching religion as a natural phenomenon equated with human society, whereby religion is seen as "a unified system of beliefs and practices relative to sacred things, that is to say, things set

---

[133] "... beatissimus Pater noster Augustinus, qui debet esse omnis nostrae actionis exemplar et regula..." *VF* 1,11 (36,32–33).

[134] "Beatissimus Pater et sacrae nostrae Religionis plantator Augustinus.... religionem suam... undavit." *VF* 1,1 (7,9–20).

[135] Weber, *Economy and Society. An Outline of Interpretive Sociology*, 2 vols., ed. Guenther Roth and Claus Wittich (Berkeley, 1978), 1:399.

[136] Durkheim, *The Elementary Forms of the Religious Life*, trans. Joseph Ward Swain (Illinois, 1926), 37.

[137] *Ibid.*

[138] Rudolph Otto, *Das Heilige. Über das Irrationale in der Idee des Göttlichen und sein Verhältnis zum Rationalen* (Breslau, 1917).

[139] Wach, *Sociology of Religion* (Chicago, 1957).

[140] Eliade, *The Sacred and the Profane. The Nature of Religion*; and *idem*, *Images and Symbols. Studies in Religious Symbolism*; and *idem*, *Myth and Reality*.

[141] Hick, *An Interpretation of Religion. Human Response to the Transcendent* (New Haven, 1992).

apart and forbidden—beliefs and practices which unite into one single moral community called a church, all those who adhere to them."[142] Weber, on the other hand, emphasized the need to analyze the meaning of religious behavior, "from the viewpoint of subjective experiences,"[143] the echoes of whose influence can be heard in Gabriel Le Bras' sociology of religious groups,[144] and when joined with that of Eliade, in the definition of religion offered by the cultural anthropologist Clifford Geertz: "... *religion* is a system of symbols which acts to establish powerful, pervasive, and long-lasting moods and motivations in men by formulating conceptions of a general order of existence and clothing these conceptions with such an aura of factuality that the moods and motivations seem uniquely realistic."[145] While sociological and anthropological approaches to religion have sought to illuminate the nature of religion *per se* and/or the meaning of religion for specific religious groups, William James, in his classic work, focused on individual religious experience, with 'religion' taken as "the feelings, acts and experiences of individual men in their solitude, so far as they apprehend themselves to stand in relation to whatever they may consider the divine."[146]

All these definitions can shed light on medieval religion approached as an object from outside, but James is of special help to us for bridging the historical abyss of over 600 years that separates us from the world of the later Middle Ages: "There can be no doubt," he notes,

> ... that as a matter of fact a religious life, exclusively pursued, does tend to make the person exceptional and eccentric. I speak not now of your ordinary religious believer, who follows the conventional observances of his country.... His religion has been made for him by others, communicated to him by tradition, determined to fixed forms by imitation, and retained by habit... We must make search rather for the original experiences which were the pattern-setters to all this mass of suggested feeling and imitated conduct. These experiences we can only find in individuals for whom religion exists not as a dull habit, but as an acute fever.[147]

Jordan was such a pattern-setter, and his "acute fever" was that of the *religio Augustini*. It has been my goal to describe, at least in part, this "fever," and the patterns that it produced, patterns that formed the "unified beliefs and practices," the "system of symbols" that established "powerful, pervasive, and long-lasting moods and motivations" for the Augustinian Order, resulting in the formulation of their conceptions of a general order of existence.

Yet as illuminating as sociological, anthropological, and pyschological definitions of religion are, they are only of partial help for interpreting late

---

[142] Durkheim, *The Elementary Forms*, 62.
[143] Weber, *Economy and Society*, 399.
[144] G. Le Bras, *Etudes de scoiologie religieuse, II. De la morphologie à la typologie* (Paris, 1956).
[145] Geertz, "Religion as a Cultural System," in *Interpretation of Culture*, 90.
[146] James, *The Varieties of Religious Experience* (New York, 1978), 42. For a comprehensive survey of modern scholarship treating religion, see the rich collection of essays edited by Frank Whaling, *Contemporary Approaches to the Study of Religion*, 2 vols., Religion and Reason 27–28 (Berlin/New York/Amsterdam, 1983 and 1985).
[147] James, *Varieties*, 24.

medieval religion. Medieval religion is a slippery concept lacking an ostensible referent, which renders the search for the *religio Augustini* precarious.[148] This is especially so since 'Religion' as an object did not exist in the Middle Ages, at least according to John Bossy. Bossy took Durkheim's equation of religion and society as his starting point for tracing the evolution of *religio*; "in classical Latin," Bossy argued, *religio*

> is a sense of duty or reverence for sacred things; derivatively, some object which inspires this frame of mind; thence a cult, or worship in general. Essentially, it is a feeling, a frame of mind... In medieval Christianity this usage disappeared. With very few exceptions, the word was only used to describe different sorts of monastic or similar rule, and the way of life pursued under them: the 'religious' were, as in subsequent Catholic usage, those who pursued such a life. The word, and its earlier meaning, were revived by fifteenth-century humanists from Lorenzo Valla to Eramus...[149]

---

[148] For an overview of the meaning of *religio* in the Middle Ages, see Ernst Feil, *Religio. Die Geschichte eines neuzeitlichen Grundbegriffs vom Frühchristentum bis zur Reformation* (Göttingen, 1986). Gavin Langmuir, in his study, *History, Religion and Antisemitism* (Berkeley, 1990), called for historians who treat religion to make explicit what they mean by the term religion, disallowing appeal to historical definitions; see *History*, 46. Langmuir distinguished between religion and religiosity, defining the latter as "the salient patterns or structures according to which the individual human organism consciously correlates all the diverse processes occuring within the organism with those that surround and impinge on it in order to develop, maintain, and ensure the coherence and continuity of the distinctive elements of its identity," (*History*, 160) while the former then is taken as comprising "those elements of religiosity that are explicitly prescribed by people exercising authority over other people." (*History*, 136) Whereas Langmuir has called for the historian to use his or her own understanding and definition of religion to explain historical religious phenomena in their own terms, this entire study is an attempt to reconstruct the meaning of the *religio Augustini* in the later Middle Ages in terms of late medieval understandings of religion. Yet to meet the challenge posed by Langmuir for historians to be forthcoming with their understanding of the term religion, for present purposes, I would define religion as social manifestations of systems of meaning by which humans relate themselves to transcendence; *cf.* John Hick, *An Interpretation of Religion*. What Langmuir termed religiosity, I consider to be spirituality, which I would define as the private and/or social manifestations of individual experience of transcendence; and theology I consider then to be written and/or spoken analysis and/or explication and/or interpretation of the foundational texts, events, and concepts upon which a theistic religion is based. To give then a final explicit definition for full disclosure, as employed in this study I use the term 'religious identity' to signify the conscious and unconscious manifestations and representations of the ideals of a group that, in the context of a group's program(s) of socialization and indoctrination, serve as the basis for an individual's self-understanding and norms of action as a member of the group, which socially manifests systems of meaning by which the members of the group relate themselves to transcendence. For an introduction to sociological approaches to religion, in addition to Whaling, *Contemporary Approaches*, 2:89–177, see Malcolm B. Hamilton, *The Sociology of Religion. Theoretical and Comparative Perspectives* (London/New York, 1995). For the most recent attempt to employ sociological perspectives for interpreting medieval religion, see Angenendt, *Geschichte der Religiosität im Mittelalter*.

[149] Bossy, "Some Elementary Forms of Durkheim," *Past and Present* XCV (1982), 3–18; 4.

Bossy put forward a threefold definition of religion and society. In the first instance, labeled definition I, religion follows the classical and early patristic understanding as worship or frame of mind. The second definition is religion as a collective term, "an objective entity, a structure or system which subsists apart from the individuals," (IIa) which only later develops into the abstract Religion with a capital 'R' (IIb).[150] The question Bossy then tries to answer is how the term 'religion' came ". . . to have the sense in which Durkheim used it, and we use it too: to get its capital 'R'."[151] The move from religion I to religion II, according to Bossy, was the development of the Reformation: "the actual motor of our change was, it seems clear, the simple existence of a plurality of embodied and embattled, faiths."[152] Whereas the emergence of Religion with a capital 'R' (IIb) was a product of early modern Europe, the Reformation brought forth the shift from religion I to religion IIa. Although religion in the Reformation came to be objectified as various systems of belief, it had not achieved its modern definition, being most often qualified as 'true' religion opposed to 'false'; it had not yet become an abstract 'thing': ". . . in the sixteenth century in general, where the Latin form *Christiana religio* is found, it must be translated 'Christian religion', not '*the* Christian religion': we have now had to invent the appalling 'religiosity' to fill the gap where 'religion' once stood."[153] Nevertheless, it was only with the Reformation that 'religion' became a system, identifiable and distinguishable in its multifarious forms, having rediscovered the classical and early patristic understanding which had been lost in the Middle Ages, when 'religion' was limited to the monastic life.[154] If Bossy's analysis is correct, then the *religio Augustini* simply means the way of life defined by the Augustinian Rule.

That Bossy had a limited view of the Middle Ages with respect to the understanding of *religio* was competently shown by Peter Biller.[155] Biller demonstrated that in lexical works such as Papias' *Elementarium* (c. 1040–1045), Huguccio's *Magnae derivationes* (c. 1200), and Balbi's *Catholicon* (1286), as well as "among academic theologians from Abelard to St. Bonaventure there is a continuity of discussion of *religio*, in its classical and patristic senses, as a virtue annexed to justice."[156] Biller then continued to argue that the Middle Ages also gave evidence of an understanding of *religio* as a system of faith

---

[150] *Ibid.*, 8; Bossy sets forth this scheme for society, but notes it is 'practically identical' with the term religion. Bossy labels the last two definitions as religion/society II(a) and II(b).

[151] *Ibid.*, 5.

[152] *Ibid.*

[153] *Ibid.*

[154] Bossy restated his position, in shortened form, in his *Christianity in the West, 1400–1700* (Oxford, 1985), 170–171. Langmuir followed Bossy for his discussion of the concept of religion in the Middle Ages, even if he based his own definition of religion on his own definition of 'religiosity', which Bossy found 'appalling'; see Langmuir, *History*, 70f.

[155] Biller, "Words and the Medieval Notion of 'Religion'," *JEH* 36 (1985), 351–369.

[156] *Ibid.*, 357.

and worship, Bossy's definition IIa, brought about by the sense of embattled faiths, although Biller does so with reference to the terms *lex*, *fides*, and *secta*, rather than to *religio*, suggesting that "men in the Middle Ages had the 'thing though they did not have the word'."[157]

Biller's investigation comes much closer to Jordan's understanding of *religio*. As already seen, Jordan defined religion as a moral virtue, and he did so calling on the authority of Cicero.[158] One can only agree with Biller when he concludes that the evidence "does not support Bossy's description of the word *religio* in the Middle Ages. The monastic sense may often have predominated, but the classical and patristic senses, far from dying out, had a strong and varied life among different sorts of people. The picture is much more complex and diverse than the one given by Bossy."[159]

The simultaneity of diverse senses in the Middle Ages, according to Biller, is recognizable not only for the term *religio*, but also for the derivative *religiosus*. As a substantive, *religiosus* most often signified a monk, or "a person following the religious life, usually under a rule," but as an adjective it is more general, meaning 'worshipful' or 'pious'.[160] John Van Engen, however, has noted that although Biller makes important points in arguing for the diversity of the meanings of *religio* in the Middle Ages, *religiosus* was defined as one who lived a 'stricter' or 'holier' life than 'normal', with the basis for comparison being the monastic life.[161] Van Engen's qualification is apparently supported by Jordan's position when he made clear in his *Expositio Orationis Dominice* that the definition of *religio* as a moral virtue was distinct from being *in statu religionis*. A *religiosus*, for Jordan, did indeed live a 'stricter' life than the normal Christian, who was only to fulfill the required obligations to God. If the term *religiosus*, both as a substantive and as an adjective, was defined based on the monastic life, then Biller's argument against Bossy loses some of its force; the fact that academic definitions of *religio* were not restricted by the walls of the monastery is an important qualification, but if 'to be religious' or 'to be a religious' in the Middle Ages was predominantly monastic, then the medieval understanding of *religio* must be interpreted within the context of monasticism, even if medieval scholars recognized the broader etymology and history of the term, and we must await the Reformation for the emergence of *religio* as a "system of faith and worship" distinct from the monastic life.[162]

---

[157] *Ibid.*, 360; *cf.* Feil, *Religio*, 126–127. Feil, however, was unaware of Bossy's and Biller's work.

[158] "Et diffinitur <religio> a Tulio in secundo *Rethorice* sue sic: Religio est virtus que cuidam nature quam divinam vocant cultum cerimoniamque affert." Jor. *Exp.* 7, fol. 83ra. The reference is to Cic. inv. 2,161 (148,11–13).

[159] Biller, "Words," 359–360.

[160] *Ibid.*, 358.

[161] John Van Engen, "The Christian Middle Ages as an Historiographical Problem," *AHR* 1987, 519–552; 546, n. 93.

[162] This seems to be the view as well of Giles Constable: "Monasticism in the Middle Ages was more loosely defined than it is today. As a term, like most modern -isms, it did not exist, and the closest equivalents were the monastic *institutio*,

716   APPENDIX A

Both Bossy and Biller, however, have left unclarified the relationship between religion I and religion IIa, with Bossy simply claiming that neither understanding was present in the Middle Ages, and with Biller arguing that both were current simultaneously. Moreover, neither analyzed the understanding of *religio* within the monastic context, leaving the monastic *religio* as a separate, independent understanding that did not merit a place within the scheme of development from religion I to religion IIa and IIb. Yet it was precisely the monastic understanding of *religio* that brought religion I and religion IIa together, as Jordan's discussions of religion illustrate.

In his *Opus Postillarum*, his first major collection of sermons, completed after 1365, Jordan included a *Tractatus de virtutibus et vitiis*, in which he gave a lengthy treatment of *religio*. Jordan's entire treatise is a summary, or even compilation, often word for word, of the *Secunda Secundae* of Thomas Aquinas' *Summa Theologiae*, although Jordan never cites Thomas by name.[163] Religion, for Jordan, is a moral virtue, a part of natural righteousness (*iustitia naturalis*), which pertains to the worship of God.[164] Closely associated with *religio* is *latria*, which is three-fold. First, latria can be understood as those acts that are offered to God in reverence and recognition of God's lordship, such as genuflection. Second, latria is the very performance of such acts. And third, latria is the habit by which such acts are more easily and quickly performed. Taken in its first sense, latria is the nature of the virtue religion; in its second sense, latria is the acts of religion; but in its third sense, it is equated with the virtue itself.[165] In this light, religion, or latria, can be understood as piety, with regard to devotion; as worship in the sense of fervent attention given to a specific object or act; as a certain 'servitude' with respect to the works that are offered to God in recognition of his lord-

---

nomen, professio, or *propositum* ... *Monachatus* was sometimes used for the state of being a monk, and *monachare* for becoming a monk, but the commonest term was *religio*, which was equivalent to monastic observance and which Aquinas defined as the obligation by which people bound themselves to serve God. Religion was a way of life, a *conversatio* or *ordo*, not a system of belief..." Constable, *Reformation*, 7. My argument is that *religio* could indeed, even if not necessarily, be based upon and thus include a 'system of belief'. *Cf.* Peter Brown, *The Rise of Christendom* (Oxford, 1996), 21–32.

[163] For Thomas, see Feil, *Religio*, 105–111.

[164] "Partes autem iustitie quasi personales sunt hee: religio, pietas et observantia, gratitudo, vindicatio, veritas, amicitia, liberalitas, que omnes annectuntur iustitie sub ratione, qua cuiuslibet debitum redditur, puta per religionem deo, per pietatem parentibus et patrie, per gratitudinem benefactoribus. Et sic de aliis, que omnes sunt sub <ratione> iustitie naturalis secundum Tullium, de quibus omnibus et similis secundum ordinem est videndum. Et primo de religione. Religio est virtus ad quam pertinet cultus deo exhibere." Jor. *OP-B*, fols. 185^{rb-va}.

[165] "Unde ad hanc virtutem [*scil.* religionem] pertinet latria. Et nota quod latria tripliciter sumitur. Uno modo sumitur pro hiis, que deo exhibentur ad reverentiam et cognitionem dominium sui, sicut sunt sacrificia genuflexionis. Alio modo pro ipsa exhibitione. Tertio modo pro habitu, quo predicti exequii exhibitio prompte et faciliter elicitur. Primo modo latria est natura virtutis, scilicet religionis; secundo modo, est actus; sed tertio modo est ipsa virtus que etiam dicitur religio." Jor. *OP-B*, fol. 185va.

ship; or as one's obligation to perform specific works for the worship of God.[166] Thus, according to Isidore, religion is derived from *re eligando*: it is the repeated "choosing" of those things pertaining to the worship of God and their repeated pondering in one's heart; or in other words, religion can be seen as coming from *religando*, by which religion binds one to God.[167] Therefore, *religio* is closely associated with *sanctitas*, and indeed, the two terms are identical in essence. Yet they differ in so far as religion concerns those acts owed God, whereas sanctity refers not only to these acts, but to the offering to God of all virtuous works, or to the means by which one disposes oneself by good works for divine worship.[168]

Jordan thus confirms Biller's point against Bossy that the broadly conceived, classical and early patristic understanding of religion as worship and as a virtue associated with justice was a continuous medieval understanding by no means *re*-discovered by later fifteenth-century humanists. Moreover, in his *Tractatus de virtutibus et vitiis* Jordan nowhere defined 'religion' as based on monastic vows. The claim that 'religion' in the Middle Ages was derived from the monastic understanding of the term is contradicted by Jordan. Religion was a moral virtue, an obligation, incumbent upon every member of society.

Yet when we turn to the question of how 'being religious' or 'being a religious' should be understood, Jordan is clear: 'being a religious' is based on the vow to live according to a rule, that is, on being *in statu religionis*, and it was this understanding of religion that both Bossy and Biller dismissed in terms of the development from religion I to religion IIa. The question is, therefore, to what extent is being *in statu religionis* to be identified with religion IIa, that is, the understanding of religion as a 'system of faith and worship', brought about by the sense of 'embattled faiths'?

---

[166] "Unde sciendum est, quod hec virtus, que etiam dicitur religio, quatuor modis nuncupatur. Dicitur enim pietas, quantum ad effectum devotionis; dicitur theosebia, idest, divinus cultus vel eusebia, idest bonus cultus, quantum ad studium attentionis id enim dicitur homo colere cui studiose intendit sicut agrum, aurum vel quamquam aliud; dicitur etiam latria idest servitus, quantum ad opera que deo exhibentur in recognitionem dominii; dicitur etiam religio in quantum homo obligatur ad aliqua determinata opera ad cultum dei exhibenda. Que tamen quatuor nomina eandem virtutem important, sed diversa." Jor. *OP-B*, fol. 185[va].

[167] "Dicitur autem religio secundum Isidorum in libro Ethymologorum, a re eligando ea que sunt divini cultus, huiusmodi etiam semper in corde revolenda vel etiam quia deum frequenter re eligere debemus... vel potest dici religio a religando, eo quod ipsa nos religat deo." Jor. *OP*, fol. 185[va–b]. The reference is to Isid. diff. 8,2,12 (295C).

[168] "Sanctitas est idem secundum essentiam quod religio sed differt ab ea ratione quia religio dicitur secundum quod exhibet deo debitum famulatum in hiis que pertinent specialiter ad cultum divinum, sicut in sacrificiis et oblationibus et aliis huiusmodi. Sanctitas autem dicitur secundum quod homo non solum hec, sed et aliarum virtutum opera refert in deum vel secundum quod homo se disponit per bona ad cultum divinum." Jor. *OP-B*, fol. 185[vb]. Having established the definition and parameters of *religio*, Jordan then enters into a discussion of the various religious acts, which he lists as *devotio, oratio, obsecratio, sacrificia, oblatio, votum, iuramentum, adjuratio*, and *laus divina*. Jor. *OP-B*, fols. 185[vb]–186[va].

Insight into this question is offered by Jordan's source for his treatment of religion, namely, Thomas' *Secunda Secundae*. In questions 81 to 91 Thomas treated religion as a virtue and discussed its various acts, before turning to what opposes religion in questions 92 to 100. In the final four questions, namely, questions 186 through 189, Thomas turned his sights on the issue of 'being a religious', that is, on the *status religionis*. In question 186 he defined *religiosi* by means of the rhetorical figure, *antonomasia*, whereby an object is named by its attributes. Thus, the *religiosi* are those "who completely give themselves over to divine service, as if offering themselves to God as a complete sacrifice."[169] He affirmed that the 'state of being a religious' is the perfect life, although not every *religiosus* has attained perfection.[170] The state of perfection consists in the vows of poverty, chastity, and obedience.[171] After treating the nature of vows and what is allowed to those *in statu religionis*, Thomas took up the issue of different religions in question 188, *De differentia religionum*. In responding to the question of the first article, "Whether there is only one religion?" (*Utrum sit tantum una religio*), Thomas affirmed that,

> ... the state of religion (*status religionis*) is a certain practice by which someone is exercised to the perfection of charity. There are, however, diverse works of charity, to which one is able to devote oneself freely in leisure, as well as diverse ways of practice. And therefore religions are able to be distinguished in two ways. First, according to their diversity to which they are ordained. Thus one religion is ordained to receiving pilgrims and the homeless with hospitality, and another to visiting or securing the release of captives. The second way religions are able to be distinguished is by their diversity of practices. Thus, for example, in one religion the body is castigated by fasting, in another by manual labor, or by nudity, or some other way of this type. But because in each religion the goal is most important, the diversity of religions is greater with respect to the diverse goals to which they are ordained, than it is regarding their diverse practices.[172]

Thus, there was most definitely a concept of various and diverse religions in the Middle Ages, when *religio* was understood in the sense of being *in*

---

[169] "Et ideo antonomastice religiosi dicuntur illi qui se totaliter mancipant divino servitio, quasi holocaustum Deo offerentes." Thom.Aq. *STh* II/II, q. 186, art. 1, resp. (2356a,39–42).

[170] Thom.Aq. *STh* II/II q. 186, art. 1, ad 3 (2356b,19–33).

[171] Thom.Aq. *STh* II/II q. 186, art. 6, resp. (2364a,30–40).

[172] "... status religionis est quoddam exercitium quo aliquis exercetur ad perfectionem caritatis. Sunt autem diversa caritatis opera quibus homo vacare potest, sunt etiam diversi modi exercitiorum. Et ideo religiones distingui possunt dupliciter. Uno modo, secundum diversitatem eorum ad quae ordinantur, sic ut una religio ordinetur ad peregrinos hospitio suscipiendos, et alia ad visitandos vel redimendos captivos. Alio modo, potest esse diversitas religionum secundum diversitatem exercitiorum, puta quod in una religione castigatur corpus per abstinentias ciborum, in alia per exercitium operum manualium, vel per nuditatem, aut per aliquid huiusmodi. Sed quia finis est potissimum in unoquoque, maior est religionum diversitas quae attenditur secundum diversos fines ad quos religiones ordinantur, quam quae attenditur secundum diversa exercitia." Thom.Aq. *STh* II/II q. 188, art. 1, resp. (2383b,29–50).

statu religionis. Moreover, such religions often acquired specific designations. The thirteenth-century chronicler Alberic de Trois-Fontaines referred to Lambert le Bègue (d. 1177), the twelfth-century preacher of religious reform in Liège, as "a fervent preacher of the new religion which filled Liège and the neighboring regions";[173] in a fourteenth-century manuscript the term *nova religio* was qualified by the phrase: "which is called the religion of the Beguines (*que vocatur religio beguinarum*)."[174] A contemporary of Alberic, Jacques de Vitry in his *Historia Occidentalis* made reference to the 'religion of the Humiliati' (*religio humiliatorum*)[175] and considered the Franciscans to have resuscitated the 'religion of the early church' (*primitive ecclesie religionem*).[176] And in the fourteenth century, Augustinus of Ancona spoke of the 'religion of Christ' and the 'religion of John the Baptist', as well as the 'religion of Benedict,' the 'religion of Francis', the 'religion of Dominic', and the 'religion of Augustine',[177] and Jordan spoke too of Augustine's religion (*religio Augustini*). In each of these cases the term *religio* was not synonymous with *regula*: neither John the Baptist nor Christ composed a monastic rule. Jacques de Vitry entitled his chapter on the Humiliati, *De religione et regula humiliatorum*. *Religio* was a 'way of life' in a broad sense, of which there were many in the Middle Ages, as Thomas made clear. Moreover, the Beguines, the Humiliati, the Franciscans, and the Augustinians all developed their distinctive ways of life in the face of opposition; it is certainly accurate to speak of the 'embattled religions' of the Middle Ages. These distinctive religions, these "micro-religions," or the *religiones particulares* as Augustinus of Ancona termed them, certainly did not challenge the "system of faith" of *Christianitas*, nor did they set themselves up as *ecclesiolae in ecclesia*, but they were *religiolae in religione*. In other words, they were religious entities that existed above and beyond their individual members, exhibiting distinctive ways of life, and even if they did not develop separate "systems of faith," they certainly did have their own systems of worship. If religion as a virtue was incumbent upon all, the diverse and distinctive *religiones* offered the opportunity for fulfilling one's obligations in a particular fashion.[178] Or in the terms of Biller and Bossy, in the Middle Ages religion IIa was a subset of religion I. A micro-religion was the social context for establishing the

---

[173] "Nove religionis que fervet in Leodio et circa partes illas ferventissimus predicator." *Chronicon, MGH.SS* 23.855, as cited by Ernest W. McDonnell, *The Beguines and Beghards in Medieval Culture* (New Jersey, 1954), 73.

[174] Paris, BnF MS lat. 4896A, as cited by McDonnell, *The Beguines*, 73, n. 16.

[175] Jac.V. *HO* 28 (144).

[176] Jac.V. *HO* 28 (158f).

[177] See Chapter One, n. 385.

[178] With reference to the discussion in note 148 above concerning definitions of religion, in keeping with my definition given there, a micro-religion then is the social manifestation of systems of meaning by which humans relate themselves to transcendence, in accordance with the parameters of an identifiable spirituality. It is most likely in this sense too that in northern Europe in the eleventh and twelfth centuries *religio* was associated with confraternities; see Susan Reynolds, *Kingdoms and Communities in Western Europe, 900–1300* (Oxford, 1997²), 69.

'religious individual'.[179] If we desire to understand the concept of religion in the Middle Ages, we cannot dismiss the monastic contribution to the development of the term.

My purpose in discussing the positions of Biller and Bossy was not to attempt to give a final answer to the meaning of 'medieval religion,' but rather to use their discussions as a wedge with which to pry open a bit further than otherwise possible a window onto the understanding of the *religio Augustini*. On the one hand, *religio* was a moral virtue consisting of everything that humans owe God. Yet on the other hand, *religio* was a specific way of life, based on a vow, defined legally as being *in statu religionis*.[180] Being *in statu religionis* incorporated fulfilling one's debt to God, that is, *religio* as a virtue.

Even though he closely followed Thomas for his understanding of *religio*, Jordan diverged from his source in two significant respects. First, for Thomas the designation *religiosus* was derived from being *in statu religionis*, which he identified with the perfect life of monastic vows. Jordan quoted Thomas' derivation of *religiosus*,[181] but explained that having a *status religionis* is not the only basis for deserving the appellation of being a religious. The Beghards, the followers of Lull, and anyone else who took a private vow were properly said to be *religiosi*, even though Matthew of Paris, for example, referred to the Beghards, who were bound by no perpetual vow, as *se asserentes religiosos*.[182] In other words, Jordan broadened the category of *religiosi* to include those not officially *in statu religionis*, many of whom were lay. To this extent, Jordan was echoed by Geert Groote, who was "repelled by the usual interpretation of *religio*,"[183] claiming that the Beguines "are just as religious as the nuns in their convents. To love God and worship him is religion, not the taking of special vows."[184] Jordan made this distinction in his *Liber Vitasfratrum* in the chapter dealing with manual labor and whether it was permitted for *religiosi* to live from alms. The *religiosi* who do not have a *status religionis* were comprised by and large of the laity and were required to live from the fruits of their own labors. The laity, Jordan affirmed with

---

[179] "The individual does, and indeed can, exist only within society. The medieval individual is absorbed into the social macrocosm via the microgroup... Each microgroup adheres to certain values which are, in part, specific to the social microcosm in question and in part common to a number of groups or for society as a whole, and the indiviudal becomes part of that culture by assimilating those values. As the individual does so, he or she becomes a personality." Gurevich, *The Origins of European Individualism*, 89.

[180] In Canon Law the term *status* was used to refer to the conditions of the Orders' instituted way of life; see, for example, Sextus 3.17.1 (Fr. 1055) and Clem. 3.10.1.9 (Fr. 1168).

[181] "Et ex hac virtute per anthonomasyam dicuntur illi religiosi qui seipsos totos tamquam holocaustum deo offerunt perpetuo." Jor. *Exp.* 7, fol. 83ra; *cf.* Thom.Aq. *STh* II/II q. 186, art. 1 resp. (2356a,39–42).

[182] MacDonnell, *Beguines*, 249.

[183] *Ibid.*, 126.

[184] As quoted by MacDonnell, *Beguines*, 126, n. 29.

appeal to Augustine, are not allowed to live from alms except in the following four cases: 1) when they are poor, infirm, or sick; 2) if their labor does not provide sufficiently for their sustenance; 3) if they do not know how to work sufficiently to sustain themselves and thus fall into serious poverty, and 4) if they give all their goods to the poor and therefore do not have sufficient resources remaining to live.[185] Given the fourth case especially, Jordan made room for all those living the apostolic life to be included in the category *religiosi* whether or not they made official profession in an approved Order.

The second respect in which Jordan deviated from the teaching of Thomas on the issue of *religio* was that Jordan nowhere equated the *status religionis* in and of itself with the perfect life. For Thomas, the *status religionis* was identified as the *vita perfecta*, consisting of the monastic vows of poverty, chastity, and obedience.[186] For Jordan, the *vita perfecta* did not enter his discussion of *religio* or of the designation *religiosi*. In the *Liber Vitasfratrum* Jordan did affirm that the anchoritic life was more perfect than the cenobitic in his general discussion of the history and development of monasticism.[187] His focus, however, was not on the perfect life, but rather on the declines and renewals of the apostolic life over time, and it is here that we find an additional component of his understanding of the *religio Augustini*. Although the anchoritic life is more perfect than the cenobitic, the cenobitic is more secure. However, the most perfect life, the *vita perfectissima*, is the combination of the anchoritic and cenobitic lives, the harmonization of the *vita contemplativa* and the *vita activa*. The *religio Augustini* was the *vita perfectissima*, lived in imitation of Augustine.[188]

In the later Middle Ages, religion was a moral virtue, incumbent upon all members of society, consisting of all acts owed to God. The micro-religions offered distinct forms for meeting one's obligation. The phenomena I have designated as micro-religions are not to be equated with sects, cults, or churches, or with the religious Orders *per se*. The term micro-religion is used to refer to the various *religiones*, the *religiones particulares*, within *Christianitas*. The micro-religions were specific subcultures within the general religious culture of the later Middle Ages.[189] Among the micro-religions, the *religiolae in religione*, the *religio Augustini* formed the *vita perfectissima*. It was a specific way of life based on the example of Augustine, consisting of ideals, institutions and regulations: the *religio Augustini* embodied the Augustinian identity.

Augustine's religion has remained an unrecognized factor in attempts to delineate the contours of late medieval Augustinianism. Yet the Order's

---

[185] *VF* 2,25 (252,40–253,52).
[186] Thom.Aq. *STh* II/II q. 186, art. 6–7 (2363b–2366a).
[187] See *VF* 1,4 (15ff).
[188] See Chapter Three above.
[189] Martha Newman has analyzed Cistercian religious culture, defined as "the public expressions of symbolic meaning through speech, action, and ritual that are a dialogue between individuals on the one hand and the traditions of religion on the other." M. Newman, *The Boundaries of Charity. Cistercian Culture and Ecclesiastical Reform, 1098–1180* (Stanford, 1996), 7.

theology, religious ideals, and pastoral endeavor can only be distinguished heuristically, keeping the broader perspective of that theology as part and parcel of Augustine's religion ever in mind. One enters the realm of ahistorical theology when one abstracts the theology of the Order in the later Middle Ages from the Order's religious culture, which included textual, sociological, psychological, historical, and theological components. These components worked together to create the Order's religious identity. The Order's elusive "group spirit" was a concrete historical reality: it was its created identity as the sons of Augustine, whose programmatic mission was to sanctify the souls of late medieval society. In imitation of Augustine, Augustine's sons were to transform both themselves and their world. A theological task it was indeed: late medieval Augustinianism was the Order's theological imperative to teach and to preach how life was to be lived.

4. Religionization

In the history of Christianity in medieval and early modern Europe, two major movements have attracted the attention of scholars: Christianization and Confessionalization. Christianization has been seen as a multifaceted and multilayered missionary venture to convert pagan Europe, reaching its culmination in the eleventh century when Christendom, in the words of John van Engen, "rooted in practice and profession and given shape by liturgical, ecclesiastical, and credal structures, included every person in medieval Europe except the Jews."[190] Confessionalization has turned to the later period, after the original upheavals of the Reformation, by tracing the religio-political dynamics by which territorial rulers established religious conformity with a given confession.[191] Religionization, however, has gone undetected in treatments of Christendom's development. Yet religionization, not limited to strict chronological boundaries, is an apt description for the continued "Christianization" of Christendom, which reached its high point in the period between the "end of Christianization" and the beginning of Confessionalization, namely, between the eleventh and early sixteenth centuries. This was a period of rich religious ferment, from the renewed emphasis on the apostolic life present in the new monasticism and the canonical movement, to the rise of the mendicant orders, the spread of individualized religious devotion, the rise of lay piety, the emergence of "semi-religious" groups such as the Beguines, confraternities, and the Modern Devotion, and finally observantism and the early Reformation. While in broad terms

---

[190] John Van Engen, "The Christian Middle Ages as an Historiographical Problem," *AHR* 1986, 519–552. See also James C. Russell, *The Germanization of Early Medieval Christianity. A Sociohistorical Approach to Religious Transformation* (Oxford, 1994).

[191] See Heinz Schilling, *Religion, Political Culture and the Emergence of Early Modern Society*, SMRT 50 (Leiden 1992); Wolfgang Reinhard and Heinz Schilling, eds., *Die Katholische Konfessionalisierung*, Schriften des Vereins für Reformationsgeschichte 198, (Heidelberg 1995).

these developments can be grouped together and labeled as the "age of reform," reform as a descriptive concept is ambiguous, referring at times to institutional reform, personal reform, monastic reform and the like, lacking the concreteness to encompass the most conscious endeavor to broaden, expand, and deepen religion itself. If the Christening of Europe, or the Christianization of Europe can be used as a helpful descriptive category of the phenomena whereby Europe emerged as the religio-political unit of Christendom, and if Confessionalization characterizes early modern political territories adopting and enforcing a given religious confession—without implying or assuming a theological, political, or economic determinism— then religionization can be introduced as a descriptive category of the development whereby the religious life was extended to include, and indeed eventually was seen as obligatory for, every member of Christendom. Increasingly the *religiosi* were considered to be not just those wearing a monastic habit, but all who lived the Christian life.

Within the general pastoral and catechetical programs of the high and later Middle Ages, religionization was the formation, cohesion and extension of micro-religions, each with its own implicit or explicit theology, whereby in the course of the later Middle Ages the definition of *religiosi* was expanded to include all true Christians. It is a descriptive term for the evolution in the definitions and expressions of 'being religious' from the eleventh to the early sixteenth century, when the category of the *religiosi* was becoming increasingly "fuzzy," leading eventually to a modified and completely altered idealized cognitive model[192] for the determination of the category. The 'proto-type' religious at the beginning of the development was clearly the monk, withdrawing from the world, seeking the world's conversion by bringing the world into the monastery, or, leaving it to its own desserts and deserts,[193] whereas in the later fourteenth and fifteenth centuries the 'proto-type' religious was a friar, or a member of the new devout, or a lay saint, or a Beguine, or a recluse, and the list could be expanded based on who might be answering the question. All these later 'proto-type' religious did not seek to bring the world within the walls of the cloister in order to "save" the world, but rather sought to sanctify society by bringing the cloister to the world. As Antonius Rampegolus made clear, being a religious was more than adherence to external, formalized factors; it was based on internal disposition. He by no means stood alone in the Middle Ages. The emphasis on the need "to be truly religious" progressed to the point that the technical definition of the *religiosi* itself was expanded to include those taking private vows and living the religious life voluntarily, as well as those who officially entered an *ordo*, with an established *regula* and *institutio*. In short, the determination of 'being religious' came to be made by the definition of *religio* itself. *Religio*, whether officially within a *status religionis*, or a personalized, internalized way of life, signified the individual's chosen and determined way for fulfilling the requirements of *religio*

---

[192] Lakoff, *Women, Fire, and Dangerous Things*.
[193] See Ludo J.R. Millis, *Angelic Monks and Earthly Men* (Woodbridge, 1992).

as part of *iustitia naturalis*, consisting of everything Christians owe their God. Jacques de Vitry had claimed that all Christians lived under a rule, the rule of Christ, the supreme abbot,[194] and Thomas Aquinas recognized the existence of multifaceted 'religions', defined by their unique "slant" on living the religious life, though for Thomas, the *religiones* were part and parcel of the *status religionis* designated as the *vita perfectiva*. Almost a century later Jordan of Quedlinburg distinguished between those *religiosi* officially *in statu religionis* and those not, without attributing the *vita perfecta* in and of itself to either category of religious. For Jordan, it was not the *vita perfecta* as such that was foremost in his concern, but the *vita perfectissima*, the Augustinians' *vita contemplativa* consisting of solitude to be sure, but solitude that led to care for society in preaching and teaching—by definition. The *vita perfectissima* for Jordan was equated with his own Order's *religio*, but not with the Order itself. Shortly after Jordan, his younger contemporary Geert Groote held up the *religio beguinarum* as equally religious as the nuns in cloisters, for 'being religious', according to Groote, was simply the attribute of those who truly loved God. Every true Christian deserved the title 'religious', just as Jordan claimed that not only the *religiosi in statu religionis*, but every Christian was to become a saint and thus to be as bright and shining as the stars.[195] Belonging to an *ordo* may have retained its privileged status, but it was no longer exclusive. Thus in c. 1430 the Dominican Johannes Nider composed his treatise *De secularium religionibus*, arguing for the importance of the religious life of the laity.[196] Joining a religious Order was a possible means of fulfilling one's religious obligations, but was no longer the sole basis for 'being religious'.[197]

---

[194] "Non solum hos qui seculo renunciant et transeunt ad religionem regulares iudicamus, sed et omnes Christi fideles, sub euangelica regula domino famulantes et ordinate sub uno summo et supremo abbate uiuentes, possumus dicere regulares." Jac.V. *HO* 34 (165,17–20). Hinnebusch notes that Gerhoch of Reichersberg held similar views in his *Liber de aedificio Dei*, 43 (*PL* 190,1302). *Cf.* Constable, *The Reformation of the Twelfth Century*, 7 and 293.

[195] Saak, "Quilibet Christianus."

[196] See John Van Engen, "Friar Johannes Nyder on Laypeople Living as Religious in the World," in *Vita Religiosa im Mittelalter. Festschrift für Kaspar Elm zum 70. Geburtstag*, ed. Franz J. Felten and Nikolas Jaspert, with Stephanie Haarländer, Berliner Historische Studien 31/Ordensstudien 13 (Berlin, 1999), 583–615. Van Engen translates *De secularium religionibus* as "laypeople living as religious in the world," yet the more literal translation is more accurate: on the religions of the laity.

[197] This development has previously been recognized with regard to the *Devotio Moderna*. My point here is that the *Devotio Moderna*, technically speaking, as Rudolph Van Dijk has recently argued, was a particular form of a more general late medieval devotional movement, itself a part of on-going religionization, which can only be detected when the existence and importance of micro-religions are acknowledged, and irrespective of whether these micro-religions were lived in the context of institutionalized orders. See R.Th.M. Van Dijk, "Die Frage einer nördlichen Variante der Devotio Moderna. Zur Interferenz zwischen den spätmittelalterlichen Reformbewegungen," in *Wessel Gansfort (1419–1489) and Northern Humanism*. Ed. F. Akkerman, G.C. Huisman, and A.J. Vanderjagt (Leiden 1993), 157–169; *cf.* K. Elm, "*Vita regularis sine regula*," 244–248, 255–264; Van Engen, "Friar Johannes Nyder," *passim*.

APPENDIX A

The Reformation of the twelfth century, combined with the "pastoral revolution" of the thirteenth, initiated a series of profound developments in the religious, social and cultural life of Europe.[198] According to Giles Constable, "The application of monastic life to all people, and the interiorization of monastic values and spirituality, eventually led to monasticizing everyone and destroying the special position held by monks in the early Middle Ages."[199] Part of this pastoral endeavor to "monasticize everyone" was the proliferation of catechetical literature. The first general programmatic wave of catechesis in the medieval West produced such works in the first half of the thirteenth century as Robert Grosseteste's *De Decem Mandatis* and Edmund of Abingdon's *Speculum Ecclesie*.[200] The second such wave was marked by the various forms of "new devotion," epitomized by the northern German-Netherlandic *Devotio Moderna*, and culminated in the early Reformation of the sixteenth century and Luther's priesthood of all believers.[201]

The general catechetical endeavor, however, should not be limited to a progressive "monasticization" of medieval society. Edmund's *Speculum*, for example, has been seen as "a skillful *summa* of Hugh's [of St. Victor] teaching on the life of meditation and contemplation which should be the ideal of the religious."[202] Yet in this treatise Edmond is not addressing monastics. He quotes Eusebius to emphasize that 'religion' offers the height of perfection, yet when he continues to describe and explain what the perfect life entails, it is not the monastic vows that he holds up, or even mentions, but the exhortation to live honorably, amicably, and humbly.[203] The treatise continues to explicate that which makes one holy, that which makes one a saint, which is defined most of all by knowledge of the truth and love of the good (ch. 3), which is then detailed in the rest of the work by expositing the seven virtues, the seven gifts of the holy spirit, the Ten Commandments, the twelve articles of faith, the four cardinal virtues, the six works of mercy, the seven petitions of the *Pater Noster*, and the eucharist. In short, Edmund's work is a catechetical treatise for the religious Christian, whereby the knowledge and following the basic doctrines of the Christian faith was equated with being a religious. There is no mention of monastic vows or monastic rules. This application of the religious life to each and

---

[198] See Constable, *The Reformation of the Twelfth Century*; and Colin Morris, *The Papal Monarchy. The Western Church from 1050–1250* (Oxford, 1989).
[199] Constable, *The Reformation of the Twelfth Century*, 7.
[200] Goss.*Dec.man.*; Edm.Ab. *Spec.*
[201] On the later phase of the general catechetical program, see Robert J. Bast, *Honor Your Fathers*. The various waves of catechesis can be illustrated by the textual history of Edmund's *Speculum Ecclesie*, which was originally composed, in Latin, and given the title *Speculum Religiosorum*; the text(s) enjoyed popularity in Latin, French and English, which in the various forms, can be seen as peaking in the late thirteenth/early fourteenth century, then again in the later fourteenth century, and finally another peak in the fifteenth century; see Edm.Ab. *Spec.* intro., 16.
[202] Edm.Ab. *Spec.* intro., 24.
[203] "Perfecte quidem vivere est . . . vivere honorabiliter, amicabiliter et humiliter." Edm.Ab. *Spec.* 2,3 (32,17–18).

every Christian was a development within the general upsurge in catechesis that I have called 'religionization,' of which 'monasticization' can be seen as one form.

Religionization, however, is not to be equated itself with the pastoral theology or with the general catechetical program of the high and later Middle Ages. Religionization was the formation, cohesion and expansion of micro religions, formal religious groups with their own distinct religious culture. As distinct religious groups in society, the micro-religions—whether they be the religious orders, or 'semi-religious' lay groups such as the Beguines, Beghards, confraternities, or the brothers and sisters of the common life[204]— espoused a particular form of religious practice, based on their group-specific ideals. Each micro-religion implicitly or explicitly exhibited a distinct theology, even if not always in keeping with the standards of university theology in the Middle Ages, or with contemporary assumptions as to what is and what is not valid theology. They also exhibited their own spirituality. Spirituality is often used by modern scholars as essentially equivalent to the medieval definition of 'religion' itself, especially in terms of the 'micro-religions'. Moreover, spirituality has been treated separately from theology proper, with the exception, perhaps, of the spirituality of mystical theology. Spirituality has been seen as the 'affective' side of religion, whereas theology is the 'rational' side.[205] Yet, theology could be affective as well; the Augustinian university theologians in the fourteenth century defined theol-

---

[204] Though scholars have studied the legal terminology and the religious content of the divergent monastic rules, orders, customs, and legal states (e.g.: *status canonicus, status monachus*), the sundry religions have not been the object of investigation. Research has, however, identified the growth of the 'semi-religious' (*Semireligiosentum*), exemplified most of all by the Brothers and Sisters of the Common Life; See Kaspar Elm, "Die Bruderschaft vom Gemeinsamen Leben. Eine Geistliche Lebensform zwischen Kloster und Welt, Mittelalter und Neuzeit," *OGE* 59 (1985), 470–496; idem, "*Vita regularis sine regula*: Bedeutung, Rechtsstellung und Selbstverständnis des mittelalterlichen und frühneuzeitlichen Semireligiosentums," in *Häresie und vorzeitige Reformation im Spätmittelalter*, ed. F. Smahel (Munich, 1998), 239–273. Elm classified the diverse forms of religious expression lived 'between the monastery and the world' as the *status medius*, a term Elm employs with reference to Gerard Zerbolt of Zutphen's treatise, *Super modo vivendi devotorum hominum*, to signify a religious commitment between the *saeculares saeculariter viventes* and the *status religiosorum*; Elm, "Die Bruderschaft," 476. Yet, as Elm admits, even given the many contributions of the last decades the phenomenon of the semi-religious is still in need of illumination; Elm, "Die Bruderschaft," 494. The problem of the semi-religious, for both medieval churchmen and modern scholars, is that most often *religio* was a distinct component of the monastic life, as was *ordo* or *regula*, yet lacked canonical definition. Consequently, whenever *religiones* emerged in the later Middle Ages, it was unclear how to describe them in legal terms. Some religions had an order, a juridical status, a rule and established codes of conduct, but others, and increasingly so in the fourteenth and fifteenth centuries, did not.

[205] See Joseph Wawrykow, "On Dispelling the Malaise in Scholastic Theology," in John Van Engen, ed., *The Past and Future of Medieval Studies* (Notre Dame, 1994), 178–189; cf. John C. Hirsh, *The Boundaries of Faith. The Development and Transmission of Medieval Spirituality*, SHCT 67 (Leiden, 1996).

ogy as *scientia affectiva*, a knowledge of the heart, rather than of the mind, and in his *Liber Vitasfratrum*, Jordan claimed the highest form of knowledge was *scientia spiritualis*, thus combining explicitly what most often by modern scholars has been kept clearly distinct. For the Augustinians, in any case, theology was affective and practical, aimed at leading to the love of God and love of neighbor. Their practical bent, their attempt to bring the riches of the contemplative life to society, their attempt to 'religionize' society, did not entail, however, a backing away from the specificity of their religion itself: it was inherent therein. The Augustinians' pastoral theology was as genuinely Augustinian as was their academic theology, and both were central components of the *religio Augustini*.

To treat late medieval theology historically, scholars must strive to perceive that within the context of the micro-religions, theology and spirituality formed a unit. Theologically religionization was virtually identical with sanctification,[206] and as Jordan insisted, every true Christian was to become a saint. Even the abstract, systematic doctrines of sanctification did not exist independently from the micro-religions in which they were developed. What from one perspective might appear as completely rational, abstract ideas, for the medieval theologians were embodied. The cognitive models for the doctrines of sanctification were the embodied, lived religious lives of the theologians in the context of the micro-religions: theologically sanctification was the theoretical expression of religionization.

Above I mentioned that religionization was the formation, cohesion and expansion of micro-religions. The religion-specific nature of theology applies to the first two aspects. The lack of specificity appears only when the level of interpretation shifts to the reception of that theology. In "going beyond the walls" of a given micro-religion, whether the walls were metaphorical or material, the micro-religion based its endeavor on religion-specific theological ideals, but the extent to which such religion-specific theology was received by the audience as such is another question.

To sketch the contours of religionization in bringing the concept and phenomenon into sharper focus, I will first mention five points to illustrate what religionization is not, before turning to the positive approach with further demarcations.

1.) Though resulting from the inherent theologies and spiritualities of the micro-religions, religionization was not synonymous with individual spirituality, devotion, or piety. Recent scholarship has highlighted the importance of lay religion, personal devotion, and popular piety in the later Middle Ages, especially in opposition to official, established religion.[207] While such study has made major contributions to the understanding of the social aspects of religious life, religionization as such is not to be identified with

---

[206] See E.L. Saak, "Quilibet Christianus."

[207] For an overview, see Robert W. Scribner, "Elements of Popular Belief," in *Handbook of European History, 1400–1600. Late Middle Ages, Renaissance and Reformation*, vol. 1: *Structures and Assertions*, ed. Thomas A. Brady Jr, Heiko A. Oberman, and James D. Tracy (Leiden, 1994), 231–262.

popular religion or personal devotion. The basic sociological premise of religionization, namely, the formation, cohesion, and expansion of micro-religions, assumes the definition that a particular micro-religion is by definition supra-individual, and is not independent from social structures, to the same extent that devotion was not completely private.

2.) Further, religionization was not codified doctrinally. This point may seem to contradict my above argument that each micro-religion implicitly or explicitly was based upon a religion-specific theology. What I mean here by stating that religionization was not codified doctrinally is that it did not receive institutional directives from the ecclesiastical hierarchy. Only when religionization came into open conflict with established hegemonic structures, did it evoke official doctrinal response, namely, when religionization was viewed as heresy. Such, for example, occurred with the micro-religion of the Cathars, and the Beguines burned as heretics. Whereas with Christianization the determinative rite was baptism, and, perhaps, confession of the creed doctrinally codified, and whereas Confessionalization was doctrinally codified in Protestant confessions or the decrees of Trent, there was no such doctrinal codification for religionization as such. The diversity of the micro-religions precluded any overarching platform of inculcation.

3.) Not only is religionization to be distinguished from individualized spirituality and personal religion, but also from popular piety or popular religion. Occurring on the micro level of social analysis, religionization is not dichotomized by categories of lay/learned or official/popular; a micro-religion could consist of what traditional analysis has termed either official or popular religion, and incorporate both lay and learned categories of membership.

4.) In contrast to Christianization and Confessionalization, religionization was not inherently political. This is not to say, however, that political aspects were not involved, such as we find in spread of Clunaic and Cistercian monasticism,[208] and in the late medieval observant reform movement;[209] territorial rulers often took active roles in religionizing their subjects by means of policy, patronage, and example. Given Jordan's, and Thomas Aquinas', definition of religion as part of *iustitia naturalis*, it is hardly surprising to recognize the political aspects of religionization. And yet, the point to be made, is that religionization was not dependent in and of itself on political policy. Religionization took place most often on a very localized level. The diversity of the micro-religions preclude any attempt to associate religionization with political strategy for a territory as such. Religionization did not play a role in the definition of political boundaries.

5.) Religionization was not dependent on institutionalization. The Augustinians had their unique *religio*, but the *religio Augustini* as such is not to be equated with the *Ordo*, or the *Institutio*, or the *Regula* of the OESA. This becomes most evident in the observant movement. In the fifteenth century the Augustinians, as all the mendicant orders, became administratively

---

[208] See, for example, Constance Bouchard, *Sword, Miter, and Cloister. Nobility and the Church in Burgundy, 980–1198* (Ithaca, N.Y., 1987).

[209] Manfred Schulze, *Fürsten und Reformation*.

divided into observant and conventual congregations. Unlike the Franciscans, however, the Augustinians never split into two distinct Orders. The conventual and observant friars shared the same rule, order, and institution: they followed different religions, or had different interpretations of the *religio Augustini*, which then became administratively distinct. *Religio* is not synonymous with *Ordo*, nor even with *Regula*, as Jordan had made clear; one could be a religious without entering the *status religionis*, which did entail an institutionalization of the *religio*. The micro-religions phenomenologically and at times sociologically were independent from legal institutionalization.

In this light, three elements of religionization can be identified. First, there was the change in the idealized cognitive model of the *religiosi*; second, the formation and cohesion of micro-religions; and third, the extension of the micro-religions based on transformational sanctity.[210] These three aspects of religionization are not to be seen as stages, but as the three foundational attributes. These foundational attributes are complimented by the following three fundamental characteristics.

1.) Religionization was implicitly gendered. The basic, defining category for tracing religionization is the meaning attributed to 'being religious'. With the micro-religions as the fundamental category for a sociology of religion, religionization precludes adopting any given norm based on theological or ecclesiological presuppositions of what 'being religious' entailed. Thus analyzing religionization by definition requires accepting as a given the gendered nature of 'being religious', whereby males and females ascribed content and meaning to the category upon which micro-religions were formed. By recognizing the fact that religionization itself led to the non-identification of 'being religious' with male norms of religio-ecclesiastic life, analysis of the process must take into account female and male religions, analyzing the means by which meaning was ascribed to a particular expression of religious life within the context of a particular micro-religion.

Moreover, in addition to particularized male and female micro-religions, religionization as such was gendered, in so far as 'being religious' became increasingly feminized in the later Middle Ages. As Carolyn Bynum has argued:

> In the twelfth and thirteenth centuries, women's piety was a special case of lay piety. Increasingly in the fourteenth century, lay piety *became* female piety and as such, of course, increasingly suspect. Thus, the religiosity of medieval women, ecstatic and self-denying, yet profoundly oriented toward service *in the world*, is a distinct socioreligious type that needs to be explored as background to the Reformation.[211]

In medieval definitions, piety was a particular act of religion and thus calls for interpretation within the perimeters of the micro-religion of which it was an expression. Given the fact that micro-religions were not identical with institutionalized structures, religionization took place on a level primary to the institutionalization of religious groups and practices, and thus

---

[210] See E.L. Saak, "Quilibet Christianus."
[211] Bynum, *Fragmentation and Redemption*, 77.

it takes into account the micro-religions independent of formal organizations, including the "ordinary experience" of women being religious. "Although male orders fought to define themselves and each other in sometimes very uncharitable polemic," Bynum notes,

> ... women floated from institution to institution. Later claimed by the various orders as Premonstratensians, Cistercians or Franciscans, a strikingly large number of women saints of the thirteenth and fourteenth centuries cannot really be seen as affiliated closely with any religious house or possessing any clear status. They were simply women in the world (in their fathers', uncles' or husbands' houses), being religious. Historians have repeatedly argued that women's failure to create or to join orders was owing to male oppression... It may be, however, that women's rather 'structureless' religion simply continued their ordinary lives... Recent research indicates that, in some instances, women who could have chosen the more formal life of the convent chose the quasi-religious status instead. In any case, if women's communities (convents or beguinages) were institutionalized liminality... that liminality was imaged as continuity with, not as reversal of, the women's ordinary experience.[212]

While women who did not enter formal, institutionalized religious organizations, those that had an *ordo, institutio,* and/or *regula,* and thus indeed lacked, on a legal ground, the 'status' of being a 'religious', or in legal terminology, they were not *in statu religionis,* Jordan himself makes clear that this did not mean that such women were relegated to a 'quasi' religious status. They could genuinely and truly be *religiosae,* precisely within their "structureless" ordinary experience. On the level of micro-religion, religionization entails accepting the distinction between the 'religious' and the 'quasi-religious' only when found in the medieval sources themselves and thus guards against a predetermined norm whereby the 'religious' are defined based on male models, with women "added to" accordingly, or categorized as only 'quasi' religious. Religionization occurred within an enlarged field of social action that not only takes into account, but presupposes as the focal point of analysis the "... locations of private, supportive, informal, local social structures," and "the interplay between informal, interpersonal networks and the formal, official social structures."[213] While we find reference to the *religio beguinarum,* we do not see the qualification of *pseudo-religio,* or *quasi-religio,* and when Matthew of Paris questioned the legitimate religious status of the Beghards, he did not refer to them as *pseudo-religiosi,* or *quasi-religiosi,* but as *se asserentes religiosos.* In short, there were no 'semi-religious' (*Semireligiosentum*), and this hold true for both male and female groups of religious: one was either a religious, or not, even if one was seen as illegitimately portraying oneself as such from the outside perspective.[214]

---

[212] Bynum, *Fragmentation and Redemption*, 46–47; cf. Elm, "*Vita regularis sine regula*," 249–250.

[213] Marcia Millman and Rosabeth Moss Kanter, "Introduction to Another Voice: Feminist Perspectives on Social Life and Social Science," in *Feminism and Methodology*, ed. Sandra Harding (Bloomington, Indiana, 1987), 29–36; 32.

[214] *Semireligiosentum* is an historiographical construct based on traditionally institu-

The micro-religions as such are gender neutral; or rather, as a concept *per se* religionization precedes the gendered historical phenomenon. This allows for a more value-free analysis of engendering particular micro-religions on the one hand, and on the other, the means by which the gendered micro-religions effected change within the religious sociological hierarchy in the later Middle Ages by focusing both on the female micro-religions themselves, and on the role of female imagery within male and female micro-religions. Bynum notes that, "Most medieval holy women in fact practiced what late medieval theorists called the 'mixed life'. They carried out both charity and a meditation that issued in mystical union. But what is more important is the fact that they understood the meaning of their lives to be such a profound combination of action and contemplation that the contrast between the categories vanishes."[215] Yet Jordan explicitly defined the *vita contemplativa* as including preaching and teaching. For Jordan, the contemplative life embraced all endeavors that pertained to the soul, the soul of oneself or of one's neighbor. The *vita activa* pertained to physical life as such.[216] Thus, the question that must be asked, is to what extent is such an understanding of the religious life, and one that surpasses the traditional calls for the 'mixed life', representative of female religion or of a particular version of male religion? Is Jordan an example of a feminization

---

tionalized, legal definitions of the *religiosi* thus delegitimizing the historical experience of the members of such micro-religions who considered themselves in fact to be *religiosi*, even if not monks, friars, or nuns, as did such established figures as Jacques de Vitry, Jordan of Quedlinburg, Geert Groote, and Johannes Nider. My argument is that we are better able to access, describe, and analyze the historical phenomena of '*Semireligiosentum*', what Hostiensis referred to as the *status religiosus largo modo*, which I would claim is better understood and described when seen as that of the *religiosi sine statu*, or the *religiones secularium* than it is as the *vita regularis sine regula*, with the concepts of micro-religion and religionization than we are with 'out-group' terms and labels in attempt to categorize and thus control. Elm has given the best encapsulation of the phenomena of the *religiosi sine statu* that I have seen: "In dieser ambivalenten Situation, die man mit Formulierungen wie *vita regularis sine regula, via media, status tertius, status medius* zu beschreiben versuchte, entstand bei aller Verschiedenheit, die nicht zu übersehen ist, eine eigene Spiritualität, ja Kultur, der sich die Forschung erst seit einigen Jahrzehnten zuwendet. Was sie ähnlich wie die übrigen Formen genossenschaftlich ausgerichteter geistlicher Gemeinschaftsbildung sowohl orthodoxen als heterodoxen Charakters kennzeichnet, ist in erster Linie die auf der Voraussetzung weitgehender 'brüderlicher' Gleichheit beruhende Organisationsstruktur, die konventikelartige Versammlung, das paraliturgische Gebet und das Verbreitung volkssprachlichen Schrifttums, und schließlich das Streben nach individueller, nicht selten den Rahmen des Üblichen, ja der Orthodoxie sprengender religiöser Erkenntnis und Erfahrung." Elm, "*Vita regularis sine regula*," 255–256; *cf.* Van Engen, "Friar Johannes Nyder," 612–613. This phenomenon, this culture, I would claim is the *religio* of the *religiosi sine statu*, which functioned on the same primary, micro-level as did the *religio* of the *religiosi in statu religionis*. The function of the micro-religions was primary to the categorizing and defining those religions' expressions and manifestations.

[215] Bynum, *Fragmentation and Redemption*, 69.
[216] E.L. Saak, "Quilibet Christianus."

of clerical piety? With his concept of the priesthood of all believers, furthermore, Luther continued an on-going development that for the two preceding centuries, at least, had been expanding the definition of the 'true Christian' to include all members of society. In this light, the question can be posed as to the extent to which the *religio Lutheri*, based on an intense personal relationship with the divine, yet one that was also designed to function in the world, was also the culmination of the "feminization" of religion that Bynum has noted as a distinct socioreligious type. In acknowledging the inherently gendered nature of the primary religious experience within the context of the micro-religions, it could well prove that the *religio Lutheri*, and indeed, the early Reformation as such, was the triumph of "feminine religion" that was only once again repressed and suppressed with the onslaught of the male dominating Confessionalization, whereby the "priesthood of all believers" became sacrificed to the dominant principle of *cuius regio, eius religio*, the institutional domination of a particular micro-religion. Answers to such questions will only be had with much detailed future research, but the point to be made, is that gender is a foundational category of analysis of religionization, which itself was implicitly and explicitly gendered.

2.) Religionization was inherently hermeneutical. The micro-religions created themselves based on ascribed meaning. Thus a corollary of this second characteristic of religionization is that it was inherently textual. Indeed, a micro-religion can be viewed as a 'textual community' of sorts, whereby the definition of 'being religious' was based on a particular reading of a given text or texts, whether these texts actually achieved written form, or remained "dramatic" texts of performance in society.[217] The *religio Augustini*, for example, was a mythic textual community based on a particular reading of Augustine's *Rule*, *Constitutions*, and the documents illustrating the history of the Order. With the emergence of the institutionalized Augustinian Observant movement in the early fifteenth century, we find new readings of the traditional texts, yielding a new definition of the *religio Augustini*, so that in terms of micro-religion, we need to speak of a *religio Augustini¹* and a *religio Augustini²*, with the first referring to the conventuals and the second to the Observants.[218] Even if the label remains the same, in point of fact, with the emergence of the Observance, there is a new micro-religion within the OESA, based upon different readings of the Order's *Rule*, *Constitutions*, and traditions.[219]

3.) Religionization, therefore, was inherently catechetical. The textualization of religionization was the basis for the extension of a given micro-religion, thus contributing to the new formation of micro-religious textual

---

[217] *Cf.* Brian Stock, *The Implications of Literacy*; *cf.* Bürkle, *Literatur im Kloster*, 159–258.

[218] Actually, a *religio Augustini* micro-religion could also be identified within the Order of Augustinian Canons, and thus, perhaps the canonical form of Augustinian monasticism could assume the designation *religio Augustini¹*, with the eremetical branches labeled as the second and third forms.

[219] See my forthcoming study, *The Failed Reformation*.

communities.[220] To this extent, religionization was "top down." In terms of the micro-religions as such, however, the 'top' was defined not by the binary oppositions of male/female, cleric/lay etc., but by the definer and teacher of the micro-religion itself. The concentric circles resulting from a stone thrown into a pond provide, perhaps, a better image for the "top down" character that I have in mind here, rather than a hierarchically vertical "flow chart." Within a given micro-religion, there were the definers and teachers on the one hand, and the followers on the other. The waves of concentric circles aptly depict a micro-religion spreading from its source. This wave-like expansion served both to give cohesion to the micro-religion and to extend the micro-religion beyond the confines of its actual boundaries. By catechetical in this light I intend the mechanisms whereby the definers and teachers of a given micro-religion sought to inculcate the ideals and practices of that micro-religion, such as Jordan's writing his *Liber Vitasfratrum* explicitly as a means by which any Augustinian friar might know if he is a true son of Augustine. The "waves" of catechesis can be recognized in the gendered textualizations of the micro-religions, which could in turn, form the basis for the formation of new micro-religions based on the hermeneutics of the given texts.

To summarize, religionization was the formation, integration, and expansion of micro-religions, based on the definition of the term 'being religious' as revealed by spiritual knowledge, and was not synonymous with individual spirituality, devotion, or piety, was not codified doctrinally, nor was it synonymous with popular piety or popular religion, was not inherently political, nor dependent on institutionalization, but was inherently gendered, hermeneutical, and catechetical.

In presenting the model of religionization for the interpretation of late medieval religious culture, I in no way intend to have presented a comprehensive account. My approach has been one of detection, rather than explication, definition, and codification, much as the astrophysicist detects black holes with reference to observations of bending light. Religionization is indeed such a "black hole," and thus I have tried to point to the evidence for its existence, rather than to explicate the 'thing' itself. But just as the effects of posited black holes can radically alter conceptions of the universe, so the effects of religionization can reform perceptions and portrayals of medieval Christianity.

Religionization entails a shift in the general focus of analysis from macro structures to micro. Scholars have described the relationships between the institutional church, academic theology, spirituality, and lay piety based on normative binaries of cleric/lay, male/female, reason/emotion, group/

---

[220] On the function of religious texts in religious communities, which bears close similarities to what I am referring to here as the 'textualization of religionization', see Nikolaus Staubach, "Von der persönlichen Erfahrung zur Gemeinschaftsliteratur. Entstehungs- und Rezeptionsbedingungen geistlicher Reformtexte im Spätmittelalter," *OGE* 68 (1994), 200–228.

individual, orthodox/heterodox, and sociologists have sought to categorize religious experience and practice with appeal to ideal types, whether they be those of Weber, of Troeltsch, or of someone else. A norm, or ideal, has been established, which then allows for measuring observed phenomena based on this norm. I am not denying the existence of such norms, and they often are indeed to be found in the sources themselves. My point is that such macro-norms and ideal types are insufficient for the basic category of analysis for medieval religion.

By recognizing the fundamental importance of micro-religions, one can analyze their hermeneutical endeavor to ascribe meaning to their determined way of life, which in turn provide the links to the macro structures. Religionization occurred on the level of individual religious experience, but it was not limited to private ideas, feelings, and beliefs. Such interiorization was placed in service of the social dimensions and existence of the given religion, linking the individualized, interiorized devotion as a religious act with the bond of socialized religion. The vast variation of religious experience operative on the level of the micro-religions forms the basic category of analysis. The phenomenon of religionization studied, for example, when the *religio Augustini* is the subject of observation is the same as when the *religio beguinarum*, or the *religio humiliatorum* are investigated, namely, the formation, cohesion and extension of micro-religions as such. The secondary level of analysis is then the inter-relationship of micro-religions, and the relationship between micro-religions and other social systems. It is at this level that religionization assumes its political characteristics, rather than being inherently political as are Christianization and Confessionalization. The determination of heresy, for example, is a secondary level interpretation of a micro-religion's primary level hermeneutical structuration.

Yet religionization entails a change in perspective not only of sociological categories for the analysis of religion in the medieval west. As a primary level classification, the micro-religions disallow the segregation of religious experience into the binary of rational/emotional, or theology/spirituality. Since religionization occurred on the level of individual religious experience, and since individuals cannot be classified as *either* rational *or* emotional, but both together in various proportions, it is fallacious to distinguish on the primary level the rational expression of that primary experience in terms of theology, and the emotional expression of the primary experience in terms of spirituality, and then on this basis to keep separate theology and spirituality as completely different religious phenomena and/or categories. It was only on the secondary, or even tertiary level that the rational expression of the primary religious experience became abstracted from that primary level and institutionalized as academic theology.

Moreover, religionization entails the reconceptualization of the "driving force" or forces in historical development. It assumes that in the normal course of events, the primary level of analysis is the most fundamental level of change, the level of the micro-religions, their individual adherents and their individual texts. To appeal again to the analogy with astrophysics, just as quantum theory is central for interpreting gravitational theory, so in historical analysis is the "quantum" level of the micro-religious central for interpreting the "gravitational" level of macro-structures. Institutional, macro-level changes do not occur independently from individual, micro-level changes. Moreover, the primary level of change occurs on the primary level of analysis, namely, micro-level change precedes macro-level change. This is in no way, however, asserting a determinism of any type. On the micro-level especially history has its own "indeterminacy principle," which is as strong a principle if not infinitely stronger, than the analogous nuclear principle. Whereas Christianization and Confessionalization were both fundamentally macro phenomena, religionization was fundamentally micro, which originated within Christianization, as a "by-product" so to speak, and eventually yielded Confessionalization, which occurred when a particular micro-religion gained such dominance that it became institutionalized and normative for the macro-structures.

These three developments, however, are not implicitly exclusive in any way, nor three successive stages of some underlying teleology. As soon as Christianization began, the issue of catechesis, and thus religionization, arose, even if looking at the long-term, broad development we can identify an emphasis on Christianization giving way to one on religionization as Europe emerged as Christendom in the course of the fifth to eleventh centuries. Religionization itself in time produced Confessionalization, yet continued on the micro-level "underneath" Confessionalization, and this occurred precisely as a new wave of Christianization began, namely, the overseas explorations and exploitations in the later sixteenth and seventeenth centuries which sought to extend once again the boundaries of *Christianitas*.

Religionization was a central factor in the transition between medieval and early modern culture. Together with the secondary, macro-level developments the primary, micro-level infra-structure was instrumental in instigating change: if the emergence of early modern Europe was based on religious change, or if religious change was perhaps the *causa efficiens* of early modern Europe, then the "efficient cause" of early modern Europe was the religionization of the medieval west.[221]

---

[221] Here I have sketched the contours of religionization with broad strokes in attempt to place the *religio Augustini* in its historical scope. The precise parameters of religionization, and indeed the concrete description of the phenomenon as such, is a task for future research.

APPENDIX B

BONIFACII VIII

*Bullae selectae spectantes
ad ordinem eremitarum Sancti Augustini*

1. Bonifacii VIII, *Ad consequendam*, 19 February 1295; Empoli *Bull.* 48B–49B; Alonso *Reg.* 73, nr. 181.

Dilectis filiis Generali, aliisque Provincialibus Prioribus ac universis fratribus ordinis eremitarum S. Augustini salutem et apostolicam benedictionem.

1. Ad consequendam gloriam celestis patrie sic divina pietas per suam gratiam humilitatem vestram cernitur allexisse, quod semper ad hoc intenti estis et vigiles, ut illam vobis et proximis per innocentis vite studium acquiratis. Hec et alia sancta pauperrime religionis vestre merita Nos inducunt, quod simus ex intimo cordis affectu soliciti, ut in omnibus, que ad laudem dei et tranquillum statum devotionis vestre cupitis, habeamus providentie studium efficacis.

2. Sane non sine quadam turbatione animi frequenter audivimus, quod inter vos et religiosos aliquos illa de causa aemulationis et dissensionis materia oritur, quod ipsi domos et ecclesias regulares iuxta loca vestra non sine gravi vestro preiudicio et scandalo manifesto quandoque construere presumebant.

3. Cum itaque ad apostolici spectet officii dignitatem de regno militantis ecclesie cuilibet scandali materiam abolere, Nos digne volentes quod huiusmodi aemulationis et dissensionis occasio per diligentie nostre studium amputetur, auctoritate presentium ordinamus et districtius inhibemus, quod nulli liceat amodo de Minorum, Predicatorum, Penitentie Iesu Christi, Sancte Marie de Monte Carmelo, Sancte Clare, aliisque ordinibus in paupertate fundatis, nullique mulierum de predictis seu quibuslibet aliis ordinibus aliquod monasterium, ecclesiam, vel oratorium edificare seu construere, nulli quoque seculari vel religioso cuiuscunque professionis ecclesiam, vel monasterium, seu oratorium iam edificatum, in aliquem transferre de ordinibus memoratis, infra spatium centum quadraginta cannarum a vestris ecclesiis mensurandarum per aërem etiam, ubi alias recte mensurari loci dispositio non permittit.

4. Preterea statuimus, ut quidquid contra huiusmodi ordinationis et inhibitionis nostre tenorem ex nunc in antea edificatum fuerit, diruatur et ne de notitia ordinum et quantitate cannarum huiusmodi aliqua possit dubitatio exoriri; illos ordines intelligi volumus in paupertate fundatos, qui ex regula vel constitutionibus suis extra septa ecclesiarum, monasteriorum suorum, vel officinarum eorum et clausuram ipsorum nullas debent possessiones habere.

5. Quod si aliquis de ordinibus ipsis possessiones in aliquibus membris suis habere, in aliis vero non habere noscatur, eum ad ordinationem et

inhibitionem huiusmodi, de predictis ordinibus in paupertate fundatis, annumerari volumus et quamlibet cannarum ipsarum octo palmorum longitudinem continere.

6. Non obstantibus varia locorum consuetudine seu privilegiis, indulgentiis, sive literis quibuscunque, tam supradictis ordinibus, quam mulieribus vel alicui eorum ab Apostolica Sede sub quacunque forma concessis, seu etiam concedendis, que de presentibus specialem et expressam non fecerint mentionem.

7. Nulli ergo omnino hominum liceat hanc paginam nostre ordinationis, inhibitionis, et constitutionis infringere vel ei ausu temerario contraire. Si quis autem hoc attentate presumpserit, indignationem omnipotentis dei et beatorum Petri et Pauli apostolorum eius se noverit incursurum.

Datum Laterani undecimo Calendas Martii, Pontificatus nostri anno primo.

2. Bonifacii VIII, *Sacre religionis merita*, 8 April 1298; Empoli *Bull.* 45; Alonso *Reg.* 80, nr. 201.

Dilectis filiis Priori Generali et fratribus eremitarum ordinis S. Augustini salutem et apostolicam benedictionem.

1. Sacre religionis merita, in qua mundanis derelictis illecebris, querentes celestia, domino militatis, exposcunt, ut Nos ordinem vestrum piis affectibus favorabiliter prosequamur.

2. Hinc est, quod Nos devotionis vestre supplicationibus inclinati, vobis et successoribus vestris, ac eidem ordini auctoritate presentium indulgemus, quod tu Generalis Prior, ac successores tui Generales Priores dicti ordinis, quorum confirmatio ad sedem apostolicam noscitur pertinere, qui pro tempore fuerint a diffinitoribus et discretis ipsius ordinis, qui secundum ipsius instituta ordinis electi fuerint, vel assumpti, absolvi possitis ab huiusmodi Generalis Prioratus officio et etiam amoveri, quodque in manus ipsorum diffinitorum et discretorum ipsum officium resignare, eisque tradere sigillum ipsius officii ad requisitionem et mandatum teneamini eorundem.

3. Nulli ergo omnino hominum liceat hanc paginam nostre concessionis infringere vel ei ausu temerario contraire. Si quis autem hoc attentare presumpserit, indignationem omnipotentis dei et beatorum Petri et Pauli apostolorum eius se noverit incursurum.

Datum Rome apud S. Petrum sexto Idus Aprilis, Pontificatus nostri anno quarto.

3. Bonifacii VIII, *Tenorem cuiusdam constitutionis*, 5 May 1298; Empoli *Bull.* 46A–47A; Alonso *Reg.* 81, nr. 205.

Universis presentes literas inspecturis salutem et apostolicam benedictionem.

1. Tenorem cuiusdam constitutionis edite a felicitatis recordationis Gregorio Papa decimo predicessore nostro in generali Concilio Lugdunensi cum

quibusdam mutationibus et detractationibus per Nos nuper Rome apud sanctum Petrum, quinto nonas Martii, Pontificatus nostri anno quarto, in eadem constitutione factis, presentibus fecimus adnotari, qui talis est.

2. Religionum diversitatem nimiam ne confusionem induceret, generale Concilium consueta prohibitione vitavit, sed quia non solum importuna petentium inhiatio illarum postmodum multiplicationem extorsit, verum etiam aliquorum presumptuosa temeritas, diversorum ordinum precipue mendicantium, quorum nondum approbationis meruere principium, effrenatam quasi multitudinem adinvenientes, apostolica constitutione districtius inhibentes, ne aliquis de cetero novum ordinem aut religionem inveniat, vel habitum nove religionis assumat.

3. Cunctos affatim religiones et ordines mendicantes post dictum Concilium adinventos, qui nullam confirmationem Sedis Apostolice meruerunt, perpetue prohibitioni subiicimus, et quatenus processerant, revocamus. Confirmatos autem per sedem eandem, post idem tamen Concilium institutos, quibus ad congruam sustentationem, redditus aut possessiones habere, professio sive regula vel constitutiones quelibet interdicunt, sed per questum publicum tribuere victum solet incerta mendicitas modo decernimus subsistere infrascripto.

4. Ut professoribus eorundem ordinum ita liceat in illis remanere sit velint, quod nullum deinceps ad eorum professionem admittant nec de novo domum aut aliquem locum acquirant, nec domos seu loca que habent alienare valeant sine sedis eiusdem licentia speciali, Nos enim ea dispositioni sedis apostolice reservamus in Terre sancte subsidium vel pauperum, vel alios pios usus per locorum ordinarios, vel eos, quibus sedes ipsa commiserit, convertenda. Si vero secus presumptum fuerit nec personarum receptio nec domorum vel locorum acquisitio aut ipsorum ceterorumque bonorum alienatio valeat et nihilominus contrarium facientes sententiam excommunicationis incurrant.

5. Personis quoque ipsorum ordinum omnino interdicimus quoad extraneos predicationis et audiende confessionis officium, ac etiam sepulturam. Sane ad Predicatorum et Minorum ordines, quos evidens ex eis utilitas ecclesie universali proveniens perhibet approbatos, presentem non patiantur constitutionem extendi. Ceterum Eremitarum Sancti Augustini et Carmelitarum ordines, quorum institutio dictum Concilium generale precessit, in solido statu volumus permanere.

6. Ad hec personis ordinum, ad Constitutio presens extenditur, transeundi ad reliquos ordines approbatos licentiam concedimus generalem, ita quod nullus ordo ad alium, vel conventus ad conventum se ac loca sua totaliter transferat, sedis eiusdem super hoc permissione spcialiter non obtenta.

Datum Rome apud S. Petrum, tertio Nonas Maii, Pontificatus nostri anno quarto.

---

4. Bonifacii VIII, *Sacer ordo vester*, 21 January 1299; Empoli *Bull.* 44B–45A; Alonso *Reg.* 82, nr. 206.

Dilectis filiis Priori Generali et universis prioribus et fratribus ordinis eremitarum S. Augustini, presentibus quam futuris religiosam vitam professis, salutem et apostolicam benedictionem.

1. Sacer ordo vester in agro dominico divina dispositione plantatus, apostolicis gratiis digne meretur attolli, cuius professores mundanis a se relegatis illecebris, celestium contemplationi vacantes, insistunt iugiter profectibus animarum. Nos autem ad dictum ordinem, quem in statu firmo, solido, et stabili decrevimus et volumus permanere, apostolice considerationis intuitum dirigentes, ad ea libenter intendimus, per que professores iam dicti nullum interne pacis patiantur excidium, nullumque religiosi status perferant detrimentum, sed eo devotius divino cultui ac salutis insistant operibus, quo quietior status fuerit eorundem, ipsique ampliori fuerint libertate dotati.

2. Eapropter dilecti in domino filii devotionis vestre precibus favorabiliter annuentes, vos et predictum ordinem, personas, et ecclesias, oratoria, domos, res alias, et loca vestra, ac spectantia ad eadem in quibus inhabitatis adpresens vel inhabitabitis in futurum, cum omnibus iuribus et pertinentiis suis ac personis degentibus in eisdem, in ius et proprietatem beati Petri et apostolice sedis assumimus, illaque a cuiuscunque Diocesani et cuiuslibet alterius potestate, iurisdictione, et dominio omnimode in perpetuum prorsus eximimus de gratia speciali. Decernentes ex nunc vos et ordinem vestrum ac personas, eccclesias, oratoria, domos, et loca prefata, ac pertinentia ad eadem, soli Romano Pontifici et dicte sedi tam in spiritualibus quam in temporalibus absque ullo medio subiacere. Ita quod nec locorum ordinarii, nec alia quevis persona ecclesiastica in vos et ordinem, personas, ecclesias, oratoria, domos, et loca predicta, utpote prorsus exempta, possint excommunicationis, suspensionis, aut interdicti promulgare sententias vel alias potestatem seu iurisdictionem aliquam exercere, quod si forsan quidquam in contrarium a quacunque fuerit attentatum, illud omnino sit irritum et inane.

3. Nulli ergo omnino hominum liceat hanc paginam nostre assumptionis exemptionis et constitutionis infringere vel ei ausu temerario contraire. Si quis autem hoc attentare presumpserit, indignationem omnipotentis dei et beatorum Petri et Pauli apostolorum eius se noverit incursurum.

Datum Lateran. duodecimo Calendas Februarii, Pontificatus nostri anno quarto.

5. Bonifacii VIII, *In causa que*, 14 March 1299; Empoli *Bull.* 49B–50A; Alonso *Reg.* 82–83, nr. 208.

Dilecto filio Archidiacone Bruliensi in ecclesia Agennensi salutem et apostolicam benedictionem.

1. In causa que inter priorem et conventum fratrum ordinis eremitarum sancti Augustini Agennensis ex parte una, et Guardianum et fratres ordinis Minorum eiusdem loci ex altera, super eo quod dicti prior et conventus proponunt dictos Guardianum et fratres quendam eorum locum de novo

edificasse propinquum oratoria dictorum prioris et conventus infra spatium centum et quadraginta cannarum contra tenorem privilegii fratribus dicti ordinis eremitarum ab apostolica sede concessi, in eorundem prioris et conventus preiudicium et gravamen vertitur seu verti speratur, dilectum filium nostrum Ioannem tituli sanctorum Marcellini et Petri presbyterum cardinalem deputavimus auditorem.

2. Verum quia ipsis Guardiano et fratribus Minoribus citatis pluries de mandato Cardinalis ipsius in audientia publica, ut est moris, ut coram ipso Cardinali per se vel per procuratorem idoneum legitime comparerent in eadem causa mediante iustitia processuri, ipsisque non comparentibus in terminis competentibus, ad hoc eis peremptorie assignatis, non potest in eadem causa procedi, discretioni tue per apostolica scripta mandamus, quatenus eosdem Guardianum et fratres ex parte nostra peremptorie citate procures, ut infra duorum mensium spatium post citationem tuam huiusmodi per procuratorem idoneum cum omnibus actis, iuribus, et munimentis causam huiusmodi contingentibus apostolico se conspectui representent, facturi et recepturi super premissis quod ordo exegerit rationis. Diem vero huiusmodi citationis et formam et quidquid inde duxeris faciendum, Nobis per tuas literas harum seriem continentes fideliter intimare procures.

Datum Laterani secundo Idus Martii, Pontificatus nostri anno quarto.

6. Bonifacii VIII, *Exhibita nuper nobis*, 15 January 1301; Empoli *Bull.* 47A–48A; Alonso *Reg.* 85, nr. 214.

Dilectis filiis priori provinciali et fratribus eremitarum ordinis sancti Augustini in provincia Thuringie et Saxonie, salutem et apostolicam benedictionem.

1. Exhibita nuper nobis vestra petitio continebat, quod vos iam quatuor anni elapsis et amplius in Castro Novo Quidelingborch Alberstadensis diocesis de consensu venerabilis fratris nostri episcopi Alberstadensis loci diocesani locum ad construendum, edificandum, inhabitandum, et permanendum pro vobis et fratribus vestri ordinis recepistis, ibique ad hoc construxistis et edificastis oratorium et domos ac ea inhabitastis et tenuistis et in habitatis etiam et tenetis. Verum Guardianus et fratres ordinis Minorum loci alterius castri quod dicitur Castrum Antiquum Quidelingborch, pretextu privilegii eis ab apostolica sede concessi, per quod aliorum religiosorum loca infra mensuram centum quadraginta cannarum prope loca ipsorum fratrum Minorum haberi vel fieri prohibentur, asserentes predictum locum vestrum de Castro Novo prope iam dictum locum eorum de Castro Antiquo infra mensuram cannarum huiusmodi esse situm, nituntur ipsum locum vestrum facere demoliri. Quare Nobis humiliter supplicastis, ut cum predicta castra sint sub diversis dominiis et iurisdictionibus constituta et flumen quoddam decurrat per medium inter ea, dictusque locus vester distet a predicto loco eorum ultra huiusmodi mensuram centum quadraginta cannarum, si per viam scilicet per quam itur de altero ad alterum eorundem et per terram tantummodo mensuretur, licet si fieret mensuratio per aerem et supra domos,

muros, et flumen, predicta mensura centum quadraginta cannarum comprehenderet loci distantiam utriusque, providere vobis super hoc de benignitate apostolica dignaremur.

2. Nos igitur intendentes ut prefatum privilegium seu cannarum terminatio vel mensura locum non habeat in religiosorum loca sita in diversis civitatibus, castris, aut terris, seu villis, et maxime consistentibus sub diversis dominiis et iurisdictionibus, sed in iis tantum religiosorum locis factis vel faciendis, que sub uno et eodem corpore alicuius civitatis vel castri seu terre vel ville comprehendere, seu attingere posset cannarum mensura vel terminatio predictarum, presentium vobis auctoritate concedimus, ut huiusmodi privilegio seu oppositione dictorum fratrum Minorum, aut quibuscumque privilegiis, gratiis, indulgentiis, et literis eis a predicta sede concessis nequaquam obstantibus positis vos et alii fratres vestri ordinis in predicto loco vestro de Castro Novo licite ac libere remanere, nec ad dirutionem seu destructionem ipsius loci vestri vel ad illum quomodolibet relinquendum aliquatenus teneamini, neque ad id a quoquam compelli, vel coarctari quomodolibet valeatis.

3. Nulli ergo omnino hominum liceat hanc paginam nostre concessionis infringere vel ei ausu temerario contraire. Si quis autem hoc attentare presumpserit, indignationem omnipotentis dei et beatorum Petri et Pauli apostolorum eius se noverit incursurum.

Datum Laterani decimo octavo Calendas Februarii, Pontificatus nostri anno sexto.

7. Bonifacii VIII, *Inter sollicitudines nostras*, 16 January 1303; Empoli *Bull.* 50B–52A; Alonso *Reg.* 91–92, nr. 236.

Dilectis filiis Generali et provincialibus prioribus fratrum eremitarum ordinis sancti Augustini, presentibus et futuris salutem et apostolicam benedictionem.

1. Inter sollicitudines nostras, illa debet esse precipua, ut super dominicum gregem commissum Nobis, observemus vigilias, indefessam exerceamus curam et exactam diligentiam apponamus, ne illum lupus rapax invadat et eius sanguis secundum prophetam de nostris, quod absit, manibus requiratur. Hoc autem bene fit, si oleo dulcedinis verbi dei foveantur subditi, increpationis vino peccatorum suorum medeantur vulnera et penitentie acrimonia purgata tegantur. Ad id vero exequendum scientia divine legis exposcitur, desideratur ordo, vite integritas flagitatur, scriptum est enim, Tu scientiam repulisti et ego te repellam, ne sacerdotio fungaris mihi quia labia sacerdotis custodiunt scientiam et legem requirunt ex ore eius; alias, prout ad eum pertinet, inter lepram et lepram non posset discernere, nec peccator existens, dei deberet narrare iustitias et testamentum illius assumere per os suum, nam cuius vita despicitur, consequens est, ut eius predicatio contemnatur.

2. Quapropter ut ipsi gregi eadem cura nostra eo plenior impendatur, quo plures operarii in agro domini fuerint constituti, vesterque ordo, qui sacerdotibus abundat et in suis fratribus viget scientia et vite sinceritate per dei gratiam pollet, in eodem agro fructus uberes afferat, tibi fili Prior Generalis,

per te vobis vero provinciales priores in provincialibus vestris capitulis cum diffinitoribus ipsorum capitulorum, fratribus eiusdem vestri ordinis sacerdotibus in sacra pagina eruditis, examinatis et approbatis a vobis predicationis et tam ipsis quam aliis fratribus dicti ordinis ad id idoneis audiendi confessiones, absolvendi confitentes, iniugendi eis penitentias salutares, officia auctoritate apostolica committendi eisdem quoque fratribus, quibus dicta officia per vos taliter commissa fuerint, quod illa libere valeant exercere, plenam tenore presentium damus et concedimus facultatem, districtius inhibentes ne quis, fratres ipsius ordinis, quibus dicta officia taliter committenda duxeritis in executione officiorum ipsorum audeat quomodolibet impedire.

3. Ad hec, sepulturam in ecclesiis et locis vestris liberam esse censemus, ut eorum devotioni et extrema voluntati, qui se illic sepeliri deliberaverint, nisi excommunicati vel interdicti aut etiam publico usurarii fuerint, nullus obsistat.

4. Statuentes, ut nulli religiosi vel seculares, vobis invitis, aliquorum corpora defunctorum in vestris cemeteriis sepelire aut in ecclesiis vestris missarum solemnia vel pro animabus eorum, qui ad loca vestra tumulandi feruntur, ibidem exequias celebrare sine vestro assensu et voluntate presumunt... constitutionem... quam super predicationibus faciendis, confessionibus audiendis, iniugendis penitentiis, absolutionibus impendendis... portione obventionum tam funeralium quam relictorum, datorum et donatorum in personis fratrum Predicatorum et Minorum ordinum olim edidimus in vobis et vestri ordinis fratribus per omnia volumus integraliter et inconcusse servari. Ita quod considerata personarum, quas ad id habueritis idoneas et cleri ac populi quantitate eorum, quos ad huiusmodi audiendarum confessionum officium eligetis, metiamini numerum, vos infra medium congruum continentes, et nunquam in aliquo excedentes, ut sic moderatione servata, nec alios, quibus hoc per eandum constitutionem nostram concessimus ad invidiam vel scandalum nec locorum episcopos, quibus a vobis electos presentare debetis ad repulsam provocetis ipsorum.

5. Nulli ergo omnino hominum liceat hanc paginam nostre dationis, concessionis, inhibitionis, constitutionis, et voluntatis infringere, vel ei ausu temerario contraire. Si quis autem hoc attentare presumpserit, indignationem omnipotentis dei et beatorum Petri et Pauli apostolorum eius se noverit incursurum.

Datum Laterani decimo septimo Calendas Februarii, Pontificatus nostri anno octavo.

APPENDIX C

AUGUSTINI DE ANCONA

Summe de potestate ecclesiastica
Epistola Dedicatoris et Tabula

Augustinus of Ancona's *Summa de potestate ecclesiastica* is an expansive treatise on Church government, explicating the implications of Christ's reign on earth. Augustinus followed by and large the canonistic tradition on the fundamental questions, which gives the work an impression of distanced political theory. Yet when one reads the text in context, it assumes a far different hue, which reveals its contemporary edges, and the abstract theory takes on an immediate, practical nature. What, however, that context was precisely is more difficult to determine. In Chapter One I argued that Augustinus was responding both to Marsilius of Padua's *Defensor Pacis* and to the *Sachsenhausen Appeal*. This is not meant to imply that Augustinus' *Summa* was composed as a point by point refutation, or, that Augustinus necessarily had either document on his desk. A detailed textual analysis of these works would shed more light on the precise relationship between them. Unfortunately, such a study is dependent on a critical edition of, and commentary on, the *Summa*, which is not forthcoming any time in the forseeable future. Thus for present purposes, I have based my reading on contextual and circumstantial arguments, which do not yield conclusive proof, and the exact context of the work remains to some degree a matter for continued speculation. The question hinges on when Augustinus composed his *Summa* and whether it was at all possible for him to have known, or to have known of, either the *Defensor Pacis* or the *Sachsenhausen Appeal*. The *terminus ad quem* for the completion of the work is the end of 1326 and John XXII's letter of acknowledgement; the *terminus a quo*, however, is more problematic.

Ulrich Horst argued for placing the *Summa* in context of the Franciscan poverty debates, thus suggesting dating the work to 1326, rather than to 1320. Horst claimed that the date of composition is controversial, namely, either in 1320, as Adolar Zumkeller put forth, or by 1326, which had been the majority opinion since the work of Ministeri.[1] Horst's contextualization is one I favor, yet the controversy he set up is one of straw. The date of 1320 was repeated by Zumkeller in his few abbreviated lines on Augustinus in the *Lexikon des Mittelalters* without any argument whatsoever.[2] Zumkeller apparently adopted the dating of the *Summa* as given by Augustinus Fivizanius,

---

[1] Horst, "Die Armut Christi," 471, and *passim*.
[2] Zumkeller, "Augustinus von Ancona," *LexMA* 1:1230.

the sixteenth-century editor of the *Summa*, who dated the work to 1320, based on an account of Augustinus' biography that was definitively corrected by Ministeri, whom Wilks followed.[3] Such an oversight on Zumkeller's part is not the basis for claiming a controversy regarding the dating of the work. Yet controversy remains.

Ministeri argued that Augustinus composed his *Summa* in response, at least in part, to the *Defensor Pacis*, a position repeated by Willigis Eckermann, in his entry on Augustinus in the *TRE*.[4] Miethke, however, challenges this position arguing that Augustinus must have completed his *Summa* by mid-1325 at the latest, based on the time required to prepare a copy for John XXII, together with the time required to send the work to Avignon, so that John could respond by the end of 1326.[5] Therefore, Miethke argues, any direct response to Marsilius by Augustinus is excluded as a real possibility,[6] especially so since the *Defensor Pacis* was not known outside of Paris before 1326.[7]

Whether knowledge of the *Defensor Pacis* was indeed confined to Parisian circles until 1326, however, needs to be questioned. Reconstructing the reception of the work based on extant manuscripts is vital, yet not definitive. The six articles condemning positions drawn from the *Defensor Pacis* are a case in point. William of Cremona finished his *Reprobatio* in late 1326 or early 1327. *Licet iuxta doctrinam* is dated 23 October 1327. If William's *Reprobatio* had reached John XXII by early October, one can, based on Miethke's argument for Augustinus' *Summa*, surmise that it had been sent several months earlier, placing the sending to c. July 1327. If we randomly take the period of composition to be one month, and the preparation for the copy sent to John to be one month, then William began his work c. May 1327. If it took John's request for a response one month to reach William, then William would have received such a request in April of 1327. The question then is when did John first become aware of the *Defensor Pacis*, and how. If John only heard of the work in 1326, then this preserves the 1326 dating of its reception outside of Paris. If, however, these most theoretical and illustrative time spans were actually extended, then it is very likely that John became aware of Marsilius' treatise in 1325, if not towards the end of 1324, which indicates that the work was known beyond Paris

---

[3] Ministeri, "De Vita et Operibus," 27–56; Wilks, *The Problem of Sovereignty*, 3–6.

[4] Ministeri, "De Vita et Operibus," 54; Eckermann, "Augustinus Triumphus," in *TRE* 4:742–744. Eckermann's entry is the best short introduction to Augustinus. The entry on Augustinus in the *Dictionary of the Middle Ages* by Lawrence Gushee should be ignored as flawed and unreliable; Gushee, "Augustinus Triumphus," *Dictionary of the Middle Ages*, ed. Joseph R. Strayer (New York, 1983): 2:1.

[5] Miethke, *De Potestate Papae*, 174.

[6] "Die allgemeine Systematik, die der Autor entwickelt, macht die Annahme schwierig, er hätte vielleicht in Opposition zu einer bestimmten Gegenposition zur Feder gegriffen. Das wenige, was sich über die Zeit des Abschlusses der Schrift ermitteln ließ, schließt jedenfalls eine direkte Bezugnahme auf Marsilius von Padua und dessen 'Defensor Pacis' wohl aus." *Ibid.*, 175.

[7] *Ibid.*, 176, n. 519.

before 1326. Even more to the point is that if William had access to a text of the *Defensor Pacis* either directly, or through report, beyond the positions of the six articles themselves, previous to or corresponding with his beginning work on his *Reprobatio*, it seems likely as well that the text was more widely known before 1326, especially if William sought further information and perhaps even a copy of the text itself, only after having received John's sollicitation for a reply, which would push the above time scheme back significantly, meaning, an earlier point of beginning, indicating again the knowledge of Marsilius previous to 1326. Thus the question becomes, what sort of knowledge of the *Defensor Pacis* did William have?

Miethke himself gives a clue, and a rule of thumb for determining direct Marsilian influence. In his Nicomachean Ethics, Aristotle had spoken of a coercive force required for a law to have the force of law (ἀναγκαστικὴ δύναμις), which Thomas of Aquinas, or William of Moerbeke, and Robert Grosseteste had translated as *vis coactiva*. Marsilius, finding in this term a key to his political theory, rendered it as *potestas coactiva*.[8] This, according to Miethke, was a unique "Marsilianism" so that one "könnte die Regel aufstellen, daß immer dort, wo in einem spätmittelalterlichen Text von *potestas coactiva* die Rede ist, ein Bezug auf Marsilius von Padua wahrscheinlich wird, sodaß diese Begriffsprägung heute geradezu als ein Schibboleth für eine unmittelbare Marsiliusrezeption dienen kann."[9]

The term *potestas coactiva* does not as such appear in the six articles. Article five, however, gets close in condemning the point that the Church has no coercive power to punish any one for crimes, unless such power is granted to the Church by the emperor (*Quinto dicunt, quod papa vel ecclesia simul sumpta nullum hominem quantumcumque sceleratum potest punire punitione coactiva, nisi imperator daret eis auctoritatem*). In his refutation of this article William argued forcefully for the pope's authority and right to punish the emperor and anyone else.[10] His reasoning was that Christ had granted Peter the jurisdiction and authority to punish evil, which Peter could not have possessed had Christ not granted him *potentia coactiva*.[11] In his treatment of the first article, in dealing with the question as to whether the emperor could appropriate Church property, as well as that of the laity, as his own, William

---

[8] Miethke, *De Potestate Papae*, 214–215.

[9] *Ibid.*, 215.

[10] "Preterea papa de iure potest punire imperatorem usque ad incarcerationem, et sibi omnem poenam citra mortem inferre immediate ex propria auctoritate, et usque etiam ad mortem, ut habet gladium materialem ad nutum, si peccati qualitas requirit." Will.Crem. *Repr.* 5,2 (92,19–22).

[11] "Unde Ambrosius super illud Lucae: 'Mitte hamum' etc., dicit: Est et aliud apostolicum piscandi genus, quo genere solum Petrum Dominus piscari iubet dicens: 'Mitte hamum, et eum piscem, qui primo ascendit, tolle.' Glossa: 'Per hamum intellige iurisdictionem, qua Petrus praefuit aliis, quia hamo, id est ferro, resecantur putridae carnes,' id est mali et vitiosi homines, quod fieri non potest nisi per potentiam coactivam, quae Petro colata fuit a Christo, cum dicit: 'Mitte hamum' etc. Ergo potest punire sceleratos punitione coactiva, esto quod imperator nullam sibi conferat puniendi auctoritatem." Will.Crem. *Repr.* 5,2 (92,36–93,45).

replied in the negative, yet left the door open, depending on how one takes the term *bona*. In one way, the goods of the Church and those of the laity are also those of the emperor. Thus, even though the emperor cannot appropriate goods as goods of the Church or of the laity as such, he can do so in so far as they fall under his jurisdiction and dominion through his jurisdictional or coercive power, *potestas sive coactiva sive iurisdictionalis*,[12] and here is the Marsilian term explicitly. If Miethke is correct in his estimation of the term *potestas coactiva*, then one must conclude that William had direct knowledge of the text of *Defensor Pacis*.[13]

The same can be said of Augustinus' *Summa*. Augustinus used the term *violenta coactio* to refer to the force of law, from which, however, the pope is free, although the pope is bound by the positive virtue of justice, which corresponds to divine law.[14] However, in discussing the extent to which Christ bound himself to the vow of obedience, Augustinus made a distinction between obedience and servitude. Obedience is the willful submission to a higher authority. Thus Christ, in his human nature, was obedient to the authority of his parents, as well as to the political authority of his time. This was a willful submission, not a coercive servitude, which implies and requires, Augustinus stated, a certain *potestas coactiva*.[15] If the term *potestas coactiva* is indeed a shibboleth of a direct reception of Marsilius' *Defensor Pacis*, then Augustinus no less than William of Cremona knew the text directly. Augustinus knew his Aristotle well and had he intended to use *vis coactiva*, he would have done so. Either he coined the term himself, or adopted it from Marsilius, which applies as well to William. *Potestas coactiva*, however, was not a central term and concept for either William or Augustinus. Yet their use of the term as such gives strong indications that

---

[12] "Bona enim laicorum et sunt ecclesiae et sunt laicorum et sunt imperatoris, sed sub alia et alia ratione, modo unusquisque debet stare in suis terminis, et ideo imperator non potest talia bona accipere, ut sunt ecclesiae, tanquam sua, nec etiam ut sunt laicorum, sed solum sub ea ratione, qua spectant ad eius dominium et potestatem sive coactivam sive iurisdictionalem." Will.Crem. *Repr.* 1,6 (33,967–973); *cf.* Miethke, *De Potestate Papae*, 215–216, n. 653.

[13] Miethke argued that there was virtually no relation whatsoever between William's *Reprobatio* and the *Defensor Pacis*; Miethke, *De Potestate Papae*, 106–108; "Daß er [William] sich nicht die Mühe gemacht hat, die von ihm inkriminierte Schrift des Marsilius zu lesen, unterscheidet ihn nicht von seinen Mitstreitern... In solchem unentschiedenen Stil ist der gesamte Text [Williams] gehalten, der keinen Vergleich mit dem *Defensor Pacis* aushält (zumal et diesen, wie gesagt, wahrscheinlich niemals zu Gesicht bekommen hat!)." *Ibid.*, 107.

[14] See Chapter One above, notes 232 and 235.

[15] "Obedientia videtur differre a subiectione et servitute, nam subiectio importat superioritatem... Servitus vero <importat> quandam coactivam potestatem... sed obedientia importat quandam placitam voluntatem. Si ergo ista referantur in christo ad personarum diversitatem neganda sunt. Non enim in christo fuit alia persona secundum quam conveniret sibi subiectio vel servitus et alia secundum quam conveniret sibi superioritas vel dominium. Hoc enim saperet errorem Arrii. Si vero referantur ad naturarum pluralitatem cum determinatione nature humane vera sunt et concessa in scriptura sacra, nam secundum quod homo fuerit subiectus patri." Aug.Anc. *Summa* 82,1 (ed. Rome, 1479), fol. 235[va].

their common source was the *Defensor Pacis*, which therefore seems to have been known outside of Paris previous to 1326.

Furthermore, Augustinus had certainly been developing his political thought since at least 1315, when he first introduced the distinction between the pope's *potestas ordinis* and *potestas jurisdictionis* in discussing what happens to papal power upon the death of the pope. In his *Summa* this distinction became the very foundation for his treatment of ecclesiastical power. Giles of Rome did not employ the distinction in his *De ecclesiastica potestate*, but William of Cremona did in his *Reprobatio*. As mentioned in Chapter One, this was a distinction that neither Augustinus nor William created themselves, but Augustinus did develop it to its highest degree. Marsilius used the term *potestas coactiva* as a central concept, but as frequently spoke of *judicium coactivum* and *jurisdictio coactiva*. Either one must consider William's and Augustinus' use of *potestas jurisdictionis* as independent of context, whereby Augustinus based on his own theoretical speculation used the distinction and developed it extensively in his *Summa*, or one must interpret Augustinus' (and William's) use of *potestas jurisdictionis* as a reply to Marsilius' denying the Church any *iurisdictio coactiva*. In short, the role of *potestas jurisdictionis* in Augustinus' *Summa* is highly suggestive that he knew the text of the *Defensor Pacis* and Marsilius' rejection of ecclesiastical coersive jurisdiction and power. Moreover, if one excludes any knowledge of the *Defensor Pacis* on the part of Augustinus, one is left having to find a real referent for those "curious and superstitious Athenians," who are only concerned for novelties, in their denying of papal supremacy, which Augustinus set forth in his dedicatory epistle to John XXII as those he was intending to refute. It could have been pure rhetoric, but the circumstantial evidence is strongly weighted toward Marsilius as the historical referent of Augustinus' comment. Unless clear proof can be established that Augustinus was ignorant of Marsilius' text, one should refrain from reading the *Summa* as an aloof, abstract, theoretical treatise having no connection with its contemporary environment. Moreover, Augustinus must have become acquainted with the *Defensor Pacis* between late 1324, when it first perhaps became known to John XXII, and mid to late 1325, the required time of completion for the work to have arrived in Avignon for John to have responded by the end of 1326, if Miethke's estimations are accurate in this case. I would argue, based on our current information and knowledge, that the *Summa* was a work that Augustinus had begun perhaps to conceive already shortly after 1315, which then received its final form in response to the *Sachsenhausen Appeal* and the *Defensor Pacis* in late 1325, which further implies, as does William of Cremona's *Reprobatio*, that Marsilius' text was indeed known beyond Paris before 1326.

The importance of Augustinus' *Summa*, however, extends far beyond offering evidence for the early reception of the *Defensor Pacis*. Augustinus' treatise, which Miethke called "a rich encyclopedic mine" (*eine enzyklopädische Fundgrube*),[16] is the most extensive ecclesiological work that had ever been written up to that time. Augustinus' dedicatory letter to John XXII and

---

[16] Miethke, *De Potestate Papae*, 175.

the *Tabula* of questions as given in the Rome, 1479 edition here follows. I have standardized the orthography, modernized the punctuation, expanded all abbreviations and contractions, and have corrected typographical errors, but otherwise the text is as printed. Foliation is given within the text, and that found in the *Tabula* refers to the text of the *Tabula* itself, not to the individual questions. It is hoped that by presenting even a skeletal view of the work's depth and breath, new interest might be generated in the *Summa*, as well as in its author.

APPENDIX C

//fol. 2ᵛᵇ// Incipit summa catholici doctoris Augustini de Ancona de potestate ecclesiastica

Sanctissimo ac reverendissimo in Christo patri ac domino, domino Johanni divina providentia pape xxii, frater Augustinus de Ancona ordinis fratrum eremitarum sancti Augustini cum omni famulatu et reverentia post pedum oscula beatorum. Quamvis dei filius humani generis naturam assumens infirma mundi elegerit, ut fortia queque confunderet, ecclesiastice tamen potestatis altitudinem suos fideles latere novit quinimo tanquam supra petram fundatam ipsam esse supra omnem principatum et potestatem, ut ei genua //fol. 3ʳᵃ// cuncta cruenter celestium, terrestrium et infernorum verbis apertissimis declaravit. Unde error est ut puto pertinaci mente non credere Romanum pontificem universalis ecclesie pastorem Petri successorem et Christi legitimum vicarium supra spiritualia et temporalia universalem non habere primatum, in quem quandoque multi labuntur dicte potestatis ignorantia, que cum sit inifinita, eo quod magnus dominus et magna virtus eius et magnitudinis eius non est finis, omnis creatus intellectus in eius perscrutatione invenitur deficere. Multi vero hominum complacentia quia sic multa de divino cultu et Christi reverentia usurpata sunt, que honoribus deferuntur humanis sive humilitate nimia sive adulatione pestifera. Multo magis hac duplici causa multa subtrahuntur de Christi vicarii dominio et potentia. Multa autem curiosa scientia et utinam non elata superbia cupientes ex quibusdam novis videri potius quam videre et sciri potius quam scire, imitantes in hoc illos curiosos et superstittiosa Athenienses qui ad nihil aliud vacabant nisi audire vel discere aliquid novi. His omnibus modis impugnatur quandoque Christi sponsa sed vinci non potest, tempestates suscipit, sed non demergitur, iacula mittuntur in eam, sed non perforatur, machinamenta preparantur, sed turris Davidica non eliditur. Huic tamen pestifero morbo salubri remedio providetur cum a sacre scripture doctoribus varia et diversa conscribuntur quia enim nullus umquam hominum ita clare locutus est ut in omnibus ab omnibus intelligi posset. Ideo utile fore censuit Augustinus diversos libros a diversis fieri etiam de eisdem questionibus diverso stilo non diversa fide, ut veritas quidem ipsa ad omnes perveniat, ad alios sic, ad alios autem sic. Nec aliud intelligo scripturam voluisse significare quod adducebantur Salomoni equi de Egypto et de cunctis regionibus terre, nisi quia summo pontifici diversi libri a cunctis Christi militibus offeruntur. Nec mirum quia lectulum eius sexaginta fortes ambiunt ex fortissimis Israel omnes tenentes gladios et ad bella doctissimi.

Summam igitur de potestate ecclesiastica //fol. 3ʳᵇ// pretitulatam sanctitati vestre dignum putavi presentandam fore ut sicut talis potentia a vobis tanquam a fonte derivatur in omnes per universalem influentiam, sic quid corrigendum est in ea vestro iudicio reservetur per discussionis prudentiam et quid tenendum est comprobetur per confirmationis sententiam.

Tabula

//fol. 319ra// Incipiunt rubrice et tituli questionum summe de ecclesiastica potestate, doctoris clarissimi fratris Augustini de Ancona ordinis fratrum heremitarum sancti Augustini.

Questio prima de potestate pape a quo est principaliter, ubi decem queruntur
    Utrum sola potestas pape sit a deo immediate effective et nulla alia
    Utrum potestas cuiuslibet pape sit a deo
    Utrum potestas pape sit universaliter maior omni alia
    Utrum aliquis possit esse equalis pape in potestate
    Utrum singularius sit a deo potestas pape quam aliqua alia
    Utrum potestas pape sit una vel plures
    Utrum sit simul sacerdotalis et regalis
    Utrum sit simul temporalis et spiritualis
    Utrum sit simul eterna et temporalis
    Utrum sit utile de tali potestate disputare

Questio ii de pape electione, ubi octo queruuntur
    Utrum conveniens sit papam fieri hominum electione, vel magis immediate a Christo
    Utrum quilibet papa post Petrum factus sit per electionem
    Utrum esset magis conveniens papam fieri per successionem quam per electionem
    Utrum due partes cardinalium debeant ad minus in eius electionem convenire
    Utrum electio pape possit in aliquo vitiari
    Utrum eius electio cadat sub examinatione sicut electio aliorum
    Utrum imperator vel alius princeps possit habere ius in electione pape
    Utrum laici possint et debeant electioni pape interesse

Questio iii de eligentium iurisdictione, ubi undecim quereuntur.
    Utrum ad collegium cardinalium solum spectat papam eligere
    Utrum deficiente collegio electio pape devolvatur ad generale concilium
    Utrum tale collegium teneatur semper eligere hominem sufficientioris scientie
    //fol. 319rb// Utrum teneatur semper eligere hominem sanctioris vite
    Utrum teneatur magis eligere hominem iuristam quam theologum
    Utrum teneatur magis eligere hominem de collegio quam extra collegium
    Utrum maiorem potestatem habeat collegium eligens quam papa electus
    Utrum papa mortuo potestas eius remaneat in collegio
    Utrum mortuo papa collegium possit quicquid potest vivens papa
    Utrum in tali electione debeat precedere tractatus et aliqua prelocutio
    Utrum tutius sit celeriter eligere vel in tali electione diu cogitare

Questio iv de pape renuntiatione, ubi octo quereuntur
    Utrum papa posset renuntiare si in papatu imprimeretur caracter

Utrum papa posset renuntiare si papatus esset nomen ordinis et non iurisdictionis
Utrum quia papatus est a solo deo papa possit ex se renuntiare
Utrum papa possit renuntiare propter votum emissum de cura ecclesie habenda
Utrum papa possit eius legitimam administrationem renuntiare
Utrum quia sacerdotium pape est eternum possit renuntiare
Utrum possit probari per rationes quod papa renuntiare potest
Utrum istud possit probari per auctoritates

Questio v de pape depositione, ubi octo queruntur
Utrum solum pro heresi papa sit deponendus
Utrum per violentiam et ignorantiam in heresim labatur sit deponendus
Utrum sit deponendus pro simonia
Utrum sit deponendus pro quocunque notorio crimine
Utrum ad depositionem eius sit necessaria productio plurium testium quam ad depositionem aliorum
Utrum ad generale concilium spectet eius depositionem pronuntiare
Utrum papa mortuus pro heresi possit condemnari
//fol. 319va// Utrum pape aperte malo sit obediendum

Questio vi de pape sententie appellatione, ubi octo queruntur
Utrum a papa possit appellari ad deum
Utrum a papa appellari ad deum sit appellari contra deum
Utrum a papa appellari ad deum talis appellatio apud deum admittitur
Utrum a papa presenti possit appellari ad futurum
Utrum a papa possit appellari ad collegium cardinalium
Utrum a papa possit appellari ad concilium generalium
Utrum papa possit facere statutum quod ad eius sententia possit appellari
Utrum sit error dicere quod a papa possit ad deum vel hominem appellari

Questio vii de pape reprehensione, ubi quatuor queruntur
Utrum ad papam se extendat fraterna reprehensio
Utrum reprehensio pape debeat fieri in secreto vel in aperto
Utrum si papa non audit reprehendentem sit dicendum ecclesie
Utrum papa de omni peccato reprehendi debeat ex precepto

Questio viii de pape representatione, ubi quatuor queruntur
Utrum papa representetur per archam Noe
Utrum papa representetur per montem Sinai
Utrum papa representet Christum quantum ad personam vel quantum ad officium
Utrum pape assistant cardinales sicut Christo astiterunt apostoli

Questio ix de pape honoris exhibitione, ubi sex queruntur
Utrum pape debeatur honor qui debetur Christo secundum quod deus
Utrum pape debeatur honor qui debetur Christo secundum quod homo

Utrum pape debeatur honor qui debetur sanctis
Utrum pape debeatur honor qui debetur angelis
Utrum pape debeatur honor qui debetur imagini Christi
Utrum pape aperte malo debeatur honor

//fol. 319^(vb)//
Questio x quomodo ad papam spectet de fide et heresi determinare, ubi sex queruntur
    Utrum ad papam spectet determinare que sunt fidei
    Utrum ad papam spectet determinare quod est heresis
    Utrum ad papam spectet circa illa que sunt fidei aliquid addere vel diminuere
    Utrum sine mandato pape aliquis possit de heresi inquirere
    Utrum sine mandato pape aliquis possit in heresi comprehensos condemnare
    Utrum sine mandato pape liceat principibus Christiane fidei capere hereticos et iudicare

Questio xi quomodo ad papam spectet determinare que pertinent ad veritatem divine essentie, ubi queruntur sex
    Utrum ad papam spectet sub articulo ponere que non possunt ab homine naturaliter cognosci
    Utrum ad papam spectet sub articulo ponere: Credo in unum deum
    Utrum ad papam spectet sub articulo ponere: unum deum esse creatorem omnium
    Utrum ad papam spectet determinare modum credendi trinitatem
    Utrum ad papam spectet determinare modum distinctionis personarum
    Utrum ad papam spectet determinare modum unitatis trium personarum

Questio xii quomodo ad papam spectet determinare que pertinent ad distinctionem personarum, ubi quatuor queruntur
    Utrum ad papam spectet sub articulo ponere patrem esse omnipotentem
    Utrum ad papam spectet determinare modum generationis filii a patre
    Utrum ad papam spectet determinare modum procedendi spiritus sancti a patre et filio
    Utrum a papam spectet plura ponere sub articulo spiritus sancti quam patris et filii

Questio xiii quomodo ad papam spectet determinare que pertinent //fol. 320^(ra)// ad naturam humanam a dei filio assumptam, ubi quinque queruntur
    Utrum ad papam spectet sub articulo ponere modum conceptionis et incarnationis Christi
    Utrum ad papam spectet sub articulo ponere modum passionis et sepultare Christi
    Utrum ad papam spectet in symbolo explicare omnes articulos fidei

Utrum ad papam spectet in symbolo explicare omnia sacramenta ecclesie
Utrum ad papam spectet determinare per quem modum corpus Christi est sub sacramento altaris

Questio xiiii de sanctorum veneratione, ubi quinque queruntur
Utrum solum ad solum papam pertineat sanctos canonizare
Utrum sicut papa universaliter ita episcopus in diocesi sua possit aliquem sanctum canonizare
Utrum papa absque requisitione collegii possit aliquem sanctum canonizare
Utrum papa canonizando aliquem sanctum possit errare
Utrum si quis non est canonizatus per papam possit pro eo officium decantari

Questio xv de causa canonizationis sanctorum, ubi quinque queruntur
Utrum papa debeat aliquem canonizare propter fructum scientie
Utrum papa debeat canonizare aliquem propter sanctitatem vite
Utrum papa debeat canonizare aliquem propter bonam famam
Utrum papa propter evidentiam miraculorum debeat aliquem canonizare
Utrum papa debeat aliquem canonizare propter donum prophetie

//fol. 320rb//
Questio xvi de modo canonizationis sanctorum, ubi quatuor queruntur
Utrum papa in canonizatione alicuius sancti debeat servare ordinem iudiciarium
Utrum papa debeat canonizare aliquem sanctum statim sibi denunciatum
Utrum papa eundum modum debeat servare in canonizatione martyris et confessoris
Utrum papa possit aliquem canonizare ad ordinem apostolorum sicut martyrum, confessorum seu virginum

Questio xvii de sanctis canonizandis, ubi sex queruntur
Utrum papa debeat canonizare omnes quos constat ecclesie esse in vita eterna
Utrum papa debeat canonizare patres veteris testamenti
Utrum preter informationem pape corpus unius sancti in pluribus ecclesiis venerari sit peccatum
Utrum omnes canonizati per papam sint in vita eterna
Utrum sine auctoritate pape possint sanctorum reliquie furtive subtrahi de loco ubi sunt
Utrum sine auctoritate pape possint sanctorum reliquie emptioni et venditioni exponi

Questio xviii de angelorum administratione, ubi quinque queruntur
Utrum papa sit maior angelo in iurisdictione
Utrum papa sit maior angelo in sacramentorum administratione

Utrum papa sit maior angelo in dominatione
Utrum papa sit maior angelo in cognitione
Utrum papa sit maior angelo in premiatione

//fol. 320va//
Questio xix de pape presidentia, ubi quinque queruntur
    Utrum solus papa sit sponsus ecclesie
    Utrum solus papa sit caput totius ecclesie
    Utrum solus papa sit episcopus cuiuslibet eccclesie immediate
    Utrum papa sit specialius episcopus Romanus quam alterius ecclesie
    Utrum papa possit immediate in qualibet diocesi et perrochia quid potest episcopus vel sacerdotus

Questio xx de modi presidendi efficacia, ubi sex queruntur
    Utrum papa presit ecclesie per potestatem clavium
    Utrum papa per potestatem clavium presit spiritualibus et temporalibus
    Utrum solus papa habeat clavium potestatem
    Utrum in papa potestas clavium sit una vel plures
    Utrum in papa potestas clavium sit potestas ordinis vel iurisdictionis
    Utrum papa in potestate clavium possit excedere vel errare

Questio xxi de pape residentia, ubi quatuor queruntur
    Utrum papa debeat semper Rome residere
    Utrum papa debeat residere in patria unde est oriundus
    Utrum papa debeat magis discurrere per mundum quam in uno loco residere
    Utrum pape tempore persecutionis antichristi solum Roma sedes sit reliquenda

Questio xxii de obedientia Christianorum, ubi septem queruntur
    Utrum pape Christiani in omnibus teneantur obedire
    Utrum pape teneantur obedire laici Christiani sicut clerici Christiani
    Utrum pape laici Christiani magis teneantur obedire quam imperatori vel regi
    Utrum pape servi Christianorum magis teneantur obedire quam propriis dominis
    Utrum papa possit servos Christianorum a servitute eximere et libertati reddere
    Utrum papa Christianos liberos possit ad //fol. 320vb// servitutem damnare
    Utrum papa Christianos existentes sub dominio infidelium debeat ab eorum dominio subtrahere

Questio xxiii de obedientia paganorum, ubi sex queruntur
    Utrum pagani de iure sint sub pape obedientia
    Utrum preter papam pagani sint imperatori immediate subiecti
    Utrum papa iuste possit dominia et iurisdictiones a paganis auferre

APPENDIX C

   Utrum papa iuste possit punire paganos agentes contra legem nature
   Utrum papa possit cogere paganos vivere lege imperiali
   Utrum papa ritum paganorum debeat tollerare

Questio xxiiii de obedientia Iudeorum, ubi decem queruntur
   Utrum papa debeat Iudeos cogere ad suscipiendam fidem
   Utrum papa debeat Iudeos cogere ad dimittendum iudaismum
   Utrum papa debeat Iudeorum filios eis invitis facere baptizari
   Utrum papa debeat Iudeos cogere ad laborandum manibus
   Utrum papa debeat Iudeos privare omni administratione officiorum super Christianos
   Utrum papa debeat Iudeos privare ut nullum dominium supra Christianos habeant
   Utrum papa debeat permittere Christianos cum Iudeis conversari
   Utrum papa debeat Iudeos punire pena spirituali qua Christianos punit
   Utrum papa debeat permittere Iudeorum oblationes et elemosinas recipi a fidelibus
   Utrum papa debeat permittere Christianos principes aliquas exactiones in Iudeos facere

Questio xxv de resistentia scismaticorum, ubi sex queruntur
   Utrum omnes resistentes pape sint scismatici
   Utrum omnes scismatici resistentes pape sint heretici
   //fol. 321ra// Utrum omnes scismaticos papa possit omni potestate privare
   Utrum papa debeat punire scismaticos gravius quam hereticos
   Utrum reputet Grecos scismaticos vel hereticos
   Utrum papa teneat Grecos esse paganos vel Christianos

Questio xxvi de resistentia tyrannorum, ubi sex queruntur
   Utrum tyranni resistentes pape sint scismatici
   Utrum tyranni resistentes pape sint heretici
   Utrum ad papam spectet punire tyrannos
   Utrum papa debeat punire tyrannos pena temporali vel spirituali solum
   Utrum papa contra tyrannos sibi resistentes debeat cruce signatos destinare
   Utrum papa in puniendo tyrannos debeat magis declinare ad misericordiam quam ad iustitiam

Questio xxvii de resistentia excommunicatorum, ubi queruntur decem
   Utrum solus papa debeat excommunicare
   Utrum papa pro quolibet peccato mortali excommunicare debeat
   Utrum papalis excommunicatio iniuste lata sit timenda
   Utrum omnes excommunicati per papam damnentur
   Utrum solus papa debeat absolvere excommunicatos a iure et iudice inferiori
   Utrum papa debeat excommunicare pro peccato fiendo sicut pro peccato iam facto
   Utrum papa totam unam universitatem resistentem sibi excommunicare debeat

Utrum per papam sint excommunicati portantes pecuniam in Alexandriam
Utrum papa debeat aliquem excommunicare nisi semel tantum
//fol. 321ʳᵇ// Utrum per papam excommunicatis scienter communicantes sint excommunicati

Questio xxviii de resistentia hereticorum, ubi queruntur octo
  Utrum omnes dubii in fide per papam sint habendi heretici
  Utrum sequentes opinionem erroneam alicuius magistri per papam sint heretici reputandi
  Utrum baptizantes imagines et violatores sacramentorum per papam sint pro hereticis iudicandi
  Utrum incidentes in adiuratam heresim per papam sint censendi relapsi
  Utrum relapsi per papam statim tradendi sint seculari iudicio
  Utrum heretici per papam puniendi sint temporali pena
  Utrum heretici in aliquo casu per papam sint tollerandi
  Utrum heretici revertentes ad fidem per papam sint recipiendi

Questio xxix de faciente indulgentiam, ubi queruntur decem
  Utrum solus papa possit dare universalem indulgentiam
  Utrum papa possit dare indulgentiam sibiipsi
  Utrum papa existens in culpa mortali possit indulgentiam dare
  Utrum papa possit indulgentiam dare illis qui sunt in purgatorio
  Utrum episcopus sine autoritate pape possit indulgentiam dare
  Utrum episcopus omnes indulgentias quas dat in consecrationibus diversarum ecclesiarum transferre possit ad consecrationem unius
  Utrum simplex sacerdos possit dare indulgentiam
  Utrum legatus pape possit dare indulgentiam si non sit sacerdos
  Utrum quilibet electus sine auctoritate pape possit dare indulgentiam
  Utrum sancti viri possint dare indulgentiam

//fol. 321ᵛᵃ//
Questio xxx de causa indulgentie, ubi sex queruntur
  Utrum papa solum pro actibus exterioribus debeat indulgentiam dare
  Utrum papa solum pro temporalibus bonis debeat indulgentiam facere
  Utrum papa debeat indulgentiam dare solum habentibus voluntatem dandi aliquid temporale sicut dantibus
  Utrum non existente iusta causa indulgentia data per papam valeat
  Utrum solum voluntas pape possit esse causa iusta faciendi indulgentiam
  Utrum questores deferentes litteras papales contineant iustam causam indulgentiam faciendi

Questio xxxi de indulgentiarum recipiente, ubi queruntur quatuor
  Utrum indulgentiam datam per papam recipiant existentes in peccato mortali
  Utrum indulgentiam datam per papam recipiant cruce signati morientes cum firmo propositio transfretandi

APPENDIX C

Utrum indulgentiam datam per papam recipiant clerici et religiosi sicut alii
Utrum indulgentiam datam per papam possit quis recipere pro patre et matre sicut pro seipso

Questio xxxii de effectu indulgentie, ubi queruntur quatuor
   Utrum papa possit facere quod duorum existentium in purgatorio in equali pena unus citius liberetur quam alius
   Utrum papa possit facere quod bona facta ab existente in peccato mortali sint meritoria illis qui sunt in purgatorio
   Utrum papa per communicationem indulgentie possit totum locum purgatorum expoliare
   Utrum papa per communicationem indulgentie possit contritos et confessos sic a tota pena et culpa absolvere ut non transeant per ignem purgatorii

//fol. 321vb//
Questio xxxiii de illis qui sunt infra terram, qui nec sunt nec fuerunt de ecclesia, ubi quatuor queruntur
   Utrum papa per communicationem indulgentie possit absolvere pueros non baptizatos
   Utrum papa per communicationem indulgentie possit absolvere pueros non circumcisos
   Utrum papa per communicationem indulgentie possit limbum puerorum expoliare
   Utrum papa per communicationem indulgentie possit pueris existentibus in limbo ianuam paradysi aperire

Questio xxxiiii de illis qui sunt infra terram, qui quandoque fuerunt de ecclesia quamvis nunc non sunt, ubi quatuor queruntur
   Utrum papa possit mandare ut quilibet teneatur potius velle ad penam inferni damnare quam peccare mortaliter
   Utrum papa possit facere quod damnati non gaudeant de penis inimicorum eorum
   Utrum papa possit aliquem iuste ad penam inferni damnare
   Utrum papa possit facere quod indulgentie et suffragia ecclesie sint meritoria illis qui sunt in inferno

Incipit secunda pars huius operis in qua nunc considerandum est de ipsa potestate ecclesiastica per comparationem ad actum ad quem ordinatur

Questio xxxv de imperatoris electione, circa quam queruntur octo
   Utrum papa per seipsum possit imperatorem eligere
   Utrum electores per quos papa imperatorem eligit debeant esse de Alamania
   Utrum papa dictos electores possit mutare
   Utrum papa predictos electores possit //fol. 322ra// de alia natione ordinare quam de Alamania

Utrum papa in electione imperatoris possit alteri parti eligentium favere
Utrum papa possit imperatorem facere per hereditariam sucessionem sicut per electionem
Utrum papa melius faceret ordinando imperium per hereditariam successionem quam per electionem
Utrum papa melius faceret ordinando plures imperatores quam unum

Questio xxxvi de imperii derivatione, ubi queruntur septem
Utrum papatus fuerit ante imperium
Utrum papatus derivatus sit ab imperio
Utrum papa saltem temporale dominium ab imperatore recognoscat
Utrum imperator in dominio temporalium sit maior papa
Utrum imperator sit maior papa in dignitate
Utrum imperator sit maior papa in causalitate
Utrum imperator sit maior papa in auctoritate

Questio xxxvii de imperii translatione, ubi queruntur sex
Utrum auctoritate pape facta sit translatio omnium regnorum
Utrum auctoritate pape imperium specialiter translatum sit ad Romanos
Utrum auctoritate pape imperium translatum sit a Romanis ad Grecos
Utrum auctoritate pape imperium translatum sit a Grecis ad Germanos
Utrum auctoritate pape imperium transferri possit a Germanis ad alios
Utrum auctoritate pape ordinandum sit studium semper sequi imperium et regalem militiam

Questio xxxviii de imperatoris confirmatione, ubi queruntur quatuor
//fol. 322rb// Utrum per papam imperator electus debeat confirmari
Utrum per papam imperator electus debeat iniungi et consecrari
Utrum per papam imperator electus debeat coronari
Utrum pape imperator electus debeat fidelitatem iurare

Questio xxxix de imperatoris administratione, ubi tria queruntur
Utrum imperator electus absque hoc quod sit per papam confirmatus possit administrare
Utrum imperator per papam electus et confirmatus absque aliqua alia solemnitate possit administrare
Utrum imperator statim electus absque pape auctoritate possit administrare saltem in regno Alamanie

Questio xl de imperatoris depositione, ubi queruntur quatuor
Utrum papa possit imperatorem deponere
Utrum papa per contumaciam imperatorem deponat
Utrum papa possit imperatorem excommunicare
Utrum papa possit imperatoris subditos a iuramento fidelitatis absolvere

Questio xli de imperatoris examinatione, ubi tria queruntur
Utrum examinatio electionis sit de iure naturali et divino

Utrum ad papam spectet imperatoris electionem examinare
Utrum ad papam spectet examinare personam electam

Questio xlii de ipsius imperii duratione, ubi duo queruntur
    Utrum Romanum imperium autoritate pape confirmatum debeat durare usque ad finem seculi
    Utrum Romanum imperium nunc divisum auctoritate pape ante finem seculo debeat reintegrari

//fol. 322va//
Questio xliii de ipsius imperatoris cessione et eius concessione, ubi tria queruntur
    Utrum Constantinus potuerit pape partem imperii concedere et partem sibi reservare
    Utrum Constantinus potuerit pape immediatam administrationem imperii concedere
    Utrum concessionem factam pape per Constantinum sequentes imperatores posssint revocare

Questio xliiii de ipsius imperatoris legum institutione, ubi octo queruntur
    Utrum imperator absque pape auctoritate possit leges condere
    Utrum leges imperiales ex precepto pape omnes teneantur observare
    Utrum leges imperiales ex precepto pape habeant homines in foro conscientie ligare
    Utrum papa leges imperiales sua auctoritate possit corrigere
    Utrum papa leges imperiales sua auctoritate possit mutare
    Utrum papa sua auctoritate possit reum impunitum dimittere quem leges imperiales condemnant
    Utrum papa absque peccato legibus imperialibus possit uti
    Utrum papa legibus imperialibus sit solutus

Questio xlv de aliorum regum subiectione, ubi tria queruntur
    Utrum omnes reges subiiciantur pape quantum ad eius mandati observationem
    Utrum omnes reges subiiciantur pape quantum ad temporalium recognitionem
    Utrum omnes reges subiiciantur pape quantum ad sententie appellationem

Questio xlvi de aliorum regum correctione, ubi tria queruntur
    Utrum papa possit omnes reges cum forefaciunt publice corrigere
    Utrum papa possit omnes reges cum //fol. 322vb// subest causa deponere
    Utrum papa possit in quolibet regno regem instituere

Questio xlvii de actu electionis quantum ad dominium spirituale, ubi octo queruntur
    Utrum papa possit aliquem suum consanguineum absque persone acceptione ad prelaturam ecclesiasticam eligere ratione qua consanguineus est

Utrum papa sine acceptione persone possit ad prelaturam ecclesiasticam eligere bonum dimissio meliori

Utrum papa sine acceptione possit ad prelaturam ecclesiasticam eligere divitem dimisso paupere

Utrum papa sine acceptione persone possit ad prelaturam ecclesiasticam eligere potentem et nobilem ratione qua potens et nobilis

Utrum papa sine acceptione persone possit ad petitionem regum et principum aliquem eligere ad prelaturam ecclesiasticam

Utrum papa semper cum acceptat personam in eligendo aliquem ad prelaturam ecclesiasticam peccet mortaliter

Utrum papa possit conferre sine peccato prelaturam ecclesiasticam petenti et procuranti ipsam

Utrum papa possit conferre magisterium sine peccato petenti et procuranti licentiam magistrandi

Questio xlviii de dispensatione primi precepti, ubi quatuor queruntur
Utrum papa possit dispensare cum demonum consultoribus qui plures deos colunt

Utrum papa possit dispensare cum astrologis et planetariis qui plures deos adorant

Utrum papa possit dispensare cum sortilegis et malificis qui unum deum non adorant

Utrum papa possit dispensare cum idolatris qui unum deum non colunt

//fol. 323ra//
Questio xlix de dispensatione secundi precepti, ubi queruntur quatuor
Utrum papa possit in iuramento dispensare
Utrum preter papam aliquis possit in iuramento dispensare
Utrum papa possit dispensare in voto continentie iuramento solemnizato
Utrum papa possit dispensare cum iurantibus per idola qui nomen dei in vanum assumunt

Questio l de dispensare tertii precepti, ubi sex queruntur
Utrum papa possit dispensare quod dies sabbati servetur secundum sensum spiritualem non litteralem

Utrum papa possit dispensare quod dies sabbati in diem dominicam sit mutata

Utrum papa possit dispensare quod in die dominico fient servilia opera

Utrum papa debeat prohibere strictius opera servilia fieri in die dominica quam fuerint prohibita in die sabbati

Utrum papa possit dispensare quod in die dominica fiat forum emptionis et venditionis

Utrum papa possit dispensare quod in die dominica committatur bellum

Questio li de dispensatione quarti precepti, ubi quinque queruntur
Utrum papa possit dispensare quod a subventione parentum absolvatur homo per introitum religionis

Utrum papa possit dispensare quod homo introitum religionis dimittat propter subventionem parentum
Utrum papa possit dispensare quod homo peregrinationem vel oblationem voto promissam dimittat propter subventionem parentum
Utrum papa possit dispensare quod homo preter honorem nullam aliam subventionem parentibus teneatur impendere
Utrum papa possit dispensare quod homo vigore precepti nullum alium teneatur honorare preter naturales parentes

//fol. 323rb//
Questio lii de dispensatione quinti precepti, ubi quinque queruntur
  Utrum papa possit dispensare quod homo occidatur absque transgressione divini precepti
  Utrum aliquis preter papam possit in homicidio dispensare
  Utrum papa possit dispensare quod homo occidens alium ne occidetur ab eo excusetur ab homicidio
  Utrum papa possit dispensare quod homo interficiens seipsum non incurrat culpam homicide
  Utrum papa possit dispensare quod homo interficiens filiam in adulterio deprehensam non incurrat culpam paricidii

Questio liii de dispensatione sexti precepti, ubi quinque queruntur
  Utrum papa possit dispensare quod unus homo habeat plures uxores
  Utrum fuerit aliquando humana auctoritate dispensatum plures uxores habere
  Utrum papa possit dispensare quod una mulier posset esse uxor plurium virorum
  Utrum papa possit dispensare quod simplex fornicatio non sit peccatum mortale
  Utrum papa possit dispensare in omni gradu consanguinitatis

Questio liiii de dispensatione septimi precepti, ubi quatuor queruntur
  Utrum papa possit dispensare in furto quod non sit peccatum mortale
  Utrum papa possit dispensare in furto in casu proprie necessitatis
  Utrum papa possit dispensare in furto in casu aliene paupertatis
  Utrum papa possit dispensare quod res furtive sublata non restituatur

Questio lv de dispensatione octavi precepti, ubi quatuor queruntur
  //fol. 323va// Utrum papa possit dispensare quod falsum testimonium non sit peccatum mortale
  Utrum papa possit dispensare quod mendacium non sit peccatum
  Utrum papa possit dispensare quod liceat mentiri mendacio officioso vel iocoso
  Utrum papa possit dispensare quod inferrendo testimonium non interveniat iuramentum

Questio lvi de dispensatione noni precepti, ubi quatuor queruntur
    Utrum papa possit dispensare in concupiscentia rei aliene auctoritate legis Moysaice
    Utrum papa possit dispensare in concupiscentia rei aliene auctoritate legis evangelice
    Utrum papa possit dispensare in concupiscentia rei aliene auctoritate legis humane
    Utrum papa possit dispensare in concupiscentia rei aliene quod non sit peccatum mortale

Questio lvii de dispensatione decimi precepti, ubi quinque queruntur
    Utrum papa possit dispensare auctoritate cuiuslibet legis ne carnalis concupiscentia sit peccatum mortale
    Utrum umquam cum aliquo sanctorum fuerit dispensatum ut esset sine peccato carnalis concupiscentie
    Utrum papa possit dispensare ut consensus carnalis concupiscentie non sit peccatum mortale
    Utrum papa possit dispensare ut morosa delectatio in concupiscentia carnali non sit peccatum mortale
    Utrum papa possit dispensare ut concupiscentia carnalis aliquibus remediis ex toto vitetur

Questio lviii de dispensatione sacramentorum, ubi octo queruntur
    //fol. 323vb// Utrum papa possit dispensare quod aliquod sacramentum do novo instituatur
    Utrum papa possit dispensare quod effectus sacramenti alicui conferatur sine sacramento
    Utrum papa possit dispensare in sacramentorum forma
    Utrum papa possit dispensare in sacramentorum materia
    Utrum papa possit dispensare in sacramentorum ritu
    Utrum papa possit dispensare in sacramentorum numero
    Utrum papa possit dispensare in sacramentorum iteratione
    Utrum papa possit dispensare in sacramentorum ordinatione

Questio lix de dispensatione articulorum, ubi queruntur quatuor
    Utrum papa possit dispensare in novi symboli editione
    Utrum papa possit dispensare in articulorum additione
    Utrum papa possit dispensare in articulorum diminutione
    Utrum papa possit dispensare in articulorum coactione

Questio lx de dispensatione legum et canonum sanctorum, ubi octo queruntur
    Utrum papa possit dispensare in lege nature
    Utrum papa possit dispensare in lege Moysaica
    Utrum papa possit dispensare in lege evangelica
    Utrum papa possit dispensare in lege humana
    Utrum papa possit dispensare in epistolis Pauli
    Utrum papa possit dispensare in dictis doctorum qui approbati sunt per ecclesiam

Utrum papa possit dispensare in canone predecessorum summorum pontificum

Utrum papa possit dispensare in ca-//fol. 324ra//-none conciliorum sanctorum patrum

Questio lxi de pape exemptione, ubi sex querunur
  Utrum papa possit in ecclesia exemptionem facere
  Utrum papa possit aliquos eximere a seipso in spiritualibus
  Utrum papa possit aliquis eximere a seipso in temporalibus
  Utrum papa debeat in ecclesia exemptionem facere vel magis eam tollere
  Utrum papa debeat aliqua collegia eximere a iurisdictione episcoporum
  Utrum papa debeat aliquos religiosos eximere a iurisdictione omnium prelatorum

Questio lxii de papa absolutione, ubi sex queruntur
  Utrum papa possit absolvere usurarium absque eo quod usuram restituat
  Utrum papa possit absolvere servum usurarum quod non teneatur ad restitutionem et absque eo quod sibi faciat relaxationem
  Utrum papa possit absolvere non rite absolutum per ratihabitionem
  Utrum papa possit absolvere habentem rem alienam post annos prescriptionis absque eo quod ipsam restituat
  Utrum papa possit absolvere simoniacum absque eo quod simoniam reddat
  Utrum papa possit absolvere ludentem ad taxillas absque eo quod restittat lucrum.

Questio lxiii de papa ligatione ubi queruntur quatuor
  Utrum preceptum pape magis liget quam ligamen legis nature
  Utrum preceptum pape magis liget quam ligamen conscientie erronee
  Utrum preceptum pape magis liget quam ligamen conscientie recte
  Utrum preceptum pape universaliter liget in omnibus

Questio lxiiii de dispensatione predicationis, ubi sex queruntur
  Utrum dispensatio predicationis in papa sit potestatis ordinis vel iurisdictionis
  Utrum sine auctoritate pape conve-//fol. 324rb//-niat episcopus predicare
  Utrum papa possit religiosos ad officium predicationis assumere
  Utrum papa religiosis petentibus et procurantibus debeat officium predicationis conferre
  Utrum sola auctoritate pape sine requisitione episcoporum et presbiterorum religiosi possint predicare
  Utrum magistris in theologia ex officio conveniat predicare sicut episcopis

Questio lxv de dispensatione confessionis, ubi sex queruntur
  Utrum papa possit facere quod quilibet christianus non confiteatur semel in anno proprio sacerdoti
  Utrum auctoritate pape religiosi possint in qualibet parochia sicut proprii sacerdotes confessionis audire
  Utrum papa possit facere quod peccata semel in anno confessa homo teneatur iterum confiteri

Utrum papa possit facere quod confessio eorundem peccatorum habeat efficaciam nisi semel
Utrum papa possit facere quod quis differat confessionem usque ad quadragesimam sine peccato
Utrum ex precepto pape sacerdos parochialis teneatur credere solo verbo suo subdito dicenti se esse confessum religioso habenti auctoritatem absolvendi

Questio lxvi de largitione privilegiorum, ubi queruntur quatuor
Utrum privilegium a papa indultum Isidorus bene diffiniat
Utrum papa privilegiorum lege in ecclesia uti debeat
Utrum solus papa privilegia concedere possit
Utrum privilegium concessum per papam per successorem possit revocari

Questio lxvii de pape interpretatione, ubi quinque queruntur
Utrum solus papa possit privilegium apostolicum interpretari
Utrum solus papa possit interpretari sacram scripturam
//fol. 324va// Utrum solus papa possit interpretari ius civile
Utrum papa possit interpretari ius naturale
Utrum papa dubia semper in meliorem partem teneatur interpretari

Questio lxviii de beneficiorum collatione, ubi quatuor queruntur
Utrum solus papa in pluralitate beneficiorum possit dispensare
Utrum sine auctoritate pape episcopus possit plura beneficia uni conferre
Utrum mortuo papa collegium cardinalium possit ecclesiastica beneficia dispensare
Utrum cum dispensatione pape licitum sit plura beneficia retinere

Questio lxix de officii administratione, ubi septem queruntur
Utrum ex precepto pape quilibet beneficiatus teneatur dicere horas canonicas
Utrum ex precepto pape beneficiatus totiens teneatur dicere horas canonicas quot habet beneficia
Utrum ex precepto pape beneficiatus teneatur dicere horas secundum consuetudinem universalis ecclesie vel illius ecclesie in qua beneficiatus est
Utrum ex precepto pape existens in sacris teneatur horas canonicas dicere
Utrum ex precepto pape beneficiatus existens in studio sit excusatur a debito dicendi horas
Utrum ex precepto papa omnes religiosi teneantur dicere horas
Utrum ex precepto pape obmittendi horas iniungendum sit quod dicat easdem horas quas dimisit

Questio lxx de translatione, ubi queruntur quinque
Utrum papa possit dispensare ut matrimonium nondum consumatum carnaliter dissolvatur per translationem ad statum religionis
Utrum papa possit dispensare ut religiosus ab observatione regule absolvatur per translationem eius ad statum prelationis

Utrum papa possit dispensare ut episcopus //fol. 324ᵛᵇ// a voto solemniter emisso absolvatur propter translationem eius ad religionis statum

Utrum papa possit dispensare ut religiosus absolvatur a voto per translationem eius ad secularem ecclesiam

Utrum papa possit dispensare ut religiosus professus in artiori regula absolvatur a voto per translationem eius ad regulam lationem

Questio lxxi de ordinatione, ubi quatuor queruntur
  Utrum ad solum papam spectet ordinatio studiorum
  Utrum ad solum papam spectet ordinatio officiorum
  Utrum ad solum papam spectet ordinatio religionum
  Utrum solum ad papam spectet ordinatio prelationum

Questio lxxii de pape provisione, ubi quatuor queruntur
  Utrum papa peccet providendo de beneficia ecclesiastico bono dimisso meliori
  Utrum papa peccet providendo compatriote domestico magis quam extraneo
  Utrum papa peccet non providendo theologis magistris religiosis unde decenter possint vivere
  Utrum si religioso per papam sufficienter est provisum elemosinam receptam iuste possit retinere

Questio lxxiii de papa concessione, ubi quinque queruntur
  Utrum papa sine peccato possit concedere in casu fieri usuras
  Utrum papa sine peccato possit concedere fieri usuras cum infidelibus et publicis hostibus ecclesie
  Utrum papa sine peccato possit alicui concedere decimas laicorum
  Utrum papa possit sine peccato regi Francie vel alteri principi concedere decimas clericorum
  Utrum papa sine peccato possit decimas ecclesiarum sibiipsi concedere in proprium usum

//fol. 325ʳᵃ//
Questio lxxiii de papa commissione, ubi quatuor queruntur
  Utrum papa possit committere totum officium papale simplici clerico vel laico
  Utrum papa possit committere totum officium epsicopale simplici sacerdoti
  Utrum papa possit committere totum officium clericale simplici laico
  Utrum papa possit committere simoniam

Questio lxxv de pape conservatione, ubi queruntur quatuor
  Utrum solum ad papam spectet omnes in suo iure conservare
  Utrum solum ad papam spectet religiosis et pauperibus conservatores dare
  Utrum conservatores dati per papam possint esse alii quam ecclesiarum prelati
  Utrum conservatores dati per papam habeant iurisdictionem nisi super manifestis iniuriis

Sequitur tertia et ultima pars ut potestas pape comperatur ad statum quem per talem potentiam homo consequitur, circa quam primo queritur de statu perfectionis primitate

Questio lxxvi de status perfectionis primitate, ubi queruntur quatuor
    Utrum omnis status perfectio sit a Christo effective inchoata
    Utrum status perfectio inchoata a Christo preferenda sit perfectioni patrum veteris testamenti
    Utrum omnis status perfectio in Christo sit demonstrata exemplo
    Utrum omnis status perfectio in Christo sit demonstrata verbo et doctrina

Questio lxxvii de Christi caritate, ubi tria queruntur
    Utrum Christus in sola caritate posuerit perfectionis statum
    Utrum perfectum modum diligendi Christus posuerit sub precepto vel concilio
    Utrum ad perfectum modum diligendi Christi aliquis perfectionis status possit attingere

//fol. 325rb//
Questio lxxviii de Christi paupertate, ubi quatuor queruntur
    Utrum Christus elegerit statum paupertatis
    Utrum paupertas fecerit in Christo perfectionis statum
    Utrum Christus sic fuerit pauper quod mendicaverit hostiatim
    Utrum Christus sic fuerit pauper quod manibus laboraret

Questio lxxix de Christi proprietate, ubi queruntur quatuor
    Utrum Christus habuerit aliquid proprium
    Utrum Christum habuerit aliquid in communi
    Utrum Christus res sibi oblatas possit convertere in proprium usum
    Utrum Christus rerum sibi concessarum habuerit dominium vel usum tantum

Questio lxxx de Christi vite communitate, ubi tria queruntur
    Utrum modus vivendi Christi servando aliquid in communi diminuerit de eius perfectionis statu
    Utrum communis modus vivendi Christi in conversatione derogaverit eius perfectionis statu
    Utrum communis modus vivendi Christi in victu et vestitu statui pefectionis eius conveniret

Questio lxxxi de Christi carnalitate, ubi quatuor queruntur
    Utrum Christus servando carnalitatem parentum fuerit in perfectionis statu
    Utrum Christus servando carnalitatem consanguineorum steterit in statu perfectionis
    Utrum Christus servando carnalitatem amicorum recesserit a perfectionis statu

Utrum Christus servando carnalitatem beneficiorum tenuerit perfectionis statum.

//fol. 325va//
Questio lxxxii de Christi obedientia, ubi quatuor queruntur
  Utrum in Christo fuerit obedientia
  Utrum Christus fuerit obediens homini vel deo solum
  Utrum obedientia in Christo fecerit perfectionis statum
  Utrum obedientia in Christ fuerit voto promissa

Questio lxxxiii de Christi continentia, ubi tria queruntur
  Utrum Christus potuerit actum coniugalem exercere
  Utrum Christus propter perfectionis statum debuerit vitare coniugium carnale
  Utrum Christus a statu perfectionis decidisset in carnali coniungio vivendo

Questio lxxxiiii de apostolorum vocatione, ubi queruntur quatuor
  Utrum apostoli prius vocati fuerint ad statum religionis quam prelationis
  Utrum apostoli post exercitationem mandatorum fuerint vocati ad religionis statum
  Utrum apostoli post eorum vocationem fuerint in perfectionis statu
  Utrum apostoli fuerint prius a Christo baptizati quam ad apostolatum vocati

Questio lxxxv de apostolorum predicatione, ubi queruntur quatuor
  Utrum per apostolos in toto orbe evangelium Christi fuerit predicatum
  Utrum apostoli predicando semper annuntiarent pacem
  Utrum apostoli predicando uterentur prudentia
  Utrum apostoli predicando libris ad predicandum indigerent

Questio lxxxvi de apostolorum conversatione, ubi quatuor queruntur
  Utrum Christus in collegio apostolorum debuerit mulierum consortium admittere
  Utrum apostolis post Christi resurrectionem licitum fuerit mulieres in eorum //fol. 325vb// conversatione habere
  Utrum Paulo licitum fuerit mulierum conversatione uti sicut aliis
  Utrum prelatis successoribus apostolorum licitum sit mulieres in eorum conversatione tenere

Questio lxxxvii de apostolorum perfectione, ubi queruntur quatuor
  Utrum status apostolorum in perfectione excesserit cuiuslibet perfectionis statum
  Utrum status apostolorum in perfectione excesserit statum omnium prelatorum
  Utrum status apostolorum Christi in perfectione excesserit statum discipulorum Johannis Baptiste

Utrum status apostolorum Christi excesserit in perfectione statum discipulorum eius quos binos misit ante faciem suam

Questio lxxxviiii de apostolorum prelatione, ubi queruntur quatuor
    Utrum solum Petrus fuerit a Christo assumptus ad prelationis statum
    Utrum perfectior fuerit in apostolis status prelationis quam religionis
    Utrum illi septuaginta duo discipuli assumpti fuerint ad statum prelationis
    Utrum illi septem diacones ad statum prelationis fuerint assumpti

Questio lxxxix de apostolorum paupertate, ubi queruntur quatuor
    Utrum apostolis fuerit interdicta possessio pecunie et rerum mobilium
    Utrum apostolis fuerit interdicta possessio rerum stabilium
    Utrum preceptum datum apostolis de non possedendis rebus temporalibus per Christum fuerit revocatum
    Utrum apostoli mendicaverint hostiatim

//fol. 326ra//
Questio xc de apostolorum continentia, ubi tria queruntur
    Utrum continentia in apostolis fecerit perfectionis statum
    Utrum coniugale vinculum diminuisset in apostolis perfectionis statum
    Utrum continentia in apostolis fuerint cum voto servata

Questio xci de apostolorum obedientia, ubi tria queruntur
    Utrum obedientia apostolos posuerit in perfectionis statum
    Utrum obedientia in apostolis magis fecerit perfectionis statum quam castitas vel paupertas
    Utrum obedientiam apostoli voto promiserunt

Questio xcii quomodo apostolorum perfectio observata est in episcopis ecclesie primitive, ubi quatuor queruntur
    Utrum episcopi in ecclesia primitiva servarent apostolorum vitam de non habendo proprium
    Utrum episcopi tunc servarent vitam apostolorum de non habendo possessiones
    Utrum episcopi et clerici ecclesie primitive tunc servarent vitam apostolorum de voto continentie
    Utrum episcopi tunc servarent vitam apostolorum de voto obedientie

Questio xciii quomodo status perfectio apostolorum observata est in presbyteris et diaconibus ecclesie primitive, ubi quatuor queruntur
    Utrum in ecclesia primitiva presbyteri essent distincti ab episcopis
    Utrum in eccclesia primitiva presbyteri et diaconi haberent perfectionis statum
    Utrum in ecclesia primitiva presbyteri et diaconi essent equalis perfectionis cum episcopis
    Utrum in ecclesia primitiva in perfectionis statu similiores essent episcopis, presbyteri et diaconi quam monachi

//fol. 326rb//
Questio xciii quomodo apostolorum pefectio observata est in martyribus, ubi quatuor queruntur
    Utrum in ecclesia primitiva martyrium posuerit martyres in perfectionis statu
    Utrum per solum supplicium mortis martyres consecuti sint statum perfectionis
    Utrum plus faciat ad perfectionis statum martyrium quam religionis votum
    Utrum semper sit perfectionis opus quod homo mortis periculo se exponat

Questio xcv quomodo apostolorum perfectio observata est in confessoribus, ubi queruntur quatuor
    Utrum sola caritas posuerit confessores in perfectionis statu
    Utrum magis amor amicitie quam concupiscentie fecerit in confessoribus statum perfectionis
    Utrum plus posuerit in perfectionis statu confessores corporis continentia quam temporalium carentia
    Utrum magis per humilitatem quam per aliam virtutem confessores consecuti sint statum perfectionis

Questio xcvi quomodo apostolorum perfectio observata est in virginibus, ubi quatuor queruntur
    Utrum virginitas sine voto servata posuerit virgines in perfectionis statu
    Utrum virginitas voto promissa fuerit apud deum maioris meriti quam sine voto
    Utrum virginibus corruptores volentes ipsas corrumpere violenter licitum fuerit eos interficere
    Utrum virgines que fuerint violenter corrupte a barbaris perdiderint aureolam

Questio xcvii quomodo apostolorum perfectio observata est in monachis manibus laborantibus, ubi sex queruntur
    Utrum monachi manibus laborantes fuerint in perfectioni statu
    //fol. 326va// Utrum illa que acquisiverunt monachi ex labore ipsorum eis vel monasterio fuerint acquisita
    Utrum fuerit licitum monachis aliquid proprium habere
    Utrum monachi solitarii fuerint in perfectiori statu quam viventes in societate
    Utrum monachorum vita quanto artior fuerit tanto perfectior
    Utrum monachis universaliter ex precepto esus carnium fuerit interdictus

Questio xcviii quomodo apostolorum perfectio observata est in monachis contemplationi vacantibus, ubi queruntur quatuor
    Utrum monachi insistentes contemplationi essent in perfectionis statu
    Utrum monachi insistentes contemplationi essent in statu magis securo quam alii
    Utrum monachi insistentes contemplationi essent in statu magis meritorio

Utrum monachi vacantes contemplationi essent in statu magis utili et necessario

Questio xcix quomodo apostolorum perfectio observata est in predicatoribus evangelii, ubi queruntur quinque
　Utrum omnes predicatores evangelii fuerint in perfectionis statu
　Utrum predicatio evangelii magis fecerit ad perfectionis statum quam alia pietatis opera
　Utrum predicare evangelium mendicando fuerit maioris perfectionis quam vivendo de communi administratione auditorum
　Utrum perfectio predicatorum fuerit in conformando se capacitati auditorum
　Utrum predicare evangelium excommunicatis ex ecclesie mandato fuerit interdictum

Questio c quomodo apostolorum perfectio observata est in doctoribus et sacre scripture expositoribus, ubi quinque queruntur
　Utrum dicta doctorum maioris autoritatis sint quam dicata summorum pon-//fol. 326vb//-tificum
　Utrum doctores et expositores sacre scripture episcopis sint preponendi
　Utrum in modo exponendi sacram scripturam ecclesia doctorum regulas debeat imitari
　Utrum solum illorum doctorum opuscula que ecclesia recipit sint approbata
　Utrum illorum doctorum opuscula quos ecclesia canonizat ex hoc ipso sint per ecclesiam approbata

Questio ci quomodo apostolorum pefectio representatur in papa, ubi octo queruntur
　Utrum papa sit in perfectiori statu quam aliquis alius episcoporum
　Utrum papa statum perfectionis Christi et apostolorum perfectiori modo representet quam aliquis religiosorum
　Utrum papa possit esse in perfectionis statu absque eo quod sit perfectus
　Utrum in papa exterior apparatus diminuat de eius perfectionis statu
　Utrum in papa administratio temporalium diminuat de perfectione status eius
　Utrum in papa determinatio causarum diminuat de eius statu perfectionis
　Utrum in papa habere dominium et usum rerum diminuat de statu perfectionis eius
　Utrum papa possit omnis perfectionis statum mutare

Questio cii quomodo status perfectionis representatur in cardinalibus, ubi queruntur quinque
　Utrum cardinales representent statum perficiendorum vel perfectorum
　Utrum cardinales in perfectionis statu preferendi sint episcopis
　Utrum abdicatio temporalium magis requiratur ad perfectionis statum cardinalium quam episcoporum
　Utrum deroget statui perfectionis cardinalium ut omnes de una patria sint electi
　Utrum legatio in cardinalibus spectet ad eorum perfectionis statum

//fol. 327ʳᵃ//

Questio ciii quomodo status perfectio representat in episcopis, ubi queruntur quinque

Utrum episcopi perfectiori modo represententent statum apostolorum quam religiosi

Utrum ad perfectionis statum acquirendum magis religio quam episcopalis prelatio sit procuranda

Utrum in episcopis cura temporalium diminuat de eorum perfectioni statu

Utrum episcopi de bonis ecclesie possint condere testatmentum

Utrum episcopi bona ecclesiastica non erogando pauperibus maneant in perfectionis statu

Questio ciiii quomodo status perfectio representatur in presbyteris et curatis, ubi queruntur quatuor

Utrum presbyteri representent statum perfectionis discipulorum Christi

Utrum presbyteri in perfectionis statu sint preferendi religiosis

Utrum presbyteri in regiminis cura preferendi sint regibus

Utrum presbyteri novi testamenti preferendi sint presbyteris veteris testamenti

Questio cv quomodo status perfectio representatur in religionis mendicantibus, ubi novem queruntur

Utrum religiosi mendicantes sint perfectioris status quam alii

Utrum religiosi mendicantes cum perfectionis statu possint esse de collegio et numero magistrorum

Utrum religiosi mendicantes cum perfectionis statu possint esse de collegio et numero studentium scholarium

Utrum plures magistros esse in una religionis collegio deroget eorum perfectionis statui

Utrum religiosi mendicantes cum perfectionis statu possint esse testamentorum executores

Utrum religiosi mendicantes cum perfectionis statu possint esse regum et reginarum confessores

Utrum religiosi mendicantes cum perfectionis statu possint esse secularium principum officiales

Utrum religiosi mendicantes cum perfectionis statu possint se de negotiis secularium intromittere

Utrum religiosi mendicantes possint cum //fol. 327rb// perfectionis statu largiores elemosinas recipere quam alii pauperes mendicantes

Questio cvi quomodo status perfectio representatur in religiosis in communi possessiones habentibus, ubi quinque queruntur

Utrum religiosi habentes possessiones in communi representat Christi et apostolorum perfectionis statum

Utrum religiosi habentes possessiones in communi sint in equali perfectionis statu cum religiosis mendicantibus

Utrum religiosi habentes possessiones in communi cum eorum perfectionis statu possint mendicando elemosinas recipere

Utrum religiosi professi in una religione cum eorum perfectionis statu possint prefici in prelaturam aliterius religionis

Utrum ingredientes religionem elapso probationis anno teneantur ex voto in religione permanere sicut professi

Questio cvii quomodo status perfectio representatur in evangelii predicatoribus, ubi queruntur quatuor

Utrum predicatores absque peccato possint in predicatione evangelii aliqua verba humane letitie immiscere

Utrum absque peccato predicatores possint conatum apponere in complacendo auditoribus

Utrum absque peccato possint curam apponere in ornatu verborum

Utrum predicatores absque peccato possint populi scelera tacere non pronunciando eis

Questio cviii quomodo status perfectio representatur in magistris et doctoribus, ubi queruntur quatuor

Utrum dignus magistrari in theologia teneatur scire omnes scientias humanas

Utrum dignus magistrari in theologia teneatur scire omnium gentium linguas

Utrum dignus magistrari in theologia teneatur scire ius canonicum

Utrum dignus magistrari in theologia si non magistratur perdet aureolam

Questio cix quomodo status perfectio representatur in medicis, ubi decem queruntur

Utrum medici sint honorandi pre aliis professoribus aliarum artium

Utrum medici si non sint de legitimo thoro nati possint sine peccato medicorum officium exercere

Utrum tutius sit quod homo medicis practicis //fol. 327va// quam theoreticis se in cura committat

Utrum tutius sit plures medicos in egritudine habere quam unum

Utrum medici peccent dantes medicinas non in debitis signis astrorum

Utrum medici peccent accipientes stipendium pro infirmitate quam sciunt esse incurabilem

Utrum medici peccent non monentes infirmos ut animarum medicos ante omnia debeant convocare

Utrum medici teneantur ex precepto pauperibus et religiosis auxilium et consilium impendere

Utrum medicine ars clericis et religiosis sit interdicta

Utrum medici dantes aliquam medicinam vel facientes aliquam incissuram ex qua sequitur mors sint irregulares

Questio cx quomodo status perfectio representatur in notariis, ubi sex queruntur

Utrum solum habens iurisdictionem temporalem possit publicos notarios facere

Utrum ad notariatus officium debeant aliqui admitti nisi iurati
Utrum notarius possit suum officium delegare
Utrum notarius gerat officium unius testis in instrumentis peractis per eum
Utrum notarius factus religiosus possit notariatus officium exercere
Utrum clerici possunt exercere notariatus officium

Questio cxi quomodo status perfectio representatur in advocatis, ubi queruntur septem
Utrum clerici absque peccato possint advocationis officium exercere
Utrum omnes laici indifferenter ad officium advocationis sine peccato possint admitti
Utrum advocati teneantur ex precepto dei non prestare patrocinium in causa iniusta
Utrum advocati sine peccato contra adversarium possint uti insidiis et fallaciis
Utrum advocati teneantur ad restitutionem recepti stipendii si ex eorum //fol. 327vb// negligentia perdatur causa quam assumunt
Utrum advocati accipientes salarium ultra quantitatem in iure taxatam teneantur ad restitutionem
Utrum advocati absque peccato possint pactum facere cum litigatore de media vel quarta portione litis

Questio cxii quomodo status perfectio representatur in iudicibus, ubi quinque queruntur
Utrum iudex possit mutare penam in lege taxatam
Utrum iudex plus ad clementiam quam ad rigidam iustitiam debeat declinare
Utrum iudex habens taxatum stipendium pro suo officio teneatur ad restitutionem eorum que aliter recipit
Utrum in eadem causa idem possit esse iudex et advocatus
Utrum iudex eodem iudicio debeat ab eterno iudice iudicari quo ipse alios iudicat et cetera

Explicit Tabula super Summa de ecclesiastica potestate clarissimi sacre theologie doctoris fratris Augustini de Ancona sacri ordinis fratrum heremitarum Aurelii doctoris et patris Augustini in questiones centumduodecim et articulos quadringentos septuaginta sex distincta.

APPENDIX D

JORDANI DE QUEDLINBURG

Vita Sancti Augustini

Paris, Bibliothèque de l'Arsenal, MS 251 is the autograph copy of Jordan of Quedlinburg's *Collectanea Augustiniana*. The parchment manuscript measures 248 x 186 mm. In addition to the 18th-century hand responsible for marginal notes periodically throughout the manuscript, two other hands can be identified. One is that of an otherwise anonymous brother Bernardus, who wrote the colophon on fol. 104rb: *Liber iste est parisiensis ordinis heremitarum sancti Augustini. Si quis furatus fuerit, anathama sit.* Fol. 104v contains numerous, miscellaneous pen-trials, among which in Bernardus' hand is found not only a trial of the colophon, but also the note: *anno domini m° cccc lxix vigilia purificationis huc accessus.* This then allows for the dating of a second series of marginalia which were made in the hand of Bernardus. Bernardus' marginalia indicate that Jordan's *Collectanea* continued to play a role in the Order's on-going conflict with the Canons. Thus c. 1469, some fifteen years before Pope Sixtus IV prohibited further discussion of the matter, in the margin on folio 7va, commenting on the fourth sermon *ad fratres in eremo, De Prudentia*, Bernardus commented: *Nota contra detractores ordinis nostri qualis fuit dux et pater heremitarum.* Yet over a century before Bernardus found in Jordan's text evidence and proof of Augustine's paternity of the Hermits, Jordan himself composed the manuscript with the same purpose and goals in mind, and his hand is the third hand identifiable in MS 251 of the Bibliothèque de l'Arsenal.

That the hand that wrote the text is that of Jordan is ascertainable from the marginal insertions. The text is written in double columns with dark brown ink. Three places in the *Vita* Jordan added text in the bottom margin, written with different ink, a light brown ink (or written with a different pen), which then he underlined in red. The first two of these insertions are combined with erasure, and are the addition of text taken from Datius' *Chronica*. Jordan cites Datius' *Chronica* three times,[1] and each time the text is an insert. The addition of Datius thus appears to have been part of the revision process, which also included marginalia indicating the works of Augustine upon which the given passage had drawn. These marginal references are likewise written with the lighter brown ink, and at times are also underlined in red. The hand of the inserts, including the additions *in rasura* in the text columns themselves emending the text to accommodate the added material, is the same hand as that of the text columns. This is

---

[1] Arbesmann, "Vita," 346–347.

highly suggestive evidence that Jordan himself was responsible for the actual writing of the entire *Collectanea*.² After having corrected and made the desired additions to the text, together with the marginal references, Jordan then went over his text a third time, indicated by additional marginal references to the works of Augustine and corrections, made in a grayish ink, yet in the same hand.

To date, Jordan's autograph has been the only known copy of his *Collectanea*. Zumkeller lists three additional manuscripts containing only the *Vita Sancti Augustini*.³ In the fifteenth century, Jordan's *Vita* served as the major source for John Capgrave's *Life of Augustine*.⁴ In 1684 J. Hommey published Jordan's *Vita Sancti Augustini*, together with the other texts of *Collectanea*, aside from the *sermones*, the *Regulae*, the *Legenda* and the *Vita Monicae*, based on the autograph.⁵ The *Catalogus Codicum Hagiographicorum Latinorum* of the Bibliothèque Nationale in Paris, however, lists manuscript lat. 5338 as containing a *Vita Sancti Augustini, de translatione ejusdem prima, de translatione secunda*, and *annotatio temporum beati Augustini episcopi*.⁶ The catalogue further notes: *Auctore, ut videtur, Jordano de Saxonia*. Paris, BnF, MS lat. 5338, fol. 1ra–108vb is actually a previously unknown fifteenth-century copy of the entire *Collectanea*. The first and last quires, however, are missing, and the *sermones* follow the other texts, rather than preceding them as in Paris, Bibl. de l'Arsenal, MS 251. The manuscript begins with the *Vita*, though lacking the first quire, the text is preserved only from the end of chapter nine, or fol. 62va of the autograph. I am currently preparing a critical edition of Jordan's *Vita Sancti Augustini*, which will include a thorough study of this manuscript, together with a detailed analysis of the construction of the autograph, a study of the *Sermones ad fratres in eremo*, complete collation of all extant textual witnesses, and discussion of all other relevant material, such as the *Legenda de Sancto Augustino* of Jordan's *Collectanea*.⁷ Paris, BnF MS lat. 5338 takes on added importance for the critical edition since quire nine of Paris, Bibl. de

---

[2] On the determination of an autograph, see M.C. Garand, *Guibert de Nogent et ses secrétaires*, Corpus Christianorum: Autograph medii aevi, 2 (Turnhout, 1995).

[3] Zumkeller *MSS* NR. 639 (287). The manuscripts are: Brussels, Bib. Royale 1351–72, 14. s., fol. 35r–47v; Toulouse, Bibl. de la Ville 169, 14. s., fols. 1 sqq.; and Vienna Kaiserl. Privatbibl. 9375.A. n. 22, 15. s., fol. 81–96. *Cf. Bibliotheca Hagiographica Latina Antiquae et Mediae Aetatis*, edd. Socii Bollandiani, 2 vols. (Bruxelles, 1898–1901); I: 125–128; *Bibliotheca Hagiographica Latina Antiquae et Mediae Aetatis. Novum Supplementum*, ed. Henricus Fros (Bruxelles, 1986), 101–105.

[4] See Arbesmann, "Vita."

[5] J. Hommey, *Supplementum Patrum* (Paris, 1684), 569–659; I have used the Paris 1696 edition of this work. Hommey's text of the *Vita*, however, is not without problems. A complete collation of Jordan's autograph with the text of Hommey yielded 278 variant readings. Many of these are simple mis-readings or eye-skips, yet others are of more substantial nature, based on what is apparently Hommey's attempts to correct and/or improve Jordan's text.

[6] *Catalogus Codicum Hagiographicorum Latinorum Antiquiorum Saeculo XVI qui asservantur in Bibliotheca Nationali Parisiensi*, ed. Hagiographi Bollandiani (Bruxellis, 1890), II, 261.

[7] See my forthcoming edition, *Jordani de Quedlinburg Opera Selecta*, vol. 2: *Jordani de Quedlinburg Vita Sancti Augustini. Introduction, Critical Edition, Translation, and Commentary*.

l'Arsenal MS 251 is missing. The text in the autograph breaks off on fol. 96vb with chapter 22 of the *translationes Sanctae Monicae* (26 chapters are listed in the *tabula* on fol. 89vb–90ra), continuing then mid-stream on fol. 97ra with the *Legenda de Sancto Augustino*. As indicated in the *Tabula* beginning the work (fol. 2^{ra-vb}), which follows Jordan's prologue, after the translations of Monica yet preceding the *Legenda de Sancto Augustino* was to be a versified life of Augustine, given the title, *Metrum pro depingenda vita Sancti Augustini* (fol. 2vb).[8] This text is preserved in BnF MS lat 5338 (fol. 48rb–51rb), which is then followed by a versified life of Paul the first Hermit (fol. 51rb–52va), not mentioned in the *Tabula* of Jordan's autograph.[9] This copy of the *Collectanea*, together with Bernardus' marginalia and John Capgrave's *Life* give evidence of the resonance Jordan's work had within the Order throughout the later Middle Ages. Moreover, Johannes von Paltz knew Jordan's *Vita*. In his defense of the Order in the *Supplementum Coelifodina* (1504), Paltz inserted a passage taken from Jordan's *Vita* word for word:

Johannes von Paltz, *Supplementum Coelifondinae*, ed. B. Hamm *et al.*, SuR 3 (Berlin, 1983), 274,5–14.

Jordan de Quedlinburg, *Vita Sancti Augustini*, 7,1 Paris, Bibl. de l'Arsenal MS 251, fol. 60ra.

Post haec autem, cum instigante eius pia mater de Mediolano recedere et ad Africam remeare disponeret, adivit sanctum Simplicianum petens, ut sibi aliquos de fratribus suis eremitis servos dei donaret, quos secum in Africam assumeret, et cum eis inibi iuxta vitam apostolicam in communi viveret et sic talem collapsam innovaret et resuscitaret. Cuius piis precibus ille pater Simplicianus annuens dedit duodecim fratres, viros religiosos. Cum quibus adiunctis sibi carissimis amicis suis, qui diu secum fuerant, Nebridio, Euodio, Alypio et Pontiano, cum matre et filio Adeodato ad Africam proficiscendi iter arripuit. De hoc ipse in sermone De tribus generibus monachorum, qui incipit >Ut nobis per litteras.<

Post hec autem cum instigante eius pia matre de Mediolano recedere et ad Africam remeare disponeret, adivit sanctum Simplicianum petens ut sibi aliquos de fratribus suis eremitis servos dei donaret, quos secum in Africam assumeret et cum eis ibi ordinem plantaret.

Cuius piis precibus pius ille pater Simplicianus annuens dedit ei duodecim fratres viros religiosos, cum quibus adiunctis sibi carissimis amicis suis qui diu secum fuerant, Nebridio, Evodio, Alipio et Pontiano, cum matre et filio Adeodato, ad Africam proficiscendi iter arripuit. De hoc ipse in sermone de tribus generibus monachorum, qui incipit *Ut nobis per litteras* . . .

---

[8] Cf. *Bibliotheca Hagiographica Latina Antiquae et Mediae Aetatis. Novum Supplementum*, 104, n. 799. For the text of Jordan's *Tabula*, see Saak, "Augustinian Identity," 253–254. The missing quire in the autograph has not previously been mentioned by scholars, nor has the *Metrum pro depingenda vita Sancti Augustini*; see for example Arbesmann, "Vita," 344 and Hümpfner, intro., xxivff.

[9] For the coherence of the *Vita* of Paul the First Hermit having been included either originally by Jordan himself, or by the scribe of Paris, BnF MS lat. 5338, see K. Elm, "Elias, Paulus von Theben und Augustinus als Ordensgründer."

Paltz had been drawing on Ambrosius de Cora's *Defensorium ordinis fratrum heremitarum sancti Augustini*, yet this section of text is to be found neither in Ambrosius' *Defensorium* nor in his *Chronica*.[10]

Since the critical edition of Jordan's *Vita Sancti Augustini* is still in preparation, presenting a working text here will enable the reader to have an established, reliable text of Jordan's work. The text of Jordan's *Vita Sancti Augustini* here presented is that of the autograph. For the present purposes and for the ease of the modern reader I have standardized the orthography and modernized the punctuation. I have used 'u' for the vowel 'u' and 'v' and 'v' for the consonant 'u' and 'v' thus printing *una*, *vita*, and *vivere* rather than *vna*, *uita* and *viuere*; I have rendered the manuscript's 'w' as 'vu' or 'v', and thus print *vult* and *evangelium* rather than *wlt* and *ewangelium*; *Yponensis* is edited as *Hipponensis* and *apud Yponem* as *apud Hipponem*; I have used -ti- for -ci- before a vowel (both are found in the manuscript) and thus print the forms *ratio*, *scientia*, *iustitia*, *etiam* etc., rather than *racio*, *sciencia*, *iusticia*, and *eciam*; i/j/y are used synonymously in the autograph, and thus I have printed *tertii* and *diabolus* rather than *tercij* and *dyabolus*; I have added an initial 'h' for clarity when called for, and thus have spelled the manuscript's *ymnus* and *ortus* as *hymnus* and *hortus*, when the latter is referring to a garden, rather than to an origin or a beginning (though Augustine's conversion having taken place in a garden, *abscessi ergo in hortum*, [Aug. conf. 8,8,19] could have overtones of Augustine's having withdrawn into his own origins as a Christian, a return to the womb for his re-birth).

Jordan systematically organized his text, which I have followed. In the manuscript chapters are clearly indicated by a decorated initial, usually accompanied by a rubricated chapter title. I have numbered the chapters with Roman numerals for ease of reference, and have supplied chapter titles within brackets <> where none are given in the text. All rubrics are

---

[10] In his *Defensorium*, Ambrosius retells the life of Augustine. This portion of the biography in Ambrosius' text reads as follows: "Et cum quamdiu sic devote ac beate in nemoribus degisset a pia rogatur parente, secum ut in Affricam redire vellet, quod recte tante matris munera nescens ac dei mandati memor, que parentes iubet a filiis honorari, ei morem genere decrevit. Ob idque a sancto Simpliciano licentiam petens, obnixe ei suplicavit, ut aliquot suis ex fratribus de quibus in Affricania oris religionem plantaret, largiretur. Cuius pius pater precibus annuens Anastasium, Fabrianum, Severum, Nicholaum, Cirillum, Stephanum, Derotheum, Issac, Nichostratum, Paulinum, Jacobum, Vitalemque viros perfecto in heremitica vita probatissimos donavit. Amicisque suis karissimis Alippio, Nebridio, Evodio, Pontiano et filio suo ingeniosissimo Adeodato divaque matre sua adiunctis Affricam petens iter arripuit, de quibus omnibus velut humilitatis magistra et omnis honestatis exemplar, Monica, ita cura gessit quasi omnes genuisset, ita serviunt quasi ab omnibus genita fuisset." Ambr. C. *Def.* (Rome, 1481), fol. 9ʳ. While there are certainly indications that Ambrosius was likewise familiar with Jordan's *Vita*, Paltz apparently took his account here directly from Jordan. The editors of the *Supplementum* can not be expected to have known this passage from Jordan. I will be treating Ambrosius, as well as Paltz, at length in volume 2, *The Failed Reformation*.

printed in small capitals. Jordan also indicated subdivisions of chapters with the paragraph sign ¶. These I have likewise numbered, though with Arabic numerals. No other paragraphization has been introduced, which at times may seem awkward to the modern reader, yet preserves the organization of the text Jordan himself provided.

To aid the reader, I have capitalized proper nouns. This includes Jordan's consistent rendering of the name of Augustine's son with three words, *a deo datus*, which I have printed as *Adeodatus*. In addition I have printed book titles and scriptural citations in italics. Quotation marks have been used only for direct quotations within the text, rather than for Jordan's own use of sources, which deserves special comment.

In addition to Augustine's *Confessiones, Retractationes, De Civitate Dei, De Trinitate*, and the *sermones* cited from his own *Collectanea*, which include two authentic sermons of Augustine, Jordan mentions drawing on the following sources: Possidius' *Vita Sancti Augustini*, a *Legenda Famosa*, and Datius' *Chronica*. The last text has not survived, except for fragments preserved in Landulfus' *Historia Mediolanensis*. The *Legenda Famosa* Jordan cites is the *Vita Sancti Augustini* of Philip of Harvengt. Not named by Jordan is the *Legenda Aurea* of Jacobus de Voragine.[11]

Jordan's *Vita Sancti Augustini* is an intricate pastiche, complied from the sources mentioned above. The following examples are illustrative:

Jor. *Vita* 2,1:

Cum igitur decem et novem esset annorum, defuncto iam patre ante biennium, quem in extremo vite sue mater quoque deo lucrata fuerat, discendi ordine pervenit in librum quemdam Ciceronis cui<us> nomen Hortensius, qui exhortationem continet ad philosophiam, in quo etiam vanitas mundi contemnenda docetur. Et ex hoc quidem liber ei plurimum placuit, sed hoc solum refrangebat, quia nomen Christi non erat ibi. Hoc enim nomen salvatoris in ipso adhuc lacte matris tenerum cor eius biberat et alte retinebat et quidquid sine hoc nomine fuisset, quamvis altum expolitum et veridicum non eum totum rapiebat, prout ipse tertio libro Confessionum refert.

In this passage Jordan weaves together the *Confessiones* with the *Legenda Aurea* and shades of Philip of Harvengt's *Vita* as well. He begins with the phrase: "Cum igitur decem et novem esset annorum," echoing Aug. conf. 3,4,7 (25): "cum agerem annum aetatis undevicensimum," which continues with the reference to his father, "iam defuncto patre ante biennium," yet Jordan's text is more closely paralleled with *LA* 120 (843,30–31): "Cum igitur esset annorum XIX." He then includes reference to Monica converting Patricius by noting: "quem in extremo vite sue mater quoque deo lucrata fuerat," drawing from Aug. conf. 9,13,37 (118): "Sit ergo in pace cum viro, ante quem nulli et post quem nulli nupta est, cui servivit fructum tibi afferens cum tolerantia, ut eum quoque lucraretur tibi." Jordan then returns to Aug. conf. 3,4,7 but seven lines previous to the ones with which he began,

---

[11] *Cf.* Arbesmann, "Vita," 45–47. Arbesmann does not mention the *Legenda Aurea*.

namely, "discendi ordine pervenit in librum quemdam Ciceronis cui<us> nomen Hortensius, qui exhortationem continet ad philosophiam"; *cf.* Aug. conf. 3,4,7 (25): "et usitato iam discendi ordine perveneram in librum cuiusdam Ciceronis, cuius linguam fere omnes mirantur, pectus non ita. sed liber ille ipsius exhortationem continet ad philosophiam et vocatur 'Hortensius'." Yet Philip's *Vita* is closer to Jordan's text: "discendi ordine pervenit in quemdam librum Tullii cuius nomen Hortensii. Ille siquidem liber ad philosophiam hortatur." Phil. vita Aug. 2 (107A). Jordan then switches to the *Legenda Aurea*, which did not mention the *Hortensius*, for the following phrase: "in quo etiam vanitas mundi contemnenda docetur et ex hoc quidem liber ei plurimum placuit, sed hoc solum refrangebat, quia nomen Christi non erat ibi"; *cf.* LA 120 (843,30–31): "in quo vanitas mundi contemnenda et philosophia appetenda dicebatur, perlegeret, ex hoc quidem liber plurimum placuit, sed quia nomen Jesu Christi, quod a matre imbiberat, ibi non erat, dolere coepit," though Jordan's text is not without influence from the *Confessiones* which he then picks up again in parallel with the *Legenda Aurea* after the "insert" from the latter, by skipping to Aug. conf. 3,4,8 (26): "et hoc solum me in tanta flagrantia refrangebat, quod nomen Christi non erat ibi." He then continues with Aug. conf. 3,4,8 (26) for the remainder of the passage in question: "quoniam hoc nomen salvatoris mei, filii tui, in ipso adhuc lacte matris tenerum cor meum pie biberat et alte retinebat, et quidquid sine hoc nomine fuisset, quamvis litteratum et expolitum et veridicum, non me totum rapiebat."

Jor. *Vita* 2,1–2:

In predicto autem errore permansit fere novem annis, ut in principio quarti libri Confessionum humiliter confitetur.

2. Mater autem eius pro eo multum flebat, amplius quam flere solent matres corporea funera, et ipsum ad unitatem fidei ducere satagebat. Cui pre dolore perditionis filii pene deficienti data est divinitus huiusmodi consolatio.

Here Jordan began by summarizing Aug. conf. 4,1,1 (33): "Per idem tempus annorum novem, ab undevicesimo anno aetatis meae usque ad duodetricesimum, seducebamur et seducebamus...," but then we find a typical example of his meshing of texts. The first sentence of 2,2 combines Aug. conf. 3,11,19 (31) with *LA* 120 (843,31); Aug. conf. 3,11,19 (31): "Et misisti manum tuam ex alto et de hac profunda caligine eruisti animam meam, cum pro me fleret ad te mea mater, fidelis tua, amplius quam flent matres corporea funera." *LA* 120 (843,31): "... mater vero eius plurimum flebat et ipsum ad veritatem fidei reducere satagebat." Jordan then brings in Phil. vita Aug. 3 (1207D): "Ipsi vero matri, prae dolore perditionis illius pene deficienti, quanta divinitus data sit consolatio."

Jor. *Vita*, 3,1:

Et venit Mediolanum ad Ambrosium episcopum in optimis notum orbi terre, et suscepit eum paterne. Cepit autem Augustinus viro dei adherere et eius predicationes frequenter audire. Primo quidem non ut veritatem audiret quod in ecclesia Christi prorsus desperabat, sed explorans utrum fame illius facundia conveniret et delectabatur suavitate sermonis, non satagens discere que dicebat. Deinde cepit paulatim animum rebus magis quam verbis applicare.

This again is a mixed passage. It begins with the Aug. conf. 5,13,23 (56): "Et veni Mediolanium ad Ambrosium episcopum, in optimis notum orbi terrae, pium cultorem tuum, cuius tunc eloquia strenue ministrabant adipem frumenti tui et laetitiam olei et sobriam vini ebrietatem populo tuo. ad eum autem ducebar abs te nesciens, ut per uem ad te sciens ducerer. suscepit me paterne ille homo dei et peregrinationem meam satis episcopaliter dilexit." *Cf.* Phil. vita Aug. 6 (1209D): "Ille vero homo Dei hunc advenientem benigne suscepit...". He then switches to *LA* 120 (844,49–51): "Coepit autem Augustinus beato Ambrosio adhaerere et eius praedicationes frequenter audire," substituting the *Legenda*'s *beato Ambrosio* with *viro dei*, drawn from the *Legenda*, though three lines earlier, referring to Ambrose as *vir dei*. Jordan then interweaves Aug. conf. 5,13,23 with Phil, vita Aug. 6; Aug. conf. 5,13,23 (56): "et eum amare coepi, primo quidem non tamquam doctorem veri, quod in ecclesia tua prorsus desperabam..."; *cf.* Phil. vita Aug. 6 (1209D–1210A): "... et iste illius primo quidem non sanctitatem, sed benignitatem erga se dilexit. Quo loquente in populo verbum Dei Augustinus frequenter aderat, non ut veritatem audiret, sed explorans utrum fame illius facundia conveniret. Audierat enim illius facundiam commendari, cui attente inhiabat, delectatus sermonis suavitate, potius quam rei veritate." Jordan then adds a phrase from Aug. conf. 5,14,24 (57): "Cum enim non satagerem discere quae dicebat..." The final sentence is directly from Phil. vita Aug. 6 (1210A): "Deinde cum frequenter interesset praedicationi, coepit paulatim animum rebus magis, quam verbis, intendere..."; *cf.* Aug. conf. 5,14,24 (57): "... veniebant in animum meum simul cum verbis quae diligebam res etiam quas neglegebam, neque enim ea dirimere poteram. et dum cor aperirem ad excipiendum quam diserte diceret, pariter intrabat et quam vere diceret..."

These examples should clearly illustrate how Jordan went about constructing his text. I do not, however, mean to imply that he consciously picked and chose individual wordings from his various sources. Most likely Jordan had read all his sources so thoroughly that they were in his own mind a mixture, reflected in his composition. Unravelling the various threads of his compilation is a task for the commentary to the critical edition. For the text that follows, I have given references in the notes only to the sources Jordan himself names, without the detailed analysis of each passage as given in these examples. For Augustine's *Confessiones*, including in the passages cited above, I have used the edition of O'Donnell to refer the reader to his excellent commentary. The intent is to provide a reliable, readable text, that of the autograph, that can be of use to scholars before the appearance of the critical edition.

//fol. 54ʳᵇ// Prologus in vitam sancti Augustini episcopi

Almi patris ac doctoris eximii Augustini Hipponensis episcopi, ortum procursumque ac finem vite auxiliante eo qui laudatur in sanctis suis fideliter descripturus, nichil huic operi inserendum censui, quod non ipsius propriis dictis, aut aliorum autenticis scriptis confirmetur. Secutus precipue vestigium illius venerandi viri sancti Possidonii Calamensis episcopi eiusdem sancti patris discipuli et in suo monasterio olim canonici, qui eius gesta prout viderat et per experientiam didicerat diffuse conscripsit, ad ea maxime se referens tempora, quibus ipse cum eo presentialiter fuerat conversatus. Neque enim tantus doctor veritatis honorari se gratum duceret laudibus falsitatis. Ipse et enim dicit in primo libro *De Trinitate*: "Malim," inquit, "me reprehendi a reprehensore falsitatis, quam ab eius laudatore laudari."[1] Porro hoc unum obsecro eum qui hec legerit, ut si qua hic scripta repererit, que in vulgatis legendis non habentur, non prius dentem mordacem exerceat quam signatarum remissionum loca studiose requirat. Nec temeritati mee quisquam ascribat quod post tam magnorum virorum studia, qui legendas eiusdem sancti doctoris conscripserunt, //fol.54ᵛᵃ// ausus sum manum ponere, quia profecto sepe inspice que maiorum metentium manus effugiunt a parvulis colliguntur.

Incipit tractatus de vita sancti Augustini episcopi.

I. <De eius iuventute>

1. Augustinus doctor egregius ex provincia Africana civitate Thagatensi, honesta prosapia de numero curialium, patre quidem adhuc gentili Patricio nomine, matre vero dicta Monica, christianissima progenitus fuit. Qui divino nescientes ducti consilio, hunc summa eorum cura et diligentia enutritum litterali inbuendum tradiderunt studio. Quem prescia futuri divina clementia, tanti ingenii ditavit perspicatia, ut non solum coevorum, verum etiam grandevorum, discendi agilitate prevolaret studia. Parentes autem eius tanto profectui congaudentes, que illi erant necessaria magna preparabant diligentia, mirantibus cunctis eorum vicinis cum attenderent, quantam illi filio inpenderent curam, non considerantes quid expenderet, dum pro voto proficeret. Una autem dierum puer nimio dolore stomachi vexatus anxius valde laborabat, hortante igitur matre ut baptizaretur sed rennuente patre, baptisma //fol. 54ᵛᵇ// dilatum est. Interim miserante dei gratia dolore quiescente sanatus est. Cuius mundatio adhuc dilata fuit, quasi necesse esset, ut adhuc sordidaretur si viveret, quia maius peccatum esset si post baptismum peccaret. Grecas sane litteras quibus docebatur oderat, Latinas vero satis diligebat, ut ipse hec memoratur in primo libro *Confessionum*.[2]

---

[1] Aug. trin. 1,3,6 (34,62–63).
[2] Aug. conf. 1,13,20 (10).

2. Parvo igitur tempore in eo quo natus est municipio et in Madauris civitate vicina quo a parentibus missus fuit, doctus est grammaticam. Inde reversus cum sextum decimum etatis sue ageret annum disposuit longius proficissi doceri rethoricam. Sed anno illo cum parentibus demoratus et interposito otio ex necessitate domestica, interim ab omni scola feriatus cum ageret annos ferventis adolescentie per devexa lascivie vagabundus ruebat, patre quidem adhuc cathecumino non multum curante, matre vero prout poterat revocante, ac ille matris monita quasi anicularia reputans, coevos et consimiles malebat audire quam matri obedire, ut ipse in secundo libro *Confessionum* humiliter confitetur.[3] Tandem valefacto parentibus Carthaginem profectus, ibi in scola cuiusdam rethoris incredibili celeritate doctus est.

II. <De eius errore>

1. Cum igitur decem et novem esset annorum, defuncto iam //fol. 55ra// patre ante biennium, quem in extremo vite sue mater quoque deo lucrata fuerat discendi ordine pervenit in librum quemdam Ciceronis cui<us> nomen *Hortensius*, qui exhortationem continet ad philosophiam, in quo etiam vanitas mundi contemnenda docetur. Et ex hoc quidem liber ei plurimum placuit, sed hoc solum refrangebat, quia nomen Christi non erat ibi. Hoc enim nomen salvatoris in ipso adhuc lacte matris tenerum cor eius biberat et alte retinebat et quidquid sine hoc nomine fuisset, quamvis altum expolitum et veridicum non eum totum rapiebat, prout ipse tertio libro *Confessionum* refert.[4] Itaque instituit animum suum intendere in scripturas sanctas, ut videret quales essent sed quia scientia sine caritate non edificat, sed inflat, ipse quia tumens erat inani philosophia reverberatus aciem in eas figere non valebat.[5] Divine ergo valefaciens scripture in Manicheorum errorem incidit, qui dei filium non verum corpus, sed fantasticum assumpsisse affirmant et carnis resurrexionem negant.[6] Ponunt etiam duo rerum principia, unum bonorum et aliud malorum. Ad has etiam nugas productus est, ut arborem fici plorare crederet cum ab ea ficus vel folium decerperetur, ut ipse in eodem libro tertio *Confessionum* refert.[7] In predicto autem errore permansit fere novem annis, //fol. 55rb// ut in principio quarti libri *Confessionum* humiliter confitetur.[8]

2. Mater autem eius pro eo multum flebat, amplius quam flere solent matres corporea funera, et ipsum ad unitatem fidei ducere satagebat. Cui pre dolore perditionis filii pene deficienti data est divinitus huiusmodi consolatio.[9]

---

[3] Aug. conf. 2,3,7 (18).
[4] Aug. conf. 3,4,7–8 (25–26).
[5] Aug. conf. 3,5,9 (26).
[6] Aug. conf. 3,6,10–3,7,12 (26–28).
[7] Aug. conf. 3,10,18 (31).
[8] Aug. conf. 4,1,1 (33).
[9] Aug. conf. 3,11,19 (31).

3. Quadam enim vice vidit se stare quasi in quadam regula lignea. Et ecce iuvenis quidam pulcherrimus cultu splendido, vultu hilari adveniens arrisit illi flenti: "Que," inquiens, "tibi causa est doloris et luctus continui?" At illa ait: "Perditio filii mei." Cui iuvenis: "Esto," inquit, "secura quia ubi tu, ibi ille." Et ecce continuo iuxta se filium suum stare vidit. Quod cum evigilans memoriter retineret ut prudens et magne fidei mulier interpretata est veraciter, plane cognoscens et asserens apud se, quia quandoque in eadem regula veritatis catholice fidei videret Augustinum in qua videbat et se. Non enim reputabat hoc tanquam somnium, sed tanquam divinum responsum dicens, *O mulier magna est fides tua, fiat tibi sicut vis*. Quocirca dum idem visum Augustino recenseret, et ille perverse interpretari conaretur dicens: "Falleris mater, non tibi sic dictum est, sed ubi ego, ibi tu," econtra illa dicebat: "Non fili michi dictum est, ubi ille, ibi tu, sed ubi tu, //fol. 55va// ibi ille."[10]

4. Accepit illa ad consolationem sui, et aliud divinitus responsum per quemdam episcopum virum catholicum et sacris litteris eruditum, ad quem cum supplex veniret plorans et devote postulans ut Augustinum conveniret, eumque ab errore suo revocans ad fidem catholicam invitaret, ille respondit: "Filius profecto tuus indocilis adhuc est, superbe tumens novitate illius heresis paratus magis questiunculas texere quam docenti acquiescere. Sustine igitur paulisper et incessanter ora, legendo enim reperiet quantum sit secta illa quam diligit execranda. Nam et ego ipse cum essem adolescentulus in eodem errore desipui et legendo et intelligendo quam fugienda esset cognovi et fugi." Que responsio cum illi non sufficeret, sed importunitate feminea cum nimia lacrimarum effusione instaret, ut cum filio suo loqui dignaretur et eum ad meliora hortaretur. Ille quasi tedio percussus: "Vade," inquit, "secura. Impossibile enim est ut filius tantarum pereat lacrimarum." Quod responsum in tantum sibi placuit, ac si de celo ei prophetia sonuisset. Hec ipse in tertio libro *Confessionum*.[11]

5. Cum autem vicesimum etatis sui annum ageret et magister Carthaginensis decem *Categorias* Aristotelis lectitaret, et illis vix intelligentibus, iste libellum accepit et solus domi legens, quidquid in eo //fol. 55vb// latebat, per se intellexit. Omnes denique libros artium liberalium quoscumque invenit, legit, quoscumque legere potuit, per seipsum intellexit, ut ipse fatetur in quarto libro *Confessionum*.[12] Demum cum iam summus philosophus et rethor luculentissimus haberetur prius in sua civitate Thagatensi scolas regens docuit grammaticam et inde regressus Carthaginem pluribus annis in ibi docuit rethoricam. Eo tempore scilicet anno suo vicesimo sexto vel vicesimo septimo scripsit tres libros *De Pulchro et Apto* ad Hierium, Romane urbis oratorem, quem non noverat facie, sed amabat hominem ex doctrine fama, ut ipse hec testatur quarto libro *Confessionum*.[13]

---

[10] Aug. conf. 3,11,19–20 (31).
[11] Aug. conf. 3,12,21 (32).
[12] Aug. conf. 4,16,28–30 (43–44).
[13] Aug. conf. 4,2,2 (33); 4,14,21 (41).

III. <De eius peregrinatione ad Italiam>

1. Anno autem undetrecesimo etatis sue venit Carthaginem quidam Manicheorum episcopus, Faustus nomine, magnus laqueus diaboli nominatissimus apud eos, quod esset honestarum omnium doctrinarum peritissimus. Qui tante fame et auctoritatis erat apud illos ut qui eum sequerentur non quemlibet hominem sed Spiritum Sanctum se sequi arbitrarentur. Ad quem cum Augustinus gratia discendi venisset, expertus est hominem gratum et iocundum verbis sed vere scientie expertem. Quapropter quia questiones quas super dubiis in lege Manicheorum Augustinus sibi collegerat, per illum talem ac tantum doctorem auctorem ducem //fol. 56ra// et principem illius secte ut diu speraverat, enodande solute non fuerunt. Nec enim ausus fuit cum Augustino sarcinam disputationis subire, nec eum puduit confiteri se illa nescire. Igitur <Augustinus> omnem conatum quo proficere in illa secta statuerat, exinde prorsus postposuit, contentus sic interim manere donec aliud melius eligendum eluceret. Hec ipse libro quinto *Confessionum*.[14] Demum quibusdam amicis persuadentibus cogitavit pergere Romam, ut potius ibi doceret quod docebat Carthagini, maxime quia audierat quietius ibi studere adolescentes et quod Carthagini satis esset inquietudo. Verum hec illius cogitatio dei erat dispensatio, cum autem inchoasset iter, secuta est eum mater usque ad mare. Sed Augustinus fefellit eam violenter se tenentem, ut aut eum revocaret aut cum ipso pergeret, finxit ergo se nolle eam deserere donec facto vento navigaret, et mentitus est matri. Nolente autem matre sine eo redire domum, vix ei persuasit ut in loco qui proximus navi illorum erat in memoriam beati Cypriani martiris, ea nocte maneret. Cumque illa paululum divertisset, ascendens ille nocte navem, clanculo profectus est. Illa autem mansit tota nocte flendo et orando ut impediretur navigium, flavit continuo ventus et implevit vela navis et litus subtraxit aspectibus //fol. 56rb// eorum. Reversa ergo illa mane ad litus ubi filium dimiserat prospiciens rem gestam, insaniebat intollerabili dolore et gemitu implebat aures dei et nesciebat quod illi deus gaudiorum facturus erat de absentia eius et ideo flebat et eiulabat, post multum vero luctum conversa rursus ad deprecandum pro eo dominum abiit ad solita. Ille autem pervenit Romam. Hec ipse libro quinto *Confessionum*.[15] Cum ergo Rome esset, incurrit egritudinem validam et hoc mater nesciebat, sed pro illo orabat absens et maiore solicitudine eum parturiebat spiritu quam carne pepererat. Cottidie elemosinam faciens et obsequia sanctis nullo die pretermittens oblationem bis in die, mane et verspere ad ecclesiam sine ulla intermissione veniens non ad vanas fabulas, sed ut dominum audiret in suis sermonibus et deus illam in suis orationibus pro salute filii sui. Retractatus ergo ex illa egritudine cepit sedule agere id propter quod venerat ut doceret Rome artem rethoricam, et congregabantur ad hospitium eius multi. Post hec missum est a Mediolano Romam ad Symacum prefectum ut previderet magistrum

---

[14] Aug. conf. 5,3,3 (46–47); 5,5,9 (40); 5,6,10 (49); 5,7,12 (50–51); 5,7,13 (51).
[15] Aug. conf. 5,8,14 (51); 5,8,15 (52–53).

rethorice artis et Mediolanum dirigeret. Tunc ergo Symacus prefectus misit
eis Augustinum probatum magistrum. Et venit Mediolanum ad Ambrosium
episcopum in optimis //fol. 56va// notum orbi terre, et suscepit eum paterne.
Cepit autem Augustinus viro dei adherere et eius predicationes frequenter   160
audire. Primo quidem non ut veritatem audiret quod in ecclesia Christi
prorsus desperabat, sed explorans utrum fame illius facundia conveniret et
delectabatur suavitate sermonis, non satagens discere que dicebat. Deinde
cepit paulatim animum rebus magis quam verbis applicare. Hec ipse <libro>
quinto *Confessionum*.[16]   165

2. Cum autem quadam die beatus Ambrosius in predicatione de incarnatione domini tractaret, Augustinus astans in populo metu dei correptus
est et oblitus sui suarumque omnium cogitationum, pallens et tremens
omnibus qui aderant videntibus obriguit. Finita ergo admonitione quam ad
populum beatus Ambrosius ministrabat, Augustinus ad eum pervenit pate-   170
faciens ei suam tam subitam mutationem. Quod audiens beatus Ambrosius
cognitoque quod in Manicheorum secta iam fluctuans pene diffideret et per
spiritum sanctum cognoscens qualiter fidelis et catholicus futurus esset, gavisus valde placidissime et multum caritative eum suscepit. Itaque letabatur
beatus Ambrosius super eum sicut in evangelio de quodam patre legitur,   175
qui cadens super collum filii sui quem perdiderat et imponens anulum digito eius plorans deosculabatur eum. Hic sanctus Datius Mediolanensis episcopus in *Chronica* sua.[17] Augustinus autem ex tunc illucescente veritate
paulisper sectam Manicheorum, quamdiu tenuerat relinquendam esse decrevit,
et tamdiu in ecclesia catholica cathecuminus esse constituit, donec plenius   180
eluceret veritas quam teneret, ut ipse habetur quinto libro *Confessionum*
humiliter confitetur.[18]

3. Inter hec venit ad eum mater pietate fortis terra marique eum sequens
et in periculis omnibus de deo secura, nam et per maxima discrimina ipsos
nautas consolabatur, pollicens eis perventionem cum salute, quia ei deus   185
hoc per visum promiserat. Invenit ergo filium qui iudicavit ei quod Manicheus
iam non esset, sed nec Catholicus. Tunc illa exilivit letitia inenarrabili cum
audisset eum licet veritatem non dum adeptum a falsitate tamen iam ereptum et pectore pleno fiducie ait: "Credo in Christo quod priusquam migrem
de hac vita visura sim meum filium fidelem Christianum," et fundebat //fol.   190
56vb// ad deum preces et lacrimas densiores ut acceleraret adiutorium suum
et illuminaret tenebras eius. Diligebat enim et ipsa Ambrosium sicut angelum
dei, quia per illum cognoverat filium suum ad illam fluctuationem iam esse
perductum. Itaque cum ad memorias sanctorum sicut in Africa solebat, panem
et pultes et merum attulisset ab hostiario prohibebatur, ac ubi hoc episcopum   195
vetuisse cognovit, obedienter amplexa est. Hoc enim egentibus tribuendum
ferebat, et pro canistro pleno terrenis fructibus, plenum purgatioribus votis
pectus, ad memoriam martirum offere didicerat. Igitur omni die dominico

---

[16] Aug. conf. 5,9,16–17 (53); 5,10,15 (54); 5,13,23–24 (56–57).
[17] Land. *Hist.* I,9 (41,33–42).
[18] Aug. conf. 6,2,2 (58–59).

audiebat Augustinus Ambrosium verbum veritatis recte populo disserentem sepiusque in suis sermonibus dicentem, *Littera occidit, spiritus autem vivificat*.[19] Et conferebat Augustinus cum carissimis amicis suis Alipio et Nebridio, multas questiones. Quorum alter Alipius scilicet ex eodem quo ipse erat ortus municipio, Nebridius autem relicta patria vicina Carthagini, atque ipsa Carthagine relicto etiam paterno rure optimo, venerat Mediolanum querens Augustinum ut secum viveret in flagrantissimo studio veritatis. Erant ergo hii tres pariter nutantes in consilio quisnam esset modus vite tenende. Et ecce iam tricenarius erat, ut ipse hec libro sexto *Confessionum* refert.[20] //fol. 57ra//

IV. De eius conversione

1. Cum autem iam via Christi sibi placeret, sed per ipsam adhuc ire pigeret, misit dominus in mentem eius, visumque est ei bonum pergere ad Simplicianum heremitam servum dei, audierat ei quod a iuventute sua devotissime deo servierat et vere sic erat. Iam vero senuerat et multa expertus, multa edoctus erat, et beatus Ambrosius vere eum ut patrem diligebat. Cui estus cordis et errorum circuitus manifestans, ipse scilicet Augustinus devote postulavit ut vir sanctus proferret ei quis esset aptus modus vivendi. Sic affecto ut ipse erat ad ambulandum in via dei, videbat enim plenam ecclesiam et alius sic ibat, alius autem sic displicebat quippe ei quidquid agebat in seculo pre dulcedine dei et decore domus eius quam dilexit. Simplicianus autem eum hortari cepit et ad humilitatem Christi precipue invitavit et inter invitandum Victorini Romani quondam rethoris conversionem in medium recitavit. Rome siquidem multis annis Victorinus ille magister fuerat, et ob insigne preclari magisterii statuam in Romano foro habere meruerat, qui tandem conversus loquacem scolam suam deserens in scola Christi humilis discipulus effectus est. Hoc exemplo commonitus Augustinus ad imitandum exarsit, et soli //fol. 57rb// deo servire proposuit.[21]

2. Interea cum quadam die essent Augustinus et Alipius pariter in domo et absens esset Nebridius, venit ad eos Pon<ti>cianus, quidam civis Africanus preclare in palatio militans, et consederunt ut colloquerentur. Et videns Pon<ti>cianus forte super mensam lusoriam que ante eos erat codicem tulit et aperuit invenitque sane inopinate Paulum Apostolum, putaverat enim aliquid esse de libris quorum professio eos continebat. Tunc arridens Augustinumque intuens gratulatorie miratus est quod eas et solas pre eius oculis litteras comperisset, Christianus quippe fidelis erat ille. Cui cum iudicasset Augustinus illis scripturis se maximam curam impendere, ortus est sermo ipso Pon<ti>ciano narrante de Anthonio Egyptio monacho, cuius nomen excellenter clarebat apud servos dei, ipsos autem usque ad illam horam latebat. Inde sermo eius devolutus est ad monasteriorum greges et incolas deserti eremi spiritu pauperes qualium est regnum celorum. Et erat

---

[19] II Cor. 3:6.
[20] Aug. conf. 6,1,1 (58); 6,2,2 (58–59); 6,4,6 (61); 6,7,11–6,16,26 (64–72).
[21] Aug. conf. 8,1,1 (89); 8,2,3 (89); 8,1,2 (88); 8,2,3–8,5,10 (89–92).

monasterium Mediolani plenum fratribus bonis extra urbis menia sub Ambrosio nutritore. Augustinus autem nichil horum noverat, et ideo intente cuncta tacitus audiebat. Addidit quoque Pon<ti>cianus quodam die cum ipse apud Treveros cum imperatore fuisset se et tres alios contubernales //fol. 57va// exisse deambulatum in hortos muris contiguos, unum secum deorsum et alios duos seorsum pariter digressos. Sed illos alios duos vagabundos irruisse in quandam casam in qua eremite quidam habitabant et invenisse ibi codicem in quo scripta erat vita Antonii eremite. Quam legere cepit unus eorum et mirari et accendi, qui ait ad socium suum: "Ego iam servire deo statui in hoc loco et hac ipsa hora aggredior si te piget immitari noli adversari." Respondit ille se velle adherere socio et sic ambo relictis omnibus secuti sunt dominum. Tunc Pon<ti>cianus et qui cum eo in alia parte deambulabant querentes eos devenerunt in eundum locum et invenientes monuerunt ut redirent quia declinasset dies, at illi narraverunt propositum suum. Isti autem illis pie congratulati fleverunt, seque eorum orationibus commendantes ad palatium abierunt. Illi vero in casa manserunt. Quod audientes sponse eorum dicaverunt et ipse virginitatem deo.[22]

3. Hiis itaque exemplis Augustinus compunctus rodebatur intus, et confudebatur pudore horribili vehementer. Nam exempla servorum dei quos de nigris lucidos et de mortuis vivos fecerat, congesta in sinum cogitationes sue urebant, et accendebant eum valde. Cumque Pon<ti>cianus abisset, Augustinus in illa grandi rixa interioris //fol. 57vb// domus sue, tam vultu quam mente turbatus, invasit Alipium et exclamavit, "Quid patimur? Quid audimus? Surgunt indocti et celum rapiunt, et nos cum doctrinis nostris ecce ubi volutamur in carne et sanguine. An quid precesserunt pudet sequi?" Et cum hec diceret, attendebat in eum Alipius attonitus, non enim solita sonabat verba plusque loquebantur anima eius frons, gene, oculi, color, modus vocis quam verba que promebat. Cum autem tali rixa intrinsecus descerperetur, hortulum hospitio suo contiguum ingressus est. At Alipius pedetentim secutus est eum. Sedereuntque quantum potuerunt remoti ab edibus. Augustinus itaque fremebat spiritu et erat turbulentissimus et accusabat se ipsum. Alipius vero affixus lateri eius tacitus eum dolens considerabat et inter verba accusantis everso fundo cordis sui et congesta ante oculos mentis universa massa miseriarum suarum, ab orta est procella ingens, ferens ingentem imbrem lacrimarum, ad quam liberius effundendam, relicto Alipio in eo quo consederunt loco paulo remotius secessit. Solitudo quippe illi ad negotium flendi aptior videbatur. Alipius vero mansit in eo quo consederunt loco nimium stupens. Augustinus autem doloris incontinens //fol. 58ra// sub quadam ficu se proiecit et lamentabiles voces dabat dicens: "Et tu domine usque quo? Quamdiu, quamdiu? Cras et cras? Quare non modo? Quare non hac hora finis turpitudinis mee?" Dum hec et hiis similia amarissima contritione cordis sui diceret, iactans voces miserabiles, repente audivit vocem quasi de vicina doma, cum repetitione crebro modulantem: *Tolle lege, tolle lege.* Statimque mutato vultu intentissimus cogitare

---

[22] Aug. conf. 8,6,14–15 (84–95).

cepit, utrum nam solerent pueri in aliquo genere ludendi tale aliquid cantitare, nec occurrebat. Intellexit igitur divinitus se moneri, ut accepto codice legeret quod primum capitulum inveniret et quod ab illo doceretur, ageret. Itaque repressis lacrimis concitus ad locum ubi sedebat Alipius rediit et arrepto codice apostolico, quem iuxta illum cum modo surgeret, dimiserat, aperuit et legit in silentio capitulum quo primum coniecti sunt oculi eius: *Non in commessationibus et ebrietatibus non in cubilibus et in puditiis, non in contentione et emulatione, sed induimini dominum Iesum Christum et carnis curam non feceritis in desideriis.*[23] Nec ultra voluit legere, nec opus erat. Statimque cum fine huius sententie quasi luce securitatis infusa cordi eius omnes dubitatis tenebre diffugerunt. Tunc interiecto digito aut nescio quo alio signo codicem //fol. 58rb// clausit et tranquillo iam vultu indicavit Alipio quid legisset. At ille petiit videre et accepto codice vidit et prospiciens quid ultraquam iste legerat haberetur; ignorabat enim Augustinus quid sequeretur, invenit ille, legit: *Infirmum autem in fide suscipite*,[24] quod Alipius ad se retulit, et Augustino hilariter aperuit et mox tali ammonitione proposito bono ei coniunctus est. Inde ad matrem Augustini pariter ingrediuntur, indicantes ei ordinem rei, ut que pro filio dolebat cum eo consolationem acciperet. At illa gaudens gratias egit deo, qui ei plusquam petisset concesserat, videbat enim illum non solum ad amorem fidei verum etiam ad contemptum seculi omnino accensum. Unde luctus eius in gaudium, planctus versus est in tripudium stante iam filio in ea regula fidei in qua ante tot annos ei fuerat revelatus. Hec ipse octavo libro *Confessionum*.[25]

V. <De eius cathecumenatu>

Iam liber erat animus eius pulsis anxietatibus curarum et suavitatibus nugarum, quibus carere suave sibi subito factum est et quas prius amittere metus fuerat, iam dimittere gaudium erat. Et placuit ei non tumultuose sed leviter se subtrahere a scolarum regimine, iam enim paucissimi dies supererant ad vindemiales ferias et statuit tollerare eas ut sollemniter abscederet. //fol. 58va// Evolutis autem diebus viginti qui ei longi et multi videbantur, pre amore libertatis otiose a professione rethorica solutus est. Et quonaim soli deo vacandi, orandi et in lege domini meditandi, toto mentis desiderio estuabat ut locus proposito conveniret tumultum civitatis deserens in rure Cassi<ci>aco prope Mediolanum per honoratum virum Verecundum nomine sibi concesso manere decrevit, donec ad baptismum aptaretur. In quo rure ab estu seculi requiescens et divinis lectionibus vacans cum Alipio et aliis amicis suis eodem desiderio flagrantibus aliquam diu commoratus est, matre sua eis semper adherente muliebri habitu, virili fide, anili securitate, materna caritate, christiana pietate, ut ipse refert nono libro *Confessionum*.[26] Ibi etiam

---

[23] Rm. 13:13–14.
[24] Rm. 14:1.
[25] Aug. conf. 8,7,18 (96); 9,2,3, (102); 8,8,19 (97); 8,11,27 (100); 8,12,28–29 (101); 8,12,30 (101–102).
[26] Aug. conf. 9,1,1 (103); 9,2,2 (103); 9,3,7–9,4,8 (105–106).

plures conscripsit libros adhuc cathecuminus, videlicet librum *De Academicis*, librum *De Ordine*, librum *Soliloquiorum* et librum *De Beata Vita*, quem librum ipse occasione tali scripsit. Olim enim multi diem natalis sui consueverunt celebrare, et ipse Augustinus ante conversionem suam hoc consuevit. Accidit autem illis diebus quibus Augustinus erat in rure ut dies natalis sui eveniret. Nolens autem ipse diem illum natalis sui de mortali vita amplius celebrare per tres dies cum sociis, quid esset beata vita sollicite disputavit //fol. 58vb// et tandem diffinitum est inter eos, quod beata vita non nisi in dei cognitione consistit et hanc disputationem continet liber iste, ut hec ipse recitat in libro *Retract<at>ionum* circa principium.[27] Iste scripsit ibidem epistulas ad Nebridium et nonnulla opuscula alia cum ibi presentibus disputata, ut ipse refert nono libro *Confessionum*.[28] Cum ergo scripturas divinas legeret earum valde afficiebatur dulcedine et accendebatur vehementer. Legebat et ardebat et dolebat quod latrasset adversus litteras de melle celi melleas et de lumine dei luminosas et cum legeret psalmos David, quartum assumens psalmum et eius singulos versus attende legens et attentius relegens a gemitu cordis sui rugiebat et cum flere non sufficeret voces dolori congruas proferebat. Perveniens autem ad illum versum, *In pace in idipsum dormiam et requiescam ut totus in devotione ardebat*, pre gaudio exclamabat: "O in pace, o in idipsum, o qui dixit dormiam et requiescam. Tu es domine idipsum valde qui non mutaris et in te solo requies." Inter hec et multa alia divine consolationis beneficia non defuerunt ei acerbe potula temptationis. Contigit enim ut gravi dentium dolore vexaretur in tantum ut pre dolore loqui non posset. Recolens itaque fideliter illum versiculum, *Dominus* //fol. 59ra// *exaudiet me cum clamavero ad eum*,[29] ascendit in cor eius admonere eos qui secum aderant ut orarent dominum pro eo. Et cum non posset loqui, scripsit hec in terra et dedit eis legere. Ut autem suppliciter cum illis ad orandum genua flecteret, dolor ille tam velociter fugit, ut ipse admirans expaverit, cum nil tale ab ineunte etate in se expertus fuerit. Et tunc insinuati sunt ei in profundo nutus divini et gaudens in fide laudavit nomen domini, demum insinuat sancto viro Ambrosio per litteras pristinos errores suos et presens votum suum ut ipse moneret quid de libris sanctis legere deberet, quo percipiende christiane gratia aptior fieret atque paratior. At ille iussit Isaiam prophetam, eo quod pre ceteris evangelii vocationisque gentium sit prenuntiator apertior. Cuius principium cum Augustinus non intelligeret totumque aliud tale esse arbitrans distulit ut illud relegeret, cum in divinis scripturis magis exercitatus esset. Inde ubi tempus advenit, quo nomen eum dare oportebat, relicto rure Mediolanum remeavit, ut hec ipse commemorat nono libro *Confessionum*.[30] Reversus itaque de rure in Mediolanum baptismum percepturus scripsit ibidem librum *De Immortalitate Anime* et libros disciplinarum, ut ipse ait in primo *Rectractationum*.[31]

---

[27] Aug. retract. I,2 (11,1–6).
[28] Aug. conf. 9,4,7 (105).
[29] Ps. 4:4.
[30] Aug. conf. 9,4,8–12 (106–108); 9,5,13–9,6,14 (108).
[31] Aug. retract. I,6 (17,40–41).

VI. De eius baptismo

1. Baptizatus est igitur Augustinus a beato Ambrosio anno etatis sue tricesimo secundo tempore pascali, ut ait Possidonius,[32] in fontibus qui beati Iohannis ascribuntur cunctis fidelibus eiusdem urbis astantibus et videntibus deumque laudantibus. In quibus fontibus Ambrosius et Augustinus prout spiritus sanctus dabat eloqui illis, hymnum *Te deum laudamus* decantantes cunctis qui aderant audientibus et mirantibus ediderunt. Qui etiam hymnus ab universa ecclesia catholica usque hodie tenetur et religiose decantatur, ut hec testatur sanctus Datius Mediolanensis episcopus //fol. 59rb// in primo libro capitulo decimo *Cronice* sue.[33]

2. Denique in eisdem fontibus simul cum ipso Augustino, Alipius et puer Adeodatus de ipso carnaliter natus, spiritualiter renati sunt. Quindecim quippe annorum erat puer ille cum in gratia baptismi factus est beato Augustino coevus tam velocis et ipse ingenii ut multos grandeve etatis et magne eruditionis agilitate intelligendi preveniret viros. Mirabatur profecto Augustinus et horrebat ob tale ingenium cum audiret illum annorum sedecim subtiliter interrogantem, interrogando arguentem, ita ut illius magis interrogationi quam sue intentus esset responsioni. Erat enim puer ille ardentissimus veritatis amator et occultorum diligens investigator. Verum cum puer ipse flagraret tam desiderio bene vivendi quam studio cito de medio sublatus est, ut ipse refert nono libro *Confessionum*.[34]

3. Accepto igitur baptismi salutaris munere quasi ditati multis divitiis et inestimabilibus margaritis mutuo in deo letantes omnium gratiarum actione cibum sumentes sicut erant magno gaudio gavisi confortati sunt. Hec sanctus Datius Mediolanensis episcopus ubi supra.[35]

4. Protinus autem in fide catholica mirabiliter confirmatus, spem omnem quam habebat in seculo dereliquit. Nec satiabatur //fol. 59va// dulcedine mirabili considerare altitudinem consilii divini super salutem generis humani. Frequentans igitur limina ecclesie et intentus modulationi hymnorum et melodie psalmorum reficiebatur delectabiliter, flebat hilariter. Hoc quippe genus consolationis recens tunc freqentare inchoaverat. Mediolanensis ecclesia quadam temporis impellente augustia, cum enim Iustina imperatrix Arrianorum errore seducta, beatum Ambrosium atrociter persequeretur, fideles cum episcopo suo mori parati in ecclesia excubabant. Tunc idem antistes aliorum magis quam sue afflictioni compatiens instituit ut secundum morem orientalium partium psalmi et hymni in ecclesia cantarentur, ut canticis spiritualibus fideles intenti meroris et tedii presentis obliviscerentur. Cessante autem persecutione nichilominus consuetudo psallendi in ecclesia remansit et usque in hodiernum diem per totum orbem diffusa est. Hiis itaque psalmorum et hymnorum cantibus Augustinus vehementer affectus illis hymnidicis angelorum choris interesse sitiens ardebat et uberrime flebat.

---

[32] Possid. vita Aug. I,6 (44,29–32; *PL* 32,35).
[33] Land. *Hist.* I,9 (41,49–42,4).
[34] Aug. conf. 9,6,14 (108–109).
[35] Land. *Hist.* I,9 (42,4–5).

Qui autem in gratia baptismi secum renati fuerant cum eo simul vivebant, consociato eis et Evodio iuvene de eodem municipio nato et prius se baptizato, //fol. 59ᵛᵇ// simul erant isti simul habitaturi placito sancto pariter servientes domino, qui habitare facit unanimes in domo. Hec ipse nono libro *Confessionum*.[36] Et quoniam exhortatione sancti senis Simpliciani et exemplis eremitarum ad fidem conversus fuerat, ad quorum etiam imitationem toto mentis desiderio estuabat.

5. Ab ipso sancto Simpliciano sancte conversationis habitum formamque vivendi accepit, quam postmodum in Africa exuberans redolevit. Unde ipse in quodam sermone suo ad presbyteros Hipponenses, qui incipit, *In omnibus operibus vestris sacerdotes carissimi*, sic dicit: "Cur murmurastis si in hiis paschalibus diebus presentialiter vobiscum non fui? Placuit enim michi segregare me a vobis et pergere ad fratres meos in solitudine, quos ut frequenter dixi tales inveni, quales invenire desideravi. Cur ergo turbamini? Nunquid non ipsi vere pauperes? Nunquid non obedientes? Nunquid non mundum et pompas eius conculcaverunt? Nunquid non in forma vivendi vos multo tempore precesserunt? Nunquid non vere fratres mei et patres sunt? Nunquid non per eorum exempla ad viam veritatis perveni? Nunquid non eos semper dilexi et eorum sanctam conversationem semper desideravi? Nunquid non etiam per Simplicianum linguriensem //fol. 60ʳᵃ// in fide instructus sum? Cur ergo murmuratis? Cur de mea absentia dolorem habere ostenditis? Facite que placita sunt michi et tunc ubicumque fuero vobiscum ero usque ad consummationem seculi."[37] Hec ipse ibi.

VII. De eius reditu in Africam

1. Post hec autem cum instigante eius pia matre de Mediolano recedere et ad Africam remeare disponeret, adivit sanctum Simplicianum petens ut sibi aliquos de fratribus suis eremitis servos dei donaret, quos secum in Africam assumeret et cum eis ibi ordinem plantaret. Cuius piis precibus pius ille pater Simplicianus annuens dedit ei duodecim fratres viros religiosos, cum quibus adiunctis sibi carissimis amicis suis qui diu secum fuerant, Nebridio, Evodio, Alipio et Pontiano, cum matre et filio Adeodato, ad Africam proficiscendi iter arripuit. De hoc ipse in sermone de tribus generibus monachorum, qui incipit *Ut nobis per litteras declaravit sanctus pater Ieronimus*, loquens de genere et ordine eremitarum sic ait: "Isti sunt viri illi perfecti quibus frequenter adhesi tempore errorum meorum per quos etiam illuminari merui. Quorum etiam sanctitatis fama ad aures meas perveniens, baptizari non diu distuli. Et pia matre me instigante apud Mediolanum, ut ad patriam remearem. Cupiens etiam eos habere in //fol. 60ʳᵇ// visceribus caritatis et cum eis pariter vivere, ad virum illum Simplicianum qui a iuventute sua deo devotissime vixerat, in omni caritate perrexi deprecans cum fletu et gemitu, ut michi quosdam de suis servos dei donaret. Et donavit eos michi

---

[36] Aug. conf. 9,6,14 (109); 9,7,15 (109); 9,7,16 (109–110); 9,8,17 (110).
[37] Jor. *Coll.* sermo 26, fol. 32ᵛᵃ⁻ᵇ; sermo 5 *PL* 40,1246.

445 paterne. Quare donavit eos michi paterne? Quia sciebat me velle monasterium in Africa edificare. Et assumptis mecum Anastasio, Fabiano, Severo, Nicolao, Dorotheo, Isaac, Nicostrato, Paulo, Cyrillo, Stephano, Iacobo et Vitali pauperculo," et infra, "hiis mecum assumptis imitari cupiebam cum carissimis meis amicis, Evodio, Alipio et Pontiano, qui diu mecum fuerant,
450 et cum ceteris duodecim quos nuper assumpseram illos quorum famam etiam sanctus pater Ieronimus michi descripserat et sic perveni in Africam."[38] Hec ipse ibi.

2. Predictis autem omnibus fratribus et amicis sancto Augustino consociatis illa pia mater ita curam gessit, quasi omnes genuisset. Ita servivit
455 quasi ab omnibus genita fuisset, ut ipse dicit nono libro *Confessionum*.[39] Transiens autem et iter faciens per Tusciam, ubi ut fertur plura erant loco eremitica, ubicumque fratres sui propositi invenit ipsos caritative visitavit et eos suis collationibus salutis pabulo dulciter recreavit. Perveniens autem Romam et audiens quod Manichei qui ibi erant multos Catholicos decipie-
460 bant, ipse eorum //fol. 60[va]// iactantiam tacitus ferre non valens contra eos ibidem disputavit et duos libros contra eos scripsit quorum unum *De Moribus Ecclesie Catholice* alterum *De Moribus Manicheorum* intitulavit. Scripsit etiam ibidem librum *De Quantitate Anime*, in quo per modum dialogi inter se et filium Adeodatum multa subtilia de anima queruntur ac disseruntur.
465 Scripsit etiam in eadem urbe librum *De Libero Arbitrio*, causam sumens ex disputationibus habitis contra Manicheos in quo questiones incidentes solvuntur, et ostenditur malum non esse exortum nisi ex libero arbitrio. Hec ipse primo libro *Retrac<ta>tionum*.[40] Deinde egressi de urbe cum essent apud Ostiam Tiberinam post longi itineris laborem instaurantes se navigationi
470 Augustinus et mater stabant soli incumbentes ad quandam fenestram, unde hortus intra domum que eos habebat prospectabatur remoti a turbis et colloquebantur soli valde dulciter de vita eterna sanctorum et inhiabant ore cordis in superna fluenta fontis vite. Erigentes se ardentiore affectu in idipsum et gradatim transcendentes cuncta corporalia attingerunt raptim toto
475 ictu cordis regionem ubertatis indeficientis <et> fontem vite eterne. Cui suspirantes et ibidem religatas primitias spiritus relinquentes ad oris colloquium redierunt, vilescebatque eis mundus iste inter //fol. 60[vb]// verba cum omnibus delectationibus suis. Tunc ait illa: "Fili mi quantum ad me attinet, nulla re iam delector in hac vita. Quid hic faciam adhuc et cur
480 hic sim nescio. Iam consumpta spe huius seculi, unum erat propter quod in hac vita aliquantulum immorari: cupiebam ut te Christianum catholicum viderem prius quam morerer. Cumulatius hoc michi deus meus prestitit ut te etiam contempta felicitate terrena servum eius videam."[41]

---

[38] Jor. *Coll.* sermo 21, fol. 26[ra-b]; sermo 21 *PL* 40,1268–1269.
[39] Aug. conf. 9,9,22 (113).
[40] Aug. retract. I,8,1 (21,1–22,3); I,9,1 (23,7–8).
[41] Aug. conf. 9,10,23–24 (113); 9,10,26 (114).

VIII. De morte matris

1. Factum est autem vix infra quinque dies ut ipsa decumberet febribus, et cum egrotaret quadam die defectum mentis passa, paululum subtracta est a presentibus. Ut autem reddita est sensui, intuens Augustinum et fratrem suum ait: "Ubi eram?" Illis vero attonitis subiunxit: "Ponite," inquit, "hoc corpus ubicumque, nichil vos eius cura conturbet. Tantum illud vos rogo, ut ad domini altare memineritis mei ubicumque fueritis." Omnem quippe iam reliquerat curam, qua prius estuaverat de sepulcro quod sibi domi iuxta corpus viri sui sumptuose preparaverat. Nam cum paulo ante ipsa cum quibusdam amicis Augustini de contemptu vite huius et de bono mortis loqueretur, illisque stupentibus virtutem femine, querentibusque annon formidaret tam longe a sua civitate sepeliri: "nichil," inquit, "longe //fol. 61ra// est deo, neque timendum est ne ille non cognoscat in fine seculi unde me resuscitet." Die ergo nono egretudinis sue, anima illa religiosa et pia, corpore soluta est. Anno etatis sue quinquagesimo sexto; etatis vero Augustini anno tricesimo tertio. Et convenerunt multi fratres et religiose femine eius exequias de more celebrantes. Hec ipse libro nono *Confessionum*.[42] Quibus peractis Augustinus cum suis in Africam reversus est. Veniensque Carthaginem, a quodam honorato viro Innocentio nomine, hospitio receptus est. Qui cum ob gravem cordis infirmitatem a medico incidi deberet Augustinus suo hospiti pie conpatiens sua oratione ipsum curavit cunctis stupentibus quod ille de tam gravi infirmitate sic subito curatus fuit. Hec ipse in libro vicesimo duo *De Civitate Dei*.[43] Inde profectus ad agros proprios propriamque domum ibi cum amicis et fratribus quos secum de Italia assumpserat, ac aliis eodem desiderio flagrantibus qui eidem adherebant, ieiuniis et orationibus vacans, venditis propriis et secundum modum et regulam sanctorum apostolorum pauperibus erogatis, pauper cum pauperibus in ordine adhuc laicali ferme per triennium conversatus est. In lege domini meditans die ac nocte et de hiis que sibi deus cogitanti atque oranti intellecta revelabat et presentes et absentes sermonibus ac libris docebat. Hec in //fol. 61rb// legenda Possidonii et in alia legenda famosa.[44] Scripsit enim ibi libros duos *De Genesi contra Manicheos*. Item librum *De Musica* sex libros continentem quos apud Mediolanum inchoaverat. In quibus presertim in sexto ostendit quomodo a corporalibus et spiritalibus sed mutubilibus numeris ad immutubiles numeros pervenitur qui iam in ipsa sunt immutabili veritate, et sic invisibilia dei per ea qua facta sunt intellecta conspiciuntur, et qui ista nunc conspicere non possunt et tamen ex fide Christi vivunt quod post hanc vitam ipsa certitudinaliter atque feliciter conspicient. Qui autem ea conspicere possunt et tamen in fide Christi non vivunt, cum tota sapientia sua in fine peribunt. Per idem etiam tempus ibidem scripsit librum *De Magistro* continentem dialogum inter

---

[42] Aug. conf. 9,11,27 (114); 9,11,28 (115); 9,12,31 (116).
[43] Aug. civ. 22,8 (816,45–818,135).
[44] Possid. vita Aug. 3,1–2 (48,1–10; *PL* 32,36); 5,1 (52,3; *PL* 32,37); 3,2 (48,7–10; *PL* 32,36); Phil. vita Aug. 18 (1218A).

se et filium Adeodatum qui eodem anno quo venit in Africam de medio
sublatus est. In quo libro ostendit non esse magistrum alium qui docet
hominem nisi deum. Eodem etiam tempore et loco scripsit librum *De Vera
Religione* in quo ostendit quod sola religio Christiana et nulla alia religio est
vera. Hec ipse in libro *Retrac<ta>tionum*.[45]

2. Verum cum lumen tante sanctitatis et doctrine latere non posset, fama
quippe eius ubique diffundebatur et in omnibus libris suis et actibus
ammirabilis habebatur. Apud Hipponem Regium erat quidam vir Christianus
magnarum opum qui ad eum misit pollicens, quod si illum videre et verbum ex ore suo audire mereretur //fol. 61va// iuxta consilium suum relicto
seculo totus ad dominum converteretur. Quod Augustinus ubi comperit
volens deo lucrari animam et nichilominus intendens querere locum aptum
ubi constituerit monasterium, in quo secretus cum fratribus suis posset deo
servire, Hipponem profectus est et virum predictum ad contemptum mundi
et amorem dei quantum deus donabat exhortatus est, cuius ille presentia
gaudens exhortationem eius gratanter accepit, sed tamen quod promiserat
occulto dei consilio adpresens implere distulit. Inane tamen esse non potuit
quod per tale vas mundum divina sapientia profudit. Hec in legenda
Possidonii.[46] Quod autem intentione constituendi monasterium Hipponem
perexerit expresse ipse idem testatur in sermone primo de communi vita
clericorum ubi sic dicit: "Ego quem deo propitio videtis episcopum vestrum
iuvenis veni ad istam civitatem ut multi vestrum noverunt. Querebam ubi
constituerem monasterium et viverem cum fratribus meis, spem quippe
seculi omnem reliqueram." Et infra: "Veni ad istam civitatem propter videndum amicum, quem putabam me posse lucrari deo ut vobiscum essem in
monasterio, quasi secretus quia locus habebat episcopum."[47] Hec ipse ibi.

IX. De institutione ordinis eremitarum et edificatione primi monasterii sui

Itaque apud Hipponem in eremo segregata a gentibus locum aptum ad
serviendum deo inveniens cum favore et subsidio sancti Valerii Hipponensis
episcopi monasterium ibidem edificavit //fol. 61vb// et in eo fratres eremitas quos undique per nemora conquisivit una cum amicis et fratribus prius
eidem adherentibus collocavit et cum eis vivere cepit secundum regulam
sub sanctis apostolis constitutam. Unde ipse in sermone supra allegato ad
presbyteros Hipponenses sic dicit: "Ego, sacerdotes dei altissimi, ut multi
vestrum viderunt et audire potuerunt, veni ad hanc civitatem cum carissimis meis amicis Evodio, Simplicio, Alipio, Nebridio et Anastasio; securus
denique veni quia sciebam presulari sanctum senem Valerium propterea
securus accessi non ut haberem in vos potestatem sed ut abiectus essem in
domo domini omnibus diebus vite mee non ut ministrari deberem sed minis-

---

[45] Aug. retract. I,11,1 (33,1–11); I,12 (36,1–5); I,13,1 (36,1–8).
[46] Possid. vita Aug. 3 (52,2–3; *PL* 32,37).
[47] Jor. *Coll.* sermo 27, fol. 33rb; Aug. sermo 355 (Lambot, 124,24–125,17)

trare et pacifice vivere optabam in solitudine, nichilque divitiarum mecum
attuli sed dei gratia me coadiuvante favoratus etiam a sancto sene episcopo
Valerio monasterium in eremo a gentibus segregatum, multo labore fatigatus edificavi et cum longiore anxietate servos dei per nemora habitantes
in unum congregavi et cum eis pariter vivere cepi, secundum modum et
regulam sub sanctis apostolis constitutam, omnia communiter habentes et
possidentes viventes in vigiliis et orationibus ultra id quod explicare possumus."[48] Hec ipse ibi. Quod autem sanctus Valerius non solum favorem
sed etiam subsidium ad structuram monasterii sibi prestiterit, testatur ipse
//fol. 62ra// in alio sermone preallegato, *Ut nobis per litteras*, ubi loquens
ad fratres suos in eodem monasterio sic ait: "Vos," inquit, "vinea mea electa
estis, in medio ecclesie paradisi plantata. Ad hanc vineam ego solus dei virtute vos congregavi et operarios meos feci ut laborantes in ea usque in
finem fructum recipiatis in tempore suo. Ad hanc vineam vos elegi, ad hanc
hereditatem vos convocavi, licet favoratus a sancto episcopo Valerio, qui
de bonis episcopatus ut monasterium in eremo edificarem multa michi donavit. Non enim satis fuit patrimonium meum vendere, nisi etiam ipse me
coadiuvasset."[49] Hec ipse ibi. In prefato autem monasterio ipse Augustinus
copiosum numerum fratrum congregavit, quibus et modum vivendi secundum formam vite apostolorum tradidit et sic ordinem eremitarum ipse instituit. Prius enim eremite per diversa nemora disiuncti singulariter alii sic,
alii sic vivebant, sed nunc per Augustinum ad communem observantiam
regule apostolice reducti, sub tanto patre in communi vivere inceperunt.
De hoc ipse in eodem sermone iam allegato sic dicit: "Perveni in Africam
pia matre defuncta et edificavi ut videtis monasterium in quo nunc sumus
in solitudine a gentibus segregatum. Et placuit deo centenarium numerum
fratrum michi donare, illuminans corda nostra non solum sanctissimos patres
//fol. 62rb// solitarios imitari, sed etiam in hac solitudine more apostolorum omnia communiter possidere nos servare et postea docere et per me
vobis precipere voluit. Sic enim videtis quod ante me multi fuerunt patres
quos sequi et imitari debemus, non tamen sicut ego secundum apostolicam
vitam, alios vivere docuerunt. Capud igitur et principium omnium vestrum
me dicere non erubesco."[50] Hec ipse ibi. Huius itaque ordinis fratrum habitus erat cuculla nigra, cincta zona pellicea id est corrigia, ut ipse refert in
preallegato sermone ad presbyteros Hipponenses, ubi comparationem faciens
inter ipsos presbyteros canonicos suos et fratres istos in eremo sic ait: "Et
si vobis grave est et molestum egredimini foras pergite ad fratres meos et
discite ab eis quia mites sunt et humiles corde pauperes spiritu et filii obedientie. Egredimini foras et quid estis et quid ipsi sunt considerare vos volo.
Nunquid enim et vos tales sicut et ipsi sunt? O utinam tales essetis sicut
ipsi sunt." Et infra: "Vos discursores civitatis et ipsi visus hominum fugiunt.
Vos pellibus cuniculorum et variorum ornati iam estis et ipsi ovino habitu

---

[48] Jor. *Coll.* sermo 26, fol. 31^{ra-b}; sermo 5 *PL* 40,1243–1244.
[49] Jor. *Coll.* sermo 21, fol. 27rb; sermo 21 *PL* 40,1270.
[50] Jor. *Coll.* sermo 21, fol. 26rb; sermo 21 *PL* 40,1269.

colore nigerrimo asperrimoque induti sunt. Vos balteis militum mundo apparere desideratis et ipsi zonis camelorum renibus succincti more Helie et Iohannis decorati sunt."[51] Hec ipse ibi. Porro //fol. 62va// hiis fratribus idem pater dedit primo certas traditiones secundum formam vite aposto-
610 lice compendiose comprehensas, quas margaritas paradisi appellat in sermone primo ad fratres eosdem, qui incipit *Fratres mei et letitia cordis mei et gaudium meum quod estis*. Demum regulam conscripsit quam ipse speculum appellat, quam et eisdem fratribus tradidit, ut habetur ex preallegato sermone *Ut nobis per litteras*.

X. Qualiter factus est presbyter

Post hec cum flagitante ecclesiastica necessitate providendum esset civitati de presbytero beatus Valerius Hipponensis episcopus comperta Augustini fama, eum ad se accersiri fecit. Cumque idem antistes de providendo et ordinando presbytero plebem alloqueretur et exhortaretur, astante in po-
620 pulo Augustino securo et ignaro quid futurm esset. Solebat enim laicus ab eis tantum ecclesiis que non haberent episcopos suam abstinere presentiam. Eum ergo tenuerunt et ut in talibus consuetum est episcopo ordinandum intulerunt omnibus id uno consensu et desiderio fieri petentibus magnoque studio et clamore flagitantibus ubertim eo flente et renitente eo quod multa
625 et magna vite sue pericula de regimine ecclesie provenire consideraret atque ideo flevit nonnullis quidem lacrimis eius superbe interpretantibus et tanquam eum consolantibus et dicentibus quia locus presbyterii licet ipse maiori dignus esset appropinquaret //fol. 62vb// tamen episcopatui. Tandem flentem et frustra renitentem beatus Valerius de turba segregavit et licet invitum
630 presbyterum ordinavit. Hec Possidonius.[52]

XI. De edificatione secundi monasterii in horto

1. Reverso itaque Augustino ad monasterium suum, non enim sine monastica disciplina voluit vivere, placuit sancto seni Valerio ordinatori eius ipsum cum suis fratribus in eremo paterne visitare et eis ad tempus pro devotione
635 commanere. Et tunc cognito proposito Augustini quod omnino cum fratribus suis nichil habentibus, nichil habens optabat vivere, monasterium autem istud in eremo nimium distabat a plebe, cuius curam ipse iam presbyter habebat gerere, dedit ei hortum civitati propinquum in quo mox monasterium edificavit et in eo de fratribus prioris monasterii quosdam secum
640 locavit, colligens nichilominus et alios eiusdem propositi fratres clericos servientes et ibidem deo pariter et in communi viventes, secundum modum et regulam sub sanctis apostolis constitutam, maxime ut nemo quidquam proprium in illa sancta societate haberet, sed eis essent omnia communia

---

[51] Jor. *Coll.* sermo 26, fol. 32rb; sermo 5 *PL* 40,1245.
[52] Possid. vita Aug. 4,1 (50,3–4; *PL* 32,37); 4,1–2 (50,7–52,15; *PL* 32,37); 4,3 (52,22–24; *PL* 32,37); 4,2 (52,15–20; *PL* 32,37).

et distribueretur unicuique sicut opus erat, quod iam ipse prior fecerat, dum de transmarinis ad sua remeasset, ut ait Possidonius.[53] Et hec predicta sunt ipsemet in preallegato sermone primo de communi vita clericorum testatur, dicens sic: "Apprehensus presbyter factus sum. Et quia hic disponebam esse cum fratribus //fol. 63ra// in monasterio cognito instituto et voluntate mea, bone memorie senex Valerius dedit michi hortulum illum in quo nunc est monasterium et cepi boni propositi fratres colligere compares meos nichil habentes sicut nichil habebam et imitantes me ut quomodo ego tenuem paupertatem meam vendidi et pauperibus erogavi sic facerent et illi qui mecum esse voluissent, ut de communi viveremus."[54] Hec ipse ibi. Hoc idem expressius dicit in sermone alio ad presbyteros Hipponenses, qui incipit *In omnibus operibus*, ubi loquens de fratribus primi monasterii sic ait: "Quorum," inquit, "fama ad aures sancti Valerii episcopi pervenit et placuit sibi in eremo nos visitare et stetit diebus tredecim donans michi hortum amenitatibus plenum in planitie positum. Et quia a gentibus erat segregatus libenter illum suscepi ut edificarem ibi etiam monasterium fratrum, quos tales inveneram, quales invenire desideravi."[55] Hec ipse ibi. Hos quoque fratres idem pater in omni disciplina et observantia regulari instruxit et nichilominus eos studio sacre scripture erudivit, ut iam non tantum sibi in simplicitate viverent sed et aliis prodesse valerent. Sanctus autem Valerius ordinator eius ut erat vir pius et timens deum exultabat uberius et deo gratias agebat, suas exauditas a domino fuisse preces quas se frequentissime fudisse narrabat, ut sibi divinitus //fol. 63rb// homo concederetur talis qui posset verbo dei et doctrina salutari ecclesiam domini edificare, cui rei se minus utilem previdebat, cum esset natura Grecus et in Latina lingua et litteris minus doctus. Quocirca Augustino potestatem contulit ut contra morem Africanarum ecclesiarum coram se in ecclesia predicaret, de quo cum multi episcopi ei derogarent, ille sciens illud in orientalibus ecclesiis ex more fieri, linguas obtrectantium non curabat, dummodo per eum fieret, quod per se fieri non valebat. Unde accensa et ardens levata *super candelabrum* lucerna *omnibus qui in domo* erant lucebat.[56] Et postmodum discurrente huiusmodi fama et bono exemplo precedente nonnulli presbyteri quibus erudita inerat facundia, accepta ab episcopo potestate ceperunt verbum dei tractare in populo, etiam in episcoporum suorum presentia. Hec Possidonius.[57] Cuius rei gratia Augustinus ordinavit ut fratres sui de secundo monsterio per eum in sacra pagina eruditi quia non tantum distabant a populo ut fratres primi monasterii verbum dei etiam publice in populo predicarent ac etiam confessiones fidelium audirent, et vita pariter et exemplo dei populum salubriter edificarent, prout ipse idem pater testatur in sermone preallegato, qui incipit *Ut bene nostis fratres*, ubi sic dicit: "Et licet fratres nostri collocati in horto sancti Valerii episcopi satis distent ab urbe, eorum tamen fama divinitus

---

[53] Possid. vita Aug. 5,1 (52,1–8; *PL* 32,37).
[54] Jor. *Coll.* sermo 27, fol. 33^{rb-va}; Aug. sermo 355 (Lambot, 125,17–27).
[55] Jor. *Coll.* sermo 26, fol. 31rb; sermo 5 *PL* 40,1244.
[56] Mt. 5:15.
[57] Possid. vita Aug. 5,2 (52,8–54,16; *PL* 32,37); 5,3 (54,16–21; *PL* 32,37); 5,4 (54,21–26; *PL* 32,37); 5,5 (54,26–31; *PL* 32,37–38).

divulgata ordinavi //fol. 63ᵛᵃ// ut verbum dei populo salubriter predicarent, animeque fidelium suam vitam et exempla audiendo et videndo, sponte redirent ad illum qui ex nichilo cuncta creavit. Ecce quomodo terram iudicant, ligant et solvunt, que volunt semper deo favente."[58] Hec ipse ibi.

2. Eo tempore in illa Hipponensi urbe Manicheorum pestilentia multos tam cives quam peregrinos infecerat, quos precipue illius heresis presbyter nomine Fortunatus loquaci versutia seduxerat, qui in eadem urbe conversans magnus apud multos habebatur. Interea multi Hipponensium tam Christiani quam Donastiste heretici, beatum Augustinum adeunt summopere postulantes, ut predictum Fortunatum conveniret et cum eo de lege domini disputaret. Ille vero paratus omni poscenti se reddere rationem de fide et spe que in ipso erat, potensque exhortari in doctrina sana et eos qui contradicunt arguere quod petebatur non renuit sed et utrum ille hoc fieri vellet sciscitatus est. At illi statim ad predictum Fortunatum accedentes, petunt instanter ut id non recuset. Ille vero quoniam apud Carthaginem sanctum noverat Augustinum, cum adhuc secum eodem errore detineretur, nisus est vitare congressum sed cogente verecundia et illorum instantia tandem promisit in commune se esse venturum, certamenque disputandi subiturum. Unde condicto die et loco convenerunt in unum //fol. 63ᵛᵇ// concurrentibus quam plurimis studiosis turbisque curiosis, apertisque tabulis notariorum ad excipienda verba singulorum. Prima die disputatio est cepta et secundo die finita. Erat autem disputationis illius questio, unde sit malum? Augustinus enim tenebat et dicebat quod malum est exortum in homine ex libero voluntatis arbitrio; Fortunatus autem tenebat quod natura mali deo est coeterna. In qua disputatione doctor ille Manicheus nec catholicam Augustini assertionem potuit infirmare nec Manicheorum sectam aminiculo veritatis potuit probare. Sed deficiens responsione et digna affectus confusione veritati volens, nolens cessit nec tamen Catholicus factus est, sed paulopost de civitate confusus abscessit. Ac sic per dei servum Augustinum de omnium cordibus, tam presentium quam absentium, ad quos illa pervenit disputatio ille error ablatus est et intimata et confirmata est catholice veritatis religio. Hec Possidonius.[59] Predictam autem disputationem Augustinus in librum contulit et plures alios libros eodem tempore prebyterii sui contra Manicheos et alios hereticos scripsit, librum etiam *De Sermone Domini in Monte* et quamplures alios edidit, ut dicit in primo libro *Retrac<ta>tionum*.[60] Predicabat autem Augustinus privatim et publice, loquens verbum //fol. 64ʳᵃ// dei cum omni fiducia, omnem hereticum destruens, Catholicos instruens infundente ei Spiritu Sancto ineffabilem gratiam, mirantibus cunctis disertam eius facundiam. Cuius famam nominis non solum ecclesia Africana, verum etiam transmarina iam noverat gaudens quod talem ei deus lucernam contulerat, cuius verbo et exemplo illuminari meruerat. Hec Possidonius.[61]

---

[58] Jor. *Coll.* sermo 13, fol. 15ᵛᵇ; sermo 14 *PL* 40,1257.
[59] Possid. vita Aug. 6,2 (56,6–10; *PL* 32,38); 6,3 (56,11–15; *PL* 32,38); 6,4–5 (56,16–58,24; *PL* 32,38); 6,6 (58,24–28; *PL* 32,38); 6,7–8 (58,28–60,44; *PL* 32,38).
[60] Aug. retract. I,16,1 (51,7–8).
[61] Possid. vita Aug. 7,1–4 (60,1–62,26; *PL* 32,38–39).

XII. Qualiter factus est episcopus

Cum vero pre ceteris senex ille Valerius exultaret, cepit ut se habet humana fragilitas formidare, ne suus ille Augustinus presbyter ab alia quereretur ecclesia, et sibi ablatus in episcopum eligeretur. Quod utique aliquando provenisset nisi hoc precognito idem episcopus illum fecisset absentari, ne quesitus posset inveniri. Unde ampliore timore concussus presertim cum et corpore esset infirmus et etate defessus, egit secrete apud primatem episcopum Carthaginensem allegans infirmitatem sui corporis etatisque gravitatem, et obsecrans ut Augustinus Hipponensis ecclesie episcopus ordinaretur, qui sue cathedre non tam succederet quam consacerdos accederet. Cuius ille piis precibus clementer annuens rescripto mediante concessit quod petebat. Demum veniente ad ecclesiam Hipponensem tunc primate Numidie, cum Megalio Orilamensi episcopo, Valerius antistes episcopis qui forte tunc aderant //fol. 64rb// et clericis Hipponensibus ac universe plebi inopinatam cunctis suam insinuat voluntatem. Omnibus igitur audientibus, gratulantibus atque id fieri perficique ingenti desiderio clamantibus, in episcopum Augustinus electus est. Sed cum hoc Augustinus vivente suo episcopo omnimode recusaret, compulsus tamen et coactus tandem subcubuit et episcopalem tam locum quam ordinem cum beato Valerio suscepit. Quod quidem non debere fieri postea dixit et scripsit, cum universalis consilii cognovisset decreta, que tunc temporis ei erant incognita, nec quod sibi factum esse doluit, aliis fieri voluit. Factus vero episcopus quo maiore dignitate refulsit, eo maiore instantia et auctoritate verbum dei predicavit, non in sua tantum civitate sed ubicumque eum ecclesiastica necessitas invitavit, vel ad instruendum Catholicos vel ad destruendum hereticos. Hec Possidonius.[62]

XIII. De edificatione tertii monasterii in episcopio

1. Videns autem beatus Augustinus quod necesse erat episcopum assiduam hospitalitatis humanitatem quibusque venientibus sive transeuntibus exhibere, quod in monasterio fratrum convenienter fieri non valebat, voluit in ipsa episcopali domo monasterium secum habere clericorum, ut qui presbyter in horto cum fratribus vixerat in episcopio nichilominus pauper cum pauperibus deo regulariter serviret. Hec in legenda famosa.[63] Unde etiam //fol. 64va// ipse in sermone primo de communi vita clericorum, qui incipit *Propter quod volui*, sic ait: "Placuit deo michi dicere sursum conscende, usque adeo timebam episcopatum, ut quia ceperat iam alicuius momenti inter servos dei fama mea in quo loco sciebam non esse episcopum, ne illo accederem cavebam, sed servus contradicere domino non debet." Et infra: "Perveni ad episcopatum, vidi necesse habere episcopum exhibere humanitatem assiduam quibuscumque venientibus sive transeuntibus, quod si non fecisset episcopus

---

[62] Possid. vita Aug. 8,1 (62,1–9; *PL* 32,39–40); 8,2 (62,9–64,16; *PL* 32,39); 8,3 (64,17–25; *PL* 32,39–40); 8,3–5 (64,25–66,35; *PL* 32,40).
[63] Phil. vita Aug 22 (1221B).

inhumanus diceretur. Si autem illa consuetudo in monasterio permissa esset, indecens esset. Et ideo volui habere in domo ista episcopi mecum monasterium clericorum."[64] Hec ipse ibi. In alio quoque sermone ad presbyteros Hipponenses, qui incipit *In omnibus operibus vestris*, sic ait: "Edificato monasterio fratrum in horto placuit ei qui me segregavit ex utero matris mee, et vocavit me per gratiam suam michi dicere, *Amice, surge et ascendi superius.*[65] Et sic cum molestia et grandi anxietate factus sum episcopus. Et quia cum fratribus meis ut hactenus feceram semper corpore habitare non poteram, propterea infra domum episcopi, vos clericos habere volui et mox vobiscum secundum formam apostolicam vivere cepi."[66] Hec ipse ibi.

2. Memorata tria monasteria per eundem sanctum patrem constructa et instructa ipse simul commemorat in sermone ad fratres suos in eremo, qui incipit *Ut bene nostis*, ubi sic dicit: "Ut bene //fol. 64vb// nostis fratres carissimi tria monasteria apud Hipponem dei gratia merui laudabiliter ad honorem sancte trinitatis construere. Quorum primum hoc est in quo iam multis annis modico pabulo contenti, alacriter commoramini bestiis associati, avibus ministrati, ciborumque spernentes delicias, visus hominum fugientes et ideo non solum ego miser sed vos sepe angelorum estis assueti colloquiis. Aliud quoque monasterium in horto edificatum est, quem michi sanctus pater noster Valerius dedit. Et quoniam postquam episcopus factus sum, nec semper hic vobiscum habitare potui nec cum fratribus qui in predicto monasterio in horto sunt, propterea intra domum episcopi mecum habere volui monasterium clericorum et cum eisdem pariter vivere secundum apostolicam traditionem."[67] Hec ipse ibi. Sane propter episcopatus dignitatem se a fratribus priorum monasteriorum suorum minime alienavit, sed apud se eorum aliquos semper esse desideravit, vel saltem se eis in pristina vita religionis quantum potuit conformavit. Unde ipse in sermone ad eosdem fratres qui incipit *Ut nobis per litteras*, sic ait: "Et ecce postquam episcopus factus sum, Vitalem, Nicolaum, Stephanum, Dorotheum, Paulum, Iacobum, Cyrilum, frequenter rogavi, ut me solum in episcopatu non dimitterent. Quia licet episcopus essem non credebam tamen paupertatem despicere sed cum Abraham, Isaac, et Iacob inter divitias vivere, aut veram paupertatem servare optabam, ut de numero eorum essem de quibus dicit Apostolus, *Tanquam nichil habentes et omnia possidentes.*[68] Hos igitur frequenter rogavi ut venirent //fol. 65ra// non ut essent rebelles eremi sed solitarie etiam in civitate viventes habitare possemus in placito sancto. Sed ecce noluerunt venire tanquam de se ipsis timentes, ne a seculo caperentur. Noluerunt venire. Quare noluerunt? Non quia non digni, sed quia non solum pauperes esse voluerunt. Sed etiam supra id quod in speculo nostro edidimus facere voluerunt, de quo nunc summum gaudium habere debemus, quia facere voluerunt que deo et michi promiserunt. Et quia solus stare non poteram

---

[64] Jor. *Coll.* sermo 27, fol. 33^{rb-va}; Aug. sermo 355,2 (Lambot, 125,8–126,5).
[65] Lc. 14:10.
[66] Jor. *Coll.* sermo 26, fol. 31rb; sermo 5 *PL* 40,1244.
[67] Jor. *Coll.* sermo 13, fol. 15va; sermo 14 *PL* 40,1257.
[68] II Cor. 6:10.

episcopus ideo rogavi sanctum senem Valerium, qui michi iam potestatem predicandi in populo dederat, ut intra domum episcopi monasterium clericorum constituerem. Et placuit sancto episcopo michi condescendere et sic cum eisdem in omni paupertate vivere cepi. Non manducamus carnes nisi dum hospites veniunt sed tantum olera et legumina absque oleo et butyro sicut ante vobiscum cum gaudio consueveram. Igitur fratres mei, licet me in cathedra episcopali videatis, paupertatem michi caram sponsam tenere congratulor, quia ipsa est etiam Christi sponsa, sanctorum possessio, beatorum vita, fidelium securitas, clericorum ornamentum, monachorum vita, nobilium pulcritudo, divitum magnificentia. Hec est illa sancta paupertas, quam qui tenet et amat, nulla indigentia laborare potest. Nec mirum fratres quia sibi datur omnium dominium possidere. Ipsa est enim sperantibus //fol. 65rb// in se thesaurus in paupertate, solatium in sollitudine, gloria in abiectione, honor in contemptu, umbraculum in omni protectione."[69] Hec ipse ibi. Sepe etiam ipse strepitum secularium negotiorum fugere volens, ad alterum monasterium fratrum in eremo declinabat et cum illis aliquibus diebus pro sua devotione et fratrum exhortatione manebat, ita ut de hoc etiam nonnunquam sui canonici murmurarent. Unde ipse in sermone ad presbyteros Hipponenses preallegato, sic ait loquens canonicis: "Cur," inquit, "murmurastis, si in hiis paschalibus diebus presentialiter vobiscum non fui? Placuit enim michi segregare me a vobis et pergere ad fratres meos in solitudine quos, ut dixi, tales inveni, quales invenire desideravi. Cur ergo turbamini?" Et infra: "Cur de mea absentia dolorem habere ostenditis? Facite que placita sunt michi et tunc ubicumque fuero, vobiscum ero, usque ad consummationem seculi. Decreveram enim cum eisdem rusticanis meis in caritate humiliter habitare usque ad festum sancte ascensionis domini, nec ad vos redire optabam, quousque vos emendatos esse cognovero. Sed quoniam Fortunatum adversarium ad partes occulte velud lupum pervenisse iam sentio, ideo compulsus reversus sum ad vos, cupiens illum videre et cum eo pariter disputare, et illum conculcare domino auxiliante, qui totis visceribus dissipare //fol. 65va// conatur, et iugulare filios quod peperi in visceribus caritatis."[70] Hec ipse ibi.

3. Fratres autem predicti sicut de presentia tanti patris potissime consolabantur, ita de eius recessu quam plurimum turbabantur. Unde ipse in sermone de prudentia ad eosdem fratres sic dicit: "Supplico vobis fratres, ut non turbemini de meo recessu, decreveram enim diu inter vos consolari et vobiscum habitare, usque ad festum dominice ascensionis. Sed quia adversarius noster Fortunatus ad partes pervenit, ideo redire Hipponem omnino compellor, cupiens illum videre, et cum illo pariter disputare."[71] Hec ipse ibi. Consolabantur nimirum memorati fratres sepius ab ipso patre non solum sua dulci presentiali conversatione et sermonum suorum suavi refectione, sed etiam caritativa temporalium provisione. Unde ipse in sermone de oratione ad eosdem fratres sic ait: "Non tedeat vos orare, quia non familiam regere

---

[69] Jor. *Coll.* sermo 21, fol. 27^{rb-va}; sermo 21 *PL* 40,1270–1271.
[70] Jor. *Coll.* sermo 26, fol. 3^{va-b}; sermo 5 *PL* 40,1246.
[71] Jor. *Coll.* sermo 4, fol. 7vb; sermo 4 *PL* 40,1242.

sed tantum deo placere debemus. Et ut bene psallere et orare possitis absque magno corporis impedimento, de bonis episcopatus ecclesie Hipponensis centum et quadraginta vestimenta cum calciamentis vobis dilectis fratribus meis deportari precopi ut tempore frigoris quantum necesse fuerit unusquisque recipiat, reponentes ea et custodientes in communi vestiario cum omni diligentia et caritate, scientes quod vera caritas non querit //fol. 65vb// que sua sunt, sed que dei."[72] Hec ipse ibi. Proficiente igitur sancti viri sana et sancta doctrina, multi divino afflati spiritu, vilefacientes seculo, ad monasteria sua confluxerunt, ibique relicta seculari proprietate et propria voluntate sub tali ac tanto patre et doctore, deo devote servierunt, quorum sancta continentia, paupertas voluntaria, humilis obedientia, longe lateque suavem odorem effudit. Unde nonnulli episcopi, tante sanctitatis emulatores effecti, multos ex eisdem monasteriis fratres sibi donare petierunt, sub quorum cura multas ecclesias ad serviendum deo commiserunt. Ex quibus etiam fere decem in episcopos sunt sublimati. Illi vero propositi sui, non immemores et doctrinam salutarem, quam a sancto viro Augustino acceperant redolentes monasteria etiam collectis fratribus instituerunt. E quibus postmodum multos proficiente eorum religione et fidelium devotione, ad instruenda alia monasteria emancipaverunt et sic non solum in Africa sed etiam in transmarinis partibus huius sancte religionis propositum dilatatum est.

4. Denique vir iste sanctus in cultu, gestu et habitu, in sermonibus et moribus, talem se exhibuit omnibus, ut ad utilitatem omnium omnia fieret omnibus. Religiosis quippe honeste maturus, secularibus vero mature iocundus aderat, ut illos in sanctitate cepta exemplo //fol. 66ra// sui confirmaret et istos ad sanctitatem congruam hilaritale invitaret. Indiscplinationes quoque et transgressiones suorum regulat recta et honesta arguebat, et tollerabat quantum decebat et oportebat in talibus precipue docens ne cuiusquam cor declinaret in verba maligna ad excusandas excusationes in peccatis. Indumenta eius et calciamenta et lectualia, ex moderato et competenti habitu erant, nec nitida nimium, nec abiecta plurimum. Plerumque enim sicut nimia vestium pulchritudo, sic arguitur earum nimia turpitudo. At ipse medium tenebat, volens etiam seipsis dare aliis formam vivendi, non materiam detrahendi. Hec Possidonius.[73] Unde ipse in sermone secundo de communi vita clericorum, qui incipit *Caritati vestre*, sic ait: "Nolo quod talia offerat sanctitas vestra, quibus ego quasi decentius utar, verbi gratia, offeratur michi byrrum pretiosum, forte deceret episcopum sed non decet Augustinum, hominem pauperem de pauperibus natum. Ne forte dicturi sint homines quod inveni pretiosas vestes, quas non possem in domo patris mei habere. Talem debeo habere, qualem si non habuerit fratri meo possim dare. Siquis in elemosinam dederit, vendo ut quando vestis non potest esse communis pretium vestis possit esse commune. Si hoc eum delectat ut habeam ego, det talem de quibus non erubescam. Fateor ego vobis quod de pretiosa veste erubesco, //fol. 66rb// quia non decet hanc ammonitionem, non decet

---

[72] Jor. *Coll.* sermo 22, fol. 20ra; sermo 22 *PL* 40,1273.
[73] Possid. vita Aug. 11,1–6 (72,1–74,31; *PL* 32,XX); 25,3 (132,9–14; *PL* 32,55).

hanc professionem, non decet hec membra, non decet hos canos."[74] Hec ipse ibi. Mensa frugali et parca semper usus est et inter olera et legumina propter infirmos et hospites, plerumque carnes habebat. Semper autem vinum habebat quo sobrie utebatur iuxta consilium Apostoli ad Timotheum scribentis, *Noli adhuc aquam bibere, sed modico vino utere propter stomachum tuum et frequentes tuas infirmitates.*[75] Pauper quippe sibi et parcus aliis dives et largus habebatur, sibi ieiunans aliis epulabatur. Ostium eius viatori patuit, mensa eius hospitibus servivit. In ipsa autem mensa, magis lectionem vel disputationem quam epulationem diligebat, et contra pestem detractionis hos versus scriptos habebat:

Quisquis amat dictis absentem rodere vitam.
Hanc mensam indignam noverit esse sibi.

Nam et aliquando cum sibi quidam familiarissimi coepiscopi ad detractionem linguam laxassent adeo dure eos redarguit, ut diceret quid nisi desisterent, aut versus ipsos deleret, aut de mensa recederet. Quod profecto aliquando contigit, ut surgens cubiculum suum ingrederetur cum in mensa aliquis plus iusto loqueretur. Quadam vice cum quosdam suos familiares ad prandium invitasset, unus eorum curiosior ceteris coquinam ingressus est. Cumque //fol. 66[va]// omnia frigida reperisset, reversus ad Augustinum interrogavit, quid ciborum pransuris paterfamilias ipse preparasset. Cui Augustinus talium epularum nequamquam curiosus respondit: "Et ego vobiscum nescio." Vasa domus eius vel marmorea vel lingnea erant vel testea, non inopia necessitatis sed proposito voluntatis. Coclearibus tantum argenteis utens conpauperum semper memor erat, eisque ex hiis que habere poterat erogabat. Nam et de vasis dominicis propter pauperes et captivos, aliquando iubebat frangi et conflari et indigentibus dispensari. Cum autem ecclesie pecunia deficeret, hoc ipsum in populo Christiano denuntiabat se non habere quod indigentibus erogaret. Consanguineis sic bene fecit, non ut divitias haberent sed ut aut non, aut minus egerent. Hec Possidonius.[76] Unde ipse in sermone ad fratres in eremo Hipponensi, qui incipit *Ut nobis per litteras*, sic ait: "Non debemus habere temporalia ad possidendum, nec ego qui episcopus sum, habere debeo, nisi tantum ad dispensandum, quia bona ecclesiarum patrimonium pauperum sunt. Unde ego, qui episcopus sum summe cavere debeo, ne res pauperum, quas Hipponensis ecclesia conservare videtur divitibus largiantur. Quod bene feci hucusque. Nam consanguineos habeo et nobiles se dicere non erubescunt ad me episcopum veniunt et aliquando cum minis, aliquando cum blandimentis dicentes, 'Da nobis aliquid //fol. 66[vb]// pater. Caro enim tua sumus,' et tamen dei gratia et vestris orationibus mediantibus aliquem consanguineum me predicasse non recolo. Cariores eos michi reputo pauperes quam divites, quia habentes victum et vestitum fideles omnes contenti esse debent. Maxime nos clerici

---

[74] Jor. *Coll.* sermo 28, fol. 38[ra-b]; Aug. sermo 356,12 (Lambot, 140,24–141,12).
[75] I Tim. 5:23.
[76] Possid. vita Aug. 22,6 (122,37–43; *PL* 32,52); 22,5 (122,32–36; *PL* 32,52); 23,1 (124,1–2; *PL* 32,52); 25,15 (130,73–75; *PL* 32,54); 24,14 (130,70–72; *PL* 32,54).

in cuius signum capita tonsa et rasa habere debemus, ne divitiarum capilli occupent mentem servorum dei."⁷⁷ Hec ipse ibi. Pupillos et viduas in tribulatione constitutos, et egrotantes postulatus visitabat eisque supplicibus manus inponens, facta oratione infirmitates eorum sanabat. Acceperat enim donum curationis ab eo qui dixit, *Super egros manus inponent et bene habebunt.* Quadam etiam vice rogatus ut pro quibusdam energuminis patientibus oraret, ipse eis compatiens et lacrimas fundens, deum pro eis oravit et demones ab illis hominibus fugavit. Hec Possidonius.⁷⁸ Ipse etiam in libro vicesimo secundo *De Civitate Dei* duo miracula de se tanquam de quodam alio refert dicens: "Hipponi quandam virginem scio, que cum oleo se perunxisset, cum pro illa orans presbyter, lacrimas suas stillavit, mox a demone fuisse sanatam." In eodem etiam libro sic ait: "Scio etiam episcopum semul pro adolescente quem non vidit orasse, illumque a demonio curavisse."⁷⁹ Nullum autem dubium videtur quin de se loquatur, sed humilitatis causa //fol. 67ʳᵃ// se ipsum non vult nominare. Senibus quoque etate defessis valde compatiens erat, quos etiam cum quadam veneratione pie subportabat. Unde ipse in sermone ad fratres in eremo Hipponensi de otiositate fugienda, qui incipit *Apostolus Petrus fratres carissimi,* sic ait: "Et si aliqui sunt ex vobis qui per annos octoginta et amplius sunt sanctissime in heremo conversati, iugo sancte obedientie, paupertatis et castitatis decorati, iam gaudeant exspectantes beatam spem et adventum domini. Isti enim ut videmus, qui amplius ieiuniis et orationibus et operibus monasterii insistere non posunt, fecerunt enim dum potuerunt. Propterea filioli mei si modo non faciunt ea que facere consueverant, non sit vobis molestum si quiescunt non miremini, si venerantur a me ut patres non tristemini quia ipsi digni sunt. Non enim dolere debetis, quia caritas non cogitat malum, gaudet autem de bono. Ideo volumus et in Christi nomine ordinamus ut et ipsi qui centum annorum sunt et amplius, *Pater Noster* sedendo in lectulo dicant et diligenter eis sine murmure serviatur, ut et ipsi pro nobis intercedant in celis, quorum habitatio iam ibi est."⁸⁰ Hec ipse ibi.

5. Denique in hiis que ecclesia possidebat implicatus amore non erat. Domum vel agrum nunquam emere volebat, multas etiam hereditates sibi dimissas respuebat, eo quod mortuorum filiis propinquis potius ipsa deberi dicebat. //fol. 67ʳᵇ// Domus curam omnemque substantiam ad vices valentioribus clericis delegabat, a quibus de perceptis et expensis completo anno rationem audiebat, nunquam clavem huiusmodi distributionum in manu habens, nec se talibus occupationibus implicans, sed in superioribus et spiritualibus suspensus, ad disponenda temporalia aliquando descendabat non propria ductus voluntate sed fratrum coactus necessitate. Hiis vero pro tempore dispositis, tamquam a spinis et tribulis evocans animum, ad superiora et interior revocabat mentis intuitum in lege domini meditans die ac nocte. Novarum quoque fabricarum studium nunquam habere volebat, devitans

---

[77] Jor. *Coll.* sermo 21, fol. 26ᵛᵃ⁻ᵇ; sermo 21 *PL* 40,1269.
[78] Possid. vita Aug. 27,1–2 (138,1–6; *PL* 32,56); 29,4 (156,16–158,20; *PL* 32,59).
[79] Aug. civ. 22,8 (821,243–247).
[80] Jor. *Coll.* sermo 16, fol. 20ᵛᵃ; sermo 17 *PL* 40,1264.

in eis implicationem sui animi, quem semper liberum habere volebat ab omni molestia corporali, ut libere vacare posset continue meditationi et assidue lectioni. Non tamen illa edificare volentes prohibebat, nisi forte immoderate fieri conspexisset.

6. Feminarum nullam umqum intra domum suam passus est conversari, nec etiam germanam sororem, aut fratris sui filias, que deo pariter serviebant. Dicebat enim quod etsi de sorore vel neptibus nulla mali possit oriri suspitio tamen quia tales persone non possunt sine aliis sibi necessariis esse et ad eas etiam alie advenirent, et viri sancti sine aliis clericis et laicis non sint ex illis possent infirmiores aut humanis temptationibus commoveri, aut certe malis hominum suspitionibus infamari. Nec umquam //fol. 67va// cum muliere solus loqui volebat etiam si secretum aliquid interesset. Eapropter si forte aliquam earum ut ei loqui dignaretur petebat, nunquam sine fratribus aut clericis testibus eam accedere permittebat. Docti ergo viri cautela magna debet nobis esse instructio. Hec Possidonius.[81] Ipse enim dixisse legitur in libro de cohabitatione clericorum et mulierum: "Experto crede, episcopus loquor coram deo non mentior. Cedros libani duces gregum sub hac peste cecidisse reperi, de quorum casu non magis suspicabar, quam Ambrosii vel Ieronimi impudica turpitudine. Quocirca familiaritatem feminarum sicut venenum fugiendam docuit, nec minus ut dicebat eo timende sunt, quia religiose videntur, quia quanto religiosiores videntur, tanto citius alliciunt et sub pretextu pietatis latet viscus libidinis."[82] Hec ipse ibi. Feminarum etiam monasteria non nisi urgentibus necessitatibus visitabat. Tria retulit se a beato Ambrosio didicisse: primum quod uxorem cuiquam nunquam peteret; secundum quod militare volentem ad hoc non commendaret; tertium quod ad convivia invitatus non iret. Causa primi est, ne si illi inter se non conveniant, sibi maledicant. Et utique satis videtur incongruum ut vir religiosus professus continentiam aliquos carnalem invitet ad copulam. Causa secundi est, ne si militantes calumniam exerceant in eum alii culpam refundant. Causa //fol. 67vb// tertii est, ne temperantie modum perdat. Omnia iuramenta etiam que a nonnullis religiosis frequentantur et a quibusdam simplicioribus iuramenta non putantur videlicet deus testis est, deus scit et cetera huiusmodi summa cura, summaque vigilantia tamquam pestem exhorruit. Et si quis commensalium suorum in aliquod huiusmodi iuramentum laberetur, statutum fuit, ut unam de statutis perderet potionem. Erat enim suis secum commorantibus et convivantibus numerus poculorum prefixus, asserebat enim summopere tenendum esse illud evangelicum: *Sit sermo vestri: est est, non non*,[83] ne consuetudine iurandi quis laqueum incidat periurandi. Laudabat vir sanctus plurimum illos quibus moriendi desiderium inerat et super hoc exempla trium episcoporum sepius recitabat. Beatus enim Ambrosius cum in extremis esset et rogaretur ut prolongationem vite sibi precibus optineret, respondit: "Non sic vixi, ut pudeat me inter vos vivere, nec mori

---

[81] Possid. vita Aug. 24,10 (128,47–49; *PL* 32,53); 24,1 (124,1–126,10; *PL* 32,53); 24,13 (130,65–70; *PL* 32,54); 26,1–3 (134,1–136,25; *PL* 32,55).
[82] *Non invenitur.*
[83] Mt. 5:37.

timeo, quoniam bonum habemus dominum." Quod responsum Augustinus mirabiliter extollebat, de quodam etiam alio episcopo retulit, quod cum ei diceretur eum ecclesie multum fore necessarium et ideo eum adhuc dominus liberaret, ait: "Nunquam bene si aliquando quare non modo?" De alio quoque episcopo aiebat Cyprianum referre, quod cum in infirmitate gravi laboraret, adhuc sibi sanitatem restitui exorabat. Cui iuvenis //fol. 68ra// speciosus apparens cum indignatione infremuit et ait: "Pati timetis exire non vultis, quid faciam vobis?" Raro pro aliquo litteris vel verbis intercedere volebat, recolens quemdam philosophum contemplatione sue fame, amicis multa non prestitisse addens quoniam plerumque potestas que petit, premit. Cum autem id faciebat, sic stilum temperabat ut onerosus non esset sed mereretur urbanitate dictaminis exaudiri volebat potius inter ignotos quam inter amicos causas audire, dicens quia inter illos libere poterat cognoscere iniquum et unum ex hiis esset amicum facturus pro quo scilicet iustitia mediante sententiam daret. Ex amicis vero esset unum perditurus, scilicet contra quem proferret sententiam.

7. Hereticos vir iste sanctus validissime confutabat, ita ut ipsi inter se publice predicarent, peccatum non esse interficere Augustinum, quem tamquam lupum occidendum esse dicebant et occisoribus omnia peccata sua a deo dimitti indubitanter asserebant. Multas ab eis insidias mortis pertulit, sed dei providentia ita pugilem suum preservavit quod nec vi nec dolo sibi nocere potuerunt. Nam aliquando cum armati in insidiis laterent et illum de more ad visitandas instruendas vel exhortandas catholicas plebes euntem occidere disponerent, contigit ut divina dispensatione sed ducatoris hominis errore recto itinere ammisso vel dimisso per aliam viam vir sanctus quo tenderat perveniret et sic presidio erroris //fol. 68rb// manus illorum evaderet. Quo postea cognito deo gratias egit. Qui quomodo vult, liberat quos salvare disponit. Verumtamen a predicatione verbi dei timore incusso propter hoc non destitit, sed semper et ubique cum tempus et locus exigeret, illorum errorem pressit et oppressit et pro eis nonnunquam damnatis apud principes seculi intercessit. Eodem siquidem tempore multe et quasi infinite hereses in Africa pullulabant, Donatiste namque velut sub professione continentium ambulantes erant, in ingenti numero per omnes ferre Africanas regiones constituti qui Circumcelliones dicebantur, superba audacia homines etiam violenter et cum armis ad suam sectam trahentes. Manichei nichilominus versuta calliditate multos seducebant. Pelagianiste similiter novas hereses publice et per domos disseminare callide conabantur. Felix etiam hereticus Maxentius, Pascentius, Felicianus, Faustus, Secundinus, Petilianus et multi alii heretici, quos enumurare longum et superfluum esset, doctrinas varias et prophanas in cordibus infirmorum seminabant. Contra quos omnes preclarissimus magister ecclesie et veritatis velut fortissimus athleta pro fidei sinceritate scriptis et dictis continue dimicavit, et eos publica disputatione confutavit. Quorum multi divina inspiratione et Augustini disputatione et predicatione ad fidem catholicam sunt conversi. Plerumque etiam ei predicanti accidit ut digressionem a materia faceret et tunc //fol. 68va// dicebat hoc deum ad profectum salutis alicuius ordinasse, sicut in quodam Manicheorum negotiatore patuit, qui in quadam predicatione Augustini ubi

ipse digressionem faciens contra hunc errorem predicaverat, conversus fuit. Concilia etiam episcoporum et synodos sacerdotum colloquia principum ab eis invitatus frequentavit a quibus non que sua, sed que Iesu Christi sunt quesivit, ut scilicet quod iustum erat confirmaretur et quod iniustum discrete corrigeretur. Hec Possidonius.[84]

8. Eodem preterea tempore scilicet episcopatus sui, multos conscripsit libros ad edificationem fidelium et roborationem fidei orthodoxe. Primo quidem scripsit librum *Ad Simplicianum*. Cum autem Augustinus eruditione Simpliciani, ut supradictum est, conversus fuisset et ipse Augustinus ad Africam remeasset, ipse Simplicianus Mediolanensis episcopus factus beato Ambrosio succedens, audivit famam celeberrimam de Augustini sapientia et eius admirabili doctrina, eumque episcopum esse factum propter quod sibi misit quasdam questiones subtiles de sacra scriptura solvendas. At Augustinus suis questionibus respondens hunc librum duos libros continentem sibi transmisit. Item scripsit librum *Confessionum* tredecim libros continentem. In quibus de malis suis propriis confitetur et de bonis deum laudat iustum et bonum. Quos quidem libros fecit ut exercitaret suum intellectum et inflammaret ad deum suum affectum. In tantum namque ipsum excitabant et inflammabant quod non est aliquis ita durus et indevotus //fol. 68[vb]// qui non excitetur ad devotionem et inflammetur ad amorem, si ipsos libros cum attentione legerit. Omnia enim verba in ipsis libris posita sunt ad dei amorem inflammantia melle divine dulcedinis condita et devotione suavissima plena. Item scripsit librum *De Opere Monachorum*. Cum enim in Africa cepissent esse multa monasteria monachorum inter eos magna questio est exorta. Quidam enim dicebant quod propriis manibus operari oportebat, iuxta verbum Apostoli dicentis: *Qui non laborat nec manducet*,[85] et iterum: *Nocte et die laborantes* fuimus, *ne vestrum* ali*quem gravaremus*.[86] Alii vero econtrario dicebant quod ipsi nichil debebant propriis manibus operari, adducentes pro se verbum evangelii dicentis: *Respicite volatilia celi*[87] etc., et iterum: *Respicite lilia agri*,[88] et in tantum augebatur ista contentio, ut ex hoc fere tota ecclesia turbaretur, aliis defendentibus istos, aliis illos. Propter quod Aurelius Carthaginensis episcopus rogavit Augustinum ut super hoc aliquid scriberet et doceret et dirigeret tam ipsos monachos quam alios. Augustinus ergo de hoc librum composuit, in quo ostendit quod certis horis et temporibus orationi est insistendum. Ostendit etiam ibi quante necessitatis et utilitatis sit propriis manibus laborare. Scripsit preterea librum *De Trinitate*, quem iuvenis incepit et senex edidit, libros quindecim continentem. Item scripsit *De Civitate Dei* continentem viginti duos libros. Cum enim Goti Romam cepissent pagani //fol. 69[ra]// et infideles insultabant Christianis et deum verbum

---

[84] Possid. vita Aug. 27,1 (138,6–8; *PL* 32,56); 25,2 (132,7–9; *PL* 32,55); 27,7 (142,32–144,34; *PL* 32,56); 27,9–11 (144,52–146,70; *PL* 32,57); 12,1–2 (76,1–12; *PL* 32,43); 13,1–21,1 (82,1–118,10; *PL* 32,44–54).
[85] II Th. 3:10.
[86] I Th. 2:9.
[87] Mt. 6:26.
[88] Mt. 6:28.

blasphemaverunt dicentes quod postquam Roma a cultura deorum recesserat et Christum coluerat, semper ab hostibus victa fuit. Unde Augustinus zelo
1105 domus dei plurimum exardescens hunc librum scripsit. In primis quinque libris repellens errorem illorum, qui dicunt quod omnia bona et omnia prospera illis accidunt, qui diversos deos colunt. In aliis quinque refellitur error illorum, qui dicunt quod in hac vita bona et mala nunquam defuerunt nec umquam deficient sed variantur diversimode secundum loca, tempora et
1110 personas. In duodecim vero aliis libris sequentibus adversa predictorum redarguit, ostendens iustos in hac vita premi et impios florere debere, ubi de duplici civitate scilicet Ierusalem et Babylonia et eorum regibus ait: "Quia rex Ierusalem Christus, rex Babylonis diabolus. Quas duas civitates, ut ibidem dicit, duo amores sibi fabricant. Quia civitatem diaboli consti-
1115 tuit amor sui crescens usque ad contemptum dei. Civitatem vero dei amor dei constituit crescens usque ad contemptum sui."[89] Hec ipse in secundo libro *Retrac<ta>tionum*. Preter hos plures alios et pene innumerabiles scripsit libros, tractatus, epistolas ad diversas personas, homelias et sermones. In tanta copia ut vix aliquis possit sufficere ad legendum, cum Augustinus
1120 sufficeret ad scribendum. Multos quidem scripsit //fol. 69rb// adhuc laicus, multos religiosus et prebyter factus, plurimosque episcopus dictavit. Hec Possidonius.[90] Cum autem ipse predictos libros et tractatus fecisset voluit relegere omnes et diligenter examinare ut si qua esset in eis non sane dicta ea provide retractaret, si qua dubia explanaret, et si qua obscura eluci-
1125 daret, maxime ea et circa ea que scripsit dum adhuc cathecuminus et secularis esset, secularis scientie consuetudine, adhuc inflatus, sicut ipse in prologo libri *Retrac<ta>tionum* refert.[91] Ut autem ad faciendum hoc magis otium haberet, maxime quia in duobus consiliis episcoporum ab omnibus coepiscopis ipsi Augustino cura de scripturis esset inposita per aliquot annos ante
1130 suum obitum petiit, humiliter a clero et populo ut per quinque dies in hebdomada liceret sibi assidue vacare otio, immo potius literali inservire negotio et in reliquos dies exteriorum negotiorum tumultus differe. Quod quidem ei concessum exstitit sed cogente necessitate frequentius irruptum fuit. Quapropter ut adhuc liberius posset vacare studio, attendensque etate se grandevum
1135 et eum qui ordine nature preteriri non potest terminum non longe abesse et timens ne post decessum suum aliquis ambitiosus vel minus idoneus cathedram episcopalem acciperet, vel forte in electionis negotio scisma in ecclesia fieret, consuluit et consulendo petiit ut eo vivente religiosum eligerent //fol. 69va// episcopum, qui eo decedente absque dissensione episcopatum
1140 susciperet. Eoque vivente ille negotia ecclesie et populi pro eo disponet et maiora cum oportunum esset suum consilium ad ipsum referret, sicque factum est, ut compromisso in Augustinum facto, ipse quemdam virum religiosum Eraclium nomine ad succedendum sibi eligeret, quem ipse Augustinus in scola Christi erudierat et tam sanctitate quam scientia adprime inbuerat.
1145 Cuius electioni tam clerus quam populus consensu unanimi acclamavit. In

---

[89] Aug. retract. II,43,1–2 (124,1–125,42).
[90] Possid. vita Aug. 28,1 (146,3–4; *PL* 32,57).
[91] Aug. retract. Prol. 3 (6,43–7,54).

quem etiam Augustinus de omnium consensu suarum occupationum sarcinam refudit. Ipse vero studio vacavit. Tunc igitur omnes libros suos revidit, relegit et examinavit atque ad unguem correxit, et sic librum *Retrac<ta>tionum* fecit. Et nichilominus plures libros postmodum conscripsit. Hec in legenda famosa.[92] Verum aliquanto post tempore cum Vandali adiunctis sibi Alanis et Gotis totam Africe provinciam occupassent, vastantes omnia nec parcentes sexui, ordini vel etati. Demum ad Hipponensem civitatem venerunt et ipsam manu valida obsederunt. Sub hac tribulatione Augustinus preceteris sue senectutis amarissimam et lugubrem duxit vitam. Fueruntque sibi lacrime sue panes die at nocte cum videret alios hostili nece extinctos alios effugatos, ecclesias sacerdotibus et ministris destitutas virginesque sacras et quosque continentes //fol. 69vb// ubique dissipatos, et in hiis alios tormentis defecisse, alios in captivitate perdita animi et corporis integritate ac fide, malo more et duro hostibus deservire hymnos et laudes dei de ecclesiis deperisse. Edificia ecclesiarum pluribus locis ignibus concremata, sollemnia divinorum desisse, sacramenta divina vel non queri vel querenti qui tradat non facile reperiri. Ipsosque ecclesiarum prepositos et clericos qui forte necem evaserant rebus omnibus spoliatos atque nudatos egentissimos mendicare si tamen essent qui eis subvenirent. Inter omnia tamen hec et multa alia mala, cuiusdam sapientis sententia se consolabatur dicentis: "Non est magnus magnum putans, quod cadunt lapides et moriuntur mortales." Convocatis autem fratribus dixit eis: "Ecce rogavi dominum ut aut nos ab istis periculis eruat, aut patientiam tribuat, aut me de hac vita suscipiat." Et hoc ipsum coepiscopi et alii qui aderant per eum exhortati a domino petiverunt. Et ecce tertium quod petivit obtinuit et tertio obsidionis mense febribus laborans et lecto decubuit.

9. Quo egrotante quidam eger ad ipsum venit et ut sibi manum inponeret et ab infirmitate curaret ipsum instanter rogavit. Cui Augustinus respondit: "Quid est hoc fili quod loqueris? Putas si tale quid facere possem, michi hoc ipsum non conferrem?" Ille autem instabat asserens sibi in visione dictum esse, "Vade ad Augustinum episcopum //fol. 70ra// ut tibi manum inponat et salvus eris." Videns autem Augustinus fidem eius, facta oratione manum egroto imponens, infirmus infirmo sanitatem restituit. Intelligens autem vir dei dissolutionem sui corporis imminere quia frequenter predicaverat non debere presbyterum et quemlibet quantumcumque laudatum Christianum de hac vita sine luctu et penitentia egredi. Hoc ipse adimplere voluit et septem psalmos penitentiales quos sibi scribi fecerat in lectulo suo contra parietem habebat, eosque legebat et relegebat et inter legendum ubertim flebat. Et ut deo vacaret liberius ac eius intentio a nullo distraheretur, ante decem dies sui obitus nullum ad se ingredi precepit nisi vel medicus ingrederetur vel cibus vel quodlibet aliud necessarium inferretur. Et per illud tempus assidue incubuit orationi et devotioni ac plorationi. Ad extremam autem horam veniens scilicet quinto calendas septembris membris omnibus sui corporis incolumis integro aspectu atque auditu fratrum

---

[92] Phil. vita Aug. 28 (1226B).

1190 conventu astante et exitum eius cum orationibus domino commendante senex et plenus dierum obdormivit in pace. Testamentum nullum fecit quia unde faceret pauper Christi non habuit. Clerum sufficientissimum et monasteria tam virorum quam feminarum plena continentibus reliquit instructa moribus et ornata libris quos ipse dictavit, in quibus nobis adhuc vivit,
1195 quamvis carne obierit. Vivit quippe deo vivit et //fol. 70rb// nobis quia et perfecte inheret deo et per scripta sua loquitur nobis, prout quidam poeta eleganter designavit, qui suis quos moriens relinquebat in tumulo suo hos versiculos scribere mandavit:

Vivere post obitum vatem vis nosse viator.
1200 *Quod legis ecce loquor, vox tua nempe mea est.*

Vixit autem in clericatu vel episcopatu annis ferme quadraginta. Etatis vero illis anni septuaginta sexta. Hec Possidonius.[93] Talem igitur virum et tantum patrem ac doctorem omnes venerentur Catholici et precipue religiosi et clerici cum et illius doctrina omnium sit instructio Catholicorum et illius
1205 vita sit forma et norma omnium religiosorum et clericorum. Ipse quippe est decus et forma huius nostre professionis ipse speculum et regula nostre religionis. Nulli dubium quin ipse iam receptus in consortium angelorum, ubi videt principium in splendoribus sanctorum, non immemor est fratrum suorum, sed quantum spero et presumo de eo nos sibi subditos reconciliabit deo, qui vivit et regnat in secula seculorum, Amen. Hec Possidonius
1210 et in legenda famosa.[94] Et sciendum quod legenda famosa appellatur hic legenda quedam sollemnis et antiqua, stilo venusto more veterum compilata a quodam qui Philipum se nominat, circa finem eiusdem legende sic dicens: "Eligant alii quod sua cuique suggerit ambitio, sed si Philipo daretur optio, mallet sanctam paupertatem qua deus pontificem ditavit Augustinum,
1215 quam regnum et divitias quibus regem extulit Alexandrum." Et habetur illa legenda in multis antiquis monasteriis canonicorum regularium et premonstratensium.[95]

---

[93] Possid. vita Aug. 28,4–7 (148,23–150,50; *PL* 32,58–58); 28,7–8 (152,51–61; *PL* 32,58); 28,9 (152,66–71; *PL* 32,58); 28,11 (154,77–80; *PL* 32,58); 29,2 (156,11–13; *PL* 32,59); 29,5 (158,26–28; *PL* 32,59); 31,6–8 (192,30–194,52; *PL* 32,63–64).
[94] Phil. vita Aug. 31–33 (1228D–1234B).
[95] Phil. vita Aug. 32 (1229A–B).

APPENDIX E

GREGORII ARIMENENSIS

Ordinationes et Litterae

The four texts here presented have all been previously published in the critical edition of Gregory's *Register*. I include them for illustrative purposes of Gregory's reform endeavors. I have divided these documents into two sections. The first consists of Gregory's circular letter, which he referred to as his *Ordinationes*. The text is that of the critical edition, Greg. *Reg.* 1 (3–8). The second section contains the text of three letters, corresponding to Greg. *Reg.* 2 (8–12); 391 (218–220); and 658 (335–336). The first is the letter Gregory sent to the convent in Avignon accompanying his *Ordinationes*. The second, is a letter sent to Frater Johannes, the prior provincial of the March of Ancona. And the third, is a letter sent to Fratres Johannes de Monte Rodono and Cicho de Aversa, visitators to the Province of Apulia. Each of these texts were discussed in Chapter Three above.

For all the documents, I have followed the text of the critical edition, including reproducing the editorial comments given in square brackets, which most often indicate a damaged part of the manuscript. For present purposes and for the ease of the reader, I have standardized the orthography. The critical edition preserves the orthography as given in the manuscript. The Latin bears clear evidence of its Italianate character. Thus we find the use of 'ç' for 'z', for example in the word *scandalizare*, the manuscript gives the form *scandaliçat*; Greg. *Reg.* 391 (220), and *zelus* as *çelus*; Greg. *Reg.* 462 (257). Further, *posscimus* is written for *possimus*, and *confexiones* for *confessiones*. For the composition of the manuscript, which was written by seven different scribes, see de Meijer's introduction, Greg. *Reg.*, viii–ix.

I.

Gregorii Arimenensis
Prioris Generalis Ordinis Fratrum Eremitarum Sancti Augustini

Ordinationes

5 Infrascripte sunt ordinationes [nostre] per provincias ordinis misse et ad provincias infrascriptas [scilicet]: Senensem, Romandiole, Marchie Anchonitane, Marchie Tarvisine, Auplee, Pisanam, Vallis Spoleti, Rheni et Sueviae, Romanam, Terre Sancte, Lombardie, Francie, Angliae, Provincie Provincie, Narbonensis, Coloniensis, Ispaniae, Bavarie, Saxoniae, Ungarie, Tholose,
10 Terre Laboris, Aragoniae, Scicilie.

Frater Gregorius prior generalis ordinis fratrum heremitarum sancti Augustini licet indignus religioso viro fratri ... priori provinciali provincie ... eiusdem ordinis salutem in Domino sempiternam.

Super nostre religionis specula licet inmeriti constituti, dum plurimos
15 immo fere omnes aspicimus ad divina desides, solicitos ad mundana, contra eorum professionem et statum proprias cumulare pecunias, perfrui deliciis, pompis seculi gloriari sicque religiositatis deserta semita vias potius incedere seculares, terret nos plurimum illa divina sententia, qua de manu negligentis speculatoris comminatur Dominus sanguinem requirere morientis.
20 Quam ob rem tuam caritatem exhortamur in Domino ut fratres tue provincie, pro quorum salute tu quoque constitutus speculator agnosceris, ab huiusmodi secularibus viis ad via, que vere religiosos decet et sanctos, summa diligentia et solicitudine studeas revocare; et ut melius id perficere valeas tibi per presentes quasdam ordinationes transmittimus, per nos etiam ad
25 omnes provincias ordinis destinandas, quas sub pena absolutionis a provincialatus officio per omnia loca tue provincie publicabis et facies ab omnibus Deo favente inviolabiliter observari, ipsarumque copiam singula tue provincie loca te iubente et ordinante habebunt, ut quolibet mense semel in eisdem conventibus ordinationes prefate legantur.
30 In primis monemus et hortamur in Domino omnes et singulos fratres tue provincie et ab eis volumus inviolabiliter observari, ut ad dicendum divinum officium tam in die quam in nocte in ecclesia conveniant prout quilibet eorum secundum suum statum convenire debet iuxta nostri ordinis instituta. Convenientes vero devote et in silentio maneant, divinum officium
35 punctatim dicant et morose tam legendo quam cantando rubricas ecclesie diligentius observantes. Deficientes vero fratres ad horas venire canonicas, si simplices conventuales fuerint vel studentes, qui ex eis fuerunt priores in aliquo convenu studii generalis vel gradum adepti sunt lectorie ad mensam nudam sedebunt, reliqui vero in terra in medio refectorii reficiendi tam isti
40 quam illi ex hiis, que discretio prioris secundum exigentiam negligentie ipsorum illis decreverit ministranda. Lectores vero actu legentes in conventu diebus dominicis [aliisque] festis duplicibus maioribus vel minoribus ad matutinum venire negligentes, pro qualibet vice sint sua septimanali provi-

sione privati, nisi ea die habeant predicare vel solemnem aliquem actum scolasticum exercere. Venerabilium vero magistrorum in sacra theologia, quorum mores et vita esse debent ceteris in exemplum, quisquis duabus diebus de predictis consequenter ad matutinum venire neglexerit, sue semptimanalis provisionis medietate privetur, nisi aliqua ipsarum [dierum] pro sermone fuerit vel pro aliquo solemni actu scolastico occupatus. Et ut hoc nostrum mandatum diligentius observetur, mandamus priori conventus et procuratori eiusdem, quod in casu negligentie nulli magistrorum vel lectorum suas septimanales provisiones tribuant, quas in fine hebdomane decernimus esse dandas, sub pena solutionis de proprio quam eum incurrere volumus ipso facto; si vero in aliquibus conventibus fuerint lectores actu legentes provisiones septimanales non recepturi, volums quod huiusmodi lectores ea pena puniantur, que lectoribus non actu legentibus superius est taxata.

Item additionem, qua cavetur quod nulli frater liceat ultra quam ter in hebdomada extra communem vitam refectorii refici quoquo modo, sic interpretamur ut ter tantummodo liceat, obtempta pro qualibet vice prioris licentia speciali; contrafacientes vero pena ibidem taxata puniantur. Si vero quisquam venerabilium in sacra pagina magistrorum aut aliquis lectorum conventus actu legentium saltem ter in septimana in communi conventus mensa non fuerit, magister medietate, lector vero tota septimanali provisione privetur sub mandato et pena prioris et procuratoris, que superius sunt expressa.

Porro cum deliciosa vita a religiosis sit penitus fugienda, presenti tenore mandamus, quatenus nullus frater nostri ordinis nisi sit infirmus, iaceat infra locum ordinis super culcitras de plumis vel pennis neque in linteaminibus lineis sub pena privationis vocis et annualis provisionis, quas contrafacientem incurrere volumus ipso facto, mandantes prioribus conventuum vel eorum vicem gerentibus ut omnes culcitras conventuum ubicumque existentes, illis dumtaxat exceptis que erunt necessarie pro infirmis, vendi faciant infra spatium trium mensium et ex ipsarum pretio fieri faciant fiscones in cellis et cameris collocandos, sub pena privationis ab officio suo, quaterque in anno visitent et scrutentur omnes conventus cameras et cellas, et si quos invenerint predicti mandati transgressores, denuntient voce ac annuali provisione privatos cum hoc culcitras et linteamina, que in lectis eorum repererint, vendi faciant, eorum pretia in fiscones similiter conversuri quibus culcitris et linteaminibus ex nunc eiusmodi privamus transgressores et conventibus applicamus.

Ceterum, quia nichil est iura condere nisi sit qui tueatur et exequatur eadem, omnibus et singulis prioribus localibus tue provincie vel eorum vicem gerentibus mandamus ut ad observandum et per alios ovservari faciendum omnia supradicta diligenter intendant et satagant cum effectu. Quod si ipsi transgressores vel negligentes fuerint reperti, per priorem provincialem, quem ad hoc inquirendum iubemus sub pena absolutionis a provincialatus officio esse solicitum, . . . [*humidatis macula scriptura non amplius legitur*] volumus esse voce privatos et cum hoc mandamus eosdem per dictum priorem provincialem ab officio prioratus vel alio quo in regimine conventus fungerentur absolvi, intimantes expresse quod [. . .] in predictis diligentiam vel desidiam favente Domino intendimus vigilare, nec id conniventibus oculis pertransire.

Verum, quia iuxta sacrorum canonum instituta abdicatio proprietatis sicut custodia castitatis annexa sunt observantie regulari, ideo iuxta tenorem constitutionum nostrarum mandamus ut omnes fratres conventuales et studentes quidquid habent in pecunia ultra valorem duorum florenorum, quod pro cottidianis necessitatibus et expensis cuilibet fratri penes se retinere permittimus, tenere debeant in archa vel capsa communi sub duabus clavibus, quarum unam prior habeat aliam procurator conventus. Et ne per ignorantiam vel exquisitam malitiam hec nostra constitutio violetur, volumus ut obvenientem pecuniam fratri titulo causa vel iure quocumque post aliam pecuniam depositam in capsa communi modo et forma premissis cum ipsa florenum excedet, simili modo in dicta capsa frater ipse deponere integraliter teneatur, ita quod nullo casu ultra valorem duorum florenorum pro suis necessitatibus et expensis quis possit aliquam pecuniam retinere.

Inhibentes insuper ut nullus frater aliquam pecunie quantitatem alicui persone extra nostrum ordinem constitute audeat mutuare, cum talis contractus propietatem de sui natura pretendat. Si quis vero in hoc trangressor extiterit, sit ipso iure tota pecunia mutuata privatus, conventui ad quem sua bona post mortem ipsius devenire debent protinus applicanda. Quod si dicta pecunia de manu debitoris pro tunc recuperari non posset, volumus quod de aliis bonis dicti fratris si qua habet vendendis equalis quantitas pecunie procuretur eidem conventui tribuenda, mandantes nichilominus eidem fratri sic mutuanti sub pena carceris, quam ipso facto incurrat, ut predictam mutuatam pecuniam recuperare studeat cum effectu.

Et quia paupertatem religiosam precipue mendicantium quedam tanto perniciosior quanto inanior curiositas permaxime dehonestat, ut qui de elymosinis vivunt cum usu vasorum de argento reficiantur, sue professionis et status immemores, idcirco omnibus et singulis fratribus dicte provincie tam conventualibus quam studentibus districtius inhibemus, quatenus vasa argentea, siphos seu tacias, gobetos vel coclearia de argento nullus de cetero apud se vel alium tenere vel habere presumat, sed infra quindenam a publicatione presentium qui habuerit penitus vendat, pecuniam inde habitam in prefata archa seu capsa communi reponat sub pena privationis ipso facto tam vocis quam ipsorum vasorum seu pretii eorundm, ultra quas penas superius pretaxatas in contemptores et transgressores huius nostre constitutionis et contentorum in ea aut alicuius eorum in ipsorum quemlibet, hac canonica monitione premissa, excommunicationis sententiam proferimus in hiis scriptis, quam eos et eorum quemlibet incurrere volumus ipso facto, absolutione nobis tantummodo reservata.

Et quia interest officii nostri ea que salutem respiciunt animarum in publicam deducere notionem, ne pretextu ignorantie illicita commitantur, ideo infrascriptam clausulam in quodam privilegio domini Alexandri pape quarti, quod in conventu nostro Senensi reperimus plumbea vera bulla bullatam, tibi presentium tenore transmittimus, fratribus tue provincie cum presentibus ordinationibus intimandam, que talis est: "Nec prior nec fratres in generali vel provinciali capitulo constituti possint alicui fratri eiusdem ordinis concedere proprium aliquod, cum sit contra substantiam ordinis, vel usufructum cuiuscumque rei mobilis vel immobilis ex testamento seu alio quocunque titulo sibi dimissum; facta vero contra hoc super hiis vel aliquo premissorum concessio habeatur irita et inanis," etc. Quam formam privilegii apostolici sequentes, omnes fratres ordinis nostri quocunque titulo vel causa aut quavis auctoritate munitos possidentes aut tenentes aliquid contra seriem privilegii supradicti, declaramus et denuntiamus licite illa possidere vel retinere non posse, et tales concessiones, privilegio ipsi contrarias, cassas et irritas atque nullas esse tenore presentium nuntiamus, districte precipiendo mandantes, ne de cetero prior aliquis provincialis aut localis seu conventus aut quisvis officialis ordinis nostri quacunque auctoritate munitus, proprium aliquod vel usufructum alicuius rei mobilis vel immobilis alicui fratri presumat concedere contra formam privilegii supradicti, nullusque aliquid tale presumat sub pena carceris temeritate propria possidere. Supradictum autem privilegium bullatum nobiscum ferre decrevimus, ut conscientias aliorum super hoc certiorare possimus.

Ceterum circa reliquarum ordinationum nostri ordinis observantiam sic per totam tibi commissam provinciam te sollicitum iugiter exhibeas et fidelem, ut ex tue sollicitudinis fructu digne apud homines laudem et apud deum premia mereraris eterna.

II.

Gregorii Arimenensis
Prioris Generalis Ordinis Fratrum Eremitarum Sancti Augustini

Litterae

A. Florence, after 17 September 1357

Infrascripte sunt constitutiones et ordinationes particulares ultra antescriptas per nos date conventui de Avinione anno domini MCCCLVII.

Frater Gregorius prior generalis etc. Religiosis viris universis et singulis fratribus conventus Avinionensis tam presentibus quam futuris conventualibus et forensibus eiusdem ordinis salutem in domino sempiternam.

Quoniam regularem vitam ducentium maxime interest ut inter ipsos iuxta apostolicum dogma omnia et recte et secundum ordinem fiant directione regiminis et vite fratrum supradicti conventus, infrascriptas ordinationes duximus statuendas.

In primis monemus et exhortamur etc., ut supra in antecedentibus constitutionibus capitulo primo.

Item ut populus istius civitatis eo numerosior et ferventior ad ecclesiam nostram conveniat ut audiat verbum dei, quo a doctoribus et peritioribus spervaverit edoceri, volumus et ordinamus ut quilibet venerabilium magistrorum in sacra theologia, cui popularis predicationis deus gratiam contulit, quolibet mense saltem semel debeat populo vulgariter predicare.

Item additionem que loquitur etc., vide in antecedentibus ordinationibus capitulo secundo.

Item propter plura inconvenientia evitanda, volumus et mandamus ut nullus venerabilium magistrorum, quando extra communem mensam reficitur, debeat aut possit aliquem fratrem, sive pro servitio sive pro societate sue refectionis, ultra duos secum tenere sine prioris pro qualibet vice obtenta licentia speciali. Possint tamen tam magistri quam lectores actu legentes invicem refici, si placuerit predictis duobus fratribus non exclusis. Famulos vero non plures sed unum tantum quilibet magistrorum teneat secundum diffinitionem capituli generalis; contrafaciens sit sua annuali provisione privatus, quam si prior vel procurator taliter contrafaciendi contulerit, de suis bonis restituere conventui teneatur.

Item ordinamus quod quilibet magistrorum sacre pagine qualibet die in prandio, quando dumtaxat infra locum reficitur, duo piceria vini puri recipiat a conventu totidemque de sero cum fuerit in loco, canapario ne plus tribuat iniugentes; de pane vero sic discrete recipiat ut de distractione non possit haberi suspitio, sic etiam de pictantiis ei volumus moderate ministrari, ut et ipse contentari rationabiliter possit et aliis murmurandi occasio subrahatur.

Item circa pictantias venerabili magistro regenti aut etiam lectori Sententiarum pro actibus fiendas scolasticis sic duximus statuendum, ut videlicet quando magister suum facit in theologia principium pro pictancia expendatur unus florenus et tantundem quando de Quolibet vel aliud solemniter disputabit; pro principio vero bachalarii legentis Sententias floreni tantummodo medietas expendatur.

Item volumus ut magistro regenti dentur singulis VII mensibus, incipiendo a kalendis octobris, libre sex candelarum de sepo vel valor ipsarum, per singulos vero sequentium mensium libre tres vel valor ipsarum. Procuratori vero ordinis pro quolibet VII mensium supradictorum libre quinque et pro quolibet quinque mensium sequentium libre tres aut valor ipsarum, prohibentes ne supradicte candele vel pecunie dentur alicui predictorum nisi pro tempore quo fuerit in conventu, nec datio ista fiat pro pluribus mensibus simul. Priori vero et cuilibet lectorum similter per singulos septem menses supradictos III libre, per singulos quinque sequentes libra una aut pretium earundem, pro tempore dumtaxat quo presens extiterit in conventu.

Item pro caligis, sutellaribus, bothis, et pro omni generaliter calciamento suo dari volumus magistro regenti quolibet anno in principio hiemis duos florenos et eodem tempore priori et cuilibet lectorum unum florenum cum dimidio.

Item magistro regenti taxamus danda pro toto anno quintalia lignorum LX et procuratori ordinis quinquaginta, secundum quod etiam fuit eis per nostrum predecessorem taxatum.

Item sicut per predecessorem nostrum prefatum taxatum fuit, ut prior conventus Avinionensis pro sua annuali provisione recipiat a conventu florenos IIII pro quolibet anno, sic et nos tenore presentium confirmamus.

Item mandamus priori qui pro tempore fuerit, quatenus pannos domini pape, qui omni anno ex parte eius fratribus amore dei donantur, ipse prior de concilio magistri regentis et lectorum conventus ac etiam procuratoris ordinis pauperioribus et magis indigentibus fratribus, tam studentibus quam conventualibus ipsius dumtaxat conventus, sic distribuere teneatur, quod qui accipiunt uno anno non recipiant alio anno immediate sequenti, et nulli plus vel minus magistrum, priorem, procuratorem ordinis vel lectorem volumus computari.

Item mandamus omnibus et singulis fratribus ipsius conventus ut quicunque habet scutellas aut alia vasa stagnea seu etiam tobaleas vel pannos aliquos pertinentes ad canipam, debeant infra tres dies a publicatione presentium restituere et assignare priori et canapario sub pena furti, cui pene subicimus ex nunc quemlibet qui huiusmodi mandati repertus fuerit esse transgressor; mandantes insuper ut post lapsum trium dierum predictorum tantum prior conventus universalem indagationem faciat diligenter, consequenter etiam districtius inhibentes sub pena premissa, quatenus nullus presumat de vasis sic restitutis aut quibuscumque stagneis dumtaxat ipsius conventus aliquod deferre ad aliquem locum preter refectorium, canipam vel coquinam nisi solus canaparius, et hoc tantum causa reparationis ipsorum vel ipsum ad vini cellerarium deferendo, de quibus vasis duabus vicibus in anno, scilicet circa festum Resurrectionis Domini et circa festum Omnium Sanctorum, teneatur ipse cellerarius priori coram procuratore conventus et duobus aliis fratribus, quos prior elegerit, distinctam reddere rationem, cogendus prorus ad sufficientem satisfactionem, si aliquod ex predictis vasis ex sua negligentia vel fraude fuerit perditum vel ammissum.

Item venerabilem magistrum regentem et lectores conventus exhortamur et monemus, ac etiam eisdem mandamus districte, quatenus circa profectum studentium diligentem curam adhibeant, continuando scilicet tam lectiones quam disputationes cottidianas et ad easdem ipsos sollicitando studentes, ex quibus, si quos adverterint negligentes et desides, faciant additionem que contra tale loquitur observari, inhibentes prefato venerabili magistro, ac etiam aliis magistris quibuscumque, ne tempore cottidianarum disputationum aliquos studentes secum in mensis detineant aut aliter occupent quominus ipsis studentes possint eiusdmodi disputationibus interesse. Declaramus insuper et statuimus, quod ex sociis cuiusquam venerabilis magistri unus tantum exemptus esse possit a debito veniendi ad chorum hiis horis et temporibus, quibus ceteri studentes venire tenentur.

Item statuto venerabilis predecessoris nostri nos conformantes, decernimus quod si plures studentes in ipso conventu de aliqua una provincia fuerint, is solus provisionem a conventu recipiat, qui prius studium occupavit, et si plures simul venerint, is tantum qui in ordine reperitur antiquior.

Item propter honestatem ordinis conservandum, volumus et mandamus per priorem inviolabiliter observari ut omnem diligentiam adhibeat, quod nulla mulier ad puteum nostrum accedat, et quod nullus secularis in refectorio commedat, nisi aliquando ex rationabili causa cum toto conventu reficeretur ibidem. Nullus etiam fratrum secularem ad cellam aliquam introducat, nisi de prioris licentia pro qualibet vice obtenta; contrafaciens per tres dies dum conventus reficitur in terra sedere cogatur, et eidem pene volumus subiacere quicumque in altera domorum seu cellarum iuxta portam loci sitarum hora aliqua commedere presumpserit seu bibere.

Item cum in nostris constitutionibus caveatur quod prior provincialis facta visitatione locorum omnium de provincia in aliquo loco non sit asiduus, ne tedio et frequentia fratrum ad eum recurrentium efficiatur alicui conventui onerosus, et hoc maxime in conventu curie propter onera multa que substinet sit vitandum, volumus et mandamus ut prior provincialis ipsius provincie non possit morari in ipso conventu plusquam per tres dies continuos pro qualibet vice qua ad dictum conventum acceserit, excepto tempore quo debeat visitare conventum, et tunc suam visitationem infra tres septimanas a die sui adventus decernimus debere finiri.

Item mandamus prior conventus ut additionem, que loquitur de fratribus forensibus debentibus solvere qualibet die conventui medium turonensem, universaliter quo ad omnes fratres tam ipsius provincie quam alterius forenses faciat inviolabiliter observari, hoc excepto, quod fratres ipsius provincie possint ea die dumtaxat qua veniunt ad conventum sine predicta sollutione manere; mandantes insuper priori, quatenus omnes fratres forenses tam solvere debentes quam non debentes in conventu residentes compellat venire ad ecclesiam, tam de die quam de nocte, illis horis exceptis quibus pro causis suis vel aliis propter que venerunt negotiis fuerint impediti.

Item quia religiosis non congruit deliciosa refectio, presenti tenore statuimus quod de cetero non ministrentur regulariter carnes reficiendis fratribus in conventu ultra quam ter in septimana in prandiis tantum, videlicet die dominico et feriis tertia atque quinta; omni vero die qua non est ieiunium

statutum ab ecclesia vel ab ordine provideatur in cena de ferculo absque
caseo; similiter etiam in prandio illis diebus quibus carnes non erunt fratribus 140
ministrande.

Item ne a predictarum ordinationum observantia possit se aliquis per
ignorantiam excusare, mandamus ut omnes ordinationes premisse in refectorio
quolibet mense legantur, ceteris ordinationibus specialiter ad istum conventum
spectantibus per predecessores nostros factis tenore presentium revocatis. 145

Item die XVII septembris misimus de Florencia nostram ordinationem
predicto conventui Avinionensi ut nullus frater ultra tres vices deberet
commedere carnes in septimana sub pena privationis vocis, quam ipso facto
contrafacientes incurrerent; delinquentes vero et vocem non habentes sint
ipso facto annuali provisione privati, infirmis dumtaxat exceptis; mandantes 150
priori dicti conventus ut ultra unam vicem delinquentes nobis debeat nuntiare.

B. Sancto Elpidio, 27 May 1358

Scripsimus fratri Iohanni provinciali provincie Marchie Anconitane litteram
de penitentiis fratrum provincie predicte fiendis in hec verba.

Discretioni tue ad maiorem cautelam fiendorum duximus infrascripta 155
annotata relinquere, que omnia et singula per obedientiam salutarem et
sub pena inobedientie nostre, quam ipso facto, si in ipsorum aliquo negligens extiteris, te sentias incurrisse, modis et temporibus in ipsis preceptis
inferius expressis in te et tuis subditis, prout te vel ipsos contingent inpreter-
misse et inviolabiliter exequeris. 160

Et primo quidem omnes et singulos infrascriptos fratres olim priores
penam quam eis, pro eo quod quadragesimam sancti Martini in suis conventibus etiam in communi servari non fecerunt, nos viva voce in presenti
provinciali capitulo publice iniunximus sustinendam, videlicet, sedendi ad
mensam nudam XV diebus continuis infra VI menses compellas penitus 165
adimplere. Nomina autem predictorum sunt hec: frater Bonifatius de Ancona,
prior olim Ancone, frater Iohannuctius de sancto Severeno, prior olim
Montemilonis, frater Matheus de Camereno, prior olim loci de Rotis, frater
Matheus de sancta Anatolia, prior olim Exii, frater Simon de Montesecuro,
prior olim Cerreti, frater Augustinus de Ausino, prior olim Ausini, frater 170
Angelus de Monte sancte Marie in Cassiano, prior olim Racaneti, frater
Iacobus de Montefortino, prior olim ibidem, frater Egidius de Macerata,
prior olim Montis Rubiani, frater Marinus de Monte Ulmi, prior olim ibidem, frater Angelus de Monte Alto, prior olim ibidem, frater Stephanus
de Pulverisio, prior olim ibidem, frater Blasius de Monte sancte Marie in 175
Georgio, prior olim Civitanove, frater Paulus de Montefortino, prior olim
in Turris Palmarum, frater Andriolus de Macerata, prior olim Montis Elperii,
frater Nicoluctius de Curinalto, prior olim ibidem, frater Floranus de Monte
Causario, prior olim ibidem, frater Lucas de sancto Genesio, prior olim
ibidem, frater Genesius de sancto Genesio, prior olim de Turris Transonis, 180
frater Nicoluctius de Fronsifronio, prior olim ibidem, frater Simon de sancto
Elpidio, prior olim ibidem, frater Iacobus de Amandula, prior olim ibidem,
frater Simon de Murro, prior olim ibidem, frater Antonius de Monte sancti

Martini, prior olim in Griptis ad mare, frater Ferrantius de Fabriano, prior olim Montis Sancti.

Consequenter vero fratres infrascriptos, pro eo quod post inhibitionem a nobis per nostras communes ordinationes factam in culcitris de plumis, vel linteaminibus de lino iacuerunt, penam in dictis nostris ordinationibus communibus contra huiusmodi transgressores appositam, sine ulla simulatione facias observare, suis enim vestimentorum provisionibus pro hoc anno ac etiam vocibus sunt privati. Nomina vero ipsorum sunt hec: frater Victor de Tollentino, prior olim in Monte sancte Marie in Cassiano, frater Matheus de sancta Anatolia, prior olim Exii, frater Iacobus de Montefortino, prior olim ibidem, frater Clemens de Urbino, frater Andreas de Monte sancte Marie in Georgio, frater Angelus de Monte sancte Marie in Georgio, frater Angelus de sancta Anatolia, frater Vannes de sancto Elpidio parvus. Si autem aliquis predictorum provisionem istius anni iam a conventu suo recepisset, cogas eundem dictam provisionem receptam infra VI menses proxime futuros ei conventui a quo recepit restituere integraliter et complete.

Insuper pecunias infrascriptas qui contra nostri ordinis constitutiones et additiones extra nostrum ordinem inventi sunt mutuasse, propter quod ipsarum constitutionum et additionum vigore eisdem mutuatis pecuniis sunt privati, ac etiam ipsas pecunias hic tibi subicimus annotatas. Frater Ieronimus de Fabriano mutuavit magistrato homini florenum I. Item duabus aliis personis secularibus anconitanos II. Item cuidam consobrine sue anconitanos VIII. Item Lallus de Montefortino anconitanos XII. Frater Vitus de Morte florenos II. Frater Antonius de sancto Severino florenos V. Frater Iacobus de sancto Severino libras V, solidos XIII. Igitur supradictas pecunias a supradictis fratribus infra mensem unum proxime futurum exigens, conventibus ad quos ipsorum bona devolvi debent post mortem, liberas applicabis. Fratres autem Mathiolum de Turri Palmarum, Ferrantinum de Fabriano et Simonem de Murro, pro eo quod non diffiniti ad populum predicare presumpserunt, XV diebus infra VI menses ad terram sedentes facias penitere.

Volumus etiam et tibi districte precipimus, quatenus in tua visitatione diligenter perscruteris contra fratres infrascriptos nobis delatos et non presentes de articulis infrascriptis. Frater Ambrosius de Fabriano delatus est nobis quod percussit fratrem Mathiolum de Pesaurio graviter in maxilla. Item quod percussit fratrem Matheum de Fronsifronio similiter in maxilla. Frater Nuçconus de Cingulo delatus est nobis, primo quod vendidit unam molam florenis VII vel circa. Item quod recepit a quodam sacerdote anconitanos LXXII. Item quod recepit de quodam testamento libras XIIII vel circa, que omnia spectant ad conventum Montis Milonis, de quibus nullam resignationem aut rationem reddidit conventui memorato. Frater Franciscus de Cingulo delatus est nobis, primo quod nescit competenter legere. Item quod recepit sacros ordines sine debita licentia. Frater Cola de Macerata delatus est nobis quod iacuit in culcitra et linteaminibus post inhibitionem a nobis generaliter promulgatam. Conventus Urbini delatus est nobis quod multas possessiones vendidit debita licentia non obtenta. Item quod de predictis possessionibus venditis non est reddita ratio competens in conventu. Frater Thomasuctius de sancta Victoria nunc apostata delatus est nobis quod proiecit malitiose fratrem Matheum de sancta Victoria de alto muro deorsum, propter quod dictus frater Matheus confractus fuit usque ad articulum mortis. Frater Bonaventura de Murro de Vallia nunc apostata delatus est nobis quod in sua apostasia nostrum ordinem multipliciter scandalizat. Frater Vitus de Firmo delatus est nobis quod non bene fideliter pertractavit bona conventus Firmi, quando dicta bona habuit pertractare. Frater Nicolaus de Monte sancte Marie in Georgio delatus est nobis quod sit infamis graviter inter fratres et seculares dicte terre, quia habuerit duas filias ex quadam vidua male fame. Frater Stephanus de Pulverisio delatus est nobis quod sit infamis de ludo taxillorum. Item quod sit blasphemator dei et sanctorum. Supradicta omnia diligenter indagabis, et ea secundum quod postulat iuris ordo, etiam data ubi danda foret purgatione canonica fideliter et attente, prout de te bene speramus, fine debito terminabis.

C. Bologna, 1 October 1358

Dicta die scripsimus fratribus Iohanni de Monte Rodono et Cicho de Aversa etc. sic.

Quamvis non possimus in nostra propria persona singulas dicti ordinis provincias ut cupimus et debemus [visitare], nolumus tamen ut ipse provincie ad quas accedere non valemus reformatione et visitatione atque correctione debitis, tam in capite quam in membris totaliter defraudentur. Et ideo vos, de quorum probitate, zelo atque prudentia, gerimus in domino fiduciam pleniorem visitatores facimus in provincia Apulee ordinis memorati dantes vobis auctoritatem et potestatem in dicta provincia et fratribus et conventibus singulis provincie supradicte inquirendi, visitandi tam in capite quam in membris atque cognoscendi tam in causis criminalibus, civilibus, spiritualibus atque temporalibus semel et pluries quotiens vobis visum fuerit opportunum, tam ex officio quam ad alterius denuntiationem vel querellam necnon etiam a fratribus dicte provincie iuramenta exigendi, per excommunicationis sententiam et alia opportuna remedia compellendi, corrigendi, conformandi, officiales etiam quoscumque lectores et studentes, ac priorem provincialem a suis officiis, lectoriis et studiis absolvendi, fratres de conventibus ad vos vocandi, de conventu ad conventum removendi atque alibi collocandi, et alia omnia et singula faciendi et exercendi in provincia et fratribus supradictis, que ad officium visitatoris pertinere noscuntur, ad correctionem fratrum provincie memorate secundum nostri ordinis instituta. Mandantes vobis in meritum obedientie salutaris, quatenus infra mensem a receptione presentium computandum iter accipere debeatis ad visitationis officium, vobis in provincia memorata commissum fideliter exequendum, iter sic inceptum consequenter postea prosequendo, quam visitationem vestram in dicta provincia vos volumus terminasse infra terminum trium mensium postquam provinciam ingressi eritis prelibatum, ad provinciam vestram evestigio reversuri. Volentes ut si quid notabile in dicta provincia facietis, nobis significare per vestras litteras debeatis.

275 Ceterum tenore presentium fratribus tam provinciali priori quam aliis universis provincie Apulee memorate, precipimus per obedientiam salutarem, quatenus vos caritative et reverenter ut visitatores nostros recipiant et pertractent et vobis et iusionibus vestris atque statutis tamquam nobis et nostris satagant inviolabiliter obedire velut obedientie et religionis filii et devoti.
280 Declarantes tenore presentium ut dicta provincia Apulee vobis in expensis necessariis tam in eundo, stando, quam etiam redeundo redeundo debeat integraliter providere.

APPENDIX F

JORDANI DE QUEDLINBURG

*Meditationum de Passione Christi Momentum
et Expositio Arboris eius*

This appendix is intended to provide documentation for Chapter Five that could not have been effectively presented in the footnotes. In the notes I have referred the reader to the appendix, citing the number of the appendix to be consulted for the requisite documentation. There are three parts in total. The first section of the appendix contains textual comparisons of Jordan's *Meditationes de Passione Christi* with Ludolph of Saxony's *Vita Christi* and Ulrich Pinder's *Speculum Passionis*. The text of article 17 of Jordan's *Meditationes* comprises the second section of the appendix, and that of the *Expositio Arboris* from Jordan's *Expositio Orationis Dominice* the third. I have standardized the orthography throughout. Source references to the texts presented are given in the appendix itself.

Medieval discussions of the Passion appear in many different forms. In Chapter Five I have used several different terms to refer to various types of 'Passion-talk', brief definitions of which, I hope, will contribute to clarity. A. *Passion Discourse*. I use Passion discourse in a non-technical sense to refer to all written material in which mention of the Passion is made in some form. This can include formal treatises on the Passion, as well as simple references to the Passion. B. *Passion Text*. The Passion text refers to the harmonized Gospel accounts of the Passion. This does not include the interpretations of that text, nor the expanded versions of that text drawn from the prophetic literature of the Hebrew Bible. In this light, *the* Passion text is used synonymously with *the* Passion narrative. C. *The Classic Text of the Passion*. The classic text of the Passion is used to refer to the standard expanded version of the Passion text, whereby the details of the Gospel accounts were filled-in based primarily on the Psalms and Isaiah. The classic text then became the basis for most treatments, expositions, interpretations, discussions, and artistic representations of the Passion. D. *Passion Narratives*. Passion narratives refer to narrative accounts of the Passion in their particular manifestation. This includes the individual narratives of the Gospels, as distinct from their harmonization, which I refer to as the Passion text, or as *the* Passion narrative. Passion narratives are not, however, limited to the individual narratives of the four Gospels. Any narrated account of the Passion is labeled a Passion narrative, such as, for example, the account given in Ludolph of Saxony's *Vita Christi*. In short, Passion narratives encompass all textualizations of the classic text of the Passion. E. *The Cultural Text of the Passion*. The cultural text of the Passion refers to all representations of Christ's Passion, written, performed, painted or sculpted, including meditations on the Passion, visions of the Passion, and discussions of the 'para-Passion', meaning, the eucharist, Mary's relationship to the Passion, the equating of Christ's birth with his Passion (*e.g.*: the first blood Christ shed for human kind is traditionally considered to have been at his circumcision; in the later Middle Ages, the birth of Christ and his Passion were intimately related), discussion of the cross, and the like. Thus I use the cultural text of the Passion as the broadest, most all-encompassing category. Whereas Passion discourse refers to all written mentions of the Passion, the cultural text of the Passion refers to all representations and manifestations of the Passion in medieval culture, whether they be that of formal theological treatises, or the magical uses of the Host to the extent that it implies the crucified body of Christ. F. *Imago Passionis*. The *imago Passionis* refers to the mental image of the Passion that formed and was formed by the cultural text. It also refers to the mental image of the Passion upon which textualizations of the classic text in Passion narratives were based. G. *Extra-Textual Dimensions of the Passion*. The extra-textual dimensions of the Passion refers to the historical crucifixion as an event, and believers' experience of that historical event in their present.

These seven terms then are used to discuss various approaches to and aspects of medieval treatments of the Passion. Although they are distinct, they are all inter-related. An account of a vision of the Passion, for example, is a Passion discourse that is a textualization of an extra-textual dimension(s) of the Passion, based upon the cultural text as related to the classic text and a given *imago Passionis*, to which then the vision contributes reciprocally, as well as to the cultural text. The place and function of the Passion in medieval culture is a morassic labyrinth. I have introduced these terms and distinctions in hope of being better able thereby to cut a path through the labyrinth that will allow for some of its structure to become apparent without becoming in the process overly bogged down or stuck in the morass itself.

This is what I tried to achieve in Chapter Five.

I. Textual Traditions

Pinder's *Speculum Passionis*	Jordan's *Meditationes*	Ludolph's *Vita Christi*
		Nunc secundum Hieronymum, aspergamus de sanguine librum nostrum... iam enim instat ut ad Passionem Domini veniamus, quam et ex affectu inspicere, et in effectu imitari debemus, juxta illud Exodi:
Inspice et fac secundum exemplar quod tibi monstratum est in monte. Exodi XXV.	*Inspice et fac secundum exemplar quod tibi in monte monstratum est,* Exodi XXV.	*Inspice et fac secundum exemplar quod tibi in monte monstratum est.*

Christus etsi persepe mons in scriptura dicatur ratione tamen summitatis excellentissime sue perfectionis, maxime in cruce exaltatus mons dicitur ratione summitatis meriti sue sacratissime passionis. In hoc ergo monte Christo videlicet crucifixo monstratum est nobis hodie exemplar, idest speculum diligenter inspiciendum et efficaciter imitandum. Non enim sufficit Christiano Christum passum inspicere, nam et hoc fecerunt Iudei et gentiles sui crucifixores. Sed exigitur etiam secundum exemplar monstratum operari et facere. Et hoc est quod indicitur cuilibet fideli in propositis verbis: Inspice videlicet et fac secundum exemplar dominice passionis, ipsam tibi per intimam compassionem visceraliter incorporando. Et fac secundum exemplar ipsum efficaciter imitando. Quorum utrumque nos docet beatus Petrus I Petri 5, *Christus* inquiens *passus est pro nobis.* Ecce primum quod est diligenter cordis oculo inspiciendum, nobis relinquens exemplum ut sequamur vestigia eius. Ecce secundum quod est efficaciter in facto imitandum. De his igitur duobus tota nostra versabitur consideratio.

Pinder *SP* (ed. Nürnberg, 1507), fol. 1ra.

Etsi Christus ubique in scriptura dicatur mons ratione summitatis sue excellentissime perfectionis, maxime tamen exaltatus in cruce mons dicitur ratione sublimitatis meriti sue sacratissime passionis. In hoc ergo monte Christo videlicet crucifixo hodie monstratum est exemplar diligenter inspiciendum et efficaciter imitandum. Non enim sufficit Christiano Christum passum inspicere, nam et hoc fecerunt Iudei et gentiles sui crucifixores, sed exigitur etiam secundum exemplar monstratum operari et facere. Et hoc est quod dicitur cuilibet fideli in verbis prepositis: Inspice et fac secundum exemplar etc, quasi dicit, Inspice exemplar dominice passionis ipsam tibi per intimam conpassionem hodie visceraliter incorporando. Et fac secundum exemplar ipsum efficaciter imitando. Et utrumque horum docet beatus Petrus Prime Petri 5, *Christus* inquam *pro nobis passus est.* Ecce primum quod est diligenter cordis occulo inspiciendum, vobis relinquens exemplum ut sequamini vestigia eius. Ecce secundum, quod esse efficaciter in facto imitandum. Igitur circa hec duo versabitur nostra consideratio in toto processu istius beate passionis . . .

Jor. *Med.* Prol., fol. 1ra.

Christus enim est tanquam liber exemplaris ad cuius exemplar totam vitam nostram ducere et corrigere debemus; etsi Christus saepius in Scriptura dicatur mons, ratione summitatis sive excellentissimae perfectionis, maxime tamen exaltatus in cruce mons dicitur ratione sublimitatis meriti suae sacratissimae Passionis. In hoc ergo monte, Christo scilicet crucifixo, monstratum est nobis exemplar diligenter inspiciendum et efficaciter imitandum. Non enim sufficit Christiano Christum passum inspicere, nam et hoc fecerunt Judaei et Gentiles sui crucifixores, sed exigitur etiam secundum exemplar monstratum operari et facere. Et hoc est quod indicitur cuilibet fideli in verbis propositis: *Inspice et fac.* Quasi diceret: Inspice exemplar Dominicae Passionis ipsam tibi per intimam compassionem visceraliter incorporando, et fac secundum illud exemplar, ipsum efficaciter imitando. Et utrumque horum docet Petrus: *Christus*, inquit, *pro nobis passus est*, ecce primum, quod est diligenter cordis oculo inspiciendum; *vobis reliquens exemplum, ut sequamini vestigia ejus*, ecce secundum, quod est efficaciter in facto imitandum.

VC II.51 (III.374–375).

Pinder's *Speculum Passionis*

Incipiendo ipsam nunc ab eo loco ubi Iohanes Christi passionem inchoat, quam et in sexaginta quinque articulos dividemus, in quibus tunc Christus aliquod notabiliter passus fuit, cum annexis sibi documentis atque orationibus, que quidem orationes cuiuscumque articuli ad duo nobis poterunt seruire: ad consummariam scilicet recollectionem eorum que tam sub illo articulo quam ipsius documento continentur; et ad legentium puta devotionem: que tunc ut magis augeatur omnia que Christus passus est ita homini debent esse cordi ac gratuita ac si pro ipsius solummodo salutari ea passus sit. Et propter hanc causam etiam orationes iste omnes in singulari numero sunt formate, ut infra patebit.

Pinder *SP* II (ed. Nürnberg, 1507), fol. 21rb.

Jordan's *Meditationes*

Incipiemus ab eo loco ubi Johannes Christi passionem inchoat, omnium nichilominus quatuor evangelistarum dictis de eadem de passione simul adfierem historie contexendo. Nec est intentionis mee circa singula gesta historie passionis in moralis, sed circa illa precipue puncta in quibus singulis Christus aliquid notabiliter passus fuit, que omnia ad lxv articulos reduncuntur... Ut autem de eisdem articulis planior evidentia habeatur cuilibet articulo premittitur unum theoreuma per modum orationis in quo utrumque premissorum, scilicet tam articulus passionis quam exemplar imitationis, substantialiter implicantur. Et hec theoreumata deserviunt nobis ad duo, videlicet ad summariam recollectionem illorum que sub illo articulo continentur... Et ut in recolendo istos articulos dominice passionis devotio magis augeatur omnia que Christus passus est, ita homini debent esse accepta et grata ac si pro ipsius salute solum modo ea sit passus.

Jor. *Med.* Prol., fol. 1ra–2vb.

A final comparison taken from the second article according to Jordan and Pinder, or the third in Ludolph's text, should suffice as evidence that Pinder was indeed drawing from Jordan's text itself, rather than simply via Ludolph.

Pinder's *Speculum Passionis*

Documenta.

Ex hoc articulo habentur tria documenta salutifera. Nam ex primo dicto, scilicet apparitionis instruimur quod nobis assistunt sancti angeli orantibus confortantibus nos in oratione.

Vnde dicitur in psalmo. Prevenerunt coniuncti psal-

Jordan's *Meditationes*

Documenta.

Ex isto articulo habentur tria documenta salutifera. Nam ex primo dicto instruimur quod sancti angeli assistunt nobis orantibus comfortantes nos in oratione. Et ideo dictum est, quod non propter se, sed propter nos et nobis orans, dominus comfortatus est ab angelo. Unde Bernar-

Ludolph's *Vita Christi*

Ex isto articulo, qui est sudoris sanguinei defluxio, habetur documentum salutiferum, quod et nos in oratione debemus ita ess intenti et fervidi, ut ex vehementia intentionis, et fervore devotionis, sudemus quasi sanguinem per configurationem Passionis Christi, et ardorem dilec-

lentibus. Et ibi: In conspectu angelorum psallam tibi.

Ex secundo vero dicto trahitur documentum quod nos in agonya vel quacumque necessitate ad orationem fugere debeamus. Et quanto necessitas maior, tanto oratio debet esse prolixior. Unde ad hoc docendum: Dominus factus in agonya prolixius orabat. Ex tertio dicto quod est principale illius articuli habetur documentum: quod nos in oratione debemus esse adeo intenti atque fervidi ut ex vehementia intentionis et fervore devotionis sudemus quasi sanguinem per configurationem passionis Christi et ardorem dilectionis ad deum. Unde glosa Romanos viii, dicit: quod charitas que in nobis per spiritum sanctum facta est ipsa gemit, ipsa orat contra quam aures cladere non novit qui eam dedit Immo etiam ipsa charitas gemit et orat usque ad guttas sanguinis quod fit dum quis in toto corde devotio accenditur quod pro amore dei si oporteret sanguinem suum fundere non veretur. Et ideo sic vel consilimi modo oret.

Pinder *SP* II (ed. Nürnberg, 1507), fol. 23vb.

dus super Canticum: Angeli psallentibus dignanter admisceri solent. Unde Ps. Prevenerunt principes coniuncti psallentibus. Et alibi, In conspectu angelorum psallam tibi . . .

Ex secundo vero dicto trahitur documentum, quod nos in agonya vel quacunque necessitate constituti, debemus confugere ad orationem. Et quanto neccessitas maior, tanto oratio debet prolixior. Unde ad hoc docendum: Dominus factus in agonya prolixius orabat. Ex tertio autem dicto, quod est principale istius articuli, habetur documentum quod et nos in oratione debemus ita esse intenti et fervidi ex vehementia intentionis et fervore devotionis sudemus quasi sanguinem per configurationem passionis Christi et ardorem dilectionis ad deum. Unde Glossa Romanos 8 dicit, quod caritas que in nobis per spiritum sanctum facta est in ipsa gemit, ipsa orat, contra quam aures cladere non novit qui eam dedit immo etiam ipsa caritas gemit et orarat usque ad guttas sanguinis quod fit dum quis orans in tanto ardore devotionis accenditur quod pro amore dei si oportet sanguinem suum fundere non veretur.

Jor. *Med.* art. 2, 5^{rb-va}.

tionis ad Deum. Quod fit, dum quis orans in tanto ardore devotionis accenditur, quod pro amore Dei, si oportet, sanguinem suum fundere non veretur; et talis sic incalescit spiritu, ut totus sanguis in corpore quasi spiritui alludens pronum et promptum se exhibeat ad exsudandum: quia vero caro ex infirmate sua tam vehementem ardorem devotionis suffere non praevalet, ideo sudorem quasi sanguinem evaporat vel saltem pro sanguine ardentes lacrymas per oculos effundat. Et quoniam nos tam vigorosam orationem effundere non valemus, adiungamus orationem nostram orationi Christi, qui est advocatus noster apud Patrem et ipse interpellat pro nobis, imo orat nobiscum. Et illa oratio est efficacissima, et Deo Patri accepta, quae scilicet in unione orationis Christi offertur. Quam efficaces etiam sint lacrymae orationis, et maxime illae quae in recordatione Passionis Christi funduntur, patet ex quadam revelatione facta cuidam personae, de qua legitur quod apparens ei Dominus in spiritu ait: Si quis in recordatione meae Passionis lacrymas cum devotione funderit, suscipere volo ac si ipse pro me passus sit.

VC II.59,11 (III.478).

Pinder nevertheless follows Ludolph in placing the prayers of each article at the end of the article, rather than at the beginning as did Jordan. Yet even here Pinder followed the text of Jordan far more closely than Ludolph, as the example from the second article illustrates:

Pinder's *Speculum Passionis*	Jordan's *Meditationes*	Ludolph's *Vita Christi*
Oratio	Theorema	
Domine Iesu christe fili dei vivi qui in oratione positus ab angelo confortari voluisti, factusque in agonya guttas sanguinis mirabiliter sudasti, da mihi per virtutem orationis tue ut oranti mihi semper assistat angelus tuus sanctus qui me confortans quatenus recordatione passionis tue dulcedine soporatus lachrymarum guttas pro sanguine in conspectu tuo merear dulciter desudare. Pinder *SP* II (ed. Nürnberg, 1507), fol. 23vb.	Iesu, qui in oratione positus ab angelo confortari voluisti, factusque in agonya guttas sanguinis mirabiliter desudasti, da mihi per virtutem orationis tue ut oranti mihi semper assistat angelus tuus sanctus confortans quatenus recordatione passionis tue spiritus meus devotionis fervore accensus amorisque tui dulcedine saporatus lacrimarum guttas pro sanguine in conspectu tuo mereatur dulciter desudare. Jor. *Med.* art. 2, fol. 4rb.	O pie Jesu, qui factus in agonia guttas sanguinis mirabiliter desudasti, da mihi ut recordatione tuae Passionis accensus, lacrymarum guttas, pro sanguine in conspectu tuo merear dulciter desudare. *VC* II.59,11 (III.478)

APPENDIX F 829

II.

Jordani de Quedlinburg, *Meditationes de Passione Christi*, art. 17, Basel, UB MS B.V. 26, fol. 14vb–15rb.

THEOREMA

Iesu, qui immundis Iudeorum sputis pulchrimam faciem tuam maculari 5
voluisti, da michi tue imaginis faciem in me nunquam meis sordidis actibus
autem cogitationibus inquinare.

Articulus XVII

Septimus decimus articulus est consputio faciei. Cum enim Iudei omnes
acclamarent eum *reum* esse *mortis*,[1] *tunc expuerunt in faciem eius*.[2] //fol.15ra// 10
Proprium enim est Iudeorum conspuere in faciem eius quem abiciebant, et
hoc in magnum vituperium et despectum. Unde etiam in lege si pater
alicuius puelle spuisset in faciem eius, ita abhominabilis reddebatur quod
ad minus septem diebus oportebat eam esse sequistratam a communione
hominum, ut habetur Deuteronimii 25.[3] Quid enim turpius, quid despec- 15
tius quid ignominiosius et vituperiosius quam exspui in faciem et maxime
in illam faciem speciosissimam in quam desiderant angeli prospicere que
plena est gratiarum et desiderata cunctis gentibus que salus est aspicien-
tium? O quam ceca emulatio infelicium Iudeorum qui non exhorruerunt
turpissimis sputis suis maculare et turpare tam amabilem faciem. Et non 20
tantum simplicibus sputis salive, sed verisimile est quod extra actiones suas
fetidissimas in faciem eius proiecerunt. Unde Matheus non dicit *spuerunt* sed
exspuerunt quasi excitando spuerunt. Et sic illa facies benedicta facta est ita
abhorriabilis quasi esset leprosa exsputis et verberibus, que ei in faciem
dederunt. Ut sequitur, unde ad impletum est in eo illud Isaie 53: *Non est* 25
ei species neque decor, audivimus eum et non erat aspectus. Et nos reputavimus eum
quasi leprosum, percussum a deo et humilitatum.[4] Et subdicit, *ipse autem vulneratus*
est propter iniquitates nostras attritus est propter scelera nostra.[5]

DOCUMENTA

Ex hoc articulo sumuntur duo documenta. PRIMUM est, quod nos diligen- 30
ter caveamus ne et nos unquam cum iudeis Christi faciem conspuamus.

---

[1] Mt. 26:66.
[2] Mt. 26:67.
[3] *Cf.* Dt. 25:9.
[4] Is. 53:2–4.
[5] Is. 53:5.

Quod fit quam ad presens quadrupliciter: primo namque secundum Hieronimum, faciem Christi conspuunt qui conscientiam suam //fol.15rb// fedis cogitationibus et actionibus polluunt. Quia enim Christus conscientiam suam
35 sanctam inhabitat in quam dei facies, id est imago, relucet. Hinc est, quod quicumque conscientiam suam peccatis polluit, quasi sputum in Christi faciem proicit. Et ideo dicit Hieronimus: Quod dominus noster in faciem suam conspui voluit, ut nos lavaret.[6] Secundo, secundum Augustinum: Illi in faciem Christi exspuunt, qui presentiam gratie eius execrandis verbis ex
40 interna cece mentis insania conceptis respuunt et eum in carne venisse negant.[7] Tertio, secundum Gregorium, faciem Christi conspuunt qui iustos et sanctos in presenti vita contumeliis afficiunt.[8] Unde Iob 30: faciem meam conspuere non verentur,[9] ubi dicit Gregorius: faciem eius conspuere, est iustos et sanctos etiam in presentia confutare, et in eorum contumelias fluxa
45 verba quasi fluentes salivas mittere.[10] Quarto potest dici, quod ad litteram Christum in faciem illi conspuunt, qui eucharistiam indigne sumunt. Quicumque enim polluta conscientia corpus Christi in os suum accipiunt, hii saliva sua peccato infecta sacramentum contingunt, malefaciunt et deglutiunt; ac per hoc quid aliud isti faciunt quam quod in faciem Christi con-
50 spuunt? Ut etiam de hiis indigne communicantibus intelligatur verbum pre alligatum, Iob: faciem meam conspuere non verentur. Item quasi in faciem Christi conspuunt qui prelatos suos contempnunt.

SECUNDUM documentum est, secundum Chrysostomum, ut nos ista sputa turpissima et alia facta exprobrabilia passionis Christi nobis ad magnam
55 gloriam reputemus.[11] Quia ut dicit Chrysostomus super Mattheum: Attende quod Evangelista //fol.15va// cum summa diligentia ea que universaliter esse exprobratissiam exponit vel ommittens autem verecundias sed gloriam existimans maximam dominatorem orbis terrarum pro nobis talia sustinere, hic nostre menti inscribamus et in hiis gloriemur. Etsique istud documen-
60 tum possit referri ad singula puncta dominice passionis precipue tamen ad istud quod sic exprobratissimum fuit.

CONFORMATIO

Ad conformandum se huic articulo, formet homo in mente sua Christum tam horribiliter sputis in facie decrepatum et regratietur sibi pro magna
65 gloria nostra. Recogitet etiam quotiens ipse faciem illam speciosissimam in conscientia sua polluit. Item quotiens indigne communicando sputi sui contactu Christum sordidaverunt, vel aliter.

---

[6] Cf. Hier. In Is.14 (590,15–20).
[7] Aug. quaest.evang. I, 44 (34,2–35,6).
[8] Greg.M. moral. 20,19,45 (1036,6–10).
[9] Iob 30:10.
[10] Greg.M. moral. 20,19,45 (1036,6–10).
[11] Chrysost. hom. in Matth. 85 (757).

III.

Jordani de Quedlinburg, *Expositionis Orationis Dominice Expositio Arboris*. Berlin, StB MS theol. lat. qu. 175, fols. 88ra–89vb.

Expositio Arboris

Ut autem exclusio vitiorum et introductio virtutum, donorum, beatitudinum et fructuum per singulas petitiones secundum adaptationes premissas //fol. 88rb// lucide et oculatim etiam rudibus et simplicibus patefiant, omnia hec in unam arborem redigere decrevi.

Ad cuius arboris notitiam pleniorem possumus dicere quod hec est arbor illa mystica, quam vidit rex Nabuchodonosor, ut legitur Danielis 4: *Videbam*, inquit, *et ecce arbor in medio terre; arbor fortis et proceritas eius contingens celum, aspectus eius usque ad terminum universe terre et folia eius pulcherrima et fructus eius nimius et esca universorum in ea. Subter eam habitabant animalia et bestie et in ramis eius conversabantur volucres celi.*[12] Arbor ista est oratio dominica ex ipso ore domini procreata, et ideo fortis est utpote ab ipsa invincibili veritate producta et plantata, ac in ipso etiam firmissime radicata. Hec arbor stare dicitur in medio terre, id est, in corde humano; cor enim medium <est> hominis. <Et> nempe non sufficit hanc orationem dicere ore nisi et intentio versetur in corde, iuxta illud <prime> Corinthiorum 14: *Psallam spiritu, psallam et mente.*[13] *Proceritas eius usque ad celum pertingit* quia ipsa mentem devotam sursum sublevat et usque ad celum pertingere facit. Ad quod designandum in summitate arboris pater celestis et due stelle celi, quasi de duabus rosis radiantes depinguntur, ut per hoc proceritas orationis dominice ad celum pertingere innuatur. In duabus quidem rosis stellatis due prime exordiales huius orationis particule describuntur, que velut quedam stelle fulgidissime divini videlicet amoris et celestis desiderii in mente orantis rutilant impetrandi fiduciam excitantes, supra quas in cacumine effigies dei patris collocatur, ad ostendum quod arbor huius orationis sicut ab ipso tota incipit, sic ad ipsum tota dirigitur et per ipsum perficitur et in ipso feliciter consumatur. Et hoc sive accipiatur hic 'pater' //fol. 88va// essentialiter sive personaliter prout supra in principio est premissum. Aspectibus eius usque ad terminos universe terre, quia ab omnibus videri et intelligi seu adipisci potest, ipsa enim tante facilitatis evidentie et compendiositatis est ut quilibet cuiuscumque status homo quantumcumque rudis eam possit aspicere, discere et etiam retinere. Unde Cyprianus in libro De Oratione Dominica: "cum dominus Iesus Christus colligens doctos pariter et indoctos omni sexui atque etati precepta salutis addiderit, preceptorum suorum grande compendium fecit ut in disciplina celesti discentium memoria non laboraret, sed quod esset simplici fidei necessarium velociter disceret."[14]

---

[12] Dn. 4:7–9.
[13] I Cor. 14:15.
[14] Cypr. domin.orat. 28 (519–524); Thom.Aq. *CA* ad Matth. 6:3 (108b).

40 Et ut aspectus huius arboris evidentius appareat, sciendum est quod in ipso trunco seu stipite arboris quasdam puellarum figuras circumambeuntibus eas circulis collocavi, que sunt septem et significat septem petitiones huius sanctissime orationis dominice, que et eisdem circulis inscribuntur. Singule etiam puelle membranas singulas tenent manibus similiter dimem-
45 bratas iuxta divisionem et dearticulationem cuiuslibet petitionis quales etiam membrane ex primis exordialibus rosis procedere demonstrantur. De qualibet autem puellarum velut ex trunco arboris procedit unus ramus continens virtutes, dona, beatitudines et fructus, que per illam petitionem introducuntur. Et ex opposita parte cuiuslibet rami est alius ramus vitio-
50 rum illorum, que per illam petitionem excluduntur, non quidem coniunctus arbori sed distanter in ore bestie illud capitale vitium representantis gestatur; et ad illam bestiam cum ramo suo propellendam est unus angelus iuxta petitionem quamlibet collocatus ad designandum quod per talem petitionem tale vitium profugatur. In exordio autem cuiuslibet rami in primo
55 folio ceteris venustiori //fol. 88vb// et maiori inscribitur una de virtutibus principalibus videlicet theologica vel cardinalis. Ex qua alie virtutes in eodem ramo consequenter posite quodam ordine velut per frondes et ramuscillos sive virgas quemadmodum pictura protendit, derivantur vel ad ipsam quomodolibet reducuntur. Hoc attento quod ubicumque videris aliquid ramo
60 superductum vel quasi ipsi ramo transfixum designat quod omnia in illo ramo consequenter exinde procedentia ab illa virtute, que illi folio inscribitur, procedunt vel sub ea qualitercumque continentur, puta sicut partes subiective vel partes potentiales sive etiam integrales. Inscribuntur autem virtutes foliis ea ratione, quia sicut folia arbori deserviunt ad duo videlicet ad arboris
65 decorationem et ad fructus protectionem, sic revera virtutes hominem bonis ornant moribus et nichilominus bonorum operum fructus a temptationum ventis et caninatibus protegunt et defendunt; et hoc est quod dicitur *folia eius pulcherrima*. In singulo quoque ramorum principalium ponuntur aliqui fructus, per quos designantur fructus spiritus, qui sunt duodecim, quos enu-
70 merat Apostolus <ad> Galatas 5. Et describuntur hii fructus per ramos singulos secundum quod quilibet ipsorum fructuum cuilibet petitioni videtur convenientius adaptari. De quibus fructibus intelligendum est quod subditur, *et fructus eius nimius*, quantum ad fructus spirituales, qui in hac vita acquiri possunt, qui sunt quedam participatio et pregustatio illius supremi
75 fructus beatitudinis eterne, qui per pomum aureum in manu dei patris designatur, ad quem quidem fructum consequendum tota hec oratio principaliter ordinatur.

Ponuntur etiam et alii fructus et immaturi velut ex floribus prodeuntes et adhuc //fol. 89ra// ipsis floribus coherentes, qui significant beatitudines,
80 que sunt quidam actus ex donis spiritus sancti procedentes neque ad hoc nomen fructus obtinentes, quarum quelibet per illam petitionem introducitur in cuius ramo ipsa crescere figuratur.

Et quoniam in hac oratione non tantum simplices et mediocres, sed et perfectissimi fructum inveniunt, ideo subicitur *et esca universorum in ea*, quia
85 cuiuscumque status et conditionis homo existat, fructum ex hac arbore carpere poterit secundum exigentiam sui status: sive iustus sive peccator,

doctus sive idiota, activus sive contemplativus, incipiens, proficiens, sive perfectus. Unde dicit *Glossa* super Mattheum: "dominus noster paucis verbis res multiplices et necessarias memorie commendavit, ut sic simplicitas fidei sufficientiam sue salutis addisceret et prudentia ingeniosorum amplius profunditate mysteriorum stupesceret."[15] Unde hec oratio est quasi quidam fluvius, in quo et agnus peditat et elephas natat sicut de sacra scriptura dicit Gregorius: "hinc Isaie sermonem," inquit, "abbreviatum faciet dominus super terram, quem ita verbis abreviavit ut memoriter capi possit, ita rebus implevit ut nemo sine gratia spiritus sancti percipere possit."[16] Quod vero subditur *subter eam habitabant animalia et bestie*,[17] refertur ad vitia et peccata sive vitiorum suggestiones, quibus orantis animus distrahitur et plerumque homo ab orationis fructu deicitur et frustratur, que tamen divina gratia per ferventis orantis dona cum virtute huius sanctissime orationis propelluntur et excluduntur ac sub affectionum pedibus penitus substernuntur. Et idcirco signanter tales bestie dicuntur subter arborem, non in arbore habitare. Nec tamen in pictura arboris nostre huiusmodi bestias subter arborem sed potius a latere //fol. 89rb// iuxta collocavi, utpote quamlibet bestiam ex adverso illius petitionis quam impugnat, quod ideo feci, ut distinctius appareat quo petitio cui vitio specialiter adversetur.

Sunt autem septem bestie secundum septem vitia capitalia: Prima est Bufo, per quem superbia vel inanis gloria designatur, quia sicut Bufo ad omnem tactum se animat et indignatur, ac per hoc turgescit amplius et inflatur, sic superbus. Versus:

Est tumide rane similata superbia plane.[18]

Et quia ruta naturaliter habet fugare Bufonem hinc est quod angelus Bufoni contrarius cum ruta est depictus.

Secunda bestia est Luter, in quo avaritia designatur. Unde versus:

Ceu Luter servat cupidus res et coacervat.

Tertia bestia est Canis, in quo designatur invidia quia:

Dum canis os rodit, socium quem diligit, odit.

Unde invidi dente canino mordere dicuntur. Unde versus:

More canis rodit mordens quos invidus odit.[19]

Quarta bestia est Ursus, in quo gula significatur, quia Ursus omnia comedit indifferenter, ut dicit Aristoteles 6 *De Animalibus*.[20] Unde versus:

Cui venter deus est velut ursus gluto vorax est.

---

[15] *Cf. Glos.ord.* ad Matth. 6:8 (ed. Strassburg, 1480/81), IV.24B; (ed. Venice, 1588), V.24F.

[16] *Non invenitur.*

[17] Dn. 4:9.

[18] After extensive search, and multiple requests of experts, I have only been able to identify one of the numerous verses Jordan includes here. I would like to thank in particular C.H. Kneepkens, Walter Simon and Manfred Schulze for their help in this regard.

[19] *Cf.* Hier. epist. 50,1 (Walter nr. 6445; ThesLL III, col. 252,57*sqq*).

[20] Arist. *De historia animalium* 8,17 (600a,27–600b,24).

Quinta bestia est Ericius aut Hyricius, in quo ira designatur, quia quando aliquid persentit statim spinas suas exasperat et in globum conversus in sua se arma recolligit. Versus:

Ericii more sevis homo stulte furore.

Sexta bestia est Sus, in quo est luxuria, ex eo quod se ceno et luto ingurgitat et in locis fetidis requiescat. Versus:

Gaudet luxosus coitu quasi spurco luto sus.

Septima <bestia> est Asinus, in quo designatur accidia, quia est animal iners et pigrum. Versus est:

Ut Asellus iners omnisque boni pigri expers.

Harum siquidem bestiarum quelibet gestat in ore ramum exustum cum foliis nigris quibus vitia inscribuntur ad designandam vitiorum deformationem. //fol. 89va// Et in primo cuiuslibet rami folio contingente ipsum ramum inscribitur vitium capitale cuius filie in sequentibus foliis insignantur.

Cuilibet etiam istorum ramorum insidet una avis utpote illius vitii maiorem similitudinem gerens, verbi gratia: Ramo superbie insidet Pavo, in quo superbia designatur propter glorificationem pennarum. Unde versus:

Extollit plana quasi pavo gloria vana.

In ramo avaritie residet Monedula, pro eo quod semper congregat et furata abscondit. Unde versus:

Que cupidus cumulat ut avara Monedula servat.

In ramo invidie <sedet> Vultur, qui est avis invidiosa in tantum quod etiam invidet propriis pullis, cum impinguantur. Unde tunc eos eicit de nido nec redire permittit. Unde versus:

Vulturis invidia proprios detrudit in ima.

In ramo gule sedet Corvus, qui est avis voracitati intenta. Unde versus:

In nimiis escis quasi Corvus gluto quiescis.

In ramo ire <sedet> Pica, que est avis rixosa. Unde versus:

Ira velut Pica rixis est semper amica.

In ramo luxurie sedet Passer, qui est avis valde libidinosa in tantum etiam quod caro eius frequenter in cibum sumpta est libidinis incitativa, ut dicit Constantinus. Unde versus:

Passer ut alatur libidine non satiatur,

'ut alatur', id est, ut incipit alas habere tunc enim incipit statim luxuriari.

<In> ramo vero accidie insidet Bubo, que est parva noctua. Est enim avis onusta quidem plumis, sed gravi semper detenta pigritia, die et nocte commorans in cavernis et sepulchris. Debilis est ad volandum et alie aves de die volant in circuitu eius et deplumant ipsum; sic est de accidiosis et de pigris. Unde versus:

Sic piger in strato quasi Bubo cumbit in antro.

Hiis avibus vitiosis adversantur columbe in ramis virtutum residentes, de quibus intelligendum //fol. 89vb// est quod subicitur, *et in ramis eius conversantur volucres celi.*[21] Per istos volucres dona spiritus sancti intelliguntur. Unde in figura columbe depinguntur tenentes singule suos flores in ore, quibus

---

[21] Dn. 4:9.

ipsa dona spiritus sancti sunt inscripta ad designandum quod hec dona spiritus sancti animam spiritualibus carismatibus floridam faciunt et fecundam. In quolibet autem ramo illarum septem principalium virtutum una columba residet, quia per quamlibet petitionem unum donum introducitur quod etiam illi virtuti specialiter coaptatur.

Hanc itaque arborem plene intelligere, et eius fructus digne carpere nobis concedat huius orationis sanctissime, sapientissimus auctor Iesus Christus, qui cum patre et spiritu sancto vivit et regnat unus deus gloriosus, per infinita secula seculorum, Amen.

Explicit expositio orationis dominice, edita et lecta in scolis Erfordis per fratrem Iordanum de Quetelingburg, ordinis heremitarum sancti Augustini, anno domini M CCC xxvii cum Mattheum ordinarie lectitaret, qui etiam ad maiorem utilitatem hanc lecturam secundum numerum decalogi decem lectionibus contentam compendiose conscribere et communicare curavit pulsatus instantibus auditorum.

BIBLIOGRAPHY

I. Primary Sources

A. *Manuscripts*

Anon. *Vita* — Anonymous, *Vita Aurelii Augustini Hipponensis Episcopi*. Florence, Biblioteca Laurenziana, MS Plut. 90. Sup. 48, fol. 1^r–13^r.

Ant.Ramp. *FB* — Antonius Rampegolus, *Figure Bibliorum*. Uppsala, UB, MS C 162, fol. 1^r–117^v; Uppsala, UB, MS C 121, fol. 1^r–148^r; The Hague, Koninklijke Bibliotheek, MS 71 G 57, fol. 1^r–114^v.

Aug.Anc. *Sup.Matth.* — Augustinus de Ancona, *Lectura super Mattheum*. Munich, BStB, MS Clm. 8334, 286 fols.

Aug.Nov. *Sermo* — Augustinus Novellus de Padua, *Sermo ad clerum in honorem S. Augustini*. Basel, UB, MS A.N. IV. 13, fol. 221^r–224^r.

Hen. *Exp.* — Henricus de Frimaria, *Expositio Orationis Dominice*. Basel, UB, MS A.X. 124, fol. 182^r–192^r.

Hen.Riet. *Quest.* — Henricus Riettmüller de Liechtstal, *Questiones Quodlibetice*. Basel, UB, MS AN.IV. 13, fol. 140^r–241^v.

Herm.Sch. *Spec.* — Hermanus de Schildis, *Speculum Manuale Sacerdotum*. The Hague, Koninklijke Bibliotheek, MS 70 G 19, fol. 7^r–20^v.

Jor. *Coll.* — Jordanus de Quedlinburg, *Collectanea Augustiniana*. Paris, Bibliothèque de l'Arsenal, MS 251, fol. 1rb–104^v.

Jor. *Exp.* — Jordanus de Quedlinburg, *Expositio Orationis Dominice*. Berlin, StB, MS theol.lat.qu. 175, fol. 73ra–89vb; Munich, BStB, MS Clm. 8151, fol. 85^r–106^r.

Jor. *Med.* — Jordanus de Quedlinburg, *Meditationes de Passione Christi*. Basel, UB, MS B.V. 26, fol. 1ra–43rb.

Jor. *OJ* — Jordanus de Quedlinburg, *Opus Jor [Sermones de tempore]*. Vatican City, Biblioteca Apostolica Vaticana, MS Pal. lat. 448, 458 fols.

Jor. *OP-B* — Jordanus de Quedlinburg, *Opus Postillarum*. Berlin, StB, MS theol. fol. 133, 217 fols.

Jor. *Vita* — Jordanus de Quedlinburg, *Vita Sancti Augustini*. Paris, Bibliothèque de l'Arsenal, MS 251, fol. 54rb–70rb.

Müntzinger *Exp.* — Johannes Müntzinger, *Expositio super oratione dominica*. Basel, UB MS A. VI. 4, fol. 59^r–65^v.

Sim.C. *OEp.* — Simon of Cremona, *Opus epistolarum dominicalium*. Tübingen, UB, MS Mc 329, 125 fols.

B. *Printed Sources*

Aeg.Rom. *De eccl.pot.* — Aegidius Romanus, *De Ecclesiastica Potestate*. Ed. Richard Scholz. Weimar, 1929; reprint: Aalen, 1961. *Giles of Rome on Ecclesiastical Power*. Translated by R.W. Dyson. Suffolk, 1986.

Aeg.Rom. *Reg.Princ.* — Aegidius Romanus, *De Regimine Principum Libri III*. Rome, 1607; reprint: Darmstadt, 1967.

Aeg.Rom. *Sent.* — Aegidius Romanus, *In primum librum Sententiarum*. Venice, 1521; reprint: Frankfurt, 1968; *In secundum librum Sententiarum*. Venice, 1581; reprint: Frankfurt, 1968.

Aeg.Vit. *Lett.Fam.* — *Egidio da Viterbo, O.S.A. Lettere Familiari*, vol. II. Ed. Anna Maria Voci Roth. Rome, 1992.

Aeg.Vit. *Lett.Gen.*   Giles of Viterbo, O.S.A., *Letters as Augustinian General.* Ed. Clare O'Reilly. Rome, 1992.

Aeg.Vit. *Or.foed.*   Aegidii Viterbiensis, *Oratio habita post tertiam Concilii Lateranesis sessionem per fratrem Aegidium Viterbiensem Ordinis Eremitarum Sancti Augustini Generalem de Iulii Pontificis et Maximiliani Imperatoris foedere in templo divae Mariae de populo,* 25 November 1512. Edited with Introduction by Clare O'Reilly, in "*Maximus Caesar et Pontifex Maximus*: Giles of Viterbo Proclaims the Alliance between Emperor Maximilian I and Pope Julius II." *Aug(L)* 1972, 80–117; text, 100–112. Translated by Maria Boulding, O.S.B. in Martin, *Friar, Reformer, and Renaissance Scholar. Life and Works of Giles of Viterbo 1469–1532.* Villanova, PA, 1992, 297–308.

Aeg.Vit. *Or.Lat.*   Aegidii Viterbiensis, *Oratio prima Synodi Lateranensis habita per Egidium Viterbiensem Augustiniani Ordinis Generalem,* 3 May 1512. Edited with Introduction by Clare O'Reilly, "'Without Councils we cannot be saved.' Giles of Viterbo addresses the Fifth Lateran Council." *Aug(L)* 27 (1977), 166–204; text, 182–204. Translated by Joseph C. Schnaubelt, O.S.A., in Francis X. Martin, O.S.A., *Friar, Reformer, and Renaissance Scholar. Life and Works of Giles of Viterbo 1469–1532.* Villanova, PA, 1992, 285–296.

Albert. *Exp.*   Albertus de Padua, *Expositio Evangeliorum Dominicalium.* Venice, 1476.

Alfon. *Sent.*   Alfonsus Vargas Toletani, *In Primum Sententiarum.* Venice, 1490; reprint: New York, 1952.

Alonso *Reg.*   C. Alonso, *Bullarium Ordinis Sancti Augustini, Registra I: 1256–1362.* Rome, 1997.

Ambr.C. *Chron.*   Ambrosius de Cora, *Chronica sacratissimi Ordinis fratrum heremitarum sancti Augustini.* Rome, 1481.

Ambr.C. *Def.*   Ambrosius de Cora, *Defensorium Ordinis fratrum heremitarum Sancti Augustini.* Rome, 1481.

Ps.Anselm. *Dial.*   Ps.Anselmus, *Dialogus Beatae Mariae et Anselmi de Passione Domini.* *PL* 159,271–289.

Ps.Anselm. *Men.Cr.*   *De Mensuratione Crucis.* *PL* 159,289–302.

Ant.Ramp. *FB*   Antonius Rampegolus, *Figure Bibliorum.* Cologne, 1505; 1609; Venice, 1500

Arist.   Aristoteles, *Opera edidit Academia Regia Borussica.* Ed. Immanuel Bekker. Vol. 1–2. Berolini, 1831.

Aug. civ.   Augustinus, *De Civitate Dei.* Ed. Bernardus Dombart et Alphonsus Kalb, 2 vols.: 1. libri I–X, *CCSL* 47; 2. XI–XXII, *CCSL* 48. Turnhout, 1955.

Aug. conf.   Augustinus, *Confessiones.* Ed. Lucas Verheijen. *CCSL* 27. Turnhout, 1981; ed. James J. O'Donnell, *Augustine Confessions,* 3 vols.; vol. 1: *Introduction and Text.* Oxford, 1992; trans.: Rex Warner, *The Confessions of St. Augustine.* New York, 1963.

Aug. c.Maximin.   Augustinus, *Contra Maximinum Arianorum episcopum.* *PL* 42,743–814.

Aug. corrept.   Augustinus, *De Correptione et Gratia.* *PL* 44,915–946.

Aug. de serm.dom.   Augustinus, *De Sermone Domini in Monte.* Ed. Almut Mutzenbecher. *CCSL* 35. Turnhout, 1967.

Aug. persev.   Augustinus, *De dono perseverantie.* *PL* 45,993–1036.

Aug. enchir.   Augustinus, *Enchiridion ad Laurentium.* Ed. E. Evans. *CCSL* 46.21–114. Turnhout, 1969.

Aug. epist.   Augustinus, *Epistolae.* Ed. Al. Goldbacher. *CSEL* 44. Lipsiae, 1904.

Aug. ieiun.   Augustinus, *De utilitate ieiunii.* Ed. S.D. Ruegg. *CCSL* 46.225–241. Turnhout, 1969.

Aug. in evang. Ioh.	Augustinus, *Tractatus in Iohannis Evangelium*. Ed. Augustino Mayer. *CCSL* 36. Turnhout, 1954.
Aug. in psalm.	Augustinus, *Enarrationes in Psalmos*. Ed. E. Eligius Dekkers et Johannes Fraipont. 3 vols.: 1. I-L, *CCSL* 38; 2. LI-C, *CCSL* 39; 3. CI-CL, *CCSL* 40. Turnhout, 1956.
Aug. lib.arb.	Augustinus, *De Libero Arbitrio*. Ed. W.M. Green. *CCSL* 29.205–321. Turnhout, 1970.
Aug. quaest.evang.	Augustinus, *Quaestiones Evangeliorum*. Ed. Almut Mutzenbecher. *CCSL* 44B. Turhout, 1980.
Aug. retract.	Augustinus, *Retractationes*. Ed. Almut Mutzenbecher. *CCSL* 57. Turnhout, 1984.
Aug. serm.	Augustinus, *Sermones*, I-CCCXL *PL* 38; CCCXLI-CCCXCVI *PL* 39,1493–1748.
Aug. trin.	Augustinus, *De Trinitate*. Ed. W.J. Mountain with Fr. Glorie. 2 vols.: 1. I-XII, *CCSL* 50; 2. XIII-XV, *CCSL* 50A. Turnhout, 1968.
Ps.Aug. cog.vit.	Ps.Augustinus, *De Cognitione Verae Vitae*. *PL* 40,1005–1032.
Ps.Aug. erem.	Ps.Augustinus, *Sermones ad fratres in eremo*. Jor. Coll., fol. 3ra–48va; *PL* 40,1233–1358.
Ps.Aug. man.	Ps.Augustinus, *Manuale*. *PL* 40,951–968.
Aug.Anc. *De dupl.pot.*	Augustinus de Ancona, *Tractatus de Duplici Potestate Prelatorum et Laicorum*. Ed. Richard Scholz. In R. Scholz, *Die Publizistik zur Zeit Philipps des Schönen und Bonifaz' VIII*. Kirchenrechtliche Abhandlungen 6/8 (Stuttgart, 1903), 486–501.
Aug.Anc. *De pot.coll.*	Augustinus de Ancona, *De Potestate Collegii Mortuo Papa*. Ed. Richard Scholz. In R. Scholz, *Die Publizistik zur Zeit Philipps des Schönen und Bonifaz' VIII*. Kirchenrechtliche Abhandlungen 6/8 (Stuttgart, 1903), 501–508.
Aug.Anc. *Summa*	Augustinus de Ancona, *Summa de Potestate Ecclesiastica*. Rome, 1479.
Bacon *Mult.Spec.*	David C. Lindberg, *Roger Bacon's Philosophy of Nature. A Critical Edition, with English Translation, Introduction, and Notes, of* De Multiplicatione specierum *and* De speculis comburentibus. Oxford, 1983.
Barth.Arn. *Resp.*	*Bartholomaei Arnoldi de Usingen O.S.A. Responsio contra Apologiam Philippi Melanchthonis*, ed. Primoz Simoniti, Cassiciacum, Supplement 7. Würzburg, 1978.
Ps.Beda *Med.*	Ps.Beda, *Meditationes Passionis Christi per septem diei horas Libellus*. *PL* 94,561–568.
Bern. *Opera*	*Sancti Bernardi Opera*. Ed. Jean Leclercq, C.H. Talbot, N.M. Rochais. 8 vols., Editiones Cistercienses. Rome, 1957–1977.
Ps.Bern. *Lam.*	Ps.Bernardus, *Lamentatio in Passionem Christi*. *PL* 184,769–772.
Ps.Bern. *Med.*	Ps.Bernardus, *Meditatio in Passionem et Resurrectionem Domini*. *PL* 184,741–768.
Ps.Bern. *Vit.Myst.*	Ps.Bernardus, *Vitis Mystica seu Tractatus de Passione Domini*. *PL* 184,635–740.
Bert. *KVA*	*Kaiser, Volk und Avignon. Ausgewählte Quellen zur antikurialen Bewegung in Deutschland in der ersten Hälfte des 14. Jahrhunderts*. Edited and translated by Otto Berthold, together with Karl Czok and Walter Hofmann. Darmstadt, 1960.
Biel *Exp.*	Gabrielis Biel, *Canonis Missae Expositio*. Ed. William J. Courtenay and Heiko A. Oberman. 5 vols. *VIEG* 31–34, 79. Wiesbaden, 1963–1976.
Bruno *In Cant.*	Bruno of Segni, *Expositio in Cantica Canticorum*. *PL* 164,1233–1288.

Bruno *In Ex.*	Bruno of Segni, *Expositio in Exodum*. *PL* 164,233–378.
Bruno *In Luc.*	Bruno of Segni, *Commentarium in Lucam*. *PL* 165,333–452.
Bruno *In Matth.*	Bruno of Segni, *Commentarium in Mattheum*. *PL* 165,63–314.
Bruno *Lib.Sent.*	Bruno of Segni, *Libri Sententiarum*. *PL* 165,875–1078.
Bruno *Resp.*	Bruno of Segni, *Responsio de statu ecclesiae*. *PL* 165,1121–1156.
Cassian. inst.	Cassianus, *De Coenobiorum Institutis*. Ed. Michael Petschenig. *CSEL* 17.1–231. Prague, 1887.
Cassian. coll.pat.	Cassianus, *Collationes Patrum*. *PL* 49,477–1328.
CDP	*Codex Diplomaticus Ordinis Eremitarum Sancti Augustini Papiae*. Vol. 1. Ed. R. Maiocchi and N. Casacca. Pavia, 1905.
Chrysost. hom.in Matth.	Chrysostomus, *Homeliae in Mattheum*. 2 vols.: 1. hom. 1–45, *PG* 57; 2. hom. 46–92, *PG* 58.
Ps.Chrysost. in Matth.	Ps.Chrysostomus, *Opus Imperfectum in Mattheum*. *PG* 56,411–428.
Cic. inv.	Marcus Tullius Cicero, *De Inventione*. Ed. Eduard Stroebel. Biblioteca Scriptorum Graecorum et Romanorum Teubneriana. Stuttgart, 1965.
Comestor *HS*	Petrus Comestor, *Historia Scholastica*. *PL* 198,1055–1722.
Comestor *Serm.*	Petrus Comestor, *Sermones in festo S. Augustini*. *PL* 198,1783–1800.
Const.Ratis.	*Constitutiones Ordinis eremitarum sancti Augustini*. Ed. Ignacio Arámburu, *Las primitivas Constituciones de los Agustinos*. Valladolid, 1966.
Cron.Cont.	*Chronici Saxonici Continuatio Erfordensis*. *Mon.Erph.*, 443–485.
Cron.Eng.	*Cronica Erfordensis Engelhusiana*. *Mon.Erph.* 784–806.
Cron.Erf.	*Cronica S. Petri Erfordensis Moderna*. *Mon.Erph.* 117–369.
Cypr. domin. orat.	Cyprianus, *De Dominica Oratione*. Ed. C. Moreschini. *CCSL* 3A.87–113. Turnhout, 1976.
Dam. fid.orth.	Iohannes Damascenus, *De Fide Orthodoxa*. *PG* 94,781–1228.
De ad.	*De adventu Ludovici Bavari in Urbem et de his quae hac occassione in Romana Provincia Ordinis Eremitarum Sancti Augustini evenerunt*, 1328. *AAug.* 4 (1911/1912), 67–70.
Denzinger *Ench.*	Heinrich Denzinger, *Enchiridion symbolorum definitionum et declarationum de rebus fidei et morum*. 38th edition, corrected, expanded, and translated into German by Peter Hünermann. Freiburg im Breisgau, Basel, Rome, Vienna, 1999.
Dion. div.nom.	Ps.Dionysius, *De Divinis Nominibus*. *PG* 3,585–996.
Documents	*Documents pour servir à l'histoire médiévale de la province augustinienne de Cologne. Extraits des registres des prieurs généraux, (1357–1506)*. Eds. Norbert Teeuwen, OESA, Albéric de Meijer, OESA. Institut Historique Augustinien. Héverlé-Louvain, 1961.
Edm.Ab. *Spec.*	Edmund of Abingdon, *Speculum Religiosorum* and *Speculum Ecclesie*. Ed. Helen P. Forshaw, S.H.C.J., Auctores Britiannici Mediii Aevi III. Oxford, 1973.
Epist.VPD	*Epistola De Vita et Passione Domini Nostri. Der Lateinische Text mit Einleitung und Kommentar*. Ed. Monica Hedlund. Kerkhistorische Bijdragen 5. Leiden, 1975.
Empoli *Bull.*	L. Empoli, *Bullarium Ordinis Eremitarum Sancti Augustini*. Rome, 1628.
Eras. *Eccl.*	*Ecclesiastes. Opera Omnia Desiderii Erasmi Roterodami*. Vol. V/IV. Ed. Jacques Chomarat. Amsterdam, 1991.
Esteban	*Acta Capitulorum Generalium et Provincialium*. Ed. E. Esteban. *AAug.* 2 (1909)–4 (1912).

FM	*Fasciculus Morum. A Fourteenth-Century Preacher's Handbook.* Ed. and trans. Siegfried Wenzel. Philadelphia, 1989.
Fr.	*Corpus Iuris Canonici.* Ed. A.L. Richter and A. Friedberg. 2 vols. Leipzig 1879; reprint: Graz, 1959.
Gerhoch *In psalm.*	Gerhoch of Reichersberg, *Expositio in Psalmos.* Gerhohi Praepositi Reichersbergensis *Opera Inedita* II/1. Eds. PP. Damiani, Odulphus van den Eynde and P. Angelinus Rijmersdael. Rome, 1956.
Gerson *Ad deum*	*The 'Ad Deum Vadit' of Jean Gerson. Published from the Manuscript Bibliothèque Nationale, Fonds Fr. 24841.* Ed. David Hobart Carnahan. Illinois, 1917.
Gest.Mag.	*Gesta Archiepiscoporum Magdeburgensium.* Ed. Guilelmus Schum. *MGH.SS* 14.361–484. Hannover, 1883; reprint: New York, 1963.
Glos.ord.	*Biblia Latina cum Glossa Ordinaria.* Facsimile Reprint of the *Editio Princeps,* Adolph Rusch of Strassburg 1480/1481. 4 vols., Turnhout, 1992; *Biblia Sacra cum Glossa interlinearia, ordinaria, Nicolai Lyrani Postilla ac Moralitatibus, Burgensis Additionibus, et Thoringi replicis.* 4 vols., Venice, 1588.
Greg.M. in evang.	Gregorius Magnus, *Liber Homiliarum in Evangelia. PL* 76,1075–1314.
Greg.M. moral.	Gregorius Magnus, *Moralia in Iob.* Ed. Marcus Adriaen. 3. vols.: 1. lib. I-X, *CCSL* 143; 2. lib. XI-XXII, *CCSL* 143A; 3. lib. XXII-XXXV, *CCSL* 143B. Turnhout, 1979–1985.
Greg.M. pastoral.	Gregorius Magnus, *Regulae Pastoralis Liber. PL* 77,9–130.
Greg.M. sacr.	Gregorius Magnus, *Liber Sacramentorum. PL* 78,9–637.
Ps.Greg. ex.Al.	*Expositio Novi Testamenti, auctore Alulfo. PL* 79,1137–1424.
Greg. *Sent.*	Gregorius Ariminensis, *Lectura Super Primum et Secundum Sententiarum.* 7 vols. *SuR* 6–12. Ed. A. Damasus Trapp, *et al.* Berlin, 1978–1987.
Greg. *Reg.*	*Gregorii de Arimino O.S.A. Registrum Generalatus, 1357–1358.* Ed. Albericus de Meijer. Fontes historiae Ordinis Sancti Augustini. Prima series, Registra Priorum Generalium 1. Institutum Historicum Augustinianum. Romae, 1976.
Gross. *Dec.man.*	Robert Gorsseteste, *De Decem Mandatis.* Ed. Richard C. Dales and Edward B. King. Auctores Britannici Medii Aevi X. Oxford, 1987.
Hen. *In mentem*	Henricus de Frimaria, *Tractaus de aventu verbi in mentem.* In *Henrici de Frimaria O.S.A. Tractatus Ascetio-Mysici.* Ed. A. Zumkeller. Würzburg, 1975, 3–61.
Hen. *Inst.*	Henricus de Frimaria, *Tractatus de quattuor instinctibus.* Ed. A. Zumkeller and Robert G. Aarnock, *Der Traktat Heinrichs von Friemar über die Unterscheidung der Geister. Lateinsch-mittelhochdeutsche Textausgabe mit Untersuchungen.* Würzburg, 1977.
Hen. *Tract.*	Henricus de Frimaria, *Tractatus de origine et progressu Ordinis Fratrum Eremitarum S. Augustini.* Ed. Rudolph Arbesmann. *Aug(L)* 6 (1956), 90–145.
Herm.Sch. *cont.neg.*	*Hermanni de Schildis O.S.A. Tractatus Contra Haereticos Negantes Immunitatem et Iurisdictionem Sanctae Ecclesiae.* Ed. Adolar Zumkeller. *CSA* 2. Rome, 1970.
Herm.Sch. *Spec.*	Hermannus de Schildis, *Speculum Manuale Sacerdotum.* Mainz, 1480.
Hier. adv.Iovin	Hieronymus, *Adversus Iovinianum. PL* 23,221–352.
Hier. in Is.	Hieronymus, *Commentariorum in Esaiam.* Ed. Marcus Adriaen. *CCSL* 73A. Turnhout, 1963.
Hier. in Matth.	Hieronymus, *Commentariorum in Matheum.* Ed. D. Hurst and M. Adriaen. *CCSL* 77. Turnhout, 1969.

Hier. in psalm.	Hieronymus, *Tractatus in Psalmos*. Ed. D. Germanus Morin. *CCSL* 78.3–446. Turnhout, 1958.
Hug. *Phys.*	Hugolinus de Urbe Veteri, *Commentarius in primam et secundam quaestionem primi libri Physicorum Aristotelis*. Ed. Willigis Eckermann, *Der Physikkomentar Hugolins von Orvieto OESA. Ein Beitrag zur Erkenntnislehre des Spätmittelalterlichen Augustinismus*. SuR 5. Berlin/New York, 1972.
Hug. *Sent.*	Hugolinus de Urbe Veteri, *Commentarius in Quattuor Libros Sententiarum*. 4 vols. Ed. Wigillis Eckermann. Würzburg, 1980–1988.
Hug.SV. *Reg.*	Hugo de S. Victore, *Expositio in Regulam Augustini*. *PL* 176, 881–924.
Hug.SV. *Ar.An.*	Hugo de S. Victore, *De Arrha Animae*. *PL* 176,951–970.
Hug.SV. *Arc.Moral.*	Hugo de S. Victore, *De Arca Noe Morali*. *PL* 176,619–704.
Ps.Hug.SV. *Med.*	Ps.Hugo de S. Victore, *De Meditando seu Meditandi Artificio*. *PL* 176, 993–998.
Initium	Anonymous, *Initium sive Processus Ordinis Heremitarum Sancti Augustini*. Ed. Balbino Rano, in "Los dos Primeras Obras Conocidas sobre el Origen de la Orden Agostiniana." *AAug*. 45 (1982), 331–351.
Innoc. *Alt.Myst.*	Innocentius, *De Sacro Altaris Mysterio*. *PL* 217,763–916.
Isid. diff.	Isidorus, *Differentiarum*. *PL* 83,9–98.
Jac.V. *HO*	*The Historia Occidentalis of Jacques de Vitry. A Critical Edition*. Ed. John Frederick Hinnebusch, O.P. Spicilegium Friburgense 17. Fribourg, 1972.
Joh.XXII *Let.*	*Lettres de Jean XXII (1316–1334). Textes et Analyses*. Ed. Arnold Fayen, 2 vols. Rome, 1908.
Jor. *OD*	Jordanus de Quedlinburg, *Opus Dan [Sermones de sanctis]*. Strassburg, 1484.
Jor. *OP*	Jordanus de Quedlinburg, *Opus Postillarum et sermonum de tempore*. Strassburg, 1483.
Jor. *OS*	Jordanus de Quedlinburg, *Opus Sermonum [Opus Dan]*. Paris, 1521.
LA	Iacopo da Verasse *Legenda Aurea*. Ed. Giovanni Paolo Maggioni. Millennio Medievale 6, Testi 3. 2 vols. Firenze, 1998.
Lambot	C. Lambot, ed. *Sermones selecti duodeviginti Sancti Augustini*. Stromata mediaevalia. Utrecht, 1950.
Land. *Hist.*	Landulfus, *Historia Mediolanensis*. Ed. L.C. Bethmann and W. Wattenbach. *MGH.SS* VIII.41–43.
Lanf. *Cor.*	Lanfrancus de Bec, *Liber de corpore et sanguine domini*. *PL* 150, 407–442.
LEC	*Licet Ecclesiae Catholicae*. Ed. Albericus de Meijer, *Aug(L)* 6 (1956), 9–13.
Lombardus	Petrus Lombardus, *Sententiae in IV Libris Distinctae*. Spicilegium Bonaventurianum 4–5. 2 vols., Grottaferrata, 1971; 1981.
Lud.IV. *App.*	Ludovicus IV, *Appellatio*. S. Baluzius, *Vitae Paparum Avenionensium*, nr. 75. Ed. G. Mollat. Vol. 3. Paris, 1921, 386–425; Berthold, *Kaiser, Volk, und Avignon*, 44–106.
Mars.Ing. *Sent.*	Marsilius of Inghen, *Questiones super Quattuor libros Sententiarum*. Strassburg, 1501; reprint: Frankfurt, 1966.
Marsilius *Def.pac.*	*The Defensor Pacis of Marsilius of Padua*. Ed. C.W. Previté-Orton. Cambridge, 1928.
Mon.Erph.	*Monumenta Erphesfurtensia, Saec. XII. XIII. XIV*. Ed. Oswaldus Holder-Edger. Hannover and Lipsia, 1899.
MVC	*Iohannis de Caulibus Meditaciones Vite Christi, olim S. Bonauenturo attributae*. Ed. M. Stallings-Taney. *CCCM* 153. Turnhout, 1997.
Neap.Ur. *Ep.*	*Neapoleon de Ursinis Cardinalis Epistola ad Philippum Regem Francorum*

	de statu Romanae Ecclesiae post Obitum Clementis V. Ed. S. Baluzius, *Vitae Paparum Avenionensium.* Ed. G. Mollat. Vol. 3. Paris, 1921, 237–241.
Nic.Al. *Sermo*	Nicolas de Alessandria, *Sermo de Beato Augustino.* Ed. Balbino Rano, in "Los dos Primeras Obras Conocidas sobre el Origen de la Orden Agustiniana," *AAug.* 45 (1982), 352–376.
Paltz *Coel.*	Johannes von Paltz, *Coelifodina.* Ed. Christoph Burger and Friedhelm Stasch, with Berndt Hamm and Venicio Marcolino. *SuR* 2. Berlin, 1983.
Paltz *Suppl.Coel.*	Johannes von Paltz, *Supplementum Coelifodinae.* Ed. Berndt Hamm, with Christoph Burger and Venicio Marcolino. *SuR* 3. Berlin, 1983.
Phil.IV. *Ep.*	*Philippi IV Regis Rancorum Epistola qua Cardinales Hortatur ad Maturandam Electionem Summi Pontificis.* Ed. S. Baluzius, *Vitae Paparum Avenionensium.* Ed. G. Mollat. Vol. 3. Paris, 1921, 241–244.
Pinder, *SP*	Ulrich Pinder, *Speculum Passionis.* Nürnberg, 1507.
Pinder, *SbL*	Ulrich Pinder, *Speculum Passionis, Das ist: Spiegel des bitteren Leydens unnd Sterbens Jesu Christi . . . Verlegt und getruckt zu Salzburg durch Johann Baptist Mayr.* Salzburg, 1663; reprinted Weisbaden, 1986 with commentary by Helmar Junghans and Christa-Maria Dreissiger.
Phil. vita Aug.	*Philippi de Harveng Abbatis Bonae Spei Vita Beati Augustini Hipponensis Episcopi. PL* 203,1205–1234.
Possid. vita Aug.	*Vita S. Augustini Episcopi Auctore Possidio, Vita di S. Agostino.* Ed. Michele Pellegrino, Verba Seniorum 4. Alba, 1955.
Prisc. gramm.	Priscianus, *Institutiones.* Vols. 2–3 of *Grammatici Latini.* Ed. Heinrich Keil. Leipzig, 1855–1880; reprint: Hildesheim, 1961.
Regula	*Regula Sancti Augustini.* Ed. L. Verheijen, *La Règle de saint Augustin.* 2 vols. Paris, 1967, 1:417–437.
R.Maur. *In Matth.*	Rabanus Maurus, *Commentarium in Mattheum. PL* 107,727–1156.
Sal.Quest.	*The Prose Salernitan Questions.* Ed. Brian Lawn. Oxford, 1979.
Schp.chron.	*Die Magdeburger Schöppenchronik.* Ed. C. Hegel, in *Die Chroniken der deutschen Städte vom 14. bis ins 16. Jahrhundert.* Vol. 7/1: *Die Chroniken der niedersächsischen Städte. Magdeburg.* Göttingen 1869; reprint Stuttgart, 1962.
Sen. epist.	Seneca, *Ad Lucilium Epistulae Morales.* Ed. L.D. Reynolds. Oxford, 1965.
Stat.Con.	*Statutum Concordiae inter Quatuor Ordines Mendicantes annis 1435, 1458 et 1475 Sancitum.* Ed. Benevenutus Bughetti, O.F.M. *Archivum Franciscanum Historicum* 25 (1932), 241–256.
Staupitz *Const.*	*Constitutiones fratrum Eremitarum sancti Augustini ad Apostolicorum privilegiorum formam pro reformatione Alemanniae.* Ed. Wolfgang Günter, in Johann von Staupitz, *Sämtliche Schriften. Abhandlungen, Predigten, Zeugnisse,* ed. Lothar Graf zu Dohna and Richard Wetzel. Vol. 5. *SuR* 17. Berlin, 2001.
Syb.B. *Repr.*	Sybert von Beek, *Reprobatio Sex Errorum.* Ed. Richard Scholz, *Unbekannte Kirchenpolitische Streitschriften aus der Zeit Ludwigs des Bayern (1327–1354). Analysen und Texte.* 2 vols. Rome, 1911–1914, 2:3–15.
Thom.Aq. *STh.*	*S. Thomae de Aquino, Ordinis Praedicatorum, Summa Theologiae,* cura et studio Instituti Studiorum Medievalium Ottaviensis. Ottawa, 1941–1945.
Thom.Aq. *CA*	*Catena Aurea in Quatuor Evangelia,* I. *Expositio in Mattheum et Marcum;* II. *Expositio in Lucam et Ioannem.* Ed. Angelici Guarienti, O.P., Taurini et Romae. Marietti, 1953.

Thom.Aq. *Sup.Matth.* Super Evangelium S. Matthaei Lectura. Ed. P. Raphaelis Cai, O.P., Taurini et Romae. Marietti, 1951.
Thom.Arg. *Sent.* Thomas de Argentina, *Commentaria in IV libros Sententiarum.* Venice, 1564; reprint: Ridgewood, 1965.
Thom.Arg. *Add.* Thomas de Argentina, *Additiones.* Ed. Ignacio Arámburu, *Las primitivas Constituciones de los Agustinos.* Valladolid, 1966.
Thom.Kemp. *Hort.* Thomas a Kempis, *Hortulus rosarum.* Ed. Paul van Geest, *Thomas a Kempis (1379/80–1471). Een studie van zijn mens-en godsbeeld.* Kampen, 1996: 343–381.
Thom.Kemp. *Vall.* Thomas a Kempis, *Vallis liliorum.* Ed. Paul van Geest, *Thomas a Kempis (1379/80–1471). Een studie van zijn mens-en godsbeeld.* Kampen, 1996: 387–432.
TSG Het Tübingse Sint-Geertruihandschrift. Hs. Tübingen, Universitätsbibliothek Me.IV.3. Ed. Hans Kienhorst and Gerard Sonnemans. Hilversum, 1996.
UkErf Urkundenbuch der Erfurter Stifter und Klöster. Ed. A. Overmann. 3 vols., Magdeburg, 1934.
UkLF Urkundenbuch des Klosters Unser Lieben Frauen zu Magdeburg. Ed. Gustav Hertel. Halle, 1878.
UkStErf Urkundenbuch der Stadt Erfurt. Teil 1. Ed. Carl Beyer. Halle, 1889.
UrkM Urkundenbuch der Stadt Magdeburg. Geschichtsquellen der Provinz Sachsen und Angrenzender Gebiete 26. Ed. Gustav Hertel. Band 1. Halle 1892; reprint: Darmstadt, 1975.
VC Ludolphus Carthusiensis, *Vita Jesu Christi ex Evangelio et approbatis ab Ecclesia Catholica Doctoribus sedule collecta.* Ed. L.M. Rigollot. 4 vols., Paris, 1878.
VF Jordani de Saxonia *Liber Vitasfratrum.* Ed. Winfridus Hümpfner and Rudolph Arbesmann. Cassiciacum 1. New York, 1943.
VP Vitae Patrum. *PL* 73.
WA D. Martin Luthers Werke. Kritische Gesamtausgabe. 61 vols., Weimar, 1883–1999
WABr D. Martin Luthers Werke. Kritische Gesamtausgabe, Briefwechsel. 16 vols., Weimar, 1930–1980.
WAT D. Martin Luthers Werke. Kritische Gesamtausgabe, Tischreden. 6 vols., Weimar, 1912–1921.
Will.Crem. *Repr.* Guillemi de Villana Cremonensis O.S.A. *Tractatus cuius Titulus Reprobatio Errorum.* Ed. Darach Mac Fhionnbhairr. *CSA* 4. Rome, 1977.
Zach.Bes. *Con.Evang.* Zachary of Besançon, *De Concordia Evangelistarum.* PL 186, 11–620.

II. SECONDARY LITERATURE

Adam, Bernd, *Katechetische Vaterunserauslegungen. Texte und Untersuchungen zu deutschsprachigen Auslegungen des. 14. und 15. Jahrhunderts.* Munich, 1976.
Aertsen, Jan, *Nature and Creature. Thomas Aquinas's Way of Thought.* STGMA 21. Leiden, 1988.
Angenendt, Arnold, *Geschichte der Religiosität im Mittelalter.* Darmstadt, 1997.
Ankersmit, F.R., *De navel van de geschiedenis. Over interpretatie, representatie en historische realiteit.* Groningen, 1990.
——, "Statements, Texts and Pictures." In *A New Philosophy of History*, ed. Frank Ankersmit and Hans Kellner. Chicago, 1995, 212–240.
Arbesmann, Rudolph, "Jordanus of Saxony's *Vita S. Augustini*: The Source for John Capgrave's Life of St. Augustine." *Traditio* 1 (1943), 341–353.

——, "Henry of Friemar's 'Treatise on the Origin and Development of the Order of the Hermit Friars and its True and Real Title.'" *Aug(L)* 6 (1956), 37–145.
——, "The 'Vita Aurelii Augustini Hipponensis Episcopi' in Cod. Laurent. Plut. 90 Sup. 48." *Traditio* 18 (1962), 319–355.
——, *Der Augustiner-Eremitenorden und der Beginn der humanistischen Bewegung*. Würzburg, 1965.
——, "A Legendary of Early Augustinian Saints." *AAug.* 29 (1966), 5–58.
——, "Some Notes on the Fourteenth-Century History of the Augustinian Order." *AAug.* 40 (1977), 62–78.
——, "The Question of the Authorship of the *Milleloquium Veritatis S. Augustini*." *AAug.* 43 (1980), 163–185.
Arendt, Hannah, *Love and Saint Augustine*. Ed. Joanna Vecchiarelli Scott and Judith Chelius Stark. Chicago, 1996.
Arquillière, H.-X., *Le plus ancien traité de l'église, Jacque de Viterbo, De Regimine Christiano (1301–1302)*. Paris, 1926.
——, *L'Augustinisme politique*. Paris, 1934.
——, "L'Essence de l'Augustinisme politique." In *Augustinus Magister*. Congrès International Augustinien. Études Augustiniennes, 3 vols. Paris, 1955, 2:991–1001.
Baier, Walter, *Untersuchungen zu den Passionsbetrachtungen in der 'Vita Christi' des Ludolf von Sachsen. Ein quellenkritischer Beitrag zu Leben und Werk Ludolfs und zur Geschichte der Passionstheologie*. 3 vols. Analecta Cartusiana 44. Institut für Englische Sprache und Literatur, Universität Salzburg. Salzburg, 1977.
Bainbridge, W. and R. Stark, *A Theory of Religion*. New York, 1987.
Ballweg, Jan, *Konziliare oder päpstliche Ordensreform. Benedikt XII. und die Reformdiskussion im frühen 14. Jahrhundert*. SuR.NR 17. Tübingen, 2001.
Bange, P. *Spiegels der Christenen. Zelfreflectie en ideaalbeeld in laat-middeleeuwse moralistisch-didactische traktaten*. Nijmegen, 1986.
Bartlett, Robert, *The Making of Europe. Conquest, Colonization and Cultural Change 950–1350*. Princeton, 1993.
Bast, Robert J., *Honor Your Fathers: Catechisms and the Emergence of a Patriarchal Ideology in Germany, c. 1400–1600*. SMRT 63. Leiden, 1997.
——, "Strategies of Communication: Late-Medieval Catechisms and the Passion Tradition." In *The Broken Body* (see MacDonald, A.A.), 133–143.
——, and Andrew C. Gow, eds., *Continuity and Change. The Harvest of Late Medieval and Reformation History*. Essays presented to Heiko A. Oberman on his 70th Birthday. Leiden, 2000.
Baxandall, Michael, *Painting and Experience in Fifteenth Century Italy. A Primer in the Social History of Pictorial Style*. Oxford, 1972. 2nd ed. Oxford, 1988.
Beckwith, Sarah, *Christ's Body. Identity, Culture and Society in Late Medieval Writings*. London, 1993.
Belting, Hans, *The Image and Its Public in the Middle Ages. Form and Function of Early Paintings of the Passion*, trans. Mark Bartusis and Raymond Meyer. New York. 1990. Originally published as *Das Bild und sein Publikum im Mittelalter: Form und Funktion früher Bildtafeln der Passion*. Berlin, 1981.
——, *Likeness and Presence. A History of the Image before the Era of Art*. Chicago, 1994. Originally published as *Bild und Kult?Eine Geschichte des Bildes vor dem Zeitalter der Kunst*. Munich, 1990.
Bestul, Thomas H., *Texts of the Passion. Latin Devotional Literature and Medieval Society*. Philadelphia, 1996.
Berg, D. *Armut und Wissenschaft. Beiträge zur Geschichte des Studienwesens der Bettelorden im 13. Jahrhundert*. Düsseldorf, 1977.
Berger, Peter L. and Thomas Luckmann, *The Social Construction of Reality. A Treatise in the Sociology of Knowledge*. New York, 1966.
Bernstein, Alan E., "Theology between Heresy and Folklore: William of Auvergne on Punishment after Death." *Studies in Medieval and Renaissance History* 5 (1982), 5–44.

Biller, Peter, "Words and the Medieval Notion of 'Religion'." *JEH* 36 (1985), 351–369.
Bizer, Ernst, *Fides ex auditu: Eine Untersuchung über die Entdeckung der Gerechtigkeit Gottes durch Martin Luther*. 3rd rev. ed., Neukirchen-Vluyn, 1966.
Black, Antony, *Political Thought in Europe, 1250–1450*. Cambridge, 1992.
Bloomfield, Martin, *The Seven Deadly Sins. An Introduction to the History of a Religious Concept, with Special Reference to Medieval English Literature*. Michigan, 1952.
——, et al. eds., *Incipits of Latin Works on the Virtues and Vices, 1100–1500 A.D., Including a Section of Incipits of Works on the Pater Noster*. The Medieval Academy of America. Cambridge, 1979.
Boase, T.S.R., *Boniface VIII*. London, 1933.
Bochet, Isabelle, *Saint Augustin et Le Desir de Dieu*. Paris, 1982.
Böhm, Sigurd, *La Temporalité dans l'Anthropologie Augustinienne*. Paris, 1984.
Boockmann, Hartmut, *Stauferzeit und spätes Mittelalter. Deutschland 1125–1517*. Berlin, 1987.
Bordier, Jean-Pierre, *Le Jeu de la Passion. Le message chrétien et le théâtre fraçais (XIIIe–XVIe s.)*. Paris, 1998.
Bouchard, Constance, *Sword, Miter, and Cloister. Nobility and the Church in Burgundy, 980–1198*. Ithaca, N.Y., 1987.
Boyle, L.E., "The Summa Confessorum of John of Freiburg and the Popularization of the Moral Teaching of St. Thomas and of some of his Contemporaries." In *St. Thomas Aquinas, 1274–1974. Commemorative Studies*. 2 vols., ed. Etienne Gilson et al. Toronto, 1974, 2:245–286.
Bossy, John, "Some Elementary Forms of Durkheim." *Past and Present* 95 (1982), 3–18.
——, *Christianity in the West, 1400–1700*. Oxford, 1985.
Bostik, Curtis V., *The Antichrist and the Lollards. Apocalypticism in Late Medieval and Reformation England*. SMRT 70. Leiden, 1998.
Brady, Thomas A., "In Search of the Godly City: The Domestication of Religion in the German Urban Reformation." In *The German People and the Reformation*. Ed. R. Po-Chia Hsia. Ithaca, N.Y., 1988, 14–31.
——, "The Holy Roman Empire's Bishops on the Eve of the Reformation." In *Continuity and Change* (see Bast), 20–47.
Brecht, Martin, *Martin Luther. His Road to Reformation, 1483–1521*. Trans. James L. Schaaf. Philadelphia, 1985.
——, *Martin Luther. Shaping and Defining the Reformation, 1521–1532*. Trans. James L. Schaaf. Philadelphia, 1990.
Brentano, Robert, *Rome Before Avignon. A Social History of Thirteenth-Century Rome*. London,1974; 2nd edition London, 1991.
Brown, Peter, *The Rise of Christendom*. Oxford, 1996.
Brundage, James, *Law, Sex, and Christian Society in Medieval Europe*. Chicago, 1987.
Burger, Christoph, "Direkte Zuwendung zu den 'Laien' und Rückgriff auf Vermittler in spätmittelalterlicher katechetische Literatur." In *Spätmittelalterliche Frömmigkeit* (see Hamm), 85–110.
Burke, Peter, *History and Social Theory*. New York, 1992.
Burr, David, *Olivi and Franciscan Poverty. The Origin of the 'Usus Pauper' Controversy*. Philadelphia, 1989.
Bynum, Caroline Walker, *Docere verbo et exemplo. An Aspect of Twelfth-Century Spirituality*. Harvard Theological Studies 31. Missoula, Montana, 1979.
——, *Jesus as Mother. Studies in the Spirituality of the High Middle Ages*. Berkeley, 1982.
——, *Holy Feast and Holy Fast. The Religious Significance of Food to Medieval Women*. Berkeley, 1987.
——, *Fragmentation and Redemption. Essays on Gender and the Human Body in Medieval Religion*. New York, 1992.
Cameron, Euan, *The European Reformation*. Oxford, 1991.
Camille, Michael, *The Gothic Idol. Ideology and Image-Making in Medieval Art*. Cambridge, 1989.

———, "Mimetic Identification and Passion Devotion in the Later Middle Ages: A Double-sided Panel by Meister Francke," in *The Broken Body* (see MacDonald, A.A.), 183–210.

Carmignac, Jean, *Recherches sur le 'Notre Pere'*. Paris, 1969. *Catalogus Codicum Hagiographicorum Latinorum Antiquorum Saeculo XIV qui asservantur in Bibliotheca Nationali Parisiensi*. Ed. Hagiographi Bollandiani. Bruxellis, 1890.

Châtillon, Jean, "La Bible dans les écoles du XIIe siècle." In *Le Moyen Age et la Bible*. Eds. Pierre Riché and Guy Lobrichon. Paris, 1984, 163–197.

———, *Le Mouvement Canonial Au Moyen Age. Réforme de l'église, spiritualité et culture*. Ed. Patrice Sicard. Paris, 1992.

Chazan, Robert, *Medieval Stereotypes and Modern Antisemitism*. Berkeley, 1997.

Christian, William A., Sr., *Doctrines of Religious Communities. A Philosophical Study*. New Haven/London, 1987.

Cipola, Carlo M., *Before the Industrial Revolution. European Society and Economy, 1000–1700*. New York, 1976.

Classen, Peter, *Gerhoch von Reichersberg. Eine Biographie mit einem Anhang über die Quellen, ihre Handschriftliche Überlieferung und ihre Chronologie*. Wiesbaden, 1960.

Cohen, Jeremy, *The Friars and the Jews. The Evolution of Medieval Anti-Judaism*. Ithaca, N.Y., 1982.

Colish, Marcia L., "Early Scholastic Angelology." *RThAM* 62 (1995), 80–109.

———, *Medieval Foundations of the Western Intellectual Tradition, 400–1499*. New Haven, 1997.

Constable, Giles, *Three Studies in Medieval Religious and Social Thought*. Cambridge, 1995.

———, *The Reformation of the Twelfth Century*. Cambridge, 1996.

Cornelis, Arnold, *Logica van het Gevoel. Filiosofie van de Stabiliteitslagen in de Cultuur*. Amsterdam, 1998.

Counihan, Cyril, "Lay and Clerical Elements in Early Augustinian History." *AAug.* 43 (1980), 304–333.

Courcelle J. and P. Courcelle, *Iconographie de Saint Augustin. Les Cycles du XVe Siècle*. Paris, 1969.

Courtenay, William J., "The 'Sentences'-Commentary of Stukle: A New Source for Oxford Theology in the Fourteenth Century." *Traditio* 34 (1978), 435–438.

———, "Augustinianism at Oxford in the Fourteenth Century." *Aug(L)* 30 (1980), 58–70.

———, *Schools and Scholars in Fourteenth-Century England*. Princeton, 1987.

———, "Spirituality and Late Scholasticism." In *Christian Spirituality. High Middle Ages and Reformation*. Ed. Jill Raitt, 109–120. London, 1987.

———, "Marsilius von Inghen (d.1396) als Heidelberger Theologe." *Heidelberger Jahrbücher* 32 (1988), 26–42.

———, "Augustine and Nominalism." In *Saint Augustine and his Influence in the Middle Ages*. Ed. Edward B. King and Jacqueline T. Schaefer (Sewanee, TN, 1988), 91–97.

———, *Capacity and Volition. A History of the Distinction of Absolute and Ordained Power*. Bergamo, 1990.

———, "Conrad of Megenberg: The Parisian Years." *Vivarium* 35 (1997), 102–124.

Cruel, R., *Geschichte der deutschen Predigt im Mittelalter*. Detmold, 1879.

Curtius, Ernst Robert, *European Literature and the Latin Middle Ages*. 7th printing with Afterword by Peter Godman. Princeton, 1990.

Dagenais, John, *The Ethics of Reading in Manuscript Culture. Glossing the* Libro de Buen Amor. Princeton, 1994.

Damiata, Marino, *Plenitudo Potestatis e Universitas Civium in Marsilio da Padova*. Florence, 1983.

Danto, Arthur C., *Narration and Knowledge*. New York, 1985.

D'Avray, David, *The Preaching of the Friars. Sermons Diffused From Paris Before 1300*. Oxford, 1985.

De Jong, Mayke, "Old Law and New-Found Power: Hrabanus Maurus and the Old Testament." In *Centers of Learning. Learning and Location in Pre-Modern Europe and the Near East*. Eds. Jan Willem Drijvers and Alasdair A. MacDonald. *BSIH* 61 Leiden, 1995, 161–176.

De Lubac, Henri, *Théologies d'occasion*. Paris, 1984.
Delumeau, Jean, *Sin and Fear. The Emergence of a Western Guilt Culture, 13th–18th Centuries*, trans. Eric Nicholson. New York, 1990.
Denifle, Heinrich, "Die Denkschriften der Colonna gegen Bonifaz VIII. und der Cardinäle gegen die Colonna." In *Archiv für Literatur- und Kirchengeschichte des Mittelalters*. Ed. Heinrich Denifle and Franz Ehrle. Vol. 5. Freiburg im Breisgau, 1889, 493–529.
———, *Luther und Luthertum in der ersten Entwicklung*. 2 vols. Mainz, 1904–1909.
Derbes, Ann, *Picturing the Passion in Late Medieval Italy. Narrative Painting, Franciscan Ideologies, and the Levant*. Cambridge, 1996.
Dibelius, O., *Das Vaterunser. Umrisse zu einer Geschichte des Gebets in der alten und mittleren Kirche*. Giessen, 1903.
Dinzelbacher, Peter, "Zur Erforschung der Geschichte der Volksreligion. Einführung und Bibliographie." In *Volksreligion im hohen und späten Mittelalter*, ed. Peter Dinzelbacher and Dieter R. Bauer, 9–27. Paderborn, 1990.
Doucet, P.V., *Commentaires sur les Sentences. Supplement au Repertoire de M. Frédéric Stegmueller*. Quaracchi, 1954.
Drewermann, Eugen, *Strukturen des Bösen*. Vol. II: *Die jawistische Urgeschichte in pyschoanalytischer Sicht*. Paderborn, 1978; fifth edition, 1988.
Drijvers Jan Willem, *Helena Augusta. The Mother of Constantine the Great and the Legend of Her Finding the True Cross*. BSIH 27. Leiden, 1992.
Duffy, Eamon, *The Stripping of the Altars. Traditional Religion in England c. 1400–c. 1580*. New Haven, 1992.
Durkheim, Emile, *The Elementary Forms of the Religious Life. A Study in Religious Sociology*, trans. Joseph Ward Swain. Illinois, 1926.
Dykema, Peter A. and Heiko A. Oberman, eds., *Anticlericalism in Late Medieval and Early Modern Europe*. SMRT 51. Leiden, 1993.
———, *Conflicting Expectations: Parish Priests in Late Medieval Germany*. Unpublished Ph.D. dissertation, University of Arizona, 1998.
———, "Handbooks for Pastors: Late Medieval Manuals for Parish Priests and Conrad Porta's *Pastorale Lutheri* (1582)." In *Continuity and Change* (see Bast). Leiden, 2000, 143–162.
Eagleton, Terry, *Ideology: An Introduction*. London, 1991.
———, *Ideology*. New York, 1994.
Eckerman, Willigis, *Der Physikkommentar Hugolins von Orvieto OESA. Ein Beitrag zur Erkenntnislehre des Spätmittelalterlichen Augustinismus*. SuR 5. Berlin and New York, 1972.
———, and Cornelius Petrus Mayer, eds., *Studien über Augustinus, den Augustinismus und den Augustinerorden. Festschrift P. Dr. theol. Dr. phil. Adolar Zumkeller OSA zum 60. Geburtstag*. Cassiciacum 30. Würzburg, 1975.
———, "Augustinus Favaroni von Rom und Johannes Wycliff. Der Ansatz ihrer Lehre über die Kirche." In *Scientia Augustiniana*, 323–348.
———, "Augustinus Triumphus." *TRE* 4:742–744.
———, ed., *Schwerpunkte und Wirkungen des Sentenzenkommentars Hugolino von Orvieto, OESA*. Cassiciacum 42. Würzburg, 1990.
———, "Simon Fidati von Cascia OESA (d. 1348). Europäische Theologie im lateinischen Mittelalter." *Aug(L)* 47 (1997), 339–356.
Ehrle, Franz, *Der Sentenzenkommentar Peters von Candia, des Pisaner Papstes Alexanders V. Ein Beitrag zur Scheidung der Schulen in der Scholastik des vierzehnten Jahrhunderts und zur Geschichte des Wegestreites*. Franziskanische Studien, Beiheft 9. Münster, 1925.
Eire, Carlos M.N., *War Against the Idols. The Reformation of Worship from Erasmus to Calvin*. Cambridge, 1986.
Eliade, Mircea, "Shamanism." In *Ancient Religions*. Ed. Vergilius Ferm. New York, 1950; first paperback ed. 1965, 299–308.
———, *A History of Religious Ideas*. Vol. 3: *From Muhammad to the Age of Reforms*. Chicago,

1985. Originally published as *Histoire des croyances et des idées religieuses*. Vol 3: *De Mahomet à l'âge des Réformes*. Paris, 1983.
——, *The Sacred and the Profane*. 1957. New York, 1987.
——, *The Myth of Eternal Return*. New York, 1954; 9th edition, New York, 1991. Originally published as *Le Mythe de l'éternel retour: archétypes et répétition*, Paris, 1949.
——, *Images and Symbols. Studies in Religious Symbolism*. Princeton, 1991. Originally published as *Images et Symboles*. Paris, 1952.
——, *Rites and Symbols of Initiation. The Mysteries of Birth and Rebirth*. New York, 1958. Trans. Willard R. Trask, with a new Forward by Michael Meade. Dallas, 1994.
Elias, Norbert, *The Civilizing Process*. 2 vols. New York, 1978.
——, *What is Sociology?* New York, 1978.
——, *The Society of Individuals*. Oxford, 1991.
Elliott, Dyan, *Spiritual Marriage. Sexual Abstinence in Medieval Wedlock*. Princeton, 1993.
——, *Fallen Bodies. Pollution, Sexuality, and Demonology in the Middle Ages*. Philadelphia, 1999.
Elm, Kaspar, *Beiträge zur Geschichte des Wilhelmitenordens*. Münstersche Forschungen 14. Köln, 1962.
——, "Verfall und Erneuerung des Ordenswesens im Spätmittelalter." In *Untersuchungen zu Kloster und Stift*, ed. Max-Planck-Institut für Geschichte. Veröfftentlichungen des Max-Planck-Instituts für Geschichte 68. Göttingen, 1980, 188–238.
——, ed., *Ordensstudien I: Beiträge zur Geschichte der Konversen im Mittelalter*. Berliner Historische Studien 2. Berlin, 1980.
——, "Mendikantenstudium, Laienbildung und Klerikerschulung im Spätmittelalterlichen Westfalen." In *Studien zum städtischen Bildungswesen des späten Mittelalters und der frühen Neuzeit*. Abhandlungen der Akademie der Wissenschaften in Göttingen Phil.-hist. Kl. III,137. Göttingen, 1983, 586–617.
——, "Die Bruderschaft vom Gemeinsamen Leben. Eine Geistliche Lebensform zwischen Kloster und Welt, Mittelalter und Neuzeit." *OGE* 59 (1985), 470–496.
——, "Elias, Paulus von Theben und Augustinus als Ordensgründer. Ein Beitrag zur Geschichtsschreibung und Geschichtsdeutung der Eremiten- und Bettelorden des 13. Jahrhunderts." In *Geschichtsschreibung und Geschichtsbewusstsein im späten Mittelalter*. Ed. Hans Patze. Vorträge und Forschungen 31. Sigmaringen, 1987, 371–397.
——, *Mittelalterliches Ordensleben in Westfalen und am Niederrhein*. Paderborn, 1989.
——, ed., *Reformbemühungen und Observanzbestrebungen im spätmittelalterlichen Ordenswesen*. Berliner Historische Studien 14/Ordensstudien 6. Berlin, 1989.
——, "*Augustinus Canonicus-Augustinus Eremita*: A Quattrocento Cause Célèbre." In *Christianity and the Renaissance. Image and Religious Imagination in the Quattrocentro*, ed. Timothy Verdon and John Henderson. New York, 1990, 83–107.
——, "Die Bedeutung historischer Legitimation für Entstehung, Funktion und Bestand des mittelalterlichen Ordenswesens." In *Herkunft und Ursprung. Historische und mythische Formen der Legitimation*. Ed. Peter Wunderli. Sigmaringen, 1994, 71–90.
——, "*De praestantia religionis S. Augustini*: Eine als verloren geltende Quaestio quodlibetica des Augustiner-Eremiten Gerhard von Bergamo (d. 1355)." In *Mittelalterliche Texte. Überlieferung&Befund&Deutungen*, Kolloquium der Zentraldirektion der Monumenta Germaniae Historica am 28./29. Juni 1996. *MGH.SS* 42, ed. Rudolf Schieffer. Hannover, 1996, 155–172.
——, "*Vita regularis sine regula*. Bedeutung, Rechtsstellung und Selbstverständnis des mittelalterlichen und frühneuzeitlichen Semireligiosentums." In *Häresie und Vorzeitige Reformation im Spätmittelalter*, ed. F. Smahel. München, 1998, 239–273.
Elm, Susanna, *'Virgins of God'. The Making of Asceticism in Late Antiquity*. Oxford, 1994.
Elssius, P., *Encomiasticon Augustinianum*. Bruxellis, 1654. Reprint. Westmead, Farnborough, Hants, England, 1970.
Elze, Martin, "Das Verständnis der Passion Jesu im ausgehenden Mittelalter und bei Luther." In *Geist und Geschichte der Reformation. Festgabe Hanns Rückert zum 65. Geburtstag*, ed. K. Scholder. Berlin, 1966, 127–151.

Erdei, Klara, *Auf dem Wege zu sich selbst: Die Meditation im 16. Jahrhundert. Eine Funktionsanalytische Gattungsbeschreibung.* Wiesbaden, 1990. *L'État Angevin. Pouvoir, Culture et Société entre XIIIe et XIVe Siècle.* Collection de l'École Française de Rome 245. Istituto Storico Italiano Per il Medio Evo. Nuovi Stuid Storici 45. Roma, 1998.
Evans, Arthur, *Mycenaean Tree and Pillar Cult.* London, 1901. *Faire Croire. Modalités de la diffusion et de la réception des messages religieux du XIIe au XVe siècle.* Table Ronde organisée par l'Ecole francaise de Rome, en collaboration avec l'Institut d'histoire médiévale de l'Université de Padoue, Rome, 22–23 juin 1979. Rome, 1981.
Feil, Ernst, *Religio. Die Geschichte eines neuzeitlichen Grundbegriffs vom Frühchristentum bis zur Reformation.* Göttingen, 1986.
Felten, Franz J. and Nikolas Jaspert eds., with Stephanie Haarländer, *Vita Religiosa im Mittelalter. Festschrift für Kaspar Elm zum 70. Geburtstag.* Berliner Historische Studien 31/Ordensstudien 13. Berlin, 1999.
Finke, Heinrich, *Aus den Tagen Bonifaz VIII. Funde und Forschungen.* Münster, 1902.
Fleith, Barbara, *Studien zur Überlieferungsgeschichte der Lateinischen Legenda Aurea.* Subsidia Hagiographica 72. Société des Bollandistes. Bruxelles, 1991.
———, "The Patristic Sources of the *Legenda Aurea*. A Research Report." In *The Reception of the Church Fathers in the West.* Ed. Irena Backus. 2 vols. Leiden, 1997, 1:231–287.
Flemming, J., "Baum, Bäume." In *Lexikon der Christlichen Ikonographie.* Ed. Engelbert Kirschbaum, et al. Rome/Frieburg/Basel/Vienna, 1968, 1:258–268.
Foucault, Michel, *The History of Sexuality.* Vol. 1: *An Introduction.* New York, 1978.
———, *Power/Knowledge: Selected Interviews and Other Writings, 1972–1977.* Ed. C. Gordon. New York, 1980.
Frank, Isnard Wilhelm, *Die Bettelordenstudia im Gefüge des Spätmittelalterlichen Universitätswesens.* Institut für Europäische Geschichte Mainz Vorträge 83. Stuttgart, 1988.
Frank, Robert Worth, Jr., "Meditationes Vitae Christi: The Logistics of Access to Divinity." In *Hermeneutics and Medieval Culture.* Ed. Patrick J. Gallacher and Helen Damico. New York, 1989, 39–50.
Frassetto, Michael, ed., *Medieval Purity and Piety. Essays on Medieval Clerical Celibacy and Religious Reform.* New York, 1998.
Freedberg, David, *The Power of Images. Studies in the History and Theory of Response.* Chicago, 1989.
Freeden, Michael, *Ideologies and Political Theory. A Conceptual Approach.* Oxford, 1996.
Freud, Sigmund, *Civilization and Its Discontents.* The Standard Edition. New York, 1989.
Füser, Thomas, "Vom *exemplum Christi* über das *exemplum sanctorum* zum 'Jedermannsbeispiel'. Überlegungen zur Normativität exemplarischer Verhaltens-muster im institutionellen Gefüge der Bettelorden des 13. Jahrhunderts." In *Die Bettelorden im Aufbau,* (see Melville, Gert), 27–105.
Gadamer, Hans-Georg, *Truth and Method.* 2nd rev. ed., trans. Joel Weinsheimer and Donald G. Marshall. New York, 1993.
Gager, J.G., *The Origins of Anti-Semitism. Attitudes toward Judaism in Pagan and Christian Antiquity.* Oxford, 1983.
Geertz, Clifford, *Local Knowledge. Further Essays in Interpretive Anthropology.* New York, 1983.
Gewirth, Alan, *Marsilius of Padua, The Defensor Pacis.* Vol. 1: *Marsilius of Padua and Medieval Political Philosophy.* New York, 1951.
Gierke, Otto, *Political Theories of the Middle Ages.* Trans. with an introduction by Frederic William Maitland. Cambridge, 1900; Beacon Paperback edition: Boston, 1960³.
Giddens, Anthony, *The Constitution of Society. Outline of the Theory of Structuration.* Berkeley, 1984.
———, *New Rules of Sociological Method. A Positive Critique of Interpretative Sociologies.* 2nd ed. Stanford, 1993.
Goebel, P. *Geschichte der Katechese im Abendlande vom Verfalle des Katechumenats bis zum Ende des Mittelalters.* Kempten, 1880.

Goering, Joseph, *William de Montibus (c. 1140–1213): The Schools and the Literature of Pastoral Care*. Toronto, 1992.
——, "The Summa *Qui bene presunt* and Its Author." In *Literature and Religion in the Later Middle Ages. Philological Studies in Honor of Siegfried Wenzel*. Eds. Richard G. Newhauser and John A. Alford. *Medieval and Renaissance Texts and Studies* 118. New York, 1995, 143–159.
Goodich, Michael, *Vita Perfecta: The Ideal of Sainthood in the Thirteenth Century*. Monographien zur Geschichte des Mittelalters 25. Stuttgart, 1982.
Gow, Andrew Colin, *The Red Jews: Antisemitism in an Apocalyptic Age 1200–1600*. SMRT 55. Leiden, 1995.
Grane, Leif, "Gregor von Rimini und Luthers Leipziger Disputation." *Studia Theologica* 22 (1968), 29–49.
——, "Divus Paulus et S. Augustinus, Interpres eius fidelissimus. Über Luthers Verhältnis zu Augustin." In *Festschrift für Ernst Fuchs*, ed., Gerard Ebeling, E. Jüngel, and G. Schunack. Tübingen, 1973, 133–146.
——, *Modus loquendi theologicus. Luthers Kampf um die Erneuerung der Theologie (1515–1518)*. Leiden, 1975.
——, "Kritische Berichte. Lutherforschung und Geistesgeschichte. Auseinandersetzung mit Heiko A. Oberman." *ARG* 68 (1977), 302–315.
Grant, Edward, "Cosmology." In *Science in the Middle Ages*. Ed. David C. Lindberg. Chicago, 1978, 265–302.
——, *Planets, Stars, and Orbs. The Medieval Cosmos, 1200–1687*. Cambridge, 1994.
Graus, Frantisek, *Pest-Geissler-Judenmorde. Das 14. Jahrhundert als Krisenzeit*. Göttingen, 1987.
Gregory, Brad S., *Salvation at Stake. Christian Martyrdom in Early Modern Europe*. Harvard Historical Studies 134. Cambridge, MA, 1999.
——, "Late Medieval Religiosity and the Renaissance of Christian Martyrdom in the Reformation Era." In *Continuity and Change*, (see Bast), 379–399.
Grundmann, Herbert, *Religiöse Bewegungen im Mittelalter*. Berlin, 1935. Reprint. Hildesheim/Zürich/New York, 1977.
Guarieneri, Romana, "Il movimento del Libero Spirito." In *Archivio Italiano per la storia della pietà* 4 (1965), 351–708.
Gurevich, Aron, *Medieval Popular Culture. Problems of Belief and Perception*. Trans. Janos M. Bak and Paul A. Hollingsworth. Cambridge, 1988.
——, *The Origins of European Individualism*. Trans. Katherine Judelson. Oxford/Cambridge, MA, 1995.
Gutiérrez, David, "De Antiquis Ordinis Eremitarum Sancti Augustini Bibliothecis." *AAug.* 23 (1954), 154–372.
——, *The Augustinians in the Middle Ages, 1357–1517*. Villanova, Penn., 1983. Originally published as *Los Agustinos en la edad media 1357–1517*. Rome, 1977.
——, *Geschichte des Augustinerordens*. V. 1/1: *Die Augustiner im Mittelalter, 1256–1356*. Würzburg, 1985.
Hackett, Jeremiah, "The Use of a text quotation from Meister Eckhart by Jordan of Quedlinburg OSA." In *Proceedings of the Patristic-Medieval and Renaissance Conference* 2. Villanova, 1977, 97–102.
——, "Verbum mentalis conceptio in Meister Eckhart and Jordanus of Quedlinburg. A Text Study." In *Sprache und Erkenntnis im Mittelalter*. Akten des VI. Internationalen Kongresses für mittelalterliche Philosophie der Societe internationale pour l'Étude de la Philosophie Médiévale, 29 August–3 September 1977. 2 vols. Berlin-New York, 1979, 2:1003–1011.
——, "Augustinian Mysticism in Fourteenth-Century Germany: Henry of Friemar and Jordanus of Quedlinburg." In *Augustine: Mystic and Mystagogue*. Ed. Frederick van Fleteren, Joseph C. Schnaubelt, OSA, Joseph Reino. New York et al., 1994, 439–456.
Haimerl, F. *Mittelalterliche Frömmigkeit im Spiegel der Gebetbuchliteratur Süddeutschlands*. München, 1952.

Hamel, Adolf, *Der junge Luther und Augustin*. Gütersloh, 1934; reprint: Hildesheim/New York, 1980.
Hamilton, Malcom B., *The Sociology of Religion. Theoretical and Comparative Perspectives*. London/New York, 1995.
Hamm, Berndt, "Frömmigkeit als Gegenstand theologiegeschichtlicher Forschung. Methodisch-historische Überlegungen am Beispiel von Spätmittelalter und Reformation." *ZThK* 74 (1977), 464–497.
——, *Frömmigkeitstheologie am Anfang des 16. Jahrhunderts. Studien zu Johannes von Paltz und seinem Umkreis*. BhTh 65. Tübingen, 1982.
——, "Normative Centering in the Fifteenth and Sixteenth Centuries: Observations on Religiosity, Theology, and Iconology." *JEMH* 3 (1999), 307–354.
——, and Thomas Lentes, eds., *Spätmittelalterliche Frömmigkeit zwischen Ideal und Praxis*. SuR.NR 15. Tübingen, 2001.
——, "Johann von Staupitz (ca. 1468–1524): spätmittelalterlicher Reformer und 'Vater' der Reformation." *ARG* 92 (2001), 6–41.
Hammerling, Roy, *The History and Interpretation of the Lord's Prayer in the Latin West from the First to the Eighth Century*. Unpublished Ph.D. dissertation, University of Notre Dame, 1997.
Handbook of European History, 1400–1600. Late Middle Ages, Renaissance, and Reformation. Eds. Thomas A. Brady Jr., Heiko A. Oberman, and James D. Tracy. 2 vols. Leiden, 1994.
Hansen, Dorothee, *Das Bild des Ordenslehrers und die Allegorie des Wissens. Ein gemaltes Programm der Augustiner*. Berlin, 1995.
Harmening, Dieter, "Katechismusliteratur. Grundlagen religiöser Laienbildung im Spätmittelalter." In *Wissensorganisierende und wissensvermittelnde Literatur im Mittelalter. Perspektiven ihrer Erforschung, Kolloquium 5.–7. Dezember 1985*. Ed. Norbert Richard Wolf. Wiesbaden, 1987, 91–102.
Harran, Marilyn J., *Luther on Conversion. The Early Years*. Ithaca, N.Y., 1983.
Hatfield, Rab, "The Tree of Life and the Holy Cross. Franciscan Spirituality in the Trecento and the Quattrocento." In *Christianity and the Renaissance*, 132–160.
Haug, Walter and Burghart Wachinger eds., *Die Passion Christi in Literatur und Kunst des Spätmittelalters*. Tübingen, 1993.
Hendrix, Scott H., *Tradition and Authority in the Reformation*. Variorum, Aldershot, 1996.
Hermans, Jos. M.M., and Aafje Lem, *Middeleeuwse Handschriften en Oude Drukken in de Collectie Emmanuelshuizen te Zwolle*. Zwolle, 1989.
Hermelink, Heinrich, *Die theologische Fakultät in Tübingen vor der Reformation, 1477–1534*. Stuttgart, 1906.
Hick, John, *An Interpretation of Religion. Human Responses to the Transcendent*. New Haven, 1992.
Hinnebusch, William A., O.P., *The History of the Dominican Order. Origins and Growth to 1500*. 2 vols. New York, 1966.
Hirsh, John C., *The Boundaries of Faith. The Development and Transmission of Medieval Spirituality*. SHCT 67. Leiden, 1996.
Hoenen, M.J.F.M., *Marsilius of Inghen. Divine Knowledge in Late Medieval Thought*. SHCT 50. Leiden, 1993.
Holly, Michael Ann, *Past Looking. Historical Imagination and the Rhetoric of the Image*. Ithaca, N.Y., 1996.
Holzapfel, Egidius, *Werner Rolevincks Bauernspiegel. Untersuchung und Neuherausgabe von 'De Regimine Rusticorum'*. FTS 76. Basel/Freiburg/Vienna, 1959.
Horst, Ulrich, "Die Lehrautorität des Papstes nach Augustinus von Ancona." *AAug*. 54 (1991), 271–303.
——, "Die Armut Christi und der Aposteln nach der Summa de ecclesiaspotestate des Augustinus von Ancona." In *Traditio Augustiniana. Studien über Augustinus und seine Rezeption*. Festgabe für Willigis Eckermann OSA zum 60. Geburtstag. Eds. Adolar Zumkeller and Achim Krümmel. Cassiciacum 46. Würzburg, 1994, 471–494.

Housley, Norman, *The Italian Crusades. The Papal-Angevin Alliance and the Crusades Against Christian Lay Powers, 1254–1343*. Oxford, 1982.
——, *The Avignon Papacy and the Crusades, 1305–1378*. Oxford, 1986.
Hsia, R. Po-chia, *The Myth of Ritual Murder. Jews and Magic in Reformation Germany*. New Haven and London, 1988.
Huizinga, J., *Herfsttij der middeleeuwen*. 1919. 22nd reprint: Amsterdam, 1997.
Hundersmarck, Lawrence F., "Preaching the Passion: Late Medieval 'Lives of Christ' as Sermon Vehicles." In *De Ore Domini. Preacher and Word in the Middle Ages*. Eds. Thomas L. Amos, Eugene A. Green, and Beverly Mayne Kienzle. Kalamazoo, 1989, 147–167.
Hyde, J.K., *Society and Politics in Medieval Italy. The Evolution of the Civil Life, 1000–1300*. London/New York, 1973.
James, William, *The Varieties of Religious Experience*. New York, 1978.
Jaye, Barbara H., *The Pilgrimage of Prayer: The Texts and Iconography of the 'Exercitium Super Pater Noster'*. Salzburg, 1990.
Jedin, Hubert, *A History of the Council of Trent. The First Sessions at Trent*. Trans., Ernest Graf. Edinburgh, 1961.
Jordan, William Chester, *The Great Famine. Northern Europe in the Early Fourteenth Century*. Princeton, 1996.
Jungmann, J.A., *The Mass of the Roman Rite: Its Origins and Development*. 2 vols. New York, 1951.
Kadlec, J., "Hermann Schwab von Mindelheim und sein Apokalypskommentar." In *Scientia Augustiniana*, (see Eckermann), 276–288.
Kantorowicz, Ernst H., *The King's Two Bodies. A Study in Mediaeval Political Theology*. Princeton, 1957.
Kehrein, Joseph, ed., *Lateinische Sequenzen des Mittelalters*. Mainz, 1873; reprint: Hildesheim, 1969.
Kieckhefer, Richard, *Repression of Heresy in Medieval Germany*. Pennsylvania, 1979.
——, *Unquiet Souls. Fourteenth-Century Saints and Their Religious Milieu*. Chicago, 1984.
——, "Major Currents in Late Medieval Devotion." In *Christian Spirituality II: High Middle Ages and Reformation*. Ed. Jil Rait, in collaboration with Bernard McGinn and John Meyendorff. *World Spirituality: An Encyclopedic History of the Religious Quest* 17. New York, 1988, 75–108.
Klapisch-Zuber, Christiane, "Plague and Family Life." In *The New Cambridge Medieval History*. Vol. VI, c. 1300–c. 1415. Ed. Michael Jones. Cambridge, 2000, 124–154.
Koch, Lucia, "'Eingezogenes Stilles Wesen'? Protestantische Damenstifte an der Wende zum 17. Jahrhundert." In *"In Christo ist weder Man noch Weyb" Frauen in der Zeit der Reformation und der katholischen Reform*. Ed. Anne Conrad. Münster, 1999, 199–230.
Kolde, Theodor, *Die deutsche Augustiner-Congregation und Johann von Staupitz. Ein Beitrag zur Ordens und Reformationgeschichte*. Gotha, 1879.
——, *Martin Luther. Eine Biographie*. Gotha, 1884.
Köpf, Ulrich, *Die Anfänge der theologischen Wissenschaftstheorie im 13. Jahrhundert*. Tübingen, 1974.
——, "Kreuz IV. Mittelalter." *TRE* 19, 732–761.
——, "Monastische Theologie im 15. Jahrhundert." *Rottenburger Jahrbuch für Kirchengeschichte* 11 (1992), 117–135.
Kunzelmann, Adolbero, *Geschichte der deutschen Augustiner-Eremiten*. Vol. 1: *Das dreizehnte Jahrhundert*. Würzburg, 1969.
——, *Geschichte der deutschen Augustiner-Eremiten*. Vol. 5: *Die Sächsisch-Thüringische Provinz und die Sächsische Reformkongregation bis zum Untergang der Beiden*. Würzburg, 1974.
——, "Die Bedeutung des alten Erfurter Augustinerkloster." In *Scientia Augustiniana*. (see Eckermann), 609–629.
Kürzinger, Josef, *Alfonsus Vargas Toletanus und seine theologische Einleitungslehre*. BGPhThMA 29. Münster, 1930.

La Capra, D., *Soundings in Critical Theory*. New York, 1989.
Ladner, Gerhart B., *God, Cosmos, and Humankind. The World of Early Christian Symbolism*. Trans. by Thomas Dunlap. Berkeley, 1992.
Lakoff, George, *Women, Fire, and Dangerous Things. What Categories Reveal about the Mind*. Chicago, 1987.
——, and Mark Johnson, *Philosophy in the Flesh. The Embodied Mind and Its Challenge to Western Thought*. New York, 1999.
Landgraf, A.M., *Dogmengeschichte der Frühscholastik*. Vol. 1/1, *Die Gnadenlehre*. Regensburg, 1952.
Langmuir, Gavin, *History, Religion and Antisemitism*. Berkeley, 1990.
——, *Toward a Definition of Antisemitism*. Berkeley, 1990.
Lawless, Georege, *Augustine of Hippo and his Monastic Rule*. Oxford, 1987.
Lawrence, C.H., *The Friars. The Impact of the Early Mendicant Movement on Western Society*. London, 1994.
Le Bras, G., *Etudes de sociologie religieuse, II. De la morphologie à la typologie*. Paris, 1956.
Le Goff, Jacques, *The Medieval Imagination*, trans. Arthur Goldhammer. Chicago, 1988.
Leclercq, Henri, "Croix et Crucifix." *DAChL* 3/2: 3045–3131.
——, "Oraison dominicale." *DAChL* 12:2244–2255.
——, "Sator-Arepo." *DAChL* 15/1:913–915.
Leclercq, Jean, "Monastic and Scholastic Theology in the Reformers of the Fourteenth to Sixteenth Century." In *From Cloister to Classroom. Monastic and Scholastic Approaches to Truth*, ed. E. Rozanne Elder. Kalamazoo, Mich., 1986, 178–201.
Lerner, Robert E., *The Heresy of the Free Spirit in the Later Middle Ages*. Berkeley 1972.
Lewis, Gertrud Jaron, *By Women, for Women, about Women: The Sister-Books of Fourteenth-Century Germany*. Toronto, 1996.
Lickteig, Franz-Bernard, *The German Carmelites at the Medieval Universities*. Textus et Studia Historica Carmelitana 13. Rome, 1981.
Lievens, Robrecht, *Jordanus van Quedlinburg in de Nederlanden. Een Onderzoek van de Handschriften*. Gent, 1958.
Little, Lester K., *Religious Poverty and the Profit Economy in Medieval Europe*. London, 1978,
Lorenz, Sönke, *Studium Generale Erfordense. Zum Erfurter Schulleben im 13. und 14. Jahrhundert*. Monographien zur Geschichte des Mittelalters 34. Stuttgart, 1989.
Luhmann, Niklas, *Soziologische Aufklärung*. 4 vols. Opladen, 1970–1987.
——, *Soziale Systeme. Grundriss einer allgemeinen Theorie*. Frankfurt, 1984.
——, *Die Wissenschaft der Gesellschaft*. Frankfurt, 1990.
Maierù, Alfonso, *University Training in Medieval Europe*, trans. and ed. D.N. Pryds. Education and Society in the Middle Ages and Renaissance 3. Leiden, 1993.
Mannheim, K., "Conservative Thought." In K. Mannheim, *Essays on Sociology and Social Psychology*. Ed. P. Kecskemeti. London, 1953.
Manselli, Raoul, *La Religion Populaire au Moyen Age. Problemes de methode et d'histoire*. Paris, 1975.
Marcolino, Venicio, "Der Augustinertheologe an der Universität Paris." In *Gregor von Rimini. Werk und Wirkung bis zur Reformation* (see, Oberman, Heiko Augustinus), 127–194.
Markus, R.A., *Saeculum: History and Society in the Theology of St. Augustine*. Cambridge, 1970.
——, "Sign, Communication, and Communities in Augustine's *De Doctrina Christiana*." In *De doctrina christiana. A Classic of Western Culture*. Ed. Duane W.H. Arnold and Pamela Bright. Notre Dame, 1995, 97–108.
Marrow, James H., *Passion Iconography in Northern European Art of the Late Middle Ages and Early Renaissance. A Study of the Transformation of Sacred Metaphor into Descriptive Narrative*. Kortrijk, Belgium, 1979.
Martin, Francis X., "The Augustinian Observance." In *Reformbemühungen und Observanzbestrebungen im spätmittelalterlichen Ordenswesen*, (see Elm), 325–345.
——, *Friar, Reformer, and Renaissance Scholar. Life and Works of Giles of Viterbo, 1469–1532*. Villanova, PA, 1992.

Martin, Herve, *Le metier de predicateur à la fin du Moyen Age, 1350–1520*. Paris, 1988.
Mathes, Fulgence, "The Poverty Movement and the Augustinian Hermits." *AAug.* 31 (1968), 5–154; *AAug.* 32 (1969), 5–116.
Matsura, Jun, "Restbestände aus der Bibliothek des Erfurter Augustinerklosters zu Luthers Zeit und bisher unbekannte eigenhändige Notizen Luthers. Ein Bericht." In *Lutheriana. Zum 500. Geburtstag Martin Luthers von dem Mitarbeitern der Weimarer Ausgabe*, ed. Gerhard Hammer and Karl-Heinz zur Mühlen, 315–330. AWA 5. Köln, 1984.
Matter, E. Ann, *The Voice of My Beloved. The Song of Songs in Western Medieval Christianity*. Philadelphia, 1990.
Matthews, Gareth B., ed., *The Augustinian Tradition*. Berkeley, 1999.
Meier, John P., *A Marginal Jew. Rethinking the Historical Jesus*, vol. 2: *Mentor, Message, and Miracles*. New York, 1994.
Meijer, Alberic de, "Saint Augustine and the Conversation with the Child on the Shore. The History Behind the Legend." *Augustinian Heritage* 39 (1993), 21–34.
Melville, Gert and Jörg Oberste, *Die Bettelorden im Aufbau. Beiträge zu Institutionalisierungsprozessen im mittelalterlichen Religiosentum*. Vita Regularis. Ordnung und Deutung religiosen Lebens im Mittelalter 11. Münster, 1999.
Mertens, Volker, and Hans-Jochen Schiewer, ed. *Die deutsche Predigt im Mittelalter. Internationales Symposium am Fachbereich Germanistik der Freien Universität Berlin von 3.–6. Oktober 1989*. Tübingen, 1992.
Michalsky, Tanja, *Memoria und Repräsentation. Die Grabmäler des Königshauses Anjou in Italien*. Veröffentlichungen des Max-Planck-Instituts für Geschichte 157. Göttingen, 2000.
Miethke, Jürgen, *Ockhams Weg zur Sozialphilosophie*. Berlin, 1969.
———, "Die Rolle der Bettelorden im Umbruch der politischen Theorie an der Wende zum 14. Jahrhundert." In *Stellung und Wirksamkeit der Bettelorden in der städtischen Gesellschaft*, (see Elm, Kaspar), 119–153.
———, *De Potestate Papae. Die päpstliche Amtskompetenz im Widerstreit der politischen Theorie von Thomas von Aquin bis Wilhelm von Ockham*. SuR.NR 15. Tübingen, 2000.
Miles, Margaret R., "Desire and Delight: A New Reading of Augustine's *Confessions*." In *Broken and Whole. Essays on Religion and the Body*. Ed. Maureen A. Tilley and Susan A. Ross. College Theological Society 39. London, 1993, 3–16.
Millis, Ludo J.R., *Angelic Monks and Earthly Men*. Woodbridge, 1992.
Millman, Marcia and Rosabeth Moss Kanter, "Introduction to Another Voice: Feminist Perspectives on Social Life and Social Science." In *Feminism and Methodology*. Ed. Sandra Harding. Bloomington, Indiana, 1987, 29–36.
Milway, Michael, "Forgotten Best-Sellers from the Dawn of the Reformation." In *Continuity and Change*, (see Bast), 113–142.
Ministeri, P.B., "De Augustini de Ancona, O.E.S.A. (d. 1328) Vita et Operibus." *AAug.* 22 (1951/1952), 7–56, 148–262.
Moeller, Bernd, "Frömmigkeit in Deutschland um 1500." *ARG* 56 (1965), 3–31.
———, "Luther und die Städte." In *Aus der Lutherforschung. Drei Vorträge*. Ed. Die Gemeinsame Kommision der Rheinisch-Westfälischen Akademie der Wissenschaften and the Gerda Henkel Stiftung, 1983, 9–26.
Mollat, G. *The Popes at Avignon. The 'Babylonian Captivity' of the Medieval Church*. Trans. from the 9th French edition by Janet Love. New York, 1963.
Moltmann, Jürgen, *Der Gekreuzigte Gott. Das Kreuz Christi als Grund und Kritik Christlicher Theologie*. Munich, 1972.
Mone, F.J., *Lateinische Hymnen des Mittelalters aus Handschriften herausgegeben und erklärt*. 3 vols., Freiburg, 1853–1855.
Moore, R.I., *The Formation of a Persecuting Society. Power and Deviance in Western Europe, 950–1250*. Oxford, 1987.
Moorman, John, *A History of the Franciscan Order, From its Origins to the Year 1517*. Oxford, 1968.
———, *Medieval Franciscan Houses*. Franciscan Institute Publications, History Series, nr. 4. St. Bonaventure, N.Y., 1983.

Morris, Colin, *The Papal Monarchy. The Western Church from 1050–1250*. Oxford, 1989.
Morrison, Karl F., *The Mimetic Tradition of Reform in the West*. Princeton, 1982.
———, *Understanding Conversion*. Charlottesville, VA, 1992.
Muir, Edward, *Civic Ritual in Renaissance Venice*. Princeton, 1981.
Mulchahey, Michele, *Dominican Education and the Dominican Ministry in the Thirteenth and Fourteenth Centuries: fra Jacopo Passavanti and the Florentine Convent of Santa Maria Novella*. Unpublished Ph.D. Dissertation, University of Toronto, 1988.
———, "The Dominican *Studium* System and the Universities of Europe in the Thirteenth Century." In *Manuels, Programmes de Cours et Techniques d'Enseignement dans les Universités Médiévales*. Ed. J. Hamesse. Louvain-la-Neuve, 1994, 277–324.
———, *"First the Bow is Bent in Study..." Dominican Education Before 1350*. Pontifical Institute of Medieval Studies: Studies and Texts 132. Toronto, 1998.
Müller, Alphons Victor, *Luthers theologische Quellen*. Giessen, 1912.
Müller, Karl, *Der Kampf Ludwigs des Baiern mit der römischen Curie. Ein Beitrag zur kirchlichen Geschichte des 14. Jahrhunderts*. Vol. 1: *Ludwig der Baier und Johann XXII*. Tübingen, 1879.
Mylonas, George Emmanuel, "Religion in Prehistoric Greece." In *Ancient Religions*. Ed. Vergilius Ferm. New York, 1950; first paperback ed. 1965, 147–167.
MacDonald, A.A., H.N.B. Ridderbos, and R.M. Schlusemann, eds., *The Broken Body. Passion Devotion in Late-Medieval Culture*. Mediaevalia Groningana 21. Groningen, 1998.
———, "Passion Devotion in Late-Medieval Scotland." In *The Broken Body*, 109–131.
MacGrade, A. Stephen, *The Political Thought of William of Ockham. Personal and Institutional Principles*. Cambridge, 1974.
McDonnell, Ernest W., *The Beguines and Beghards in Medieval Culture*. New Jersey, 1954.
McGann, Jerome, *The Textual Condition*. Princeton, 1991.
McGinn, Bernard, *The Presence of God. A History of Western Christian Mysticism*. Vol. 1: *The Foundations of Mysticism. Origins to the Fifth Century*. New York, 1994; vol. 2: *The Growth of Mysticism. Gregory the Great Through the 12th Century*. New York, 1996.
McGrath, Alister E., "Augustinianism? A Critical Assessment of the so-called 'Medieval Augustinian Tradition' on Justification." *Aug(L)* 31 (1981), 247–267.
McIlwain, C.H., *The Growth of Political Thought in the West*. London, 1932.
McNeil, M.G., *Simone Fidati and his De gestis Domini Salvatoris*, Washington, D.C., 1950.
Newhauser, R., *The Treatise on Vices and Virtues in Latin and the Vernacular*. Typgologie des sources du Moyen Age occidental, fasc. 68. Turnhout, 1993.
Newman, Martha, *The Boundaries of Charity. Cistercian Culture and Ecclesiastical Reform, 1098–1180*. Stanford, 1996.
Newton, Adam Zachary, *Narrative Ethics*. Cambridge, MA, 1995.
Nirenberg, David, *Communities of Violence. Persecution of Minorities in the Middle Ages*. Princeton, 1996.
Oberman, Heiko Augustinus, *Archbishop Thomas Bradwardine. A Fourteenth-Century Augustinian*. Utrecht, 1958.
———, *The Harvest of Medieval Theology. Gabriel Biel and Late Medieval Nominialism*. Cambridge, 1963; reprint: Durham, N.C., 1983.
———, *Forerunners of the Reformation*. Philadelphia, 1966; reprint: Philadelphia, 1981.
———, "Headwaters of the Reformation: Initia Lutheri—Initia Reformationis." In *Luther and the Dawn of the Modern Era: Papers for the Fourth International Congress for Luther Research*, ed. H.A. Oberman. SHCT 8. Leiden, 1974, 40–88.
———, *Werden und Wertung der Reformation. Vom Wegestreit zum Glaubenskampf*. Tübingen, 1977. 2nd ed. Tübingen, 1979. Trans. by Denis Martin under the title *Masters of the Reformation. The Emergence of a New Intellectual Climate in Europe*. Cambridge, 1981.
———, "Reformation: Epoche oder Episode." *ARG* 68 (1977), 56–109.
———, ed., *Gregor von Rimini. Werk und Wirkung bis zur Reformation*. SuR 20. Berlin-New York, 1981.
———, *Luther. Mensch Zwischen Gott und Teufel*. Berlin, 1982.

——, *The Roots of Anti-Semitism in the Age of Renaissance and Reformation*. Philadelphia, 1984.
——, *The Dawn of the Reformation. Essays in Late Medieval and Early Reformation Thought*. Edinburgh, 1986.
——, *The Impact of the Reformation*. Grand Rapids, MI., 1994.
——, "Hus and Luther: Prophets of a Radical Reformation." In *The Contentious Triangle: Church, State, and University. A Festschrift in Honor of Professor George Huntston Williams*. Ed. Rodney L. Peterson and Calvin Augustine Pater. Sixteenth Century Essays & Studies 51. Kirksville, MO, 1999, 135–166.
——, *The Reformation. From the Last Days to the Beginning of the New World: Luther's Beachhead and the Shores of America*. Ed. Donald Weinstein. Forthcoming, New Haven.
Ocker, Christopher, "Augustinianism in Fourteenth-Century Theology." *Augustinian Studies* 18 (1987), 81–106.
——, *Johannes Klenkok: A Friar's Life, c. 1310–1374*. Transactions of the American Philosophical Society. Vol. 38, part 5. Philadelphia, 1993.
Offler, H.S., "The 'Influence' of Ockham's Political Thinking: The First Century." In *Die Gegenwart Ockhams*. Eds. Wilhelm Vossenkuhl and Rolf Schönberger. Weinheim, 1990, 338–365.
Ossinger, J., *Bibliotheca Augustiniana*. Ingolstadt, 1768; reprint: Torino, 1963.
Otto, Rudolph, *Das Heilige. Über das Irrationale in der Idee des Göttlichen und sein Verhältnis zum Rationalen*. Breslau, 1917.
Owens, Joseph, "Faith, ideas, illumination, and experience." In *Cambridge History of Later Medieval Philosophy*, ed. Norman Kretzmann, Anthony Kenny, and Jan Pinborg, ass. ed., Eleonore Stump. Cambridge, 1982, 440–459.
O'Malley, John W., *Giles of Viterbo on Church and Reform. A Study of Renaissance Thought*. SMRT 5. Leiden, 1968.
Partner, Peter, *Renaissance Rome, 1500–1559*. Berkeley, 1976.
Paton, Bernadette, *Preaching Friars and the Civic Ethos: Siena, 1380–1480*. London, 1992.
Patze, Hans, and Walter Schlesinger, ed., *Geschichte Thüringens*. Vol. 2/2, *Hohes und Spätes Mittelalter*. Köln/Wien, 1973.
Pauler, Roland, *Die Deutschen Könige und Italien im 14. Jahrhundert. Von Heinrich VII. bis Karl IV*. Darmstadt, 1997.
Pelikan, Jaroslav, *The Christian Tradition. A History of the Development of Doctrine*. Vol. 1: *The Emergence of the Catholic Tradition (100–600)*. Chicago, 1971.
Pelzer, A., "Prosper de Reggio Emilia des Ermites de Saint-Augustin et le manuscrit latin 1086 de la Bibilothèque Vaticane." *Revue néo-scholastique* 30 (1928), 316–351.
Pennington, Kenneth, *The Prince and the Law, 1200–1600. Sovereignty and Rights in the Western Legal Tradition*. Berkeley, 1993.
Petroff, Elizabeth Alvilda, *Medieval Women's Visionary Literature*. Oxford, 1986.
Pickering, F.P., *Literatur und darstellende Kunst im Mittelalter*. Berlin, 1966.
——, "The Gothic image of Christ. The sources of medieval representations of the crucifixion." In F.P. Pickering, *Essays on Medieval German Literature and Iconography*. Cambridge, 1980, 3–30.
Piur, Paul, *Petrarcas 'Buch Ohne Namen' und die Päpstliche Kurie. Ein Beitrag zur Geistesgeschichte der Frührenaissance*. Halle, 1925.
Pryds, Darleen N., *The King Embodies the Word. Robert d'Anjou and the Politics of Preaching*. SHCT 93. Leiden, 2000.
Ramakers, B.A.M., *Spelen en Figuren. Toneelkunst en processiecultuur in Oudenaarde tussen Middeleeuwen en Moderne Tijd*. Amsterdam, 1996.
Rano, Balbino, "Las dos Primeras Obras Conocidas sobre el Origen de la Orden Augstiniana." *AAug*. 45 (1982), 331–376.
——, "San Agustín y los orígenes de su Orden. Regla, Monasterio de Tagaste y Sermones ad fratres in eremo." In *San Agustín en el XVI Centenario de su Conversion 386/87–1987, La Ciudad de Dios, Revista Agustiniana* CC (1987). El Escorial, 1987, 649–727.

——, "San Agustin y su Orden en Algunos Sermones de Agustinos del Primer Siglo (1244–1344)." *AAug.* 53 (1990), 7–93.
Rapp, Francis, *L'Eglise et la vie religieuse en occident à la fin du Moyen Age.* Paris, 1971.
Reames, Sherry L, *The* Legenda aurea. *A Reexamination of Its Paradoxical History.* Madison, WI, 1985.
Reeves, Marjorie, "Joachimist Expectations in the Order of Augustinian Hermits." *RThAM* 25 (1958), 111–141.
Reinhard, Wolfgang and Heinz Schilling, eds., *Die Katholische Konfessionalisierung.* Schriften des Vereins für Reformationsgeschichte 198. Heidelberg, 1995.
Rennhofer, F., "Jordan v. Quedlinburg (J.v. Sachsen)." *LThk* 5:1120.
Reynolds, Susan, *Kingdoms and Communities in Western Europe, 900–1300.* Oxford, 1984; 2nd ed. 1997.
Rhodes, J.T., "Prayers of the Passion: From Jordanus of Quedlinburg to John Fewterer of Syon." *Durham University Journal* LXXXV #1; n.s. LIV #1 (1993), 27–38.
Richstaetter, Carl, *Christusfrömmigkeit in ihrer historischen Entfaltung: Ein quellenmässiger Beitrag zur Geschichte des Gebetes und des mystischen Innenlebens der Kirche.* Köln, 1949.
Ricoeur, Paul, *The Conflict of Interpretations.* Evanston, Ill, 1974.
——, *Time and Narrative.* 3 vols. Chicago, 1984–1988.
——, *Lectures on Ideology and Utopia.* Edited by George H. Taylor. New York, 1986.
Ridderbos, Bernhard, "The Man of Sorrows: Pictorial Images and Metaphorical Statements." In *The Broken Body* (see MacDonald, A.A.), 145–181.
Riffaterre, Michael, "The Mind's Eye: Memory and Textuality." In *The New Medievalism.* Eds. Marina S. Brownlee, Kevin Brownlee, and Stephen G. Nichols. Baltimore, 1991, 29–45.
Rigaudière, Albert, "The Theory and Practice of Government in Western Europe in the Fourteenth Century." In *The New Cambridge Medieval History,* vol. VI: c. 1300–c.1400. Ed. Michael Jones. Cambridge, 2000, 17–41.
Rivière, Jean, *Le Problème de l'Église et de l'État au Temps de Philippe le Bel. Étude de Théologie positive.* Paris, 1926.
Roest, Bert, *Reading the Book of History. Intellectual Contexts and Educational Functions of Franciscan Historiography, 1226–ca. 1350.* Groningen, 1996.
——, "A Meditative Spectacle: Christ's Bodily Passion in the *Satirica Ystoria.*" In *The Broken Body* (see MacDonald, A.A.), 31–54.
——, *A History of Franciscan Education (c. 1210–1517).* ESMAR 11. Leiden, 2000.
Roth, Francis, "The Great Schism and the Augustinian Order." *Aug(L)* 8 (1958), 281–298.
Rubin, Miri, *Corpus Christi. The Eucharist in Late Medieval Culture.* Cambridge, 1991.
——, *Gentile Tales. The Narrative Assault on Late Medieval Jews.* Yale, 1999.
Rudolf, R., *Thomas Peutners Betrachtungen über das Vater unser und das Ave Maria, nach österreichischen Handschriften hrsg. und untersucht.* Vienna, 1953.
Ruh, Kurt, "Zur Theologie des mittelalterlichen Passionstraktates." *Theologische Zeitschrift* 6 (1970), 17–39.
Ruokanen, Miikka, *Theology of Social Life in Augustine's* De Civitate Dei. Forschungen zur Kirchen- und Dogmengeschichte 53. Göttingen, 1993.
Rupp, Gordon, *The Righteousness of God.* London, 1953.
Russell, James C., *The Germanization of Early Medieval Christianity. A Sociohistorical Approach to Religious Transformation.* Oxford, 1994.
Rüther, Andreas, "La participation des ordres mendiants au soutien spirituel dans les campagnes d'Alsace." In *La christianisation des campagnes.* Ed. J.-P. Massaut et M.-E. Henneau. Bruxelles-Rome, 1996, 127–138.
Saak, Eric Leland, "The *Figurae Bibliorum* of Antonius Rampegolus: MS Uppsala C 162." In *Via Augustini. Augustine in the Later Middle Ages, Renaissance, and Reformation. Essays in Honor of Damasus Trapp, O.S.A.,* ed. Heiko A. Oberman and Frank A. James, III, in cooperation with Eric Leland Saak. SMRT 48. Leiden, 1991, 19–41.

——, *Religio Augustini: Jordan of Quedlinburg and the Augustinian Tradition in Late Medieval Germany*. Unpublished Ph.D. Dissertation. University of Arizona, 1993.
——, "*Quilibet Christianus*: Saints in Society in the Sermons of Jordan of Quedlinburg, OESA." In *Models of Holiness in Medieval Sermons*. Fédération Internationale des Instituts d'Études Médiévales, Texts et Études du Moyen Âge 5. Ed. Beverly Mayne Kienzle, with Edith Wilks Dolnikowski, Rosemary Drage Hale, Darleen Pryds and Anne T. Thayer. Louvain-la-Neuve, 1996, 317–338.
——, "The Reception of Augustine in the Later Middle Ages." In *The Reception of the Church Fathers in the West*. Ed. Irena Backus. 2 vols. Leiden, 1997, 1:367–404.
——, "The Creation of Augustinian Identity in the Later Middle Ages." *Aug(L)* 49 (1999), 109–164; 251–286.
——, "Aegidius Romanus." In *Augustine Through the Ages. An Encyclopedia*. Ed. Allan D. Fitzgerald, O.S.A. *et al.* Grand Rapids, MI, 1999, 14–15.
——, "*Milleloquium Sancti Augustini*." In *Augustine Through the Ages*, 563.
——, "Scholasticism, Late." In *Augustine Through the Ages*, 754–759.
——, "Pelagian/Anti-Pelagian Preaching: Predestination, Grace, and Good Works in the Sermons of Jordan of Quedlinburg, OESA (d. 1380)." Forthcoming in *Aug(L)*.
Sandy, Peggy Reeves, *Divine Hunger. Cannibalism as a Cultural System*. Cambridge, 1986.
Scheff, Thomas, *Microsociology. Discourse, Emotion and Social Structure*. Chicago, 1990.
Scheible, Heinz, "Aristoteles und die Wittenberg Universitätsreform. Zum Quellenwert von Lutherbriefen." In *Humanismus und Wittenberger Reformation. Festgabe anläßlich des 500. Geburtstages des Praeceptor Germaniae Philipp Melanchthon am 16. Februar 1997*, ed. Michael Beyer and Günter Wartenberg, with Hans-Peter Hasse. Leipzig, 1996, 123–144.
Schilling, Heinz, *Religion, Political Culture and the Emergence of Early Modern Society*. SMRT 50. Leiden, 1992.
——, "*Vita Religiosa* des Spätmittelalters und frühneuzeitliche Differenzierung der *christianitas*—Beobachtungen zu Wegen und Früchten eines Gesprächs zwischen Spätmittelalter- und Frühneuzeithistorikern." In *Vita Religiosa* (see Felten), 785–796.
Schleusener-Eichholz, Gudrun, *Das Auge im Mittelalter*. 2 vols., Münstersche Mittelalter-Schriften 35/II. München, 1985.
Schmitt, Jean C., "Religion populaire et culture folklorique. A propos d'une reedition: 'La piete populaire au Moyen Age'." *Annales E.S.C.* 31:5 (1976), 941–953.
Schmidt, Tilmann, *Der Bonifaz-Prozess. Verfahren der Papstanklage in der Zeit Bonifaz' VIII. und Clemens' V*. Forschungen zur Kirchlichen Rechtsgeschichte und zum Kirchenrecht 19. Cologne, 1989.
Schneyer, J.-B., *Repertorium der Lateinischen Sermones des Mittelalters für die Zeit von 1150–1350*. 11 vols., BGPhThMA 43. Münster, 1969–1990.
Schnurr, Klaus, *Hören und Handeln. Lateinische Auslegungen des Vaterunsers in der Alten Kirche bis zum 5. Jahrhundert*. FTS 132. Freiburg/Basel/Wien, 1985.
Scholz, Richard, *Die Publizistik zur Zeit Philipps des Schönen und Bonifaz' VIII. Ein Beitrag zur Geschichte der politischen Anschauungen des Mittelalters*. Stuttgard, 1903.
——, *Unbekannte Kirchenpolitischen Streitschriften aus der Zeit Ludwigs des Bayern (1327–1354). Analysen und Texte*. 2 vols. Rome, 1911–1914.
Schrama, Martijn, "*Studere debemus eam viriliter et humiliter*. Theologia Affectiva bei Hugolin von Orvieto (d. 1373)." *Bijdragen. Tijdschrift voor filosofie en theologie* 53 (1992), 135–151.
——, "*Theologia Affectiva*. Traces of Monastic Theology in the Theological Prolegomena of Giles of Rome." *Bijdragen. Tijdschrift voor filosofie en theologie* 57 (1996), 381–404.
Schreckenberg, H., *Die christlichen Adversus-Judeos-Texte und ihr literarisches und historisches Umfeld (1.–11. Jh.)*. Frankfurt am Main, 1982; 2nd rev. ed., 1990.
Schulze, Manfred, "Via Gregorii in Forschung und Quellen." In *Gregor von Rimini.Werk und Wirkung*, (see Oberman, Heiko A.), 1–126.
——, *Fürsten und Reformation. Geistliche Reformpolitik weltlicher Fürsten vor der Reformation*. SuR.NR 2. Tübingen, 1991.

Schuppisser, Fritz Oskar, "Schauen mit den Augen des Herzens. Zur Methodik der spätmittelalterlichen Passionsmeditation, besonders in der Devotio Moderna und bei den Augustinern." In *Die Passion Christi in Literatur und Kunst des Spätmittelalters.* Eds. Walter Haug and Burghart Wachinger. Tübingen, 1993, 169–210.

Schürer, M., "Die Dominikaner und das Problem der *generationes venturae.* Zu Traditionsbildung und -vermittlung in der Frühphase der Institutionalisierung des Predigerordens." In *Die Bettelorden im Aufbau,* (see Melville, Gert), 169–214.

Schwab, F.M., *David of Augsburg's 'Pater Noster' and the Authenticity of His German Works.* Munich, 1971.

Scribner, Bob, *Popular Culture and Popular Movements in Reformation Germany.* London, 1987.

———, "Das Visuelle in der Volksfrömmigkeit." In *Bilder und Bildersturm im Spätmittelalter und in der frühen Neuzeit,* ed. Bob Scribner. Wolfenbütteler Forschungen 46. Wiesbaden, 1990, 9–20.

———, "Elements of Popular Belief." In *Handbook of European History, 1400–1600. Late Middle Ages, Renaissance and Reformation,* vol. 1: *Structures and Assertions.* Eds. Thomas A. Brady Jr, Heiko A. Oberman and James D. Tracy. Leiden, 1994, 231–262.

———, *Religion and Culture in Germany (1400–1800).* Ed. Lyndal Roper. SMRT 81. Leiden, 2001.

Seegets, Petra, *Passionstheologie und Passionsfrömmigkeit im ausgehenden Mittelalter. Der Nürnberger Franziskaner Stephan Fridolin (gest. 1498) zwischen Kloster und Stadt.* SuR.NR 10. Tübingen, 1998.

Shank, Michael, *'Unless You Believe, You Shall Not Understand.' Logic, University, and Society in Late Medieval Vienna.* Princeton, 1988.

Shannon, Joseph L., *Good Works and Predestination According to Thomas of Strassburg, O.S.A.,* Baltimore, 1940.

Smalley, Beryl, "Oxford University Sermons, 1290–1293." In *Medieval Learning and Literature. Essays Presented to Richard William Hunt,* ed. J.J.G. Alexander and M.T. Gibson. Oxford, 1976, 307–327.

———, *The Gospels in the Schools c. 1100–c. 1280.* London, 1985.

Sorabji, Richard, *Time, Creation and the Continuum. Theories in Antiquity and the Early Middle Ages.* New York, 1983.

Southern, R.W., *The Making of the Middle Ages.* New Haven and London, 1953.

Spiegel, Gabrielle M., *The Past as Text. The Theory and Practice of Medieval Historiography.* Baltimore, 1997.

Spruit, Leen, *'Species Intelligibilis'. From Perception to Knowledge.* 2 vols., BSIH 48–49. Leiden, 1994.

Stakemeier, Eduard, *Der Kampf um Augustin auf dem Tridentinum.* Paderborn, 1937.

Stamm, Heinz-Meinholf, *Luthers Stellung zum Ordensleben.* VIEG 101. Wiesbaden, 1980.

Stange, Carl, "Über Luthers Beziehungen zur Theologie seines Ordens." *NKZ* 11 (1900), 574–595.

———, "Luther über Gregor von Rimini." *NKZ* 13 (1902), 721–727.

———, *Studien zur Theologie Luthers.* Gütersloh, 1928.

Staubach, Nikolaus, "Von der persönlichen Erfahrung zur Gemeinschaftsliteratur. Entstehungs- und Rezeptionsbedingungen geistlicher Reformtexte im Spätmittelalter." *OGE* 68 (1994), 200–228.

Stauch, Liselotte, and Walther Föhl, "Baum." In *Reallexikon zur Deutschen Kunstgeschichte,* ed. Otto Schmitt. 2 vols. 1:63–90. Stuttgart, 1948.

Stegmüller, Friedrich, *Repertorium Commentariorum in Sententias Petri Lombardi.* 2 vols. Würzburg, 1947.

———, *Repertorium Biblicum Medii Aevi.* 11 vols. Madrid, 1949–1980.

Steinmetz, David C., *Misericordia Dei. The Theology of Johannes von Staupitz in its Late Medieval Setting.* SMRT 4. Leiden, 1968.

———, "Luther and the Late Medieval Augustinians: Another Look." *CTM* 44 (1975), 245–260.

———, *Luther and Staupitz. An Essay in the Intellectual Origins of the Protestant Reformation.* Duke Monographs in Medieval and Renaissance Studies 4. Durham, N.C., 1980.
Stock, Brian, *The Implications of Literacy. Written Language and Models of Interpretation in the Eleventh and Twelfth Centuries.* Princeton, 1983.
———, *Listening For The Text. On the Uses of the Past.* Baltimore, 1990.
———, *Augustine the Reader. Meditation, Self-Knowledge, and the Ethics of Interpretation.* Cambridge, MA, 1996.
Streveler, Paul A., "Gregory of Rimini and the Black Monk on Sense and Reference: An Example of Fourteenth-Century Philosophical Analysis." *Vivarium* 18 (1980), 67–78.
Stritzky, Maria-Barbara von, *Studien zur Überlieferung und Interpretation des Vaterunsers in der frühchristlichen Literatur.* Münster, 1989.
Stroick, Clemens, *Heinrich von Friemar. Leben Werke, philosophisch-theologische Stellung in der Scholastik.* FTS 58. Freiburg, 1954.
Swanson, R.N., "Passion and Practice: the Social and Ecclesiastical Implications of Passion Devotion in the Late Middle Ages." In *The Broken Body* (see MacDonald, A.A.), 1–30.
Tachau, Katherine, *Vision and Certitude in the Age of Ockham. Optics, Epistemology and The Foundations of Semantics, 1250–1345.* STGMA 22. Leiden, 1988.
Taylor, Miriam S., *Anti-Judaism and Early Christian Identity. A Critique of the Scholarly Consensus.* Studia Post-Biblica 46. Leiden, 1995.
Tentler, Thomas N., *Sin and Confession on the Eve of the Reformation.* Princeton, 1977.
Terpstra, Nicholas, "Introduction: The Politics of Ritual Kinship." In *The Politics of Ritual Kinship. Confraternities and Social Order in Early Modern Italy.* Ed. Nicholas Terpstra. Cambridge, 2000.
Tierney, Brian, *Foundations of the Conciliar Theory. The Contribution of the Medieval Canonists from Gratian to the Great Schism.* Cambridge Studies in Medieval Life and Thought 4. Cambridge, 1955.
———, *Origins of Papal Infallibility, 1150–1350. A Study on the Concepts of Infallibility, Sovereignty and Tradition in the Middle Ages.* SHCT 6. Leiden, 1972.
Tolan, John, *Petrus Alfonsi and His Medieval Readers.* Gainesville, Florida 1993.
Trapè, Agostino, "Scuola Teologica e Spiritualia nell'Ordine Agostiniano." In *Sanctus Augustinus Vitae Spiritualis Magister.* 2 Vols. Rome, 1959, 2:5–75.
Trapp, A. Damasus, "Hiltalinger's Augustinian Quotations." *Aug(L)* 4 (1954), 412–449.
———, "Augustinian Theology of the Fourteenth Century. Notes on Editions, Marginalia, Opinions and Booklore." *Aug(L)* 6 (1956), 146–274.
———, "Peter Ceffons of Clairvaux." *RThAM* 24 (1957), 101–154.
———, "Gregory of Rimini Manuscripts, Editions, and Additions," *Aug(L)* 8 (1958), 425–443.
———, "La tomba bisoma di Tommaso da Strasburgo e di Gregorio da Rimini." *Augustinianum* 6 (1966), 5–17.
———, "Dreistufiger Editionsprozess und dreiartige Zitationsweise bei den Augustinertheologen des 14. Jahrhunderts?" *Aug(L)* 25 (1975), 283–292.
———, "A Round-Table Discussion of a Parisian OCist-Team and OESA-Team about AD 1350." *RThAM* 51 (1984), 206–222.
Trextler, Richard, *Public Life in Renaissance Florence.* New York, 1980.
Troeltsch, Ernst, *Augustin, die christliche Antike und das Mittelalter. Im Anschluss an die Schrift "De Civitate Dei".* Berlin,1915.
Turner, Victor W., *The Ritual Process. Structure and Anti-Structure.* Chicago, 1969.
Tyler, J. Jeffrey, *Lord of the Sacred City. The 'Episcopus Exclusus' in Late Medieval and Early Modern Germany.* SMRT 72. Leiden, 1999.
Van der Eerden, Peter, "Engelen en demonen." In *De middeleeuwse ideeënwereld, 1000–1300.* Ed. Manuel Stoffers. Hilversum, 1994, 117–143.
Van Dijk, R.Th.M., "Die Frage einer nördlichen Variante der Devotio Moderna.

Zur Interferenz zwischen den spätmittelalterlichen Reformbewegungen." In *Wessel Gansfort (1419–1489) and Northern Humanism*. Ed. F. Akkerman, G.C. Huisman, and A.J. Vanderjagt. *BSIH* 40. Leiden, 1993. 157–169.

Van Engen, John, *Rupert of Deutz*. Berkeley, 1983.

———, "The Christian Middle Ages as an Historiographical Problem." *AHR* 1987, 519–552.

———, "Friar Johannes Nyder on Laypeople Living as Religious in the World." In *Vita Religiosa*, (see Feltsen), 583–615.

Van Geest, Paul, *Thomas a Kempis (1379/80–1471). Een studie van zijn mens-en godsbeeld*. Kampen, 1996.

Van Oort, Johannes, *Jerusalem and Babylon. A Study into Augustin''s 'City of God' and the Sources of his Doctrine of the Two Cities*. Supplements to Vigiliae Christianae 14. Leiden, 1991.

Van Os, Henk, *Gebed in Schoonheid. Schatten van privé-devotie in Europa, 1300–1500*. Amsterdam, 1994.

Vauchez, André, *Religion et Societé dans l'Occident Médiéval*. Torino, 1980.

Verdon, Timothy, "Christianity, The Renaissance, and the Study of History: Environments of Experience and Imagination." In *Christianity and the Renaissance. Image and Religious Imagination in the Quattrocento*. Ed. Timothy Verdon and John Henderson. Syracuse, N.Y., 1990, 1–37.

Verheijen, L., *La Règle de saint Augustin*. Vol. 1: *Tradition manuscrite*; vol. 2: *Recherches historiques*. Paris, 1967.

———, *Nouvelle Approche de la Règle de saint Augustin*. Abbaye de Bellefontaine, 1980.

Vovelle, Michel, *Ideologies and Mentalities*. Trans. Eamon O'Flaherty. Oxford, 1990.

Wach, Joachim, *Sociology of Religion*. Chicago, 1957.

Whaling, Frank, ed., *Contemporary Approaches to the Study of Religion*. 2 vols. Religion and Reason 27–28. Berlin/New York/Amsterdam, 1983 and 1985.

Walsh, Katherine, "The Observance: Sources for a History of the Observant Reform Movement in the Order of Augustinian Friars in the Fourteenth and Fifteenth Centuries." *Rivista Di Storia Della Chiesa in Italia* 31 (1977), 40–67.

———, "Papal Policy and Local Reform: A) The Beginning of the Augustin Observance in Tuscany," B) *Congregatio Ilicetana*: The Augustinian Observant Movement in Tuscany and the Humanist Ideal." *Römische Historische Mitteilungen* 21 (1979), 35–57; 22 (1980), 105–145.

———, *Richard Fitz Ralph in Oxford, Avignon and Armagh. A Fourteenth-Century Scholar and Primate*. Oxford, 1981.

———, "Wie ein Bettelorden zu (s)einem Gründer kam. Fingierte Traditionen um die Entstehung der Augustiner-Eremiten." In *Fälschungen im Mittelalter*. Internationaler Kongress der Monumenta Germaniae Historica, München, 16.–19. September 1986. Teil V: *Fingierte Briefe, Frömmigkeit und Fälschung. Realienfälschungen. MGH.SS* 33/V. Hannover, 1988, 585–610.

Warnar, Geert, *Het Ridderboec. Over Middelnederlandse literatuur en lekenvroomheid*. Amsterdam, 1995.

Wawrykow, Joseph, "On Dispelling the Malaise in Scholastic Theology." In *The Past and Future of Medieval Studies*. Ed. John Van Engen. Notre Dame, 1994,178–189.

Weber, Max, *Economy and Society. An Outline of Interpretive Sociology*. Ed. Guenther Roth and Claus Wittich. Berkeley, 1978.

Weber, Philip E., "Varieties of Popular Piety Suggested by Netherlandic *Vita Christi* Prayer Cycles," *OGE* 64 (1990), 195–226.

Weidenhiller, P. Egino, *Untersuchungen zur deutschsprachigen katechetischen Literatur des späten Mittelalters, Nach den Handschriften der Bayerischen Staatsbibliothek*. Munich, 1965.

Weinbrenner, Ralph, *Klosterreform im 15. Jahrhundert zwischen Ideal und Praxis*. SuR.NR 7. Tübingen, 1996.

Weinstein, Donald, *Savonarola and Florence. Prophecy and Patriotism in the Renaissance*. Princeton, 1970.

Weiss, Ulmann, *Die frommen Bürger von Erfurt. Die Stadt und ihre Kirche im Spätmittelalter und in der Reformationszeit*. Weimar, 1988.
Wenzel, Horst, *Hören und Sehen, Schrift und Bild. Kultur und Gedächtnis im Mittelalter*. München, 1995.
Wenzel, Siegfried, *Verses in Sermons. "Fasciculus Morum" and Its Middle English Poems*. Cambridge, MA., 1978.
——, *Preachers, Poets, and the Early English Lyric*. Princeton, 1986.
Werner, Karl, *Die Scholastik des späteren Mittelalters*. Vol. 3: *Der Augustinismus in der Scholastik des späteren Mittelalters*. Wien, 1883.
Wesjohann, Achim, "*Simplicitas* als franziskanisches Ideal und der Prozeß der Institutionalisierung des Minoritenordens." In *Die Bettelorden im Aufbau*, (see Melville, Gert), 107–168.
White, Hayden, *The Content of the Form. Narrative Discourse and Historical Representation*. Baltimore, 1987.
Willeumier-Schalij, J.M., "De LXV Artikelen van de Passie van Jordanus van Quedlinburg in Middelnederlandse handschriften." *OGE* 53/1 (1979), 15–35.
Wilks, Michael, "*Papa est nomen iurisdictionis*: Augustinus Triumphus and the Papal Vicariate of Christ." *Journal of Theological Studies* 8 (1957), 71–91, 256–272.
——, *The Problem of Sovereignty in the Later Middle Ages. The Papal Monarchy with Augustinus Triumphus and the Publicists*. Cambridge, 1963.
Wilson, Katharina M., *Medieval Women Writers*. Athens, Georgia, 1984.
Winterhagen, Wilhelm E., "Martin Luther und das Amt des Provinzialvikars in der Reformkongregation der deutschen Augustiner-Eremiten." In *Vita Religiosa*, (see Feltsen), 707–738.
Wriedt, Markus, "Via Guilelmi—Via Gregorii: Zur Frage einer Augustinerschule im Gefolge Gregors von Rimini under besonderer Berücksichtigung Johannes von Staupitz." In *Deutschland und Europa in der Neuzeit. Festschrift für Karl Otmar Freiherr von Aretin zum 65. Geburtstag*. Ed. Ralph Melville, Claus Scharg, Martin Vogt, and Ulrich Wengenroth. *VIEG* 134. Mainz, 1988, 111–131.
——, *Gnade und Erwählung. Eine Untersuchung zu Johann von Staupitz und Martin Luther*. *VIEG* 141. Mainz, 1991.
Ypma, Eelcko, *La Formation des Professeurs chez les Ermites de Saint-Augustin de 1256 à 1354*. Paris, 1956.
——, "Les *cursores* chez les Augustins." *RThAM* 26 (1959), 137–144.
——, "La Promotion au lectorat chez les Augustins et le *De lectorie gradu* d'Ambroise de Cora." *Aug(L)* 13 (1963), 391–417.
——, "Recherches sur la productivité littéraire de Jacques de Viterbe jusqu'a 1300." *Aug(L)* 25 (1975), 230–249.
——, "Jacques de Viterbe témoin valable?" *RThAM* 52 (1985), 232–234.
Zschoch, Hellmut, *Klosterreform und monastische Spiritualität im 15. Jahrhundert. Conrad von Zenn OESA (d. 1460) und sein Liber de vita monastica*. *BhTh* 75. Tübingen, 1988.
Zumkeller, Adolar, *De Doctrina Sociali Scholae Augustinianae Aevi Medii*. *AAug*. 22 (1952), 57–84.
——, *Hermann v. Schildesche O.E.S.A. (d. 8 Juli 1357), zur 600. Wiederkehr seines Todestages*. Cassiciacum 14. Würzburg, 1957.
——, "Die Lehrer des geistlichen Lebens unter den deutschen Augustinern vom dreizehnten Jahrhundert bis zum Konzil von Trient." In *Sanctus Augustinus, vitae spiritualis magister*. 2 vols. Rome, 1959, 2:239–338.
——, "Das Ungenügen der menschlichen Werke bei den deutschen Predigern des Spätmittelalters." *ZKTh* 81 (1959), 265–305.
——, *Schrifttum unde Lehre des Hermann von Schildesche*. Cassiciacum 15. Würzburg, 1959.
——, "Martin Luther und sein Orden." *AAug*. 25 (1962), 254–290.
——, "Die Augustinertheologen Simon Fidati von Cascia und Hugolin von Orvieto und Martin Luthers Kritik an Aristoteles." *ARG* 54 (1963), 15–37.
——, "Joachim von Fiore und sein angeblicher Einfluss auf den Augustiner

Eremitenorden (Kritische Bemerkungen zu einer Untersuchung M. Reeves)." *Augustinianum* 3 (1963), 382–388.

———, "Die Augustinerschule des Mittelalters: Vertreter und Philosophisch-Theologische Lehre." *AAug.* 27 (1964), 167–262.

———, *Manuskripte von Werken der Autoren des Augustiner-Eremitenordens in mitteleuropäischen Bibliotheken*. Cassiciacum 20. Würzburg 1966.

———, "Hermann von Schildesche." *VerLex* 3:1107–1112.

———, "Jordan von Quedlinburg (Jordanus de Saxonia)." *VerLex* 4:853–861.

———, "Jourdain de Saxe ou de Quedlinburg, ermite de Saint-Augustin, vers 1300–1380 (1370?)." *DSp* 8:1423–1430.

———, "Jordan(us) von Quedlinburg (von Sachsen). Augustiner-Eremit, geistlicher und homiletischer Schriftsteller, c. 1300–1380." *NDB* 10:597–598.

———, "Der Augustinertheologe Johannes Hiltalingen von Basel (d. 1392) über Urstand, Erbsünde, Gnade und Verdienst." *AAug.* 43 (1980), 57–162.

———, "Augustinerschule." *LexMA* 1:1222–1223.

———, *Leben, Schrifttum und Lehrrichtung des Erfurter Universitätsprofessors Johannes Zachariae O.S.A. (d. 1428)*. Cassiciacum 34. Würzburg, 1984.

———, *Erbsünde, Gnade, Rechtfertigung und Verdienst nach der Lehre der Erfurter Augustinertheologen des Spätmittelalters*. Cassiciacum 35. Würzburg, 1984.

———, "The Spirituality of the Augustinians." In *Christian Spirituality. High Middle Ages and Reformation*. Ed. Jill Raitt. London, 1987, 63–74.

———, "Der 'Liber de Vita Monastica' des Conradus de Zenn O.E.S.A. (d. 1460) und die Spiritualität der spätmittelalterlichen 'Observantia Regularis'." *Revista Agustiniana* 33 (1992), 921–938.

———, *Johannes von Staupitz und Seine Christliche Heilslehre*. Cassiciacum 45. Würzburg, 1994.

———, *Theology and History of the Augustinian School in the Middle Ages*. The Augustinian Series 6. Ed. John E. Rotelle, O.S.A., Villanova, 1996.

Zur Mühlen, K., "Affekt II." *TRE* 1:600–605.

INDEX

Aachen, 42
Aarnock, Robert G., 352n
Achatio, Frater, OESA, 654
Acre, 16
Ad consequendam, 25, 736f
Adam, Bernd, 427n, 563n, 565n
Adeodatus (son of Augustine), 191, 210, 229, 288–290, 778, 790–792, 794
Aertsen, J., 399n, 496n, 497n, 571n, 573n, 574n
Agnes von Bilzheim, OP, 511, 513, 518, 559
Alan of Lille, 478n
Alanus Angelicus, 77n, 101n
Alaric, 46
Alberic de Trois-Fontaines, 719
Albert the Great, OP, 364n
Albert of Padua, OESA, 244, 367, 380, 416, 439n, 444n, 453n, 684n
Albertus, OESA, 166
Alexander III (Pope), 101n, 200
Alexander IV (Pope), 5, 48, 113, 195, 200, 202, 207, 208, 216–218, 230, 232, 280, 313, 314, 336, 814
Alexander of Hales, OFM, 364n
Alexander of San Elpidio, OESA, 58n, 64, 65n, 113, 145, 157, 158, 237, 291, 378
Alexander, J.J.G., 380n
Alfonso of Aragon, 16, 113
Alipius, 191, 210, 229, 786–788, 791, 792, 794
Alphonsus Vargas, OESA, 363, 365, 686, 688, 699
Altenburg, 623, 640, 643
Alvarus Pelagius, OFM, 28
Ambrose, St., 181, 184, 190, 191, 203, 209, 211, 213, 227, 228, 290, 491, 780, 785–787, 789, 790, 805
Ambrosius de Cora, OESA, 188, 189n, 240, 585, 586, 615n, 679, 777
Amsterdam, 521
Anagni, 16, 19, 39, 40, 41, 71
Anastasius, 794
Andreas, Frater, OESA, 337f
Andreas Bodenstein von Karlstadt, 665, 669, 670, 693

Andreas de Saxonia, OESA, 699
Andreas of Recanati, OESA, 237–239
Andreas Proles, OESA, 701n
Angelo, Frater, OESA, 323, 336
Angelucio, Frater, OESA, 335, 336
Angelus, Frater, OESA, 336
Angelus, Prior in Cassiano, OESA, 319
Angelus de Cortanio, OESA, 250n, 316, 322, 342
Angelus Dobelinus, OESA, 689n, 699
Angenendt, Arnold, 8n, 713n
Angermünde, 265
Ankersmit, F., 485n
Annibaldo Annibaldi, 47
Anonymous Florentine (author of *Vita Sancti Augustini* and *Initium*), 189ff, 194ff, 210, 215, 222, 232, 313
Anselm, St., 506, 531
Anthony, St., 189, 191, 192, 195, 201, 202, 210, 276, 786, 787
Antonius, Frater, OESA, 319f
Antonius de Iaquinto, OESA 338
Antonius Rampegolus, OESA, 219n, 300, 301n, 399n, 516, 529–535, 543, 561, 576, 577, 581, 594–618, 679, 723
Antonius Sucquet, 500n
Antonius Terre Senesis, OESA, 530n
Antwerp, 531, 619, 651
Apulia, 321
Aquila, 321
Aragon, 16, 17
Arbesmann, Rudolf, OSA, 141n, 174n, 189n, 190–193, 200n, 206n, 210, 214, 215n, 216, 219, 265n, 272, 286n, 687n, 774n, 776n, 778n
Arendt, Hanna, 6n
Aristotle, 56n, 57n, 58n, 63n, 77n, 123, 141, 254, 255, 303, 304, 351, 364n, 374, 381, 491, 492, 495, 496, 704, 706n, 745, 746, 783, 833
Arnald de Conbello, OESA, 328, 329
Arnold von Haldensleben, 259
Arnold of Regensburg, OESA, 323, 324
Arquillière, H.-X., 28n, 157n
Asti, 593

Augsburg, 257n, 531, 625n, 643, 644, 645n, 646, 648, 653

Augustine, St., Bishop of Hippo, 4, 6, 7, 9, 10, 12–14, 40, 46, 78, 79n, 123, 140–142, 144, 147, 149, 150, 153, 157–160, 163–165, 167–169, 171–213, 215–220, 223–226, 228–233, 235, 239, 243, 245, 247, 264–269, 273–276, 278–291, 294, 299, 302n, 304, 305, 307, 313, 314, 330, 331, 337, 343, 348, 351, 352, 355–357, 360, 366–368, 372, 381, 387, 395, 396, 402, 410, 412, 421n, 424, 429–434, 436, 441, 451n, 464n, 468, 469, 471n, 474, 476, 479, 481n, 483, 488, 491, 495n, 514, 516, 531, 538, 541, 559, 565, 571n, 572, 575–579, 581, 583, 584, 586, 592, 600, 614, 615n, 625, 626, 629, 632, 633, 635, 636, 640–642, 652, 657, 672–675, 679, 680, 683, 686, 688, 691–693, 694, 695, 697–699, 701, 702, 704, 705, 706n, 707, 708, 721, 722, 732, 733, 774–815, 830

Augustine's Religion (*religio Augustini*), 7, 145, 232, 268, 269, 271, 273, 280, 283, 286, 308, 310, 312–314, 343, 351, 358, 367, 368, 382, 429, 469, 501, 559, 560, 567n, 574–577, 579, 581, 583–585, 657, 674, 679, 699, 700, 703–705, 707, 708, 710–714, 719–722, 724, 727, 728, 732, 734, 735n, 810

Augustinian Observance, 8n, 12, 325, 586, 587, 593–596, 618, 631, 641, 645, 700, 701, 728, 732

Augustinian Platform, 3, 4, 6–8, 12–16, 22, 30, 43, 157, 158, 162, 174, 239, 243, 266, 306, 346, 351, 355, 357, 468, 473, 474, 503, 583, 584, 586–588, 590, 618, 620, 625, 628, 670–675, 677, 679, 699, 701

Augustinian Regular Canons, Order of, 9, 10n, 160, 163–169, 171–175, 178, 179, 182, 183, 193–196, 199–202, 205–208, 215, 219–221, 223, 225, 226, 231, 232, 234, 235, 246, 258n, 263, 272–276, 289, 307, 313, 732n, 774

Augustinian School, 6n, 348–350, 411, 466, 684, 685, 687–691, 695, 698, 699

Augustinianism, Late Medieval, 8n, 9, 10, 56n, 58n, 157, 158n, 264, 308, 313, 315, 346, 350, 351, 355, 365, 366, 377, 583, 683, 685–708, 721, 722

Augustinians (OESA), 1–6, 8–12, 13, 14, 19–30, 40, 41, 43, 46, 48, 60, 71, 113, 114, 128, 138, 140–142, 144, 145, 148, 156–160, 162–176, 178, 179, 183, 187–197, 199–203, 205–209, 211, 213–221, 223–226, 229–237, 239–247, 253, 254, 256, 258, 263–276, 279–283, 286, 289, 291–294, 298, 301–310, 312, 313, 315, 317–320, 324, 329–332, 334–336, 339–344, 348–350, 352, 355–358, 360, 361, 363, 365–373, 375–380, 382–384, 385n, 386, 402, 404, 411, 429, 452, 468, 469, 473, 475, 476, 492, 505, 534, 541, 542, 559, 574, 575, 577–579, 581–584, 586, 588, 591, 593, 594, 605, 612, 615, 619n, 625, 628, 632, 633, 635–639, 641, 644, 647–649, 651, 652, 656, 660, 661, 663, 669, 670, 671, 673–675, 679, 684, 686–693, 698–702, 705, 707, 708, 710, 712, 721, 722, 727–729, 732, 736–742, 774, 776

Augustino de Penna, OESA, 322

Augustinus Favaroni, OESA, 408, 445n, 590, 591, 593–596, 618, 693, 696, 699, 700

Augustinus Fivizanius, 743

Augustinus of Ancona, OESA, 5, 7n, 29, 30, 40, 41, 43, 44, 48–51, 53, 55, 56, 58n, 65, 69–80, 82, 84–126, 128–149, 151, 153–158, 163, 171, 206, 235, 367, 386n, 403, 406, 417, 463, 562n, 569, 585, 589, 596, 605, 615n, 628, 639, 673, 679, 680, 684n, 719, 743, 744, 746, 747, 749

Augustinus Novellus de Padua, OESA, 188

Augustinus of Orvieto, OESA, 379n

Augustinus Panizarius, 167f

Aurelius, Bishop of Carthage, 807

Ausculta fili, 18

Avignon, 41n, 42n, 49, 50, 67, 68, 109, 111, 112, 134, 137, 162, 231, 267, 270, 320, 327–331, 369n, 474, 587, 591, 592, 605, 747

Azzo Visconti, 172

Backus, Irena, 9n, 183n
Baden, 341
Baier, Walter, 477n, 478n

INDEX

Bainbridge, W., 579n
Baldus de Ubaldis, 43
Ballweg, Jan, 44n, 156n
Bamberg, xiii, 384n
Bange, P., 542n
Barfleur, 252, 265
Bartholomew, Frater, OESA, 336
Bartholomew Arnoldi von Usingen, OESA, 621f
Bartholomew Brancasolus, OESA, 340
Bartholomew of Urbino, OESA, 141, 142n, 314, 337, 367
Bartholomew of Venice, OESA, 591, 594
Bartlett, Robert, 545n
Bartolus of Sassoferrato, 43
Basel, xiii, 670
Basel, Council of, 585, 615n
Basil, St., 195, 202, 206
Bast, Robert J., 257n, 475n, 546n, 555n, 725n
Battista degli Aloysi, OESA, 241n
Bauer, Dieter R., 563n
Baxandall, Michael, 489n, 709
Beckwith, Sarah, 516n
Bede (the Venerable), 506
Belting, Hans, 489n, 500n, 506n
Benedict Caetani (see Boniface VIII)
Benedict, St., 145, 150
Benedict XII (Pope), 44n, 156n, 168
Benedictines (OSB), 48, 148, 195, 351, 361, 385n, 548, 649, 651–653, 655, 656, 667, 670
Berg, Dieter, 368n
Bergamo, 172
Berger, Peter L., 312n
Bergundius de Tortis, 166
Berlin, xiii, 338, 385n, 562
Bernard of Clairvaux, St., 50, 141, 184, 337, 349, 477, 506, 531, 536, 538, 541, 545, 548
Bernard of Manso, OESA 327
Bernard Muricula, 169
Bernardus, Frater, OESA, 774
Bernardus de Albia, 239n
Bernstein, Alan, xii, 488n
Bertold Puchhauser of Regensburg, OESA, 591, 594, 596, 700
Bertold of Regensburg (OFM), 10n
Bertold Ronebiz, 259
Bertrand del Poggetto, Cardinal, 168
Bertrand du Poujet, 112
Bestul, Thomas H., 354n, 507n, 546, 547, 551, 555n
Betterton, Maria Luisa, xii

Biller, Peter, 714–717, 719, 720
Bizer, Ernst, 534n
Black, Antony, 28n, 41n
Bloomfield, Morton, 385n, 564n
Boase, T.S.R., 17n, 24n, 40n, 42n
Bobbio, 172
Boccacio, 43
Bochet, Isabelle, 431n
Boethius, 254n
Böhm, Sigurd, 282n, 431n
Bologna, 183, 220, 223, 226, 244, 245, 253–256, 341, 370, 383, 492, 588, 590, 591, 594
Bonagratia of Bergamo, OFM, 67, 68
Bonaventure, St., OFM, 243, 245, 364, 506
Bonaventure of Padua, OESA, 591, 592n
Boniface VIII (Pope), 6n, 12, 16, 17, 18, 19, 20, 24–28, 30, 39, 40, 41, 52, 53, 54, 55, 71, 105, 113, 144, 156n, 157, 158, 367, 470, 586, 618, 675, 736–742
Boniface IX (Pope), 589
Boockmann, Hartmut, 161n
Bossy, John, 713–717, 719, 720
Bostick, Curtis, 604n
Bouchard, Constance, 728n
Bourges, 18, 19, 20, 24n, 25
Boyle, Leonard, OP, 514n
Brady, Thomas A., 241n, 257n
Brecht, Martin, 623n, 630n, 631n, 633n, 636n, 638n, 640n, 644n, 645n, 660n, 665n, 671n
Bremen, 619, 651
Brentano, Robert, 45n, 47n, 48, 53, 54n
Brescia, 172
Brethren of Favali, 5, 200
Brictinenses, 5, 200
Brothers and Sisters of the Common Life (*Devotio Moderna*), 385n, 722, 724n, 725, 726
Brothers of the Sack, 20
Brown, Peter, 288n, 291n, 716n
Bruges, 239n, 326, 585
Brundage, James, 292n
Brünn, 175n
Bruno Berndes, 259
Bruno of Segni, OSB, 508, 509, 520, 543, 548–555
Brussels, 775n
Burchard, Archbishop of Magdeburg, 256–262, 264, 265, 293, 364
Burger, Christoph, 348n, 470n
Bürkle, Susanne, 511n, 732n

Burr, David, 402n
Busso, Count of Mansfeld, 261
Bynum, Carolyn Walker, 179, 283n, 534n, 564n, 729–732

Calbe, 261
Cambridge, 382
Cambrai, 179
Camille, Michael, 491n, 517n
Cameron, Euan, 534n
Carmelites (OCarm.), 8n, 25, 368n, 387n, 669, 689, 736, 737
Carmignac, J., 564n
Carpentras, 328
Carthusians (OCarth.), 11, 195, 351, 385n, 667
Cassiodorus, 58
Catherine of Siena, St., 592n
Celestine V (Pope), 17, 24
Centumcellae, 197, 203–205, 212, 213, 227, 233, 276
Charles II (King of Naples), 28, 134
Charles IV (Emperor), 164n, 171, 257n
Charles V (Emperor), 620
Charles of Calabria, 49
Chasseguet-Smirgel, Janine, 294n
Châtillon, Jean, 9n, 515n
Chazan, Robert, 546n
Chicago, xiii
Christ, Dorothea A., xii
Christian, William A., 308n
Christman, Robert, xii
Chrysostomus, 830
Church, 1, 2, 6, 11, 13, 14n, 15, 23, 24, 27, 28, 30, 31, 34–40, 46, 51, 53, 54, 56, 58–64, 66, 68–72, 76–82, 85, 87, 89–93, 101–106, 108, 109, 111, 112, 114, 116, 119, 122, 123, 125, 129–131, 133, 134, 137–140, 142–146, 149, 150, 156, 161, 165, 172, 176, 177, 184, 186, 190, 196, 209, 211, 218, 236, 237, 239, 257n, 260, 262, 267, 269, 270, 279–282, 286, 304, 314, 340, 345–347, 356, 358, 360, 366, 404, 416, 433, 463, 464, 469, 474, 554, 589, 592, 596, 598, 601, 602, 604–609, 611, 616–618, 620–622, 624, 639, 640, 745–747
Cicero, 48, 138, 514, 715, 779, 782
Cicho de Aversa, OESA, 342
Cipolla, Carol M., 241n
Cistercians (OCist.), 195, 721n, 730
Classen, Peter, 552n, 555n

Clericis laicos, 18, 24
Clemen, Otto, 623n
Clement V (Pope), 18n, 41, 42, 49, 66n, 127, 128n, 134, 239n
Clement VI (Pope), 269
Clement VII (Pope), 587, 591, 592, 687
Clement, Frater, Prior General OESA, 378
Cobello Carociali, OESA, 316
Cohen, Jeremy, 546n
Colish, Marcia, 8n, 9n, 426n
Cologne, 260, 325–328, 352, 353, 383, 530n, 531, 597n
Como, 172
Confessionalization, 4
Conrad II (Emperor), 163
Conrad, Frater, OESA, 326
Conrad, OPraem. (Provost in Magdeburg), 258, 263
Conrad of Megenberg, 384n
Conrad of Zenn, OESA, 353, 615n
Constable, Giles, 354n, 520n, 542n, 544n, 545, 715n, 716n, 724n, 725
Constance, 257n
Constance, Council of, 530, 585, 587, 591–594
Constantine (Emperor), 48, 53, 84, 89–92, 93n, 94n, 138
Constantine of Erfurt, 265
Cornelis, Arnold, 306n
Counihan, Cyril, 5n
Courcelle, J., 468n
Courcelle, P., 468n
Courtenay, William J., xii, 38n, 253n, 255n, 362, 363n, 368n, 376n, 384n, 389n, 689, 690
Cousins, Ewert, 505n
Cum inter nonnullos, 67, 69, 121, 144
Curtius, Ernst Robert, 543n
Cyprian, 80n, 420n, 452n, 463n, 561n, 784, 806, 831

Dagenais, John, 544n
Dales, Richard C., xii
Damiata, Marino, 56n, 65n
Danielou, Jean, 564n
Dante, 40n, 43
Danto, Arthur C., 189n
Datius, Bishop of Milan, 227, 774, 776, 785, 790
D'Avray, David, 380n
De Jong, Mayke, 508n
De Lubac, Henri, 158n
De Meijer, Alberic, OSA, xii, 5

INDEX

De Vries, Jan, 241n
Decot, Rolf, xiii
Delumeau, J., 503
Demandt, Alexander, 368n
Denifle, Heinrich, OP, 24n, 692, 693n
Denzinger, Heinrich, 60n, 65n
Derbes, Anne, 489n, 506n, 579n
Dibelius, O., 565n
Dictatus papae, 30
Dinzelbacher, Peter, 563n
Dionysius Carthusiensis, OCarth., 445n
Dionysius de Burgo, OESA, 605
Dionysius de Florentina, OESA, 384n
Dionysius of Nursia, OESA, 315
Dohna, Lothar, Graf zu, 641n
Dolnikowski, Edith Wilks, 7n
Dominic, St., 8n, 142, 145, 194, 206, 719
Dominicans (OP), 8, 9, 23, 25, 27, 173, 183, 193–195, 200, 202, 216n, 217, 241–243, 272, 273, 279, 294, 303, 307, 364, 368n, 385n, 387n, 534, 615, 669, 685, 689, 736, 738, 742
Dominicus, Frater, OESA, 379n
Dominicus Schleupner, 627
Donatus, 250
Doucet, P.V., 384n
Dresden, 672
Drewermann, Eugen, 294n, 345, 565n
Drijvers, Jan Willem, 547n
Duffy, Eamon, 515n
Durkheim, Emile, 501n, 711, 713, 714
Dykema, Peter, xii, 264n, 352n, 386n
Dyonisius of Viterbo, OESA, 380

Eagelton, Terry, 709n
Eberhard von der Mark (Count), 353
Eckbert of Schönau, 547
Eckermann, Willigis, OSA, 41n, 141n, 383n, 539n, 589n, 591n, 744
Edmund of Abingdon, 725
Edward I (King of England), 95n
Edward II (King of England), 127, 134
Ehrle, Franz, SJ, 685–687, 689, 691, 692, 699
Eindhoven, xiii
Eire, Carlos, 490n
Eisleben, 645
Elder, E. Rozanne, 362n
Eliade, Marcia, 14n, 174n, 307n, 445n, 565n, 566n, 711, 712
Elias, 195
Elias, Norbert, 308n, 310n, 312n
Elizabeth of Rabenswald (Countess), 353

Elliot, Dyan, 292n, 298, 299n
Elm, Kaspar, xii, 5, 29n, 162n, 173n, 220n, 250n, 280n, 347, 350, 368n, 382n, 618n, 724n, 726n, 730n, 731n, 776n
Elm, Susanna, 291n
Elze, Martin, 409n, 503n
Erasmus of Rotterdam, 385, 386, 540, 713
Erdei, Klara, 483n, 506n
Erfurt, 11, 42, 141, 223, 226, 233, 244n, 254, 256–258, 264, 265, 275, 292, 344, 351–353, 359, 361, 364, 368, 369n, 370, 383, 385, 388, 403, 411, 466, 470, 471, 478n, 490, 503, 504, 560, 562, 568, 574, 588, 589, 591, 620, 621, 630, 643, 645, 646, 689, 691, 693, 700, 705, 835
Erlenborn, Neal, xii
Ernst Hunger, 259
Eusebius, 725
Evans, Arthur, 565n
Evodius, 184, 228, 791, 792, 794
Exhibita nuper nobis, 26, 740f
Exiit qui seminat, 67, 121, 144
Ezzelino of Romano, 113

Fabriano, 70
Feil, Ernst, 713, 716n
Feraria, 343
Ferarra, 341, 357n
Ferm, Vergilius, 565n
Fermo, 70
Fernandus de Hispania (Bishop of Avignon), 175n
Finke, Heinrich, 17n, 20n, 24n, 27n, 40n, 594n
Firmano, 337
Fitzgerald, Allan D., 19n
Flanders, 30, 239n
Fleith, Barbara, 183n
Flemming, J., 565n
Florence, 17, 114, 141n, 145, 163, 189, 190, 202n, 233, 237, 247n, 253–255, 320, 321, 324, 331, 341, 358, 359, 369n, 370, 374, 378, 408n, 529n, 585, 684
Foligno, 321
Föhl, Walter, 565n
Fortunatus, 798, 801
Foucault, Michel, 16n, 305n
Fowler, Murray, 565n
Francis Caetani, Cardinal-Deacon, 27n
Francis Carrara, 592n

Francis of Assisi, St., 8n, 44, 67, 142, 144, 145, 149, 214–216, 232, 235, 239, 279, 506, 524, 548, 719
Franciscans (OFM), 8, 11, 23, 25–27, 47, 59, 67–69, 144, 146, 149, 153, 155, 156, 162, 163, 195, 200, 202, 215, 217, 235–237, 239, 241, 242, 244, 270, 279, 294, 303, 307, 364, 368n, 385n, 387n, 402, 534, 542, 548, 615, 669, 689, 719, 729, 730, 736, 738–742
Franciscus de Roma, OESA, 379n
Franciscus of Viterbo, OESA, 380
Frank, Isnard, 368n
Frank, Robert, 506
Frasseto, Michael, 289n
Frederick II (Emperor), 52, 64n
Frederick of Austria, 59, 127, 172
Freedberg, David, 478n, 481n, 490n, 499n, 500n
Freeden, Michael, 709
Freud, Sigmund, 306
Friedrich Peypus, 535
Friedrich the Wise (Elector of Saxony), 535, 623, 640
Frömmigkeit/Frömmigkeitstheologie, 347–351, 355, 394, 470, 476, 677, 689, 697, 700, 701
Frymire, John, xii
Fulconus de Duce, 168
Füser, Thomas, 23n, 183n, 200n, 223n

Gabriel Biel, 404n, 409n, 461, 462, 515, 642, 693, 706n
Gabriel de Cantiana, OESA, 335, 337
Gabriel Zwilling, OESA, 640
Gadamer, Hans-Georg, 309n, 517n, 709n
Gager, J.G., 547n, 556n
Gagliardus de Tolosa, OESA, 328, 329
Galeazzo Visconti, 59, 170, 172
Galganus, Blessed, 215
Garand, M.C., 775n
Gaspar of Orvieto, OESA, 585
Geary, Patrick, xiii
Geert Groote, 720, 724, 731n
Geertz, Clifford, 309n, 489n, 712
Genoa, 17, 163, 168, 183, 371, 530, 594, 595, 612
Geoffrey Hardeby, OESA, 270n
Georg Spalatin, 623, 626, 627, 640, 642, 645, 646, 705
Gerard of Bergamo, OESA, 219, 220, 234, 279

Gerard of Siena, OESA, 684
Gerard Zerbolt of Zutphen, 726n
Gerhoch of Reichersberg, OSB, 552n, 554n, 724n
Gewirth, Alan, 55n, 56n, 57n, 58n, 128n
Ghent, 585
Gibson, M.T., 380n
Giddens, Anthony, 307n, 709n
Gierke, Otto, 53n
Giles of Rome, OESA, 3n, 5, 6, 13, 18–25, 28–32, 34, 35, 38–41, 44, 48, 49, 55, 58, 62, 64, 71, 78, 79n, 84n, 96, 105, 138, 157, 158n, 163, 235, 242, 243, 245, 267, 272n, 284n, 292, 331, 358, 360, 365–367, 375, 383, 398n, 404–408, 422n, 424, 425n, 426n, 427, 430, 445n, 463, 569, 579, 586, 605, 628, 633, 661, 673–675, 679, 680, 684–688, 690–692, 747
Giles of Viterbo, OESA, 1–4, 6, 13, 45, 112, 243, 671, 679
Gilson, Etienne, 514
Giotto, 43
Giovanni Andrea, 43
Giovanni Colonna, 47
Girard, OESA, 166
Goebel, P., 565n
Goering, Joseph, 475n, 509n
Goldhammer, Arthur, 291n
Göller, E., 258n
Godman, Peter, 543n
Goodich, Michael, 272n
Gottschalk Hollen, OESA, 699f
Gow, Andrew, xii, 257n, 555n
Grane, Leif, 694–696, 702
Grant, Edward, 425n
Grasse, 201
Gratian, 32, 126n, 140
Graus, Frantisek, 161n, 501
Great Schism, 12, 43, 162, 584, 586–588, 591–595, 604, 618, 701
Green, Rosalie B., 506n
Gregory, Brad S., xii, 675n
Gregory VII (Pope), 5, 30, 548, 553
Gregory IX (Pope), 47, 67, 200, 592
Gregory X (Pope), 25, 737
Gregory XII (Pope), 592
Gregory the Great, St., 184, 420n, 478, 491, 521, 830
Gregory of Rimini, OESA, 234, 243, 250, 253n, 266, 267, 271, 315–343, 359, 362n, 365–367, 369n, 370,

INDEX

378n, 380n, 383, 384n, 387, 395n, 411, 442, 474, 529n, 530n, 579, 587, 618, 671, 673, 674, 679, 680, 684–687, 689–694, 696–699, 702, 705–708, 811–822
Griffiths, Gordon, xii
Groningen, xi, xiii
Grundmann, Herbert, 564n
Guarnieri, Romana, 265n
Guilio Mancini, 499n
Gurevich, Aaron, 10n, 312n, 489n, 503n, 564n, 720n
Gushee, Lawrence, 744n
Gutiérrez, David, 20n, 22n, 159n, 240, 241n, 243n, 529n, 586n, 591n, 593n, 595n, 618n

The Hague, xi, xiii, 99n, 529n, 530n
Halberstadt, 26
Hale, Rosemary Drage, 7n
Halle, 26, 261
Hamel, A., 672n, 694n, 705n
Hamese, J., 368n
Hamilton, Malcom B., 713n
Hamm, Berndt, xii, 348–350, 394n, 437n, 452n, 470n, 471n, 503n, 517n, 586n, 641n, 699, 700
Hammer, Gerhard, 705n
Hammerling, Roy, 565n
Hansen, Dorothee, 357n
Harding, Sandra, 730n
Harmening, Dieter, 474n
Harran, Marilyn J., 630n
Hartmut de Gotha, OESA, 511, 513, 518, 519
Hatfield, Rab, 565n
Hatlie, Peter, xii
Haug, Walter, 354n
Heliodorus, 499n
Heloise, 245
Henderson, John, 506n
Hendrix, Scott, 619n
Henricus Rietmüller, OESA, 303, 304n, 387n
Henry VII, Count of Luxemburg (Emperor), 42, 66n, 127, 163, 172
Henry of Cambia, OESA, 323
Henry of Cremona, 28, 29, 58n
Henry of Ghent, 19
Henry of Friemar, OESA, 174n, 189, 200, 208–219, 222, 223, 225, 228, 230, 232, 233, 235, 256, 258, 263, 264, 265n, 266n, 272n, 273–276, 280n, 302n, 313, 314, 351, 352, 355, 357n, 367, 369n, 370, 380, 400n, 439n, 445n, 456n, 469, 474, 512n, 563n, 571n, 572n, 577, 615n, 679, 684n, 704
Heraclius, Bishop of Hippo, 180, 808
Herford, 383n
Hermann of Mindelheim, OESA, 590, 596, 700
Hermann of Schildesche, OESA, 55, 60n, 65, 71, 140, 141, 157, 256, 273, 292, 293n, 351–353, 355, 360, 367, 401n, 473, 474, 515n, 615n, 679
Hermans, Jos. M.M., xii, 244n
Hermelink, Heinrich, 692
Hick, John, 711, 713n
Hildegard of Bingen, 491
Hildesheim, 260
Himanen, Katja, xii
Hinnebusch, William A., OP, 242n, 724n
Hippo Regius, 176, 177, 180, 181, 184, 185, 199, 205, 206, 227, 229, 231, 280, 474
Hirsh, John C., 726n
Hoenen, M.J.F.M., 496n
Holly Michael, 510
Holzapfel, Egidius, 567n
Hommes, Hilly, xii
Hommey, J., 775
Honorius IV (Pope), 48
Honorius Augustodunensis, 531n
Horlings-Brandse, Norry, xii
Horst, Ulrich, 41n, 69n, 71, 72n, 116n, 123n, 144, 155n, 743
Hostiensis, 77n, 87n, 731n
Housley, Norman, 42n, 70n, 112n, 115n, 136n, 258n
Hsia, R. Po-chia, 491n, 547n
Hugh of St. Cher, 445n
Hugh of St. Victor, 29, 50, 63, 78, 359, 397n, 448n, 464n, 543, 548, 633, 725
Hugolino of Orvieto, OESA, 188, 365n, 366, 383, 693, 698, 699
Huguccio of Pisa, 50
Huizinga, J., 476, 477, 503, 505
Hümpfner, Winfridus, OSA, 216n, 218n, 219–222, 223n, 224n, 226, 243n, 265n, 266n, 271, 272n, 273n, 274n, 286n, 312n, 415n, 477n, 478n, 482, 560n, 776n
Hundersmarck, Lawrence F., 507
Hungary, 17
Hurcker, Bernd Ulrich, 383n
Hyde, J.K., 163n, 164n

In causa que, 739f
Innocent III (Pope), 5, 23, 45, 47, 51, 52, 54, 95n, 200, 216n, 279
Innocent IV (Pope), 77n, 279, 338
Innocent VIII (Pope), 586
Innocentius, 181, 793
Inter sollicitudines nostras, 26, 28, 741f
Isidore of Seville, 514, 543

Jacob Pérez of Valencia, OESA, 693
Jacob Propst, OESA, 619, 620, 651
Jacob Sassi, OESA, 237
Jacobus de Voragine, OP, 175, 183, 184–187, 227, 547, 778
Jacques de Vitry, 179, 719, 724, 731n
Jacques le Grand, OESA, 699
James of Aquaviva, St., 214, 214
James of Viterbo, OESA, 5, 28–30, 49, 58, 65, 157, 367, 384n, 605, 684n
James, William, 712
Jean de Meun, 245
Jean Gerson, 243, 348, 349, 355, 356, 445n, 510, 556, 557, 584, 699
Jedin, Hubert, 693n
Jensen, Richard, xii
Jerome, St., 184, 195, 201, 277, 499n, 509, 510, 538, 541, 549, 551n, 552n, 792, 805, 830
Jerome Emser, 628, 647
Jerome of Pistoia, OESA, 593
Jerome Schurf, 659
Jerome Seripando, OESA, 3n, 693
Jerusalem, 546
Jews, 11, 12, 15, 102–105, 162, 300, 439, 440, 480, 546–558, 580, 602, 604, 614, 661, 722
Joachim of Fiore, 200, 206, 208, 214
Joan of Arc, 585
John XXII (Pope), 12, 30, 41–43, 49, 50n, 59, 60, 64–71, 75n, 90, 94, 95, 101n, 108, 109, 112–117, 119, 121, 122, 134–140, 144, 148, 149, 156, 158–160, 164–66, 168–71, 173, 213, 214, 233, 234, 235–240, 246, 256, 257n, 259–263, 272, 352, 357, 367, 586, 675, 743–745, 747, 749
John, Frater, OESA, 323
John Bonus, Friar, 5, 200
John Capgrave, OESA, 775, 776
John Cassian, 248, 277n, 360, 361, 565
John de Castello de Mutina, OESA, 318
John de Civita de Boiano, OESA, 317
John of Constantinople, 592
John of Basel, OESA, 231, 267, 315, 329, 330, 369, 383, 591, 592, 673, 686, 687, 690, 699
John of Bohemia (King), 169, 171, 172, 235
John Dominici, Cardinal, 592
John of Foligno, OESA, 326
John of Jandun, 65n
John of Lucino, OESA, 317
John of Machelinea, OESA, 325
John of Monte Rodono, OESA, 315, 316, 342
John of Murro, OFM, 19
John of Saints Marcellinus and Peter, Cardinal, 26
John of Salisbury, 29
John of Swabia, OESA, 593
John Whitering, OSB, 510
John Wycliff, 243, 270n, 585
Johann Baptist Mayr, 536, 538n
Johann Weseke, 259
Johannes Bindus, OESA, 250
Johannes de Caulibus, OFM, 507, 579
Johannes Eck, 628
Johannes de Lanna, OESA, 256
Johannes de Fonte, OFM, 384n
Johannes Dorsten, OESA, 349n, 401n, 700
Johannes Greffenstein, OESA, 632, 633
Johannes Hoffmeister, OESA, 693
Johannes Hus, 531, 585, 591, 594, 626, 641, 642, 644
Johannes Klenkok, OESA, 266n, 383, 699
Johannes Lang, OESA, 644, 645
Johannes Müntzinger, 427n
Johannes Nider, OP, 724, 731n
Johannes von Paltz, OESA, 348, 349, 452, 470, 471, 473, 474, 477n, 487, 503n, 560n, 586n, 615n, 669, 679, 699, 700, 701n, 708, 776, 777
Johannes Staupitz, OESA, 349, 408, 409, 411, 445n, 626, 631, 632n, 639, 641–662, 679, 691, 693, 696–699, 702, 708
Johannes Sulpitius Verulanus, 531n
Johannes Zachariae, OESA, 401n, 588–591, 593, 594, 596, 618, 673, 679, 700
Johnson, Mark, 306n
Jones, Michael, 43n, 326n
Jordan of Quedlinburg, OESA, 7n, 10–12, 141, 164, 169, 171, 179, 183, 187–189, 200, 208, 210, 216–234, 243–258, 261, 263–303,

305–314, 324, 330, 334, 337, 344, 351–361, 364, 366–369, 371, 373, 379n, 381, 383–404, 406–425, 427–466, 468, 469, 471, 474, 476–498, 500–505, 509–511, 514–516, 518–520, 523, 539–541, 544, 555–579, 581, 582, 584, 592, 596, 604, 615n, 620, 633, 637n, 641, 642, 671–674, 679, 680, 699, 703, 704, 708, 710–712, 715–721, 724, 727, 728, 730, 731, 733, 774–780, 823–835
Jordan of Saxony, OP, 223
Jordan, William Chester, 42n
Judelson, Katherine, 10n
Julius II (Pope), 1, 112, 675
Junghans, Helmar, 536, 539n
Jungmann, J.A., SJ, 563n
Justinian, 136

Kadlec, J., 591n
Kanter, Rosabeth Moss, 730n
Kantorowicz, Ernst H., 32n, 40n, 46, 47n, 52, 53n, 95n
Karl von Miltitz, 623, 643
Katharina, Sister (Dominican in Unterlinden), 511, 519
Katherine von Bora, 619
Kaufmann, Walter, 294n
Kehrein, Joseph, 480n
Keller, Hans, 485n
Kenny, Anthony, 496n
Kieckhefer, Richard, 265n, 477n, 505n, 511n, 513, 515
Kienzle, Beverly Mayne, 7n
Klapisch-Zuber, Christiane, 326n
Kneepkens, C.H., xii, 833
Knights Templars, 17
Knoll, Paul W., xii
Koch, Lucia, 640n
Koenker, Ernest B., xii
Kolde, Theodor, 568n, 636n, 641n, 691, 692, 694, 698, 699
Konrad Mach (burgher of Magdeburg), 293
Köpf, Ulrich, 362n, 364n, 532n, 539n
Kramer, Femke, xii
Kretzmann, Norman, 496n
Krümmel, Achim, 41n
Kuiters, Rafael, 5n
Küng, Hans, 345
Kunzelmann, A., OSA, 5n, 27, 243n, 244n, 265n, 352n, 588n
Kürzinger, Josef, 175n

Ladner, Gerhart B., 565n
La Kapra, D., 709n
Lakoff, George, 306n, 492n, 515n, 723n
Lambert le Bègue, 719
Landgraf, A.M., 395n, 397n, 399n
Landulfus, 778
Lanfranc of Bec, 515
Lanfranc of Milan, OESA, 167, 168, 173, 234
Langmuir G., 546n, 580n, 713n, 714n
Lateran III (Council), 45
Lateran IV (Council), 45, 52, 217, 279
Lateran V (Council), 1, 45
Lavoro, 317
Lawless, George, OSA, 9n, 204n
Lawrence, C.H., 8n, 575n
Le Bras, Gabriel, 712
Leclercq, Henri, 564n
Leclercq, Jean, 362n
Le Goff, Jacque, 291n
Leipzig, 471, 705
Lem, Aafje, 244n
Lentes, Thomas, 348n
Leo I (Pope), 531
Leo X (Pope), 3, 623, 625n, 627, 628, 638, 639, 648, 675
Leonardo de Vilaco, OESA, 323
Lerner, Robert E., 265n, 271n
Lewis, Gertrude Jaron, 511n
Lewis, Helen B., 310n
Licet ecclesie catholice, 5, 144
Licet iuxta doctrinam, 60, 65n
Lickteig, Franz-Bernard, 368n
Lievens, Robrecht, 244n, 354n
Limoges, 546
Lindberg, David C., 425n
Lippstadt, 383n
Little, Lester K., 546n
Lobrichon, Guy, 515n
Lombardy, 43, 57, 66, 135, 136, 163, 166, 167, 169–171, 180
London, 242n
Lorenzo Valla, 627, 713
Louis X (King of France), 134
Louis of Bavaria (Emperor), 12, 30, 40n, 42, 49, 50, 57, 59, 65–72, 90, 94, 95, 111, 112, 118, 120–122, 127, 136, 138, 139, 144, 155, 156, 158, 170–172, 235–238, 256, 257n, 260–262, 266
Louis Peresi, OFM, 564n
Love, Ron, xii
Lucca, 172
Luckmann, Thomas, 312n

Ludolph of Saxony, OCarth., 355n, 477n, 478n, 507, 520, 539–541, 544, 549, 555, 556, 579, 823–828
Luhmann, Niklas, 307n, 312n
Luigi Marsili, OESA, 689n
Luitbrand, King of Lombards, 163, 180
Luther, Martin, OESA (see Martin Luther, OESA)
Lüttich, 353
Lyon, 531
Lyon, Second Council of, 25, 27, 217, 737

MacDonald, A.A., 354n, 355n
Mac Fhionnbhairr, Darach, 61n
MacGrade, A. Stephen, 69n
Magdeburg, 11, 42, 222, 223, 254, 257–265, 293, 352, 364, 379n, 501, 574
Maierù, Alfonso, 254n, 255n, 380n
Mainz, xi, xiii, 473n, 546
Maitland, Frederic William, 53n
Mamilianus, Blessed, 202
Mannheim, K., 709
Manselli, Raoul, 564n
Mantua, 172
March of Ancona, 70, 238, 321, 323, 329, 336, 339, 340
March of Treviso, 321, 343
Marco Antonio Sabellico, 241n
Marcolino, Venicio, 376n, 384n
Margarite Porete, 42
Margherita Colonna, 47
Markus, R.A., 282n, 431n, 708
Marrow, James H., 485n, 486n, 505n, 517n
Marsilius of Inghen, 499, 689, 690
Marsilius of Padua, 30, 42, 55, 56, 57, 58, 59n, 60, 61n, 62, 63, 65, 68–72, 74, 75, 82n, 84, 85, 87, 90, 92, 93, 94, 95n, 96, 101, 111, 112, 113, 128, 134, 144, 146, 155, 156, 170, 743, 744–747
Martin V (Pope), 587, 593
Martin, Francis X., OSA, 2, 13n, 240n, 241n, 243, 618n
Martin, Hervé, 564n
Martin Luther, OESA, 2, 3, 8n, 10, 12, 13, 409n, 417, 472–474, 534n, 535, 619–675, 679, 680, 684, 691–694, 696–700, 702, 705–708, 732
Masteo della Scala, 172
Matelica, 323
Mathes, Fulgence, OSA, 144n, 270n

Matsura, Jan, 705
Matteo Visconti, 170
Matter, E. Ann, xii, 554
Matthäus Lang, Cardinal-Archbishop of Salzburg, 647, 648, 651, 653–655, 661
Matthew, Frater, OESA, 339
Matthew of Amelia, OESA, 335
Matthew of Ascoli, OESA, 529n
Matthew of Paris, 720, 730
Matthews, Gareth B., 4n
Maximillian (Emperor), 1
May, Gerhard, xiii
Mayer, Cornelius Petrus, OSA, 589n
McCreight, Tom, xii
McDonnell, Ernest W., 719n, 720n
McGann, J., 707n
McGinn, Bernard, 10n, 360n, 483n
McIlwain, C.H., 41n
McNiel, M.G., 579n
Meier, John P., 564n
Melfi, 158
Melville, Gert, 8n
Messina, 163
Michael, Frater, OESA, 334, 680
Michael of Cesena, OFM, 67, 68
Michael of Placentia, OESA, 320
Michalsky, Tanja, 50n
Miethke, Jürgen, 6n, 24n, 29n, 31n, 41n, 56n, 57n, 69n, 141n, 158n, 159n, 744–747
Milan, 30, 59, 163, 170, 172, 184, 197, 203, 204, 210, 230, 235, 265, 317, 531
Miles, Margaret R., 289n
Millis, Ludo J.R., 723n
Millman, Marcia, 730n
Milway, Michael, 531n
Ministeri, P.B., OSA, 41n, 49n, 50n, 51n, 65n, 126, 141n, 159n, 585n, 743, 744
Modena, 172
Moeller, Bernd, 503n, 568n
Mollat, G., 41n, 170n, 172n, 236
Moltmann, Jürgen, 467n, 489n
Monachus Niger, OSB, 362
Mone, F.J., 189n, 480n
Monica, St. (mother of Augustine), 184, 198, 204, 218, 227–229, 290, 304, 776, 781–785, 788, 791–793, 795
Mons Pisanus, 197, 202
Montecassino, 548
Montefeltro, 7
Montepessulano, 113

Montpellier, 319, 378
Moore, R.I., 545n, 546n
Mooreman, John, OFM, 241n, 242n
Morris, Colin, 5n, 292n, 725n
Morrison, Karl, 517n, 570n, 629n
Moses de León, 565
Mulchahey, Michele, 368n
Müller, Alphons Victor, 692, 693
Müller, Karl, 49n, 59n, 127n, 134n, 172n, 236n
Munich, 69, 140, 175n, 239, 385n
Mylonas, George Emmanuel, 565n

Naendrup-Reimann, Johanna, 257n
Naples, 16, 17, 49, 50, 135, 137, 158, 300, 315, 316, 318n, 321, 334, 338, 340, 371n, 529, 531, 587, 595, 605, 612–614
Napoleon Ursini (Cardinal), 127, 134
Nebridius, 184, 191, 228, 786, 789, 791, 794
Newhauser, R., 465n
Newman, Martha, 721n
Newton, Adam Zachary, 189n
Nicelosinus, Frater, OESA, 529n
Nicholas III (Pope), 67, 121, 144
Nicholas IV (Pope), 17, 19, 24, 47, 67
Nicholas V (anti-Pope), 42, 170, 236, 238
Nicholas, Bishop of Ancona, OFM, 27n
Nicholas, Frater, OESA, 339, 699
Nicholas Clavo, OESA, 323
Nicholas of Alessandria, OESA, 189, 200–208, 210, 212, 214–217, 222, 226, 228, 232–235, 273, 289, 313, 314, 357, 679, 704
Nicholas of Fabriano, OESA, 236–239, 378
Nicholas of Frusten, OESA, 323
Nicholas of Sarvar, OESA, 322–324
Nicholas of Tolentino, St., OESA, 271f
Nicol, Martin, 483n
Nicolas Amsdorf, 659, 660n
Nicolaus of Lyra, 352n
Nicolaus de Waradino, OESA, 331n
Nicolinus, Frater, OESA, 529n
Nietzsche, Friedrich, 294
Nirenberg, David, 545n, 546n, 556
Nisio de Arcochis, OESA, 338
Norbert of Xanten, 179
Novara, 168, 172
Nürnberg, 383, 531, 535, 538
Nursia, 321

Oberman, Heiko A., xii, 3n, 241n, 264n, 388n, 396n, 404n, 408, 409, 416n, 461n, 462n, 546n, 551n, 555n, 586n, 592n, 597n, 620n, 626n, 630n, 637, 638, 640n, 641n, 648n, 655n, 657, 658n, 659n, 660n, 661, 664n, 684n, 693–696, 702, 705n
Oberste, Jörg, 8n
Occhioni, Nicola, OESA, 272n
Ocker, Christopher, 266n, 697n
Odo Rigaldi, OFM, 364n
Offler, H.S., 59n, 69n
Oignies, 179
O'Malley, John W., S.J., 2
Origen, 531
Orlamunda, 670
Orléans, 546
Orvieto, 22n
Osimo, 70
Osnabrück, 383n
Ossinger, J.F., OSA, 594n
Ostia, 112, 204, 205n, 227
Otto, Archbishop of Magdeburg, 258, 261, 263
Otto, Rudolph, 711
Overmann, A., 369n
Owens, Joseph, CSSR, 496n
Oxford, 9, 255, 270, 362, 367, 372, 376n, 382, 383, 466, 588, 684, 699

Pachomius, St., 202
Padua, 128, 163, 254, 327, 357n, 373, 374
Paris, xiii, 9, 17, 19, 20, 30, 42, 126–128, 134, 141, 176n, 201, 204n, 208, 215, 218–222, 226, 231, 233, 242n, 244–247, 249n, 250, 252–256, 265, 271, 272n, 273n, 292, 314, 315, 317, 318, 323, 337, 344, 351, 352n, 357, 358, 362, 364, 367, 369, 370, 372, 375, 376, 377n, 381–383, 386n, 466, 492, 506n, 531, 568, 592, 685, 687, 699, 704, 719n, 744, 747, 774, 775, 776n
Parma, 172
Partner, Peter, 45n
Passion of Christ, 11, 12, 35, 39, 40, 299n, 301, 354, 355, 416, 450, 451, 468–472, 474, 476–483, 484n, 485, 486, 489, 490, 492, 500–549, 551, 552, 554–560, 567, 571, 578–582, 584, 595, 636, 650, 671, 675, 680, 823–830
Pastoralis cura, 66n

Paton, Bernadette, 8n
Patricius (father of Augustine), 184, 781
Paul III (Pope), 620
Paul the First Hermit, St., 190–192, 195, 201, 202, 210, 276, 277, 776n
Paul Lulmeus of Bergamo, OESA, 585
Paul Vivaldi, OESA, 595
Pauler, Roland, 163n, 170n, 172n
Paulus de Spoleto, OESA, 530n
Pavia, 160, 163, 164, 166–174, 180, 199, 201, 219, 223, 235, 237, 247, 263, 293, 385, 592n, 594n
Pelikan, Jaroslav, 4n
Pelzer, A., 383n
Pennington, Kenneth, 18n, 42n, 87n, 136n
Perugia, 321, 322
Peter Abelard, 245
Peter Aureolus, OFM, 690
Peter Ceffons, OCist., 362
Peter Comestor, 175, 179, 508, 509, 531
Peter de la Palu, OP, 28
Peter Flotte, 18, 39
Peter Lombard, 9, 255, 315, 351, 363, 381, 383, 399, 403, 405, 408, 424, 426n, 433, 465, 694n, 699, 700, 704, 707
Peter Marone, OFM, (see Celestine V)
Peter of Spain, 250
Peter unter dem Ufer, 259
Petrakopoulos, Anja, xii
Petrakopoulos, Iris, xii
Petrarch, 43, 605, 606
Petroff, Elizabeth, 512
Petrus Alfonsi, 547
Petrus de Brunniquello, OESA, 384n
Petrus de Lutre, OPraem., 60n
Peter of Candia (Pope Alexander V), 685
Petrus of Viterbo, OESA, 380
Philip (Abbot), 166, 167
Philip III, 20, 95n
Philip IV (the Fair), 6n, 12, 17, 18, 20, 24, 30, 38, 41, 71, 127, 128, 134, 158, 239n, 267
Philip Melanchthon, 621, 659
Philip of Harvengt, OPraem., 175, 179–186, 199, 205, 210, 226, 227, 778–780, 799, 809, 810
Philippo de Mantua, OESA, 322
Pickering, F.P., 485n, 517n, 518
Pierre Bertrand, 43
Pierre d'Ailly, 584
Pierre Dubois, 30
Pietro da Corbara, OFM (see Nicholas V)

Pietro de Narnia, 49
Pinborg, Jan, 496n
Pisa, 67, 68, 163, 214, 215, 250, 272n, 292, 316, 321
Piur, Paul, 605n
Ponticianus, 210, 229, 786, 787, 791, 792
Porphory, 254n
Port-Royal, 4
Porto del Popolo, 46
Possidius (Bishop of Calamo), 175–186, 191, 192, 196–199, 204, 205, 212, 213, 227, 230, 289, 778, 781, 790, 794, 796–799, 802–805, 807, 808, 810
potestas iurisdictionis, 72–74, 80, 82, 108, 109, 111, 126, 132–134, 154
potestas ordinis, 72, 82, 108, 111, 126, 132–134
Praemonstratensians, Order of, 9, 179, 263, 272
Prague, 591
Priebsch, Robert, 518n
Prosper of Aquitaine, 184
Prosper of Regio, OESA, 244, 370, 383, 684n
Pryds, Darleen, xii, 7n, 50n, 254n
Pseudo-Dionysius, 29, 35

Quedlinburg, 26, 243–245, 740

Rabanus Maurus, 508
Ragusa, Isa, 506n
Rahner, Karl, 689
Rainaldus, OESA, 168
Rait, Jill, 362n
Ramakers, B.A.M., 503n, 543, 544
Rano, Balbino, OSA, 5n, 178n, 185n, 189n, 195, 201, 204n, 208n, 222, 357n
Rapp, Francis, 564n
Rau, Suse, xii
Raymund Lull, 720
Reames, Sherry L., 183n, 185n
Recanati, 70, 238, 322
Reeves, Marjory, 214n, 604n
Regensburg, 21, 22n, 254, 373
Reggio, 172
Reid, Jonathan, xii
Reinhard von Laudenburg, OESA, 538, 539, 541
Reinhard, Wolfgang, 722n
Reinink-Sirag, Angeniet, xii
religio, 145–147, 148n, 150–152, 154, 195n, 217, 281, 314, 343, 356, 358, 430, 475, 476, 487, 488, 513, 514,

520, 557, 563, 564n, 577–583, 613–618, 631, 646, 683, 701, 704, 710–735, 794, 798
Religionization, 581–584, 674, 677, 683, 701, 705, 707, 722–735
Remigius of Auxerre, 184
Remigius of Florence, OESA, 320, 680
Renner-van Niekerk, Justa, xii
Rennhofer, F., 244n
Reuther, Rosemary Radford, 345
Reynolds, Susan, 719n
Rhodes, J.T., 354n
Ricardus de Duce, 168
Ricardus de Ianua, OESA, 529n
Riccardo Annabaldi, 47, 48, 51, 158, 280
Richard FitzRalph, Bishop of Armaugh, 269–271, 320, 343, 579
Riché, Pierre, 515n
Richstaetter, Carl, 505n
Ricoeur, Paul, 189n, 294n, 517n, 709n
Ridderbos, H.N.B., 354n, 489n
Riffaterre, Michael, 529n
Rigaudière, Albert, 43n
Rimini, 253, 321, 322, 324, 328, 341, 370, 371
Ripa, 323
Rivière, Jean, 18n, 28n, 52n
Robert, Count of Flanders, 239n
Robert Ciboule, 564n
Robert d'Anjou (King of Naples), 42, 49, 50, 94, 111–113, 115, 127, 134, 170, 172, 173, 605
Robert de Bardis (Chancellor of Paris), 221f
Robert Grosseteste, 725, 745
Robert of Pisa, OESA, 327, 329
Robin Archamonus, OESA, 340
Roest, Bert, 368n, 507n
Roger Bacon, OFM, 491, 492n
Rome, xi, xiii, 1, 2, 5, 13n, 16, 30, 32n, 42–50, 53, 68, 70, 83, 109–112, 115, 122, 123, 127, 132, 134, 137, 138, 157, 202, 203, 220, 236–238, 256, 285, 286, 319–322, 370n, 378n, 379n, 380, 585–587, 605, 623
Roper, Lyndal, 479n
Ross, Susan A., 289n
Roth, Francis, OSA, 591n, 592n, 593n
Rouen, 546
Rubin, Miri, 11n, 503n, 516n, 526n, 546n, 555n
Rublack, Hans-Christoph, xii

Rudiger, Bishop of Speyer, 546
Rudolf, R., 565n
Rufinus, OESA, 166
Rufus, St., 193, 194, 200, 206
Ruh, Kurt, 505n
Ruokanen, Mikka, 431n
Rupert of Deutz, OSB, 548
Rupp, Gordon, 693n
Ruprecht, King of Bavaria, 590
Russel, James C., 722n

Saak, E.L., 7n, 9n, 10n, 11n, 19n, 142n, 174n, 182n, 192n, 196n, 207n, 210n, 212n, 214n, 216n, 219n, 227n, 282n, 284n, 351n, 353n, 357n, 399n, 417n, 430n, 466n, 469n, 529n, 530n, 531n, 534n, 535n, 576n, 578n, 581n, 594n, 595n, 596n, 614n, 707n, 724n, 727n, 729n, 731n, 776n
Sacer ordo vester, 25, 113, 738f
Sacrae religionis merita, 25, 737
Salzburg, 536, 645–647, 649, 651, 654, 656, 657
Salze, 261
Sandy, Peggy Reeves, 580n
San Elpidio, 322
San Pietro in Ciel d'Oro, 160, 163–165, 167–173, 180, 199, 223, 234, 263, 293
San Trifone, 48, 237, 238
Santa Maria in Aracoeli, 48
Santa Maria del Popolo, 1, 5, 46, 48, 585
Santa Maria Maggiore, 44, 47
Santa Maria Virginis (Magdeburg), 258, 263
Santa Mustiola, 164, 166
Santa Prassede, 47
Santo Spirito, 190, 194
Santos, Manuel, xii
Sardinia, 180, 202
Saxony-Thuringia, Augustinian Province of, 26
Scheff, Thomas, 308n, 310n
Scheible, Heinz, 706n
Schilling, Heinz, 587n, 722n
Schleusener-Eichholz, Gudrun, 491n
Schlusemann, R.M., 354n
Schmidt, Tilmann, 18n, 42n
Schmitt, J.C., 488n
Schnurr, Klaus, 565n
Scholder, K., 409n
Scholz, Richard, 6n, 18n, 20n, 24n, 28n, 40n, 41n, 60n

Schömberger, Rolf, 59n
Schrama, Martijn, OSA, xii, 365n
Schreckenberg, H., 547n
Schulze, Manfred, xii, 395n, 585n, 587n, 696–698, 728n, 833
Schuppisser, Fritz Oskar, 539n
Schüssler-Fiorenza, Elizabeth, 345
Schürer, Markus, 23n, 223n
Schwab, F.M., 565n
Scott, Joanna Vecchiarelli, 6n, 56n
Scribner, Robert, 478, 479n, 491n, 492n, 493n, 502, 567n, 727n
Seegets, Petra, 477n
Shank, Michael, 365n
Shannon, Joseph L., 690n
Sicard, Patrice, 10n
Sicily, 16, 43n, 113
Siena, 8n, 234, 250, 254, 265, 315, 321, 322, 336, 338, 342, 373, 374, 379n, 474, 529n, 593
Sigismund (Emperor), 585, 593
Sigismund, King of Hungary, 590
Simon de Bruna, OESA, 175n
Simon de Cramaud, 585
Simon Fidati of Cascia, 538, 539n, 541, 579, 693, 698
Simon of Cremona, OESA, 188
Simon, Walter, xii, 833
Simone Martini, 43
Simplicianus, 203, 209–211, 213, 215, 216, 227, 228, 230, 232, 278, 786, 791, 794, 807
Sixtus IV (Pope), 585, 586, 774
Smalley, Beryl, 380n, 508n, 548
Society of Jesus (SJ), 620
Sorabij, Richard, 492n
Southern, Richard, 505n
Spain, 587
Speranza, 70
Speyer, 546
Spiegel, Gabrielle M., 189n, 708n
Spoleto, 70, 317, 321, 334, 335
Spruit, Leen, 492n
St. Gertrude Cloister (Second Order of St. Francis/Augustinian Canonesses), 521f
St. John the Lateran, 2, 44, 48
St. Peter's (Vatican), 236
St. William, Order of, 5
Stakemeier, Eduard, 693
Stamm, Heinz-Meinholf, 640n
Stange, Carl, 692, 694
Stark, Judith Chelius, 6n
Stark, R., 579n
status perfectionis, 146, 149, 151, 152, 154, 155

Staubach, Nikolaus, 733n
Stauch, Liselotte, 565n
Stegmüller, F., 384n, 385n
Steinmetz, David C., 408, 641n, 684n, 696–699
Stephanus de Pulverisio, OESA, 339
Stock, Brian, 483n, 544n, 732n
Stoffers, Manuel, 426n
Strassburg, 254, 303, 329, 385n, 387n, 531, 670
Streveler, Paul A., 362n
Stroick, Cl., 352n
studia, 9, 22, 128, 157, 190, 218, 231, 246, 249n, 254n, 255, 256, 314, 315, 319, 329, 357, 361, 367–377, 380, 382–387, 403, 411, 466, 473, 476, 504, 529, 562, 563, 568, 577, 578, 581, 583, 588, 592, 612, 698, 700, 701, 703–705, 708
Stump, Eleonore, 496n
Super Cathedram, 269
Swanson, R.N., 513n
Sybert von Beek, OCarm., 60n, 62n, 64n
Sylvester (Pope), 48, 90, 91, 92n, 94n, 138
Symmachus (Roman senator), 784, 785
Symon, Frater, OESA, 379n

Tachau, Katherine, 493n
Taylor, Miriam S., 547n
Tenerem cuiusdam constitutionem, 25, 737f
Tentler, Thomas N., 563n
Terpstra, Nicholas, 14n
Thagaste, 181, 184, 185
Theobaldus Coci de Miltenberg, OESA, 384n
Thomas a Kempis, 516
Thomas Aquinas, St., OP, 6n, 29, 243, 245, 254, 357n, 364, 391, 398, 408n, 445n, 459n, 464n, 513, 514, 518, 520, 523, 544, 547n, 557, 571n, 685, 716, 718–721, 724, 728, 745
Thomas de Aretio, OESA, 250, 316
Thomas Bradwardine, 387, 388, 684, 685, 690, 693
Thomas Fabri, OESA, 593
Thomas Müntzer, 647, 665, 669
Thomas of Strassburg, OESA, 255, 319, 331, 341, 342, 364, 366, 374n, 375n, 379n, 380, 381n, 383, 399, 465, 466n, 684n, 686, 688, 690, 699
Thomasuctius, Frater, OESA, 339
Tierney, Brian, 29, 42n, 51n, 53n, 58n, 63n, 66n, 67, 68, 69n, 77n,

78n, 80n, 96n, 101n, 106, 107n, 121n, 126n
Tilley, Maureen A., 289n
Tillich, Paul, 345
Todi, 237, 335
Tolan, John, 547n
Torringa, Marion, xii
Tosci, 335
Toulouse, 194, 328, 775n
Tournai, 239n
Tracy, David, 345
Trano, 338
Trapè, Agostino, OSA, 687, 688
Trapp, Damasus, OSA, xi, 188n, 342n, 362n, 384n, 592, 686–688, 689n, 690n, 694, 701n
Trask, Willard R., 14n
Trent, 170
Trent, Council of, 620, 685, 693, 728
Treviso, 341, 374
Trier, 394
Troeltsch, Ernst, 6, 158n, 707, 734
Troyes, 180
Tübingen, xi, xiii, 189n, 384n, 515, 521, 523, 657
Turner, Victor W., 491n
Tyler, J. Jeffery, 257n

Ulm, 531
Ulpian, 136
Ulrich of Trent, OESA, 343
Ulrich Pinder, 535–542, 549, 556, 557, 561, 582, 823–828
Ulrich von Hutten, 627
Unam sanctam, 28, 39, 40n, 41, 55, 618
Unterlinden, 511
Uppsala, 529n, 530n, 615n
Urban VI (Pope), 587, 589, 591, 592, 594
Urbino, 70

Valentino de Crisio, OESA, 234
Valerius (Bishop of Hippo), 176, 181, 182, 184, 191, 198, 199, 205, 212, 213, 215, 229, 794–797, 799, 801
Van der Eerden, Peter, 426n
Van der Velden, Jacoba, xii
Van Dijk, R.Th.M., 724n
Van Engen, John H., 362n, 548, 715, 722, 724n, 726n, 731n
Van Gerven, R., 51n
Van Moé, E., 51n
Van Neer, Ingrid, xiii
Van Oort, Johannes, 431n
Van Os, Henk, 513n

Vauchez, André, 563n, 564n
Veneranda sanctorum, 160, 164–166, 168, 170–172, 174, 233, 263, 357
Venice, 163, 254, 341, 373, 386n, 531
Vercelli, 172
Verdon, Timothy, 506n
Verecundus, 788
Vergil, 48, 138
Verheijen, Luc, OSA, 9n, 178, 192n
Verona, 172
Vezey, Elsie, xii
vicarius Christi, 52, 53, 55, 61, 64, 65, 73, 77, 80–83, 85, 92n, 95, 96, 105, 106, 119, 121, 122, 127, 129, 131, 134, 137, 145, 155, 157, 625
vicarius dei, 35, 38, 40, 52, 55, 75, 79
Victorinus, 210, 228, 786
Vienna, 323–325, 341, 342, 591, 775n
vita perfectissima, 283, 286, 429, 432n, 474, 583, 584, 674, 704, 721, 724
Viterbo, 202, 203, 250, 322, 359n
Vogelsang, Erich, 672
Volmarch, 341
Von Stritzky, Maria-Barbara, 565n
Vossenkuhl, Wilhelm, 59n
Vovelle, Michel, 709n

Wach, Joachim, 711
Wachinger, Burghart, 354n
Waldemar, Markgrave of Brandenburg, 259, 260
Walsh, James J., 43n
Walsh, Katherine, 221, 222, 269, 270n, 331, 593n, 594n, 595
Walter, Frater, OESA, 317, 335
Warner, Geert, 564n
Wawrykow, Joseph, 726n
Weber, Max, 711, 712, 734
Weber, Philip E., 354n
Weidenhiller, P. Egino, 475
Weinbrenner, Ralph, 312, 353n, 578n, 618n, 701n
Weinstein, Donald, xii, 630n
Weiss, Ulmann, 256n
Wenceslaus, King of Bohemia, 590
Wendelin Steinbach, 693
Wenzel, Horst, 479n, 489n, 491n, 497n, 521, 568n
Wenzel, Siegfried, 523n, 529n
Wenzeslaus Link, OESA, 619, 637, 638, 646, 650, 659, 670
Werner, Karl, 684, 685, 688, 691, 692, 698, 699
Werner Rolevinck, OCarth., 567n
Wesjohann, Achim, 23n, 200n

Whaling, Frank, 712n, 713n
White, Hayden, 189n, 708, 709
Wieland, Georg, xii
Wilhelm of Melitona, OFM, 364n
Wilks, Michael, 6n, 29, 40n, 41n, 43, 50n, 51n, 65n, 70n, 71, 77n, 83, 84n, 126, 128, 129, 130, 132, 133, 744
Willeumier-Schalij, J.M., 354n, 478n
William, Blessed, 215
William Becchi, OESA, 699
William of Cremona, OESA, 55, 59n, 60–64, 71, 157, 159, 167, 169, 171, 172, 201, 202, 208n, 223, 224, 234, 235, 245–250, 252, 266, 358, 359, 370, 372, 375n, 403, 586, 587, 673, 679, 680, 744–747
William of Gravelgem, OESA, 239n
William of Moerbeke, 63, 745
William Nogaret, 30, 39
William of Ockham, OFM, 6n, 30, 59n, 67–69, 71, 126, 140, 156, 684, 685, 705
Williamites, 200
Wilson, Katharina M., 42n
Winand of Diedenhofen, OESA, 631–633, 635, 636
Winterhager, Wilhelm E., 641n
Wittenberg, 12, 471, 642–644, 646, 649, 650, 652, 654, 655, 657, 660, 671, 673, 693, 697, 702, 705, 706n

Wolf, Norbert Richard, 474n
Wolfenbüttel, xiii, 384n
Wolfgang Capito, 660, 661
Wolfgang Schenck, 470
Worms, 625n
Wriedt, Markus, xii, 445n, 641n, 697, 698
Würzburg, 352

Ypma, Eelcko, OSA, xii, 245n, 253n, 254, 368n, 370n, 371n, 374n, 375n, 376n, 377n, 380n, 381n, 382n, 384n, 385n, 474n, 700
Yun, Bartolomé, 241n

Zachary of Besançon, 509
Zcinke, Herr, 490
Zschoch, Hellmut, 353n, 615n
Zumkeller, Adolar, OSA, xi, 6n, 41n, 50n, 60n, 141n, 175n, 188n, 214n, 243n, 256n, 266n, 273n, 292n, 352n, 353n, 354n, 383n, 384n, 385n, 386n, 401n, 403n, 415n, 416n, 466n, 478n, 515n, 530n, 538n, 577n, 588n, 589n, 591n, 592n, 596n, 604n, 641n, 688–692, 698n, 699, 743, 744, 775
Zur Mühlen, Karl-Heinz, 421n, 705n

STUDIES IN MEDIEVAL
AND REFORMATION THOUGHT

FOUNDED BY HEIKO A. OBERMAN †
EDITED BY ANDREW COLIN GOW

1. DOUGLASS, E. J. D. *Justification in Late Medieval Preaching.* 2nd ed. 1989
2. WILLIS, E. D. *Calvin's Catholic Christology.* 1966 *out of print*
3. POST, R. R. *The Modern Devotion.* 1968 *out of print*
4. STEINMETZ, D. C. *Misericordia Dei.* The Theology of Johannes von Staupitz. 1968 *out of print*
5. O'MALLEY, J. W. *Giles of Viterbo on Church and Reform.* 1968 *out of print*
6. OZMENT, S. E. *Homo Spiritualis.* The Anthropology of Tauler, Gerson and Luther. 1969
7. PASCOE, L. B. *Jean Gerson: Principles of Church Reform.* 1973 *out of print*
8. HENDRIX, S. H. *Ecclesia in Via.* Medieval Psalms Exegesis and the *Dictata super Psalterium* (1513-1515) of Martin Luther. 1974
9. TREXLER, R. C. *The Spiritual Power.* Republican Florence under Interdict. 1974
10. TRINKAUS, Ch. with OBERMAN, H. A. (eds.). *The Pursuit of Holiness.* 1974 *out of print*
11. SIDER, R. J. *Andreas Bodenstein von Karlstadt.* 1974
12. HAGEN, K. *A Theology of Testament in the Young Luther.* 1974
13. MOORE, Jr., W. L. *Annotatiunculae D. Iohanne Eckio Praelectore.* 1976
14. OBERMAN, H. A. with BRADY, Jr., Th. A. (eds.). *Itinerarium Italicum.* Dedicated to Paul Oskar Kristeller. 1975
15. KEMPFF, D. *A Bibliography of Calviniana.* 1959-1974. 1975 *out of print*
16. WINDHORST, C. *Täuferisches Taufverständnis.* 1976
17. KITTELSON, J. M. *Wolfgang Capito.* 1975
18. DONNELLY, J. P. *Calvinism and Scholasticism in Vermigli's Doctrine of Man and Grace.* 1976
19. LAMPING, A. J. *Ulrichus Velenus (Oldřich Velenský) and his Treatise against the Papacy.* 1976
20. BAYLOR, M. G. *Action and Person.* Conscience in Late Scholasticism and the Young Luther. 1977
21. COURTENAY, W. J. *Adam Wodeham.* 1978
22. BRADY, Jr., Th. A. *Ruling Class, Regime and Reformation at Strasbourg, 1520-1555.* 1978
23. KLAASSEN, W. *Michael Gaismair.* 1978
24. BERNSTEIN, A. E. *Pierre d'Ailly and the Blanchard Affair.* 1978
25. BUCER, Martin. *Correspondance.* Tome I (Jusqu'en 1524). Publié par J. Rott. 1979
26. POSTHUMUS MEYJES, G. H. M. *Jean Gerson et l'Assemblée de Vincennes (1329).* 1978
27. VIVES, Juan Luis. *In Pseudodialecticos.* Ed. by Ch. Fantazzi. 1979
28. BORNERT, R. *La Réforme Protestante du Culte à Strasbourg au XVIe siècle (1523-1598).* 1981
29. SEBASTIAN CASTELLIO. *De Arte Dubitandi.* Ed. by E. Feist Hirsch. 1981
30. BUCER, Martin. *Opera Latina.* Vol I. Publié par C. Augustijn, P. Fraenkel, M. Lienhard. 1982
31. BÜSSER, F. *Wurzeln der Reformation in Zürich.* 1985 *out of print*
32. FARGE, J. K. *Orthodoxy and Reform in Early Reformation France.* 1985
33. 34. BUCER, Martin. *Etudes sur les relations de Bucer avec les Pays-Bas.* I. Etudes; II. Documents. Par J. V. Pollet. 1985
35. HELLER, H. *The Conquest of Poverty.* The Calvinist Revolt in Sixteenth Century France. 1986

36. MEERHOFF, K. *Rhétorique et poétique au XVIe siècle en France.* 1986
37. GERRITS, G. H. *Inter timorem et spem.* Gerard Zerbolt of Zutphen. 1986
38. ANGELO POLIZIANO. *Lamia.* Ed. by A. Wesseling. 1986
39. BRAW, C. *Bücher im Staube.* Die Theologie Johann Arndts in ihrem Verhältnis zur Mystik. 1986
40. BUCER, Martin. *Opera Latina.* Vol. II. Enarratio in Evangelion Iohannis (1528, 1530, 1536). Publié par I. Backus. 1988
41. BUCER, Martin. *Opera Latina.* Vol. III. Martin Bucer and Matthew Parker: Florilegium Patristicum. Edition critique. Publié par P. Fraenkel. 1988
42. BUCER, Martin. *Opera Latina.* Vol. IV. Consilium Theologicum Privatim Conscriptum. Publié par P. Fraenkel. 1988
43. BUCER, Martin. *Correspondance.* Tome II (1524-1526). Publié par J. Rott. 1989
44. RASMUSSEN, T. *Inimici Ecclesiae.* Das ekklesiologische Feindbild in Luthers "Dictata super Psalterium" (1513-1515) im Horizont der theologischen Tradition. 1989
45. POLLET, J. *Julius Pflug et la crise religieuse dans l'Allemagne du XVIe siècle.* Essai de synthèse biographique et théologique. 1990
46. BUBENHEIMER, U. *Thomas Müntzer.* Herkunft und Bildung. 1989
47. BAUMAN, C. *The Spiritual Legacy of Hans Denck.* Interpretation and Translation of Key Texts. 1991
48. OBERMAN, H. A. and JAMES, F. A., III (eds.). in cooperation with SAAK, E. L. *Via Augustini.* Augustine in the Later Middle Ages, Renaissance and Reformation: Essays in Honor of Damasus Trapp. 1991 *out of print*
49. SEIDEL MENCHI, S. *Erasmus als Ketzer.* Reformation und Inquisition im Italien des 16. Jahrhunderts. 1993
50. SCHILLING, H. *Religion, Political Culture, and the Emergence of Early Modern Society.* Essays in German and Dutch History. 1992
51. DYKEMA, P. A. and OBERMAN, H. A. (eds.). *Anticlericalism in Late Medieval and Early Modern Europe.* 2nd ed. 1994
52. 53. KRIEGER, Chr. and LIENHARD, M. (eds.). *Martin Bucer and Sixteenth Century Europe.* Actes du colloque de Strasbourg (28-31 août 1991). 1993
54. SCREECH, M. A. *Clément Marot: A Renaissance Poet discovers the World.* Lutheranism, Fabrism and Calvinism in the Royal Courts of France and of Navarre and in the Ducal Court of Ferrara. 1994
55. GOW, A. C. *The Red Jews: Antisemitism in an Apocalyptic Age, 1200-1600.* 1995
56. BUCER, Martin. *Correspondance.* Tome III (1527-1529). Publié par Chr. Krieger et J. Rott. 1989
57. SPIJKER, W. VAN 'T. *The Ecclesiastical Offices in the Thought of Martin Bucer.* Translated by J. Vriend (text) and L.D. Bierma (notes). 1996
58. GRAHAM, M.F. *The Uses of Reform.* 'Godly Discipline' and Popular Behavior in Scotland and Beyond, 1560-1610. 1996
59. AUGUSTIJN, C. *Erasmus. Der Humanist als Theologe und Kirchenreformer.* 1996
60. McCOOG S J, T. M. *The Society of Jesus in Ireland, Scotland, and England 1541-1588.* 'Our Way of Proceeding?' 1996
61. FISCHER, N. und KOBELT-GROCH, M. (Hrsg.). *Außenseiter zwischen Mittelalter und Neuzeit.* Festschrift für Hans-Jürgen Goertz zum 60. Geburtstag. 1997
62. NIEDEN, M. *Organum Deitatis.* Die Christologie des Thomas de Vio Cajetan. 1997
63. BAST, R.J. *Honor Your Fathers.* Catechisms and the Emergence of a Patriarchal Ideology in Germany, 1400-1600. 1997
64. ROBBINS, K.C. *City on the Ocean Sea: La Rochelle, 1530-1650.* Urban Society, Religion, and Politics on the French Atlantic Frontier. 1997
65. BLICKLE, P. *From the Communal Reformation to the Revolution of the Common Man.* 1998
66. FELMBERG, B. A. R. *Die Ablaßtheorie Kardinal Cajetans (1469-1534).* 1998

67. CUNEO, P. F. *Art and Politics in Early Modern Germany.* Jörg Breu the Elder and the Fashioning of Political Identity, ca. 1475-1536. 1998
68. BRADY, Jr., Th. A. *Communities, Politics, and Reformation in Early Modern Europe.* 1998
69. McKEE, E. A. *The Writings of Katharina Schütz Zell.* 1. The Life and Thought of a Sixteenth-Century Reformer. 2. A Critical Edition. 1998
70. BOSTICK, C. V. *The Antichrist and the Lollards.* Apocalyticism in Late Medieval and Reformation England. 1998
71. BOYLE, M. O'ROURKE. *Senses of Touch.* Human Dignity and Deformity from Michelangelo to Calvin. 1998
72. TYLER, J.J. *Lord of the Sacred City.* The *Episcopus Exclusus* in Late Medieval and Early Modern Germany. 1999
74. WITT, R.G. *'In the Footsteps of the Ancients'.* The Origins of Humanism from Lovato to Bruni. 2000
77. TAYLOR, L.J. *Heresy and Orthodoxy in Sixteenth-Century Paris.* François le Picart and the Beginnings of the Catholic Reformation. 1999
78. BUCER, Martin. *Briefwechsel/Correspondance.* Band IV (Januar-September 1530). Herausgegeben und bearbeitet von R. Friedrich, B. Hamm und A. Puchta. 2000
79. MANETSCH, S.M. *Theodore Beza and the Quest for Peace in France, 1572-1598.* 2000
80. GODMAN, P. *The Saint as Censor.* Robert Bellarmine between Inquisition and Index. 2000
81. SCRIBNER, R.W. *Religion and Culture in Germany (1400-1800).* Ed. L. Roper. 2001
82. KOOI, C. *Liberty and Religion.* Church and State in Leiden's Reformation, 1572-1620. 2000
83. BUCER, Martin. *Opera Latina.* Vol. V. Defensio adversus axioma catholicum id est criminationem R.P. Roberti Episcopi Abrincensis (1534). Ed. W.I.P. Hazlett. 2000
84. BOER, W. de. *The Conquest of the Soul.* Confession, Discipline, and Public Order in Counter-Reformation Milan. 2001
85. EHRSTINE, G. *Theater, culture, and community in Reformation Bern, 1523-1555.* 2001
86. CATTERALL, D. *Community Without Borders.* Scot Migrants and the Changing Face of Power in the Dutch Republic, c. 1600-1700. 2002
87. BOWD, S.D. *Reform Before the Reformation.* Vincenzo Querini and the Religious Renaissance in Italy. 2002
88. PELC, M. *Illustrium Imagines.* Das Porträtbuch der Renaissance. 2002
89. SAAK, E.L. *High Way to Heaven.* The Augustinian Platform between Reform and Reformation, 1292-1524. 2002

Prospectus available on request

BRILL — P.O.B. 9000 — 2300 PA LEIDEN — THE NETHERLANDS